Administrative Law
in Context

THIRD EDITION

EDITED BY
COLLEEN M FLOOD
Faculty of Law, University of Ottawa

LORNE SOSSIN
Osgoode Hall Law School, York University

Toronto, Canada
2018

Emond Montgomery Publications Limited
60 Shaftesbury Avenue
Toronto ON M4T 1A3
http://www.emond.ca/lawschool

Printed in Canada.

We acknowledge the financial support of the Government of Canada. Canadä

Emond Publishing has no responsibility for the persistence or accuracy of URLs for external or third-party Internet websites referred to in this publication, and does not guarantee that any content on such websites is, or will remain, accurate or appropriate.

Vice president, publishing: Anthony Rezek
Publisher: Danann Hawes
Director, development and production: Kelly Dickson
Production supervisor: Laura Bast
Copy editor: Tom Penner
Permissions editor: Lisa Brant
Typesetters: SPi Global, Janette Thompson
Proofreaders: Valerie Adams, Darryl Kamo, and Rose Knecht
Indexer: Paula Pike

Library and Archives Canada Cataloguing in Publication

Administrative law in context / edited by Colleen M. Flood, Lorne Sossin. — Third edition.

ISBN 978-1-77255-306-2 (hardcover)

1. Administrative law—Canada—Textbooks.   I. Flood, Colleen M. (Colleen Marion), 1966-, editor   II. Sossin, Lorne Mitchell, 1964-, editor

KE5015.A845 2018   342.71'06   C2017-906758-3
KF5402.A845 2018

Foreword to Third Edition

Once again I am delighted to say a few words about the third edition of *Administrative Law in Context*. It must be gratifying to the editors and contributors to see the emergence of a third edition—a deserved recognition in itself for their collective efforts.

While not abandoning the many positive features of previous editions, there are major themes that come to my mind with the third edition that can be summarized by three words: completeness, coherence, and collaboration.

Through the substantial expansion of some chapters, the addition of new chapters, and the reorganization of other topics, this edition incorporates major recent developments that have occurred since the second edition.

In a major work that deals with different topics by different authors, the third edition aims to build more coherence among the various subjects and chapters. This is easy to say but difficult to achieve; however, this approach will be of great help to the readers of the book by having more ties that bind together the various chapters. An impressive example is the treatment of Aboriginal administrative law and its interrelationship with Canadian public law.

The theme of collaboration is present in the first two editions of the book but is even more robust and ambitious in the third edition. I greatly admire the cross-country representation of the editors and contributors—who can be compared to transnational chefs in a national kitchen with agreed upon views for the advancement of the public good. Congratulations again to the editors and contributors for another outstanding effort.

Frank Iacobucci

Foreword to the Second Edition

It is a pleasure and honour for me to continue my association with *Administrative Law in Context* by providing these remarks for its second edition. Two factors are especially important behind the appearance of a second edition. One is explained by the organic nature of the law, whether legislative or judicially inspired, in that it develops and changes rapidly, and administrative law is no exception. The other factor is that the work in question merits a second edition as judged by the response to the first edition; as such, this second edition is praiseful recognition for the editors and contributors who have toiled to produce this very helpful volume.

The second edition has retained all of the virtues of the first edition that I mentioned in my Foreword and indeed has added special attractions by the inclusion of new chapters on Aboriginal administrative law and on the Federal Court and administrative law. As well, the editors and contributors have reordered many of the chapters, changed many of the titles, as well as updating the commentary that follows, and welcomed some new contributors into their scholarly midst. All of this with no loss in the coverage, calibre, utility, or lucidity of the book. Put another way, the bottles, labelling, and packaging may have changed in some respects, but the wine tastes as good as ever, and some new vintages have been added!

I congratulate the editors and contributors for another excellent effort.

Frank Iacobucci

Foreword to the First Edition

Having spent close to 50 years in the law, I have been a witness to the remarkable growth and development of administrative law in Canada and abroad. In my student days, the administrative law syllabus was rather thin compared with the course topics and materials found in the contemporary administrative law course. There are many reasons for this turn of events, but chief among them is the tremendous proliferation of boards, tribunals, and agencies brought about by the perceived needs and preferences of the modern regulatory state. As a lawyer in the private and public sectors, law professor, member of an administrative tribunal, judge, and now back to being a lawyer, I have been privileged to have an almost front-row seat to view the parade of administrative law developments and growth. It is that perspective which causes me to state that I enthusiastically welcome the arrival of *Administrative Law in Context*. Allow me to explain my enthusiasm.

I agree with the basic premise of this volume that for many years excessive emphasis has been placed on judicial review of administrative tribunals. Indeed, in the beginning years of the subject, and for too long, there was, in my view, far too much attention paid to legal controls of administrative action, as reflected, for example, in the views of AV Dicey[1] and Lord Hewart of Bury,[2] and not enough attention to what might be called a realistic approach to the subject, as reflected in the writings of John Willis.[3]

Granted, lawyers must obviously be attuned to judicial review since legal remedies and oversight are part of the tool kit for every lawyer in advising clients. Consequently (and most appropriately), the book includes chapters on remedies, the rule of law, the duty of fairness, and judicial review. But the book goes well beyond those topics to give the reader a better understanding of what tribunals do, the complexities they face, and how they reach decisions and shape policy. Also explored are a number of theoretical issues on the legitimacy of public authority; the interplay among law, regulations, and guidelines; the choice of regulatory instruments; and other topics.

The manner of presentation of the various chapters is also noteworthy. Some 17 scholars from across the country have combined to provide a highly readable text, with a range of diversity reflected in the transnational backgrounds of the authors, and this has resulted in a menu of innovative and instructive commentary.

---

1   AV Dicey, *An Introduction to the Study of the Constitution* (London: MacMillan & Co, 1885 and subsequent editions).

2   Lord Hewart of Bury, *The New Despotism* (London: E Benn, 1929).

3   See, for example, John Willis, *Three Approaches to Administrative Law* (1935/36) 1 UTLJ 53; John Willis, 1974 Cecil Wright Memorial Lecture, University of Toronto Faculty of Law (later published as "Canadian Administrative Law in Retrospect" (1974) 24 UTLJ 225); and John Willis, "Administrative Law in Canada" (1961) 39 Can Bar Rev 251.

In short, the collection appropriately takes a broad view of the subject and does so in an informative and well-structured manner. I have no doubt that the book will accomplish the goal of its authors to serve as a primary resource for administrative law students throughout Canada. But the book is also an important scholarly contribution to the field in a variety of topics that will be of great benefit to lawyers and judges. And for all that, I wish to commend and thank the contributors for their efforts.

Frank Iacobucci

Preface

This is the third edition of *Administrative Law in Context*. As with previous editions, we hope that this volume contributes to the growing recognition that administrative law happens outside the courtroom—in government departments, agencies, boards, commissions and tribunals—affecting the experience of all those involved. Apart from emphasizing the context of administrative law on the ground, our goal has been to create an accessible, readable text that reflects the many perspectives in administrative law. We are proud to include in this volume scholars and teachers from across Canada, with some of the most experienced voices in the field, as well as some new ones. Because administrative law is ever evolving, a further goal was to create a flexible, living text. To this end, the book is accompanied by a website, at <adminlawincontext.emond.ca>, where both students and teachers can find edited and full-text cases for each chapter, recommendations for additional readings, and important additions, clarifications, and updates to the published text. Readers will also find chapters from earlier editions that they may wish to review at <emond.ca/adminlaw3e>.

It became clear after discussion with our various authors that the subject matter of administrative law is itself so vibrant and full of flux that every author would need to reinvent their chapter to take account of changing case law. In some areas we added new chapters, while in others new authors took on existing chapters. In the end, every chapter in the volume was substantially revised for the third edition. We hope this format—an edited collection spanning the breadth and depth of administrative law, combined with online resources—will continue to do justice to the dynamic nature of the field. Our heartfelt thanks to our various contributors in this edition and in the previous editions for their hard work and fantastic chapters.

In addition to our contributors we wish to thank many individuals at Emond Publishing who have done so much to get this book, and this third edition, to print, particularly Danann Hawes, Kelly Dickson, Laura Bast, and Paul Emond. We are also grateful for the administrative and research assistance provided by Greg Hinds and Oscar Cabrera (first edition), Marcelo Rodriguez Ferrere and Ryan MacIsaac (second edition), and Richard Schuett, Devon Kapoor, and Marleigh Dick (third edition). We also wish to express special thanks to Sujith Xavier and Bryan Thomas (first edition), Arthur Wilson (second edition), and Bryan Thomas (third edition)—research managers during different phases of this book's development. We are grateful to Osgoode Hall Law School for hosting a workshop in the fall of 2016 as we began discussions on the third edition, as well as the Faculty of Law at the University of Toronto, who hosted similar workshops for the previous two editions of the book.

Finally, as ever, we would like to thank all students of administrative law—past, present, and future—who stimulate and engage us, and always hold our feet to the fire.

Colleen M Flood and Lorne Sossin

Summary Table of Contents

Detailed Table of Contents

Chapter Thirteen The Charter and Administrative Law Part II:
Evan Fox-Decent, Alexander Pless

List of Contributors

WA Bogart

Online chapter: The Tools of the Administrative State and the Regulatory Mix, <www.emond.ca/adminlaw3e>.

WA (Bill) Bogart, BA, LLB (University of Toronto) LLM (Harvard), is a distinguished university professor of law at the University of Windsor (ret). Bill has held several SSHRC grants to support his research, has been a Virtual Scholar in Residence for the Law Commission of Canada, and has been a frequent government consultant. He is an author/editor of eight books—*Off the Street: Legalizing Drugs* (Dundurn, 2016) is his latest. He blogs regularly for the *Huffington Post* and comments frequently for the media.

Geneviève Cartier

Online chapter: Administrative Discretion: Between Exercising Power and Conudcting Dialogue, <www.emond.ca/adminlaw3e>.

Geneviève Cartier is a professor of law at the University of Sherbrooke. She holds a PhD from the University of Toronto and an MA from Cambridge University. A member of the Consultative Committee of the Law Commission of Canada from 2003 to 2006, she teaches and researches in the areas of public law and jurisprudence. Her work focuses on administrative discretion, the rule of law, and common law constitutionalism, and she is currently working on the question of prerogative powers. From 2012 to 2015, she was the full-time research director of the Commission of Inquiry into the granting and administration of government contracts in the construction industry, set up by the government of Québec. Her recent contributions include a chapter on deliberative constitutionalism in the administrative state, and reflections on policy and ethical aspects of public commissions of inquiry through her coordination of a special issue of the *McGill Law Journal*, dedicated to the celebration of the 50th anniversary of the Supreme Court decision in *Roncarelli v Duplessis*.

Peter Carver

Peter Carver, MA (Toronto), LLB (McGill), LLM (UBC) is a Faculty of Law professor at the University of Alberta, and Editor-in-Chief of the *Review of Constitutional Studies*. Professor Carver teaches and does research in the areas of Canadian constitutional, administrative, immigration, and mental health law. Before coming to the University of Alberta, Professor Carver served as a member of the Immigration and Refugee Board and practised law in British Columbia. His recent publications include "'A Principle of Vital Importance': The Supreme Court of Canada's Approach to Purposeful Limits on Expression in Section 2(b) of the Charter" (2017) 75 Supreme Court L Rev 191-219; "A Failed Discourse of Distrust Amid Significant Procedural Change: The Harper Government's Legacy in Immigration and Refugee Law" (2017) 21:2 Rev of Constitutional Studies 209-234; and with Isabel Grant, "*PS v Ontario*: Rethinking The Role of the Charter in Civil Commitment" (2016) 53:3 Osgoode Hall LJ 999-1032. Professor Carver wrote the chapter "Getting the Story Out" concerning administrative law and public inquiries in the first two editions of *Administrative Law in Context*.

Jennifer Dolling

Jennifer Dolling is a sole practitioner. She holds a BA in Criminology with high distinction from the University of Toronto (1996); an LLB from Queen's University (1999); and an LLM with a specialty in Health Law and Policy from the University of Toronto (2009), for which she was awarded a Canadian Institutes of Health Research Training Program Fellowship. After her call to the Ontario Bar in 2001, Jennifer practised for several years in the areas of medical malpractice, professional negligence and liability, health disciplines defence, insurance defence, and personal injury. She has appeared before administrative tribunals such as the Health Professions Appeal and Review Board. After completing her LLM, Jennifer worked as a research associate with the Faculty of Law at the University of Toronto. She was a member of the Research Ethics Board at Mount Sinai Hospital from 2007 to 2012. Prior to starting her own practice, she was research counsel in the Samuel Lunenfeld Research Institute at Mount Sinai Hospital. She has been a Council Member of the College of Physiotherapists of Ontario since 2015.

Colleen M Flood

Colleen M Flood FRSC is a professor at the University of Ottawa and a University Research Chair in Health Law & Policy. She is inaugural director of the Ottawa Centre for Health Law, Policy and Ethics. From 2000 to 2015 she was a Professor and Canada Research Chair at the Faculty of Law, University of Toronto with cross-appointments to the School of Public Policy and the Institute of Health Policy, Management & Evaluation. From 2006 to 2011 she served as a Scientific Director of the Institute for Health Services and Policy Research, one of the Canadian Institutes of Health Research.

Her two most recent books are *The Right to Health at the Public/Private Divide* (2014) (co-edited with Aeyal Gross and published by Cambridge University Press) and *Law & Mind: Mental Health Law and Policy in Canada* (2016) (co-edited with Jennifer Chandler and published by LexisNexis, Canada).

Craig Forcese

Craig Forcese is a professor with the Faculty of Law (Common Law Section), at the University of Ottawa. He teaches national security law, public international law, administrative law, and public law/legislation. Much of his current research and writing relates to national security, human rights, and democratic accountability. Craig is the co-author of *False Security: The Radicalization of Canadian Anti-terrorism* (Irwin Law, 2015); *National Security Law: Canadian Practice in International Perspective* (Toronto: Irwin Law, 2007); and co-editor of *The Human Rights of Anti-terrorism* (Toronto: Irwin Law, 2008). He is also co-editor and co-author of *International Law: Doctrine, Practice, and Theory* (Toronto: Irwin Law, 2014, 2d Ed); co-managing editor of *Public Law: Cases, Materials, and Commentary*, 3rd ed (Toronto: Emond, 2015); and co-author of *The Laws of Government: The Legal Foundations of Canadian Democracy*, 2nd ed (Toronto: Irwin Law, 2011). Before joining the law school faculty, Craig practised law at the Washington, DC office of Hughes Hubbard & Reed LLP, specializing in international trade and commercial law. He has a BA from McGill University (1992), an MA from the Norman Paterson School of International Affairs, Carleton University (1997), an LLB (summa cum laude) from the University of Ottawa (where he shared the gold medal for the best graduating average of his class) (1997), and an LLM from Yale University (2001). He is a member in good standing of the bars of Ontario, New York, and the District of Columbia.

Cristie Ford

Dr Cristie Ford is Associate Professor and Director at the Centre for Business Law at the Peter A Allard School of Law, UBC. Her research focuses primarily on regulatory theory and administrative law as they relate to international, US, and Canadian financial and securities regulation. She has authored multiple articles and two books: *Innovation and the State: Finance, Regulation, and Justice* (Cambridge University Press, 2017); and, with His Excellency the Right Honourable David Johnston and Kathleen Rockwell, the leading text, *Canadian Securities Regulation* (5th ed, 2014). Prior to joining UBC, Professor Ford practised in securities regulation and administrative law, including several years at Davis Polk and Wardwell LLP in New York. She obtained her graduate degrees from Columbia Law School, where she also taught in a variety of capacities. She sits on a number of editorial and academic advisory boards, and has served on several occasions as a consultant to the Canadian Department of Finance. She has lectured in law schools and to academic audiences across North America, Europe, and elsewhere.

Evan Fox-Decent

Evan Fox-Decent is a professor at McGill University, Faculty of Law. He teaches and publishes in legal theory, administrative law, First Nations and the law, immigration law, agency law, international law, and the law of fiduciaries. His first book, *Sovereignty's Promise: The State as Fiduciary* (Oxford: Oxford University Press, 2011), explores the implications of viewing the state and its institutions as fiduciaries of the people subject to their power. Among these implications is a distinctive interpretation of common law constitutionalism, called "administrative law as solicitude." His second monograph, with Evan J Criddle, is *Fiduciaries of Humanity: How International Law Constitutes Authority* (New York: Oxford University Press, 2016). This work develops an account of sovereignty under international law that aspires to reconcile the autonomy international law confers on states with legal responsibilities that arise from the possession of public powers.

Kate Glover

Kate Glover, BA (McGill), LLB (Dalhousie), LLM (Cambridge), DCL (McGill), of the Bar of Ontario, is an assistant professor in the Faculty of Law at Western University. Kate teaches courses in the areas of constitutional law, administrative law, and advanced public law, and has been recognized for her teaching with the Western Law Award for Teaching Excellence in 2015–16 and the J. McLeod Professor of the Year Award in 2016–17. Her research focuses on constitutional and administrative law, with particular focus on questions of constitutional reform, constitutional structuralism, institutional design, and procedural fairness. Some of her recent publications appear in the *McGill Law Journal*, the *Supreme Court Law Review*, the *Review of Constitutional Studies*, the *Alberta Law Review*, and *Foundations and Traditions of Constitutional Amendment*, edited by Richard Albert, Xenophon Contiades and Alkmene Fotiadou, and published by Hart Publishing in 2017. She has been invited to present her research widely, including at national and international conferences, as an expert witness before the Special Senate Committee on Senate Modernization, and in professional education programs for provincial law societies and bar associations. Kate was called to the Bar of Ontario in 2007, after which she served as law clerk to the Honourable Justice Abella of the Supreme Court of Canada and practised civil and public law litigation at Borden Ladner Gervais. Further, prior to joining Western Law, Kate was a Vanier Scholar, an O'Brien Fellow in Human Rights and Legal Pluralism, and the Ian Pilarczyk Teaching Fellow at McGill University's Faculty of Law. During her time at McGill, she also served as co-counsel for the *amicus curiae* in the *Senate Reform Reference* before the Supreme Court of Canada in 2013 and as Executive Director of the International Criminal Justice Clinic.

Angus Grant

Angus Grant, BA (Trent), JD/MSW (Toronto), PhD (Osgoode) is a lawyer and visiting professor of law at Osgoode Hall Law School, York University. Angus has practiced in the areas of immigration, refugee and constitutional law for many years and has appeared before a variety of Canadian appellate courts, including the Supreme Court of Canada. He has also taught administrative law, immigration law and refugee law at Osgoode Hall and at Queen's University.

Andrew Green

Andrew Green is an associate professor at the University of Toronto, Faculty of Law. His research and teaching interests focus on administrative law, environmental law, international trade (including how international trade rules constrain a country's ability to implement domestic environmental policy), and judicial decision-making. His most recent book *Commitment and Cooperation on High Courts: A Cross-Country Examination of Institutional Constraints on Judges* (with Ben Alarie) (Oxford University Press, 2017) examines how differences in the design of high courts across countries impact how judges make decisions. He holds an LLB from the University of Toronto and an LLM and JSD from the University of Chicago. Before joining the Faculty, Professor Green practised environmental law in Toronto.

Gerald Heckman

Gerald Heckman is an associate professor at the Faculty of Law, University of Manitoba where he teaches administrative, constitutional and advanced public law. After receiving his LLB from the University of Toronto, he clerked for Justice Marc Noël at the Federal Court of Canada, obtained an LLM in administrative law from Queen's University, Kingston and practiced labour, employment, and human rights law. He earned his PhD at Osgoode Hall Law School, York University. His research interests focus on public law, and include the role of international human rights norms in Canadian administrative and constitutional law, migration law, and the empirical analysis of delay in administrative decision-making. He is co-editor of *Administrative Law: Cases, Text and Materials* with Professors David J Mullan, Gus Van Harten and Janna Promislow. He is the recipient of several faculty and university teaching awards.

Justice Grant Huscroft

Online chapter: From Natural Justice to Fairness: Thresholds, Content, and the Role of Judicial Review, <www.emond.ca/adminlaw3e>.

Grant Huscroft is a Justice of the Court of Appeal for Ontario, a professor of law at Western University and was formerly a member of the Faculty of Law at the University of Auckland. He is co-director of the Public Law and Legal Philosophy Research group at Western, where his research focuses on constitutional law and judicial review in Canada and the Commonwealth. He is co-author of the treatise *The New Zealand Bill of Rights* (Melbourne: Oxford

University Press, 2003) (with Paul Rishworth, Richard Mahoney, and Scott Optican) and has edited or co-edited seven collections of essays, including *The Challenge of Originalism: Theories of Constitutional Interpretation* (York: Cambridge University Press, 2011) (with Bradley Miller); *Expounding the Constitution: Essays in Constitutional Theory* (New York: Cambridge University Press, 2008); *A Simple Common Lawyer: Essays in Honour of Michael Taggart* (Oxford: Hart Publishing, 2008) (with David Dyzenhaus and Murray Hunt); *Inside and Outside Canadian Administrative Law: Essays in Honour of David Mullan* (Toronto: University of Toronto Press, 2006) (with Michael Taggart); *Constitutionalism in the Charter Era* (Toronto: LexisNexis-Butterworths, 2004) (with Ian Brodie); *Litigating Rights: Perspectives from Domestic International Law* (Oxford: Hart Publishing, 2002) (with Paul Rishworth); and *Rights and Freedoms* (Wellington, NZ: Brookers, 1995) (with Paul Rishworth).

Laverne Jacobs

Laverne Jacobs is an associate professor and the Director of Graduate Studies at the University of Windsor's Faculty of Law. She holds degrees in Common Law and Civil Law from McGill University and a doctorate from Osgoode Hall Law School. She researches and teaches in the areas of administrative law, transparency in governance, and empirical research methodologies. She also has a particular interest in disability rights and social justice and runs a research and advocacy project called Law, Disability and Social Change at Windsor Law.

Professor Jacobs recently held the Fulbright Visiting Research Chair in Canadian Studies at the University of California, Berkeley, and, while holding this Chair, completed the first stage of a multi-year research study on disability rights and administrative law regulation. Her earlier qualitative research on administrative justice has explored meanings of the concept of "tribunal independence" within Canadian access to information and privacy commissions, and examined the effectiveness of ombuds-officer oversight for regulating access to information. Among other publications, she has co-edited a book on comparative administrative process, *The Nature of Inquisitorial Processes in Administrative Regimes: Global Perspectives* (Surrey, UK: Ashgate, 2013) (with Sasha Baglay).

Dr Jacobs' scholarship aims to bridge the gap between public law jurisprudence and public law realities through empirical inquiry. She is particularly interested in the ways in which ethnography, legal anthropology, and examinations of the intersection of law norms and informal order serve to give insight into the on-the-ground work of administrative bodies.

Outside of the university, Dr Jacobs has held public appointments as a member of the Advisory Council to the Ontario Minister responsible for the *Accessibility for Ontarians with Disabilities Act, 2005*, and as a part-time member of the Human Rights Tribunal of Ontario between 2005 and 2010. She is active in the Canadian Institute for the Administration of Justice, where she sits on its Administrative Tribunals Committee, and has served on the Board of Directors of the Income Security Advocacy Centre.

Justice Freya Kristjanson
Online chapter: Advocacy Before Administrative Tribunals, <www.emond.ca/adminlaw3e>.

Justice Freya Kristjanson was appointed to the Ontario Superior Court of Justice, Toronto Region, in June 2016. Prior to her appointment, Justice Kristjanson practiced administrative and civil litigation. In December 2016 the Society of Ontario Adjudicators and Regulators awarded Justice Kristjanson the SOAR Medal for her outstanding contributions to the Ontario administrative justice community.

Mary Liston

Mary Liston, BA (Western), MA (York), PhD (Toronto), Postdoctoral Fellowship in Law and Ethics (Toronto) LLB (Toronto), Peter A Allard School of Law, University of British Columbia. Professor Liston's research focuses on advanced and comparative public law, Canadian administrative law, Aboriginal administrative law, theories of the rule of law, and law and literature. Her work has been cited by the Supreme Court of Canada. She is a co-author along with Craig Forcese, Adam Dodek, Philip Bryden, Peter Carver, Richard Haigh, and Constance MacIntosh of *Public Law: Cases, Commentary and Analysis*, 3rd ed (Toronto: Emond, 2015). Her publications are available at: http://ssrn.com/author=91545.

Audrey Macklin

Audrey Macklin is the director of the Centre for Criminology and Sociolegal Studies, Professor of Law and Chair in Human Rights at University of Toronto. Professor Macklin also served as a member of Canada's Immigration and Refugee Board from 1994 to 1996. Her research and writing interests include transnational migration, citizenship, administrative law and business and human rights. She is co-author of *Immigration and Refugee Law: Cases, Materials, and Commentary*, 2nd ed (Toronto: Emond, 2015) and *The Governance Gap: Extractive Industries, Human Rights and the Home State Advantage* (London: Routledge, 2014).

Leslie McIntosh

Online chapter: Advocacy Before Administrative Tribunals, <www.emond.ca/adminlaw3e>.

Leslie McIntosh, BA (University of Toronto, 1974), LLB (University of Western Ontario, 1977), LLM in administrative law (Osgoode Hall Law School, 2003), is an adjunct professor of Administrative Law at Osgoode Hall Law School. Leslie was called to the Bar of Ontario and started her career with the Ontario Ministry of the Attorney General in 1979. Initially, she was seconded to the Ministry of Community and Social Services, where she appeared before a broad range of administrative tribunals. In 1982, she transferred to the Crown Law Office, Civil, of the Ministry of the Attorney General, where she was subsequently appointed General Counsel. She retired from the public service in 2011. Her practice consisted mainly of appellate work in the Supreme Court of Canada, the Court of Appeal, and the Divisional Court in the areas of civil litigation and administrative law. She was counsel for the Province of Ontario at the Inquiry into the Actions of Canadian Officials in Relation to Maher Arar, and is counsel in the SARS actions. From 2007 to 2011, Leslie was an adjunct professor of Administrative Law at the University of Toronto Law School. She is the author of numerous articles and publications, and a regular speaker at the Ontario Bar Association and other continuing legal education events.

Naiomi Metallic

BA (Dalhousie), LLB (Dalhousie), LLL (Ottawa) and LLM (Osgoode), is an associate professor at the Schulich School of Law at Dalhousie University, where she holds the Chancellor's Chair in Aboriginal Law and Policy. She was a law clerk for the Honourable Michel Bastarache at the Supreme Court of Canada, and authored a new chapter on Aboriginal language rights in his text *Les Droit Linguistiques au Canada*, 3rd ed (Thomson Reuters, 2013). After articling, Naiomi practised law for nearly a decade with Burchells LLP, in Halifax, and was an active member of the firm's Aboriginal Law practice group, appearing before the courts of Nova Scotia, New

Brunswick and the Federal courts for First Nations clients. She has been named on the Best Lawyer in Canada list in Aboriginal law since 2015. As an emerging legal scholar, she is most interested in writing about how the law can be harnessed to promote the well-being of Indigenous peoples in Canada and conveying this information in accessible ways.

Alexander Pless

Alexander Pless, BA Hon, BCL/LLB (McGill), MPA (Harvard), is General Counsel at Canada's Department of Justice, National Litigation Sector. He practices constitutional law, administrative law, Crown liability, and national security matters. He teaches constitutional law, administrative process, and judicial review of administrative action at McGill University. His writing and academic interests include all of these areas. He is a member of the Quebec bar and has acted for the Attorney General of Canada before all levels of court in Canada.

Janna Promislow

Janna Promislow, BA (Alberta), LLB (Victoria), LLM (York), PhD (York), is an associate professor at Thompson Rivers University, Faculty of Law. Before her appointment at Thompson Rivers University, Janna clerked with the Law Courts of Alberta, practised law with Davis & Company in the Northwest Territories, and served as a policy advisor for the Government of Ontario on consultation with Aboriginal communities. Janna's teaching and research interests encompass constitutional and administrative law, Aboriginal law, colonial legal history, indigenous–settler relations, and legal pluralism. She has published on the historical development of intersocietal law between Indigenous and European fur traders, treaty relationships and interpretation, and Aboriginal administrative law.

Lorne Sossin

Lorne Sossin, BA (McGill), MA (Exeter), PhD (Toronto), LLB (Osgoode), LLM, JSD (Columbia), of the Bar of Ontario, is a professor and Dean of Osgoode Hall Law School, York University. Before this appointment, Sossin was a professor with the Faculty of Law at the University of Toronto, where he served as Associate Dean and as the inaugural director of the Centre for the Legal Profession.

Sheila Wildeman

Sheila Wildeman, BA (University of Toronto), MA (Columbia), LLB (Dalhousie), LLM (University of Toronto) is an associate professor at Dalhousie University's Schulich School of Law. Professor Wildeman's teaching areas include public law, administrative law, and jurisprudence. Her research and writing has focused on consent and capacity law, and more broadly, on how legal subjects are constituted at the intersection of human rights, medical knowledge, and administrative law. Her publications in this regard have appeared in legal and medico-legal journals and in edited collections including *Being Relational: Reflections on Relational Theory and Health Law and Policy* (Jocelyn Downie and Jennifer Llewellyn, eds) (Vancouver: UBC Press, 2011).

Table of Cases

CHAPTER ONE

A Historical Map for Administrative Law: There Be Dragons

Colleen M Flood
Faculty of Law, University of Ottawa

Jennifer Dolling*
LLM, University of Toronto

* This version of our chapter was revised from the earlier edition by Colleen M Flood. She thanks Professor Bryan Thomas for his insightful editorial comments and Richard Schuett for his excellent research support. From the earlier edition of this chapter, we also thank Ryan MacIssac, Arthur Wilson, and Marcelo Rodriguez Ferrere for their assistance.

1

Administrative boards play an increasingly important role in our society. They regulate many aspects of our life, from beginning to end. Hospital and medical boards regulate the methods and practice of the doctors that bring us into this world. Boards regulate the licensing and the operation of morticians who attend to our mortal remains. Marketing boards regulate the farm products we eat; transport boards regulate the means and flow of our travel; energy boards control the price and distribution of the energy we use; planning boards and city councils regulate the location and types of buildings in which we live and work. In Canada, boards are a way of life. Boards and the functions they fulfill are legion.[1]

I. INTRODUCTION

If you are a student, you may be somewhat hazy about what administrative law is and its relationship to other areas of law—for example, constitutional law and private law. You may also have little sense of the relevance of administrative law to your future clients or to Canadian society. If you are an expert in your field, but new to administrative law, you may find that familiar words like "fairness" and "reasonableness" take on new and sometimes unfamiliar meanings in the administrative law context. In this introduction, we hope to give you a framework for approaching administrative law that will guide you through the other chapters of this text, representing a collaboration of leading scholars and teachers across Canada. As the text unfolds, you will see that we stress the importance of administrative decision-making in the lives of Canadians, the endless variety of administrative decision-making, and the relationship of administrative decision-making to public policy. In what follows, we attempt to help guide you in your study of administrative law by:

1. providing a brief history in Canada of both the administrative state and administrative law;
2. highlighting some of the big themes and contests that have arisen over the course of history that have rendered administrative law an area still in flux;
3. illustrating further the history of administrative law by discussing the role of remedies over time and the constitutional foundation for judicial review on the part of section 96 courts, which are provincial superior courts that have been found to have inherent jurisdiction to review administrative decision-making;
4. providing a high-level overview of the major parts of this text—namely, procedural and substantive review; and
5. outlining two case studies, concerning deportations and pipeline approvals, that will be referred to in subsequent chapters.

As a student, you may be taking administrative law because it is compulsory or because it is viewed as a core course whose absence from your transcript will be suspicious when you enter the job market. You may not be approaching the course eagerly, having heard, perhaps, that it is complex, dull, and tedious. With respect to complexity, administrative law is guilty as charged. Much of administrative law—particularly substantive review—is still in flux, which can be frustrating for a student looking for clear-cut answers, not endless puzzles and riddles (indeed, hence the title "There Be Dragons"). But administrative law is certainly

---

1   *Newfoundland Telephone Co v Newfoundland (Board of Commissioners of Public Utilities)*, [1992] 1 SCR 623 at 635-36.

anything but dull and tedious—it is effervescent—and the tensions and puzzles that arise go to the very heart of different views on the part of judges about what amounts to good governance and how governments, the executive, those empowered to act on the part of government, and courts should function together. Part of the problem with the image of administrative law (or "admin law" as most of you will start calling it) is its name— "administration" sounds bureaucratic and boring. A far better name for this course would be "the citizen and the state," "law for ordinary people," or "public justice." Most people will never see the inside of a courtroom, but they will be affected in a multitude of ways by decisions of administrative bodies of a seemingly endless variety.

A. A Brief Primer on the Canadian State

Before delving into the history of administrative law, it may be helpful for you to briefly review how the Canadian state is organized, as later chapters will often reference the three branches of government. As Laverne Jacobs notes in Chapter 7 of this volume, "[p]ortrayed in artistic terms, the administrative state is a pastiche: It is made up of a plurality of structures and decision-making methods, stemming from the legislature, the executive, and administrative bodies themselves." So it is important at the outset to firmly grasp the roles played by these different branches.

As you know, the legislative branch is responsible for making rules and legislation, but also regularly passes legislation that delegates powers to the executive branch.[2] This perhaps is where your knowledge becomes foggier, as the executive branch, responsible for administering and enforcing legislation, includes the Crown (represented by the governor general), the governor in council (the prime minister and Cabinet, advising the governor general),[3] and ministers delegated executive powers by the legislature to make decisions. The executive branch also includes the plethora of independent boards and tribunals of all shapes and sizes, such as Alberta's Energy and Utilities Board, the National Energy Board, the Competition Tribunal, the Immigration and Refugee Board, and so on. Where the executive branch is vested with powers in a given domain, they can enact subordinate legislation (i.e., rules and regulations) without the usual parliamentary scrutiny. Acts that delegate rule-making powers in this way are variously called enabling acts, empowering acts, or home statutes. Lastly, the judicial branch is made up of various

---

2 David Phillip Jones & Anne S de Villars, *Principles of Administrative Law*, 5th ed (Toronto: Carswell, 2009) at 85-97.

3 It should be noted that the governor in council acts on advice of the Privy Council and has been used interchangeably with Cabinet. In practice, governor in council decisions require only the prime minister and Cabinet. The Cabinet includes the prime minister and ministers appointed to policy portfolios. The Privy Council includes Cabinet ministers, former Cabinet ministers, the Chief Justice of the Supreme Court, former chief justices, former speakers of the House of Commons and the Senate, former governors general, and distinguished Canadians. See e.g. Canada, *House of Commons Procedure and Practice*, 2nd ed (House of Commons, 2009). online: <http://www.ourcommons.ca/procedure-book-livre/Document. aspx?sbdid=5328c93e-9ddb-4ae5-b9ba-059234896bd0&Language=E&Mode=1>. See also the Government of Canada's website on governor in council appointments: <https://www.appointments-nominations.gc.ca/prsnt.asp?menu=2&page=gicIntro&lang=eng>. See also the Government of Canada's "Guide to Making Federal Acts and Regulations: Part 3—Making Regulations": <http://www. pco-bcp.gc.ca/index.asp?lang=eng&page=information&sub=publications&doc=legislation/part3-eng. htm>.

courts. The judicial branch is responsible for ensuring that laws are upheld, and determining whether laws have been contravened.[4]

The separation of powers between these branches is not always obvious or airtight. Notably, administrative bodies exist *within* the executive branch—in the form of tribunals, commissions, committees, boards, and so on—that are charged with implementing the legislature's directives as set out in their enabling acts. Typically, these administrative bodies act at arm's length, meaning that they are independent of Cabinet and the legislature, and can make decisions independent of ministers or Cabinet, but are still only empowered to the extent allowed by their governing legislation and must adhere to their designated roles.[5] These bodies often play a quasi-judicial and/or quasi-legislative role, creating, interpreting, and applying laws and regulations in particular cases. A key question in administrative law concerns the degree of deference owed by courts to these court-like creatures of the executive branch.[6] But, keep in mind that the courts may also review ministerial actions and the actions of other actors in the executive branch to make sure that they act only within the scope of their delegated authority.

To get a sense of the enormous variety of administrative decision-making and, in particular, the various independent boards and tribunals and their role in your day-to-day life, take a look at the examples listed in the Appendix to this text and, if possible, see an administrative board or tribunal in action. This will help you get a far better understanding of the world of administrative decision-making than is possible from reading court judgments alone, and of the extent to which our everyday lives are regulated by the administrative state and the relevance of administrative law. Whether we know it or not, we all become enmeshed with the administrative state—and thus administrative law—at some point in our lives.

As you come to grips with the breadth of this topic, reflect as well on the wide range of tools available to the administrative state, as it pursues its policy objectives, which include rule-making, licensing regimes, investigatory and disciplinary processes, tax incentives, adjudication, audits, and so on. These diverse mechanisms can be helpfully arrayed along a spectrum from "soft" to "hard" regulatory interventions. Consider, for example, tobacco regulations, which range from the "nudge" of health warnings on cigarette packs, to the incentive-based tool of "sin taxes," to the imposition of criminal sanctions on those caught selling cigarettes to minors. The tools or interventions chosen by the administrative state in a given policy area will, one hopes, evolve through trial and error, and by learning from the successes and failures of comparator countries. It is often claimed that the administrative state has evolved in recent decades, away from reliance on "command and control" tools, and toward flexible, market-based, or self-regulatory approaches. Whether this move toward so-called new governance represents a paradigm shift, or simply a change of emphasis is open to debate.

---

4   Canada, *House of Commons Procedure and Practice, supra* note 3, ch 2.

5   Assistant Secretary to the Cabinet Machinery of Government Privy Council Office, "Public Sector Organizations," in *Guide Book for Heads of Agencies: Operations, Structures and Responsibilities of the Federal Government* at 8-9, online: <http://www.pco-bcp.gc.ca/docs/information/publications/guide2/docs/guide-eng.pdf>.

6   As Mary Liston discusses in Chapter 4, there is an ongoing contest as to the division of power between the legislature and the courts and as a consequence the balance between defence and oversight of administrative decision-making is also an ongoing contest.

PART 1: THE ORIGINS OF ADMINISTRATIVE LAW

II. THE BEGINNINGS OF ADMINISTRATIVE LAW

Some of the complexities and flux we find in administrative law jurisprudence may be con-nected to its relative newness as a field of study. Today, "[w]e are only three generations re-moved from the great British constitutional authority, AV Dicey, who could assert that "[t]he words 'administrative law' … are unknown to English judges and counsel, and are in them-selves hardly intelligible without further explanation."[7] Mike Taggart noted that the first book in Britain with the words "administrative law" in the title did not appear until 1928, and the first comprehensive textbook on the topic was published as late as 1959. In Canada, it took longer still.[8] Notwithstanding this late start, Canadian administrative law has come a long way since Dicey uttered those words. To understand administrative law, it is helpful to know something about that history[9]—both the legal context and the "parallel growth of government agencies and independent agencies."[10] So we will start with explaining the rise of the Canadian administrative state throughout the 19th and 20th centuries. Note that, in doing so, we are relying heavily on the work of others and are synthesizing their interpreta-tion of the primary material.

III. THE CONSTITUTION

Forsey notes that, by the time of Confederation in 1867, responsible government had been operating in most of what is now central and eastern Canada for almost 20 years.[11] As such, in drafting the Constitution, the architects of Confederation simply continued the system that was already working.[12] This meant responsible government: formal executive authority vested in the Queen (and exercisable by her representative, the governor general), "a cabinet responsible to the House of Commons, and the House of Commons answerable to the people."[13]

The Canadian Constitution today "is a collection of 25 primary documents outlined in the *Constitution Act, 1982*"[14] including, of course, the *Constitution Act, 1867*,[15] which brought Canada into existence.[16] However, the formal written Constitution "is only part of our whole

---

7   Law Reform Commission of Canada, Working Paper 25: *Independent Administrative Agencies* (Ottawa: Minister of Supply and Services Canada, 1980) at 1, online: <http://www.lareau-legal.ca/LRCWP25.pdf> [LRC], citing AV Dicey, *An Introduction to the Study of the Law of the Constitution*, 7th ed (1908) at 330.

8   Michael Taggart, "Prolegomenon to an Intellectual History of Administrative Law in the Twentieth Century: The Case of John Willis and Canadian Administrative Law" (2005) 43 Osgoode Hall LJ 223 at 228-29 [Taggart, "John Willis"].

9   LRC, *supra* note 7 at 17.

10 *Ibid* at 18.

11 Eugene A Forsey, *How Canadians Govern Themselves*, 7th ed (Ottawa: Minister of Public Works and Government Services Canada, 2010) at 3, online: <https://lop.parl.ca/About/Parliament/senatoreugene-forsey/book/preface-e.html>.

12 *Ibid*.

13 *Ibid* at 1.

14 Schedule B to the *Canada Act, 1982* (UK), 1982, c 11; Forsey, *supra* note 11 at 10.

15 *Constitution Act, 1867*, 30 & 31 Vict, c 3 (UK) (consolidated with amendments) [*Constitution Act, 1867*].

16 Forsey, *supra* note 11 at 11.

working Constitution, the set of arrangements by which we govern ourselves. It is the skeleton; it is not the whole body."[17] The Constitution does not mention the basic features of Canada's system of government, those being responsible government, the national Cabinet, the bureaucracy, and political parties.[18] "The flesh, the muscles, the sinews, the nerves of our Constitution have been added by legislation, … by custom, … by judgments of the courts, … and by agreements between the federal and provincial governments."[19] Thus, the Constitution is the latticework on which the vines of the administrative state and administrative law grow. In essence, administrative law concerns the "supervision" (although this word is unduly loaded) by courts of decision-making made pursuant to statute or the royal prerogative. Administrative boards and tribunals (such as those listed in the Appendix to this text), ministers, and departmental officials have no inherent power to make decisions that affect people's lives but only those powers set out in their enabling statute. Thus, the role of the court in administrative law's outer frame is to make sure, at a minimum, that decision-makers do not step outside the boundaries of what they are legally empowered to do.

If we fast-forward for a moment to 1982, we must also acknowledge the profound impact that the *Canadian Charter of Rights and Freedoms*[20] has had on administrative decision-making through judicial review and vice versa. This topic is fully explored by Alexander Pless and Evan Fox-Decent in Chapters 6 and 13. For present purposes, the interaction between Charter rights and administrative law, both in procedural and substantive review, is a deeply complex issue that courts continue to struggle with. Nowhere is that interaction more complex and fascinating than when it intersects with the rights of Indigenous Peoples, a subject explored fulsomely by Janna Promislow and Naiomi Metallic in Chapter 3.

IV. THE EXPANSION OF FORMAL POST-COLONIAL GOVERNMENT

A. The Early Years: 1850-1913

In the decades preceding and following Confederation, "the federal government and its administrators were preoccupied with the extension and protection of the frontier and the development of a national economy."[21] Then, efforts to connect Canada through its nascent railway industry first revealed the need for new decision-making structures.[22] Well before Confederation, the *Railway Act* of 1851 was enacted, from which sprang what became known as the Railway Committee of the Privy Council.[23] At this time, the committee was composed of Cabinet ministers, but the early 1870s brought about pressure for change.[24] "In a period of economic recession, many farmers and merchants blamed the railways for charging excessive or discriminatory rates and blamed the government for doing nothing about

---

17   *Ibid* at 10.

18   *Ibid.*

19   *Ibid.*

20   Part I of the *Constitution Act, 1982*, being Schedule B to the *Canada Act 1982* (UK), 1982, c 11.

21   LRC, *supra* note 7 at 20-21.

22   *Ibid* at 21.

23   *Ibid.*

24   Bernard J Hibbitts, "A Change of Mind: The Supreme Court and the Board of Railway Commissioners, 1903-1929" (1991) 41 UTLJ 60 at 62.

the problem."[25] These concerns drove calls to establish an apolitical regulatory tribunal, independent from Cabinet, modelled along the lines of the English Railway Commission, with the hope that it would do a better job of setting prices on a non-discriminatory basis.[26]

The idea of creating a railway regulatory body or commission *independent* from Cabinet was, however, rejected by the Galt Royal Commission Report of 1888,[27] which felt that the concept of an independent body responsible for decision-making was inconsistent with the Canadian system of responsible government and represented "a rejection of the legislature as the locus of the regulatory enterprise"[28] and "a rejection of the common law courts as legitimate arbiters of regulatory issues."[29] As we will see throughout this text, these kinds of concerns are still present in modern-day debates over the legitimacy of administrative decision-making. In the late 1800s, "the tradition of patronage in the public service of the day gave rise to fears that designated departmental personnel might have inappropriate backgrounds or lack the technical capacity to deal with the kinds of issues being raised in the context of railway regulation."[30] Nonetheless, the Galt Commission recognized the limitations of Cabinet ministers as regulators—Railway Committee members served part-time only, were based in Ottawa, lacked expertise, and were vulnerable to political pressure.[31]

It would be another decade before serious consideration was given to the concept of a non-elected, full-time body outside any departmental structure to regulate railways.[32] Sir Wilfrid Laurier appointed a one-man commission of inquiry, SJ McLean, to legitimize the notion of an independent railway board.[33] McLean's reports, tabled in 1902, concluded that the Railway Committee was "over-worked and ill-equipped to deal with its responsibilities"[34] and recommended the appointment of an independent commission to take its place.[35] And so came the *Railway Act*[36] of 1903, which established a new administrative agency, the Board of Railway Commissioners,[37] followed six years later by the International Joint Commission (IJC) with the United States to handle boundary waters issues.[38] By appointing experts to decide rather than merely to advise,[39] the IJC "marked a further important step in establishing a framework for government regulation in Canada."[40] In 1912, "the *Canada Grain Act*[41] established a Board of Grain Commissioners charged with the administration of

---

25 *Ibid* at n 17.
26 *Ibid*.
27 LRC, *supra* note 7 at 21.
28 Hibbitts, *supra* note 24.
29 *Ibid*.
30 LRC, *supra* note 7 at 22.
31 *Ibid* at 21.
32 *Ibid* at 22.
33 Hibbitts, *supra* note 24 at 64.
34 *Ibid* at 64-65; McLean's two reports were titled "Railway Commissions, Railway Rate Grievances," and "Regulative Legislation."
35 LRC, *supra* note 7 at 22.
36 SC 1903, 3 E VII, c 58.
37 LRC, *supra* note 7 at 23.
38 *Ibid*.
39 *Ibid* at 24.
40 *Ibid* at 23.
41 SC 1912, c 27.

terminal warehouses and generally all matters related to the inspection, weighing, trading and storage of grain."[42] Relevant Supreme Court cases at this time focused on issues of jurisdiction—for example, in *Montreal Street Railway v Montreal Terminal Railway*,[43] the court upheld a challenge to the jurisdiction of the Board of Railway Commissioners when the board attempted to make orders that contradicted provincial law, and in *Re Canadian Northern Railway*,[44] when the board made a general order regarding the erection of fences to prevent livestock from straying onto the tracks.

Inquiries, the modern versions of which are discussed by Peter Carver, "Getting the Story Out: Accountability and the Law of Public Inquiries" (available on the companion website to this text at <www.emond.ca/adminlaw3e>), also formed part of Canada's early administrative law history. *An Act Respecting Inquiries Concerning Public Matters*, given Royal Assent in 1868, gave the governor in council the power to summon witnesses to testify under oath and produce whatever documents were requested by the commissioners when the governor in council deemed it "expedient to cause inquiry to be made into and concerning any matter connected with the good government of Canada, or the conduct of any part of the public business thereof."[45] Since 1868, by our count, there have been 370 commissions of inquiry at the federal level alone.[46]

Without a doubt, this early period of administrative action was an exciting period in Canada's history, when major economic and societal changes were occurring.[47] "By 1900, the major economic and political problems that had precipitated Confederation had been resolved—the frontiers had been established and guaranteed, transportation and communication links had been forged, and our national political and legal institutions had been established."[48] The first part of the 20th century saw "intense economic development, stimulated by waves of immigration [and] integration with the American economy."[49] Immigration rose from 49,000 in 1901 to 402,000 in 1913.[50] Then came the First World War.[51]

B. The First World War and the Growth of Economic Controls

The commencement of the First World War and Canada's commitment to the war effort brought about increased intervention in the economy by the federal government, including rent and price controls and the prevention of hoarding.[52] As its reach expanded, it became logistically impossible for the government to centrally administer all aspects and so arose the advent of administrative agencies such as the Board of Grain Supervisors (succeeded in

---

42   LRC, *supra* note 7 at 24.
43   [1905] 36 SCR 369.
44   [1909] 42 SCR 443.
45   Law Reform Commission of Canada, Working Paper 17, *Commissions of Inquiry: A New Act* (Law Reform Commission of Canada, Ottawa: 1977) at 7.
46   We calculated this using statistics provided by the Privy Council Office, online: Government of Canada <http://www.pco-bcp.gc.ca/index.asp?lang=eng&page=information&sub=commissions&doc=archives/comm-eng.htm>.
47   LRC, *supra* note 7 at 24.
48   *Ibid.*
49   *Ibid.*
50   *Ibid.*
51   *Ibid.*
52   *Ibid.*

1919 by the Canadian Wheat Board), the Food Control Board (later called the Canada Food Board), the Wage Trade Board, and the municipal Fair Price Committees.[53] The government also made major inroads in health and welfare, with a Board of Pension Commissioners established in 1916, the Department of Soldiers' Civil Re-establishment in 1918, and the Department of Health in 1919.[54] The rationale for the creation of these new administrative agencies was not clearly articulated, but it was likely a combination of the need for arm's-length decision-making and specialized expertise and/or simply that the volume and complexity of matters before government required separate attention and leadership.

The administrative state was professionalized as it grew. The federal civil service was placed on more of a professional footing[55] with the *Civil Service Act* of 1918,[56] and "the Civil Service Commission assumed responsibility to pass upon the qualifications of candidates for admission to and classification, transfer, and promotion in the civil service."[57] "To finance the expansion of the public sector, direct taxation was introduced [by way of] an excess business profits tax in 1916 and an income tax on individuals and corporations in 1917,"[58] with income tax "providing guaranteed means for [future] bureaucratic growth."[59]

Thus, Canada emerged from the First World War in 1918 "profoundly changed";[60] one consequence of the war was a massive expansion of government and a corresponding "increase in the extent of governmental intervention in the daily economic life of [the citizenry]."[61] This new era of government set the stage for subsequent contests of the appropriate role for courts in reviewing delegated decision-making, because such decisions were not subject to the sunlight of scrutiny through the legislative process—a topic we return to below in Section V, "Conflicts and Tensions in Theories of Administrative Law and the Source of the Dragons."

C. The Inter-War Period

From the period following the First World War until the Depression, the federal government was more preoccupied with war debts and issues related to its absorption of the railways than with expanding its scope of regulatory control.[62] However, with the Depression of the 1930s came renewed federal legislative efforts[63] and "massive changes in regulation, both in degree and in kind."[64] The turbulent 1930s witnessed skyrocketing unemployment rates and plummeting international trade: "The federal government intervened with regulatory measures in several fields including agriculture, culture, finance, transportation, and social

---

53 *Ibid* at 24-25.

54 *Ibid* at 25.

55 *Ibid*.

56 SC 1918, c 12.

57 LRC, *supra* note 7 at 25.

58 *Ibid*.

59 *Ibid*.

60 Bernard J Hibbitts, "A Bridle for Leviathan: The Supreme Court and the Board of Commerce" (1989) 21 Ottawa L Rev 65 at 67.

61 *Ibid*.

62 LRC, *supra* note 7 at 26-27.

63 *Ibid* at 27.

64 RCB Risk, "Lawyers, Courts, and the Rise of the Regulatory State" (1985) 9 Dal LJ 31 at 39-40 [Risk, "Rise of the Regulatory State"].

security";[65] "In 1931 the Tariff Board was created as an independent agency to carry out advisory and quasi-judicial functions";[66] The Canadian Broadcasting Corporation was created in 1932,[67] and the Ontario Securities Commission followed a year later.[68] In 1935, the Canadian Wheat Board was given responsibility for marketing wheat in interprovincial and export trade[69] and, in the same year, legislation equivalent to the American "New Deal" was enacted, resulting in a number of new regulatory and adjudicatory agencies.[70] As legal historian Blake Brown notes, the consistent theme of judicial review cases at this time reflected an inseparable intertwining of constitutional and administrative law history in Canada: challenges were against the jurisdiction of these administrative boards on constitutional grounds.[71] They were simple jurisdiction arguments, challenging either on the basis of the strict construction of federal legislation or on the basis of an alleged conflict with the then-named *British North America Act 1867*.[72] For example, in *British Columbia Electric Railway v Canadian National Railway*,[73] a successful challenge prevented the Board of Railway Commissioners from exercising jurisdiction over a foreign-owned BC rail operator (the board's jurisdiction was found to be limited to railways provided for by federal legislation). Similarly, in *Halifax (City) v Halifax Harbour Commissioners*, the court prevented a provincial act from taxing federal property and the province from taking action against a federal agency under that act.[74]

D. The Second World War and Its Aftermath

During the Second World War, the federal government again took more direct control of the economy.[75] However, unlike most of the agencies created in the First World War, many of the agencies created during the Second World War continued to operate after the war's end[76] and, in the post-war period, governmental organizations proliferated,[77] with the creation of specialized bodies, such as the Atomic Energy Control Board (1946).[78] It was during this period that welfare programs were developed or significantly expanded; at the federal level, the following all came into effect: the Family Allowances Plan (1944), the Old Age Security Pension (1952), and

---

65 Jamie Benidickson, "From Empire Ontario to California North: Law and Legal Institutions in Twentieth-Century Ontario" in DeLloyd J Guth & W Wesley Pue, *Canada's Legal Inheritances* (Winnipeg: Canadian Legal History Project, 2001) 620 at 636.

66 LRC, *supra* note 7 at 28.

67 *Ibid*.

68 Risk, "Rise of the Regulatory State," *supra* note 64 at 636.

69 LRC, *supra* note 7 at 28.

70 *Ibid* at 27.

71 R Blake Brown, "The Canadian Legal Realists and Administrative Law Scholarship, 1930-1941" (2000) 9 Dal J Leg Stud 36 at 38.

72 *Constitution Act, 1867*.

73 [1932] SCR 161 (*sub nom In re Orders Nos. 42808 and 44417 of the Board of Railway Commissioners for Canada / British Columbia Electric Ry Co, Ltd v Canadian National Ry Co*).

74 [1935] SCR 215, applied in *Oatway v Canada Wheat Board*, [1945] SCR 204.

75 LRC, *supra* note 7 at 28.

76 *Ibid* at 29.

77 *Ibid*.

78 *Ibid*.

the Canada Pension Plan (1965).[79] With the proliferation of administrative agencies, "many people [began] to ask if what we [had] planted [was] a garden or a jungle."[80]

Marketing boards also spread across Canada during the economic booms of 1946-1949 and during the Korean War.[81] In 1952, in *PEI Potato Marketing Board v Willis*,[82] the Supreme Court held "that regulatory power within the jurisdiction of the federal government could validly be delegated to boards created and operated by a provincial government, and vice versa."[83] This, in turn, spurred the establishment of yet more independent administrative agencies.[84]

The 1960s and 1970s witnessed further "rapid growth in the public sector and an increasing complexity in the matters dealt with by government"[85] and "the rise of a large number of semi-independent boards, commissions, agencies, tribunals, and Crown corporations."[86] As we shall see, at this time, some profound changes arose in the approach to administrative law with, for example, the landmark case of *CUPE*[87] and increasing self-reflection on the part of courts as to their appropriate role in reviewing administrative action.

E. A Closer Look at the Reasons for the Expansion of Government Activity

As we can see from the above, the emergence of a large and complex administrative state in Canada was not created according to a blueprint.[88] Rather, it evolved organically in response to problems as they arose over the years.[89] The choice of certain types of bodies to perform particular functions appears to have been ad hoc, with "[t]he selection of a non-departmental rather than a departmental body to regulate, or an administrative tribunal rather than the courts to adjudicate, ... hav[ing] been influenced ... by the exigencies of the case and existing institutional precedents rather than by an overall plan."[90] But some of the reasons cited for devolving responsibility to independent, arm's-length agencies are still important today and include:[91]

1. the desire to depoliticize certain decisions;
2. the need for greater specialization and technical or subject-matter expertise to make decisions than is possible or feasible to collect and retain within central government;
3. a reluctance to enmesh courts in matters not suitable to judicial review because of their specific nature or the volume of decisions that have to be made; and

---

79 *Ibid* at 30.
80 Robert Reid, "Administrative Tribunals Under Review in Ontario" (1958) 1:4 Can Bar J 57.
81 LRC, *supra* note 7 at 29.
82 [1952] 2 SCR 392, 4 DLR (2d) 146.
83 LRC, *supra* note 7 at 30.
84 *Ibid*.
85 Law Reform Commission of Canada, Study Paper, *Parliament and Administrative Agencies* (Ottawa: Law Reform Commission of Canada, 1982) at 5.
86 *Ibid*.
87 *CUPE v NB Liquor Corporation*, [1979] 2 SCR 227 [*CUPE*].
88 LRC, *supra* note 7 at 17.
89 *Ibid*.
90 *Ibid*.
91 Law Reform Commission of Canada, *Independent Administrative Agencies*, Report 26 (Ottawa: Law Reform Commission of Canada, 1985) at 5.

4. because the persons subjected to decision-making viewed the courts as antithetical or unhelpful to achieving their aspirations (for example, labour unions).

Notwithstanding the good and pragmatic reasons for the rise of the administrative state, concern arose about the proliferation of administrative agencies and the legitimacy of their decisions. This was due to the significant impact a decision could have on an individual and the fact that boards and tribunals are not publicly accountable in the same way that government is when, for example, passing legislation.

V. CONFLICTS AND TENSIONS IN THEORIES OF ADMINISTRATIVE LAW AND THE SOURCE OF THE DRAGONS

In the following section, we canvass in broad strokes some of the ideas that shaped administrative law over the 20th century to help us understand how we got to where we are, where these ideas may be taking us, and how the history of these ideas will affect the development of administrative law into the future.[92]

During the late 19th century, English legal thought was the predominant model for Canadian lawyers.[93] English, and consequently Canadian, legal professionals were affected by the rise of legal formalism, a concept characterized by adherence to four principles. First, legal formalists held the "belief that law was composed of 'scientific' legal rules that could be discovered by a careful study and application of legal principles."[94] Second, as Blake Brown has identified, they believed that these rules were best discerned by a close examination of previously decided cases.[95] Third, they thought legal documents spoke for themselves, so that judges could interpret the meaning of legal documents by simply looking for the "plain meaning" of the words.[96] Last, judges could all but ignore the policy implications of their impartial rulings.[97] Under legal formalism, "decisions were to be made on the basis of scientific legal doctrines" with little regard for equitable outcomes.[98] The leader of legal formalism was AV Dicey, a law professor at the University of Oxford in the late 19th century, who "emphasized individual rights and the role of courts as the upholder of these rights."[99] In Chapter 4, Mary Liston provides a thorough discussion of Dicey and the rule of law and other competing theorists.[100]

The expanding welfare state described earlier met resistance on the part of the English legal establishment.[101] The best-known opponent in the common law world of "the pretensions and encroachments of bureaucracy"[102] was Lord Hewart, the Lord Chief Justice

---

92 See Taggart, "John Willis," *supra* note 8 at 233.

93 RCB Risk, "Canadian Law Teachers in the 1930s: 'When the World Was Turned Upside Down'" (2004) 27 Dal LJ 1 at 8 [Risk, "Canadian Law Teachers"].

94 Blake Brown, *supra* note 71 at 39.

95 *Ibid.*

96 *Ibid.*

97 *Ibid.*

98 *Ibid.*

99 *Ibid.*

100 See also *Administrative Law Today: Culture, Ideas, Institutions, Processes, Values: Essays in Honour of John Willis* [special issue] (2005) 55:3 UTLJ.

101 RCB Risk, "My Continuing Legal Education" (2005) 55:3 UTLJ 313 at 324 [Risk, "My Continuing Legal Education"].

102 Lord Hewart of Bury, *The New Despotism* (London: Ernest Benn, 1929).

of England and Wales, whose 1929 book *The New Despotism* "issued a clarion call to lawyers around the common law world to rise up and protect the rule of law against the executive and the bureaucracy, which were taking liberties with the citizens' liberties."[103] For Lord Hewart, "despotism" meant placing government departments and agencies "above the Sovereignty of Parliament and beyond the jurisdiction of the Courts" and he was dismayed at the delegation by Parliament of legislative powers to government departments and administrative agencies.[104]

In Canada, the English concept of legal formalism was virtually the only lens through which to review administrative action from the late 19th century to the late 1920s.[105] Although Canadian courts in the late 19th century had interpreted the Constitution to permit the existence of administrative bodies, by the turn of the century, formalism had begun to affect constitutional interpretation such that administrative decisions were increasingly challenged as being outside the jurisdiction (that is, *ultra vires*) of the federal or provincial legislature that created the agency in question.[106] The underlying theme in these challenges was a general concern and resistance toward the increasing size of the administrative state.[107] Legal formalists argued that tribunals had the effect of reducing the primacy of courts and were less likely to protect individual rights because they employed procedures different from those used in the courts.[108] Formalists also complained that "[t]ribunals were free to disregard precedents and interpreted statutes by explicitly considering policy ramifications."[109]

Challenges to the formalist mode of thinking began in the United States in the late 19th century and grew stronger early in the 20th century.[110] Shaped by pragmatism, the social sciences, political turmoil, and calls for a new social order, a new group of scholars named the "Progressives" emerged. Two major figures in this group were Roscoe Pound and Benjamin Cardozo. Pound argued that "common law reasoning should be instrumental and seek social welfare,"[111] while Cardozo argued that "[t]he final cause of law is the welfare of society."[112]

Despite this new line of thinking more supportive of administrative institutions and the progressive goals they aspired toward, many Canadian lawyers and judges remained unenthused[113] and continued to be "clouded by their reverence for tradition and their romanticized perception of the English system."[114] Concerned about the erosion of traditional legal principles, they challenged the growth of government regulation and the increasing use of

---

103 Michael Taggart, "From 'Parliamentary Powers' to Privatization: The Chequered History of Delegated Legislation in the Twentieth Century" (2005) 55(3) UTLJ 575 at 576 [Taggart, "Chequered History"].

104 *Ibid* at 576, citing Hewart, *supra* note 102 at 14.

105 Risk "Canadian Law Teachers," *supra* note 93 at 9.

106 Blake Brown, *supra* note 71 at 38 and 40.

107 *Ibid* at 40.

108 *Ibid* at 39.

109 *Ibid*.

110 Risk, "Canadian Law Teachers," *supra* note 93 at 10.

111 *Ibid*.

112 Benjamin N Cardozo, *The Nature of Judicial Process* (New Haven, CT: Yale University Press, 1921) at 66, cited in Risk, "Canadian Law Teachers in the 1930s," *supra* note 93 at 10.

113 Benidickson, *supra* note 65 at 633.

114 CI Kyer & JE Bickenbach, *The Fiercest Debate: Cecil A Wright, the Benchers, and Legal Education in Ontario 1923-1957* (Toronto: Published for the Osgoode Society by University of Toronto Press, 1987) at 272.

administrative bodies to implement new social and economic policies.[115] In 1934, Chief Justice Mulock described tribunals as "non-judicial bod[ies], often ignorant of the law, bound by no law, free to disregard the evidence and the law, and practically at [their] own will, to dispose finally of [the citizen's] rights."[116] Many Canadian lawyers in the 1930s felt that "to deny to the individual his traditional right of access to the courts threatens to undermine the achievements of centuries."[117] They felt that "the sacred rights of individuals [were] often entrusted to the whims of officials whose main qualification [was] political loyalty."[118] Accordingly, the key complaint was that tribunals "recklessly intruded upon liberty, by mistake or through excessive zeal."[119] However, once it became clear that such tribunals were a permanent fixture, lawyers grudgingly adopted a more conciliatory tone: A 1941 special committee of the Canadian Bar Association urged its members to, simply, "under this situation ... make the best of [tribunals] that is possible."[120]

As Blake Brown identifies, in the late 1920s and, particularly, the 1930s, several Canadian legal academics began to reconceptualize the relationship between state and citizen by questioning commonly held assumptions about the law.[121] Kerry Rittich explains: "What was at stake was a choice between a laissez-faire state, whose limits were policed by a judiciary steeped in common law rights, on the one hand, and the newly emerging regulatory state, on the other."[122] These scholars were "in direct opposition to the prevailing orthodoxy of analytical legal positivism, underpinned by the political values of classical liberalism and exemplified in the work of AV Dicey."[123] Dicey would have thought that "liberty" imposed a negative obligation on government: Not to interfere with individuals and their actions, whereas these new scholars believed that liberty imposed a positive obligation on government: To provide individuals with the basic qualities of human life and thus give them the freedom to reach their potential.[124] They "embraced the [new welfare and regulatory] state and the politics it expressed,"[125] and believed that this new state came about as a result of a fundamental change in social values and demands.[126] They viewed delegated legislation as essential to the achievement of the goals of social welfarism.[127] Moreover, they "identified that the Depression was a time of change—a terrifying time, but also a time of experimentation in public law."[128] Canadian scholars Bora Laskin, John Willis, and Cecil "Caesar" Wright chose to reject the past, with respect to both its way of thinking about the law and its politics, and instead look for "new ways of thinking about the law that would be ...

---

115 Blake Brown, *supra* note 71 at 36.
116 Rt Hon Sir W Mulock, "Address of the Chief Justice of Ontario" (1934) 12 Can Bar Rev 35 at 38.
117 HG Sparling, "Editorial: Views of the Profession" (1937) 2 Sask Bar Rev 23 at 29.
118 *Ibid.*
119 Risk, *"My Continuing Legal Education," supra* note 101 at 326.
120 Benidickson, *supra* note 65 at 633, citing "Report of Special Committee on Administrative Tribunals and Law Reform" (1941) 25 CBA Proceedings 208 at 209.
121 Blake Brown, *supra* note 71 at 44.
122 Kerry Rittich, "Functionalism and Formalism: Their Latest Incarnations in Contemporary Development and Governance Debates" (2005) 55:3 UTLJ 853 at 858.
123 Martin Loughlin, "The Functionalist Style in Public Law" (2005) 55:3 UTLJ 361 at 362.
124 *Ibid* at 367.
125 Risk, "Canadian Law Teachers," *supra* note 93 at 38.
126 *Ibid* at 41.
127 Blake Brown, *supra* note 71 at 69.
128 *Ibid* at 72.

'functional' and 'realistic,' and that would serve the changing needs of modern society."[129] In doing so, they sought to escape from the basic principle that the courts alone must determine and implement the intent of the legislature.[130]

Although the above gives a taste of changing legal thought in the 1930s, no discussion of administrative law theory from this period would be complete without specific mention of John Willis. In Canada, he was "the most important proponent of the dissenting tradition"[131] and a "zealous proponent of the administrative state."[132] He wrote in an era of "continuous and often dramatic expansion of the administrative state,"[133] and was part of the generation of 1930s legal scholars who supported new instruments for achieving the public agenda.[134] Willis believed that "[i]f the state was to look after its subjects from the cradle to the grave— which was the wish of the voters,"[135] then sweeping delegations of parliamentary power to administrative tribunals was both necessary and inevitable for the regulatory or welfare state to operationalize itself.[136] He supported the establishment of commissions or "governments in miniature" to hear disputes about policy.[137] He believed that courts and legislatures were "inadequate to perform the tasks required of a government of the twentieth century"[138] and "consigned the courts to the dust heap of history, too old-fashioned and set in their ways to be willing or able to adjust to the new facts of government."[139] He argued that the development of administrative government departments should "be designed and assessed to serve current, concrete social need and not some abstract ideal."[140] Willis was a self-declared "government man,"[141] who invested a lot of energy into arguing against court intervention in administrative action so as to create a "wide discretionary latitude for bureaucrats ... to get things done."[142] Although "Willis recognized the problem of unlimited administrative discretion, [he] believed that the courts were not well suited to considering appeals from tribunals"[143] because then "the amateur is asked to upset the expert."[144] For Willis, judicial review "would always be 'sporadic' and, in any event, the judges' ignorance of policy should disqualify them from a major role."[145] Instead of having courts review administrative decisions, "Willis advocated for the creation of a special administrative review

---

129   Risk, "My Continuing Legal Education," *supra* note 101 at 313.
130   RCB Risk, "Here Be Cold and Tygers: A Map of Statutory Interpretation in Canada in the 1920s and 1930s" (2000) 63 Sask L Rev 195 at 196.
131   JM Evans, HN Janisch, David Mullan, & RCB Risk, *Administrative Law: Cases, Text, and Materials*, 5th ed (Toronto: Emond Montgomery, 2003) at 30.
132   Blake Brown, *supra* note 71 at 45.
133   David Szablowski, "John Willis and the Challenges for Public Law Scholarship in a Neoliberal Globalizing World" (2005) 55:3 UTLJ 869 at 870.
134   Roderick A Macdonald, "Call-Centre Government: For the Rule of Law, Press #" (2005) 55:3 UTLJ 449 at 454.
135   Taggart, "Chequered History," *supra* note 103 at 585.
136   *Ibid*; G Blaine Baker, "Willis on 'Cultured' Public Authorities" (2005) 55:3 UTLJ 335 at 348 [Baker, "Willis"].
137   Blake Brown, *supra* note 71 at 50.
138   J Willis, ed, *Canadian Boards at Work* (Toronto: Macmillan, 1941).
139   Taggart, "John Willis," *supra* note 8 at 248.
140   Risk, "My Continuing Legal Education," *supra* note 101 at 326.
141   Szablowski, *supra* note 133 at 870.
142   Baker, "Willis," *supra* note 136 at 335.
143   Blake Brown, *supra* note 71 at 50.
144   *Ibid* at 51.
145   Taggart, "John Willis," *supra* note 8 at 247.

court, which, like the lower tribunal, possessed specialized knowledge of the subject area within its jurisdiction."[146] He believed it important that such a body have experience of the actual exercise of policy and administrative decision-making, and thus have less of a focus on legal doctrine and judicial decision-making.

The arguments of the scholars mentioned above represented an important shift in thinking about the administrative state in Canada.[147] Indeed, they "helped undermine the traditional ways of thinking about the administrative state, and, more importantly, about the basic functioning of the law."[148] They quieted many of the fears about the growing administrative state, and in doing so, accomplished a difficult goal: "[B]y convincing Canadian lawyers that discretion existed in administrative and judicial processes, and that policy implications were inherent in any decision, these academics opened the door for future debate and scholarship in administrative law."[149] As we will discover throughout the following chapters, the tension between the appropriate role for governments, administrative agencies, and courts—and which set of decision-makers are accountable to others—is still a strongly contested area in administrative law. We will also see shifting views on the appropriateness of roles, depending on the nature of the case in question with, for example, proponents arguing for a much greater role for administrative action when it comes to progressive distribution of benefits in a welfare state or the resolution of labour disputes, but being far less comfortable with administrative action that seeks to curtail access to the courts for vulnerable individuals—for example, immigrants and refugees. Also, we will see questions about the extent to which administrative action is necessarily instrumental to a more progressive agenda and how views on this score impact on how searching a court should be as it conducts judicial review.

VI. FROM A FOCUS ON REMEDIES TO A FOCUS ON REVIEW

We now shift our focus to the question of remedies and their role in the history of administrative law; doing so illustrates not only the importance of the common law of judicial review but also the essentiality of statutory interpretation and reform to this area of law. Reflecting the importance of remedies in the story of administrative law, in Chapter 2 Cristie Ford illuminates their integral role, not only in terms of judicial review, but also in terms of administrative decision-making itself.

This issue of remedies is related to the source of power that courts may have to review. Where do courts get the power to review administrative decision-making? There are three sources of review power: original jurisdiction; right of appeal; and, most important for our purposes, courts' inherent judicial review jurisdiction. These are explained, in turn, below.

1. *Original jurisdiction:* The ordinary courts have jurisdiction over the decisions of administrative decision-makers when they are challenged by way of direct actions by a citizen in contract or tort on the ground that the state has infringed an individual's private legal right. For example, in 2004, the Ontario Court of Appeal allowed Granite

---

146 Blake Brown, *supra* note 71 at 51.
147 Risk, "Rise of the Regulatory State," *supra* note 64.
148 Blake Brown, *supra* note 71 at 72.
149 *Ibid.*

Power to sue, in part, in tort on the basis that they had the exclusive right to supply power to Gananoque, and that the government breached this right by opening up the electricity market to competition.[150]

2. *Statutory right of appeal:* Many students assume there is always a right of appeal. In fact, there is no automatic right to appeal the substance of an administrative decision to the courts. A right to appeal must be provided for in a statute. A critically important first lesson for all students of administrative law is to review the statute establishing the administrative agency and see whether any right of appeal is provided for and on what grounds.

3. *Courts' inherent judicial review jurisdiction:* Third, and most important from our perspective, the superior courts in each province (the judges appointed by the federal government) may review administrative decisions through the courts' inherent judicial review jurisdiction. The constitutional guarantee of this jurisdiction is discussed below in the context of s 96 courts.

The words "inherent jurisdiction" refer to the fact that the jurisdiction of the superior courts is normally broader than whatever may be conferred by statute. Superior courts may hear any matter unless there is a specific statute that says otherwise or grants exclusive jurisdiction to another court or tribunal. As Craig Forcese discusses in Chapter 15, superior courts have greater freedom to craft remedies and grant relief than courts created by statute, such as the federal courts. However, inherent jurisdiction is not jurisdiction for a general appeal; thus, a court cannot simply substitute its own decision for that of an agency's—it is a bit more complicated than that.

The inherent jurisdiction of our superior courts was inherited from the United Kingdom in the 16th and 17th centuries from the Royal Court in Westminster. The Royal Court reviewed the legality of decision-making by a whole host of what were then front-running administrative tribunals such as the Bridge Commission, the Poor House Commissions, and the Sewer Commission.[151] Here is where we circle back to the issue of remedies; historically, courts' inherent "supervisory" power over administrative decision-makers had to be exercised through the remedies available—if there was no appropriate remedy, then the administrative action could not be challenged. As Cristie Ford discusses in Chapter 2, the relevant remedies were known as the prerogative writs and were once tremendously important in administrative law. These prerogative writs were *certiorari* (to quash or set aside a decision), prohibition (to order a tribunal not to proceed), *mandamus* (to order the performance of a public duty), and *habeas corpus* (to order the release of the unlawfully imprisoned). These writs were used by the Royal Courts in England, and subsequently by the superior provincial courts in Canada, to ensure that administrative bodies and tribunals did not exceed their legal powers and encroach on powers or matters that were the responsibility or privilege of central government. Before the 1970s, administrative law was about trying to squeeze cases into one or more of the prerogative writs, and courts made fine distinctions about, for example, whether or not a writ would lie. There were thousands of cases dealing with these

---

150 *Granite Power Corp v Ontario*, 2004 CanLII 44786, 72 OR (3d) 194 (CA), leave to appeal to SCC dismissed [2004] SCCA No 409 at paras 37-39 [*Granite Power*].

151 Jerome J Hanus, "Certiorari and Policy-Making in English History" (1968) 12 Am J Legal Hist 63, n 2; SA de Smith, *Judicial Review of Administrative Action*, 4th ed by J Evans (London: Stevens & Sons, 1980) at 584 (Appendix 1) and 596 (Appendix 2).

fine distinctions. Determining whether an issue was a question of *vires* could be critical to the substantive outcome of the case. If an administrative decision was *intra vires*, a reviewing court could only apply one of the writs if the lower decision was so "patently unreasonable" (a term that, as Audrey Macklin and Sheila Wildeman discuss in Chapters 11 and 12, respectively, has now been abandoned, although it still exists in a number of statutes) that it caused the administrative decision-maker to lose jurisdiction.[152] Conversely, if a decision had been *ultra vires* the administrative decision-maker, the reviewing court could make an order of *certiorari*, prohibition, or *mandamus* in favour of the person challenging the decision.[153]

As discussed in the preceding section, Canadian courts reacted defensively against governments perceived as giving their jurisdiction away to administrative agencies.[154] The legislatures inserted "privative clauses" into the statutes in an attempt to stop courts from reviewing the decisions of administrative decision-makers, but the courts responded in turn by either ignoring such clauses or interpreting them in a very restrictive way[155] and squeezed as many cases as possible into the old prerogative writs.[156] In so doing, the concept of jurisdictional error became so distorted that the courts were able to review administrative decisions just like they would review a lower court decision.[157] If you did not like an administrative decision, you would argue before the courts that the administrative decision-maker had exceeded its jurisdiction: the words *"ultra vires"* became so common that their original meaning was all but lost. But change was on the way.

The McRuer Commission[158] was a watershed moment in the administrative law revolution that took place during the 1960s and 1970s.[159] It was "set up in 1964 in response to opposition criticism of a [provincial] government bill that would have conferred broad-ranging investigatory powers on the Ontario Police Commission."[160] The McRuer Commission helped to bring about a basic codification of procedures for administrative tribunals in a number of provinces.[161] For example, in 1966, the *Administrative Procedures Act*[162] was enacted in Alberta[163] and, in 1971, the *Statutory Powers Procedure Act*[164] was enacted in Ontario.[165]

McRuer also made several recommendations with respect to the scope of judicial review.[166] He wanted to extend the availability of judicial review, "in terms of both the grounds

---

152   See e.g. *Jarvis v Associated Medical Services, Inc*, [1964] SCR 497 [*Jarvis*]. The contrast between the majority and dissenting reasons in this case is particularly illustrative of the liberties that judges would take with the *vires* approach.

153   *Granite Power, supra* note 150.

154   *Ibid.*

155   *Ibid.*

156   *Ibid.*

157   I.e., on a "correctness" standard of review: Evans et al, *supra* note 131 at 698.

158   Ontario Royal Commission, *Inquiry into Civil Rights* (JC McRuer Commissioner, 1968) [McRuer Commission].

159   David J Mullan, "Willis v McRuer: A Long-Overdue Replay with the Possibility of a Penalty Shoot-Out" (2005) 55:3 UTLJ 535 at 535 [Mullan, "Willis v McRuer"].

160   *Ibid.*

161   McRuer Commission, *supra* note 158.

162   SA 1966, c 1.

163   Evans et al, *supra* note 131 at 302.

164   SO 1971, c 47.

165   Evans et al, *supra* note 131 at 302.

166   Mullan, "Willis v McRuer," *supra* note 159 at 550.

on which it [was] available and the ease with which it [could] be sought procedurally."[167] In 1971, Ontario enacted the *Judicial Review Procedure Act*,[168] which established rules for courts reviewing errors of both law and fact (Peter J Carver provides a helpful primer on this distinction in Chapter 14). For questions of law, courts could now review the decisions of any statutory authorities that determined rights and interests of an affected party.[169] For questions of fact, courts could now review the decisions of those charged with making a "statutory power of decision" on the basis of the evidence presented and facts of which they could take official notice; this meant most judicial or quasi-judicial bodies.[170] Over the next 30 years, nearly all of the provinces and territories enacted statutes that replaced the old common law writs (the remedies) with a single application for judicial review.[171] However, the old remedies were mostly subsumed into these acts and were—and in many jurisdictions still remain—"[s]treamlined versions of the old prerogative writs (along with declaratory and injunctive relief)."[172]

As Craig Forcese discusses in Chapter 15, one of the most significant changes was the enactment of the *Federal Courts Act*[173] in 1970,[174] which allowed for the almost complete transfer of "remedial jurisdiction over federal statutory decision makers … from the provincial superior courts to the newly created Federal Court of Canada, a court that replaced the former Exchequer Court of Canada, which had had only very limited judicial review jurisdiction."[175] It was thought that by relocating jurisdiction over judicial review of federal administrative action to a federal court "there would be greater assurance of the development of an appropriate level of judicial expertise respecting the federal administrative process."[176] "Almost contemporaneously, Ontario … [conferred] most judicial review authority onto a three-judge bench of the then Ontario High Court, the Divisional Court."[177]

The importance of these new statutes cannot be understated. Previously, judicial review of administrative decisions was defined by the common law—more specifically, by the ancient prerogative writs. Now, in many cases, statutes allowed an application for "judicial review," organized the procedure to be followed, and specified which court would have jurisdiction to review. The content of judicial review of both procedural fairness and substantive error is introduced in the second half of this chapter. To sum up, administrative law moved from a pure common law regime to a simpler statutory-based regime informed by the common law.[178] But the relationship between statutes and the common law is not an easy one—as we will see when we get to evolutions of the standard of review jurisprudence following the Supreme Court's decision in *Dunsmuir*.[179]

---

167   *Ibid.*
168   SO 1971, c 48 (now RSO 1990, c J.1) [JRPA].
169   Mullan, "Willis v McRuer," *supra* note 159 at 556.
170   *Ibid.*
171   David Mullan, *Administrative Law* (Toronto: Irwin Law, 2001) at 12, 405 [Mullan, *Administrative Law*].
172   *Ibid* at 405-6; see e.g. JRPA, s 2(1).
173   RSC 1985 c F-7.
174   Evans et al, *supra* note 131 at 1135.
175   Mullan, *Administrative Law, supra* note 171 at 404.
176   *Ibid* at 425.
177   *Ibid* at 404.
178   Evans et al, *supra* note 131 at 1087.
179   *Dunsmuir v New Brunswick*, 2008 SCC 9, [2008] 1 SCR 190 [*Dunsmuir*].

VII. SECTION 96 AND THE COURTS' CONSTITUTIONAL RIGHT TO REVIEW ADMINISTRATIVE DECISIONS

We now digress from our brief history of Canada's administrative state and the evolution of administrative law to provide a bit more detail on a topic not otherwise covered in the rest of the text—namely, the nature of s 96 courts and the constitutional basis for judicial review of administrative action. As we discussed earlier, a privative or preclusive clause is a way in which the legislature attempts to stop the courts from reviewing the decisions of administrative boards or tribunals. As you will see in the jurisprudence, courts made every effort to largely ignore or otherwise narrowly interpret these kinds of clauses: "For decades such clauses were largely ignored by the courts, despite much critical commentary by academic writers such as the late Chief Justice Laskin, before he was appointed to the bench,"[180] and courts did not accept even strongly worded privative clauses as ousting their authority to review administrative decision-making for excess of jurisdiction.[181] Why is this?

Because administrative agencies and tribunals have only those powers conferred by legislation, their powers are legally limited. Courts have long seen their role as one of patrolling the borders of those legal limits to make sure that an administrative agency does not step outside its jurisdiction and exercise power that it does not have. Because privative clauses essentially prevent the court from undertaking this role, courts historically gave such clauses short shrift.

So why do "superior" courts undertake this role of keeping "inferior" administrative boards and tribunals in check, even when the legislature has told them not to? And how tightly should courts police the boundaries of administrative decision-making? Part of the answer is that, through their approach to statutory interpretation, courts have wide discretion in how they approach their role—a topic that a number of contributors to this volume discuss, including Mary Liston in Chapter 4 and Sheila Wildeman in Chapter 12. However, there are also constitutional grounds for the oversight of administrative decision-makers by superior courts.

The superior courts' role, however, creates a constitutional tension. Can a provincial legislature or the Parliament of Canada have the constitutional capacity to exclude *all* kinds of judicial review of decisions made by an administrative agency? On the one hand, the doctrine of parliamentary supremacy means that there is nothing preventing legislatures from enacting whatever they wish, including privative clauses. But what happens when those privative clauses step on the toes of the superior courts and their constitutional role? There is nothing *explicitly* said about this in the *Constitution Act, 1867*. However, there is an argument for implying a constitutionally guaranteed right to judicial review of administrative action by superior courts—one that trumps parliamentary supremacy in the context of a privative clause that seeks to preclude such review—and it has centred on the provisions of the *Constitution Act, 1867*, ss 96-101.

---

180 Andrew J Roman, "The Pendulum Swings Back: Case Comment WW Lester (1978) Ltd v UA, Local 740," (1991), 48 Admin LR 274 at 283.

181 *Ibid* at 284. See also e.g. *Jarvis, supra* note 152; David Mullan, "Dunsmuir v New Brunswick, Standard of Review and Procedural Fairness for Public Servants: Let's Try Again!" (2008) 21 Can J Admin L & Prac 117 at 128.

The starting point of this argument is s 96 of the *Constitution Act*, which provides that the appointment of superior court judges is the sole responsibility of the federal government. Remember from our discussion above that superior courts have an inherent jurisdiction to review administrative decision-making. However, another important aspect of the superior courts created under s 96 is that they themselves are immune from judicial review, because they do not have jurisdiction to judicially review *other* superior courts: They can only review "inferior" administrative tribunals.

Provinces do not have the jurisdiction to create s 96 courts. However, for various reasons, they may want to give administrative tribunals the same immunity from judicial review that s 96 courts have. If so—the argument goes—provinces have created de facto s 96 courts under the guise of an administrative tribunal. "Real" superior courts have not appreciated the provinces' attempts to create unreviewable tribunals and have developed a three-part test (below) to determine whether an administrative tribunal is actually acting like a s 96 court. If a court finds that a tribunal is acting as a s 96 court then, notwithstanding a privative clause, tribunal decisions may be subjected to review and the privative clause either read down or of no effect, because the province was without jurisdiction to create it. The three-part test is as follows:

1. *Historical inquiry:* Is the administrative decision in question similar to one that, at the time of Confederation, would have been exclusively within the power of a superior, district, or county court to make? (The jurisprudence suggests that this should be interpreted broadly so as to ensure the protection of s 96 courts.)

2. *Judicial versus legislative or administrative power:* Is the impugned power a "judicial" power as opposed to a legislative or an administrative power? A judicial power is one where there is a private dispute between parties, adjudicated through the application of a recognized body of rules and in a manner consistent with fairness and impartiality.

3. *Contemporary character:* Even if the decision-making power was historically under the jurisdiction of a superior, district, or county court, has the decision-making power in its contemporary institutional setting sufficiently changed its character such that it cannot conform to the jurisdiction of a court? For example, it was noted in *Tomko v Labour Relations Board (NS)*,[182] while referring to the Nova Scotia Labour Relations Board, that the adjudicative functions of such a board were part of its broader administrative and policy-making role as administrator of the labour relations legislation. Thus, it was agreed that one could not compare a labour relations board's cease and desist order with the jurisdiction of a superior court to issue mandatory injunctions to halt illegal activities.

The leading case on administrative tribunals masquerading as s 96 courts is *Crevier*,[183] a Supreme Court of Canada decision from 1981. In this case, Quebec legislation created a Professions Tribunal to hear appeals from discipline committees of most statutory professional bodies in Quebec. The tribunal was composed of provincially appointed judges. The

---

182 *Tomko v Labour Relations Board (NS)*, [1977] 1 SCR 112, as referenced in *Re Residential Tenancies Act, 1979*, [1981] 1 SCR 714 at 731-32.

183 *Crevier v AG (Québec)*, [1981] 2 SCR 220 [*Crevier*].

act included a privative clause stating, in effect, that the tribunal's decisions were final, even those about the reach of the tribunal's own jurisdiction.

The Supreme Court asked the following question: Was the Quebec Professions Tribunal acting like a s 96 court? Chief Justice Laskin, for the court, noted that a provincial government, in creating an administrative tribunal, could include a privative clause if it allowed superior court jurisdiction to review questions of jurisdiction even if there was limited judicial review of all other kinds of decisions from the tribunal. But, if the wording of a privative clause tried to oust review by courts over even strict jurisdictional questions, as was the case in *Crevier*, then the clause was not constitutionally valid, because the province had de facto created a s 96 court.[184] The court concluded that to give a provincial tribunal unlimited jurisdiction to interpret and apply law and then preclude any supervision by provincial superior courts created a s 96 court.

Crevier is a landmark case for the proposition that there is a constitutionally recognized right to judicial review, at least of questions of jurisdiction, that cannot be displaced by a privative clause, no matter how strongly worded. For example, following *Crevier*, Beetz J said in *Bibeault* that "[t]he role of the superior courts in maintaining the rule of law is so important that it is given constitutional protection."[185] The Supreme Court confirmed this proposition in *MacMillan Bloedel Ltd*.[186] At stake here were provisions in federal legislation that attempted to give provincial youth courts the exclusive jurisdiction to try youths for *ex facie* contempt of superior courts. The Supreme Court agreed that, although it was permissible to confer jurisdiction over such matters on courts staffed by provincial appointees, that jurisdiction could not be to the exclusion of the superior courts. A superior court has a constitutionally guaranteed entitlement to try youths for flouting an injunction issued by it. According to Lamer CJ:

> The superior courts have a core or inherent jurisdiction which is integral to their operations. The jurisdiction, which forms this core, cannot be removed from the superior courts by either level of government, without amending the Constitution. Without this core jurisdiction, section 96 could not be said to either ensure uniformity in the judicial system throughout the country or to protect the independence of the judiciary.[187]

To conclude, as recognized in *Crevier*, *Bibeault*, and *MacMillan Bloedel*, superior courts have a constitutional role and inherent jurisdiction to judicially review administrative decision-making, at least with respect to questions of jurisdiction. The way they protect this role is by ignoring provincial legislatures' privative clauses and completely excluding judicial review of administrative tribunals as an unconstitutional attempt to create a de facto superior court. A superior court, even in the face of the most strongly worded privative clause, is constitutionally entitled to check the jurisdiction of an administrative board or tribunal.

---

184 This argument was recognized five years earlier by Stephen A Scott, "The Supreme Court and Civil Liberties" (1976) 14 Alta L Rev 97 at 132: "It is one thing to admit a power to *curtail* the jurisdiction of the superior courts. It is another to admit a power to turn inferior into superior courts" (emphasis in original).

185 *UES, Local 298 v Bibeault*, [1988] 2 SCR 1048 at 1090, citing *Crevier, supra* note 183.

186 *MacMillan Bloedel Ltd v Simpson*, [1995] 4 SCR 725, [1996] 2 WWR 1.

187 *Ibid* at para 15.

PART 2: AN INTRODUCTION TO MODERN ADMINISTRATIVE LAW

VIII. WHERE TO START?

Having considered the constitutional basis by which superior courts may review administrative boards and tribunals, in the second half of this chapter we provide a high-level overview of the various parts of this book (and by extension, administrative law). The context of administrative decision-making is extremely important to the resolution of issues in this field, and a variety of sectors and kinds of decisions are examined in this book. However, we must leave the particular valleys and mountains of, for example, immigration law, labour law, and securities law for other texts. Here we concentrate on the general principles of administrative law. Our analysis focuses on how courts review decision-making on the part of those delegated power by the legislature, but we also hope to capture to a much greater extent the real world and context of administrative decision-making itself.

Historically, as discussed somewhat above, the stance of courts toward administrative agencies has been negative: to limit, to reign in, to supervise, to oversee, and to constrain. As Mary Liston describes in Chapter 4, this historical orientation of the courts toward administrative agencies and tribunals, best captured in the writings of AV Dicey on the rule of law, was one that was largely antithetical to the administrative state. As we hinted at earlier, perspectives on the rule of law and the appropriate relationships between courts, Parliament, Cabinet, and delegated decision-makers like boards and tribunals have changed over time and continue to fluctuate. The emphasis has shifted so that courts will tend to be deferential to administrative boards and tribunals where it seems that this was what Parliament intended. However, battles and differences in opinion over the appropriate balance between parliamentary sovereignty and the rule of law continue to play out in the jurisprudence, as do battles between progressive and more libertarian stances toward claims for, for example, social services. There is still no satisfactory resolution of all the various theoretical and political complexities and, in the absence of an agreed on and coherent framework, there is room for courts to obtain (or appear to obtain) the results they prefer.

Like most administrative law texts, this book looks carefully and critically at how courts review, view, and interact with administrative agencies. In addition, we try to convey a much greater sense of how administrative boards and tribunals work in practice. In Chapter 9, Angus Grant and Lorne Sossin look at how people access administrative tribunals and how decisions on budgets, staffing, websites, and translation can make all the difference between real justice and injustice. Similarly, in Chapter 2, Cristie Ford explores remedies not only from the perspective of judicial review but the varied approach to remedies available and employed by different administrative decision-makers. In Chapter 8, Andrew Green focuses on delegation of rule or regulatory making ability to a swath of different administrative decision-makers. Administrative law scholars and teachers from across Canada have joined together to work on this text to provide multiple voices, perspectives, and approaches to administrative law and to convey a greater sense of the real world of administrative decision-making. We leave it to those authors and the chapters that follow to illuminate this world. The remainder of this introduction provides a basic overview of the core features of administrative law to help guide the reader through subsequent chapters.

The core function of judicial review of administrative action is to examine how and why the courts decide to intervene in the administrative process. Administrative law is roughly divided into three parts:

1. *Procedural fairness:* First, is this an issue courts should review and, if so, did the administrative decision-maker use the proper procedures in reaching a decision?
2. *Substantive review:* Regarding the decision itself, did the administrative decision-maker make an error of the kind or magnitude that the court is willing to get involved in?
3. *Remedies and the legitimacy of judicial review:* If there are procedural or substantive defects in the decision, should the court intervene and, if so, how?

Having covered, from a bird's-eye view at least, the issue of remedies and the constitutional basis for judicial review, below we provide a snapshot of review for procedural fairness and substantive review.

IX. REVIEW FOR PROCEDURAL FAIRNESS

Chapters 5 (Kate Glover), 6 (Alexander Pless and Evan Fox-Decent), and 7 (Laverne Jacobs) all deal with aspects of procedural fairness, both in the common law and pursuant to the Charter. When it comes to the common law of procedural fairness or natural justice as required by s 7 of the Charter, the court, in reviewing the actions of the tribunal, is not interested in the actual decision that the tribunal came to in the end (the substance), but in the *procedures* followed by the tribunal in coming to the decision. As you review this discussion, consider the extent to which ensuring fair procedures is the best way to ensure good decision-making and, also, the extent to which courts believe that court-like procedures are "fair," and to what extent this belief is true.

There are several parts to this focus on procedure: the threshold question, the content of procedural fairness, bias and independence, and institutional decision-making. What follows is a simplified summary; the hard work and necessary detail are provided in Chapters 5, 6, and 7.

A. Threshold Question

First, a court should ask itself what is called the "threshold" question: Is this the kind of decision that should attract some kind of procedural right? At this stage, the court is not asking what those rights would encompass, but only the preliminary question of whether there should be any entitlement to procedural fairness at all. To put it another way, the court is asking whether it should review the administrative decision-maker's procedures or whether it is more appropriate to conclude that whatever the decision-maker decides to do by way of procedure is sufficient. Generally, if, as a result of delegation by the legislature of governmental power, a decision is made that affects an individual's rights or interests, there will be some minimum entitlement to procedural fairness, but there are still some exceptions. Kate Glover explores them in Chapter 5. Exceptions include situations where the decision is a legislative or policy decision or preliminary or investigative (and then there are the exceptions to the exceptions). Exceptions relating to policy-making may apply most frequently to ministers or the governor in council.[188] Another issue to consider here is the doctrine of legitimate expectation and in what circumstances, if any, an individual should be entitled to certain procedural rights if a representation of some form has been made that such rights would be forthcoming.

Traditionally, the determination of whether the threshold had been passed (after which there was some entitlement to procedural fairness) was carried out at common law. The earliest such example is *Cooper*, an English case from 1863.[189] In *Cooper*, the plaintiff had built a house without giving the requisite notice to the district board. The board was entitled by statute in this situation to demolish the plaintiff's house, which it did. The court unanimously held that the plaintiff should have been given at least some procedural fairness because the board's decision to demolish a house has a huge impact on the person affected. Willes J in *Cooper* stated that the rule that the threshold can be passed even when the statute does not require fairness is "of universal application, and founded upon the plainest principles of justice."[190] Note that, although the statute was silent about the right to procedural fairness, the court nonetheless "read in" these duties.

A century later in *Ridge v Baldwin*,[191] the House of Lords held that a public office-holder had a common law entitlement to reasons and a chance to respond before being dismissed from office. The case involved a police constable who had been charged with but acquitted of several crimes. The relevant statute empowered the Watch Committee[192] with discretion to dismiss the constable, which it did, but did not provide any rights to, for example, a hearing or reasons. The House of Lords held first that the constable was not employed "at pleasure," nor was he employed in a master-servant relationship, so there had to be some intelligible reason to fire him. Second, this made the Watch Committee's decision "quasi-judicial," and in discharging a quasi-judicial task, the committee had to adhere to the principles of natural justice—that is, it owed the constable a duty of fairness and was required to provide him with some reasonable opportunity to be heard.

Fast-forward to 1979 and Canada, where the Supreme Court introduced the duty of fairness owed to public office-holders in a watershed case—*Nicholson*.[193] The *Nicholson* majority, written by Laskin CJ, held that a police constable employed during a probationary period could not be dismissed arbitrarily without being given any reasons. A decade later, the Supreme Court in *Knight*[194] expanded that duty of fairness to include even those office-holders who were employed "at pleasure." Kate Glover explains these developments in Chapter 5

---

188 David Mullan notes that the Federal Court of Appeal judgment in *Gitxaala Nation v Canada*, 2016 FCA 187, [2016] 4 FCR 418 [*Gitxaala Nation*], which entertained the claim of bias or impartiality on the part of the Governor in Council in the context of a pipeline decision adversely affected Indigenous Peoples is suggestive that the judgment of Estey J in *Canada (Attorney General) v Inuit Tapirisat of Canada*, [1980] 2 SCR 735 can no longer be taken as authority for the absolute immunity of the governor in council with respect to administrative decision-making—see D Mullan, "2016 Developments in Administrative Law Relevant to Energy Law and Regulation" (2017) 5:1 Energy Regulation Quarterly, online: <http://www.energyregulationquarterly.ca/articles/2016-developments-in-administrative-law-relevant-to-energy-law-and-regulation#sthash.htF0Dna3.dpbs>.

189 *Cooper v Wandsworth Board of Works* (1863), 14 CB (NS) 180 (Ct of Common Pleas) [*Cooper v Wandsworth*].

190 *Ibid* at 190.

191 *Ridge v Baldwin (No 1)*, [1964] AC 40, [1963] UKHL 2 [*Ridge v Baldwin*].

192 *Municipal Corporations Act 1882*, 1882, c 50 (Regnal 45 and 46 Vict), s 191(4), cited in *ibid*, *Ridge v Baldwin*.

193 *Nicholson v Haldimand-Norfolk Regional Police Commissioners*, [1979] 1 SCR 311.

194 *Knight v Indian Head School Division No 19*, [1990] 1 SCR 653.

and how in *Dunsmuir*[195] the Supreme Court retreated from earlier jurisprudence to find that, in the case of a public employee under contract, the contract itself, rather than the common law of procedural review, determined what (if any) procedural rights an employee is entitled to. This wrinkle aside, the basic principle remains that a fair process may be required even if it is not specifically provided for in a statute and will be "read in."

In recent years, another component of the threshold discussion has been the Charter. In Chapter 6, Alexander Pless and Evan Fox-Decent explore the kinds of actions or decisions that fall under s 7 of the Charter. They examine in detail how the guarantee that one is not to be deprived of life, liberty, or security of the person except in accordance with fundamental justice (s 7) relates to the common law of procedural fairness and the synergistic (and complicated) relationship between the two.

An exciting area in development is the intersection of public administrative law and private law. What happens when the government and an individual have a contract that purports to govern procedural fairness? Some examples include bids for government procurement contracts (see *Irving Shipbuilding*[196]), employment contracts for civil servants (see *Dunsmuir*[197]), and contracts between immigration sponsors and the Department of Immigration (see *Mavi*[198]). Do the terms of the contract trump statutory or common law duties of fairness? Can a decision be so important to the individual that fairness is required no matter what the contract says? Does it matter whether the terms of the contract flow completely from statute? Moreover, the privatization, corporatization, and outsourcing of government services and programs have raised questions concerning the continued applicability of the principles of administrative law.[199] If a province hands over the operation of juvenile correctional facilities to the private sector, to what extent do the rules of procedural fairness still apply?[200] Further, Alexander Pless examines in Chapter 10 whether the general principles of administrative law should be adapted into assessing whether the Crown can be liable in tort law and questions the courts' resistance to viewing the legality of administrative actions as relevant to assessing tort liability.

As you progress through the cases, you will notice that the division into two separate questions of the threshold and the content of procedures is often rather artificial. It is not easy to separate the questions whether the threshold has been passed and, if so, what procedures are appropriate.

B. The Content of Procedural Fairness

If a court determines that the threshold for some form of procedural fairness has been met, it must then address what those procedures will be. The common law traditionally looked to how much of an impact the administrative decision would have on the affected individual's life. Thus, in *Cooper*, the court held that the plaintiff should have been given notice of the board's decision to demolish his house and an opportunity to respond to that notice.[201] There were many possible excuses why the plaintiff defaulted by failing to tell the board that he planned to build his new house, and he ought to have been given a chance to explain the default.[202]

---

195 *Dunsmuir, supra* note 179.
196 *Irving Shipbuilding Inc v Canada (Attorney General)*, 2009 FCA 116, [2010] 2 FCR 488, 314 DLR (4th) 340, leave to appeal refused, [2009] 3 SCR vii.
197 *Supra* note 179.
198 *Canada (Attorney General) v Mavi*, 2011 SCC 30, [2011] 2 SCR 504.
199 Mullan, *Administrative Law, supra* note 171 at 5.
200 *Ibid.*
201 *Cooper v Wandsworth, supra* note 189.
202 *Ibid*, Erle CJ.

The Supreme Court of Canada, in *Baker*,[203] identified the following five factors as relevant in determining the general level of procedural fairness: the nature of the decision and the process followed in making it; the nature of the statutory scheme; the importance of the decision to the individual affected; the legitimate expectations of the parties; and the procedures chosen by the tribunal.

Having determined the general level of procedural fairness, the court will then decide from a range of possibilities what specific procedures are required. There are a variety of possibilities and combinations of possibilities:

- *notice* that the decision is going to made;
- *disclosure* of the information on which the tribunal will base its decision;
- some opportunity to *participate* or make views known;
- a full *hearing* similar to that which occurs in a court;
- an opportunity to give *evidence* and cross-examine;
- right to *counsel*; and
- oral or written *reasons* for its decision.

You may notice that many of these possibilities seem to be a way of asking, "[t]o what extent must the administrative decision-maker act like a court?" We also need to think about who is better situated to determine what various procedures the tribunals should follow: The tribunals or the courts? Can courts really understand the day-to-day reality, costs, and impact of requiring different procedures from those that a tribunal would select itself? Justice Abella explained, "administrative tribunals ... were expressly created as independent bodies for the purpose of being an alternative to the judicial process, including its procedural panoplies. Designed to be less cumbersome, less expensive, less formal, and less delayed, these impartial decision-making bodies were to resolve disputes in their area of specialization more expeditiously and more accessibly, but no less effectively or credibly."[204] Given the myriad access to justice issues that plague the courts, we may also question generally the notion that the procedures courts adopt in fact reflect an idealized notion of fairness.

If your client asks whether he or she has a right to be represented by legal counsel before an administrative board or tribunal, to where should you turn first? Students often overlook the most important aspect of administrative law—namely, the necessity for closely examining the legislation setting up the board or tribunal, often referred to as the "enabling statute." It is possible that the common law may expand on these, but the first port of call should be the statute itself. Additionally, as discussed above, the 1970s saw the establishment of umbrella statutes that codified administrative procedure. It is important to check whether your province has such an umbrella statute that sets out the types of procedures that must be made available for all or specific types of boards and tribunals—for example, Ontario's *Statutory Powers Procedures Act*,[205] Alberta's *Administrative Procedures and Jurisdiction Act*,[206] and Quebec's *Administrative Justice Act*.[207] In British Columbia, the *Administrative Tribunals Act*[208] focuses on empowering the tribunal to enact its own rules. It is critical to remember that where a statute—be it umbrella or specific to the tribunal—specifies a certain kind of procedural right or

---

203 *Baker v Canada (Minister of Citizenship and Immigration)*, [1999] 2 SCR 817 [*Baker*].
204 *Rasanen v Rosemount Instruments*, (1994) 17 OR (3d) 267 (CA) at para 35 [*Rasanen*].
205 RSO 1990, c S.22.
206 RSA 2000, c A-3.
207 RSQ, c J-3.
208 SBC 2004, c 45.

specifically denies a procedural right that would otherwise have been available in the common law, the statute prevails over the common law. Where there is no such specificity, however, the common law may be "read in" to supplement the provisions of the statute.

In addition to the statutory regime, in practice, it is also important to check the rules pursuant to which the board or tribunal operates (these binding rules or regulations or non-binding guidelines go beyond the content of the enabling statutes). As Andrew Green discusses in Chapter 8, such rules and guidelines are critical to the day-to-day operation of boards and tribunals and, in reality, the decisions of the hundreds of boards and tribunals across the country have a far greater impact on Canadians than the relatively few decisions that are taken on judicial review to the general courts. For example, guidelines issued by the minister of immigration set out the basis on which immigration officers are to determine whether an individual deserves humanitarian and compassionate consideration, and these guidelines were central to the resolution of the *Baker* decision, which we discuss below.[209]

C. Bias, Independence, and Institutional Decision-Making

Another aspect of the part of this text that focuses on procedures is the idea of bias and the related concepts of independence and institutional decision-making, which are more fully explored by Laverne Jacobs in Chapter 7. If a decision-maker acts in a biased manner, favouring one party over another, what then? And what do we mean by bias? Do we mean that we have actual evidence that the decision-maker has already made up his or her mind or has been bribed to decide in a particular way? Or is it enough that, given all the circumstances, there is an appearance of bias?

Related to the issue of bias is independence, which, as mentioned above, is a key feature of most boards and tribunals and one of the original rationales for their creation (independence being seen as important to ensure non-political, fair decision-making). Institutional independence is related to the concept of bias, but is more about the systemic structure of a board or tribunal as opposed to individual decision-making. In the context of independence, we ask questions such as: Do the members of the tribunal have financial security or do they have security of tenure? A related issue is whether they are so dependent on or connected to the government that, if appointed, they cannot be perceived as being sufficiently able to make an independent decision.

With respect to institutional decision-making we explore the thorny issue of the extent to which boards and tribunals can consult with others to whom the person affected will not have had the opportunity to present his or her case. For example, is it acceptable that, in order to deal with a heavy caseload, a board has set up a process whereby just one member of the board hears an application or case, but the full board is involved in the final decision? If so, in what circumstances is it acceptable?

X. SUBSTANTIVE REVIEW: THE STANDARD OF REVIEW AND APPLICATION

Historically, administrative law has focused primarily on procedural review, on the implicit assumption that if a sound process is followed, a fair decision will be reached, and perhaps

---

209   Cited in *Baker, supra* note 203.

a further assumption that, while courts may lack expertise on specialized content, they are nevertheless experts on process. The second major focus of administrative law is substantive review and, here, the courts look at the decision itself, not just at the procedures that were followed in reaching the decision. Recall from the discussion above of the *intra vires-ultra vires* era that courts were extremely eager to assert their influence in the administrative sphere. However, this began to change in the deference revolution that took place in the 1960s and 1970s. The culmination of the changes was the landmark Supreme Court decision *CUPE v NB Liquor Corporation*,[210] which acknowledged that, often, there was no one right answer in terms of legal interpretation, but a range of different reasonable interpretations, and that the interpretation followed by an administrative decision-maker may be as legitimate as that of a court. *CUPE* ushered in the beginning of a new era of judicial deference toward administrative tribunals—although, as we shall see, this path has been twisted, rocky, and tentative—often two steps forward and one step back. The main thing to remember as you dive into this part of the text is that there are two parts to substantive review:

a. First, setting the "standard" of review. This is the question of the extent and degree to which a court will scrutinize a decision by an administrative decision-maker. If you think about advising your best friend on whether he or she looks great in a wedding outfit, setting the standard of review is akin to whether you stand well back and give it a quick look over, or instead get right up close and peer at the stitching, the quality of the fabric, and the fit and pronounce yes/no depending on whether you would wear it yourself.[211]

b. Second, once the "standard" of review is set, it then has to be *applied* to the specific context of the administrative decision-maker and the decision made.

As we will see, an awful lot of ink has been spilled on the first part of the inquiry, but the real action and focus of scholarly and judicial attention is now shifting to the second part. Subsequent chapters will provide a more detailed map of the rocky terrain covered by and the location of many dragons.[212]

As mentioned, the first aspect of reviewing an administrative decision is for a court to determine the standard of review by which it will regard the decision; in other words, how big an error must the tribunal make before the court will get involved? How much deference—or respect—should a court offer to the decision of an administrative decision-maker

---

210 *Supra* note 87.

211 Thanks to Audrey Macklin for this metaphor.

212 In Chapters 11 and 12, Audrey Macklin and Sheila Wildeman, respectively, set out the history of the development of the tests for the standard of review and the modern test in its application to varied decision-makers and decisions in all its myriad twists, turns, and agonies. Discussion includes for example, how historically there was a separate test for review of discretion, whereas discretionary decision-making is now folded into the new "simplified" test. (For the law of review of discretionary decision-making prior to *Dunsmuir,* see Geneviève Cartier, "Administrative Discretion: Between Exercising Power and Conducting Dialogue," available on the website <www.emond.ca/adminlaw3e>.) Evan Fox-Decent and Alexander Pless explain the differing impact of challenging the fairness of a decision employing the Charter as opposed to administrative law in Chapters 6 and 13. And Peter Carver in Chapter 14 helps the student reader bring this all together with a short chapter summarizing the essentials to better arm the student reader heading into his or her exam. Like Peter Carver, in what follows we attempt to provide a higher mapping of the issues to initiate you into some of the concepts.

on any particular issue?[213] Setting the standard of review brings to the surface all the tensions we have discussed earlier with respect to preserving the rule of law, showing respect for parliamentary sovereignty as expressed in the desire to delegate powers to administrative decision-makers, and more ends-oriented perspectives on whether administrative decision-making is overall a good thing for individuals and society. In *Dunsmuir*, the Supreme Court discussed the balance to be struck:

> As a matter of constitutional law, judicial review is intimately connected with the preservation of the rule of law. It is essentially that constitutional foundation which explains the purpose of judicial review and guides its function and operation. Judicial review seeks to address an underlying tension between the rule of law and the foundational democratic principle, which finds an expression in the initiatives of Parliament and legislatures to create various administrative bodies and endow them with broad powers. Courts, while exercising their constitutional functions of judicial review, must be sensitive not only to the need to uphold the rule of law, but also to the necessity of avoiding undue interference with the discharge of administrative functions in respect of the matters delegated to administrative bodies by Parliament and legislatures.... . Judicial review is the means by which the courts supervise those who exercise statutory powers, to ensure that they do not overstep their legal authority. The function of judicial review is therefore to ensure the legality, the reasonableness, and the fairness of the administrative process and outcomes.[214]

In *Dunsmuir*, the Supreme Court of Canada sought to provide a "principled framework that is more coherent and workable" for the judicial review of administrative decisions.[215] Audrey Macklin in Chapter 11 outlines the important history preceding *Dunsmuir*—in a sense you can't really understand this decision and what it really means without wading through the historical twists and turns. So, to grossly oversimplify, prior to *Dunsmuir* there were three standards of review: (1) patent unreasonableness (the most deferential standard of review—where you stand way back assessing your friend's wedding outfit); (2) reasonableness *simpliciter* (less deferential—you are up closer but you are looking at it from your friend's perspective); and (3) correctness (the most searching standard of review—this outfit has to be something that you yourself would wear to your own wedding). *Dunsmuir* eliminated the standard of patent unreasonableness, thus "simplifying" the standard of review to a choice between reasonableness and correctness.

The correctness standard of review should be relatively easy to grasp, as it is the stance you would normally expect of an appeal court reviewing the decisions of a lower court. This standard of correctness, when applied to a decision, is one in which there is only one defensible answer—the same answer that the reviewing court would have reached.[216] To try to simplify things for everyone, *Dunsmuir* set out the types of decisions where the correctness standard should automatically be applied: (1) where the administration decision-maker is answering constitutional questions regarding the division of powers; (2) "true questions of jurisdiction or *vires*"; (3) questions of general law that are "both of central importance to the

---

213   David Dyzenhaus, "The Politics of Deference: Judicial Review and Democracy" in M Taggart, ed, *The Province of Administrative Law* (1997) 279 at 286 (quoted with approval in *Baker, supra* note 203 at para 65, L'Heureux-Dubé J; *Law Society of New Brunswick v Ryan*, 2003 SCC 20, [2003] 1 SCR 247 at para 49; *Dunsmuir, supra* note 179 at para 48).

214   *Dunsmuir, supra* note 179 at paras 27-28.

215   *Ibid* at para 32.

216   *Wilson v Atomic Energy of Canada Ltd*, 2016 SCC 29, [2016] 1 SCR 770 at para 23 [*Wilson*].

legal system as a whole and outside the adjudicator's specialized area of expertise"; and (4) "questions regarding the jurisdictional lines between two or more competing specialized tribunals."[217] As you can probably guess, there is a lot of contestation involved in defining these categories (for example, what is meant by "true questions of jurisdiction") and there is also overlap across these categories.

Understanding the "reasonableness" standard is a much more complicated business. But you should grasp that adopting a "reasonableness" standard is intended as a mark of respect to the decision-making capabilities of the decision-maker, at least vis-à-vis the particular decision under review. The reasonableness standard acknowledges the legislature's desire that the administrative agency's expertise be applied to the question and not that of the courts. The reasonableness standard also admits of the fact that certain questions do not have a single, ineluctable answer, but may give rise to a number of possible, reasonable conclusions. A court reviewing on a standard of reasonableness is concerned with the existence of "justification, transparency, and intelligibility within the decision-making process," and ensuring that the "decision falls within a range of possible, acceptable outcomes which are defensible in respect of the facts and law."[218] As Chief Justice McLachlin noted in *Catalyst Paper Corp v North Cowichan (District)*, reasonableness "must be assessed in the context of the particular type of decision-making involved and all relevant factors" and "takes its colour from the context."[219]

In *Dunsmuir*, the Supreme Court again tried to simplify standard of review test by stating that, where the question is one of fact, discretion, or policy, the standard of reasonableness will usually apply. The reasonableness standard also applies to the review of questions where the legal and factual issues are intertwined and cannot be readily separated.[220] *Dunsmuir* further stated that deference (i.e., a standard of reasonableness) will usually apply where a tribunal is interpreting its home statute, or where an administrative tribunal has developed expertise in the application of a common law or civil law rule specific to its statutory context.[221] In a series of post-*Dunsmuir* rulings, a majority of the Supreme Court has aspired to make reasonableness the default standard to be applied unless the decision falls into one of the four correctness standard categories described above. Such a move is not without controversy—to say the least. For present purposes all you need to grasp is that if the presumption of reasonableness is rebutted, the court will engage in a more exacting analysis. If you are representing the individual challenging the administrative decision, and want to overturn it, then you will be arguing for a standard of review that is "correctness" (a more searching standard) as opposed to "reasonableness" (more deferential). But having "won" in terms of securing a more searching standard of review does not mean you have won the case—the court must now turn to apply the selected standard of review to the decision before it.

---

217 *Dunsmuir, supra* note 179 at paras 58-61; and, general comment: while the Supreme Court stated that this list was non-exhaustive, it has generally been considered exhaustive as there are very few other categories where the correctness standard can apply.

218 *Ibid* at para 47.

219 *Catalyst Paper Corp v North Cowichan (District)*, 2012 SCC 2, [2012] 1 SCR 5 at paras 18 and 23.

220 *Ibid* at para 53.

221 *Ibid* at para 54.

To add further complexity to what is already a complex path, there is a further test that may have to be applied in determining the standard of review, namely, the "pragmatic and functional test" that existed pre-*Dunsmuir*. The Supreme Court has said that where a particular case does not clearly map on to the guidelines provided in *Dunsmuir*, a reviewing court is instructed to weigh four non-exhaustive factors to determine which standard of review is applicable:[222]

1. the presence or absence of a privative clause;
2. the purpose of the tribunal as determined by interpretation of enabling legislation;
3. the nature of the question at issue; and
4. the expertise of the tribunal.

Fortunately, courts are not required to apply these factors as a strict code and do not need to exhaustively analyze all of them if this is not needed for the particular context of the administrative decision.[223] Still, the potential addition of this test, beyond the guidance laid out in *Dunsmuir*, adds further complexity to an already challenging task.

What lurks behind all of the problems we see springing from *Dunsmuir* (and its antecedents and progeny) are profound disagreements between judges regarding the appropriate balance to be set between the rule of law and deference as respect for administrative decision-making. For example, with respect to interpretation of an agency's home statute, which *Dunsmuir* told us should be reviewed under the reasonableness standard, there has been a sharply divided court on whether the correctness standard should instead apply.[224] Thus, lower courts and academic commentators have highlighted that *Dunsmuir* has not simplified but in fact further complicated administrative law, claiming the categorical approach is unworkable, and the standard of reasonableness is impractical. And some claim judicial deference has been applied inconsistently across courts and within courts themselves.[225] On top of all this, simplifying the standard does not mean that the conflicts won't resurface when it comes to the *application* of the reasonableness standard. It may be that simplifying the standard of review test merely shifts all the contestation, complexities, and tensions into applying the standard once it is set.

Let us look for example at *Wilson v Atomic Energy of Canada Ltd*, in which the majority of the Supreme Court held in a 6-3 decision that the reasonableness standard of review was appropriate, whereas the dissent would have applied the correctness standard.[226] At issue in this case was whether showing deference to the adjudicator would be appropriate in administrative decisions on questions of law. Justice Abella, writing for the majority, rejected the

---

222   *Ibid* at para 64.

223   For a full review of these guidelines, and their further contrasting with the correctness standard, see Gerald P Heckman, "Substantive Review in Appellate Courts since Dunsmuir" (2009) 47:4 Osgoode Hall LJ 756-758.

224   See *Commission scolaire de Laval v Syndicat de l'enseignment de la région de Laval*, 2016 SCC 8, [2016] 1 SCR 29; *Wilson, supra* note 216; and *Edmonton (City) v Edmonton East (Capilano) Shopping Centres Ltd*, 2016 SCC 47, [2016] 2 SCR 293.

225   David Mullan, *Administrative Law: Cases, Texts and Materials*, 5th ed (Toronto: Emond Montgomery, 2003) at vi.

226   *Supra* note 217. See also David Phillip Jones, "Administrative Law in 2016: Update on Caselaw, Recent Trends and Related Developments" (Paper delivered at the Federal Court Judges' Annual Education Seminar Mont St-Hilaire, Quebec, 28 September 2016) [unpublished] at 31 [Jones 2016].

Federal Court of Appeal's application of the correctness standard and found that reasonableness was appropriate in the circumstances.[227] In contrast, the dissent argued that the correctness standard applied, as the issue fell under more than one adjudicator's jurisdiction, and the matter had applicability to the general rule of law. The dissent argued that inconsistent decisions between tribunals with overlapping jurisdiction could undermine the rule of law, and therefore should not be afforded deference.[228]

But, again, it is critical to remember that, despite the angst and hand-wringing, setting the standard of review is not determinative of whether or not the administrative decision is overturned. A reviewing court must always then apply that standard to the decision in question, be it a decision taken by a minister, a municipality, a board, or a tribunal. Even if a court has determined that the correctness standard applies, in reviewing the decision it may nonetheless determine that the standard has been met. Likewise, if the court determines that the reasonableness standard applies, this does not necessarily mean the decision will stand; it may be that the court finds that no reasonable decision-maker could have reached that conclusion because the conclusion did not fall within a range of reasonable alternative decisions. For example, in the case of *Del Vecchio v Canada*,[229] the Federal Court found with respect to decisions on prisoner transfers from the United States to Canada that the minister of public safety had a high degree of discretion and was owed deference—the court should apply a standard of reasonableness to test the minister's decision. However, in arbitrarily refusing to allow Mr Del Vecchio to transfer into a Canadian prison while letting Mr Del Vecchio's criminal accomplices transfer, the minister's decision was deemed to fall outside the range of reasonable alternatives. The court set aside the minister's original order and ordered him to make a new, reasonable decision.

Judicial review of substantive error can and does occasionally overlap with the other main branch of administrative law, judicial review of procedural fairness.[230] Recall that an element of procedural fairness is the duty to give reasons. But a failure to give reasons, or a failure to give reasons that sufficiently explain the decision, can also lead to a finding of unreasonableness. To go back to our example of *Del Vecchio v Canada*,[231] the minister's decision appeared arbitrary to the court (and to Mr Del Vecchio) because the minister had failed to explain why Mr Del Vecchio was being treated differently than his accomplices. The minister had provided some reasons, meaning that procedural fairness was met, but those reasons were inadequate, meaning that the decision was unreasonable. Had the minister paid better attention to procedural fairness—the duty to give reasons—his decision may not have appeared arbitrary and may, in fact, have been found to be reasonable.

And unfortunately, all of these questions concerning the standard of review and its application may then be further complicated when it comes to constitutional questions. The Supreme Court's 2012 decision in *Doré v Barreau du Québec*[232] changed the approach used to review administrative decisions where the plaintiff alleges a Charter infringement, stating that the standard of review approach described above should be used in place of the *Oakes* test normally

---

227 *Wilson, supra* note 216, at paras 21-22, 39.
228 *Ibid* at paras 88-91.
229 *Del Vecchio v Canada (Public Safety and Emergency Preparedness)*, 2011 FC 1135 [*Del Vecchio*].
230 Diana Ginn, "New Words for Old Problems: The Dunsmuir Era" (2010) 37 Advocates' Q 317 at 334-37.
231 *Supra* note 229.
232 2012 SCC 12.

employed in Charter cases.[233] The Supreme Court found that the standard of review in the case of administrative decisions engaging Charter interests and values will be reasonableness, with the concept of "proportionality" helping to determine what is in fact reasonable. This allows the administrative decision-maker to consider how best to protect the particular Charter interest or value at stake while balancing against the objectives of their home statute. As with many Supreme Court decisions in administrative law attempting to address difficult problems, *Doré* leaves much unresolved. For example, to what extent does this new approach allow judicial reconsideration and re-weighing of values as part of the "reasonableness" review? And to what extent will the shift in the onus of proof—under the reasonableness test in administrative law the onus lies with claimants, while under s 1 of the Charter, the onus is on government—have an impact on how well administrative law serves to uphold Charter values?

A. Pipelines Case Study

Since the publication of the last edition of this volume, one of the most compelling legal and political issues in the sphere of administrative law and justice has been that of proposals to build pipelines or repurpose existing pipelines. These proposals bring together a number of substantive fields, including energy and environmental law, Indigenous treaty and constitutional rights, the principles of Canadian federalism, and the separation of powers. Administrative law has been at the heart of disputes over pipelines, both with respect to reviewing the process of decision-making and the decision itself. Who makes decisions about pipelines and what constitutes a fair process for such decision-making? And where decisions about pipelines are challenged, what are the grounds for a court to intervene in this process, and on what standard of review?

Our Pipelines Case Study is perhaps best exemplified by the case of *Gitxaala Nation v Canada*,[234] which examines the duty to consult with and accommodate Indigenous Peoples in approving pipeline projects. The context for *Gitxaala* was legislation, passed in 2012, reconfiguring the decision-making process for *National Energy Board Act*[235] pipeline applications and designated projects under the *Canadian Environmental Protection Act, 1999*.[236] The *Gitxaala* decision attracted much public attention because the applicants succeeded in derailing a major pipeline initiative on grounds that the governor in council failed to consult adequately with affected Indigenous Peoples.

Beyond *Gitxaala*, there is a cluster of other relevant pipeline cases by courts at all levels in Canada, as well as tribunals such as the National Energy Board (NEB), that will be touched on by various contributors.[237] These cases speak to the courts' comfort level in reviewing decisions made by the governor in council or a minister, and the legitimacy of delegation of duties to consult to administrative agencies like the National Energy Board or even private actors, such as mining companies. *Gitxaala* and other pipeline cases engage the rights of Indigenous Peoples and raise intriguing questions at the intersection of administrative law

---

233 *Multani v Commission scolaire Marguerite Bourgeoys*, 2006 SCC 6, [2006] 1 SCR 256.

234 *Gitxaala Nation*, *supra* note 188.

235 RSC 1985, c N-7.

236 SC 1999, c 33.

237 The National Energy Board itself provides a helpful chart of ongoing litigation: see online: <https://www.neb-one.gc.ca/pplctnflng/crt/index-eng.html>

and constitutional law. The fraught and troubled history of relations between the Crown and Indigenous Peoples tests all of our assumptions about the benefits of decisions made by administrative actors and the appropriateness of deference.

The Supreme Court addressed these complex relationships in *Chippewas of the Thames First Nation v Enbridge Pipelines Inc.*[238] In *Chippewas*, the NEB was the final decision-maker on an application by Enbridge Pipelines Inc for a modification that would reverse the flow of part of a pipeline. The NEB issued notice to Indigenous groups, including the Chippewas of the Thames First Nation (CTFN), informing them of the project, and provided them funding to participate in the NEB's upcoming hearing process. The CTFN submitted evidence and made oral submissions outlining their concerns, particularly the risks involved in the potential of oil spills resulting from pipeline failures or accidents to adversely affect the community's land use. The NEB nonetheless approved the project, and indicated that potentially affected Indigenous Peoples had received adequate information and had the opportunity to share their views. The NEB also found that potential project impacts on the rights and interests of Indigenous Peoples would likely be minimal and would be appropriately mitigated.

The CFTN appealed the NEB decision on the basis that the Crown could not delegate its duty to consult. A majority of the Federal Court of Appeal (FCA) dismissed the CTFN's appeal and the FCA's decision was in turn upheld by the Supreme Court. Karakatsanis and Brown JJ, writing for a unanimous court, held that in a case such as this where an independent administrative body (the NEB) has jurisdiction over a decision that could impact Indigenous Peoples' rights, the NEB's actions constitute Crown conduct for purposes of discharging the Crown's constitutional duty to consult and accommodate. The Supreme Court held that the Crown may rely on an agency like the NEB to discharge its obligations provided that, under the particular circumstances, the agency possesses the statutory powers to fulfill the requirements of the duty to consult, and affected Indigenous groups are aware that the Crown is relying on this process to fulfill its duty. In this context, it does not matter whether the government directly participated in the hearing process. The court noted, however, that should an agency's statutory powers be insufficient, or where the agency does not provide adequate consultation and accommodation, the Crown must provide further avenues for meaningful consultation and accommodation prior to project approval. In this case, the court found the NEB's statutory authority was sufficient to satisfy the duty to consult and that, based on its reasons and the evidence before the court, it met the burden of consultation in fact.

The Pipelines Case Study also raises interesting questions of bias and impartiality, more fully explored by Laverne Jacobs in Chapter 7. The Energy East pipeline hearings, for example, were disrupted over allegations of impartiality involving former Premier Jean Charest's talks with the Joint Review Panel, notwithstanding his paid advocacy role with TransCanada, causing the panellists to recuse themselves from all subsequent decision-making and the resulting suspension of the NEB process in August 2016.[239] Allegations of political interference arose when Prime Minister Harper alleged in 2012 that people seeking to be

---

238   2017 SCC 41 [*Chippewas*]. See also the companion case of *Clyde River (Hamlet) v Petroleum Geo-Services Inc*, 2017 SCC 40.

239   Shawn McCarthy, "Energy East hearings put on hold over complaints against NEB members," *The Globe and Mail* (30 August 2016), online: <http://www.theglobeandmail.com/report-on-business/industry-news/energy-and-resources/national-energy-board-suspends-future-hearings-into-energy-east-pipeline/article31610177/>.

heard in the Northern Gateway NEB hearings were "radicals" funded by US environmental groups.[240] Against the backdrop of delays and perceived deficiencies in the environmental assessment process, the federal government passed legislation now known as the *Jobs, Growth and Long-Term Prosperity Act*,[241] which expanded the minister's discretion over project approvals (among other streamlining of the assessment process), amended/repealed over ten pieces of federal environmental legislation and reformed NEB operations.[242] As well, the legislation amended the charity provisions of the *Income Tax Act*,[243] which have had negative implications for many of Canada's environmental organizations.[244]

Most recently, Prime Minister Trudeau announced in November 2016 the decision to approve Kinder Morgan's Trans Mountain pipeline and Enbridge's Line 3, and reject the proposed Northern Gateway, the latter being a proposed 1,177-kilometre pipeline that would have carried oil from Bruderheim, Alberta, to an export terminal in Kitimat, British Columbia.[245] This raises important questions about the appropriate roles for different decision-makers (PMO, Cabinet, NEB, etc.) as well as the courts' role in supervising these decision-making processes and outcomes.

The NEB had previously determined there were significant but mitigatable environmental issues with the Kinder Morgan project, and former Conservative Prime Minister Harper had approved the project in 2014, setting out over 200 preconditions. The Federal Court overturned that approval in 2016, as it found the federal government had not adequately consulted Indigenous Peoples. Instead of pursuing these consultations, Prime Minister Trudeau opted, as noted above, to cancel the Kinder Morgan project stating: "The Great Bear Rainforest is no place for a pipeline and the Douglas Channel is no place for oil tanker traffic."[246] To what extent did Prime Minister Trudeau's decision need to rest on actual evidence of environmental harm versus political preference under the *Canadian Environmental Assessment Act*?[247] To what extent should courts review this kind of discretionary decision-making?[248]

---

240 Peter O'Neil, "Rae: PM Out of Line Saying Pipe Critics 'Radicals,'" *Vancouver Sun* (11 January 2012), online: <https://www.pressreader.com/canada/vancouver-sun/20120111/281771331056910>.

241 SC 2012, c 19.

242 For example, see the repeal of certain NEB sections in *ibid*, ss 68-99, among others including amendments to: The *Species at Risk Act*, SC 2002, c 29, which permits the NEB to issue certificates when required to do so by the governor in council; the *National Energy Board Act*, which allows the governor in council to make decisions regarding the issuance of certificates for major pipelines among others, revises the environmental assessment review process with timelines, and limits which parties are allowed to participate by defining "interested parties" left to the discretion of the reviewing panel or environmental agency; and the *Canadian Environmental Assessment Act*, which allows the governor in council to exclude a project from application under the Act if it is determined that a province will undertake an equivalent review.

243 RSC 1985, c 1 (5th Supp).

244 See e.g. Carol Goar, "Stephen Harper intimidates charities into silence: Goar," *The Toronto Star* (15 July 2014), online: <https://www.thestar.com/opinion/commentary/2014/07/15/stephen_harper_intimidates_charities_into_silence_goar.html>.

245 John Paul Tasker, "Trudeau Cabinet approves Trans Mountain, Line 3 Pipelines, Rejects Northern Gateway," *CBC News* (29 November 2016), online: <http://www.cbc.ca/news/politics/federal-cabinet-trudeau-pipeline-decisions-1.3872828>.

246 *Ibid*.

247 SC 2012, c 19, s 52.

248 Similar questions swirled around the two other projects approved by the Trudeau government (1) Line 3—a 1,659-kilometre project that will carry oil from a terminal near Hardisty, Alberta, through northern Minnesota to Superior, Wisconsin, and (2) the Trans Mountain Pipeline—a $6.8-billion, 1,150-kilometre twinned pipeline will move a mix of oil products from Edmonton to a terminal in Burnaby, BC; Tasker, *supra* note 245.

This brief introduction to some of the administrative law issues surrounding pipeline decision-making is intended to be a point of departure for the chapter-specific references to pipeline decision-making and litigation, most of which are new to this volume. Many chapter authors also will return to new developments in the area of deportation, a topic featured in previous editions of the book, which we now turn to describe.

B. Deportation Case Study

The second case study is centred on decisions with respect to deportation, for example, with respect to unsuccessful immigration and refugee claimants seeking an exemption on humanitarian and compassionate grounds, such as in the case of *Baker*[249] and more recently in 2015, *Kanthasamy* v *Canada (Citizenship and Immigration)*.[250]

Further complicating both the decision-making process itself and review of deportation decisions by courts is that security and anti-terrorism concerns have come to be closely associated with the issue of deportations, especially in cases such as *Suresh v Canada (Minister of Citizenship and Immigration)*,[251] *Ahani v Canada (Minister of Citizenship and Immigration)*,[252] and *Agraira v Canada (Public Safety and Emergency Preparedness)*,[253] and related cases concerning deportation of non-citizens following criminal convictions, as explored in *Canada (Citizenship and Immigration) v Khosa*.[254]

Whether in refugee, humanitarian and compassionate leave, or national security contexts, the deportation case study focuses on the complexities of ministerial discretion, where a minister or his or her delegates has broad authority to apply a relatively open, legal standard. For example, s 25.1 of the *Immigration and Refugee Protection Act*[255] provides:

> 25. (1) Subject to subsection (1.2), the [Minister] must, on request of a foreign national in Canada who applies for permanent resident status and who is inadmissible or does not meet the requirements of this Act, and may, on request of a foreign national outside Canada who applies for a permanent resident visa, examine the circumstances concerning the foreign national and may grant the foreign national permanent resident status or an exemption from any applicable criteria or obligations of this Act if the [Minister] is of the opinion that it is justified by humanitarian and compassionate considerations relating to the foreign national, taking into account the best interests of a child directly affected.
>
> • • •
>
> 25.1 (1) The [Minister] may, on the [Minister's] own initiative, examine the circumstances concerning a foreign national who is inadmissible or who does not meet the requirements of this Act and may grant the foreign national permanent resident status or an exemption from any applicable criteria or obligations of this Act if the [Minister] is of the opinion that it is justified by humanitarian and compassionate considerations relating to the foreign national, taking into account the best interests of a child directly affected.

The legal questions surrounding issues of discretionary decision-making are many. How should discretion of this kind be structured? Can different ministerial delegates approach broad terms such as "humanitarian and compassionate" or "national interest" in entirely

---

249 *Supra* note 203.
250 2015 SCC 61, [2015] 3 SCR 909.
251 2002 SCC 1, [2002] 1 SCR 3.
252 2002 SCC 2, [2002] 1 SCR 72.
253 2013 SCC 36, [2013] 2 SCR 559.
254 2009 SCC 12, [2009] 1 SCR 339.
255 SC 2001 c 27.

different ways or is some consistency necessary? What are the requirements of procedural fairness in these settings? To what extent must affected parties understand the "case to meet" before an opportunity to make submissions or be "heard" can be said to be effective? What role do ministry guidelines play in setting out the criteria for such discretionary decisions? Where a discretionary decision on deportation is challenged, what is the appropriate standard of review? What role, if any, do international law and conventions play in the legal framework for ministerial discretion?

The Supreme Court's ruling in *Baker* centred on legal accountability for exercises of ministerial discretion over humanitarian and compassionate exemptions, as permitted under provisions quoted above.[256] This case concerned a woman, about to be deported for overstaying, who requested that the minister use his discretionary power to allow her, on humanitarian and compassionate grounds, to remain in Canada with her four Canadian-born children while she applied for permanent residency. Her application was denied. As a practical matter, immigration officers (not the minister) exercised the power to grant humanitarian and compassionate exemptions in individual cases. An immigration officer had written up inflammatory notes about the merits of Ms Baker's application. Despite the relatively informal nature of these notes, the Supreme Court accepted these sufficed as "reasons" for the decision. (For a fuller summary of the facts, see Kate Glover's discussion in Chapter 5.)

Important issues covered in *Baker* that will be the focus of attention throughout this text include what fairness requires in terms of Ms Baker's procedural rights to participate in the decision-making process—for example, the right to make her case and have an oral hearing; the duty to give reasons and the scope of that duty; bias; the role of guidelines that had been developed to structure the exercise of discretion on the part of immigration officers who had been delegated this power by the minister of immigration; and the relevance of international treaties ratified but not yet incorporated in domestic law. In terms of substantive review, the *Baker* ruling provided a new test for determining the standard of review for discretionary decisions such as those made by the minister of immigration—since supplanted by the test set out in *Dunsmuir*[257] and its progeny.

For administrative law redux, read *Baker* and attempt to answer the following questions in relation to the case.

QUESTIONS

SOURCE OF LAW

1. What sources of law did the Supreme Court consider in reaching its decision?

THE SCOPE OF THE APPEAL

2. What are the arguments for and against the Supreme Court's decision to use the certification of "a question of general importance" to be the trigger to review the whole decision? How should the courts approach statutes that preclude an administrative decision-maker being reviewed by the general courts?

---

256 *Baker, supra* note 203.
257 *Dunsmuir, supra* note 179.

PROCEDURAL FAIRNESS

3. Madam Justice L'Heureux-Dubé said that the duty of fairness required that Ms Baker be accorded more than "minimal" procedural rights even though she was seeking a highly discretionary benefit. How should the principles of procedural fairness be applied to those, like Ms Baker, seeking a highly discretionary benefit? How does one decide what procedural rights should be available generally? What do you think of the test laid out?

4. What procedural rights was Ms Baker found to have had? Do you think they were satisfactory? Why or why not? When do you think an oral hearing should be required?

5. Prior to *Baker,* there was division of opinion over the requirement of statutory or prerogative decision-makers to provide reasons for their decisions. On what grounds was Ms Baker found to be entitled to reasons? Why does this illustrate the absence of a bright line between procedural and substantive review? What do you think is the nature of the relationship between reviewing discretionary decision-making and the requirement to give reasons?

6. The notes of Immigration Officer Lorenz were taken to be sufficient reasons for the decisions. On what grounds did the court decide that this was sufficient? Why is the court's requirement for reasons such an important finding?

7. One of several factors identified by L'Heureux-Dubé J as helpful in determining the scope of the duty of fairness is "legitimate expectation."
   a. How did she interpret the doctrine of legitimate expectation in terms of its ramifications for procedural and substantive rights?
   b. The court found that the federal government signature to the *Convention on the Rights of the Child* should *not* be viewed as a representation. What would have been the implications if the court had viewed this as a representation?
   c. Do you think Ms Baker should have had to know of the existence of the *Convention on the Rights of the Child* in order to make an argument in legitimate expectation?

8. What is the test for establishing bias? At what point does a decision-maker's obvious lack of sympathy give rise to a reasonable apprehension of bias?

SUBSTANTIVE REVIEW AND ABUSE OF DISCRETION

9. *Baker* is an important decision because it is a step toward reconciling the theory on which the courts review decisions for error of law and jurisdiction and the theory on which they review for abuse of discretion. *Baker* resulted in the folding of all questions of review of discretion into the general law of review using a "pragmatic and functional" analysis (which was later modified in *Dunsmuir* to become the "standard of review analysis"[258]). What were the factors relied on in *Baker* to determine what the standard of review should be? What concerns arise in applying these factors to discretionary decisions?

10. With regard to review of discretionary decision-making, what three standards of review did the Supreme Court acknowledge? What standard of review did Ms Baker

---

258 *Dunsmuir, supra* note 179.

seek, and what standard was found? How will you know when you should apply one standard as opposed to another?

11.   As a result of *Baker*, what advice would you give clients who ask you about the impact of international agreements that Canada has ratified but not incorporated into domestic law? How does this affect discretionary decision-making?

XI. CONCLUSION

Administrative law today cannot be properly understood without knowing at least something about its historical evolution. What began as limited prerogative writs developed over the 20th century into a whole category of law on par with contract or criminal law. Catalysts for this exponential growth included the two world wars, the expansion of the welfare state, and the introduction of the Charter. As the executive branch of government grew more and more powerful, the need for a judicial check on that power grew accordingly. Of course, the courts were probably also concerned that these new things called "administrative tribunals" were getting to wade into their turf and make quasi-judicial decisions or would make decisions that were not subject to the sunlight of scrutiny in the House of Commons.

Today, administrative law is pervasive, not only encompassing judicial review of administrative decision-making, but also informing the way decisions are made in the first instance. How courts approach the review of this enormously variable set of administrative decisions depends on the type of administrative agency, the type of decisions being made by the agency, and the impact of those decisions. Some agencies appear more court-like in nature, adjudicating on particular disputes and having a deep impact on particular individuals. These kinds of agencies arguably should be required to act more like courts in terms of the type of processes that they follow in order to ensure the highest possible standard of decision-making, although this requirement may have to be balanced against the volume of decisions to be adjudicated on (for example, in the immigration area). However, many agencies and tribunals combine adjudicative-like functions with broad-based policy-making where it seems much less appropriate to restrict the agency or tribunal to a court-like process. What is fair in terms of processes in this case?

One thing that has not changed since the beginnings of administrative law is the basic tension in "the constitutional divide between the executive and judicial branches of government."[259] On the one hand, as AV Dicey would say, the executive (including tribunals) has to play by the rules of the law just like anyone else. On the other hand, John Willis might retort, the democratically elected executive has to be allowed leeway in order to get things done and look after its citizens. The difficulty often is that, when a court reviews the actions of an administrative tribunal, the court holds the tribunal up to the standard that it expects of other courts and, unsurprisingly, frequently finds that administrative decision-makers fall short of this mark. At the same time, the courts have to be respectful of democratic will. This requires courts to respect the purpose for which administrative tribunals have been established and the fact that these functions have explicitly *not* been delegated to courts for a reason. As a student you may hope for yes-or-no answers to questions, but that is simply not

---

259   *Ocean Port Hotel Ltd v British Columbia (General Manager, Liquor Control and Licensing Branch)*, 2001 SCC 52, [2001] 2 SCR 781.

possible in administrative law given the myriad contexts of administrative decision-making. Justice Iacobucci highlights this in commenting on the difficulties we experience with applying a common standard of review framework to the myriad contexts of administrative decision-making:

> The complexity lies not with the conceptual framework of acknowledging that a spectrum of standards of review exists, but rather with its application to our complicated world of delegated powers. The complexity was created not by courts but by the legislatures, who wisely decided that not all administrative agencies would operate in the same way. It is a complexity that the courts must attempt to deal with and it would be irresponsible simply for judges to wish it away.[260]

Administrative decision-making and the courts' responses thereto are critical to the effective implementation of public policy and the efficient and just operation of public programs. Administrative law peers over the shoulder of every administrative decision-maker in Canada, inculcating the norms of fairness and transparency. In what follows we hope to convey to you the complexities and challenges in administrative law, the importance of administrative decision-making and administrative law in the lives of many Canadians, and the tools to better understand this ever-evolving field. We hope you find this text useful and easy to follow and that it stimulates a passion for administrative law. We value your feedback and thoughts on improvement for subsequent editions; you can provide feedback by contacting the publisher at <emond.ca/contact-us.html>. Administrative law is not for the faint-hearted and "there be dragons" at almost every turn. While it may be no salve for the frustration you feel, you will be a better navigator of these complexities if you understand that what underlies repeated attempts by the courts to improve administrative law are contests over the appropriate role of courts in relationship to the myriad types of administrative decision-making that exist.

SUGGESTED ADDITIONAL READINGS

CASES

Baker v Canada (Minister of Citizenship and Immigration), [1999] 2 SCR 817.

Crevier v AG (Québec), [1981] 2 SCR 220.

---

260 The Honourable Frank Iacobucci, "Articulating a Rational Standard of Review Doctrine: A Tribute to John Willis" (2002) 27: Queen's LJ 859 at 866.

CHAPTER TWO

Remedies in Administrative Law: A Roadmap to a Parallel Legal Universe

Cristie Ford

Peter A Allard School of Law, University of British Columbia

I. INTRODUCTION

The Northern Gateway pipeline saga introduced in this book's first chapter is a case study in how administrative law operates in Canada, and the crucially important subjects, on the border between law and policy, that get decided through administrative law means.

The saga also helps shed light on the role of the courts, vis-à-vis the executive, and in particular on the kinds of remedies that courts are able to impose.

Gitxaala Nation[1] is generally considered at least a qualified victory for the several First Nations that brought the matter to the Federal Court of Appeal. The Gitxaala Nation had alleged that the federal Crown had failed in its duty to consult and, if necessary, to accommodate their interests during the Northern Gateway pipeline approval process. A majority of the Federal Court of Appeal held that they were right: that at key points, Canada had offered "only a brief, hurried, and inadequate opportunity … to exchange and discuss information and dialogue," and that the consultation process fell "well short of the mark."[2]

In many respects, the majority's decision looks like any appellate decision (albeit a long one, weighing in at almost 140 pages). It reviews the facts and the decisions reached below, analyzes the case law, and develops a lengthy set of reasons for deciding in the way it did. Yet in other ways, it looks different. For example, Gitxaala Nation are styled as both "appellants"—appealing a National Energy Board (NEB) decision to issue regulatory certificates approving key pieces of the pipeline project—and as "applicants" on "judicial review," challenging an Order in Council made by the Governor in Council (i.e., federal Cabinet, or the "GIC"), directing the NEB to issue those certificates. Is there a meaningful difference between an "applicant" and an "appellant"? How exactly does a court acquire the authority to oversee the actions of the NEB, or of federal Cabinet? The Federal Court of Appeal also made observations about its role that were very different from what any appellate court would normally have made in reviewing a trial court decision. It said things like, "the Governor in Council is entitled to a very broad margin of appreciation in making its discretionary decision upon the widest considerations of policy and public interest."[3]

Perhaps more importantly, although the Gitxaala were seen to have enjoyed a victory, the remedy they received was confusing. The court did not make a decision about whether, on its merits, the Northern Gateway pipeline project should proceed. It did not give it the go-ahead, nor order that it had to be stopped. It did not order sanctions or money damages against the GIC for proceeding with the project on the basis of what it had held to be inadequate consultation. Instead, it "quashed" the earlier GIC decision and sent it back, *again to the GIC*, for reconsideration. The majority held that Canada would have to go back and adequately consult with the relevant First Nations, but once it had done so (something the court did not think would take long) it was apparently free to continue with the approval process.

None of this seems very familiar or necessarily, at first glance, very satisfactory. What was going on? Why did this outcome count as a success for the Gitxaala Nation at all, if it failed to stop the pipeline, imposed no damages, and put the ultimate approval decision back with the GIC itself? Was this the most they could have hoped for? Understanding how the remedies operated in this case involves understanding how administrative law remedies have evolved to be something separate from what we normally expect from courts—something that recognizes the particular role of administrative decision-makers, like the GIC and many others, and that draws on a particular tradition, and a particular understanding of court authority.

---

1   *Gitxaala Nation v Canada*, 2016 FCA 187, [2016] FCJ No 705 (QL) [*Gitxaala Nation*].
2   *Ibid* at para 325.
3   *Ibid* at para 152.

Even starting with a court decision as we have done, however, can obscure what goes on before a party like the Gitxaala get to court. Administrative law does not begin at the point where a party to an administrative action seeks judicial review of that action through the courts. The scope of administrative law begins much earlier, and also encompasses administrative decision-making processes that may take policy into account, or operate under a different mandate, or otherwise look quite different from what a court is likely to produce. Most other tribunals, to be sure, are not as purely political as the GIC, but nor are they courts.[4] Rich forms of action are possible in these forums. A tight focus on court action thus misses the hugely important first step in real-life administrative action: the varied and sometimes creative remedies that a tribunal itself may impose.

Let us, then, start at the beginning. This chapter provides an overview of administrative law remedies as a whole, including not only judicial review but also front-line tribunal remedies, internal and external appeals, enforcement mechanisms, and extralegal strategies. Discussing remedies near the beginning of an administrative law textbook may seem unconventional. We have chosen this approach because understanding the available remedies is an important part of understanding what one is getting into in administrative law, and it provides a broad structural framework on which subsequent chapters can build. This chapter is meant to operate almost as a decision tree, to help guide students through the different stages where remedies issues arise. Figure 2.1 sets out the broad outlines of the chapter.

The chapter is divided into three main sections. Section II, "Remedial Options at the Tribunal Stage," Section III, "Enforcing Tribunal Orders Against Parties," and even the first part of Section IV, "Challenging Administrative Action Without Going to Court" have not traditionally been located in the "remedies" chapter of administrative law texts (if they appear at all). As we shall see in Section II, remedial options available to administrative agencies at the first stage differ from those available to courts and reflect the different composition of tribunals. The remedies available at the administrative stage are both more limited (in terms of the tribunal's statute-derived authority to impose them) and, potentially, more expansive (as a consequence of tribunals' particular expertise and their ability to remain seized of a matter over time). Section III looks at the ability of a party or tribunal to *enforce* a tribunal order against another party, either civilly or criminally. Section IV considers parties' ability to *challenge* tribunal action. This includes internal appeal options, extralegal options, appeal to the courts, and, finally, the classic administrative law remedy of judicial review (which, as discussed below, is not the same thing as appeal to the courts). In addressing these three aspects in a single chapter, the goal is to provide the reader, in a systematic and chronological fashion, with a conceptual frame of reference that includes the full range of remedial options available to parties before administrative tribunals.

---

4 The GIC is not a tribunal at all, but it is the exception in this chapter. For simplicity I use the term "tribunal" throughout to refer to the full range of administrative agencies, commissions, and other bodies, but generally not including Cabinet. This is an oversimplification because many administrative decision-makers do not take a tribunal form. Many administrative decisions are made by bureaucrats without a hearing or the court-style structure of a tribunal; administrative agencies also regularly make policy decisions that affect individual and social interests. However, the tribunal is perhaps the prototypical administrative structure for the purpose of understanding the remedies available to a party to tribunal action.

Figure 2.1

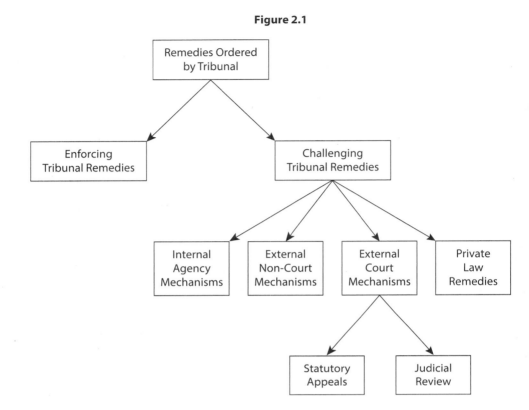

II. REMEDIAL OPTIONS AT THE TRIBUNAL STAGE

Administrative tribunals are as varied as the topics on which they adjudicate, and it would be unwise to generalize about the remedial powers available to them. However, two general comments about available remedies can safely be made. First, because a tribunal does not have the general jurisdiction that a court does, the power to impose a particular remedy must be provided for in the tribunal's enabling statute. Whether a tribunal can order that, for example, money damages be paid, an administrative penalty be imposed, or an individual be stripped of a licence will depend on the remedial powers the statute provides to it. Second, most tribunals' composition, structure, and mandates are different from courts', and their approach to remedies reflects those differences. For example, certain tribunals' expertise with a more limited subject matter may help them to identify systemic problems or recurring patterns across multiple individual disputes. Their ability to stay involved in (that is, to remain "seized" or to "have seizin" of) a dispute over a longer period of time is well established, and many tribunals are less constrained by formal rules than courts are in developing remedies. Together, on occasion, these factors allow tribunals to conceptualize and implement novel remedial strategies aimed at addressing the systemic problems they see.

A. **Statutory Authority**

As a creature of statute, a tribunal cannot make orders that affect individuals' rights or obligations without authority from its enabling statute.[5] Therefore, the first step in determining a tribunal's remedial options is to look at the statute itself. If a tribunal makes orders outside the scope of its enabling statute, it is exceeding its jurisdiction, and those orders will be void.[6]

Many enabling statutes set out express lists of the remedies a tribunal may order. For example, tribunals often have the power to make declaratory orders, to order a party to repair a problem or to mitigate damage, or to order a party to comply with the tribunal's enabling statute. Licensing powers may also be given to tribunals in statutory regimes designed to protect the public (for example, through professional licensing qualifications or requirements for corporations issuing securities to public investors), or to manage natural resources (for example, fishing and forestry licences). Some tribunals can appoint conciliators and otherwise assist in settling matters before them.[7] Some enabling statutes empower tribunals to impose significant fines and possible incarceration, or provide for more serious quasi-criminal offences that must be prosecuted by the Crown.[8]

Other statutes accord their tribunals broad, discretionary power to fashion the remedies they see fit. For example, the Ontario *Human Rights Code* gives the Ontario Human Rights Tribunal the discretion to order a party who has been found to discriminate to "do anything that, in the opinion of the tribunal, the party ought to do to achieve compliance with this Act, both in respect of the complaint and in respect of future practices."[9]

Even where a tribunal's remedial power is less certain (that is, its enabling statute does not expressly permit a particular remedy and the tribunal has no broad discretionary power), one may try to argue that, as a matter of practical necessity, a tribunal must have the remedial power to do the things its statute requires it to do.[10] However, orders for the payment of money, such as compensation or damages, fines, fees and levies, and costs, can generally only be ordered by tribunals that have the express statutory authority to do so. Tribunals also lack the equitable jurisdiction to order interim injunctions, although they may be given statutory authority to seek an injunction in court to enforce a statute. Finally, whether a tribunal has the power to grant remedies under the *Canadian Charter of Rights and Freedoms*[11] is a separate question. As Evan Fox-Decent and Alexander Pless explain in Chapter 13, The Charter and Administrative Law Part II: Substantive Review, a separate test determines whether particular administrative tribunals can grant remedies under s 24(1) of the Charter.[12]

---

5 *Att Gen of Can v Inuit Tapirisat*, [1980] 2 SCR 735, [1980] SCJ No 99 (QL).

6 When two tribunals share jurisdiction over a particular statutory provision (e.g., a workers' compensation tribunal and a human rights tribunal considering a statutory provision that concerns them both), a tribunal can also be found to exceed its jurisdiction if it deals with a claim that has already been "appropriately dealt with" by the other relevant tribunal. See *British Columbia (Workers' Compensation Board) v Figliola*, 2011 SCC 52, [2011] 3 SCR 422.

7 E.g. *Canadian Human Rights Act*, RSC 1985, c H-6, ss 47-48; BC *Employment Standards Act*, RSBC 1996, c 113, s 78 [BC ESA].

8 See e.g. BC *Securities Act*, RSCBC 1996, c 418, s 155.

9 *Human Rights Code*, RSO 1990, c H.19, s 41(1)(a).

10 *ATCO Gas and Pipelines Ltd v Alberta (Energy & Utilities Board)*, 2006 SCC 4, [2006] 1 SCR 140.

11 Part I of the *Constitution Act, 1982*, being Schedule B to the *Canada Act 1982* (UK), 1982, c 11 [Charter].

12 See *R v Conway*, 2010 SCC 22, [2010] 1 SCR 765.

Moreover, some provinces have now enacted statutes that explicitly bar at least some tribunals from considering Charter issues.[13]

B. What Makes Administrative Tribunals Unique

Administrative tribunals and agencies vary widely in their structures and functions, but collectively they also differ from courts in important ways. The particular structures and qualities of administrative tribunals equally affect the kinds of remedies they are inclined, and empowered, to grant. This part of the chapter seeks to set out in broad strokes the kinds of remedies that tribunal-type administrative bodies in particular are likely to grant. The kinds of functions performed by tribunal-type administrative bodies—namely, party-on-party dispute resolution, party-versus-agency enforcement and disciplinary proceedings, and other similar forms of hearings and decision-making—tend to be the most common ways in which members of the public engage with administrative bodies. These functions also square especially well with the concept of a "remedy," defined by *Black's Law Dictionary* as "the means by which the violation of a right is prevented, redressed, or compensated."[14]

However, the reader should be aware that tribunal-type administrative agencies are only one version of administrative agency operations. Parties may interact, be answerable to, and seek to influence administrative law agencies in other ways. Agencies' policy-making functions, in particular, are outside the scope of this chapter but should not be outside one's field of vision.[15] Through their statutory drafting choices, legislators regularly delegate detailed policy-making decisions to administrative tribunals. Many larger administrative agencies have formal policy-making departments, which generally operate at some remove from their tribunal departments. Administrative policy instruments can range from formal, binding interpretive releases to relatively informal, non-binding administrative guidance. Policy releases and guidelines have a direct impact on regulated entities. They are publicly available, and regulated entities are expected to know about them. Their release can be preceded by formal public consultation, providing those affected with a chance for input in advance.

Moreover, even when acting in their tribunal capacity, administrative tribunals often do, and should, take a broader perspective on a dispute than courts necessarily will. One way to understand the difference is in terms described by an American scholar, Abram Chayes, in the mid-1970s.[16] Chayes talked about courts, not administrative agencies. Nevertheless, his

---

13 See e.g. the BC *Administrative Tribunals Act*, SBC 2004, c 45 [ATA], which provides that the majority of provincial tribunals do not have discretion to consider either constitutional questions generally, or at least constitutional questions relating to the Charter. The statute establishes a mechanism for referring constitutional questions to the courts. Sections 46.1-46.3 of the Act impose similar restrictions on many tribunals' jurisdiction to apply the BC *Human Rights Code* to any matter before them on the basis that the Human Rights Tribunal is the more appropriate forum.

14 *Black's Law Dictionary*, 10th ed, *sub verbo* "remedy."

15 See Chapter 8, Delegation and Consultation: How the Administrative State Functions and the Importance of Rules.

16 Abram Chayes, "The Role of the Judge in Public Law Litigation" (1976) 89 Harv L Rev 1281; see also DM Gordon, "'Administrative' Tribunals and the Courts" (1933) 49 LQ Rev 94 (defining a judicial function as one that determines "pre-existing" rights and liabilities by reference to a "fixed objective standard," as contrasted to an administrative function, in which rights and liabilities are created by "policy and expediency").

point illuminates the distinction between the two. Chayes described an emerging dichotomy between traditional conceptions of adjudication and an emerging judicial role in what he described as public law litigation. In traditional adjudication, a suit involves only the private parties before the court. It is self-contained and party-initiated. A dispassionate judge identifies the private right at issue on the basis of doctrinal analysis and retrospective fact inquiry. The judge imposes relief, understood as compensation for the past violation of an identifiable existing right. (This portrayal describes party-on-party dispute resolution, but this sort of rights-based approach also underpins tribunal-on-party regulatory action, such as a self-regulatory profession's disciplinary proceeding against one of its members.) By contrast, in public law litigation, Chayes argued that the debate is more focused on the vindication of broader statutory or constitutional policies. The lawsuit is not self-contained. The judge must manage complex trial situations involving not only the parties to the dispute but also the many and shifting parties not before the court who nevertheless may be affected by the suit's outcome. Fact inquiry is predictive, not retrospective. Through a combination of party negotiation and continuing judicial involvement, the judge fashions relief that is ad hoc, ongoing, and prospective. On the Chayes model, judges can become change agents under whose management specific cases can have far-reaching effects.

Like Chayes's public law adjudicatory model, administrative agencies—even when acting as tribunals rather than policy-making bodies—may have a broader mandate, and the ability to leverage a broader range of tools than a traditional assertion of rights-based claims provides. Chayes's point was somewhat aspirational when it came to courts, but it is accurate in describing how at least some tribunals function. Many administrative bodies are explicitly charged with managing complex and often "polycentric" problems in a comprehensive manner. The Supreme Court of Canada has recognized this, pointing out that "while judicial procedure is premised on a bipolar opposition of parties, interests, and factual discovery, some problems [assigned to tribunals by their enabling statutes] require the consideration of numerous interests simultaneously, and the promulgation of solutions which concurrently balance benefits and costs for many different parties."[17]

This has a few implications. First, it means that relative to courts, administrative tribunals have stronger theoretical justifications for remaining seized of a case over a longer period of time.[18] Second, it means that administrative tribunals may try to develop remedies that address underlying structural or systemic problems, in a forward-looking rather than retrospective, rights-oriented way. This is not to say that courts may not also sometimes craft systemic, forward-looking remedies. Indeed, Chayes's point is that they may.[19] However, relative to courts, administrative tribunals may be especially well placed to develop and implement novel remedies thanks to their subject-specific expertise, their field sensitivity, and their particular statutory mandates.

---

17 *Pushpanathan v Canada (Minister of Citizenship and Immigration)*, [1998] 1 SCR 982 at para 36, [1998] SCJ No 46 (QL); see also *Catalyst Paper Corp v North Cowichan (District)*, 2012 SCC 2, [2012] 1 SCR 5 at paras 17-25 [*Catalyst Paper*]; *Canada v Kabul Farms Inc*, 2016 FCA 143, [2016] FCJ No 480 (QL) at paras 24-25.

18 See e.g. *Ontario (Ministry of Correctional Services) v Ontario (Human Rights Comm)* (2001), 39 CHRR 308 (Ont Sup Ct), aff'd [2004] OJ No 5051 (CA) (holding that the Human Rights Tribunal of Ontario had extensive supervisory jurisdiction over its orders and could remain seized of a matter to recast its orders to deal with ongoing systemic racism at correctional facilities).

19 *Doucet-Boudreau v Nova Scotia (Minister of Education)*, 2003 SCC 62, [2003] 3 SCR 3, provides justification for structural injunction-style remedies by courts.

Just as importantly, administrative tribunal members are a more diverse group than judges are, especially in terms of their training and expertise. Many tribunal members are not legally trained. Some tribunals' enabling statutes stipulate that a certain portion of their tribunal members should be laypersons. For example, the federal *Competition Tribunal Act*[20] stipulates that the tribunal shall consist of not more than six members who are Federal Court judges, and not more than eight other "lay" members. The statute goes on to say that the Governor in Council should establish an advisory council, "to be composed of not more than ten members who are knowledgeable in economics, industry, commerce or public affairs,"[21] to advise the Minister of Industry with respect to the appointment of lay members. The result is a tribunal with substantial expertise in economics and in commerce.[22] The tribunal's expertise also makes it more likely that its members will devise remedies that reflect their training and perspective, and that may be more economic than legal.

Sometimes, the composition of tribunal membership reflects an explicit attempt to represent different interest groups, perhaps especially in subject areas where there is a perception that judges historically have been unsympathetic or not alive to some of the issues at stake. A classic example is a tripartite labour board, on which a representative of labour, a representative of management, and a third member must sit. A further example of a tripartite structure is the BC Review Board, charged under the *Criminal Code*[23] with making dispositions with respect to individuals found unfit to stand trial or not criminally responsible on account of mental disorder. The BC *Mental Health Act*[24] requires that each panel of the Review Board consist of a doctor, a lawyer, and a person who is *neither* a doctor *nor* a lawyer.[25] The kinds of remedies that such boards devise are likely to reflect the particular priorities and assumptions of its members, and may not be limited to the set of strictly legal remedies that spring most easily to the legally trained mind.

Administrative law has also been affected by what is variously called "new public management" theory, neoliberalism, or administrative structures that "span the public-private divide." Effectively, these are mechanisms by which public structures, such as administrative tribunals, retain ultimate accountability for their programs but "outsource" the implementation of those programs to private or third-party actors. For example, hundreds of standards developed by private bodies are incorporated into law and used for enforcement and compliance purposes.[26] Regulators also delegate enforcement and compliance functions to private bodies. For example, the Technical Standards and Safety

---

20   RSC 1985, c 19 (2nd Supp), s 3(2) [CTA].

21   *Ibid*, s 3(3).

22   *Canada (Director of Investigation and Research) v Southam Inc*, [1997] 1 SCR 748. Separately, note that expertise is not only based on qualifications. Tribunal members also gain expertise through familiarity and experience with their fields.

23   RSC, 1985, c C-46.

24   RSBC 1996, c 288 [BC MHA].

25   BC MHA, s 24.1(3). Additional guidelines on qualifications for part-time members of the board can be found in "Recruitment, Screening and Appointment Procedures" (Vancouver: British Columbia Review Board, 2004), online: British Columbia Review Board <http://www.bcrb.bc.ca/BCRB%20Recruitment%20Procedures%202011.pdf>.

26   For example, since 1927, the Canadian Standards Association's Canadian Electrical Code, Canadian Standards Association Standard C22.1-06, has provided the standards for addressing shock and fire hazards of electrical products in Canada. It has been incorporated by reference into provincial regulations across the country: see e.g. *Electrical Safety Regulation*, BC Reg 100/2004, s 20.

Association (TSSA) is a delegated administrative authority for safety regulation in Ontario covering elevating devices, amusement rides, boilers, and other products. The various provincial securities commissions also delegate the regulation of investment dealers and mutual fund dealers to their respective self-regulated organizations, the Investment Industry Regulatory Organization of Canada (IIROC) and the Mutual Fund Dealers Association (MFDA). Many professionals, including doctors and lawyers, are regulated in Canada by their self-governing professional bodies, which are not government agencies.

These are deeply embedded features of Canadian law, especially in fields where there are highly technical product or process issues to be regulated. They are also controversial, particularly as their use becomes more widespread and it becomes clear that "technical" standards are not so easily divorced from larger social and policy considerations. Proponents of public–private coordination in regulation argue that delegated implementation is the best way forward for administrative agencies that are otherwise at risk of being ineffective and out of touch; that it allocates action to those bodies best equipped and with the greatest information to perform tasks effectively; that public–private partnerships are capable of accomplishing public ends more efficiently than the public sector could acting alone; and that such partnerships do not eliminate the public state, but rather "save" it from its own bureaucratic flaws.[27] Those opposed argue that these mechanisms are privatization by another name; that they reduce accountability and the public sector's responsibility for what should be publicly provided goods and services; and that they "hollow out" the state in potentially irretrievable ways.[28] We must leave this important debate for another day. At a practical level, though, parties to administrative actions should be aware that a constellation of ostensibly private actors may play more or less formal roles in real-life public administration.

As well, both tribunal-side and policy-side administrative functions have been affected by globalization. The effects of globalization mean that domestic administrative tribunals no longer act entirely free of international and transnational agreements, organizations, standard-setting bodies, and commitments. Some of the most notable international examples come out of the European Union, whose policy and harmonization directives and court decisions have, over the last several decades, had a direct impact on European nation states' domestic administrative law. In Canada, as well, international obligations have had an impact on, for example, federal labour policies and their subsequent administration through a variety of public bodies.[29] International human rights norms have also influenced the substantive review of administrative decisions.[30] Relevant international or transnational standards are sometimes set by governments acting together (such as the North American Free Trade Agreement [NAFTA] and its associated side agreements) and sometimes by independent, private, or non-governmental bodies filling lacunae in international law (as is the case

---

27　Jody Freeman, "Private Parties, Public Functions, and the New Administrative Law" (2000) 52 Admin L Rev 813; Richard Stewart, "Administrative Law in the Twenty-First Century" (2003) 78 NYUL Rev 437.

28　See e.g. Harry Arthurs, "Public Law in a Neoliberal Globalized World: The Administrative State Goes to Market (and Cries 'Wee, Wee, Wee' All the Way Home)" (2005) 55 UTLJ 797.

29　Canada, Commission on Labour Standards Review, *Fairness at Work: Federal Labour Standards for the 21st Century* (Gatineau: Human Resources and Skills Development Canada, 2006) at 51-52, online: <http://publications.gc.ca/collections/collection_2008/hrsdc-rhdsc/HS24-31-2006E.pdf>.

30　See Chapter 16, International Human Rights Norms and Administrative Law.

with forest practices certification).[31] Looking at these developments, some scholars have even begun to herald the birth of a "global administrative law."[32]

Thus, the conversation about proper tribunal action spans multiple disciplines—law, public policy, and organizational and political theory—and it is taking place at the levels of practice and theory, both within tribunals and with respect to them. The forces that influence tribunals produce remedies that can be more dynamic and varied than the ones we are accustomed to seeing in the courts. Courts' review of administrative action—the piece of the puzzle that gets so much attention in mainstream Canadian administrative law courses—is only one facet of administrative law.

C. Systemic Remedies at the Tribunal Level

Some of the factors described above—ongoing seizin, a broad mandate, different expertise, public–private coordination, and transnational linkages—have led some tribunals to create innovative remedies. For example, one cluster of innovations incorporates an independent third party in trying to develop and implement remedial measures within a subject organization or corporation where systemic problems seem to be significant. These remedies try to effectuate meaningful systemic change within the organization through sustained engagement with the problem by an impartial outsider. They have become fairly common, particularly among securities and other corporate regulators in the United States and Australia, as well as Canada.[33] An important function of the third party in this context is to facilitate a deliberative process within the organization itself—that is, to help the troubled organization confront and work through its problems internally. Some scholars argue that transparent, accountable, and broadly participatory dialogue of this nature, potentially facilitated by such third parties, is the most legitimate and most effective mechanism for making decisions in complex organizational structures.[34]

---

31 Errol Meidinger, "The Administrative Law of Global Private-Public Regulation: The Case of Forestry" (2006) 17 EJIL 47.

32 Benedict Kingsbury, Nico Krisch & Richard B Stewart, "The Emergence of Global Administrative Law" (2005) 68 Law & Contemp Probs 15.

33 In the United States, corporate monitorships have been imposed on dozens of corporations under the terms of deferred criminal prosecution agreements or regulatory enforcement settlements. On the effectiveness of corporate monitorships in that context, see Cristie Ford & David Hess, "Corporate Monitorships and New Governance Regulation: In Theory, in Practice, and in Context" (2011) 33:4 Law & Pol'y 509. The Australian Competition and Consumer Commission was a pioneer in developing what are known there as "enforceable undertakings": Christine Parker, "Restorative Justice in Business Regulation? The Australian Competition and Consumer Commission's Use of Enforceable Undertakings" (2004) 67 Mod L Rev 209. Canadian examples include Settlement Agreement, Mackie Research Capital Corporation, 2010 BCSECCOM 646 (22 November 2010), online: <http://www.bcsc.bc.ca/Enforcement/Settlements/PDF/2010_BCSECCOM_646_pdf/>; Settlement Agreement, *In the Matter of Union Securities Ltd and John P Thompson* (18 April 2006), online: <http://docs.iiroc.ca/DisplayDocument.aspx?DocumentID=71522F-D9816A452F8246B58D8776B613&Language=fr>; Order, *In the Matter of Agnico-Eagle Mines Limited* (28 April 2005), online: Ontario Securities Commission <http://www.osc.gov.on.ca/en/10499.htm>.

34 See e.g. Amy Gutmann & Dennis Thompson, *Why Deliberative Democracy?* (Princeton, NJ: Princeton University Press, 2004); but see César A Rodríguez-Garavito, "Global Governance and Labor Rights: Codes of Conduct and Anti-Sweatshop Struggles in Global Apparel Factories in Mexico and Guatemala" (2005) *Politics & Society* 203.

One effort at creating such a deliberative, third-party facilitated process took place within Ontario's Ministry of Correctional Services, as a response to a long-standing human rights complaint by an employee of the ministry. The complainant in that case, Michael McKinnon, was a correctional officer of Indigenous ancestry working within the Ministry of Correctional Services. In 1998, the Human Rights Tribunal of Ontario (then called the Board of Inquiry) found that Mr McKinnon suffered discrimination and harassment at his workplace, the Toronto East Detention Centre, because of his race, ancestry, and ethnic origin. In response, the tribunal ordered a number of systemic remedies to address the "poisoned atmosphere" at the facility, Toronto East, and within corrections generally. Among other things, the tribunal ordered that certain individual respondents be relocated, that the tribunal's order be publicized among corrections employees, and that a human rights training program be established. The tribunal reconvened the hearing in 2002 because of Mr McKinnon's allegations that the poisoned work environment had not improved. The issue for the tribunal at that point was not whether the existing systemic remedies had been implemented in a strict sense, but whether they had been carried out in good faith.

 After dealing with the question whether it could remain seized of the matter—finding that it could, as affirmed later by the Ontario Court of Appeal[35]—the tribunal ordered an additional range of remedies, including training for ministry and facility management; establishing a roster of external mediators to deal with discrimination complaints; and appointing, at the ministry's expense, an independent third-party consultant nominated by the Ontario Human Rights Commission (OHRC) to develop and oversee the delivery of training programs. The third-party consultant was to be nominated by the OHRC, to be paid for by the ministry, and to report to the tribunal.

What makes these remedies interesting is that they are so different in character from traditional legal remedies, such as damages (in the civil context) or quashing of ministry or Facility decisions (in the administrative law context). This looks like Chayes's public law litigation model: these remedies are prospective, open-ended, and subject to ongoing revision and elaboration. The tribunal's remedial orders—the emphasis on training, and bringing in the expertise of external human rights consultants to work with the Ministry in developing that training—seem geared less toward redressing the wrongs against Mr McKinnon in particular, and more toward effecting wide-ranging and permanent *systemic* change to institutional culture.

The *McKinnon* case became the longest-running human rights case in Canada, but ultimately after a protracted and difficult run, it had a somewhat happy ending. As of May 2005, the parties were still arguing over the scope of the third-party consultant's responsibilities, with the consultant alleging that the ministry was attempting to gain control over the process. The process of defining the consultant's mandate seemed itself to have become an adversarial contest that did not bode well for the consultant's ability to catalyze the hoped-for meaningful dialogue within the ministry.[36] By 2007, the tribunal found that the ministry had not been implementing the tribunal's previous orders in good faith,[37] and in February

---

35 *Ontario v McKinnon*, [2004] OJ No 5051 (QL) (CA) [*McKinnon*].

36 Human Rights Tribunal of Ontario, Interim Decisions and Rulings, *Ontario Human Rights Commission and Michael McKinnon and Ontario Ministry of Correctional Services*, 2005 HRTO 15 (19 May 2005), online: <http://www.canlii.org/en/on/onhrt/doc/2005/2005hrto15/2005hrto15.html>.

37 *McKinnon v Ontario (Correctional Services)*, 2007 HRTO 4.

2011 the tribunal found that a *prima facie* case had been made out that the deputy minister was in contempt for failing to implement the earlier orders. The tribunal exercised its discretion to state a case for contempt to the Ontario Divisional Court.[38] (As we see below, this is a tribunal's last resort in trying to get its orders followed.)

Before that case could be heard, however, and after 23 years of litigation, Michael McKinnon and the ministry finally reached a settlement. Under the August 2011 settlement agreement, the OHRC, the Ministry of Community Safety and Correctional Services, and the Ministry of Government Services all signed on to a three-year Human Rights Project, which established mechanisms targeting accountability, operations, learning, and complaint management within correctional services.[39] Despite progress, however, a pervasive "organizational culture" remained a barrier to effecting "long-term, systemic, or broad-based human rights improvements."[40] In the agreement's final year, the parties formulated a "Multi-Year Plan" to "crystalize the extensive work" done to date and to "sustain change" into the future.[41]

The *McKinnon* settlement and the efforts that continue to follow it are cause for some optimism, but a satisfactory result was never, and is still not, a foregone conclusion. The 2011 settlement might not have happened in the absence of a factor external to the tribunal process—the appointment of a new Deputy Minister of Corrections with a mandate to professionalize the service and improve its record.[42] Nor is a 23-year-long litigation matter ever really a victory, no matter what its outcome. Thus, *McKinnon* raised and still leaves us with some challenging questions: Is it possible to effect real, substantive "good faith" compliance in a truly recalcitrant employer? Is it appropriate to use law to simultaneously enforce rights, redress wrongs, and "cure" systemic problems? Is it appropriate for a tribunal to continue crafting new orders in an effort to achieve an optimal outcome? Can external third

---

38   *McKinnon v Ontario (Correctional Services)*, 2011 HRTO 263.

39   OHRC, "Organizational change in Correctional Services—the MCSCS Human Rights Project Charter," online: <http://www.ohrc.on.ca/en/annual-report-2012-2013-rights-partners-actions/organizational-change-correctional-services-%E2%80%93-mcscs-human-rights-project-charter>. The executive committee receives advice from an Aboriginal advisory subcommittee, an external advisory group, and several working groups. Committee members receive *Human Rights Code* training, and the ministry discloses relevant internal operations data to the OHRC. See OHRC, "Correctional Services: Update on the MCSCS Human Rights Project Charter," online: <http://www.ohrc.on.ca/en/annual-report-2011-2012-human-rights-next-generation/correctional-services-update-mcscs-human-rights-project-charter>.

40   *Ibid.*

41   OHRC, "Reaching new milestones with the Human Rights Project Charter," online: <http://www.ohrc.on.ca/en/annual-report-2013-2014-ohrc-today/organizational-change-page>. A phased implementation strategy focuses on embedding human rights and Aboriginal expertise, service delivery, building competencies, maintaining an inclusive workplace, and complaint management."

42   The Toronto East Detention Centre is not the only Ontario facility at which correctional officers have alleged that they suffer discrimination and harassment based on their race or ancestry. See e.g. *Cox v Ontario (Community Safety and Correctional Services)*, 2014 HRTO 286, an ongoing matter involving an allegation of a hate mail campaign directed at African-Canadian corrections officers going back to 2004. Mr Cox claims that the mail is coming from fellow correctional officers. Like Mr McKinnon, Mr Cox alleges that his employer has not taken adequate affirmative steps to respond to the problem, and that the majority of Don Jail correctional officers do not participate in its ostensibly mandatory human rights training program. He also alleges, *inter alia*, that the Ontario Public Service Employees Union actively undermined an earlier investigation into the incidents. See Jasmin Seputis, "Toronto Jail Guard Seeks Workplace Racism Investigation,"*CBC News* (5 March 2012), online: <http://www.cbc.ca/1.1129238>.

parties really change culture and create meaningful dialogue? If not, what legal options do we have left—through tribunal remedies or otherwise?

Moreover, we should not overestimate courts' comfort with broader remedial orders by tribunals that aim to address systemic problems. Court review of tribunal remedies by means of judicial review serves a valuable validation function, based on important rule-of-law values. It also introduces some difficult tensions. As we have identified, cases like *McKinnon* straddle what Chayes might describe as the boundary between party-on-party dispute resolution and public law litigation. As we know, when courts engage with systemic issues, they run quickly into public policy choices, public law separation-of-powers concerns, and legitimacy concerns. Tribunals, too, may quickly run into the limits of their statutory authority. This is as it should be. And yet, for these reasons, judicial review may always serve as a brake on tribunals' more ambitious efforts to effect systemic change.

For example, in *Moore v British Columbia (Education)*,[43] the court reviewed the BC Human Rights Tribunal's decision that the failure to provide educational support to Jeffrey Moore, a child with dyslexia, constituted discrimination on the basis of disability. The tribunal had considered not only Jeffrey's personal damages but also the fact that the BC Ministry of Education had implemented a fixed cap on special education funding, below the actual incidence rate; and the school district's decision, faced with those funding constraints, to close its Diagnostic Centre, which provided support to dyslexic students, without providing an adequate substitute.

At the Supreme Court of Canada, writing for a unanimous court, Abella J upheld the Human Rights Tribunal's findings of discrimination against Jeffrey by the district, and the personal damages it awarded. However, the tribunal's systemic remedies were held to be too remote from the scope of the complaint.[44] They were "quashed," or invalidated. The court observed that a remedy afforded by the tribunal to an individual claimant could still have a systemic impact, but that

> The remedy must flow from the claim. In this case, the claim was made on behalf of Jeffrey, and the evidence giving concrete support to the claim all centred on him. While the Tribunal was certainly entitled to consider systemic evidence in order to determine whether Jeffrey had suffered discrimination, it was unnecessary for it to hold an extensive inquiry into the precise format of the provincial funding mechanism or the entire provincial administration of special education in order to determine whether *Jeffrey* was discriminated against. *The Tribunal, with great respect, is an adjudicator of the particular claim that is before it, not a Royal Commission.*[45]

Abella J also set aside the tribunal's remedial orders against the Ministry on the basis that the connection between province-wide fixed cap funding and closure of the Diagnostic Centre was too remote. Moreover, Abella J found no need for the tribunal to remain seized "on behalf of an individual student who has finished his high school education and will not re-enter the public school system."[46] The sharp contrast in *Moore* between the tribunal's conception of its mandate, consistent with the Chayes public law litigation model, and the

---

43   2012 SCC 61, [2012] 3 SCR 360 [*Moore*].

44   *Catalyst Paper, supra* note 17 at para 56. The relevant standard of review was patent unreasonableness, which exists in British Columbia under the BC ATA.

45   *Moore, supra* note 43 at para 64 (emphasis added).

46   *Ibid* at para 66.

Supreme Court's retrospective, party-focused analysis underscores both the possibilities, and limitations, of novel remedial strategies in effecting systemic change.

III. ENFORCING TRIBUNAL ORDERS AGAINST PARTIES

After a tribunal makes a decision and imposes an order, assuming no one challenges that decision,[47] another set of administrative law remedies becomes available: the enforcement powers. These may be invoked where a tribunal needs to enforce its order against a party that is not complying with the order. This is not uncommon among self-regulatory organizations such as professional licensing bodies, where the tribunal acts against particular individuals rather than adjudicating disputes between parties. Alternatively, a party to a multiparty dispute before a tribunal may want to enforce the tribunal's order against another party on which the order was imposed. Criminal prosecution is also a possibility. Of course, regardless of any broader social patterns or systemic factors operating, tribunal orders can only be enforced against the parties on which they are imposed.

A. The Tribunal Seeks to Enforce Its Order

Rarely, a tribunal may enforce its own orders. One tribunal that has the power to enforce its own orders—for example, an order for civil contempt—is the federal Competition Tribunal.[48] Some other tribunals are also given the authority to enforce monetary obligations, such as requiring unpaid wages or family maintenance to be paid, imposing liens, making garnishment orders, seizing assets, or even suspending driving privileges.[49] However, any enforcement powers a tribunal has must be granted to the tribunal in its enabling statute, and that delegation of enforcement power must pass constitutional scrutiny. For example, a provincially created tribunal cannot have criminal (and therefore federal) enforcement powers.[50]

In British Columbia, certain sections of the *Administrative Tribunals Act* are intended to assist tribunals in obtaining compliance with their orders. For example, s 18 permits certain tribunals to schedule a hearing, make a decision, or dismiss an application if a party fails to comply with an order (presumably, an order to appear). Section 31(1)(e) permits some tribunals to dismiss an application if the applicant fails to comply with a tribunal order. Section 47, which permits some tribunals to make orders for payment of costs, also allows some tribunals, under s 47(1)(c), to require a party to pay the *tribunal's* actual costs "if the tribunal considers the conduct of a party has been improper, vexatious, frivolous or abusive." Orders for

---

47 See Section IV.

48 CTA, s 8(1). See *Chrysler Canada Ltd v Canada (Competition Tribunal)*, [1992] 2 SCR 394 (4th) [*Chrysler Canada*] (holding that clear and unambiguous statutory language can override the common law rule that only superior courts have the power to punish for contempt and that the wording of the CTA, s 8(1) (as it then was), which conferred on the tribunal jurisdiction "to hear and determine all applications made under Part VIII of the *Competition Act* and any matters related thereto," constituted such clear and unambiguous statutory language); also *Lymer v Jonsson*, 2016 ABCA 76 at paras 11-13 (re registrar in bankruptcy).

49 E.g., BC ESA, ss 87-101; *Maintenance Enforcement Act*, SNS 1994-95, c 6, ss 19, 27-30.

50 *MacMillan Bloedel Ltd v Simpson*, [1995] 4 SCR 725, [1996] 2 WWR 1; *United Nurses of Alberta v Alberta (Attorney General)*, [1992] 1 SCR 901, 89 DLR (4th) 609 [*United Nurses of Alberta*].

costs, on being filed in the court registry, have the same effect as a court order for the recovery of a debt (s 47(2)).

More commonly, the tribunal must make an application in court to enforce any order it makes. Where a party has disobeyed a tribunal order, the statute provides that the tribunal may apply to court for an order requiring the person to comply.[51] The tribunal's order is presumed to be valid and correct if the party disobeying it failed to file an appeal (if one is available) or if the party appealed and lost.[52] Other statutes allow tribunal orders to be registered with the court, sometimes only with leave.[53] In Quebec, a distinct procedure known as homologation gives courts the authority to compel individuals to fulfill tribunal orders. Courts can only access homologation if it is expressly provided for in the tribunal's enabling statute.[54] The omnibus *Statutory Powers Procedure Act* in Ontario allows tribunals to state a case for contempt to the Ontario Divisional Court, as happened in the *McKinnon* case in 2011.

Once a tribunal has successfully converted its order into a court order through one of the mechanisms above, the order can be enforced in the same manner as a court judgment. Among other things, this means that the court can initiate contempt proceedings if the party continues to disregard the order.[55] Contempt proceedings may be available if a party fails to abide by a tribunal's procedural order (for example, by failing to appear as a witness or to produce documents) or a tribunal's final substantive order.[56] Contempt can be civil or, where the conduct constitutes an intentional public act of defiance of the court, criminal.[57] In a contempt proceeding, the judge does not inquire into the validity of the tribunal's underlying order. However, only violations of "clear and unambiguous" tribunal orders will form the basis of a contempt order.[58] A court can also refuse to hold a party in contempt until an appeal or judicial review application (discussed in Section IV below) is completed, although parties can be required to pay moneys into court in the meantime.[59]

Note that legislators seem content to house tribunal order enforcement powers in the courts, even while using clauses to try to limit the availability of judicial review from administrative tribunals (known as "privative clauses").[60] For the legislative drafter, then, access to courts to *enforce* tribunal orders seems to be acceptable, while access to courts to *challenge* tribunal orders is less so. There is history at work here, along with separation-of-powers concerns and the legislator's appreciation for courts' existing enforcement powers. Arguably, this drafting choice also signals that legislators may be most concerned about conserving

---

51 See e.g. *Statutory Powers Procedure Act*, RSO 1990, c S 22 [SPPA], ss 13 and 19, respectively.

52 *Estevan Coal Corp v Estevan (Rural Municipality No 5)*, [2000] 8 WWR 474.

53 See e.g. ATA, ss 47, 54.

54 See e.g. *Regulation respecting the conciliation and arbitration procedure for the accounts of members of the Corporation professionnelle des physiothérapeutes du Québec*, RRQ, c C-26, r 141.1.

55 Tribunals themselves may have the power to make orders for *in facie* contempt (contempt "in the face of" the court during the proceedings) because this power is implicit in the designation of a tribunal as a court of record. If a tribunal is not designated as such, then the power to punish for *in facie* contempt, like the power to punish for *ex facie* contempt (contempt outside the proceedings), must be explicitly conferred by the enabling statute. See *Chrysler Canada, supra* note 48.

56 See e.g. SPPA, s 13.

57 *United Nurses of Alberta, supra* note 50; also *Re Cowan*, 2010 ONSC 3138.

58 *Chrysler Canada, supra* note 48; *Bell ExpressVu Limited Partnership v Corkery*, 2009 ONCA 85 at paras 24-28.

59 *Boucher v Logistik Unicorp Inc*, [2001] JQ No 64 (QL) (CA), leave to appeal to SCC refused, [2001] CSCR No 115; *Sodema Inc v Sarafian*, 2006 QCCA 816, [2006] JQ No 5460 (QL).

60 On privative clauses and substantive fairness, see Chapter 11, Standard of Review: Back to the Future?

scarce judicial resources when those judicial resources might be deployed to undermine, rather than buttress and reinforce, the authority of the tribunals the legislation creates.

B. A Party Seeks to Enforce a Tribunal's Order

A party to an administrative action may also, exceptionally, bring an action against another party in court to enforce the tribunal's order. For example, a group of teachers successfully sought to enforce an arbitrator's order that a school board annually set aside certain funds for teachers' professional development.[61] Sara Blake has suggested that the party's success "may depend on whether the tribunal order is of a type that a court would enforce, and whether the court believes it should enforce the tribunal order in the absence of any statutory procedure for obtaining court assistance."[62] In other words, courts may be more likely to grant a private application to enforce a tribunal order where the court recognizes the tribunal's order as similar to the kind of order that a court might make. However, the private applicant will first have the difficult task of convincing the court that it should intervene in this way, even though there may be no statutory provision explicitly empowering it to do so.

C. Criminal Prosecution

Many statutes provide for quasi-criminal prosecution of persons who disobey tribunal orders. Quasi-criminal offences are prosecuted by the federal or provincial Crown, as appropriate, and they carry penalties that include fines and imprisonment. For example, a person who commits an offence under s 155 of the BC *Securities Act*[63] is liable to a fine of not more than $3 million, to imprisonment for not more than three years, or both. Indictable offences under the federal *Fisheries Act*[64] may attract, at their upper end, fines of up to $500,000 or imprisonment for up two years, or both.[65]

In the absence of other provisions, it is a criminal offence to disobey a lawful order of a federal or provincial tribunal. The federal *Criminal Code* states:

> 127(1) Every one who, without lawful excuse, disobeys a lawful order made by a court of justice *or by a person or body of persons authorized by any Act to make or give the order*, other than an order for the payment of money, is, *unless a punishment or other mode of proceeding is expressly provided by law*, guilty of
>> (a) an indictable offence and liable to imprisonment for a term not exceeding two years; or
>> (b) an offence punishable on summary conviction.[66]

The *Criminal Code* provision is only available where no other penalty is expressly provided by law. What does this mean? Superior courts' own contempt powers do not generally count

---

61   *Melia v Moose Jaw Roman Catholic Separate School District No 22* (1979), 108 DLR (3d) 113, [1979] SJ No 568 (QL) (CA).

62   Sara Blake, *Administrative Law in Canada*, 4th ed (Markham, Ont: LexisNexis Butterworths, 2006) at 226.

63   BC *Securities Act*

64   *Fisheries Act*, RSC 1985, c F-14.

65   *Fisheries Act,* s 78(b).

66   *Criminal Code*, s 127(1) (emphasis added).

as an "other mode of proceeding" for purposes of this section.[67] Most administrative tribunals do not have the ability to make contempt orders on their own. Therefore, the *Criminal Code* provisions should apply where no "punishment or other mode of proceeding" is explicitly set out in the *tribunal's enabling statute*. This has been held not to violate the constitutional separation of powers, even when dealing with provincial tribunals, on the basis that the provincial tribunal is still making orders that are non-criminal. Parliament, acting within its sphere, is the one that has decided that breach of those provincial provisions is a criminal offence.[68]

IV.　CHALLENGING ADMINISTRATIVE ACTION WITHOUT GOING TO COURT

A party to an administrative action may also decide to challenge that administrative action itself. The possible bases for a party's challenge are described in other chapters in this text. For example, a party may challenge the tribunal's jurisdiction, its procedure, its impartiality, or the substance of its final decision. Each of these usually amounts to a direct or indirect challenge to the remedies or orders the tribunal imposes. Sometimes, these challenges are made through applications for what in administrative law is called "judicial review." However, applications for judicial review, like litigation generally, can be expensive and drawn-out affairs. Moreover, it is important to be realistic about what can be achieved through judicial review. In order to bring a successful judicial review application, a challenger must be aware of the specific remedial mechanisms available and how those mechanisms will help them achieve the result that they want. For example, as the *Gitxaala Nation* example shows, a motion to quash a tribunal decision, if successful, will usually only lead to the court sending the matter back to the original tribunal for rehearing.[69] This result may not satisfy the challenger. Even assuming that proper procedure is observed the second time, there is no guarantee that the party will receive the substantive outcome they seek.

For these reasons, parties seeking to challenge administrative action should consider their options carefully. This part of the chapter outlines the various review mechanisms available, including both non-court mechanisms and court-based mechanisms. We begin first with mechanisms that are internal to the administrative apparatus itself, then move to mechanisms that exist externally to both the administrative agency and courts (for example, ombudspersons), finally turning to court-based mechanisms. Here we distinguish between appeals and judicial review, and discuss private law or alternative monetary remedies that may exist against administrative decision-makers.

67　*R v Gibbons*, 2012 SCC 28, [2012] 2 SCR 92 (holding that s 127 applies "where there is an express alternative statutory response to failures to obey court orders," and that the Ontario Rules of Civil Procedure are not such an alternative); but see *R v Nielsen*, 2014 ABCA 173, 575 AR 197 (determining, for purposes of granting leave to appeal, that there is a "real issue" as to whether the Alberta Rules of Court would constitute such an exception).

68　*United Nurses of Alberta*, *supra* note 50.

69　See Kate Glover, Chapter 5, The Principles and Practices of Procedural Fairness.

A. Internal Tribunal Mechanisms

A party considering a challenge to tribunal action will need to understand the particular tribunal's structure and capacity, as established by its enabling statute. All tribunals can fix certain things, such as clerical errors or factual errors due to mistake or dishonesty, without express statutory authority. This is sometimes called the "slip rule."[70] Tribunals can also "change their minds" until the time a final decision is made. Therefore, what constitutes a "final decision" is important. For example, if a statute provides that final decisions must be in writing, then only written decisions will constitute final decisions. Preliminary rulings can also be changed until the final decision on a matter has been made.[71]

Some enabling statutes specifically provide tribunals with the ability to reconsider and rehear decisions they have made. This is most common where a particular tribunal has ongoing regulatory responsibility over a particular domain, such as public utilities regulation or employer–employee relations. For example, the *Public Service Labour Relations Act* provides, "[s]ubject to subsection (2) [prohibiting retroactive effect of any rights acquired], the Board may review, rescind or amend any of its orders or decisions, or may rehear any application before making an order in respect of the application."[72] Absent such express statutory authority, however, for policy reasons that favour finality of proceedings, a tribunal cannot reconsider or alter a final decision made within its jurisdiction. Once it has made a final decision, the tribunal is *functus officio*.[73]

As a next-best alternative for challenging a tribunal decision, consider that some administrative tribunals are part of multi-tiered administrative agencies. Those tribunals' enabling statutes may provide for appeals internal to the administrative agency itself. For example, parties appearing before Canada's Immigration and Refugee Board Immigration Division may appeal to its Immigration Appeal Division.[74] Similarly, provincial securities acts across the country provide that persons directly affected by decisions made by Securities Commission staff may appeal to (or, in some statutes, seek "review" from) the commission itself, to which staff report.[75] Again, parties should be aware that internal appellate structures may not look much like courts.

These internal review proceedings do not preclude subsequent appeals to the courts. Indeed, the various provincial securities acts mentioned above provide for appeals under limited conditions from their internal appellate bodies to the courts. These are called "statutory appeals." Where the statute does not provide for an appeal to the courts, the parties' only access to the courts is by means of judicial review. However, as discussed in more detail below, where a statute provides for reconsideration or internal administrative appeals within

---

70 See e.g. *Chandler v Alberta Association of Architects*, [1989] 2 SCR 848 at 861 [*Chandler*]; *Muscillo Transport Ltd v Ontario (Licence Suspension Appeal Board)* (1997), 149 DLR (4th) 545 at 553 (ONSC), aff'd [1998] OJ No 1488 (QL) (CA).

71 *Comeau's Sea Foods Ltd v Canada (Minister of Fisheries and Oceans)*, [1997] 1 SCR 12.

72 *Public Service Labour Relations Act*, SC 2003, c 22, s 43.

73 *Chandler*, *supra* note 70. Because rights of appeal from tribunals tend to be more limited than from courts, the *functus officio* doctrine should be more flexible and less formulistic for such tribunals.

74 *Immigration and Refugee Protection Act*, SC 2001, c 27 [IRPA], ss 62-71, 174-75. Recourse to the courts is only available with leave of the Federal Court: *ibid*, s 72.

75 See e.g. Ontario *Securities Act*, RSO 1990, c S 5, s 8(2); Alberta *Securities Act*, RSA 2000, c S-4 [AB *Securities Act*], s 35(1); BC *Securities Act*, ss 165(3), 167(1).

a multi-tiered agency, a challenger will generally be expected to exhaust those avenues before making an application for judicial review.

One of the more interesting innovations in internal administrative appeals was created in 1996, with the passage of Quebec's *Administrative Justice Act*.[76] The statute creates the Tribunal administratif du Québec (TAQ), a supertribunal that hears "proceedings" brought against almost all administrative tribunals and public bodies in the province, including government departments, boards, commissions, municipalities, and health care bodies.[77] As a practical matter, this means that there is now one main appellate/review body for administrative matters in the province. According to the Act, the tribunal's purpose is "to affirm the specific character of administrative justice, to ensure its quality, promptness and accessibility and to safeguard the fundamental rights of citizens."[78] It is an administrative (that is, executive branch) institution, not a judicial one, but its remedial powers include judicial review-style options and (surprisingly for common law administrative lawyers) the ability to substitute its decision for an original tribunal's: "[i]n the case of the contestation of a decision, the Tribunal may confirm, vary or quash the contested decision and, if appropriate, make the decision which, in its opinion, should have been made initially."[79] Where the TAQ has jurisdiction to consider a proceeding, claimants should exhaust the remedies available from it rather than trying to circumvent the administrative process.[80] Avenues of appeal from the TAQ to the Superior Court of Quebec are limited.[81]

B. External Non-Court Mechanisms

A party considering a challenge to administrative action should also not overlook non-legal avenues. For example, ombudspersons or similar positions exist by statute in every Canadian province. There is no overarching federal ombudsperson, but some federal departments and subject areas have their own specialized ombudspersons. Generally, the mandate of an ombudsperson is to provide a forum for citizens to bring their complaints regarding the way that government departments and agencies have dealt with them. There is no charge to make a complaint to an ombudsperson. Ombudspersons have discretion as to whether or not they will investigate a complaint.

An ongoing issue has been the degree to which an ombudsperson can assert jurisdiction with respect to administrative tribunal decisions and processes (as opposed to the general

---

76 *An Act Respecting Administrative Justice*, RSQ, c J-3.

77 *Ibid*, s 14. The use of the word "proceedings" rather than "appeal" or "review" indicates that the tribunal can hear appeals in the traditional sense, but it can also hear various demands that look more or less like review or *révision*. The scope and nature of the available proceedings depend on the wording of each tribunal's enabling statute.

78 *Ibid*, s 1.

79 *Ibid*, s 15.

80 *Okwuobi v Lester B Pearson School Board; Casimir v Quebec (Attorney General); Zorrilla v Quebec (Attorney General)*, 2005 SCC 16, [2005] 1 SCR 257.

81 The tribunal is composed of four divisions (social affairs, immovable property, territory and environment, and economic affairs), but, per s 159 of the Act, an appeal to the court is only available from the immovable property division and from decisions regarding the preservation of agricultural land. This tracks the appeals that were available from those tribunals before the TAQ was created; the TAQ replaced a plethora of administrative appeal bodies, but was not intended to increase the number of available appeals to the courts.

run of government departments and ministries—that is, public servants not possessing the statutorily created decision-making structure that tribunals have). Most legislation defines the ombudsperson's jurisdiction as being over "matters of administration," and courts have tended to define "administration" expansively as involving generic administrative processes, not simply as the antonym of "judicial" processes.[82] Among the tribunals themselves, the range of bodies subject to an ombudsperson's investigatory powers can be quite broad. In Ontario, for example, the courts have held that even largely independent bodies can be subject to ombuds review if the government pays its members' wages.[83] However, most ombuds statutes provide that an ombudsperson is not authorized to investigate a tribunal's decision until after any right of appeal or review on the merits has been exercised or until after the time limit for doing so has expired.[84]

Several other public officials similar to ombudspersons also exist, including freedom of information and privacy commissioners, the auditor general, provincial auditors, and human rights commissioners. While harder for individuals to instigate, public inquiries are another mechanism for challenging government conduct.[85]

C. Using the Courts

Finally, there are the courts. The ability to challenge administrative action in the courts is a mixed, but necessary, blessing. On the downside, even leaving aside some very serious concerns about costs and access to justice, courts may be reluctant to embrace novel, non-courtlike, yet potentially effective remedies devised by specialized tribunals. The richness and creativity that may characterize administrative law remedies could be stifled by potentially over-judicialized, overly interventionist court scrutiny. This is one reason that the internal appeal mechanisms described above, which permit decisions to be reviewed by higher-level bodies within the administrative agency structure itself, make sense. On the other hand, there are times—among others, during national emergencies—when executive action unquestionably needs to be subject to the rule of law, as applied by independent courts.[86] As with so many things in administrative law, context matters in thinking about the legitimacy of each alternative. There may be times when it makes sense to maintain the integrity of the administrative regime through all internal appeal stages. There may also be

---

82 For example, in *British Columbia Development Corporation v Friedmann (Ombudsman)*, [1984] 2 SCR 447, the Supreme Court ruled that policy-making activities of provincial Crown corporations were "matters of administration" for the purposes of the *Ombudsman Act*. The Ontario Court of Appeal has interpreted the ombudsperson's jurisdiction over "administration of a government agency" to include investigations into matters determined by administrative tribunals: *Ombudsman of Ontario v Ontario (Labour Relations Board)* (1986), 44 DLR (4th) 312 (Ont CA).

83 *Ontario (Ombudsman) v Ontario (Health Disciplines Board)* (1979), 104 DLR (3d) 597 (Ont CA).

84 See e.g. the Yukon *Ombudsman Act*, RSY 2002, c 163, s 12. The Manitoba *Ombudsman Act*, CCSM c O45, s 18(d) and the Saskatchewan *Ombudsman and Children's Advocate Act*, RSS 1978, c O-4, s 15(1)(d) provide that rights of appeal or review preclude an ombudsperson's intervention "unless the Ombudsman is satisfied that in the particular case it would have been unreasonable to expect the complainant to resort to the tribunal or court," although the time limitation for appeal or review must still have run.

85 See Peter Carver, Getting the Story Out: Accountability and the Law of Public Inquiries, <www.emond.ca/adminlaw3e>.

86 See Chapter 4, Administering the Canadian Rule of Law. The national security context is also treated differently: consider *Canada (Prime Minister) v Khadr*, 2010 SCC 3, [2010] 1 SCR 44 [*Khadr*].

times when what is required is faster and unapologetic recourse to the courts—for example, allowing a party to "leapfrog" the internal appeals and proceed directly to judicial review.

There are two main ways by which a party to a tribunal action can access the courts to challenge that action: appeal and judicial review. Appeal mechanisms—either to internal administrative appellate bodies or to courts—are provided for in the statutory scheme itself. The scope of a possible appeal is confined to what the statute expressly provides. Courts still struggle sometimes with knotty issues in taking appeals from administrative tribunals, but relative to judicial review it is easier to determine whether internal appeals or statutory appeals to the courts are available: one just has to read the statute. By contrast, judicial review is an exceptional remedy that goes beyond what the statute provides for.[87] Significantly, judicial review is also discretionary. Judicial review doctrine is the product of decades of contentious court battles, modified from time to time by statute, directly pitting "legal" values of justice and the rule of law against "democratic" values and legislative intent, as well as "bureaucratic" values such as efficiency and expertise. Even the seemingly basic questions of whether judicial review is available in a particular situation, and what remedies are available, have been shaped by these contests.

Regardless of whether a party exercises a statutory right of appeal, where available, or seeks judicial review, that court decision can be appealed further up the judicial hierarchy.[88]

1. Statutory Rights of Appeal to the Courts

Below are the major questions a party must ask to determine whether an appeal from a tribunal to the courts is available to them.

a. Does the Tribunal's Enabling Statute Provide for a Right of Appeal?

Courts have no inherent appellate jurisdiction over administrative tribunals.[89] A tribunal's enabling statute may provide for a right to appeal to the courts. If it does not, then quite simply there is no such appeal. A dissatisfied party could only access the courts by way of the exceptional remedy of judicial review, described below. Moreover, parties generally may not appeal interlocutory rulings (for example, on jurisdiction, procedural or evidentiary issues, or bias).[90] To be appealable, the tribunal's decision must decide the merits of the matter or otherwise be a final disposition of it.[91]

---

87   David J Mullan, *Administrative Law* (Toronto: Irwin Law, 2001) at 462.

88   When reviewing a statutory appeal from an administrative actor or a judicial review, an appellate court should "step into the shoes" of the court that initially conducted the judicial review, determining whether the judge selected the appropriate standard of review and applied it correctly: *Agraira v Canada (Public Safety and Emergency Preparedness)*, 2013 SCC 36, [2013] 2 SCR 559 at paras 46-47.

89   *Medora v Dental Society* (1984), 56 NBR (2d) 145 at 147, [1984] NBJ No 236 (QL) (CA).

90   *Mary & David Goodine Dairy Farm v New Brunswick (Milk Marketing Board)*, 2002 NBCA 38, 217 DLR (4th) 708, [2002] NBJ No 177 (QL); *Roosma v Ford Motor Co of Canada Ltd* (1988), 66 OR (2d) 18 (Div Ct); *Newfoundland Transport Ltd v Newfoundland (Public Utilities Board)*, [1983] NJ No 92, 45 Nfld & PEIR 76 at 78 (CA); *contra, Fox v Registered Nurses' Assn*, 2002 NSCA 106, 207 NSR (2d) 330.

91   *Ontario (Human Rights Commission) v Ontario Teachers' Federation*, 19 OR (3d) 371, [1994] OJ No 1585 (QL) (Div Ct); *Prince Albert (City) v Riocan Holding Inc*, 2004 SKCA 73, 241 DLR (4th) 308 (CA).

Usually, a tribunal's enabling statute will also set out the court to which tribunal orders may be appealed. For federal tribunals, appeals are usually taken to the Federal Court or the Federal Court of Appeal.[92] Appeals from provincially constituted tribunals may be taken, depending on what the enabling statute says, to the province's trial court of general jurisdiction,[93] to a divisional court,[94] or to a court of appeal.[95] Rarely, a statute will provide a right (seldom exercised) to appeal a tribunal decision to Cabinet itself.[96]

b. What Is the Scope of Available Appeal?

Just as the enabling statute determines whether a statutory appeal is available in the first place, the enabling statute entirely determines its scope. That scope varies from tribunal to tribunal. Some statutes permit complete *de novo* review of a tribunal's decision, while others will be limited to issues of law based entirely on the record. In other words, an appellate court's jurisdiction in reviewing *tribunal* decisions may be different in scope from an appellate court's jurisdiction in reviewing lower *court* decisions. A court that has been designated to take appeals from a tribunal's decision must look to the tribunal's enabling statute to determine the breadth and scope of its appellate powers. Often, for example, enabling statutes will provide for a statutory right of appeal from an administrative decision-maker only on questions of law or jurisdiction.[97]

Arguably, the scope of an available appeal is determined by how closely the tribunal's subject matter, and its expertise, mirror the mandate and expertise of general courts. Statutes are more likely to provide a right of appeal to the courts where the tribunal has the power to affect individual rights (for example, human rights tribunals, land-use planning tribunals, and professional licensing). Labour relations and employment-related matters, which have long been adjudicated by tripartite boards with specialized expertise and which involve claims by organized labour to which courts were historically perceived to be hostile, cannot generally be appealed to the courts.[98] The same considerations affect the scope of available appeal. A statute is more likely to provide for a right of appeal to the courts where

---

92 Respectively, see e.g. *Trade-marks Act*, RSC 1985, c T-13, s 56; and CTA, s 13.

93 See e.g. Nunavut's *Travel and Tourism Act*, RSNWT 1988, c T-7, s 8.

94 See e.g. Ontario's *Expropriations Act*, RSO 1990, c E26, s 31.

95 See e.g. Newfoundland and Labrador's *Law Society Act, 1999*, SNL 1999, c L-9.1, s 55.

96 See e.g. *Broadcasting Act*, SC 1991, c 11, s 28.

97 In *Edmonton (City) v Edmonton East (Capilano) Shopping Centres Ltd*, 2016 SCC 47, [2016] 2 SCR 293 at para 29 [*Edmonton East*], the majority pointed to six recent Supreme Court of Canada decisions involving statutory rights of appeal. In five of those cases, as well as in the *Edmonton East* context itself, the statutes in question provided for leave to appeal to the relevant court only on questions of law or jurisdiction. In one case, *Sattva Capital Corp v Creston Moly Corp*, 2014 SCC 53, [2014] 2 SCR 633, a statutory appeal was available on a question of law, with leave and subject to potential conditions, effectively where the court had determined that the point of law was of particular importance to the parties, to a group of individuals, or to the public generally: *Arbitration Act*, RSBC 1996, c 55, s 31(2). It is not surprising that arbitrators would be treated differently than tribunals in this regard.

98 Gus Van Harten et al, *Administrative Law: Cases, Text, and Materials*, 7th ed (Toronto: Emond Montgomery, 2015) at 17. While Canadian courts were historically not friendly to organized labour, they were not as hostile to it as US courts were: John Godard, "Labour Law and Union Recognition in Canada: A Historical-Institutionalist Perspective," (2013) 38:2 Queen's LJ 391-418 at 400.

individual rights are at stake. For example, statutes generally provide for a broad power to appeal from certain professional disciplinary tribunals on questions of fact and law, where professionals risk losing their ability to practise their profession,[99] and from human rights tribunals adjudicating on violations of human rights codes.[100]

Yet even where the appeal rights are broad, courts will show deference to a tribunal's decisions, in order to respect the legislative intention to give a specialized tribunal responsibility for a particular statutory regime, and because of the tribunal's expertise and its familiarity with its own legislative scheme. Note that the standard of review on a statutory appeal from an administrative decision is generally "reasonableness." That is, unlike an appeal from a trial court to an appellate court, the question is not whether the original decision-maker made an error of law, or committed a palpable and overriding error of fact.[101] Most of the time, the question on a statutory appeal from an administrative decision-maker, as it is on judicial review, is not whether the decision-maker's decision was correct, but whether it was *reasonable*.[102] Standard of review is discussed in detail in Chapters 13 and 14 of this text.

Below are a few more considerations relevant to statutory appeals from administrative tribunals.

c. Is an Appeal Available as of Right, or Is Leave Required? If Leave Is Required, Who May Grant It?

Appeals can be as of right or require leave. Where leave must be obtained, it can be the leave either of the original decision-maker or, more frequently, of the appellate body (that is, the court). For example, British Columbia's *Forest Practices Code of British Columbia Act*[103] provides for an appeal as of right from the Forest Appeals Commission to the BC Supreme Court on questions of law or jurisdiction. By contrast, a person affected by a decision of the BC

---

99   See e.g. *Ontario College of Teachers Act, 1996*, SO 1996, c 12, s 35(4). See also *Reddall v College of Nurses of Ontario* (1983), 149 DLR (3d) 60, 42 OR (2d) (CA). Ontario statutes in particular tend to provide explicitly for appeal from various tribunals "on questions of law or fact or both."

100 See e.g. Ont HRC, s 42(3); also *Zurich Insurance Co v Ontario (Human Rights Commission)*, [1992] 2 SCR 321 at 336-38.

101 In *Wilson v Atomic Energy of Canada Ltd*, 2016 SCC 29, [2016] 1 SCR 770 [*Wilson*] at paras 14-16, the Court stated that the standard of review on an appeal from a judicial review was still reasonableness (overruling the Federal Court of Appeal in *Wilson v Atomic Energy of Canada Limited*, 2015 FCA 17, which had held at paras 25-26 and 34 that the normal appellate standard applied).

102 *Mouvement laïque québécois v Saguenay (City)*, 2015 SCC 16, [2015] 2 SCR 3 at paras 38, 46 ("Where a court reviews a decision of a specialized administrative tribunal, the standard of review must be determined on the basis of administrative law principles ... regardless of whether the review is conducted in the context of an application for judicial review or of a statutory appeal," and "on judicial review of a decision of a specialized administrative tribunal interpreting and applying its enabling statute, it should be presumed that the standard of review is reasonableness"); also *Edmonton East, supra* note 97 at paras 22-31. In *Edmonton East*, the Court split 5:4, with a forceful dissent, on the question of whether the standard of review was necessarily reasonableness, when the statutory regime provided for a right of appeal from the administrative decision-maker to the courts. However, all judges apparently agreed that statutory appeals from administrative decision-makers should be conducted on the basis of administrative law principles.

103 RSBC 1996 [*Forest Practices Code*].

Securities Commission may appeal to the BC Court of Appeal only with leave of a justice of that court.[104] Sometimes, additional statutory criteria must also be met before such leave will be granted.[105]

d. Is a Stay of Proceedings Automatic, or Must One Apply for It?

The rules governing stays of proceedings vary between jurisdictions and even tribunals. Specific enabling statutes may expressly empower their tribunals or the appellate bodies (internal or court) to which they appeal to stay enforcement of the tribunal order pending appeal.[106] The Ontario *Statutory Powers Procedure Act* establishes a default rule that an appeal operates as a stay of a tribunal's proceedings.[107] The BC ATA, by contrast, provides that "the commencement of an appeal does not operate as a stay or suspend the operation of the decision being appealed unless the tribunal orders otherwise."[108] In the Federal Court, as well, stays of proceedings are usually discretionary.[109] Unless a statute specifically excludes it, as BC's ATA does, the superior court that is the tribunal's designated appellate court has the inherent authority to grant a stay.[110]

Like the legislative decision to permit appeals as of right or only with leave, a legislative decision to make a stay automatic or not says something about how the legislature views the tribunals in question. Requiring potential appellants to apply for leave to appeal places an additional hurdle before them. Automatically staying a tribunal's decision holds its powers in abeyance while a court checks the tribunal's decision. Where the legislature decides that stays will not be automatic, the legislature may choose to allocate the power to order a stay either to the tribunal or to a court. These statutory drafting decisions reflect the legislature's assessment of the proper balancing of rule-of-law and efficiency concerns, the balance between tribunal expertise and judicial oversight, and the legislature's comfort with granting broad autonomy to the relevant tribunal.

---

104 Compare *Forest Practices Code*, s 141 with BC *Securities Act*, s 167.

105 For example, an appeal to the Federal Court of Appeal from judicial review by the Federal Court on immigration matters may be made only if the Federal Court judge certifies that "a serious question of general importance" is involved. See IRPA, s 74.

106 See e.g. *Re Hampton Court Resources Inc*, 2006 ABASC 1447 (June 13, 2006) (holding that, taken together, s 38(5) of the AB *Securities Act* and the provisions of the Alberta Rules of Court require that a stay of a commission decision be sought in the first instance from the commission).

107 SPPA, s 25.

108 ATA, s 25.

109 *Federal Courts Act*, RSC 1985, c F-7, s 50(1) [FCA]; but see s 50.1 concerning mandatory stays of claims against the Crown under certain conditions. In *Cardoza Quinteros v Canada (Citizenship and Immigration)*, 2008 FC 643 at paras 10, 13, the Federal Court noted that the granting of a stay requires (1) a serious issue to be tried; (2) that irreparable harm would be suffered if no stay were granted; and (3) that the balance of convenience favour granting the order. The Court also noted that the serious issue threshold "cannot automatically be met simply by formulating a ground of judicial review which, on its face, appears to be arguable."

110 *Kooner v College of Physicians and Surgeons of Ontario* (2002), 213 DLR (4th) 707 (Ont Div Ct).

D. Using the Courts: Judicial Review

Now, finally, we discuss judicial review, the parallel universe under whose rules the outcome in *Gitxaala Nation* could be considered some sort of victory for the Gitxaala.

Judicial review has long been the fixation of administrative law, at the expense of tribunal-based and extralegal mechanisms and statutory appeals—not to mention the hugely important arena of administrative rulemaking—in part because administrative law is created primarily by judges, lawyers, and legal scholars. The legal training these individuals receive is, understandably, preoccupied with legal mechanisms and, in particular, with courts and the common law. This makes for an overly narrow lens. And yet, having placed judicial review in its broader context, it nonetheless deserves careful attention. Judicial review can be conceptually and logistically complex, and it differs from a straightforward appeal. The outcome in *Gitxaala Nation* was a function of the available judicial review remedies.

As we shall see throughout this volume, the basic nature of judicial review is different from statutory or internal tribunal appeals because, at its root, judicial review is about the inherent jurisdiction of courts to oversee and check administrative (that is, executive) action in the interest of the rule of law. This makes it a potentially sweeping remedy. Unlike appeals from tribunals, which are statutorily created, judicial review is the review of executive action *beyond* what the legislature provided for.

Here are four things to know about judicial review: first, courts always and fundamentally retain the discretion to hear, or not to hear, an application for judicial review. Second, in addition to overcoming the fundamentally discretionary nature of judicial review, an applicant will need to cross some specific thresholds in order to be heard. Third, the historical development of the remedies available through judicial review has actively shaped, and limited, the possibilities and potential of judicial review itself. In spite of statutory reform and evolving case law, the ancient prerogative writs that were the original forms of judicial review continue to haunt its present forms. And finally, in response to the apparent disconnect between what some parties may want by way of remedies and what they can obtain on judicial review, some interesting private law and monetary damages-oriented remedies have sprung up around the edges of judicial review. Each of these points is developed in more detail below.

1. Discretionary Bases for Refusing a Remedy

A court's decision whether to grant judicial review is intimately bound up with the core tension that underlies all of administrative law—what the Supreme Court has called "an underlying tension between the rule of law and the foundational democratic principle, which finds an expression in the initiatives of Parliament and legislatures to create various administrative bodies and endow them with broad powers."[111] Courts are the indispensable guardians of the rule of law, but they still need to operate within their sphere of authority. This means respecting the fact that, through enabling statutes, legislatures grant authority over certain things to administrative tribunals, *and not to the courts*. A lot of administrative

---

111 *Dunsmuir v New Brunswick*, 2008 SCC 9, [2008] 1 SCR 190 at para 27 [*Dunsmuir*].

law jurisprudence is devoted to trying to negotiate a path through the difficult territory on the borders of the branches' spheres of authority. What concerns us here is the threshold question of whether to grant judicial review at all—before considering the merits of the case, before figuring out the standard of review, and before determining the degree of procedural fairness a party is entitled to. Judicial review is fundamentally discretionary in a way that appeals are not. A court has the discretion to refuse to grant a remedy even where one seems clearly warranted on the facts.[112]

The original set of discretionary grounds for refusing relief derive from common law and equity, and they have survived the statutory reform of judicial review. They are reminiscent of similar equity-based grounds in civil procedure, such as laches (unreasonable delay), or unconscionability:

1. The most important basis for refusing to grant a remedy in judicial review is discussed in more detail below: that *adequate alternative remedies are available.*[113] Parties should exhaust all other legal avenues for review before proceeding to the "last resort" of judicial review.

2. Judicial review applications that are brought before tribunal proceedings have been concluded are usually dismissed as being *premature.* This includes challenges to the tribunal's interim procedural and evidentiary rulings. The policy rationales that underlie dismissals for prematurity include: (a) that administrative action is meant to be more cost-effective than court proceedings, and interim judicial review fragments and protracts those proceedings; (b) that preliminary complaints may become moot as the proceedings progress; and (c) that the court will be in a better position to assess the situation once a full and complete record of tribunal proceedings exists.[114] A judge on judicial review retains the discretion to hear an early application; there is no "hard and fast rule" that prevents reviewing interim decisions.[115] However, to obtain judicial review of a tribunal's preliminary or interim ruling, an applicant must generally show exceptional circumstances, the presence of which mean the applicant should not be forced to wait until the administrative proceeding concludes. This is particularly true where the evidentiary record is not complete, factual issues have not been resolved, or the tribunal's expertise has not yet been brought to bear on relevant issues.[116] Evidence of irreparable harm, prejudice, costs, or delay, or the absence of an appropriate remedy at the end of the proceedings may constitute special or exceptional circumstances.[117] Concerns that do not qualify include those about procedural fairness or bias, jurisdictional issues, the presence of an important legal or

---

112 *Strickland v Canada (Attorney General)*, 2015 SCC 37, [2015] 2 SCR 713 at paras 37-45 [*Strickland*]; *Immeubles Port Louis Ltée v Lafontaine (Village)*, [1991] 1 SCR 326 [*Immeubles Port Louis*].

113 See *infra* notes 147 to 149 and accompanying text.

114 *Halifax (Regional Municipality) v Nova Scotia (Human Rights Commission)*, 2012 SCC 10, [2012] 1 SCR 364.

115 *British Columbia (Ministry of Public Safety and Solicitor General) v Mzite*, 2014 BCCA 220.

116 *Ibid*.

117 *Ibid*; *Manitoba Hydro-Electric Board v Consumers' Association of Canada (Man) Inc*, 2012 MBCA 1, 275 Man R (2d) 60; *Calgary (City) v Alberta (Human Rights and Citizenship Commission)*, 2011 ABCA 65, 39 Alta LR (5th) 104; *Volochay v College of Massage Therapists of Ontario*, 2012 ONCA 541, 111 OR (3d) 561 [*Volochay*].

constitutional issue, or the fact that all parties have consented to seeking judicial review early.[118]

3. Even if statutory time limits for filing a judicial review application have been met, parties must be aware that *delay and acquiescence* may be grounds for a reviewing court to refuse a remedy.[119] Parties should object promptly to any perceived impropriety on the part of the tribunal. Similarly, choosing not to attend a hearing could waive any right to judicial review.

4. A remedy in judicial review will not be granted where the issues are *moot*. This may be the case where a dispute is over or has not yet arisen, where a tribunal's order has expired or no longer affects the applicant, or where the litigant no longer actually wants the remedy that the tribunal might have granted had it not erred.[120]

5. The court will use its discretion to refuse to grant a remedy on judicial review where the party making the judicial review application *does not come with clean hands*. This could include seeking a remedy to facilitate illegal conduct or to obtain an unfair advantage, or flouting the law or making misrepresentations.[121]

By the 1990s, these long-standing grounds for refusing relief came to be overlaid with a different vision of judicial review that reflected a new sensitivity to separation of powers issues, and increased deference toward administrative tribunals. The overarching presumption of judicial deference toward administrative decision-making percolated throughout the judicial review process, eventually reaching the discretionary grounds for granting relief in the first place. In other words, even where the five original grounds above were not present, courts began to recognize that it could sometimes be appropriate to refuse to grant judicial review out of deference to tribunals' unique institutional roles. Perhaps the most forceful statement about the contingent nature of judicial review remedies from this era comes from *Domtar Inc v Quebec*.[122] In deciding not to intervene to resolve a conflict in legal interpretation between two tribunals construing the same statutory language, the Supreme Court of Canada stated, "[t]he advisability of judicial intervention in the event of conflicting decisions among administrative tribunals, even when serious and unquestionable, cannot, in these circumstances, be determined solely by the 'triumph' of the rule of law."[123] The court went on to articulate what was then a novel, and striking, notion: that even the most deeply cher-

---

118 *Canada (Border Services Agency) v CB Powell Limited*, 2010 FCA 61, [2011] 2 FCR 332, leave to appeal to SCC refused, 2011 SCCA No 267, at para 33 [*CB Powell*].

119 *Immeubles Port Louis, supra* note 112; *2122157 Ontario Inc v Tarion Warranty Corporation*, 2016 ONSC 851 (Div Ct).

120 *Borowski v Canada (Attorney General)*, [1989] 1 SCR 342 at 353; but see *Mission Institution v Khela*, 2014 SCC 24, [2014] 1 SCR 502 at paras 13-14 [*Khela*] (agreeing to hear a *habeas corpus* appeal in spite of its factual mootness, given the time it takes to pursue such an application); *Attawapiskat First Nation v Canada*, 2012 FC 948 at paras 41-48 [*Attawapiskat First Nation*] (exercising discretion to hear judicial review in spite of technical mootness, where parties are in an ongoing relationship, and same issue will arise in other similar relationships).

121 See e.g. *Gazlat v Canada (Citizenship and Immigration)*, 2008 FC 532, [2008] FCJ No 677 (QL). Courts may still exercise their discretion to grant judicial review even if an applicant does not come with clean hands: *Canada (Minister of Citizenship and Immigration) v Thanabalasingham*, 2006 FCA 14, 263 DLR (4th) 51.

122 *Domtar Inc v Quebec (Commission d'appel en matière de lésions professionnelles)*, 1993 SCC 106, [1993] 2 SCR 756 [*Domtar*].

123 *Ibid* at 795.

ished rule-of-law values will not always point the way to the only, or perhaps even the most appropriate, response to a problem in administrative law:

> [C]ertainty of the law and decision-making consistency are chiefly notable for their relativity. Like the rules of natural justice, these objectives cannot be absolute in nature regardless of the context. The value represented by the decision-making independence and autonomy of the members of administrative tribunals goes hand in hand here with the principle that their decisions should be effective. In light of these considerations we must conclude that, *for purposes of judicial review, the principle of the rule of law must be qualified*. This is consistent with the continuing evolution of administrative law itself.[124]

Consistent with this, in 1999, then Chief Justice McLachlin set forth a vision of a "new rule of law," which would

> [make] it possible for institutions other than courts to play key roles in maintaining it. It opens the door to the idea that courts do not necessarily have a monopoly on the values of reasons and fairness ... [C]ontrary to Dicey's view that the courts' primary role is to constrain, limit and, if possible eliminate administrative power, the new Rule of Law allows courts to respect and advance the roles of administrative tribunals. The courts' role shifts from being a brute guardian of an artificial and restrictive Rule of Law to that of a partner.[125]

In this way, courts moved past the restrictive traditional grounds for refusing to exercise discretion to grant judicial review. They did so in the service of a more respectful relationship with the other branches of government, and particularly with administrative tribunals. But to the extent that this shift could be read as introducing some poorly defined, deferential "X factor" into the decision-making process, it risked exempting courts from the very ethos of justification that tribunals were expected to observe in their decision-making. Surely this would be a misreading. The fact that judicial review is discretionary does not mean that courts should refuse to grant judicial review solely on the basis of some abstract ideal of partnership with administrative tribunals, or a relative and qualified rule-of-law value. Respecting, protecting, and adhering to the rule of law means that judges should base even their discretionary decisions on identifiable reasons.

Today, in deciding whether to exercise its discretion to grant judicial review, a court adopts a multi-factorial, contextual approach that nevertheless draws some insight from the traditional grounds described above. Deference to tribunals at the point of deciding whether to grant judicial review is understood to be consistent with normal judicial review analysis, which generally aims to strike the balance between the courts' essential role in upholding the rule of law, while avoiding "undue interference" with administrative powers.[126] While the factors to be considered in exercising the discretion "cannot be reduced to a checklist or a statement of general rules,"[127] there is guidance to be had. In *Khosa*, the court

---

124   *Ibid* at 799-800 (emphasis added).

125   Beverley McLachlin, "The Roles of Administrative Tribunals and Courts in Maintaining the Rule of Law" (1998-1999) 12 CJALP 171-89 at 175. This article is also an early statement of the Chief Justice's concept of the "ethos of justification" that underlies the rule of law, and this concept continues to be a vital part of contemporary jurisprudence.

126   See especially *Dunsmuir, supra* note 111 at paras 20-24.

127   *Strickland, supra* note 112 at para 45 (in considering whether adequate alternative remedies had been exhausted).

stated that the discretion to grant or withhold judicial review "must be exercised judicially and in accordance with proper principles."[128] In setting out those proper principles, the court identified the standard of review principles that govern administrative law generally, and which are discussed in other chapters of this book, plus the traditional grounds as identified and described above: "other factors such as an applicant's delay, failure to exhaust adequate alternate remedies, mootness, prematurity, bad faith and so forth."[129] In *MiningWatch* (*per coram* with Rothstein J writing), the court added another consideration. It is one that has been rising in salience since *Khosa*: the balance of convenience to the various parties.[130] In an interesting juxtaposition to the *Domtar* language, which had proposed that the rule of law must sometimes be qualified, *MiningWatch* observes that, because the discretionary power to refuse judicial review "may make inroads upon the rule of law, it must be exercised with the greatest care."[131]

2. Is Judicial Review Available? Threshold Questions

Leaving to one side what the cases above have said about the discretionary nature of judicial review writ large, the unique history, purpose, and mechanics of judicial review also mean that whether it will be available in any particular situation depends on a set of considerations particular to administrative law.[132]

One of the key threshold questions is whether the tribunal whose actions are being challenged is, in fact, a public body. Judicial review is available to check executive action. Therefore, only public bodies can be subject to judicial review.[133] While this may sound straightforward, some organizations in Canadian society exercise some degree of "public" function, yet operate at considerable distance from government. Others seem private, but

---

128 *Canada (Citizenship and Immigration) v Khosa*, 2009 SCC 12, [2009] 1 SCR 339 at para 40 [*Khosa*].

129 *Ibid* at para 51.

130 *MiningWatch Canada v Canada (Fisheries and Oceans)*, 2010 SCC 2, [2010] 1 SCR 6 at para 52 [*MiningWatch*]; see also *Khosa, supra* note 128 at paras 36, 133-35. In that case, the balance of convenience justified reducing the impact of the remedy granted, from relief in the nature of *certiorari* and *mandamus* to a declaration. (These specific forms of relief are discussed below.)

131 *MiningWatch* at para 52.

132 For this chapter's purposes, we will assume that the court in question has the jurisdiction to grant judicial review. Note, however, that preliminary objections about a subject's justiciability have been raised in the Crown prerogative context: in *Hupacasath First Nation v Canada (Foreign Affairs and International Trade Canada)*, 2015 FCA 4, 379 DLR (4th) 737 [*Hupacasath First Nation*], a First Nation alleged that a foreign investment agreement between Canada and the People's Republic of China might affect Aboriginal rights and interests that it had asserted over territory in British Columbia, and that Canada had a duty to consult with it and if necessary to accommodate its concerns before the agreement came into force. Canada argued that decisions to enter into international agreements and treaties are exercises of federal Crown prerogative power, over which the Federal Court has no jurisdiction. In its decision, the Federal Court of Appeal declined to follow Ontario Court of Appeal jurisprudence holding that the Federal Courts had no jurisdiction over exercises of the Crown prerogative, and further held that exercises of pure federal Crown prerogative are justiciable. For more on the interplay between aboriginal law and administrative law, see Chapter 3, Realizing Aboriginal Administrative Law. The fact that government is exercising the Crown prerogative can also affect the scope of remedies a court is prepared to grant: see *Khadr, supra* note 86, in which it limited the appropriate remedy to a declaration.

133 Private actors may also owe a duty of fairness that can be enforced through the private law remedies of declaration and injunction; however, these remedies are outside the scope of this chapter.

have some connection to public authority. For example, stock exchanges regulate the conduct of their members and issue and revoke licences, and their operations clearly go to the protection of the public. However, their authority to act as they do derives from a compact with their members rather than from any statutory grant of authority. Similarly, one should distinguish between government-acting-as-the-state, and government-acting-as-private-contracting-party. As a general matter, a private party will have difficulty seeking judicial review of a government board's decision not to award it a particular contract.[134] As well, public employees with employment contracts will have their employment relationships governed by private (contract) law, not public (administrative) law.[135]

Various factors go into determining whether a particular tribunal is a private body or a public one. Relevant considerations include whether the matter at issue is of a more public or more private character; the nature of the decision-maker and the nature of its relationships to a statutory scheme or to government action; whether the decision being challenged was authorized by a public source of law; and whether public law remedies would be "suitable."[136]

In addition to determining whether a tribunal is a sufficiently "public" body, a party seeking to challenge administrative action should determine whether they have *standing* to challenge a tribunal decision. The answer will be straightforward for individuals who are actual parties to an administrative action, but other persons may have a collateral interest in the same matter and may want to challenge a tribunal order that does not directly affect them.[137] There is also discretionary "public interest standing," under which an individual or group may be able to challenge administrative action on behalf of others.[138] Given that tribunals are expected to maintain a degree of impartiality, courts will also exercise their discretion in deciding whether, and to what degree, a tribunal should be able to participate when a party challenges its administrative action.[139] Angus Grant and Lorne Sossin discuss standing in greater detail in Chapter 9, Fairness in Context: Achieving Fairness through Access to Administrative Justice.

---

134   But consider the improper purpose doctrine: *Shell Canada Products Ltd v Vancouver (City)*, [1994] 1 SCR 231.

135   *Dunsmuir, supra* note 111 especially at paras 79-83, 112-17.

136   *Air Canada v Toronto Port Authority*, 2011 FCA 347 at para 60; see also *McDonald v Anishinabek Police Service* (2006), 83 OR (3d) 132 (Div Ct) (decisions by the chief of a police service created through a combination of contract and statute could be judicially reviewed); *Attawapiskat First Nation, supra* note 120 at paras 50-62; *Setia v Appleby College*, 2013 ONCA 753 (a private high school's decision to expel a student could not be judicially reviewed); *West Toronto United Football Club v Ontario Soccer Association*, 2014 ONSC 5881 (a provincial soccer association's decision to intervene in a disputed match decision was judicially reviewable).

137   See e.g. *Globalive Wireless Management Corp v Public Mobile Inc*, 2011 FCA 194.

138   The leading case is *Canada (Attorney General) v Downtown Eastside Sex Workers United Against Violence Society*, 2012 SCC 45 at para 37, under which the test is: "(1) whether there is a serious justiciable issue raised; (2) whether the plaintiff has a real stake or a genuine interest in it; and (3) whether, in all the circumstances, the proposed suit is a reasonable and effective way to bring the issue before the courts."

139   Considerations include whether there is any other party with the necessary knowledge and expertise to stand in opposition to the party challenging the administrative action; whether the tribunal has a more policy-oriented or adjudicatory, dispute resolution oriented role; and what limits need to be imposed to ensure that the tribunal is not "bootstrapping" a weak decision by, e.g., introducing new arguments after the fact: *Ontario (Energy Board) v Ontario Power Generation Inc*, 2015 SCC 414, [2015] 3 SCR 147 at paras 52-59, 63-69.

Third, a party seeking to challenge administrative action should determine to which court they should apply for judicial review. Both the provincial superior courts and the federal courts have judicial review jurisdiction. Although a tribunal's enabling statute will generally set out which court has jurisdiction to hear a statutory *appeal* to the courts, this is not the case for judicial review. (This makes sense, because judicial review is an extraordinary remedy that the enabling statute does not provide for in the first place.) Typically, the choice of courts is determined by whether the source of the impugned authority's power is provincial or federal.[140] Some overarching provincial statutes, such as Ontario's *Judicial Review Procedure Act*, stipulate the particular provincial court to which judicial review applications should be brought.[141]

Fourth, a party should ensure that they have not missed any deadlines. Some statutes impose time limits within which a party must file an application for judicial review. For example, the *Federal Courts Act* states that a judicial review application from a federal tribunal to the Federal Court must be made within 30 days of the time the underlying decision or order is first communicated.[142] In Alberta, the rules impose a six-month time limit on all applications for judicial review, except *habeas corpus* applications.[143] Nova Scotia precludes all applications for judicial review after the earlier of six months following the decision, or 25 days after the decision is communicated to the person.[144] In British Columbia, the general time limit is 60 days.[145] Parties should therefore check all applicable statutes, including the tribunal's enabling statutes, global procedural and judicial review acts, and rules of court, for time limits affecting judicial review. However, courts are often statutorily empowered to extend the time limit for making a judicial review application—for example, where there is a reasonable explanation for the delay, where no substantial prejudice or hardship would result from such an extension, or where the party can demonstrate *prima facie* grounds for relief.[146]

---

140 There are some exceptions. Provincial superior courts have concurrent or exclusive jurisdiction over some specific aspects of federal statutory regimes, as a result of both the *Constitution Act, 1982*, being Schedule B to the *Canada Act 1982* (UK), 1982, c 11, and the *Federal Courts Act*. In particular, provincial superior courts have concurrent jurisdiction where Charter issues are raised in attacks on federal legislative regimes (*Reza v Canada*, [1994] 2 SCR 394) and—although this is private law, not judicial review—over damages actions in which relief is sought against the federal Crown (*Canada (Attorney General) v TeleZone Inc*, 2010 SCC 62, [2010] 3 SCR 585 [*TeleZone*]). On the Crown prerogative see also *Hupacasath First Nation, supra* note 132, and on concurrent jurisdiction more generally, see also *Strickland, supra* note 112 at paras 16-33 (affirming the Federal Court's refusal to hear a judicial review of family law child support guidelines on the basis that the provincial superior courts were the more appropriate forum).

141 Ontario *Judicial Review Procedure Act* RSO 1990, c J 1 [Ont JRPA], s 6 says that judicial review applications shall be made to the Divisional Court, unless "the case is one of urgency and … the delay required for an application to the Divisional Court is likely to involve a failure of justice," in which case an application may be made to the Superior Court of Justice.

142 FCA, s 18.1(2). The deadline can be extended: see e.g. *Canada (Attorney General) v Larkman*, 2012 FCA 204.

143 Rule 3.15 of the *Alberta Rules of Court* (Alta Reg 124/2010) imposes this time limit where the relief sought is the setting aside of a decision or act.

144 Rule 7.05(1), *Nova Scotia Civil Procedure Rules*, 2008, imposes the time limit on applications for relief in the nature of *certiorari*, online: <http://www.courts.ns.ca/Civil_Procedure_Rules/CPRs_in_html/Rule_07.htm#Rule7.05>.

145 BC ATA, s 57(1). Note, however, that the ATA does not apply to all tribunals in BC.

146 E.g. Ont JRPA, s 5; BC ATA, s 57(2). The *Federal Courts Act* does not set out the conditions that must be met in order for the court to grant an extension of time: FCA, s 18.1(2).

The final threshold matter that a party must establish before gaining access to judicial review is that they have exhausted all other adequate means of recourse for challenging the tribunal's actions.[147] Depending on the tribunal's enabling statute, other means of recourse may include almost any of the legal remedies above: reconsideration by the same tribunal, appeals to internal appellate tribunals and other intra-agency mechanisms such as grievance arbitration, and appeals to a court. However, not all other means of recourse will necessarily be adequate. Considerations include "the convenience of the alternative remedy; the nature of the error alleged; the nature of the other forum which could deal with the issue, including its remedial capacity; the existence of adequate and effective recourse in the forum in which litigation is already taking place; expeditiousness; the relative expertise of the alternative decision-maker; economical use of judicial resources; and cost."[148] In balancing these factors, a court should engage in a broad inquiry that considers not only whether some other remedy is adequate but whether—taking into account the purposes and policy considerations underpinning the legislative scheme, the balance of convenience to the parties, and other factors the court may consider relevant—granting judicial review in the circumstances would be appropriate.[149]

Courts will not find existing non-court appeal mechanisms to be inadequate based only on unproven allegations that an appellate tribunal will suffer from the same errors[150] or biases[151] as the original tribunal. Nor can challengers circumvent available appeals in favour of judicial review by consent, or simply by raising apparent issues with the original tribunal's procedure or jurisdiction.[152] Also, at least in the context of Aboriginal self-government in the taxation field, the fact that appellate tribunal members lack indicia of institutional independence—that is, they may not be paid, they lack security of tenure, and they are appointed by the people whose claims they have to adjudicate—will not make that appellate body "inadequate" without concrete evidence that independence is lacking in practice.[153]

Parliament and several provinces have also legislated in this area. For example, the *Federal Courts Act* prohibits *judicial review* by the Federal Court where an available appeal of a tribunal's decision to the Federal Court exists.[154] Quebec's *Code of Civil Procedure* also prohibits a superior court from applying Quebec's version of *certiorari* to a tribunal decision where an appeal is available, unless the tribunal lacked or exceeded its statutory au-

---

147   *Harelkin v University of Regina*, [1979] 2 SCR 561, 96 DLR (3d) 14 [*Harelkin*].

148   *Strickland, supra* note 112 at para 42.

149   *Ibid* at paras 43-44.

150   *Harelkin, supra* note 147.

151   *Turnbull v Canadian Institute of Actuaries* (1995), 129 DLR (4th) 42 (Man CA); but see, *contra, Re Batorski v Moody* (1983), 42 OR (2d) 647 (Div Ct).

152   *CB Powell, supra* note 118, at para 33. ("Concerns about procedural fairness or bias, the presence of an important legal or constitutional issue, or the fact that all parties have consented to early recourse to the courts are not exceptional circumstances allowing parties to bypass an administrative process, as long as that process allows the issues to be raised and an effective remedy to be granted ... [T]he presence of so-called jurisdictional issues is not an exceptional circumstance justifying early recourse to courts.")

153   *Canadian Pacific Ltd v Matsqui Indian Band*, [1995] 1 SCR 3.

154   FCA, s 18.5. For a more extensive discussion of access to judicial review in the Federal Court, see *Canada (National Revenue) v JP Morgan Asset Management (Canada) Inc*, 2013 FCA 250, [2014] 367 DLR (4th) 525.

thority. On the other hand, Ontario's *Judicial Review Procedure Act* and Prince Edward Island's *Judicial Review Act* both permit judicial review notwithstanding any other right of appeal to the courts.[155] Of course, the fact that a court *may* grant judicial review, even where a right of appeal exists, does not mean that it *will* do so. As we might expect, courts are reluctant to do so.[156]

E. Remedies on Judicial Review

The remedies available on judicial review have their roots in the ancient prerogative writs, discussed further below. Over time, those became unwieldy. In many provinces they were modified by statute to redress problems arising from the writs' extreme technicality and unjustified narrowness. However, it is still necessary to understand the ancient writs to understand the scope and range of remedies available on judicial review. For example, neither the old writs nor the reform statutes, which are based on the old writs, permit a court on judicial review to substitute its views on the substance of a matter for the tribunal's views. The old writs also continue to operate in some provinces, albeit in a more limited way.[157]

A party contemplating judicial review should also be aware that, unlike an appeal, an application for judicial review usually does *not* automatically stay the enforcement of the underlying tribunal order, although the tribunal or the court or both may have the power to stay the tribunal's order on application.[158] The legislative decision to make stays automatic for many appeals but not for judicial review applications is consistent with the "last resort" nature of judicial review. The rules regarding stays vary from jurisdiction to jurisdiction and from tribunal to tribunal, so parties seeking a stay should be sure to review the relevant enabling statute, as well as the rules of court and any omnibus statutes governing procedure or judicial review.

---

155   See, respectively, *Code of Civil Procedure*, RSQ, c C-25, art 846; Ont JRPA, s 2(1); and *Judicial Review Act*, RSPEI 1988, c J-3, s 4(2) [PEI JRA].

156   See e.g. *Volochay*, *supra* note 117 at para 70, *Anne & Gilbert Inc v Government of PEI*, 2012 PECA 4, 320 Nfld & PEIR 99.

157   For example, the "direct action in nullity" is a judicial review remedy that predates the Quebec *Code of Civil Procedure*, RSQ 1977, c C-25, and is not referred to in it, yet it continues to operate: *Immeubles Port Louis*, *supra* note 112. In New Brunswick, one cannot apply specifically for the traditional prerogative writs of *certiorari*, *mandamus*, or prohibition, which are now available simply as judicial review. However, a range of "alternative" remedies echoing the old prerogative writs continues to exist. See e.g. *Sullivan v Greater Moncton Planning District Commission* (1993), 132 NBR (2d) 285 (TD). Manitoba's Court of Queen's Bench Rules, Man Reg 553/88, Rule 68.01 states only that "[a] Judge on application may grant an order of *mandamus*, prohibition, *certiorari* or *quo warranto*." Yukon Territory has not enacted any statutory changes to the common law writs.

158   See e.g. Ontario SPPA, s 25 (an appeal acts as a stay, but judicial review is not an appeal for that purpose); New Brunswick *Energy and Utilities Board Act*, SNB 2006, c E-9.18, s 52(2) (judicial review does not automatically stay an order, but the board itself or the Court of Appeal may stay it). Indeed, one federal statute that establishes securities clearing houses and banking and payment systems stipulates that *no* stay shall be granted for a judicial review application related to the government's administration of those systems: *Canadian Payments Act*, RSC 1985, c C-21, s 46.

The following sections introduce the prerogative writs and subsequent statutory reform. Because judicial review remains a fundamentally discretionary power, the bases on which courts have refused to grant a remedy are also discussed.

1. Introduction to the Prerogative Writs

Certiorari is the most commonly used prerogative remedy, both historically and today. *Certiorari* ("cause to be certified") is a special proceeding by which a superior court requires some inferior tribunal, board, or judicial officer to provide it with the record of its proceedings for review for excess of jurisdiction. It was the established method by which the Court of King's Bench in England, from earliest times, checked the jurisdiction of inferior courts and maintained the supremacy of the royal courts. In the United States, the vast majority of applications to the US Supreme Court are still made by way of a petition for *certiorari*. A successful *certiorari* application results in the "quashing" (effectively, the invalidating) of a tribunal's order or decision. It is an *ex post facto* remedy. Note, however, that generally the court cannot substitute its decision for the decision of a tribunal that the court finds had erred, because the court has not been granted the statutory decision-making authority.[159] Quashing the existing decision effectively means that the matter is remitted to the administrative decision-maker, who still retains the statutory jurisdiction to decide. This is what happened in *Gitxaala Nation*.

The related writ of *prohibition* is another special proceeding, issued by an appellate court to prevent a lower court from exceeding its jurisdiction, or to prevent a non-judicial officer or entity from exercising a power. Prohibition is a kind of common law injunction to prevent an unlawful assumption of jurisdiction. Unlike *certiorari*, which provides relief after a decision is made, prohibition is used to obtain relief pre-emptively. It arrests the proceedings of any tribunal, board, or person exercising judicial functions in a manner or by means not within its jurisdiction or discretion.

Mandamus (literally, "we command") is a writ issued by a superior court to compel a lower court or a government agency to perform a duty it is mandated to perform. It can be combined with an application for *certiorari*. *Certiorari* would be used to quash a decision—for example, for a lack of procedural fairness—while *mandamus* would be used to force the tribunal to reconsider the matter in a procedurally fair manner. A variation on *mandamus* gives the court the ability to send a matter back to a tribunal for reconsideration with directions. Superior courts have the inherent power to order reconsideration with directions, and several provincial statutes and rules of court, as well as the *Federal Courts Act*, also grant this power. If the court issues directions, it must clearly state what the original panel is to do or what it must refrain from doing. These directions may only protect against unfair procedures or excess of power and cannot tell the tribunal how it must decide. In particular, the general rule is that *mandamus* cannot be used to force an administrative decision-maker to exercise

---

159   In exceptional circumstances, a court will nevertheless make the decision that it finds the original tribunal ought to have made. See e.g. *Renaud v Québec (Commission des affaires sociales)*, [1999] 3 SCR 855, 184 DLR (4th) 441, [1999] SCJ No 70 (QL); *Corp of the Canadian Civil Liberties Assn v Ontario (Civilian Commission on Police Services)* (2002), 61 OR (3d) 649 (CA); *Allman v Amacon Property Management Services Inc*, [2007] BCJ No 1144 (QL) (CA).

its discretion in a particular way, although exercises of discretion cannot be unlawful and must always conform to the constitution.[160]

A *declaration* is a judgment of a court that determines and states the legal position of the parties, or the law that applies to them. There are two kinds of declarations: the public law kind, used to declare some government action *ultra vires*, and the private law kind, used to clarify the law or declare a private party's rights under a statute. The public law kind is the main concern of administrative law. Declarations are not enforceable, and they cannot require anyone to take or refrain from taking any action. Historically, this made declarations useful in actions against the Crown itself because the traditional common law position was that relief in the nature of *mandamus* was not available against the Crown. It was not thought appropriate for a court to order enforcement against the Crown, because the Crown was the source of its own authority. (These prohibitions on remedies against the Crown itself were substantially, though not completely, relaxed over the course of the 20th century.) The non-coercive nature of the remedy has not often proven to be a problem, because court declarations against government bodies in particular tend to be respected.[161] Where a declaration does not produce a government response, however, as happened in the *Khadr* case,[162] the declaration may look like a distinctly second-rate remedy relative to *mandamus*. At least where the Crown prerogative over foreign affairs is concerned, an aggrieved party may find himself or herself having a right without a remedy—or, more accurately, having a right for which a meaningful remedy exists only in the political, and not the legal, arena.

---

160 In the special circumstances of the so-called *Insite* case, which concerned a safe drug injection site in Vancouver's Downtown Eastside neighbourhood, the Supreme Court of Canada held that the province's Minister of Health had not exercised its discretion in a manner consistent with the Charter when he refused to exempt Insite from certain criminal law provisions. The Court found that sending the matter back to the Minister for reconsideration would be inadequate in view of the attendant risks and delays, and that "the only constitutional response to [Insite's exemption application] was to grant it." It therefore took the rare step of issuing an order in the nature of *mandamus*, *compelling* the Minister to exercise its discretion so as to issue an exemption to Insite: *Canada (Attorney General) v PHS Community Services Society*, 2011 SCC 44, [2011] 3 SCR 134 at para 150. The Federal Court of Appeal has done the same in some recent cases in which it held that there was "only one lawful way" in which the decision maker's discretion could be exercised: *Canada (Public Safety and Emergency Preparedness) v LeBon*, 2013 FCA 55; or, pushing the concept further, in "exceptional" cases in which, for example, "there has been substantial delay and the additional delay caused by remitting the matter to the administrative decision-maker for re-decision threatens to bring the administration of justice into disrepute": *D'Errico v Canada (Attorney General)*, 2014 FCA 95 at paras 16-18.

161 *Lount Corp v Canada (Attorney General)*, [1984] 1 FC 332 at 365 (TD) (noting that "by long tradition, the executive abides by declarations of the Court even though not formally or specifically directed to do so"); aff'd *sub nom Canada (Attorney General) v Lount Corp*, [1985] 2 FCR 185.

162 *Khadr*, *supra* note 86. In 2008 the Supreme Court of Canada determined that Omar Khadr had been deprived of his s 7 Charter rights by Canadian officials operating at the Guantanamo Bay detention facility, who shared transcripts of their interviews of Mr Khadr with US authorities. The Court ordered that the Canadian authorities produce those transcripts to Mr Khadr, which they did, but the Prime Minister refused requests to seek his repatriation from the United States to Canada. In its 2010 decision, the Supreme Court of Canada held that, notwithstanding the violation of Mr Khadr's s 7 Charter rights, it would not order the Canadian government to request his repatriation. In light of the Crown prerogative over foreign affairs, the court concluded that the appropriate remedy was a declaration that Canada had infringed Mr Khadr's s 7 rights, leaving it to the government to decide how best to respond. The government did not seek Mr Khadr's repatriation.

Less common these days are the writs of *habeas corpus* and *quo warranto*. *Habeas corpus* (literally, "produce the body") is a writ employed to bring a person before a court, most frequently to ensure that the person's imprisonment or detention is not illegal. Like *certiorari*, *habeas corpus* continues to live an active life in the United States, where it is the primary mechanism for challenging state-level death penalty sentences in the federal courts. In Canada, *habeas corpus* applications are fairly rare. Most are brought by prisoners detained in correctional institutions and by police, immigration, child welfare, and mental health detainees. Unlike the other prerogative writs, *habeas corpus* is not inherently discretionary. It issues "as of right if the applicant proves a deprivation of liberty and raises a legitimate ground upon which to question the legality of the deprivation."[163] *Quo warranto* ("by what warrant?" or "by what authority?") is a writ used to inquire into what authority existed to justify acts by or powers claimed by a public office. It is rarely used today, and some provinces have abolished it by statute.[164]

2. Statutory Reform

Over time, each of the prerogative writs above came to be characterized by technical complexity and arcane rules. Potentially meritorious applications were dismissed because the applicant had petitioned for the wrong writ, or because the claim was barred by some technical limitation. For example, although court decisions later re-expanded the writ's scope, a number of cases in Canada in the 1960s and 1970s held that *certiorari* and prohibition were only available to address "judicial" or "quasi-judicial" (as opposed to "administrative") final decisions that affected the rights of citizens. As the case law became more arcane and the practical injustices more obvious, policy reasons for maintaining the distinction between the various writs eroded.

The result, in many provinces and at the Federal Court,[165] was statutory reform. Some provinces enacted omnibus statutes governing judicial review or statutory/civil procedure,[166] while others used their rules of court to enact changes.[167] Only Yukon Territory seems to have

---

163   *Khela, supra* note 120 at paras 38-50. In other ways, as well, *habeas corpus* has developed to be a speedier and more accessible remedy for those who claim to have been unlawfully deprived of their liberty. On the Federal Court's jurisdiction, see also *infra* note 173.

164   E.g. PEI JRA, s 11; BC *Judicial Review Procedure Act*, RSBC 1996, c 241, s 18 [BC JRPA]. These statutes provide that certain remedies for what would have been an information in the nature of *quo warranto* are still available. However, *quo warranto* is still used in Quebec and New Brunswick to challenge the authority of municipal councillors on the basis of a prohibited conflict of interest. See e.g. *R v Wheeler*, [1979] 2 SCR 650.

165   FCA, s 18(1) provides that the Federal Court has exclusive original jurisdiction "to issue an injunction, writ of *certiorari*, writ of prohibition, writ of *mandamus*, or writ of *quo warranto*, or grant declaratory relief, against any federal board, commission or other tribunal." Note that *habeas corpus* is not included in the list. Jurisdiction to grant *habeas corpus* in, e.g. federal penitentiaries, which are otherwise subject to Federal Court review, remains with the provincial superior courts: *Khela, supra* note 120 at paras 31-35.

166   Ontario JRPA, BCJRPA, PEI JRA, Quebec *Code of Civil Procedure*, RSQ, c C-25. Ontario and British Columbia have enacted the most comprehensive reforms. Be aware that, apart from *habeas corpus*, terminology in Quebec is different. For example, prohibition and *certiorari* are codified under "evocation" and "revision" in s 846 of the *Civil Code*. Remedies equivalent to *quo warranto* and *mandamus* are codified under ss 838 and 844ff, respectively, and the terms "*quo warranto*" and "*mandamus*" are used in practice, but they do not appear in the Code. There also exists the "declaratory judgment in motion," codified at s 453, which allows a party to have their rights "declared."

167   Alberta, Manitoba, New Brunswick, Newfoundland, Northwest Territories, Nova Scotia, Nunavut, and Saskatchewan.

left the common law untouched. The details vary from one statutory scheme to another, but key statutes that may apply are the *Federal Courts Act*, the Ontario and BC *Judicial Review Procedure Acts*, the Ontario *Statutory Powers Procedure Act*, the BC *Administrative Tribunals Act*, the PEI *Judicial Review Act*, Quebec's *Code of Civil Procedure*, and the rules of court in other provinces and territories. These important statutes have sought to clarify procedure surrounding judicial review. Some have also sought to change the substantive shape of judicial review itself. Therefore, parties considering challenging a tribunal order must be aware of the relevant statutes' provisions, in addition to the provisions of the tribunal's own enabling statutes. Statutory reforms commonly provide for the following:

1. Simplified application procedures. For example, a statute may state that applications for orders "in the nature of" *mandamus*, prohibition, or *certiorari* shall be deemed to be applications for judicial review, to be brought by way of an originating notice or petition. The new judicial review application combines, and in the process supersedes, the old writs of *certiorari*, prohibition, *mandamus*, public law declaration, and injunction. (Some statutes include *quo warranto* and *habeas corpus* within the ambit of the statute; some abolish *quo warranto*; some provinces have a dedicated *Habeas Corpus Act*.) It is sufficient for a party to set out the grounds on which relief is sought and the nature of the relief sought, without having to specify under which particular writ they might have proceeded at common law.

2. Simplified remedies including, for example, the power to set aside a decision or direct the tribunal to reconsider its decision, with or without directions. Some statutes also expressly give courts the authority to ignore technical irregularities or defects in form if the court finds no substantial wrong or miscarriage of justice has occurred.

3. Greater clarity as to who may be parties to a hearing—for example, decision-makers whose exercise of statutory authority is being questioned. Generally, judicial review statutes also provide that notice must be given to the Attorney General, who is entitled as of right to be heard on the application.

4. A right of appeal. Judicial review applications are generally made to provincial superior courts, and the statutes provide for a subsequent right of appeal to the provincial Court of Appeal.

5. Judicial review mechanisms to challenge interlocutory orders and to resolve interim issues. At common law, *certiorari* was only available with respect to "decisions"—that is, final orders. However, the BC and Ontario JRPAs use the words "exercise of statutory power," rather than the word "decision," thereby expanding the range of judicial review to include any exercise of statutory power.[168] Other statutes permit a tribunal itself to refer a "stated case" to the courts for determination of a question of law, after which the case can go back to the original tribunal for determination of the ultimate issues.[169] For example, BC tribunals that do not have jurisdiction over constitutional questions under the ATA can issue a stay and refer a constitutional question to a court of competent jurisdiction.[170] Enabling statutes must authorize stated cases.

---

168 BC JRPA, s 3; Ontario JRPA, s 2.
169 E.g. FCA, s 18.3; BC ATA, s 43.
170 BC ATA, ss 44, 45.

F. Private Law Remedies

As noted above, a tribunal's enabling statute may give it the power to order a range of remedies, including money damages. Courts on judicial review do not have the same ability. The difficulty is that neither the old prerogative writs, nor the new statutory remedy of judicial review, allow a party to obtain monetary relief through judicial review. In some circumstances, unhappy parties would probably prefer monetary relief to any other remedy. Attempts to obtain private law remedies from public bodies has put considerable momentum behind the development of the law in this area, and courts have responded in two main ways.

The first has been to clarify and elaborate upon those instances where public bodies, like administrative agencies, can be subject to purely private law remedies outside the scope of administrative action and judicial review. The Crown and its servants can be liable to private parties for monetary relief,[171] although some statutes limit individual administrative tribunal members' liability.[172] However, to seek monetary relief, an aggrieved party must initiate a separate civil action for restitution or damages alongside, or in lieu of, a judicial review application.

Government agencies can be sued, for example, for breach of contract, for the tort of negligence, or the special tort of misfeasance in (or abuse of) public office. The first two are straightforward private law actions. The third, as a potential source of money damages against public actors acting in their public capacity, has attracted some interest lately. The threshold is high, however. To succeed in an action for tort of misfeasance in public office, the plaintiff must establish, in addition to the basic elements of negligence, (1) deliberate and unlawful conduct by someone in public office, and (2) the public officer's subjective knowledge that the conduct was unlawful and likely to harm the plaintiff. Because this tort alleges bad faith on the part of a public official, "clear proof commensurate with the seriousness of the wrong" is required.[173] Because a public officer must be able to make decisions that are adverse to some peoples' interests, in the service of broader public policy goals, mere knowledge of that harm is insufficient. The public officer must "deliberately engage in conduct that he or she knows to be inconsistent with the obligations of the office."[174]

The leading case on the tort of misfeasance in public office, *Odhavji*, involved an action for damages against police officers and the chief of the Toronto Police Service by the estate of an individual shot by the police. The plaintiffs alleged that the police officers involved in the shooting did not promptly or fully comply with their statutory duty to cooperate with an ensuing investigation, and that the chief of police did not adequately compel them to

---

171   The Federal Court has concurrent original jurisdiction over all actions for damages against the federal Crown. See *supra* note 109. Individual servants of the Crown, including ministers, are also liable for breaches of private law duties on the same basis as other individuals. However, "core policy matters" are protected from suit: *R v Imperial Tobacco Canada Ltd*, 2011 SCC 42, [2011] 3 SCR 45 at para 90 [*Imperial Tobacco*]. A more in-depth discussion is contained in Chapter 15, Making a Federal Case Out of It: The Federal Court and Administrative Law.

172   E.g. BC ATA, s 56.

173   *Powder Mountain Resorts Ltd v British Columbia*, 2001 BCCA 619 at para 8.

174   *Odhavji Estate v Woodhouse*, 2003 SCC 69, [2003] 3 SCR 263 at para 28 [*Odhavji*]. For his perspective on the tort's value as a practical tool for enhancing state accountability in the UK context, notwithstanding its rather poor fit with the conceptual underpinnings of modern tort law, see John Murphy, "Misfeasance in a Public Office: A Tort Law Misfit?" (2012) 32 Oxford J Leg Stud 51.

cooperate. The case made its way to the Supreme Court of Canada on the defendant's motion to dismiss the plaintiff's claim, where the court determined that the plaintiff had made out a cause of action and that the matter should be allowed to proceed. In other words, the court held that there was such a thing as the tort of misfeasance in public office. Subsequent cases have considered allegations of tort of misfeasance in public office against a range of public actors including provincial and federal departments or ministries, federal penitentiary staff, hospital boards, and racing commissions.[175]

As these cases make clear, some torts overlap with a potential judicial review application while others do not. Judicial review was not a possibility in a case like *Odhavji*, because there was no administrative decision to challenge. It was about police action. In other cases, like one involving Health Canada's handling of a drug approval application, or a hospital board's revocation of a doctor's privileges, an administrative actor's conduct may be precisely what is being challenged.

The relationship and potential overlap between private rights of action and judicial review applications was a cause for concern for a number of years. Then, in 2010, in a case concerning private law claims for breach of contract, negligence, and unjust enrichment, the Supreme Court of Canada made it clear that parties do not need to seek judicial review *before* they can bring a private law action for damages, and the private law action does not constitute a collateral attack on government conduct.[176] Alexander Pless discusses this and other cases in greater detail in Chapter 10, Crown Liability for Negligent Administrative Action. Following *TeleZone*, if a party has a fundamentally private law claim arising from an administrative decision, and primarily wants monetary damages, that party may proceed directly by way of private action. As Binnie J points out, though, "no amount of artful pleading in a damages case will succeed in setting aside the order said to have harmed the claimant or enjoin its enforcement. ... The claimant must ... be content to take its money (if successful) and walk away leaving the order standing."[177] Note that, while *TeleZone* makes

---

175 Some have succeeded, including *Apotex Inc v Canada*, 2017 FCA 73 (Health Canada deliberately evaluated drug approval application against inappropriate standard, and attempted to conceal or dissemble that fact); *Rosenhek v Windsor Regional Hospital*, 2010 ONCA 13, [2010] OJ No 129 (QL), leave to appeal refused, [2010] SCCA No 89 (hospital revoked a doctor's privileges for ulterior purpose, not for the public good, and in bad faith); *Ontario Racing Commission v O'Dwyer*, 2008 ONCA 446, 293 DLR (4th) 559 (Racing Commission frustrated raceway employee's efforts to pursue a complaint about Commission employee's prior conduct, which had led to employee's firing); *JP v British Columbia (Children and Family Development)*, 2015 BCSC 1216 (ministry employee approached child protection file with a closed mind, wilfully and deliberately behaving unlawfully and not in best interests of the children); *McMaster v The Queen*, 2009 FC 937, [2009] FCJ No 1071 (QL) (long and apparently intentional delay by Corrections and prison staff in getting a prisoner new shoes, resulting in prisoner's injury while exercising). See also *Carhoun & Sons Enterprises Ltd v Canada (Attorney General)*, 2015 BCCA 163 [*Carhoun*] (motion to strike dismissed, where respondent alleged unreasonable delay by government in carrying out an environmental assessment). Others have failed: see e.g. *Harrison v British Columbia (Children and Family Development)*, 2010 BCCA 220, 319 DLR (4th) 251, leave to appeal refused, [2010] SCCA No 293 (no evidence of targeted malice by social worker who disclosed unsubstantiated complaint of child abuse to employer of alleged abuser, who worked in youth support services).

176 *TeleZone, supra* note 140. The courts retain the residual discretion to stay a damages action if the claim being made is actually "in its essential character" an application for judicial review. *TeleZone, ibid* at para 78; on this point see also *Manuge v Canada*, 2010 SCC 67, another of the five companion cases released alongside *TeleZone*.

177 *TeleZone, supra* note 140 at para 75.

clear that parties do not need to seek judicial review before they can bring an action for damages, that case still allows the Crown to raise the legality of the decision as a defence to the damages action.[178]

A second and genuinely novel response to the question of when damages could be available against administrative authorities would be to develop a claim for monetary relief grounded entirely in public, as opposed to private, law. This is what a majority of the Federal Court of Appeal recently did, in *obiter*, in *Paradis Honey*.[179]

The case involved a claim by a group of Canadian beekeepers that the respondents, the Minister of Agriculture and Agri-food and the Canadian Food Inspection Agency, were negligent in imposing a blanket prohibition on importing honey bee "packages" from the United States. (Bees can be imported in "packages," which hold a queen and a small colony, or simply as a "queen," a much smaller container holding a queen bee and a few attendant bees. Replacing a failed bee colony with a package, as opposed to a queen, is more efficient and less risky.) The appellant beekeepers argued that the minister had adopted a blanket policy of issuing no permits for importing bee packages, even though the relevant statute and regulations gave the minister the authority to issue permits to import animals (in this case, bees) in any kind of packaging *so long as* doing so would not introduce disease or toxic substances into Canada. The appellants argued that the prohibition exceeded the minister's lawful authority. They further argued that in prohibiting packages while still permitting queens to be imported, the respondents were using their permit-granting authority in bad faith or for an improper purpose, and impermissibly favouring some parts of the Canadian beekeeping community over others. The decision occurred at the motion to dismiss stage, meaning that the majority of the Federal Court of Appeal held only that, assuming the facts as pleaded were all true, it was not plain and obvious that the appellant beekeepers' claims would fail.

The appellants sought money damages to compensate them for the costs they incurred as a result of the blanket prohibition on importing bee packages. Because they were seeking damages, they had to establish a claim in private law—in this case, primarily in negligence.[180] As the majority pointed out in *obiter*, the tort of negligence is indeed a poor fit for a situation in which parties have been harmed by impermissible government action. It is grounded in proximity and the concept of what one owes to one's neighbour—admittedly,

---

178 *TeleZone, supra* note 140 at para 46. The precise role of legality or illegality in an action for damages is a little more complicated in practice than this, and is explored in more detail in Chapter 10.

179 *Paradis Honey Ltd v Canada*, 2015 FCA 89, 382 DLR (4th) 720 [*Paradis Honey*]. The majority's reasons (by Stratas JA for himself and Nadon JA) were based on the beekeepers' claims in negligence and bad faith against the respondents: see paras 88-111 (among other things, forcefully criticizing the ban on private suits against government "policy" decisions, following *Imperial Tobacco, supra* note 171 at paras 102-110). The majority then went on to observe that "were it necessary," they would also have concluded that the facts pleaded supported a claim for monetary relief in public law. Pelletier JA, dissenting, would have confirmed the Federal Court's dismissal of the beekeepers' statement of claim. The matter was subsequently certified as a class action: *Paradis Honey Ltd v Canada*, 2017 FC 199.

180 Both majority and minority agreed that the appellants' allegations, if proved, would have given them an administrative law remedy such as *certiorari* and *mandamus: ibid* at paras 1, 76, 112. The appellants also argued that the respondents had acted in bad faith or pursuant to an improper purpose, and the majority of the Federal Court of Appeal declined to strike those claims: *ibid* at para 87.

a strange way to conceptualize the relationship between citizens and the state.[181] To make a claim, therefore, the appellants had to plead that their rights were particularly well-defined, based on specific legislative criteria, and that the respondents had specifically assured them that imports that affected their economic interests would only be banned where there was scientific evidence of risk.[182]

After dealing with the negligence claim, the majority of the court goes on to consider a matter not pleaded: the novel possibility of a *public law* claim for monetary damages, which the majority describes as a "responsible, incremental change to the common law founded upon legal doctrine and achieved through accepted pathways of legal reasoning ... [which] does not throw into doubt the outcomes of previous cases, but rather offers better explanations for them, leading us to a more understandable, more coherent law of liability for public authorities."[183] Rather than trying to adapt ill-fitting private law principles to public law contexts (or, in their words, "using a screwdriver to turn a bolt"),[184] the majority argues for drawing on underlying principles of administrative law and judicial review to create a new test: that as a matter of public law, courts should grant relief, including monetary relief, when (1) "a public law authority acts unacceptably or indefensibly in the administrative law sense," and when (2) "as a matter of discretion, a remedy should be granted."[185] The majority insists that, the limits of the prerogative writs and judicial review aside, underlying public law principles support courts' discretion to grant monetary relief. Moreover, there are times when the goal of adequately compensating the harmed, or perhaps the quality of a public authority's conduct (if it is, for example, exceptionally poor or clearly in violation of a duty), justifies a court exercising its discretion to grant a new species of *public* law monetary damages.

The *obiter* in *Paradis Honey* has begun to provoke discussion, as was surely its intention, not only about the imperfections of existing private law jurisprudence vis-à-vis public actors, but also about the public law foundations on which administrative law rests, and about the limits of the prerogative writs and judicial review.[186] It is too soon to say whether Justice

---

181   *Ibid* at paras 119-130.

182   *Ibid* at paras 90-91.

183   *Ibid* at para 118; see also para 145.

184   *Ibid* at para 127.

185   *Ibid* at para 132. The content of the first requirement—what constitutes unacceptable or indefensible action in administrative law—is the subject of most of the rest of this textbook. Basically, it usually requires that the administrative actor act outside the range of reasonableness. The content of the second requirement—the fact that judicial review and its remedies are discretionary—has been discussed above.

186   See e.g. *Patrong v Banks*, 2015 ONSC 3078 at paras 69-78 (partially endorsing the majority's argument and arguing for a broader understanding of the state's private law liability); but see *Carhoun, supra* note 175 (citing *Paradis Honey, supra* note 179 before proceeding with a conventional tort law analysis); Paul Daly, "Rethinking Public Authority Liability in Tort: *Paradis Honey Ltd v Canada*, 2015 FCA 89" (13 April 2015) at Administrative Law Matters, online: <http://www.administrativelawmatters.com/blog/2015/04/13/rethinking-public-authority-liability-in-tort-paradis-honey-ltd-v-canada-2015-fca-89/>. Justice Stratas's reasons in the case have also attracted interest for his discussion at paras 134-137, of how the "margin of appreciation" that courts grant administrative decision-makers on judicial review may be narrower or wider, depending on the nature of the decision-maker. Thus far, the Supreme Court has taken a dim view of this suggestion, preferring an approach that seems more focused on the nature of the question at issue: *Wilson, supra* note 101 at paras 18-39. For more on this, see Chapters 11 (Standard of Review: Back to the Future?) and 12 (Making Sense of Reasonableness).

Stratas's argument in favour of a public law monetary damages remedy will gain traction. What we can say at this stage is that the proposed change would not be incremental, at least at the level of theory. At the level of application, though, it may be: recognizing a public law remedy in money damages may actually provide us with a more coherent and explicit explanation for outcomes that courts already sometimes reach. Given the ongoing desire by parties for a remedy in money damages and given the narrowness of the tort of misfeasance in public office, we can expect more action around this issue.

V. CONCLUSION

A goal of this chapter has been to locate judicial review within the larger administrative law landscape. By understanding the concerns that animate administrative law generally, we can begin to understand the outlines of this parallel universe of actions and remedies. Administrative law remedies are the product of history, and of democratic and rule-of-law priorities, often acting in tension with each other. They need to be considered in light of the tug of war between courts and legislators as demonstrated by, for example, legislators' creation of internal appeal mechanisms and courts' periodic circumvention of those internal appeals in favour of immediate judicial review. Another recurring theme is the tug of war between tribunals and the courts that oversee them, in terms of courts' willingness to recognize and give effect to potentially creative and uncourtlike tribunal remedies. These tensions are emblematic of a deeper contest between deeply held values around the rule of law on the one hand, and administrative expertise, efficiency, and democratic accountability on the other.

Administrative law remedies are also path-dependent, meaning that they have been shaped by their historical origins in the prerogative writs and by subsequent, sometimes piecemeal, attempts to modify judicial review. If we were to design a set of remedies out of whole cloth today, it is not obvious that we would decide to set up two separate mechanisms for accessing the courts (that is, statutory appeals and judicial review). We might create an overarching administrative review tribunal like Quebec's instead. Perhaps, as well, there was an earlier juncture at which we could have developed a public law remedy for monetary damages, and perhaps it would have spared us a bit of confusing caselaw along the way. Freed of the historical baggage of the prerogative writs, a court might have even imposed monetary damages on the Crown for its failure to consult and accommodate in the *Gitxaala Nation* case. Yet without genuinely sweeping reform, administrative law remedies will continue to be influenced by their historical roots, and the scope of those remedies in turn will continue to influence the development of administrative law as a whole. Even as these remedies continue to evolve, they will be informed by the particular history and rules that govern this parallel legal universe.

In part as a corrective to the heavy conventional emphasis on judicial review and its idiosyncrasies, this chapter tries to situate judicial review remedies within a larger context. Myriad other remedies are available at different stages of administrative action. Rich debate exists concerning appropriate tribunal functioning and the proper scope of tribunal action. Tribunals develop remedies that are novel, by court standards, because they are differently constituted than courts are. It is in part the heterogeneity and depth of this experience that underlies the modern instinct that courts should show some respectful deference in exercising judicial review of tribunal decisions. Regardless of how we may feel about any particular decision, this chapter also counsels respect for that difference. A conversation about administrative law remedies illustrates the larger point that animates much of this volume: judicial review and court-centred processes, which make up the bulk of this book, are nevertheless just one, final stage of administrative law and practice. It should not limit our appreciation of, and approach to, the complex and varied forms that front-line administrative action can represent.

SUGGESTED ADDITIONAL READINGS

CASES

Canada (Attorney General) v PHS Community Services Society, 2011 SCC 44, [2011] 3 SCR 134 ("the *Insite* case").

Canada (Prime Minister) v Khadr, 2010 SCC 3, [2010] 1 SCR 44.

Harelkin v University of Regina, [1979] 2 SCR 561, 96 DLR (3d) 14.

McKinnon v Ontario, [2003] OJ No 893 (QL) (Div Ct).

Paradis Honey Ltd v Canada, 2015 FCA 89, 382 DLR (4th) 720.

Setia v Appleby College, 2013 ONCA 753.

STATUTES

Federal Courts Act, RSC 1985, c F-7.

Students should also be familiar with any omnibus statutes or rules of court governing judicial review in their provinces. See Section IV.E.2, "Statutory Reform," above.

CHAPTER THREE

Realizing Aboriginal Administrative Law

Janna Promislow
Thompson Rivers University Faculty of Law

Naiomi Mettalic
Schulich School of Law, Dalhousie University

I. INTRODUCTION

Situated near the beginning of this textbook, this chapter introduces an area of administrative law that is both distinctive and that we aspire to have embedded throughout this book. Aboriginal administrative law is defined by intersections, and in particular the intersection of three areas of Canadian public law: administrative law, constitutional law, and Aboriginal law. These areas in turn intersect with Indigenous law, which encompasses multiple Indigenous traditions of public law-making, legality, fairness, and accountability. None of these areas of law or traditions exist in isolation from each other, and all continue to evolve both separately and in relation to each other. Our task is not to define the boundaries of the field as much as to gather the issues and areas that can benefit from being understood in conversation with each other.

Before explaining the reasons for treating a field of "Aboriginal administrative law" separately and introducing the scope of the chapter, it will be helpful to address the terminology we use and our choice to continue to describe this emerging field as *Aboriginal* administrative law. A symptom of the rapid evolution of this area of law and public policy is that the accepted ways to refer to the descendants of the original peoples of North America living within the territory we now call Canada are also evolving rapidly. The term "aboriginal," used in s 35(2) of the *Constitution Act, 1982*, has become outdated. The current preference for a "pan" term is "Indigenous" rather than "Aboriginal" (both capitalized to demonstrate that a word that is otherwise an adjective is being used to signify a name), a preference that grounds the identification of these peoples and their rights beyond the Canadian Constitution with reference to international law, and the United Nations Declaration on the Rights of Indigenous Peoples (UNDRIP),[1] which supports a principle of Indigenous Peoples identifying and defining themselves.[2] The naming of the three identities within the umbrella of "aboriginal" in s 35(2)[3]—"'aboriginal peoples of Canada' includes the Indian, Inuit and Métis peoples of Canada"—is similarly outdated, and particularly the term "Indian." With respect to the particular identity indicated as one of the three constitutional peoples, "First Nations" has long replaced this term, used both in policy and more recent legislation, referring primarily (but not exclusively) to communities with reserve lands under the *Indian Act* (a First Nation) and their members (First Nations people).[4] As part of larger efforts toward decolonization, attention is focused on how individuals, communities, and nations self-identify, and often the choice is for names from their own languages over names attributed to them by colonial history, law, and policy. For example,

---

1   United Nations Declaration on the Rights of Indigenous Peoples, GA Res 61/295, UNGAOR (2007), online: <www.un.org/esa/socdev/unpfii/documents/DRIPS_en.pdf> [UNDRIP].

2   For a brief discussion, see Benjamin J Richardson, Shin Imai & Kent McNeil, "Indigenous Peoples and the Law—Historical, Comparative and Contextual Issues" in Benjamin J Richardson, Shin Imai & Kent McNeil, *Indigenous Peoples and the Law: Comparative and Critical Perspectives* (Oxford: Hart Publishing, 2009) 3 at 12. See also, Pam Palmater, "Terminology," online: <http://www.pampalmater.com/terminology/>; Brittany Luby, Kathryn Labelle & Alison Norman, "(Re)naming and (De)colonizing the (I?)ndigenous People(s) of North America—Part II" (8 November 2016), *Active History.ca*, online: <http://activehistory.ca/2016/11/renaming-and-decolonizing-the-indigenous-peoples-of-north-america-part-i/>; and Bob Joseph, "Indigenous or Aboriginal. Which is Correct?" (5 January 2016), online: <https://www.ictinc.ca/blog/indigenous-or-aboriginal-which-is-correct>.

3   These terms—"Indian"/"First Nation," "Inuit," and "Métis"—obscure the fact that Canada is home to between 50 and 70 distinct Indigenous Peoples with multiple communities and ways of organizing themselves within the larger people or national group. And while these three "umbrella" identity groups have distinct origins and histories, boundaries between them can also be porous and fluid, given changes in legal definitions and recognition, and given the significant shared experience and kin-relationships existing between them. The naming of these three groups in s 35(2) is thus also best understood as representing a moment in history and not as representing classifications of any definitive legal nature or a reality of identities to be found in lived experience. A few examples of related literature and views: Chris Anderson, *Métis: Race, Recognition, and the Struggle for Indigenous Peoplehood* (Vancouver: UBC Press, 2014); âpihtawikosisân (Chelsea Vowel), "Pan-Indianism, Pan-Métisism" (2 May 2011), online: <http://apihtawikosisan.com/2011/05/pan-indianism-pan-metisism/>; and Brent Olthuis, "The Constitution's Peoples: Approaching Community in the Context of Section 35 of the Constitution Act, 1982" (2009) 54 McGill LJ 1.

4   For titles of legislation using the term "First Nations," see *infra* note 32. Most recently, and in relation to s 91(24) of the *Constitution Act, 1867*, demarcating federal jurisdiction over "Indians and Lands Reserved for Indians," the Supreme Court has confirmed that "Indians" is a pan-Aboriginal term in this context: *Daniels v Canada (Indian Affairs and Northern Development)*, 2016 SCC 12 [*Daniels*].

people who belong to the Cree nation might still use this English word of colonial origins, but they might also prefer to signify their ethnic, cultural, and political belonging with "Nehiyaw," their people's own word for themselves from their own language.[5] With the resurgence of Indigenous Peoples' legal traditions and efforts to revive Indigenous languages, we can expect continued evolution in the identification and naming of Indigenous Peoples. As we proceed to use all of these terms in rapid succession in the paragraphs that follow, it may be helpful to keep in mind that the complexity of decolonization begets complexity, and that when we refer to a community, group, or nation, the terms we use connote a specific perspective and historical moment.

When used to refer to areas of law, "Aboriginal" and "Indigenous" also signify distinct systems of law. "Indigenous law" is increasingly used as an umbrella term encompassing the specific legal orders of Indigenous nations. These orders are among Canada's founding legal orders and continue to grow, evolve, and govern affairs in Indigenous communities today.[6] On the other hand, "Aboriginal" remains the language of the Constitution, language that is not so easily changed. When used to refer to an area of law, "Aboriginal" signifies that the law of the Canadian state is the subject at hand.[7] Our use of the term "Aboriginal" to connote this

---

5 For discussion of the politics of "naming," see Brittany Luby, Kathryn Labelle & Alison Norman, "(Re)naming and (De)colonizing the (I?)ndigenous People(s) of North America-Part I" (7 November 2016), *Active History.ca*, online: <http://activehistory.ca/2016/11/renaming-and-decolonizing-the-indigenous-peoples-of-north-america-part-ii/>.

6 For further discussion of the terminology and nature of Indigenous legal orders, see John Borrows, *Canada's Indigenous Constitution* (Toronto: University of Toronto Press, 2010); Gordon Christie, "Culture, Self-Determination and Colonialism: Issues Around the Revitalization of Indigenous Legal Traditions" (2007) 6 Indigenous LJ 13; Hadley Friedland & Val Napoleon, "Gathering the Threads: Indigenous Legal Methodology" (2015) 1:1 Lakehead LJ 16; Aaron Mills, "The Lifeworlds of Law: On Revitalizing Indigenous Legal Orders Today" (2016) 61 McGill LJ 847; Robert Yelkátte Clifford, "Listening to Law" (2016) 33 Windsor YB Access Just 47; and Hadley Friedland, "Wanisk?: Reimagining the Future with Indigenous Legal Traditions" (2016) 33 Windsor YB Access Just 85.

7 Aboriginal law is itself both a subfield of Canadian public law and a field of law that is broader than public law. It encompasses the Aboriginal and treaty rights protected by s 35 of the *Constitution Act, 1982*, federal jurisdiction under s 91(24) of the *Constitution Act, 1867*, and other constitutional authorities and restraints (e.g., the Royal Proclamation of 1763, s 109 of the *Constitution Act, 1867*, the *Manitoba Act, 1870*, the *Constitution Act, 1930*, and s 25 of the *Constitution Act, 1982*); the policies, prerogative authorities, and legislative frameworks addressing the resolution of historical grievances, self-government rights, and the relationship between the Crown and Indigenous Peoples more generally; the interpretation and application of the *Indian Act*, RSC 1985, c I-5 [*Indian Act*]; the interpretation and application of other legislation particular to Aboriginal peoples or with provisions specific to Aboriginal people—for example, the *Metis Settlements Act*, RSA 2000, c M-14, the *First Nations Oil and Gas and Moneys Management Act*, SC 2005, c 48 [*First Nations Oil and Gas*], the *Inuit Language Protection Act*, SNu 2008, c 17, *Family Homes on Reserves and Matrimonial Interests or Rights Act*, SC 2013, c 20, s 718 [*Family Homes on Reserves*], s 2(e) of the *Criminal Code*, RSC 1985, c C-46, and s 29.1 of the *Environmental Assessment Act*, SBC 2002; and common law concepts that continue to have importance within these areas, such as *sui generis*, fiduciary duty, the honour of the Crown, customary law, and the doctrine of discovery. These diverse legal instruments and doctrines structure both public and private relationships, including, with respect to the latter, rights of contract (e.g., creditor–debtor relationships on reserves), torts (e.g., *Saik'uz First Nation and Stellat'en First Nation v Rio Tinto Alcan*, 2015 BCCA 154, *Uashaunnat (Innus de Uasshat et de Mani-Utenam) c Companie minière IOC inc (Iron Ore Company of Canada)*, 2016 QCCS 5133), and property rights (e.g., the right to acquire and transfer property, matrimonial real property on reserve and residential tenancies). They bring together a field in which Indigeneity is a factor that impacts the applicable law in a given situation.

diverse field of administrative law thus anchors this area in the language of the Canadian Constitution and Canadian law more generally. It also serves to distinguish this field of law from Indigenous law. The Truth and Reconciliation Commission (TRC) explains, "[a]ll Canadians need to understand the difference between Indigenous law and Aboriginal law ...; each Indigenous nation has its own laws and legal traditions. Aboriginal law is the body of law that exists within the Canadian legal system."[8] As we describe in Section IV, Indigenous law informs and intersects with Aboriginal administrative law, but is not (or is not yet) central to it. As we toggle between Indigenous and Aboriginal law, it may be helpful to recall that while systems of law influence each other, with concepts borrowed from one area to another even within a system of law (with many examples to be described in this textbook), the distinctive systems denoted by Indigenous versus Aboriginal law are grounded in distinctive worldviews.

Aboriginal administrative law requires its own treatment for at least three reasons. First, history suggests that the fit of Indigenous Peoples within the administrative state has been poorly understood and poorly executed. Starting from a history that stretches back much further than the emergence of the welfare state detailed by Colleen M Flood and colleagues in Chapter 1, the aims of colonial policy—dispossessing Indigenous lands and assimilating Indigenous Peoples into extinction[9]—meant that the administration of government in Indigenous contexts was always an afterthought. Without wholesale reform, coloniality continues to manifest in the irregularity of government programs and services for Indigenous Peoples, particularly for First Nations living on reserves recognized under the *Indian Act*,[10] and the reluctant and piecemeal recognition and implementation of Indigenous laws and jurisdictions. In these contexts, over-reliance on policy and discretion over legislative frameworks dominates, and First Nations struggle to access the benefit of the rule of law through judicial review. We outline this history and highlight some ongoing issues in Section II, "Administrative Law as Arbiter Between Indigenous Peoples and the Crown."

Second, administrative law is critical to the implementation of Aboriginal rights and self-determination. Canadian jurisprudence on Aboriginal rights and self-government has not repudiated colonial policy and doctrines at the foundations of Crown sovereignty, a

---

8 Truth and Reconciliation Commission of Canada, *The Final Report of the Truth and Reconciliation Commission of Canada*, vol 6: Reconciliation (Montreal and Kingston: McGill-Queen's University Press, 2015) at 45.

9 See Truth and Reconciliation Commission of Canada, *Honouring the Truth, Reconciling for the Future-Summary of the Final Report of Truth and Reconciliation Commission of Canada* (2015) [TRC Summary Report] Chapter 1, "Introduction" at 1: "For over a century, the central goals of Canada's Aboriginal policy were to eliminate Aboriginal governments; ignore Aboriginal rights; terminate the Treaties; and, through a process of assimilation, cause Aboriginal peoples to cease to exist as distinct legal, social, cultural, religious, and racial entities in Canada. The establishment and operation of residential schools were a central element of this policy, which can best be described as "cultural genocide."'

10 The *Indian Act* defines "reserves" as "a tract of land, the legal title to which is vested in Her Majesty, that has been set apart by Her Majesty for the use and benefit of a band": see ss 2(1), 18.

subject of significant critique.[11] Administrative law in relation to implementing Aboriginal rights and self-government is often characterized by the concerns and limitations raised in these critiques. Aboriginal rights and self-determination, however, are also rooted in Indigenous law and governance. The administrative law relating to the implementation of rights reflects both the colonial and Indigenous origins of these rights by considering adaptations of Canadian administrative law to serve policy objectives of reconciliation,[12] including a rule of law that recognizes Indigenous law as a foundational legal tradition within Canada.[13] Within this aspect of the field, there are several developing areas of law: tribunals and negotiations processes to resolve historical and current disputes about Aboriginal rights, land, treaty promises, governance, and the duty to consult and accommodate Indigenous Peoples. These areas are canvassed in Section III of this chapter, "Recognizing and Implementing Aboriginal Rights." Section IV, "Administrative Law in Indigenous Governance," picks up the discussion with an examination of Indigenous governance bodies, their relationships to the state, and the treatment of their decisions on judicial review—the latter being a subject that remains nascent. This section will explain that Indigenous governance encompasses a spectrum of decision-makers, including ones with authority under Canadian statutes, bodies constituted by communities and nations and given authority through negotiated agreements, bodies jointly constituted by Indigenous nations and government, and Indigenous decision-makers that are founded in Indigenous law and sit outside the recognition policies of the Canadian governments.

---

11 See TRC Summary Report, *supra* note 9 at 183-200 and Call to Action #45, calling on Canada to develop a new Royal Proclamation on Reconciliation that would include repudiation of the doctrine of discovery and *terra nullius*, adoption and implementation of the *United Nations Declaration on the Rights of Indigenous Peoples* as the framework for reconciliation, and the renewal and establishment of treaty relationships. See also: Borrows, 2010, *supra* note 6; Robert Miller, Jacinta Ruru, Larissa Behrendt & Tracy Lindberg, *Discovering Indigenous Lands. The Doctrine of Discovery in the English Colonies* (New York: Oxford University Press, 2010); Felix Hoehn, "Back to the Future—Reconciliation and Indigenous Sovereignty after Tsilhqot'in" (2016) 67 UNB LJ 109; James Anaya, *Indigenous Peoples in International Law*, 2nd ed (New York: Oxford University Press, 2004); Mark D Walters, "'Looking for a Knot in the Bulrush': Reflections on Law, Sovereignty and Aboriginal Rights" in Patrick Macklem & Douglas Sanderson, eds, *From Recognition to Reconciliation: Essays on The Constitutional Entrenchment of Aboriginal and Treaty Rights* (Toronto: University of Toronto Press, 2016) 35; and Jeremy Webber, "We Are Still in the Age of Encounter: Section 35 and a Canada Beyond Sovereignty" in Patrick Macklem & Douglas Sanderson, eds, *ibid*, 62.

12 See for example, *Kainaiwa/Blood Tribe v Alberta (Energy)*, 2017 ABQB 107 [*Kainaiwa/Blood Tribe*]; Nigel Bankes, "Reasons, Respect and Reconciliation" (3 March 2017), ABlawg.ca, online: <http://ablawg.ca/2017/03/03/reasons-respect-and-reconciliation/>.

13 See Borrows, 2010, *supra* note 6; Royal Commission on Aboriginal Peoples, *Report of the Royal Commission on Aboriginal Peoples* (Ottawa: Minister of Supply and Services, 1996) [RCAP Report], vol 2, ch 3 "Governance"; and TRC Summary Report, *supra* note 9, "Revitalizing Indigenous Laws: Truth, Reconciliation and Access to Justice" at 202-7 and Call to Action #50 calling on Canada to fund the establishment of Indigenous law institutes for the development, use, and understanding of Indigenous laws and access to justice in accordance with the unique cultures of Aboriginal peoples in Canada.

With further detail on the relevant doctrines and issues being picked up in later chapters, our discussion of these developing areas will primarily highlight how Aboriginal law presents distinctive problems for the rule of law, and the reach and potential limitations of judicial review principles. Our discussion of these areas will also highlight the creativity and flexibility of administrative law, including the potential for Aboriginal administrative law to both inform the evolution of principles in other areas of administrative law and foster a more pluralistic approach to the rule of law.

Third, treating Aboriginal administrative law as a distinctive and emerging field serves to reinforce and supplement key administrative law themes about the rule of law and flexible, contextual analysis, while also posing challenging questions about whether the principles of judicial review are up to the task of reconciliation or, alternatively, whether new adaptations and directions are required. Thus, a key task for Aboriginal administrative law is to help frame evaluation and critique the application of judicial review principles and other aspects of administrative law in Indigenous contexts. The aim for any such evaluation is to consider directions that will ensure administrative law evolves to support reconciliation and remedies the harms of colonization, and how administrative law may improve relationships between Canada and Indigenous Peoples. The adaptation of administrative law to Indigenous contexts, along with potential learning and influence from Indigenous law and governance, may in turn be applied to push the evolution of administrative law in other contexts. These themes and questions will inform the discussion throughout the chapter and come into focus again in the conclusion.

A final word before turning to Section II. Administrative law is undeniably a difficult subject, with doctrines bridging the abstract concerns for the rule of law and the separation of powers with the practical concerns of individuals and groups who are aggrieved by government decisions. Aboriginal administrative law augments the difficulty level a notch or two. To the "regular" complexities of administrative law, Aboriginal administrative law layers on more theoretical and practical tensions; Indigenous actors affected by government action are still individuals and groups aggrieved by government decisions, but their actions and grievances are often contextualized by legislation and policy (or an absence of these), arising from or attempting to address colonial history, and also by Indigenous ideas of law and governance. This chapter sits near the beginning of this textbook because administrative law in Indigenous contexts is and must be understood as part of the larger field. Nevertheless, as this chapter attempts to present, this context requires sufficient background to contextualize issues that arise in Indigenous contexts, and to anticipate the unique dimensions this context might bring to judicial review and administrative law more generally. However, the irregularities that arise in Indigenous contexts also present new complexities through the discussion of how administrative law principles transfer to address the particular issues that arise in this context. It is difficult to follow some of these discussions without first becoming well versed in the principles of judicial review addressed in the chapters that follow. As a result, Aboriginal administrative law is a great way to "test" your understanding of what administrative law is all about, and we invite you to return to this chapter toward the end of your course.

II. ADMINISTRATIVE LAW AS ARBITER BETWEEN INDIGENOUS PEOPLES AND THE CROWN

Much has been written about the role of s 35 of the *Constitution Act, 1982* in mediating the relationship between the Crown—federal and provincial governments and their delegates—and Indigenous Peoples in Canada. In most Canadian law schools, you will find a portion of a constitutional law course, or even entire courses, dedicated to this subject. By comparison, very little attention has been paid to the role—actual or potential—that administrative law plays in reconciling the relationship between Indigenous Peoples and the Crown. As explained further below, the Crown—especially the federal government—both in the past and even in the present, exercises a significant amount of legislative and discretionary control over nearly all aspects of the lives of Indigenous Peoples.[14]

As a student of administrative law, you will learn that, at its root, administrative law is aimed at providing legal doctrines and remedies to supervise the machinery of government and to hold governments accountable to the rule of law.[15] As you read this section, keep in mind these overarching objectives and critically consider whether there is a role for administrative law in reconciling the relationship between Indigenous Peoples and the Crown. If so, have administrative law doctrines and remedies been effective in this relationship so far? To the extent that Indigenous Peoples have sought accountability through judicial review, are there ways to make these doctrines and remedies more effective? Likewise, can the emerging field of "Aboriginal administrative law" inspire adaptations or transformations that further reconciliation, decolonization, and justice?

A. The Relationships Between the Administrative State and Indigenous Peoples

This section will focus on the post-Confederation relationship between Indigenous Peoples and the Crown. For the better part of this relationship (about a century), the Crown's approach toward Indigenous Peoples was characterized as one of "domination and assimilation."[16] It is important to recall, however, that the first two centuries of relations between Indigenous Peoples and European explorers and settlers who came to North American have been characterized as having a "nation-to-nation" quality.[17] The point is that the relationship can change. For the past 30 years or so, Canada has been in transition from

---

14 The significant level of discretionary control exercised over First Nations child welfare programs was the recent subject of comment by the Canadian Human Rights Tribunal in *First Nations Child and Family Caring Society of Canada v Attorney General of Canada (for the Minister of Indian and Northern Affairs Canada)*, 2016 CHRT 2 at paras 105-106 [*Caring Society*].

15 See Chapter 2, Remedies in Administrative Law: A Roadmap to a Parallel Legal Universe. See also *Martineau v Matsqui Inmate Disciplinary Board*, [1980] 1 SCR 602, at 621; *Baker v Canada (Minister of Citizenship and Immigration)*, [1999] 2 SCR 817, 174 DLR (4th) 193 at para 56; *Dunsmuir v New Brunswick*, 2008 SCC 9, [2008] 1 SCR 190 at para 28; and *Catalyst Paper Corp v North Cowichan (District)*, 2012 SCC 2, [2012] 1 SCR 5 at para 10.

16 See RCAP Report, *supra* note 13, vol 1, "Looking Forward, Looking Back," ch 5, "Stage Two: Contact and Co-operation."

17 *Ibid*.

domination and assimilation to an era of renewal and reconciliation.[18] However, as the 2015 *Final Report of the Truth and Reconciliation Commission* (TRC) of Canada reveals, there is still much work to be done.[19]

At Confederation, s 91(24) of the *Constitution Act, 1867* assigned exclusive legislative jurisdiction over "Indians and Lands reserved for the Indians" to the federal government.[20] While today our Constitution recognizes that the Aboriginal peoples of Canada includes "the Indian [First Nation], Inuit and Métis peoples of Canada,"[21] following Confederation, the federal government recognized jurisdiction only in relation to Indians/First Nations. Canada denied responsibility toward both the Inuit and the Métis until the Supreme Court of Canada affirmed these groups fell within Canada's jurisdiction in 1939 and 2016, respectively.[22] Due to Canada's attempts to minimize its responsibilities to different Indigenous groups in Canada, the history of the relationship between the Canadian administrative state and Indigenous Peoples relayed below will primarily focus on First Nations living on reserve. This is because First Nations living on reserve are the *one* Indigenous group Canada *has* historically exercised control over, though, as will be seen, neglect and minimization of responsibility is a theme underlying this relationship as well.

Canada's "Indian policy" over First Nations for the first 70 years following Confederation was animated by an objective of assimilation. Colonial governments sought to segregate First Nations on small and less-than-desirable parcels of land (reserves), hoping they would eventually become extinct from disease and starvation or subsumed into mainstream culture.[23] On reserves, First Nations were prevented from exercising their traditional subsistence livelihoods and government rations to alleviate starvation were provided sparingly, generally only to the elderly, ill, and the infirm.[24] Further, the federal government pursued a policy of cultural genocide, through sending thousands of Indigenous children to Indian

---

18 *Ibid.*

19 See TRC Summary Report *supra* note 9 at 6-8: "To the Commission, reconciliation is about establishing and maintaining a mutually respectful relationship between Aboriginal and non-Aboriginal peoples in this country. In order for that to happen, there has to be awareness of the past, acknowledgement of the harm that has been inflicted, atonement for the causes, and action to change behaviour. We are not there yet. ... The urgent need for reconciliation runs deep in Canada. Expanding public dialogue and action on reconciliation beyond residential schools will be critical in the coming years. Although some progress has been made, significant barriers to reconciliation remain. The relationship between the federal government and Aboriginal peoples is deteriorating. Instead of moving towards reconciliation, there have been divisive conflicts over Aboriginal education, child welfare, and justice. ... Too many Canadians know little or nothing about the deep historical roots of these conflicts. ... Too many Canadians still do not know the history of Aboriginal peoples' contributions to Canada, or understand that by virtue of the historical and modern Treaties negotiated by our government, we are all Treaty people. History plays an important role in reconciliation; to build for the future, Canadians must look to, and learn from, the past."

20 *Constitution Act, 1867* (UK), 30 & 31 Vict, c 3, s 91(24), reprinted in RSC 1985, Appendix II, No 5 [*Constitution Act, 1867*].

21 *Constitution Act, 1982*, s 35(2), being Schedule B to the *Canada Act 1982* (UK), 1982, c 11.

22 See *Reference re: British North America Act*, 1867 (UK), s 91, [1939] SCR 104 (*Re Eskimo Reference*) and *Daniels, supra* note 4. Despite these decisions, Canada has never passed legislation in relation to the Inuit or Métis, although it has negotiated modern treaties with Inuit groups in recent decades. How Canada will react to the recent ruling that Métis peoples fall within its jurisdiction remains to be seen.

23 See RCAP Report, *supra* note 13, ch 6, "Displacement and Assimilation" at 136.

24 H Shewell *"Enough to Keep Them Alive"—Indian Welfare in Canada, 1873-1965* (Toronto: University of Toronto Press, 2004) at 327.

residential and day schools,[25] as well as revoking the "Indian status" of thousands of First Nations men, women, and children through several arbitrary identity laws,[26] among other assimilatory policies.[27]

Many of these policies were legislated in the *Indian Act*, which was first enacted in 1876 and has continued in force until the present day.[28] The *Indian Act* has been amended over time with the last major overhaul of the law occurring in 1951.[29] It is a common misconception that the *Indian Act* is a comprehensive statute covering all manner of subjects having to do with First Nations people.[30] In fact, the scope of the *Indian Act* is narrow. Specifically, it contains laws regarding: (1) Indian registration and band membership rules; (2) Indians' collective interests in reserve lands (how they can be surrendered, transferred, leased, expropriated, etc.) and a quasi-private property regime for band members; (3) Indian wills and estates; (4) taxation of Indians and exemption from seizure of property on reserve; (5) election of band councils; and (6) by-laws that can be enacted by band councils.[31] Outside of the *Indian Act*, there are a handful of stand-alone federal laws on specific topics relating to First Nations, all of which have been enacted in the past 20 years. Most of them deal with issues of land, money, or taxation.[32]

Aside from the *Indian Act*, and the limited number of modern statutes passed in the last two decades, the most striking feature of the relationship between First Nations and the federal government—for administrative law purposes—is the absence of legislation with only policy manuals and discretion operating in lieu. Most notably, there is an absence of any legislation having to do with the provision of essential services in First Nations communities, such as in the areas of social assistance, child welfare, child care, health, education, police,

---

25 See TRC Summary Report, "The History," *supra* note 9 at 37-135.

26 See P Palmater, *Beyond Blood: Rethinking Indigenous Identity* (Purich Publishing, 2011); B Lawrence, *"Real" Indians and Others: Mixed-Blood Urban Native Peoples and Indigenous Nationhood* (Vancouver: UBC Press, 2004); and V Napoleon, "Extinction by Number: Colonialism Made Easy" (2001) 16 No 1 CJLS 113.

27 This includes banning spiritual practices, replacing traditional governments with *Indian Act* Chief and Councils, and preventing bands from hiring lawyers to prosecute land claims. See RCAP Report, *supra* note 13, vol 1, ch 6 and TRC Summary Report, *supra* note 9 "Introduction" at 1.

28 *Indian Act*, SC 1876, c 18.

29 See *Indian Act*, SC 1951, c 29. There have since been some smaller amendments to the Indian registration and membership provisions with *An Act to Amend the Indian Act*, SC 1985, c 27 (Bill C-31) and Bill C-3: *Gender Equity in Indian Registration Act*, SC 2010, c 18, as well as some smaller amendments to remove provisions deemed antiquated or paternalistic through *An Act to amend the Indian Act (publication of by-laws) and to provide for its replacement*, SC 2014, c 38.

30 Indeed, it is often stated that the *Indian Act* is "cradle to grave" legislation, controlling all aspects of First Nations peoples' lives: see, for example, R Kuppa & R Potts, *Law & Anthropology: An Introduction* (Kluwer Law International, 1996) at 150.

31 *Indian Act*, ss 5-14; ss 18-41, and 53-60; ss 42-52; ss 87 and 89-90; ss 74-80 and ss 81-86.

32 See *First Nations Land Management Act*, SC 1999, c 24; *First Nations Fiscal Management Act*, SC 2005, c 9; *First Nations Financial Transparency Act*, SC 2013, c 7; *First Nations Goods and Services Tax Act*, SC 2003, c 15, s 67; and *First Nations Oil and Gas*, *supra* note 7. Two statutes enacted in 2013 address two subjects that First Nations had long maintained were neglected areas (among many) requiring legislative action: matrimonial property and drinking water on reserve. See *Family Homes on Reserves*, *supra* note 7; and the *Safe Drinking Water for First Nations Act*, SC 2013, c 21. A statute allowing bands to opt into an alternative election process to that set out in the *Indian Act* was passed in 2014: the *First Nations Elections Act*, SC 2014, c 5.

fire, and emergency services. The reasons for this appear to be related to neglect rather than design as explained further below.

To a certain extent, the provinces can also pass laws that apply to First Nations living on reserve. The law in this regard is complex, but the basic constitutional principles are that provincial laws apply on reserve if they (1) are of general application, (2) do not single out First Nations, (3) do not conflict with provisions in the *Indian Act* or another federal law, and (4) do not touch on a subject that goes to the "core of Indianness."[33] The classic example are provincial traffic laws; they are of general application and do not conflict with the *Indian Act* or other federal laws, nor do they go to the "core of Indianness." They therefore apply on reserve.

These constitutional principles prevent some, but not all, provincial laws from applying on reserve. Most provincial statutes having to do with land (which are based on a model of individual ownership), conflict with the land provisions in the *Indian Act* that attempt to preserve the collective interests of the band in reserve land. This therefore precludes provincial statutes on such subjects such as wills and estates, land registries, land assessment, liens, municipal zoning, and construction, etc., from applying on reserve. Sometimes provincial laws are incapable of applying on reserve even where there is no similar law in the *Indian Act*, but the subject matter is a subject at the "core of Indianness" in which the federal government *could* legislate (but chooses not to).[34] This includes areas such as matrimonial property, in relation to which legislation was only recently passed to address this gap,[35] and residential tenancy laws on reserve, in relation to which the legislative gap continues.[36]

For the most part, these constitutional rules prevent the application of provincial laws of general application touching on land. Beyond this, there are no strict prohibitions on the application of provincial laws on reserve. However, there are a number of areas in which

---

33 For an extensive review of the law in this regard, see P Hogg, *Constitutional Law of Canada*, 5th ed (Scarborough, Ont: Carswell: 2007) (loose-leaf), ch 28, "Aboriginal Peoples."

34 This is otherwise known as the constitutional doctrine of interjurisdictional immunity (IJI). In *Tsilhqot'in Nation v British Columbia*, 2014 SCC 44 at paras 128-152 [*Tsilhqot'in Nation*], the Supreme Court of Canada clarified that, although Aboriginal and Treaty rights and Aboriginal title are at the "core of Indianness," the IJI doctrine is to be construed narrowly and does not prevent provincial laws from applying to Aboriginal title lands, preferring that any incursions instead be justified under the justification test set out *R v Sparrow*, [1990] 1 SCR 1075 [*Sparrow*]. See also *Grassy Narrows First Nation v Ontario (Natural Resources)*, 2014 SCC 48. For further commentary on the application of IJI in the Aboriginal context, see: Bruce McIvor & Kate Gunn, "Stepping into Canada's Shoes: Tsilhqot'in, Grassy Narrows and the Division of Powers" (2016) 67 UNB LJ 146; John Borrows, "The Durability of *Terra Nullius: Tsilhqot'in Nation v British Columbia*" (2015) 48 UBC Law Review 701 [Borrows, 2015]; and K Wilkins, "*R v Morris*: A Shot in the Dark and Its Repercussions" (2008) 7 Indigenous LJ 1.

35 See *Derrickson v Derrickson*, [1986] 1 SCR 285, which confirmed that provincial matrimonial property legislation could not apply on reserve. Canada was slow to rectify the legislative gap resulting from the court's decision. It took decades of advocacy by First Nations organizations, in particular First Nations women's groups, decrying the impact such a gap had on vulnerable women on reserve to convince the federal government to act: see Library of Parliament, "Legislative Summary of Bill S-2: "Family Homes on Reserves and Matrimonial Interests or Rights Act"; *Family Homes on Reserves*, *supra* note 7. The *Family Homes on Reserves and Matrimonial Interests or Rights Act*, SC 2013, c 20, was finally passed in 2013. Several Aboriginal organizations, including the Native Women's Association of Canada, have been quite critical of this legislation.

36 See *Matsqui Indian Band v Bird*, 1992 CanLII 1225 (BCSC); *Sechelt Indian Band v British Columbia (Manufactured Home Park Tenancy Act, Dispute Resolution Officer)*, 2013 BCCA 262.

provinces could enforce their laws on reserve, including in the area of essential services.[37] However, all of the provinces, except for Ontario (for reasons explained below) generally refrain from doing so.

Following the Second World War came the rise of the administrative state in Canada, and both the federal and the provincial governments found themselves legislating over a range of essential services within their own fields of jurisdiction.[38] Yet neither could agree on who would be responsible for providing services to First Nations on reserve; the provinces argued that First Nations were a federal responsibility, and the federal government urged that provision of services to First Nations was a provincial responsibility. While federal–provincial disputes over jurisdiction are common, in this case it was a fight to avoid responsibility. In 1950, a Joint Committee of the Senate and the House of Commons on Indian Affairs reported that First Nations peoples on reserves were excluded from many federal social programs and most provincial and territorial services.[39] The committee recommended that the provinces and territories be more involved in delivering and funding social services to First Nations.[40]

In response to this recommendation, in 1951, along with the other amendments to the *Indian Act* noted above, the federal government added a provision allowing provincial laws of general application to apply to Indians whenever the *Indian Act*, its regulations, or a treaty were silent.[41] This was a unilateral attempt by the federal government to give jurisdiction over services for First Nations to the provinces. However, this failed in having the intended effect, since the provinces would not be forced to extend program benefits to First Nations, and the provinces were unwilling to do so unless the federal government reimbursed them.[42] Thus, the federal government was forced to pursue a different tactic and instead, in the 1950s and 1960s, sought to negotiate with the provinces for their assumption of jurisdiction over providing essential services to First Nations.[43] In this regard, the federal government even legislated a mechanism facilitating such jurisdictional agreements.[44] However,

---

37 Some have dubbed this "regulatory abandonment": see Constance MacIntosh, "Testing the Waters: Jurisdictional and Policy Aspects of the Continuing Failure to Remedy Drinking Water Quality on First Nations Reserves" (2007-2008) 39 Ottawa L Rev 63; David R Boyd, "No Taps, No Toilets: First Nations and the Constitutional Right to Water in Canada" (2011) 57 McGill LJ 81.

38 The provinces were legislating in the areas of social assistance, child welfare, child care, and the provisions of health and education services, as well as fire and police services, while Canada passed national legislation such as the *Family Allowance Plan*, the *Old Age Security Act*, and the *Canada Pension Plan*: see also Chapter 1 of this volume.

39 H Shewell & A Spagnut, "The First Nations of Canada: Social Welfare and the Quest for Self-Government" in J Dixon & RP Scheurell, eds, *Social Welfare with Indigenous Peoples* (London: Routledge, 1995) at 3.

40 Canada, INAC, *Income Assistance Program—National Manual, January 2012*, at 13 [INAC Manual 2012], online: <https://www.aadnc-aandc.gc.ca/DAM/DAM-INTER-HQ-HB/STAGING/texte-text/hb_sp_npm_mnp_1335464147597_eng.pdf>.

41 *Indian Act*, 1951, s 87 (now *Indian Act*, RSC 1985 c I-5, s 88).

42 Kerry Wilkins, "'Still Crazy After All These Years': Section 88 of the *Indian Act*" (2000) 38:2 Alta LR 458 at 460.

43 See Canada, Department of Indian Affairs, *Income Assistance Program National Manual* (Ottawa: Public Works and Government Services Canada, 2005) at 13. For a more extensive account of this history, see H Shewell, *"Enough to Keep Them Alive": Indian Social Welfare in Canada, 1873-1965* (Toronto: University of Toronto Press, 2004).

44 In 1966, Parliament enacted the *Canada Assistance Plan*, 1966 SC c 45 [Plan]. Part II of Plan, which was entitled "Indian Welfare," gave legislative authority to the federal government to enter into agreements with the provinces to extend provincial welfare programs to Indians ordinarily resident on reserves, provided such agreements were consented to by the First Nations.

only one such agreement was ever signed, and this was between Canada and the province of Ontario in 1965.[45]

While it was attempting to negotiate with the provinces in the 1960s, due to growing public outcry over poverty in First Nations communities,[46] the federal government was finally compelled to provide for a system of social services on reserve. This was not done by means of legislation, however. Instead, the Department of Indian Affairs (INAC)[47] obtained a Treasury Board Directive in 1964 to spend federal funds for social assistance on reserves using the rates and standards enacted by the provinces.[48] Department staff adapted provincial laws and policies in order to create federal policy manuals to apply on reserves in different provinces.[49] Although intended as a temporary measure, this practice of "regulating" via policy manuals has continued to the present day and has been expanded to all services provided on reserve, including child welfare, assisted living, education, policing, emergency services, health, day care, housing, and infrastructure.[50] Further, although relevant Treasury

---

45 See the *1965 Memorandum of Agreement Respecting Welfare Programs for Indians* between the Government of Canada and the Government of Ontario, which instituted a cost-sharing arrangement respecting the application of provincial welfare laws to Indian reserves in the province. See also the *Indian Welfare Services Act*, RSO 1990, c I.4. The agreement relates to social assistance, daycare, and child welfare, but not other essential services like health and education. See *Brown v Canada (Attorney General)*, 2017 ONSC 251, for a recent discussion of the 1995 agreement (in the context of a class action relating to the so-called Sixties Scoop).

46 Shewell & Spagnut, *supra* note 39 at 4.

47 The name of the government department (or ministry) responsible for federal authority under s 91(24) has changed over time, reflecting the dynamics of naming discussed in the introduction. The department name is currently Indigenous and Northern Affairs Canada. For convenience and to avoid confusion, we have adopted the abbreviation INAC to refer to this department, regardless of its name at a given moment of time.

48 Citizenship & Immigration, Indian Affairs Branch, "Authority to Introduce Increased Rates of Assistance to Indians—Details of Request to the Honourable the Treasury Board," Ottawa, 16 June 1964; Treasury Board Minute, TB 627879, dated 23 July 1964.

49 Department of Citizenship and Immigration, "Circular 107-Application of Provincial General Welfare Assistance Programs," Ottawa, 20 July 1964; see for example INAC, *Atlantic Regional Office, 1967 Social Welfare Regulation*; and INAC, 1991 *New Brunswick Social Assistance Manual—First Nations Social Development Manual*; and see also INAC Manual 2012, *supra* note 40.

50 For example, here is a list of current INAC policies applicable to First Nations and incorporated by reference in the current funding agreements: (1) the *Band Employee Benefits Program Policy*; (2) the *Band Support Funding Program Policy*; (3) the *Professional and Institutional Development Program Guidelines*; (4) the *Indian Registry Report Manual*; (5) the *Elementary and Secondary Education Program National Program Guidelines*; (6) the *High-Cost Special Education National Program Manual*; (7) the *New Paths for Education National Program Guidelines*; (8) the *Success Program National Program Guidelines*; (9) the *Education Partnerships Program National Program Guidelines;* (10) the *Summer Work Experience Program*; (11) the *Skills Link Program National Program Guidelines;* (12) the *Post-Secondary Student Support Program and University and College Entrance preparation Program National Program Guidelines*; (13) the *Post-Secondary Partnerships Program National Program Guidelines*; (14) the *First Nation and Inuit Cultural Education Centres Program National Program Guidelines*; (15) the *Social Programs-National Manual*; (16) the *Lands and Economic Development Services Program Guidelines*; (17) the *Land Management Manual*; (18) the *Community Opportunity Readiness Program Guidelines*; (19) the *Strategic Partnerships Initiative Program Guidelines*; (20) the *Protocol for AANDC-Funded Infrastructure*; (21) the *Interim Resources Management Assistance (IRMA) Program Guidelines*; and (22) *DIAND Search and Recovery Guidelines*.

Board authorities have been updated periodically, comparability with provincial/territorial standards has generally remained the governing delivery standard.[51]

Moreover, while federal government staff initially delivered these essential services in First Nations communities, over time the federal government introduced funding agreements that permitted First Nations governments to hire their own staff to deliver such services. This is known as "program devolution" or "self-administration."[52] These agreements are in the nature of "contribution agreements," meaning they provide little flexibility in terms program design and delivery to First Nations.[53] Indeed, it is the federal government that dictates the terms and conditions under which programs are offered,[54] as well as onerous reporting and accountability requirements.[55] If a First Nation defaults on any requirements of their agreement, Canada is entitled to step in and take control of the First Nation's financial management or even cancel the agreement.[56]

The federal approach to delivery of essential services on reserve—now in place for over 50 years—has become the subject of growing criticism,[57] some of it directly relevant to the role of administrative law, which will be discussed further below. Beyond this, the approach

---

51 See "Memorandum of Understanding between the Department of Indian and Northern Development and the Treasury Board," August 1990.

52 Program devolution was conceived to give greater priority to Aboriginal concepts of community priorities into the 1970s and 1980s. Generally, there are two types of funding agreements: (1) comprehensive funding agreements (CFAs) and (2) Block Agreements. See Institute of Governance, *Special Study on INAC's funding arrangements-Final Report* (22 December 2008) at 13 [IOG Report]. CFAs are one-year funding agreements, while block agreements can be multi-year agreements. The most significant difference between them, however, is that First Nations in block agreements can shift any surpluses in funding from one program to another (e.g., a surplus in housing could be shifted to education), whereas First Nations in CFAs must return any surpluses to the department. Beyond this, the agreements are largely similar. See J Rae, "Program Delivery Devolution: A Stepping Stone of Quagmire for First Nations?" (2009) 7:2 Indigenous LJ 1 at 6; see also Stephen Cornell, Catherine Curtis, & Miriam Jorgensen, "The Concept of Governance and Its Implications for First Nations" (2004) No 2004-02 Joint Occasional Papers on Native Affairs 1 at 8.

53 Using contribution agreements to fund First Nations programming, instead of more flexible funding mechanisms, such as grants or interprovincial transfers that give funding recipients far more latitude, has been criticized: see Treasury Board of Canada Secretariat, *From Red Tape to Clear Results—The Report of the Independent Blue Ribbon Panel on Grant and Contribution Programs*, December 2006 at 3.

54 IOG Report, *supra* note 52 at 13. Such program terms and conditions are those set by treasury board approvals, which, as discussed above, for virtually every essential service on reserve requires "comparability" with provincial and territorial standards, as well as any additional requirements imposed by INAC policies.

55 A 2002 Auditor General's report found that the average First Nation was required to complete 168 reports annually just to keep funding for basic services flowing to their community: Office of the Auditor General, *2002 December Report of the Auditor General of Canada, Chapter 1—Streamlining First Nations Reporting to Federal Organizations* at 8. In addition to these reports, the agreements require First Nations to prepare annual consolidated financial statements and disclose these to community members upon request, in addition to the band's conflict of interest policy, annual report of activities, and fiscal plans. See DIAND/First Nation Funding Agreement, 2007-2008, clause 4.6 and 4.7.

56 See IOG Report, *supra* note 52 at 15. See also INAC, Directive 205—Default Prevention and Management (2013).

57 See Rae, 2009, *supra* note 52.

has been charged as being assimilative and culturally inappropriate,[58] coercive (since First Nations have little choice in having agreements to fund essential services or say in the content of these agreement),[59] and not premised on true self-government or a nation-to-nation relationship.[60] In 2011, the Auditor General of Canada went so far as to say that this approach "severely limit[s] the delivery of public services to First Nations communities and hinder[s] improvements in living conditions on reserves."[61] This observation is borne out by statistics that continue to demonstrate significant socio-economic gaps between First Nations and the rest of Canadians.[62]

Calls to overhaul First Nations' current relationship with the administrative state and to replace it with its only viable alternative—self-government—were raised as early as 1983 in the *Penner Report*,[63] and again in the *Royal Commission Report on Aboriginal Peoples* (RCAP) in 1996,[64] though neither was ultimately acted upon. Expectations of resolution through s 35 have proven misplaced, as judicial recognition of self-government rights under s 35 has been very restricted, with equally limited progress having been made under negotiations policies. Sections III and IV of this chapter pick up the story regarding the implementation of s 35 rights and self-government.

---

58 In *Caring Society*, *supra* note 14, the Canadian Human Rights Tribunal found that child welfare services on reserve replicated the residential school system by contributing to overrepresentation of First Nations children in state care, and that the "reasonable comparability" standards violated substantive equality by failing to ensure that programming for First Nations children and families met their distinct needs and circumstances of First Nations children and families living on reserve—including their cultural, historical, and geographical needs and circumstances—see paras 423-427 and 464-465.

59 In *Attawapiskat First Nation v Canada*, 2012 FC 948 [*Attawapiskat*], the Federal Court described comprehensive funding agreements (CFAs) as "adhesion contracts" imposed as a condition of receiving funding for services that "are the life blood of the community" over which there was "no evidence of real negotiation" and was illustrative of "[t]he power imbalance between government and this band dependent for its sustenance" on the CFA (see paras 58-59). See also IOG Report, *supra* note 52 at 31.

60 Canada, House of Commons, *Report of the Special Committee on Indian Self-Government in Canada*, 32nd Parl, 1st Sess, 1980-81-82-83 at 20 [Penner Report], online: <http://caid.ca/PennerRep1983.pdf>; Shewell & Spagnut, *supra* note 39 at 21-22; Rae, 2009 *supra* note 52 at 7.

61 Office of the Auditor General of Canada, *2011 Status Report of the Auditor General of Canada to the House of Commons* (June 2011) at 8.

62 While only making up 7 percent of the population, Aboriginal children make up 48 percent of children in foster and permanent care. Secondary school completion rate for First Nations students on reserve is only 49 percent. The number of First Nations adults that live in overcrowded homes is 23.4 percent. Nearly 32.2 percent of household water is unsafe to drink, and 34 percent of communities still get water by truck, from wells, or collected from rivers, lakes or water plants. Thirty-seven point three percent of First Nations households require major repairs. In 2006, the unemployment rate for First Nations people living on reserve was 25 percent, approximately three times the rate for non-Aboriginal Canadians. Suicide rates among First Nations youth are five to seven times higher than other young non-Aboriginal Canadians. See Statistics Canada, "Living arrangements of Aboriginal children aged 14 and under" (13 April 2016); and Assembly of First Nations, "Fact Sheet-Quality of Life of First Nations" (July 2011).

63 The Penner Report, *supra* note 60, was extremely critical of devolution and called on the government to immediately implement self-government both through constitutional amendment and legislation.

64 RCAP concluded that Aboriginal people possess inherent self-government jurisdiction over core areas, including matters vital to the life, welfare, culture, and identity of their peoples and local matters, which could be exercised unilaterally by First Nations without negotiation with other governments. See RCAP Report, *supra* note 13, vol 2 at 159.

B. Themes Arising from the Relationship

1. *Violation of the Rule of Law and Overbroad Discretion*

Generally in administrative law, much flows from the fact that administrative boards and tribunals are empowered and circumscribed by their own overarching legislation. In contrast, it is extremely important to appreciate that the vast majority of modern services provided to First Nations are provided in the absence of a legislative framework. The system runs only on Treasury Board authorities, policies, and funding agreements. The only law that can be linked to Canada's provision of services on reserve is the very general authorization given to INAC under its enabling legislation, the *Department of Indian Affairs and Northern Development Act*, to act in relation to "Indian Affairs."[65]

Canada's ad hoc response to the provision of services and rights to Indigenous Peoples, absent any governing legislation, is at complete odds with the rule of law, in particular the "principle of legality." This principle expresses the notion that, within a legal system, published laws should exist in order to bind both ordinary citizens and government alike. Having published laws serves to (1) protect against arbitrary exercises of power by the government, and (2) inform citizens of the standards governing themselves and others.[66] When there is no law, what exists in its place is discretion.[67] Although it is generally accepted that discretion plays a central and necessary role in the day-to-day functioning of the modern administrative state,[68] what is needed is a balance between law (clear rules) and discretion. Ronald Dworkin analogizes the appropriate ratio between law and discretion to a doughnut: "Discretion, like the hole in a doughnut, does not exist except as an area left open by the surrounding belt of restriction. It is therefore a relative concept. It always makes sense to ask, 'Discretion under what standards?' or 'Discretionary as to which authority?'"[69] This analogy frames discretion as appropriately restricted by a fairly robust (or doughy) belt or framework of laws that provides checks and balances to curb the likelihood of arbitrary exercises of power. Thus, a proper balance of laws and discretion would resemble a collection of doughnuts, side by side, representing several delegations of discretion, each defined and constrained by law. By comparison, and adhering to Dworkin's analogy, the exercise of discretion over essential services on reserve by Canada is more a like hula hoop than a doughnut. The restrictive belt of law, instead of being robust or doughy, is flimsy, plastic and hollow: the only legislative provision authorizing the exercise of discretion is bare grant of power in the *Department of Indian and Northern Affairs Act*. There are zero restrictions included in this delegation of authority and no other laws in the area of essential services to further constrain it.

---

65 *Department of Indian Affairs and Northern Development Act*, RSC 1985, c I-6, ss 2(1), 4. Canada's legislative jurisdiction of "Indians and lands reserved for Indians" stems from s 91(24) of the *Constitution Act, 1867.*

66 *Re Manitoba Language Rights*, [1985] 1 SCR 721 at paras 59-60.

67 See AV Dicey, *An Introduction to the Study of the Law of the Constitution*, 6th ed (1902) at 184. For Dicey, the primary purpose served by the rule of law is to limit the exercise of arbitrary power by government. The basic notion is that laws serve to limit arbitrary actions by officials by constraining the exercise of discretion.

68 Geneviève Cartier, "Administrative Discretion: Between Exercising Power and Conducting Dialogue" in *Administrative Law in Context*, 2nd ed (Toronto: Emond Montgomery, 2013) at 403.

69 R Dworkin, *Taking Rights Seriously* (Cambridge, MA: Harvard University Press, 1977) at 31.

Where a government official possesses far too great a level of discretion over the lives of Indigenous Peoples, this can create opportunities for abuse of power.[70] Documented allegations of such abuse of power by Canadian administrative officials in relation to First Nations include refusals by INAC to accept funding agreements accompanied by letters from bands stating they felt coercion to sign.[71] Too large a measure of discretion creates opportunities for significant variances in interpretation of key program terms and requirements by different government staff, leading to inconsistent positions, confusion, and uncertainty, which can all impact the quality and level of services received by the end user, in the present case First Nations individuals, families, children, and communities. This was evident in a series of cases involving INAC's interpretation of its "reasonable comparability" standard. In one case, INAC alleged that this standard required First Nations to strictly adhere to provincial rates in the delivery of social assistance on reserve with no room for flexibility (that resulted in harmful overall reduction of basic benefits received by First Nations),[72] where in another case being heard during the same time period, the department argued that "reasonable comparability" did not require it to provide the same level of child welfare services or disability services as in the provinces.[73]

2. Lack of Accountability by Canada

Discretion and the lack of legislation reduces oversight of the actions of government officials by Parliament. In the recent *Caring Society* decision, the Canadian Human Rights Tribunal found that Canada had knowingly underfunded child welfare services on reserves for well over a decade, yet the government had failed to effectively correct the problem.[74] Lack of laws and legislated oversight mechanisms have undoubtedly contributed to the underfunding that plagues the delivery of services to First Nations across the board. In this regard, as early as 1994, the Auditor General of Canada suggested that INAC should have clear and substantive legislative authority for carrying out major program activities on reserve, such

---

70   AV Dicey wrote that "wherever there is discretion there is room for arbitrariness." See AV Dicey, *supra* note 67, at 184.

71   Mia Rabson, "Agreement with Feds Signed 'Under Duress': First Nation," *Winnipeg Free Press* (24 April 2013); Frank Molley "Harper Government Pressures Poorest Community to Sign Agreement Despite Court Injunction," *Wabanaki Press* (15 March 2013); "Esgenoopetitj First Nation in 'Lose-Lose' Over Federal Funding," *CBC News*, online: <http://www.cbc.ca/1.1340403> (19 March 2013); "Membertou Refusing to Renew Federal Funding Agreement," *CBC News*, online: <http://www.cbc.ca/1.1331319> (25 March 2013); Michael Harris, "Fiscal 'Blackmail' in Canada's Poorest Quarter," *iPolitics* (17 March 2013), online: <http://ipolitics.ca/2013/03/17/fiscal-blackmail-in-canadas-poorest-quarter/>.

72   *Simon v Canada (Attorney General)*, 2013 FC 1117; rev'd 2015 FCA 18 [*Simon*].

73   *Caring Society*, *supra* note 14, and *Pictou Landing Band Council v Canada*, 2013 FC 342 [*Pictou*].

74   See *Caring Society*, *supra* note 14 at para 267, where the tribunal cited internal departmental memos from 2006 acknowledging that if its current social programs were administered by the provinces this would result in a significant increase in costs for AANDC. In conclusion, the tribunal found that: "Overall, AANDC's method of providing funding to ensure the safety and well-being of First Nations children on reserve and in the Yukon ... falls far short of its objective. In fact, the evidence demonstrates adverse effects for many First Nations children and families living on reserve and in the Yukon, including a denial of adequate child and family services, by the application of AANDC's FNCFS Program, funding formulas and other related provincial/territorial agreements" (para 393).

as social assistance.[75] The Auditor General would reiterate the need for legislation over essential services again in reports in 2006, 2011, and 2013, respectively.[76] The Assembly of First Nations has also called on the federal government to provide "a legislative funding base to provide First Nation governments with a predictable and secure foundation upon which to make strategic decisions."[77]

Despite these calls, Canada has done little to address these recommendations.[78] Not having legislation has allowed Canada to minimize its responsibility toward First Nations. For years, the government has maintained that its provision of services on reserves is strictly a voluntary exercise of the federal spending power done as a matter of good public policy, and that it has no obligation to provide services pursuant to its constitutional jurisdiction over Indians.[79] In court, the department has tried to maintain that it is only a "funder," and the provision of essential services on reserves is in reality a provincial responsibility.[80] In the circumstances, there is little scope for real accountability by anyone to First Nations governments or communities. In lieu of governmental accountability, the formal lines of accountability instead flow "down" from INAC and on to the bands for program expenditures. In turn, INAC accounts to Parliament for its spending. Independent reports show that INAC does poorly at obtaining data on outcomes, and consequently its reports to Parliament do not show where the gaps are and where progress can be made.[81] Among the dangers identified by the Auditor General of Canada, vis-à-vis not legislating with respect to programs on reserve, was an undermining of Parliament's control and accountability.[82] This is borne out by the observation about the quality of reports going to Parliament from INAC; if Parliament is not getting regular reports on outcomes (but only data on dollars spent), it cannot engage in a well-informed policy debate about the programs it provides on reserves, what is the appropriate role for INAC and whether it is meeting this role, and what long-term outcomes Canada wants to achieve in terms of the well-being of First Nations. When this does not occur, debate on First Nations policy is likely to be mostly reactive, responding to crises as they arise.[83]

---

75 Auditor General of Canada, *1994 Report of the Auditor General of Canada to the House of Commons*, vol 14, ch 23, "Indian and Northern Affairs Canada—Social Assistance."

76 Auditor General of Canada, *2006 Report of the Auditor General of Canada*, Chapter 5, "Management of Programs for First Nations," at 2-3 and 9; Auditor General of Canada, *2013 Status Report of the Auditor General of Canada*, ch 6, "Emergency Management on Reserves" at 5. Auditor General, *supra* note 57 at 5.

77 Assembly of First Nations, Transforming the Relationship—Sustainable Fiscal Transfers for First Nations, Pre-Budget Submissions, 2010 (13 August 2010).

78 The only essential service area Canada has attempted to legislate was education during the Harper administration. The government *First Nations Education Act* was extremely contentious, drawing criticism that it gave too much control to the federal government. On this, see Michael Mendelson, "A Second Look at the *First Nations Control of Education Act*," Caledon Institute of Social Policy, August 2014.

79 Shewell & Spagnut, *supra* note 39 at 15; C MacIntosh, "Jurisdictional Roulette: Constitutional and Structural Barriers to Aboriginal Access to Health" in *Frontiers of Fairness* (Toronto: University of Toronto Press, 2005) at 6-7.

80 Canada has taken this position in both the *Caring Society*, *supra* note 14 and *Simon*, *supra* note 72, decisions.

81 IOG Report, *supra* note 52 at 37.

82 Auditor General, *supra* note 75 at 14-15.

83 For example, we saw this play out in April 2016 in response to a rash of suicide attempts in the Attawapiskat First Nation: see Susana Mas & Peter Zimonjic, "Attawapiskat Suicide Crisis: MPs Hold Emergency Debate Over Suicide Attempts," *CBC News* (13 April 2016), online: <http://www.cbc.ca/1.3531829>.

3. Lack of Access to Justice

Despite the lack of legislation, recently some First Nations have been successful in seeking judicial review against Canada, with courts drawing on a broad understanding of what constitutes a reviewable decision in order to find jurisdiction to review Canada's actions[84] and drawing on policy guides, public commitments, and even international law to supply norms and standards to assess government conduct.[85] Although in recent years, some First Nations have been able to successfully challenge INAC's abuse of discretion in the courts using administrative law,[86] this is the exception and not the rule.[87] There are likely many more instances of abuse of power that go unchallenged. First Nations are among the poorest and most marginalized people in Canada. Historic neglect and mistreatment at the hands of government can create conditions where Indigenous groups are rendered powerless to challenge government decisions.[88]

Many First Nations lack the financial resources to proceed with legal action. Judicial review can easily cost in the tens of thousands of dollars, if not more, and Canada tends to vigorously defend such actions and this can serve to increase legal costs significantly.[89] In addition, some First Nations have been dissuaded from seeking redress due to concerns that, by proceeding with litigation, they may experience retaliation from government. One substantiated instance of retaliation was found against Canada for its treatment of Dr Cindy Blackstock, the lead complainant in the *Caring Society* case, who was put under government

---

84 *Day Star First Nation v Canada (Attorney General)*, 2003 SKQB 261 [*Day Star*] at para 17; *Nolan v Canada (Attorney General)* (1998), 155 DLR (4th) 728 (Ont SC) [*Nolan*]; *Pikangikum First Nation v Canada (Minister of Indian and Northern Affairs)*, 2002 FCT 1246 [*Pikangikum*]; *Nunavut Tunngavik Inc v Canada (Attorney General)*, 2004 FC 85 at para 9; and *Tsawout First Nation v Canada (Indian Affairs and Northern Development)*, 2008 FC 207 at para 16.

85 *Pikangikum*, *ibid* (Default Intervention policy); *Mohawks of the Baie of Quinte v Canada*, 2013 FC 669 (Specific Claim policy); *Pictou*, *supra* note 73 (Jordan's Principles); *Simon*, *supra* note 72 (FC decision) (commitments to involve First Nations in policy development, as well as the provision in the *United Nations Declaration on the Rights of Indigenous Peoples* regarding meaningful participation of Indigenous Peoples in administrative decisions). On the relationship between administrative and international law, human rights law, and particularly declarations, see Chapter 16, Section II of this volume.

86 See *Attawapiskat*, *supra* note 59 and *Pictou*, *supra* note 73.

87 *Lac Seul First Nation v Canada (Minister of Indian Affairs & Northern Development)*, 2004 FC 1183 [*Lac Seul*]; *Songhees Indian Band v Canada (Minister of Indian Affairs and Northern Development)*, 2006 FC 1009; *Alexis Nakota Sioux Nation v Canada (Minister of Indian Affairs and Northern Development)*, 2006 FC 721; *Simon*, *supra* note 72; and *Shiner v Canada (Attorney General)*, 2017 FC 515.

88 See T Alfred, "Colonialism and State Dependency," prepared for the National Aboriginal Health Organization Project, *Communities in Crisis*.

89 If legal fees can be used as an illustration, in the 2012-2013 fiscal year, INAC had the highest litigation expenses ($104 million) of any federal department (almost doubling the budget of the second-place department, the Canada Revenue Agency [$66 million]). See Yamri Taddese, "Feds Pouring Big Money into Aboriginal Litigation," *Law Times* (11 November 2013). It has also been reported that Canada spent over $5.3 million in legal fees on the *Caring Society* decision alone. See Tim Fontaine, "Canada Discriminates Against Children on Reserves, Tribunal Rules," *CBC News* (26 January 2016), online: <http://www.cbc.ca/1.3419480>. For further discussion of access to administrative justice, see Chapter 9. In other contexts, redress through the courts is also very expensive and can take years if not decades in some cases; see note 117 for an example.

surveillance and also barred from certain government meetings, due to her involvement in the case.[90]

Aside from the serious access to justice issues that are always present for First Nations, the lack of a legislative framework with respect to core programming on reserve adds several additional barriers. To begin with, there are limited avenues for redress. The template model for funding agreements has always included dispute resolution provisions, but the breadth of exceptions to this clause (which make budget decisions made in accordance with program terms and conditions, the amount of funding provided by Canada under the agreement, default or remedial decisions, and matters of policy all off-limits) essentially hollow out the alternative dispute resolution option and render it meaningless.[91]

Beyond alternative dispute resolution mechanisms, hope for justice for Indigenous Peoples rests then with access to the general courts and human rights tribunals. And yet here again there are many problems. The recent *Caring Society* decision is proof that human rights challenges against Canada relating to services on reserve is a viable option for redress. In this case, the Canadian Human Rights Tribunal found that Canada had knowingly underfunded First Nations child and family services for over a decade and that this constituted discrimination.[92] But this is the first decision of its kind, succeeding only after a nine-year battle during which Canada aggressively defended the claim, seeking to block the complaint at almost every turn.[93] Turning to the general courts, the types of legal challenges that can be made are limited, partly because the lack of clear legislative frameworks gives the courts little to work with as we discuss further below. Attempts to address disputes between Canada and First Nations regarding services and funding based on arguments on s 35 of the *Constitution Act, 1982*, s 15 of the *Charter*, or claims based in Canada's fiduciary duty, have all been unsuccessful to date.[94] Arguments based on administrative law, namely breach of procedural fairness and

---

90   See Amnesty International Canada, Press Release, "Invasive surveillance of human rights defender Cindy Blackstock" (29 May 2013); *First Nations Child & Family Caring Society of Canada v Attorney General of Canada (for the Minister of Indian and Northern Affairs Canada)*, 2015 CHRT 14 (CA). Other examples include anecdotes that Indigenous groups have been concerned that the federal government would pull out of self-government or other negotiations if litigation was initiated, or First Nations otherwise being subject to adverse treatment, such as in the case of *Attawapiskat*, where the First Nation alleged that Canada retaliated against it for publicly linking its housing crisis to chronic underfunding by unilaterally taking control of the band's financial management. See *Attawapiskat, supra* note 59. While this was alleged by the First Nation, the Federal Court of Canada was reluctant to make a finding of retaliation by the prime minister or the department.

91   First Nations for the IOG Report, *supra* note 52 at 38, specifically raised their desire to have an independent and enforceable dispute resolution mechanism between First Nations and the federal government regarding funding agreements.

92   *Caring Society, supra* note 14.

93   To read about Canada's attempts to derail the case on procedural grounds, see *First Nations Child and Family Caring Society of Canada and Assembly of First Nations v Attorney General of Canada (representing the Minister of Indian Affairs and Northern Development)*, 2011 CHRT 4; and *Canada (Human Rights Commission) v Canada (Attorney General)*, 2012 FC 445, aff'd 2013 FCA 75.

94   *Mousseau v Canada (Attorney General)* (1993), 126 NSR (2d) 33 (NSCA) (decision regarding housing services on reserve); *Nolan, supra* note 84 changes to employment programming for off-reserve Aboriginal groups); *Ochapowace Indian Band No 71 v Canada* (1998), 167 Sask R 167 (auditing of bands in Comprehensive Funding Agreements); *Day Star* (changes to post-secondary funding for First Nations); *Micmac First Nation v Canada (INAC)*, 2007 FC 1036 aff'd 2009 FCA 377 (decision to stop education funding to landless band).

substantive unreasonableness have met with greater success,[95] but here too we find many problems. First, administrative law remedies can sometimes be ineffective in addressing the true scope of the dispute between a First Nation and the department. Consider the case involving the Thunderchild First Nation, where the Federal Court dismissed the First Nations challenge to set aside INAC's decision to take control of the band's financial management.[96] The First Nation was one of the five Manitoba bands over which Canada asserted control over the band's financial management after the band refused to sign its annual funding agreements. The refusal was based on the band's disagreement with unilateral changes imposed by Canada, as well as systemic underfunding of services in the community. The Federal Court found that INAC's intervention policy permitted it to take control over the band's finances where they refused to sign and there was a limited duty to consult about the decision to do so. Thus, the Federal Court's decision was unable to address the broader justice issues the First Nations were concerned about, namely unilateral and arbitrary action by INAC in changing its funding agreements and chronic underfunding.

Further, as mentioned earlier, there been have cases where the courts have suggested that administrative law remedies were not available due to the fact that INAC's activities did not arise out of legislative enactments.[97] In these and other cases, government lawyers strenuously argue that, because INAC's activities arise from the exercise of discretion and relate to policy, they are either immune from judicial review, or INAC is entitled to a significant amount of deference.[98] In addition to immunity and deference to discretion, government lawyers advance other arguments related to the irregular nature of service delivery on reserve in attempts to block legitimate claims. For example, in one case INAC argued that the fine print in funding agreements meant that the First Nations had "agreed" to the particular decision the bands were challenging in court (cuts to social assistance), and therefore their claim was moot.[99] In another case, Crown lawyers advanced the argument that the funding agreements between First Nations and Canada meant that the relationship between them was purely contractual in nature and therefore precluded public/administrative law challenges.[100] Both arguments were ultimately unsuccessful, but there is always the risk that a future court, with a judge unfamiliar with these issues, would accept such arguments. Many questions arise from the Crown making these sorts of arguments:

- Discussed below in relation to Aboriginal rights, how do the "honour of the Crown" and reconciliation objectives condition the administration and review of policy-based decisions?

---

95 *Pikangikum, supra* note 84 (decision to place band in co-management); *Attawapiskat, supra* note 59 (decision to place band in third-party management); *Simon, supra* note 72 (decision to cut social assistance), which was overturned on appeal.

96 *Thunderchild First Nation v Canada (Indian Affairs and Northern Development)*, 2015 FC 200.

97 See *Lac Seul, supra* note 87 at para 13 (changes to child welfare prevention services on reserve); and in *Simon, supra* note 72 at para 30, the applications judge suggested that without a specific statutory provision, review was not possible.

98 The arguments were advanced in *Simon, ibid.*

99 *Ibid* at paras 50-60.

100 See *Attawapiskat, supra* note 59 at paras 50-62 and see *Canada (Attorney General) v Simon*, 2012 FCA 312 at paras 28-31. In the latter case, the Federal Court of Appeal specifically noted the lack of any legislative framework as the *raison d'être* of the funding agreements, and therefore this could not preclude public law remedies (at para 30).

- How are such principles incorporated within the principles of judicial review, or do they require a distinctive approach to be developed?
- Should deference to the expertise and procedural choices of the executive apply in the context of this imbalance of power between "contracting parties"?
- Do formalist concerns for not judicially supervising policy decisions apply? Or is it the reverse—should courts be uninhibited to intervene to uphold principles of accountability and fairness in these contexts where legislative intent is unexpressed and Crown discretion is therefore unstructured?

Even as a novice in the field of administrative law, it is likely clear to you by now that judicial reviews in this context are extremely difficult cases to bring before the courts. The reasons for this difficulty are many, including:

1. *Lack of statutory norms/objectives*—There is no statute to easily point to in order to establish what the statutory objectives of a given program or the applicable program standards are. However, as noted above, some judges have looked to such things as policies, public statements, and international human rights instruments to supply standards for government conduct.[101]
2. *Complexity*—Instead of clear statutory provisions, there can be an overwhelming and confusing paper trail of dense, unclear, and inconsistent funding authorities, policies, funding agreements, departmental reports, and other departmental correspondence that form the record of decision. It can be difficult for even a judge desirous of justice and reconciliation of making headway through this morass. To illustrate the problem of having multiple disparate documents as evidence of the government's intentions, there have been recent instances of relevant undisclosed documents from the government coming to light near the end of, or even after, a case.[102]
3. *Reticence to address socio-economic claims*—Some judges are uncomfortable in wading into cases about government decisions over program benefits and socio-economic rights, and would prefer to leave such issues to the politicians, especially when the evidentiary record is so voluminous and complex.
4. *Undue deference to government*—In circumstances of a complex, fact-heavy claim raising socio-economic dimensions, it can be tempting for judges to place reliance on INAC and their counsel and to trust the narrative of events they present instead of wading into what can sometimes be multi-volume books of the evidence containing

---

101 See note 87 for policies, public statements, and international law that judges have looked at to supply standards for government conduct.

102 See *First Nations Child and Family Caring Society of Canada v Attorney General of Canada*, 2013 CHRT 16, where, through an ATIP request, Cindy Blackstock found additional documents not disclosed by Canada in the human rights complaint, after which the department further advised that it would seek to adduce an additional 50,000 additional documents. In *Simon, supra* note 72, a researcher conducting independent research for the Assembly of Nova Scotia Mi'kmaq Chiefs uncovered Circular 107 at the National Archives, which had never been disclosed in the case and is relevant to the long-standing interpretation by Canada of its 1964 Treasury Board authority and other similar funding authorities. See Mi'kmaq Rights Initiative, Press Release, "Document Shows that the First Nations' Social Case Would Have had a Different Outcome" (1 December 2015), and *CBC News*, "Mi'kmaq Welfare Fight With Federal Government Given New Life" (2 December 2015), online: <http://www.cbc.ca/1.3347957>.

the record. This can put First Nations at a significant disadvantage because the record of decision on judicial review is prepared by the government, and there are limits on additional evidence that claimants may adduce.[103]

Overall, the history described above reveals troubling irregularities in the current relationship between the Crown and Indigenous Peoples, particularly with respect to service delivery in First Nations communities. These irregularities are in tension with fundamental principles of administrative law, such as the rule of law, supervision of the machinery of government, accountability, and access to justice. If true, one might ask, then, why has administrative law not been used more readily to address disputes between Indigenous People and Canada regarding conditions in First Nations communities? As suggested above, access to administrative justice is a significant obstacle. But the other obstacles identified are more at the level of principle, raising the types of concerns and obstacles that might be lessened by understanding these challenges to government action (and inaction) in their proper context. To this end, Aboriginal administrative law locates these grievances in relation to continuing colonial relationships, a critical factor that weighs against deferring to government in what administrative law otherwise characterizes as policy decisions over which the government holds superior expertise and competence. By doing so, the aim is to identify when attention to unique factors and principles is required (such as attention to colonial relationships and the honour of the Crown). This "extra" contextualization also serves, we hope, to render Indigenous grievances over government action (and inaction) more understandable as part of the domain of public law and therefore more amenable to the pursuit of administrative law remedies.

III.   RECOGNIZING AND IMPLEMENTING ABORIGINAL RIGHTS

Administrative law is also important in the processes of recognizing and implementing the constitutional rights of Aboriginal peoples. As you will learn in Chapters 6 and 13 by Evan Fox-Decent and Alexander Pless, the intersection of constitutional rights and administrative decision-makers has many facets. To appreciate this intersection in relation to Aboriginal rights, it will be helpful to first canvass a small part of the history of s 35 of the *Constitution Act, 1982* and the mechanisms available to address the content of these rights, relative to Charter rights.

As detailed in Section II, Canada's colonial history has left many outstanding and ongoing issues regarding the relationship between Indigenous Peoples and the Crown. The resolution of issues of land, governance, and the foundations of Canadian sovereignty are ongoing concerns that have been known and considered by governments for as long as the British colonies and interests in what is now Canada have existed. While engagement in Aboriginal rights requires awareness of this long history, our chapter will pick up the story

---

103 Indeed, the rules of court in some jurisdictions prevent applicants from adducing any additional evidence. In the duty to consult context, this has operated to prevent First Nations from putting forward compelling evidence of their Aboriginal and treaty rights impacted by a project and consequently preventing the courts from properly assessing the level of consultation they were owed under the Crown's constitutional duty to consult and accommodate. See e.g. *Martin v Province of New Brunswick and Chaleur Terminals Inc*, 2016 NBQB 138.

with the modern administrative state and more recent issues relating to the adoption and implementation of constitutional protection for Aboriginal rights through s 35 of the *Constitution Act, 1982*, rights that had previously been recognized and protected by the common law and policy.[104]

The implementation of this constitutional protection has not followed the same path as the implementation of Charter rights. One example of how Charter rights have been implemented is that review of proposed legislation for consistency with the Charter is institutionalized as a responsibility of the minister of justice under s 4.1 of the *Department of Justice Act*.[105] In spite of a recommendation to adopt the same approach for s 35 rights by the Standing Senate Committee on Legal and Constitutional Affairs in 2007,[106] there is no parallel responsibility for the minister of justice with respect to Aboriginal rights.[107] How do we explain this difference of treatment? The difference relates to fundamentally different starting points. Charter rights are assumed to exist, and judicial interpretation then focuses on whether the rights have been engaged, the scope of those rights, and whether the government action in question has infringed the right. By contrast, the existence of Aboriginal rights is not assumed and must be proven on a case-by-case basis.[108]

The "empty box" approach to Aboriginal rights[109] originates in political negotiations leading up to the patriation of the Constitution in 1982. Political agreement among the provinces (without Quebec) and the federal government was reached only with respect to recognizing and affirming "the *existing* aboriginal and treaty rights of the aboriginal

---

104 An exception are treaty rights that were "modified" and became constitutionally protected by the *Natural Resources Transfer Agreements* between the federal and prairie provincial Crowns in 1930: *R v Horseman*, [1990] 1 SCR 901. For discussion see Kerry Wilkins, "Unseating Horseman: Commercial Harvesting Rights and the *Natural Resources Transfer Agreements*" (2007) 12 Review of Constitutional Studies/Revue d'études constitutionnelles 135. Regarding the pre-1982 status of Aboriginal rights in Canada, see Kent McNeil, *Common Law Aboriginal Title* (New York: Oxford University Press, 1989); Paul G McHugh, *Aboriginal Societies and the Common Law: A History of Sovereignty, Status, and Self-Determination* (Oxford: Oxford University Press, 2004); Kent McNeil & David Yarrow, "Has Constitutional Recognition of Aboriginal Rights Adversely Affected their Definition?" (2007) 37 SCLR (2d) 177.

105 RSC 1985, c J-2. The success or significance of this mandatory review is certainly debatable. Nevertheless, it is a tangible government action taken in the wake of the adoption of the Charter in 1982, involving a conversation within the executive about the nature of the Minister's and the executive's duties in relation to vetting legislation for Charter violations; see *Schmidt v Canada (Attorney General)*, 2016 FC 269 at paras 241-247.

106 *Taking Aboriginal Rights Seriously: Non-Derogation Clauses Relating to Aboriginal and Treaty Rights*, Final Report of the Standing Senate Committee on Legal and Constitutional Affairs, December 2007, online: <https://sencanada.ca/content/sen/committee/392/lega/rep/rep05dec07-e.pdf> [Senate Report, 2007]. See Recommendation 3, at 25-26 and preceding discussion at 20-25.

107 To the extent that Aboriginal rights have been considered in the daily business of the federal Department of Justice, the approach has been to insert "non-derogation" clauses in legislation acknowledged to have a potential effect on Aboriginal rights. Such clauses provide that "the act in question [is] not to be interpreted 'so as to abrogate or derogate from any existing aboriginal or treaty rights of the aboriginal peoples of Canada under section 35 of the *Constitution Act, 1982.*'" See discussion in Senate Report, 2007, *ibid*.

108 For a contrary approach which identifies "generic" rights held by all Aboriginal peoples in Canada and "specific" rights that must be proven by an individual rights-holding group, see Brian Slattery, "The Generative Structure of Aboriginal Rights" (2007) 38 SCLR (2d) 593.

109 Ardith Walkem & Hallie Bruce, eds, *Box of Treasures or Empty Box? Twenty Years of Section 35* (Vancouver: Theytus, 2003).

peoples of Canada" (emphasis added), as the language of s 35(1) ultimately provided, and not to any rights of autonomy and self-determination as the Indigenous parties were seeking. The language of s 35 reflected legal and political debates about the nature of Indigenous rights; the provinces considered such rights to be sufficiently protected through legislation and demanded further definition of the "additional rights" Indigenous leaders were seen as seeking.[110] The lack of definition of Aboriginal rights in s 35 became the judiciary's problem following the failure of post-1982 constitutional discussions and proposals that included robust definitions of Aboriginal self-government.[111] However, the Supreme Court promptly laid waste to any assumptions that the pre-1982 status quo was preserved by s 35.[112]

Left in the hands of the judiciary, Aboriginal, treaty, and title rights jurisprudence focuses on describing and proving these rights (as well as infringements and justification of infringements by the Crown). These rights have been defined as modern expressions of historical practices, customs, or traditions (e.g., harvesting rights[113] and a limited notion of self-government),[114] historically provable occupation of land (Aboriginal title),[115] or the modern expression of a right negotiated at a historic moment in time (historic treaty rights).[116] Consequently, proving these rights involves an enormous commitment of time and resources by the claimant community, as well as long trials and commitments of public resources.[117] The case-by-case basis for proving Aboriginal rights coupled with the difficult burdens involved in litigating these rights have impeded the integration of protection for these rights into the day-to-day business of government. Further, legal arguments are available to deny the existence of rights in some cases, or for a reduced scope of the right in others. Such legal advice, along with risk management strategies

---

110   Douglas E Sanders, "The Indian Lobby," in Keith Banting & Richard Simeon, eds, *And No One Cheered: Federalism Democracy and the Constitution Act* (Toronto: Methuen, 1983) 301 at 320, detailing the discussions and the proposal by Alberta Premier Peter Lougheed to add the word "existing" to the proposed clause. See also Michael Woodward & Bruce George, "The Canadian Indian Lobby of Westminster 1979-1982" (1983) 18 J of Cdn St 119; and Peter H Russell, *Constitutional Odyssey: Can Canadians Become a Sovereign People?* 2nd ed (Toronto: University of Toronto Press, 1993) at 122; and, more recently, Madeline Rose Knickerbocker & Sarah Nickel, "Negotiating Sovereignty: Indigenous Perspectives on the Patriation of a Settler Colonial Constitution, 1975-83" (2016) 190 BC Studies 67.

111   Russell, *supra* note 110, Chapters 10 and 11, with the text of the self-government proposal in the *Charlottetown Accord* reproduced at 255. See also Jeremy Webber, "After Patriation: Aboriginal Rights, Meech Lake, and Charlottetown, 1982-1992" in *Reimagining Canada: Language, Culture, Community and the Canadian Constitution* (Montreal and Kingston: McGill-Queen's University Press, 1994) 122.

112   *Sparrow, supra* note 34. The Supreme Court rejected the federal government's argument that the scope of the right was defined by the manner in which it was regulated prior to 1982. For discussion, see Brian Slattery, "Making Sense of Aboriginal and treaty Rights" (2000) 79 Can Bus Rev 196 at 205-6.

113   *R v Van der Peet*, [1996] 2 SCR 507 [*Van der Peet*]; *Lax Kw'alaams Indian Band v Canada (Attorney General)*, 2011 SCC 56, [2011] 3 SCR 535; *R v Powley*, 2003 SCC 43, [2003] 2 SCR 207 [*Powley*].

114   *R v Pamajewon*, [1996] 2 SCR 821 [*Pamajewon*].

115   *Delgamuukw v British Columbia*, [1997] 3 SCR 1010; *Tsilhqot'in Nation, supra* note 34.

116   *R v Badger*, [1996] 1 SCR 771 [*Badger*]; *R v Marshall*, [1999] 3 SCR 456 [*Marshall*].

117   For example, the trial in *Tsilhqot'in Nation, supra* note 34 took 339 days, with the litigation originating with a claim filed in 1989: Woodward & Company, "Blazing a Trail for Reconciliation, Self-Determination & Decolonization: *Tsilhqot'in Nation v British Columbia and Canada*," online: <http://www.woodwardand company.com/?page_id=87>.

and lack of political will, has not facilitated discussions or action on the *implementation* of Aboriginal rights.[118]

The lack of implementation of Aboriginal rights results in regulations that affect Indigenous livelihoods—such as regulation of hunting, fishing, and gathering—that might be challenged for failure to consider and accommodate the constitutional protection for Aboriginal rights. For example, an early fishing rights case, *R v Adams*,[119] challenged a regulation in which the Aboriginal right was accommodated only by the issuance of a subsistence permit at the minister's discretion. The court found that the Crown could not justify this infringement, signalling that governments should legislate how Aboriginal rights will be addressed within the larger scheme:

> In a normal setting under the Canadian Charter of Rights and Freedoms, where a statute confers a broad, unstructured administrative discretion which may be exercised in a manner which encroaches upon a constitutional right, …the proper judicial course is to find that the discretion must subsequently be exercised in a manner which accommodates the guarantees of the Charter. [T]he same approach should not be adopted in identifying infringements under s 35(1) of the Constitution Act, 1982. In light of the Crown's unique fiduciary obligations towards aboriginal peoples, Parliament may not simply adopt an unstructured discretionary administrative regime which risks infringing aboriginal rights in a substantial number of applications in the absence of some explicit guidance. If a statute confers an administrative discretion which may carry significant consequences for the exercise of an aboriginal right, the statute or its delegate regulations must outline specific criteria for the granting or refusal of that discretion which seek to accommodate the existence of aboriginal rights. In the absence of such specific guidance, the statute will fail to provide representatives of the Crown with sufficient directives to fulfil their fiduciary duties, and the statute will be found to represent an infringement of aboriginal rights under the Sparrow test.[120]

Where courts might ordinarily defer to reasonable legislative and executive choices regulating matters such as access to natural resources, the court has made it clear that the choice to regulate Aboriginal rights through unstructured discretion does not attract deference.[121] Deference, then, must be applied cautiously in a context where the constitutional rights at stake have not been actively considered and accommodated in policy formation and the legislative process, and protection for rights may yet depend on the goodwill of the sovereign.

---

118 Kerry Wilkins, "Reasoning with the Elephant: The Crown, Its Counsel and Aboriginal Law in Canada" (2016) 13 Indigenous LJ 27. The current Liberal government has announced intentions to implement UNDRIP and, in doing so, address Aboriginal rights in a holistic manner; see Honourable Carolyn Bennett, Minister of Indigenous and Northern Affairs, "Speech to United Nations Permanent Forum on Indigenous Issues, 16th Session," United Nations Headquarters, New York, New York, 25 April 2017: "In direct response to the Declaration, the Prime Minister has mandated the Minister of Justice and Attorney General for Canada to chair a working group to review all federal laws and policies related to indigenous peoples, to reverse the colonial and paternalistic approaches. This is about breathing life into Section 35 of Canada's Constitution which formally entrenches the rights of indigenous people in Canadian law, and yet for far too long has not been lived up to."

119 [1996] 3 SCR 101 [*Adams*].

120 *Ibid* at paras 53-54. In *Haida Nation v British Columbia (Minister of Forests)*, 2004 SCC 73, [2004] 3 SCR 511 at para 51 [*Haida Nation*], the court softened this statement by suggesting that a policy guideline "may guard against unstructured discretion and provide a guide for decision-makers."

121 Returning to the Charter context, the court in *Carter v Canada (Attorney General)*, 2015 SCC 5, [2015] 1 SCR 331, articulated a principle that bears some relation to the view expressed in *Adams, supra* note 119, when it said the choice for an absolute prohibition was not a "complex regulatory response" to the issue of assisted suicide and therefore should not attract deference from the court (at paras 87-98).

A. Settling Aboriginal Rights: Negotiations Policies and Tribunals

The different starting points between Charter and Aboriginal rights—assumed existence versus a need to prove existence—create a world of difference in terms of how government understands its responsibilities with respect to the implementation of these rights and the nature of the judicial role when disputes reach that arena. With judicial emphasis on the need for negotiated settlements of Aboriginal rights, one might expect to find a programmatic attempt to resolve Aboriginal rights reflected in legislative frameworks enabling specialized and independent tribunals with a mandate to support negotiations, make recommendations for, and/or adjudicate the expedient settlement of claims. Any such attempt would draw on administrative law to inform the design of such tribunals, and again in judicial review of their decisions.

Tribunals and commissions have played important roles in this area, but fall far short of a programmatic effort to settle Aboriginal rights.[122] The Royal Commission on Aboriginal Peoples (RCAP)—itself a commission—recommended that an "Aboriginal Lands and Treaty Tribunal" be established and related proposals are raised from time to time.[123] The TRC emphasized the implementation of the United Nations Declaration on the Rights of Indigenous Peoples (UNDRIP), which includes, in Article 40, an Indigenous right "to access to and prompt decision through just and fair procedures for the resolution of conflicts and disputes with States" and decisions that "give due consideration to the customs, traditions, rules, and legal systems of the indigenous peoples concerned and international human rights."[124] In contrast to such recommendations, there are two provincial treaty commissions that focus on education and research about historic treaties and treaty relationships rather than prompt

---

122 See generally Michael Coyle, "ADR Processes and Indigenous Rights: A Comparative Analysis of Australia, Canada and New Zealand" in Richardson et al, *supra* note 2 at 371.

123 RCAP recommended both the creation of treaty commissions as "permanent, independent and neutral forums where negotiations as part of treaty processes can take place," including mediation and binding or non-binding arbitration on matters, and conducting expert fact-finding (see RCAP Report, *supra* note 13, vol 2, ch 3, at 85 and 87) and the Aboriginal Lands and Treaties Tribunal, which RCAP recommended as an adjudicative body to support treaty processes and a mandate over good faith in negotiations processes, an ability to order interim relief, and to hear appeals on funding matters (*ibid*, vol 2, ch 3, at 88). In his review of the Comprehensive Land Claims Policy in 1985, a task force chaired by Murray Coolican recommended that a commission be created to monitor negotiation and report annually to Parliament (*Living Treaties, Lasting Agreements: Report of the Task Force to Review Comprehensive Claims Policy*) [Coolican Report]. Recently, David Rosenberg and Tim Dickson called for a joint First Nation and government body to be created to map lands in BC that are subject to Aboriginal title: "Mapping Aboriginal Title in British Columbia" (2016) 7 Advocate 505 at 514. See also Shin Imai, "Sound Science, Careful Policy Analysis, and Ongoing Relationships: Integrating Litigation and Negotiation in Aboriginal Lands and Resources Disputes" (2003) 41 Osgoode Hall L J 587.

124 Truth and Reconciliation Commission of Canada, *Calls to Action* (2015) Calls to Action #48 and #50, online: <http://www.trc.ca/websites/trcinstitution/File/2015/Findings/Calls_to_Action_English2.pdf>. The TRC also recommended the adoption by governments of "legal principles" regarding the proof of Aboriginal title (Call to Action #52), and transparency regarding federal legal opinions on the scope and extent of Aboriginal and Treaty rights (Call to Action #51); the lack of availability of an effective remedy within Canadian domestic law was sufficiently made out in a case brought by the Hul'qumi'num Treaty Group that the Inter-American Commission on Human Rights accepted their case for a hearing on the merits without requiring them to pursue a case in Canadian courts first: *Hul'qumi'num Treaty Group v Canada*, Organization of American States Inter-American Commission on Human Rights, Case No 12.374, Report on Admissibility No 105/09.

and fair resolution of claims.[125] One tribunal has been created with authority to adjudicate: the Specific Claims Tribunal (SCT), established in 2008, has a legislative mandate to resolve claims arising from historic grievances.[126] Responding to long-standing criticisms of the Crown's policy-based approaches to the negotiated settlement of these grievances, including concerns over the conflicted nature of the process in which the Crown is both a party to the dispute and decision-maker regarding the acceptance of claims for negotiation,[127] the SCT's mandate focuses on historic breaches of duty regarding the Crown's implementation of treaty promises, creation of reserve lands, and other legal obligations.[128] The tribunal's mandate notably excludes claims based on Aboriginal rights, and title or treaty rights of an ongoing nature (e.g., harvesting rights) and allows only monetary remedies.[129] Within this narrow scope, the joint work of the Crown and the Assembly of First Nations to establish the SCT to provide an adjudicated resolution where a negotiations process fails[130] has been a significant step forward, one that embraces the creative possibilities and ideas of improving access to dispute resolution through specialized tribunals.[131]

Since it began taking cases in 2011, ten applications for judicial review of SCT decisions have been filed at the Federal Court of Appeal (as set out under s 34(1) of the SCT Act) resulting in three decisions.[132] The first of those judicial reviews to reach the Supreme Court of Canada was heard in April 2017. The anticipated decision in *Williams Lake Indian Band v Canada* will likely focus on the tribunal's expertise in questions of fiduciary duty and raise issues about the "margins of appreciation" in a contextual approach to reasonableness

---

125   Canada currently has treaty commissions relating to historic treaties in Saskatchewan (Office of the Treaty Commissioner: <http://www.otc.ca/>), Manitoba (Treaty Relations Commission of Manitoba: <http://www.trcm.ca/>). Both of these commissions are created by "memoranda of agreement" between the federal Department of Indigenous and Northern Affairs and regional political-territorial representatives of First Nations. A legislatively established treaty commission was recommended by Justice Linden in the *Report of the Ipperwash Inquiry*, 2007, at 99-101, online: <https://www.attorneygeneral.jus.gov.on.ca/inquiries/ipperwash/report/vol_4/pdf/E_Vol_4_B_Policy.pdf>. Discussions to create this commission between the Chiefs of Ontario and the Ontario government are ongoing. Contrast this with the Waitangi Tribunal in New Zealand/Aeotearoa, which has a mandate to inquire into and make recommendations on the settlement of claims arising from breaches of the Treaty of Waitanti and was established by legislation in 1975, see "About the Waitangi Tribunal," online: <https://waitangitribunal.govt.nz/about-waitangi-tribunal/>.

126   The *Specific Claims Tribunal Act*, SC 2008, c 22 [SCT Act].

127   For a succinct review of the history leading up to the establishment of the SCT, see Mary C Hurley *Legislative Summary: Bill C-6: The Specific Claims Resolution Act* (Ottawa: Library of Parliament, Law and Government Division, 2002 [revised 2003], online: <https://lop.parl.ca/About/Parliament/Legislative Summaries/bills_ls.asp?ls=c6&Parl=37&Ses=2&Language=E>.

128   SCT Act, s 14.

129   *Ibid*, ss 15(f), (g).

130   First Nations must first attempt to have their claims settled through negotiations under Canada's *Specific Claims Policy and Process Guide* (Ottawa: Minister of Indian Affairs and Northern Development, 2009), online: <https://www.aadnc-aandc.gc.ca/eng/1100100030501/1100100030506> [*Specific Claims Policy*].

131   Notably, the SCT has discretion to hold hearings in communities (SCT Act, s 18). For a description of the adaptations of the SCT to the context of the disputes it hears, see Alisa Lombard, "Specific Claims Adjudication Processes and Cultural Diversity: Reconciling Societal Traditions" (2016) 29 Can J Admin L & Prac 187.

132   According to information tracked by the SCT, see online: <http://www.sct-trp.ca/DecisionCourt/index_e .htm>.

review. It will be a perfect vantage point to assess the adaptation of the concept of deference to the reconciliation aims and context of the SCT.

The legislative framework for the SCT is one of two exceptions in the landscape of resolving Indigenous land, rights, and governance claims. The other exception is the British Columbia Treaty Commission (BCTC), which, as a tripartite body, is constituted by federal and provincial legislation as well as by resolution of the BC First Nations Summit, but understood to be a provincial entity.[133] The BCTC plays a central role in the facilitation of treaty negotiations as well as a public education function. Apart from this facilitative role (without an arbitral or dispute resolution function), the panoply of negotiations occurring around Aboriginal rights in the country occur under policy frameworks and presumably under the prerogative authority of the Crown. Although exercises of prerogative authority are reviewable by the courts, they generally demark decisions that are political in character or have strong political elements to them.

Federally, these policies include the Comprehensive Claims Policy, the current version of which has been in place since 1986 and has recently been modified by an "interim policy" following an assessment of the process in 2015.[134] The Comprehensive Claims Policy permits the negotiation of modern treaties respecting Indigenous claims to land, resources, and self-government. Indigenous groups that did not sign historic treaties that ceded land can pursue treaties under this policy.[135] In 1995, following the failure of post-1982 constitutional negotiations intended to provide greater definition to the constitutionally protected s 35

---

133 *British Columbia Treaty Commission Act*, SC 1995, c 45; see s 4(2) regarding the entity operating as a provincial entity; *Treaty Commission Act*, RSBC 1996, c 461; see s 3(2) regarding the commission operating as a provincial entity. For information on the First Nations Summit, see online: <http://www.fns.bc.ca /about/about.htm>.

134 For the Comprehensive Claims Policy, see online: <https://www.aadnc-aandc.gc.ca/eng/140569340991 1/1405693617207> [*Comprehensive Claims Policy*]. For the "interim policy" see online: <https://www. aadnc-aandc.gc.ca/eng/1405693409911/1405693617207>. For the evaluation report leading to the interim policy, see Douglas Eyford, *Renewing the Comprehensive Claims Policy: Towards a Framework for Addressing Section 35 Aboriginal Rights*, online: <https://www.aadnc-aandc.gc.ca/eng/1408631807053/1 408631881247> [Eyford Report].

135 The comprehensive claims policy has the most relevance in British Columbia, in the Ottawa valley, and in the northern territories, including Nunavut, the creation of which was the result of the settlement of Inuit claims. In the Atlantic region, a distinct set of negotiations are underway in light of the text of the historic treaties, which did not "cede and surrender" Indigenous lands, and Supreme Court recognition of treaty rights to harvesting and trading in pursuit of a "moderate livelihood"; see Indigenous and Northern Affairs Canada, "Fact Sheet Progress Report on Aboriginal and Treaty Rights Negotiations in the Maritimes and the Gaspésie," online: <http://www.aadnc-aandc.gc.ca/eng/1100100028644/1100100028 645> [offline as of November 2017]. Regarding Aboriginal title claims in the region, see Robert Hamilton, "After *Tsilhqot'in Nation*: The Aboriginal Question in Canada's Maritime Provinces" (2016) 67 UNBLJ 58. And since the *Manitoba Métis Federation v Canada (Attorney General)*, 2013 SCC 14, [2013] 1 SCR 623 [*MMF*] and the *Daniels* (*supra* note 4) decision in 2016, the federal government is paying greater attention to settling distinctive Métis claims (see Thomas Isaac, *A Matter of National And Constitutional Import: Report of the Minister's Special Representative on Reconciliation with Métis: Section 35 Métis Rights and the Manitoba Métis Federation Decision* (June 2016), online: <https://www.aadnc-aandc.gc.ca/eng/14676417 90303/1467641835266#chp5g>), although Métis communities have been signatories to northern claims agreements; see Larry Chartrand, "Métis Land Claim Participation in the North: Implications for Southern Canada" (2017) 4 Northern Public Affairs, online: <http://www.northernpublicaffairs.ca/index/magazine/ volume-4-issue-2/metis-land-claim-participation-in-the-north-implications-for-southern-canada/> .

rights and self-government in particular, the federal government also adopted a policy recognizing the inherent right of self-government as a s 35 right (the Inherent Rights Policy or IRP). The IRP also set out the parameters and scope of negotiations in relation to areas of jurisdiction the federal government is willing to transfer, as well as the negotiations process.[136] Like other areas of federal negotiations policies, the IRP has resulted in remarkably few agreements over the years.[137]

The criticism of these policies is legion, including concerns of expense, debt burdens for participating nations, clashes on principles and mandates such as the required extinguishment or modification of Aboriginal rights in exchange for "certainty" under the Comprehensive Claims Policy, lack of accountability measures, and a general lack of progress. However, since this chapter is not the appropriate forum to delve into these critiques and dynamics, we will refer you elsewhere[138] and instead focus on concerns that reiterate our general concern for the over-reliance on policy and discretion in the field. One concern is the lack of an independent body or commissioner to supervise negotiations, promote accountability, and report to Parliament on progress.[139] A second concern is the contradiction between policy statements that assure that negotiation processes are intended to address constitutional rights,[140] and Crown (federal and provincial in BC) mandates for negotiations premised on government policy and not rights. As Eyford describes the situation, "Canada does not recognize the existence of an Aboriginal group's specific s 35(1) rights at the outset of modern treaty negotiations .... Canada's negotiation mandates are not informed by an Aboriginal group's pre-existing Aboriginal rights. Canada is prepared to make a general recognition that a treaty group has Aboriginal rights, including title in the preamble to a treaty but is not prepared to provide the specific recognition

---

136 Indigenous and Northern Affairs, "The Government of Canada's Approach to Implementation of the Inherent Right and the Negotiation of Aboriginal Self-Government" [*Self-Government Policy*], online: <http://www.aadnc-aandc.gc.ca/eng/1100100031843/1100100031844#PartI>. The IRP allows for a variety of negotiations, involving individual First Nations with reserve lands, First Nations who have signed land claim agreements without accompanying self-government negotiations, and regional groups or Indigenous Peoples without a land base.

137 A 2015 Fact Sheet from Indigenous and Northern Affairs Canada indicates 22 self-government agreements have been concluded, 18 of which are part of comprehensive claims agreements, online: <https://www.aadnc-aandc.gc.ca/eng/1100100016293/1100100016294>.

138 Especially in relation to the Comprehensive Claims Policy. See Eyford Report, *supra* note 134. See also Arthur Manuel & Grand Chief Ronald M Derrickson, *Unsettling Canada: A National Wake-Up Call* (Toronto: Between the Lines, 2015), ch 15 "No Half Measures: The Price of Uncertainty"; Colin Samson, "Canada's Strategy of Dispossession: Aboriginal Land and Rights Cessions in Comprehensive Land Claims" (2016) 31 CJLS 87; and Andrew Woolford, "Transition and Transposition: Genocide, Land and the British Columbia Treaty Process" (2011) 4:2 New Proposals: J of Marxism & Interdisciplinary Inquiry 67.

139 See Eyford Report, *supra* note 134. The BCTC model is considered too toothless to "meaningfully supervise negotiations" (*ibid*).

140 For example, the Comprehensive Claims Policy indicates it aims to address the "unfinished business of treaty-making in Canada" where "Aboriginal land rights have not been dealt with by treaties or through other legal means" (Eyford Report, *supra* note 134), while the Self-Government Policy recognizes "the inherent right" through negotiations which are "the most practical and effective way to implement the inherent right of self-government" (see *Self-Government Policy*, *supra* note 136).

sought by some Aboriginal groups."[141] Echoing the debate that followed the Supreme Court's decision in *Doré v Barreau du Québec*[142] regarding reasonableness review of discretionary decisions where Charter rights have been implicated (a topic that will be discussed in Chapter 13 by Evan Fox-Decent and Alexander Pless), it is difficult to have a conversation about implementing a constitutional right when the parties do not first address the presence and scope of that right. As Vickers J commented in the trial decision of *Tsilhqot'in Nation*, in relation to the duty to consult (to which we will turn next), "British Columbia ... refused to acknowledge title and rights during the process of consultation .... A statement to the effect that a decision is made 'without prejudice' to Aboriginal title and rights does not demonstrate that title and rights have been taken into account, acknowledged, or accommodated."[143]

B. The Duty to Consult and Accommodate: Remedies for Reconciliation?

The irregularity of Aboriginal rights—the protection of which is realized only following epic litigation or negotiation in a Crown-controlled policy environment—sets the stage for the Supreme Court decision in *Haida Nation*, which established a Crown obligation to consult and, if appropriate, accommodate Aboriginal rights prior to the proof or settlement of those rights.[144] Building on an existing Crown obligation in relation to proven rights, the revamped *Haida Nation* duty borrows heavily from traditional administrative law concepts of procedural fairness to respond to the issues with the availability of effective and timely remedies for Aboriginal rights holders discussed above. The *Haida Nation* duty to consult and accommodate aims to preserve Aboriginal and treaty rights while the processes to determine, recognize, and respect these rights, and ultimately achieve the reconciliation of Aboriginal claims with the "sovereignty of the Crown," continue to play out.[145]

The source of this duty to consult is the "honour of the Crown," an archaic common law principle that has been revived in Aboriginal law and has been accorded status as a principle

---

141   Eyford Report, *supra* note 134. In a 2006 audit of the British Columbia process, the auditor general made a similar observation: "For example, the two governments base their participation in the treaty process on their own policies, and do not recognize the Aboriginal rights and title claimed by the First Nations. Many First Nations base their participation in the process on the assertion that they have Aboriginal rights under Canada's Constitution and that these rights should be acknowledged before negotiations begin." (See *2006 November Report of the Auditor General of Canada*, ch 7, online: <http://www.oag-bvg .gc.ca/internet/English/parl_oag_200611_07_e_14975.html#ch7hd3b>.)

142   2012 SCC 12, [2012] 1 SCR 395.

143   *Tsilhqot'in Nation v British Columbia*, 2007 BCSC 1700 at paras 1136-1137 [*Tsilhqot'in Nation (BCSC)*].

144   *Haida Nation, supra* note 120; *Taku River Tlingit First Nation v British Columbia (Project Assessment Director)*, 2004 SCC 74, [2004] 3 SCR 550 [*Taku River Tlingit*]. The obligation also applies in the context of historic treaty rights, regulating the interplay between First Nations' rights to their livelihoods over unoccupied Crown lands and the government right to take up lands for settlement and development: *Mikisew Cree First Nation v Canada (Minister of Canadian Heritage)*, 2005 SCC 69, [2005] 3 SCR 388 [*Mikisew Cree*]; and further applies to interpreting modern treaties, supplying a duty to consult to gaps in the treaty rather than only finding a duty to consult as explicitly provided for in the treaty text: *Beckman v Little Salmon/ Carmacks First Nation*, 2010 SCC 53, [2010] 3 SCR 103 [*Little Salmon/Carmacks*].

145   *Haida Nation, supra* note 120, at paras 25-27; *Mikisew Cree, supra* note 144 at paras 54-57.

of constitutional law.[146] The Supreme Court has explained that this principle arises "from the Crown's assertion of sovereignty over an Aboriginal people and *de facto* control of land and resources that were formerly in the control of that people"[147] and which, in Aboriginal law contexts, dates back to the *Royal Proclamation of 1763* and the principles of protection offered to Indigenous Peoples in that proclamation.[148] As a constitutional principle, the honour of the Crown governs Crown–Indigenous relations and gives rise to specific obligations such as the duty to consult. These obligations currently include purposive interpretation of treaties and statutes to reflect the assumption that the Crown always "intends to fulfil its promises";[149] honourable Crown conduct in the negotiation and implementation of treaty commitments; and diligent efforts to fulfill constitutional obligations.[150] In the context of the duty to consult, the principle means that

> the Crown ... cannot cavalierly run roughshod over Aboriginal interests where claims affecting these interests are being seriously pursued in the process of treaty negotiation and proof .... To unilaterally exploit a claimed resource during the process of proving and resolving the Aboriginal claim to that resource, may be to deprive the Aboriginal claimants of some or all of the benefit of the resource. That is not honourable.[151]

Nevertheless, and in contrast to at least a cursory reference to the UNDRIP standard of consultation of "free prior and informed consent" (Article 32.2 and elsewhere),[152] the Supreme Court has been equally adamant that the honour of the Crown does not require the Crown to obtain Indigenous consent before making decisions to exploit a resource, except in the clearest of title cases.[153] As the court said in *Haida Nation*, consultation "does not

---

146 *Haida Nation, ibid* at paras 16-25; *Little Salmon/ Carmacks ibid*, at para 42. In *R v Marshall, supra* note 116, the Supreme Court cited a 17th century doctrinal rule of construction of land grants as authority for the honour of the Crown principle (at para 43, and discussed in Jamie Dickson, *The Honour and Dishonour of the Crown: Making Sense of Aboriginal Law in Canada* (Vancouver: Purich Publishing, 2015)). Timothy McCabe has remarked: "The honour of the Crown as a principle by which court may measure and regulate conduct of the government in relation to aboriginal peoples is almost entirely a creation of the Supreme Court of Canada since 1982" (*The Honour of the Crown and its Fiduciary Duties to Aboriginal Peoples* (Toronto: LexisNexis Canada, 2008) at 53).

147 *Haida Nation, ibid* at para 32.

148 *MMF, supra* note 135 at para 66.

149 *Badger, supra* note 116 at para 41.

150 *MMF, supra* note 135 at 73-83. For discussion, see Brian Slattery, "Aboriginal Rights and the Honour of the Crown" (2005) 29 SCLR (2d) 433; see also McCabe and Dickson, both *supra* note 146.

151 *Haida Nation, supra* note 120 at para 27.

152 The meaning of the standard of prior, informed consent, and the identification of the rights to which it applies is a matter of developing international law jurisprudence and custom. See Gerald Heckman, Chapter 16 in this text regarding international human rights and administrative law generally. Regarding UNDRIP and the issue of consent specifically, see Michael Coyle, "From Consultation to Consent: Squaring the Circle?" (2016) 67 UNBLJ 235 [Coyle, 2016]; Anaya, *supra* note 11; Dwight G Newman, *Revisiting the Duty to Consult Aboriginal Peoples* (Vancouver: Purich, 2014) at 147-153; Paul Joffe, "UN Declaration on the Rights of Indigenous Peoples: Canadian Government Positions Incompatible with Genuine Reconciliation" (2010) 26 NJCL 121; and Penelope Simons & Lynda Collins, "Participatory Rights in the Ontario Mining Sector: An International Human Rights Perspective" (2010) 6 JSDLP 177.

153 While the Court suggested consent was required in relation to proven Aboriginal title in *Tsilhqot'in Nation*, it also allowed for the possibility of an infringement to be justified without such consent: *Tsilhqot'in Nation, supra* note 34 at para 76. For commentary, see Val Napoleon, "Tsilhqot'in Law of Consent," (2015) 48 UBC L Rev 873 and Borrows, 2015, *supra* note 34.

give Aboriginal groups a veto over what can be done with land pending final proof of the claim."[154] Instead, what the honour of the Crown requires as a measure of consultation is "meaningful consultation," and good faith efforts on the part of both the Crown and Indigenous parties toward "seeking compromise in an attempt to harmonize conflicting interests and move further down the path of reconciliation."[155]

As both source and standard, the honour of the Crown mediates the line between law and politics. As source, the principle draws upon an account of Crown sovereignty as potentially just, and serves to bridge the gap until Canada's foundations in *de facto* assertions of authority can be righted through reconciliation; namely, the settlement and recognition of Aboriginal rights through treaties.[156] The honour of the Crown is thus a stop-gap principle, providing a remedy in law in the meantime and governing the processes of reconciliation such as the implementation of negotiated rights.[157] It also serves as a reminder that without some meat on the bones of s 35 rights (at least), Canada remains a country founded on a colonial rule of law.[158] As standard, the honour of the Crown calls upon government to "balance Aboriginal concerns ... with other societal interests,"[159]

---

154 *Haida Nation*, *supra* note 120 at para 48.

155 *Ibid* at paras 41, 42, 49. For critiques of this standard, see Gordon Christie, "Developing Case Law: The Future of Consultation and Accommodation" (2006) 39 UBC L Rev 139 [Christie, 2006]; Kaitlin Ritchie, "Issues Associated with the Implementation of the Duty to Consult and Accommodate Aboriginal Peoples: Threatening the Goals of Reconciliation and Meaningful Consultation" (2013) 46 UBC L Rev 397; and E Ria Tzimas, "To What End the Dialogue?" (2011) 54 Sup Ct L Rev (2d) 493.

156 *Haida Nation*, *supra* note 120 at paras 20, 32. For discussion see, Walters, 2016, *supra* note 11, and "The Morality of Aboriginal Law" (2006) 31 Queen's L J 470; Hoehn, *supra* note 11.

157 Recent challenges to the effectiveness of this remedy have failed: see *Prophet River First Nation v Canada (Attorney General)*, 2017 FCA 15 [*PRFN*, FCA], leave to appeal to the SCC dismissed, 2017 CanLII 40511 (SCC), and *Prophet River First Nation v British Columbia (Environment)*, 2017 BCCA 58, leave to appeal to the SCC dismissed, 2017 CanLII 40513 (SCC). These cases attempted to argue that cumulative impacts on treaty rights infringe those rights by leaving the "meaningful" exercise of livelihood rights jeopardized. Consultation itself was either not challenged or found to be adequate under the *Haida Nation/Mikisew Cree* framework, and the environmental assessment process did not provide for addressing rights infringement. The Federal Court of Appeal stated that as a summary proceeding, "judicial review is not the proper forum to determine whether the appellants' rights are unjustifiably infringed" (*PRFN*, FCA, *ibid*, at para 78).

158 See literature noted at note 11, *supra*. Many Indigenous and other scholars do not see recognition through s 35 rights (or the honour of the Crown) as a path to decolonization or justice. See e.g. Glen Coulthard, *Red Skin White Masks—Rejecting the Politics of Recognition* (Minneapolis: University of Minnesota, 2014); Mariana Valverde, "The Crown in a Multicultural Age: The Changing Epistemology of (Post)colonial Sovereignty" (2012) 21 Social & Legal Studies 3; and Christie, 2006, *supra* note 155.

159 *Haida Nation*, *supra* note 120 at para 50. It is worth noting that the more archaic version of the principle also incorporated a notion of balancing reliance on the Crown's honour to give effect to the concerned interest against other interests within the scope of the Crown's responsibilities to the broader public: "Where nothing would pass by a construction against the grantee, a charter is construed liberally in his favour, because it is not consistent with the honour of the Crown to suppose a grant with the intention of passing nothing; but where, as in this case, the franchise is perfect, and the question is whether the prerogative is to be restrained, a contrary rule prevails and the construction is against the grantee, because the prerogative of the Crown is in truth the privilege of the subject, and it is not to be presumed from doubtful expressions that the Crown, when granting a privilege to one subject, intended to interfere with the rights of others" (*Eastern Archipelago Company v the Queen* (1853), 2 E&B 857 at 1009).

recalling both the court's concerns for its institutional competence in a field that requires negotiated solutions and the court's timidity around assigning significant content to Aboriginal rights ahead of the political field. The perennial question surrounding the duty to consult is whether the court prescribed enough content to tilt the risk management equation in favour of the protection of Aboriginal rights, and cast a long enough shadow to improve the political climate for negotiations.

In spite of the distinctive source and foundations for the duty to consult, the duty nevertheless has much in common with judicial review for procedural fairness, described more fully by Kate Glover in Chapter 5. As a matter of source, the requisite honourable conduct by the Crown—and the related assumption that Crown promises are intended to be fulfilled—shares more than a passing resemblance to this statement of a basic principle of the rule of law:

> In a nation governed by the rule of law, we assume that the government will honour its obligations unless it explicitly exercises its power not to. In the absence of a clear express intent to abrogate rights and obligations—rights of the highest importance to the individual—those rights remain in force. To argue the opposite is to say that the government is bound only by its whim, not its word. In Canada this is unacceptable, and does not accord with the nation's understanding of the relationship between the state and its citizens.[160]

It is also similar to articulations of legitimate expectations, and particularly Evans JA's discussion of the purposes of legitimate expectations potentially applying to create consultation obligations prior to the passing of regulations in *Apotex Inc v Canada (Attorney General)*, beyond the ordinary reach of the duty of fairness:[161]

> [W]here the legitimate expectation arises from a promise or undertaking, categorically and specifically given to an individual or a defined group, the rationale for holding the government to it derives from the individual's reliance interest or, in the absence of a detrimental reliance, from the individual's right to expect that, in the absence of a compelling reason for not so doing, the government will act with basic decency by keeping promises that it makes to individuals.[162]

In other words, while the "mystical," "archaic," or "moralistic" tones of the honour of the Crown principle can distract,[163] and while the contemporary applications of the honour of the Crown are evolving in a uniquely Aboriginal law history and context, the principle protects values well known in a country governed by the rule of law. Seeing these theoretical and policy-based connections facilitates an evaluation of judicial review for a breach of

---

160 *Wells v Newfoundland*, [1999] 3 SCR 199 at para 46.

161 [2000] 4 FCR 264, 2000 CanLII 17135 [*Apotex*].

162 *Ibid* at para 122. For a discussion of this decision and, more generally, a comparison between the s 35 duty to consult and other public law consultation obligations, see Peter Carver, "Comparing Aboriginal and Other Duties to Consult in Canadian Law" (2012) 49 Alta LR 855 at 861.

163 See for example Valverde's criticism of the honour of the Crown in Valverde, *supra* note 158. See also Slatter J's criticism in *R v Lefthand*, 2007 ABCA 206 at para 75, leave to appeal to refused, 2008 CanLII 6384 (SCC).

obligations specific to Aboriginal peoples—the duty to consult—against and in relation to judicial review for breach of more broadly applicable government obligations.[164]

The duty to consult conditions the legality of government decisions in a manner that parallels, both structurally and purposively, the duty of procedural fairness[165] and the procedural obligations embedded in fundamental justice in s 7 of the Charter (outlined by Fox-Decent and Pless in Chapter 6). The court has been explicit about relying on familiar concepts and techniques to flesh out the content of the duty, at least up to the point of the duty to accommodate. In *Haida Nation*, for example, the court stated, "In discharging [the duty to consult], regard may be had to the procedural safeguards of natural justice mandated by administrative law."[166] And in *Little Salmon/Carmacks*, the court rejected the argument that administrative law principles "are not tools toward reconciliation of Aboriginal people and other Canadians," and instead stated that "[a]dministrative law is flexible enough to give full weight to the constitutional interests of the First Nation."[167] Thus, the court has mandated an approach to the duty to consult and accommodate that understands this specific obligation as embedded within the values, techniques, and rights that condition the legality of executive action in Canada.

The court has similarly mandated an approach to carrying out of these obligations that relies on embedding the duty within existing regulatory frameworks. In *Haida Nation*, the court stated that "[i]t is open to governments to set up regulatory schemes to address the procedural requirements appropriate to different problems at different stages, thereby strengthening the reconciliation process and reducing recourse to the courts."[168] Similarly, in *Taku River Tlingit*, the court found that the province was not required to develop special consultation measures to address the First Nation's concerns, since the BC environmental assessment scheme and decision in issue "specifically set out a scheme that required consultation with affected Aboriginal peoples."[169] And in *Rio Tinto Alcan Inc v Carrier Sekani Tribal*

---

164 This discussion is not intended to suggest that the limitations of the legitimate expectations doctrine be transferred to the context of the honour of the Crown, although interesting comparisons might be made on this point as well. As discussed in Chapter 5, establishing a legitimate expectation provides a basis for procedural rights but not a substantive one. The duty to consult *and accommodate* is, in name, also substantive in nature; for discussion of the substantive aspect of this duty, see Veronica Potes, "The Duty to Accommodate Aboriginal Peoples Rights: Substantive Consultation?" (2006) 17 J of Env Law & Practice 27 and Lorne Sossin, "The Duty to Consult and Accommodate: Procedural Justice as Aboriginal Rights" (2010) 23 Cdn J Admin L & Prac 93-113. Further comparison can also be pursued in relation to whether legitimate expectation arguments may be made to push the limits of the duty of fairness to apply to "legislative" decisions, as in *Apotex* (*supra* note 161). By comparison, the issue of whether the duty to consult applies to legislative decisions is, at the time of writing, before the Supreme Court to be decided: *Canada (Governor in Council) v Mikisew Cree First Nation*, 2016 FCA 311, leave to appeal to SCC granted, 2017 CanLII 29943.

165 John Willis argued that natural justice should be considered as having a quasi-constitutional character: see "Administrative Law in and the British North America Act" (1939) 53 Harvard LR 251.

166 *Haida Nation, supra* note 120 at para 41.

167 *Little Salmon/Carmacks, supra* note 144 at paras 45, 47.

168 *Haida Nation, supra* note 120 at para 51.

169 *Taku River Tlingit, supra* note 144 at para 40. But note that engagement through a broad public process that does not directly engage affected Indigenous Peoples will note satisfy the duty: *Mikisew Cree, supra* note 144 at para 64. See generally, Neil Alastair Craik, "Process and Reconciliation: Integrating the Duty to Consult with Environmental Assessment" (2016) 53 OHLJ 632.

Council,[170] the Supreme Court relied on *Paul v British Columbia (Forest Appeals Commission)*[171] and *R v Conway*[172] regarding tribunal jurisdiction over constitutional questions and remedies to delineate the approach to determining the role of administrative bodies in determining the adequacy of Crown consultation and/or the obligation of carrying out the duty itself.[173] As in those cases, the authority of the administrative body depends on the language of the statute interpreted in accordance with principles of administrative law.[174]

Most recently, in *Clyde River (Hamlet) v Petroleum Geo-Services Inc*[175] and *Chippewas of the Thames First Nation v Enbridge Pipelines Inc*,[176] the Supreme Court considered the role of tribunals, and specifically the National Energy Board (NEB), in regulatory processes where the NEB had final approval authority without involvement of a ministry of the Crown. In these cases, the court largely confirmed the approach to tribunal jurisdiction as set out in *Haida Nation*, *Taku River Tlingit*, and *Carrier Sekani*, described above. The court's approach, however, also indicates that there are limits to the parallels between tribunal jurisdiction in relation to the duty to consult and established approaches to tribunal jurisdiction over Charter rights and remedies. In relation to the obligation to determine Charter matters, Charter jurisdictions are "delegated" to tribunals along with delegations of authority to decide questions of law and/or remedial measures, and tribunals are understood as part of an undifferentiated branch of government generally referred to as the executive. By contrast, the obligation for all matters relating to consultation ultimately rests with the Crown, which may "rely on steps taken by an administrative body to fulfil its duty to consult."[177] In this "reliance" approach, the Crown is differentiated from tribunals that operate at arm's length from government ministries, which nevertheless act "on behalf" of the Crown in carrying out their regulatory processes and approvals.[178] Where the tribunal's authority is insufficient to meet the Crown's constitutional obligations, the Crown must work around the regulatory process to fulfill its duty, and the tribunal "must withhold project approval" until that obligation is satisfied.[179] This approach is, on the one hand, responsive to Indigenous Peoples' arguments to the extent that it preserves their relationship as with the

---

170 2010 SCC 43 [*Carrier Sekani*].

171 2003 SCC 55 [*Paul*].

172 2010 SCC 22 [*Conway*].

173 *Carrier Sekani*, *supra* note 170 at paras 56-58.

174 See Chapter 13 by Evan Fox-Decent and Alexander Pless for further discussion of tribunal authority over constitutional questions and remedies. For commentary on these issues in the context of s 35 rights specifically, see see Kirk N Lambrecht, *Aboriginal Consultation, Environmental Assessment and Regulatory Review in Canada* (Regina: University of Regina Press, 2013); Janna Promislow, "Irreconcilable? The Duty to Consult and Administrative Decision Makers" (2013) Cdn J Admin L & Prac 251; David Mullan, "The Supreme Court and the Duty to Consult Aboriginal Peoples: A Lifting of the Fog?" (2011) 24 Cdn J Admin L & Prac 233; Sari Graben and Abbey Sinclair, "Tribunal Administration and the Duty to Consult: A Study of the National Energy Board" (2015) 65 UTLJ 382; Matthew Hodgson, "Pursuing a Reconciliatory Administrative Law: Aboriginal Consultation and the National Energy Board" (2016) 54 OHLJ 125; Michael McClurg, "A Pragmatic Approach: The Nunavut Wildlife Management Board and the Duty to Operationalize Consultation" (2010) 9 Indig LJ 77.

175 2017 SCC 40 [*Clyde River*].

176 2017 SCC 41 [*Chippewas*].

177 *Chippewas*, *ibid* at para 32; *Clyde River*, *supra* note 175 at para 30.

178 *Chippewas*, *ibid* at para 31.

179 *Clyde River*, *supra* note 175 at para 39.

Crown and not with arm's length regulatory agencies such as the NEB.[180] On the other hand, this approach treats Aboriginal constitutional rights differently than other constitutional rights without a principled explanation of this difference. Moreover, the court may have removed the possibility that an administrative process might be found to itself be a breach of the duty to consult, since in this approach the Crown can (indeed, must) correct any flaws in the consultation process without requiring a change of the legislative structure that would ensure a process designed with the duty to consult in mind.[181] Once again, there is a preference for policy solutions over legislative frameworks that institutionalize Indigenous interests.

Reliance on established administrative law principles raises other questions as well, and particularly questions regarding the fit of the duty to consult with other public law obligations. For example, in *Gitxaala Nation v Canada (Attorney General)*,[182] the Federal Court of Appeal quashed Cabinet's approval of the Northern Gateway pipeline project on the basis of a breach of the duty to consult but would have upheld the decision on substantive review of the merits. While all parties agreed that the duty owed to Indigenous parties in the circumstances were deep, the court reviewed the adequacy of the consultation and found that the implementation of the consultation plan fell "well short of the mark."[183] The court further required that reasons be given for this decision to ensure that impacts on Aboriginal rights are not lost in the balancing of multiple interests inherent in the approval of a major interprovincial pipeline project.[184] By contrast, the FCA upheld Cabinet's approval of the project, reasoning that it fell within the "very broad margin of appreciation" allowable for Cabinet in this policy decision context.[185] It is difficult to square the findings within the same judicial review decision that the Crown did not attend sufficiently to Indigenous interests in its balancing exercise (or at least did not sufficiently explain how it balanced the competing interests), and that the Crown's decision to approve the pipeline was reasonable in light of the balancing of interests at stake. As the Supreme Court recently stated in *Clyde River*, "[a] project that breaches the constitutionally protected rights of Indigenous Peoples cannot serve

---

180   It might also be noted that the federal Crown's argument in the case supported a reliance approach, whereby the responsibility for the duty to consult ultimately rests with ministries of the Crown.

181   The possibility that the duty to consult might invalidate legislation was considered in *Ross River Dena Council v Government of Yukon*, 2012 YKCA 14, in which the Yukon Court of Appeal said: "[s]tatutory regimes that do not allow for consultation and fail to provide any other equally effective means to acknowledge and accommodate Aboriginal claims are defective and cannot be allowed to subsist" (at para 37). It is not clear whether the Supreme Court's approach is consistent with this statement, since it relies on efforts beyond the legislative framework to provide the effective means of acknowledging and accommodating Aboriginal claims. Comparing to *Singh v Canada (Minister of Employment and Immigration)*, [1985] 1 SCR 177, in which half the court held that s 7 rights invalidated a legislative regime that determined refugee applications without adequate hearing rights, raises questions and a need to explain the apparent weakness of consultation obligations relative to the procedural rights provided by fundamental justice.

182   2016 FCA 187, [2016] FCJ No 705 (QL) [*Gitxaala Nation*].

183   *Ibid* at paras 186, 230, 266.

184   *Ibid* at paras 311-324. The Federal Court of Appeal's reasoning also connects to the discussion earlier in this section about the difficulty of negotiations about Aboriginal rights when the rights themselves are not acknowledged. See also *Kainaiwa/Blood Tribe, supra* note 12, regarding the connection between reasons and the honour of the Crown.

185   *Ibid* at para 152.

the public interest."[186] Perhaps this example makes the point that review for procedural errors—including alleged breaches of the duty to consult—should generally precede reviews on the merits of the decisions.[187] Nevertheless, the decision in *Gitxaala Nation* highlights another reconciliation project—the reconciliation of s 35 obligations within the larger body of administrative law.[188]

IV. ADMINISTRATIVE LAW IN INDIGENOUS GOVERNANCE

Like other public decision-makers, Indigenous governments may be subject to judicial review for breaches of procedural fairness, lack of jurisdiction, and the legality of their decisions more generally. But unlike other administrative decision-makers, Indigenous governments have varied and often multiple sources of authority, including Indigenous law, that add complexity to questions of amenability to judicial review and the approach to deference required by the reviewing judge. Issues relating to the "fit" of Indigenous governments within the doctrines of judicial review intersect with the constitutional law issues relating to the definition and recognition of an inherent right of self-government. Further, administrative law (and its relatives within Indigenous legal orders) has an important role within Indigenous governments, addressing how these governments make decisions, resolve disputes, and carry out their work. For these reasons, we will start this section with a primer on Indigenous self-government in Canada.

Indigenous Peoples have always understood themselves as self-determining. The British colonial project in North America began with relationships between sovereign nations giving rise to treaties and other forms of mutual recognition.[189] Later colonial policy ceased to recognize Indigenous polities and instituted a number of governmental policies that created intrusive federal supervisory authorities over Indigenous communities and people and created disjunctures between these peoples and their governments. The common law arguably maintained some recognition of Indigenous self-government through this period in the pre-1982 concept of Aboriginal (or Native) title, but judicial recognition of this inherent right of self-government, or indeed any rights of self-government, under s 35 remains ephemeral at

---

186   *Clyde River, supra* note 175 at para 40.

187   See the discussion of the duty of fairness as stand-alone grounds for judicial review that presumes that proper process will affect outcome without presuming what the effect will be in *Cardinal v Director of Kent Institution*, [1985] 2 SCR 643, discussed by Kate Glover in Chapter 5.

188   For further commentary on this case, see Martin Olyznski, "Northern Gateway: Federal Court of Appeal Applies Wrong CEAA Provisions and Unwittingly Affirms Regressiveness of 2012 Budget Bills" (5 July 2016), *Ablawg*, online: <http://ablawg.ca/2016/07/05/northern-gateway-federal-court-of-appeal-wrong -ceaa-provisions/>.

189   See RCAP Report, *supra* note 13. See also Mark D Walters, "Promise and Paradox: The Emergence of Indigenous Rights Law in Canada" in Richardson et al, *supra* note 2 at 21; Brian Slattery, "The Organic Constitution: Aboriginal Peoples and the Evolution of Canada" (1996) 34 Osgoode Hall L J 101; Robert A Williams Jr, *Linking Arms Together. American Indian Treaty Visions of Law and Peace, 1600-1800* (New York & Oxford: Oxford University Press, 1997); James [sákéj] Youngblood Henderson, "Empowering Treaty Federalism" (1994) 58 Sask L Rev 241; Janna Promislow, "Treaties in Law and History" (2014) 47 UBCLR 1183; James Tully, *Strange Multiplicity: Constitutionalism in an Age of Diversity* (Cambridge: Cambridge University Press, 1995).

best.[190] As noted above in Section III, constitutional negotiations post-1982 failed, including a robust proposal to define Aboriginal self-government as a third order of constitutionally secured governance.[191] The existing jurisprudence on self-government as a s 35 right defines the right so narrowly that negotiations with government are rendered the more promising route for achieving a state-recognized form of self-government.[192] Since the failure of the proposed constitutional amendments, the key platforms for negotiated self-government have been the comprehensive claims and self-government (IRP) policies canvassed in Section III.

The right of a people to self-determine is a foundational principle in international human rights law.[193] As the long-standing federal self-government policy suggests,[194] self-government for Indigenous Peoples in Canada—meaning at least the authority to make rules and decisions and resolve internal disputes[195]—is well accepted as an important step toward remedying colonial legacies and reconciliation. The contentious issues remain ones of process,

---

190 *Campbell v British Columbia*, [2000] 4 CNLR 1 (BCSC) [*Campbell*]. For discussion, see Kent McNeil, "Judicial Approaches to Self-Government Since Calder: Searching for Doctrinal Coherence" in Hamar Foster, Heather Raven & Jeremy Webber, eds, *Let Right Be Done: Aboriginal Title, the Calder Case and the Future of Indigenous Rights* (Vancouver: UBC Press, 2007) 129; Mark D Walters, "The 'Golden Thread' of Continuity: Aboriginal Customs at Common Law and Under the *Constitution Act, 1982*" (1999) 44 McGill L J 711; McNeil & Yarrow, *supra* note 104.

191 See the text of the Charlottetown Accord, Part IV, available from *The Canadian Encyclopedia*, *sub verbo* "Charlottetown Accord Document," online: <http://www.thecanadianencyclopedia.ca/en/article/charlottetown-accord-document/>. See also Peter H Russell, *Constitutional Odyssey: Can Canadians Become a Sovereign People?* 3rd ed (Toronto: University of Toronto Press, 2004); and Bradford W Morse, "Regaining Recognition of the Inherent Right of Aboriginal Governance" in Yale Belanger, ed, *Aboriginal Self-Government in Canada: Current Trends and Issues*, 3rd ed (Saskatoon: Purich Publishing, 2008) 55-84.

192 *Pamajewon*, *supra* note 114, *Mitchell v MNR*, 2001 SCC 33, [2001] 1 SCR 911. For critique of this jurisprudence see: Bradford W Morse, "Permafrost Rights: Aboriginal Self-Government and the Supreme Court in *R v Pamajewon*" (1997) 42 McGill LJ 1011; PJ Vicaire, "Two Roads Diverged: A Comparative Analysis of Indigenous Rights in a North American Constitutional Context" (2013) 58 McGill LJ 607 at 656-657; JE Dalton, "Exceptions, Excuses and Norms: Aboriginal Self-Determination in Canada: Protections Afforded by the Judiciary and Government" (2006) 21 No 1 Can JL & Soc'y 11 at 19-20; McNeil, 2007, *supra* note 107; and, D Moodie, "Thinking Outside the 20th Century Box: Revisiting *Mitchell*—Some Comments on the Politics of Judicial Law Making in the Context of Aboriginal Self-Government since *Calder*: Search for Doctrinal Coherence" (2003-2004) 35 Ottawa LR 1.

193 See Anaya, *supra* note 11, ch 3. Article 1 of the *International Covenant on Economic, Social and Cultural Rights* and the *International Covenant on Civil and Political Rights* both state: "All peoples have the right of self-determination. By virtue of that right they freely determine their political status and freely pursue their economic, social and cultural development." Article 3 of the UNDRIP states: "Indigenous peoples have the right to self-determination. By virtue of that right they freely determine their political status and freely pursue their economic, social and cultural development."

194 Debates in international law, and around UNDRIP, respond to state concerns about using the language of "self-determination" in relation to sub-state nations (peoples). Anaya, *supra* note 11, addresses the false equation between self-determination and statehood. See also Joffe, *supra* note 151; Brenda Gunn, "Overcoming Obstacles to Implementing the UN Declaration on the Rights of Indigenous Peoples in Canada" (2013) 31 Windsor YB Access to Just 147; Brian Slattery, "The Paradoxes of National Self-Determination" (1994) 32 OHLJ 703; and Karlo Bastra, John McGarry & Richard Simeon, eds, *Territorial Pluralism: Managing Difference in Multinational States* (Vancouver: UBC Press, 2015). We use the language of self-government here as it is commonly used in relation to the discussions within Canada, but this use of familiar language does not signal acceptance of the limitations of the concept as defined by government policy.

195 Cornell et al, *supra* note 52 at 5.

scope, constitutional fit, and increasingly, also implementation.[196] As noted in Section III, only a handful of self-government agreements have been completed under this policy, with the majority of comprehensive self-government agreements being achieved through the negotiation of modern treaties. Nevertheless, and as described in Section II, the delivery of some public services has been devolved to Indigenous communities (both on reserve and off). Further, the difficulties involved in replacing the *Indian Act*[197] in tandem with the slow progress of treaty and self-government negotiations have contributed to the emergence of two other trajectories for self-government, particularly for First Nations. One is "opt-in" legislation increasing the authority of *Indian Act* band councils in some areas of jurisdiction; the most prominent among these is the *First Nations Land Management Act*.[198] The second is the emergence of reconciliation and other intergovernmental agreements, particularly at the provincial level, which address consultation protocols; decision-making with respect to certain lands, waters, or resources; revenue sharing; and intergovernmental relations more generally.[199]

---

196 For discussion, see Naomi Metallic, "Ending Piecemeal Recognition of Indigenous Nationhood and Jurisdiction: Returning RCAP's Aboriginal Nation Recognition and Government Act" in *Redefining Relationships: Indigenous Peoples and Canada* (Saskatoon: Native Law Centre, *forthcoming*). Regarding implementation, see e.g. *Nunavut Tunngavik Incorporated v Canada (Attorney General)*, 2014 NUCA 2, in which the representative of the beneficiaries of the Nunavut Final Agreement is pursuing the federal Crown for failure to implement the terms of that agreement, including provisions relating to the establishment of an environmental monitoring program. See generally, the Land Claims Agreements Coalition, "Implementation Issues," online: <http://www.landclaimscoalition.ca/implementation-issues/>.

197 The current federal Liberal government has committed to tackling this long-standing reform project. In a speech by Justice Minister Wilson-Raybould, she cautions that reform will not be fast: "What we need is an efficient process of transition that lights a fire under the process of decolonization but does so in a controlled manner that respects where Indigenous communities are in terms of rebuilding. As was described to me by one chief when I was BC Regional Chief, rather than popping the balloon that is the *Indian Act*, we need to let the air out slowly in a controlled and deliberate manner—slowly until it is all gone and when it is all out what replaces it will be strong and healthy First Nation governments—governments that design and deliver their own programs and services." See the Honourable Jody Wilson-Raybould, PC, QC, MP, "Speech to Assembly of First Nations Annual General Assembly, Scotiabank Convention Centre, Niagara Falls, ON" (12 July 2016). For discussion, see John Borrows, "Seven Generations, Seven Teachings: Ending the Indian Act" (May 2008) *National Centre for First Nations Governance*, online: <http://fngovernance.org/resources_docs/7_Generations_7_Teachings.pdf>.

198 The *First Nations Land Management Act*, SC 1999, c 24, allows bands to pass laws on land development, conservation, protection, management, use and possession of First Nation land, environmental assessment, matrimonial property, laws to manage natural resources of reserve lands and other land related issues. See also legislation noted in *supra* note 32

199 See, for example, the range of agreements being negotiation in British Columbia: "First Nations Negotiations," online: <http://www2.gov.bc.ca/gov/content/environment/natural-resource-stewardship/consulting-with-first-nations/first-nations-negotiations>. Some specific examples from other provinces include: *Protocol Agreement on Government to Government Relations between Chiefs of the First Nations of Alberta and the Government of Alberta*, 22 May 2008 (sets out a process for meetings between the Grand Chiefs and Premier to discuss issues of common interest, consultation procedures with First Nations regarding land and resource development, and establishment of sub-tables); *City of Regina and File Hills Qu'Appelle Tribal Council Protocol Declaration of Understanding*, 5 June 2007 (to formalize a constructive working relationship between the City of Regina and the File Hills Qu'Appelle Tribal Council on such things as quality of life for urban First Nations people residing within Regina, cooperation on service delivery and enhancing communication and consultations); and *The Agreement Respecting a New Relationship Between the Cree Nation and the Government of Quebec (La Paix des Braves)*, 7 February 2002 (establishes revenue sharing with respect to mining, hydroelectric development, and forestry carried out on the traditional lands of the Cree People, online: <http://www.gcc.ca/issues/paixdesbraves.php>).

In light of the many options emerging in response to the limitations of policy platforms, limitations of public and community resources, and other obstacles, it is fair to say that the route to self-determination in Canada follows a piecemeal, winding path with more than a few forks in the road. The products of this policy and jurisprudential landscape are several different models or approaches to governance, ranging from councils that roughly approximate municipal governments, to governments that have a nation-to-nation (or "government-to-government") relationship with Canada.[200] The former is often associated with *Indian Act* band councils, which courts have recognized as delegated statutory decision-makers with subordinate law-making authority as defined in statutes.[201] The latter is often associated with modern treaties and the governments recognized and established through those agreements, such as the Nisga'a Lisims government. Such agreements also outline the Indigenous government's areas of primary jurisdiction, and the relationship of its laws to federal and provincial statutes through mechanisms such as paramountcy rules, and avenues of appeal and judicial review from the decisions of the Indigenous party's government, administration, and dispute resolution mechanisms. Between these "poles," or possibly on a different scale, sit forms of self-government that involve Indigenous participation within public institutions of government. These forms of participation include Indigenous participation in land and resource management through representation in regulatory agencies, such as the Mackenzie Valley Environmental Impact Review Board (MVEIRB) in the Northwest Territories,[202] and Indigenous participation in public government, as illustrated by the government of Nunavut over which Inuit control is, at least for now, secured by the demographics of the territory.

Political scientists describe the status of self-government in Canada as "multilevel governance." As Martin Papillion explains, the approach to self-government is an adaptation of federalism that occurs

---

200   RCAP suggested three models of Aboriginal government: the nation government model, the public government model, and the community of interest model. In each of these models, an Aboriginal government, "would have powers and authorities in respect of law making (legislative); administration and policy making (executive); and interpretation, application and enforcement of law (judicial)" (RCAP Report, *supra* note 13, "Models of Aboriginal Government: An Overview," vol 2, ch 3). Other approaches include Frances Abele and Michael Prince's delineation of four "pathways" to self-determination: (1) "mini-municipalities" embedded in federalism-as-usual; (2) new subnational entities in a modest adaptation of Canadian federalism (adapted federalism); (3) a fully developed third order of government in the federation (trilateral federalism); (4) Aboriginal governments as part of a treaty-based alliance between the Aboriginal governments and the Crown in Canada (nation-to-nation). (Frances Abele & Michael J Prince, "Four Pathways to Aboriginal Self-Government in Canada" (2006) 36 American Rev of Can Studies 568 at 570). See also Shin Imai, "Indigenous Self-Determination and the State" in Richardson et al, *supra* note 2 at 285, adopted in the previous version of this chapter: Janna Promislow & Lorne Sossin, "In Search of Aboriginal Administrative Law" in Colleen Flood & Lorne Sossin, eds, *Administrative Law in Context*, 2nd ed (Toronto: Emond Montgomery, 2013) 449.

201   *Gabriel v Canatonquin*, [1978] 1 FC 124 (TD), aff'd [1980] 2 FC 792 (CA); *Sparvier v Cowessess Indian Band No 73*, [1993] 3 FCR 142, 13 Admin LR (2d) 266 (TD) [*Sparvier*]. This status is also true for Métis settlement councils under Alberta's *Métis Settlements Act*, RSA 2000, c M-14. For discussion of the scope of *Indian Act* band council authority, see text accompanying footnotes 30 to 32 in Section II.

202   For evaluation, see Geneviève Motard, « Des competences legislatives personnelles en matière d'activités de chasse, de pêche et de piégeage dans les ententes de revendications territoriales : les limites de la cogestion » (2016) 61 McGill LJ 907 and Sari Graben, "Living in Perfect Harmony: Harmonizing Sub-Arctic Co-Management through Judicial Review" (2011) 49 Osgoode Hall LJ 199.

less through the recognition of indigenous governments as co-sovereigns, as indigenous claims would suggest, than through the layering of new multilevel governance (MLG) regimes that coexist with the existing division of powers and intergovernmental relation systems of the two countries. As a result, indigenous governance in Canada … is characterized today by a multiplication of decision-making spaces and processes that often exist in tension with the existing federal structure without altering it.[203]

As suggested by this description, the range of bodies and modes of expressing self-government do not permit a linear approach or a ranking of the "degree" of self-government achieved through each. Indeed, there is no agreement among commentators on the nature of the sovereignty or status of the governments achieved through treaty negotiations,[204] and the few judicial decisions on the issue also emphasize different sources of authority for these governments.[205] Equally importantly, the goals and priorities of different Indigenous communities and nations are not uniform.[206] Additional complexities around the recognition and pursuit of negotiated self-government arrangements are found when one considers Indigenous law regarding the proper governing body or individual, and particularly that the appropriate decision-maker(s) may not map easily with centralized and delegated decision-making in the administrative state or assumptions of territorially defined jurisdictions.[207] Thus, what is clear from this very brief survey of approaches to Indigenous governance is that a simplification or rationalization of the landscape is not on the horizon.

---

203 Martin Papillon, "Adapting Federalism: Indigenous Multilevel Governance in Canada and the United States" (2012) 42 *Publius* 289-312, doi: 10.1093/publius/pjr032.

204 It is also fair to say there is no agreement on the criteria of evaluation. A few examples: Tracie Lea Scott, *Postcolonial Sovereignty? The Nisga'a Final Agreement* (Saskatoon: Purich Publishing, 2012); Sari Graben, "The Nisga'a Final Agreement: Negotiating Federalism" (2007) 6 Indig LJ 63; and Special Rapporteur Miguel Alfonso Martinez, *Study on Treaties, Agreements and Other Constructive Arrangements between States and Indigenous Populations*, UN Economic and Social Council, Commission on Human Rights, Sub-Commission on Prevention of Discrimination and Protection of Minorities, 51st Sess (1999) at para 145 (Comprehensive claims agreements as limited in terms of the reach of the negotiations (capable of establishing only delegated governmental powers), in contradistinction to the constitutional nature and international status of historic treaties which, in his assessment, were recognized under the Law of Nations).

205 In *House of Sga'nisim v Canada (Attorney General)*, 2013 BCCA 49, [2013] 2 CNLR 226, leave to appeal refused, [2013] SCCA No 44 [*Chief Mountain*], the court did not overturn *Campbell* (*supra* note 190), which recognized the inherent source of Nisga'a authority, but decided the matter on the more limited basis that the Nisga'a government can be understood as exercising delegated authority. For commentary, see Joshua Nichols, "A Reconciliation without Recollection? *Chief Mountain* and the Sources of Sovereignty" (2015) 48 UBC L Rev 515; and Kent McNeil, "The Jurisdiction of Inherent Right Aboriginal Governments," Research Paper for the National Centre for First Nations Governance (2007) at 15, online: <http://fngovernance.org/ncfng_research/kent_mcneil.pdf>.

206 Cornell et al, *supra* note 52 at 15.

207 For a review of the relevant jurisprudence, see Kent McNeil, "Aboriginal Title and Indigenous Governance: Identifying the Holders or Rights and Authority" (2016) *All Papers*, Paper 264, online: <digitalcommons.osgoode.yorku.ca/cgi/viewcontent.cgi?article=1263&context=all_papers>. This issue is identified as the problem of overlapping territories in the context of treaty negotiations. See Eyford Report, *supra* note 134.

A. The Context of Self-Government and Review of Indigenous Governments and Decision-Makers

These debates and issues are important background for understanding the type or types of authority being exercised by an Indigenous government or other body. A field of Aboriginal administrative law requires that this context be carried forward when addressing traditional administrative law questions about the exercise of authority by Indigenous governments in accordance with administrative law values of fairness, accountability, transparency, and legality more generally.[208] Corresponding with the pluralist view of Canada as tri-juridical,[209] an additional contextual factor is awareness of potential Indigenous laws and values informing the parameters of public decision-making by Indigenous governments.

Indigenous legal traditions are often rich in mechanisms that reflect administrative law values.[210] For example, Val Napoleon's work on Gitksan law and legal theory demonstrates concerns for transparency, accountability, and accessibility in the requirement that most community business—whether decisions about access or ownership of resources, or about changes in leadership, or about resolving disputes within a house (the main governance institution)—be conducted openly at a community feast. Moreover, such decision-making is supported by extensive consultation with those impacted by the issue beforehand, as well as the formal appointment of individuals to witness the proceedings, thereby creating a public record and ensuring the decisions reached are accessible to all.[211] Witnesses are selected from guests at the feast whose lineages are unrelated to the hosts, and are given roles and degrees of responsibilities that depend on their relationship to the host group.[212]

In spite of rich traditions of "administrative justice," the decisions and laws made by Indigenous governments, and particularly those formed under statutes and agreements, will not necessarily rely or rely exclusively on Indigenous legal traditions. As critics of modern treaty processes have identified, participating in land claims and self-government processes involves discourses of governance that are foreign to Indigenous practices and lifestyles and, consequently, can transform Indigenous governance and law.[213] Although

---

208   Lorne Sossin, "Indigenous Self-Government and the Future of Administrative Law" (2012) 45 UBCLR 595; Promislow & Sossin, *supra* note 200.

209   See RCAP Report, *supra* note 13. Legal pluralism here is more than the "fact" of Indigenous legal orders, but also normative, making a claim on the content and application of the rule of law. For discussion of the difference between descriptive and normative approaches to legal pluralism, see Kirsten Anker, *Declarations of Interdependence: A Legal Pluralist Approach to Indigenous Rights* (Farnham: Taylor and Francis, 2014).

210   See e.g. Shuswap Nation Tribal Council and Indigenous Law Research Unit (University of Victoria), *Secwépemc Lands and Resources Law Research Project* (2017) at 18, online: <http://shuswapnation.org/wordpress/wp-content/uploads/2017/04/Secwepemc-Land-Laws-1.pdf>. See also Cornell et al, *supra* note 52, who emphasize the importance of accountability (to one's own citizens) as critical to good governance for Indigenous Peoples.

211   Val Napoleon, *Ayook: Gitksan Legal Order, Law, and Legal Theory* (PhD Thesis, University of Victoria Faculty of Law, 2009) [unpublished]. See especially the cases Napoleon outlines in ch 3, and at 309, where Napoleon defines "public witnessing and accountability" as a general working principle of Gitksan legal theory and the steps involved in managing disputes among the Gitksan.

212   *Ibid* at xv, citing Richard Overstall, "Encountering the Spirit in the Land: 'Property' in a Kinship-Based Legal Order" in John McLaren, Andrew R Buck & Nancy E Wright, eds, *Despotic Dominion: Property Rights in British Settler Societies* (Vancouver: UBC Press, 2004) 22 at 28.

213   See e.g. Paul Nadasdy, *Hunters and Bureaucrats: Power, Knowledge and Aboriginal-State Relations in the Southwest Yukon* (Vancouver: UBC Press, 2003), and Alan Hanna, "Spaces for Sharing: Searching for Indigenous Law on the Canadian Legal Landscape" (2017, under review). Related concerns are expressed by Aaron Mills, *supra* note 6, in relation to teaching Indigenous legal traditions in Canadian law school.

transformation and change should not be presumed to produce negative outcomes,[214] Indigenous communities and critical scholars have earned their skepticism regarding the assimilative nature of the interaction and the potential to re-inscribe the harms of colonial impositions. Further challenges in drawing on Indigenous legal traditions include their grounding in supporting decentralized, non-state governance to inform governance institutions that parallel or share jurisdiction with the institutions of the Canadian state, which are hierarchically organized and highly centralized. In addition, many communities have had knowledge and dissemination of their law severely disrupted by residential schools and colonial policy more generally, such that the work of "accessing and articulating Indigenous laws … at this point of time … must start in a space of a 'deep absence' constructed by colonialism."[215] In the context of modern treaties in particular, the political choices of Indigenous communities to enter into such treaties and establish legislatures and judicial councils for the work of dispute resolution may involve more or less explicit political choices to adopt laws and strategies that re-invent or depart from their Indigenous legal traditions.[216] Other communities or nations may choose to protect their traditions and governance authority by not housing certain aspects of governance within the entities and jurisdictions recognized through intergovernmental agreements.[217]

---

214 For discussion, see William Twining, "Social Sciences and the Diffusion of Law" (2005) 32 J Law & Society 203 at 232, 237 and Nicole Roughan, "The Association of State and Indigenous Law: A Case Study in 'Legal Association'" (2009) 59 UTLJ 135.

215 Friedland & Napoleon, *supra* note 6, citing Boaventura de Sousa Santos for the idea of "deep absence." See also the TRC Summary Report, *supra* note 9 at 259.

216 The decision of the Tsawwassen First Nation Judicial Council on an election appeal in *Baird v Mack* (11 December 2012), online: <http://www.tsawwassenfirstnation.com/pdfs/TFN-Government/Judicial-Council/12.11.12_Decisions_re_2012_Election_Appeal.pdf> provides an interesting example. The Judicial Council is constituted by members and lawyers (non-members) of the Tsawwassen First Nation, and the decision is heavily reliant on Canadian election law. Nevertheless, the decision to find the general election to have been invalid relies on evidence admitted through adaptations to Canadian law to permit "the traditional approach in the Tsawwassen First Nation of elder family members speaking for those in their families" and to allow the admission of what would otherwise be hearsay evidence "because of the oral traditions of this Nation" (at 21-22). See also Kim Baird, "Self-Governing First Nations: What Are the Considerations" (Presented at *Aboriginal Administrative Law*, Continuing Legal Education Society of British Columbia Conference, Vancouver, 19 June 2015) [unpublished].

217 See e.g. the proposal of the Gitxsan Treaty Team, "Alternative Governance Model: Gitxsan Reconciliation (15 May 2008), in which the Gitxsan Treaty Team proposes an end to *Indian Act* governance, the adoption of provincial and federal governance with respect to matters of the state, and accommodation and recognition of their Aboriginal rights to "maintain a relationship with the entire 33,000 kilometres of traditional territory. The economic value of our collective inherited interest (which is neither fee simple nor sovereign but is certainly real, court-ordered and subject to definition) is to be realized by the process of accommodation articulated by the Supreme Court of Canada. In practical terms, this will presumably be effected by a combination of own investment, arrangements with external investors, and revenue sharing agreements with governments, especially the provincial in the case of resources" (at 6-7). A further complexity relates to questions of the body or collective that is authorized to make such choices on behalf of a community and/or nation. In the case of the Gitxsan, these debates erupted into litigation in which Gitxsan government, including *Indian Act* band councils and several hereditary chiefs (traditional leaders), challenged the authority of the Gitxsan Treaty Society (a body incorporated by hereditary chiefs) to make such a proposal and enter into treaty negotiations with the Crown: *Spookw v Gitxsan Treaty Society*, 2017 BCCA 16.

Emerging debates about the aims and methodologies of revitalizing Indigenous law and their application[218] are part of the context and complexity of the field encompassed within Aboriginal administrative law. However, there is no need to import the externally defined, pre-contact notion of "aboriginality" from Aboriginal rights jurisprudence.[219] Like other areas of administrative law, judicial review within Aboriginal administrative law encompasses a broader scope of decisions than judicial review for consistency with Aboriginal rights.[220] Thus, while revitalization of Indigenous law and incorporation of Indigenous law and values in the approach to administrative justice may be critically important to the self-governance aims of Indigenous communities,[221] the significance of these issues in Aboriginal administrative law is considering the space and support provided for the evolution of Indigenous law in government negotiations and implementation policies, and how Indigenous law informs the context of judicial review of decisions by Indigenous governments. In such contexts, review of the decisions of Indigenous decision-makers must proceed in an informed and deeply contextual manner to identify the source (or sources) of authority, whether that authority has been exercised in accordance with requirements and restrictions of a "multilevel" or plural rule of law, and attend to not re-inscribing the harms of colonialism on Indigenous laws and governments by ensuring a full and equal treatment of Indigenous law where relevant.[222]

One example of the need for such a contextualized approach is the treatment of the authority of *Indian Act* band councils. While these councils are understood to be "creatures of statute" for the purpose of judicial review,[223] a more informed and nuanced approach is reflected by courts that have recognized that the governance authority exercised by these councils may also be founded on inherent authority. As Marceau JA explained in *Canadian Pacific v Matsqui Indian Band*,[224]

---

218 For a very brief description of the scope of such debates, see Fraser Harland, "Introduction [to the Special Issue on Indigenous law and legal pluralism]: Moving from the Why to the How of Indigenous Law" (2016) 61 McGill LJ 721.

219 *Van der Peet, supra* note 113. In the context of Métis rights, the timeline is adjusted to before "effective control": *Powley, supra* note 113 at para 37. The pre-contact timeline and other aspects of the test have been repeatedly criticized. For one recent discussion, see John Borrows, "(Ab)Originalism and Canada's Constitution" (2012) 58 SCLR (2d) 351-398.

220 See e.g. *Blencoe v British Columbia (Human Rights Tribunal)*, 2000 SCC 44, [2000] 2 SCR 307.

221 Cornell et al, *supra* note 52 emphasize the importance of "culturally appropriate" institutions as more likely to be effective.

222 Consider Justice Lance SG Finch, "The Duty to Learn: Taking Account of Indigenous Legal Orders in Practice" (Presented at *Indigenous Legal Orders and the Common Law*, British Columbia Continuing Legal Education Conference, Vancouver, November 2012).

223 *Supra* note 201. For an overview of *Indian Act* band governments relative to Canadian public administration more generally, with attention to the imposition of *Indian Act* council structures on pre-existing governance structures and bodies of First Nations peoples, see Frances Abele, "Like an Ill-Fitting Boot: Government, Governance and Management Systems in the Contemporary Indian Act," (2008) National Centre for First Nations Governance, online: <http://fngovernance.org/ncfng_research/frances_able.pdf>.

224 [2000] 1 FCR 325 at para 29, 176 DLR (4th) 35 [*CP v Matsqui* (FCA)].

[I]t appears to me quite inappropriate to apply to Indian bands' new [taxation] by-law powers the principles of interpretation developed in municipal law. There is a big difference between municipalities and Indian bands in that the existence of the Indian groupings is not like that of municipal units, wholly dependent on an act of government authority, and the rationale behind the granting of taxation powers to both such bodies is clearly not the same. The devolved taxation powers of municipalities exists, to my mind, only to further governmental objectives of efficiency in operation and administration. The recent granting of taxation powers to Indian bands has a much broader and humane objective, which can only be seen in the context of furthering the ability of natives to govern themselves and thus, to a certain extent, invokes rights and responsibilities that predate all Indian acts.[225]

It is equally important to recognize that devolving service delivery and government program administration to First Nations through bilateral or tripartite government agreements can create complexities in understanding not only the authority under which decision-makers operate, but also the nature of the decision-maker itself. Band councils are not the only actors involved. Indigenous decision-makers in these contexts may be tribal councils, non-profit societies or for-profit corporations, specially constituted child welfare or educational agencies, individual officers within such organizations, or, as will be further discussed below, representatives of constitutional rights holders that have no corporate or statutory form under Canadian law.[226]

To date, and perhaps for obvious reasons, judicial review has focused on review of band council decisions with an emerging but still very small jurisprudence reviewing decisions of judicial councils and bodies constituted under land claim or self-government agreements. In reviewing the decisions of band councils and related decision-makers, some judges have expressed concern that the exercise of self-governing authorities should not preclude or outweigh the rights of both band members and individuals affected by band decisions to procedural fairness in decisions affecting them.[227] In the context of negotiated self-government, concern for the individual member's rights remains, but judicial awareness and concern to defer to the processes and decision-makers established under a treaty is

---

225 *Ibid* at para 29. See discussion in Mark D Walters, "Promise and Paradox: The Emergence of Indigenous Rights Law in Canada" in Richardson et al, *supra* note 2, where he favours the approach taken in *Bone v Sioux Valley Indian Band No 290*, [1996] 3 CNLR 54 (FCTD) (authority from inherent governance powers; context of a dispute regarding custom election code) over the approach in *Heron Seismic Services Ltd v Muscowpetung Indian Band*, [1991] 2 CNLR 52 (Sask QB) (authority from statute; context of a dispute over an account for work done drilling wells on reserve).

226 See *McDonald v Anishinabek Police Service* (2006), 83 OR (3d) 132 (Div Ct), noted in relation to the issue of the scope of judicial review by Cristie Ford in Chapter 2 in this volume. An example of a body with no status granted by Canadian law is the Council of the Haida Nation, discussed below.

227 *Sparvier, supra* note 201 at para 47. See also the decision of Lamer CJ in *Canadian Pacific v Matsqui Indian Band*, [1995] 1 SCR 3 at para 74 (not the majority on this point): "The fact that tribunals have been constituted within the context of a federal policy promoting Aboriginal self-government does not, in itself, dilute natural justice."

strong.[228] In either context, a construction of an "either/or" should be avoided; respect for Indigenous governance does not mean an absence of procedural and substantive fairness. The concern, instead, is for a contextual treatment of the potentially different processes and considerations at stake in what constitutes a fair and reasonable decision. As the governments recognized through negotiations increase and the authorities of governments with statutory anchors evolve, more issues will arise, and judicial reviews of Indigenous governments will increase. Specific approaches to independence or fairness, for example, may develop.[229] It will be critical to understand the context of Indigenous decision-makers to consider the possibility of multiple sources of authority for decisions, to take into account the influence and applicability of Indigenous law in understanding the rights of individuals and the authority and intent of decision-makers, and to balance such factors with the intent of the Indigenous nation or group in entering into the governance arrangement.

B. Beyond (or Before) Judicial Review: Recognizing the Authority of Indigenous Law

The final topic in this section addresses the need for a plural rule of law most directly: the presence and emergence of Indigenous governance with authority founded in Indigenous law that is asserted and expressed without concern for obtaining recognition through self-government agreements or legislation. Sometimes called the "just do it" approach, this approach refers to Indigenous nations that "simply [begin] to exercise decision-making authority in a particular policy area."[230] While such approaches may emerge out of frustration with government negotiations policies and the lack of other ways to achieve a sufficient

---

228   See e.g. *Lafferty v Tlicho Government*, [2009] 3 CNLR 151 (NWTSC), appeal dismissed on grounds of mootness, 2010 NWTCA 4. The case involved a challenge to a law passed by the Tlicho Assembly by dissident chiefs, and the challenge process established under the Tlicho constitution was to the same assembly. The challengers' attempt to have the court reverse the decision of the Assembly to not strike the law was rebuffed, with Richard J commenting, "[w]hile it may appear an anomaly to have a legislative body … re-constitute itself into an adjudicative body (the Tlicho assembly under section 13.3) to hear a challenge to the validity of one of its own laws, that is the process that the Tlicho people decided upon in adopting the Tlicho Constitution" (at para 23). A similar reinforcement of appeal/review mechanisms established under a treaty is found in *Edzerza v Kwanlin Dün First Nation*, 2008 YKCA 8, which stated the principle that "[i]t has been agreed and legislated that Kwanlin Dün is to be a self-governing first nation, and [its constitution] should not be given a narrow interpretation that restricts the ability of Kwanlin Dün to be self-governing" (at para 26). A more complex set of facts and issues is found in *Kwanlin Dün First Nation v Kwanlin Dün First Nation Judicial Council*, 2016 YKSC 35. In this case, Veale J decided a jurisdictional challenge to a decision to overturn the First Nation's eviction of two tenants from housing on settlement land pursuant to Yukon landlord–tenant legislation. The decision that was challenged was taken by the Judicial Council constituted under the First Nation's self-government agreement with original jurisdiction to review and provide relief from decisions of the Kwanlin Dün government. The First Nation's challenges to the Council's exercise of authority in the case related to the effect of laws of general application on the jurisdiction of the Judicial Council. Veale J upheld portions of the Judicial Council's decision, commenting, "it would take too narrow a view of the KDFN Constitution to decide that a law of general application displaces Judicial Council's jurisdiction to rule on KDFN's consideration of Constitutional values and procedural rights in the context of reviewing an administrative decision" (at para 53).

229   Sossin, *supra* note 208.

230   Cornell et al, *supra* note 52 at 15.

measure of self-determination,[231] they do not imply an isolationist approach. As rights holders who are owed consultation and accommodation, Indigenous nations can demand the attention of governments without government acceding to the scope or expression of those rights nor recognizing the body asserting them as an Indigenous government. Furthermore, as noted above, Indigenous nations may prefer to avoid seeking "official" recognition for their governance institutions and laws to avoid colonial dynamics that do violence to their legal orders.[232]

The Haida Nation, as an example, have confidently asserted their authority grounded in their own law and nationhood through the formation of the Council of the Haida Nation (CHN) in 1974.[233] As described by Terri-Lynn (gid7ahl-Gudsllaay) Williams-Davidson, the CHN's authority comes from the land:

> The governance structure set out in the Haida Nation's Constitution is what may be described as an inverted governance structure, with the land at the top. Immediately below are the citizens of the nation who hold the law-making authority. CHN is not a Tribal Council or a Band Council; its authority is not derived from the Government of Canada. It is not a society, governed by provincial or federal society law. Its authority is derived from the land itself…[234]

Beyond Aboriginal rights and title litigation,[235] the CHN has worked over the years to protect Haida lands and waters through many agreements with federal, provincial, and local governments implementing shared management regimes and protected areas. Signed in 2009, their protocol with the Province of British Columbia has become a well-known example of the potential for working relationships that allow for shared and joint decision-making even while issues of sovereignty, ownership, and governance authority remain disputed and subject to litigation.[236] Called the Kunst'aa Guu-Kunst'aayah Reconciliation Protocol, with the Haida words meaning "The Beginning,"[237] the agreement creates a commitment to joint decision-making over forestry allowances with space to add on additional sectors and processes over time.

The language around and mode of implementing this commitment are notable. In the preamble to the Protocol, the parties plainly state their differences over their claims to

---

231   With the absence of federal legislation recognizing Métis status or governance, and in light of relatively weak attention to Métis claims in negotiations policies, such an approach is especially relevant for Métis. See e.g. Larry Chartrand "'We Rise Again': Métis Traditional Governance and the Claim to Métis Self-Government" in Yale Belanger, ed, *Aboriginal Self-Government in Canada: Current Trends and Issues*, 3d ed (Vancouver: Purich Publishing Ltd, 2008) and Janique Dubois & Kelly Saunders, "'Just do it!' Carving Out Space for the Métis in Canadian Federalism" (2013) 46 Cdn J of Poli Sci 187.

232   Coulthard, *supra* note 158. See also Mills, *supra* note 6, specifically in relation to teaching Indigenous law in Canadian law schools.

233   See online: <http://www.haidanation.ca>.

234   Gid7ahl-Gudsllaay (Terri-Lynn) Williams-Davidson, "Weaving Together Our Future: The Interaction of Haida Laws to Achieve Respectful Co-Existence" (Prepared for the Continuing Legal Education Society of British Columbia, November 2012) at 6.2.4, online: <http://www.whiteravenlaw.ca/wp/wp-content/uploads/Weaving-Together-Our-Future.pdf>.

235   The CHN was the named litigant in *Haida Nation*, *supra* note 120.

236   See discussion in Webber, 2016, *supra* note 11 at 75-76.

237   Williams-Davidson, *supra* note 234 at 6.2.7.

sovereignty and control of the territory and waters at issue.[238] In spite of the stark differences between these assertions, the preamble ends with a commitment to "a more productive relationship" through shared decision-making with respect to land and resource management in Haida Gwaii. This commitment is then manifested in the establishment of the Haida Gwaii Management Council (HGMC) through the joint operation of the *Haida Gwaii Reconciliation Act*[239] and a resolution of the Haida Nation.[240] Further, the preamble to the *Haida Gwaii Reconciliation Act* acknowledges the disagreements documented in the Protocol and the expectation that under that Protocol, Haida Nation and BC "will operate under their respective authorities and jurisdictions." From the presentation of the competing claims in the Protocol side by side, to the language of the constituting legislation, the parties have paid close attention to the detail required to represent a non-hierarchical relationship emerging out of a colonial past.

With such dual authorities empowering its work, the HGMC is clearly different than co-management boards established through federal or provincial legislation, even if pursuant to land claims agreements. However, its distinctiveness fades when the parameters within which HGMC operates are considered. Similar to the land claims co-management boards, the HGMC consists of two members appointed by resolution of the Haida Nation after consultation with BC, two members appointed by the Lieutenant Governor in Council after consultation with the Haida Nation, and a chair appointed by resolutions of each party.[241] HGMC members are required to adhere to natural justice, impartiality, and procedural fairness in their work, but will also function on a consensus decision-making model with allowances for a majoritarian approach and a tie-breaking vote by the chair when consensus cannot be reached.[242] The authorities granted by both Haida and BC governments include

---

238 The Haida Nation asserts that Haida Gwaii is subject to the "rights, sovereignty, ownership, jurisdiction and collective Title of the Haida Nation" and that Haida Gwaii will be managed in accordance with Haida "laws, policies, customs and traditions." Directly contradicting these assertions, British Columbia lists its assertions that Haida Gwaii is Crown land, subject to "private rights or interests, and subject to the sovereignty of Her Majesty the Queen and the legislative jurisdiction of the Parliament of Canada and the Legislature of the Province of British Columbia." Kunst'aa guu—Kunst'aayah Reconciliation Protocol (14 December 2009), between the Haida Nation and Her Majesty the Queen in Right of the Province of British Columbia, online: <http://www2.gov.bc.ca/assets/gov/zzzz-to-be-moved/9efbd86da302a0712e-6559bdb2c7f9dd/9efbd86da302a0712e6559bdb2c7f9dd/agreements/reconciliation_haida.pdf>.

239 SBC 2010, c 17, s 3 [HGRA].

240 Referred to as the Stewardship Law (KaayGuu Ga ga Kyah ts'as—Gin 'inaas 'laas 'waadluwaan gud tl'a gud giidaa) on the Council of the Haida Nation, online: <http://www.haidanation.ca/wp-content/uploads/2017/03/dec.10.pdf> at 6 and HGMC websites.

241 Haida Gwaii Management Council, Frequently Asked Questions, online: <http://www.haidagwaiimanagementcouncil.ca/faqs.html> [FAQ document]. By contrast, the members of the MVEIRB are all appointed by the federal INAC minister, who appoints these members based on an equal number of nominations from the federal and territorial governments on the one hand, and from Aboriginal land claimant organizations on the other hand. The chair is generally appointed based on the nomination of the other review board members. Mackenzie Valley Review Board, "About Us," online: <http://www.reviewboard.ca/about/>.

242 See British Columbia Board Resources and Development Office, Directory of Agencies, Haida Gwaii Management Council, online: <http://www.brdo.gov.bc.ca/boardView.asp?boardNum=215137>. See also, HGRA, s 3(3) and FAQ document, *ibid*. The MVEIRB has well developed rules of procedure, as mandated by statute, in which the application of the common law duty of procedural fairness is confirmed. Mackenzie Valley Review Board, "Rules of Procedure," online <http://www.reviewboard.ca/upload/ref_library/MVEIRB_RulesofProcedure_0505.pdf>.

establishing, implementing, and amending land use objectives, determining the allowable annual cut for Haida Gwaii, the approval of management plans for protected areas, and developing policies and standards for the identification and conservation of heritage sites.[243]

To date, no judicial review of any HGMC decision has been launched.[244] If and when it happens, the reviewing judge will potentially face several unique challenges, such as giving weight to the dual authorities for the HGMC in light of the basis for judicial review, interpreting and applying Indigenous law, and considering what a plural, *non-hierarchical* rule of law demands.

The Haida Nation–BC Protocol and the HGMC is not the only example of Indigenous governance founded on Indigenous law with administrative law implications. In British Columbia, several nations have undertaken their own development assessment processes in relation to major natural resource projects.[245] Drawing more or less on Indigenous legal traditions in relation to process and decision-makers, and with diverse approaches to involving project proponents, non-Indigenous parties, and coordination with provincial and federal government processes, these assessments respond to gaps and concerns about current environmental assessment processes. They allow the nations to satisfy their questions about the developments by calling upon independent experts and considering the impacts of the proposed project in relation to their constitutional rights. They further allow the nations to express their consent or disapproval of a project on their own terms. While clearly capable of having political impact, the legal significance of these processes in the context of judicial review of environmental assessment decisions has yet to arise.[246]

If a government decision contradicts the results of one of these processes—i.e., if government approves a project that the Indigenous assessment process recommends rejecting—and Indigenous or other parties seek a review of that decision, what weight

---

243 FAQ document, *supra* note 241.

244 But see *Taan Forest Limited Partnership v United Steelworkers, Local 1-1937*, 2017 CanLII 5278 (BC LRB), a labour arbitration about a dispute arising from forestry work in the TFL area in issue in *Haida Nation*, and in which the arbitrator gave the Haida–BC Protocol interpretive relevance to the question of the applicability of previous collective agreement provisions and letters of understanding to the new Haida company that now carries the employer obligations.

245 See, for example, the Tsleil-Waututh Sacred Trust Initiative, which conducted an assessment of the expansion of the TransMountain Pipeline by Kinder Morgan (report may be requested online: <https://twnsacredtrust.ca/kinder-morgan-assessment-report/). See also the Stk'emlupsemc te Secwepemc assessment of the proposed Ajax Cooper-Gold Mine, adjacent to the City of Kamloops, Announcement of Process: <http://stkemlups.ca/files/2015/09/SSN-Media-Release-SSN-Project-Assessment-Process-for-Ajax-Project_Sept-10-2015.pdf> and decision summary: <http://stkemlups.ca/files/2013/11/2017-03-ss-najaxdecisionsummary_0.pdf>; and see the development assessment process run by the Squamish Nation for major projects proposed with Squamish Territory, conducted through contractual relationships with the project proponent: Aaron Bruce & Emma Hume, "The Squamish Nation Assessment Process: Getting to Yes" (Materials prepared for *Aboriginal Administrative Law*, Continuing Legal Education British Columbia Conference, June 2015).

246 The judicial reviews launched by the Tsleil Waututh First Nation and others in response to the National Energy Board and then the federal government's approval of the proposed TransMountain Pipeline Project may provide the first instance of an Indigenous assessment decision being entered into court. For an overview of the status of these challenges at the time, see West Coast Environmental Law Association and Tsleil Waututh Nation Sacred Trust Initiative, "Kinder Morgan Canada Limited: Brief on Legal Risks for Trans Mountain" (29 May 2017), online: <https://www.wcel.org/sites/default/files/publications/2017-05-kml-legalbrief-final.pdf>.

should the court place on the Indigenous assessment decision?[247] Short of a court recognizing the Indigenous decision, grounded in Indigenous law, as equal to that of the provincial and federal jurisdictions over environment, there are still many points in which such processes may be taken into account within the existing procedural and substantive grounds for a remedy on judicial review. For example, a contradictory decision by an Indigenous authority will not change the duty to consult principles that Indigenous consent is not required, but a comprehensive Indigenous-run and designed consultative process may arguably influence the "margin of appreciation" available to define the reasonableness of a consultation process and outcome, an argument that also appeals to UNDRIP Article 32 for interpretive support, which states that not only is the consent of affected Indigenous Peoples required but that they must do so in good faith and through the representative institutions of those peoples. Beyond creating new context for informing reasonableness, when entered into the court record on judicial review these decisions provide evidence that might be used by non-Indigenous petitioners to reflect on the reasonableness of the result, if the result itself does not already narrow or alter the shape of the policy decision to approve a given project.[248] Indeed, project proponents may also find occasion to rely on these processes to evidence adequate consultation.[249] There is much potential for interesting and challenging intersections in such a case, pushing the creative capacity of administrative law to adapt to new contexts and testing its potential to serve the aims of reconciliation.

V. CONCLUSION

In this chapter, we have seen that administrative law has several potential roles vis-à-vis Indigenous Peoples. It can be another tool in the arsenal of Indigenous Peoples to mediate disputes with state governments to address abuses of power in the provision of programs and services by the federal government. It can also be used to enrich and cross-pollinate the development of legal doctrines and forums to advance inherent rights and constitutional protections of those rights, such as informing the development of the duty to consult and accommodate and the creation of tribunals to resolving outstanding land claims. Finally, it can be employed to review the decisions of Indigenous governments pursuant to powers derived from statute, self-government agreements, or their inherent rights and legal orders. Deploying familiar administrative law concepts and principles in all of these areas will also open them up to renovation from new applications and new sources relevant in Indigenous contexts.

For administrative law to be used well in these areas—to facilitate reconciliation and decolonization—the essential administrative law tool of contextual analysis is key. The factors relevant in contextual analysis in this field of administrative law, however, may be less familiar and less well known. Moreover, the paradigm of deference may not be well-suited to problems—such as in the delivery of services and the implementation of Aboriginal rights—that the responsible governments and legislatures have yet to address through the

---

247   This brief analysis proceeds from the assumption that the report and decision of the Indigenous assessors are entered and accepted as evidence in the provincial or federal environmental assessment process.

248   See related comments on *Gitxaala Nation*, above.

249   Bruce & Hume, *supra* note 245 at 2.1.9-2.1.10.

ordinary democratic processes of law-making. Finally, negotiated forms of government and the presence of a third pillar of Canadian law in Indigenous traditions also potentially alter the dimensions of deference to executive actors.

Describing Aboriginal administrative law as a distinctive field addresses this need for context. By addressing how the history of colonialism has shaped the past and influenced current interactions between the Crown and Indigenous Peoples, as well as the policies, law, and constitutional doctrines relating to Indigenous Peoples and their rights, this field places us in a better position to evaluate the application of administrative law in Indigenous contexts. For students anxious to learn the basic principles they will need to know to survive administrative law, Indigenous contexts highlight critical absences and irregularities in the rule of law, thereby providing students with some perspective to evaluate and appreciate how judicial review works in non-Indigenous contexts. With that perspective acquired, students can then return to the issues arising in Indigenous contexts to more fully appreciate the work ahead in realizing Aboriginal administrative law.

CHAPTER FOUR

Administering the Canadian Rule of Law

Mary Liston
Peter A Allard School of Law, University of British Columbia

I. THE RULE OF LAW LEGALLY, PRACTICALLY, AND THEORETICALLY

This chapter aims to explain the idea of the rule of law in a nutshell. It also seeks to illustrate how this foundational concept animates and unifies Canadian administrative law. Although we can trace the origins of the concept back to ancient philosophical thought, for our purposes we will take 19th-century Britain as the historical starting point.[1] There, the content and purpose of the rule of law were debated legally, philosophically, and politically. These

---

1 Aristotle famously defined a well-ordered political community as one where the laws, not men, rule. We can also go back to 1215 and *Magna Carta* for an embryonic form of the British rule of law.

debates continue to inform our understanding of the necessary features of the rule of law and its relationship with different notions of justice. By focusing on British constitutionalism, the chapter does not mean to suggest that other Western legal systems or non-Western Indigenous legal orders do not share the concept of the rule of law. A civilian[2] or an Indigenous legal order,[3] however, may rank the importance of the rule of law differently or can be distinguished by a different cultural attitude toward the role of law in that society.

After reading this chapter, you should be able to comprehend the basic meaning of the principle of the rule of law, as well as understand why the rule of law does not have one simple definition because disagreement exists about its core content both in and outside of law. This chapter also sets out what judicial review is and is not about in administrative law and aims to help you recognize the legal tools and techniques that protect or pose risks for the rule of law. Viewing the rule of law as an institutional project not solely "owned" by judges and lawyers invites us to see how the executive and legislative branches also participate in upholding the rule of law. Finally, the chapter seeks to identify some current problems for the rule of law in administrative law. Because the chapter presents a comprehensive overview of the rule of law, it may be helpful for you to return to different sections of this chapter as you progress in your learning of administrative law.

SCENARIO AND QUESTIONS

1. What does the rule of law mean to you? Take five minutes and write down your initial understanding. Then think about this scenario.

2. Imagine that you are the owner of a thriving restaurant called Baker's in Vancouver. You have been in business for over 15 years, and there is no economic reason why your success should not continue. In your private life, you are a member of a religious community called the True Believers. This religious community faces a great deal of discrimination from the larger society and by the government of the day. Sometimes members are held without charges or are asked to pay hefty sums of money for bail because their proselytizing is believed to disturb both the peace and the larger public good. Because you are a person of some means, and in good standing with both the True Believers' community and the larger community, you are able to assist by posting bail for your fellow Believers who cannot afford to pay bail. In general, however, you are careful to keep your religious beliefs separate from your business activities.

The provincial government recently passed legislation giving expanded powers to an administrative agency, the BC Liquor Control Board (BCLCB), which is in charge of regulating the sale of liquor in the province. It is headed by a commissioner. Shortly after this legislation is passed, the minister—to whom the board is responsible—phoned the Commissioner of the BCLCB and, during the course of the conversation, suggested that when your liquor licence comes up for renewal, the commissioner might want to cancel it because your actions are interfering with public morals and the administration of justice in the province. You, of course, have no knowledge about this phone call.

The BCLCB cancels your liquor licence, but in the form letter you receive notifying you of this decision, you are not given any reasons. Moreover, no procedure exists through which

---

2   Analogous, but not equivalent, expressions of the rule of law in civilian systems include "l'État de droit" in France and "Rechtsstaat" in Germany.

3   For a discussion of Indigenous legal orders in Canada, see Chapter 3, "Realizing Aboriginal Administrative Law."

you can ask the BCLCB to reconsider its decision. Your livelihood is clearly imperilled due to the loss of customers and profits from your restaurant if you cannot serve alcohol.

At this time, imagine there is no written constitutional bill of rights, but the common law and a federal human rights statute do recognize some basic rights such as freedom of expression as well as prohibitions against expropriation of property without due process and fair compensation. Also at this time, imagine that public officials such as the minister have immunity from being sued civilly for damages or tried criminally. The Commissioner of the BCLCB can be sued civilly, but unfortunately only with permission of that same minister.

3. On the basis of this scenario, now revisit your understanding of the rule of law and identify two problems from this scenario that challenge your definition of the rule of law. For example, you may identify a procedural problem or a rights violation.

A. Instituting the Rule of Law

The part of our legal system that is derived from Western sources contains several features that inform a basic conception of the rule of law. First, legal institutions can be clearly differentiated from other institutions, such as those found in the executive and legislative branches: this is what we call the **doctrine of the separation of powers**.[4] Second, legal doctrine forms the basis of knowledge in our legal institutions as opposed to political will or individual judgment. Third, law is contained in a system comprised of an organic, evolving body of principles and rules that strives for coherence. Lastly, legal institutions are staffed by individuals with specialized training (that is, judges, lawyers, police, etc.). These features are the institutional foundation of the rule of law.

LEGAL PRINCIPLES

A legal principle is a binding normative standard. Unlike a rule, it does not dictate the legal result (for example, the rule "three strikes and you're out"). A principle serves to guide the judgment and discretion of public officials, especially judges. Principles possess weight and are crucial tools for statutory interpretation. When principles intersect or conflict, they do not cancel each other out. Instead, the decision-maker must take into account the relative weight she has assigned to each principle. She then must either reconcile these principles by balancing them or give one more weight than the other.

In basic terms, the **principle** of the rule of law offers four essential guarantees to legal subjects: (1) that all persons will be considered formally equal under the rule of law, including those holding public power; (2) that public standards will guide the creation, enactment, revision, and enforcement of all laws; (3) that the government and the legal system will treat individuals fairly; and (4) that an existing legal system enables access to legal processes for all persons in order to resolve complaints (this is more colloquially known as "access to

---

4   For judicial discussion of the separation of powers, see *Newfoundland (Treasury Board) v NAPE*, 2004 SCC 66, [2004] 3 SCR 381; *Doucet-Boudreau v Nova Scotia (Minister of Education)*, 2003 SCC 62, [2003] 3 SCR 3; *Cooper v Canada (Human Rights Commission)*, [1996] 3 SCR 854 [*Cooper*]; *Wells v Newfoundland*, [1999] 3 SCR 199 [*Wells*]; and *Operation Dismantle v The Queen*, [1985] 1 SCR 441.

justice"). Because the rule of law stands for the supremacy of law over unconstrained political power, a state committed to the rule of law will go some distance to guarantee that public officials are both authorized and bound by law in the exercise of their functions and powers. The institutional features discussed above, combined with the basic content discussed here, aim to constrain the exercise of public power throughout the state.

These features and guarantees are embedded in our written constitution (though not fully), realized through our institutions of government, and correspond to the notion of the rule of law held in Canadian society. Notably, these features and guarantees also comport with the jurisprudential definition of the rule of law as currently articulated by the Supreme Court of Canada: (1) it is supreme over private individuals as well as over government officials, who are required to exercise their authority non-arbitrarily and according to law; (2) it requires the creation and maintenance of a positive order of laws; (3) it requires the relationship between the state and the individual to be regulated by law; and (4) it is linked to the principles of judicial independence and access to justice.[5]

Before turning to an early, influential thinker about the rule of law, we should briefly think about the way our Westminster system of government actually works.[6] Take a look at Figure 4.1.

Figure 4.1

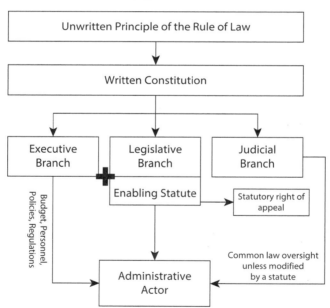

---

5   These propositions are affirmed in the following cases: *Roncarelli v Duplessis*, [1959] SCR 121 at 140 [*Roncarelli*]; *Reference re Language Rights Under s 23 of Manitoba Act, 1870 and s 133 of Constitution Act, 1867*, [1985] 1 SCR 721 at paras 55-66 [*Manitoba Language Rights Reference*]; *British Columbia v Imperial Tobacco Canada Ltd*, 2005 SCC 49, [2005] 2 SCR 473 at para 58 [*ImperialTobacco*]; *Reference re Remuneration of Judges of the Provincial Court (PEI)*, [1997] 3 SCR 3 at para 123; and *Trial Lawyers Association of British Columbia v British Columbia (Attorney General)*, 2014 SCC 59, [2014] 3 SCR 31 at paras 38-39.

6   If you need a refresher on Canadian parliamentary democracy, see Eugene Forsey, *How Canadians Govern Themselves*, 9th ed (Ottawa: Her Majesty the Queen in Right of Canada, as represented by the Minister of Public Works and Government Services Canada, 2016), online: <https://lop.parl.ca/About/Parliament/SenatorEugeneForsey/book/preface-e.html>.

In this chapter, we will work with this simplified depiction of our system of government. According to the doctrine of the separation of powers, sovereign power is divided and housed within the three different branches of government, each with its own function and personnel: the executive, the judiciary, and the legislature. As the Supreme Court wrote in the *Wells* decision:

> The doctrine of separation of powers is an essential feature of our constitution. It maintains a separation of powers between the judiciary and the other two branches, legislature and the executive, and to some extent between the legislature and the executive. ... The separation of powers is not a rigid and absolute structure. The Court should not be blind to the reality of Canadian governance that, except in certain rare cases, the executive frequently and *de facto* controls the legislature.[7]

The executive tends to be the most powerful branch in our system of government. When a majority government prevails, the government of the day (or the political executive) may dominate the legislature (but for confidence votes), and can largely control the legislative agenda. Despite being a product of the legislative branch, we therefore cannot forget that statutes bear the stamp of the executive branch, particularly in majority governments. We should also remember that in parliamentary systems such as Canada's, the executive branch exerts considerable influence in appointing appellate-level judges, including Supreme Court justices.

JURISDICTION IN ADMINISTRATIVE LAW

The basic meaning of jurisdiction in administrative law is that administrative decision-makers neither enjoy unlimited power (even if discretionary) nor do they have final say on questions regarding the scope of their delegated authority. The statutory delegate must interpret its authority (located in its home statute) in scope and in purpose so as not to assume a power that was not intended by the legislature. Administrative decision-makers can lose their jurisdiction in two ways: (1) a legal defect or error can prevent them from acquiring jurisdiction in the first place; or (2) they can properly acquire jurisdiction at the onset, but a legal error may subsequently cause them to "step outside of" or lose their jurisdiction.

This blurriness permeates administrative bodies, which are usually comprised of differing combinations of executive, legislative, and judicial functions.[8] In Figure 4.1, we can see that the executive branch is directly involved with administrative bodies by providing a budget,

---

7 *Wells, supra* note 4 at paras 52, 54.
8 Administrative bodies such as agencies, boards, and commissions possess differing combinations of policy-making, rule-making, and adjudication, which make their purposes and functions difficult to separate. This is why John Willis—an important early Canadian public law scholar—called them "governments in miniature." See "Three Approaches to Administrative Law: The Judicial, the Conceptual and the Functional" (1935) 1 UTLJ 53 at 73. Because administrative tribunals are creatures of statute that "span the constitutional divide between the judiciary and the executive" and have a significant policy-making role, their independence will be much less protected than that of the courts. See *Ocean Port Hotel Ltd v British Columbia (General Manager, Liquor Control and Licensing Branch)*, 2001 SCC 52, [2001] 2 SCR 781 at para 24. Though it is impossible to isolate law from politics completely, a complex institutional structure helps guarantee impartiality and fairness in administrative decision-making. See also the discussion of administrative independence in Chapter 7.

appointing personnel, devising policies, and enacting or endorsing regulations. Legislatures are also involved. Legislatures delegate power to administrative officials through statutes—this is why these persons are called "statutory delegates." The types of powers and the terms in which these powers are delegated in the statute are what we call their **jurisdiction** in administrative law. Politically, an administrative agency is *directly accountable* to the executive, usually to a particular minister who is responsible for that policy portfolio (for example, energy or telecommunications). Legally, if the administrative agency steps outside of, or goes beyond, the jurisdiction given by its enabling statute, its actions may be invalidated or quashed in administrative law. In this way, an administrative agency is held *indirectly accountable* when applicants seek court processes to challenge administrative decisions and procedures through administrative law. More will be said below about litigation in administrative law, but here simply note that two ways exist for an applicant to get their administrative law complaint into court: through common law judicial review (if granted), or by way of a statutory appeal (which may limit the scope of judicial oversight by setting out the grounds and conditions of appeal).

Unlike a presidential system, Canada's Westminster system of government cannot be characterized by bright-line distinctions among the three branches nor even within the executive branch—particularly, the political executive or cabinet, the bureaucracy, and administrative agencies. Cabinet, which is the political apex of the executive branch, clearly exemplifies this fusion of executive and legislative functions. Walter Bagehot (another influential Victorian British constitutionalist) defined cabinet as "… a combining committee—a *hyphen* which joins, a *buckle* which fastens, the legislative part of the State to the executive part of the State. In its origins it belongs to one, in its functions it belongs to the other."[9] Ministers possess two kinds of power: prerogative and statutory. Prerogative powers are those powers originally held by the Crown and were traditionally beyond legal control. In modern democratic states, they are now subject to common law, constitutional, and statutory constraints.[10] Ministers are also delegated powers through statutes and several important administrative law cases involve the legal and political tensions these cases pose for courts who must treat ministers with respect under the separation of powers, but must also ensure that these officials act fairly and reasonably by adhering to their authorized duties and powers. Later in this chapter, we will see an example of this tension in Section I.C's discussion of the *Insite* case.

Finally, two legal components surround and infuse the entire legal and political system: a written constitution (which is supreme law); and the unwritten principle of the rule of law (which is part of the common law or unwritten constitution originating from the United

---

9 Walter Bagehot, *The English Constitution*, ed Paul Smith (Cambridge: Cambridge University Press, 2001) at 10.

10 See *Black v Canada (Prime Minister)* (2001), 54 OR (3d) 215 (ON CA) and *Canada (Prime Minister) v Khadr*, 2010 SCC 3, [2010] 1 SCR 44. Courts also review decisions from Governor in Council, which is cabinet as a whole acting as a decision-making body. See *Canadian National Railway Co v Canada (Attorney General)*, 2014 SCC 40, [2014] 2 SCR 135. Too much deference to ministers or Cabinet can imperil the rule of law's accountability function. *See Attorney General of Canada v Inuit Tapirisat of Canada*, [1980] 2 SCR 735 and *Thorne's Hardware Ltd v The Queen*, [1983] 1 SCR 106.

Kingdom).[11] Because of the prodigious powers of the executive branch, the ability to access administrative law is crucial for the realization of the rule of law.

With our system of government in mind, we'll now turn to one of the most influential interpretations of the rule of law in administrative law: Victorian-era legal scholar Albert Venn Dicey. His conception of the rule of law heavily pervaded early 20th-century British and Canadian jurisprudence.[12] In Dicey's view, the rule of law possessed three features: (1) the absence of arbitrary and discretionary authority in government, but especially in the executive branch and the administrative state; (2) formal legal equality so that every person—including and especially public officials—would equally be subject to the law; and (3) the existence of constitutional law as a binding part of the ordinary law of the land.[13] The Diceyan model saw the judiciary as guardians of common law checks—or, in his words, "regular law" constraints—on the arbitrary power of the executive and its statutory delegates in order to protect individual rights. Dicey therefore considered the courts to be the chief rule-of-law check on the executive arbitrariness in a Westminster system of government and the primary means to control delegations of power to administrative bodies.

Common law courts, in this model, provide the institutional connection between rights and remedies and are the site for the development of the general principles of the common law constitution. According to Dicey, judge-made law combined with an unwritten constitution represented a better mode of legal constraint than written codes and constitutions because this combination was believed to be less vulnerable to executive attempts to suspend or remove rights. To take away the right to individual freedom in the English constitution, Dicey wrote, would require "a thorough revolution in the institutions and manners of the nation."[14] In a common law constitutional system like Britain's, the constitution is not the source, but the result of individual rights being defined and enforced by the common law courts. Dicey argued that this particular institutional advantage of the courts meant that they were best placed not only to control the political executive in the name of the rule of law, but also to provide superior protection of common law rights like liberty and property in the English system. The justification for judicial intervention rested on a number of grounds, including: (1) the institutional role of the courts as the principal external check on

---

11 Canada, as a former British colony, not only possesses a written constitution, but has also inherited the "unwritten" British constitution. In Britain, the constitution is said to be unwritten because no single document defines its constitutional system. Instead, a collection of statutes, decrees, conventions, customs or traditions, and royal prerogatives comprise the constitution. Seen from this perspective, it would be a mistake to think that a single document, even if comprehensive, could ever capture an entire constitution. For most countries, a constitution comprises a mix of written and unwritten sources including customary law, conventions, treaties, and other legal documents.

12 His influence and his politics endure, despite Harry Arthurs's concession that to talk about Dicey is to "belabour a horse which is thought to have died so long ago, after assaults so numerous and savage, that humane considerations might dictate another line of investigation"—see HW Arthurs, "Rethinking Administrative Law: A Slightly Dicey Business" (1979) Osgoode Hall LJ 1 at 4.

13 Ordinary law usually means domestic law, and international law only if it has been incorporated into domestic law by Parliament. This chapter focuses on domestic law. Chapter 16 explores the relationship between international human rights norms and administrative law. This term carried special meaning for Dicey as he considered the rule of law to be a distinctively British achievement which made Britain superior to all other nations.

14 Albert V Dicey, *Introduction to the Study of the Law of the Constitution*, 8th ed (London: MacMillan, 1926; reprinted 1996, Holmes Beach, FL: Gaunt) at 197.

executive and agency powers; (2) the specific task allocated to the courts through administrative law to constrain administrative discretion by ensuring that an administrative body did not overstep the jurisdiction that the legislature had set down in the statute; and (3) the judicial perception that a fundamental role of courts was to protect and vindicate the private autonomy of affected individuals, primarily through common law rights derived from contract, tort, and property law.

One key consequence of the Diceyan model was that administrative bodies—for more than half of the 20th century—were viewed with distrust as almost inherently lawless forms of governance and should be shown no curial deference in the review of their decisions.[15] In matters of agency interpretation of their statutory grants of power, his theory of the rule of law argued for the primacy of a correctness standard of review, created by judges in the common law to scrutinize administrative decisions on their merits, and meant that courts need not defer to, or show respect for, the decisions made by administrative bodies that implicated common law rights. This perception worsened when it became clear that a 20th-century Parliament could no longer provide proper oversight of the complex of administrative agencies in a modern state through regular legislative scrutiny or through political practices like ministerial responsibility.

Finally, in the traditional Diceyan model, Parliament was held to be institutionally sovereign and supreme over the other two branches of government. Parliament was considered the primary source of law—not the common law courts—as well as the source of most government power. If the use of public power was not authorized by Parliament, or if a decision-maker had acted beyond the powers delegated to it, then these actions would be considered *ultra vires* by the courts.[16] In the legal hierarchy that existed before a written constitution, Parliament (or a provincial legislature) could create statutes that conformed with, contradicted, or even overrode the common law. The rule of law required, however, that if a government wished to enact a valid legislation overriding the common law, the statute must contain language clearly expressing this purpose. If the statute contained such language, then judges could not refuse to recognize the language and were compelled to interpret and apply the statute as intended by Parliament.

SCENARIO AND QUESTIONS: NEXT STEPS

We are going to return to the scenario above, but this time with a Diceyan conception of the rule of law in mind.

At the same time as your restaurant's liquor licence was cancelled, you saw the minister on TV announcing his intention to respond to numerous complaints from the public by cracking down on members of your organization's proselytizing. He announced a new

---

15 Dicey's political views can be labelled classical liberalism, which aligns with some varieties of libertarianism. See, for example, a complementary view held by political economist Friedrich Hayek: "When the administration interferes with the private sphere of the citizen ... the problem of discretion becomes relevant to us; and the principle of the rule of law, in effect, means that the administrative authorities should have no discretionary powers in this respect." See Friedrich A von Hayek, *The Constitution of Liberty* (Chicago: University of Chicago Press, 1978) at 213 [*Hayek*].

16 For a more detailed exposition of the implications of Dicey's *ultra vires* model, see Paul P Craig, "The Nature and Purpose of Administrative Law" in *Administrative Law*, 8th ed (London: Sweet & Maxwell, 2016).

policy aimed to "stamp out" True Believers' disruptive and disorderly activities such as pamphleteering, going door-do-door to promote their religious views, and posting bail. He warned that no person would be beyond reach of the government. Later he tweeted the names of True Believers who he viewed as particularly problematic—yours was one of them.

After this, you visit a lawyer to seek advice. The lawyer tells you that the applicable statute, *An Act Concerning the Responsible Provision of All Liquor in the Province*, contains the following provisions:

> 5. The ultimate exercise of the functions, duties and powers of the British Columbia Liquor Board shall be vested in one person with the title of Commissioner.
>
> 10. The Board is authorized to grant, refuse or cancel liquor permits and may refuse to grant any permit for any reason at any time.
>
> 15. The Board may cancel any permit at its discretion.
>
> 35. The Board has exclusive jurisdiction to determine the extent of its jurisdiction under this Act or the regulations, to determine a fact or question of law necessary to establish its jurisdiction, and to determine whether or in what manner it shall exercise its jurisdiction.[17]
>
> 36. Except to such extent as the responsible Minister may order otherwise, all awards, orders and any other decisions of the Board shall not be subject to appeal or be liable to be questioned in any court.[18]

1. How would you characterize the rule of law problem(s) in this part of the scenario? Go back and look at your definition of the rule of law. Does it apply here? Why or why not?

2. What problems for the rule of law might Dicey identify in this scenario? For example, have your common law rights been negatively affected by the BCLCB's decision? By the minister's actions?

3. Can you take either the BCLCB or the minister to court? What are the barriers you face? How might they be overcome?

4. Do you want any other outcome or remedy?

B. Arbitrariness and the Rule of Law

The ever-present political and legal problem of the arbitrary use of public power profoundly animates rule-of-law attempts to ensure the legality, reasonableness, and fairness of administrative processes and their outcomes. In administrative law, the principle of the rule of law seeks to prevent illegality and constrain arbitrariness in the exercise of public authority by political and legal officials in terms of their jurisdiction over process and substance.

All branches of government—executive, legislative, judicial, administrative—can behave arbitrarily in relation to the other branches of government as well as to particular individuals. For example, if the federal or a provincial government acts in contravention of the constitutional division of powers, it is acting arbitrarily and will be found *ultra vires* its jurisdiction. If one branch of government attempts to monopolize government power, or encroaches on the powers or jurisdiction of another branch, the action will offend the doctrine of the separation of powers. If a decision-maker in government uses statutory powers outside the purpose of the enabling statute, the decision-maker will have acted outside of its jurisdiction and the decision will be invalidated because it is incorrect or unreasonable in administrative law.

---

17 This statutory provision is called a privative clause.
18 This is another kind of privative clause, called an ouster clause.

Arbitrariness commonly connotes indifference by the decision-maker about the **procedures** chosen to reach an outcome. Indifference about the procedures used to make a decision makes it more likely that the result will be unjust or unfair. In Canada, it is a generally held belief that all government decisions should be made using processes that put relevant considerations before decision-makers who must strive to achieve the best possible outcomes. As Binnie J wrote regarding procedural fairness in the *Mavi* decision: "it is certainly not to be presumed that Parliament intended that administrative officials be free to deal unfairly with people subject to their decisions ... [because the] simple overarching requirement is fairness, and this 'central' notion of the 'just exercise of power'..." motivates both good governance and judicial oversight.[19] In cases involving procedural fairness, then, we must always ask the question: "Is this a just exercise of power?" We would therefore likely think that it is inappropriate for an Immigration and Refugee Board member to select a coin toss as a procedure to decide something as important as a refugee claim. Arbitrariness can also be associated with a unilateral method of decision-making such as one that is not sufficiently consultative or participatory.

In addition to the examples concerning procedure and jurisdiction, a decision may be found arbitrary in **substance** because it is biased, illogical, unreasonable, or capricious. In other words, it will offend what appear to be shared standards of reasonableness, rationality, or morality. Such a decision may exhibit a lack of care, concern, or good judgment on the part of the decision-maker toward the affected individual or group. It can, instead of a justified response, show mere opinion, preference, stereotyping, or negative discrimination. Decision-makers act arbitrarily when they treat individuals with a lack of respect, ignore dignity interests, or deny the equal moral worth that we all share as members of the Canadian political community.[20] Arbitrariness can also suggest that a decision-maker possesses unconstrained discretionary powers, such that he or she alone can decide on how to use these expansive powers. Historically, this type of arbitrariness has been associated with the type of untrammelled power wielded by absolute monarchs. A decision, for example, may exhibit unilateralness to a degree that becomes oppressive and will therefore be considered an abuse of power or made in bad faith. This understanding informs familiar criticisms of majority decision-making that infringes minority rights.

Finally, arbitrariness seems to suggest the absence of a rule, but it should be remembered that judges or administrators can arbitrarily apply a valid rule. For example, a common rule is that a contract must be in writing. But what if the person to whom the rule applies cannot write (perhaps due to a lack of education or because of a physical disability). The rule, if applied rigidly and without exception in this context, could be deemed arbitrary.

Dicey's conception of the rule of law, albeit important, is rather skeletal. We will briefly turn to other thinkers—two legal scholars and a judge—to put more flesh on the bones, or more content into this rule of law story. In contrast to Dicey's common law model that offers institutional control of executive discretion through the judiciary, other theories of the rule of law recommend a legal system that aspires to realize a set of formal attributes that

---

19　*Canada (Attorney General) v Mavi*, 2011 SCC 30, [2011] 2 SCR 504 at paras 39 and 42 [*Mavi*].

20　The benefits of the rule of law can extend to non-citizens who are present in Canadian territory. Cases like *Baker v Canada (Minister of Citizenship and Immigration)*, [1999] 2 SCR 817, [*Baker*] which involve non-citizens in the immigration and refugee context, have posed challenges for, and often been the source of extensions to the scope of, procedural fairness in administrative law. See the cases examined in Chapter 6.

can guide the conduct of all legal subjects, including public officials. A common set of principles has evolved over time and includes those enunciated by Lon Fuller, Joseph Raz, and, more recently, British jurist Lord Bingham (former Master of the Rolls and Lord Chief Justice of England and Wales). See Figure 4.2 for a comparison of these principles.

The presumed virtue of these formal requirements rests on the belief that they permit individuals to predict state officials' responses to their behaviour, thereby allowing them to avoid sanctions and benefit from a known ambit of freedom. Such a presumption is

Figure 4.2   Some Other Attributes of the Rule of Law

	Lon Fuller's Eight Principles of Legality[21]	Joseph Raz's Incomplete List of Rule-of-Law Principles[22]	Lord Bingham's Primary Rule and Sub-Rules[23]
Where do you see overlap and differences: • with Dicey's definition? • with the Supreme Court of Canada's definition? • among these three thinkers? Note how the number of requirements has grown over time.	• laws should be general • laws should be promulgated so that citizens might know the standards to which they are being held • retroactive rule-making and application should be minimized • laws should be understandable • laws should not be contradictory • laws should not demand the impossible, requiring conduct beyond the abilities of those affected to meet	• laws should be prospective, open, and clear • laws should be relatively stable • the making of particular laws should be guided by open, stable, clear, and general rules • judicial independence should be guaranteed • procedural fairness must be observed by public officials in their decision-making • courts should have review powers over the implementation of the other principles	Primary rule: all persons, public or private, should be bound by, and entitled to benefit from, promulgated, prospective laws publicly administered in the courts Subrules: • laws should be accessible, intelligible, clear and predictable (so far as possible) • questions of legal right and liability should ordinarily be resolved by the application of law, not the exercise of discretion • laws should apply equally to all except where objective differences require differentiation • ministers and all public officials must exercise public powers in good faith, fairly, for the purposes conferred, reasonably, and within jurisdiction

21   See Lon L Fuller, *The Morality of Law*, rev ed (New Haven & London: Yale University Press, 1969) at 39, 46-90 [Fuller].

22   Joseph Raz, "The Rule of Law and Its Virtue," in *The Authority of Law: Essays on Law and Morality* (Oxford: Clarendon Press, 1979) at 214-19 [Raz, 1979].

23   Tom Bingham, *The Rule of Law* (London: Allen Lane, 2010) at 37 [Bingham].

- there should be congruence between the laws as announced and their actual administration

- courts should be easily accessible[24] and have effective remedies[25]
- the discretion of crime-preventing agencies should be constrained

- laws should adequately protect fundamental rights
- dispute resolution processes, without prohibitive cost or undue delay, should be provided when parties cannot resolve matters themselves
- adjudicative procedures provided by the state should be fair
- the state should comply with its obligations in international law

---

especially important for criminal law.[26] People can also interact with each other secure in the knowledge that they know in advance the rules that will likely apply to their behaviour should a dispute arise between them. Advance knowledge is, of course, not empirically true, and this claim relies on the ability of the law to align with other co-existing normative orders (for example, shared general norms, customs, etiquette, religious, or business norms) and to have access to this knowledge through the services of a legal professional. Individuals can also rely on a certain determinacy in the application of law so that like cases will be treated alike. In this minimalist form, the rule of law can be equated with **legal formalism** because adherence to the rule of law does not mean that the resulting laws are substantively just, only that they are valid and meet the minimum legal conditions considered essential for the realization of procedural justice. These principles guide law-making wherever it is found in the state: legislative, judicial, and administrative. Notably, unlike

---

24 Raz offers no views on how such access should be realized in practice, and whether or not access to the courts constitutes a positive duty on government. He writes: "Long delays or excessive costs may effectively turn the most enlightened law into a dead letter and frustrate one's ability effectively to guide oneself by the law (Raz, 1979, *supra* note 22 at 217). For judicial treatment of undue delay, see the discussion of *Blencoe v British Columbia (Human Rights Commission)*, 2000 SCC 44, [2000] 2 SCR 307 in Chapter 6 as part of the duty of fairness. For a discussion of our current access to justice crisis in Canada, and the important role of the administrative state in providing access, see Chapter 9.

25 Raz emphasizes the necessity for a legal system to provide effective remedies so that affected legal subjects can vindicate their rights. Chapter 2 discusses the variety of administrative law remedies a tribunal might impose as well as those available through judicial review.

26 These principles differ according to the specific area of law. The principle of legality in criminal law, for example, includes the prohibition against retroactive criminalization or *ex post facto* laws as well as the void for vagueness doctrine with respect to provisions within criminal statutes. See *R v Grant*, 2009 SCC 32, [2009] 2 SCR 353, where the Supreme Court explains the relationship between the principles of the administration of justice and the rule of law in a case concerning improper police conduct and the admission of evidence. On the relationship between the rule of law and vagueness, see Marc Ribeiro, *Limiting Arbitrary Power: The Vagueness Doctrine in Canadian Constitutional Law* (Vancouver: University of British Columbia Press, 2004).

Dicey, these other conceptions do not assume that administrative bodies are inherently lawless. Rather, if they follow these principles, they too may be more likely to engage in lawful activity, and reviewing bodies, like the courts, may be obliged to show deference to their decisions.

Behind Lon Fuller's principles of legality lies a vision of the relationship between a government and the citizenry as a "kind of reciprocity" because the enterprise of law is not a "one-way projection of authority" onto legal subjects as in authoritarian regimes; rather, it respects people's fundamental autonomy.[27] For example, the principle of publicity guides accountability and transparency in government decision-making because secret laws undermine legality and frustrate the citizen's ability to know where he or she stands in relation to a system of rights, benefits distribution, and/or enforcement and punishment. To take another example, the principle of congruency ensures a match between the rules as announced and the rules as applied in order to avoid a legal system composed of arbitrary decrees or ad hoc directives. This last principle deeply informs discretionary decision-making in the administrative state.

Joseph Raz, though following Fuller in many respects, believes it is possible to reduce the rule of law to one basic idea: law must be capable of guiding the behaviour of its subjects.[28] Raz further claims that most of the requirements we associate with the rule of law can be derived from this one basic idea in which the rule of law as the principle of legality acts as a practical guide for making effective law, thereby minimizing the harms that the legal system might itself create. For example, overbreadth in a statutory provision is a deficiency that makes it more likely that the law will cause harm by: (1) not adequately constraining the use of power; (2) not providing guidance for individual behaviour; or (3) widening the potential to infringe a specific right, such as individual liberty. Vagueness in statutory language may present similar risks. A lack of generality in a statute, on the other hand, may violate legal equality or individual dignity interests because the classification or categorization may disproportionately "single out" a particular segment of the population. A lack of generality may also indicate negative discrimination on the grounds of race, sexual preference, or other enumerated grounds. Think here of US President Trump's travel ban that affects only Muslim citizens from six listed countries. Raz's approach therefore places a great value on the role of well-crafted legislation in modern societies, and his rule-of-law model emphasizes how statutes can provide guidance and constrain discretion through preambles, purposes, enumerated lists of examples, and other techniques. Raz's principles aim to guide both the formation and application of law, but he also emphasizes that his theory does not enumerate all of the possible principles associated with the rule of law.

Lord Bingham provides an interesting complement to legal philosophers Fuller and Raz partly because his is a current and influential judicial view.[29]

.

---

27 Fuller, *supra* note 21 at 39, 207.

28 Raz, 1979, *supra* note 22 at 214.

29 The European Commission on Democracy through Law (Venice Commission) endorsed Lord Bingham's list of essentials in its *Report on the Rule of Law* (Adopted by the Venice Commission at its 86th plenary session, 25-26 March 2011).

APPLY THESE THINKERS TO THE SCENARIO

Return to the full scenario presented above. Consider the legal deficiencies in the scenario from the perspective of each thinker. Imagine how each thinker might proscribe one solution or remedy for an identified flaw.

C. Politics and the Rule of Law

The legal significance of the rule of law remains undisputed in Canada. As a foundational principle, the rule of law is both part of the written and unwritten constitution. As an unwritten principle, the rule of law implicitly appears in the preamble to the *Constitution Act, 1867*, where it states that Canada will have a "Constitution similar in principle to that of the United Kingdom."[30] The rule of law also appears as an explicit principle in the preamble to the *Constitution Act, 1982*: "Whereas Canada is founded upon principles that recognize the supremacy of God and the rule of law."[31] Whether implicit or explicit, then, the principle of the rule of law applies to the entire constitutional order and every part of government.[32] In addition to the basic attributes identified in Section I.B above, the Supreme Court of Canada in the *Manitoba Language Rights Reference* case described the rule of law as a "highly textured expression ... conveying ... a sense of orderliness, of subjection to known legal rules and of executive accountability to legal authority."[33] For the court, Canada is a "society of legal order and normative structure"[34] where the rule of law is recognized as a "fundamental postulate of our constitutional structure"[35] and exemplified by the **principle of legality**. As an expression of a commitment to peace, order, and good government over violence, anarchy, and arbitrary power, the rule of law, to the court's mind, represented a "philosophical view of society" that "in the Western tradition is linked with basic democratic notions."[36] Just how the principle of legality is linked to basic democratic notions was not spelled out fully in the *Manitoba Language Rights Reference* and we will return to the question of how the principles of democracy and the rule of law are related to each other in Section II.C below.

---

30   Preamble to the *Constitution Act, 1867* (UK), 30 & 31 Vict, c 3, reprinted in RSC 1985, App II, No 5.

31   Preamble to the *Constitution Act, 1982*, being Schedule B to the *Canada Act 1982* (UK), 1982, c 11.

32   The deepest and broadest articulation of the unwritten principle of the rule of law in the Canadian order appears in two reference cases: the *Manitoba Language Rights Reference, supra* note 5, and the *Reference re Secession of Quebec*, [1998] 2 SCR 217 [*Secession Reference*].

33   *Manitoba Language Rights Reference, supra* note 5 at para 62. In the *Manitoba Language Rights Reference*, the Supreme Court invoked the rule of law to conclude that the Manitoba government's repeated failure to respect the mandatory requirement of bilingual enactment of provincial laws rendered all subsequent unilingual legislation invalid. In order to avoid creating legal chaos in Manitoba, however, the rule-of-law principle also justified the creation of a new remedy—the delayed declaration of invalidity—which the court used to maintain the existence of the unconstitutional legal order, while giving the province time to comply by re-enacting all offending legislation.

34   *Ibid* at para 64.

35   *Ibid* at para 63.

36   *Ibid* at para 61.

As mentioned earlier, Dicey's definition of the rule of law is skeletal. Looking to richer accounts from Fuller and Raz, we see they focus on the forms that law must take and the procedures that must be used to produce valid law. But here too, in these more formalistic conceptions of the rule of law, the content has also deliberately been minimized. Without *obiter dicta* from cases included, the Supreme Court's actual legal definition of the rule of law is equally skimpy, telling us little about the kind of laws that regulate the relationship between the state and the individual or what the principle of independence and impartiality demands in *this* administrative procedure. We find the most complete account from Lord Bingham. These differences in definition, and paucity of content in the definitions provided, return us to the importance of acknowledging disagreements about the meaning of the rule of law, because it affects how we understand legal arguments and judicial interpretation. Any legal interpreter—including counsel, appellate-level judges, and adjudicators—must inevitably go "outside" law in order to determine what the rule of law means in a particular context. Because several competing conceptions of the rule of law currently exist, the interpreter must therefore choose one interpretation over another and ideally justify that choice in law.

According to Raz, the rule of law has an instrumental role as a means to realizing other important ends such as democracy, equality, and human rights—but the rule of law is not synonymous with these other goods.[37] This is because, in a society characterized by deep diversity like ours, we may agree on a common set of values that we hold important, but we will not all or always agree how these fundamental values should be ranked or weighted in relation to each other.[38] Because we live in a modern, technologically advanced pluralistic society, we require both democracy and the rule of law and this fact underscores the importance of democratic legislation in responding to different interests, perspectives, subcultures, and continuous social and economic change.[39] Judicial respect for legislation is grounded in pluralist democracy—and this respect, as will be discussed later, extends to administrative decision-makers in the executive branch. The relative autonomy of law from politics, for which Raz seems to be the strongest advocate, is a central requirement of the rule of law, but one that poses a number of challenges for the administrative state and public law.

---

37 Raz controversially states that "[a] non-democratic legal system, based on the denial of human rights, on extensive poverty, on racial segregation, sexual inequalities, and religious persecution may, in principle, conform to the requirements of the rule of law better than any of the legal systems of the more enlightened Western democracies. This does not mean that it will be better than those Western democracies. It will be an immeasurably worse legal system, but it will excel in one respect: in its conformity to the rule of law." Raz, 1979, *supra* note 22 at 211. He therefore rejects the natural law maxim that "an unjust law is no law at all."

38 In modern societies, fundamental values may conflict with or be incommensurable with each other and therefore involve tough choices or sacrifices in order to resolve the conflict. Sometimes, a constitution will select our values for us, but rank them equally in terms of importance. Consider, for example, how the Charter ranks equality and liberty equally, but explicitly excludes property interests. In a democracy, the political process is the chief forum for us to argue and collectively deliberate about which values we hold most important. These value conflicts inevitably arise in legal decisions, illustrated especially in cases involving dissents and concurrences.

39 Joseph Raz, "The Politics of the Rule of Law" (1990) 3:3 *Ratio Juris* 331 at 335 [Raz, 1990].

Raz's views resonate in Canadian jurisprudence on the rule of law. Major J, writing for the court in *Imperial Tobacco*,[40] also focused on the debates concerning the meaning of the rule of law and what principles it might incorporate, noting with approval Strayer JA's dictum that "[a]dvocates tend to read into the principle of the rule of law anything which supports their particular view of what the law should be."[41] In *Imperial Tobacco*, the Supreme Court affirmed that the rule of law does not require that legislation be prospective (except in criminal law), or general, does not prohibit the conferral of special privileges on the government, and—most surprisingly—does not ensure a fair civil trial. The court claimed that to affirm these features constitutionally, as the tobacco companies had argued, would be tantamount to endorsing one particular conception of the rule of law, thereby seriously undermining the legitimacy of judicial review.[42] Protection from unjust or unfair legislation "properly lies not in the amorphous underlying principles of our Constitution, but in its text and the ballot box."[43]

The principle of the rule of law therefore normally remains *subterranean* in most legal cases. It is like an underground stream that occasionally burbles up into full sight. When in full sight, it can be given more content, but only in connection to positive legal materials. However, it constantly informs the interpretive backdrop that judges, counsel, and claimants bring to cases.

INSIGHTS ABOUT *INSITE*?

Read the *Insite*[44] case and think about it in terms of arbitrariness and disagreements about the meaning of the rule of law. Consider especially the distinctive role of ministers in our system of government, which was discussed earlier in Section I.A.

1. According to the Supreme Court of Canada, how exactly did the minister of health act arbitrarily? To answer this question, consider the nature of the statutory provision (s 56) that conveyed his discretionary authority.

---

40 *Imperial Tobacco*, *supra* note 5, concerned a statute enacted by the province of British Columbia that permitted the province to sue manufacturers of tobacco products for compensation of tobacco-related health care costs incurred by individuals exposed to tobacco products. The statute benefited the provincial government by allowing not only the recovery of current and future costs, but also to recover costs retroactively from the past 50 years. The statute also changed rules of civil procedure in order to counter the systemic advantages that tobacco manufacturers enjoy in private law litigation by shifting the onus of proof from the government to the tobacco manufacturers. Tobacco companies had to prove, on a balance of probabilities, that their products did not cause harm. The tobacco companies argued that the shift of the evidentiary burden interfered both with the guarantee of a fair trial and the ability of judges to assess and weigh relevant evidence.

41 *Ibid* at para 33 citing *Singh v Canada (Attorney General)*, [2000] 3 FCR 185.

42 *Ibid* at para 65. Although the rule of law possesses several additional principles, there is one key attribute that it does not possess: the ability to strike down legislation. The principle must be attached to a specific constitutional provision. When legislatures use their powers validly, but from some perspectives arbitrarily, and the content of such legislation does not engage an express constitutional provision, then citizens must look to other forms of government accountability as well as the democratic process of elections for correction, not to the courts.

43 *Ibid* at para 66. See also *Bacon v Saskatchewan Crop Insurance Corp* (1999), 180 Sask R 20 at paras 30, 36 (CA).

44 *Canada (Attorney General) v PHS Community Services Society*, 2011 SCC 44, [2011] 3 SCR 134 [*Insite*]. This case concerned North America's first government-sanctioned safe injection facility, located in Vancouver, which provides medical supervision to intravenous drug users. The federal minister of health decided not to renew the exemption protecting the provincial facility from federal drug laws concerning possession and trafficking. The lack of an exemption meant that the facility would have to close.

2. A statute can indicate a ranking of values—for example, the statute in *Insite* prioritized both medical and scientific purposes as well as public health and safety. How did the judiciary, through statutory interpretation, reconcile this value conflict?

FUTURE-ORIENTED QUESTION

Recall Chapter 2 on remedies, and think again about the actual remedy that the Supreme Court employed in *Insite*. The court used the common law remedy of *mandamus* to order the minister of health to grant the exemption. This is an unusually strong remedy to use against a high-ranking public official like a minister who was delegated broad discretionary powers to make this decision. What might some of the legal or political considerations be behind the reviewing court's use of this remedy to compel the minister of health to fulfill his statutory duties in the way the court deemed to be non-arbitrary?

D. Founding the Administrative Rule of Law

The marked difference between formal (i.e., Diceyan) and more substantive approaches to the rule of law (e.g., Fuller, Raz, and Bingham) can be seen in an early administrative law case, *Roncarelli v Duplessis*,[45] which contains several examples of arbitrary power. *Roncarelli* fully illustrates one of the primary functions of the rule of law: the control of executive arbitrariness. The judgment is a complex one containing a majority decision with three concurring judgments and three dissents. We will focus only on three—the majority (Martland, Locke JJ, and Kerwin CJ), Rand J (concurring), and Cartwright J (dissent). Both the majority and the dissent represent, to equal degrees, the prevailing judicial attitudes in administrative law at the time. Rand J's decision is a creature of a different kind. His judgment anticipates another influential rule of law thinker—Ronald Dworkin—whose explicitly substantive conception of the rule of law we will turn to in a moment.[46]

READ *RONCARELLI V DUPLESSIS*

As you are reading, think about the following:

- Note the similarities and some of the differences between the scenario presented above and the actual case.
- Note how each of the three decisions characterizes the nature of the legal harm done by Duplessis differently. Consider how this matters for the rule of law.
- Finally, note how Rand J's judgment links together arbitrariness, discretion, and the rule of law.

1. What is the legal significance of the fact that Premier Duplessis acted as both premier of the province and attorney general?
2. How does the majority's decision exhibit a formalist conception of the rule of law?

---

45 *Supra* note 5.
46 Recall the definition of a legal principle at the beginning of this chapter. This definition heavily relies on Dworkin's work concerning legal principles, interpretation, and adjudication in modern legal systems.

3. How does Cartwright J's dissent map onto a Diceyan conception of the rule of law? Even if you do not agree with his line of reasoning, identify one positive feature of his judgment.

4. If the relevant statutory provisions indicated the grounds for cancellation, such as stating that the decision-maker could take "moral and religious considerations" into account, would Rand J's judgment have to change?

FUTURE-ORIENTED QUESTION

When you get to Chapter 12, think about how a contemporary court would characterize and assess Chairman Archambault's decision under the current reasonableness standard of review.

The Supreme Court examined the actions of Maurice Duplessis and found them invalid. Invoking the unwritten principle of the rule of law, the court held that no public official is above the law. Duplessis had stepped outside of his own jurisdiction (that is, the authorized bounds of his power as attorney general) by ordering the revocation of Roncarelli's liquor licence.[47] He also inappropriately exercised the jurisdiction that was properly given to the chairperson of the Quebec Liquor Commission (QLC) by the enabling statute. For the majority, the main legal wrong committed against the rule of law was the violation of the legal principle of validity. Because every official act must be justified by law or be found *ultra vires*, the decision could not be considered valid because the statute did not give the power to cancel licences to either the premier or the attorney general.[48]

Cartwright J's dissent emphasizes parliamentary supremacy in the Diceyan model in order to come to the opposite conclusion to that of the majority. For him the legislature had clearly spoken by being silent on any rules, standards, or other forms of guidance that could constrain the broad statutory grant of discretion. His dissent was, of course, legally sound at the time. Consider how the Charter has now minimized the reach of this model of judicial decision-making—for example, by enumerating a guaranteed set of rights (such as freedom of religion and association) that cannot be limited by state action unless the limits are justifiable under s 1.

Finally, notice how Rand J starts in a similar place as the majority by suggesting that Duplessis dictated Chairman Archambault's decision, thereby usurping the authority delegated to the QLC. But what if, as David Dyzenhaus has asked in his scholarship, Archambault had acted entirely on his own in cancelling Roncarelli's licence?[49] Had Archambault not consulted Duplessis, his decision would have at that time been found valid, particularly because the enabling statute granted Archambault seemingly unfettered discretion. On this basis, only when an administrative authority acts beyond the power given to it by Parliament can the courts legitimately enforce the rule of law or reaffirm the separation of powers. Perhaps for this reason, Rand J's judgment diametrically counters Cartwright J's dissent and goes much further than the majority and the other concurrence. His judgment exemplifies

---

47   The attorney general, at most, could only provide advice on the matter. The involvement of a premier was, however, extraordinary in legal terms.

48   This is also the view taken by Peter Hogg, *Constitutional Law of Canada: 2011 Student Edition* (Toronto: Carswell, 2011) at 34-4.

49   David Dyzenhaus, "The Deep Structure of Roncarelli v Duplessis" (2004) 53 UNBLJ 111 at 125.

a more value-laden substantive conception of the rule of law and one that anticipates Ronald Dworkin's "rights conception of the rule of law."[50]

For Dworkin, the rule of law necessarily entails the judicial determination of rights through principled interpretation in hard cases where a legal answer must be crafted by judges from existing legal sources (for example, statutes, regulations, constitutional documents, and case law) and principles of political morality (this means the basic tenets of modern liberalism for Dworkin). His legal subject is an individual bearer of rights who is entitled to demand the resolution of disputes over the content of these rights through the legal system—specifically through courts, which he calls the "independent forum of principle."[51] A principled interpretation must fit the existing positive law, but it also must be compatible with select principles from a larger political morality. Government respect for individual freedom, freedom of association, and equality, for example, would be principled requirements of this larger political morality. A key consequence is that judges, not legislators, are ultimately charged with guarding the integrity of the constitutional order because, as the chief political actors in the forum of principle, they possess the knowledge and the skills—honed through their unique access to the interpretation of the law—to be the better articulators of a constitutionalized public morality.[52] Dworkin's theory of adjudication has as its central focus a conception of justice designed to further political principles of autonomy, dignity, equality, and liberty for all individuals in the political community. Politics, on his account, should be held to a higher standard because we ought to prioritize the pursuit of justice in society. Of all of the theories we have considered, Dworkin's gives the judiciary the most power and potentially sanctions what some critics call "judicial activism."[53]

Rand J might be seen to fit this model. His judgment states that public authorities, especially those with broad discretionary powers, are always constrained by the unwritten principle of the rule of law, even when a statute contains no explicit or written constraints:

> In public regulation of this sort there is no such thing as absolute and untrammelled "discretion," that is that action can be taken on any ground or for any reason that can be suggested to the mind of the administrator; no legislative Act can, without express language, be taken to contemplate an unlimited arbitrary power exercisable for any purpose, however capricious or irrelevant, regardless of the nature or purpose of the statute. … "Discretion" necessarily implies good faith in discharging public duty; there is always a perspective within which a statute is intended to operate; and any clear departure from its lines or objects is just as objectionable as fraud or corruption.[54]

---

50 Two significant texts for this argument are Dworkin's *A Matter of Principle* (Cambridge, MA: Harvard University Press, 1985) at 30-32 and *Law's Empire* (Cambridge, MA: Harvard University Press, 1986).

51 See *A Matter of Principle*, *ibid*, and specifically, chapter 2, "The Forum of Principle."

52 Contrary to Dworkin, the authority of the courts in Raz's model to constrain legislation does not come from their superior wisdom or from their guardianship of superior law. Raz, 1990, *supra* note 39 at 336.

53 Many democratic theorists have criticized Dworkin's theory of adjudication and his conception of the rule of law, see: Allan C Hutchinson & Patrick Monahan, eds, *The Rule of Law: Ideal or Ideology* (Toronto: Carswell, 1987); Jeremy Waldron, *Law and Disagreement* (Oxford: Oxford University Press, 1999); Christopher Manfredi, *Judicial Power and the Charter: Canada and the Paradox of Liberal Constitutionalism*, 2d ed (Toronto: Oxford University Press, 2001); and Ran Hirschl, *Towards Juristocracy: The Origins and Consequences of the New Constitutionalism* (Cambridge, MA: Harvard University Press, 2004).

54 *Roncarelli*, *supra* note 5 at 140.

Second, even if Chairman Archambault had acted on his own in cancelling Roncarelli's licence, he would have used his discretionary powers inappropriately. Regardless of who actually was the ultimate decision-maker, the decision offended the rule of law because being a Jehovah's Witness was not a relevant factor for a decision concerning the continuation of a liquor licence for operating a restaurant. The true nature of the decision was to punish Roncarelli for exercising his civil right to post bail.

Lastly, according to Rand J the decision contradicted the substantive content of the rule of law:

> That, in the presence of expanding administrative regulation of economic activities, such a step and its consequences are to be suffered by the victim without recourse or remedy, that an administration according to law is to be superseded by action dictated by and according to the arbitrary likes, dislikes and irrelevant purposes of public officers acting beyond their duty, would signalize the beginning of disintegration of the rule of law as a fundamental postulate of our constitutional structure. An administration of licences on the highest level of fair and impartial treatment to all may be forced to follow the practice of "first come, first served," which makes the strictest observance of equal responsibility to all of even greater importance.[55]

Conventionally in public law, the rule of law's constraints on government actors seeks to prevent such "[virtual] vocation outlawry" through enforcement of the purpose of the statute and good faith decision-making achieved through the use of fair procedures.[56] Rand J added more judicial content: the administrative tribunal violated Roncarelli's fundamental rights—freedom of religion, freedom of expression, freedom to pursue his livelihood—thereby damaging the normative relationship between the state and the citizen. Rand J did so, perhaps controversially, without access to a constitutionalized bill of rights like the Charter. For that reason, Rand's account of the rule of law should give pause for thought about the scope of judicial power in a democracy.

On a formalist account, administrative law concerns the written statutes, rules, and principles that govern public decision-makers. Public decision-makers must not act outside their authority, must not abuse their authority, and must be seen not to do so. Judicial scrutiny within administrative law focuses on the limits on the authority given to decision-makers by statute or prerogative. On the more substantive account, such authority is bound by the purpose and terms of the statute, by regulations and guidelines, by the constitution, by written and unwritten legal principles, and by a broadly accepted public morality. Formally valid exercises of discretion can offend the rule of law and can subsequently be determined to be a legal wrong as an abuse of power. *Roncarelli* still stands as a paradigmatic example of a deeper principled and purposive approach to understanding how the rule of law animates administrative law.

The rule of law, like other foundational philosophical concepts (for example, democracy, freedom, autonomy, and equality) can be considered essentially contested.[57] Legal and

---

55 *Ibid* at 142.
56 *Ibid* at 141.
57 See Jeremy Waldron, "Is the Rule of Law an Essentially Contested Concept (in Florida)?" (2002) 21 Law & Phil 137. Waldron discusses how disagreements about underlying normative issues—issues such as what values the rule of law is meant to promote or what are its most important features—are pervasive and predictable. Such disagreements inform how arguments are framed in litigation and in government policy-making.

political theories like those canvassed above constitute the often unstated background assumptions that inform judicial understandings of the rule of law and appear either implicitly or explicitly in specific cases. Deeply embedded within any discussion of the rule of law is a debate about the legitimate scope and content of judicial power, particularly in a democratic state.

The growth of the regulatory state and administrative tribunals underscores the importance of bureaucratic justice and the expectation that one can "conduct one's life without being frustrated by governmental arbitrariness or unpredictability."[58] As Raz argued, implementing the principle of the rule of law in modern government requires an elaborate institutional complex staffed by competent and relatively impartial officials, using predictable and fair procedures in order to make reasoned and public decisions that, if an individual wishes to dispute, can potentially be argued by specially trained legal professionals and reviewed by an independent judiciary. In Canada, the ethos behind this elaborate institutional complex is characterized by two phrases: "deference as respect" and "institutional dialogue."

II. DEFERENCE AS RESPECT: THE CANADIAN MODEL OF ADMINISTRATIVE LAW

In Section I, we saw how the rule of law acts as a foundational metaprinciple[59] for the entire legal system by organizing and knitting together an open set of other related principles such as the principle of legality, the principle of the separation of powers, the principle of judicial independence, the principle of access to justice, the principles of fundamental justice, the principle of the honour of the Crown,[60] and so on. In the Canadian context, the rule of law has a core jurisprudential meaning—the principle of legality—which succinctly conveys the basic intuition that law should always authorize, and minimize the risks of arbitrariness, in public power. Views from several prominent legal theorists as well as key Supreme Court decisions were invoked to illustrate how this principle of legality procedurally restrains arbitrary power in three ways: first, by guiding and constraining the actions of public officials; second, by regulating the activity of law-making; and third, by seeking to minimize harms that may be created by the law itself. When it comes to controlling for substantive arbitrariness, we looked to Rand J's judgment as invoking a more modern rule of law that potentially authorizes greater judicial intervention based on public law principles and values, not purely based on private law rights as with Dicey's earlier model.

While the rule of law traditionally serves as a bulwark against the executive branch of government and supports judicial oversight of broad statutory grants of discretion, this role becomes more complicated in the modern administrative state with powers

---

58 Raz, 1990, *supra* note 39 at 332.

59 I am paraphrasing Hayek here, who calls the rule of law a "meta-legal doctrine." See Hayek, *supra* note 15 at 206 and all of Chapter 14.

60 Chapter 3 examines the rule-of-law dimensions of the honour of the Crown in Aboriginal administrative law and the duty to consult and accommodate Indigenous interests in decision-making processes. The Supreme Court confirmed the principle of the honour of the Crown and its supporting doctrine of the duty to consult as constitutional limits on executive discretion in *Beckman v Little Salmon/Carmacks First Nation*, 2010 SCC 53, [2010] 3 SCR 103.

legislatively delegated to different kinds of administrative bodies. The role of courts can be understood in two contrasting ways. On the one hand, courts provide an essential accountability function by policing the exercise of delegated powers to ensure that they are confined to terms and purposes specified by the authorizing statute—in other words, jurisdiction. On the other hand, judges are conscious of the separation of powers and, given their lack of expertise in determining the merits of certain policy-making exercises, are themselves under rule-of-law constraints to respect the legislative and executive branches.

Many of the authors in this textbook allude to the lengthy and complex history in relations among the administrative state, democracy, and the rule of law. As discussed earlier in Chapter 1, at the beginning of the 20th century the emerging administrative state was often seen as a threat both to parliamentary sovereignty and to the rule of law because delegated powers from the political executive operated outside legislative scrutiny.[61] Not only did these new administrative bodies possess substantial powers to restrict freedom, redistribute property, and make decisions on matters relating to individual rights, but they also handled many more cases than courts did. Governments—particularly the executive—could control these new bodies through the appointments process and had significant influence over delegated policy areas. The growth of regulatory law also meant an expanded scope of discretion for government officials in interpreting standards and defining goals in various statutory schemes and executive regulations. This development was extremely worrisome for those concerned with accountability because Parliament, the responsible minister, and the courts together could not provide full oversight, given their lack of specialized policy knowledge and the sheer quantity of cases that the administrative state generated (especially in areas such as immigration or social security).

The early history of the relations between the courts and the other branches of government in administrative law began as a bipolar relationship: courts showed greater deference to executive decision-making and prerogative powers, as well as to legislation, but were highly antagonistic toward decisions made by actual administrative bodies that were not seen as credible or competent decision-makers on questions of law. The history of this bipolar relationship is nowhere better exemplified than in the courts' treatment of statutory delegates with a significant democratic pedigree. Judicial review of municipal by-laws fluctuated between extreme deference on the basis that municipal councils were accountable to their electorate and pointed intervention on the basis that the contested by-law was patently unreasonable on rule-of-law grounds.[62]

As a result of the expansion of the administrative state, and well before the Charter, administrative law had to struggle to construct a relationship with the modern state that respected the expertise and policy choices of various administrative agencies and boards

---

61 Chapter 1 explains how Canadian courts gradually became aware of the problems of legitimacy when intervening in decisions made by administrative agencies and sought to set some limits to the exercise of their own reviewing powers.

62 Recent jurisprudence holds that, though municipalities are often given broad legislative discretion, their discretion is not unfettered, and their decision-making must provide reasonable grounds for courts to defer. See *Catalyst Paper Corp v North Cowichan (District)*, 2012 SCC 2, [2012] 1 SCR 5. These considerations will also inform judicial scrutiny of elected school boards and First Nations' band council decisions.

while simultaneously recognizing the legitimacy and effectiveness of parallel bodies of justice, such as administrative tribunals and labour adjudicators. The older and classical liberal view of the minimal state, like Dicey's, no longer matched reality, and courts had to change their institutional practices to acknowledge the legitimacy of the welfare state. McLachlin CJ drew on this historical context in *Alberta v Hutterian Brethen*: "Concern about overextension of regulatory authority is understandable. Governments should not be free to use a broad delegated authority to transform a limited-purpose licensing scheme into a *de facto* universal identification system beyond the reach of legislative oversight. ... [H]ostility to the regulation-making process is out of step with this court's jurisprudence and with the realities of the modern regulatory state."[63] Because so many of these administrative bodies—labour and marketing boards, for example—were created to respond to political pressures and regulatory problems, courts, through administrative law, had to rethink their attitude in relation to them in the post-war era. This attitude was usually characterized by the term "deference."

In administrative law, the attitude of courts to other branches now aspires to be a kind of respectful deference. The phrase originates in an academic article by legal scholar David Dyzenhaus where he contrasts the principle of *"deference as respect"* to the more traditional Diceyan approach, which he labels *"deference as submission."*[64] For Dyzenhaus, Cartwright J's dissent in *Roncarelli* exemplifies deference as submission because the legal order at that time required judges to capitulate to problematic legislative intent out of obedience to the principle of parliamentary supremacy; in this sense, Parliament was akin to an absolute monarch. The phrase—deference as respect—was first cited with approval by L'Heureux-Dubé J in the landmark *Baker*[65] case:

> In my opinion, the approach taken to the children's interests shows that this decision was unreasonable. ... The officer was completely dismissive of the interests of Ms Baker's children. As I will outline in detail in the paragraphs that follow, I believe that the failure to give serious weight and consideration to the interests of the children constitutes an unreasonable exercise of the discretion conferred by the section, notwithstanding the important deference that should be given to the decision of the immigration officer. Professor Dyzenhaus has articulated the concept of "deference as respect" as follows:
>
> > Deference as respect requires not submission but a respectful attention to the reasons offered or which could be offered in support of a decision ...
>
> > The reasons of the immigration officer show that his decision was inconsistent with the values underlying the grant of discretion. They therefore cannot stand up to the somewhat probing examination required by the standard of reasonableness.

The **key take-away** from the *Baker* case is that the phrase "deference as respect" justifies an attitude of judicial humility and respect toward other decision-makers when their procedures and resulting decisions are fair, reasonable, proportionate, and communicated through quality reasons.

---

63 *Alberta v Hutterian Brethren of Wilson Colony*, 2009 SCC 37, [2009] 2 SCR 567 at para 40.

64 David Dyzenhaus, "The Politics of Deference: Judicial Review and Democracy" in Michael Taggart, ed, *The Province of Administrative Law* (Oxford: Oxford University Press, 1997) at 286.

65 *Baker, supra* note 20 at para 65.

JUDICIAL REVIEW

Judicial review is both: (1) an institutional procedure; and (2) a remedy in itself. Courts do not have inherent appellate jurisdiction over administrative tribunals like they do with lower courts: a statute must provide a right of appeal. If no right of appeal exists, then the person must apply for judicial review. Despite the fact that courts may review executive action using administrative law, judicial review is considered an exceptional, discretionary remedy. In other words, it is neither automatic, nor is it an individual right.

Deference is a requirement of the law of **judicial review** and supports the separation of powers. The function of reviewing courts is not to routinely "second guess" substantive outcomes made by public authorities in the executive branch. Deference is not owed only in the face of a privative clause—discussed further below—but also to the special role some actors perform, to their function, and to their expertise in fact-finding, policy formation, knowledge, and interpretative skills. This attitudinal disposition also demands that a reviewing court properly construct and follow legislative intent. Judicial deference, then, clearly informs the principle of modern statutory interpretation.[66] Finally, the relationship of courts to the other two branches has been characterized as an "institutional dialogue" or a joint effort in governance amongst three counterparts who share equal responsibility for maintaining the requirements of the rule of law and the constitution as part of a less adversarial understanding of the doctrine of the separation of powers.[67]

This section now turns to several cases that illustrate how reviewing courts attempt to reconcile and implement the rule of law through the lens of deference as respect. The cases concern both procedural and substantive fairness. After considering deference within judicial review for procedural fairness, we will turn to substantive review and examine the following legal markers of deference as respect: privative clauses; expertise; statutory interpretation and the reasonableness standard of review; and adequate reasons. We will then examine how deference as respect guides proportionality review and reinforces the relationship between the rule of law and democracy in administrative law. The section concludes by briefly presenting non-deference or correctness review in administrative law.

A. The Presumptions of Deference

1. Procedural Fairness

As Chapter 5 explores, courts fiercely protect the **duty of fairness** in administrative procedures. Indeed, this is an area of administrative law where the judiciary may feel most confident and expert to intervene and recommend improvements in what they view as a deficient

---

66   See *McLean v British Columbia (Securities Commission)*, 2013 SCC 67, [2013] 3 SCR 895 at para 40.

67   On institutional dialogue, see: TRS Allan, "Constitutional Dialogue and the Justification of Judicial Review"(2003) 23 Oxford J Leg Stud 563; Stephen Gardbaum, *The New Commonwealth Model of Constitutionalism* (Oxford: Oxford University Press, 2013); Peter W Hogg & Allison A Bushell, "The Charter Dialogue Between Courts and Legislatures (or Perhaps the Charter of Rights Isn't Such a Bad Thing After All)" (1997) 35 Osgoode Hall LJ 75; Christopher P Manfredi, "The Life of a Metaphor: Dialogue in the Supreme Court, 1998-2003" (2004) 23 Sup Ct L Rev (2d) 105; Kent Roach, *The Supreme Court on Trial: Judicial Activism or Democratic Dialogue* (Toronto: Irwin Law, 2001); and Jeremy Waldron, "Some Models of Dialogue Between Judges and Legislatures" (2004) 23 Sup Ct L Rev (2d) 7.

decision-making process. This is because the common law has long held that a duty lies on all public authorities, independent of any statute or written constitution, to recognize the individual's right to be heard (the first principle of fairness) and right to an independent, impartial, and unbiased decision-maker (the second principle of fairness). The standard that a court applies to review the process used to make a decision is rigorous. Nevertheless, the principle of deference as respect informs procedural fairness.

READ THE *KHELA*[68] DECISION

Now consider the following questions:

1. What procedural obligations did the warden owe to Khela under the statute? What kinds of exceptions to procedural fairness did the statute contain?

2. How were Khela's rights, interests, and/or privileges affected by the decision to transfer him involuntarily?

3. What do you think a reviewing court might want to think about specifically in relation to the prison context? In what ways, for example, are courts more expert than the warden, and how is the warden more expert than the courts about prisons and the procedures used to make decisions in them?

4. On what basis did the Supreme Court find the warden's decision to be an unjust exercise of power? What procedural improvements did the court require?

Khela is one of the Supreme Court's major prison cases—you will encounter several more in Chapter 5. Note, however, that the remedy Khela requested was one of the oldest common law writs—*habeas corpus* (a remedy used to bring a person before a court to ensure that his or her detention or imprisonment is not illegal)—found in *Magna Carta* and long part of the British conception of the rule of law. This remedy is further discussed in Chapter 2.

After reading *Khela*, it would be tempting to conclude that no deference is owed under procedural fairness, but this would be a mistake. Lebel J, writing for the court, clearly states:

> Section 27(3) authorizes the withholding of information when the Commissioner has "reasonable grounds to believe" that should the information be released, it might threaten the security of the prison, the safety of any person or the conduct of an investigation. The Commissioner, or his or her representative, is in the best position to determine whether such a risk could in fact materialize. As a result, the Commissioner, or the Warden, is entitled to a *margin of deference* on this point. Similarly, the Warden and the Commissioner are in the best position to determine whether a given source or informant is reliable. Some deference is accordingly owed on this point as well. If, however, certain information is withheld without invoking s 27(3), deference will not be warranted, and the decision will be procedurally unfair and therefore unlawful.
> I should point out that not all breaches of the *CCRA* or the *CCRR* will be unfair.[69]

---

68 *Mission Institution v Khela*, 2014 SCC 24, [2014] 1 SCR 502 [*Khela*]. Khela was a federal inmate serving a life sentence for first-degree murder in a maximum-security prison. Shortly after he was transferred to a medium-security prison, a fellow inmate was stabbed. The prison's Security Intelligence Officer subsequently received anonymous information that Khela was involved in the stabbing. As a result of this and other information—not all of which was disclosed to Khela—the warden changed Khela's security classification, and he was involuntarily transferred back to the maximum-security facility on an "emergency basis." Khela claimed that the transfer was unlawful because it was procedurally unfair.

69 *Ibid* at paras 89-90 (emphasis added).

LEGAL PRESUMPTIONS

You will encounter a number of presumptions in administrative law. Here is one of the first. A presumption is a legal inference or assumption that a fact exists—for example, that administrative decision-makers have expertise in creating and implementing their own procedures. The adversely affected party will have to adduce concrete and contrary evidence in order to displace the presumption.

A **presumption** therefore exists that administrative decision-makers are "masters of their own procedures" unless the legislature indicates otherwise. A reviewing court will accord a "margin of deference" to the expertise that informs particular procedures, especially when discretion is present. If, however, the decision-maker acts unfairly, reviewing courts will not defer.

2. Privative Clauses

Privative clauses, like those we have seen in the scenario above, have historically posed challenges for the rule of law. Several types of privative clauses exist, but the general form is a statutory provision protecting the decisions made by public officials in boards, tribunals, and ministries either from further dispute internally (that is, a finality clause) or from external judicial review (that is, an ouster clause).[70] Privative clauses have given rise to an animated jurisprudential debate about the constitutional basis for deference.

A FULL PRIVATIVE CLAUSE

Except as provided in this Act, every order, award, direction, decision, declaration or ruling of the Board is final and shall not be questioned or reviewed in any court.

No order shall be made or process entered, and no proceedings shall be taken in any court, whether by way of injunction, judicial review, or otherwise, to question, review, prohibit or restrain the Board in any of its or his proceedings.

1. What is the "plain meaning" of this statutory language? What does this interpretation entail for the rule of law in administrative law?

Historically, the powers conferred on administrative agencies through privative clauses were often conveyed in absolute terms and, therefore, agency decisions were meant to be positively final.[71] The institutional result of privative clauses was a system of competing and irreconcilable supremacies between the legislative and judicial branches of government. It

---

70   For further discussion of privative clauses in administrative law, see Chapter 1. For a detailed analysis of the history, types, and constitutional effects of privative clauses, see David Dyzenhaus, "Disobeying Parliament? Privative Clauses and the Rule of Law" in Richard W Bauman & Tsvi Kahana, eds, *The Least Examined Branch: The Role of Legislatures in the Constitutional State* (Cambridge: Cambridge University Press, 2006) at 499.

71   The motive behind privative clauses was not simply to oust judicial meddling, but to direct judicial respect for the relative expertise of the administrative body and to provide efficient resolution of disputes and allocate scarce judicial resources by restricting access to the courts that usually, but not always, benefitted the better-resourced party.

produced a classic showdown between parliamentary sovereignty and the rule of law. Not wanting to be snookered by this dilemma, courts approached the interpretation of privative clauses in several different ways: reading them out of the statute if a jurisdictional error was implicated in the case, deferring to Parliament's intent to oust judicial oversight, and later developing methods of statutory interpretation grounded in the common law presumption that Parliament always intends to respect the principles of legality and the rule of law, even with respect to statutorily delegated powers with broad scope.[72] This last creative approach laid the basis for deference as respect, found in the foundational *CUPE*[73] decision, in which the privative clause came to be viewed as a communication from the legislature that courts should recognize the interpretive authority of the tribunal within its area of expertise, but that judges could exercise their rule-of-law powers of oversight on constitutional and jurisdictional matters. The resolution is now embedded in the legal presumption that reviewing courts will select the reasonableness standard in substantive review rather than a correctness standard that demands greater intrusiveness and no deference.

RECONCILING PRIVATIVE CLAUSES AND THE RULE OF LAW

In the *Dunsmuir*[74] decision, Binnie J captures the tension that privative clauses pose for the rule of law and explains how this tension can be reconciled:

> The existence of a privative clause ... helps to calibrate the intrusiveness of a court's review. It signals the level of respect that must be shown. Chief Justice Laskin during argument once memorably condemned the quashing of a labour board decision protected by a strong privative clause, by saying "what's wrong with these people [the judges], can't they read?" A system of judicial review based on the rule of law ought not to treat a privative clause as conclusive, but it is more than just another "factor" in the hopper ... Its existence should presumptively foreclose judicial review on the basis of *outcome* on substantive grounds unless the applicant can show that the clause, properly interpreted, permits it or there is some legal reason why it cannot be given effect.[75]

Now consider this testy exchange between Rothstein and Binnie JJ in the *Khosa*[76] decision concerning the constitutional basis for deference in administrative law.

First, Rothstein J:

> ... "Full" or "strong" privative clauses that purport to preclude the judicial review of a question brought before a reviewing court give rise to this judicial-legislative tension, which deference and standard of review were developed to resolve ...

---

72 See Chapter 1 for a discussion of privative clauses and Chapter 5 for a discussion of procedural fairness.

73 *CUPE v NB Liquor Corporation*, [1979] 2 SCR 227 [*CUPE*]. Chapter 11 on the standard of review presents *CUPE* in greater detail. In brief, *CUPE* signalled the beginning of the end of the Diceyan model for administrative law in Canada. It concerned a labour relations tribunal, the Public Service Staff Relations Board of New Brunswick, which had to interpret a poorly worded provision in its enabling statute concerning the meaning of the word "employee." On review, the Supreme Court held that deference was owed to the tribunal based on its expertise, the privative clause, and the reasonableness of its determination. In cases of statutory ambiguity, and where there are multiple interpretations that are reasonable, a reviewing court should defer to the interpretation of an expert tribunal. *CUPE* has been celebrated as *the* case that recognized that too much judicial intervention would "straightjacket" the flexible regulation needed in a complex industrial state.

74 *Dunsmuir v New Brunswick*, 2008 SCC 9, [2008] 1 SCR 190 [*Dunsmuir*].

75 *Ibid* at para 143.

76 *Canada (Citizenship and Immigration) v Khosa*, 2009 SCC 12, [2009] 1 SCR 339 [*Khosa*].

The question is, however, whether the creation of expert tribunals automatically meant that there was to be some limitation on the judicial review role of the courts, in particular on questions of law. Where the legislature enacted strong privative clauses precluding review for legal error, there is no doubt that this was the legislative intent. In my opinion, the same limit on judicial review cannot be inferred merely from the establishment of a tribunal when the legislature did not seek to immunize the tribunal's decisions from judicial review. In those cases, the creation of an administrative decision-maker did not by itself give rise to a tension with the supervisory role of the courts.[77]

And now Binnie J again:

I do not share Rothstein J's view that absent statutory direction, explicit or by necessary implication, no deference is owed to administrative decision-makers in matters that relate to their special role, function, and expertise. *Dunsmuir* recognized that with or without a privative clause, a measure of deference has come to be accepted as appropriate where a particular decision had been allocated to an administrative decision-maker rather than to the courts. This deference extended not only to facts and policy but to a tribunal's interpretation of its constitutive statute and related enactments because "there might be multiple valid interpretations of a statutory provision or answers to a legal dispute and that courts ought not to interfere where the tribunal's decision is rationally supported" (*Dunsmuir*, at para 41). A policy of deference "recognizes the reality that, in many instances, those working day to day in the implementation of frequently complex administrative schemes have or will develop a considerable degree of expertise or field sensitivity to the imperatives and nuances of the legislative regime" (*Dunsmuir*, at para 49, quoting Professor David J Mullan, "Establishing the Standard of Review: The Struggle for Complexity?" (2004), 17 CJALP 59, at p 93). Moreover, "[d]eference may also be warranted where an administrative tribunal has developed particular expertise in the application of a general common law or civil law rule in relation to a specific statutory context" (*Dunsmuir*, at para 54).

1. Despite the fact that you are still in an early stage of this introduction to administrative law, form a preliminary opinion about this disagreement (which has not yet been resolved in the jurisprudence). Do you agree with Binnie J that courts should defer to administrative bodies when there is a privative clause and on the basis of relative expertise? Or do you agree with Rothstein J that courts should only defer when the legislature has inserted a privative clause into a statute that communicates, among other things, expertise?

3. Expertise

A privative clause supports a presumption of deferential review on a reasonableness standard. Expertise, arguably, also provides a presumption of deferential substantive review. Due to the fundamental nature of this jurisprudential debate about the constitutional basis for deference, it is clear that administrative agencies and their counsel would be wise to demonstrate and emphasize their expertise because that may affect the level of deference a reviewing court may accord. To date, however, the Supreme Court of Canada has not provided much guidance on what expertise means or how administrative agencies can demonstrate it. Nevertheless, we may still, like legal scholar Harry Arthurs, have justifiable skepticism that

---

77   *Ibid* at paras 74, 77.

judges and lawyers should presumptively be considered all-around experts when compared to administrative decision-makers:

> There is no reason to believe that a judge who reads a particular regulatory statute once in his life, perhaps in worst-case circumstances, can read it with greater fidelity to legislative purpose than an administrator who is sworn to uphold that purpose, who strives to do so daily, and is well-aware of the effect upon the purpose of the various alternate interpretations. There is no reason to believe that a legally trained judge is better qualified to determine the existence or sufficiency or appropriateness of evidence on a given point than a trained economist or engineer, an arbitrator selected by the parties, or simply an experienced tribunal member who decides such cases day in and day out. There is no reason to believe that a judge whose entire professional life has been spent dealing with disputes one by one should possess an aptitude for issues which arise often because an administrative system dealing with cases in volume has been designed to strike an appropriate balance between efficiency and effective rights of participation.[78]

READ *NATIONAL CORN GROWERS*[79]

This case contextualizes what expertise means in relation to a statute concerning domestic and international trade.

1. Identify some of the important economic and political factors in this context.
2. The enabling statute contained a full privative clause (s 76(1)). Recall what this means.
3. Read the following provision from the enabling legislation and describe what information Parliament is communicating, particularly regarding its temporal dimension:

> 42. (1) The Tribunal ... shall make inquiry with respect to such of the following matters as is appropriate in the circumstances, namely,
>
> (a) ... whether the dumping or subsidizing of the goods
>
> (i) has caused, is causing or is likely to cause material injury or has caused or is causing retardation ...

To assist with the interpretation of this provision, the CIT considered the international *General Agreement on Tariffs and Trades* (GATT), which Canada had signed and incorporated into the SIMA. The GATT contained a similar provision with similar language:

---

78 HW Arthurs, "Protection against Judicial Review" (1983) 43 R du B 277 at 289.

79 *National Corn Growers Assn v Canada (Import Tribunal)*, [1990] 2 SCR 1324 [*National Corn Growers*]. This case concerned a decision, following an inquiry, by the Canadian Import Tribunal (CIT) that determined that American subsidizing of US corn would cause economic injury to Canadian producers. This was because American producers would be able to sell corn at lower prices in Canada (also known as "dumping") unless Canadian growers responded by reducing their prices. The enabling statute, the *Special Import Measures Ac*, RSC 1985, c S-15 [SIMA], permitted Canada to impose a countervailing duty on foreign-subsidized goods entering the Canadian market. The CIT's decision reaffirmed the preliminary decision of the Deputy Minister of National Revenue for Customs and Excise, and the Deputy Minister then used the CIT's decision to justify imposing a provisional duty on American corn imports. The National Corn Growers, a powerful American lobbying organization, challenged the CIT's decision as patently unreasonable on the grounds that it made erroneous findings of fact by: using GATT as an interpretive aid; interpreting goods to include imported goods; relying on potential imports and not just data about actual imports; finding material injury in an absence of an actual increase in imports; and relying on an absence of evidence connecting subsidized US corn to economic injury to Canadian corn producers in the Canadian market.

6. (a) No contracting party shall levy any anti-dumping or countervailing duty on the importation of any product of the territory of another contracting party unless it determines that the effect of the dumping or subsidization, as the case may be, is such as to cause or threaten material injury to an established domestic industry, or is such as to retard materially the establishment of a domestic industry.

4. How did the CIT interpret "goods"? How did the CIT interpret "material harm" to the Canadian market?

5. Gonthier J for the majority did not find the CIT's decision to be patently unreasonable. To do this, he closely examined the tribunal's reasoning. On what bases did Gonthier J find the CIT's decision to be wholly reasonable? Regarding scrutiny of the tribunal's reasons, he wrote:

I would add one final observation. In the course of these reasons, I have at times dealt in some detail with the manner in which the Tribunal arrived at its conclusion. Unlike my colleague, Wilson J, I do not think that the Tribunal's references to the provisions of the GATT, as well as all other aspects of the reasoning by which it arrived at its interpretation of SIMA, are totally irrelevant to a determination of an application for judicial review. With respect, I do not understand how a conclusion can be reached as to the reasonableness of a tribunal's interpretation of its enabling statute without considering the reasoning underlying it ... I would however note that this consideration must be undertaken in light of the overall question for determination, namely, whether or not the interpretation ultimately arrived at is patently unreasonable.[80]

6. Wilson J, in a concurrence, agreed with the majority's conclusion, but disagreed with the approach taken, arguing that it was not deferential enough:

Finally, it seems to me that to embark upon a detailed analysis of the extent to which the evidence will support the Tribunal's finding in the face of a privative clause is to engage in the very kind of meticulous analysis of the Tribunal's reasoning that ... courts should not conduct. The legislature has created the Canadian Import Tribunal in part so that it may review the Deputy Minister of Revenue's determinations. In the process, the legislature has made clear that neither this court nor the Federal Court of Appeal is to act as a normal appellate court in connection with the Canadian Import Tribunal's findings. In my view, this means that it is not open to us to evaluate the correctness of the Tribunal's assessment of the Deputy Minister's conclusions concerning whether particular trade practices have given rise to a "material injury." Faced with the highly charged world of international trade and a clear legislative decision to create a tribunal to dispose of disputes that arise in that context, it is highly inappropriate for courts to take it upon themselves to assess the merits of the Tribunal's conclusions about when the government may respond to another country's use of subsidies. If courts were to take it upon themselves to conduct detailed reviews of these decisions on a regular basis, the Tribunal's effectiveness and authority would soon be effectively undermined.[81]

7. Do you agree with Gonthier J or with Wilson J? Why?

Wilson J would have confined judicial review to the reasonableness of the tribunal's interpretation of s 42, but not a detailed analysis of the factual findings. One reason she gave for her worries regarding the potential for too intensive judicial scrutiny of the tribunal's findings was that:

Canadian courts have struggled over time to move away from the picture that Dicey painted toward a more sophisticated understanding of the role of administrative tribunals in the modern

---

80   *Ibid* at 1383.
81   *Ibid* at 1349-50.

Canadian state. Part of this process has involved a growing recognition on the part of courts that they may simply not be as well equipped as administrative tribunals or agencies to deal with issues which Parliament has chosen to regulate through bodies exercising delegated power, e.g. labour relations, telecommunications, financial markets, and international economic relations. Careful management of these sectors often requires the use of experts who have accumulated years of experience and a specialized understanding of the activities they supervise.[82]

The most recent Supreme Court statement on expertise comes from Karakatsanis J in *Capilano Shopping Centres*,[83] where she explains the relationship between the presumption of reasonableness and expertise:

> The presumption of reasonableness is grounded in the legislature's choice to give a specialized tribunal responsibility for administering the statutory provisions, and the expertise of the tribunal in so doing. Expertise arises from the specialization of functions of administrative tribunals like the Board which have a habitual familiarity with the legislative scheme they administer: "in many instances, those working day to day in the implementation of frequently complex administrative schemes have or will develop a considerable degree of expertise or field sensitivity to the imperatives and nuances of the legislative regime ...." Expertise may also arise where legislation requires that members of a given tribunal possess certain qualifications. However, as with judges, expertise is not a matter of the qualifications or experience of any particular tribunal member. Rather, *expertise is something that inheres in a tribunal itself as an institution*: "at an institutional level, adjudicators ... can be presumed to hold relative expertise in the interpretation of the legislation that gives them their mandate, as well as related legislation that they might often encounter in the course of their functions" (*Dunsmuir*, at para 68). As this court has often remarked, courts "may not be as well qualified as a given agency to provide interpretations of that agency's constitutive statute that make sense given the broad policy context within which that agency must work."[84]

Several recent cases, including a robust dissent in *Capilano Shopping Centres*,[85] have raised jurisprudential concerns that according expertise to a decision-maker simply on the basis of the existence of a privative clause, and without further contextual analysis of statutory language indicating that the decision-maker does indeed work with specialized knowledge, pays mere lip service to legislative intent and risks sweeping too many issues into a single standard.[86] The result, it is feared, may be arbitrary judicial decisions upholding arbitrary administrative interpretations. Nevertheless, the presumption of deference to expertise, including interpretive expertise in relation to a home statute, continues to hold for now.

---

82   *Ibid* at 1336.
83   *Edmonton (City) v Edmonton East (Capilano) Shopping Centres Ltd*, 2016 SCC 47, [2016] 2 SCR 293 [*Capilano Shopping Centres*].
84   *Ibid* at para 33 citing *McLean, supra* note 66 at para 31, which itself is quoting *National Corn Growers, supra* note 79 at 1336, per Wilson J (emphasis added).
85   *Ibid* at paras 63-125.
86   On this point, see: Deschamps J's concurring judgment in *Smith v Alliance Pipeline Ltd*, 2011 SCC 7, [2011] 1SCR 160; the dissent penned by Côté and Brown JJ in *Wilson v Atomic Energy of Canada Ltd*, 2016 SCC 29, [2016] 1 SCR 770; and the more recent dissent also by Côté and Brown JJ in *Capilano Shopping Centres, supra* note 83.

FUTURE-ORIENTED QUESTION

When you read Chapters 11-13 on the standard of review, revisit the disagreement between Gonthier and Wilson JJ and think about how Gonthier J's reasoning perhaps foreshadows the creation of the intermediate standard of review, reasonableness. When deciding to simplify administrative law, partly to make it more compatible with the rule of law, the Supreme Court in *Dunsmuir* eliminated the most deferential standard of review—patent unreasonableness. If you were a judge participating in further reform in this area, and wanted to better realize deference as respect within the rule of law, would you: (a) bring back the patent unreasonableness standard; (b) eliminate correctness review; or (c) have one standard of review and, if so, which one? How does your choice map onto your conception of the rule of law?

4. Interpreting Reasonableness

We have seen that courts must be bound by legislative intent as expressed in statutory provisions and purposes. But, you also know that statutory language can be highly ambiguous and conflicting and, further, may not have anticipated the issues a court is reviewing. But despite the somewhat fictive nature of legislative intent, courts and other interpreters are obliged to construct the meanings and purposes so far as that intention is discoverable from the language of the provision at issue and in the context of the statute as a whole. Where the text is unclear or ambiguous, and the ordinary meaning cannot be determined, judges may draw on other materials to assist in the interpretive effort, including legal principles, parliamentary debates, ministerial statements regarding statutory purposes, legislative history, agency interpretations, commission reports, policy manuals, international law, and scholarly opinion. After this often in-depth, creative, textual, and contextual exercise, they will then impute the meaning and purpose as legislative intent and analyze intent in relation to the particular statute under consideration. This account of statutory interpretation seems at odds with a formalist understanding of the rule of law. But, as Ruth Sullivan argues, the attraction of the less formalistic, more contextual view is that it "openly acknowledges that interpreting statutes is a complex and creative activity that is not reducible to the mechanical application of fixed legal rules. And it raises an important question: namely, whether the persons who are given power to interpret legislation—police officers and bureaucrats as well as members of administrative tribunals and courts—are appropriately chosen and adequately prepared for the task."[87]

Invoking the democratic principle and the principle of judicial restraint, the Supreme Court has affirmed that interpreters cannot ignore the words chosen by Parliament and rewrite legislation according to the interpreter's perspective concerning how the legislative purpose should be better promoted. If the statutory words are precise and unequivocal, then the ordinary meaning dominates. If the words can support more than one reasonable interpretation, then the ordinary sense plays a lesser role, but the interpreter must construct an interpretation that best fulfills the purpose(s) of the statute. In these situations, courts must follow the modern approach to statutory interpretation.[88] Finally, some statutes demand a broad and liberal reading—human rights legislation, for example—because they deal with fundamental rights or are quasi-constitutional. The key tension for the rule

---

87   Ruth Sullivan, *Statutory Interpretation* (Toronto: Irwin Law, 1997) at 39.

88   Recollect that this purposive approach to interpretation constructs legislative intent by reading statutory words: in their entire context; in their grammatical and ordinary sense when not defined; and harmoniously with the scheme, purpose, or object of the Act. See *Rizzo & Rizzo Shoes Ltd (Re)*, [1998] 1 SCR 27 at para 21.

of law centres on the question of how much actual law-making courts engage in under the guise of interpretation. Remember that it is only with a constitutionalized bill of rights that courts are explicitly authorized to replace legislative content with judicially created content.

In the transformative *Dunsmuir* case, the Supreme Court invoked rule-of-law values and attributes to justify reducing the standards of review in administrative law from three to two: correctness and reasonableness, with reasonableness subsuming the most deferential standard of patent unreasonableness.[89] The court's goal in this judgment was to provide greater guidance for reviewing courts, counsel, litigants, and decision-makers by striving to introduce clarity, consistency, and simplicity into administrative law. The Supreme Court introduced a new two-step test in which review would proceed first by examining past jurisprudence to see what level of deference was owed. If past jurisprudence did not address the question satisfactorily, then the standard of review analysis would be used to contextually analyze and determine legislative intent regarding the nature and scope of agency jurisdiction and expertise within the home statute. At least four factors guide this analysis: (1) the presence or absence of a privative clause; (2) the purpose of the tribunal from an interpretation of enabling legislation; (3) the nature of the question at issue (fact, law, mixed fact and law); and (4) the expertise of the tribunal. As you now know, several of these factors strongly point toward deferential review. With a re-crafted standard of review, the court suggested that it had reconciled the rule of law and democracy by respecting parliamentary sovereignty, placing effective limits on judicial discretion, recognizing expertise, and rejecting a "court-centric" conception of the rule of law.[90]

READ PARAGRAPHS 1-22 OF *CELGENE*[91]

This case illustrates how an interpretive disagreement is resolved under the reasonableness standard of review adhering to deference as respect. It also underscores public law scholar John Willis's wry observation that "the words are ambiguous enough to induce two people to spend good money in backing two opposing views as to their meaning."[92]

1. How would you describe the context in this case?
2. Read the following provision from the enabling legislation:

80. (1) A patentee of an invention pertaining to a medicine shall, as required by and in accordance with the regulations, provide the Board with such information and documents as the regulations may specify respecting ...

(b) the price at which the medicine is being or has been sold in any market in Canada and elsewhere ...

---

89 *Dunsmuir, supra* note 74.
90 *Ibid* at paras 27-33.
91 *Celgene Corp v Canada (Attorney General)*, 2011 SCC 1, [2011] 1 SCR 3 [*Celgene*]. The Patented Medicine Prices Review Board is authorized to investigate the pricing of medicines in the Canadian market. If the board determines that a particular price is excessive, the statute delegates to it the power to order a price reduction. Because it did not receive a Notice of Compliance from Health Canada for its pharmaceutical Thalomid, Celgene, since 1995, had to sell the drug to doctors through a Special Access Programme. Under this arrangement, the medicine is packed and shipped from the United States and paid for in US dollars, without Canadian taxes being applied to the transaction. In 2006, Celgene obtained a Canadian patent for Thalomid. The board believed it had the jurisdiction to obtain all pricing information since Thalomid was first sold in Canada. Although it initially complied with the board's pricing request, Celgene then argued that it did not have to provide further information because, under commercial law principles, the medicine was "sold" in New Jersey, not Canada.
92 John Willis, "Statute Interpretation in a Nutshell" (1938) 16 Can Bar Rev 1 at 4-5.

3.   What does Parliament intend? Here is a list of possible interpretations. Which, to your mind, best expresses the meaning of "sold in any market in Canada"?
- medicine sold IN CANADA;
- medicine *sold* [which is a legal term of art with a dominant private law, commercial meaning] in Canada;
- medicine sold IN ANY MARKET [including Canada];
- medicine sold [including by foreign sellers] in any market in Canada;
- medicine sold [restricted to medicine that is regulated by Canadian law, delivered to and used in Canada, and paid for by Canadians] in any market in Canada;
- medicine sold [though a head office in New Jersey and therefore NOT] in Canada.

Now read paragraphs 23-35.

4.   How, according to Abella J, did the Patented Medicine Prices Review Board's statutory mandate supply the key to the interpretation problem?

As the case went up through the courts, different standards of review were selected and applied (note that this phenomenon is not uncommon). Abella J, however, agreed with Evans JA in Federal Court of Appeal that the board's interpretation and resulting decision was "unassailable" under either the reasonableness or correctness standard of review.

According to *Dunsmuir* and illustrated by cases like *Celgene*, reasonableness (contextually applied) will be the presumptive standard of review *and the conclusion* when a specialized or expert tribunal interprets its enabling statute (or closely related statutes). It must correctly apply all legal principles or tests and construct an interpretation that falls within the range of possible acceptable interpretations. It should usually (but not always) communicate the decision through the provision of adequate reasons, and the outcome should be defensible in respect of the facts and the law. In return, the reviewing court should recognize the decision-maker's margin of appreciation within the range of acceptable interpretations and possible reasonable outcomes. When these conditions are met, deference as respect is achieved because courts are not micro-managing the state, and administrative actors are respecting rationality, rights, and responsibilities. As Chapter 12 discuses more fully, most of the post-*Dunsmuir* action in administrative law is now in reasonableness review.

5.   (In)Adequate Reasons

Reasons are where the rule-of-law rubber hits the administrative law road: they are fundamentally important in order to justify both state action and the Canadian model of deference as respect. Recollect that, in the *Baker* case, Mavis Baker and her counsel were lucky to gain access to the "reasons" for the negative decision—in her case the immigration officer's unadulterated, unofficial notes which the Supreme Court retroactively deemed as the reasons for the decision. As a result of the *Baker* decision, the court imposed a duty on statutory and prerogative decision-makers to give reasons in certain administrative contexts when important individual interests are at stake. When administrative decision-makers provide adequate reasons for their decisions, they contribute to the legal order by justifying the exercise of public power to affected persons. According to then Chief Justice Beverley McLachlin, when administrative officials provide adequate reasons for their decisions, they too participate in an "ethos of justification" just as courts do:

> Where a society is marked by a culture of justification, an exercise of public power is only appropriate where it can be justified to citizens in terms of *rationality and fairness*. Arbitrary decisions

and rules are seen as illegitimate. ... Indeed, most importantly, the ability to call for such a justification as a precondition to the legitimate exercise of public power is regarded by citizens as their *right* ... The Rule of Law, in short, can speak in several voices so long as the resulting chorus echoes its underlying values of fairness and rationality. ... Fair procedures, equitable treatment, and responsiveness to the public are the cornerstones of a system of administrative tribunals built according to the Rule of Law.[93]

The duty to give reasons has the potential to advance restraint and respect, thereby simultaneously facilitating rule-of-law concerns and administrative legitimacy. The actual provision of reasons represents an opportunity for the administrative decision-maker to show its expertise vis-à-vis a reviewing court, but also to demonstrate the adequacy of its concern for affected individuals by observing procedural fairness or reasonableness.

Reasons generally serve three functions: (1) they disclose expertise in the subject area of the home statute "using concepts and language often unique to their areas and rendering decision that are often counter-intuitive to a generalist";[94] (2) they justify the decision using transparent and intelligible reasoning that all audiences—counsel, affected persons, and especially the losing party, reviewing courts, other agencies, and the general public—can understand; and (3) they illustrate that the outcome is also reasonable when, as is often the case in administrative decision-making, more than one reasonable result is possible.

READ THE *MCLEAN* CASE[95]

This case concerns the initial absence of reasons, which the administrative decision-maker was able to "cure" at judicial review. In its very brief order, the British Columbia Securities Commission did not explain its interpretation of the limitation period provision (s 159)—an interpretation that allowed it to initiate secondary proceedings against McLean. It simply made an order barring McLean from activities in British Columbia for the same time period she was barred from activities in Ontario.

1. Consider McLean's interests as well as the public interest in securities regulation and enforcement across Canada (note also that Canada does not—yet—have a national securities regulator).

2. *McLean* involves two diametrically opposed interpretations. The majority held that both interpretations of the statutory provision were reasonable. Do you agree with the majority or do you agree with Karakatsanis J that only one reasonable interpretation existed? How might reasons have helped clarify this matter?

---

93 Honourable Madam Justice Beverley McLachlin, "The Roles of Administrative Tribunals and Courts in Maintaining the Rule of Law" (1999) 12 Can J Admin Law & Prac 171 at 174-75, 186.

94 *Newfoundland and Labrador Nurses' Union v Newfoundland and Labrador (Treasury Board)*, 2011 SCC 62, [2011] 3 SCR 708 at para 13 [*Newfoundland Nurses' Union*].

95 *McLean, supra* note 66. In 2008, McLean entered into settlement agreement with the Ontario Securities Commission because of improper conduct that had occurred in 2001. In 2010, the British Columbia Securities Commission (BCSC) initiated secondary proceedings against McLean based on the Ontario settlement agreement. The BCSC's home statute contained a limitations period provision barring the Commission from commencing proceedings more than six years after the date of "the events" giving rise to initial proceedings. Were "the events" the underlying misconduct which ended in 2001 or the settlement agreement in 2008? If the first interpretation held, the BCSC could not initiate secondary proceedings.

3. The commission gave no reasons, but it was subsequently able to advance interpretation arguments in court. The Supreme Court then supplemented the reasons by engaging in a statutory interpretation exercise on the commission's behalf. How does this raise concerns for the rule of law and reason-giving? Should reviewing courts show no deference when there are no or otherwise completely inadequate reasons? Is this really reasonableness review when courts actually construct the reasons?

The subsequent trajectory of the duty to give reasons has taken several twists since *Baker*. An emerging problem for the rule of law hinges on what the role of the courts should be when faced with inadequate reasons.[96] In *Newfoundland Nurses' Union*, Abella J noted that even if the reasons do not seem wholly adequate to support the decision, a reviewing court must first seek to "supplement them before it seeks to subvert them."[97] Other chapters explore reason-giving in more detail.

FUTURE-ORIENTED QUESTION

An open question remains whether or not authorizing reviewing courts to supplement reasons is only a superficial form of deference. An even bigger question asks how appropriate it is for courts to write improved or substitute new reasons or for administrative decision-makers. Does this judicial practice of supplementation violate the ethos of justification within the Canadian rule of law?

B. Discretion and Deference

The interpretive role of the courts in public law means that they must provide cogent and coherent justifications that explain the nature of the conflict and the appropriateness of the decision in favour of one right or one balance over another, especially when confronted with decisions involving broad grants of discretionary power. In administrative law, this kind of activity is particularly controversial if it means judges can "re-weigh" the factors that administrative decision-makers use, factors which are based on their expertise and experiential knowledge. In *Baker*, for example, L'Heureux-Dubé J affirmed that: "I believe that the *failure to give serious weight and consideration to the interests of the children constitutes an unreasonable exercise of the discretion* conferred by the section, notwithstanding the important deference that should be given to the decision of the immigration officer."[98] Those who support this conclusion argue that the Charter reinforces the constitutional commitment that all persons—individuals, corporations, groups, and state actors—must adhere to the rule of law and respect fundamental constitutional values. *Baker* therefore represents an important link in the rule-of-law narrative that can be traced back to *Roncarelli*. Like *Roncarelli*, *Baker*

---

96   Other recent cases involving inadequate reasons include: *Alberta (Information and Privacy Commissioner) v Alberta Teachers' Association*, 2011 SCC 61, [2011] 3 SCR 654; *Agraira v Canada (Public Safety and Emergency Preparedness)*, 2013 SCC 36, [2013] 2 SCR 559; *Sattva Capital Corp v Creston Moly Corp*, 2014 SCC 53, [2014] 2 SCR 633; and, *Kanthasamy v Canada (Citizenship and Immigration)*, 2015 SCC 61, [2015] 3 SCR 909.

97   *Newfoundland Nurses' Union, supra* note 94 at para 12. In doing so, Justice Abella referred to the work of Professor David Dyzenhaus on this point.

98   *Baker, supra* note 20 at para 65 (emphasis added).

discloses that administrative and constitutional law are attuned to underlying fundamental values such as basic concerns for human dignity, the vindication of rights, and the effects of political power on individuals.

Doré v Barreau du Québec brings the issue of re-weighing right to the surface. In *Doré*, the Supreme Court changed the methodological approach used to review discretionary decisions involving Charter rights and values.[99] Overturning precedent, the court rejected the use of the *Oakes* test to review these types of discretionary decisions. Instead, a parallel proportionality framework was constructed under the reasonableness standard of review.[100] We are still early on in the post-*Doré* jurisprudence and other chapters will explore the most recent line of cases. You will be able to confirm for yourself whether or not you agree with the justification that the court gave in *Doré* for this major change—that this promotes a "richer conception" of administrative law because it confirms "administrative decisions are always required to consider fundamental values."[101]

FUTURE-ORIENTED QUESTION

In light of recent post-*Doré* cases, has the Supreme Court successfully harmonized the rule of law with deference as respect when reviewing discretionary decisions?

C. Democracy, Deference, and the Rule of Law

Throughout this chapter, we have seen that the principles of democracy and the rule of law have had a complementary and mutually supportive relationship while, at other times, an antagonistic and undermining relationship. Reconciling the two is a permanent project. In the *Secession Reference*,[102] the Supreme Court declared that democracy cannot exist without the rule of law:

> To be accorded legitimacy, democratic institutions must rest, ultimately, on a legal foundation. That is, they must allow for the participation of, and accountability to, the people, through public institutions created under the Constitution. Equally, however, a system of government cannot survive through adherence to law alone. A political system must also possess legitimacy, and in our political culture, that requires an interaction between the rule of law and the democratic principle. ... Our law's claim to legitimacy also rests on an appeal to moral values, many of which are embedded in our constitutional structure. It would be a grave mistake to equate legitimacy with the "sovereign will" or majority rule alone, to the exclusion of other constitutional values.

This vision of democratic constitutionalism also finds its expression in administrative law.

---

99 *Doré v Barreau du Québec*, 2012 SCC 12 [*Doré*]. For further discussion, see Chapter 1.

100 *Doré* overturned *Multani v Commission scolaire Marguerite-Bourgeoys*, 2006 SCC 6, [2006] 1 SCR 256, [*Multani*]. In *Doré*, the court used the concurrence from *Multani* to draw a strong jurisprudential line between a "law" (i.e., law means a norm of general application produced by a legislative body, a definition which includes statutes, regulations, and by-laws) and decisions and orders made by administrative bodies.

101 *Doré, supra* note 99 at para 35.

102 *Supra* note 32 at paras 67, 68.

READ THE *COOPER* DECISION[103]

This case contains a spirited disagreement about the rule of law, the role of administrative tribunals, and access to justice.

1. Identify the three types of reasons Lamer CJ gives to argue why administrative tribunals should not have the jurisdiction to consider the constitutionality of their enabling statutes: the legislative intent argument; the separation of powers argument; and the parliamentary democracy argument.

2. Note how both Lamer CJ (concurring) and La Forest J (for the majority) agreed that administrative bodies like the human rights tribunal possess no relative expertise when it comes to interpreting law, especially constitutional law. Do you agree that human rights tribunals have no special expertise regarding questions of law? LaForest J's judgment, however, comes up the middle by suggesting that the enabling statute can grant jurisdiction to administrative decision-makers. Track how this view has changed in the jurisprudence discussed in Chapters 11-13.

3. Look at how the dissent written by McLachlin J (as she then was) and L'Heureux-Dubé J focuses on access to justice in the administrative state. The Canadian Human Rights Commission (CHRC) did not refer the pilot's complaint to the Canadian Human Rights Tribunal (CHRT) because it considered the retirement provision to be a *bona fide* occupational requirement and they were bound by previous judicial decisions on this point. The case is actually a judicial review of the CHRC's decision not to refer the complaint to CHRT. Consider the options that existed for the CHRC at the time:

- refer the Charter issue to the CHRT—knowing that a legal challenge concerning jurisdiction is certain;
- refuse to refer because no inquiry is warranted (which is what occurred);
- refuse to consider the matter at all because neither the CHRC nor the CHRT have the jurisdiction to consider the Charter since they are not courts of law; and
- refer the matter to Federal Court for a declaration the statute offends the Charter.

Keeping in mind both access to justice and the rule of law, if you were the head of the CHRC, which option would you select and why?

In their robust dissent written for the *Cooper* decision, McLachlin J (as she then was) and L'Heureux-Dubé J criticized Lamer CJ's "holy grail" conception of the rule of law:

> The *Charter* is not some holy grail which only judicial initiates of the superior courts may touch. The *Charter* belongs to the people. All law and law-makers that touch the people must conform to it. Tribunals and commissions charged with deciding legal issues are no exception. Many more citizens have their rights determined by these tribunals than by the courts. If the *Charter*

---

103   *Cooper, supra* note 4. This case concerns the fundamental question of whether or not human rights tribunals have the authority to determine the constitutionality of provisions in their enabling statutes. In *Cooper*, airline pilots challenged the normal age of retirement exemption in the *Canadian Human Rights Act* that forced them to retire at the age of 60, unlike the majority of employees at the time who could retire at 65. They argued that this provision violated the Charter's s 15 equality guarantee. The Canadian Human Rights Tribunal had to decide whether or not it had the authority to determine that this provision was unconstitutional. If the provision were found to be unconstitutional, the remedy would not be striking down the provision (as courts do under s 52), but refusing to apply the unconstitutional provision in the particular case at bar. It would then be up to the legislature to respond by amending the statute. This type of interaction exemplifies institutional dialogue.

is to be meaningful to ordinary people, then it must find its expression in the decisions of these tribunals.[104]

The dissent in *Cooper* expresses a vision of democratic constitutionalism that respects the legitimacy of the administrative state. This vision of Canadian constitutionalism relies on a democratic interpretation of the separation of powers and therefore recognizes the appropriate role of administrative tribunals—particularly human rights tribunals—in determining the content and scope of fundamental legal norms. On this account, administrative agencies as constitutional partners do exhibit rule-of-law attributes, have embraced rule-of-law values, and can facilitate access to justice for the benefit of citizens and other affected persons. In Raz's model of the rule of law, for example, each institution mutually supports the other. Legislatures satisfy this ideal when they make reasonably clear laws that are coherent and transparent in their purposes. Democratic legislatures go further when they respect the rights and interests of minorities or balance them properly with legitimate statutory objectives. An open and public administration conforms to the rule of law when it employs fair procedures, applies law faithfully, openly, and in a principled way in order to facilitate legislative purposes, and produces reasonable decisions and outcomes. Legal institutions will be loyal to democratic legislation through interpreting intent while rejecting inconsistent purposes.[105] Nevertheless, if courts should respect pluralism as a political fact, and ideological pluralism in particular, their job is not to endorse wholeheartedly one particular substantive political morality: that, many critics of Dworkin argue, is typically seen as the legitimate role of the legislature.

Democracy literally means "rule by the people."[106] What distinguishes democracy from other forms of government is the participation of citizens in producing the laws that bind the entire community. Democracy presupposes that we have processes for arriving at binding decisions that take everyone's interests into account. This is another reason why citizens' participation in the administrative state is so crucial. But, though all members may possess equal constitutional rights to participate politically—the s 3 right to vote in the Charter, for example—the democratic process may not represent all interests equally as a result of continuing historical exclusions and deep socio-economic divides. Public policy-making, for example, may be undermined by active minorities such as interest or lobby groups who can "capture" particular policy areas and legislative outcomes—think of the National Corn Growers case here. But, as the Supreme Court emphasizes above, the principles of democracy and the rule of law can, under the right conditions, work in harmony to secure accountability and legitimacy in public institutions.

Both democracy and the rule of law justify the creation of institutional mechanisms for citizens and affected persons to prevent or challenge the abuse of power by public officials.

---

104 *Ibid* at para 70.
105 Raz distinguishes between conflicting and inconsistent purposes. Conflicting purposes are endemic to pluralistic societies and require compromise. But "no rational society should entertain inconsistent [values]": for example, a state cannot endorse the indissolubility of marriage while, at the same time, permit divorce on demand. Inconsistent purposes and values are a form of conflict that is logical, not political. Raz, 1990, *supra* note 39 at 337.
106 For a helpful overview of the concept of democracy, see Amy Gutmann, "Democracy" in Robert E Goodin, Philip Pettit, & Thomas Pogge, eds, *A Companion to Contemporary Political Philosophy*, 2nd ed, vol 2 (Malden, MA: Blackwell Publishing, 2007) at 521-31.

As we have seen, the rule of law supports the creation of procedures that treat individuals fairly when their rights, interests, and privileges are affected in public decision-making. These institutional spaces for participation aim to secure legitimacy, justice, and administrative efficiency. Some processes will be open to all, while others may engage only certain stakeholders or interest groups. Participants may simply offer information on paper or take positions, exchange reasons, and influence substantive policy matters. The rule of law also supports judicial review of administrative decisions on their merits and greater access to the courts through the expansion of standing and intervener status. The aspiration here is that judicial deliberation will lead to better and more reasonable decision-making processes and policy outcomes. A participatory democracy will create conduits for direct participation in political decision-making through, for example, public hearings. The hope is that greater participation will lead to greater accountability and less abuse of power through public oversight. A deliberative democracy supports the creation of open, deliberative processes for public reasoning and debate on political issues. Rather than continual direct political participation, then, deliberative democracy seeks ongoing accountability about public issues. The goal is better justified public policy. Contemporary governance therefore offers a range of institutional possibilities for public participation on democracy and rule-of-law grounds.

FUTURE-ORIENTED QUESTION

Several chapters discuss administrative law and the national dynamics of, and controversies over, pipelines in Canada—Northern Gateway, Energy East, Line 9, and TransMountain. The focal administrative body here has been the National Energy Board (NEB). Current litigation involves all aspects of administrative law. Not only is the public interest implicated, but specific groups such as Indigenous Peoples on whose land pipelines may be built are seriously affected. Consider how democracy and the rule of law interact in this contentious area. For example, will the duty to consult and accommodate serve to uphold Indigenous rights or undermine them? To take another example, think about the legal challenges based on the NEB's narrow interpretation of its enabling legislation which had the effect of reducing citizen's participation in public hearings and the pipeline decision-making process. See, in particular, Chapters 3 and 8.

D. Non-Deference and the Rule of Law

Non-deference in substantive review occurs in two ways: legitimately and illegitimately. The illegitimate way occurs when courts use statutory interpretation, ostensibly in reasonableness review, to construct what they believe to be the single right answer (see *McLean* above). The legitimate way is to review using a correctness standard—a standard whose use has been radically curtailed since *Dunsmuir*.

Post-*Dunsmuir*, correctness review is now limited to: (1) a constitutional issue; (2) a question of general law that is both of central importance to the legal system as a whole *and* outside the specialized area of expertise of the administrative decision-maker; (3) drawing jurisdictional lines between two or more competing specialized tribunals; or (4) a "true" question of jurisdiction or *vires*. According to the majority, rule-of-law values such as universality, consistency, uniformity, predictability, and stability justify the unique role of the courts in reviewing tribunal decisions on a correctness standard in these circumstances.

So, for example, although a post-*Cooper* administrative tribunal may have the jurisdiction to consider Charter challenges to its enabling legislation and to award Charter remedies under s 24(1), the particular decision will not be binding authority as precedent for future cases; and, in subsequent judicial review, because the decision involves a question of constitutional law, it will be subject to a standard of correctness, ensuring that it receives little or no curial deference.[107]

III. OTHER ROUTES TO ACCOUNTABILITY IN THE ADMINISTRATIVE STATE

Judicial review represents an important, but not the sole, route to securing administrative accountability. Courts should be seen as one among the many means by which we hold government to account. Moreover, it will be better for the legitimacy of courts if we recognize them as one among a "family" of legitimate routes to securing accountability within a liberal democratic state: public inquiries, royal commissions, task forces, departmental investigations, special legislative officers, and ombudsmen. The rule of law will also inform the various institutional alternatives to judicial review of government action.

IV. CONCLUSION: A DEMOCRATIC RULE OF LAW IN THE ADMINISTRATIVE STATE

In administrative law, the concept of the rule of law is much like the Dude's carpet in *The Big Lebowski*: it ties the room together. Although it is unlikely that the rule of law will constitute a direct and complete basis for answering a law exam question, the puzzles that administrative law evokes cannot be understood without recourse to this foundational concept.

This chapter discussed the rule of law and explored its relevance for Canadian administrative law. Section I presented several of the main features of the rule of law: the rule of law as a foundational legal principle, the rule of law as a political ideal concerning proper institutional relations and competencies, and the rule of law as a distinctive political morality. Section II presented the Canadian articulation of the rule of administrative law: the "deference as respect" model. It then examined some of the legal indicators signalling a presumption of deference such as privative clauses and expertise. Defence and non-deference were examined in procedural fairness, substantive review under a reasonableness or a correctness standard, and the new intermediate form of deference applied in the proportionality analysis of discretionary decisions. In the conclusion to Section II, I argued that Canadian administrative law is committed to a distinctive form of the rule of law, which simultaneously attempts to ensure rule-of-law accountability and democratic accountability in all parts of government.

---

107   See *Nova Scotia (Workers' Compensation Board) v Martin; Nova Scotia (Workers' Compensation Board) v Laseur*, 2003 SCC 54, [2003] 2 SCR 504 [*Martin*]. Chapter 13 provides a discussion of agency jurisdiction under the Charter. See *R v Conway*, 2010 SCC 22, [2010] 1 SCR 765 and Chapter 2 on the expansion of the ability of tribunals to award Charter remedies. Parliament and provincial legislatures, however, retain the power to make it clear in the enabling legislation that statutory delegates do not have the power to consider the Charter, other constitutional issues, or issue Charter remedies.

How a judge understands the rule of law, and his or her role in upholding it through judicial review, will necessarily shape how he or she approaches the review of decisions made by public officials. How legal counsel frames rule of law arguments in litigation may significantly influence judicial decision-making. Judicial temperament is not completely predictable: Judges may conceive of themselves as the Diceyan defenders of the rule of law against a lawless administrative state. They may view themselves as Dworkinian Herculean legal guardians of the constitution, committed to upholding the rights conception of the rule of law. They may perhaps see their role as the Fullerian cooperative partner who recognizes democratic initiatives, but still maintains institutional fidelity to rule-of-law principles. Lastly, they may perceive themselves as the Razian interpreters of guided discretion and judicial faithfulness to coherent legislative purposes. The government of the day, including the officials in the administrative state, may also hold their own interpretations about what the rule of law requires (or map on to one of these approaches without expressly knowing them).

Finally, this chapter explained how the concept of the rule of law and its associated principles are fundamental to understanding the complex relationship between courts and administrative bodies. This multiplicity of institutional environments means that the rule of law will require different responsibilities and restraints for different institutional actors and practices. Though this makes administrative law a difficult field of study, and provides unending complications for judicial review of administrative decision-making, one positive reading of such complexity suggests that this is a necessary consequence of the interaction between the rule of law and democracy. Institutional dialogue and deference as respect stand as distinctive forms of the commitment to judicial restraint in Canadian administrative law—a restraint that simultaneously attempts to ensure judicial accountability and larger democratic accountability. Nevertheless, the modern development of deference and respect for administrative tribunals is both an ongoing and vulnerable achievement.

RECAP: THE VOCABULARY OF ADMINISTRATIVE LAW

This chapter aimed to introduce you to, and help you understand, these key administrative law terms:

- Arbitrariness
- Correctness review
- Deference and deference as respect
- Democracy
- Discretion
- Enabling or home statute
- Expertise
- Fairness
- Guidance
- Judicial activism and restraint
- Judicial review
- Jurisdiction
- Legal formalism
- Legality
- Legislative intent
- Parliamentary supremacy
- Principles
- Privative clauses
- Procedural fairness
- Reasonableness review
- Rule of law
- Separation of powers
- Statutory interpretation
- Weight

SUGGESTED ADDITIONAL READINGS

BOOKS AND ARTICLES

CANADIAN

Huscroft, Grant, Bradley W Miller & Grégoire Webber, eds, *Proportionality and the Rule of Law* (Cambridge and New York: Cambridge University Press, 2014).

Huscroft, Grant, & Michael Taggart, eds, *Inside and Outside Canadian Administrative Law* (Toronto: University of Toronto Press, 2006).

Lewans, Matthew, *Administrative Law and Judicial Deference* (Oxford and Portland: Hart, 2016).

McLachlin, Honourable Madam Justice Beverley "The Role of Administrative Tribunals and Courts in Maintaining the Rule of Law" (1999) 12 Can J Admin L & Prac 171.

Sullivan, Ruth, *Statutory Interpretation* (Toronto: Irwin Law, 1997).

Van Harten, Gus, et al, *Administrative Law: Cases, Text, and Materials*, 7th ed (Toronto: Emond Montgomery, 2015).

INTERNATIONAL

Allan, TRS, *Constitutional Justice: A Liberal Theory of the Rule of Law* (Oxford: Oxford University Press, 2001).

Bauman, Richard W, & Tsvi Kahana, eds, *The Least Examined Branch: The Role of Legislatures in the Constitutional State* (Cambridge: Cambridge University Press, 2006).

Bellamy, Richard, ed, *The Rule of Law and the Separation of Powers* (Aldershot, UK: Ashgate/ Dartmouth, 2005).

Bingham, Tom, *The Rule of Law* (London: Allen Lane, 2010).

Craig, Paul P, *Administrative Law*, 8th ed (London: Sweet & Maxwell, 2016).

Daly, Paul, *A Theory of Deference in Administrative Law: Basis, Application and Scope* (Cambridge: Cambridge University Press, 2012).

Dworkin, Ronald, *A Matter of Principle* (Cambridge, MA: Harvard University Press, 1985).

Dyzenhaus, David, ed, *Recrafting the Rule of Law: The Limits of Legal Order* (Oxford: Hart, 1999).

Harlow, Carol, & Richard Rawlings, *Law and Administration*, 3rd ed (Cambridge: Cambridge University Press, 2009).

Raz, Joseph, "The Politics of the Rule of Law" (1990) 3:3 *Ratio Juris* 331.

Shapiro, Ian, ed, *NOMOS XXXVI: The Rule of Law* (New York and London: New York University Press, 1994).

Tamanaha, Brian Z, *On the Rule of Law: History, Politics, Theory* (Cambridge: Cambridge University Press, 2004).

CASES

British Columbia v Imperial Tobacco Canada Ltd, 2005 SCC 49, [2005] 2 SCR 473.

Canada (Attorney General) v PHS Community Services Society, 2011 SCC 44, [2011] 3 SCR 134.

Canada (Citizenship and Immigration) v Khosa, 2009 SCC 12, [2009] 1 SCR 339.

Celgene Corp v Canada (Attorney General), 2011 SCC 1, [2011] 1 SCR.

Cooper v Canada (Canadian Human Rights Commission), [1996] 3 SCR 85.

Dunsmuir v New Brunswick, 2008 SCC 9, [2008] 1 SCR 190.

McLean v British Columbia (Securities Commission), 2013 SCC 67, [2013] 3 SCR 895.

Mission Institution v Khela, 2014 SCC 24, [2014] 1 SCR 502.

National Corn Growers Assn v Canada (Import Tribunal), [1990] 2 SCR 1324.

Roncarelli v Duplessis, [1959] SCR 121.

CHAPTER FIVE

The Principles and Practices of Procedural Fairness

Kate Glover*
Faculty of Law, Western University

I. INTRODUCTION

Fairness in administrative law is concerned with procedure rather than outcomes. It is concerned with, for example, whether the National Energy Board properly consults with affected parties before approving an application to construct a pipeline[1] and not whether the board decides to approve the application. Similarly, it is concerned with whether an individual who is deemed inadmissible to Canada on security grounds has been provided with sufficient

* Thank you to the editors of this volume and to the participants in the Administrative Law in Context workshop in September 2016 for valuable insight and comments. Thank you also to Sean Blakeley for his outstanding research assistance.

1 See e.g. *Gitxaala Nation v R*, 2016 FCA 187; *Clyde River (Hamlet) v Petroleum Geo-Services Inc*, 2017 SCC 40 [*Clyde River*]; *Chippewas of the Thames First Nation v Enbridge Pipelines Inc*, 2017 SCC 41 [*Chippewas of the Thames*].

information to know the case against her, and not with the decision of the minister of immigration, refugees, and citizenship to issue a security certificate.[2] Further, it is concerned with whether parties to a grievance arbitration are entitled to be represented by counsel and not whether a labour arbitrator ultimately accepts the grievance.[3] In each of these examples, the relevant inquiry is whether the decision-maker acted fairly in making her decision and not whether the final decision itself is fair.

In order to act fairly, an administrative decision-maker must comply with the applicable procedural obligations set by law. These obligations are informed by principles of fairness and entail a diverse range of practices. This chapter canvasses these obligations, principles, and practices in the pages that follow. Section II of the chapter deals with the principles. It explores the aims and aspirations of fairness in administrative law. It is these aims and aspirations that should guide administrative decision-makers as they resolve disputes and make decisions about procedure. This section contends that fairness is shaped by five core ideas: the inherent value of fairness, access to administrative justice, the enfranchisement of affected parties, context-dependence or flexibility, and the rule of law. Each of these ideas underlies the law of fairness in the administrative context, as it strives to nurture a culture of good public decision-making.

Section III then deals with the practices of fairness. It considers the specific procedural steps that an administrative decision-maker must follow in order to act lawfully and identifies frameworks for determining what procedural duties are owed to whom, and when. These frameworks canvass obligations that apply to administrative decision-makers by virtue of statute, the Constitution, and the common law. These obligations govern the ways in which affected individuals are able to participate in decision-making processes (for example, in person, in writing, through counsel, in open forums, in closed forums, with notice, with disclosure of materials, with opportunities for cross-examination of other parties, and so on); the modes of decision-making that are available to public authorities (for example, consultation, deliberation, adjudication, mediation, arbitration, investigation, policy-making, regulation, negotiation, and so on); and the forms through which administrative decisions should be communicated to the affected parties and the public (for example, written reasons, oral reasons, surrogate forms of reasons, public notices, private communications, interim reasons, final reports, by issuing a licence or some other action,[4] and so on).

Finally, Section IV deals with unfairness. It asks what can be done when an administrative decision-maker fails to fulfill her procedural obligations. This section points to issues that arise in challenging unfairness through judicial review, and points to other chapters of this volume that provide further guidance on challenging unfair administrative action.

Sections II, III, and IV of this chapter review a range of procedural norms and principles, setting out the particulars and situating them within their philosophical, jurisprudential, and factual contexts. Across this review of the law, you will notice four themes that are particularly prominent.

First, cultivating fair public decision-making entails attention to good procedural design. One of the challenges for jurists in the realm of procedural design is abandoning the notion

---

2   See e.g. *Charkaoui v Canada (Citizenship and Immigration*, 2007 SCC 9 [*Charkaoui*] and *Canada (Citizenship and Immigration) v Harkat*, 2014 SCC 37.

3   See e.g. *Ontario Men's Clothing Manufacturers Assn v Arthurs* (1979), 104 DLR (3d) 441 (Ont Div Ct).

4   Such actions could include issuing a passport under the *Canadian Passport Order* SI/81-86 or granting a dealer's licence under the *Alberta Barley Commission Regulation*, Alta Reg 122-1999, s 7(1).

that the ideal of fairness is a trial-like process. Administrative law operates on the premise that fairness comes in many forms, and thus a fair procedure is one that is tailored to the context in which a decision is made. The context of administrative decision-making often differs in meaningful ways from the context of judicial decision-making. Accordingly, the design of fair procedures in administrative law must resist the impulse to replicate judicial processes unless called for in the circumstances.

Second, and relatedly, a process that is fair in one administrative context might be unfair or unsuitable in another. For example, in *Hoffman-La Roche v Delmar Chemical Ltd*,[5] it was held that the commissioner of patents acted fairly when he refused to hold an oral hearing on applications for compulsory patent licences, yet in *Khan v University of Ottawa*,[6] it was unfair for a university grades committee not to hold an oral hearing when the credibility of a student appealing her grade was at stake. Similarly, in *Canada (AG) v Mavi*,[7] it was fair for the government of Ontario not to provide reasons for its decision to collect debts from sponsoring relatives in the immigration context and in *Service Corp International (Canada) Inc v Burnaby (City)*[8] for a municipality not to provide reasons explaining its planning decisions. However, in *Cardinal v Director of Kent Institution*,[9] it was held to be unfair for the director of a penitentiary not to provide reasons to two inmates who were kept in solitary conditions even after the Segregation Review Board had recommended they be transferred back into the general prison population. The differing results in these examples point to the importance of context when determining what procedures an administrative decision-maker must follow in order to act fairly. Throughout this chapter, we will be reminded that fairness cannot be assessed in abstraction. Fairness and unfairness are matters deeply entwined with the lived experience of decision-makers and of the parties affected by their decisions.

Third, the law of procedure in administrative contexts is often discussed primarily through the lens of *Baker v Canada (Minister of Citizenship and Immigration)*,[10] a case to which you were introduced in Chapter 1. *Baker* remains the leading authority on the common law duty of fairness and will be addressed in some detail below. However, as you will see in this chapter, as well as in Chapters 6, 7, and 8, the procedural obligations that bear on administrative decision-makers are not located solely in the common law; they are also grounded in statute, in subordinate legislation, in soft law instruments, and in constitutional and quasi-constitutional sources. Moreover, the process by which decisions are made is also informed by custom, institutional practice, and informal influences that operate within an organization.[11] Accordingly, despite the enduring guidance that remains to be found in *Baker*, it is neither the first nor last stop in assessing the procedural norms that govern administrative decision-making.

Finally, this chapter is framed primarily in terms of assessing the procedural *obligations* of administrative decision-makers. These obligations are sourced in statute, the Constitution,

---

5   [1965] SCR 575.
6   (1997), 34 OR (3d) 535 (CA) [*Khan*].
7   2011 SCC 30 [*Mavi*].
8   (1999), 9 MPLR (3d) 242, [2000] BCWLD 396 (BCSC).
9   [1985] 2 SCR 643 [*Cardinal*].
10 [1999] 2 SCR 817 [*Baker*].
11 See e.g. Roderick Alexander Macdonald, "Old Guards," in Roderick Alexander Macdonald, *Lessons of Everyday Law* (Montreal & Kingston: McGill-Queen's University Press, 2002) 130.

and the common law. Moreover, as we will see, fairness is a legal duty that binds administrative decision-makers in the exercise of their statutory mandates. This chapter will canvass the particulars of this legal duty. It will consider: Why does the law require public actors to decide fairly? What is the legal meaning of fairness? Who bears the duty of fairness and in what circumstances? To whom is the duty owed? How can the duty be fulfilled? In exploring these questions, we will see that, as a general rule, all public decision-makers who make administrative decisions that affect the rights, interests, and privileges of an individual must decide fairly.[12]

However, this chapter could just as easily have been framed in terms of the procedural *entitlements* of the parties who are affected by public decisions. Procedural obligations are manifestations of a belief that affected parties are entitled to the just exercise of public power. It is thus these parties who enjoy rights of participation in the decision-making process and who are entitled to know why a particular decision was made. It is also these parties who have an enforceable right to a decision that is unbiased and open. And it is the significance of the impact of public decisions on these affected parties that determines the stringency of procedural obligations that administrative decision-makers must follow. Thus, throughout reading this chapter, it should be kept top of mind that the procedural demands on administrative decision-makers reflect rights and privileges of citizens that the law seeks to protect.

II. THE PRINCIPLES OF FAIRNESS

Our study begins by looking to the principles that underlie the law of procedure in the administrative context. It is to these principles that advocates look when crafting submissions on new issues. It is on these principles that administrative decision-makers rely when resolving disputes and justifying their assessment of affected interests. It is in these principles that judges find the aims of procedural justice when applying and developing the law of procedure. Even when these principles are not expressly invoked by administrative actors or judges in their decision-making, administrative decisions can often be explained and illuminated, as well as assessed and critiqued, by reference to these orienting ideas.

The discussion below focuses on five core principles—the inherent value of fairness, the rule of law, access to administrative justice, enfranchisement of affected parties, and flexibility or context-dependence. This is a non-exhaustive list. Other principles—such as federalism,[13] the public/private divide,[14] and proportionality[15]—are also relevant to resolving procedural disputes in administrative law. Additional principles of significance may emerge in the future. But the ideas canvassed here are well-established as foundational and aspirational in administrative law's approach to procedure in Canada.

With the exception of the inherent value of fairness, the core principles are discussed below in pairs. The rule of law is considered alongside access to justice; enfranchisement is examined alongside flexibility. This approach is deliberate. It is intended to remind us that the core ideas captured by each individual principle are best understood in relation to

---

12   *Cardinal, supra* note 9 at para 14.
13   See e.g. *P&S Holdings Ltd v Canada*, 2017 FCA 41 at paras 30-37.
14   See e.g. *Air Canada v Toronto Port Authority*, 2011 FCA 347.
15   See e.g. *Singh v Minister of Employment and Immigration*, [1985] 1 SCR 177 [*Singh*].

each other. No single ambition trumps the others, and there is no fixed relationship between them. Instead, the weight and persuasive force of any individual principle, or any combination thereof, will vary depending on the facts and issues of the particular case being considered.

Discussing the principles in clusters also helps to show the ways in which the core ideas of fairness are in tension with each other and with other considerations that carry weight in administrative law, such as efficiency and government policy agendas. These tensions are reminders that no single principle can be relied upon as determinative of a particular result. In every attempt to design an administrative procedure or enforce procedural expectations, it will be necessary to balance the competing interests in order to ensure that the procedural entitlements of the affected parties account for the daily realities of the decision-maker, as well as the overarching aims of administrative law. Indeed, one of the joys, but also one of the challenges, of resolving procedural questions in administrative law is developing the capacity to grapple with a constellation of competing contextual interests—interests that ask us to adopt both a microscopic and telescopic perspective—in order to determine the specific procedures that an administrative decision-maker should follow to make decisions and resolve disputes fairly.

A. The Inherent Value of Fairness

Fairness is a founding principle of administrative law. Indeed, the common law rules of procedural fairness are, in the words of the Supreme Court of Canada, citing Professor Hogg, "basic tenets of the legal system."[16] They are a touchstone of our justice system mixed and made from the "ingredients of fundamental justice," which are enshrined in s 7 of the Charter.[17]

In part, the importance of fairness in administrative law reflects the belief that fair decision-making processes lead to high-quality decisions. In this sense, fair procedure is valuable because it promotes sound outcomes. However, administrative law does not treat fairness as merely a means to substantive ends or outcomes. Rather, administrative law seizes the constitutional spirit of fairness and affirms that fair process is, on its own, an indispensable good in public decision-making. In this sense, fair procedure is valuable because it expresses a commitment to integrity in exercises of public power and a respect for the dignity of the parties affected by state action. Fairness is, in this way, an end worthy of pursuit in and of itself, a matter central to the notion of administrative justice that is independent of the merits of final decisions or outcomes.[18]

We can see the law's recognition of the inherent value of fairness in the following two examples from the common law: first, the courts' extension of the reach of procedural obligations beyond judicial and quasi-judicial decisions; and second, the significant consequences that the courts attach to unfairness.

---

16   *Suresh v Canada (Minister of Citizenship and Immigration)*, 2002 SCC 1 at para 113, citing Peter Hogg, *Constitutional Law of Canada* (Scarborough, Ont: Carswell, 1992) (loose-leaf updated 2002), vol 2, ch 44 at 44.20 [*Suresh*].

17   *Ibid. Canadian Charter of Rights and Freedoms*, Part I of the Constitution Act, 1982, being Schedule B to the *Canada Act 1982* (UK), 1982, c 11.

18   *Dunsmuir v New Brunswick*, 2008 SCC 9 at para 90 [*Dunsmuir*].

1. Extending the Reach of Procedural Obligations

In past eras of administrative law, only judicial and quasi-judicial decisions triggered procedural obligations.[19] These types of decisions were subject to the principles of natural justice, namely *audi alteram partem* (hear the other side) and *nemo judex in sua causa* (no person can be the judge in her own cause). All other public decisions—such as a school board's denial of a student's request to wear religious objects at school[20] or a prison official's discipline of an inmate[21]—were deemed administrative and thus could be made without the burden of common law procedural obligations.[22]

In a series of cases in the last decades of the 20th century, the courts began to move away from the distinction between judicial, quasi-judicial, and administrative decisions as determinative.[23] The move unfolded in two stages. First, the Supreme Court held that a "duty of fairness" applied to administrative decisions. Chief Justice Laskin, for a 5-4 majority in *Nicholson v Haldimand-Norfolk (Regional) Police Commissioners*, explained that the recognition of this duty was necessary both for conceptual clarity and to promote justice:

> [T]he classification of statutory functions as judicial, quasi-judicial or administrative is often very difficult, to say the least; and to endow some with procedural protection while denying others any at all would work injustice when the results of statutory decisions raise the same serious consequences for those adversely affected, regardless of the classification of the function in question.[24]

At this first stage, judicial and quasi-judicial decisions were still subject to the demands of natural justice, while administrative decisions were bound by the duty of fairness. In Chief Justice Laskin's words, "in the sphere of the so-called quasi-judicial the rules of natural justice run, and … in the administrative or executive field there is a general duty of fairness."[25] According to the courts, the duty of fairness that applied to the making of administrative decisions provided for a flexible set of procedural obligations that were less onerous than natural justice, but clearly more stringent than the void of obligations that had attached to administrative decisions in the past.

Over time, the courts' approach evolved a second time. They came to accept that all decision-makers, whether exercising judicial, quasi-judicial, or administrative powers, should be subject to the same, flexible duty of fairness.[26] There was no longer a need to distinguish

---

19　See, generally, David Phillip Jones & Anne S de Villars, *Principles of Administrative Law*, 6th ed (Toronto: Carswell, 2014) ch 8.

20　This was the type of decision at issue in *Multani v Commission scolaire Marguerite-Bourgeoys*, 2006 SCC 6.

21　See e.g. *Martineau v Matsqui Institution*, [1980] 1 SCR 602 [*Martineau*].

22　Legislative decisions, some Cabinet decisions, and ministerial decisions of pure policy would also not have been subject to the common law procedural obligations of administrative law, as is still the case today. See e.g. *Martineau, ibid; Att Gen of Can v Inuit Tapirisat*, [1980] 2 SCR 735, [1980] SCJ No 99 (QL) [*Inuit Tapirisat*]; and *Wells v Newfoundland*, [1999] 3 SCR 199 [*Wells*].

23　See e.g. *Syndicat des employés de production du Québec et de l'Acadie v Canada (Human Rights Commission)*, [1980] 2 SCR 879.

24　*Nicholson v Haldimand-Norfolk (Regional) Police Commissioners*, [1979] 1 SCR 311 at 325, 88 DLR (3d) 671 [*Nicholson*]; *McCarthy v Calgary Roman Catholic Separate School District No 1* (1979), 145 DLR (3d) 765. The majority in *Nicholson* followed the lead of the House of Lords in *Ridge v Baldwin*, [1964] AC 40 (HL).

25　*Nicholson, supra* note 24.

26　*Knight v Indian Head School Board Division No 19*, [1990] 1 SCR 653 [*Knight*].

between natural justice and the duty of fairness. As Justice Dickson, on behalf of a minority of the court in *Martineau*, noted, "in general, courts ought not to seek to distinguish between the two concepts, for the drawing of a distinction between a duty to act fairly, and a duty to act in accordance with the rules of natural justice, yields an unwieldy conceptual framework."[27] With this approach, which continues to apply today, the expanded duty of fairness provides for a spectrum of procedural obligations. At the low end of the spectrum, a decision-maker is bound by minimum procedural duties, such as providing notice to affected parties. At the high end, a decision-maker must follow a more onerous set of procedures that may, in some cases, replicate the procedures followed in a civil or criminal trial.

The extension of the reach of procedural obligations was an important development in administrative law. The problem was more than just an "unwieldy conceptual framework." Rather, given the expansion of the regulatory state, it was difficult to defend an approach to public decision-making that was indifferent to procedural concerns in the vast majority of cases. As the regulatory state grew, its impact on the lives and rights of individuals also grew. Many of the decisions that the law had cast outside the realm of natural justice dealt with core matters of social welfare, including housing, employment, health care, immigration, and the environment. Thus, the law allowed many government decisions having a major impact on the rights and lives of individuals to exist outside the realm of enforceable and stringent procedural obligations. In shifting their approach, the courts reflected a concern with access to justice, as well as an admission that fairness is not synonymous with judicial process.

On these grounds, the courts eventually came to the conclusion that public decision-makers should not be immune from common law procedural obligations simply by virtue of the type of decision being made—judicial decisions versus administrative decisions. Nor should some types of government decisions automatically trigger a lower set of procedural duties. Rather, all decisions and all decision-makers should be subject to procedural obligations, the applicability and stringency of which should be assessed using a single set of considerations. With this expansion of the reach of procedural obligations and the harmonization of the law's approach to fairness, administrative law affirmed that procedural integrity was central to the exercise of public power in its respect for affected parties and a striving for good public administration, two valuable public goods.

2. *The Legal Consequences of Unfairness*

The second example that reflects the inherent value of procedural fairness in administrative law is found in the consequences of unfairness. As a general rule, the law treats administrative decisions that are tainted by unfairness as void. This means that an administrative decision that is made in breach of the duty of fairness cannot stand, even if the merits of the decision are substantively sound. Justice LeDain explained this position in *Cardinal*. In this case, two inmates of the Matsqui Institution, Mr Cardinal and Mr Oswald, were charged with criminal offences related to a hostage-taking at the prison and were subsequently transferred to Kent Institution, where they were placed in segregation on the director's oral instructions. The solitary confinement of these men continued, on the director's instructions, despite the Segregation Review Board's recommendation that they be returned to the

---

27   *Martineau, supra* note 21 at 629.

general population of the prison. When deciding to continue the segregation order, the director did not provide Mr Cardinal or Mr Oswald with reasons for their continued isolation or an opportunity to address the board's recommendation.

On appeal, the Supreme Court held that the director's failure to provide reasons and his failure to afford Mr Cardinal and Mr Oswald the opportunity to make submissions, even informally, was a breach of the duty of fairness. On the issue of whether this unfairness was sufficient to render the continued segregation unlawful, Justice LeDain wrote, "the denial of a right to a fair hearing must always render a decision invalid, whether or not it may appear to a reviewing court that the hearing would likely have resulted in a different decision. The right to a fair hearing must be regarded as an independent, unqualified right which finds its essential justification in the sense of procedural justice which any person affected by an administrative decision is entitled to have. It is not for a court to deny that right and sense of justice on the basis of speculation as to what the result might have been had there been a hearing."[28] In other words, a decision made unfairly cannot stand.[29]

As you'll see in the discussion that follows, the question in many cases is whether the principle of fairness, an inherently valuable part of our legal system, has been realized in practice. Is, for example, the flexible approach to fairness in the everyday operations of public decision-making a justified expression of access to justice, or does it diminish the value of fairness as an ideal? One might also ask why procedural fairness is not constitutionalized more broadly, beyond circumstances engaging life, liberty, and security of the person as guaranteed in s 7 of the Charter, if it is truly a necessary condition of justice. Professor Mullan argues that there is room, albeit limited room, to argue that procedural fairness has acquired some free-standing constitutional status independent of s 7.[30] This argument, contends Mullan, could find its footing in Justice L'Heureux-Dubé's claim in *Knight* that there may be "a general right to procedural fairness, autonomous of the operation of any statute."[31] Further, he argues, "given the recent resurgence in Supreme Court recognition of underlying constitutional values, there may, even now, still be a slight possibility that, by reference to process values recognized as part of the United Kingdom's unwritten constitution in 1867, the Preamble to the Canadian *Constitution Act* of that year

---

28 *Cardinal, supra* note 9 at 661.

29 In exceptional cases, relief may be withheld if the procedural error is "purely technical and occasions no substantial wrong or miscarriage of justice": *Canada (Citizenship and Immigration) v Khosa*, 2009 SCC 12 at para 43 [*Khosa*], citing *obiter* in *Pal v Canada (Minister of Employment and Immigration)* (1993), 24 Admin LR (2d) 68 at para 9; *Pannu v Canada (Minister of Employment and Immigration)* (1993), 42 ACWS (3d) 1064 (FCTD); *Pasco Pla v Canada (Minister of Citizenship and Immigration)*, 2012 FC 560. Further, relief may be denied, despite a finding of procedural unfairness, if "the demerits of the claim are such that it would in any case be hopeless" and thus "impractical" and "nonsensical" to grant relief: *Mobil Oil Canada Ltd v Canada-Newfoundland Offshore Petroleum Board*, [1994] 1 SCR 202. Moreover, notwithstanding the general rule, an administrative decision that is made unfairly at the administrative level may well be upheld on appeal if the appellate body holds a hearing *de novo* and does not import the tainted decision into its reasoning. The procedural protections offered by the fresh consideration of the issues are deemed to overcome the unfairness at the first level of decision-making: See *Harelkin v University of Regina*, [1979] 2 SCR 561; *Khan, supra* note 6; *McNamara v Ontario Racing Commission* (1998), 164 DLR (4th) 99 (Ont CA).

30 David J Mullan, *Administrative Law* (Toronto: Irwin Law, 2001) at 155.

31 *Knight, supra* note 26 at 668.

could become the source of guarantees of procedural protections, guarantees that can withstand legislative abrogation."[32]

Adding additional support to Mullan's position, the Supreme Court has continued to affirm that constitutional values, unwritten principles, and structural dimensions of the Constitution have normative consequences.[33] Further, in *Suresh*, the court explained that the principles of fundamental justice and the ideals of procedural fairness come from common stock.[34] That said, in *Knight*, Justice L'Heureux-Dubé went on to consider whether the common law procedural protections were abrogated by legislation, an analysis that would be uncalled for if procedural fairness enjoyed independent constitutional status. Moreover, on the whole, there has been little appetite by the courts to constitutionalize procedural protections in state decision-making beyond those guaranteed by s 7 of the Charter. Evan Fox-Decent and Alexander Pless further discuss the procedural implications of the Charter for administrative decision-makers in Chapter 6.

B. The Rule of Law and Access to Justice

You are already familiar, from Mary Liston's discussion in Chapter 4, with the rule of law and how it is realized within a democratic culture. As you read, the rule of law is a shared project in which public power is distributed across a sprawling, horizontal network of actors. Many institutions—legislatures, the executive, the courts, and the expanse of actors operating within the administrative state—participate in implementing, advancing, upholding, and, at times, diminishing the values that the rule of law seeks to protect. Private actors also play a role in upholding the rule of law by having high expectations of good public administration and holding public decision-makers to account when those expectations are not met.

What implications does this conception of the democratic rule of law have for understandings of procedural justice and fairness in administrative law? And how does the rule of law interact with the ambition for access to administrative justice? There are at least three responses to these questions.

First, as already mentioned, upholding the democratic rule of law is a responsibility shared by a range of public institutions. The primary institutions of Canadian state governance—legislatures, courts, the executive, and administrative actors—each have their individual roles to play. The responsibility for the rule of law is thus not only shared by various institutions, but also differentiated between the various institutional actors. Each institution has its own way of contributing to the maintenance of the rule of law. Indeed, as was highlighted in Chapter 4, the courts and administrative actors each play a unique role in upholding the rule of law. The courts provide independent oversight of state power; administrative actors provide specialized decision-making in multiple sectors. In light of this differentiation of roles, neither the design nor operation of administrative decision-making should replicate the design or operation of judicial decision-making, unless called for in the specific circumstances. Each decision-making context calls for a procedural arrangement that is tailored to

---

32   Mullan, *supra* note 30 at 151.
33   See e.g. *Reference re Secession of Quebec*, [1998] 2 SCR 217; *Reference re Supreme Court Act*, ss 5 and 6, 2014 SCC 21; *Reference re Senate Reform*, 2014 SCC 32.
34   *Suresh, supra* note 16 at para 113.

the realities of the decision-maker, the intent of the legislature, the types of decisions being made, and the impact on the parties. When the approach to administrative decision-making slides into that of judicial decision-making, and vice-versa, the diffusion of power at the heart of the democratic rule of law is undermined.

Differentiation as between institutions is also, in its ideal form, a means of furthering access to justice. In *Rasanen v Rosemount Industries*, Justice Abella explained that administrative tribunals were "expressly created as independent bodies for the purpose of being an alternative to the judicial process, including its procedural panoplies. Designed to be less cumbersome, less expensive, less formal and less delayed, these impartial decision-making bodies were to resolve disputes in their area of specialization more expeditiously and more accessibly, but no less effectively or credibly."[35] This observation highlights the foundational character of access to justice as a value of administrative justice; it is an orienting idea of the administrative state. It should, therefore, inform the meaning of fairness in administrative law.

Procedural design and the interpretation of fairness can have a meaningful impact— either positive or negative—on access to justice. At their core, procedural matters are all matters of access. The law of fairness is concerned with an affected party's right to be represented by counsel, the legal effect of delay, the extent of duties of notice and disclosure, the availability of interpretive services, and so on. On the one hand, stringent procedural obligations ensure that government decision-making respects the dignity interests of citizens affected by public power. On the other hand, stringent procedural obligations can undermine access to justice if they delay or prolong decision-making, increase the cost of pursuing administrative justice, or create other barriers to entry or use of the administrative decision-making system. Such barriers can prevent affected parties from exercising their rights of participation and, ultimately, from securing substantive justice. Between these two extremes, administrative law can strive to ensure that the legal meaning of fairness is attentive to the inextricable connection between procedural integrity and the full inclusion of affected parties in public decision-making. Angus Grant and Lorne Sossin, in Chapter 9 of this book, discuss in greater detail the extent to which the administrative state succeeds in advancing access to justice. Further, in Chapter 3, Janna Promislow and Naiomi Metallic examine the failures of the rule of law, accountability, and access to justice in the relationship between Indigenous Peoples and the Canadian state.

Second, the democratic rule of law not only entails a differentiation of responsibilities and roles between institutions, it also demands that those who wield public power are held accountable when they act unlawfully. In the administrative context, acting unlawfully includes the contravention of procedural duties. There are multiple routes by which citizens can hold public decision-makers accountable for the shortcomings of their procedural decisions. The formal and informal routes described by Cristie Ford in Chapter 2 are available to remedy instances of procedural unfairness. Depending on the issue at stake and the applicable statutory scheme, citizens can seek remedies through judicial review, statutory appeals to a court, private law claims, and claims for public law damages,[36] as well as through public inquiries, inquests, special task forces, royal commissions, departmental investigations,

---

35   *Rasanen v Rosemount Industries* (1994), 17 OR (3d) 267 (CA) at para 35 [*Rasanen*].
36   See e.g. *Paradis Honey Ltd v Canada*, 2015 FCA 89.

ombudspersons, specialized appeal tribunals,[37] "supertribunals" like the tribunal administrative du Quebec,[38] internal powers of reconsideration,[39] and the media. In upholding procedural fairness through this range of accountability mechanisms, administrative law contributes to the preservation of the democratic rule of law.

Third, the democratic rule of law can be upheld not only by formal mechanisms of accountability and oversight, but also by a culture of decision-making that reflects fundamental values and the norms of good public administration. Decision-makers who operate within this culture will internalize its norms and values, replicating them through their practices of decision-making and exercises of judgment. On this model, the norms of the rule of law and good decision-making are "enforced" and upheld through practice, from the bottom up rather than the top down.

A core element of the culture of the rule of law is the quality and character of practices of justification.[40] As explained in Chapter 4, the democratic vision regards the "justificatory exercise of reason-giving ... as an essential component of the rule of law."[41] That is, within this "culture of justification," public decision-makers must provide responsive reasons for their decisions.

When we think about the culture of justification and the quality of reasons, we tend to focus on the adequacy or substance of those reasons. The Supreme Court of Canada has held, however, that questions about adequacy and substance are not matters of procedural fairness.[42] Rather, procedural fairness is concerned only with whether a decision-maker has a duty to provide reasons and whether that duty has been fulfilled.[43] This distinction between the duty to provide reasons and the adequacy of those reasons does not render fairness irrelevant within the culture of justification—quite the opposite. When we affirm that justificatory practices are essential to the rule of law, we must also conclude that the duty to provide reasons should apply widely. A culture of justification can take hold only when the decision-makers who bear the biggest share of legal decision-making (that is, administrative decision-makers) are required to explain and justify their decisions through the provision of reasons. In this sense, fairness lies at the heart of the culture of justification.

Historically, the common law did not require public decision-makers to provide reasons for their decisions. This approach was altered in *Baker.* Justice L'Heureux-Dubé held that an administrative decision-maker is under a duty to provide "some form of reasons" when "the decision has important significance for an affected party, when there is a statutory right of appeal, or in other circumstances."[44] As is consistent with a strong commitment to the

---

37 See e.g. the Immigration Appeal Board, as provided for in *Immigration and Refugee Protection Act*, SC 2001, c 27, s 62, 67(1)(b) [IRPA].

38 *An act respecting Administrative Justice*, CQLR c J-3, r 2, s 14 [AJA].

39 *Ibid*, s 154(3). See also *Chandler v Alberta Association of Architects*, [1989] 2 SCR 848 at 861.

40 David Dyzenhaus, "Constituting the Rule of Law: Fundamental Values in Administrative Law" (2002) 27 Queen's LJ 445 at 502.

41 *Ibid* at 501-02.

42 *Newfoundland and Labrador Nurses' Union v Newfoundland and Labrador (Treasury Board)*, 2011 SCC 62 [*Newfoundland Nurses*].

43 *Ibid.*

44 *Baker, supra* note 10 at para 43.

culture of justification, these standards have been interpreted broadly and thus, the duty to provide reasons applies widely.[45]

In *Baker* and subsequent cases, the courts have recognized that only "some form" of reasons are required under the duty of fairness. On this standard, the informal notes of a junior immigration officer have been held to constitute reasons,[46] as has the record of a licence hearing before the Manitoba Taxicab Board.[47] In the former, the notes of the junior officer were held out as reasons by the final decision-maker and no other options were available.[48] In the latter, the record of the hearing contained a transcript of the proceedings, as well as disclosure and communications between the board and the parties. The Manitoba Court of Appeal held that the record "acted as a sufficient surrogate for formal, written reasons, so that a person could understand the rationale behind the Board's decision."[49] This flexibility with the form that reasons take is consistent with the principle of contextuality, as well as access to justice, as it avoids imposing a burden on decision-makers to provide written or judge-like reasons in all instances of decision-making. At the same time, if flexibility is maximized such that the bar for what counts as reasons is so low as to be effectively meaningless, we must ask whether the aims of access to substantive justice, as well as the integrity of the culture of justification, are compromised.

The gains for the culture of justification that accompany a broad interpretation of the duty to provide reasons might be attenuated by the Supreme Court's stance on implied decisions and reasons that "could be offered" for decisions. The Supreme Court has held that in some cases, the courts will review the reasons that an administrative decision-maker *could have* given, rather than actually gave, for her decision.[50] Further, the court has held that upon judicial review of an administrative decision-maker's implied decisions, a court is entitled to either "remit the issue back to the tribunal to allow the tribunal to provide reasons" or, if there is "a reasonable basis for the decision ... apparent to the reviewing court," to uphold the implied decision as reasonable.[51] While the court's comments regarding the review of implied decisions were made in the context of substantive review, the question remains as to their effect in the procedural realm. How can the procedural duty be met in these cases? Even if reasons can come in many forms, a meaningful duty to give reasons, one consistent with access to justice and the rule of law, seems to be one that cannot be satisfied

---

45   In *Mavi*, *supra* note 7 at para 45, the Supreme Court explained that reasons were not required given the context of the debt collection in question: "Given the legislative and regulatory framework, the non-judicial nature of the process and the absence of any statutory right of appeal, the government's duty of fairness in this situation does not extend to providing reasons in each case .... This is a situation, after all, merely of holding sponsors accountable for their undertakings so that the public purse would not suffer by reason of permitting the entry of family members who would otherwise not qualify for admission."

46   *Baker*, *supra* note 10.

47   *2127423 Manitoba Ltd o/a London Limos v Unicity Taxi Ltd*, 2012 MBCA 75 [*London Limos*].

48   *Baker*, *supra* note 10.

49   *London Limos*, *supra* note 47. Does the standard applied by the court in *London Limos*—understanding the rationale for the decision-maker's decision—constitute an assessment of the adequacy of the reasons? If so, is the court undertaking substantive review rather than assessing the procedural question? See e.g. *Wall v Office of the Independent Policy Review Director*, 2014 ONCA 884.

50   *Dunsmuir*, *supra* note 18 at para 48; *Newfoundland Nurses*, *supra* note 42, citing David Dyzenhaus, "The Politics of Deference: Judicial Review and Democracy" in Michael Taggart, ed, *The Province of Administrative Law* (Oxford: Hart, 1997) 279 at 286.

51   *Alberta (Information and Privacy Commissioner) v Alberta Teachers' Association*, 2011 SCC 61 at para 55.

by either implication or assumptions about what the decision-maker could have or must have been thinking. For further analysis of the duty to give reasons, see the discussion of procedural obligations arising from the Charter by Evan Fox-Decent and Alexander Pless in Chapter 6.

C. Enfranchisement and Flexibility

In "A Theory of Procedural Fairness," Roderick Macdonald argues that there is no single, universal feature of a fair process.[52] Rather, the specific procedures that comprise a process that is, on the whole, fair, will always depend on the context. The relevant context includes the type of decision being made and the type of decision-maker making it. But, Macdonald argues, every fair process must include steps that fall into two broad categories: first, steps concerned with "the quality of participation afforded to persons affected by [the] decision" and, second, steps concerned with "the kinds of reasons which may be offered to justify the decision itself."[53] Put another way, according to Macdonald, making decisions fairly demands attention to modes of participation and modes of justification. Further, on Macdonald's model, fairness requires that modes of participation and justification be tailored to the particular decision-making context in question. There is no form of participation or reason-giving that will universally satisfy the demands of fairness.

The notion of procedural fairness in Canadian administrative law reflects these concerns with participation, justification, and contextuality. As explained above, the two maxims of natural justice, *audi alteram partem* and *nemo judex in sua causa*, are the precursors of the Canadian approach to procedural fairness. These two maxims call on decision-makers to "hear the other side" and "not to be the judge in one's own case." In modern administrative law, these two maxims have evolved into concerns with the rights of affected parties to participate in decision-making (participatory rights) and with ensuring impartiality and independence in government decision-making, both real and apprehended (rules against bias). The law treats both participatory rights and protections from bias as vital to the integrity and fairness of public decision-making. A true enfranchisement of citizens in government decision-making requires that citizens be allowed to participate in the decisions that affect their interests. It also requires that participation not be undermined by perceptions or actual instances of bias in the decision-making process.

Participatory rights and the rules against bias are the core concepts of the law of procedural fairness. Both must be satisfied in order for a procedure to be fair in the eyes of the law. The thresholds that must be met are well-established. In *Baker*, Justice L'Heureux-Dubé articulated the legal standard for assessing whether modes of participation are fair. "Administrative decisions," she held, must be "made using a fair and open procedure, appropriate to the decision being made and its statutory, institutional, and social context, with an opportunity for those affected by the decision to put forward their views and evidence fully and have them considered by the decision-maker."[54] The standard for disqualifying bias is equally well-established. It was set out in *Committee for Justice & Liberty v Canada (National*

---

52 Roderick A Macdonald, "A Theory of Procedural Fairness" (1981) 1 Windsor YB Access Just 3.
53 *Ibid* at 33.
54 *Baker, supra* note 10 at para 22.

Energy Board), a case dealing with allegations of bias against the National Energy Board.[55] Writing in dissent on other points, Justice de Grandpré held that to determine whether a decision-maker is tainted by a reasonable apprehension of bias, we should ask what an "informed person, viewing the matter realistically and practically—and having thought the matter through—would conclude."[56] The question is: Would the informed person think that it is "more likely than not" that the decision-maker would not decide fairly?[57]

There is no set or checklist of procedures that will automatically meet the standards set in *Baker* or *National Energy Board* in all cases. The standards are intentionally general. Because they must apply to all cases of administrative decision-making, the standards must be sufficiently abstract to capture all administrative decision-making contexts, ranging from the National Energy Board's decisions on pipeline applications to the minister of immigration, refugees, and citizenship's determinations of admissibility to university grievance committees' adjudication of student grade appeals. The specific procedures that must be followed in order to satisfy the demands of fairness in each case will always depend on the circumstances. The circumstances are equally relevant to determining the proper modes of participation and what is necessary to avoid perceptions of bias. Justice L'Heureux-Dubé explained in *Baker* that "the concept of procedural fairness is eminently variable and its content is to be decided in the specific context of each case."[58] She went on to highlight that this variability arises across all questions of procedure. "[T]he standards for reasonable apprehension of bias," she wrote, "may vary, like other aspects of procedural fairness, depending on the context and the type of function performed by the administrative decision-maker involved."[59] The demands of fairness, in other words, cannot be assessed in abstraction. Fairness and unfairness attach as decision-making plays out on the ground.

The contextual factors that are relevant to distinguishing between fairness and unfairness in relation to participatory rights are discussed below, while the contextual factors relevant to identifying instances of bias are discussed fully by Laverne Jacobs in Chapter 7. Before turning to the discussion of the particulars of participatory rights, it is worth reiterating once more the guidance expressed in *Rasanen v Rosemount Industries*, above.

In *Rasanen*, we are reminded that context is an important element of fairness not simply to ensure that an administrative decision-maker has the practical capacity to carry out the procedures demanded of it, but also to ensure that administrative decision-makers are able to fulfill their role in the structure of governance, namely as legal decision-makers that resolve disputes for which courts are not well-suited. The enfranchisement of citizens in administrative decision-making does not, therefore, necessarily require the same form of participation called for by a criminal trial. The context of administrative decision-making will only call for these high procedural requirements in rare circumstances. Further, the context in which we assess the procedural obligations in administrative decision-making must be sensitive to, and consistent with, the statutory scheme within which a particular

---

55   *Committee for Justice & Liberty v Canada (National Energy Board)*, [1978] 1 SCR 369 [*National Energy Board*].
56   *Ibid* at 394.
57   *Ibid*. See also *Baker, supra* note 10 at para 46.
58   *Baker, supra* note 10 at para 21, citing *Knight, supra* note 26 at 682.
59   *Baker, supra* note 10 at para 47.

decision-maker operates.[60] That scheme is the foundation of a decision-maker's world and thus sets the structural parameters within which fairness should be assessed for each individual decision-maker.

Arguments in favour of maximizing participation should, however, also reflect a respect for access to justice, as discussed above. Enfranchisement and access to justice may have the greatest potential for tension. For instance, as a general rule, the greater the impact of a decision, the greater the procedural entitlements and participatory rights of affected parties.[61] However, as the stringency and complexity of procedural obligations expand, access to justice may diminish. In *Mavi*, Justice Binnie, writing on behalf of the Supreme Court, emphasized the need for the law's understanding of fairness to appreciate the intersection of access and good governance. "In determining the content of procedural fairness," Justice Binnie wrote, "a balance must be struck. Administering a 'fair' process inevitably slows matters down and costs the taxpayer money. On the other hand, the public also suffers a cost if government is perceived to act unfairly, or administrative action is based on 'erroneous, incomplete or ill-considered findings of fact, conclusions of law, or exercises of discretion.'"[62]

As a result, whenever we assess the procedural demands that attach to a decision-making process, the need for robust procedural protections must be weighed against competing needs for efficiency and access. As the process becomes more complicated and stringent, it expands the investments of time, money, and public resources necessary to achieve administrative justice. Such expansion may be justified in some circumstances, such as when liberty or security is at stake, but indefensible in others, such as when the procedural demands create insurmountable obstacles for individuals seeking justice from public officials. Again, this potential for tension between the foundational principles of fairness is not a reason to discard any single principle. Instead, it calls on us to interpret each principle in relation to the others, weighing and managing the competing interests in order to realize fairness, in both principle and practice, in government decision-making.

III. THE PRACTICES OF PROCEDURAL FAIRNESS

With this knowledge of the principles underlying fairness in Canadian administrative law, we can now turn to the practices of fairness. In this part of the chapter, we are concerned with what fairness looks like on the ground. We will explore what procedures an administrative decision-maker must follow in order to act fairly. The focus is on action and practice; the results should account for both principle and context.

The question about how to realize procedural fairness in practical terms can be framed in two different ways. From the perspective of the decision-maker, the underlying question is:

---

60   See e.g. *Mavi*, *supra* note 7. See also *Roncarelli v Duplessis*, [1959] SCR 121.

61   Paul Daly, "Administrative Law: A Values-Based Approach" in John Bell, Mark Elliott, Jason Varuhas & Philip Murray eds, *Public Law Adjudication in Common Law Systems: Process and Substance* (Oxford: Hart, 2015); *Baker*, *supra* note 10.

62   *Mavi*, *supra* note 7 at para 40, citing Donald JM Brown & John M Evans, with the assistance of Christine E Deacon, *Judicial Review of Administrative Action in Canada* (Toronto: Canvasback, 1998) (loose-leaf updated July 2010), ch 7 at 7-3; see also Mullan, *supra* note 30 at 178.

What procedural obligations does *this* decision-maker, making *this* decision, owe to *this* party? This way of framing the question focuses on obligations. From the perspective of parties affected by a decision, the core question is slightly different: To what is *this* individual entitled from *this* decision-maker making *this* decision? This question focuses on rights and entitlements.

Both of these perspectives are correct ways of thinking about the practices of procedural fairness. Both lead to the same conclusions, and they both entail an analysis of the statutory, constitutional, and common law sources of procedure that apply to a decision-maker. Thus, in terms of the legal analysis, there may be little consequence of which way you choose to articulate the issue. That said, from the perspectives of an advocate, a law student, or a legal scholar, it is important to keep in mind that the way that you frame the question reflects the position you hold, and it will affect your approach to crafting arguments. Thus, when responding to any question of procedural fairness, you should be mindful of the perspective from which you pose the inquiry—obligations or entitlements. This will not only help you to craft persuasive arguments, but will also remind you to anticipate the counter-arguments that can be made from the opposing perspective.

In order to determine the specific procedures that any administrative decision-maker must follow, we must always look to three types of sources: statutes and subordinate instruments, the Constitution, and the common law. The discussion below explores the obligations that arise from each of these sources.

A. Procedural Obligations Arising from Statute, Regulations, Rules, and Guidelines

1. Enabling and Internal Instruments

As is often true in administrative law, the first place to look for obligations that bind a decision-maker is the decision-maker's enabling statute. The enabling statute may set out no, some, or a complete code of procedural obligations for the decision-maker to follow when making decisions. Barring any constitutional concerns,[63] the obligations set out in the enabling statute will be binding on the decision-maker. Further, unless the enabling statute provides for a complete code of procedure,[64] the procedures set out in the enabling statute will only be a minimum set, which can then be fortified and supplemented with additional obligations found in any or all of the other sources discussed below.

In some cases, a statute may provide for multiple decision-making bodies within a single public organization. In such arrangements, each internal decision-making body will have its own unique function and, as a result, its own procedural obligations. The Immigration and Refugee Board is one example. The board is a large organization comprised of four unique, independently operating decision-making bodies—the Refugee Protection Division, the Refugee Appeal Division, the Immigration Division, and the Immigration Appeal Division.[65] Each division is bound by a unique set of legislative and regulatory procedural rules when

---

63 Constitutional concerns are addressed in Section III.B and in greater detail in Chapter 6.
64 *Singh*, *supra* note 15.
65 IRPA, s 2(1).

carrying out its mandate.[66] Provincial law societies are another example. The law societies are created by statute to serve multiple functions.[67] They are charged with establishing standards of professional competence and practice, investigating complaints against members of the profession, resolving complaints and disputes, imposing sanctions, accrediting legal education programs, creating and administering professional training programs, choosing leaders, and so on. These tasks are performed using various modes of decision-making—investigation, adjudication, deliberation, elections, managerial decision-making, and policy-based modes of reasoning. Because of this diversity in function and mode of decision-making, it would be inefficient and ineffective for a single decision-maker to perform all of a law society's mandated tasks. Accordingly, the provincial statutes that create the law societies provide for the societies themselves, as well as various internal decision-making bodies that are tasked with fulfilling the societies' many roles. For instance, in Nova Scotia, the *Legal Professions Act* establishes the Nova Scotia Barristers' Society, but also provides for a Complaints Investigation Committee, a Hearing Committee, a Fitness to Practice Committee, the Council of the Society, the Executive Director of the Society, and more.[68] Each of these decision-makers is then subject to unique procedural rules set out in the *Legal Professions Act* and its regulations.[69] When multiple decision-makers exist within a large, overarching organization, it is imperative to parse the enabling statute carefully to ensure that you are attaching the proper procedures to each particular decision-making body.

In many cases, a decision-maker's enabling statute will not set out a complete code of procedure for decision-making and, instead, the legislature will delegate the authority to establish additional procedural obligations to an executive actor, such as the governor in council (at the federal level), the lieutenant governors in council (in the provinces), a minister, or the decision-making body itself. These additional obligations can be established by rule or regulation, depending on the language of the statutory delegation. For instance, under the *Immigration and Refugee Protection Act*, the governor in council is broadly authorized to make regulations dealing with procedure and the minister of citizenship and immigration is authorized to propose regulations to the House of Commons on a range of matters, including procedure.[70] Both the governor in council and the minister have exercised these powers in order to enact the *Immigration and Refugee Protection Regulations*.[71] The *Immigration Refugee Protection Act* also authorizes the chairperson of the Immigration and Refugee Board to make rules regarding the procedures that will be followed by the Refugee Protection Division, the Refugee Appeal Division, the Immigration Division, and the Immigration Appeal Division.[72] These rules can address "the activities, practice and procedure of each of the Divisions of the Board, including the periods for appeal ... the priority to be given to proceedings, the notice that is required and the period in which notice must be given," as well as the "conduct of persons in proceedings before the Board, as well as the

---

66 See e.g. *Immigration Division Rules*, SOR/2002-229; *Immigration Appeal Division Rules*, SOR/2002-230; *Refugee Protection Division Rules*, SOR/2012-256; *Refugee Appeal Division Rules*, SOR/2012-257.

67 See e.g. *Legal Professions Act*, SNS 2004, c 28, s 4 [LPA].

68 LPA, ss 6(1), 9(1), 34, 34A, 41(1).

69 See e.g. LPA, ss 11, 34(1), 34A(2), 42(1); Regulations made pursuant to the *Legal Profession Act*, SNS 2004, c 28 [LPA Regs].

70 See e.g. IRPA, ss 5(1), (2).

71 *Immigration and Refugee Protection Regulations*, SOR/2002-227 [IRP Regs].

72 IRPA, s 161(1).

consequences of, and sanctions for, the breach of those rules."[73] According to the Act, these rules are subject to the approval of the Governor in Council and must be made in consultation with the deputy chairpersons of the divisions of the board.[74] The Chairperson has exercised this rule-making power when enacting the *Immigration Division Rules*, the *Immigration Appeal Division Rules*, the *Refugee Protection Rules*, the *Refugee Protection Division Rules*, and the *Refugee Appeal Division Rules*.[75] As a general rule, the obligations prescribed by these delegated forms of authority will be binding on the decision-maker.[76]

In addition to obligations set by statute, rules, and regulations, an administrative decision-maker may also establish internal policies, guidelines, and practice directions that govern its processes of decision-making (frequently known as "soft law"). For instance, the National Energy Board has issued a "Filing Manual" that sets out extensive procedures that are to be followed by applicants and the board in relation to the vast range of projects and disputes that fall within the board's jurisdiction, including applications to construct or modify a pipeline.[77] As another example, the chairperson of the Immigration and Refugee Board is authorized to "take ... any action that may be necessary to ensure that the members of the Board carry out their duties efficiently and without undue delay" and to "issue guidelines in writing to members of the Board ... to assist members in carrying out their duties."[78] The chair has issued many guidelines under this authority, including Guideline 8, the *Guideline on Vulnerable Persons*, issued in 2006 and amended in 2012.[79] This guideline offers guidance to board members when vulnerable persons appear before them. Section 1.1 provides that the intention of the *Guideline on Vulnerable Persons* is to "provide procedural accommodation(s) for individuals who are identified as vulnerable persons by the Immigration and Refugee Board of Canada." Section 4.2 advises the members of the board that they have the discretion to respond to the individual circumstances of the parties involved in their hearings and accommodate those circumstances by modifying the procedures they follow:

> 4.2 The IRB has a broad discretion to tailor procedures to meet the particular needs of a vulnerable person, and, where appropriate and permitted by law, the IRB may accommodate a person's vulnerability by various means, including:
>   a. allowing the vulnerable person to provide evidence by videoconference or other means;
>   b. allowing a support person to participate in a hearing;
>   c. creating a more informal setting for a hearing;

---

73 IRPA, ss 161(1)(a.2), (b).

74 IRPA, s 161(1).

75 *Supra* note 66. As another example, turning back to the Nova Scotia Barristers' Society, the provincial legislature has delegated to the Council of the Society authority to make regulations regarding a host of issues, including decision-making procedure. More specifically, the LPA empowers the Council to make regulations prescribing the procedures for each of the Society's internal decision-makers, including the Investigation Committee, the Hearing Committee, the Fitness to Practice Committee, and the Council itself: LPA, ss 6(1), 9(1), 11, 34, 34A, 41(1); LPA Regs. The Council has exercised this regulation-making power by enacting the LPA Regs.

76 For further discussion of the delegation of rule-making power, see Chapter 8.

77 See National Energy Board, "Filing Manual" (Ottawa: National Energy Board, 2016).

78 IRPA, s 159(1)(h).

79 Guideline issued by the Chairperson pursuant to paragraph 159(1)(h) of the *Immigration and Refugee Protection Act* [*Guideline on Vulnerable Persons*].

    d. varying the order of questioning;

    e. excluding non-parties from the hearing room;

    f.   providing a panel and interpreter of a particular gender;

    g. explaining IRB processes to the vulnerable person; and

    h. allowing any other procedural accommodations that may be reasonable in the circumstances.[80]

The normative character of guidelines, manuals, policies, and other "soft law" instruments produced internally by decision-making bodies is somewhat ambiguous. Research shows that "soft law" instruments developed by a decision-maker are powerful sources of authority for front-line decision-makers and have been treated as *de facto* binding on the ground.[81] Further, the courts have held that, in the realm of substantive decision-making, interpretive guidelines can helpfully assist decision-makers, parties, and courts.[82] However, guidelines are not legally binding on a decision-maker making these substantive decisions. Also, the courts have explained that treating soft law instruments as binding would "elevate [executive] directions to the level of law and fetter the [decision-maker] in the exercise of his discretion."[83] Neither the elevation nor the fettering are consistent with the rule of law. (See also the discussion on fettering by Andrew Green in Chapter 8).

This same reasoning applies when decision-makers exercise discretion in relation to procedural choices. Indeed, the rule that guidelines are not legally binding has also been applied in cases dealing with procedural fairness.[84] That said, in practice, the rule may not operate as rigidly when it comes to procedural guidelines as it does with guidelines dealing with substantive matters. For example, in *Bezaire v Windsor Roman Catholic Separate School Board*, ministerial guidelines and a school board policy on school closures were, in effect, treated as binding.[85] The court relied on the guidelines and policy as persuasive evidence of the procedures required by the common law duty of fairness. Thus, the guidelines and policy, despite being "soft law," supplied the basis for enforceable rights.[86]

Further, guidelines established by administrative decision-makers may be effectively binding by virtue of the doctrine of legitimate expectations. In *Agraira v Canada (Public Safety and Emergency Preparedness)*,[87] Mr Agraira, a citizen of Libya, had been living in Canada since 1997. In 2002, he was found to be inadmissible on security grounds. Mr Agraira applied to the Minister of Public Safety and Emergency Preparedness for relief from this finding. When his application was denied, Mr Agraira applied for judicial review of the minister's decision. Mr Agraira claimed, among other things, that the minister failed to follow guidelines that had been established by Citizenship and Immigration Canada and which set

---

80 *Ibid.*

81 See Laura Pottie & Lorne Sossin, "Demystifying the Boundaries of Public Law: Policy, Discretion, and Social Welfare" (2005) 38 UBC L Rev 147.

82 See e.g. *Baker, supra* note 10.

83 *Maple Lodge Farms Ltd v Canada*, [1982] 2 SCR 2 at 7. See also *Kanthasamy v Canada (Citizenship and Immigration)*, 2015 SCC 61.

84 See e.g. *Huron East (Municipality) v Avon Maitland District School Board*, [2002] OJ No 2697 (QL) (Div Ct); *DeLarue v Kawartha Pine Ridge District School Board*, 2012 ONSC 3349; *Thamoranthem v Canada (Minister of Citizenship & Immigration)*, 2007 FCA 198, [2008] 1 FCR 385.

85 (1992), 9 OR (3d) 737 (Div Ct).

86 *Ibid.* See also *Ross v Avon Maitland District School Board*, [2000] OJ No 1714 (QL) (Sup Ct J).

87 2013 SCC 36, [2013] 2 SCR 559 [*Agraira*].

out the process by which applications for ministerial relief would be assessed. Mr Agraira argued that he had a legitimate expectation that the guidelines would be followed. Justice LeBel, writing for the Supreme Court, accepted that guidelines established by an administrative decision-maker can give rise to a legitimate expectation that a particular procedure will be followed and had done so in this case.[88] Justice LeBel summarized the doctrine of legitimate expectations as follows:

> If a public authority has made representations about the procedure it will follow in making a particular decision, or if it has consistently adhered to certain procedural practices in the past in making such a decision, the scope of the duty of procedural fairness owed to the affected person will be broader than it otherwise would have been. Likewise, if representations with respect to a substantive result have been made to an individual, the duty owed to him by the public authority in terms of the procedures it must follow before making a contrary decision will be more onerous.
>
> The specific conditions which must be satisfied in order for the doctrine of legitimate expectations to apply are summarized succinctly in a leading authority entitled *Judicial Review of Administrative Action in Canada*:
>
>> The distinguishing characteristic of a legitimate expectation is that it arises from some conduct of the decision-maker, or some other relevant actor. Thus, a legitimate expectation may result from an official practice or assurance that certain procedures will be followed as part of the decision-making process, or that a positive decision can be anticipated. As well, the existence of administrative rules of procedure, or a procedure on which the agency had voluntarily embarked in a particular instance, may give rise to a legitimate expectation that such procedures will be followed. Of course, *the practice or conduct said to give rise to the reasonable expectation must be clear, unambiguous and unqualified.*[89]

According to the court, a "clear, unambiguous and unqualified" representation is one that if made "in the context of a private law contract, would be sufficiently certain to be capable of enforcement."[90] In Mr Agraira's case, the guidelines met the standard of a "clear, unambiguous and unqualified" representation regarding the procedural framework that the minister would follow when assessing applications for relief. Accordingly, a legitimate expectation arose. Justice LeBel explained that the guidelines were publicly available and were a "relatively comprehensive procedural code" for dealing with relief applications.[91] Further, although the guidelines were published by Citizenship and Immigration Canada, which is not the department of the Minister of Public Safety and Emergency Preparedness, it was "clear that [the guidelines] are 'used by employees of [both] CIC and the CBSA for guidance in the exercise of their functions and in applying the legislation.'"[92] Thus, evidence of the decision-maker's usual practice was relied on to ground the procedural obligations applicable to the minister.

In the end, although Mr Agraira successfully established a legitimate expectation as to the procedure that would be followed when his application was assessed, he had failed to

---

88   *Ibid* at para 98.
89   *Ibid* at paras 94-95, citing Brown & Evans, *supra* note 62, ch 7 at 17-10 (emphasis added by Justice LeBel); see also *Mount Sinai Hospital Center v Quebec (Minister of Health and Social Services)*, 2001 SCC 41 at para 29, [2001] 2 SCR 281; *Mavi, supra* note 7 at para 68.
90   *Mavi, supra* note 7 at para 69; *Agraira, supra* note 87 at para 96.
91   *Agraira, supra* note 87 at para 98.
92   *Ibid*, citing the respondent's factum at para 108.

show that the minister did not follow that procedure. Justice LeBel held that on the evidence, the procedural protections set out in the guidelines were provided to Mr Agraira. Accordingly, the legitimate expectation was fulfilled.

Agraira suggests that the doctrine of legitimate expectations can operate in a way to render guidelines (or presumably other "soft law" instruments) binding in practice and in legal effect. In this sense, *Agraira* seems to be at odds with the principles against elevation and fettering of discretion mentioned above. The analysis of the procedural obligations in *Agraira* also suggests that the doctrine of legitimate expectations is a stand-alone procedural right. That is, Justice LeBel's reasoning indicates that had Mr Agraira successfully shown that his legitimate expectation had not been met, then he would have been entitled to relief. However, this differs from the approach set out in *Baker*, discussed in greater detail below, which provides that legitimate expectations are just one factor to consider when determining the procedural obligations that an administrative decision-maker must follow when making decisions. There is support for both the *Baker* and *Agraira* approaches in the jurisprudence, and thus we are left with some flexibility as to the effect of legitimate expectations on the procedural obligations of public decision-makers.

The mechanics, virtues, and limits of delegating rule-making power to executive and administrative actors, as well as further commentary on the ways delegated and informal authority is exercised, are discussed by Andrew Green in Chapter 8. For our purposes, it is sufficient to summarize the discussion above by noting that the procedures that an administrative decision-maker must follow often include obligations prescribed by the decision-maker's enabling statute, as well as in subordinate legislation and administrative policy and practice. Together, these statutory, subordinate, and internal instruments can create a dense web of procedures that an administrative decision-maker must—either legally or normatively— follow when making decisions. Thus, in determining a decision-maker's obligations, each of these sources must be canvassed thoroughly. In intricate regulatory regimes like immigration or the pipeline approval process, it may take some effort to determine the matrix of procedures prescribed by the various sources and assess their normative ordering. Further, as we see from the discussion above, to fully appreciate, implement, and apply the obligations set out in enabling and internal instruments, we must also direct our attention to the case law and the context. That is, the statutory and subordinate sources cannot be interpreted and understood in a contextual or jurisprudential vacuum.

2. General Procedural Codes

In addition to procedural obligations set out in the enabling statutes, regulations, rules, policies, and practices unique to a decision-maker, some administrative decision-makers are also subject to procedural obligations set out in general procedural statutes. General procedural codes have been enacted in four provinces—Quebec,[93] Ontario,[94] Alberta,[95] and British Columbia.[96] These statutes set out common procedures that govern the decision-making bodies that fall within the scope of the statutes. The notion of common procedures is somewhat at odds with the

---

93   AJA.
94   *Statutory Powers Procedure Act*, RSO 1990, c S 22 [SPPA].
95   *Administrative Procedures and Jurisdiction Act*, RSA 2000, c A-3 [APJA].
96   *Administrative Tribunals Act*, SBC 2004, c 45 [ATA].

principles of flexibility and contextuality, which are premised on a respect for the diverse real-ities of administrative decision-makers. To maintain this respect, and accommodate the tension between generality and specificity in procedural design, the legislatures must approach ques-tions about the scope and design of the general statute with care.

The jurisdictions that have adopted the general procedural codes take different ap-proaches to application. Alberta's *Administrative Procedures and Jurisdiction Act* (APJA) applies to tribunals designated by the Lieutenant Governor in Council[97] or by express terms of a decision-maker's enabling statute.[98] The APJA does not relieve a tribunal from complying with procedures in other applicable statutes;[99] it can operate in conjunction with other statu-tory procedural schemes. Similarly, British Columbia's *Administrative Tribunals Act* applies only when adopted, in whole or in part, in another statute.[100] Quebec's *An Act Respecting Adminis-trative Justice* applies to decisions of the "Administration." The Administration is defined as "the government departments and bodies whose members are in the majority appointed by the Government or by a minister and whose personnel is appointed in accordance with the Public Service Act"[101] and the relevant decisions are those "individual decisions made in respect of a citizen."[102] Finally, Ontario's *Statutory Powers Procedure Act* (SPPA) applies to a "proceeding by a tribunal in the exercise of a statutory power of decision" where the tribunal is required by statute or otherwise by law to hold a hearing or give the parties an opportun-ity for a hearing.[103] While Ontario's open, conceptual approach all but guarantees the need for litigation to assist in resolving disputes about when a tribunal is exercising a "statutory power of decision," it offers the benefit, like Quebec's Act, of capturing new decision-makers without the need for further legislative or executive action.[104] The SPPA is the only general procedural code that provides that in the event of a conflict with another statute (or regu-lations, rules, or by-laws made under it), the SPPA prevails, unless the other statute (or regulations, rules, or by-laws made under it) provide otherwise.

The four general procedural codes also represent different approaches to the appropriate level of specificity in a common set of procedures. Quebec's Act tends toward general prop-ositions, while Ontario's is quite specific. The codes in the other provinces fall somewhere in between. Given the few jurisdictions that have enacted common codes and given the number of exemptions from Ontario's code, it is arguable whether the legislatures have adopted the best allocation of responsibility over ad hoc procedural design or struck the

---

97 APJA, s 2.

98 See e.g. *Individual Rights Protection Act*, RSA 1980, c I-2, s 29(2).

99 APJA, s 8.

100 ATA, s 1.1(1). Parts of the Act have been incorporated into the enabling statutes of, for example, the Human Rights Commission (*Human Rights Code*, RSBC 1996, c 210, s 32), the Securities Commission (*Securities Act*, RSBC 1996, c 418, s 4.1), the Employment Standards Tribunal (*Employment Standards Act*, RSBC 1996, c 113, s 74(1)(a)), the Utilities Commission (*Utilities Commission Act*, RSBC 1996, c 473, s 2.1), and the Environmental Appeal Board (*Environmental Management Act*, SBC 2003, c 53, s 93.1).

101 AJA, s 3.

102 AJA, s 1.

103 SPPA, s 3(1). "Statutory power of decision" is defined in s 1 as "a power or right, conferred by or under a statute, to make a decision deciding or prescribing, (a) the legal rights, powers, privileges, immunities, duties or liabilities of any person or party, or (b) the eligibility of any person or party to receive, or to the continuation of, a benefit or licence, whether the person is legally entitled thereto or not."

104 See Brown & Evans, *supra* note 62 (loose-leaf updated May 2016), ch 8 at 8-8, n 71.

best balance between flexibility and fairness.[105] Ultimately, regardless of their desirability and success, if you practise in, or encounter the decision-making processes of administrative actors in Quebec, Ontario, Alberta, or British Columbia, it will be imperative to familiarize yourself with the procedural protections and obligations prescribed by the general codes.

As a final note, be aware that the common law duty of fairness (discussed below in Section III.C) can add to the obligations required by statute, but it cannot override statutory obligations. Barring a constitutional or quasi-constitutional challenge, a statutory obligation will be binding even if it is inconsistent with the common law duty of fairness. In effect, statutory procedures need not be fair in the legal sense, unless required by a constitutional or quasi-constitutional source.

B. Procedural Obligations Arising from the Constitution

There are many ways in which constitutional and quasi-constitutional sources may have an impact on a decision-maker's procedural obligations. For example, obligations that are set by statute, regulation, rules, or policies may be challenged on the grounds that they are inconsistent with the structural and unwritten dimensions of the Constitution, the division of powers, or the rights and freedoms guaranteed by the *Charter of Rights and Freedoms*. Further, in the federal sector, procedural obligations set by statute, regulation, rules, or policies can also be challenged on the ground that they are contrary to the procedural protections guaranteed by the *Bill of Rights*.[106] Further still, in Quebec, such a challenge could also be grounded in the *Quebec Charter of Human Rights and Freedoms*.[107] In any of these cases, the affected party would seek relief from either the administrative decision-maker or the courts. In addition to being struck down or declared inapplicable, the procedural obligations of administrative decision-makers can also be supplemented or bolstered by the guarantees set out in the Canadian or Quebec charters or the *Bill of Rights*. These types of claims, and the contexts in which they arise, are all discussed in greater detail in Chapters 6 and 7.

Leaving those claims to subsequent chapters, this chapter can focus on the procedural obligations that flow from a single constitutional feature, namely, the unwritten principle of the honour of the Crown, now also enshrined in s 35 of the *Constitution Act, 1982*. The Canadian courts have identified this principle as the source of major legal obligations that have enforceable practical effects on the process of state decision-making, namely the Crown's duty to consult Indigenous Peoples whose rights may be adversely affected by Crown conduct and the duty to accommodate the concerns established during processes of consultation.

In Chapters 3 and 8 of this volume, Janna Promislow, Naiomi Metallic, and Andrew Green offer greater detail and critical commentary on the background of the duty to consult, the practice of consultation on the ground, and the role of administrative decision-makers in both carrying out consultation and holding other state actors to account for their duties of consultation. The exploration in this chapter is a more modest part of understanding the duty

---

105 For brief discussions of the case for general statutory procedural codes, see Mullan, *supra* note 30 at 222-25 and Gus Van Harten et al, *Administrative Law: Cases, Text, and Materials*, 7th ed (Toronto: Emond Montgomery, 2015) at 274-77.

106 *Canadian Bill of Rights*, SC 1960, c 44, ss 1, 2(e).

107 *Charter of Human Rights and Freedoms*, RSQ, C-12.

to consult. This chapter situates the duty to consult within the framework of statutory, consti-tutional, and common law procedural protections that public actors must address in order to comply with the current state of Canadian law. Further, it presents the doctrinal framework developed by the Supreme Court for determining when the duty to consult and accommo-date applies and whether it has been satisfied. As discussed in greater detail below, the framework calls for a two-step analysis: Is the duty triggered? And, if so, what does it entail? As we will see in Section III.C, this analytical framework mirrors the framework to be followed when determining the obligations that arise under the common law duty of fairness.

The contemporary understanding of the duty to consult and accommodate in Canadian constitutional and administrative law was born of cases in the 1980s, but matured somewhat in a trilogy of cases decided by the Supreme Court in 2004 and 2005: *Haida Nation*,[108] *Taku River Tlingit First Nation*,[109] and *Mikisew Cree First Nation*.[110] As noted above, according to the Supreme Court in these decisions, the duty to consult and accommodate is rooted in the honour of the Crown, an unwritten constitutional principle that gives rise to concrete obli-gations and legally enforceable rights for Indigenous peoples and communities.[111] The court explained in *Haida Nation* that, on its understanding, the honour of the Crown is rooted in an aspiration for reconciliation:

> The historical roots of the principle of the honour of the Crown suggest that it must be under-stood generously in order to reflect the underlying realities from which it stems. In all its deal-ings with Aboriginal peoples, from the assertion of sovereignty to the resolution of claims and the implementation of treaties, the Crown must act honourably. Nothing less is required if we are to achieve "the reconciliation of the pre-existence of aboriginal societies with the sover-eignty of the Crown": *Delgamuukw* [[1997] 3 SCR 1010], at para 186, quoting *Van der Peet* [[1996] 2 SCR 507], at para 31.[112]

According to the court, acting honourably means that the Crown "cannot cavalierly run roughshod over Aboriginal interests where claims affecting these interests are being ser-iously pursued."[113] To give practical effect to the admonition against "running roughshod" over Indigenous interests, the trilogy established that the Crown has a constitutional duty to actively consult Indigenous peoples whose rights may be adversely affected by Crown conduct, as well as a duty to then accommodate concerns and claims raised in the process of consultation.[114] This duty to consult and accommodate is, according to the Supreme Court, an attempt by the law to "protect Aboriginal and treaty rights while furthering

---

108   *Haida Nation v British Columbia (Minister of Forests)*, 2004 SCC 73 [*Haida Nation*].

109   *Taku River Tlingit First Nation v British Columbia (Project Assessment Director)*, 2004 SCC 74 [*Taku River*].

110   *Mikisew Cree First Nation v Canada (Minister of Heritage)*, 2005 SCC 69 [*Mikisew Cree*].

111   *Haida Nation, supra* note 108 at para 16.

112   *Ibid* at para 17.

113   *Ibid* at para 27.

114   In 2005, the SCC confirmed that the duty to consult applies to treaty rights: *Mikisew Cree, supra* note 110 at para 55. Justice Binnie explained that historic treaties do not offer the Crown an excuse to avoid con-sultation where it would normally be appropriate. In modern treaties, the duty to consult is still oper-ational and parties cannot contract out of it: *Beckman v Little Salmon/Carmacks First Nation*, 2010 SCC 53 at para 61 [*Little Salmon/Carmacks*]. Nevertheless, the court has held, as parties to modern treaties are adequately represented, and as the treaties are exemplars of "precision and sophistication," the parties to modern treaties may shape the duty to consult: *Little Salmon/Carmacks, ibid* at paras 54, 61.

reconciliation between Indigenous peoples and the Crown."[115] Both the analysis and the practice of the duty to consult are to be animated by the overarching goal of pursuing reconciliation between Indigenous Peoples and the state.

As noted above, the particulars of the duty to consult—when it applies and what it entails—are assessed by asking two questions: Is the duty to consult and accommodate triggered? If so, what does it entail? The answers to these questions have significant practical consequences for public decision-making. To understand these consequences and the law's approach to the duty to consult, we will explore each of the two questions in greater detail.

The first question asks whether the duty to consult and accommodate has been triggered. To answer this query, the law turns to another question: In the circumstances, does the Crown have "actual or constructive knowledge of a potential Aboriginal claim or Aboriginal or treaty rights that might be adversely affected by Crown conduct"?[116] For the Crown to meet this standard, three distinct elements must be satisfied:

- First, the Crown must have knowledge, real or constructive, of a right or a claim. Real knowledge exists when a "claim has been filed in court" or is indicated during negotiations; constructive knowledge arises when "lands are known or reasonably suspected to have been traditionally occupied by an Aboriginal community or an impact on rights may be reasonably anticipated."[117]
- Second, the Crown must be contemplating action that may cause an adverse effect on Aboriginal rights or title, or a claimed right or title.[118] The contemplated action can come in many forms. It might be the exercise of statutory authority or "strategic, higher level decisions."[119] Further, it could be action with an immediate effect on the interests of Indigenous communities or a decision with the potential for future adverse impacts.[120] Examples of action that has triggered the duty to consult include the transfer of logging licences for old growth forest,[121] "the approval of a multi-year forest management plan for a large geographic area,"[122] "the establishment of a review process for a major gas pipeline,"[123] and the issuance of a project approval certificate for the construction of a road to service the reopening of a mine.[124] In addition, the Supreme Court has recently confirmed that "Crown conduct which would trigger the duty is not restricted to the exercise by or on behalf of the Crown of statutory powers or of the royal prerogative."[125] Rather, the category of "Crown conduct" that can trigger the duty includes regulatory processes carried out by independent administrative agencies. While a regulatory agency that exer-

---

115 *Clyde River, supra* note 1 at para 19.
116 *Clyde River, supra* note 1 at para 25, citing *Haida Nation, supra* note 108 at para 35.
117 *Rio Tinto Alcan Inc v Carrier Sekani Tribal Council*, 2010 SCC 43 at paras 40-41 [*Carrier Sekani*].
118 *Ibid* at paras 42-44.
119 *Ibid* at para 44.
120 *Ibid*.
121 *Haida Nation, supra* note 108.
122 *Carrier Sekani, supra* note 117 at para 44, citing *Klahoose First Nation v Sunshine Coast Forest District (District Manager)*, 2008 BCSC 1642.
123 *Carrier Sekani, supra* note 117 at para 44, citing *Dene Tha' First Nation v Canada (Minister of Environment)*, 2006 FC 1354, aff'd 2008 FCA 20.
124 *Taku River, supra* note 109.
125 *Clyde River, supra* note 1 at para 25.

cises executive power authorized by the legislature is not technically "the Crown" or an agent of the Crown, it is a "vehicle through which the Crown acts."[126] A decision of such an agency can therefore constitute Crown action that triggers the duty to consult. The guiding concern when identifying Crown conduct is adverse impacts, "however made,"[127] not the precise legal boundaries of which actors constitute "the Crown."

- Third, the "claimant must show a causal relationship between the proposed government conduct or decision and a potential for adverse impacts on pending Aboriginal claims or rights."[128] This requirement is to be interpreted generously in recognition of the irreversible adverse effects that action can have on Aboriginal rights, Aboriginal title, or treaty rights before they are proven.[129] However, the impact must be more than speculative and must have an effect on the future exercise of the right.[130]

Once each of these three elements is satisfied, the duty to consult is triggered and must be actively fulfilled in order for the Crown to be acting in a way that is consistent with the Constitution.

When the duty to consult is triggered, we must then ask what it entails in the circumstances. In other words, in light of the particular decision being made or action being taken, what must the Crown do, in the eyes of Canadian state law, to act honourably? Given the origins of the duty to consult, this question must also be interpreted in light of the aspiration of reconciliation. That said, the courts have not, by any measure, expected or imagined that the Crown will achieve perfect consultation and accommodation. Moreover, the Crown is under no legal duty to agree with or adopt the positions submitted by Indigenous individuals or groups during consultation. Rather, under Canadian law, the Crown is only legally obligated to act in good faith and ensure meaningful consultation and responsive action:[131]

> The common thread on the Crown's part must be "the intention of substantially addressing [Aboriginal] concerns" as they are raised … through a meaningful process of consultation. Sharp dealing is not permitted. However, there is no duty to agree; rather, the commitment is to a meaningful process of consultation. As for Aboriginal claimants, they must not frustrate the Crown's reasonable good faith attempts, nor should they take unreasonable positions to thwart government from making decisions or acting in cases where, despite meaningful consultation, agreement is not reached … . Mere hard bargaining, however, will not offend an Aboriginal people's right to be consulted.[132]

According to the Supreme Court, meaningful and responsive consultation requires that the Crown discharge its obligations to consult before the impugned government action takes place.[133] If consultation takes place after a decision is made—after a logging licence is granted, for example, or after a pipeline is constructed—the title or right that the Indigenous community is seeking to enforce may be compromised or rendered meaningless. Moreover, consultative processes that are undertaken at the insistence of the courts rather than as a

---

126   *Clyde River, supra* note 1 at para 29. See also *Chippewas of the Thames, supra* note 1.
127   *Ibid* at para 25.
128   *Carrier Sekani, supra* note 117 at para 45.
129   *Ibid.*
130   *Ibid* at para 46.
131   *Haida Nation, supra* note 108 at para 41.
132   *Ibid* at para 42.
133   *Tsilhqot'in Nation v British Columbia*, 2014 SCC 44, [2014] 2 SCR 257 at para 78 [*Tsilhqot'in Nation*].

manifestation of Crown impulse are at odds with the conciliatory spirit that is to animate Crown action in its relationship with Indigenous Peoples:

> True reconciliation is rarely, if ever, achieved in courtrooms. Judicial remedies may seek to undo past infringements of Aboriginal and treaty rights, but adequate Crown consultation *before* project approval is always preferable to after-the-fact judicial remonstration following an adversarial process. Consultation is, after all, "[c]oncerned with an ethic of ongoing relationships" (*Carrier Sekani*, at para 38, quoting DG Newman, *The Duty to Consult: New Relationships with Aboriginal Peoples* (2009), at p 21). As the Court noted in *Haida*, "[w]hile Aboriginal claims can be and are pursued through litigation, negotiation is a preferable way of reconciling state and Aboriginal interests" (para. 14). No one benefits—not project proponents, not Indigenous peoples, and not non-Indigenous members of affected communities—when projects are prematurely approved only to be subjected to litigation.[134]

Further, meaningful and responsive consultation has been interpreted to mean that the Crown must do more than just listen. While there is no duty for the parties engaged in consultation to reach an agreement, the obligation to act honourably calls on the Crown to take steps to understand the concerns of the Indigenous Peoples whose rights are at stake and to make real efforts to address those concerns.[135]

In the eyes of the courts, the extent of the consultation and accommodation that the Crown must undertake, and the combination of practices that constitute meaningful consultation in the circumstances, exist across a spectrum.[136] The spectrum ranges from limited to deep consultation, depending on two factors: (1) the severity of the potential impact of the government action on the claimed Aboriginal or treaty right, and (2) the strength of the Indigenous community's claim to the right. When the claim is thought to be weak and the negative effects are thought to be limited, "the only duty on the Crown may be to give notice, disclose information, and discuss any issues raised in response to the notice."[137] In the converse scenario, "deep consultation, aimed at finding a satisfactory interim solution, may be required."[138] Such deep consultation may entail that Indigenous Peoples and groups are provided the opportunity to make submissions, present evidence, and offer a final argument; formal participation in the decision-making process and funding to support that participation; an oral hearing; access to material submitted by other parties, which accounts for potential barriers created by language and access to technology; and written reasons that show that concerns of Indigenous Peoples were considered and disclose the impact of those concerns on the outcome.[139] This non-exhaustive list is not a checklist, but rather a collection of possible modes of consultation. What the Constitution requires in any particular case will, as always, depend on the circumstances.

The duty to accommodate has come to be associated with the higher end of the spectrum. That is, when a strong *prima facie* case for an Aboriginal right exists and the potential adverse effects are significant, a duty to accommodate may arise. The duty to accommodate calls on the Crown to take steps or change the course of its intended path in order to avoid

---

134   *Clyde River, supra* note 1 at para 24.
135   *Haida Nation, supra* note 108 at para 49.
136   *Ibid* at paras 42-43.
137   *Ibid* at para 43.
138   *Ibid* at para 44.
139   *Clyde River, supra* note 1 at para 24.

irreparable harm or to minimize the effects of government action on Aboriginal rights, Aboriginal title,[140] and treaty rights.[141] The content of the duty to accommodate in each particular case depends on the outcome of a proportionality assessment:

> Balance and compromise are inherent in the notion of reconciliation. Where accommodation is required in making decisions that may adversely affect as yet unproven Aboriginal rights and title claims, the Crown must balance Aboriginal concerns reasonably with the potential impact of the decision on the asserted right or title and with other societal interests.[142]

The content of the duty is to be interpreted in accordance with the principles of flexibility and contextuality.[143] Accordingly, the particulars of the duty to consult and accommodate for the Crown, making a particular type of decision, will depend on a keen appreciation of the context. Again, and most fundamentally within Canadian state law, this appreciation must be animated by the honour of the Crown and the goals of reconciliation.

Looking to the cases, we see an example of a duty at the high end of the spectrum in *Tsilhqot'in.* In that case, the duty to consult was triggered when Crown officials began plans to remove timber from land subject to a claim of Aboriginal title and when the province allowed third parties to forest and develop the traditional territory of the Tsilhqot'in First Nation. In deciding the content of the duty, the court held that the "Tsilhqot'in had a strong *prima facie* claim to the land at the time of the impugned government action and the intrusion was significant."[144] Accordingly, the duty to consult fell at the high end of the spectrum described in *Haida Nation* and called on the Crown to undertake "significant consultation and accommodation in order to preserve the Tsilhqot'in interest."[145] The Court concluded that the duty to consult was not fulfilled: "The inclusion of timber on Aboriginal title land in a timber supply area, the approval of cut blocks on Aboriginal title land in a forest development plan, and the allocation of cutting permits all occurred without any meaningful consultation with the Tsilhqot'in."[146]

In contrast, we see an example of the duty to consult at the lower end of the spectrum in *Little Salmon/Carmacks.* In this case, the duty to consult was triggered by an application for an agricultural land grant. The land covered by the application included a small portion (one-third of one percent) of the trapline of a member of the Little Salmon/Carmacks First Nation. Justice Binnie, for the majority of the court, held that this quantitatively small

---

140 With respect to government action that relates to land over which Aboriginal title has been established, the duty to consult applies, embedded within an exercise of proportionality reasoning. The Supreme Court summarized the procedural obligations in such cases as follows: "Aboriginal title confers on the group that holds it the exclusive right to decide how the land is used and the right to benefit from those uses, subject to one carve-out—that the uses must be consistent with the group nature of the interest and the enjoyment of the land by future generations. Government incursions not consented to by the title-holding group must be undertaken in accordance with the Crown's procedural duty to consult and must also be justified on the basis of a compelling and substantial public interest, and must be consistent with the Crown's fiduciary duty to the Aboriginal group": *Tsilhqot'in Nation, supra* note 133 at para 88.

141 *Haida Nation, supra* note 108 at para 47.

142 *Ibid* at para 50.

143 *Ibid* at para 45.

144 *Tsilhqot'in Nation, supra* note 133 at para 93.

145 *Ibid.*

146 *Ibid* at para 96. For another example that fell at the high end of the spectrum, see *Clyde River, supra* note 1.

impact on the First Nation's rights as protected by Treaty 8 positioned the case at the low or light end of the spectrum of consultation. Further, Justice Binnie held, the duty to consult had been satisfied. The First Nation received notice of the decision and had the opportunity to submit written objections to the land grant. The Director of the Agricultural Branch had the First Nation's submissions before him when he approved the application. According to the court, "[n]either the honour of the Crown nor the duty to consult required more."[147]

A commitment to contextuality in relation to the duty to consult has also entailed that the Crown must regularly reassess its duties as it moves through various stages of a decision-making process. Public decision-making in relation to land and resources, such as the approval of a pipeline, the extraction of resources from a territory, the building of a road, or the granting of harvesting licences, is often long and proceeds through many stages. As time marches on and circumstances change, the Crown is expected to monitor and reassess its duties of consultation and accommodation. The Crown should actively and regularly reflect on the ways in which its conduct measures up against the ideals of honour and reconciliation. The court described the significance of this ongoing reflection in *Tsilhqot'in*, in relation to the facts of that case:

> The practical result may be a spectrum of duties applicable over time in a particular case. At the claims stage, prior to establishment of Aboriginal title, the Crown owes a good faith duty to consult with the group concerned and, if appropriate, accommodate its interests. As the claim strength increases, the required level of consultation and accommodation correspondingly increases. Where a claim is particularly strong—for example, shortly before a court declaration of title—appropriate care must be taken to preserve the Aboriginal interest pending final resolution of the claim. Finally, once title is established, the Crown cannot proceed with development of title land not consented to by the title-holding group unless it has discharged its duty to consult and the development is justified pursuant to s 35 of the *Constitution Act, 1982*.[148]

Much of the jurisprudence discussed above helps to provide insight into the duties of the Crown in relation to consultation and accommodation. Thus, you may be feeling somewhat comfortable assessing the consultative obligations of, for example, Cabinet ministers or executive actors exercising the Crown prerogative, who clearly count as "the Crown." And yet, at the same time, you may be left wondering about the role of the broader category of administrative agencies in processes of consultation. Do regulatory processes, like the pipeline approval process conducted by the National Energy Board, for example, trigger the duty to consult? Can such processes be relied on to fulfill the Crown's duty to consult? Further, are administrative agencies authorized to determine whether the Crown has satisfied its duty? Are regulatory bodies themselves bound by the duty to consult when they are the final decision-maker in respect of a project that could impact Indigenous or treaty rights?

While these questions have generated some uncertainty in the past, the Supreme Court has recently offered some insight. In *Clyde River*, the National Energy Board (NEB) authorized a group of corporate actors to conduct offshore seismic testing for oil and gas resources in Nunavut. It was undisputed that the testing could negatively impact the treaty rights of the Inuit of Clyde River. Under the *Nunavut Land Claims Agreement*, the Inuit of Clyde River had

---

147   *Little Salmon/Carmacks, supra* note 114.
148   *Tsilhqot'in Nation, supra* note 133 at para 91.

ceded certain rights and interests in the Settlement Area, which included Clyde River, in exchange for treaty rights. These rights included the right to harvest marine mammals. Seeking to protect these rights, the Inuit of Clyde River opposed the proponents' application to conduct testing and, in challenging the NEB's decision, alleged that the Crown's duty to consult had not been fulfilled. The Supreme Court unanimously agreed that the duty to consult had not been fulfilled in this case. In reaching this decision, the Court clarified the NEB's role in relation to the Crown's duty.

First, Justices Karakatsanis and Brown, writing for the Court, held that the NEB's approval process triggered the duty to consult. The judges explained that the duty is ultimately and always owed by the Crown and that "strictly speaking," the NEB is neither the Crown nor an agent of the Crown given that "no relationship of control exists between them."[149] However, they held, it would improperly favour form over substance to conclude that the conduct of the NEB did not in effect constitute Crown action:

> Put plainly, once it is accepted that a regulatory agency exists to exercise executive power as authorized by legislatures, any distinction between its actions and Crown action quickly falls away. In this context, the NEB is the vehicle through which the Crown acts. Hence this Court's interchangeable references in *Carrier Sekani* to "government action" and "Crown conduct" (paras 42-44). It therefore does not matter whether the final decision maker on a resource project is Cabinet or the NEB. In either case, the decision constitutes Crown action that may trigger the duty to consult.[150]

Second, Justices Karakatsanis and Brown confirmed the conclusion in *Carrier Sekani* that the Crown may rely on steps undertaken by a regulatory agency to fulfill the duty to consult, either in whole or in part. Whether the Crown can do so depends on "whether the agency's statutory duties and powers enable it to do what the duty requires in the particular circumstances."[151] Indeed, the court held that even an agency, like the NEB, that was established before judicial recognition of the duty to consult, can be relied on to fulfill the duty as long as its enabling statute affords it the power to provide the requisite level of consultation and accommodation. That said, when relying on a regulatory process to fulfill its duties, either in whole or in part, the Crown must advise affected Indigenous groups of this reliance. Further, when the regulatory process being relied on falls short of the constitutional standard, the Crown must step in to fill the gaps, either on a case-by-case basis or more systemically through legislative or regulatory amendments.[152] In examining the statutory scheme of the NEB, Justices Karakatsanis and Brown concluded that the Crown could rely on the NEB's process to completely or partially fulfill its duty because the NEB was imbued with the both the "procedural powers necessary to implement consultation" and "the remedial powers to, where necessary, accommodate affected Aboriginal claims, or Aboriginal and treaty rights."[153]

Third, the court considered whether the NEB was authorized to assess the adequacy of the consultation prior to authorizing the testing. Citing *Conway*, Justices Karakatsanis and Brown confirmed that the general rule for constitutional jurisdiction applies in the duty to

---

149   *Clyde River, supra* note 1 at para 29.
150   *Ibid* at para 29.
151   *Ibid* at para 30.
152   *Ibid* at para 22.
153   *Ibid* at para 34.

consult cases.[154] They explained that "[r]egulatory agencies with the authority to decide questions of law have both the duty and authority to apply the Constitution, unless the authority to decide the constitutional issue has been clearly withdrawn."[155] It follows, they concluded, that these agencies "must ensure their decisions comply with s 35 of the *Constitution Act, 1982*.[156] In looking at the jurisdiction of the NEB, Justices Karakatsanis and Brown had no difficulty concluding that the NEB had broad powers to hear and determine all relevant matters of fact and law and that there had been no express or implied withdrawal of the constitutional jurisdiction. Accordingly, they held that NEB decisions must be consistent with s 35(1) of the *Constitution Act, 1982* and that the NEB is authorized to determine whether the Crown's duty to consult has been fulfilled.[157] They went on to summarize how the NEB should proceed when the issue of consultation is raised and the consequences for failing to follow this guidance:

> If the Crown's duty to consult has been triggered, a decision maker may only proceed to approve a project if Crown consultation is adequate. Although in many cases the Crown will be able to rely on the NEB's processes as meeting the duty to consult, because the NEB is the final decision maker, the key question is whether the duty is fulfilled prior to project approval (*Haida*, at para 67). Accordingly, where the Crown's duty to consult an affected Indigenous group with respect to a project under *COGOA* remains unfulfilled, the NEB must withhold project approval. And, where the NEB fails to do so, its approval decision should (as we have already said) be quashed on judicial review, since the duty to consult must be fulfilled prior to the action that could adversely affect the right in question (*Tsilhqot'in Nation v British Columbia*, 2014 SCC 44, [2014] 2 SCR 257, at para 78).[158]

---

154 *R v Conway*, 2010 SCC 22, [2010] 1 SCR 765 at para 77 [*Conway*]. For greater discussion of the constitutional jurisdiction of administrative decision-makers, see Chapter 6.

155 *Clyde River*, *supra* note 1 at para 30. See also the court's explanation in *Carrier Sekani*, *supra* note 117 at para 69: "The power to decide questions of law implies a power to decide constitutional issues that are properly before it, absent a clear demonstration that the legislature intended to exclude such jurisdiction from the tribunal's power (*Conway*, *supra* note 154 at para 81; *Paul v British Columbia (Forest Appeals Commission)*, 2003 SCC 55, [2003] 2 SCR 585, at para 39). '[S]pecialized tribunals with both the expertise and authority to decide questions of law are in the best position to hear and decide constitutional questions related to their statutory mandates': *Conway*, at para 6."

156 *Clyde River*, *supra* note 1 at para 30. Professor Promislow has pointed to examples suggesting that some decision-makers are reluctant to accept that questions about the duty to consult are within their jurisdiction, even when they have jurisdiction to decide questions of law: Janna Promislow, "Irreconcilable? The Duty to Consult and Administrative Decision Makers" (2013) 22:1 Constitutional Forum 63 at 69. Such reluctance amounts to differential treatment of the duty to consult in comparison to other types of constitutional questions that arise in administrative proceedings, which have long been dealt with by the "questions of law" threshold. The legislatures could respond by either expressly including or excluding tribunals' jurisdiction over the duty to consult, leaving Indigenous parties to enforce their rights to consultation in the courts. With respect to a legislative response, it remains unknown whether an inclusive or exclusive approach to jurisdiction would be beneficial to Indigenous parties or project proponents. The exclusive approach would be at odds with the access to justice concerns underlying *Martin*, *Conway*, and *Paul*. As Professor Promislow contends at 71, whatever the ultimate approach, a legislative response should be "a matter determined through dialogue with affected Indigenous groups, ensuring that Indigenous communities have sufficient access to regulatory or other decision-makers to allow for regular oversight and dispute resolution with respect to consultation processes."

157 *Clyde River*, *supra* note 1 at para 30.

158 *Ibid* at para 39.

Finally, Justices Karakatsanis and Brown concluded that when the adequacy of Crown consultation is raised before a regulatory agency, the agency "must usually" address the issue in reasons. This is particularly true when the project in question calls for deep consultation. According to the Court, written reasons are consistent with the spirit of reconciliation that underlies the duty to consult. "Written reasons foster reconciliation," Justices Karakatsanis and Brown wrote, "by showing affected Indigenous peoples that their rights were considered and addressed … Reasons are 'a sign of respect [which] displays the requisite comity and courtesy becoming the Crown as Sovereign toward a prior occupying nation.'"[159]

On the facts of the case, the court concluded that the duty to consult had not been satisfied. The Crown agreed that given the strength of the Inuit of Clyde River's treaty rights and the potential severity of the seismic testing on the marine mammals harvested by the Inuit for spiritual, cultural, and economic well-being, deep consultation was required. Such a high level was not met on the facts. The NEB failed to assess the impact of the seismic testing on the treaty rights of the Inuit of Clyde River, independent from the environmental impact of the testing writ large. Further, the Crown failed to inform the Inuit that it was relying on the NEB's processes to fulfill the duty to consult. Finally, the process provided by the NEB did not fulfill the obligation to conduct deep consultation. No oral hearing was held. The Inuit were not provided with funding to support their participation in the process. And answers to questions posed by the Inuit regarding basic elements of the testing and their implications were not made accessible to the Inuit. The Crown was thus found in breach of its duty, and the NEB's authorization of the project was quashed.

The decisions in *Clyde River* and its companion case of *Chippewas of the Thames* offered some meaningful clarity and positive developments on lingering questions regarding the role of administrative agencies in triggering, carrying out, and assessing the fulfillment of the duty to consult. Of course, questions and mixed messages remain. For example, the court in *Chippewas of the Thames* held that the duty to consult is "not the vehicle to address historical grievances."[160] At the same time, the court affirmed that the cumulative effects and historical context of an ongoing project, a project that may have been initiated historically without consultation, for instance, is an important component of understanding the impact of a project on Indigenous rights and interests. Without providing further guidance, the court indicated that these historical factors "may … inform the scope of the duty to consult."[161] We will have to wait to determine the extent to which cumulative and historical contextual factors, which seem critical to appreciating the significance of current projects on Indigenous rights, lives, and communities and vital to the goals of reconciliation, are accounted for in government consultation processes and practices going forward.

With respect to the duty to consult and Crown conduct more broadly, despite advancement in the law of the duty to consult in Canadian constitutional and administrative law in recent years, significant questions remain regarding its character, principles, and practices. As noted above, Chapters 3 and 8 discuss these questions in greater detail. This section thus concludes with a simple doctrinal query for you to reflect upon as you move to the next section of the chapter, which deals with the common law duty of fairness. The question is

---

159 *Clyde River, supra* note 1 at para 41, citing *Kainaiwa/Blood Tribe v Alberta (Energy)*, 2017 ABQB 107 at para 117).

160 *Chippewas of the Thames, supra* note 1 at para 41.

161 *Ibid* at para 42.

whether, and in what ways, the obligations associated with the duty to consult mirror or differ from the obligations flowing from the common law duty. After *Little Salmon/Carmacks*, some commentators suggested there was ultimately no difference between the two duties, and that such an "impoverished view of the duty to consult is hardly likely to contribute to the constitutional goal of inter-societal reconciliation."[162] To what extent do the sources and aims of the constitutional and common law duties differ and to what end? Do the practical manifestations of these duties successfully achieve their goals?

Underlying this query is a curiosity about the most useful way to understand the relationship between administrative law principles of fairness and approaches to procedure, on the one hand, and constitutional principles and approaches to proper procedure, on the other. In *Little Salmon/Carmacks*, the majority of the Supreme Court rejected the argument that there is a "bright line" between the constitutional duty to consult and administrative law principles such as procedural fairness.[163] Instead, the latter seems to be relied upon to inform the obligations entailed by the former. That is, administrative decision-makers are always bound to act within the limits set by the Constitution.[164] Such limits include the honour of the Crown and the duty to consult.[165] In determining the content of the duty and in discharging the obligations, the courts have held that the Crown may have regard to "the procedural safeguards of natural justice mandated by administrative law."[166] The relevant "procedural safeguards" include not only the more narrow doctrine of natural justice but also the broader understanding of procedural fairness that has developed in contemporary administrative law.[167] The query to be determined in each case of decision-making then becomes how these common law safeguards can and should be relied upon to inform the constitutional obligation of consultation. Ultimately, what is the best way to understand the relationship between administrative and constitutional approaches? Are these helpful legal distinctions and if so, in what ways?

C. Procedural Obligations Arising from the Common Law

So far, this part of the chapter has addressed the procedural obligations that apply to administrative decision-making pursuant to statute, subordinate legislation, internal instruments, and the Constitution. This final section considers the procedural obligations that apply by way of the common law. While these common law obligations cannot override legislative and constitutional procedures, the common law can supplement the procedures required by statute and the Constitution.

This section presents the analytical framework for determining when the common law duty of fairness applies to a decision-maker and what the duty entails. This framework, set out in the leading case of *Baker*, is well-established in Canadian administrative law. *Baker* is a

---

162 Nigel Bankes, "Little Salmon and the Juridical Nature of the Duty to Consult and Accommodate" (2010), ABlawg.ca archives, online: <http://ablawg.ca/2010/12/10/little-salmon-and-the-juridical-nature-of-the-duty-to-consult-and-accommodate>.

163 *Little Salmon/Carmacks, supra* note 114 at para 45.

164 *Slaight Communications v Davidson*, [1989] 1 SCR 1038; *Doré v Barreau du Québec*, 2012 SCC 12, [2012] 1 SCR 395.

165 *Little Salmon/Carmacks, supra* note 114 at para 45.

166 *Haida Nation, supra* note 108 at para 41.

167 *Little Salmon/Carmacks, supra* note 114 at para 46.

case dealing with fairness in the deportation context, and as further exploration of this case-study weaves throughout this volume, we will closely examine the facts of Ms Baker's case and explore how the Supreme Court sought to ensure that Ms Baker was treated fairly by officials within Citizenship and Immigration Canada.

As is discussed in detail below, in order to determine what procedural obligations an administrative decision-maker must follow under the common law, we must ask two questions. First, is the duty of fairness triggered? In other words, is the decision being made one that should be made fairly? If the answer is no, the analysis ends and the decision-maker can, as a matter of law, proceed without the responsibility of common law obligations. If the answer is yes, we move to the second question: What does the duty entail? In other words, what is the content of the duty? As we will see, answering this question calls for a close assessment of the context.

As is the case with many issues in administrative law, the two-step framework is best understood in the context in which it arose, namely in the Supreme Court's consideration of *Baker v Canada (Minister of Citizenship and Immigration)*. At the time of the litigation, Mavis Baker lived in Canada but was not a Canadian citizen or a permanent resident. She arrived as a visitor from Jamaica, her country of citizenship, in 1981 and stayed in Canada thereafter. During her time in the country, Ms Baker was employed and was a mother to four children, all Canadian-born. In 1992, a deportation order was issued for Ms Baker on the grounds that she had worked illegally and had overstayed her original visitor's visa.

In 1993, Ms Baker began the process of acquiring permanent resident status. As a general rule, applicants for permanent resident status must apply from outside of Canada. This requirement meant that Ms Baker had to return to Jamaica in order to apply to stay in Canada. However, the legislative scheme also provided for an exception to the general rule. Pursuant to the IRP Regs, the minister of citizenship and immigration could grant exemptions from the "outside" rule if the minister was "satisfied that ... the person's admission should be facilitated owing to the existence of compassionate or humanitarian considerations." Ms Baker applied to the minister for such an exemption on humanitarian and compassionate grounds. Through written submissions, she argued that the application of the general rule would have grave consequences for both herself and her children. She submitted that leaving the country would jeopardize her health, as she was receiving treatment for mental illness in Canada, and such medical care might not be available in Jamaica. Further, Ms Baker's application established her care-giving and nurturing roles for her children and also indicated that she would suffer emotional hardship if separated from her family. Ms Baker's application was supported by submissions from her lawyer, her doctor, and a social worker with the Children's Aid Society.

In April 1994, Ms Baker received a letter from Citizenship and Immigration Canada, signed by Immigration Officer Caden. The letter stated that Ms Baker's application for an exemption had been denied. No reasons were provided. Upon requesting reasons, Ms Baker was provided with the notes of another Immigration Officer. Officer Caden had relied upon these notes when assessing Ms Baker's application and reaching a decision on the minister's behalf. The notes included the following appraisal of the file:

> PC is unemployed - on Welfare. No income shown - no assets. Has four Cdn.-born children- four other children in Jamaica- HAS A TOTAL OF EIGHT CHILDREN
>> Says only two children are in her "direct custody." (No info on who has ghe [*sic*] other two).

There is nothing for her in Jamaica—hasn't been there in a long time—no longer close to her children there—no jobs there—she has no skills other than as a domestic—children would suffer—can't take them with her and can't leave them with anyone here. Says has suffered from a mental disorder since '81—is now an outpatient and is improving. If sent back will have a relapse.

Letter from Children's Aid—they say PC has been diagnosed as a paranoid schizophrenic.— children would suffer if returned—

Letter of Aug. '93 from psychiatrist from Ont. Govm't.

Says PC had post-partum psychosis and had a brief episode of psychosis in Jam. when was 25 yrs. old. Is now an outpatient and is doing relatively well—deportation would be an extremely stressful experience.

Lawyer says PS [sic] is sole caregiver and single parent of two Cdn born children. Pc's mental condition would suffer a setback if she is deported etc.

This case is a catastrophy [sic]. It is also an indictment of our "system" that the client came as a visitor in Aug. '81, was not ordered deported until Dec. '92 and in APRIL '94 IS STILL HERE!

The PC is a paranoid schizophrenic and on welfare. She has no qualifications other than as a domestic. She has FOUR CHILDREN IN JAMAICA AND ANOTHER FOUR BORN HERE. She will, of course, be a tremendous strain on our social welfare systems for (probably) the rest of her life. There are no H&C factors other than her FOUR CANADIAN-BORN CHILDREN. Do we let her stay because of that? I am of the opinion that Canada can no longer afford this type of generosity. However, because of the circumstances involved, there is a potential for adverse publicity. I recommend refusal but you may wish to clear this with someone at Region.

There is also a potential for violence—see charge of "assault with a weapon"

[Capitalization in original.]

After receiving these "reasons," Ms Baker was served with another deportation order.

Ms Baker applied for judicial review of the minister's decision to reject her application for an exemption. She argued, among other things, that the minister had failed to comply with the requirements of the duty of fairness.[168] Ms Baker contended that, pursuant to the common law duty of fairness, she was entitled to an oral interview with the decision-maker; her children and their other parent were entitled to notice of the interview and the opportunity to make submissions; and the other parent of her children was entitled to appear at the interview with counsel. Ms Baker also argued that she was entitled to reasons for the minister's decision and that the notes she had received gave rise to a reasonable apprehension of bias.

Ms Baker's application for judicial review was unsuccessful at the Federal Court—Trial Division, and her appeal to the Federal Court of Appeal was dismissed.[169] On appeal to the Supreme Court, the court held that the common law duty of fairness applied to "humanitarian and compassionate decisions." Further, it held that the duty owed to Ms Baker by the

---

168   These matters are addressed in Chapters 7 and 15.

169   Pursuant to s 83(1) of the *Immigration Act*, a judgment of the Federal Court—Trial Division could be appealed to the Federal Court of Appeal only if the Trial Division certified and stated a serious question of general importance that was at stake in the case. Simpson J of the Trial Division had certified the following question in Ms Baker's case: "Given that the Immigration Act does not expressly incorporate the language of Canada's international obligations with respect to the International Convention on the Rights of the Child, must federal immigration authorities treat the best interests of the Canadian child as a primary consideration in assessing an applicant under s 114(2) of the *Immigration Act*?"

minister was more than minimal. This meant that the minister (or the officers in the department) had to consider the issues and evidence fully and fairly and that both Ms Baker and "others whose important interests were affected by the decision in a fundamental way" had to have a meaningful opportunity to present the evidence relevant to their case.[170] According to the court, an oral interview was not required to meet this standard. Ms Baker had had the opportunity to provide the decision-maker with all of the relevant information and arguments. Ms Baker was, however, entitled to written reasons for the minister's decision, given the "profound importance" of the decision to those affected.[171] Demonstrating its flexibility in relation to reasons, the court concluded that the duty to provide reasons was fulfilled when Ms Baker was given the notes of Officer Lorenz.

There is much for us to draw from the judgment of Justice L'Heureux-Dubé, writing for the court on the issue of procedural fairness, in *Baker*. The case provides guidance on the general principles governing the duty of fairness and on the two-step analytical framework that governs when determining the common law procedural obligations owed by a decision-maker to affected parties. Recall from above that procedural fairness encompasses both participatory rights and rules against bias (see Section I). The discussion in this section focuses on the guidance that *Baker* offers regarding participatory rights. The insight of *Baker* for the law of impartiality and independence is discussed in Chapter 7.

1. Step 1: Is the Duty of Fairness Triggered?

The first issue for the court to decide in *Baker* was whether the minister was subject to the duty of fairness when considering Ms Baker's application for an exemption. In other words, was the duty of fairness triggered in this case? As a general rule, first set out in *Cardinal*, the duty of fairness applies to "every public authority making an administrative decision which is not of a legislative nature and which affects the rights, privileges or interests of an individual."[172] This rule is interpreted broadly. It is intended to ensure that the duty of fairness has expansive application and is not used to narrow the reach of procedural fairness. Both the parties and the court agreed that this standard was met in *Baker*. As Justice L'Heureux-Dubé explained, "Clearly, the determination of whether an applicant will be exempted from the requirements of the Act falls within this category, and it has been long recognized that the duty of fairness applies to H&C [humanitarian and compassionate] decisions."[173] Thus, both an independent assessment of the facts and the leading precedents established that the minister (and his subordinates carrying out the decision-making) were legally required to act fairly in assessing Ms Baker's application.

Despite the broad application of the general rule and the inherent value of fairness in public decision-making, there are some limits to the reach of the duty of fairness. In other words, there are exceptions and considerations that complicate the general rule. These exceptions and considerations most often emerge in relation to three matters: the nature of the decision being made, the relationship between the administrative decision-maker and

---

170   *Baker, supra* note 10 at para 32.
171   *Ibid* at para 43.
172   *Cardinal, supra* note 9 at 653.
173   *Baker, supra* note 10 at para 20.

the affected party, or the effect of the decision on the affected party's rights.[174] Let's consider these matters more closely.

Looking to the nature of the decision being made, we find our first exception to the general rule: when exercising legislative functions, legislatures need only comply with constitutional requirements; additional procedural obligations under administrative law do not apply.[175] As the Supreme Court held in *Wells v Newfoundland*, "[l]egislatures are subject to constitutional requirements for valid law-making, but within their constitutional boundaries, they can do as they see fit. The wisdom and value of legislative decisions are subject only to review by the electorate."[176] Thus, in *Wells*, Mr Wells's argument that he was entitled to procedural fairness when the House of Assembly of Newfoundland and Labrador passed legislation that had the effect of eliminating Mr Wells's employment was rejected. The legislature had followed the constitutional requirements for valid law-making and thus had acted lawfully.

Wells seems to suggest that, as another rule, decisions of a legislative nature are not subject to the common law duty of fairness. Indeed, the general rule from *Cardinal* provides that "every public authority making an administrative decision *which is not of a legislative nature* and which affects the rights, privileges or interests of an individual" is subject to the duty of fairness.[177] However, in light of the jurisprudential evolution away from the distinction between administrative, quasi-judicial, and judicial decisions, *Wells* and *Cardinal* should likely not be read as a categorical exemption from the duty of fairness for all legislative decisions. Rather, in every instance of decision-making, the nature of the decision being made should be closely examined to determine its true character and whether it is the type of decision that should be immune from the common law duty of fairness. Such close examination was called for in *Homex Realty and Development Co v Wyoming (Village)*.[178] In that case, Homex Realty, a real estate and development business, challenged a municipal by-law on fairness grounds. The first issue was whether the duty of fairness had been triggered, and the court held that it had. Despite first appearances, the by-law was not, Justice Estey wrote on behalf of the majority, of a truly legislative character: "The by-law had some characteristics of a community interest by-law ... but it also represented the purported culmination of an *inter partes* dispute conducted on adversarial lines between Homex and the Council."[179] In other words, the town council had used the by-law to target Homex Realty because of an ongoing dispute between the municipality and the developer. Accordingly, Justice Estey

---

174 *Knight, supra* note 26.
175 *Wells, supra* note 22; *Authorson v Canada (Attorney General)*, 2003 SCC 39.
176 *Ibid* at para 59. The constitutional obligations may, however, include the duty to consult under s 35(1) of the *Constitution Act, 1982*: see e.g. *Courtoreille v Canada (Aboriginal Affairs and Northern Development)*, 2014 FC 1244. Some decisions by Cabinet may also be taken as "legislative" and thus not subject to the duty of fairness. See e.g. *Inuit Tapirisat, supra* note 22 (in relation to a statutory appeal to Cabinet under the *National Transportation Act*, RSC 1970, c N-17) and *Canadian Doctors for Refugee Care v Canada (Attorney General)*, 2014 FC 651 (in relation to orders in council passed by Cabinet), in which Cabinet was held not to be subject to the common law duty of fairness. Contrast these cases with *Desjardins v Bouchard*, [1983] 2 FC 641 (TD), in which a majority in the Federal Court of Appeal held that "the Governor in Council may not revoke a pardon under s 7 [of the *Criminal Records Act*, RSC 1970, c 12 (1st Supp)] without giving the person concerned an opportunity to be heard."
177 *Cardinal, supra* note 9 (emphasis added).
178 *Homex Realty and Development Co v Wyoming (Village)*, [1980] 2 SCR 1011.
179 *Ibid* at 1031.

concluded, "the action taken by the Council was not in substance legislative but rather quasi-judicial in character."[180] As a result, the duty of fairness applied.

Justice Dickson, writing in dissent on another point, agreed that the municipality was bound by the duty of fairness in passing this by-law. He was moved in particular by the effect of the by-law:

> The Court of Appeal noted that the municipality was acting out of what it conceived to be the public interest. I have no doubt this is true. Council was seeking to protect members of the public from potential injury in the purchase of unserviced land and to protect its ratepayers from paying the costs of servicing. But that is no answer to the case made by the appellant. What we have here is not a by-law of wide and general application which was to apply to all citizens of the municipality equally. Rather, it was a by-law aimed deliberately at limiting the rights of one individual, the appellant Homex.[181]

In light of the by-law's targeted effect on Homex Realty, Justice Dickson was of the view that the by-law was not legislative or general. It followed that Homex, as the party whose interests were affected, was entitled to procedural safeguards when the municipal council enacted the by-law. The reasoning of both Justices Dickson and Estey shows that when it comes to determining whether the duty of fairness is triggered, substance is more important than form.

We find a second exception to the general rule when we look to the nature of the relationship between the decision-maker and the individual who is claiming procedural rights. One prominent, but "rather narrow"[182] type of relationship that prevents the duty of fairness from being triggered is a contractual employment relationship. This may be somewhat surprising as the foundational cases on the duty of fairness are *Nicholson* and *Knight*, both of which deal with the dismissal of public office holders and in both of which the duty of fairness applied. But the more recent case of *Dunsmuir*, which you will read about in greater detail throughout the chapters of this volume, held that "[w]here a public employee is protected from wrongful dismissal by contract, his or her remedy should be in private law, not in public law."[183] In other words, public employees, employed under contract, are not entitled to procedural protections at common law when they are dismissed from their jobs.

The court in *Dunsmuir* expressed the assumption that most public employment relationships are contractual. In such circumstances, the majority held, "disputes relating to dismissal should be resolved according to the express or implied terms of the contract of employment and any applicable statutes and regulations, without regard for whether the employee is an office holder."[184] According to the court, the parties should be subject to the law that reflects the nature of the relationship that they chose for themselves, namely the private law of contract, rather than the public law of administration. Justices Bastarache and LeBel explained, "[a] public authority which dismisses an employee pursuant to a contract of employment should not be subject to any additional public law duty of fairness. Where the dismissal results in a breach of contract, the public employee will have access to ordinary contractual remedies."[185]

---

180   *Ibid.*
181   *Ibid* at 1052.
182   *Mavi, supra* note 7 at para 51, provides that *Dunsmuir, supra* note 18, creates a "rather narrow ... employment contract exception from the obligation of procedural fairness."
183   *Dunsmuir, supra* note 18 at para 114.
184   *Ibid* at para 113.
185   *Ibid.*

It is important to note that *Dunsmuir* does not rule out the application of the duty of fairness in all public employment contexts. The majority points to two situations in which the duty of fairness will still apply. First, when, despite appearances to the contrary, the employee is not actually protected by an employment contract, the duty of fairness still governs. Ministers and judges are examples of these types of office holders, as are employees who hold their office "at pleasure." In these circumstances, "[b]ecause [the] employee … is truly subject to the will of the Crown, procedural fairness is required to ensure that public power is not exercised capriciously."[186] Second, the duty of fairness will apply, despite the holding in *Dunsmuir*, by "necessary implication from a statutory power governing the employment relationship."[187] This determination will depend on the wording of the statute and the remaining contextual factors, as discussed below.

From these two exceptions to the *Dunsmuir* principle, we see that *Dunsmuir* reiterates the lesson learned in *Wells*: when determining whether the duty of fairness is triggered, substance prevails over form. Accordingly, the analysis of whether the duty of fairness has been triggered must not rely on superficial or unexamined descriptions of the type of relationship or decision under consideration.

The examples in *Wells* and *Dunsmuir* add nuance to the first step of the common law analysis by limiting the situations in which the duty of fairness is triggered. On the one hand, these limits and considerations could be read as undermining administrative law's claim to the inherent value of procedural fairness.[188] The decisions of legislatures, municipalities, and public employers are the work of public decision-makers; indeed they are some of our most powerful public decision-makers. And yet, the law allows these actors to operate outside of the procedural obligations set by the common law. This seems somewhat at odds with the claim that just decision-making entails fairness.

But, on the other hand, these contexts also serve as a reminder that procedural obligations and mechanisms of accountability for unfairness come in many forms, many of which find their authority and legitimacy outside the realm of administrative law. Indeed, constitutional and private law norms also play a role in ensuring the integrity of public decision-making and protecting the procedural rights of public citizens. So too do informal pressures coming from public outcry, the media, and political channels.[189] Indeed, when we recall the range of accountability mechanisms discussed by Cristie Ford in Chapter 2, we are reminded that instances of unfairness can be remedied by both formal and informal means, depending on the needs and preferences of the affected parties. The duty of fairness is not the only source of procedural protection.

---

186   *Ibid* at para 115.
187   *Ibid* at para 116. See also *Ouellette v Saint-André*, 2013 NBCA 21.
188   See e.g. Roderick Macdonald, "*AG Canada v Inuit Tapirisat of Canada*—The Limits of Procedural Fairness: Executive Action by the Governor in Council" (1981-82) 46 Sask L Rev 187.
189   See, for instance, the effect of allegations of bias in the National Energy Board's consideration of the Energy East pipeline project: Benjamin Shingler, "Denis Coderre Calls for Suspension of Energy East Hearings over Charest Affair," *CBC News* (26 August 2016), online: <http://www.cbc.ca/news/canada/montreal/denis-coderre-energy-east-pipeline-1.3736653>; Shawn McCarthy, "Energy East Hearings Put on Hold over Complaints Against NEB Members," *The Globe and Mail* (30 August 2016), online: <http://www.theglobeandmail.com/report-on-business/industry-news/energy-and-resources/national-energy-board-suspends-future-hearings-into-energy-east-pipeline/article31610177/>, which resulted in the board's process being put on hold in August 2016.

2. Step 2: What Does the Duty Entail?

In *Baker*, Justice L'Heureux-Dubé reminds us that the "existence of a duty of fairness ... does not determine what requirements will be applicable in a given set of circumstances."[190] Thus, once the common law duty is triggered, we turn to a second question: What does the duty entail? Put another way, what specific procedures must a decision-maker follow in order to satisfy the duty of fairness? The case law indicates that answering this question is to be guided by the purpose of participatory rights and a set of five non-exhaustive criteria, which are discussed below.

a. The Purpose of Participatory Rights

We already know that the duty of fairness is vital—a "cornerstone"—in modern Canadian administrative law.[191] Its observance is, as Justices Bastarache and LeBel observed in *Dunsmuir*, "central to the notion of the 'just' exercise of power."[192]

"Participatory rights" is a broad category of entitlements that falls under the umbrella of the duty of fairness. Participatory rights aim to bring fairness to life by providing for the enfranchisement of affected parties in public decision-making. The purpose of participatory rights is to ensure that "administrative decisions are made using a fair and open procedure, appropriate to the decision being made and its statutory, institutional, and social context, with an opportunity for those affected by the decision to put forward their views and evidence fully and have them considered by the decision-maker."[193] All analyses of participatory rights should strive to realize this purpose.

The purpose of participatory rights set out in *Baker* highlights not only the importance of sound procedure in public decision-making, but also the significance of context when deciding what constitutes fairness. The jurisprudence suggests that keeping context front and centre ensures that fairness is attuned to the realities of the decision-maker, the efficiency goals of the administrative state, and the rule of law. As Justice L'Heureux-Dubé explains in *Knight*:

> It must not be forgotten that every administrative body is the master of its own procedure and need not assume the trappings of a court. The object is not to import into administrative proceedings the rigidity of all the requirements of natural justice that must be observed by a court, but rather to allow administrative bodies to work out a system that is flexible, adapted to their needs and fair. As pointed out by de Smith ... the aim is not to create 'procedural perfection' but to achieve a certain balance between the need for fairness, efficiency and predictability of outcome.[194]

b. The Contextual Factors

Recall that at the second step of the analysis, we are trying to determine what the duty of fairness entails. In *Knight*, Justice L'Heureux-Dubé observed that "the concept of procedural

---

190   *Baker, supra* note 10 at para 21.
191   *Dunsmuir, supra* note 18 at para 79.
192   *Ibid* at para 90.
193   *Baker, supra* note 10 at para 22.
194   *Knight, supra* note 26 at 685.

fairness is eminently variable and its content is to be decided in the specific context of each case."[195] She reiterated the point in *Baker*, noting that "all of the circumstances must be considered" when determining the content of the duty of fairness in a particular case.[196] On its face, such a claim is daunting. It suggests that decision-makers and counsel must turn their minds to a sweeping set of considerations in order to fully assess the context of decision-making and the content of the duty of fairness.

Helpfully, the assessment of context has been channelled into a workable framework. In *Baker*, Justice L'Heureux-Dubé identified five factors that are often relevant to deciding the content of the duty of fairness in a particular case. An assessment of these factors, along with others that are meaningful in the circumstances, establishes where a particular decision-making context falls on the spectrum of fairness.

The five factors set out in *Baker* are as follows:

(1) **The nature of the decision being made and the process followed in making it.** This factor asks us to classify the decision in question as administrative, judicial, or somewhere between the two extremes. As Justice L'Heureux-Dubé explained in *Baker*, "[t]he more the process provided for, the function of the tribunal, the nature of the decision-making body, and the determinations that must be made to reach a decision resemble judicial decision-making, the more likely it is that procedural protections closer to the trial model will be required by the duty of fairness."[197]

(2) **The nature of the statutory scheme and the terms of the statute pursuant to which the body operates.** This factor asks us to consider the role of the particular decision within the overall statutory scheme within which the decision-maker operates. There is no exhaustive list of indicators that we are looking for in this reading of the statutory scheme; however, greater procedural protections are generally required when the decision in question cannot be appealed or when the decision is determinative of an issue, and there is no possibility for further requests for relief.[198] Lower procedural protections are usually indicated when the decision in question is investigative, fact-finding, or preliminary to a further stage of decision-making or when a party is seeking an exemption rather than application of a general rule.[199]

(3) **The importance of the decision to the individual or individuals affected.** This factor is quite simple. The greater the significance of the decision to the affected parties, the more stringent the required procedures should be.[200] Decisions regarding professional discipline and membership, as well as deportation, will, for example, give rise to significant procedural entitlements.[201]

(4) **The legitimate expectations of the person challenging the decision.** As discussed above (in Section III.A), the doctrine of legitimate expectations holds public decision-makers to their procedural promises, but does not guarantee or protect

---

195   *Ibid* at 682.
196   *Baker, supra* note 10 at para 21.
197   *Ibid* at para 23.
198   *Ibid* at para 24.
199   *Ibid*.
200   *Ibid* at para 25.
201   See e.g. *Kane v Bd of Governors of UBC*, [1980] 1 SCR 1105; *Baker, supra* note 10.

substantive outcomes. In *Baker*, Justice L'Heureux-Dubé explains the general rules as follows:

> If the claimant has a legitimate expectation that a certain procedure will be followed, this procedure will be required by the duty of fairness .... Similarly, if a claimant has a legitimate expectation that a certain result will be reached in his or her case, fairness may require more extensive procedural rights than would otherwise be accorded.[202]

In *Baker*, the doctrine of legitimate expectations is presented as one factor to be considered in determining applicable procedures. *Baker* provides that the doctrine "is based on the principle that the 'circumstances' affecting procedural fairness take into account the promises or regular practices of administrative decision-makers, and that it will generally be unfair for them to act in contravention of representations as to procedure, or to backtrack on substantive promises without according significant procedural rights."[203] While, as discussed above, there is some uncertainty about the implications of a legitimate expectation, it is, at a minimum, a well-established part of the *Baker* analysis. Further, it is well-settled in recent jurisprudence that the affected party need not prove that he or she relied on the decision-maker's representation in order to invoke the doctrine of legitimate expectations.[204]

(5) **The choices of procedure made by the decision-maker itself.** In *Baker*, Justice L'Heureux-Dubé noted that "important weight must be given to the choice of procedures made by the agency itself and its institutional constraints."[205] This weight will be particularly great when the decision-maker is authorized by statute to choose its own procedures or when it has an expertise regarding its own procedural design.[206]

This factor is a meaningful affirmation of the notion that an "administrative body is the master of its own procedure"[207] and a statement about who is best suited to make decisions about the procedures that will be followed in decision-making—the administrative actor making the decision, who is intimately familiar with the daily realities of decision-making in its statutory context, or the courts. This is a theme to which we will return below in Section IV of this chapter. Here, it is worth noting that the decision-maker's choices are just one factor among many that are to be accounted for when deciding what procedural obligations apply.

In a manner consistent with the overall theme of flexibility and contextuality, the list of factors to be considered when determining the content of the duty of fairness is elastic and itself subject to modification when the context calls for it. Indeed, the list of factors is non-exhaustive[208] and is meant to assist in determining the applicable procedures in a given case, rather than exhaust our procedural imaginations or understandings of the relevant context. In *Mavi*, Justice Binnie describes it as "obvious" that "the requirements of the duty in particular cases are driven by their particular circumstances. The simple overarching

---

202 *Baker, supra* note 10 at para 26.
203 *Ibid.*
204 *Mavi, supra* note 7 at para 68.
205 *Baker, supra* note 10 at para 27.
206 *Ibid* at para 29.
207 *Knight, supra* note 26 at 685.
208 *Baker, supra* note 10 at para 28.

requirement is fairness, and this 'central' notion of the 'just exercise of power' should not be diluted or obscured by jurisprudential lists developed to be helpful but *not* exhaustive."[209] Despite these affirmations of the elasticity of the framework, in practice, the five factors set out in *Baker* have been relied on heavily and, often, exclusively.[210]

An assessment of the *Baker* factors leads to a determination of the measure of fairness owed in the circumstances. The analysis is qualitative. The goal is to gauge where a particular decision-making context falls on a spectrum of fairness. As you consider each factor, and again when you examine the factors in the aggregate, you are seeking to determine whether, in the circumstances, the burden of fairness is heavy, light, or somewhere between the two ends of the spectrum.

Once the weight of the burden of fairness is determined, you then decide which specific procedures will satisfy the duty of fairness in the circumstances. This determination is, again, context-specific, and the range of possible procedures to be canvassed and considered is open and flexible as the administrative state allows for a diversity of modes of participation, modes of decision-making, and modes of reason-giving. The usual range of possibilities includes procedures dealing with notice, disclosure, hearings (which raises questions about the form of the hearing—oral, written, electronic, open, closed, etc.), the right to representation, opportunities to call evidence and cross-examine witnesses, deadlines and the relevance of timeliness, the duty to give reasons, and so on.

The determination of which specific procedures apply in any particular set of circumstances cannot be made in the abstract. Rather, we must always look to the context and consider what the affected parties might need or request. Indeed, recalling the overarching purpose of participatory rights, the essential query is: considering all of the circumstances, what procedures must be followed to ensure that those whose interests are affected have a meaningful opportunity to present their case fully and fairly?

Ultimately, while a usual range of options has developed, the common law duty of fairness is, at least in principle, infinitely plastic. It allows—and strives for—the most fitting procedures in a particular decision-making context. That said, on the whole, the flexibility of procedural fairness has not led to or been confronted with particularly imaginative procedural design in administrative decision-making.

This chapter does not canvass the law on all of the specific procedures that could be implemented in the administrative context. However, a few general points will provide guidance on the types of concerns to which you should turn your mind as you consider which procedures apply in a specific case. (Further guidance on the specific procedures required under the Charter is found in Chapter 6).

First, notice is the most fundamental of the participatory rights. Without notice, it is impossible for an affected party to exercise her other rights of participation except by chance. Indeed, it is difficult to imagine how an affected party could seize an opportunity to put her views and evidence before a decision-maker without notice that a decision is to be made.

---

209 *Mavi, supra* note 7 at para 42.

210 In *Archer v Luterbach* (2001), 199 FTR 96 (CA), a case dealing with a decision to remove buffalo due to concerns with mad cow disease, the Federal Court held that in "cases where time is an issue, the right to participate could be tailored to fit the circumstances" (at para 39). In *Miel Labonté Inc v Canada (Attorney General)*, 2006 FC 195, Justice Noël cited *Archer* and noted that time constraints could constitute a "sixth [*Baker*] factor" (para 66).

As Brown and Evans explain, "[n]otice must be adequate in all circumstances in order to afford to those concerned a reasonable opportunity to present proofs and arguments, and to respond to those presented in opposition."[211] Jones and de Villars describe the general rule at common law as follows: "an administrator must give adequate notice to permit affected persons to know how they might be affected and to prepare themselves adequately to make representations."[212] In other words, adequate notice is that which is consistent with the enfranchisement of affected parties in public decision-making.[213] Assessing the adequacy of notice will, unsurprisingly, be a matter that depends on the context. Issues of the form, timing, and content of the notice will have to be considered, all of which must be sufficient to enable the affected parties to fully participate. For instance, in circumstances in which decisions affect a defined population, personal notice may not be required, but rather general dissemination of information within a territory or through channels accessible to the population may be sufficient.[214] Further, notice must be given with sufficient time for a party to prepare, although the amount of preparation time that is called for will depend on the type of decision being made.[215] Finally, the content of the notice must give sufficient information for individuals to know they are affected and prepare submissions. What counts as sufficient may depend not only on the type of decision being made, but also the knowledge and experience of the person receiving the information.[216]

Second, in line with the principle of contextuality and access to justice, it is only in rare cases that a decision-maker is required to hold an oral hearing. Recall that the range of administrative decision-making contexts is sweeping and includes such diverse settings as the granting of hunting licences, the issuance of security certificates, the enactment of municipal by-laws, and professional discipline hearings against lawyers. In many instances, an oral hearing would be inappropriate to the decision being made and would impose too great of a burden on decision-makers. Often, a decision-maker is able to properly assess the relevant information, evidence, and arguments on a written record alone. As discussed below, the court held that the facts in *Baker* were one such instance. The common law will, however, require an oral hearing in some circumstances. For example, in *Khan*, the success of a student's grade appeal turned on whether the student had handed in a fourth exam booklet, which the professor contended had not been submitted. As this was an issue requiring an assessment of the student's credibility, the student was entitled to appear before the university committee in person.[217] For further discussion of when oral hearings might be required

---

211   Brown & Evans, *supra* note 62, ch 9 at 9-1200.

212   Jones & de Villars, *supra* note 19 at 272.

213   With respect to having important information about the decision being made, the entitlement to disclosure is also a particularly important entitlement. It enables an affected party to know the case she has to meet. See e.g. *May v Ferndale Institution*, 2005 SCC 82; *Mission Institution v Khela*, 2014 SCC 24, [2014] 1 SCR 502 [*Khela*] (corrections); *Sriskandarajah v United States of America*, 2012 SCC 70 (extradition); *Charkaoui, supra* note 2 (immigration); *Pritchard v Ontario (Human Rights Commission)*, 2004 SCC 31 (disclosure and privilege).

214   See e.g. *Hardy v Minister of Education* (1985), 22 DLR (4th) 394 (BCSC), dealing with decisions regarding school closures, and *Re Joint Board under the Consolidated Hearings Act and Ontario Hydro* (1985), 19 DLR (4th) 193 (Ont CA), dealing with a combination of personal notice and published newspaper announcements regarding decisions about the location of electrical lines.

215   See e.g. *Zeliony v Red River College*, 2007 MBQB 308.

216   See e.g. *R v Ontario Racing Commission, ex parte Taylor*, [1971] 1 OR 400 (CA).

217   *Khan, supra* note 6.

in administrative settings, see the discussion of Evan Fox-Decent and Alexander Pless in Chapter 6. In addition, further discussion of fairness concerns in oral hearings is found in Laverne Jacobs's examination of bias in Chapter 7.

Third, as noted above (in Section II.B), the common law has not historically required decision-makers to provide reasons for their decisions.[218] However, this rule was modified in *Baker*. After weighing the benefits of reasons against concerns about placing unreasonable burdens on decision-makers, Justice L'Heureux-Dubé concluded that it was "now appropriate to recognize that, in certain circumstances, the duty of procedural fairness will require the provision of a written explanation for a decision."[219] Such circumstances include: "where the decision has important significance for the individual, when there is a statutory right of appeal, or in other circumstances."[220] Ultimately, this change to the rule was compelled by weighing competing concerns of access to justice. On the one hand, reasons "foster better decision-making by ensuring that issues and reasoning are well articulated and, therefore, more carefully thought out. The process of writing reasons for decision by itself may be a guarantee of a better decision."[221] Moreover, reasons "allow parties to see that the applicable issues have been carefully considered, and are invaluable if a decision is to be appealed, questioned, or considered on judicial review."[222] Further still, when a decision-maker provides reasons for its decision, those affected "may be more likely to feel they were treated fairly and appropriately."[223] On the other hand, a reasons requirement could inappropriately burden administrative decision-makers, thereby adding time and cost to the process of administrative justice. Further, there was a concern that requiring reasons may conduce a lack of candour on the decision-makers' part.[224]

In weighing the competing claims, Justice L'Heureux-Dubé concluded that the benefits of a general duty to provide "some form of reasons" in the circumstances listed above outweighed the concerns. Indeed, the concerns could be mitigated by ensuring that the common law duty to provide reasons is applied in a manner consistent with the principle of contextuality, such that it "leaves sufficient flexibility to decision-makers by accepting various types of written explanations for the decision as sufficient."[225] As you assess and reflect upon the way in which the duty to provide reasons is applied on the ground, consider whether the rule of law, access to justice, and contextuality concerns that underpin the reasons requirement set out in *Baker* are furthered in the current state of Canadian administrative law. You will find further discussion of these questions on the duty to provide reasons in Chapter 6, which considers the issue through the lens of the Charter.

---

218 *Baker, supra* note 10 at para 37, citing *Northwestern Utilities Ltd v City of Edmonton* (1978), [1979] 1 SCR 684; *Supermarchés Jean Labrecque Inc v Flamand*, [1987] 2 SCR 219 at 233; *Public Service Board of New South Wales v Osmond* (1986), 159 CLR 656 (HCA) at 665-66.

219 *Baker, supra* note 10 at para 43.

220 *Ibid.*

221 *Ibid* at para 39.

222 *Ibid.*

223 *Ibid.*

224 *Ibid* at para 40.

225 *Ibid.* On this flexibility, see also Roderick A Macdonald & David Lametti, "Reasons for Decision in Administrative Law" (1990) 3 CJALP 123.

c. Applying the Contextual Factors

In *Baker*, Justice L'Heureux-Dubé relied on the contextual factors to determine what procedural steps the minister was legally bound to follow when assessing Ms Baker's application for an exemption on humanitarian and compassionate grounds. The process that had been followed consisted of submission of a written application, with supporting documents, by Ms Baker; review of the file by a junior officer, who summarized the application and made a recommendation; and consideration of all of the material by a senior officer, who then made the decision. Ms Baker argued that the decision-making context called for additional procedures—namely, an oral hearing and notice to herself and her children.

Justice L'Heureux-Dubé noted that in deciding Ms Baker's appeal, the overarching inquiry was "whether, considering all the circumstances, those whose interests were affected had a meaningful opportunity to present their case fully and fairly."[226] Turning to the contextual factors, Justice L'Heureux-Dubé concluded that the humanitarian and compassionate grounds decision was not a judicial decision, but rather a polycentric discretionary decision. The minister had to consider many factors in assessing Ms Baker's application. Further, within the statutory scheme, the minister's decision dealt with the application of an exception from the general principles of Canadian immigration law. In Justice L'Heureux-Dubé's view, these two considerations supported the conclusion that the duty of fairness called for "more relaxed requirements" in this case.[227] However, other factors suggested more stringent obligations: first, the statute did not provide for an appeal procedure for the humanitarian and compassionate grounds decision, although judicial review was available; second, the decision was of "exceptional importance" to Ms Baker and her family; and, third, the statutory scheme empowered the minister with significant discretion to decide the procedure to be followed. As a matter of practice, interviews were not held in all cases. According to Justice L'Heureux-Dubé, the "institutional practices and choices made by the minister are significant, though of course not determinative factors to be considered in the analysis."[228]

Upon balancing the factors, Justice L'Heureux-Dubé concluded that Ms Baker was entitled to a level of fairness that was more than minimal. The context required that the minister, or his officers, consider the issues and evidence fully and fairly and that Ms Baker and other parties whose "important interests are affected by the decision in a fundamental way must have a meaningful opportunity to present the various types of evidence relevant to their case."[229] Ultimately, Justice L'Heureux-Dubé held, this standard was met. True to the principle that administrative decision-makers need not replicate judicial processes in order to be fair, an oral hearing or interview was not required. According to the court, Ms Baker and her children had the opportunity to put forward, in writing, all of the information and argumentation relevant to the application. Thus, the decision-makers had the information needed to make a fully informed decision. This, Justice L'Heureux-Dubé held, "satisfied the requirements of the participatory rights required by the duty of fairness in this case."[230]

---

226   *Baker, supra* note 10 at para 30.
227   *Ibid* at para 31.
228   *Ibid*.
229   *Ibid* at para 32.
230   *Ibid* at para 34.

On the issue of providing reasons, Justice L'Heureux-Dubé held that the minister's decision was of such "profound importance" to Ms Baker and her family that the duty to provide reasons was triggered. "It would be unfair," Justice L'Heureux-Dubé explained, "for a person subject to a decision such as this one which is so critical to their future not to be told why the result was reached."[231] However, in Ms Baker's case, the duty to provide reasons was fulfilled when Ms Baker was provided with the notes of Officer Caden. According to the court, this conclusion was consistent with the reality of the decision-making context. There was no other record explaining the outcome, and thus the notes must be taken as the reasons for the minister's decision. Further, accepting the notes as reasons reflected the flexible, contextual posture that we must take when determining the requirements of procedural fairness in a particular decision-making context. This posture must attend to the "day-to-day realities of administrative agencies and the many ways in which the values underlying the principles of procedural fairness can be assured."[232] This reasoning was seen, in the court's eyes, as doing justice to the inherent value of fairness while also accounting for the need for flexibility and contextuality. These latter principles remind us, as did Justice L'Heureux-Dubé, that "transparency may take place in various ways."[233]

The facts and issues at stake in *Baker* provide a rich opportunity for considering the meaning of fairness in Canadian public law. It is a set of circumstances that forces us to confront fundamental questions about procedural justice in a context that implicates individual interests, dignity, family, human rights, marginalization on multiple fronts, health, and personal security. From these circumstances, the court constructed an analytical framework that continues to prevail today. This stability is unusual in administrative law.[234] Perhaps you will ask yourself whether this long-standing quality of *Baker* is justified. Does it structure our thinking such that we are directed to the most important considerations? Does it help us to realize the aspirations of procedural justice? Does it promote enfranchisement and access to justice in the realm of public decision-making?

One point to notice from the *Baker* framework is the prominent place of legislative intent and statutory interpretation within the contextual analysis. Knowing what the common law requires will always call for a nuanced and deep understanding of the statutory scheme within which an administrative decision-maker operates. In this sense, an analysis of the common law duty of fairness is always a balancing of views on how a decision-maker must act in order to be fair. Deference to legislative intent is reflected in the importance of the statutory scheme to shape the common law duty of fairness, as expressly implicated in the first two *Baker* factors. Respect for the views of administrative decision-makers is reflected in the fourth and fifth *Baker* factors, which direct our attention to the choices and practices of administrative actors. Further, respect for judicial views is reflected in the value attributed to the common law duty of fairness in administrative law and in the heavy reliance on jurisprudence to determine the procedural obligations to which decision-makers are held. Do you think that the proper balance has been struck in showing deference to these multiple views? Which institutional actor is in the best position to decide what is fair?

---

231   *Ibid* at para 43.
232   *Ibid* at para 44.
233   *Ibid*.
234   David Stratas, "The Canadian Law of Judicial Review: A Plea for Doctrinal Coherence and Consistency" (2016) 42:1 Queen's LJ.

As we conclude this section on the common law duty of fairness, it is worth circling back to the underlying principle of participatory rights, which the contextual factors are supposed to help us achieve. The principle provides that public decisions must be made "using a fair and open procedure, appropriate to the decision being made and its statutory, institutional, and social context, with an opportunity for those affected by the decision to put forward their views and evidence fully and have them considered by the decision-maker."[235] This quote from *Baker* has become a catchphrase in administrative law. On the one hand, it offers clear guidance on the procedural obligations of administrative decision-makers. It signals many of the core values of fairness in administrative decision-making—openness, contextuality, enfranchisement, justification, integrity, and respect for human dignity. It also sets the general legal standard to which processes of administrative decision-making will be held—the standard of a fair and open procedure. On the other hand, this quote may have become so ubiquitous that it has lost some of its rhetorical force. The words of Justice L'Heureux-Dubé may, because of their familiarity and because of the long-standing status of *Baker* as the leading case on procedural fairness, no longer inspire critical reflection on the fundamental ideas they seek to capture.

Such apathy about fairness in the administrative context must be resisted. Complacency regarding fairness jeopardizes the integrity of the administrative system as a whole and undermines the legitimacy of particular instances of administrative decision-making. It is with this appreciation for the significance of fair process in mind that we must always undertake our analyses of the common law duty of fairness and assess the decisions of public officials and courts on matters of fairness.

IV. CHALLENGING UNFAIRNESS

Now that you are familiar with the principles and practices of procedure in administrative law, you have the foundation of knowledge necessary to identify and challenge unlawful and unfair procedural action by administrative decision-makers. Chapter 2 of this volume deals with remedies and the mechanisms available for challenging administrative decisions. These remedies and mechanisms apply, subject to any statutory constraints applicable to a particular decision-maker and in a particular jurisdiction, when seeking to challenge administrative action on procedural grounds. As is true in every case, the suitability of any particular mechanism and any particular remedy will depend on the needs and interests of the affected parties. Further, with respect to judicial review of administrative action, Chapter 2 deals with the availability of judicial review, including when it is available on procedural grounds. As you know from Cristie Ford's discussion in that chapter, a decision-maker must constitute a "public" actor in order for its decisions to be subject to judicial review on administrative law grounds. This qualitative assessment determines which actors are sufficiently "public" that they can be governed by the duty of fairness and that their breaches of the duty can be enforced through administrative review.[236]

---

235   *Baker, supra* note 10.
236   The case of *Wall v Judicial Committee of the Highwood Congregation of Jehovah's Witnesses*, 2016 ABCA 255, suggests that private actors may be subject to the duty of fairness. The appeal of this decision will be argued on 2 November 2017 before the Supreme Court of Canada.

Further, in Chapters 11, 12, 13, and 14, Audrey Macklin, Sheila Wildeman, Evan Fox-Decent, Alexander Pless, and Peter Carver deal with the history, meaning, and application of standards of review in the realm of substantive fairness. These chapters speak to the measure of deference that courts should show to administrative decision-makers when engaged in review of substantive decisions. But what is the standard of review when judicial review of administrative action is sought on procedural grounds? This chapter briefly considers this question here to ensure that, from this volume as a whole, you not only have the knowledge necessary to identify unfairness in the eyes of the law, but also have the foundation necessary to pursue meaningful remedies. Thus, to the comprehensive discussions of remedies and the standard of review in Chapters 2, 11, 12, 13, and 14, this part will add some considerations in relation to the judicial review of procedural obligations, in particular in relation to the applicable standard of review.

First, recall the discussion above in Section II of this chapter regarding the legal consequences of unfairness, namely that the decision is rendered void. Absent exceptional circumstances, the usual remedy for a finding of unfairness is a quashing of the administrative decision. This was true historically as a decision made by virtue of poor procedure was treated as outside the jurisdiction of the decision-maker, and thus void. Further, as the courts bear the constitutional responsibility to ensure that statutory decision-makers act within their jurisdiction, matters of unfair procedure could not be protected by a privative clause.[237]

Second, when procedural decisions are under scrutiny in the context of judicial review, they will be reviewed, as a general rule, on a standard of correctness.[238] An error of procedure is deemed to be an error of law and, thus, a matter reviewed on correctness.

And yet, this general, long-standing rule is not as strict as it seems. As you know from Section III.C of this chapter, the *Baker* analysis entails that in the context of judicial review, deference is to be shown to the choices of procedure made by the decision-maker. According to Justice L'Heureux-Dubé, such choices should be given "important weight."[239] Other cases support this show of deference to administrative decision-makers in relation to their procedural choices. In *Council of Canadians with Disabilities v VIA Rail Canada Inc*, Justice Abella explains, for the majority, that "[c]onsiderable deference is owed to procedural rulings made by a tribunal with the authority to control its own process. The determination of the scope and content of a duty to act fairly is circumstance-specific, and may well depend on factors within the expertise and knowledge of the tribunal, including the nature of the statutory scheme and the expectations and practices of the Agency's constituencies."[240] The Federal Court of Appeal has agreed with this approach. In *Re: Sound v Fitness Industry Council of Canada*, Justice Evans wrote:

> In short, whether an agency's procedural arrangements, general or specific, comply with the duty of fairness is for a reviewing court to decide on the correctness standard, but in making that determination it must be respectful of the agency's choices. It is thus appropriate for a reviewing court to give weight to the manner in which an agency has sought to balance maximum participation on the one hand, and efficient and effective decision-making on the other.

---

237 Mullan, *supra* note 30 at 228-29. *Newfoundland Telephone Co v Newfoundland (Board of Commissioners of Public Utilities)*, [1992] 1 SCR 623 at 645.
238 *Newfoundland Nurses, supra* note 42; *Khela, supra* note 213 at para 79.
239 *Baker, supra* note 10 at para 27.
240 2007 SCC 15 at para 231.

In recognition of the agency's expertise, a degree of deference to an administrator's procedural choice may be particularly important when the procedural model of the agency under review differs significantly from the judicial model with which courts are most familiar.[241]

Indeed, the Federal Court of Appeal has accepted that some decisions of a procedural nature by the National Energy Board are reviewable on a standard of reasonableness.[242] In relation to the board's design of its "Application to Participate Form" (the Form), Justice Stratas, writing for the court, undertook an analysis of the context and concluded that a "significant margin of appreciation" was owed to the NEB in the circumstances.[243] The context included the NEB's "considerable experience and expertise in conducting its own hearings and determining who should not participate, who should participate, and how and to what extent."[244] Further, *Baker* indicated that the board's procedural choices regarding the design of the Form and the requirement that it be completed were entitled to deference, in particular given the board's statutory discretion over these decisions. Finally, the board's decisions were protected by a privative clause. In light of these factors, Justice Stratas concluded that the board's procedural choices regarding the Form were entitled to deference. He then upheld the design of the Form to be reasonable. Rejecting an argument that the Form was too complicated, the Court of Appeal held that the Form was consistent with the board's statutory mandate regarding the participation of parties not directly affected by a project. Justice Stratas concluded that the board is "entitled to take the position that, consistent with the tenor of section 55.2 of the National Energy Board Act, *supra*, it only wants parties before it who are willing to exert some effort."[245] Further, the "rigorous" form was commensurate with the statutory requirement that applicants for intervenor status have "relevant information or experience."[246] Justice Stratas also concluded that the standard of reasonableness applied to the board's decision to deny an application for intervenor status. Here, the decision at issue was both procedural and substantive in nature. Moreover, it called for an exercise of the board's experience and expertise in managing its own proceedings. Accordingly, this decision-making context called for a margin of appreciation to be shown to the board.[247]

These cases demonstrate that questions remain regarding the standard of review that applies when courts review administrative decisions on procedural grounds. As it now stands as a matter of doctrine, the general rule favouring a correctness standard continues to apply. However, there is significant movement in this area. An approach to the standard of review for questions of procedural fairness that is attentive to the context, including the nature of the decision-maker's statutory scheme, is consistent with the approach in the substantive realm and the principles set out in *Dunsmuir*.[248] Further, it reflects the developing principles regarding the standard of review on questions about the duty to consult. On

---

241   2014 FCA 48 at para 42.
242   *Forest Ethics Advocacy Association v National Energy Board*, 2014 FCA 245.
243   *Ibid* at para 72.
244   *Ibid*.
245   *Ibid* at para 75.
246   *Ibid* at para 77.
247   *Ibid* at paras 78-84.
248   Paul Daly, "Canada's Bipolar Administrative Law: Time for Fusion" (2014) 40:1 Queen's LJ 213.

judicial review of matters related to the duty to consult, the applicable standard of review varies according to the question at stake. In *Carrier Sekani*, the chief justice explained that "some deference is appropriate on matters of mixed fact and law, invoking the standard of reasonableness."[249] However, she cautioned that "this, of course, does not displace the need to take express legislative intention into account in determining the appropriate standard of review on particular issues."[250] Thus, in *Little Salmon/Carmacks*, the applicable standard of review changed to accommodate the issue at stake:

> In exercising his discretion under the Yukon *Lands Act* and the *Territorial Lands (Yukon) Act*, the Director was required to respect legal and constitutional limits. In establishing those limits no deference is owed to the Director. The standard of review in that respect, including the adequacy of the consultation, is correctness. A decision-maker who proceeds on the basis of inadequate consultation errs in law. Within the limits established by the law and the Constitution, however, the Director's decision should be reviewed on a standard of reasonableness: *Dunsmuir v New Brunswick*, 2008 SCC 9, [2008] 1 SCR 190, and *Canada (Citizenship and Immigration) v Khosa*, 2009 SCC 12, [2009] 1 SCR 339. In other words, if there was adequate consultation, did the Director's decision to approve the Paulsen grant, having regard to all the relevant considerations, fall within the range of reasonable outcomes?[251]

One final issue with respect to challenging decisions regarding procedural obligations: Is a breach of the duty to consult subject to judicial review by virtue of administrative law? This query returns us to the relationship between administrative law analyses and constitutional approaches. With respect to the proper route for challenging the Crown's failures to consult, the majority in *Little Salmon/Carmacks* was satisfied that administrative law was sufficiently nimble to account for a breach of the duty to consult. Justice Binnie noted that the parties in *Little Salmon/Carmacks* proceeded by virtue of an ordinary application for judicial review, which is an administrative law remedy. In his view, this was the appropriate way to proceed:

> Such a procedure was perfectly capable of taking into account the constitutional dimension of the rights asserted by the First Nation. There is no need to invent a new "constitutional remedy." Administrative law is flexible enough to give full weight to the constitutional interests of the First Nation. Moreover, the impact of an administrative decision on the interest of an Aboriginal community, whether or not that interest is entrenched in a s 35 right, would be relevant as a matter of procedural fairness, just as the impact of a decision on any other community or individual (including Larry Paulsen) may be relevant.[252]

While the analysis of the duty to consult may fit within the administrative law approach, the courts have also held that the constitutional obligations flowing from the duty to consult may not exhaust the obligations of consultation that a decision-maker must follow in carrying out its mandate. Rather, the common law duty of fairness may require consultation, even if a claim of the duty to consult is unsuccessful.[253]

---

249   *Carrier Sekani*, *supra* note 117 at para 65.
250   *Ibid*.
251   *Little Salmon/Carmacks*, *supra* note 114 at para 48.
252   *Ibid* at para 47.
253   See e.g. *Taku River Tlingit First Nation v British Columbia (Minister of the Environment)*, 2014 BCSC 1278.

V. CONCLUSION

Our public officials must act fairly when exercising their mandates. To act fairly, an official must be animated by the principles of fairness and make decisions in accordance with the applicable procedural obligations set by statute, regulations, rules, policies, the Constitution, and the common law. In their ideal manifestation, these obligations are informed by principle, are well-tuned to the realities of the particular decision-making context, and, as a result, are conducive to conditions in which affected parties experience public decision-making processes as fair, even when those parties do not agree with a substantive decision. In practice, designing workable and meaningful procedural structures using the legislative, constitutional, common law, and institutional sources available will always be a matter of trial and error, as there is much to learn about fairness from witnessing administrative decision-making in action. That said, as we know from this chapter and others, when we are confronted with unfairness, there are mechanisms available for reform, revision, and remedies.

As you read this chapter, you may have found yourself questioning whether the distinctions between principle and practice and between procedure and outcome are as stark as they first seemed. This is an intuition worth pursuing. Much of the discussion in this chapter suggests that the practices of fairness are better understood through the lens of contextuality, access to justice, the rule of law, enfranchisement, and reconciliation. Similarly, much of the discussion indicates that the principles of fairness are more richly conceptualized when informed by the practical realities of administrative decision-making.[254] Further, this chapter has also emphasized that, in any particular case, the type of decision being made and the significance of that decision on the affected parties—which are clearly matters related to substance—play a meaningful part in designing a fair process for making the decision. Again, the law will better calibrate the norms and expectations of fairness when it does not assess fairness in abstraction from the practical questions and disputes that must be resolved, but rather appreciates that procedural fairness cultivates the conditions in which the pending questions and disputes can be resolved. It follows that it is somewhat misleading to suggest that a concern with procedure is not also a concern with substance; the two are intimately, and indeed inextricably, knitted together.

When reading this chapter, you may have also questioned whether the law can exhaust the meaning of fairness. Indeed, the study of fairness reveals that the practice of acting fairly is not merely a matter of following prescribed rules. Acting fairly calls upon administrative decision-makers to marshal their capacities for ethical reasoning and judgment in order to bring fairness to life. While the formal rules of law cannot fully capture or prescribe these capacities, we can seek to ensure that legal rules and judgments are guided by commitments to, and a weighing of, the value of fairness, the rule of law, participation, flexibility, access to justice, in its many forms, and other commitments necessary to achieve administrative justice. It is in the attempt to realize these commitments in practical instances of decision-making that we find the law's capacity for fairness. These commitments can offer a common foundation on which decisions in the diverse contexts of administrative decision-making can be made. Further, they can afford parties a baseline for assessing rights

---

254   On the relationship between practice, principle, and institutional design, see Lon Fuller, "Means & Ends" in Kenneth I Winston, ed, *The Principles of Social Order: Selected Essays of Lon L Fuller*, revised ed (Oxford: Hart Publishing, 2001) 61.

and entitlements, illuminate routes of argumentation and advice for counsel as they help their clients navigate administrative processes, offer legislators a conceptual framework to work within when they codify procedural obligations, guide judges as they review the lawfulness of administrative decision-making procedures, and furnish scholars and students with a structure through which to appraise the law governing procedural fairness and all of its shortcomings.

Questions of procedural fairness can seem difficult at times because, as is discussed in this chapter, there are often multiple competing interests at stake. For instance, heavy procedural obligations on decision-makers can come at a cost to access to justice for affected parties. However, lighter procedural burdens may sacrifice access to substantive justice and compromise the rule of law if opportunities for participation and expectations of reason-giving are constrained. Further, the rule of law demands that the courts both oversee the exercise of public power and show some measure of deference to administrative decision-makers. A commitment to access to justice also gives rise to these competing demands.

These tensions and competing interests need not be an obstacle to realizing procedural fairness in the administrative context, nor to your understanding of administrative law. Instead, these tensions can be embraced as part of the richness of fairness. When we wrestle with questions of procedural fairness, the aim is to understand and be alert to the diverse goals of administrative decision-making and to find the balance that best appreciates the particular context. Indeed, given the importance of context and circumstances when it comes to procedural fairness, whatever your future role might be in the administrative state—whether citizen, counsel, decision-maker, judge, or reformer—your capacity to make effective arguments about procedural rights and obligations will be strengthened if you are willing to immerse yourself in the particular context in which decisions are made. This entails familiarizing yourself with the intricacies and realities of the administrative context in which you are working and crafting arguments that are tailored to those realities. Further, it entails internalizing the principles and rules of administrative procedure, appreciating their virtues, and challenging their limits. With this deep understanding of the context of decision-making and the landscape of the law, you will be nimble across decision-making contexts and in response to procedural questions of any kind.

CHAPTER SIX

The Charter and Administrative Law Part I: Procedural Fairness

Evan Fox-Decent[*]

Faculty of Law, McGill University

Alexander Pless[†]

Department of Justice, Government of Canada

I. INTRODUCTION

Armed with an understanding of how courts treat procedural review of administrative decisions, it is now necessary to examine the court's approach when an administrative decision appears to engage a Charter protected right. When reading this chapter, consider the affinity the duty of procedural fairness has to the duty to consult in the First Nations context, as discussed by Janna Promislow and Naiomi Metallic in Chapter 3, Realizing Aboriginal Administrative Law.

This chapter sets out various ways in which judicial review of procedure at common law has influenced understandings of the Charter, as well as the manner in which the Charter has influenced review of administrative decisions when a Charter right is clearly at stake. As we

---

[*] We are indebted to Patrick Baud, Colleen Flood, Robert Leckey, Mary Liston, Sara Gauthier, and Lorne Sossin for valuable comments and suggestions, some on past versions, others on this one.

[†] The views expressed in this chapter are my own and do not necessarily reflect those of my employer, the Department of Justice, or the Attorney General of Canada.

shall see, the courts rely explicitly on the common law doctrine of procedural fairness to interpret the principles of fundamental justice set out in s 7 of the Charter.[1] Indeed, this chapter is largely about the relationship between the common law duty of procedural fairness and the principles of fundamental justice of s 7.

II. PROCEDURAL FAIRNESS AND THE PRINCIPLES OF FUNDAMENTAL JUSTICE

As discussed by Kate Glover in Chapter 5, The Principles and Practices of Procedural Fairness, the duty of procedural fairness in administrative law requires decision-makers to provide a fair hearing to individuals subject to their authority. At a minimum, this usually means that front-line decision-makers must hear the other side and decide the matter before them impartially and independently. The duty does not mean that the individual must receive an oral hearing (very often written submissions are enough), but the individual must receive notice of the proceedings and have a full and fair opportunity to respond to the facts and contentions on which the decision-maker may ultimately rely. Implicit in the duty to hear the other side is a duty to disclose all facts and contentions, barring considerations such as privacy and national security, which may justify non-disclosure. In some cases, the individual may have a right to legal counsel. These safeguards are frequently referred to as participatory rights, and they apply before the decision has been made. If the decision affects an important interest, such as continued residency in Canada, the decision-maker owes the individual reasons for the decision. The duty to give reasons applies after the decision has been made.

In addition to the duty of fairness that applies at common law to a vast array of public entities—probably any entity that exercises statutory powers[2]—a duty of fairness may also be owed under the Charter. The class of entities to which the Charter applies may be narrower than those captured by the common law duty of fairness.[3] Where the Charter does apply, the duties are considerable.[4] What does the Charter require in terms of procedural fairness or a fair hearing? The Charter stipulates that "[e]veryone has the right to life, liberty and security of the person and the right not to be deprived thereof *except in accordance with the principles of fundamental justice.*"[5] Section 7 is the only rights-conferring provision in the Charter that refers to the principles of fundamental justice, and, within the Charter's substantive rights-conferring provisions, only these principles have been found to include

---

1   *Canadian Charter of Rights and Freedoms*, Part I of the *Constitution Act, 1982*, being Schedule B to the *Canada Act 1982* (UK), 1982, c 11 [Charter].

2   See e.g. the definition of "federal board, commission or other tribunal" in s 2 of the *Federal Courts Act*, RSC 1985, c F-7 and the discussion in BJ Saunders, DJ Rennie, & G Garton, *Federal Courts Practice 2017* (Toronto: Carswell, 2016).

3   Charter, ss 30, 32(1).

4   Compare, for example, *McKinney v University of Guelph*, [1990] 3 SCR 229, where the court concludes that the Charter does not apply to a university, with *Kane v Bd of Governors of UBC*, [1980] 1 SCR 1105, where a university is found to owe a duty of fairness.

5   Charter, s 7 (emphasis added).

procedural fairness.[6] The presence of the principles of fundamental justice within s 7 has led to that section's emergence as the primary source of procedural safeguards within the Charter.[7]

To access procedural safeguards in the context of s 7, complainants must first cross the "threshold" of establishing that their "life, liberty or security" interests are impaired by the relevant decision. Section 7 only applies to legislation or decisions that impair a person's interests in their life, liberty, or security of the person.[8] The right to life has been interpreted to mean one's right to live and be free of state conduct that increases the risk of dying. The right to liberty implies at least two elements: freedom from physical restraint and freedom to make fundamental life choices. The right to security of the person has both a physical and a psychological component. The physical component is engaged where there is a threat of physical harm. The psychological component is engaged only where the state imposes (or threatens to impose) severe psychological harm.[9] If the affected individual cannot establish that an impugned decision touches a s 7 interest, procedural fairness may still be due, but as a matter of common law, or the *Canadian Bill of Rights*, rather than as a consequence of s 7 and the principles of fundamental justice.

A further important threshold issue in this context concerns the relationship of procedural fairness to legislation. Legislation can (and often does) determine the content of available procedures.

The common law does not empower judges to impose procedures in the face of clear statutory language that dictates less stringent (or even no) procedural safeguards.[10] Under s 7, however, the procedural requirements of the principles of fundamental justice are constitutional requirements. In other words, if a s 7 interest is engaged, procedural fairness comes into play by means of the principles of fundamental justice, and legislation must conform to them in order to be lawful.[11] Other non-Charter sources of procedural safeguards that ordinary

---

6   Arguably, s 1 of the Charter implicitly contains procedural fairness (or something much like it) within the idea that infringements of rights must be limited to those that can be "demonstrably justified in a free and democratic society." Similarly, the preamble to the Charter refers to the rule of law, and procedural fairness might also be inferred from that principle. See Mary Liston, Chapter 4, Administering the Canadian Rule of Law, for discussion of the sense in which procedural fairness informs the rule of law and the idea of a common law constitution.

7   Sections 8 though 14 are sometimes regarded as elaborations of the principles of fundamental justice in the detention context. Naturally, the courts look to the common law to guide their interpretation of these procedural rights. But these rights are parasitical on invasive state action, and so in this sense they are not substantively "right-conferring" in the sense in which s 7 guarantees to everyone the right to life, liberty, and security of the person independently of anything the state does.

8   *Carter v Canada (Attorney General)*, 2015 SCC 5 at para 55, [2015] 1 SCR 331 [*Carter*].

9   *Ibid* at paras 62, 64.

10 *Ocean Port Hotel Ltd v British Columbia (General Manager, Liquor Control and Licensing Branch)*, 2001 SCC 52, [2001] 2 SCR 781 [*Ocean Port*].

11 The Supreme Court's decision in *Doré v Barreau du Québec*, 2012 SCC 12, discussed in Chapter 13, The Charter and Administrative Law Part II: Substantive Review, adds a wrinkle to the application of s 7 procedural rights. The requirements of procedural fairness are typically reviewed on the standard of correctness. *Doré* establishes that administrative decisions raising Charter concerns are evaluated on the standard of reasonableness. If a decision involves establishing procedures in a case that engages s 7 rights, it might be argued that it should be reviewed on the standard of reasonableness. The question remains unresolved. But see Paul Daly, "Canada's Bi-Polar Administrative Law: Time for Fusion" (2014) 40:1 Queen's LJ 213 at 236, who suggests that "[s]auce for the *Charter* goose should be sauce for the procedural fairness gander."

legislation cannot oust would be the *Bill of Rights*,[12] the doctrine of the honour of the Crown under s 35 of the *Constitution Act, 1982*,[13] and fiduciary obligations owed by the Crown to Aboriginal peoples under that same section of the *Constitution Act, 1982* (see Janna Promislow and Naiomi Mettalic's discussion in Chapter 3, Realizing Aboriginal Administrative Law).

The *Bill of Rights* is rarely argued. Presumably because its early jurisprudence created a number of unusual and complex restrictions to its application, it is perceived as ineffective. But litigants ignore it at their peril. Where it applies, the *Bill of Rights* provides procedural safeguards that cannot be overridden "unless it is expressly declared by an Act of the Parliament of Canada that it shall operate notwithstanding the *Canadian Bill of Rights*."[14] It is worth remembering that half the court in *Singh* found the very same procedural guarantees for the applicant in the *Bill of Rights* that the other half found in s 7.[15] The important difference is that under the *Bill of Rights* it is not necessary to show that life, liberty, or security of the person is at stake in order to obtain the relevant procedural protection.[16]

Ocean Port is often cited for the proposition that clear statutory requirements can oust common law guarantees of procedural fairness. However, it is important to note that this is only true in jursidictions that do not have quasi-constitutional procedural guarantees like those guaranteed by the *Bill of Rights* or Quebec's *Charter of Human Rights and Freedoms*.[17] Any decision taken under statutory authority conferred by Parliament, for example, may potentially give rise to procedural rights under the *Bill of Rights*.[18]

---

12   *Canadian Bill of Rights*, SC 1960, c 44, reprinted in RSC 1985, Appendix III [*Bill of Rights*].

13   Being Schedule B to the *Canada Act 1982* (UK), 1982, c 11.

14   *Bill of Rights*, s 2.

15   In *Singh*, *infra* note 20, only six judges participated in the decision. Beetz, Estey, and McIntyre JJ relied on s 2(e) of the *Bill of Rights*: "2. Every law of Canada shall, unless it is expressly declared by an Act of the Parliament of Canada that it shall operate notwithstanding the *Canadian Bill of Rights*, be so construed and applied as not to abrogate, abridge or infringe or to authorize the abrogation, abridgment or infringement of any of the rights or freedoms herein recognized and declared, and in particular, no law of Canada shall be construed or applied so as to .... (e) deprive a person of the right to a fair hearing in accordance with the principles of fundamental justice for the determination of his rights and obligations."

16   See e.g. *Hassouna v Canada (Citizenship and Immigration)*, 2017 FC 473 at paras 70-126, where the Federal Court concludes that ss 10(1), (3), and (4) of the *Citizenship Act*, RSC 1985, c C-29, are inoperative under s 2(e) of the *Bill of Rights* because they provide no right to a fair hearing before revoking Canadian citizenship for "false representation or fraud or ... knowing conceal[ment of] material circumstances."

17   At the federal level, the *Bill of Rights* functions like the Quebec *Charter of Human Rights and Freedoms*, CQLR, c C-12, functioned in *2747-3174 Québec Inc v Quebec (Régie des permis d'alcool)*, [1996] 3 SCR 919 [*Régie*], to fix quasi-constitutional guarantees of procedural fairness that cannot be varied except where the statute is expressly declared to operate notwithstanding the *Bill of Rights*. Notice that in a jurisdiction with no such quasi-constitutional guarantee, the common law yields to a clear statutory requirement. See the discussion in *Ocean Port*, *supra* note 10 at para 28 explaining why *Régie* does not apply in British Columbia.

18   Unwritten constitutional principles may also complicate the usual story of the supremacy of clear legislation over the common law. A court of appeal has imposed a duty to give reasons where an unwritten constitutional principle was at stake (protection of minorities), and the relevant legislation was silent on the issue: *Lalonde v Ontario (Commission de restructuration des services de santé)* (2001), 56 OR (3d) 577 (CA). It remains to be seen whether they would do the same in similar circumstances if confronted with express legislation that barred the imposition of such a duty. In two cases in which the rule of law was alleged to operate as an unwritten constitutional principle, the Supreme Court declined to invalidate the impugned legislation: *British Columbia v Imperial Tobacco Canada Ltd*, 2005 SCC 49, [2005] 2 SCR 473; *British Columbia (Attorney General) v Christie*, 2007 SCC 21 [*Christie*]. For discussion of the rule of law cases, see Mary Liston, Chapter 4.

The remainder of this section now examines the content of the principles of fundamental justice in various statutory contexts. As we shall see, the common law of procedural fairness informs both the specific content of the principles (for example, oral hearings, disclosure, the duty to give reasons, and timely decision-making) and the reasons for interpreting them to have particular contents in some decision-making contexts but not in others.[19] And as in the common law context, the specific procedural requirements of the principles of fundamental justice in s 7 are determined flexibly but on a standard of correctness.

A. Oral Hearings and the Scope of Section 7

In 1985, *Singh v Minister of Employment and Immigration*[20] established that the principles of fundamental justice include procedural fairness. *Singh* involved seven refugee claimants who had no opportunity to present their cases in oral hearings before either the decision-maker at first instance (formally the minister, acting on the recommendation of the precursor to today's Immigration and Refugee Board, the Refugee Status Advisory Committee) or the Immigration Appeal Board (IAB) on appeal. The statutory scheme at the time provided for the possibility of an oral hearing, but only before the IAB on appeal, and *only* if the IAB concluded on the basis of the asylum seeker's written submissions that there were reasonable grounds to believe that the claimant could make a successful claim at an oral hearing. Thus, the statutory scheme precluded the IAB from granting an oral hearing to claimants who failed to set out "reasonable grounds." Because the statutory scheme excluded the possibility of an oral hearing in these cases, the common law of procedural fairness could not "supply the omission of the legislature";[21] there was no omission but rather a clear exclusion.

Six judges took part in the judgment: three found an infringement of s 7 of the Charter and three found an infringement of s 2(e) of the *Canadian Bill of Rights*. Wilson J wrote the Charter portion of the judgment, finding that "everyone" in s 7 includes "every human being who is physically present in Canada,"[22] and that the security interest "must encompass freedom from the threat of physical punishment or suffering as well as freedom from such punishment itself."[23] As a consequence, Wilson J held that s 7 applied to Singh (the threshold was crossed), and, although he did not have a constitutional right to remain in Canada per se, he did have a constitutional right to have his claim determined in accordance with the principles of fundamental justice. Wilson J concluded that the interests protected under s 7 are of such importance that generally an oral hearing will be required when those interests are engaged. Where credibility is at stake, as it almost always is in refugee cases, she found it "difficult to conceive of a situation"[24] in which the claimant would not be entitled to prior discovery of the minister's case and an oral hearing. She affirmed the conventional wisdom that resort to the Charter should be reserved for cases in which ordinary statutory interpretation cannot provide a remedy. She held that this was one such case because the principles

---

19 For an earlier, but still exemplary, discussion of the relationship between the common law and the principles of fundamental justice, see JM Evans, "The Principles of Fundamental Justice: The Constitution and the Common Law" (1991) 29 Osgoode Hall LJ 51.

20 [1985] 1 SCR 177 [*Singh*].

21 *Cooper v Wandsworth Board of Works* (1863), 14 CB (NS) 180, 143 ER 414 (CP) at 420.

22 *Singh*, *supra* note 20 at para 35.

23 *Ibid* at para 47.

24 *Ibid* at para 59.

of fundamental justice in the context of a refugee claimant require an oral hearing, and the statute itself expressly barred some refugee claimants from receiving such a hearing. *Singh* remains a vivid example of how review under the Charter can overcome clear legislation, usually an insurmountable obstacle to relief at common law.

Singh is also a foundational case in Canadian immigration law for both its recognition that s 7 applies to non-citizens and its impact on Canada's statutory and institutional framework regarding refugee claimants. At no small cost, the government overhauled the statutory scheme and established the Immigration and Refugee Board to ensure that all refugee claimants will receive a fair hearing in accordance with the principles of fundamental justice.

Notice, however, that although the constitutional status of the Charter is required to overcome the language of the statutory scheme then in place, Wilson J relies on the common law idea from civil and criminal procedure that credibility is best assessed through an evaluation of oral testimony. In other words, the Charter can take a complainant across the normally insuperable threshold of a clear statutory bar to certain procedures; however, once the threshold is crossed, it is still the common law that determines the content that the procedure must have to pass constitutional muster.

B. Incorporation of the Common Law Framework Under Section 7

Chapter 1 by Colleen Flood and Jennifer Dolling and Chapter 5 by Kate Glover have already described the landmark case of *Baker v Canada (Minister of Citizenship and Immigration)*[25] in which the Supreme Court drew together a wide body of jurisprudence to establish a framework for determining the content of procedural fairness in a particular case. Recall that the framework the court established in *Baker* for determining the content of procedural fairness ("the *Baker* framework") is composed of five non-exhaustive contextual factors, none of which is necessarily determinative. The first concerns the nature of the decision: the more the decision can be said to be judicial or quasi-judicial in nature, adjudicative rather than administrative, the weightier the procedural safeguards must be. The second factor is the role and place of the decision within the statutory scheme. For example, if the decision constitutes an exception to the general principles of the scheme, fewer protections are due. On the other hand, if procedural safeguards are present elsewhere in the Act, and if the decision is final, these considerations would militate in favour of more stringent procedures. The third factor is the importance, in practical terms, of the decision to the individual affected. The fourth is legitimate expectations. Legitimate expectations can arise as a result of past practices or representations of public officials that, if present, may provide a basis for procedural safeguards that would not otherwise be available. The fifth factor calls for a measure of deference to the minister's or agency's choice of procedure.

The court in *Baker* applied this framework to determine only the content of Ms Baker's participatory rights; she had a right to make written submissions and to have those submissions fully considered, but she was not entitled to an oral hearing. As well, her children were denied independent standing on the grounds that their interest in the proceedings could be communicated to the minister and defended by Baker's legal counsel. The court considered the issues of bias and the duty to give reasons independently of the *Baker* framework and

---

25   [1999] 2 SCR 817 [*Baker*].

found that both are required under the common law duty of procedural fairness. However, as we shall now see in *Suresh v Canada (Minister of Citizenship and Immigration)*,[26] where the *Baker* framework is applied in the context of a s 7 claim, it creates a stronger duty to give reasons as a principle of fundamental justice. The court finds in Suresh that the reasons must emanate from the decision-maker herself (e.g., the minister).[27] So, for example, in *Baker* the court accepts that the minister endorsed a recommendation and treated the recommendation as the reasons for decision. In *Suresh* the court finds that where s 7 is at issue, the reasons for decision must be written by the person who takes the decision. *Suresh* involved a convention refugee detained on a security certificate for alleged links with the Liberation Tigers of Tamil Eelam (LTTE). The Federal Court upheld the certificate and, in the subsequent deportation hearing, the adjudicator found Suresh to be inadmissible as a refugee on grounds of membership in a terrorist organization. Pursuant to s 53(1)(b) of the *Immigration Act* in force at the time,[28] the minister proceeded to issue an opinion that Suresh constituted a danger to the security of Canada and should be deported, notwithstanding an acknowledgment that Suresh would face a risk of torture upon his return to Sri Lanka. Suresh challenged the minister's decision on constitutional and administrative law grounds. The court held that "barring extraordinary circumstances, deportation to torture will generally violate the principles of fundamental justice protected by s 7 of the *Charter*,"[29] but ultimately the case was decided in Suresh's favour because the minister had breached the s 7 principles of fundamental justice by failing to provide Suresh with adequate procedural safeguards and reasons for the decision.

Unlike the statutory provisions under scrutiny in *Singh*, s 53(1)(b) of the *Immigration Act* did not require the minister to adopt or follow any particular procedure. The minister notified Suresh that she intended to consider issuing a "danger opinion" against him and gave him the opportunity to make submissions to her. Those submissions were considered by an immigration officer who weighed the importance of Canada's commitment to fight terrorism against the risk of torture to Suresh. The officer recommended in a memorandum to the minister that she issue an opinion under s 53(1)(b) that Suresh constitutes a danger to Canada. Suresh did not have an opportunity to see or respond to the officer's memorandum, which the court described as "more like a prosecutor's brief than a statement of reasons for a decision."[30]

Without the guidance of statute, the court turned to the *Baker* framework to assess the adequacy of the procedure afforded Suresh: "Insofar as procedural rights are concerned, the common law doctrine summarized in *Baker*, properly recognizes the ingredients of fundamental justice."[31] It is worth noting that despite its reliance on *Baker* to determine the content of the s 7 guarantee, the court emphasizes that "the common law is not constitutionalized."[32]

---

26 2002 SCC 1, [2002] 1 SCRS 3 [*Suresh*].

27 *Ibid* at para 126.

28 RSC 1985, c I-2 (superseded by the *Immigration and Refugee Protection Act*, SC 2001, c 27).

29 *Suresh, supra* note 26 at para 76. This is a notable instance in which the principles of fundamental justice are deemed to contain substantive as well as procedural guarantees. It is also an instance in which international law guides the court's interpretation of the Charter. The international/domestic law nexus is explored by Gerald Heckman in Chapter 16, International Human Rights Norms and Administrative Law. Examination of the substantive guarantees implicit in the principles of fundamental justice is more a matter of constitutional than administrative law and, generally, beyond the scope of this book.

30 *Ibid* at para 126.

31 *Ibid* at para 113.

32 *Ibid* at para 114.

It would seem that the court perceives the possibility of cases where the procedural require-ments of fundamental justice would be different under s 7 and the common law. Yet it is diffi-cult to imagine circumstances where this would be the case. If s 7 is engaged, procedural requirements are likely to be very significant, but it does not follow that the common law an-alysis would not produce the same result. What is safe to conclude from the court's comment it that the requirements of s 7 can only be the same or greater than the requirements of com-mon law.

C. The Duty to Disclose and the Right to Reply

Weighing together the five factors referred to above, the court concluded that Suresh did not have a right to an oral hearing, but he did have the right to disclosure of the materials on which the minister would base her decision, including the memorandum from the immigra-tion officer who initially reviewed Suresh's case under s 53(1)(b) of the *Immigration Act*. Suresh also had the right to reply to the claims set out in the memorandum, including claims relevant to the threat he posed to Canada and the risk of torture he would face if deported. The min-ister then had an obligation to consider Suresh's submissions as well as those of her staff.

Let us now explore further the interaction between the Charter, statutes, and the common law by considering what would have happened if the immigration officer who prepared the memorandum was a lawyer whose legal advice the minister explicitly sought and whether his report to the minister could be fairly characterized as a legal opinion. The court said that Suresh was entitled to disclosure "[s]ubject to privilege or similar valid reasons for reduced disclosure, such as safeguarding confidential public security documents."[33] In *Pritchard v Ontario (Human Rights Commission)*[34] (a case of judicial review at common law rather than review under the Charter), the court held that the common law doctrine of solicitor–client privilege barred a complainant before the Ontario Human Rights Commission from obtaining disclosure of a legal opinion drafted by the commission's in-house counsel.[35]

In principle, an ordinary statute can oust privilege when privilege is asserted as a doctrine of the common law (the ouster must be clear and explicit, and the court in *Pritchard* said that any such legislation would be interpreted restrictively). It seems to follow that a duty to disclose found to inhere in the principles of fundamental justice could also reduce the effect of privilege. However, the Court in *Pritchard* found that meeting the requirements of proced-ural fairness does not require the disclosure of a privileged legal opinion. Thus, if the reason disclosure is required in *Suresh* is that procedural fairness is a feature of the principles of fundamental justice, and procedural fairness does not require disclosure of a legal opinion, then the immigration officer's memorandum may not be discoverable if the minister can convince a court that the memorandum is, in substance, a legal opinion. To pierce privilege, a complainant would have to distinguish procedural fairness at common law (the context in *Pritchard*) from procedural fairness under s 7.

---

33   *Ibid* at para 122.
34   2004 SCC 31, [2004] 1 SCR 809 [*Pritchard*].
35   The issue whether the minister could use solicitor–client privilege to block disclosure of the immigration officer's memorandum did not arise in *Suresh* because the minister simply did not disclose the report prior to making her decision. Although the report was drafted prior to the decision, it was provided to Suresh only after the decision was made, apparently as reasons for the decision.

D. The Duty to Give Reasons

Another area of procedural fairness influenced by *Suresh* is the duty to give reasons. *Baker* established that the requirements of procedural fairness may include a duty to provide reasons in certain circumstances, such as when the decision has "important significance for the individual, when there is a statutory right of appeal, or in other circumstances."[36] In *Baker*, the notes and recommendation of a junior officer were deemed to satisfy the reasons requirement because the senior officer and formal decision-maker followed the recommendation, and no other reasons were provided. The notes were so riddled with stereotypes and prejudice that the court found that they gave rise to a reasonable apprehension of bias. After *Baker*, some courts interpreted the duty to require no more than a symbolic or even box-ticking exercise,[37] while others interpreted the obligation to require a substantive justification of the impugned decision.[38] As discussed above, in *Suresh*, the court held that the minister herself (not a delegated officer) must provide "responsive" reasons that demonstrate both that the individual is a danger to Canada and that there are no substantial grounds to believe he or she would be subject to torture. Unlike *Baker*, the court did not separate its discussion of participatory rights from its treatment of the duty to give reasons; both were informed by contextual analysis conducted under the *Baker* framework. Specifically, the court made much of the importance of the security interest arising from torture to justify its expansive reading of the duty to give reasons. The court's attentiveness to the sheer brutality of torture suggests that the justificatory burden under the duty to give reasons is likely to become heavier in rough proportion to the significance of the interest, even in non-Charter contexts.

Because the duty to give reasons is part of the duty of procedural fairness, it is reviewed on a standard of correctness. This means that a decision will be quashed if the reviewing court considers that the procedure followed failed to respect the requirements of procedural fairness. No deference is owed to the decision-maker on questions of procedural fairness. Moreover, the correctness standard is brought to bear on procedural questions without application of the context-sensitive approach the courts have developed to determine the standard of review applicable to particular substantive decisions. In the wake of *Dunsmuir v New Brunswick*,[39] two standards of review are now available, correctness and reasonableness. For discussion of these standards, see Chapters 11 and 12 by Audrey Macklin and Sheila Wildeman, respectively. While a deferential standard would ordinarily apply to the outcome (the substance) of a decision, *Suresh* suggests a non-deferential approach to deterimining whether the reasons are "responsive."

However, the court's decision in *Newfoundland and Labrador Nurses' Union v Newfoundland and Labrador (Treasury Board)*[40] raises serious doubt that inadequate reasons will give rise to a violation of procedural fairness. Although the decision arises in a non-constitutional context, the court's reasons are likely to be applicable if the issue were to arise under s 7. In this case, Abella J, writing for a unanimous court, rejects the proposition that the

---

36 *Baker, supra* note 25 at para 43.
37 *Liang v Canada (Minister of Citizenship and Immigration)*, [1999] 4 FC D-54, [1999] FCJ No 1301 (QL) (TD).
38 See e.g. *VIA Rail Canada Inc v National Transportation Agency*, [2001] 2 FC 25 (CA); and *Gray v Director of the Ontario Disability Support Program* (2002), 59 OR (3d) 364 (CA), 212 DLDR (4th) 353.
39 2008 SCC 9, [2008] 1 SCR 190.
40 2011 SCC 62, [2011] 3 SCR 708.

inadequacy of reasons is a stand-alone basis for quashing a decision.[41] The assessment of the reasonableness of an outcome, she explains, is not to be undertaken in two steps. It had been argued that regardless of the reasonableness of the outcome, the reasons provided were inadequate and therefore failed to meet the requirements of procedural fairness. She explains that the assessment is instead a "more organic exercise."[42] She goes on to say that "it strikes me as an unhelpful elaboration on *Baker* to suggest that alleged deficiencies or flaws in the reasons fall under the category of a breach of the duty of procedural fairness and that they are subject to a correctness review."[43] The net result of this is that if reasons are provided at all, it seems that the duty has been complied with, and that the adequacy of those reasons will be assessed together with the outcome in the substantive review on a reasonableness rather than correctness standard of review.

E. The Right to State-Funded Legal Counsel

In the administrative realm, the presence of lawyers is sometimes viewed as a hindrance to speedy, inexpensive, and conciliatory dispute resolution, and procedural fairness does not necessarily entail a right to legal counsel even at one's own expense.[44] The Supreme Court has held that neither procedural fairness nor the rule of law in the administrative setting requires the state to fund legal representation.[45]

In certain circumstances, however, where a decision impairs a s 7 interest, the state must provide the individual with legal counsel in order to satisfy the requirements of the principles of fundamental justice. In *New Brunswick (Minister of Health and Community Services) v G(J)*,[46] the New Brunswick minister of health and community services sought to extend for six months a previous custody order over an indigent complainant's three young children. Lamer CJ for the majority and L'Heureux-Dubé J for the concurring minority held that a forced separation would have "a serious and profound effect"[47] on the parent's psychological integrity and stigmatize her, thereby engaging her right to security of the person.[48] Furthermore, the custody hearing in such cases is adversarial and held in a court of law. Given the seriousness of the interest, the complexity of the proceedings, and the limited capacities of the individual, Lamer CJ found that the principles of fundamental justice required a fair hearing and that in these circumstances a fair hearing required the Crown to provide legal aid to the parent.

---

41 *Ibid* at para 14.

42 *Ibid*.

43 *Ibid* at para 21.

44 *Re Men's Clothing Manufacturer's Association of the Ontario and Toronto Joint Board, Amalgamated Clothing and Textile Worker's Union* (1979), 222 LAC (2d) 328 (H W Arthurs), quashed (1979), 104 DLR (3d) 441 (Ont Div Ct).

45 *Christie, supra* note 18. At a more general level, *Christie* may also be read to suggest that the Supreme Court will not use unwritten constitutional principles (in this case the rule of law) to invalidate legislation. In *Christie*, a provincial tax scheme was alleged to impair the ability of the underprivileged to obtain legal representation and access to the courts.

46 [1999] 3 SCR 46 [*G(J)*].

47 *Ibid* at para 60.

48 *Ibid* at paras 60-61 and 116.

G(J) also offers insight into why a majority of the Supreme Court has never found an infringement of s 7 to be justified under s 1. Lamer CJ notes that s 7 infringements are not easily saved under s 1 because the rights protected under s 7 are very significant, and because "rarely will a violation of the principles of fundamental justice, specifically the right to a fair hearing, be upheld as a reasonable limit demonstrably justified in a free and democratic society."[49] Although the court in *Suresh* insisted that "the common law [of procedural fairness] is not constitutionalized" but rather "is used to inform the constitutional principles that apply,"[50] there is no question that enfolding procedural fairness into the s 7 principles of fundamental justice has elevated the duty of fairness to new heights. The consistent refusal of a majority of the Supreme Court to find a s 7 infringement justified under s 1 signals the remarkable extent to which the right to a fair hearing has in fact been constitutionalized.[51]

F. Undue Delay

A further element of procedural fairness concerns the timeliness with which administrative proceedings are conducted. The Constitution does not refer explicitly to unreasonable delays before administrative agencies, but in *Blencoe v British Columbia (Human Rights Commission)*,[52] Bastarache J, speaking for the majority, acknowledged the possibility that an undue delay in the resolution of a human rights complaint could infringe the security of the person of interest protected under s 7. Specifically, it is possible that an inordinate and undue delay could result in stigmatization and an impairment of the psychological integrity of the alleged wrongdoer, but, as we shall see, the threshold to cross is set very high, to the point of it being difficult to imagine a delay that could actually constitute an infringement of s 7.

Blencoe had been a minister in the government of British Columbia in March 1995, when one of his assistants accused him of sexual harassment. A month later the premier removed him from Cabinet and the New Democratic Party caucus. In July and August 1995, two women filed sexual harassment complaints against Blencoe with the BC Council of Human Rights (later the BC Human Rights Commission). Hearings were eventually scheduled before the BC Human Rights Tribunal in March 1998, after the commission had completed its preliminary investigation and some 30 months after the initial complaints were filed. Media attention was intense. The court recognized that Blencoe's career as a politician was finished, that he suffered clinical depression, that his financial resources were depleted, and that he and his family had moved twice to flee the stigmatizing effects of the outstanding complaints. Nonetheless, Bastarache J found that even on the assumption that the delay was a cause of Blencoe's grief, "[t]he state has not interfered with the respondent and his family's ability to make essential life choices,"[53] and so the state did not infringe Blencoe's s 7 security interest.

---

49 *Ibid* at para 99. It is also noteworthy that Lamer CJ finds the infringement unjustifiable solely on the basis of the legal aid policy's deleterious effects; in other cases in which the court refers to deleterious effects, the reference comes only after the court has already determined that the Crown failed to satisfy some other aspect of the test from *Oakes* (for example, lack of minimal impairment).

50 *Suresh*, *supra* note 26 at para 114.

51 But see *Carter*, *supra* note 8 at para 95, where the Supreme Court notes that although "[i]t is difficult to justify a s 7 violation ... in some situations the state may be able to show that the public good ... justifies depriving an individual of life, liberty or security of the person."

52 2000 SCC 44, [2000] 2 SCR 307.

53 *Ibid* at para 86.

Wareham v Ontario (Ministry of Community and Social Services)[54] reveals a potentially more liberal approach to issues of delay and abuse of process. Janice Wareham brought a class action on behalf of persons with disabilities. She claimed that she and the class she represented suffered maladministration under the Ontario Disability Support Program (ODSP). The province brought a motion to strike the statement of claim as disclosing no cause of action. The Ontario Court of Appeal allowed the plaintiffs to amend the s 7 aspect of their claim to include an attack on the process used to determine eligibility for ODSP benefits. The plaintiffs had alleged that, in practice, the ODSP eligibility determination process was Kafkaesque. The court referred to Lorne Sossin's finding that the process was a case study of "bureaucratic disentitlement," which is "a series of structural and situational features of the welfare eligibility process which together have the effect of discouraging applicants and demoralizing recipients."[55] In other words, the cumulative effect of the various steps in the ODSP eligibility procedure was to cause such delay and hardship for applicants that conceivably the overall procedure itself constitutes an infringement of the principles of fundamental justice.

G. *Ex Parte, in Camera* Hearings

In the wake of the events of September 11, 2001, many liberal democracies, including Canada, enacted legislation to give police and security services added powers to investigate and prosecute terrorism. Canada, however, already had comprehensive legislation in place within its *Immigration and Refugee Protection Act* (IRPA)[56] that permitted the detention of foreign nationals and permanent residents (not citizens) suspected of terrorism or of having an association with terrorist organizations. Detainees under the IRPA are not charged criminally and do not benefit from a presumption of innocence and other due process guarantees that permeate the criminal justice system. This scheme eventually gave rise to *Charkaoui v Canada (Citizenship and Immigration).*[57]

Canadian security agencies alleged that Adil Charkaoui, Hassan Almrei, Mohamed Harkat, Mohamed Zeki Mahjoub, and Mahmoud Jaballah were involved with terrorist organizations. Charkaoui is a permanent resident. The others are foreign nationals who had been recognized as convention refugees. The minister of citizenship and immigration and the minister of public safety and emergency preparedness issued security certificates against them pursuant to s 77 of the IRPA, leading to their detention pending deportation.

Under ss 78-84 of the IRPA, the detention and the reasonableness of security certificates are subject to review by the Federal Court. During the review process, prior to amendments to the IRPA enacted in 2008, *ex parte* and *in camera* hearings (closed-door hearings in which neither the person named on the certificate nor his or her lawyer is present) were held at the request of the Crown if the judge believed that disclosure of some or all of the evidence on which the certificate was based could undermine national security. The judge then provided to the named person a summary of the evidence, but not its sources or any other details that

---

54   2008 ONCA 771. The case seems not to have been tried on the merits.

55   *Ibid* at para 30, citing Lorne Sossin, "Boldly Going Where No Law Has Gone Before: Call Centres, Intake Scripts, Database Fields, and Discretionary Justice in Social Assistance" (2004) 42 Osgoode Hall LJ 363 at 399.

56   *Supra* note 28.

57   2007 SCC 9, [2007] 1 SCR 350 [*Charkaoui*].

might compromise national security. The judge could receive and rely on evidence withheld from the named person that would be inadmissible in a court of law, such as uncorroborated hearsay evidence provided by foreign security agencies known to use torture. If the judge determined that the certificate was reasonable, there was no appeal or opportunity for further judicial review.

McLachlin CJ, for a unanimous Supreme Court, found that these proceedings doubly engaged s 7 because persons subject to security certificates face detention pending deportation (the liberty interest), and because the person's removal may be to a place where his or her life or freedom would be threatened (the security interest). The court held that the review procedure violated the principles of fundamental justice because it denied the named person a fair hearing. A fair hearing, the court said, requires a judge to decide the case on the basis of all the relevant facts and law. Unlike an inquisitorial system in which judges play an investigative role, in an adversarial system such as ours, judges do not have the power to investigate and gather evidence. Without such powers, the court found, Federal Court judges may have to decide on the reasonableness of the Crown's case without the benefit of having the evidence adequately tested. The named person is precluded from raising legal objections to the evidence, or from basing legal arguments on it. As a result, the judge may have to decide the matter without a full and fair appraisal of all the facts and law at issue.

A further implication of the secrecy required by the statutory scheme is that the named person may never know the case that he or she has to meet because it may be based, in whole or in part, on undisclosed material. In perhaps the sharpest language in her judgment, the chief justice said that the "principle [of knowing the case to meet when liberty is in jeopardy] has not merely been limited; it has been effectively gutted."[58]

An important aspect of the court's ruling on the principles of fundamental justice concerns the issue, whether reviewing judges may balance the interests of the individual against those of society at the s 7 stage of determining the content of the principles of fundamental justice. In *Thomson Newspapers Ltd v Canada (Director of Investigation and Research, Restrictive Trade Practices Commission)*,[59] La Forest J wrote as part of the majority and found that determining their content requires a "just accommodation between the interests of the individual and those of the state."[60] Similarly, in *Ruby v Canada (Solicitor General)*, Arbour J, writing for the court, held that "[i]n assessing whether a procedure accords with the principles of fundamental justice, it may be necessary to balance the competing interests of the state and the individual."[61] In *Charkaoui*, however, the court affirmed its more recent holding in *R v Malmo-Levine* that s 7 does not permit "a free-standing inquiry ... into whether a particular legislative measure 'strikes the right balance' between individual and societal interests in general."[62] Such balancing, the court said, should be conducted under s 1. Nonetheless, in *Khawaja v Canada (Attorney General)*,[63] Richard CJ of the Federal Court of Appeal relied heavily

---

58 *Ibid* at para 64.

59 [1990] 1 SCR 425 [*Thomson*].

60 *Ibid* at para 176.

61 2002 SCC 75, [2002] 4 SCR 3 at para 39 [*Ruby*].

62 *R v Malmo-Levine; R v Caine*, 2003 SCC 74, [2003] 3 SCR 571 at para 96, cited in *Charkaoui, supra* note 57 at para 21.

63 *Khawaja v Canada (Attorney General)*, 2007 FCA 388, [2008] 4 FCR 3, leave to appeal to SCC refused, 2008 CanLII 18970 (SCC) [*Khawaja*].

on *Ruby* and *Thomson* when he balanced the interests of the state and the individual within s 7 in favour of the state. *Khawaja* came down just months after *Charkaoui* and upheld the constitutionality of *ex parte* sessions mandated under s 38 of the *Canada Evidence Act*[64] for the purpose of reviewing sensitive information that the government wishes to keep secret.

To remedy the procedural shortcomings of the statutory scheme in *Charkaoui*, the court suggested that a special advocate (an independent, security-cleared lawyer) could be appointed to represent the named person during *in camera* proceedings. The Crown's failure to incorporate such a measure, or to otherwise correct the procedural defects referred to above, led the court to conclude that the violation of s 7 could not be saved under s 1 because the infringement did not minimally impair the right at stake. Parliament has since amended the IRPA to provide for a special advocate.[65] The advocate, however, once he or she goes behind closed doors, is not permitted to communicate with the named person except with the judge's authorization. As a result, the advocate may not be able to ask the named person for an explanation of facts or events presented as grounds for detention, such as trips to the Middle East or central Asia, visits to certain websites, or apparent associations with terror suspects. Exculpatory explanations may exist and be forthcoming but for the shroud of secrecy that still envelops security certificate proceedings.

In *Canada (Citizenship and Immigration) v Harkat*, the court concluded that the communications restrictions on special advocates do not violate s 7 of the Charter, largely because of the designated judge's responsibility to ensure that the named person receives sufficient disclosure.[66] The court's endorsement of the special advocate process is not unequivocal. They recognize that in a given case, it may not meet the requirements of procedural fairness. In such a case, a judge hearing the matter would have a duty to stay proceedings under s 24 of the Charter.[67] The court also concluded that designated judges could, albeit sparingly, allow special advocates to interview and cross-examine the human sources of the Canadian Security Intelligence Service (CSIS) during *in camera* proceedings.[68] Shortly after judgment in *Harkat*, Parliament responded by amending the *Canadian Security Intelligence Service Act* to extend a class privilege to CSIS's sources, which prevents special advocates from examining sources in most circumstances.[69]

Interestingly, the court's original endorsement of the use of a special advocate system in *Charkaoui* takes place in its s 1 analysis and not in the analysis of the requirement of natural justice under s 7.[70] As a result, it is unclear whether the court is of the view that using special advocates is consistent with the principles of fundamental justice, or whether the special advocate system is inconsistent with s 7 but justified under s 1. This marks the first time the court has seriously entertained an infringement of s 7 being saved by s 1. Moreover, this may mean that a special advocate program in a non-constitutional context would not be

---

64   RSC 1985, c C-5.

65   *Immigration and Refugee Protection Act*, SC 2001, c 27, ss 83-87.2, as amended by *An Act to amend the Immigration and Refugee Protection Act (certificate and special advocate) and to make a consequential amendment to another Act*, SC 2008, c 3.

66   *Canada (Citizenship and Immigration) v Harkat*, 2014 SCC 37, [2014] 2 SCR 33 [*Harkat*] at paras 60, 64, 69-70, 76-77.

67   *Ibid* at para 77

68   *Ibid* at paras 88-89.

69   RSC 1985, c C-23, s 18.1.

70   *Charkaoui*, *supra* note 57 at paras 70-87.

consistent with the common law duty of fairness, because the content of the common law duty informs and so is similar to the procedural content of s 7. If this is so, such a program could be upheld only if supported by clear statutory language that explicitly limited the reach of the common law of procedural fairness.

In the 2008 case *Charkaoui v Canada (Citizenship and Immigration) (Charkaoui II)*,[71] the Supreme Court reviewed CSIS's policy of destroying operational notes, including notes relied on to issue a security certificate against Charkaoui. The court held that the Crown has an obligation to retain (not destroy) such documents because they must be available for assessment by the reviewing judge. Speaking more generally to the duty to disclose, the court said that the security certificate procedure brings s 7 interests into play, and as a result a "form of disclosure of all the information that goes beyond the mere summaries which are currently provided by CSIS to the ministers and the designated judge is required to protect the fundamental rights affected by the security certificate procedure."[72]

Charkaoui and *Charkaoui II* figure in a line of cases stretching back to *Singh*, in which s 7 has provided procedural safeguards to non-citizens who historically were vulnerable to unstructured discretionary authority subject only to limited review. Nonetheless, the bigger question that is easily lost in the minutiae of Charter review of specific statutory provisions, and which was never asked by the court, is whether it is at all just to incarcerate foreign nationals and permanent residents without the protection of fundamental criminal law principles, such as the rules of evidence, the idea that the Crown must prove its case beyond a reasonable doubt, the proscription against double jeopardy, and the presumption of innocence. These principles lie at the heart of our justice system because they are constitutive of the rule of law, and because deprivations of liberty arising from detention are so serious. Sections 7 through 14 of the Charter reflect and embody these principles, and those sections are supposed to apply to "everyone," regardless of civil and political status. They remain in place for citizens. But for others who have yet to attain citizenship, and who are subject to security certificates rather than criminal law, the Charter's safeguards against arbitrary prosecution are silenced because, in the case of security certificates, there is no prosecution at all.

III. CONCLUSION

In many respects, the requirements of procedural fairness under s 7 of the Charter are the same as at common law. Fortunately for litigants and students, the *Baker* analysis is central to the analysis in both cases. The result depends on the context. There are, however, some important differences. Most notably, where s 7 is engaged, the requirements of natural justice cannot be removed or reduced by express statutory language. Statutory procedures that are inconsistent with the requirements of the Charter are void.[73] As a result, it is important to determine whether or not the facts of the case are sufficient to trigger a s 7 claim if the procedure at issue is established by statute.

---

71 *Charkaoui v Canada (Citizenship and Immigration)*, 2008 SCC 38, [2008] 2 SCR 326. [*Charkaoui II*].

72 *Ibid* at para 50.

73 Section 52, *Constitution Act, 1982*. As discussed above, similar protections are guaranteed where the *Canadian Bill of Rights*, or similar provincial statutes apply. See for example Quebec's *Charter of Human Rights and Freedoms*, RSQ 1977, c C-12.

We also observed that the content of procedural fairness may vary in the s 7 context. For example, in *Singh* the court suggested that the duty to provide reasons may be particularly intense where s 7 interests are engaged. It will be interesting to see as the jurisprudence develops whether the procedural requirements of s 7 track those of the common law or take on a character of their own.

SUGGESTED ADDITIONAL READINGS

BOOKS AND ARTICLES

Daly, Paul, "Canada's Bi-Polar Administrative Law: Time for Fusion" (2014) 40:1 Queen's LJ 213

Evans, JM, "The Principles of Fundamental Justice: The Constitution and the Common Law" (1991) 29 Osgoode Hall LJ 51.

Van Harten, Gus, Gerald Heckman, David Mullan & Janna Promislow, *Administrative Law: Cases, Text, and Materials*, 7th ed (Toronto: Emond Montgomery, 2015) 871-76.

CASES

Canada (Attorney General) v PHS Community Services Society, 2011 SCC 44, [2011] 3 SCR 134.

Canada (Prime Minister) v Khadr, 2010 SCC 3, [2010] 1 SCR 44.

Charkaoui v Canada (Citizenship and Immigration), 2007 SCC 9, [2007] 1 SCR 350.

Conway, R v, 2010 SCC 22, [2010] 1 SCR 765.

Doré v Barreau du Québec, 2012 SCC 12.

Lake v Canada (Minister of Justice), 2008 SCC 23, [2008] 1 SCR 761.

Mills v The Queen, [1986] 1 SCR 863.

Multani v Commission scolaire Marguerite-Bourgeoys, 2006 SCC 6, [2006] 1 SCR 256.

Newfoundland and Labrador Nurses' Union v Newfoundland and Labrador (Treasury Board), 2011 SCC 62.

Nova Scotia (Workers' Compensation Board) v Martin; Nova Scotia (Workers' Compensation Board) v Laseur, 2003 SCC 54, [2003] 2 SCR 504.

Singh v Canada (Minister of Employment and Immigration), [1985] 1 SCR 177.

Slaight Communications Inc v Davidson, [1989] 1 SCR 1038.

Suresh v Canada (Minister of Citizenship and Immigration), 2002 SCC 1, [2002] 1 SCR 3.

Wareham v Ontario (Ministry of Community and Social Services), 2008 ONCA 771.

CHAPTER SEVEN

The Dynamics of Independence, Impartiality, and Bias in the Canadian Administrative State

Laverne Jacobs*

Faculty of Law, University of Windsor

* I am grateful to the co-contributors and editors of this volume for their feedback on this chapter. Thanks also to Cameron Taylor (JD '18) and Christina Loebach (JD '15) for their research assistance.

I. INTRODUCTION

This chapter addresses the controversial issues of tribunal[1] independence, impartiality, and bias. It is useful at the outset to define the relationship between these three concepts, although this relationship is discussed in greater detail below. Put simply, independence, impartiality, and bias all centre on the notion of fairness in the administrative decision-making process. Key characteristics of a fair proceeding before an administrative body are that the decision-maker and the decision-making process not grant undue preferential or adverse treatment nor be driven by preconceived notions. These characteristics are vital not only to the litigants before the tribunal, but also to the public's confidence in the administration of justice. Most certainly, the general public would lose faith in public decision-makers if it perceived that their decisions were based on irrelevant considerations, such as relationships with the litigants before them, prejudice, or undue pressure from government. A full and fair hearing will also result in better decision-making.[2] Our legal tradition has gone to great lengths to protect this fundamental tenet of fairness. Consequently, regardless of what the reality may be in any given administrative decision-making process, the mere perception of partiality toward a particular outcome, or *bias*, provided that the perception is reasonable, is enough to have a decision overturned.

If bias is the evil that we are trying to avoid, *impartiality* refers to the ideal state of the decision-maker or decision-making institution. An impartial decision-maker is one who is able to make judgments with an open mind—that is, one who comes to the decision-making table without their "mind already made up" or without connections that improperly influence the decision-making process. Finally, *independence* is said to be a means of achieving impartiality. For example, by ensuring through legislation that an administrative tribunal is not too dependent on government for the necessities of its day-to-day functioning, it is theoretically less likely that government officials can pull decision-making strings.

Canadian administrative law jurisprudence shows a continual ebb and flow between allowing deference to the nature of administrative bodies and legislative choices, on the one hand, and asserting judicial paradigms as ideal forms for resolving issues of administrative independence, impartiality, and bias, on the other hand. This chapter argues that, when it comes to the administrative state, the process of developing appropriate juristic tools such as "guarantees of independence" and "the rule against bias" requires a perspective that is always situated between a court-derived model and the wide variety of administrative actors that exist.

II. SOURCES OF THE GUARANTEE OF AN INDEPENDENT AND IMPARTIAL TRIBUNAL

The guarantee of a proceeding before an independent and impartial tribunal stems from common law, and from constitutional or quasi-constitutional principles. This chapter thus

---

1   The term "tribunal" is a contested one by some decision-making bodies within the administrative justice system. It is used here generically to encompass all statutory administrative bodies (variously termed, for example, agencies, boards, or commissions), not simply those that are adjudicative in a court-like sense or those that render binding decisions.

2   On the merits of fair proceedings leading to better decision-making, see Chapter 5 in this volume.

builds on the concepts of procedural fairness discussed by Kate Glover in Chapter 5, The Principles and Practices of Procedural Fairness, and by Evan Fox-Decent and Alexander Pless in Chapter 6, The Charter and Administrative Law Part I: Procedural Fairness. At common law, the principles of natural justice are encapsulated in two central ideas. The first is that a decision-maker should neither judge their own cause nor have any interest in the outcome of a case they are deciding. This idea is generally known as the rule against bias and is often summarized in a Latin maxim: *nemo judex in sua causa debet esse* (no one is fit to be the judge in their own cause). The second idea requires the decision-maker to hear and listen to both sides of the case before making a decision. This requirement has been summarized by the maxim *audi alteram partem* (hear the other side). Both the *nemo judex* and the *audi alteram partem* principles inform the right to an independent and impartial proceeding. The *nemo judex* rule aims to avoid circumstances in which the decision-maker acts as both prosecutor and judge in the same matter or decides for personal gain or benefit. Similarly, by requiring the decision-maker to listen to all sides of a dispute, the *audi alteram partem* rule seeks, in part, to encourage the decision-maker to focus on the facts of the dispute and the relevant law, and not on extraneous, or irrelevant, considerations.[3]

In addition to these common law principles, some have argued—with limited success—that the promise of an independent and impartial administrative tribunal is also guaranteed by unwritten constitutional principles and the rule of law.[4] What is more certain is that a determination by an independent and impartial tribunal is guaranteed in some cases through the *Canadian Charter of Rights and Freedoms*.[5] The table on the following page indicates the wording of the guarantees provided by various enactments.

The most striking features of this comparative table are the differences in wording, the seeming variation in the rights protected, and the collection of standards employed to protect them. For example, although the Canadian *Bill of Rights* and the *Alberta Bill of Rights* make "due process of law" the decisive factor for determining whether one has been legally or illegally deprived of his or her rights, s 7 of the Canadian Charter speaks of "principles of fundamental justice." To what extent are the two expressions coterminous? Is one concept broader than the other? And how do concepts such as "due process of law," and "fundamental justice" relate, if at all, to the common law principle of natural justice? These are all questions with which the courts, lawyers, academics, and students have grappled.[6]

---

3   I discuss the interplay of these ideas in Laverne A Jacobs, "Tribunal Independence and Impartiality: Rethinking the Theory After *Bell* and *Ocean Port Hotel*—A Call for Empirical Analysis" in Laverne A Jacobs & Anne L Mactavish, eds, *Dialogue Between Courts and Tribunals: Essays in Administrative Law and Justice (2001-2007)* (Montreal: Les Éditions Thémis, 2008), online: <https://papers.ssrn.com/sol3/papers.cfm?abstract_id=2332875> [Jacobs & Mactavish].

4   *Ocean Port Hotel Ltd v British Columbia (General Manager, Liquor Control and Licensing Branch)*, 2001 SCC 52, [2001] 2 SCR 781 [*Ocean Port*] and *McKenzie v Minister of Public Safety and Solicitor General*, 2006 BCSC 1372, 61 BCLR (4th) 57; 2007 BCCA 507, 71 BCLR (4th) 1, appeal to the SCC dismissed without reasons, [2007] SCCA No 601 (QL), after the BC Court of Appeal determined the issue to be moot because of legislative amendment [*McKenzie*]. Both cases are discussed below.

5   Part I of the *Constitution Act, 1982*, being Schedule B to the *Canada Act 1982* (UK), 1982, c 11 [Charter].

6   See e.g. *Singh v Minister of Employment and Immigration*, [1985] 1 SCR 177 [*Singh*], an immigration case in which the Supreme Court of Canada held that, at a minimum, "fundamental justice" included the notion of procedural fairness.

Statute	Section(s)	Guarantee Provided
Canadian Charter of Rights and Freedoms	s 7	Everyone has the right to life, liberty and security of the person and the right not to be deprived thereof except in accordance with the principles of fundamental justice.
Canadian Charter of Rights and Freedoms	s 11(d)	Any person charged with an offence has the right ... to be presumed innocent until proven guilty according to law in a fair and public hearing by an independent and impartial tribunal.
Quebec *Charter of Human Rights and Freedoms*[7]	s 23	Every person has a right to a full and equal, public and fair hearing by an independent and impartial tribunal, for the determination of his rights and obligations or of the merits of any charge brought against him.
Canadian *Bill of Rights*[8]	ss 1(a)	[T]he right of the individual to life, liberty, security of the person and enjoyment of property, and the right not to be deprived thereof except by due process of law.
Canadian *Bill of Rights*	2(e)	[N]o law of Canada shall be construed or applied so as to ... deprive a person of the right to a fair hearing in accordance with the principles of fundamental justice for the determination of his rights and obligations.
Alberta *Bill of Rights*[9]	s 1(a)	[T]he right of the individual to liberty, security of the person and enjoyment of property, and the right not to be deprived thereof except by due process of law.

Moreover, it is clear from the table that many situations trigger the right to what we might call globally "an independent and impartial proceeding." What is not always clear is how smoothly these situations translate to the various instances of socio-economic regulation that are addressed by administrative actors in the administrative state. For example, s 11(d) of the Canadian Charter has been held to require penal consequences before it can be

---

7   RSQ, c C-12 [Quebec Charter].
8   SC 1960, c 44, C-12.3.
9   RSA 2000, c A-14.

applied outside the context of courts.[10] And while s 23 of the Quebec Charter seems all-encompassing insofar as it allows for a fair hearing by an independent and impartial tribunal for the mere determination of the individual's rights and obligations, this seemingly low threshold is elevated by a legislated definition of "tribunal." The Quebec Charter defines "tribunals" as being adjudicative bodies only.[11] The acceptable degree of independence and the way in which impartiality is understood may be quite different for hearings before a body in Quebec that is established to set prices and develop policy in the natural resources sector than for hearings before a human rights tribunal.

Generally, these variations, whether they stem from legislative enactments, the common law, or from judicial interpretations of both, indicate a context-driven and, at times, uneven promise of independence and impartiality. To predict the degree of independence that any administrative body should exhibit and the ways in which impartiality and bias should be understood within the context of that body's functioning, it is important to have a thorough understanding of not only the law but also the nature, purpose, and practical ways that the administrative body in question operates.

III. WHAT IS "TRIBUNAL INDEPENDENCE" AND WHY IS IT IMPORTANT?

Challenging administrative tribunals for lack of independence has been a highly litigated area in administrative law. Indeed, since the advent of the Canadian Charter, some have characterized this new preoccupation with independent decision-making as providing "a more extensive basis for challenging adjudicators and statutory regimes than has been envisaged under traditional common law conceptions of bias."[12] Because independence has attracted such attention as a means of challenging administrative regimes, this chapter focuses first on arguments regarding lack of independence as a reason for alleging reasonable apprehension of bias on the part of individual administrative decision-makers or of administrative decision-making institutions.

The notion of tribunal independence raises several questions. To what extent should tribunals and other administrative bodies be independent of the branches of government that have created them? How can a tribunal (and its members) best fulfill the often competing functions for which it has been created while maintaining an appropriate distance from government, litigants, and other stakeholders? And how do we define "appropriate" in this context? In this chapter, we explore the various relationships that affect the independence of tribunals and their individual decision-makers, and the ways that independence may be,

---

10   See *Alex Couture Inc v Canada (Attorney General)* (1991), 83 DLR (4th) 577 (Qc CA), leave to appeal denied, [1992] 2 SCR v, at 91 DLR (4th) vii [*Couture*]; *Chrysler Canada Ltd v Canada (Competition Tribunal)*, [1992] 2 SCR 394. Section 7 of the Charter seems to offer more fertile ground and has been used with some success in deportation matters (see *Charkaoui v Canada (Citizenship and Immigration)*, 2007 SCC 9, [2007] 1 SCR 350, but see also *Suresh v Canada (Minister of Citizenship and Immigration)*, 2002 SCC 1, [2002] 1 SCR 3).

11   Section 56 of the Quebec Charter reads: "In sections 9, 23, 30, 31, 34 and 38, in Chapter III of Part II and in Part IV, the word 'tribunal' includes a coroner, a fire investigation commissioner, an inquiry commission, and any person or agency exercising quasi-judicial functions."

12   See Gus Van Harten, Gerald Heckman & David J Mullan, *Administrative Law: Cases, Text, and Materials*, 6th ed (Toronto: Emond Montgomery, 2010) at 444.

or perceived to be, compromised. These relationships are examined critically from both the perspective of jurisprudential debates and the practical realities of daily tribunal operations. Specific tensions include the appointments process, removal of members, tribunals as a function of policy-making, internal interactions among tribunal members and staff, and the vexing question of the extent to which explicit and implicit constitutional, structural guarantees of independence do or should apply to tribunals.

By design, administrative decision-making bodies in Canada have been created in a way that leaves them connected to government. Most have a link with the executive branch of government through a minister of Cabinet. Generally, under their enabling statutes, tribunals, or at least their chairs, are required to maintain some contact with this minister. At the very least, they are obliged to file annual reports to this minister.[13] They may also have additional statutory obligations that force them to interact with the minister and the minister's department. For example, they may be asked to provide advice to the minister or additional information on developments in the regulation of the industry or sector under their supervision.[14] Finally, the minister will certainly be involved in the process of appointing and removing members of the tribunal. In Ontario, with the enactment of the *Adjudicative Tribunals Accountability, Governance and Appointments Act, 2009* (ATAGAA), the chair of an adjudicative tribunal must interact with the minister responsible for the tribunal or with the executive branch of government in order to recommend the appointment or reappointment of tribunal members.[15] The design of the Canadian administrative state differs markedly from that of some jurisdictions. For example, in the United Kingdom, recent tribunal reform has resulted in all administrative tribunals interacting with an executive agency called Her Majesty Courts and Tribunal Service, instead of with host departments.[16] The institutional arrangements within the administrative justice systems of different jurisdictions are discussed in greater detail in Section IV.D below.

Given the political nature of the executive branch of government and, in particular, its responsibility to create and promote the government's policies, one can easily see how members of the general public may be wary that inappropriate interference may stem from the regular interactions between government departments and tribunals. For instance, users of the tribunal might be concerned that the minister might use these opportunities to dictate, whether explicitly or implicitly, how particular files should be decided. This concern can be particularly acute in situations where the government is frequently an

---

13 A typical provision imposing the obligation to file an annual report to the minister can be found in the *Residential Tenancies Act, 2006*, SO 2006, c 17, s 180. The *Adjudicative Tribunals Accountability, Governance and Appointments Act, 2009*, SO 2009, c 33, Schedule 5 [ATAGAA], requires adjudicative tribunals in Ontario to report to their responsible ministers on a wide array of matters relating to tribunal internal governance. These matters include the development and maintenance of consultation policies, ethics plans, and codes of conduct. ATAGAA is discussed in greater detail below. See *infra* note 15 and accompanying text.

14 See e.g. *Alcohol and Gaming Regulation and Public Protection Act, 1996*, SO 1996, c 26, Schedule, s 3(4).

15 ATAGAA. See, generally, L Jacobs, "A Wavering Commitment? Administrative Independence and Collaborative Governance in Ontario's Adjudicative Tribunals Accountability Legislation" (2010) 28:2 Windsor YB Access to Just 285.

16 Although one must be careful in making sweeping comparisons because the terminology in different jurisdictions varies for different administrative bodies.

opposing party before the tribunal—for example, in immigration matters or disputes relating to social benefits.

These introductory paragraphs point us in the direction of an initial understanding of the concept of tribunal independence and why it is important. When we speak of "independence," we are referring to the tribunal's ability to decide matters free of inappropriate interference or influence. The executive branch of government may be one source of interference in the administrative law context, but several other sources—including litigants, other tribunal members, and staff—may also exist. As in the case of judicial decisions made in the criminal law context or in civil matters, the independence of the administrative decision-maker is valued as an aspect of the rule of law. In theory, when decision-makers are in an insulated zone, the public will have greater confidence that the decision being rendered is based only on relevant considerations, such as the facts of the case and the law. In the context of the administrative state, however, difficulty arises in determining what constitutes "relevant" considerations or "inappropriate" interference.[17] Some of the most interesting tensions in administrative law arise in the clash between the day-to-day realities of the work of administrative tribunals and judicial understandings of how the administrative state should work. This chapter argues that the law on tribunal independence is no exception. Arguably, it is one of the richest areas in which to explore these tensions. By focusing primarily on judicial review of administrative action, administrative law has, to date, given privilege to judicial conceptions of independence while failing to adequately integrate those judicial understandings with on-the-ground tribunal realities.

The following discussion provides an overview of the historical development of the law on tribunal independence and the relationship between independence and the concept of impartiality. It explores administrative law's understandings of independence from both judicial and tribunal perspectives, using the appointment and removal of tribunal decision-makers as an example. The chapter then examines some alternate modes of institutional arrangement that exist in various jurisdictions in order to contemplate possible means of improving the independence of the administrative justice system in Canada. The purpose of this discussion is not to suggest that judicial paradigms form the most appropriate backdrop for the decision-making of administrative tribunals but to offer the reader information so that they may reflect on how administrative tribunal practices might be served if these models were adopted.

Finally, we take a solid look at the concept of disqualifying bias—the second major component of this chapter—and examine the legal principles and practical realities surrounding it. At the end of the chapter, we circle back to highlight the connections between adjudicative independence and disqualifying bias in the everyday tribunal context. To do this, we examine some of the common institutional practices used by "multifunctional" bodies to promote consistency and policy-making as they administer across diverse contexts.

---

17 The fact that the enabling legislation may sometimes provide a role for government to play in the decision-making process as a party—for example, in contexts such as immigration, or social benefits litigation—sometimes also contributes to rendering complex the question of what constitutes relevant or irrelevant considerations.

IV. THE DEVELOPMENT OF THE LAW OF TRIBUNAL
INDEPENDENCE IN CANADA

The jurisprudence on tribunal independence in Canada is easiest understood as having developed through a series of three waves. The first wave of jurisprudence used the independence of the judiciary as a foundation on which to mould the concept of administrative tribunal independence. The second wave, marked by the decision in *Ocean Port*,[18] affirmed the hybrid nature of tribunals and maintained that there is no general constitutional guarantee of independence where tribunals are concerned. The third wave served as a retrenchment: litigants once again pushed to have judicial declarations that administrative tribunal independence is guaranteed by the Constitution.

A. The First Wave of Tribunal Independence Jurisprudence: Laying the Groundwork

1. The Theory of Judicial Independence

A discussion about the independence of administrative bodies is best started with an overview of the theory of judicial independence. This is because modern administrative law theory in Canada has developed tribunal independence on the foundation of judicial independence. At its core, judicial independence is a means of ensuring that judges act free from any interference or influence. In Australia, Sir Guy Green has described judicial independence as the capacity of the courts "to perform their constitutional function free from actual or apparent dependence upon any persons or institutions."[19] Chief Justice Dickson, speaking for the majority of the Supreme Court in *The Queen v Beauregard* offered this useful definition:

> Historically, the generally accepted core of the principle of judicial independence has been the complete liberty of individual judges to hear and decide the cases that come before them: *no outsider—be it government, pressure group, individual or even another judge—should interfere in fact, or attempt to interfere, with the way in which a judge conducts his or her case and makes his or her decision.* This core continues to be central to the principle of judicial independence.[20]

How is this "complete liberty" to be ascertained? Although it is certainly impossible to monitor all the contacts and communications of every judge, when it comes to assuring independence from government (the first of the outside interferences noted by Dickson CJ), three objective structural conditions have been identified as necessary to guarantee independence: security of tenure, financial security, and administrative (or institutional) control. These three conditions serve to reassure the public that the possibility of interference in judicial decision-making by the executive and legislative branches of government has been reduced, if not eliminated.

With respect to security of tenure, the type of interference targeted is the ability of the government to remove a judge for such things as rendering decisions that do not meet the

---

18   *Ocean Port, supra* note 4.

19   Sir Guy Green, "The Rationale and Some Aspects of Judicial Independence" (1985) 20 ALR 135. Sir Guy Green's formulation of the concept of judicial independence was endorsed by the Supreme Court of Canada in *Valente v The Queen*, [1985] 2 SCR 673 at para 18, LeDain J [*Valente*].

20   [1986] 2 SCR 56 at para 21 (emphasis added) [*Beauregard*].

government's approval. As a result, the condition that a judge's tenure be secure mandates that a judge be removed only for cause. Security of tenure is guaranteed by the Constitution, which provides that judges of the superior courts shall hold office during good behaviour or until they reach the age of 75.[21] Moreover, before removal, judges must be provided with an opportunity to respond to the allegations against them.[22] Consequently, "at pleasure" appointments, which allow judges to be removed at the request of Cabinet, without pre-specified cause and without necessarily allowing the judge to be heard, have been rendered invalid.

"Financial security" aims to satisfy two goals. The first is a guarantee that, although the government is responsible for the remuneration of judges, it will not alter their pay for arbitrary reasons such as its discontent with decisions rendered. To accomplish this goal, judges are guaranteed a fixed salary under the Constitution.[23] As well, more recently, compensation commissions have been set up to help facilitate negotiations in judges' pay and pay-related matters, such as pensions.[24] The second goal is a promise that the amount that judges are paid will be sufficient to keep them from seeking alternative means of supplementing their income. Security of tenure and financial security have historical roots dating back to 13th-century England.[25] The concepts evolved from experiences in which the King manipulated the judiciary in order to ensure that the bench was sympathetic toward him, and from the problem of bribery caused by the underpayment of court officials, including judges.

Administrative or institutional control is the third objective guarantee of independence. Institutional control deals with the manner in which the affairs of the court are administered—from budgetary allocations for buildings and equipment to the assignment of cases. It addresses how responsibility for such administration should be divided between the judiciary and the other branches of government. Although questions about, for example, the allocation of court cases have clearly been determined to fall properly within the ambit of the chief justice of the court,[26] other matters, such as obtaining budgetary allocations for equipment, are more problematic.[27] For example, allowing judges to obtain their own funding for resources, instead of asking them to go through a Cabinet minister such as the attorney general, might appear to be an approach that fosters the independence of the judiciary; however, this method could result in judges soliciting funds from the government or others, which is unseemly from the perception of administrative control. For the Supreme

---

21   See *Constitution Act, 1867* (UK), 30 & 31 Vict, c 3, reprinted in RSC 1985, Appendix II, No 5, s 99.

22   An example of this is found in the federal *Judges Act*, RSC 1985, c J-1, s 64; see also Canadian Judicial Council, online: <http://www.cjc-ccm.gc.ca>, which outlines the complaints procedure and inquiry process for the investigation of federally appointed judges. For a recent example of the judicial inquiry process in action, see *The Honourable Justice Bernd Zabel—Reasons for Decision* (11 September 2017) Ontario Judicial Council, online: <http://www.ontariocourts.ca/ocj/ojc/public-hearings-decisions/d2017/zabel/>.

23   See *Constitution Act, 1867*, s 100.

24   See e.g. *Provincial Court Judges' Assn of New Brunswick v New Brunswick (Minister of Justice); Ontario Judges' Assn v Ontario (Management Board); Bodner v Alberta; Conférence des juges du Québec v Quebec (Attorney General); Minc v Quebec (Attorney General)*, 2005 SCC 44, [2005] 2 SCR 286.

25   See WR Lederman, "The Independence of the Judiciary" (1956) 34 Can Bar Rev 769, 1139.

26   See *Valente, supra* note 19.

27   See Martin Friedland, *A Place Apart: Judicial Independence and Accountability in Canada* (Ottawa: Canadian Judicial Council, 1995); see also Jules Deschênes and Carl Baar, *Masters in Their Own House* (Ottawa: Canadian Judicial Council, 1981).

Court, the Federal Courts, and the Tax Court, issues of institutional control that rely on a government allocation of resources have been addressed through the use of a negotiating office called the Federal Commissioner of Judicial Affairs.[28] The problem of balancing judicial independence and judicial administration is particularly acute at the provincial and territorial level where, as a result of our constitutional division of powers, the administration of the court system requires some involvement by the provincial legislature and executive.[29]

As with security of tenure and financial security, administrative control is concerned with making sure that judges are not put in compromising situations where they might choose to make decisions to protect their own employment and interests, rather than for the sake of rendering decisions solely on the basis of their legal judgment. However, unlike the first two guarantees of independence, the nature of administrative control is primarily institutional as opposed to individual. Although there may be implications that affect an individual judge, it is not the individual judge and their relationship with the government that is at issue, but the relationship between the government and the court as an institution.

Finally, the jurisprudence has come to recognize a fourth type of independence—that is, independence from interference in deliberations, commonly known as adjudicative independence. Referenced briefly in the Supreme Court's decision in *Beauregard*,[30] the concept of adjudicative independence embodies the ability of a decision-maker to decide, free of inappropriate interference by other decision-makers. Such inappropriate interference may include, for example, pressure to decide a certain way or substitution of another's decision for one's own. Unlike security of tenure, financial security, and administrative control, adjudicative independence is not structural in nature. It does not relate to the design of the institution by the government. Adjudicative independence deals with relational matters and the internal process of deliberation by individual decision-makers. Adjudicative independence is one guarantee of independence that is frequently called into question in the administrative state, especially as a result of institutional practices used to develop policy and consistency such as full board meetings in which all adjudicators in a tribunal convene to discuss the possible implications of a draft decision on the tribunal's jurisprudence. We examine adjudicative independence in greater detail when we discuss institutional bias.

As alluded to in the introduction, the purpose of judicial independence is to help boost public confidence in the justice system. Judicial independence has the protection of the public in mind, not the protection of the judges. The mere appearance of inappropriate interference with the decision-making process is enough to engender a loss of public confidence in decision-making.[31] On a micro level, whether the duty of fairness has been breached in any given proceeding is generally foremost on the minds of particular litigants. Some would also argue that a reasonable perception of interference may threaten public acceptance of the law itself. In this light, independence is not a goal in and of itself; rather, judicial independence serves as a cornerstone to protect other values that are considered important within our system of justice. Most commonly, independence is said to be maintained in order to provide an appearance of impartiality in the decision-making process. Providing guarantees of judicial independence aims to assure the public that

---

28   Established under Part III of the *Judges Act*.
29   See *Constitution Act, 1867*, s 92(14).
30   See *Beauregard, supra* note 20 and accompanying text.
31   See *R v Sussex Justices, ex parte McCarthy*, [1924] 1 KB 256

decision-makers are in a position to make decisions impartially. The independence of administrative tribunals seeks to achieve the same goal while also allowing tribunal members to use their expertise and analytical capacities to reach the best decisions.

2. From Judicial Independence to Tribunal Independence

Over time, for better or for worse, the criteria guaranteeing independence of the judiciary have served as a foundation from which courts have determined whether administrative tribunals are also sufficiently independent. *Valente* was the first Supreme Court case in Canada to suggest that the guarantees for judicial independence could also be applied to a variety of tribunals.[32] Since that time, litigants have pushed for tribunals to be held to the same degree of independence as the courts. These litigants have argued that various constitutional safeguards (namely, ss 7 and 11(d) of the Canadian Charter as well as the unwritten constitutional principle of judicial independence) and quasi-constitutional provisions (such as s 23 of the Quebec Charter and the Canadian *Bill of Rights*) guarantee tribunal independence.[33]

Over the years, the test for adequate tribunal independence has developed to be whether a reasonable, well-informed person having thought the matter through would conclude that an administrative decision-maker is sufficiently free of factors that could interfere with his or her ability to make impartial judgments.[34] The standard for tribunal independence is not as strict as it is for judicial independence. Administrative tribunals do not have to meet the same degree of independence as the courts. The methodological approach taken by the courts when the independence of an administrative tribunal is challenged consists of applying the guarantees of tribunal independence in a flexible way to account for the functions performed by the tribunal under scrutiny. This method was stated concisely in *Canadian Pacific Ltd v Matsqui Indian Band*[35] by Lamer CJ:

> [W]hile administrative tribunals are subject to the *Valente* principles, the test for institutional independence must be applied in light of the functions being performed by the particular tribunal at issue. The requisite level of institutional independence (i.e. security of tenure, financial

---

32 *Valente* was the first Supreme Court case to deal with the question of judicial independence in Canada. The question at issue was whether a provincial court judge, appointed under the *Provincial Courts Act*, RSO 1980, c 398 and sitting as the Ontario Provincial Court (Criminal Division), could be considered an independent tribunal under s 11(d) of the Charter.

33 See e.g. with respect to the Charter, s 7, *Singh*, *supra* note 6 and, with respect to s 11(d) of the Charter, *R v Généreux*, [1992] 1 SCR 259; *Ruffo v Quebec (Conseil de la magistrature)*, [1991] AQ No 1101 (QL) (Sup Ct)—the argument relating to s 11(d) of the Charter was abandoned at the higher levels of court; *Couture*, *supra* note 10; in relation to the unwritten constitutional principles stemming from the preamble of the Constitution, see *Ocean Port*, *supra* note 4, and *McKenzie* (Sup Ct J), *supra* note 4, decision on appeal; as regards s 23 of the Quebec Charter, see *2747-3174 Québec Inc v Quebec (Régie des permis d'alcool)*, [1996] 3 SCR 919 [*Régie*], and *Montambeault v Brazeau*, [1996] AQ No 4187 (QL) (Qc CA).

34 This test, generally referred to as the "reasonable apprehension of bias" test, has many purposes. It is used to determine whether a reasonable apprehension exists that an administrative decision-maker has acted partially or exhibited bias. Moreover, it has been applied to evaluate administrative bodies as a whole in order to determine whether the institution can be said to exhibit a lack of independence or impartiality in a substantial number of cases. The test is discussed below in Section V, "Reasonable Apprehension of Bias."

35 [1995] 1 SCR 3 [*Matsqui*].

security, and administrative control) will depend on the nature of the tribunal, the interests at stake, and other indices of independence such as oaths of office.[36]

A tribunal's operational context is identified not only through an examination of its enabling legislation, but also through an examination of how it functions in practice. In *Matsqui*, the need to see the tribunal in practice was a point of division between the majority and minority decisions. While all the judges who addressed the issue of independence agreed with the theoretical approach set out by Lamer CJ, outlined above, the majority opinion on this issue maintained that the test should be deferred until the tribunals had actually been up and running in order to have the benefit of knowing how they operated in practice.[37]

The principles developed in *Matsqui* were applied in *2747-3174 Québec Inc v Quebec (Régie des permis d'alcool)*,[38] a case argued under s 23 of the Quebec Charter. In *Régie*, it was held that the decision-makers of Quebec's liquor licensing board possessed sufficient security of tenure despite the fact that their terms of office were limited. The Supreme Court of Canada held that the requirements of tribunal independence do not necessitate that administrative actors, like judges, hold office for life. The court reasoned that what must be avoided, however, is that adjudicators face the possibility of being simply dismissed at the pleasure of the executive branch of government. The fixed-term appointments in *Régie* were acceptable because they provided expressly that the decision-makers (called "directors" in *Régie*) could be dismissed only for specific reasons. The directors could also contest any dismissals in court. Sanctions were therefore available for any arbitrary interference by the executive in a director's term of office.

The respondent in *Régie* also challenged the board's administrative control. It argued that there were so many points of contact between the liquor board and the minister responsible for the board's enabling legislation that the board's institutional independence was threatened. However, the court held that administrative control was also sufficient. The court reasoned that it was not unusual for a minister to have many points of contact with a tribunal under its responsibility. The court noted further that no evidence had been provided to show that the minister could affect the decision-making process.[39]

---

36 *Ibid* at para 83.

37 *Ibid* at paras 116-17. For further discussion, see Laverne Jacobs, "From Rawls to Habermas: Toward a Grounded Theory of Impartiality in Canadian Administrative Law" (2014) 51:2 Osgoode Hall LJ 543.

38 *Régie*, *supra* note 33.

39 Nevertheless, the Supreme Court of Canada held that the liquor licensing board lacked the requisite degree of impartiality to meet the requirements of s 23 of the Quebec Charter. This is because it was possible for one single employee to participate at every stage of the process leading up to the cancellation of a liquor permit, from investigation to adjudication. The possibility that an employee who had made submissions to the directors might then advise them in respect of the same matter was held to be problematic as it puts the same individual into conflicting roles within the institution. There was also no evidence of on-the-ground measures being put in place to prevent a single employee from playing multiple and possibly conflicting roles; see also *Brosseau v Alberta Securities Commission*, [1989] 1 SCR 301 [*Brosseau*].

It is easy to state the test for tribunal independence and to give illustrations of how the test has been applied in the jurisprudence. It is more challenging, however, to explain why flexibility is needed when applying the criteria for judicial independence to tribunals. Standard explanations point to the wide range of tribunal structures, the various ways that tribunals are connected to government, the great divergence in the nature and work of administrative bodies, and the many functions that any one administrative body may be asked to perform in tandem. These standard explanations also emphasize that the test for independence is often a way of investigating whether a reasonable apprehension of bias exists in a particular administrative context. Although such explanations take us to a certain point, they do not explain why tribunals ought not to have the same guarantees of structural independence—security of tenure, financial security, administrative control—as a court. Perhaps the best judicial attempt to explain normatively why the objective guarantees of judicial independence need not apply to administrative tribunals comes from the Supreme Court of Canada's decision in *Ocean Port*,[40] discussed in the next section.

In many cases, the objective guarantees of independence for the judiciary do not meet anything near a complete match for tribunals. With regard to administrative control, similar to courts, most tribunal chairs, like chief justices, are responsible for distributing their own caseload and for tribunal management. As well, the tribunal chair usually has the authority to allocate budgetary resources as effectively as possible. In the administrative justice system, balancing cost efficiencies with independence is often a preeminent preoccupation. One mechanism designed to achieve this balance is the Administrative Tribunals Support Service of Canada (ATSSC).[41] Adopted by the federal government in 2014, the ATSSC aims to "strengthen capacity to meet tribunal needs"[42] by providing secretarial, human resource, and other types of administrative support centrally to 11 different administrative tribunals.[43] We see more divergence, however, between courts and administrative tribunals when it comes to financial security and security of tenure. Although the pay for a tribunal member is normally set by legislation, for part-time members in particular, the pay is often disproportionate to the skill contributed. Generally, tribunal service is seen as a type of public service, done more for honour than for glory or riches.[44] In the administrative tribunal context, security of tenure shows a similar marked difference from the judiciary. Tribunal members can be appointed for a variety of terms. Some statutes provide for fixed-term appointments, varying from months to years. In some cases, appointments are renewable; in others, the statute gives no mention of renewal; and in others still, appointments are not renewable at

---

40   *Ocean Port, supra* note 4.
41   See the *Administrative Tribunals Support Service of Canada Act*, SC 2014, c 20, s 376.
42   See the Department of Justice Canada's archived press release on the ATSSC, online: <http://news.gc.ca/web/article-en.do?nid=897239>.
43   See the website of the Administrative Tribunals Support Service of Canada: <https://www.canada.ca/en/administrative-tribunals-support-service.html>.
44   See online: Ontario Public Appointments Secretariat <http://www.pas.gov.on.ca/scripts/en/home.asp>.

all. That there can be wide variation in appointments is illustrated in a 2014 study of 28 Québec administrative tribunals.[45]

One type of appointment, termed an "at pleasure" appointment because it allows the government to appoint a member for as long as the government deems fit, has generated significant controversy in administrative law jurisprudence. In essence, "at pleasure" appointments theoretically enable the government to remove a decision-maker whose decisions are not in line with its expectations. Given that tribunals are to be independent or "at arm's length" from government, "at pleasure" appointments open the door to the possibility of governmental interference with tribunal decision-making. The issue of whether "at pleasure" appointments fail to provide adequate guarantees of independence from arbitrary interference from the executive branch of government was addressed in *Ocean Port*. The issues surrounding "at pleasure" appointments were not resolved, however, as the more recent case of *Keen v Canada (Attorney General)*[46] demonstrates. For more than one reason, *Ocean Port* forms a turning point in the jurisprudence on the independence of administrative tribunals. It constitutes the second wave of jurisprudence in this area. We address it next, along with the practical risks of "at pleasure" appointments, illustrated by the later case of *Keen*.

B. The Second Wave: Parliamentary Supremacy Versus Warding Off Interference

1. *Ocean Port*

Ocean Port is at the heart of the second wave of tribunal independence jurisprudence for two reasons. In its narrowest sense, the Supreme Court of Canada decision in *Ocean Port* is significant because it attempted to lay to rest the controversial issue of whether "at pleasure" appointments provide a satisfactory degree of independence for decision-makers sitting on tribunals that impose penalties. This was the Supreme Court's first opportunity to address the crucial question of whether "at pleasure" appointments, which were clearly not as secure as fixed-term appointments, could provide an adequate image of independence from government. From a broader perspective, *Ocean Port* is an important administrative law case because it offers definitive opinions regarding the constitutional nature of courts and tribunals and the distinction between the two. On both levels, the court's *dicta* offer reasons why administrative tribunals should not need the same degree of independence as courts.

---

45 See Pierre Noreau, France Houle, Martine Valois & Pierre Issalys, *La justice administrative: entre indépendance et responsabilité. Jalons pour la création d'un régime commun des décideurs administratifs indépendants* (Cowansville: Éditions Yvon Blais, 2014) [Noreau et al]. A concise summary of the study is provided in France Houle, et al, "Administrative Justice: Independence and Responsibility—Towards a Common Regime for Independent Adjudicators" (2014) 27 Can J Admin L & Prac 219 [Houle, "Independent Adjudicators"]. For a chart that provides an overview of the appointment and renewal possibilities for these tribunals, see Society of Ontario Adjudicators and Regulators, "Results of research into the process of appointments and re-appointments to administrative tribunals in Québec" (by Zinejda Rita) at 6, online: <https://soar.on.ca/2016/04/results-and-research-of-appointments-and-re-appointments -to-administrative-tribunals-in>.

46 2009 FC 353, [2009] 342 FTR 270 [*Keen*].

Ocean Port dealt with the BC Liquor Appeal Board, a liquor-licensing body that could impose sanctions and remove licences upon finding that a licensee had contravened the province's *Liquor Control and Licensing Act*.[47] The Royal Canadian Mounted Police (RCMP) had reported that Ocean Port Hotel was responsible for five incidents that had violated the Act, the regulations enacted under the statute, and the terms of its liquor licence. The Liquor Control and Licensing Branch, a regulatory branch established under the Act, consequently imposed a two-day suspension on Ocean Port's liquor licence. The Liquor Appeal Board, the appellate body that existed at the time under the statutory regime,[48] held a hearing *de novo* and confirmed the suspension, finding that the evidence supported four of the five alleged infractions.

On appeal to the BC Court of Appeal, Ocean Port Hotel argued that the Liquor Appeal Board lacked sufficient independence to render a fair hearing.[49] The Act indicated that the chair and the members of the board were to serve "at the pleasure of the Lieutenant Governor in Council." The Court of Appeal held that the Liquor Appeal Board members required more security of tenure than what was offered through "at pleasure" appointments in order to be (and appear to be) sufficiently independent of governmental influence of their decision-making.

At the appeal before the Supreme Court of Canada, Ocean Port Hotel added a new dimension to its argument. It submitted that, as an administrative tribunal exercising adjudicative functions, the Liquor Appeal Board required the same degree of independence guaranteed to the courts. The independence of the superior courts of inherent jurisdiction is enshrined in the Constitution. The hotel relied on *Reference re Remuneration of Judges of the Prov Court of PEI; Ref re Independence and Impartiality of Judges of the Prov Court of PEI*.[50] In *PEI Reference*, the Supreme Court of Canada held that judicial independence is an unwritten

---

47 RSBC 1996, c 267.

48 The Liquor Appeal Board has since been removed. Under reforms to the liquor licensing regime in British Columbia that came into effect in 2017, the general manager has the power to reconsider enforcement decisions in certain circumstances (where there is substantial, previously unavailable material evidence, errors of law and/or breach of procedural fairness). Outside of these situations, and for further relief, a person with standing must seek judicial review. See *Liquor Control and Licensing Act*, SBC 2015, c 19, ss 53.1, 72.

49 Ocean Port Hotel submitted that the Board's decision was therefore invalid. The hotel took issue with the terms of appointment of the members of the Liquor Appeal Board. In analyzing the question, the BC Court of Appeal in *Ocean Port Hotel* focused on the similarities between the BC Liquor Appeal Board and its sister institution in Quebec. This comparison could be made easily, given that the Supreme Court of Canada decision in *Régie* had just come down. Gonthier J in *Régie* had determined that the fixed-term appointments held by the directors of the Régie des permis d'alcool would not have been valid had they allowed the directors to be removed without cause—that is, at the pleasure of the executive branch of government. Because *Régie* was a judgment dealing with a body mandated to control the same industry and with adjudicative tasks similar to those of the BC Liquor Appeal Board, the Court of Appeal held that the Liquor Appeal Board members must also require more security of tenure than what was offered through "at pleasure" appointments. In its decision, the BC Court of Appeal stated that the decision to suspend a licence closely resembles a judicial decision and that the penalty was one of serious economic consequence. The BC Court of Appeal also took into account that the same contraventions of the *Liquor Control and Licensing Act* could have been prosecuted in the Provincial Court, where a greater level of independence would have been guaranteed. Moreover, the statute provided a lesser penalty for offences prosecuted in the Provincial Court.

50 [1998] 3 SCR 3 [*PEI Reference*].

constitutional principle that applies not only to the superior courts of inherent jurisdiction but also extends to the Provincial Court of summary jurisdiction. In the *PEI Reference*, Lamer CJ held further that this unwritten constitutional principle is affirmed by the preamble of the Constitution, which indicates that Canada's Constitution is "similar in Principle to that of the United Kingdom."[51] Ocean Port Hotel argued that this unwritten, constitutional principle guaranteeing judicial independence should be interpreted to extend to administrative tribunals as well.

The Supreme Court of Canada disagreed. The Supreme Court asserted that there is no freestanding constitutional guarantee of administrative tribunal independence and that the enshrined constitutional protection of judicial independence could not be translated to the context of administrative decision-making bodies. In its reasons, the court emphasized that judicial independence has historically developed to protect the judiciary from interference from the executive branch of government. By contrast, administrative tribunals are not separate from the executive. In the court's words, administrative tribunals may be seen as "spanning the constitutional divide between the executive and judicial branches of government."[52] Tribunals are created precisely for the purpose of implementing the policies of the executive branch of government. In so doing, they may be required to make quasi-judicial decisions. However, their primary function as policy-makers and their status as extensions of the executive branch of government, make the degree of their independence a question most appropriately determined by Parliament or legislature. It is up to Parliament or the legislature to determine the structure, responsibilities, and degree of independence required of any particular tribunal. In this way, the Supreme Court in *Ocean Port* asserted that the legislature will should prevail in determining how much independence any given tribunal should have.

Furthermore, the court reminded us that tribunal independence is a common law principle of natural justice. As with all principles of natural justice, the degree of independence required at common law could be ousted by express statutory language or necessary statutory implication, so long as the statute is constitutionally valid. As a general rule, administrative tribunals do not attract Charter or quasi-constitutional requirements of independence. However, by virtue of the nature of their work, some tribunals may be subject to these protections. This was the characteristic that distinguished the liquor board in *Régie* from the one in *Ocean Port*.[53] In Quebec, adjudicative bodies had all been made subject to the Quebec Charter's quasi-constitutional guarantee of independence, which ultimately required them to possess a greater guarantee of independence. Such a quasi-constitutional requirement did not exist in British Columbia. Finally, the court pointed out that the *PEI Reference* made no assertions that the unwritten constitutional guarantees of judicial independence were to apply to administrative tribunals as well. In sum, *Ocean Port* affirmed that there is no general constitutional guarantee of independence for administrative tribunals. The only way that constitutional or constitution-like protections can be afforded to a tribunal is if the actions

---

51   The British *Act of Settlement* of 1701 was the historical inspiration for the judicature provisions of our Constitution.

52   *Ocean Port*, *supra* note 4, at para 24.

53   For more details about how this issue was handled in *Régie*, see the discussion at *supra* note 49 and accompanying text.

of the particular tribunal trigger the protections offered by the Canadian Charter or by one of the provincial or federal quasi-constitutional statutes.[54]

On a theoretical level, it is up to the legislature or Parliament to create enabling statutes that foster independent decision-making when legislating for a variety of different tribunals. *Ocean Port* affirms this and implicitly encourages legislative policy-makers to consider the specificities of various tribunals, to retain and promote factors that foster independence, and to eliminate those that do not. In some circumstances, use of the judicial conditions of independence may be effective. But policy-makers should be open to considering factors that actually affect the independence of administrative decision-makers in various contexts. One wonders whether it may be useful to examine different types of tribunals according to their statutory nature. For example, in the case of parliamentary officers—access-to-information and privacy commissioners and ombudsmen—these bodies have a more direct link to the legislature than to an executive government department. This can lead to the presence or absence of particular challenges with respect to independence that are specific to them. As well, the perception of what a tribunal does and to whom it owes its allegiance may also affect its independence. This may be best reflected in the culture of the institution itself. Empirical exploration of these issues would undoubtedly prove fruitful.[55]

Even as early as *Valente*, the first Supreme Court decision to deal with the issue of judicial independence, the court noted that the three criteria identified to guarantee independence were not fixed or exhaustive and may evolve over time. *Ocean Port* seems to have opened the door to allowing us to determine more genuine and accurate criteria of independence for administrative tribunals.

2. *Keen v Canada*

Although *Ocean Port* represents the first time that the Supreme Court addressed the question of whether there is a freestanding constitutional guarantee of tribunal independence that could guarantee security of tenure to the same degree as their judicial counterparts, it was not the first time that inherent problems with "at pleasure" tribunal appointments had been raised. Several cases prior to *Ocean Port* had addressed the question tangentially.[56] In these cases, the main issue had been whether compensation was owed to appointees whose terms had been terminated early because of restructuring of government tribunals. In determining that compensation was owed, some lower courts had admonished the government for interfering with terms that had been set through order in council.[57] These decisions stressed that the appearance of independence would be undermined if the government could freely change terms of appointments. Yet, neither *Ocean Port* nor the prior lower-court decisions addressed the fundamental problem with "at pleasure" appointments—that the

---

54 See the table and accompanying discussion in Section II, "Sources of the Guarantee of an Independent and Impartial Tribunal."

55 Laverne Jacobs, *Fashioning Administrative Independence at the "Tribunal" Level: An Ethnographic Study of Access to Information and Privacy Commissions in Canada* (PhD dissertation, York University, Osgoode Hall Law School, 2009) [unpublished].

56 See e.g. *Hewat v Ontario* (1997), 32 OR (3d) 622 (Div Ct); varied (1998), 37 OR (3d) 161 (CA) [*Hewat*]; *Dewar v Ontario* (1996), 30 OR (3d) 334 (Div Ct); (1998), 37 OR (3d) 170 (CA); *Wells v Newfoundland*, [1999] 3 SCR 199; *Preston v British Columbia* (1994), 92 BCLR (2d) 298.

57 See, in particular, *Hewat*, *ibid*.

government *is not legally prevented* from removing appointees for the decisions they make. No clearer example of this exists than the case of Linda Keen.

Uproar ensued when Canada's Nuclear Safety Commission President Linda Keen was removed from her job over a decision to keep a nuclear power plant closed for its failure to meet safety standards. The Nuclear Safety Commission regulates all nuclear facilities and activities in Canada to ensure their compliance with health, safety, security, and environmental standards as well as with Canada's international obligations. It does not have jurisdiction over the medical health care of Canadians. The commission reports to Parliament through the minister of natural resources.[58] In 2007, the commission decided to keep closed a nuclear power plant that had been temporarily shut down for routine maintenance because of its failure to meet safety standards. This nuclear reactor, however, was also a primary source for the production of medical isotopes used in health care in the country and around the world.

Natural Resources Minister Gary Lunn was concerned that the commission had not reopened the nuclear power plant in question. The closure had caused a severe shortage of critical medical isotopes necessary for the critical health care of many Canadians and people around the world. The minister participated in conference calls with the president of the commission, members of the commission, and the licence holder, at which he requested that a hearing be convened immediately in order to approve the restart of the reactor. Minister Lunn then availed himself of the statutory directive power under the *Nuclear Safety and Control Act*[59] to require the commission to take into account, in its decision-making, "the health of Canadians who, for medical purposes, depend on nuclear substances produced by nuclear reactors." Yet, the directive power allows only for directives of "general application on broad policy matters" to be issued to the commission.[60] Finally, the minister brought about the emergency enactment of a piece of legislation (a step that is always open to governments to do) that forced the reactor to remain open for a period of time.[61]

About two weeks after these events had occurred, the minister wrote to the president of the commission, asking her to explain why certain evidence had not been taken into account in the commission's decision-making and why the directive issued by his office had been ignored. In his letter,[62] Minister Lunn questioned Ms Keen's judgment and whether she was duly executing the requirements of the position. In his opinion, her decision demonstrated a grave inability to manage risk to the health of Canadians. Minister Lunn indicated that he

---

58 More information about the work of the Nuclear Safety Commission can be found online: Canadian Nuclear Safety Commission <http://www.nuclearsafety.gc.ca/eng>.

59 SC 1997, c 9.

60 With respect to directives from Cabinet to the Canadian Nuclear Safety Commission, s 19 of the *Nuclear Safety and Control Act, ibid*, is the relevant provision. It reads: "DIRECTIVES 19(1) The Governor in Council may, by order, issue to the Commission directives of general application on broad policy matters with respect to the objects of the Commission. (2) An order made under this section is binding on the Commission. (3) A copy of each order made under this section shall be (a) published in the Canada Gazette; and (b) laid before each House of Parliament."

61 *An Act to permit the resumption and continuation of the operation of the National Research Universal Reactor at Chalk River*, SC 2007, c 31 (12 December 2007), Department of Justice Canada online: <http://laws-lois.justice.gc.ca/eng/acts/N-15.8/FullText.html>.

62 At one point, the letters between Linda Keen and Gary Lunn were posted on the Internet.

was considering asking the governor in council to remove Ms Keen from her position as president, and asked for her comments.

Ms Keen responded to Minister Lunn's letter, refuting his assertions. Ms Keen was also scheduled to appear before a parliamentary committee to explain her position on the matter. However, on the night before the parliamentary hearing, her position as president was officially terminated. The order in council that removed Ms Keen stated that the governor in council had considered her letter, but found that she had failed to demonstrate the necessary leadership to address the isotope crisis in a timely way. It stated further that the governor in council had lost confidence in her. The termination cut short Ms Keen's second five-year term of appointment as president. Ms Keen was removed as president and relegated to an ordinary member of the commission, but she resigned from the commission several months later.

Ms Keen applied to the Federal Court for judicial review.[63] At issue was whether she received adequate procedural fairness in the manner of her dismissal. The court held that the circumstances of her termination were sufficient to satisfy the requirements of fairness for an "at pleasure" appointment (which is how her appointment as president was characterized). The governor in council's dismissal was therefore upheld.

How should the messages from *Ocean Port* and *Keen* be reconciled? *Ocean Port* affirmed that a variety of tribunal appointments can satisfy the requirement of security of tenure so long as there are no constitutional standards at play and the terms of the appointment derive from constitutionally valid legislation. However, cases such as *Keen* show that, as a practical reality, governments still can, and do, interfere with administrative decision-making because of improper understandings about tribunal accountability. In particular, there is a strong argument that the minister misunderstood the nature of the relationship between the executive and the commission. The commission was not accountable to the minister for the decisions rendered in individual cases. Individual cases are not subject to ministerial oversight, and their outcomes are not meant to be dependent on ministerial input or, worse, ministerial pressure. Legislative design would have been necessary to support such ministerial intervention and without it, the "at pleasure" appointment simply facilitated Ms Keen's removal.

The Federal Court decision also raises concerns. The Federal Court was faithful to the Supreme Court's guidance in *Dunsmuir*,[64] which provided that a lower level of procedural fairness is required on termination of an "at pleasure" appointee than on the dismissal of an appointee instated on terms of good behaviour. *Dunsmuir* had specified that, with respect to "at pleasure" appointments, procedural fairness is needed "to ensure that public power is not exercised capriciously."[65] In this light, the Federal Court held that Ms Keen had been provided with adequate procedural fairness for an "at pleasure" appointment. It was enough that the minister had written to Ms Keen advising her that he was contemplating recommending to the governor in council that her position as president be terminated, that he had provided her with the reasons for his concern, and that he had offered her an opportunity to respond. The Federal Court also noted that the order in council terminating Ms Keen's appointment stated that the governor in council had "carefully considered [her] submission."[66]

---

63 *Keen, supra* note 46, Hughes J.
64 See *Dunsmuir v New Brunswick*, 2008 SCC 9, [2008] 1 SCR 190.
65 *Ibid* at para 115.
66 *Keen, supra* note 46 at para 54.

Can one genuinely say, however, that the exchange of correspondence and the wording in the order in council served to ensure that the Crown had not acted capriciously? Moreover, this is a situation in which reasons could be beneficial. One would expect that someone in the position of Ms Keen, who has suffered a significant impact from the loss of her livelihood, could, practically, benefit from knowing the final reason for her termination. At the very least it would allow her to use that knowledge on further review. The loss of livelihood is a factual element that also seems to fit well with a *Baker* assessment for a higher duty of procedural fairness.

In the 2000s, some provincial jurisdictions reinforced their legislative enactments to ensure that tribunal members have fixed terms of appointment. For example, in British Columbia, the *Administrative Tribunals Act* (ATA)[67] was created to provide guiding principles and uniformity to various aspects of the administrative justice system in the province. Section 3 of the ATA suggests that tribunal members be appointed for an initial term of two to four years with reappointment for additional terms of up to five years. An even more profound example is found in Quebec. In 2005, the enabling statute of the Administrative Tribunal of Quebec (ATQ) was modified so that members would hold tenure during good behaviour. The ATQ is a conglomerate appeal tribunal that hears decisions in five main sectors of activity (social assistance, education, economic affairs, immovable property, and mental health). Essentially an appointment for life, tenure at the ATQ is at the highest level of tenure possible and comparable to that of the judges of the courts of inherent jurisdiction.[68] Recent jurisprudence in Quebec has also shown success in extending similar permanency of tenure to another adjudicative body, the Commission des lésions professionnelles.[69] Outside Canada, the United Kingdom enacted legislation in 2007 that grants administrative tribunal decision-makers the same guarantees of structural independence as judges and aims to bring tribunals within the realm of the judiciary.[70] Finally, some authors have raised the question of whether administrative independence in Canada meets international law standards.[71]

C. Third Wave—Reasserting the Push for Independence: Unwritten Constitutional Principles, Tribunal Independence, and the Rule of Law

The Supreme Court of Canada in *Ocean Port* clearly indicated that there is no freestanding constitutional guarantee of independence for administrative tribunals.[72] As noted above, this is because administrative tribunals form part of the executive branch of government. The court held that because constitutional guarantees of independence serve primarily to

---

67   SBC 2004, c 45 [ATA].

68   See the *Administrative Justice Act*, RSQ, c J-3, s 38, as am 1996, c 54, s 38; 2005, c 17, s 2. For a description of the ATQ's work, see also generally: <http://www.taq.gouv.qc.ca/en/about/the-tribunal/origin-and-role>.

69   See *Association des juges administratifs de la Commission des lésions professionnelles c Québec (Procureur général)*, 2011 QCCS 1614 (decision on appeal). See generally, on the independence of the ATQ, *Barreau de Montréal v Québec (Procureure générale)*, [2001] JQ No 3882 (QL) (CA).

70   See the *Tribunals, Courts and Enforcement Act 2007*, c 15 [TCEA], s 1. See also Lord Justice Carnwath, "Tribunals and the Courts—the UK Model" (2011) 24 Can J Admin L & Prac 5.

71   See Gerald Heckman & Lorne Sossin, "How Do Canadian Administrative Law Protections Live Up to International Human Rights Standards? The Case of Independence" (2005) 50 McGill LJ 193.

72   *Ocean Port*, *supra* note 4 at paras 20-24.

protect the judiciary from interference by the executive, they cannot work to protect tribunals from the branch of government of which they are a part. At the same time, Supreme Court and other Canadian jurisprudence has shown a willingness to expand the notion of "court" to allow litigants before some lower judicial entities the benefits of constitutional guarantees of independence. The third wave of tribunal independence jurisprudence is marked by litigants reasserting a push for tribunals to have the same independence as courts. Despite the holding in *Ocean Port*, advocates maintain that this independence can be guaranteed by the unwritten constitutional principles that protect our courts of inherent jurisdiction—principles that stem from the UK *Act of Settlement, 1701*.

In the 2006 BC Supreme Court decision in *McKenzie*,[73] the petitioner argued that the unwritten constitutional guarantees of independence should be expanded to apply to residential tenancy arbitrators. Her arguments asserted that such arbitrators were at the high end of the adjudicative spectrum. Decided shortly after *Ocean Port*, *Bell Canada v Canadian Telephone Employees Association*[74] had suggested a spectrum of decision-making types in which highly adjudicative tribunals endowed with court-like powers and procedures could require more stringent requirements of procedural fairness, including a higher degree of independence.[75] The petitioner in *McKenzie* argued that, because other adjudicators seemingly on the outer edge of the judiciary, such as justices of the peace and deputy judges, had been deemed to attract unwritten constitutional guarantees of independence, residential tenancy arbitrators, because of the nature of their work, should also attract such guarantees. The petitioner, a residential tenancy arbitrator who had had her appointment rescinded mid-term, also argued that it would be a clear violation of the rule of law if such guarantees were not given to administrative bodies at the high end of the adjudicative spectrum—for example, residential tenancy arbitrators.[76] The respondents contended that a provision of the provincial *Public Sector Employers Act*[77] allowed for this rescission. The court addressed two main issues in *McKenzie*: (1) a narrow question interpreting the *Public Sector Employers Act*, and (2) a much broader question determining whether the position of residential tenancy arbitrators was protected from interference by constitutional guarantees, including guarantees of their security of tenure.[78]

The BC Supreme Court agreed with the petitioner's argument. McEwan J first set out the principles laid down in the *PEI Reference*, which held that judicial independence not only stemmed from specific provisions of the Charter—namely, ss 7 and 11(d)—but also derived from unwritten constitutional principles dating back to the UK *Act of Settlement, 1701*. That these principles applied in Canada was evident from the preamble to the Constitution, which referred to "a Constitution similar in principle to that of the United

---

73 *McKenzie, supra* note 4.

74 2003 SCC 36, [2003] 1 SCR 884 [*Bell Canada*].

75 By contrast, the court held that tribunals falling at the other end of the spectrum that dealt primarily with developing or supervising the implementation of particular government policies may not need to offer as high a degree of procedural protection and require less independence from the executive.

76 The concept of the rule of law is discussed in Chapter 4, Administering the Canadian Rule of Law.

77 RSBC 1996, c 384.

78 Indeed, one wonders whether the Court needed to address this broader constitutional question at all. From the way that it framed the issues, it might have been sufficient, once it had determined that the statute did not allow for the rescission, to end its judicial analysis at that point. See the BCSC decision in *McKenzie, supra* note 4 at para 5.

Kingdom."[79] Second, the BC Supreme Court noted that the Supreme Court of Canada, in *Ell v Alberta*,[80] had determined that these unwritten constitutional principles serve to protect the judicial independence of justices of the peace, a class of decision-makers for whom the issue of independence had been debatable for some time. McEwan J also noted that in Ontario, the Court of Appeal had found that deputy judges in the small claims court also attracted such constitutional guarantees.[81] In light of the extension of the principles of independence to classes of adjudicators other than superior and provincial court judges, the BC Supreme Court found that judicial independence should apply to residential tenancy arbitrators as well. Moreover, the jurisdiction of residential tenancy arbitrators had been taken directly from the courts of civil jurisdiction. Justice McEwan reasoned that the rule of law required this result because the same matter would have been decided by decision-makers endowed with greater independence if landlord and tenant cases had not been carved out of the courts. Later cases, however, such as the Saskatchewan Court of Appeal decision in *Saskatchewan Federation of Labour v Government of Saskatchewan*,[82] have declined to apply *McKenzie's* constitutional interpretation, opting instead to adhere to the more restrictive interpretation of the Constitution put forward by the Supreme Court of Canada in *Ocean Port*.

Though *McKenzie* now stands as an anomalous decision, one still wonders what implications would have flowed from an interpretation of the Constitution put forward by *McKenzie*. For example, the reasoning of the case lay partly in the fact that residential tenancy arbitrators are similar to courts in most of the work that they do. Although some argue for judicial independence for "purely adjudicative" administrative decision-making bodies,[83] what about administrative bodies endowed with both adjudicative and policy-making functions? Would it ever be possible for constitutional guarantees to attach solely to the adjudicative functions of a multifunctional tribunal? Moreover, in light of the holding in *Ocean Port*, can any tribunal be said to be purely adjudicative such as to attract an unwritten constitutional guarantee of independence? Through their decision-making, all tribunals are said to create policy. Was the Supreme Court in *Ocean Port* correct in its assertion that all tribunals create policy through their decision-making?

McKenzie also alludes to a number of practical questions in the debate on tribunal independence. As part of its reasoning, the court asserted that the rule of law, through the affirmation of the principles of judicial independence, would serve to keep the legislature from inappropriately vesting tribunals with diminished forms of natural justice if budgetary or other pressures make it convenient to do so. Is the court's approach one of judicial functionalism, as McEwan J seemed to assert, or does this reasoning imply an interference by the courts with the operation of the legislature? The court's reasoning also raises a much wider question of judicial activism that is often seen in judicial review matters. This is the question of who, as between the legislature in creating the tribunal and the judiciary in reviewing its

---

79   See *PEI Reference, supra* note 50; see also preamble to *Constitution Act, 1867*.

80   2003 SCC 35, [2003] SCR 857.

81   See *Ontario Deputy Judges' Association v Ontario (Attorney General)* (2006), 210 OAC 94, 80 OR (3d) 481 (CA).

82   2013 SKCA 61.

83   See e.g. S Ronald Ellis, "The Justicizing of Quasi-Judicial Tribunals (Part I)" (2006) 19 Can J Admin L & Prac 303.

functioning, is in the best position to dictate the normative aspects of the administrative justice system.

D. Strengthening Independence Through Policy Reform? Comparing Institutional Arrangements Across Jurisdictions

1. Institutional Arrangements

Institutional arrangements can be broadly understood as the ways in which the institutions of governance are designed to interact with one another. Institutions of governance include courts, tribunals, and the legislature, among others. The institutional arrangements of other jurisdictions present different options for preserving and promoting the independence of decision-makers within administrative justice systems. Some of these arrangements are significantly more robust than what we have seen in our jurisprudence and, in many cases, than what exists on the ground in Canada.

Discussions about tribunal independence can be confusing because there are several intertwined issues, the scopes of which are often not clearly distinguished, making them difficult to unravel and to evaluate independently. When it comes to institutional arrangements, the debates over which public policy changes may bring about greater tribunal independence rest on three principal issues. The first is how to insulate administrative decision-makers so that they are not removed for decisions that displease the executive or legislative branch of government that has appointed them. It is important to keep in mind that issues about how an adjudicator is treated focus not so much on the treatment of the adjudicator as a person (though that can be an important, separate problem involving potential issues of discrimination, fairness, etc.) but on the impact that the treatment has on the public's confidence in the administrative justice system. In other words, it is important to step back and ask, "in what way(s) does the action of the government show that a particular result is being sought for reasons that do not emerge from a fair hearing of the merits of the case?" An illustration can be found in the *Keen* case where the reasons for Ms Keen's removal seem to deal with the minister's inability to obtain a desired outcome, although the matter should have been left in the hands of those legally appointed to review and evaluate the relevant material. Another vibrant example arises from the first hundred days of the Trump administration—the firing of FBI Director James Comey. Although Comey is not a decision-maker in the quasi-judicial sense,[84] reports of his removal hint that warding off an investigation into possible Russian interference in the national election (an incident that could have significant negative effects on the US president's position) may have been a source of the sudden dismissal.

Insulation from improper removal has been addressed by two types of policy reform. The lifetime appointment is one type of policy reform. This structural development can be seen in the United Kingdom and here in Canada with the Administrative Tribunal of

---

84 For an informative overview of the independence of administrative judges and administrative law judges in the United States and the nature of their roles, see Russell L Weaver and Linda D Jellum, "Neither Fish Nor Fowl: Administrative Judges in the Modern Administrative State" 28 Windsor YB Access to Just 243 and James E Moliterno, "The Administrative Judiciary's Independence Myth" 41 Wake Forest L Rev 1191.

Québec. Prior to 2007, tribunals in the United Kingdom were commonly overseen and managed by the government departments that rendered the initial decisions that they reviewed. In 2007, a radical transformation of structural independence occurred with the enactment of the *Tribunals, Courts and Enforcement Act 2007*. Tribunals were moved out of the executive branch of government and into the judiciary. The Ministry of Justice became responsible for the administration of all tribunals, through an agency that was originally entitled Tribunals Service and renamed the Her Majesty's Courts and Tribunals Service (HMCTS) in 2011.[85] They have the same term of appointment as judges, which is essentially a lifetime appointment. In Québec, the decision-makers of the Administrative Tribunal of Québec have lifetime appointments although they are still members of the executive branch of government. Although lifetime appointments for tribunal appointees certainly stave off the arbitrary dismissals, a disadvantage is that the changeover of perspectives that comes with fixed shorter-term appointments become less frequent and firmly entrenched views on the socio-economic issues before the tribunal may have the potential to last for quite some time.

The second type of policy reform has kept tribunals within the executive branch of government but created fixed terms of appointment. An interesting illustration of this structural reform can be found in Ontario, where the Management Board of Cabinet has implemented a graduated maximum term of renewals that became effective in 2006.[86] Commonly called the "Ten-year Rule," the directive mandates that appointments to administrative tribunals and regulatory agencies should not exceed ten years in total. For tribunal members, associate chairs, and vice chairs, the ten years consist of an initial two-year appointment, followed by eligibility for reappointment for a three-year term, and then eligibility for a further five-year reappointment.[87] Appointments beyond ten years are to be made only in exceptional circumstances. This approach enables a greater changeover of perspectives in decision-making, addressing the disadvantage of lifetime appointments. However, it, too, is subject to much debate within the administrative justice community. For example, the Society of

---

85   See HM Courts & Tribunals Service, *Framework Document* (July, 2014), s 1.7, online: <https://www.gov.uk/government/publications/hm-courts-and-tribunals-service-framework-document>, which states: "HM Courts & Tribunals Service provides the system of support, including infrastructure and resources, for the administration of the business of the courts in England and Wales and those tribunals throughout the United Kingdom, for which the Lord Chancellor is responsible. The agency provides the support necessary to enable the judiciary, tribunal members and magistracy to exercise their judicial functions independently."

86   See Ontario, Management Board of Cabinet, *Agencies & Appointments Directive* (October, 2015), online: <https://www.ontario.ca/page/agencies-and-appointments-directive>. See also Public Appointments Secretariat—Corporate Policy, Agency Governance and Open Government Division, *Q&A, The Agencies & Appointments Directive 10-Year Maximum Appointment to Adjudicative Tribunals and Regulatory Agencies* [*Agencies & Appointments Directive*] (August 2015), online: <https://goo.gl/6eV2WA>.

87   For executive chairs and chairs of administrative tribunals and regulatory agencies, the initial two-year term may be waived by the responsible minister. If that occurs, the executive chair or chair will be eligible for an additional five-year term once a period of time totalling five years has elapsed since their initial appointment. See s 3.2.2 "Term of Appointment—Adjudicative Tribunals and Regulatory Agencies" in *Agencies & Appointments Directive, ibid*.

Ontario Adjudicators and Regulators (SOAR) conducted a study in 2015,[88] the findings of which suggest that some of the larger administrative tribunals in the province[89] may suffer a profound loss of experienced adjudicators at the end of the first ten-year year period. They express concern that the quality of expert decision-making will be reduced, that newer appointees will not have the wealth of training resources due to the exit of ten-year appointees, and that a large number of new appointees will need to be recruited at the end of the ten-year period which will occasion a high expenditure of resources.

A second principal issue entangled in the debate about how, structurally, to ensure greater independence is the question of how to reduce interference by government with adjudicative independence when decisions are being rendered. The minister's attempts to participate in and influence the Nuclear Safety Commissions' decision-making about whether or not to keep the reactor closed in *Keen* is a useful illustration of the problem. In the United Kingdom, a greater separation between decision-makers and subject matter ministries or departments was specifically contemplated when tribunals were moved to the judiciary in the 2000s. In Ontario, clustering (which is the bringing together of tribunals for efficiency) has also been used to reduce accountability connections between subject matter ministries and tribunals reviewing decisions of those ministries or their responsible ministers.[90] Responsibility for Ontario's Environmental and Land Tribunals Cluster (ELTO), for example, now resides with the Ministry of the Attorney General instead of with the Ministry of the Environment. A memorandum of understanding between the responsible minister and the executive chair of ELTO has been signed (as required by ATAGAA) to ensure even greater independence in the decision-making of the tribunals of the cluster.[91] The Australian Appeals Tribunal (AAT), established in 1976, presents one of the earliest examples of centralizing administrative responsibility for tribunals in one agency distanced from the subject matter jurisdictions addressed by the tribunal itself.[92]

The third principal issue is how to design appointment and reappointment processes that support and promote the principles that ground independence, such as transparency and competence. This issue is more subtle, as the connection between appointment/reappointment processes and the independence of adjudicators has not been fleshed out well in the literature. People often emphasize the need to have merit-based appointments. However, the relationship between merit-based appointments and independence can be further unpacked. In a study published in 2014, a group of professors at the University of Montréal determined that transparency, legitimacy, and competence are preconditions to adjudicator independence.[93] Through empirical data, they found that lack of transparency in the rules

---

88 "Study on the Impact of the Government Directive on Term Limits for OIC Appointments" (February 2015), online: <https://soar.on.ca/images/Files_Not_in_Doc_Library/SOAR_Report_on_the_impact_of_the_Directive-on_term-limits-for_tribunal_members.pdf>.

89 SOAR has defined larger tribunals as those tribunals with 20 or more order-in-council appointees as well as a chair or executive chair. These tribunals totalled 17 in the province at the time of their study.

90 This may not have been the original intention of clustering, but the wording of ATAGAA does not make its intention clear. See ATAGAA, ss 15-19.

91 See ELTO's Public & Governance Accountability Documents, online: <http://elto.gov.on.ca/public-and-governance-accountability-documents/>.

92 For a discussion of centralized oversight of the development of regulations see Chapter 8, Delegation and Consultation: How the Administrative State Functions and the Importance of Rules.

93 See Noreau et al, *supra* note 45, and Houle, "Independent Adjudicators," *supra* note 45.

used to find and appoint adjudicators can leave appointment processes open to manipulation by those who would like to use them for political patronage or to appoint individuals who do not have the qualifications for the job. Even more interestingly, through their study they found that systems that provide gaps for illegitimate appointments create an organizational atmosphere in which adjudicators without appropriate competence rely on stronger members (for example, on decision-making panels). This system of dependence can undermine the real independence of the weaker members who, instead of adjudicating the merits of the case based on their expertise vis-à-vis the subject matter and law, find themselves relying on the input of other members in making their decisions.

One way of addressing this challenge is to ensure not only that appointment processes are transparent, but also that there is a roster of competent individuals available to be selected from when openings arise on tribunals. In 2017, a bill was presented in the Québec National Assembly which, if it had passed, would have created a secretariat to ensure transparent, formal processes for the selection of appointees to tribunals.[94] The secretariat's role would have been to create a nonpartisan committee to review all applicants, to administer aptitude tests for the positions, and to maintain a roster of eligible names for the tribunals.[95]

In summary, it is noteworthy that although security of tenure, financial security, and administrative control may figure within the independence issues discussed, they do not form the main organizing axes of the challenges to independence and impartiality that arise in the everyday work of tribunals. Appointments, adjudicative independence, and managing necessary interactions with the executive branch of government are among the central independence-related concerns in a tribunal's regular operational context. This is one example of how elements of the judicial paradigm may not reconcile easily with the daily operational context of administrative tribunals. A second broad example can be found in the nature of bias in the administrative state. As we will see in the next section of this chapter, determining when disqualifying bias exists in the administrative state also (like independence) requires the consideration of several contextual factors, including the nature and functioning of the particular administrative body under scrutiny.

V. REASONABLE APPREHENSION OF BIAS

Challenges for reasonable apprehension of bias arise from a variety of administrative law situations. These situations relate to perceived partiality either on the part of an individual decision-maker or on an institutional level. Traditional concerns about bias—for example, that the decision-maker has a direct, pecuniary interest in the outcome—stem from easy-to-understand occurrences that would be fatal to any decision-making system, including the judiciary. Others stem from the very nature of the administrative state, which itself comprises a wide range of administrative actors, from government ministers to adjudicative bodies, with very different natures and purposes. Included in the list of situations that have

---

94 See Projet de loi n°792: *Loi sur la procédure de sélection et de nomination des décideurs administratifs indépendants et de renouvellement de leur mandat*, online: <http://www.assnat.qc.ca/fr/travaux-parlementaires/projets-loi/projet-loi-792-41-1.html>.

95 Finally, a robust blueprint to address, cohesively, the issues that plague the structural independence of adjudicative tribunals has been suggested by lawyer and former tribunal member, Ron Ellis, in his recent book, *Unjust by Design: Canada's Administrative Justice System* (Vancouver: UBC Press, 2013).

been attacked for reasonable apprehension of bias are the appearance of perceived attitudinal bias in the decision-making process and concern about the practices used by administrative bodies to promote consistency and efficiency within their work. Two such administrative practices that have prompted challenges for reasonable apprehension of bias in the jurisprudence are full board meetings and the use of "lead cases," discussed in Section V.B.3 below. Most recently, the rise in self-represented litigants has corresponded to an increased concern about reasonable apprehension of bias, both by the litigants and by adjudicators, as self-represented litigants may not fully comprehend the tribunal's process and may perceive bias on the part of adjudicators. Adjudicators, by contrast, may be concerned about balancing a desire to assist the self-represented litigant with avoiding the appearance of partiality. Issues relating to reasonable apprehension of bias have also arisen in contemporary times due to the use of social media by tribunal members, such as the use of Twitter by adjudicators to share opinions on topics related to the matter at issue.

A. The Rule Against Bias

As discussed at the beginning of this chapter, the *nemo judex* rule aims to maintain public confidence in the administration of justice. Like independence, the rule against bias aims to preserve the appearance of impartiality in the decision-making process. The rule against bias contributes to this function by ensuring that decision-makers are not reasonably perceived to be deciding matters that will benefit them or those with whom they have significant relationships. The rule seeks equally to avoid decision-making partiality that will result in negative treatment of a party occurring as a result of a decision-maker's interests and relationships. Finally, the rule against bias serves generally to prevent decision-makers from making decisions based on factors that are irrelevant to the decision-making process. The concern regards the decision-maker's current or prior knowledge, relationships, actions, or practices. Allegations of reasonable apprehension of bias exist in two major forms in administrative law: (1) *perceptions of individual bias*, which deal with the impartiality of individual decision-makers; and (2) *perceptions of institutional bias*, which deal with whether reasonable perceptions of partiality regarding the decision-making body as a whole can be raised in a substantial number of cases.

There have been over 600 challenges stemming from perceived bias brought before administrative boards and tribunals in the past five years.[96] The rule against bias is one of the oldest common law doctrines. Yet, reasonable apprehension of bias is clearly still a common challenge raised in the current practice of administrative law. All administrative actors required to meet the standards of procedural fairness—including administrative tribunals, ministers, and other public officials—are subject to the rule against bias.[97] The party alleging perceived bias must bring this concern to the attention of the particular decision-maker on the first available occasion. If the claim is successful, its effect will be to quash any decisions

---

96   A search on Quicklaw of decisions by all boards and tribunals across the country between January 1, 2011 and December 31, 2016 produced 659 cases dealing with allegations of reasonable apprehension of bias.

97   For a discussion of the central features of procedural fairness in administrative law, see Chapter 5, The Principles and Practices of Procedural Fairness.

made and have the proceedings reheard by an alternative decision-maker or a newly constituted panel.

In this section, we consider the common law test (and its variations) for determining
whether disqualifying bias exists in an administrative decision-making process. We examine
the most common situations in which a reasonable apprehension of bias has been found to
arise, including the recent phenomenon of self-represented litigants and the use of social
media by tribunal members. We also discuss various practices of tribunals and other administrative actors that have incited allegations of reasonable apprehension of bias. Throughout
this section, we consider the issue of bias from the perspectives of actors within the administrative state and of the courts.

B. The Reasonable Apprehension of Bias Test

The test for bias relies on perception. Whether bias *actually* exists in a decision-making
context is not the question; to have a decision quashed, it is sufficient that a reasonable
person with an informed understanding of how the tribunal functions perceive that the
decision-making is biased. The classic test was formulated in *Committee for Justice and
Liberty v National Energy Board*,[98] a 1970s case in which the chair of a panel of the National
Energy Board was responsible for receiving applications and issuing certificates for a pipeline. The Chair, Mr Crowe, had previously been involved in a study group that had put in an
application for consideration. The majority of the Supreme Court of Canada held that there
was a reasonable apprehension of bias with respect to Crowe's participation as Chair.

The test for determining reasonable apprehension of bias was formulated in the dissenting opinion of Justice DeGrandpré. However, it has been used consistently by the
Supreme Court and lower courts since that time. DeGrandpré J articulated the test in the
following way:

> [T]he apprehension of bias must be a reasonable one held by reasonable and right-minded
> persons, applying themselves to the question and obtaining thereon the required information.
> In the words of the Court of Appeal, that test is "what would an informed person, viewing the
> matter realistically and practically—and having thought the matter through—conclude. Would
> he think that it is more likely than not that Mr Crowe, whether consciously or unconsciously,
> would not decide fairly?"[99]

Moreover, the grounds for the apprehension of bias must be substantial. A real likelihood or probability of bias should be demonstrated. Mere suspicion of bias is insufficient
for the test to be met. The courts often talk of demonstrating the likelihood of bias on a
balance of probabilities. The reasonable, well-informed person is also not one who is overly
sensitive.[100] The application of the test has broadened to encompass not only individual
decision-makers but also decision-making institutions. The institutional aspect of bias was
first recognized in *Lippé*, where the test was identified as determining whether there could

---

98   [1978] 1 SCR 369 [*Committee for Justice and Liberty*].

99   *Ibid* at 394.

100 See generally, on the test for reasonable apprehension of bias and the standard that must be met,
     Committee for Justice and Liberty, *supra* note 98 at 394-95; *Bell Canada*, *supra* note 74 at para 50; *R v S (RD)*,
     [1997] 3 SCR 484 at paras 31 and 112 [*S (RD)*].

be "a reasonable apprehension of bias in the mind of a fully informed person *in a substantial number of cases.*"[101]

The standard for bias varies, depending on context. What will give rise to a reasonable apprehension of bias in one administrative decision-making context may not do so in another. For example, although both cases dealt with a decision-maker's prior involvement with a particular matter, the Supreme Court of Canada held that the involvement of the National Energy Board's chair caused a reasonable apprehension of bias in *Committee for Justice and Liberty*, discussed above, but found differently when the Quebec minister of the environment ordered a company to prepare a site characterization study and decontamination measures in *Imperial Oil Ltd v Quebec (Minister of the Environment).*[102] The difference is explained by the central idea animating procedural fairness in administrative law: the nature and context of the decision-making process drives the content of procedural fairness, including what constitutes impartiality. Primarily because of the quasi-judicial nature of the National Energy Board's functions in determining applications, the court in *Committee for Justice and Liberty* found that Mr Crowe's involvement in the decisions leading up to one party's application to the board was enough to suggest that he might make a biased appraisal in his adjudicative capacity. By contrast, the nature of the work done by the minister in *Imperial Oil* did not require him to act in a truly adjudicative capacity. His work was of a political nature and in the public interest. In this way, the minister's prior involvement in decontaminating a site over which lawsuits had been brought against him did not cause him to be in a conflict of interest when he later exercised statutory authority to order a company to remedy the contamination.[103]

Determining which procedural safeguards, including the degree of independence and impartiality, are needed in any particular administrative context is a matter of balancing several factors including the nature of the decision being made, the nature of the statutory scheme, and the agency's choice of procedures.[104]

Allegations of reasonable apprehension of bias exist in two major forms in administrative law—individual bias and institutional bias. In the following sections, we examine each of these forms of disqualifying bias and explore the variations in the standard used to determine the existence of a reasonable apprehension of bias in different contexts.

---

101 See *R v Lippé*, [1991] 2 SCR 114 at para 59 [*Lippé*] (emphasis added). See also *Matsqui, supra* note 35, where the Court confirmed the test for the administrative context.

102 2003 SCC 58, [2003] 2 SCR 624 [*Imperial Oil*].

103 *Ibid*.

104 The Supreme Court presented a non-exhaustive list of factors in *Baker v Canada (Minister of Citizenship and Immigration)*, [1999] 2 SCR 817 [*Baker*]. These factors include (1) the nature of the decision being made and the process followed in making it; (2) the nature of the statutory scheme and the terms of the statute pursuant to which the body operates; (3) the importance of the decision to the individual or individuals affected; (4) the legitimate expectations of the person challenging the decision; and (5) the choices of procedure made by the agency itself. For a broader discussion of these factors see Grant Huscroft's "From Natural Justice to Fairness: Thresholds, Content, and the Role of Judicial Review," available at <http://www.emond.ca/adminlaw3e>, and *IWA v Consolidated-Bathurst Packaging Ltd*, [1990] 1 SCR 282 [*Consolidated-Bathurst*].

1. Perceptions of Individual Bias

Administrative law jurisprudence has established four situations in which a reasonable apprehension of bias may arise vis-à-vis an individual decision-maker. These are situations in which the decision-maker may reasonably be perceived to have:

1. a pecuniary or material interest in the outcome of the matter being decided;
2. personal relationships with those involved in the dispute;
3. prior involvement in or knowledge or information about the matter in dispute; or
4. an attitudinal predisposition toward an outcome.

Each of these is discussed in turn. An allegation can be brought on more than one ground—for example, prior involvement and attitudinal bias, or personal relationship and material interest.

a. Pecuniary or Material Interest in the Outcome

i. Pecuniary Interest

The existence of a decision-maker's direct pecuniary interest in the outcome of a case is one of the clearest circumstances giving rise to disqualification for reasonable apprehension of bias. The *nemo judex* maxim is designed to prohibit an administrative actor from making decisions that advance his or her own cause. Standing to receive a monetary gain fits the notion of advancing one's cause in an archetypical way. The seminal case setting out the common law's strict stance against pecuniary interest is *Dimes v Grand Junction Canal Co*,[105] in which a decision of the Lord Chancellor of England was set aside because of his shareholder interest in a company that was a party to the proceedings.

Although the common law may be unequivocal when it comes to disqualifying a decision-maker who has a direct pecuniary interest, it becomes more flexible when dealing with cases in which the financial interest is indirect. Consider the example of *Energy Probe v Canada (Atomic Energy Control Board)*.[106] There, the Atomic Energy Control Board renewed the operating licence of a nuclear generating station run by Ontario Hydro. A part-time member of the panel was also the president of a company that supplied cables to nuclear power plants. This member had also been a past director and shareholder of the company. The company had supplied cables to Ontario Hydro in the past after having successfully completed a competitive tender process. Energy Probe contested the decision to renew Ontario Hydro's licence, arguing that the decision should be quashed because of the member's participation. The majority of the Federal Court of Appeal was of the opinion that a reasonable apprehension of bias had not been established. They adopted the reasons of Justice Reed, who, at first instance, had held that a pecuniary interest must be direct and certain in order to give rise to a reasonable apprehension of bias. On the date of the hearing relating to the licences, the part-time member in question did not have a contract with Ontario Hydro or one that would take effect during the life of the new licence. He also was

---

105   [1852] Eng R 789, 10 ER 301, 3 HLC 759.
106   [1984] 1 FC 563, 15 DLR (4th) 48 [*Energy Probe*].

not a shareholder at the time of the hearings. Justice Reed held that his interest was therefore not direct. Moreover, there was no certainty that the part-time member would sell cables to Ontario Hydro in the future. The contracts that the company had held in the past had been contingent on success in a tendering process. *Energy Probe* therefore stands for the proposition that only direct and certain financial interest can constitute pecuniary bias. However, Justice Heald, for a minority of the Federal Court of Appeal, would have held that instead of focusing on directness and certainty, a more rational test would have determined whether the benefits in question stemmed from the decision to be rendered, and whether the benefits would be so sufficiently likely to occur that they would "colour" the case in the eyes of the decision-maker.

In some cases, pecuniary interest may be held not to give rise to a reasonable apprehension of bias if the decision-maker's gain is no more than that of the average person in a widespread group of benefit recipients.[107] Last, we know that, as a general principle, the common law must cede to legislative will. The law relating to pecuniary interest in reasonable apprehension of bias is no different. Statutory authorization that allows for indirect pecuniary benefit has prevailed over the common law rule against bias in contexts such as the regulation of egg marketing[108] and for some self-regulated discipline committees.[109] In these contexts, the legislation usually requires that members be drawn from the professional community, and the courts generally find that the prospect of such members deciding in a manner that would undermine competition for their own self-interest to be too speculative and remote to incite a reasonable apprehension of bias.[110]

ii. Non-Pecuniary Material Interest

Although monetary interest is the classic personal interest giving rise to a reasonable apprehension of bias, other forms of material interest have also led to disqualification. For example, a decision of a band council to evict a band member so that his house could be given to a larger family was set aside because an intended resident of the home was one of the councillors.[111] The case of *Service Employees International Union, Local 204 v Johnson*,[112] a case discussed in detail below in relation to prior knowledge, presents a more involved example. There, the members of the Ontario Labour Relations Board had a potential interest in a case before them dealing with the circumstances in which the government could terminate their appointments.

---

107 Exclusions from the general rule have been created by legislation and at common law. See e.g. *Municipal Government Act*, RSA 2000, c M-26, s 170(3)(i) and *R v Justices of Sunderland*, [1901] 2 KB 357 (Eng CA).

108 *Burnbrae Farms v Canadian Egg Marketing Agency*, [1976] 2 FC 217 (CA).

109 *Pearlman v Manitoba Law Society Judicial Committee*, [1991] 2 SCR 869.

110 See also *Matsqui, supra* note 35, where this idea was most explicitly stated by Lamer CJ. Municipal law is another area in which pecuniary interests are legislatively addressed. See e.g. the Alberta *Municipal Government Act*.

111 *Obichon v Heart Lake First Nation No 176*, [1988] FCJ No 307 (QL), 21 FTR 1 (TD). For a discussion of Indigenous Administrative Law, see Chapter 3 by Janna Promislow and Naomi Metallic, Realizing Aboriginal Administrative Law.

112 (1997), 35 OR (3d) 345 (Gen Div), 1997 CanLII 12280 (Ont Sup Ct) [*SEIU*]. This case is discussed in detail below because it relates to reasonable apprehension of bias arising from prior knowledge.

b. Personal Relationships with Those Involved in the Dispute

When we speak of the personal relationships of decision-makers giving rise to a reasonable apprehension of bias, it is not only their relationships with the parties that can be disqualifying. Significant relationships between administrative actors and others involved in the matter—for example, counsel and witnesses[113]—must also be taken into account. Key factors to consider are whether the relationship presents a significant enough interest to affect the impartiality of the decision-maker and the amount of time that has passed—that is, whether the relationship is current enough to reasonably pose a significant threat to impartiality.

Although it is outside the administrative law context, a basic example of a personal relationship giving rise to reasonable apprehension of bias is found in the House of Lords' decision in *In re Pinochet*.[114] The *Pinochet* application asked the House of Lords to determine whether former Chilean head of state Augusto Pinochet was protected by a continued immunity or could be extradited to stand trial for crimes against humanity committed in Chile. Pinochet was in England at the time for medical treatment. At the proceedings, Amnesty International, a major intervener, argued in support of Pinochet's extradition. Unbeknown to Pinochet, a member of the House of Lords, Lord Hoffman, had connections with Amnesty International at the time of the hearing. Lord Hoffman was not only a director and chair of Amnesty International Charity Limited, his wife also did administrative work for Amnesty International's press and publications department. The matter was quashed for reasonable apprehension of bias and a new hearing was held. The House of Lords held that, although he was not technically a party to the matter before the Law Lords, Lord Hoffman's involvement with an affiliated charity that was mandated to promote the same goals as the intervener was sufficient to show a relationship between the two, even giving rise to reasonable apprehension of bias. Because Lord Hoffman's connections were sufficiently disqualifying, the Law Lords did not need to examine whether Lady Hoffman's connections with Amnesty International would also be disqualifying.[115]

How far can arguments for reasonable apprehension of bias regarding personal relationships be stretched? A case from the BC Human Rights Tribunal illustrates an attempt to push the idea of a personal connection in a novel way. In *Brar v College of Veterinarians of British Columbia*,[116] the appointment of the adjudicator assigned to the case expired before the end of the hearing. By that time, over 200 days of hearings had already taken place and an estimated additional year and a half would be required for hearing completion and a decision to be rendered. Only three weeks before her appointment ended, the adjudicator received notice that her appointment would not be renewed. The adjudicator therefore adjourned the proceedings for the balance of the month, and asked that the parties maintain the

---

113   For two interesting and contrasting cases concerning expert witnesses before tribunals who were subsequently appointed to the tribunals before the tribunal's decision was rendered, see *Li v College of Physicians & Surgeons (Ontario)* (2004), 21 Admin LR (4th) 270 (Ont Div Ct) and *Stetler v Ontario (Agriculture, Food & Rural Affairs Appeal Tribunal)* (2005), 76 OR (3d) 321 at paras 90-97 (CA). In these cases, the issue at hand was whether the tribunal would give more weight to the testimony of the expert witnesses because of their elevation to the position of tribunal member.

114   [1999] UKHL 52.

115   See also *Poitras c Bellegarde*, 2011 FCA 317.

116   2010 BCHRT 308, aff'd 2011 BCSC 486.

hearing dates already scheduled for later that year and that they await further notice from the tribunal. She stated that her decision was based on the uncertainty of the situation and reasoned that it would be inappropriate and unfair for the parties to continue to spend resources to continue the hearing at the time. She was concerned, for example, that if the parties raised interim applications before the expiry of her appointment, she might not be able to fully adjudicate them during the short time remaining. She also indicated that she had asked the Ministry of the Attorney General about reappointment approximately nine months before the expiry date, with repeated follow-up inquiries sent by the tribunal chair.

Shortly thereafter, the complainants sent a letter to each of the tribunal chair and the ministry, requesting the tribunal member's reappointment for another term or, at the very least, her appointment for enough time to complete the decision.[117] The complainants alleged government interference with the decision-making independence of the tribunal member. The respondents sent a reply letter to each of the tribunal chair and the ministry and submitted an application for reasonable apprehension of bias before the tribunal. With respect to reasonable apprehension of bias, they argued that counsel for the complainants had taken up the cause of the tribunal member concerning her reappointment. They therefore argued that the tribunal member should not now be reappointed to continue hearing the matter because she could be perceived to be indebted to counsel to the complainant. The tribunal, and the Superior Court on judicial review, found that no reasonable apprehension of bias had been established. Despite the respondents' argument that the complainants' decision to champion the tribunal member's reappointment had been incited by the tribunal member's comments when she adjourned, the respondents had submitted no evidence in support of their assertion.

Given that the reasonable apprehension test requires the strong likelihood of an informed person seeing a reasonable risk of partiality, what type of evidence could be brought by respondents in a situation like *Brar*? The common law maintains a strong presumption of impartiality for adjudicators, offers immunity for tribunal members, and protects deliberative secrecy. In light of these tenets of administrative law, it may be a formidable task, even with significant supporting evidence, to launch a successful challenge along the lines of that of the respondents in *Brar*.

As emphasized throughout this book, appreciating context in administrative law is vital; it is equally so in determining disqualifying bias. As Lord Steyn stated about reasonable appearances of bias in *Man O'War Station Ltd v Auckland City Council (Judgment No 1)*: "This is a corner of the law in which the context, and the particular circumstances, are of supreme importance."[118] Lord Steyn's observation is reflected in the fact that there are a myriad of circumstances that may give rise to the reasonable apprehension of bias, especially in the Canadian administrative state where there is a diversity of decision-making bodies. The nature of the tribunal itself can sometimes have an impact on whether an allegation of bias is reasonable. For example, labour arbitration panels traditionally comprise three members, two representing each of labour and management and one neutral chair. Connections between practising lawyers in the field and members from labour or management are

---

117 The ATA allows for such extensions under ss 6 and 7.
118 [2002] 3 NZLR 577, [2002] UKPC 28 at para 11.

almost inevitable.[119] Moreover, nominees are chosen because of their sympathy to the interests of the party that nominated them. Nevertheless, determining whether a reasonable apprehension of bias exists within the tripartite labour context is a matter of balancing a legislated desire to have representative experts populate decision-making panels and the Supreme Court's firm counsel that nominated arbitrators "are to exercise their function not as the advocates of the parties nominating them, and *a fortiori* of one party when they are agreed upon by all, but as free, independent, and impartial minds as the circumstances permit."[120]

Finally, there are additional contextual factors that may diminish an apprehension of bias. The amount of time that has passed between the member's active association with the person involved in the dispute and the member's appointment to the tribunal is one such factor. In *Marques v Dylex*,[121] a labour board member who had previously been a lawyer with the firm acting for an earlier iteration of the union appearing before his panel was not disqualified for appearance of bias. The Divisional Court noted that over a year had passed since the member had been involved with the law firm or had had anything to do with the predecessor of the union. Necessity—which sometimes arises in smaller jurisdictions where members of a very small bar may be required to fill legislated roles—can also be a relevant factor.[122] Last, keep in mind that, although Canadian common law is grounded in an Anglo-European notion of impartiality in which decisions are considered fair when made by those who are at a distance from the parties and the matter at interest, other conceptions of justice also exist. Some Indigenous communities, for example, consider decisions to be fair when rendered by non-strangers whom they know and trust.[123]

c. *Prior Knowledge or Information About a Matter in Dispute*

Generally speaking, in deciding whether a reasonable apprehension of bias exists because of a decision-maker's prior involvement with a matter, tribunals, and courts on review, will focus on the nature and extent of the decision-maker's previous involvement. The Supreme Court of Canada articulated this general principle most forcefully in the 2003

---

119 See "Nominee Bias" in MR Gorsky et al, *Evidence and Procedure in Canadian Labour Arbitration* (Scarborough, Ont: Carswell, 1991). A critique of the approach of the courts is offered by TS Kuttner, "Is the Doctrine of Bias Compatible with the Tri-Partite Labour Tribunal?" (1986) 19 Admin LR 81-98.

120 *Szilard v Szasz*, [1955] SCR 3. See also *Black & McDonald Ltd v Construction Labour Relations Association of British Columbia* (1986), 19 Admin LR 73 (BCCA); *UFCW, Local 1252 v Prince Edward Island (Labour Relations Board)* (1998), 31 Admin LR 196 (PEICA) (debating whether indirect interest can avoid disqualifying bias for labour tribunal members with connections to parties). For a recent case illustrating the bias issues relating to tripartite arbitration boards and how they may be handled on the ground by the labour arbitrator at first instance, see *Fredericton (City) v International Assn of Fire Fighters, Local 1053 (Collective Agreement Grievance)*, [2008] NBLAA No 17 (QL), MJ Veniot.

121 (1977), 81 DLR (3rd) 554 (Ont Div Ct).

122 See e.g. *Kalina v Directors of Chiropractic*, [1981] OJ No 3219 (Div Ct) (QL) [*Kalina*].

123 On this idea, see Janna Promislow and Lorne Sossin, "In Search of Aboriginal Administrative Law" in *Administrative Law in Context*, 2nd ed (Toronto: Edmond Montgomery Publications, 2013). For a discussion of Indigenous administrative law see Chapter 3, Realizing Aboriginal Administrative Law.

decision of *Wewaykum Indian Band v Canada*.[124] The general principles from *Wewaykum* serve as a foundation for deciding reasonable apprehension of bias claims for both judicial and administrative actors with prior knowledge of a matter. *Wewaykum* was a property dispute involving two First Nations bands. In *Wewaykum*, Mr Justice Binnie's previous employment as associate deputy minister of justice from 1982 to 1986 was challenged as giving rise to reasonable apprehension of bias. During that time, he had been responsible for almost all litigation against the government of Canada and had supervisory authority over thousands of cases. An access-to-information request showed that in late 1985 and early 1986, he had participated in a meeting at which the current case was discussed and had received some information about one of the bands' claims. The bands sought to set aside the court's unanimous judgment in the matter, which had been made some nine months earlier.[125]

The parties argued that the memoranda demonstrated that Binnie J had been involved in developing the Crown's litigation strategy against them.[126] The Supreme Court carefully examined the 14 memoranda that had been revealed by the access request. There were pieces of correspondence in which Binnie J was involved, either directly or indirectly. After this examination, the court held that, although his connection to the file might have been greater than simply pro forma management, he was never counsel of record and played no active role in the dispute after the claim was filed. The court also noted that the file was transferred to the Vancouver regional office to be handled by a lawyer located there. The court therefore found the parties' argument that Binnie J had been involved in the litigation in a material way to be unsubstantiated.[127]

In the context of the administrative state, reasonable apprehension of bias arising from prior knowledge has sometimes led to severe consequences. For example, in *SEIU*,[128] the entire Ontario Labour Relations Board was found to be disqualified to hear a case before it because of information received earlier at a plenary meeting of the vice chairs. The members of the board were prevented by oath of office from revealing what they knew, but indicated that the information that was received contradicted one or more of the parties' representations. In Ontario, the *Public Officers Act*[129] allows for the Divisional Court to appoint a disinterested person to adjudicate a matter in circumstances where the public officer empowered

---

124 2003 SCC 45, [2003] 2 SCR 259 [*Wewaykum*]. Of course, the classic case on the matter is *Committee for Justice and Liberty*, *supra* note 98. See, more recently, *Terceira v Labourers International Union of North America*, (2014) 122 OR (3d) 521 (CA) and *Tolias (Re)*, [2016] OJ No 3118 (CA).

125 *Wewaykum Indian Band v Canada*, 2002 SCC 79, [2002] 4 SCR 245.

126 In further support of their allegation of a reasonable apprehension of bias, the parties had also pointed to Binnie J's long-standing interest in First Nations matters and to prior decisions that he had made. The court held, however, that all that was relevant in deciding whether a reasonable apprehension of bias existed was Binnie J's involvement in the file at issue as the head of litigation at the Department of Justice.

127 See, by contrast, *Canadian Union of Postal Workers v Canada Post Corporation*, 2012 FC 975.

128 *Supra* note 112. See also *Jogendra v Ontario (Human Rights Tribunal)*, [2011] OJ No 2518 (QL) (Sup Ct J).

129 RSO 1990, c P.45.

to perform the functions is disqualified.[130] That was the outcome in *SEIU*.[131] More often, issues surrounding prior knowledge arise when a tribunal adjudicator is asked to hear an appeal or a subsequent proceeding of a matter that they originally decided.[132] The common law concept of mediation privilege, which precludes a tribunal member from adjudicating a case that he or she has mediated, is an attempt to avoid the reasonable apprehension of bias issue that may come with prior knowledge. Mediation privilege may be directed by statute,[133] but, even where statutes do not explicitly provide for mediation privilege, some administrative bodies will ensure through their formal or informal practice that mediators do not sit in further deliberation of a matter with which they have dealt.[134] Sometimes a statute will authorize a multiplicity of functions that may countenance an administrative actor's prior knowledge from his or her involvement in an earlier stage of the process. We examine multiplicity of functions when we discuss institutional bias.

d. Attitudinal Predisposition Toward an Outcome

Predispositions giving rise to a reasonable apprehension of bias have been gleaned from decision-makers' comments and attitudes in both the course of the hearing and outside the proceedings. During the hearing, antagonism toward litigants, *ex parte* communications, and irrelevant or vexatious comments, as well as the adjudicator or any other member of the tribunal taking an unauthorized role as an advocate to the proceeding before it, have all given rise to a reasonable apprehension of bias.

An on-the-ground example comes from *Law Society of Upper Canada v Cengarle*.[135] The original hearing panel in this disciplinary matter had been particularly interventionist. As the appeal panel asserted in *Cengarle* in summarizing the current state of the law, "[t]he effect of interventions by a tribunal on the appearance of fairness in any given case must be assessed in relation to the unique facts and circumstances of the particular hearing."[136] The appeal

---

130 Section 16, *ibid*, indicates that the person being replaced must be disqualified "by interest" from acting, and there must be no other person empowered to perform the function. This compares to the situation in which there is an absence of legislation governing the complete disqualification of all tribunal members. In such cases, necessity may require an impugned tribunal member to serve. See e.g. *Kalina, supra* note 122.

131 Although the court is not altogether clear in its reasoning. On the one hand, because the matter before the board also dealt with the government's ability to terminate appointments mid-term, the court structured its analysis around the interest of the vice-chairs. In other words, the Divisional Court reasoned that the vice-chairs had an interest in the outcome of the matter as it might have affected their security of tenure. However, through the course of the decision, that reason was supplanted by the court's focus on the prior knowledge of the board and how that prior knowledge disqualified the entire board from hearing the matter. See *SEIU, supra* note 112 at paras 29-57.

132 See e.g. the debate between the majority and dissenting judges in *Law Society of Upper Canada v French*, [1975] 2 SCR 767, in which members of the discipline committee for the law society also sat on appeals by convocation. The majority decision did not find disqualifying bias. However, the *Law Society Act* was modified in 1998, removing the adjudicative role of convocation and splitting the body so that there is no overlap between the original disciplinary committees and those hearing appeals.

133 See e.g. *Health Insurance Act*, RSO 1990, c H.6, s 23.

134 An example is the Office of the Information and Privacy Commissioner of Ontario, which separates mediators and adjudicators through informal but strict practice.

135 [2010] LSDD No 61 (QL) [*Cengarle*].

136 *Ibid* at para 21.

panel held that the sheer volume of interventions was not the marker of whether the process had been tainted by a reasonable apprehension of bias. However, they examined all the interjections made by the first instance panel and found that 16 of the 56 interventions gave a cumulative appearance of reasonable apprehension of bias. These interventions showed the first instance panel to have descended into the arena and assumed the role of a prosecuting advocate. More specifically, the appeal panel found that the chair of the original hearing had intervened excessively during the examination-in-chief of certain witnesses and had done so in a manner that, to a reasonable person, appeared to cross-examine them.[137]

Cases such as *Cengarle* raise the issue of how to draw the line between valid non-adversarial or "inquisitorial" processes (sometimes called "active adjudication") and, the appearance of partisan interference by the tribunal.[138] Compare, for example, the concerns in *Cengarle* with the Federal Court of Appeal holding in *Thamotharem*,[139] where a guideline ("Guideline 7") set out by the chair of the Immigration and Refugee Board directed refugee protection officers or, in their absence, a member of the board to begin the questioning at a hearing.[140] Guideline 7 prompted litigious controversy over the fairness of the procedure. Ultimately, the Federal Court of Appeal held that this process—an inquisitorial one—showed no transgression of the duty of fairness owed by the decision-maker. Although "relatively unfamiliar to common lawyers" who are steeped in the adversarial tradition, an inquisitorial process (which originated in the Civil Law tradition) in and of itself presents no challenges to notions of fairness. Equally important, the Board's choice of an inquisitorial method fit comfortably within the structure that Parliament had designed for it under the *Immigration and Refugee Protection Act*.[141] Is Guideline 7 simply another instance of statutory authorization permitting divergence from a judicial common law standard? Is it greater recognition that administrative decision-making is not always best suited to a traditional common law adversarial context?[142]

Other situations in which decision-maker's comments have given rise to reasonable apprehension of bias include *ex parte* communications (that is, where the decision-maker chooses to speak privately with one party)[143] and cases in which sexist, condescending, or other irrelevant comments have been made.[144] Although decisions made by the decision-maker in previous unrelated cases will generally not give rise to a reasonable apprehension of bias, comments in a decision showing a predisposition toward an outcome in a specific case before the decision-maker have been held to give rise to reasonable apprehension of

---

137 An older case that illustrates similar issues of a tribunal descending into the role of advocate is *Golomb and College of Physicians and Surgeons of Ontario* (1976), 12 OR (2d) 73 (Div Ct).

138 See generally, Laverne Jacobs & Sasha Baglay, eds, *The Nature of Inquisitorial Processes in Administrative Regimes: Global Perspectives* (Surrey, UK: Ashgate, 2013) [Jacobs & Baglay]. On active adjudication, see Samantha Green & Lorne Sossin, "Administrative Justice and Innovation: Beyond the Adversarial/Inquisitorial Dichotomy" in Jacobs & Baglay, *ibid*.

139 *Thamotharem v Canada (Minister of Citizenship and Immigration)*, 2006 FC 16, [2006] 3 FCR 168, aff'd 2007 FCA 198, [2008] 1 FCR 385.

140 See also the discussion of *Thamotharem* in Chapter 9 by Angus Grant and Lorne Sossin "Fairness in Context: Achieving Fairness through Access to Administrative Justice."

141 SC 2001, c 27.

142 See, generally, Jacobs & Baglay, *supra* note 138.

143 See e.g. *Law Society of Alberta v Merchant*, [2011] LSDD No 29 (QL).

144 *Yusuf v Canada (Minister of Employment and Immigration)*, [1992] 1 FC 629; see also, generally, *Sawridge Band v Canada (CA)*, [1997] 3 FC 580 and *Rutigliano v Ontario (Provincial Police)*, 2012 ONCA 484.

bias.[145] At the same time, it is important to note that it is possible for comments made by a decision-maker to show understanding of or to take judicial notice of the broader social context without necessarily giving rise to a reasonable apprehension of bias.[146]

A decision-maker's alleged attitude or predisposition to the outcome of a case has also been said to arise through comments expressed outside the hearing room about the on-going case. In these circumstances, the administrative law jurisprudence has held that the standard for determining whether disqualifying bias exists should be whether the adjudica-tor has a closed mind. In other words, what is central is whether the decision-maker is amenable to persuasion or whether their comments indicate "a mind so closed that any submission [by the parties] would be futile."[147] The test has led to permissible variation in the degree to which a decision-maker may be wedded to a position held prior to making a de-cision on the outcome. The degree to which a court will accept a prior, fixed view on the part of a decision-maker is determined by the nature and function of the decision-making pro-cess. For example, in *Old St Boniface Residents Assn Inc v Winnipeg (City)*, the Supreme Court of Canada held that, because of the nature of municipal governance, it is to be expected that municipal councillors would have advocated a position during election time or before dif-ferent committees prior to sitting on municipal council in the final decision of the same issue.[148] The court held that the reasonable apprehension of bias standard could not apply to a situation of municipal government such as the one in *Old St Boniface*. Instead, the Supreme Court held that a more appropriate test in light of the nature and function of mu-nicipal council is that a councillor be disqualified for bias only if it can be established *in fact* that a councillor has such a closed mind on a matter that any representations made would be futile.[149] In a related case, decided on the same day and reaching the same result, judges for the minority expressed concern that the standard articulated by the court could lead to posturing on the part of municipal decision-makers.[150]

In the later case of *Newfoundland Telephone*,[151] the court indicated that a multifunctional administrative body may have varying standards depending on the function being per-formed. Administrative bodies that conduct policy functions will be subject to the closed-mind standard established in *Old St Boniface*.

The recent case of *Gitxaala Nation v Canada*[152] offers an example of this standard's appli-cation as well as an illustration of how the determination of whether disqualifying bias exists depends on context. In *Gitxaala Nation*, the Gitxaala Nation argued that the process used by the governor in council (i.e., Cabinet) in approving a pipeline was procedurally flawed for a

---

145 *Alberta Teachers' Association v Alberta (Information and Privacy Commissioner)*, 2011 ABQB 19. This case is related to the Supreme Court of Canada decision that held that the commissioner's implied decision to extend the timeline that the office would follow in rendering its decision was subject to and met the *Dunsmuir* standard of reasonableness: see *Alberta (Information and Privacy Commissioner) v Alberta Teachers' Association*, 2011 SCC 61, [2011] 3 SCR 654.

146 *S (RD)*, *supra* note 100.

147 See *Newfoundland Telephone Co v Newfoundland (Board of Commissioners of Public Utilities)*, [1992] 1 SCR 623 [*Newfoundland Telephone*].

148 See *Old St Boniface Residents Assn Inc v Winnipeg (City)*, [1990] 3 SCR 1170 [*Old St Boniface*] at para 45.

149 *Ibid* at para 57. See also, more recently, *Rainbow Beach Developments Inc v Parkland (County)*, 2013 ABCA 205.

150 See *Save Richmond Farmland Society v Richmond (Township)*, [1990] 3 SCR 1213.

151 *Newfoundland Telephone*, *supra* note 147.

152 2016 FCA 187 [*Gitxaala Nation*].

variety of reasons.[153] One of these reasons was that a previous minister of natural resources (who was, at the time, also a member of Cabinet) had stated in the media that the pipeline under consideration was in the national interest, along with other comments that appeared to favour approving the pipeline. The Gitxaala Nation argued that Cabinet had prejudged the matter, essentially approving the pipeline before receiving the necessary evaluative reports and holding the required consultations with affected Indigenous Peoples. However, the Federal Court of Appeal rejected this argument, holding that "evidence of one Minister's comment made years before the decision at issue is insufficient to establish that the outcome of the governor in council's decision was predetermined."[154] The lack of connection between the former minister's comments and the decision under scrutiny led to the court's finding that there was no disqualifying bias, both because the minister who made the comments was no longer in the position and because of the length of time that had passed. In making this decision, the Federal Court of Appeal also took into account the nature of the governor in council's work. This work involves balancing many different, and often conflicting considerations, over highly politically charged issues. The context was far from an adjudicative one (which would have attracted a reasonable apprehension of bias standard); instead, the closed-mind standard established in *Old St Boniface* was appropriate because of the policy-driven context.[155] Interestingly, by allowing the bias arguments to be made in this context, *Gitxaala Nation* shows a move towards greater reception of the duty of procedural fairness in policy-making. Since the decision in *Inuit Tapirisat*, Canadian administrative law jurisprudence has generally shown reluctance to admit that Cabinet owes a duty of procedural fairness to parties affected by its actions. Undoubtedly, the duty to consult Indigenous Peoples has helped bring about this change.[156]

Moreover, administrative bodies that perform multiple functions including investigations, policy-making, and adjudication, may be afforded more freedom to hold a fixed view during an investigative or policy-making stage than at an adjudicative stage, so long as there are no constitutional contraventions. Despite this general principle, however, the jurisprudence is not always straightforward as to when the reasonable apprehension of bias test should apply and when the closed-mind test should apply. For example, in *Chrétien v Canada (Ex-Commissioner, Commission of Inquiry into the Sponsorship Program and Advertising Activities)*,[157] a reasonable apprehension of bias standard was used to evaluate comments made to the media by the commissioner of a public inquiry. The applicant, former Prime Minister Jean Chrétien, was successful in having the factual findings in the public inquiry set aside because the commissioner's media comments made during the inquiry showed prejudgment of the matter. This was surprising because public inquiries aim to determine the facts and do not have binding, enforceable impact. On the basis of Supreme Court jurisprudence, one would have expected the investigatory nature to require a closed-mind test.

---

153   These reasons dealt with the government's failure to satisfy its duty to consult with Indigenous Peoples. For a fuller discussion of *Gitxaala Nation*, see Chapter 3, Realizing Aboriginal Administrative Law.

154   *Gitxaala Nation* at para 200.

155   *Ibid* at paras 198-99.

156   See the discussion of when the duty of fairness is triggered in Chapter 5, The Principles and Practice of Procedural Fairness. With respect to the duty to consult and its impact, see Chapter 3, Realizing Aboriginal Administrative Law.

157   2008 FC 802, [2009] 2 FCR 417, aff'd 2010 FCA 283.

In light of these cases, one is left wondering about the conceptual framework that can be used to understand when and why the different tests for disqualifying bias should be applied. First, the Supreme Court cases regarding municipal councillors such as *Old St Boniface* suggest that legislative functions will not attract a high degree of scrutiny from the perspective of procedural fairness. Similarly, cases such as *Newfoundland Telephone* seem to reassert a traditional common law idea that investigative work does not attract the highest degree of procedural fairness because the impact on the individual is not binding. Whereas the first approach may gain purchase from constitutional doctrines relating to the separation of powers, the latter idea is more questionable. Impact on the individual should be measured in ways that extend past the existence or absence of a binding order. It could be argued that that in some circumstances, such as public inquiries where the impact on one's reputation can be quite significant, reasonable apprehension of bias may be more appropriate because of its more objective and possibly easier evidentiary standard to meet.

Should public advocacy, such as academic publications, which take a specific view on an issue or area of law, be held to give rise to a reasonable apprehension of bias? The question arose in the case of *Great Atlantic & Pacific Co of Canada v Ontario (Human Rights Commission)*,[158] when a professor who had written extensively against gender discrimination was appointed as a board of inquiry to adjudicate human rights applications. Because there was also a distinct, more immediate factor present that had the potential to cause disqualifying bias, the court held that the issue of the professor's advocacy did not need to be determined. As such, the question has remained relatively outstanding in our jurisprudence. But with the advent of social media, the question arises more frequently now in relation to adjudicators who are or were academics and have expressed their views via their postings to the Internet or social media sites. We discuss social media and tribunal adjudication below. Given that administrative tribunals are designed to be expert tribunals, it is natural that members will be chosen from realms in which their expertise has been shown, such as academia, practice, or otherwise. Having part-time members who are also active in the field through academic writing or as practitioners can be useful so long as they are not also engaged as counsel, parties, interveners, etc., while serving as decision-makers in any given case.[159]

In conclusion, whereas the reasonable apprehension of bias test has been held to apply in individual bias cases, the closed-mind test, which supports a different evidentiary burden, is generally used in conjunction with policy-making and investigatory functions. What is interesting about these tests is not only the variation in standards themselves, but the conceptual rationale(s) underpinning their application.

2. Social Media and Disqualifying Bias

The administrative law jurisprudence has only started to develop principles regarding whether and how the use of social media by adjudicators may signal a reasonable apprehension of bias. Though there are a variety of forms of social media, there are two principal ways in which adjudicator activity on social media raises concerns about potential disqualifying

---

158   (1993), 13 OR (3d) 824 (Div Ct).
159   *Ibid.*

bias: (i) through online comments suggesting a predisposition toward a party or cause before them,[160] and (ii) by connections with others online, suggesting a personal relationship that may influence the adjudicator in that person's favour.[161]

In the context of the administrative state, adjudicators are drawn from worlds where they have developed and demonstrated their expertise. In the modern age, this expertise is frequently disseminated through comments on current topics of the day via Facebook, Twitter, and other social media outlets. It is not unusual for an allegation of disqualifying bias to arise with respect to expert adjudicators who are or were formerly academics (where there is a natural expectation that they will comment on current events in their academic roles) or because they have connections (such as Facebook friends) with prominent members of government in their area of expertise.

In *Hirsch v Ontario (Environment and Climate Change)*,[162] a member of the Environmental Review Tribunal, who was also a university professor, had posted a link regarding the Ontario government's climate change policy on her Twitter account. In response to an allegation of reasonable apprehension of bias, the tribunal held that the Twitter posting was informational. The Twitter post did not express any opinion on the part of the adjudicator. It also did not deal with any matter that was before the adjudicator or that could come before the tribunal. The tribunal noted that the posting had been made while the adjudicator was a full-time professor with a part-time appointment to the tribunal and well before the hearing had arisen. However, even if the adjudicator had held a full-time appointment to the tribunal at the time of posting, one can see from the tribunal's analysis that what is most important is the potential for the post to reveal a state of mind of the adjudicator that was not impartial.

While the jurisprudence on adjudicators and social media is still nascent, some tribunals provide guidance to their adjudicators on how to manage same. For example, the *Member Social Media and Social Networking Policy of the BC Workers' Compensation Appeal Tribunal* (WCAT)[163] advises its tribunal members that their outside activities should generally not interfere with the impartial, effective, and timely performance of their responsibilities.[164] Among the specific pieces of guidance offered in relation to independence, impartiality, and integrity are that adjudicators should refrain from posting anything that detracts from the dignity of WCAT or publishing anything that may reflect adversely on the tribunal. Tribunal members are advised not to "friend" (through Facebook, etc.) representatives who appear before the tribunal. If a tribunal member is a "friend" with a representative, they are in a conflict of interest. Adjudicators should also avoid commenting on social media in a way that shows an association with issues that may come before the tribunal or with

---

160 *Hirsch v Ontario (Environment and Climate Change)*, 2016 CanLII 1702 (Ont ERT).
161 See e.g. *Riach v Canada (Attorney General)*, 2011 FC 1230; *Canadian Union of Postal Workers v Canada Post Corp*, 2012 FC 975, *DeMaria v Law Society of Saskatchewan* 2015 SKCA 106; and *Heffel v Registered Nurses Assn of the Northwest Territories and Nunavut*, 2015 NWTSC 16.
162 *Supra* note 160.
163 Available as Annexe 3 in *Utilisation des Médias Sociaux par les Officiers Judiciaires Canadiens*, online: <https://www.cacp.ca/comit%C3%A9-sur-les-amendements-l%C3%A9gislatifs-activit%C3%A9s.html?asst_id=845>.
164 *Ibid*. Reproducing WCAT Code of Conduct for Members at s 2.7, "Outside Activities."

organizations that frequently come before the tribunal.[165] A final, interesting piece of advice is that adjudicators should consider where they post material on the Internet and whether their posting site or the networks that they join give the appearance of undermining their independence, impartiality, and/or integrity.[166]

However, issues about bias in social media cut two ways. Adjudicators must refrain from using the Internet in ways that are inappropriate, especially when viewed by parties and the general public. But there is also a deeper concern relating to bias, which is that adjudicators should not use the Internet to learn information about parties that has not come to them in the record. This long-standing principle of fairness, which requires adjudicators to decide matters from information brought to them through proper channels and processes, is reflected in the WCAT social media policy as well.[167]

3. Perceptions of Institutional Bias

The need for institutional policy-making, collaboration, and consistency is an element that distinguishes administrative tribunals from courts. This section takes a look at some of the ways in which apprehensions of bias have arisen in response to institutional practices developed by tribunals for these purposes. As you read this section, consider the connection between institutional bias and adjudicative independence.

Finally, please keep in mind the pipeline case study relating to the National Energy Board (NEB), which was discussed in Chapter 1, and consider what legal principles should apply to the allegation of disqualifying bias on the part of the board members who met with Jean Charest. More specifically, in 2016, the NEB was conducting its National Engagement Tour, which, according to an NEB news release, was designed to improve relationships with municipalities and Indigenous Peoples, as well as to improve pipeline safety and environmental outcomes.[168] During this tour, the chair and vice-chair met with Jean Charest, a former premier of Québec, who was, at the time of the meeting, a consultant for one of the applicants for the pipeline project under consideration. Initially, the chair and vice-chair reported that they had not discussed the pipeline with Mr Charest at the meeting. However, it was later revealed that that was not the case. In what circumstances should institutional consultations be said to give rise to a reasonable apprehension of bias? Did the meeting meet that threshold?[169]

---

165   *Ibid.*

166   *Ibid.*

167   *Ibid* at "(e) Fairness."

168   NEB news release, "Energy East Hearing Panel Steps Down," online: <http://news.gc.ca/web/article-en.do?nid=1122609>.

169   In this regard, see the excellent analysis of the issues by David Mullan, "Bias, the National Energy Board and the Energy East Hearings" in D Mullan, "2016 Developments in Administrative Law Relevant to Energy Law and Regulation" (2017) 5:1 Energy Regulation Q, online: <http://www.energyregulationquarterly.ca/articles/2016-developments-in-administrative-law-relevant-to-energy-law-and-regulation#sthash.htF0Dna3.dpbs>. The NEB chair and vice-chair decision A79374-1(9 September 2016) to recuse is available for download at: <https://apps.neb-one.gc.ca/REGDOCS/Item/Filing/A79374>.

a. Bias, Adjudicative Independence, and Policy-Making (and Whose Policies Are They Anyway?)

Policy-making is generally accepted as being central to tribunal existence. This is because unlike courts, tribunals have been created to manage and oversee areas that are often polycentric in nature. The policy-making function of administrative tribunals attracted a significant increase in attention after MacLachlin CJ's postulate in *Ocean Port* that every tribunal, no matter how adjudicative it appears, has some role in implementing a government policy.[170] Tribunals create policy in their day-to-day work in several ways. Focusing primarily on adjudicative bodies, Houle and Sossin identify three modes of policy-making by administrative tribunals: decision-making; informal rule making through the use of such soft law as guidelines, bulletins, and manuals; and formal rule making through delegated legislation.[171] Generally, the policies that administrative bodies make, whether primarily adjudicative or otherwise, serve to further the objectives of the statute that the tribunal has been mandated to administer, to promote consistency in the decisions rendered by the tribunal's various members, and to render the tribunal more efficient in its decision-making process. Although it can be argued that courts also further the policy of legislation simply by rendering decisions under a statute, the methods used to create policy and the function of policy-making itself are distinctive characteristics of administrative bodies. In the context of the administrative state, policy-making relates to the expertise (in the subject matter or in managing the subject matter) possessed by the tribunals that administer and further the objectives of a particular statute.

Tensions arise, however, when the methods used by tribunals in their policy-making activities appear to infringe on the adjudicative independence of any individual tribunal decision-maker. Adjudicative independence is one guarantee of independence that is frequently called into question in the administrative context. Referenced briefly in the Supreme Court's decision in *Beauregard*,[172] the concept of adjudicative independence embodies the ability of a decision-maker to decide free of inappropriate interference by other decision-makers. Such inappropriate interference may include, for example, pressure to decide a certain way or substitution of another's decision for one's own. Of all the guarantees of independence, adjudicative independence is a value that is particularly delicate in the administrative law context. There is often a tension between the need for tribunal members to collaborate to further the law as an institution and the need to give each decision-maker space to render his or her rightful decisions. This tension has shown up most frequently with respect to the use of full board meetings to promote consistency in tribunal decision-making. Nevertheless, policy-making practices have come up against adjudicative independence more recently in other key ways. In addition to full board meetings, two additional tribunal practices discussed in this section are using lead cases to promote adjudicative efficiency and consistency, and assisting the executive branch of government to develop its policy.

---

170 See *Ocean Port*, *supra* note 4 at para 24.
171 See France Houle & Lorne Sossin, "Tribunals and Policy Making" in Jacobs & Mactavish, *supra* note 3. Rule making is also discussed in Chapter 8, Delegation and Consultation: How the Administrative State Functions and the Importance of Rules.
172 See *Beauregard*, *supra* note 20 and accompanying text.

b. Full Board Meetings

In administrative law, the methods used to promote consistency in decision-making across tribunals as institutions have given rise to allegations of reasonable apprehension of bias. At the heart of the debate over consistency is whether the adjudicative independence of any individual member has been compromised. The tools used to promote consistency often involve the input of tribunal members other than those charged with determining a specific claim. As a consequence, allegations of reasonable apprehension of bias have been made by litigants concerned that the adjudicators deciding their claims have based their decisions on considerations that they themselves did not come across in the course of their adjudications.

The challenge of fostering coherence has become all the more important with the proliferation of larger boards across the country. Such boards can have several members—sometimes in the hundreds—in various parts of the country who may each have distinct views on how the law under the legislation should be developed. Similar decisions in similar cases show the general public how a tribunal has chosen to apply its statutes in various factual situations. The "policy" that consistent decisions develop is a form of non-binding guideline that tribunal users can refer to in deciding how to manage their affairs in the industry or sector regulated by the tribunal. It can help them determine, for example, whether to bring a matter before the tribunal or to settle. If tribunals were without a means of promoting consistency, the general public using tribunal services would be at a disadvantage in anticipating how their affairs will be regulated and such randomness in result would undermine trust in the administrative state. In a trilogy of cases (*IWA v Consolidated-Bathurst Packaging Ltd*,[173] *Tremblay v Quebec (Commission des affaires sociales)*,[174] and *Ellis-Don Ltd v Ontario (Labour Relations Board)*),[175] the Supreme Court of Canada set out the guidelines that tribunals should follow so that members can collaborate within their institution to promote consistency of outcome without compromising the adjudicative independence of any one decision-maker or fairness to the parties.

In *Consolidated-Bathurst*, the Ontario Labour Relations Board held a meeting of the full labour board to discuss the draft reasons of one of its three-member panels. The purposes of such meetings were to facilitate understanding and appreciation throughout the board of policy developments and to evaluate the practical consequences of proposed policy initiatives on provincial labour relations and the economy. At this particular meeting, the decision discussed dealt with whether a legal test the board had established through its jurisprudence should be replaced by another. At issue before the Supreme Court was whether full board meetings constitute a breach of the natural justice principle that "they who hear must decide," by placing the decision-makers in a situation where others who have not heard the evidence or arguments can influence them on the particular matter. It was also argued that such meetings are unacceptable because they do not provide the parties with adequate opportunity to answer issues that may be voiced by board members who had not heard the case. The appellant's arguments were therefore cast as a matter of improper

---

173   *Consolidated-Bathurst*, *supra* note 104.
174   [1992] 1 SCR 952 [*Tremblay*].
175   2001 SCC 4, [2001] 1 SCR 221 [*Ellis-Don*].

encroachment on the adjudicative independence of the actual decision-makers and of lack of opportunity to know the full case to be met.

The Supreme Court acknowledged the need for full board meetings to ensure consistency. In the majority's opinion, such meetings allowed the members of a large board[176] with a heavy case load[177] to benefit from the acquired expertise of the collective. As well, consultation was useful in achieving the board's mandate. The structure of the board was conducive to exchanges of opinions between management and union (as evidenced by its tripartite nature) in order to use its combined expertise to regulate labour relations in a prompt and final manner.[178] The majority also saw coherence as a goal to be fostered so that the outcome of disputes did not depend on the identity of the decision-maker. And last, in the majority's view, the fact that a privative clause protects the board's decisions made it even more incumbent on the board to take measures to avoid conflicting results.

At the same time, the court recognized that fostering coherence should not compromise any panel member's capacity to decide in accordance with his conscience and opinions. The court laid down the following guidelines governing intra-agency consultation:

> It is obvious that no outside interference may be used to compel or pressure a decision maker to participate in discussions on policy issues raised by a case on which he must render a decision. It also goes without saying that a formalized consultation process could not be used to force or induce decision makers to adopt positions with which they do not agree. Nevertheless, discussions with colleagues do not constitute, in and of themselves, infringements on the panel members' capacity to decide the issues at stake independently. A discussion does not prevent a decision maker from adjudicating in accordance with his own conscience and opinions nor does it constitute an obstacle to this freedom. Whatever discussion may take place, the ultimate decision will be that of the decision maker for which he assumes full responsibility.[179]

The court held that the relevant issue is whether there is *pressure* on the decision-maker to decide against his or her own conscience and opinions. It outlined the following conditions for the holding of such meetings so that natural justice would not be breached: that the discussions be limited to law or policy and not factual issues, and that the parties be given a reasonable opportunity to respond to any new ground arising from the meeting. In this regard, the court approved of the checks and balances put in place by the Labour Relations Board—for example, not keeping minutes of the meeting, not keeping attendance, and not holding a vote at the end of the discussion.

Tremblay was decided a few years after *Consolidated-Bathurst*. In *Tremblay*, the court clarified that the imposition of consultation meetings by a member of the board who was not on the panel could amount to an inappropriate constraint. The court also held that, even in situations where the consultation process is said to be voluntary, it is important to determine whether the operational practice of the tribunal shows evidence that the consultation, in fact, comprises systemic pressure.

In *Tremblay*, the consultation process was quite different from that in *Consolidated-Bathurst*. Although the consultations were optional in theory (they were to be called by the

---

176 There were 48 members in 1982-83.
177 At the time, there were approximately 266 cases a year.
178 *Ellis-Don, supra* note 175 at para 80.
179 *Consolidated-Bathurst, supra* note 104, paras 70-73.

decision-making member of the commission), the practice at the Commission des affaires sociales (CAS) made consultation compulsory when a proposed decision was contrary to previous decisions.

Another factor that gave an appearance of constraint and an apparent lack of decisional independence at the CAS was that the president could refer a matter before another member for plenary discussion. The Supreme Court noted that, in such circumstances, a decision-maker may not feel free to refuse to submit a question to the consultation process. Because the statute expressly indicated that the individual decision-makers must decide matters, imposing group consultation on them amounted to an act of compulsion and went against legislative intent. As well, the plenary meetings aimed to reach a consensus. Overall, many of the protective mechanisms that the court had approved in *Consolidated-Bathurst* simply did not exist at the CAS. In particular, unlike the practice of the Ontario Labour Relations Board, CAS took attendance, voted by a show of hands, and kept minutes of the meetings. These aspects created an appearance of "systemic pressure."

Finally, at issue in *Ellis-Don* was whether facts had been discussed at a full labour board meeting, contrary to the jurisprudential rules governing institutional decision-making set out in *Consolidated-Bathurst* and *Tremblay*. Although *Ellis-Don* focused only on the issue of providing the parties with a full opportunity to respond to matters discussed at a plenary meeting and did not deal with the questions of pressure and independence, it is useful because it reiterates the jurisprudential guidelines governing intra-agency consultation as set out by the Supreme Court in *Consolidated-Bathurst* (above).

c. Lead Cases

Since the time of the *Consolidated-Bathurst* trilogy, other tribunal practices for garnering consistency, developing policy, and addressing *efficiency* (another perennial concern in the face of the heavy workloads of tribunals) have come to the attention of the courts. One recent development is the use of lead cases. In the decision of *Geza v Canada (Minister of Citizenship and Immigration)*,[180] the Immigration and Refugee Board instituted a procedure through which it attempted to select one of several similar refugee claims to create a full evidential record for all. The purpose of the lead case initiative was to enable the board to have one case in which there were informed findings of fact and a relatively thorough analysis of the relevant legal issues.[181] The board was attempting to deal efficiently with a large influx of refugee claims by the Hungarian Roma. Although chosen before many Roma had had their claims heard, the claim chosen was to be representative of the issues that typically recurred when the Hungarian Roma were seeking refugee status. The case used as the lead case was selected with the participation of the lawyer who had the largest inventory of pending Hungarian Roma claims. The minister of citizenship and immigration was invited to participate in the hearings. This claim was then heard by an experienced panel of the board chosen for its familiarity with the relevant country conditions and experience with case management

---

180   [2005] 3 FCR 3 (Fed Ct), rev'd [2006] 4 FCR 377 (CA) [*Geza*].

181   In a similar vein, see also *Thamotharem*, *supra* note 139 (CA), and *Benitez v Canada (Minister of Citizenship and Immigration)*, 2007 FCA 199, [2008] 1 FCR 155, in which allegations of reasonable apprehension of bias were brought against the Immigration and Refugee Board for its creation of procedural guidelines that suggested the manner in which adjudicators should conduct their hearings.

of the Roma cases, and drawn from different regions of Canada. The appellants argued that the lead case initiative was designed to reduce the number of successful Roma refugee applications, and therefore showed bias. For the Court of Appeal, Evans JA held that, based on the entire factual matrix, a reasonable person would conclude that the lead case initiative was designed not only to generate consistency but also to reduce the number of positive decisions that might be rendered in favour of the 15,000 Roma claimants and to deter future claims. Justice Evans held that, although there was no single fact that alone established a reasonable apprehension of bias, there were several facts that contributed collectively to a reasonable apprehension of bias. The decision in *Geza* is useful both for showing the boundaries between tribunal efficiency and bias, and for indicating that a reasonable apprehension of bias can arise from the totality of evidence, as opposed to a single, determinative fact.

d. Adjudicative Independence and the Legislative Process

In *Communications, Energy and Paperworkers Union of Canada, Local 707 v The Alberta Labour Relations Board*,[182] the Alberta Labour Relations Board was consulted for its knowledge of the field by the executive branch of government in order to help the government implement a new legislative policy. As a result, the board faced a legal battle in which it was said to lack independence and impartiality with respect to any matter it had to deal with touching on the labour law policy, and experienced a grave loss of confidence by the unions affected by the policy. To many, this occurrence may ring contradictory in light of McLachlin CJ's now famous dicta in *Ocean Port* that all tribunals exist precisely to further the policy of the executive branch of government.[183] *Alberta Labour Relations Board* raises a fresh and interesting question of independence in administrative law—namely, how should feedback on the industry be transferred to the executive department that has responsibility for the tribunal? The question turns on how a tribunal can communicate such information while preserving its impartiality and independence from the executive branch of government.

e. Multifunctionality

The expertise required of the tribunal members and staff is not only juristic expertise, which is needed to interpret the statute, but may also include expertise in the particular technical subject area.[184] The appointments process often reflects this diversity through requirements that a tribunal be composed of experts drawn not only from lawyers but also from other fields and sometimes even from the general public. For example, the Complaint Review Committee established under the Alberta *Architects Act* is composed of at least three registered architects and one licensed interior designer.[185] These experts are mandated to

---

182 [2004] AJ No 83 (QL) [*Alberta Labour Relations Board*].

183 *Ocean Port, supra* note 4 at para 24. See also Lorne Sossin & Charles W Smith, "The Politics of Transparency and Independence Before Administrative Boards" (2012) Sask L Rev 13.

184 France Houle provides a thoughtful definition of what it means to be an "expert" in the administrative law sense in France Houle, "Le fonctionnement du régime de preuve libre dans un système non-expert: Le traitement symptomatique des preuves par la Section de la protection des réfugiés" (2004) 38 RJT 263. See also, generally, L Jacobs & T Kuttner, "The Expert Tribunal" in Jacobs & Mactavish, *supra* note 3.

185 *Architects Act*, RSA 2000, A-44, s 36.

investigate and hold hearings into complaints about the conduct of architects.[186] Similarly, appointees to the Practice Review Board, which assesses the practice and educational standards of the architects, must be registered architects, interior designers, individuals who are able to assess academic qualifications, and members of the public.[187] The Alberta *Natural Resources Conservation Board Act* has a provision allowing for the appointment of technical experts who, on the approval of the Lieutenant Governor in Council may sit with the board to assist with technical information in a matter or may report to the Board.[188] It is not just the appointment of experts to a tribunal, however, that serves to reflect a tribunal's polycentric nature. The structure of many enabling statutes themselves reflects the polycentric nature of the tribunal through the plurality of functions that the tribunal may be asked to perform.

For example, the Canadian International Trade Tribunal (CITT) is endowed with both broad powers of policy development and adjudicative powers. The CITT conducts inquiries and provides advice on economic, trade, and tariff matters as referred to it by the minister of finance or the governor in council. It also hears appeals of decisions made under various statutes by the Canada Revenue Agency.[189] This type of plurality of function has been called into question by litigants on judicial review in cases where staff research was not revealed to all the parties, raising issues of procedural fairness.[190] Many tribunals make available to the public their staff reports, research, and even training manuals and adjudicator decision-making guides, most often by posting them on their websites.[191] Some tribunals try to maintain a de facto separation of powers within their work, seemingly to avoid allegations that one aspect of the tribunal's work has had an inappropriate interference with another aspect of its work, causing a reasonable apprehension of bias.[192]

The most common complaint in relation to a tribunal's multiplicity of functions stems from a perception by the user that a tribunal has the potential to act as both prosecutor and judge in the same matter. Generally, it has been held that overlapping functions are not a problem so long as sanctioned by a statute that is in conformity with the Constitution or applicable quasi-constitutional enactment.[193]

---

186 *Ibid*, s 37.

187 *Ibid*, s 38.

188 See *Natural Resources Conservation Board Act*, RSA 2000, c N-3, s 23.

189 *Canadian International Trade Tribunal Act*, RSC, 1985, c 47 (4th Supp), ss 16, 18, 19. See also the mandate of the Canadian International Trade Tribunal, online: Canadian International Trade Tribunal <http://www.citt.gc.ca>.

190 See, in particular, *Toshiba Corp v Canada (Anti-Dumping Tribunal)* (1984), 8 Admin LR 173 (FCA).

191 See e.g. the publications of the Immigration and Refugee Board, which include policies, procedures, and research reports on various countries, online: Immigration and Refugee Board of Canada <http://www.irb-cisr.gc.ca/Eng/BoaCom/pubs/Pages/index.aspx>.

192 Such allegations have been made in the literature: see e.g. Colin J Bennett, "The Privacy Commissioner of Canada: Multiple Roles, Diverse Expectations and Structural Dilemmas" (2003) 46:2 Canadian Public Administration 218.

193 See the discussion of *Régie, supra* note 33 and accompanying text, and *Brosseau, supra* note 39 (holding that, if authorized by a constitutionally valid statute, the multiplicity of rules in one administrative body does not give rise to reasonable apprehension of bias). At issue in *Brosseau* was whether there was a reasonable apprehension of bias arising from the multiple roles, including investigation and adjudication, at the Alberta Securities Commission. The litigation was prompted by the fact that the Commission chair, in his investigative capacity, had received a report prior to the hearing from the deputy director of enforcement. See also *Cantelo v New Brunswick (Police Commission)*, 2007 NBQB 32.

In some cases, tribunals may take their own proactive measures to reduce the appearance or reality that relations are too close between those acting in a prosecutorial fashion and those performing adjudicative functions. Should such proactive measures be taken into account in determining whether a reasonable person could find a lack of impartiality vis-à-vis the tribunal? *Lippé* had indicated that the test for impartiality on an institutional level is whether the system is structured in a way that creates a reasonable apprehension of bias in a substantial number of cases.[194] Several factors could be considered to decide whether such bias exists. Determining which factors to use was held to be a matter of looking at the tribunal in question, the way that it operates in practice, and any safeguards that may exist to prevent incidents of bias in practice. In the Federal Court decision of *Sam Lévy & Associés Inc v Mayrand*,[195] the court held that although the superintendent of bankruptcy was statutorily endowed with powers of investigation and adjudication, the fact that he used his delegation powers to hive off adjudicative responsibilities was sufficient to avoid a reasonable apprehension of institutional bias and a violation of the right to a fair hearing under the federal *Bill of Rights*. The Alberta Queen's Bench decision of *Currie v Edmonton Remand Centre*[196] illustrates how operational practice may have a negative effect on the outcome. In *Currie*, the court found institutional bias from the overlapping functions of the prison guards and the disciplinary board members. *Currie* dealt with the question of whether disciplinary hearings used in a provincial prison exhibited signs of institutional bias in a substantial number of cases. The disciplinary hearings were used to determine whether prisoners had committed breaches of acceptable standards of conduct within the prison and the appropriate punishment for contraventions of the rules and regulations of the correctional institution. However, those who were responsible for maintaining order in the institution were also placed on the disciplinary panels. This caused an appearance of conflict—in particular, an appearance that the institution's primary decision would be maintained at the expense of the prisoner having a fair opportunity to contest it.

The applicants argued that the provisions of the Alberta *Corrections Act*[197] and the Alberta *Correctional Institution Regulation*,[198] which allowed for this decision-making structure to exist, were contrary to ss 7 and 11(d) of the Charter. The Alberta Queen's Bench found that, although s 11(d) did not apply in this case, there was indeed a breach of s 7 of the Charter. In addition to finding that none of the traditional guarantees of independence existed in this case, the court's holding was also based, in part, on the fact that the culture of the institution and these types of hearings within them made it impossible for a prisoner to assert their side of the story.

In summary, multifunctionality is a current concern of many administrative bodies. Often, tribunals will use their own de facto methods of reducing the appearance of bias, which can be raised by the enabling statute. The degree to which these practices will or should be taken into account is a matter of debate, and the effect that these practices have on the outcome can be quite significant.

---

194 *Lippé, supra* note 101.
195 2005 FC 702, [2006] 2 FCR 543, Martineau J.
196 2006 ABQB 858, 276 DLR (4th) 143 [*Currie*].
197 RSA 2000, c C-29, s 15.
198 Alta Reg 205/2001, ss 43, 44(3), 44(5), 45.

4. Self-Represented Litigants and Reasonable Apprehension of Bias

There has been a marked increase in the number of self-represented litigants appearing before courts and tribunals. This is due mainly to the inability to afford the expense of a lawyer.[199] In the context of the administrative state, administrative tribunals were originally designed to be expert decision-making bodies that could be navigated by everyday individuals. Reducing complexity in procedure in order to ensure accessibility was one of the original aims of the administrative state.[200]

The growth of self-represented litigants raises concerns about whether the administrative justice system can be truly designed to be more user-friendly.[201] Inevitably, part of rendering the administrative justice system more user-friendly should be an attempt to demystify the processes and institutional design of administrative tribunals themselves. A significant number of motions for recusal for perceptions of bias are brought by self-represented litigants in the tribunal process. As one analysis has shown, these allegations are often prompted by a misunderstanding of how the tribunal functions.[202] Self-represented litigants may misunderstand the steps of a tribunal's procedure or the roles of various players within the tribunal's institutional design.[203] For example, it can be confusing to lawyers, let alone self-represented litigants, to see a tribunal adjudicator seek advice from counsel to the tribunal.[204] Similarly, co-location of different arms of an administrative regime may give the appearance that there is the possibility of improper sharing of information between them unless the protections against information sharing are themselves made known to the public.[205] The increase in self-represented litigants coupled with limits on legal aid should encourage administrative tribunals to develop ways to simplify their processes and to educate the public about how they function.

VI. CONCLUSION

This chapter has provided an historical overview of the law of tribunal independence in Canada, linking it to its jurisprudential roots in judicial independence and its stated goals of preserving impartiality and avoiding bias. It has also offered a critical look at current situations that have given rise to allegations of individual and institutional bias in the Canadian administrative state. The chapter illustrates that, although security of tenure, financial security, and administrative control—the central tenets of judicial independence—may figure in

---

199 See Julie Macfarlane, "The National Self-Represented Litigants Project: Identifying and Meeting the Needs of Self-Represented Litigants: Final Report (May 2013) and Michelle Flaherty (2014) "Self-Represented Litigants: A Sea Change in Adjudication" in Peter Oliver and Graham Mayeda (eds), *Principles and Pragmatism: Essays in Honour of Louise Charron* (Toronto: LexisNexis, 2014) 323-346.

200 See *Final Report of the Agency Cluster Facilitator for the Municipal, Environment and Land Use Planning Tribunals* (Toronto: Agency Cluster Project, 22 August 2007) (Facilitator: Kevin Whitaker).

201 See e.g. Lorne Sossin, "Designing Administrative Justice," Osgoode Legal Studies Research Paper No 26/2017, online: <https://papers.ssrn.com/sol3/papers.cfm?abstract_id=2906784>.

202 See Emily Lawrence and Adam Stikuts, "Allegations of Bias in Administrative Law Proceedings: A Review of Recent Cases" (2017) 30 CJALP 145. These authors provide an excellent survey of cases, including cases filed by self-represented litigants. I draw on a few of the cases they discuss as examples.

203 *Ibid.*

204 See e.g. *Stephenson v Municipal Property Assessment Corporation*, 2015 CanLII 43401 (Ont ARB).

205 See e.g. *Perry v Nova Scotia Barristers' Society*, 2016 NSSC 121.

the problems of independence, impartiality, and bias affecting administrative tribunals, they are by no means the main issues of independence, impartiality, and bias currently affecting tribunals in their everyday operational contexts. Portrayed in artistic terms, the administrative state is a pastiche: it is made up of a plurality of structures and decision-making methods, stemming from the legislature, the executive, and administrative bodies themselves. The context of any administrative body, therefore, needs to be taken into account in determining the standard to apply when bias is alleged.

In addition to the many contexts of administrative decision-making, ranging from ministers to adjudicative tribunals, there are also external contextual factors that can have an impact on whether an administrative actor is affected by disqualifying bias. As illustrated in this chapter, in current times, these external contexts can include the ability of a self-represented litigant to have an appropriate appreciation of the nature and processes of the administrative actor with which it is dealing, and the details of social media engagement in a particular case.

Moving forward, practitioners and students of administrative law will need to consider the tension between what a reasonable person can expect in terms of fairness in any given context and the necessary institutional constraints that the administrative actor may face either individually or institutionally. A balance between these two underlying principles should inform adjudication regardless of which of the variations of the test for disqualifying bias is applicable.

On the level of administrative law theory, one wonders whether a fundamental reconceiving of the nature and purpose of administrative tribunals is a necessary precondition to guaranteeing impartiality in the administrative state, whether the concepts of independence and impartiality need a fresh look within the administrative context, or both. This chapter serves as both a call for a greater empirical understanding of the true challenges to the work of administrative tribunals and for a more genuine reflection of these challenges in legislative policy, measures of reform, and judicial review.

SUGGESTED ADDITIONAL READINGS

BOOKS AND ARTICLES

Bryden, Philip, "Structural Independence of Administrative Tribunals in the Wake of *Ocean Port*" (2003) 16 Can J Admin L & Prac 125.

Carnwath, Lord Justice, "Tribunals and the Courts—the UK Model" (2011) 24 Can J Admin L & Prac 5.

Comtois, Suzanne, "Le contrôle de la cohérence décisionnelle au sein des tribunaux administratifs" (1990) 21 RDUS 77.

Ellis, Ron, *Unjust by Design: Canada's Administrative Justice System* (Vancouver: UBC Press, 2013).

Heckman, Gerald, & Lorne Sossin, "How Do Canadian Administrative Law Protections Live Up to International Human Rights Standards? The Case of Independence" (2005) 50 McGill LJ 193.

Houle, France, et al, "Administrative Justice: Independence and Responsibility—Towards a Common Regime for Independent Adjudicators" (2014) 27 Can J Admin L & Prac 219.

Jacobs, Laverne, "From Rawls to Habermas: Toward a Grounded Theory of Impartiality in Canadian Administrative Law" (2014) 51:2 Osgoode Hall LJJ 543-594.

Jacobs, Laverne, "A Wavering Commitment?: Administrative Independence and Collaborative Governance in Ontario's Adjudicative Tribunals Accountability—Legislation" (2010) 28:2 Windsor YB Access Just 285.

Jacobs, Laverne, & Sasha Baglay, eds, *The Nature of Inquisitorial Processes in Administrative Regimes: Global Perspectives* (Surrey, UK: Ashgate, 2013).

Jacobs, Laverne, "Tribunal Independence and Impartiality: Rethinking the Theory after Bell and Ocean Port Hotel—A Call for Empirical Analysis" in Laverne A Jacobs & Anne L Mactavish, eds, *Dialogue Between Courts and Tribunals: Essays in Administrative Law and Justice (2001-2007)* (Montreal: Éditions Thémis, 2008) 45, online: <https://papers.ssrn.com/sol3/papers.cfm?abstract_id=2332875>.

Kligman, Robert D, *Bias* (Toronto: Butterworths, 1998).

Macdonald, Roderick A, "The Acoustics of Accountability—Towards Well-Tempered Tribunals" in András Sajó, ed, *Judicial Integrity* (Leiden: M Nijhoff Publishers, 2004) 141.

Moliterno, James E, "The Administrative Judiciary's Independence Myth" 41 Wake Forest L Rev 1191.

Mullan, David J, "Chapter 14: Bias and Lack of Independence" in *Administrative Law* (Toronto: Irwin Law, 2001).

Mullan, David J, "2016 Developments in Administrative Law Relevant to Energy Law and Regulation" (2017) 5:1 Energy Regulation Q, online: <http://www.energyregulationquarterly.ca/articles/2016-developments-in-administrative-law-relevant-to-energy-law-and-regulation#sthash.htF0Dna3.dpbs>.

Noreau, Pierre, France Houle, Martine Valois & Pierre Issalys, *La justice administrative: entre indépendance et responsabilité. Jalons pour la création d'un régime commun des décideurs administratifs indépendants* (Cowansville: Éditions Yvon Blais, 2014).

Sossin, Lorne, "Administrative Law at Pleasure: *Keen v Canada*," available online: <www.emond.ca/adminlaw3e>.

Sossin, Lorne, & Jamie Baxter, "Ontario's Administrative Tribunal Clusters: A Glass Half-Full or Half-Empty for Administrative Justice?" (2012) 12 OUCLJ 157.

Sossin, Lorne, & Charles W Smith, "The Politics of Transparency and Independence Before Administrative Boards" (2012) Sask L Rev 13.

Weaver, Russell L & Linda D Jellum, "Neither Fish Nor Fowl: Administrative Judges in the Modern Administrative State" 28 Windsor YB Access Just 243.

Whitaker, K, M Gottheil & M Uhlmann, "Consistency in Tribunal Decision Making: What Really Goes on Behind Closed Doors ..." in Laverne A Jacobs & Anne L Mactavish, eds, *Dialogue*

Between Courts and Tribunals: Essays in Administrative Law and Justice (2001-2007) (Montreal: Les éditions Thémis, 2008).

Wyman, KM, "The Independence of Administrative Tribunals in an Era of Ever Expansive Judicial Independence" (2001) 14 Can J Admin L & Prac 61.

CASES

2747-3174 Québec Inc v Quebec (Régie des permis d'alcool), [1996] 3 SCR 919.

Association des juges administratifs de la Commission des lésions professionnelles c Québec (Procureur général), 2011 QCCS 1614 (decision on appeal).

Beauregard v Canada, [1986] 2 SCR 56.

Bell Canada v Canadian Telephone Employees Association, [2003] 1 SCR 884.

Brosseau v Alberta Securities Commission, [1989] 1 SCR 301.

Canadian Pacific Ltd v Matsqui Indian Band, [1995] 1 SCR 3.

Chrétien v Canada (Commission of Inquiry into the Sponsorship Program and Advertising Activities, Gomery Commission), 2008 FC 802, [2009] 2 FCR 417; aff'd 2010 FCA 283.

Committee for Justice and Liberty v National Energy Board, [1978] 1 SCR 369.

Communications, Energy and Paperworkers Union of Canada, Local 707 v the Alberta Labour Relations Board (2004), 351 AR 267 (QB).

Ellis-Don Ltd v Ontario (Labour Relations Board), 2001 SCC 4, [2001] 1 SCR 221.

Energy Probe v Canada (Atomic Energy Control Board) (1984), 15 DLR (4th) 48 (FCA).

Geza v Canada (Minister of Citizenship and Immigration), [2005] 3 FCR 3 (Fed Ct); rev'd [2006] 4 FCR 377 (CA).

International Woodworkers of America, Local 2-69 v Consolidated-Bathurst Packaging Ltd, [1990] 1 SCR 282.

Keen v Canada (Attorney General), 2009 FC 353.

McKenzie v Minister of Public Safety and Solicitor General, 2006 BCSC 1372, 61 BCLR (4th) 57, leave to appeal to the SCC dismissed without reasons, (2007), 71 BCLR (4th) 1 (CA), [2007] SCCA No 601 (QL).

Newfoundland Telephone Co v Newfoundland (Board of Commissioners of Public Utilities), [1992] 1 SCR 623.

Ocean Port Hotel Ltd v British Columbia (Gen Manager Liquor Control), 2001 SCC 52, [2001] 2 SCR 781.

Old St Boniface Residents Assn Inc v Winnipeg (City), [1990] 3 SCR 1170.

R v Lippé, [1991] 2 SCR 114.

R v S (RD), [1997] 3 SCR 484.

Reference Re Remuneration of Judges of the Provincial Court (PEI), [1997] 3 SCR 3.

Sam Lévy & Associés Inc v Mayrand, [2006] 2 FCR 543 (Fed Ct).

Save Richmond Farmland Society v Richmond (Township), [1990] 3 SCR 1213.

Thamotharem v Canada (Minister of Citizenship and Immigration), 2006 FC 16, [2006] 3 FCR 168, 2007 FCA 198, [2008] 1 FCR 385.

Tremblay v Québec (Commission des affaires sociales), [1992] 1 SCR 952.

Valente v The Queen, [1985] 2 SCR 673.

STATUTES

Adjudicative Tribunals Accountability, Governance and Appointments Act, 2009 (ATAGAA), SO 2009, c 33, Schedule 5.

Administrative Tribunals Act (ATA), SBC 2004, c 45.

Alberta Bill of Rights, RSA 2000, c A-14, s 1(a).

Canadian Bill of Rights, SC 1960, c 44, ss 2(e), (f), reprinted in RSC 1985, App III.

Canadian Charter of Rights and Freedoms, Part I of the *Constitution Act, 1982*, being Schedule B to the *Canada Act 1982* (UK), 1982, c 11, ss 7, 11(d).

Charter of Human Rights and Freedoms, RSQ, c C-12, s 23.

CHAPTER EIGHT

Delegation and Consultation: How the Administrative State Functions and the Importance of Rules

Andrew Green

Faculty of Law, University of Toronto

I. INTRODUCTION

In November 2016, Prime Minister Justin Trudeau made a series of controversial announcements. His government ordered the National Energy Board to allow Kinder Morgan's Trans Mountain pipeline project and Enbridge's Line 3 pipeline project to move ahead but at the same time rejected the Northern Gateway pipeline proposal. Trudeau claimed his government's decision was based on science and evidence, even bringing his own credibility into play by stating that if he thought the Kinder Morgan project was unsafe for the BC coast, he would reject it.

These choices about pipelines had to be made in the face of uncertainty and conflict. On one side was the threat that without the pipelines the economy would falter, not only in

Alberta but across the country. On the other lay the risks from climate change, oil spills, and tanker traffic if the pipelines were built. Both sides marshalled evidence to support their predictions and were backed by strident voices.

So, who should decide how to balance these interests, and how should we resolve the uncertainty? In Canada, the classic story about how decisions are made, such as whether to approve a pipeline, how to determine if a substance is toxic, or whether to admit a refugee, is straightforward. The public elects representatives to the legislature. These representatives hold reasoned debates about policy and enact laws based on those debates. The laws enacted may be broad, such as the *Canadian Environmental Assessment Act, 2012*[1] establishing a process to review projects for their environmental impacts before they are approved. They may also be more closely tailored, such as the *Species at Risk Act*,[2] which addresses only certain species (those "at risk").

These elected representatives, however, seek all manner of policy solutions to issues in such varied areas as the environment, the economy, health care, and food labels. There is too much to do and too much to know for elected representatives, so they do what we all often do in such situations—they delegate to someone else—and this act of delegation and its exercise is the realm of administrative law. Legislators enact statutes to delegate decisions to some part of the executive, whether it is the governor in council (also known as Cabinet), a particular minister, a civil servant, or some board or other decision-maker.[3] The party who is given the power will use its knowledge and expertise to gather evidence, analyze the relevant issues, and make a reasoned decision based on the direction given by the legislators in the relevant statute. The courts are in a position to ensure that executive decision-makers follow fair procedures and stay within the powers given by statute. Behind all this lies the public who will hold their representatives accountable at voting time for any decisions made.

So, that's the classic story—the legislature delegates power to some part of the executive, which makes decisions, as empowered by its statute and informed by expertise, and is monitored by the courts. There is some truth in this simple story; however, as with much of administrative law, the actual story is more complicated.[4] Consider the Northern Gateway pipeline decision. Under the *National Energy Board Act*, Parliament did delegate the power to decide to the executive—but, specifically, delegated power to Cabinet, a body subject to political accountability and with members of diverse backgrounds, but not specific expertise in energy.[5] It granted Cabinet the power to decide "on the widest considerations of policy

---

1   SC 2012, c 19.

2   SC 2002, c 29.

3   See Chapter 1, A Historical Map for Administrative Law: There Be Dragons, for a discusson of who is included in the "executive."

4   For a discussion of the differences in the United States between the assumptions about how administrative law works and the actual day-to-day workings of the administrative state, see Daniel A Farber and Anne Joseph O'Connell, "The Lost World of Administrative Law" (2014) 92 Texas Law Review 1137. They see key assumptions in the United States as "that statutes delegate authority to particular agencies (rather than, for example, to the Executive Branch as a whole); that agency decisions through discrete actions are based on evidence rather than political perspectives and that we can identify the particular evidence before the agency (aka 'the record'); that certain kinds of reasons and only those reasons are allowed; that one agency, rather than many, makes the decision; and that the output of the administrative process consists of discrete, severable decisions."

5   *National Energy Board Act*, RSC 1985, c N-7, s 54.

and public interest assessed on the basis of polycentric, subjective, or indistinct criteria and shaped by its view of economics, cultural considerations, environmental considerations, and the broader public interest."[6] Parliament included an expert body as part of the decision-making process—the National Energy Board—which gathered information and was part of a public hearing process that resulted in a report to Cabinet recommending approval of the pipeline. The board established general rules for itself about how the hearings should take place, as well as rules (subject to Cabinet approval) about how pipelines are to be constructed.[7] Despite the statute and powers delegated to Cabinet to make decisions regarding the pipeline, environmental and Indigenous groups challenged the report and the Cabinet decision in court. Based on the extremely broad nature of the delegated power and the role played by Cabinet, the Federal Court of Appeal gave Cabinet the "widest margin of appreciation over these questions."[8] It found Cabinet's decision to be reasonable as "[t]o rule otherwise would be to second-guess the governor in council's appreciation of the facts, its choice of policy, its access to scientific expertise and its evaluation and weighing of competing public interest considerations, matters very much outside of the ken of the courts."[9] It did, however, find that the Cabinet had failed to fulfill its duty to consult Indigenous Peoples in its initial approval of the Northern Gateway pipeline.

The federal government's Northern Gateway pipeline decision thus involved a combination of one-off discretionary decisions (the Cabinet "may" direct the board to issue a certificate or dismiss the application), rules governing how the decision is to be made and how to construct pipelines, public hearings, and judicial review by a court of the administrative process and decision. While Parliament formally gave Cabinet the power to decide, different parties took part in the decision using different types of processes. Administrative law is about how such powers are and should be employed and ultimately whose decision prevails. While the classic story tells of a dominant legislature with strong though subordinate partners in the executive and the courts, in fact, power can shift between these bodies over time and across issues. At times in the past, the courts have taken a strong role in deciding policy, although they are ostensibly backing off such a role recently. At other times, the executive (or, more properly, some part of the executive) runs with the power given to it by the legislature beyond what would seem to be the natural limits of its mandate.

This chapter focuses on a particularly important, though underappreciated, aspect of how power is allocated under administrative law in Canada—the ability of an administrative decision-maker to make and apply rules or soft law (such as guidelines). Before going any further, however, it is important to be clear on terminology. **Rules** are legally binding requirements and, as such, the legislature has to expressly grant to the decision-maker in a statute the power to make rules.[10] In this chapter, all binding requirements are termed "rules," including rules and regulations as well as other forms of binding requirements such

---

6 *Gitxaala Nation v Canada*, 2016 FCA 187 at para 154 [*Gitxaala Nation*].
7 National Energy Board Rules of Practice and Procedure, 1995 (SOR/95-208) and National Energy Board Onshore Pipeline Regulations (SOR/99-294).
8 *Gitxaala Nation, supra* note 6 at para 155.
9 *Ibid* at para 157.
10 Both regulations and rules are legally binding and arise from a statutory power. The federal *Statutory Instruments Act*, RSC 1985, c S-22, includes both in the term "statutory instruments." The term "regulation" is generally used in statutes where there is a delegation of the power to fill in detailed requirements. Rules and regulations are also sometimes called "delegated legislation."

as municipal by-laws and certain orders in council made by Cabinet. They cover such diverse issues as permissible levels of pollution, the required content of a prospectus, working conditions in mines, and record-keeping requirements for beekeepers.

Soft law, on the other hand, is also developed by administrative decision-makers but is not legally binding. However, as we will see, soft law, which includes guidelines or policies, plays an important role in how decisions are made, both procedurally and substantively.[11] Guidelines may, for example, structure how an immigration officer views whether an individual deserves humanitarian and compassionate consideration, potentially altering the course of the individual's life.[12] As we will discuss, soft law may or may not be made following a formal process where the public or others have input. Further, as they are not directly legally binding in that they do not directly impose a legal requirement, the power to make soft law does not have to be expressly provided for in a statute.

Both rules and soft law are intended to give general guidance on how to make future decisions. They are key to understanding how policy is set because they fill in gaps in statutes. Rules and soft law may relate to process, such as in the case of National Energy Board (NEB) where the Act empowers the board to hold hearings concerning pipelines, but allows the board broad discretion over how those hearings are to take place.[13] They may also deal with substance, such as regulations exempting certain industrial activities from having to comply with species-at-risk requirements.[14]

Rules and guidelines are in theory different than adjudication. Adjudication deals with one-off disputes: Did this individual commit insider trading? Or does this person satisfy the requirements to stay in the country as a refugee? However, rules and adjudication blend into each other, and the line between them can be hard to see. Both require expertise. Further, rules can be quite specific, such as a regulation that the tariff provisions of the *National Energy Board Act* apply to anyone who was operating a pipeline on November 2, 1959.[15] On the other hand, what may be categorized as adjudication may have broad implications, such as a pipeline hearing in which a board panel concludes that upstream greenhouse gas emissions are not part of its mandate. Adjudication is well covered in the rest of this book, but rules require separate consideration given their importance.

Before we discuss how rules and guidelines are made, we begin in Section II by discussing why we may want legislators to delegate power to others to make detailed policy decisions and, in particular, the need to take advantage of the expertise and experience of different decision-makers. We then turn in Section III to the risks raised by delegation, where the party

---

11   See e.g. Lorne Sossin & Charles Smith, "Hard Choices and Soft Law: Ethical Codes, Policy Guidelines, and the Role of Law in Regulating Government" (2003) 40 Alta L Rev 867; France Houle & Lorne Sossin, "Tribunals and Guidelines: Exploring the Relationship Between Fairness and Legitimacy in Administrative Decision-Making" (2006) 46 Can Pub Admin 283.

12   See *Baker v Canada (Minister of Citizenship and Immigration)*, [1999] 2 SCR 817 [*Baker*]. For a more recent example (discussed further below), see *Kanthasamy v Canada (Citizenship and Immigration)*, 2015 SCC 61 [*Kanthasamy*].

13   *National Energy Board Act*, RSC 1985, c N-7, s 8 and National Energy Board Rules of Practice and Procedure, 1995 (SOR 95/-208).

14   *Wildlands League v Ontario (Natural Resources and Forestry)*, 2016 ONCA 741 [*Wildlands League*] (upholding regulations under Ontario's *Species at Risk Act*, SC 2002 c 29, exempting certain activities from the prohibitions under the Act on harming species at risk or their habitat).

15   National Energy Board Order No MO-62-69, CRC, c 1055.

delegating the power loses some control over how the resulting policy decisions actually turn out. In Section IV we look at delegation of the power to make rules and how these benefits and risks are dealt with in Canada—focusing on the key issues of how much power is delegated, to whom the power is given, what processes are used to make rules, and, finally, what type of oversight is necessary. The issue of delegation is common across all regulatory systems, but different countries balance the benefits and risks in different ways, both as a matter of where the emphasis lies in administrative law and because of the nature of the background institutions (such as whether it is a Parliamentary system, such as it is in Canada, or a Presidential system, as it is in the United States). To give a point of comparison, we will look at some of the ways the United States attempts to solve the problem of delegation. Finally, in Section V we will discuss the need to balance power across the different players and how the allocation of power changes over time. The executive generally plays a dominant role in shaping policy in many areas in Canada, with the legislature and the courts at times seeming to take subordinate roles.

II. WHY DO LEGISLATURES DELEGATE TO ADMINISTRATIVE DECISION-MAKERS?

When you examine the range of issues that are covered by rules or soft law, it becomes immediately apparent how important they are to our lives.[16] Yet despite their importance, legislatures do not make these detailed prescriptions about our lives but instead delegate this power to members of the executive, including ministers, boards and tribunals, and self-regulating bodies like the Law Society of Ontario.

Why do legislators give others the power to make such important policy decisions?[17] The primary reason legislators delegate power is *expertise*.[18] They cannot possibly have sufficient expertise to understand and evaluate all the various, detailed requirements in the vast range of areas that comprise the regulatory and welfare state. Such expertise requires education and training as well as experience in dealing with a particular issue. For example, developing the appropriate procedures for an immigration hearing may require the expertise of individuals who have been involved in many such hearings. Developing air pollution standards requires an understanding of science as well as of the manner in which industries use and dispose of various pollutants. Developing rules for a securities market requires knowledge of how these markets function, the role of the consumer, and the manner in which corporations make decisions. Although individual legislators may have some information on these

---

16 Taggart states that "[i]t is trite to observe that delegated legislation ... often has more impact on the lives of ordinary citizens than do most full-blown Acts of Parliament." Michael Taggart, "From 'Parliamentary Powers' to Privatization: The Chequered History of Delegated Legislation in the Twentieth Century" (2005) 55 UTLJ 575.

17 Such shifting of responsibility raised concerns about the constitutionality of delegated powers when it became increasingly common in the early part of the 20th century. See *ibid* for a discussion of the history of delegated legislation.

18 As a result, expertise is an important concept in administrative law. As Kate Glover discusses in Chapter 5, expertise underlies the tests related to procedural fairness and, as Audrey Macklin discusses in Chapter 11, it has been crucial in the determination of the standard of review courts use when reviewing the substance of administrative decisions.

issues, the concern is that legislators cannot make optimal decisions in all these areas because of their lack of expertise. The argument, therefore, is that legislators should delegate the power to fill in the details to individuals or groups who do have the expertise.

There is, however, a related reason for delegation. Even if they had the expertise, legislators lack the *time and information* to make all the decisions necessary for the functioning of the current regulatory and welfare state. They lack the time to think through all the different ways in which specific provisions should be structured, relate to other provisions, and may apply in particular circumstances. For example, in regulating professions such as optometry, legislators may enact a broad provision that a member of the College of Optometry may be found guilty of professional misconduct if he or she contravenes a requirement specified in regulations and then delegate the power to make the regulation to the college itself. Even if it were possible to do so, legislators do not have the time to consider all the potential ways in which an optometrist might engage in professional misconduct.

The lack of time raises the related point that, even with time and expertise, legislators never have complete information about the future. They cannot possibly know all the new ways in which optometrists may think to act unprofessionally, or all the different pollutants that may be invented, or the different types of securities that may be developed. Legislation is therefore necessarily and unavoidably incomplete. Because legislation can be difficult and time-consuming to alter, legislators may delegate the power to fill in requirements in order to increase *flexibility*—to allow the requirements to be changed as new information arises. This flexibility is particularly important in rapidly changing areas such as environmental and securities regulation.

When delegating power, legislators have to decide whether to grant the power to adjudicate disputes between parties and/or to make rules about, for example, the process of decision-making or how policy decisions must be taken. As we discussed, the line between adjudication and rule making is not clearcut, and both require expertise. However, a key difference is that adjudication is more flexible and allows fine tailoring to different fact situations, while rules bring more certainty and consistency because of their more general nature.

These issues of expertise, time, and information also explain why there is soft law. While not legally binding, soft law such as policies and guidelines can have significant impacts on people's lives. For example, guidelines were central to *Baker*.[19] In that case, Ms Baker was an overstayer in Canada and had been ordered deported. She applied to the immigration minister to exercise his discretion under the *Immigration Act*[20] to grant humanitarian and compassionate exemptions. She was seeking to stay in Canada pending determination of her application for permanent residency.[21] As a practical matter, immigration officers (not the minister) exercised the power to grant humanitarian and compassionate exemptions in individual cases. However, the minister had issued guidelines setting out the bases on which immigration officers should decide whether the individual deserved humanitarian and compassionate consideration. Although these guidelines were not legally binding, the Supreme Court of Canada took them into account in deciding that the officer had not acted reasonably in failing to exercise the humanitarian and compassionate power in favour of Ms Baker. These guidelines were therefore important to the court in deciding the limits on

---

19   *Supra* note 12.
20   SC 1976-77, c 52.
21   For a discussion of the facts of *Baker*, see Kate Glover, Chapter 5.

the discretion of the minister (delegated to an immigration officer) to be exercised under the *Immigration Act*.

Soft law has some advantages over rules. Both provide a greater measure of certainty to those who come before regulatory decision-makers. However, soft law is much more easily adaptable to changing circumstances, as making soft law is less likely to involve time-consuming and costly procedural steps than rule making. As we will discuss below, regulation-making involves mandatory procedures (such as pre-publication) whereas guidelines come in a variety of forms and result from a range of different types of processes, some of which are informal and non-public. As the Federal Court of Canada stated:

> Effective decision-making by administrative agencies often involves striking a balance between general rules and the exercise of ad hoc discretion or, to put it another way, between the benefits of certainty and consistency on the one hand, and of flexibility and fact-specific solutions on the other. Legislative instruments (including such non-legally binding "soft law" documents as policy statements, guidelines, manuals and handbooks) can assist members of the public to predict how an agency is likely to exercise its statutory discretion and to arrange their affairs accordingly, and enable an agency to deal with a problem comprehensively and proactively, rather than incrementally and reactively on a case by case basis. ... Because "soft law" instruments may be put in place relatively easily and adjusted in the light of day-to-day experience, they may be preferable to formal rules requiring external approval and, possibly, drafting appropriate for legislation.[22]

While soft law may have some advantages over rules from an efficiency perspective because they are easily altered, this ease of adjustment raises concerns about democratic legitimacy as it may stem from a lack of procedural safeguards.

Legislators therefore may want to set out broad policy decisions in legislation. They leave these decisions necessarily incomplete, either because they lack the expertise to make the decisions or because they lack the time and information needed to make the requirements at the time of enactment. Legislators delegate the power to make rules and soft law in order to allow others to fill in the gaps left in the legislation.

III. THE RISKS OF DELEGATION

While there are benefits to the legislature delegating power, delegation is not without its risks, nor is it necessarily always benign. Delegation raises the risk that those who are making the rules or soft law are not following the wishes or expectations of those who delegated the power. This risk arises because of a *principal–agent problem* inherent in such delegation.[23] The principal–agent problem arises in all sorts of settings when one party (the principal) gives another party (the agent) the power to undertake some task on the principal's behalf. For example, the principal–agent problem arises when you (as a principal) put your faith in

---

22 *Canada (Minister of Citizenship and Immigration) v Thamotharem*, 2007 FCA 198 at paras 55-56 [*Thamotharem*].
23 For a good discussion of the principal–agent problem and its relationship to administrative law, see Matthew D McCubbins, Roger G Noll & Barry R Weingast, "Administrative Procedures as Instruments of Political Control" (1987) 3 JL Econ & Org 243. See also Adrian Vermeule, "The Administrative State: Law, Democracy, and Knowledge" in Mark Tushnet, Mark Graber & Sanford Levinson, eds, *The Oxford Handbook of the US Constitution* (New York: Oxford University Press, 2015).

a real estate agent to do the best possible job for you, but you cannot know if the agent is devoting as much time to your house as she should, as there may be other higher-valued houses that she would make more money from selling. In the administrative law context, this principal–agent problem arises because the administrative agent who makes the rules or soft law may not be following the wishes of the legislature (which can be termed "the principal").

We discussed above the reasons why legislatures (the principal) both need and wish to delegate powers to administrative decision-makers (agents) for reasons of expertise, information, and time. The risks arise from the same features that make principals want to have agents undertake the task for them. The principal's lack of expertise, information, or time means that he or she has difficulty ensuring that the agent is actually acting in his or her best interests in carrying out the task.

Two concerns arise when legislators delegate power to the executive to adjudicate or to make rules or soft law. First, the agent (for example, the party making the rules or soft law) may follow its own views and values rather than the legislators' views or values in exercising the power. Because legislators often enact legislation setting out only broad directions for policy, a ministry or agency making regulations under such legislation has considerable scope to determine the content of the detailed rules. The rule-maker may, however, have very different views from the legislators of what constitutes the appropriate rule or guideline in particular cases.[24] Legislators do not have the expertise, time, or information to monitor the content of each rule or guideline. The agent may in such cases be attempting to further the public interest but is doing so in the way it (as opposed to the legislature) believes is best.

Second, the administrative agent may not even be attempting to further the public interest; it may, instead, be seeking to further its own interest. For example, if regulated parties such as a particular industry group are able to offer some form of inducement to members of the Ontario Securities Commission (such as future job opportunities), these members may be influenced in how they make rules or soft law. Such influence by private actors is often termed "capture." Capture arises "where organized interest groups successfully act to vindicate their goals through government policy at the expense of the public interest," such as through long-term relationships with regulators or provision of biased information.[25] Such capture can be by industry groups but also by groups favouring greater regulation, such as environmental groups or labour organizations. Alternatively, the agent may in some cases simply not want to expend the effort to regulate in a particular area or may seek to use its power to pursue projects or regulations that further its own ends (such as greater job security, power, or resources) rather than the public interest.

---

24   As discussed below, the impact of such a divergence in views will depend in part on the institutional structures in place. For example, in a Westminster system, the legislature and the executive are to some extent connected. Cabinet decides in large part how much detail is provided in legislation and how much is delegated to others to fill in. The minister is then responsible to Parliament for the resulting regulation. Although this system may provide a more direct connection and different dynamic between the rule-maker and the legislatures than the stricter separation of power in the United States, the lack of time, expertise, and information affect legislators' ability to monitor and control rule-makers in both systems.

25   Michael A Livermore & Richard L Revesz, "Regulatory Review, Capture and Agency Inaction" (2013) 101 Georgetown LJ 1337 at 1340.

Similarly, legislators themselves may delegate in order to further their own interests, such as where they enact broad legislation and delegate rule-making powers to avoid blame for stringent regulations or to get credit for seeming to take strong action but not actually doing anything. The legislature could, for example, enact very broad, tough-sounding pollution control legislation and then delegate the details to Cabinet to work out. Cabinet could then exempt or "grandfather" certain parties, such as particularly powerful industry groups. The legislators seek credit for enacting strong legislation but also are able to satisfy politically powerful parties.[26]

This principal–agent problem arises in any delegation of power where it is difficult for the principal to monitor the actions of the agent. The extent of the problem will vary depending on the relationship between the principal and the agent. The close connection between ministers and their ministries at least provides some (though at times weak) accountability to legislators for those making rules in ministries. The problem may become worse as the power to make rules is delegated to parties more independent of government. As Taggart notes, one of the trends of most concern in delegated legislation is the involvement of private parties (including regulated parties) in making rules. For example, governments in recent years have contracted out public services to private actors, giving rise to questions about the accountability of, and control by, legislators over these actors.[27]

IV. ALLOCATING POWER AND CONTROLLING RISKS

The Canadian administrative state is built on the core principle of legislative supremacy. Elected legislators have the principal power to determine policy and to decide who makes particular decisions. As the Supreme Court of Canada has noted, there is a "foundational democratic principle, which finds an expression in the initiatives of Parliament and legislatures to create various administrative bodies and endow them with broad powers."[28]

So how then should these powers to set policy be allocated to take advantage of the strengths of delegation in terms of leveraging expertise, experience, and flexibility, while at the same time minimize the risks from delegation, for example, that an administrative decision-maker will make choices that do not align with what the legislature intended? As we have seen, legislators can delegate the power to adjudicate disputes or to make more general rules. We will focus in this section on delegation of the power to make rules and soft law. In order to get a sense of how power is allocated and the steps that can be taken to control the risks, we need to think about some key questions:

- How much power should be delegated?
- To whom should the power be given?
- How should the power be exercised?
- How should we monitor how the powers are being used?

---

26 See for example, Matthew C Stephenson, "Legislative Allocation of Delegated Power: Uncertainty, Risk, and the Choice Between Agencies and Courts" (2006) 119 Harv L Rev 1035.

27 Taggart, *supra* note 16.

28 *Dunsmuir v New Brunswick*, 2008 SCC 9, [2008] 1 SCR 190 at para 27 [*Dunsmuir*].

These questions are all inter-related and cannot be cleanly separated. However, to get a sense of the issues around delegated rule-making power, it is useful to at least initially deal with them individually.

A. How Much Power Should Be Delegated?

One obvious question legislators must ask is how much power should they exercise them-selves and how much should they delegate. An Act may grant broad powers to make regu-lations. Under the *Food and Drugs Act*, Cabinet "may make regulations for carrying the purposes and provisions of this Act into effect" including "prescribing standards of compos-ition, strength, potency, purity, quality or other property of any article of food, drug, cos-metic or device."[29] Or even more broadly, under the *Competition Act*, "The Governor in Council may make such regulations as are necessary for carrying out this Act and for the ef-ficient administration thereof."[30] Legislators may delegate the power to make rules about substance—such as the composition of food—or process. For example, under the *National Energy Board Act*, the board "may make rules respecting ... the procedure for making appli-cations, representations and complaints to the Board and the conduct of hearings before the Board, and generally the manner of conducting any business before the Board."[31]

While legislators may grant broad powers to make rules, they may at the same time at-tempt to structure how an Act is interpreted including how the regulation-making powers will be viewed. One way they may try to structure interpretation is by setting out the pur-poses of the Act. The *Competition Act*, for example, states:

> The purpose of this Act is to maintain and encourage competition in Canada in order to pro-mote the efficiency and adaptability of the Canadian economy, in order to expand opportun-ities for Canadian participation in world markets while at the same time recognizing the role of foreign competition in Canada, in order to ensure that small and medium-sized enterprises have an equitable opportunity to participate in the Canadian economy and in order to provide con-sumers with competitive prices and product choices.[32]

Such purpose sections aid those making regulations—and to a certain extent the courts, as we will see, in overseeing the actions of administrative decision-makers—in understanding how broad regulatory powers should be used. However, statutes often do not have such clear statements, and, even when they do, the statements themselves may be very broad and bring in competing considerations.

In addition to purposes sections, legislators may place more particular limitations on how the power to make rules is to be exercised. The Harper government, for example, amended

---

29   RSC 1985, c F-27, s 30(1).
30   RSC 1985, c C-34, s 128(1).
31   RSC 1985, c N-7, s 8.
32   *Competition Act*, RSC 1985, c C-34, s 1.1. Others set out the underlying policy directly, such as the *Canada Transportation Act,* which declares a National Transportation Policy in the Act that "a competitive, eco-nomic and efficient national transportation that meets the highest practical safety and security stan-dards and contributes to a sustainable environment and makes the best use of all modes of transportation at the lowest total cost is essential to serve the needs of its users, advance the well-being of Canadians and enable competitiveness and economic growth in both urban and rural areas in Canada." See *Canada Transportation Act*, SC 1996, c 10, s 5.

the *Fisheries Act* to constrain the power to make certain regulations.[33] Under s 35 of the Act, "No person may carry on any work, undertaking or activity that results in serious harm to fish that are part of a commercial, recreational or Aboriginal fishery, or to fish that support such a fishery," except in certain circumstances. One of those circumstances is that the work, undertaking, or activity is prescribed by regulation, and the minister is empowered to make regulations exempting works, undertakings, and activities from this prohibition on serious harm to fish. However, ss 6 and 6.1 of the Act state that

6 Before recommending to the Governor in Council that a regulation be made in respect of section 35 … the Minister shall consider the following factors:
(a) the contribution of the relevant fish to the ongoing productivity of commercial, recreational or Aboriginal fisheries;
(b) fisheries management objectives;
(c) whether there are measures and standards to avoid, mitigate or offset serious harm to fish that are part of a commercial, recreational or Aboriginal fishery, or that support such a fishery; and
(d) the public interest.
6.1 The purpose of section 6, and of the provisions set out in that section, is to provide for the sustainability and ongoing productivity of commercial, recreational and Aboriginal fisheries.

These provisions give greater guidance to the minister as to what types of regulations are consistent with the Act and to the courts, if called upon to review the decision, as to whether the minister has stayed within her powers.

Soft law, as we discussed, does not require a statutory basis, as it is not legally binding. However, in some cases, legislators do explicitly provide for guidelines within legislation. For example, the *Immigration and Refugee Protection Act* creates an Immigration and Refugee Board, which hears a range of reviews and appeals relating to such matters as individuals claiming refugee status or admissibility decisions for foreign nationals.[34] The Refugee Appeal Division alone resolved 3,000 appeals of refugee protection claims in 2016.[35] Given the large number of cases, the possibility exists for a huge variation in decisions. For example, when a non-Canadian is detained for an immigration infraction, the board may review the detention. On one report, board members in Ontario were almost three times more likely to release detained individuals than members in the rest of Canada.[36] One method to attempt to reduce such variance across decision-makers is through guidelines that aim to bring some uniformity in approach. The Act states that the chairperson of the board "may issue guidelines in writing to members of the Board and identify decisions of the Board as jurisprudential guides, after consulting with the Deputy Chairpersons, to assist members in

---

33 RSC 1985, c F-14.
34 SC 2001, c 27.
35 Immigration and Refugee Board of Canada, *2017-18 Departmental Plan—Part III*, online: <http://www.irb-cisr.gc.ca/Eng/BoaCom/pubs/Pages/DpPm1718partIII.aspx>.
36 Adrian Humphreys, "Immigration and Refugee Board in Ontario Less Likely to Release Detainees Than in Rest of Canada: Analysis" *National Post* (7 March 2017), online: <http://nationalpost.com/news/canada/refugee-board-in-ontario-much-less-likely-to-release-detainees-than-in-rest-of-canada-analysis/wcm/e2b9a860-4fd9-49fc-95cc-88c2379d16e4>. Note that this analysis does not appear to account for various factors that could account for differences across regions such as differences in types of cases that come before the board in each region.

carrying out their duties."[37] The chair has issued nine guidelines covering issues from how to approach detention decisions to, most recently, promoting greater understanding of cases involving sexual orientation and gender identity and expression.[38]

The breadth of the power the legislature delegates to others will depend on a number of factors, such as the capacity of the legislature to make detailed statutory rules.[39] If the members of the legislatures have the time, resources, and expertise to make particular rules, they will be more likely to set out detailed requirements in legislation. The willingness of the legislature to delegate powers will also depend on its confidence in the party exercising the power and that there are controls on the exercise of discretion, such as what processes they have to follow and what oversight exists. We turn to these issues next.

B. To Whom Should the Power Be Given?

Legislators will be more likely to delegate broad powers to make rules the more they trust the agent making the rules to follow their policy preferences. This trust will vary according to such factors as the level of control the legislators have over those making the policy. For example, in Canada legislators may delegate rule-making powers in broad terms because Cabinet (whose members are generally part of both the legislature and the executive) may either be making the rules or have some control over the ministry or other body making the rules. This element of trust, however, raises a second type of principal–agent problem: trust between the public and elected officials. The ability of Cabinet to both set the scope of discretion and control the exercise of that discretion provides the party in power a significant ability to steer the details of policy at the expense of other elected members of the legislature.[40] How much power the legislature delegates may therefore depend on whether there is a majority or minority government. In a minority government situation, for example, the opposition parties have greater bargaining power and, thus, may be less likely to grant broad discretion to ministries controlled by the ruling party.[41]

As we have seen, legislatures often choose to delegate to Cabinet—the most powerful part of the executive. In fact, Cabinet holds the power to make a wide range of regulations under many different statutes at the federal level from the *Canada Business Corporations Act*[42] and the *Controlled Drugs and Substances Act*[43] to the *Youth Criminal Justice Act*[44] and the

---

37   SC 2001, c 27, s 159(1)(h).

38   The Chairperson's Guidelines for the Immigration and Refugee Board can be found at <http://www.irb-cisr.gc.ca/Eng/BoaCom/references/pol/GuiDir/Pages/index.aspx>.

39   See, for example, John D Huber, Charles R Shipan & Madelaine Pfahler, "Legislatures and Statutory Control of Bureaucracy" (2001) 45 Am J Pol Sci 330 (discussing some of the factors influencing the degree of discretion granted by legislatures including bargaining costs, legislative capacity, and the availability of non-statutory means of control).

40   David Mullan, *Administrative Law* (Toronto: Irwin Law, 2001) and Taggart, *supra* note 16.

41   An example is the *Kyoto Protocol Implementation Act*, SC 2007, c 30, which was a federal private member's bill aimed at reducing the discretion of the executive in the area of climate change, ostensibly by requiring the government to develop and implement a plan to meet Canada's emission reduction commitments under the Kyoto Protocol. The Federal Court, however, held these requirements to be non-justiciable: *Friends of the Earth v Canada (Governor in Council)*, 2008 FC 1183, [2009] 3 FCR 201.

42   RSC 1985, c C-44.

43   SC 1996, c 19.

44   SC 2002, c 1.

Yukon First Nations Land Claims Settlement Act.[45] At the other end of the spectrum, legislators may delegate the power to make rules to a relatively arm's-length body, such as the Office of the Superintendent of Financial Institutions, which regulates banks. The superintendent has protections under its enabling statute to foster independence such as holding office for a term of seven years (so longer than the election cycle).[46] The superintendent has the power to make numerous decisions that have significant impacts on the Canadian economy and has used its powers to make guidelines about important matters such as the capital requirements of banks.

However, even where legislators delegate power to a relatively independent body, they often ensure that Cabinet retains some control. In the case of the NEB making regulations about pipeline safety, for example, the board may make the regulations, but they are subject to approval by Cabinet. In other cases, the legislature mixes responsibility, such as in the case of the *Species at Risk Act*. Cabinet has discretion as to whether to order a species be added to the "List of Wildlife Species at Risk" under the *Species at Risk Act*.[47] Listing triggers various protections for the species and its habitat under the Act. An expert body (the Committee on the Status of Endangered Wildlife in Canada, or COSEWIC) makes a recommendation to place a species on the list. COSEWIC is an advisory panel of academics, consultants, and biologists who are elected by their peers. If COSEWIC recommends placing a species on the list, Cabinet has nine months to decide whether to add the species to the list or not. If it chooses not to add the species to the list, Cabinet must give reasons for not adding the species. If it takes no actions within the nine months, the minister must add the species to the list. Elgie calls this "constrained discretion," as Cabinet discretion is constrained by having to give reasons for going against the expert recommendations and must act within a specific period of time with the default being listing of the species.[48]

Legislatures may also attempt to indirectly control the exercise of discretion through the choice of body that is granted the discretion.[49] Consider the decision about whether to approve the Kinder Morgan pipeline. The outcome may be different or at least influenced depending on whether the decision is delegated to a body whose mandate mainly concerns energy regulation (such as the National Energy Board), which may frame the issue around trade, energy, and economic growth, as opposed to an agency whose key function is to regulate environmental issues (in which case the regulatory discourse may be shaped around scientific knowledge) or a body whose function is to bring about reconciliation between the Crown and Indigenous Peoples. Each of these bodies may have the expertise to make the rules or soft law, but their actual policy preferences may differ depending on their mission or composition.

Further, the legislature may attempt to steer how the powers are used by determining the composition of the body that is exercising the discretion, such as by specifying that the

---

45   SC 1994, c 34.

46   *Office of the Superintendent of Financial Institutions Act*, RSC 1985, c 18 (3d Supp), Part I, s 5.

47   *Species at Risk Act*, SC 2002, c 29, s 27 contains the requirements on amending the "Species at Risk List."

48   For a discussion of this "constrained discretion," see Stewart Elgie, "Statutory Structure and Species Survival: How constraints on Cabinet discretion affect Endangered Species Listing Outcomes" (2008) 19 J Envtl L & Prac 1.

49   David B Spence, "Managing Delegation Ex Ante: Using Law to Steer Administrative Agencies" (1999) 28 J Legal Stud 413.

decision-making body be composed of representatives of different groups. For example, the *Law Society Act* in Ontario provides that the Law Society of Ontario is to be governed by Convocation, which is composed of benchers. Convocation has the ability to make different types of rules such as by-laws to set the qualifications for those who may be licensed to practice law in Ontario and to make certain regulations (subject to approval of the provincial Cabinet) including about the appointment of a Complaints Resolution Commissioner.[50] The Act provides that 40 persons who are licensed to practise law in Ontario and five persons who are licensed to provide legal services shall be elected to Convocation.[51] In addition, the provincial Cabinet may appoint eight non-licensees to Convocation as lay-benchers.[52] The legislature thus may influence the content of the rules by diversifying (at least slightly) the composition of Convocation—on the assumption that a more representative Convocation is less likely to adopt self-interested or inefficient regulations. Similarly under the *Canada Labour Code*, the Canada Industrial Relations Board is to be composed of a chair and a number of vice chairs, all of whom "must have experience and expertise in industrial relations."[53] It is also to include an equal number of representatives of employees and employers. The board has broad powers to make regulations, such as rules of procedure, determination of collective bargaining units, criteria for determining whether an employee is a member of a trade union, and the conditions for valid strike or lockout votes.[54]

So, legislators paint the broad strokes of who is to exercise rule-making power. However, there is still significant work to be done to fill in the outline, work that is typically done by Cabinet. The *National Energy Board Act*, for example, establishes the National Energy Board and states that the board is to consist "of not more than nine members to be appointed by the Governor in Council."[55] It places some weak constraints on who can be a member, including that members must be Canadian citizens or permanent residents and cannot be engaged in the business of producing, selling, buying, or dealing in hydrocarbons or electricity.[56]

Beyond these weak constraints, however, the Cabinet has broad discretion over appointments to these bodies. It may then be able to steer the exercise of discretion by assigning people with particular beliefs or skills to the positions. A body composed of former energy industry executives may decide differently than a body of environmental scientists. As is discussed further by Laverne Jacobs in Chapter 7, The Dynamics of Independence, Impartiality, and Bias in the Canadian Administrative State, the Cabinet may also possibly remove members of different decision-making bodies, though often not easily. Legislators may set different constraints on removing members of boards or tribunals from office. In the case of the Canada Industrial Relations Board, for example, chairs and vice chairs are appointed for terms of five years and are to hold office during good behaviour though they are subject to removal at any time for cause.[57] National Energy Board members are appointed for terms of

---

50   *Law Society Act*, RSO 1990, c L.8, ss 62 and 63.

51   *Ibid*, ss 15 and 16.

52   *Ibid*, s 23.

53   *Canada Labour Code*, RSC 1985, c L-2, s 9 [*Canada Labour Code*].

54   *Ibid*, s 15.

55   RSC 1985, c N-7, s 3(1) [*National Energy Board*].

56   *Ibid*, s 3(4).

57   *Canada Labour Code*, s 9.

seven years during good behaviour, though they "may be removed at any time by the Governor in Council on address of the Senate and House of Commons."[58] The Cabinet then can potentially use its power to appoint, and with more difficulty its power to remove, decision-makers who will make rules in line with its preferences.

Even more broadly, the legislature can attempt to keep other bodies from having any input into the exercise of discretion. One of the most important examples—discussed in earlier chapters—is of the legislature attempting to protect the decisions of its delegates from review by the courts. Legislators may insert privative clauses of various strengths into statutes that may, for example, state that the decision of a body is final and not reviewable by any court. Courts have been reticent to give full effect to such clauses.[59] However, they can have the effect of making courts more hesitant to intervene or raise the costs of individuals accessing the courts. Some Acts such as the *National Energy Board Act* add another wrinkle. The Act allows for appeals to the Federal Court of Appeal but makes it more difficult to get a hearing by requiring that an appeal receive leave of the court.[60] This screen on accessing judicial reviews raises the direct costs of launching an appeal (as there is an extra step in the process) and all other things being equal reduces the probability of a review being heard.[61]

The identity of the rule-maker therefore may be important to the resulting rules. The choice can influence the resulting rules both through the mandate of the rule-maker as well as its expertise (or lack thereof). Legislature and Cabinet may also take other measures to either enhance or hamper the attributes of the decision-maker and its processes, such as through the resources given to the rule-maker. Delegating rule-making power to an under-resourced body, even an expert one, can lead to fewer rules and/or a reliance by the body on information from parties who have a vested interest in the outcome (such as an environmental assessment body relying heavily on information from a proponent of a project).

C. How Should the Power Be Exercised?

Decisions can be influenced not only by who makes them, but also by how they are made. There is a wide range of processes that a body creating rules could follow. At one extreme, it could make the rules based on no external information and no consultation with any other group. At the other, the body could hold a full hearing on the rule, taking submissions from different groups and engaging in consultations over draft rules. Actual decision-making processes generally fall somewhere between these extremes. This section first discusses why process, and in particular public consultation, is important. It then looks at how rule-making processes are set by the legislature, the executive, and the courts as well as the important shift in process to encompass the duty to consult.

---

58 *National Energy Board*, s 3(2).

59 See the dicussion in Chapter 1 on discussing privative clauses.

60 *National Energy Board*, s 22(1).

61 See also the *Immigration and Refugee Protection Act*, SC 2001, c 27 [IRPA] on requiring leave to seek judicial review. These provisions concerning leave have resulted in a high variance in leave grants by particular judges in the context of refugee determinations: Sean Rehaag, "Judicial Review of Refugee Determinations: The Luck of the Draw?" (2012) 38:1 Queens LJ 1.

1. Why Consult?

Making rules or guidelines may involve many different processes to gather and analyze information and formulate appropriate rules. A key feature of these processes is the extent of public participation. Why might we want to have a process that includes public participation? The principal reason is that it may result in better rules or guidelines. First, process requirements may ensure that those making the rules or guidelines have all the relevant information. This information may, for example, be about the costs and the benefits of a particular rule, such as how much it would cost regulated parties to comply with the rule (for example, the cost of putting safety equipment on all machines to protect workers) or how the regulated activity affects the general public (such as the impact of noise pollution on their daily activities). It may also provide information on how the public and the regulated party value the changes proposed under the rule. Consider a rule limiting greenhouse gas emissions. Public consultation may provide the party making the rule with a better understanding of the extent to which the public cares about and is willing to bear costs of addressing climate change. This additional information may reduce the mistakes made by the party making the rule about either the extent of the problem or the values of the public regarding the issue.

Second, instead of merely gathering information, such processes may promote active deliberation where issues are debated and ideas exchanged. Such debate may lead not only to better understanding of the issues but also to the growth of shared values and goals. For example, deliberation on the rules about public schools in Alberta may lead to new shared values or goals for education for citizens of the province. Some jurisdictions, such as British Columbia, have experimented with "citizen juries" for developing policies. These juries are made up of a number of citizens who are given information on an issue (or set of issues) and time to debate. The hope is that the exchange of ideas will lead to a better, more considered decision on the policy.

More formal processes for making rules or guidelines therefore potentially lead to better decisions through increased information for the rule-makers or more thoughtful deliberation by citizens. Better information and deliberation may reduce the probability of mistakes by rule-makers. Further, the involvement of the public increases the openness of the process to scrutiny, which may reduce the probability that those making the rules or guidelines act on their own view of the public interest (as opposed to that of the legislators or the public). It may also reduce the ability of interest groups to pressure those making the rules or guidelines to decide in their favour (and against the interests of the public more generally).[62]

However, more formal processes are not without their risks. First, making proposals and holding hearings or consultations to obtain public input can be expensive and time-consuming. Perhaps more important, public consultation can considerably lengthen the time it takes to make a rule or guideline. Formal processes have been blamed, in part, for the inflexibility and slow-changing nature of the US regulatory system. An example of the time that consultations can add to rule making is the air pollution standards process in Ontario. In the 1970s, the Ontario government made standards setting out permissible levels of emissions of particular substances. The Ministry of the Environment decided to revise those standards in the late 1980s. It engaged in public consultations from 1987 to 1990, but was unable to obtain agreement and stopped the process. It began again in 2001 and went through a

---

62   See e.g. Richard Stewart, "The Reformation of American Administrative Law" (1975) 88 Harv L Rev 1669.

series of proposals and different efforts at getting public comments. This process continued over four years before new standards were in force.[63]

Second, while formal processes may provide transparency that reduces interest group power, the processes at the same time provide another avenue through which interest groups can pressure those making the rules or guidelines. It is important to consider who is using the process and the nature of that group's involvement. Is a particular group able to use its resources to dominate the process? Little research has been done on this issue in Canada. Third, and relatedly, those making the rules or guidelines may not actually attend to the public participation. They may simply go through the motions in the process and not substantively change their views.

Finally, public participation may be detrimental if the public itself makes mistakes. Many of the issues that are addressed through rules and guidelines are highly technical or based on complex science. Individual members of the public may make mistakes in understanding and expressing opinions about an issue. These mistakes can lead individuals to believe that a risk is greater than it actually is. For example, individuals tend to perceive the risk of a car accident to be greater if they have seen a car accident recently. Individuals may also perceive risks to be less than they actually are. For example, individuals tend to be overly optimistic about their own personal risks of accident. Most believe they have above-average skills and are less likely than average to have a workplace accident. Further, many of these mistakes concern the types of issues that involve regulatory choices that are difficult for individuals to understand. Individuals have difficulty, for example, understanding very small probabilities of catastrophic harm, such as a catastrophic shift in climate. They tend to ignore these very small probability risks even though they should be taken into account.[64]

A related concept is that individuals often do not invest the time or resources necessary to become informed on an issue. Instead, they may base their decisions on decisions of others. If some individuals believe, for example, that the use of a hormone in the production of meat is carcinogenic (even though there is no evidence to that effect), other people may adopt the same position, purely on the basis that the first individuals believed it. More may come to the same belief on the basis of the now greater number of people who believe that hormones are harmful. These "information cascades," where people come to believe something on the basis that others believe it, can lead to dramatic shifts in public opinion on issues.[65]

The possibility of such mistakes has led to different types of proposals for structuring decision-making. Some commentators have called for the isolation of regulatory decision-makers from the public because of these mistakes—that is, they argue that decisions should be made largely by experts as opposed to through "deliberation," which is likely to be based on mistaken understandings.[66] Others claim that any such isolation is inherently undemocratic and that the mistakes can be reduced through an appropriately deliberative process.[67]

---

63 Environmental Commissioner of Ontario, *Annual Report 2004-2005* at 55-58, online: <http://docs.assets. eco.on.ca/reports/environmental-protection/2004-2005/2004-05-AR.pdf>.

64 Richard Posner, *Catastrophe: Risk and Response* (Oxford: Oxford University Press, 2004).

65 Cass Sunstein, *Risk and Reason* (Cambridge: Cambridge University Press, 2002).

66 Cass Sunstein, *Law of Fear* (Cambridge: Cambridge University Press, 2005).

67 See Dan Kahan, "Fear of Democracy: A Cultural Evaluation of Sunstein on Risk" (2006) 119 Harv L Rev 1071.

2. Legislating Process

Given these benefits and costs related to the process for making rules or guidelines, what have we done in Canada to address these issues? Legislatures may use either a general statute or a more specific, substantive statute to set the process by which the discretion is to be exercised. For example, Parliament enacted the *Statutory Instruments Act*, which provides some general process requirements for how rules are made.[68] The Act requires that any proposed regulation be sent to the Clerk of the Privy Council (a civil servant whose function is to advise Cabinet) so that the Clerk and the Deputy Minister of Justice can review the proposed regulation to ensure it is authorized by statute and does not unduly trespass on Charter rights. It also mandates that regulations be published in the *Canada Gazette*.[69] However, in terms of general process, the *Statutory Instruments Act* is quite thin. Further, the legislature sometimes exempts certain regulations from the requirements of the *Statutory Instruments Act*.[70] As we will see, Cabinet itself generates many of the requirements on regulation-making.

The United States has taken the opposite approach. The federal *Administrative Procedures Act* (APA) imposes significant requirements on the making of rules.[71] It establishes two main processes for making rules. There is a formal process under which there is a hearing requirement for some rules. The hearing involves almost court-like procedures including presentation of evidence and cross-examination. Most often, however, regulatory agencies use a more informal process—notice and comment rule making which, as its name suggests, involves the decision-maker giving relevant parties notice of the proposed rule and interested persons the opportunity to comment on the proposal. While it seemed more informal than a full hearing, the courts have over time increased the requirements on those making rules. Consequently, the notice and comment process is now very process-heavy and legalized. It has also led to considerable litigation about both the content and substance of rule making.[72] The key point, though, is that the United States has taken a different tack than Canada, as the legislature has set detailed procedural requirements for rule making.

In addition to general statutes such as the Canadian *Statutory Instruments Act* and the American APA, legislators may impose procedural requirements on rules or guidelines made under particular statutes. For example, under the Ontario *Securities Act*, the Ontario Securities Commission has the power to make rules about a variety of matters such as regulating the distribution of securities and public reporting by public companies.[73] The Act imposes detailed requirements on the commission to publish proposed rules, including

---

68   RSC 1985, c S-22.

69   Since the mid-1980s, the publication of proposed regulations in the *Canada Gazette* has been accompanied by a regulatory impact-analysis statement. The statement sets out the rationale for the regulation and attempts to measure the costs and benefits of the regulation. There is a more general statute in Quebec. See Hudson Janisch, "Further Developments with Respect to Rulemaking by Administrative Agencies" (1995) 9 Can J Admin L & Prac 1 for a general discussion of rule making in Canada.

70   See, for example, s 35(4) of the *Fisheries Act*, RSC 1985, c F-14, which specifies that regulations exempting parties from the prohibition on works, undertakings, or activities that cause serious harm to fish that are part of a fishery are themselves exempt from certain requirements of the *Statutory Instruments Act*.

71   5 USC S500 et seq.

72   See Daniel A Farber & Anne Joseph O'Connell, "The Lost World of Administrative Law" (2014) 92 Tex L Rev 1137 (discussing concerns about the US *Administrative Procedures Act*).

73   RSO 1990, c S.5, s 143 [*Ontario Securities Act*].

publishing a statement of the purpose of the rule, a discussion of alternatives to the proposed rule and reasons for not adopting them and a description of the anticipated costs and benefits of the proposed rule. The commission then has to invite and give a reasonable opportunity to interested persons and companies to comment on the proposal and may only make a rule after "considering all representations made."[74] The Act further requires that the commission provide the rule to the minister along with any comments and the commission's response to any significant concerns and the minister then has the power to approve or reject the rule or return it to the commission for further consideration.[75]

Ontario has enacted similar requirements in other areas. For example, the Ontario *Environmental Bill of Rights*[76] creates procedural rights surrounding government decisions in the environmental area, including the making of rules. The Bill provides for the creation of an online registry of all proposed rules and instruments (including regulations, formal rules, policies, orders, and approvals). There are different notice and comment procedures for different types of decisions (with, for example, longer comment periods for decisions that may have a greater impact on the environment). The minister of the environment and climate change is to "take every reasonable step to ensure that all comments relevant to the proposal that are received as part of the public participation process ... are considered when decisions about the proposal are made."[77] The government can be taken to court for failure to fulfill statutory procedural requirements.[78]

These procedures imbedded in either general or specific legislation are a way for the legislature to ensure there is a form of accountability in the making of rules or guidelines. It allows the public to know what the decision-maker is doing and potentially have some input into its decisions. The public then provides a check on the principal–agent problem more directly when the details of the policy are being worked out.

3. Executive Action

The executive, and in particular federal and provincial cabinets, may also attempt to control how rules and guidelines are made. The federal Cabinet has at times structured the making of rules and regulations through Cabinet directives, which are guidelines that are for all intents and purposes mandatory on other members of the executive. These Cabinet directives have been very controversial. In 2007 the Cabinet put in place the Cabinet Directive on

---

74 *Ibid*, s 143.2. See Janisch, "Further Developments re Rulemaking by Administrative Agencies," *supra* note 69, and Mullan, *supra* note 40, for a discussion of the history behind the procedural rules for the OSC.

75 *Ontario Securities Act*, s 143.3. The Act provides for similar processes if the commission makes a policy about the principles or criteria to be considered in its exercise of discretion or the manner in which the commission interprets the Act, the regulations or the rules (s 143.8).

76 SO 1993, c 28.

77 *Ibid*, s 35.

78 See for example, *Enbridge Gas Distribution Inc v Ontario Energy Board* (2005), 74 OR (3d) 147 (CA) (upholding the Ontario Energy Board's rule making under the Act, noting that if the legislature was concerned that the board engaged in "thoughtless rule-making, it would surely have imposed a requirement to give reasons for rule-making, if indeed it left the Board with any rule-making power at all" (at 160)). See also *Hanna v Ontario (AG)*, 2011 ONSC 609 (court reviewing wind power regulations under the *Canadian Environmental Protection Act, 1999*, SC 1999, c 33, to determine whether the statutorily required process was followed).

Streamlining Regulation, replacing the former Government of Canada Regulatory Policy. The Cabinet directive emphasized the importance of identifying interested and affected persons when making regulations and providing them with meaningful opportunities and information for participation. However, it also was criticized for non-transparency and an emphasis on economic factors.[79]

The Harper government replaced that directive with the Cabinet Directive on Regulatory Management in 2012. The 2012 directive includes the requirement that regulatory agencies undertake a regulatory impact analysis of any proposed regulation. The process is to include notification and consultation with any interested and affected parties and an assessment of the costs and benefits of any regulation. It also has a substantive element in that it mandates that in developing the option "to maximize net benefits," the decision-maker is to limit the burden imposed on Canadians and businesses, and in particular small businesses, as well as prevent or mitigate adverse impacts and enhance the positive impacts on health, safety, security, and the environment.

The United States has taken a similar approach but with a more formalized process. The structure of agencies and decision-makers is somewhat different. However, for those over which the president has control, various presidents have imposed requirements on rule making through executive orders, including mandating detailed cost-benefit analysis and extensive participation.[80] In fact, because the statutory process requirements under the APA are so onerous, rule-making agencies often attempt to avoid these processes, with the result that these executive orders may in practice be more influential than the statutory processes.[81]

The decision-makers themselves may also make rules or guidelines about the process they will follow in making decisions (either in adjudication or in making rules). For example, as we saw, the chair of the Immigration and Refugee Board makes guidelines to aid in adjudicating the large number of cases the board hears each year. The board also has a "Policy on the Use of Chairperson's Guidelines" that sets out the circumstances in which the chairperson will create guidelines.[82] Although the resulting guidelines are not binding, these circumstances show their potentially broad reach, as the policy states that the chairperson may make guidelines to, among other things, resolve an ambiguity in the law or inconsistency in decision-making, establish "legal interpretations as preferred positions" and set preferred approaches to the exercise of discretion. The policy on the use of guidelines sets out a process for creating guidelines, though the process is vague. The enabling legislation requires the chairperson to consult with deputy chairpersons before making guidelines.[83] The policy adds that "[o]ther consultation shall also take place, that is appropriate for the nature of the issue or matter being addressed in the guidelines, including consultation with

---

79 The Cabinet directive also sets out process requirements, such as analysis of the costs and benefits of proposed regulations. See Cabinet Directive on Streamlining Regulation (April 2007), online: Treasury Board of Canada Secretariat <http://www.tbs-sct.gc.ca/ri-qr/directive/directive00-eng.asp>.

80 Cass Sunstein, "The Office of Information and Regulatory Affairs: Myths and Realities" (2013) 126 Harv L Rev 1838 [Sunstein, "Office of Information"].

81 Daniel A Farber & Anne Joseph O'Connell, "The Lost World of Administrative Law" (2014) 92 Tex L Rev 1137.

82 Immigration and Refugee Board, "Policy on the Use of Chairperson's Guidelines," online: <http://www.irb-cisr.gc.ca/Eng/BoaCom/references/pol/pol/Pages/PolGuideDir.aspx>.

83 IRPA, s 159(1)(h).

the Executive Director" and that "[e]xternal consultation shall also take place, the extent of which shall be determined at the discretion of the Chairperson." There is therefore some process involved in making these guidelines, although fairly minimal and discretionary given the importance of the resulting guidelines.

4. Judicial Review of Process

So far, we have discussed the role of the legislature and executive in the making of rules and soft law. The third broad actor in administrative law is the courts. The courts are an obvious candidate for oversight of rules and soft law. In theory, they are an independent third party that can monitor or review the rules that are made. Such monitoring may keep the agent within the bounds of the power delegated to it by the legislature and control the agent where it makes mistakes, substitutes its own views of the public good, or acts in its own self-interest.

Courts may review either the process by which rules or soft law are made or the substance of the rules themselves. We will discuss judicial review of substance in the section on oversight. In terms of process, courts could potentially review how the rules were developed and create a common law set of procedures that must be followed when making rules under delegated powers. However, as Kate Glover explains in Chapter 5, there is no common law requirement of procedural fairness where a decision is of a "legislative and general" nature.[84] Because rules are typically general (that is, apply to many parties), they tend to fall under this exception to procedural fairness.

"Legislative" in this context does not necessarily mean "by the legislature." In *Att Gen of Can v Inuit Tapirisat*,[85] the Inuit Tapirisat challenged a rate increase for telephone services supplied by Bell Canada. The Canadian Radio-television and Telecommunications Commission (CRTC) implemented the rate increase following hearings in which the Inuit Tapirisat had participated. The CRTC approved the rate increase without attaching the conditions that the Inuit Tapirisat had requested. The Inuit Tapirisat appealed to the federal Cabinet under provisions of the *National Transportation Act*[86] to have the CRTC decision set aside. As part of this appeal, the CRTC made submissions to Cabinet through the Department of Communications. The Inuit Tapirisat was not allowed to review or respond to the CRTC submission. Cabinet rejected the appeal.

The Inuit Tapirisat sought judicial review, claiming it had been denied procedural fairness in its appeal because the CRTC had made submissions to which it did not have access. The Supreme Court of Canada, however, found that Cabinet did not owe the Inuit Tapirisat procedural fairness in this case. Among other things, Estey J found that setting rates was "legislative action in its purest form" because it affected many Bell subscribers.[87] He pointed to, among other things, the fact that the legislation created procedural rules for the CRTC but

---

84 *Knight v Indian Head School Division No 19*, [1990] 1 SCR 653.

85 [1980] 2 SCR 735 [*Inuit Tapirisat*]. See also *Denby v Dairy Farmers of Ontario*, 2009 Carswell Ont 6924 (Sup Ct J (Div Ct)) (no procedural fairness due for creation of new dairy quota policy by the Dairy Farmers of Ontario because the decision was of a legislative nature).

86 SC 1996, c 10.

87 *Inuit Tapirisat, supra* note 85 at 754.

not for Cabinet appeals. In the end, he found that there was no obligation on Cabinet to provide procedural fairness, such as notice, a hearing, or reasons.

Inuit Tapirisat shows that for a decision to be "legislative" in nature, the body making the decision does not have to be the legislature. The decision itself must have this "legislative and general" character. Although this legislative and general category is not self-evident, it appears to exclude rules aimed at a single party. For example, *Homex Realty v Wyoming*[88] involved a dispute between a municipality and a developer over who should pay the costs of installing services for a new subdivision. After extended and bitter negotiations, the municipality used its powers to make by-laws to designate the developer's subdivision plan not to be a "registered plan." It did so without notice to the developer. If the by-law was valid, the developer would have to obtain permission from the municipality to sell parts of the development and, before providing consent, the municipality would impose conditions (such as installing services). The developer challenged the by-law on the ground that the municipality did not act fairly in enacting the by-law. Estey J held that the by-law was not general in nature, but was aimed at resolving a dispute with one party—the developer. The municipality therefore owed a duty of fairness in such situations. Dickson J, in dissent, also agreed that there was duty on the municipality to provide procedural fairness. He stated, "[w]hat we have here is not a by-law of wide and general application which was to apply to all citizens of the municipality equally. Rather, it was a by-law aimed deliberately at limiting the rights of one individual."[89]

The Federal Court more recently considered the issue of the scope for procedural review of regulations in *Canadian Society of Immigration Consultants v Canada (Citizenship and Immigration)*.[90] The court found that a decision to terminate the mandate of the existing body regulating immigration consultants and replace it with a new body was "essentially a 'legislative' action (whether it results from an Act of Parliament or from a regulation made by the Executive branch)."[91] The fact that the regulation was aimed at one particular body (the Canadian Society of Immigration Consultants) did not make it an "individual" decision so as to make it non-legislative in nature. As a result, the duty of fairness did not apply to the regulation-making process at issue. The court did open the door to the possibility of the application of the doctrine of legitimate expectations to the regulation-making process, but found that, even so, there was no breach of the Society's legitimate expectations.

5. Duty to Consult and Accommodate in Rule Making?

The courts then have taken only a limited role in establishing common law requirements for the process of making rules. There is, however, increasing recognition of a constitutional constraint on rule making that courts have become involved in defining—the duty to consult and accommodate Indigenous Peoples in decisions that affect them. As discussed in Chapter 3, this duty arises under s 35 of the Constitution. The Supreme Court has stated that

---

88   [1980] 2 SCR 1011.

89   *Ibid* at 1052. The majority and the dissent, therefore, agreed that the developer was owed a duty of fairness because the by-law was not "legislative" or general. They differed on whether they should, in their discretion, grant the remedy requested by the developer. The majority held that the court should not grant the remedy because of the actions of the developer during the negotiations and litigation.

90   2011 FC 1435, [2013] 3 FCR 488.

91   *Ibid* at para 113.

it is "a procedural duty that arises from the honour of the Crown,"[92] although there is also an accommodation requirement that may arise in certain circumstances.[93]

The Supreme Court has stated that the duty to consult not only arises in individual decisions that impact Aboriginal rights, but also in "strategic, higher level decisions."[94] The Federal Court of Appeal recently decided that the duty to consult does not extend as far as legislative action. In *Canada (Governor General in Council) v Mikisew Cree First Nation*, the court dismissed an appeal of a Federal Court decision finding that the federal government had breached its duty to consult the Mikisew Cree in developing and introducing certain aspects of two omnibus bills amending the *Canadian Environmental Assessment Act*, the *Fisheries Act*, the *Species at Risk Act*, the *Canadian Environmental Protection Act* and the *Navigable Waters Protection Act*.[95] The Mikisew Cree argued that the amendments would reduce their ability to participate in decisions that affect their treaty rights and that the Crown should have consulted them in the developing the amendments. The court, however, found that legislative action itself does not fall within the scope of the duty to consult.

However, the courts have found that the duty to consult arises in general decisions that may affect Indigenous or treaty rights. These decisions include various types of plans such as for forest stewardship and municipal land use. Further, the Alberta Court of Appeal addressed the duty to consult in making a water management plan made under the *Water Act*.[96] Under s 9 of the *Water Act*, the minister of the environment had the discretion to require a director or other person to develop a water management plan. The lieutenant governor in council was empowered to approve any such plan under the Act. The Tsuu T'ina Nation claimed the Crown had failed to adequately consult and accommodate them in making the plan. The court found that the fact that the plan was adopted by an order in council (that is, by Cabinet) does not take it outside the scope of the duty to consult in appropriate circumstances. The court stated, "even if the Legislature itself does not have a duty to consult prior to passing legislation, the duty may still fall upon those assigned the task of developing the policy behind the legislation, or upon those who are charged with making recommendations concerning future policies and actions."[97] The duty to consult on this view would then appear to apply to delegated legislation such as orders in council.[98]

The federal government has adopted the "Aboriginal Consultation and Accommodation: Updated Guidelines for Federal Officials to Fulfill the Duty to Consult,"[99] which provides step-by-step guidance for how federal departments and agencies are to interpret and fulfill

---

92 *Tsilhqot'in Nation v British Columbia*, 2014 SCC 257 44, [2014] 2 SCR 257 at para 78.

93 See Chapter 3, Realizing Aboriginal Administrative Law.

94 *Rio Tinto Alcan Inc v Carrier Sekani Tribal Council*, 2010 SCC 43 at para 44.

95 *Canada (Governor General in Council) v Mikisew Cree First Nation*, 2016 FCA 311.

96 *Tsuu T'ina Nation v Alberta (Environment)*, 2010 ABCA 137; *Water Act*, RSA 2000, c W-3.

97 *Ibid* at para 55.

98 The Federal Court of Appeal in *Mikisew* distinguishes *Tsuu T'ina Nation* from the challenge to the omnibus bills noting that "the consultations in *Tsuu T'ina Nation* occurred outside the legislative context, as they were to be conducted well after the enactment of the legislation" (*supra* note 95 at para 50). See also *Adams Lake Indian Band v British Columbia*, 2011 BCSC 266.

99 Indigenous and Northern Affairs Canada, "Aboriginal Consultation and Accommodation—Updated Guidelines for Federal Officials to Fulfill the Duty to Consult," online: <http://www.aadnc-aandc.gc.ca/eng/1100100014664/1100100014675#chp1_6_1>. Provincial governments also have various guidelines on the duty to consult and accommodate.

the duty. In terms of rule making, the guidelines note that "[g]overnment actions that may adversely impact Aboriginal and Treaty rights can include ... change in regulation or policy that may restrict land use," indicating that the federal government may see rule making as encompassed by the duty.

6. Consultation and Interest Group Power

Much of the formal consultation in rule making in Canada established either by legislation or guideline consists of the provision of notice of the proposed rule and the opportunity for those affected to comment on the proposal. How do such "notice and comment" require-ments fit with our discussion of the benefits and risks of process? They are beneficial in that they ensure that those affected have some information about the proposed rule and the regulators potentially receive information back about the costs and benefits of and trade-offs in making the rule. Further, the cost of these requirements is relatively low.

However, notice and comment requirements have a number of drawbacks. First, they can cause delay because those making the rules need to give notice of and time to comment on any proposed material change to a rule. Second, while notice and comment rules potentially open the rule-making process up to a greater range of parties, it is not clear who can partici-pate. It may be that the comment process is dominated by certain parties and, in particular, the regulated parties. Certain groups may be able to make more detailed and effective comments if they have resources and are willing to invest in the process. If significant costs may be imposed on relatively few parties, they have greater incentive to invest resources to oppose the rule than if the benefits (or costs) are spread over a larger number of parties. Finally, notice and comment rules do not provide scope for deliberation. The comments of each individual are provided to the government, but there is no exchange of ideas between those making the comments.[100]

The process of making rules can therefore aid in controlling the actions of the "agent." It can potentially reduce mistakes in rule making by increasing the flow of information to rule-makers. It can also provide some transparency that may reduce the rule-makers' ability to make rules that do not follow the interests of legislators but rather their own idiosyncratic view of the public good or their own self-interest (such as where they seek to favour certain parties because of the rewards those parties can provide to them). Legislators may even be able to use the process to aid in ensuring that rules have a particular substantive content by altering procedures to favour certain parties.[101] For example, procedures that favour or encourage submissions by environmental groups may lead to rules that tend to favour their interests.

However, there is no necessary connection between these processes and results, or a reduction in interest group power. As noted above, much depends on the relative resources of the parties and the willingness of parties to become involved in the rule making. It also depends on the willingness of the rule-maker to take the comments of interested parties into account. Interestingly, there may be a connection between these process requirements

---

100   See Andrew Green, "Creating Environmentalists: Environmental Law, Identity and Commitment" (2006) 17 J Envtl L & Prac 1 for a discussion of administrative law, deliberation, and the formation of shared values or identities.

101   McCubbins, *supra* note 23.

and substantive review by the courts. If a rule-maker follows expansive procedures (including public participation), courts may be more willing to defer to the resulting decisions (rules) because, for example, the use of the procedures is a signal of better-quality decisions.[102] Courts, however, may not know if as a result of the notice and comment process that the quality of decisions *actually* is improved and that the rule-makers *actually* do take public comments into account. Part of the answer may be to require the rule-maker to provide reasons in the hope that it will be held accountable, either by the public or by legislators. However, such accountability can be a weak constraint where time, expertise, and information costs hinder monitoring.

D. How Should We Monitor How the Powers Are Being Used?

We have so far looked at issues around the scope of the delegated power to make rules, the identity of the rule-maker and the process for making rules. A further, related issue is whether anyone reviews the proposed or actual rules or guidelines. We will look at two sources of such monitoring: legislative or executive oversight and judicial review.

1. Legislative and Executive Oversight

Instead of indirectly attempting to ensure that the power it delegates conforms to its views, the legislature could directly control the discretion by reviewing the resulting rules or soft law. The legislature itself, or more likely a committee, could examine the rules or soft law and decide whether to approve, disapprove, or amend them. Such legislative committees have been used at both the federal and the provincial level in Canada to examine regulations. For example, at the federal level, a joint committee of the Senate and House of Commons reviews regulations, although the intent is to review the form of the regulation and not the underlying reasons for it.[103] More generally, many boards or other bodies have to report annually on their activities, which provides an opportunity for the legislature to consider their rule making. Although legislative committees may review rules and regulations, there is generally no legislative oversight of soft law.

However, the use of legislative committees to review regulations only goes part of the way to solving the principal–agent problem. As a committee, it may have some time to examine regulations that are made but, absent a significant allocation of resources, still less time than the agency or ministry, particularly if there is a desire to review not only formal regulations but all rules and even soft law. Further, it exacerbates the problem of time in some ways because it creates a system where regulations go back and forth between the legislators and the agency or rule-making authority. This oversight causes delay in implementation. More importantly, however, legislative review does not solve the problems concerning expertise and information. Members of the legislature are unlikely to have

---

102 Matthew Stephenson, "The Strategic Substitution Effect: Textual Plausibility, Procedural Formality, and Judicial Review of Agency Statutory Interpretations" (2006) 120 Harv L Rev 528.

103 *Statutory Instruments Act*, s 19. See Mullan, *supra* note 40, describing the federal and provincial committees that have been set up to review regulations. And Taggart, *supra* note 16 at 624, notes that the second half of the 20th century "was dominated by the attempt to enhance parliamentary safeguards against potential and actual 'abuses' of these delegated powers."

enough information or expertise to adequately review the regulations. This lack of expertise and information is often one of the main reasons for delegation in the first place. Legislators are likely either to largely defer to the rule-making authority, in which case the purpose of review is lost, or to take a hard look and be willing to substitute their own views, in which case the potential for errors increases significantly. Finally, legislative review does little to aid in the principal–agent problem between the public and the legislature/executive.

Centralized oversight within the executive itself has perhaps greater implications. The starkest example is the Office of Information and Regulatory Affairs (OIRA) in the United States. Starting in the 1980s, most federal agencies had to submit proposed rules to OIRA, a strong central oversight body within the executive, for approval. This requirement is in addition to following the procedures under the APA discussed above. OIRA reviews proposals based on cost-benefit analysis undertaken by the agency.

The Canadian equivalent arises under the Cabinet Directive on Regulatory Management. In addition to the procedural steps discussed in the previous section, the Cabinet directive imposes further accountability requirements such as the obligation on decision-makers to develop regulatory plans and submit them to the Treasury Board. The Treasury Board is, in essence, a committee of Cabinet. The Treasury Board is also given an oversight role to review the proposed regulations and ensure the requirements of the directive have been met and to promote "regulatory reform."

Central oversight involving a separate check through a body such as Cabinet composed of elected officials may allow for greater democratic accountability for rules.[104] Further it may reduce capture, which as we noted above is where interest groups sway public powers for private purposes. Centralized oversight may reduce capture to the extent the oversight body's mandate is general in nature, rather than specific to one particular industry. Close relationships between a regulator and the regulated industry may give rise to concerns about the nature of the resulting rules. General centralized oversight may avoid such a close relationship. Centralized oversight may also result in better rules to the extent it allows the central body to help "collect widely dispersed information" both inside and outside government, and to coordinate across different government departments and decision-makers.[105]

The difficulty, of course, lies in the fact that the effort to check or review agency decisions to overcome capture may itself give rise to capture.[106] The central oversight body is another route for regulated parties or others to stop new regulatory measures or to steer them in their interests. As such, centralized review may stymie regulation, particularly as such review tends to focus on regulatory action rather than inaction.

---

104   For arguments in favour of centralized oversight, see Michael A Livermore & Richard L Revesz, "Regulatory Review, Capture and Agency Inaction" (2013) 101 Georgetown LJ 1337.

105   Sunstein, "Office of Information," *supra* note 80.

106   Livermore and Revesz, *supra* note 104 at 1340. See also Lisa Heinzerling, "Classical Administrative Law in the Era of Presidential Administration" (2014) 92 Tex L Rev 171 (arguing that central oversight by OIRA actually enlarges the group that can delay or stop rules that favour the public interest, and that the expansion of people involved and the lack of transparency favour regulated interests).

2. *Judicial Review of Substance*

In addition to review by the legislature or the executive, courts may oversee the content of rules or soft law. One of the seminal cases in Canada is *Thorne's Hardware Ltd v The Queen*.[107] In that case, the federal governor in council (Cabinet) made an order in council under the *National Harbours Board Act* extending the boundaries of the Port of Saint John, New Brunswick. The applicant challenged the order in council on the basis that it was made in bad faith. It argued that Cabinet extended the boundaries in order to increase the revenues of the National Harbour Board and that such a purpose was not within the scope of Cabinet's powers under the Act. The Act provided that the boundaries of the Saint John harbour were those set out in a schedule "or as may be determined from time to time by order of the Governor in Council."[108]

The Supreme Court, however, held that while it was possible to strike down an order in council on "jurisdictional or other compelling grounds," "it would take an egregious case to warrant such action. This is not such a case."[109] It refused to examine the evidence of bad faith that the applicant provided, stating that "the government's reasons for expanding the harbour are in the end unknown. Governments do not publish reasons for their decisions; governments may be moved by any number of political, economic, social, or partisan considerations."[110] As a result, the court found against the applicant, stating that the harbour extension was an issue of "economic policy and politics" for which Cabinet "quite obviously believed [it] had reasonable grounds" and the court "cannot enquire into the validity of those beliefs."[111]

The court in *Thorne's Hardware* therefore took a strong position against examining the actions of Cabinet in making orders in council (a form of delegated rule making). However, as discussed in Chapters 11 and 12, the Supreme Court of Canada more recently established a broad default of reasonableness review following *Dunsmuir*.[112] One question was whether this reasonableness framework applied to rule making. At first, it appeared it would. In *Catalyst Paper Corp v North Cowichan (District)*, the Supreme Court undertook a reasonableness review of a municipality's by-laws, noting that,

> review of municipal bylaws must reflect the broad discretion provincial legislators traditionally accorded to municipalities engaged in delegated legislation. Municipal councils passing bylaws fulfill a task that affects their community as a whole and is legislative rather than adjudicative in nature. Bylaws are not quasi-judicial decisions. Rather, they involve an array of social, economic, political, and other non-legal considerations.[113]

---

107 [1983] 1 SCR 106 [*Thorne's Hardware*].

108 *National Harbours Board Act*, RSC 1970, c N-8, s 7(2).

109 *Thorne's Hardware*, *supra* note 107 at 111.

110 *Ibid* at 112-13.

111 *Ibid* at 115. The Supreme Court applied the principle in *Thorne's Hardware* in refusing to allow an applicant to examine members of a city council to determine their motives in creating a board of inquiry: *Consortium Development (Clearwater) Ltd v Sarnia (City of)*, [1998] 3 SCR 3. But see *Catalyst Paper Corp v North Cowichan (District)*, 2012 SCC 2 at para 14 [*Catalyst Paper*] ("this attempt to maintain a clear distinction between policy and legality has not prevailed").

112 *Dunsmuir*, *supra* note 28.

113 *Catalyst Paper*, *supra* note 111 at para 19.

In applying the reasonableness framework to its review of the by-laws, the court was very deferential to the municipality. The court noted that courts reviewing by-laws "must approach the task against the backdrop of the wide variety of factors that elected municipal councillors may legitimately consider in enacting bylaws" and the test is "only if the bylaw is one no reasonable body informed by these factors could have taken will the bylaw be set aside."[114] Here the court found the substance must conform to the rationale of the statutory regime, and, given it is a legislative process, the municipality was not required to give reasons or formally explain the basis of the by-law, as it may consider objective factors but also "broader social, economic and political factors that are relevant to the electorate."[115] After briefly reviewing the process and content of the by-laws, the court held that the by-laws were within a reasonable range of outcomes.

However, the Supreme Court elected not to bring regulations under the standard of review framework in *Katz Group Canada Inc v Ontario (Health and Long-Term Care)*.[116] In that case, the court was faced with a challenge by Shoppers Drug Mart and other drug stores against Ontario government regulations aimed at prices of generic drugs. The drug stores argued that regulations were inconsistent with the purpose of the provincial drug statutes aimed at reducing drug prices, as there was no evidence the regulations would lead to lower prices.

Rather than folding the test for regulations in the standard of review analysis, as was done with by-laws in *Catalyst Paper*, the court adopted an approach in line with *Thorne's Hardware*. The court noted that regulations "benefit from a presumption of validity," which means that the challenger has to demonstrate the invalidity of the regulation and courts "where possible" are to construe the regulation so that it is valid.[117] The court adopted language from an Ontario Court of Appeal decision, which stated that challenges to regulations are "usually restricted to the grounds that they are inconsistent with the purpose of the statute or that some condition precedent in the statute has not been observed."[118] The court noted that:

> It is not an inquiry into the underlying "political, economic, social or partisan considerations" (*Thorne's Hardware Ltd v The Queen*, [1983] 1 SCR 106, at pp 112-13). Nor does the vires of regulations hinge on whether, in the court's view, they will actually succeed at achieving the statutory objectives. ... They must be "irrelevant," "extraneous" or "completely unrelated" to the statutory purpose to be found to be ultra vires on the basis of inconsistency with statutory purpose.... In effect, although it is possible to strike down regulations as ultra vires on this basis, as Dickson J observed, "it would take an egregious case to warrant such action" (*Thorne's Hardware*, at p 111).[119]

The court found that, in this case, the regulations accord with the purpose of the relevant statutes which, was to control and reduce drug prices and "[w]hether they will ultimately prove to be successful or represent sound economic policy is not the issue."[120]

---

114 *Ibid* at para 24.
115 *Ibid* at para 30.
116 *Katz Group Canada Inc v Ontario (Health and Long-Term Care)*, 2013 SCC 64 [*Katz Group*].
117 *Ibid* at para 25.
118 *Ibid* at para 27, citing *Ontario Federation of Anglers & Hunters v Ontario (Ministry of Natural Resources)* (2002), 211 DLR (4th) 741 (Ont CA).
119 *Ibid* at para 28.
120 *Ibid* at para 39.

Following *Katz Group*, then, courts are not to review the reasonableness of the substance of regulations in the *Dunsmuir* sense, but instead whether the regulations appear "completely unrelated" to the statutory purpose. A more recent case in Ontario dealt with the connection of regulations with the statutory purpose but also with the second important factor referred to by the court in *Katz Group*—that the maker of the regulation fulfills any condition precedent in the statute before making the regulation. In *Wildlands League v Ontario (Natural Resources and Forestry)*, the Ontario Court of Appeal dismissed a challenge by environmental groups to regulations made under Ontario's *Endangered Species Act* (ESA)[121] that exempt certain industrial activity from prohibitions on killing, harming, harassing, or capturing listed species at risk (SAR) or destroying or damaging their habitat.[122]

The Wildlands League argued first that the regulations were aimed at cost savings and as such were inconsistent with the purpose of the Act to protect and promote the recovery of SAR.[123] Following the *Katz Group* approach, the court held that, "[w]hile the motive for the regulation may well have been a concern for administrative efficiency and cost savings, the limitations, conditions, exceptions and scoping of the exemptions contained in the regulation are directed toward the protection of SAR. The regulation is therefore not 'irrelevant,' 'extraneous' or 'completely unrelated to' the purpose of the ESA and its scheme."[124]

The Wildlands League then argued that the minister, in making the regulations, had failed to observe a condition precedent. Under s 57(1) of the ESA, before making an exemption regulation, the minister must consult with an expert on the possible effects of the proposed regulation on a species if "the Minister is of the opinion that the regulation is likely to jeopardize the survival of the species in Ontario or to have any other significant adverse effect on the species." The Wildlands League argued that the minister had failed to fulfill this condition as he did not assess the effect of the regulation on each species listed as at risk under the Act. They contended that the minister's determination under s 57 should be reviewed by the court under a standard of correctness or at least reasonableness. The court, however, took a very light hand on the necessity of observing conditions precedent, finding that:

> Where a statutory condition precedent itself requires an opinion to be reached or a determination to be made, it is beyond the scope of judicial review to assess whether the determination was objectively correct or reasonable. At the same time, it is not sufficient that the decision-maker purported to make the determination. The determination must have been made in good faith and based on the factors specified in the enabling statute.[125]

In this case, the court found evidence that the minister had considered how the regulation affected each species.

---

121 *Wildlands League v Ontario, supra* note 14, leave to appeal to Supreme Court of Canada denied May 5, 2017; *Endangered Species Act, 2007*, SO 2007, c 6.

122 ESA, ss 9 and 10.

123 ESA, s 1 states, "The purposes of this Act are: 1. To identify species at risk based on the best available scientific information, including information obtained from community knowledge and aboriginal traditional knowledge. 2. To protect species that are at risk and their habitats, and to promote the recovery of species that are at risk. 3. To promote stewardship activities to assist in the protection and recovery of species that are at risk."

124 *Wildlands League, supra* note 14 at para 98.

125 *Ibid* at para 56.

As a result of *Katz Group* and its progeny, it is hard to challenge regulations. Even though the substance of regulations could in theory be subject to the reasonableness standard of review under the *Dunsmuir* approach, the courts have taken an even lighter hand.[126] In part, such light review in the context of regulations may be due to the fact that in *Katz Group* the regulations were made by Cabinet, which is composed of elected officials. The courts may see less of a need to review (or legitimacy in reviewing) such regulations as there is more clearly an alternate source of accountability than the courts.[127]

However, while the courts may undertake only a light review of regulations made by Cabinet, they may be more likely to review under the *Dunsmuir* framework other types of rules made by other types of bodies such as boards or tribunals. For example, the Supreme Court in *Green v Law Society of Manitoba* recently considered whether the Law Society of Manitoba could impose rules that couple a mandatory continuing professional development program with a possible suspension for not complying with the program.[128] Under Manitoba's *Legal Profession Act*, the Law Society "must ... establish standards for the education, professional responsibility and competence of persons practicing or seeking the right to practice law in Manitoba."[129] The Act provides that "[i]n addition to any specific power or requirement to make rules under this Act, the benchers may make rules to manage the society's affairs, pursue its purpose and carry out its duties."[130]

The majority of the court found that the *Dunsmuir* framework applied and that the applicable standard of review was reasonableness. It found that the rule will only be set aside if it "is one no reasonable body informed by [the relevant] factors could have [enacted]" (citing *Catalyst Paper*) meaning "that the substance of [law society rules] must conform to the rationale of the statutory regime set up by the legislature" (citing *Catalyst Paper* and *Katz Group*). The court held that reasonableness was appropriate as, among other things, the legislature had given the Law Society a broad discretion to regulate the legal profession in the public interest and the power to "make rules of general application to the profession, and in doing so, the benchers act in a legislative capacity."[131] In addition, the benchers are elected by and accountable to the members of the legal profession. The court found the

---

126   See Paul Daly, "The Scope and Meaning of Reasonableness Review" (2014-15) 52 Alta L Rev 799 (arguing against a fragmented approach to judicial review where regulations are reviewed under a different framework than other administrative decisions).

127   But see *Canadian National Railway Co v Canada (Attorney General)*, 2014 SCC 40, [2014] 2 SCR 135, in which the court reviewed a decision by Cabinet to rescind a Canadian Transportation Agency decision regarding a fuel surcharge. The court adopted the *Dunsmuir* framework, noting that "[t]he precedents instruct that the *Dunsmuir* framework applies to administrative decision-makers generally and not just to administrative tribunals. The *Dunsmuir* framework thus is applicable to adjudicative decisions of the Governor in Council" (at para 54). It distinguished *Katz Group* by stating, "[u]nlike cases involving challenges to the vires of regulations, such as *Katz Group* ..., the Governor in Council does not act in a legislative capacity when it exercises its authority under s 40 of the CTA to deal with a decision or order of the Agency" (at para 51).

128   *Green v Law Society of Manitoba*, 2017 SCC 20 [*Green*].

129   *The Legal Profession Act*, CCSM c L107, s 3(2).

130   *Ibid*, s 4(5). Section 4(6) provides that the rules are binding on the law society, the benchers, the members and everyone who practices or seeks the right to practise law under the Act.

131   *Green, supra* note 128 at para 22. In support of the standard of reasonableness, the court also pointed to the fact that the Law Society was acting pursuant to its home statute and has expertise in regulating the legal profession (paras 24 and 25). The dissent also applied a reasonableness standard of review.

rules reasonable after construing the scope of the Law Society's statutory mandate to be to protect the public interest in the delivery of legal services and determining that the suspension for breach of the rules was reasonable in light of the Law Society's statutory mandate.

Courts therefore have been very deferential in reviewing the substance of rules, particularly when reviewing regulations as opposed to other forms of rules. They will of course review rules for other reasons. For example, courts will assess whether a rule violates the *Canadian Charter of Rights and Freedoms*.[132] Evan Fox-Decent and Alexander Pless examine substantive judicial review and the Charter in Chapter 13.

Courts have been even more reluctant to review soft law.[133] One exception to this reluctance is review for "fettering." Fettering occurs where a decision-maker does not exercise her discretion in a matter but instead follows a guideline or policy that she views as mandatory or binding because of its language or practical effect.[134] In *Kanthasamy v Canada (Citizenship and Immigration)*, the court reviewed a decision by an officer in Citizenship and Immigration Canada denying Kanthasamy, then a 17-year-old, an exemption on humanitarian and compassionate grounds to apply for permanent resident status from within Canada.[135] Under s 25(1) of the *Immigration and Refugee Protection Act*, the minister has the discretion to provide such an exemption "if the Minister is of the opinion that it is justified by humanitarian and compassionate considerations relating to the foreign national, taking into account the best interests of a child directly affected." The minister had put in place guidelines to aid in determining whether there were sufficient humanitarian and compassionate grounds. These guidelines stated that the applicant must show either "unusual or undeserved" or "disproportionate" hardship and set out a list of non-exhaustive factors that may be relevant (such as ties to Canada, the best interests of any children affected, and health considerations). According to the guidelines, an officer considering an application for relief under s 25(1) must assess all the facts and undertake a "global assessment" of the considerations. The officer relied on the language of the guidelines in denying Kanthasamy the exemption.

Abella J, writing for the majority, found that the guidelines are useful in indicating a reasonable interpretation of s 25(1) but, as they are not legally binding, officers should not "fetter" their discretion by treating them as mandatory requirements. Instead the officers should consider the guidelines as descriptive but consider and weigh all the relevant factors in the particular case. In this case, Abella J found that the officer failed to sufficiently consider a number of considerations such as Kanthasamy's age and mental health concerns and took the elements of the guidelines as distinct legal tests rather than as descriptive aids to fulfilling the provision's equitable purpose (para 45). As the officer failed to consider the

---

132 Part I of the *Constitution Act, 1982*, being Schedule B to the *Canada Act 1982* (UK), 1982, c 11 [Charter]. For a discussion of some of the grounds of review, see Mullan, *supra* note 40, Chapter 7 (including that the party making the rule must act in good faith, for a proper purpose, and on relevant considerations). On the Charter and regulations, see *Eldridge v British Columbia (Attorney General)*, [1997] 3 SCR 624.

133 For example, for a discussion of soft law and the Charter, see e.g. *Little Sisters Book and Art Emporium v Canada (Minister of Justice)*, [2000] 2 SCR 1120, and Lorne Sossin, "Discretion Unbound: Reconciling Soft Law and the Charter" (2002) 45 Can Pub Pol'y 465.

134 See e.g. *Thamotharem*, *supra* note 22 (finding a guideline specifying reverse-order questioning for refugee protection hearings did not constitute an unlawful fetter because it expressly directed panel members to consider the particular facts of each case to determine whether there should be an exception to this order of questioning).

135 *Kanthasamy*, *supra* note 12.

evidence as a whole, Abella J found that the officer's "approach unduly fettered her discretion and, in my respectful view, led to its unreasonable exercise."[136]

In summary, courts have tended to take a fairly light review of rules and soft law (with the exception of fettering). Yet even if courts were willing to review rules or soft law substantively, is this something we should want them to do? There are three principal reasons why we may not. First, judicial review can be time-consuming and expensive. In some cases, there are only a few parties who bear the costs from a new rule, while the benefits are spread across many people. For example, if the Ontario Ministry of the Environment makes a rule limiting sulphur dioxide emissions, the rule may impose significant costs on a few industries or firms but provide benefits (in terms of lower levels of air pollution or acid rain) to a large number of people (both within and potentially outside the province). In such a case, the industries or firms affected may have the incentive to challenge the rule in court (and be willing and able to expend the resources to do so), while those who benefit individually receive too little benefit to take on the expense of becoming involved in the application. The government agency that created the rule would have to represent the interests of those whom the rule benefits. Conversely, if the costs are spread over a large number of people (for example, a rule imposing a tariff on an imported consumer product), there may be no one person who is sufficiently harmed to bear the costs of challenging the government decision. As a result, this check on government rules depends, in part, on such factors as how many parties benefit or bear costs and the resources of those parties.

The second concern with substantive judicial review is that, even if the "appropriate" challenges come before the courts, the courts often do not have the expertise to review the rules. There is therefore a large potential error cost from substantive judicial review—that is, courts might be less likely than the administrative decision-maker to determine the "right" answer.[137] Generalist courts that are "compulsorily ignorant" may not have the knowledge, experience, or technical expertise to review the often very detailed, technical rules.[138] For example, in *Katz Group*, how can a court determine the appropriateness of a rule concerning pricing structures for generic drugs or even the appropriate interpretation of the purposes of the legislation? The expertise of the ministry in these issues would aid in making these determinations. A court could defer to the decisions of the rule-maker, in which case there is no real check on the principal–agent concern. Alternatively, the court could take a hard look (potentially substituting its own view of the appropriate policy), in which case there is an increased risk that the wrong rule will be chosen. As with legislative review, the check on the principal–agent concern comes at the cost of loss of expertise.

Finally, even if the courts have the expertise to review administrative rules, this discussion of the courts' role in reviewing administrative rules has implicitly assumed that courts are attempting to determine the best possible interpretation of legislative power and the appropriateness of the challenged rule. However, judges also have their own policy

---

136   *Ibid* at para 60.
137   Stephenson, *supra* note 26.
138   See Taggart, *supra* note 16 at 589 (discussing the distaste of administrative law scholar John Willis for judicial review).

preferences.[139] Judicial review, therefore, gives rise to a concern that judges' discretion over policy outcomes (the content of rules) creates a further principal–agent problem as judges seek to implement their own views of appropriate policy.[140]

The issue of the extent of desirable substantive review by courts of administrative decisions has long vexed courts, legislators, and legal scholars. This issue is more fully addressed in other chapters in this book. However, there is an interesting connection between judicial review and the discussion above of structural approaches to controlling delegated decision-making. In order to increase the likelihood that rules will align with their preferences, legislators may wish a particular agency, rather than courts, to interpret legislative provisions in making rules.[141] For example, legislators who are favourable to unions or workers may believe that a Ministry of Labour interpretation of a rule-making power is more likely to favour unions or workers than a court's interpretation. Thus, in such cases, they may seek to limit judicial review. In other cases, the legislators may believe that courts' interpretations are more likely to be in accordance with their preferences and seek to expand judicial review. Such limitation or expansion of judicial review could come, for example, through a privative clause or a right to appeal, or through other cues as to who the legislature wishes to set policy. However, given the lack of clarity in how the courts interpret their "expertise" relative to that of administrative decision-makers, legislators can never be sure that their choice of delegate (either administrative decision-maker or court) will prevail over time.[142]

V. THE SEARCH FOR A BALANCE

While adjudication tends to get more attention in administrative law, rules and soft law are critical to the operation of the administrative state. There are few areas of practice that are not at least touched, if not dominated, by them. If you are in private practice, rules and soft law will determine or at least influence many of your clients. To be effective, you need to understand how they are made and how they can be challenged to be in a position to aid your clients' interests. If you are working for the government, you may have to draft, apply, or follow a wide range of rules and soft law. You need to ensure they are developed and applied fairly and are safeguarded to the extent possible from judicial review.

---

139 See generally, Jeffrey A Segal & Harold J Spaeth, *The Supreme Court and the Attitudinal Model Revisited* (Cambridge: Cambridge University Press, 2002) and Thomas J Miles & Cass R Sunstein, "Do Judges Make Regulatory Policy? An Empirical Investigation of Chevron" (2006) 73 U Chicago L Rev 823. For an application of the attitudinal model of judicial decision-making in the Canadian context, see e.g. Benjamin Alarie & Andrew Green, "Policy Preference Change and Appointments to the Supreme Court of Canada" (2009) 47:1 Osgoode Hall LJ 1.

140 See e.g. Stephenson, *supra* note 26 (discussing the possible differences in policy preferences between legislatures, agencies, and courts).

141 See e.g. *ibid* (arguing that legislators may wish to delegate the power to interpret legislation to agencies, if they wish to produce consistent interpretation across issues, or to the courts, if they wish to produce consistent interpretation across time—that is, even when other legislators are in power).

142 Adrian Vermeule, "The Delegation Lottery" (2006) 119 Harv L Rev 105 (arguing that the choice of who interprets legislation is as much of a "lottery" for legislators as is the ultimate rule or decision that a delegate makes on the basis of broad legislative provisions). See also Chapters 9 and 10 in this book discussing the Supreme Court's approach to determining the standard of review.

Legislators delegate the power to make rules and soft law to widely different types of decision-makers—from Cabinet and individual ministers to independent boards and tribunals or self-regulating bodies. These rules and soft law give guidance on procedural matters as well as substantive issues, such as how to interpret a legislative provision or the factors to consider in exercising a discretionary power. In delegating the power to make rules and soft law, legislators gain the use of the expertise of these other parties. Further, they expand the reach of their regulatory powers because they would not otherwise have the time to make rules in all the areas that are encompassed by a modern welfare and regulatory state. However, at the same time, they relinquish a significant amount of power to parties they cannot fully control because of the information and time costs of monitoring them. This difficulty in monitoring creates the principal–agent problem.

Administrative law is in part about this struggle to take advantage of the benefits of delegation while minimizing the risks. Different countries have sought different means of resolving this struggle, and even in the same country the trade-offs made will change over time with different governments and altered contexts. In Canada, the executive has tended to hold considerable sway in developing rules and soft law. The centralized control by Cabinet has the potential to meld expertise with greater political accountability to the electorate. However, in practice such accountability depends on the issue, as the public tends to react sporadically, focusing on certain issues for a time before a different set of concerns catches its attention. Rule making is particularly technical and complex, and as such, the public may have difficulty sustaining attention over the vast array of rules and soft law that make up the modern regulatory state. In recent years, the courts have generally tended to take a more deferential role in reviewing government decisions. This deference is particularly evident in the review of rule making, especially in the review of the substance of regulations. The executive then often plays a central role in monitoring itself, and often does not execute the role very well.

The result is a system in which elected officials delegate broad powers to make rules and (directly or indirectly) soft law, but with varying degrees of oversight of their creation and use. The difficulty in challenging rules and soft law after they are made points to the need to consider getting involved in the process of creating them. These rules and soft law are central to the ultimate distribution of power—they shape who gets to stay in the country, which species are protected, and what health services people receive. Given their importance in the lives of Canadians, rules and soft law are woefully understudied and their significance underappreciated. The struggle over how to allocate decision-making powers continues.

CHAPTER NINE

Fairness in Context: Achieving Fairness Through Access to Administrative Justice

Angus Grant and Lorne Sossin*
Osgoode Hall Law School, York University

I. INTRODUCTION

In Chapter 5 of this volume, Kate Glover sketches out the essential features of procedural fairness in administrative law. In this chapter, we further elaborate on these principles by examining the everyday practice of administrative justice and the various contexts in which fairness concerns may arise. One important prism through which we will examine the lived experience of fairness is that of access to administrative justice. To elaborate on this perspective on fairness in administrative justice, we will be drawing on the case study of deportation and the setting of immigration and refugee determinations.

* We are indebted to the contributors to this volume for constructive comments on the chapter, and to Marleigh Dick for her helpful research assistance.

As is by now apparent, a primary aim of administrative law is to provide efficient and fair procedures to a vast array of decisions that governments make every day. For the community at large generally and for vulnerable communities specifically, it is far more likely that a person's rights and important interests will be at stake in an administrative proceeding than a judicial one. As the chief justice of Canada has observed, "Many more citizens have their rights determined by these tribunals than by the courts."[1] Yet, remarkably, until recently, texts on administrative law rarely canvassed questions of access to administrative justice as an essential aspect of the fairness analysis. While rule of law concerns and the ideal of one's "day in court" have come to characterize "access to justice," it is less clear what this means in the diverse variety of settings where vulnerable people come before administrative decision-makers.

Rights and important interests are often at stake in administrative justice, whether before a human rights tribunal, an immigration board, or a securities commission. Access to a decision-maker may make the difference between justice and injustice. The rule of law is no less significant in an administrative hearing room or decision-making process than a courtroom, and arguably, as we discuss below, it may be more so. In this sense, fairness ought to be seen not just as a set of rules governing how affected parties may participate in public decisions but also as a claim about people's experiences in this process. If I am afforded a hearing but cannot understand the proceeding, and do not know what I need to show in order to obtain the outcome I wish, has the decision-maker discharged the duty of fairness?

How tribunals make policy, how tribunal members are appointed, the resources available for parties before tribunals, and the fairness and quality of decision-making provided by those tribunals all form part of the core concern of administrative justice. While these issues could arise in a myriad of administrative settings, our analysis in this chapter will be concerned primarily with administrative law settings that adjudicate claims related to individual rights and interests.[2]

In what follows we will explore what "access to justice" means in the context of administrative tribunals and how we measure "fairness" in the myriad contexts of administrative law. As we shall see, there is no one answer to these questions, and the comparison of administrative tribunals to courts sometimes obscures more than it reveals. In this chapter, we canvass the contexts of fairness and access from the perspective of those affected by administrative decisions. This perspective requires that attention be paid not just to the statutory provisions that empower tribunals, or the court decisions that interpret those provisions, but also to the everyday practice before tribunals.

For example, in empowering the Immigration and Refugee Board to determine refugee claims and other immigration matters, the *Immigration and Refugee Protection Act* states that the board "shall deal with all proceedings before it as informally and quickly as the

---

1   *Cooper v Canada (Human Rights Commission)*, [1996] 3 SCR 854 at 899-900, McLachlin J (as she then was) (dissenting).

2   In other words, we focus here on tribunals whose primary purpose is the impartial resolution of disputes or the determination of an individual's status, such as labour boards, immigration processes, human rights tribunals, and worker compensation appeal boards. We do not mean to suggest there are no access concerns for other kinds of agencies, boards, and commissions, but the intersections of access and justice are at their clearest where the subject matter of a tribunal is primarily adjudicative. For a discussion on classifying tribunals as adjudicative and non-adjudicative, see Ed Ratushny, *The Independence of Federal Administrative Tribunals and Agencies in Canada* (Ottawa: Canadian Bar Association, 1990) at 46-47.

circumstances and the considerations of fairness and natural justice permit."[3] It is clear from this provision that the board is given considerable leeway to determine what fairness means and requires in the context of the proceedings that come before it. It is also clear from the legislation that fairness in this context is framed in light of a corresponding legislative requirement for speed in decision-making. These twin imperatives of efficiency and fairness lie at the very heart of administrative law. Negotiating the tension between them is correspondingly a central concern of administrative lawyers and tribunals alike.

While we do not suggest that this list is exhaustive, it is possible to approach our topic from at least three distinct perspectives:[4]

1. *Access to the tribunal*
   How do parties find the tribunal—is it accessible in person through an office open to the public? If so, is the tribunal housed in a single office or in multiple offices in a range of communities? Is video conferencing available for those unable or unwilling to travel to attend a hearing? Is the tribunal accessible through telephone and/or Internet services, and if so, are these points of contact made available in the languages spoken by users of the tribunal?

2. *Access to legal or other knowledge necessary to obtain tribunal services*
   How do parties learn what they need to know to be able to contribute to the proceedings and to support their claims? Are the relevant legislative provisions and regulations setting out the powers of a tribunal publicized to parties? Are the prior decisions of the tribunal available and accessible? Have guidelines been developed to set out the standards by which decisions will be reached, and if so, have those guidelines been made available to the public? Are tribunal staff available to assist with filling out forms or to assist in preparing parties' submissions? Again, are guidelines and/or tribunal staff available in languages spoken by users of the tribunal?

3. *Access to resources needed to navigate tribunal system*
   How do people present their positions before a tribunal? Is there a right to state-funded legal representation? Do fees create barriers and if so is there a procedure for waiving fees? Are previous decisions of the tribunal available, and if so, are they in a form that can be searched and sorted through by self-represented parties? Is there access to mediation, dispute resolution, or settlement services? Are interpreters available?

In the following analysis, we explore each of these ways of addressing access to administrative justice.

---

3 *Immigration and Refugee Protection Act*, SC 2001, c 27, s 162(2).

4 For a helpful conceptual review of "access to justice," see Rod McDonald, "Access to Justice in 2003: Scope, Scale and Ambitions" in J Bass, WA Bogart & FH Zemans, eds, *Access to Justice for a New Century—The Way Forward* (Toronto: Irwin, 2005). McDonald sets out that "commentators identify a broad inventory of features that would characterize an accessible justice system: (1) just results, (2) fair treatment, (3) reasonable cost, (4) reasonable speed, (5) understandable to users, (6) responsive to needs, (7) certain, and (8) effective, adequately resourced and well-organized. But, as the experiences of the last four decades illustrate, these are not features of an accessible justice system; [these] are merely features of an accessible dispute resolution system. These experiences point to two main organizing themes of a comprehensive access to justice strategy: the strategy must be multi-dimensional; and it must take a pluralistic approach to the institutions of law and justice": at 23-24.

II. ACCESS TO ADMINISTRATIVE JUSTICE: THE TRIBUNAL

In *Baker v Canada (Minister of Citizenship and Immigration)*, the Supreme Court of Canada noted that the bedrock underlying virtually all questions of fairness in administrative procedures is the requirement that administrative decisions are made using procedures appropriate to the decision-making context, with an opportunity for those affected by the decision to put forward their views and evidence fully and have them considered by the decision-maker.[5]

When we think of the mandate of a tribunal, we are often referring to its powers, its jurisdiction, and its statutory purposes. We rarely think of this mandate in terms of the things that matter most to those who come before the tribunal, such as: How do I find the tribunal? Where is it located? Can I initiate proceedings, and if so, how is this done? How much will it cost? Will I have a hearing? If so, what will I have to say? Is it accessible to people living with physical or mental disabilities? Who will help me if I get confused or cannot understand what is expected of me or what I can expect of others in the process?

These concerns do not typically arise in academic discussions of procedural fairness, which tend to be rooted in the more formal language of the right to be heard by an impartial and independent tribunal. Yet for many people, particularly those without legal representation (further discussed below), tangible impediments to even beginning to seek administrative justice, let alone obtaining it, can be formidable.

While the governing statute of a tribunal (and its subordinate legislation—regulations and rules) typically sets out the powers of a tribunal, it is often left to the tribunal itself to decide what face it presents to the public. There are two aspects to this perspective we wish to explore—first, the issue of standing before a tribunal, and second, the issue of whether a tribunal will hold oral or written hearings, and, if oral hearings, whether those hearings are in person or via other technological means.

A. Standing

The first aspect of this perspective on access is standing. Who serves as the gatekeeper for administrative justice? This question may have several answers, depending on one's perspective. We begin here by examining standing before administrative tribunals, then move on to outline standing before the courts, where administrative matters are frequently litigated through to their conclusion.

In administrative law, the first sense in which standing is understood is the standing to access the tribunal. Tribunals, unlike courts, have no inherent jurisdiction. The standing to bring a matter to a tribunal must be found in the tribunal's governing statute (or some other statutory authority).

As Robert Macaulay and James Sprague have noted, "There are a number of cases on standing before administrative agencies in Canada, but each of them relies so specifically on the mandating legislation of that agency, or at least upon the interpretation of some judicially-oriented chairperson, that they are not really very helpful as a general guide."[6] For example, the *Ontario Residential Tenancies Act, 2006*, establishing the Landlord Tenant Board,

---

5   [1999] 2 SCR 817 at para 22 [*Baker*].

6   R Macaulay & J Sprague, *Practice and Procedure Before Administrative Tribunals* (Toronto: Carswell, 2001) (looseleaf) 9.7(b).

sets out that "[t]he parties to an application are the landlord and any tenants or other persons directly affected by the application."[7] Ontario also has a general procedural statute for administrative proceedings, the *Statutory Power Procedures Act*, which provides that

> The parties to a proceeding shall be the persons specified as parties by or under the statute under which the proceeding arises or, if not so specified, persons entitled by law to be parties to the proceeding.[8]

The Alberta *Administrative Procedures Act*[9] does not address standing, but a report of the Alberta Law Reform Institute entitled "Powers and Procedures of Administrative Tribunals"[10] recommended the following standing provision:

Parties
(1) A tribunal must grant standing in proceedings before it to the following:
  (a) persons who have standing under the enabling enactment;
  (b) persons whose rights or obligations will be directly varied or affected by the tribunal's determination of the matter before it.

With respect to who is entitled by law to be parties to a proceeding before a tribunal, David Mullan has observed that the issue of standing before tribunals has become more important as the duty of fairness has been interpreted more expansively in the wake of cases such as *Nicholson v Haldimand-Norfolk (Regional) Police Commissioners*.[11] One might imagine even more pressure for generous approaches to standing as the scope of fairness continues to expand,[12] and tribunal jurisdiction over the *Canadian Charter of Rights and Freedoms* has been approached more generously.[13]

However, the point of departure for who is entitled to fairness remains the tribunal's governing statute. Returning to the Ontario Landlord and Tenant Board, for example, the Act provides: "The Board shall adopt the most expeditious method of determining the questions arising in a proceeding that affords to all persons directly affected by the proceeding an adequate opportunity to know the issues and be heard on the matter."[14] As can be seen from this context, the enabling statute sets the parameters for access, but it also provides a measure of discretion to the board to determine both *who* is directly affected by its proceedings and what amounts to an adequate opportunity to be heard.

Historically, the kinds of tribunals where standing has been an issue were either regulatory tribunals (for example, an energy board or competition tribunal) or tribunals whose decisions touched many people indirectly (for example, a municipal planning board) or labour tribunals

---

7 SO 2006, c 17, s 187(1).
8 RSO 1990, c S.22, s 5 [SPPA].
9 RSA 2000, c A-3.
10 Consultation Memorandum No 13 (2008), online: <https://www.alri.ualberta.ca/docs/cm013.pdf>.
11 [1979] 1 SCR 311. See David Mullan et al, *Administrative Law: Cases, Text and Materials*, 5th ed (Toronto: Emond Montgomery, 2005) at 1247-48.
12 *Baker*, *supra* note 5, and see also *Ontario (Energy Board) v Ontario Power Generation Inc*, 2015 SCC 44, [2015] 3 SCR 147.
13 See *Martin v Nova Scotia (Workers' Compensation Board); Nova Scotia (Workers' Compensation Board) v Laseur* [2003] 2 SCR 504; *Paul v British Columbia (Forest Appeals Commission)*, [2003] 2 SCR 585; *R v Conway*, [2010] 1 SCR 765; and *PS v Ontario*, 2014 ONCA 900. See also the discussion of the Charter and administrative law by Evan Fox-Decent and Alexander Pless (Chapters 6 and 13) in this volume.
14 *Ontario Residential Tenancies Act, 2006*, s 183. See also Chapter 5 in this volume.

(where the rights of some employees may have an impact on a much wider group of employees). In regulatory cases, boards typically work out representative compromises, whereby a ratepayers association or citizens group is granted standing to represent the interests of those indirectly affected by board decisions (these groups will sometimes be referred to as interveners as well). This practice may raise accountability questions as the tribunal rarely inquires into the representative character of public interest groups.

In the labour board setting, standing issues often involve third-party employees who are affected by another employee's grievance—for example, where an incumbent employee would potentially be displaced following a successful grievance. Should the incumbent employee be given the opportunity to participate in the grievance to protect her rights? The answer would appear to be "no, except in limited circumstances."[15] As one labour arbitrator observed, "If the rights of individual employees who are directly or indirectly affected by the outcome of arbitration proceedings were granted standing in all cases where their individual rights were affected, the numbers of potentially affected employees would be quite large, arbitration hearings would become lengthy and more expensive, and employees would come to feel some obligation to be separately represented."[16]

The second and related sense in which standing arises in administrative law is the question of a party's standing to challenge an administrative decision in court.[17] While superior courts have inherent jurisdiction to determine standing, as opposed to administrative bodies such as tribunals whose standing is a matter for their governing statutes, the principles developed by courts in relation to this gatekeeping role may well influence tribunals. In particular, the broadening of public interest standing, discussed below, has broad application to a number of tribunal contexts, where adjudicators will often have a residual discretion to permit standing or intervention where it is in the public interest to do so.[18]

Under the historical regime of prerogative writs, discussed in Chapter 2 of this volume, standing was limited to those directly affected by state action. To the extent that state action concerned the public interest, remedial authority lay with the attorney general. This approach is also captured in the *Federal Courts Act*, which provides standing to the attorney general or to any party "directly affected" by state action.[19]

It remains the case that not every citizen is entitled, as of right, to challenge administrative action. Judicial review of administrative action is generally reserved for those who are found to have a sufficient legally recognized interest in the matter to justify the judicial review application. It is said that the test for standing is whether the applicant is a "person aggrieved" by the administrative decision. It has been said that a person aggrieved is one who will suffer some "peculiar grievance of their own beyond some grievance suffered by them in common with the rest of the public."[20]

---

15 See *CUPW v Canada Post Corp (Hall Grievance)* (2006), 149 LAC (4th) 306.

16 *Re Royal Victoria Hospital and ONA* (O'Dwyer) (1993), 30 CLAS 355.

17 See, for example, David Mullan, *Administrative Law* (Toronto: Irwin, 2001), ch 18.

18 See Robert MacAulay and James Sprague, *Practice and Procedure before Administrative Tribunals*, vol 2 (Toronto: Carswell, 2004) (looseleaf) ch 9.7 (2013 - Rel. 7).

19 *Federal Courts Act*, RSC 1985, c F-7, ss 18(1), 28(2). See Craig Forcese's discussion of the Federal Court in Chapter 15 of this volume.

20 See, for example, *Friends of the Oldman River Society v Association of Professional Engineers, Geologists and Geophysicists of Alberta* (1997), [1998] 5 WWR 179 (Alta QB), rev'd on other grounds, 2001 ABCA 107. See also TA Cromwell, *Locus Standi: A Commentary on the Law of Standing in Canada* (Toronto: Carswell, 1986) at 106-108.

These limits on standing were justified on the basis that they promoted the efficiency of administrative action by keeping the administration free from artificial or academic challenges to administrative action, while still respecting the rights of third parties. In many cases where the applicant for judicial review cannot show that he or she is directly affected or aggrieved by the challenged administrative act, there will in fact be third parties in the community who are directly affected or aggrieved. The general policy of the court is not to decide issues in the absence of the parties whose rights are most directly affected by the court's decision. In other words, if those who are most directly affected by the administrative decision are content to "live with it," the court will not permit curious busybodies to bring applications for judicial review in their stead. If, on the other hand, those most directly impacted or "aggrieved" wish to challenge the administrative action, they should be able to do so free from interference.[21] While an aggrieved party may wish to challenge an administrative decision in the courts, few have the financial resources to launch a judicial review. For this reason, one of the most significant developments in Canadian public law is the concept of discretionary public interest standing, which may allow a "test" applicant or NGO to launch judicial review proceedings on behalf of a broader group.

The justification for discretionary public interest standing can be readily illustrated by recourse to the immigration context. Non-citizens facing removal may wish to challenge some aspect of the removal scheme. However, because of the mechanics of Canadian immigration law, the individual may be removed from Canada before a decision can be made on the challenge. When this happens, the courts have frequently declined to render a decision on the merits of the case, because the outcome has become moot; win or lose, the applicant has still been deported. The matter would not be moot, however, for a public interest group that represents the interests of non-citizens generally. This ability of advocacy organizations to sustain a legal challenge throughout the lengthy litigation process makes public interest standing an important option in cases where removal may occur.

Alternatively, an immigration provision that is constitutionally suspect may go unchallenged because suitable litigants are either outside Canada or are living "underground" and may fear coming forward to challenge the law in court. Where the vulnerability of a disadvantaged group prevents members of that group from accessing the courts, it may be appropriate for public interest organizations to step forward. This was the situation in the leading case on public interest standing, *Canada (Attorney General) v Downtown Eastside Sex Workers United Against Violence Society*,[22] which involved a challenge to the constitutionality of *Criminal Code* provisions relating to prostitution.

In the *Downtown Eastside* case, the parties challenging the provisions consisted of a former sex worker and an organization whose mandate was to improve the conditions for female sex workers in the Downtown Eastside of Vancouver. At the outset of the litigation, the attorney general of Canada sought to have the case dismissed on the basis that the parties lacked standing before the courts. The British Columbia Supreme Court accepted this position and dismissed the case on this basis, but the British Columbia Court of Appeal overturned this decision. In later upholding the Court of Appeal decision, the Supreme Court of Canada indicated that a liberal approach to the issue of public interest standing may frequently best serve

---

21 For discussion, see *Alberta Liquor Store Assn v Alberta (Gaming and Liquor Commission)*, 2006 ABQB 904 at paras 10-11.

22 2012 SCC 45 [*Downtown Eastside*].

the interests of justice. The *Downtown Eastside* case affirmed the test for determining standing that had previously been established in the jurisprudence, but underscored that the discretion to grant public interest standing should be exercised in a broad, generous, and liberal manner.[23] The test for public interest standing remains threefold:

1. Is the matter serious and justiciable?
2. Is the party seeking standing genuinely interested in the matter?
3. Is there any other reasonable and effective way for the matter to be adjudicated?[24]

The only source of controversy between the parties in the *Downtown Eastside* case related to the third factor. In previous cases, this factor had been viewed as a strict requirement that the party seeking standing had to establish that there was essentially *no* other reasonable and effective manner in which the issue could be brought before the courts. The Supreme Court of Canada, however, concluded that the third factor would be better expressed as requiring that the proposed proceeding be, in light of various pragmatic considerations, a reasonable and effective means of bringing the case to court.

In considering whether there are other reasonable and effective ways of bringing an issue before the courts, judges should adopt a pragmatic point of view, particularly on the question as to whether, practically speaking, other litigants who have standing as of right are likely to bring the matter to court on their own. As well, even where there are other litigants with a direct interest in the proceedings, a court may consider whether a public interest organization will bring any particularly useful or distinct perspectives to the issue at hand.[25] In 2013, the Supreme Court of Canada relied on this aspect of the *Downtown Eastside* decision to grant public interest standing to a representative Métis organization in a groundbreaking case on Métis rights. In that case, the court granted standing to the Manitoba Metis Federation, despite the fact that there were other individual litigants involved in the case who had, in fact, brought forward the litigation on their own.[26]

In reinforcing a liberal approach to the question of public interest standing, the court in the *Downtown Eastside* case characterized the issue in part as one of access to justice. Writing for the court, Cromwell J articulated several considerations for determining public interest standing matters, including the following:

> The court should consider whether the case is of public interest in the sense that it transcends the interests of those most directly affected by the challenged law or action. Courts should take into account that one of the ideas which animates public interest litigation is that it may provide access to justice for disadvantaged persons in society whose legal rights are affected. Of course, this should not be equated with a licence to grant standing to whoever decides to set themselves up as the representative of the poor or marginalized.[27]

---

23   *Ibid* at para 35, citing *Canadian Council of Churches v Canada (Minister of Employment and Immigration)*, [1992] 1 SCR 236.

24   This test was first developed in a trilogy of public interest standing cases—see *Thorson v Canada (Attorney General)*, [1975] 1 SCR 138; *Nova Scotia Board of Censors v McNeil*, [1976] 2 SCR 265; *Canada (Minister of Justice) v Borowski*, [1981] 2 SCR 575.

25   *Downtown Eastside*, *supra* note 22 at para 51.

26   *Manitoba Metis Federation Inc v Canada (Attorney General)*, 2013 SCC 14.

27   *Downtown Eastside*, *supra* note 22 at para 51.

In another case that arose shortly after the Supreme Court's *Downtown Eastside* decision, a trio of groups, together with individual litigants, initiated a challenge to changes that the federal government had made to health care funding for certain categories of non-citizens.[28] In seeking standing, the groups adduced evidence indicating the efforts they had made to identify individual litigants who were directly affected by the health care changes. The evidence also revealed that most of the individuals identified were unwilling to participate in the litigation. Among other practical impediments, some potential applicants were too physically or mentally ill to participate in a challenge. Others were facing removal from Canada and, therefore, may not have been present to see the litigation through to its conclusion. Finally, the groups demonstrated the more general reluctance of vulnerable applicants to publicly challenge the Government of Canada while their immigration status remained uncertain.

The Federal Court granted standing to the groups, noting that, in addition to the difficulties faced by individual litigants in challenging the health care changes, the public interest groups had the capacity and resources to present the issues concretely in a well-developed factual setting.[29] Allowing the groups to participate as parties to the litigation also had the potential to avoid a multiplicity of challenges and a correspondingly unnecessary expenditure of scarce judicial resources.[30]

Complex Charter litigation increasingly requires the production of a large record of supporting evidence. Indeed, in numerous cases the courts have refused to consider Charter-based arguments without a fulsome factual background and evidentiary record.[31]

This leads to an uncomfortable irony for many vulnerable groups as they engage with the administrative state: they seek the protection of the Charter to help address the causes and consequences of their vulnerability, yet to do so requires access to resources that they frequently lack. This is precisely why public interest standing can play a crucial role in administrative justice.

In the *Canadian Doctors* case, the public groups adduced a comprehensive body of evidence that would have been impossible for individual litigants to obtain—evidence documenting the lived experiences of a wide swath of individuals who had lost health care coverage, evidence of doctors, public health experts, historians, health policy and health economics experts, and survey data analysis experts. On the basis of this evidentiary foundation, the Federal Court concluded that the health care changes amounted to cruel and unusual treatment contrary to s 12 of the Charter and also violated the equality provisions of the Charter under s 15.

In addition to challenging allegedly unconstitutional laws, discretionary public interest standing also has been applied to challenge the decision-making of administrative bodies in court. The leading case in this area remains *Finlay v Canada (Minister of Finance)*.[32] In granting public interest standing to a claimant challenging a decision by the federal government not to impose penalties on Manitoba for garnishing benefits of a social welfare recipient in apparent breach of the Canada Assistance Plan provisions, the Supreme Court of Canada

---

28 *Canadian Doctors for Refugee Care v Canada (AG and MCI)*, 2014 FC 651 [*Canadian Doctors*].
29 *Ibid* at para 347.
30 *Ibid* at para 344.
31 *Mackay v Manitoba*, [1989] 2 SCR 357; *Laidlow v Canada (Citizenship and Immigration)*, 2012 FCA 256.
32 [1986] 2 SCR 607.

accepted that this form of standing would be available to challenge administrative action and not simply legislation.

In *Finlay*, the court applied the three-part test for standing in order to grant standing to a recipient of social benefits and allow that recipient to challenge the conduct of the federal government toward the province of Manitoba under the Canada Assistance Plan. The applicant not only raised a serious issue with respect to the legality of the government's action (or, in this case, its inaction in failing to penalize a province for breaching the conditions of the plan), but the applicant was also a recipient of the benefit in question, and was, therefore, genuinely interested in the case. Because neither the federal government nor the provinces had an interest in compelling a penalty from the federal government, the court also concluded that there was no reasonable alternative by which the challenge would reach court (even though this standard was lowered in the *Downtown Eastside* case).

The court has elsewhere affirmed that the purpose of granting status is to "prevent the immunization of legislation or public acts from any challenge,"[33] and that public interest standing is available in the context of challenges that arise out of administrative tribunals,[34] but there is some suggestion that the scope of such challenges may be limited to legislative provisions and public acts of a legislative character, which would exclude most tribunal decision-making.[35]

On access grounds, tribunals have also sought standing before courts where their decisions are judicially reviewed. In *Children's Lawyer for Ontario v Goodis*,[36] the Ontario Court of Appeal considered a case where the Information and Privacy Commissioner responded to a judicial review application by the Office of the Children's Lawyer of Ontario, as the successful requestor chose not to participate in the judicial review proceedings. As Goudge JA observed, s 9(2) of the *Judicial Review Procedure Act* entitles an administrative tribunal to be a party to the proceedings but leaves to the court's discretion the scope of its standing. The court found that context is central to the exercise of this discretion, and that in settings where a party is unable or unwilling to participate in a judicial review, as in the *Children's Lawyer* setting, tribunal standing is needed to ensure that the court has an adequate legal and factual basis upon which to make an impartial and reasoned decision.[37]

As these examples illustrate, and as explored by Kate Glover in Chapter 5 in this volume, the tension between fairness and efficiency is an enduring theme in settings of access to administrative justice. On the one hand, expanding the scope of those entitled to participate in judicial review processes may be resisted on the basis that the increased complexity and evidentiary burden this places on the courts belies the very purpose of administrative efficiency and judicial review. On the other hand, any substantive understanding of fairness reveals that vulnerable populations may frequently be both unable and unwilling to shoulder the heavy burden of challenging laws that may very well infringe important, constitutionally protected rights.

---

33   *Canadian Council of Churches v Canada (Minister of Employment and Immigration)*, supra note 23 at para 252.

34   See *Vriend v Alberta*, [1998] 1 SCR 493 at 528.

35   See *Canadian Bar Assn v British Columbia*, 2006 BCSC 1342 at paras 41 and 42. For further discussion, see L Sossin, "The Justice of Access: Who Should Have Standing to Challenge the Constitutional Adequacy of Legal Aid?" (2007) 40 UBC L Rev 727.

36   (2005), 75 OR (3d) 309 (CA) [*Children's Lawyer*].

37   See *ibid* at para 48.

And as the courts have recently noted, there may frequently be efficiency gains by allowing public interest standing where doing so can help to consolidate legal challenges and avoid a multiplicity of challenges, all based on an inferior evidentiary record.

B. Hearings

The second aspect of the perspective on access to administrative justice is how parties will interact with the tribunal. Will the tribunal conduct its process entirely in writing or will there be an opportunity for a hearing of some kind? As discussed earlier in this volume, full oral hearings are not required in all administrative law contexts; rather, the specific format of proceedings that tribunals incorporate into their decision-making processes, and the discretion available to tribunals to control their processes, will normally be set out in empowering statutes.[38] Commencing with the seminal decision of the Supreme Court of Canada in *Singh v Canada (Minister of Employment and Immigration)*,[39] Canadian courts have frequently elaborated on hearing requirements from the traditional perspectives of procedural justice (in the common law) and fundamental justice (pursuant to s 7 of the Charter).

Courts have less frequently considered the practical barriers that many individuals face in seeking a fair hearing process. Administrative tribunals, like courts, need to be accessible to all. Various pieces of federal and provincial legislation mandate that tribunals and regulatory bodies comply with a series of uniform standards.[40] Accessibility may mean a ramp to the hearing room and wheelchair accessible washrooms, while in other cases it will mean access to materials to those with visual disabilities or sign language interpretation for the hearing impaired during a proceeding. Accessibility standards also apply to digital materials and proceedings. Various human rights codes also apply to ensure a standard for accommodation and an enforcement mechanism.[41]

While accessibility for parties with physical disabilities is a pressing concern, accessibility for parties living with mental or cognitive disabilities is an emerging concern as well. These accessibility issues typically are more difficult to identify and more challenging to accommodate.[42] Tribunals are responding with enhanced training and education for members and staff, dedicated accessibility officers, and accessibility plans. Some tribunals permit parties to bring support persons with them, while others emphasize their flexibility as between written, electronic, and in-person hearings to accommodate different kinds of special needs.

For example, in 2006, the Immigration and Refugee Board (IRB) issued Guideline 8 aimed to assist decision-makers in accommodating the needs of vulnerable persons.[43] Among

---

38 For further discussion on the fairness requirement of hearings in administrative law, see Kate Glover's discussion in Chapter 5.

39 [1985] 1 SCR 177.

40 For example, the *Ontarians with Disabilities Act, 2005*, SO 2005, c 11, mandates a series of customer service standards, which are being developed on a sector-by-sector basis.

41 See e.g. BC *Human Rights Code*, RSBC 1996, C 210, s 8.

42 See L Sossin, "Mental Health and Administrative Justice" (Paper presented at Canadian Institute for the Administration of Justice, "Mental Health and the Justice System: Barriers and Solutions" (26 September 2011) (unpublished, on file with author).

43 Immigration and Refugee Board, *Chairperson Guideline 8: Procedures with Respect to Vulnerable Persons Appearing Before the IRB* [Guideline 8] (amended 15 December 2012), online: <http://www.irb-cisr.gc.ca/Eng/BoaCom/references/pol/GuiDir/Pages/GuideDir08.aspx>.

other things, Guideline 8 defines vulnerability and sets out a variety of accommodations that may be appropriate, ranging from providing gender-specific interpreters and decision-makers, to varying the formality of the hearing process to appointing a designated representative who, among other things, may testify on the claimant's behalf. Guideline 8 is born of an important recognition that an administrative tribunal's choice of hearing procedures may differentially impact different persons. While general procedures may satisfy basic fairness criteria, such procedures may, depending on the circumstances, impose significant barriers on particular individuals.

Other approaches to accessibility emphasize access for parties in remote areas or where physical presence in a hearing room would be prohibitively expensive. The Ontario Landlord and Tenant Board, among other province-wide bodies, has instituted video conferencing as a substitute for in-person hearings. On the one hand, this measure provides much greater access to hearings without the long travel time and dislocation previously associated with attending hearings in person. On the other hand, many report disadvantages of a hearing by video, some of which may go to the fairness of the proceeding.[44] For this reason, s 5.2(2) of the SPPA states that a tribunal *shall not* hold an electronic hearing if a party satisfies the tribunal that holding an electronic rather than an oral hearing is likely to cause the party significant prejudice.

In addition to the location of hearings, tribunals also face other questions of how to ensure full and fair access to the public, while optimizing efficiency. The proliferation of technology has only added to these questions. Is it important that a tribunal have a physical presence at all or will a "virtual" tribunal which is accessible through the Internet be sufficient? In the United Kingdom, a recent report urged the government to shift many civil matters to virtual courtrooms and to an Internet-based dispute resolution system.[45]

The Supreme Court of Canada has also recently contemplated the importance for the justice system to be receptive to new modes of hearing cases. In *Hryniak v Mauldin*, Karakatsanis J noted:

> The balance between procedure and access struck by our justice system must come to reflect modern reality and recognize that new models of adjudication can be fair and just.[46]

Furthermore, these issues arise not as an abstract question of fairness but as a concrete trade-off involving resources. Video conferencing, for example, is far less expensive than maintaining an office in remote centres or obtaining facilities for in-person hearings. Of course, a hearing by teleconference would be even less expensive. The question is when efficiency or cost-cutting measures begin to erode the fairness of a decision-making process and undermine the likelihood that the decision reached is the right one.

---

44 For discussion, see L Sossin & Z Yetnikoff, "I Can See Clearly Now: Videoconference Hearings and the Legal Limit on how Tribunals Allocate Resources" (unpublished paper, 2006). This is particularly the case in hearings involving credibility assessments. Evaluating the spontaneity of an individual's responses to questions or the subtle aspects of their demeanour, for example, can be challenging in a video conferencing environment.

45 Owen Bowcott, "Online Court Proposed to Resolve Claims of up to £25,000" (16 February 2015), *The Guardian*, online: <https://www.theguardian.com/law/2015/feb/16/online-court-proposed-to-resolve-claims-of-up-to-25000>. While such a shift may in some ways enhance access, it may also pose barriers, for example, for those without access to technology or for those unfamiliar with how to use it.

46 *Hryniak v Mauldin*, 2014 SCC 7 at para 2.

III. ACCESS TO ADMINISTRATIVE JUSTICE: INFORMATION AND KNOWLEDGE

Some would argue that accessing a tribunal itself is far less difficult than accessing the legal expertise necessary to succeed at a tribunal. The way in which a tribunal communicates the information and knowledge necessary to access its services or remedies varies and will rarely be set out in an empowering statute. The wave of legislative initiatives related to accountability has, in some parts of the country, led to greater transparency requirements on tribunals. For example, the Ontario *Adjudicative Tribunals Accountability, Governance and Appointments Act, 2009*[47] requires that tribunals publish "public accountability documents" that include, among other things, consultation policies, service standards to the public, and conflict-of-interest guidelines. While such common informational templates may assist with accountability, they offer little in the way of relevant information for the individual party seeking a remedy before the tribunal. In this, as in so many areas affecting access to administrative justice, it is the policies of the tribunal itself, not those of the government, that will be determinative.

A. Guidelines

As discussed above and by Andrew Green in Chapter 8 in this volume, many tribunals develop guidelines to ensure consistency and to structure discretion.[48] Transparency with respect to the standards of decision-making represents an emerging aspect of access to administrative justice. For this reason, it is important that guidelines are developed that set out these standards; and where this occurs, it is equally important that these guidelines are made publicly available. One interesting question is whether it can be said to be a requirement of fairness that a tribunal with significant discretion actually structure that discretion in some fashion. To date, the farthest a court has been willing to go is to state that where guidelines are in place, it may be a breach of fairness for the decision-making body to ignore those guidelines without justification.[49]

Because tribunals are bound only by statutory provisions, it is not open to a tribunal to develop binding guidelines on their own initiative.[50] This issue has arisen in the context of the Immigration and Refugee Board (IRB).

The IRB issued *Chairperson Guideline 7: Concerning Preparation and Conduct of a Hearing in the Refugee Protection Division* in accordance with the legislative authority conferred to the Chairperson of the IRB by s 159 of the *Immigration and Refugee Protection Act*.[51] Guideline 7 circumscribes inquiry powers of IRB members so that they can limit the scope of the inquiry,

---

47   SO 2009, c 33, Schedule 5. See online: <https://www.ontario.ca/laws/statute/09a33>.

48   See F Houle & L Sossin, "Tribunals and Guidelines: Exploring the Relationships Between Fairness and Legitimacy in Administrative Decision-Making" (2006) 46 Canadian Public Administration 282 at 294-300.

49   *Bezaire v Windsor Roman Catholic Separate School Board* (1992), 9 OR (3d) 737 (Div Ct).

50   See *Little Sisters Book and Art Emporium v Canada (Minister of Justice)*, 2000 SCC 69 at para 85. Because they are not considered binding as law, guidelines are not subject to Charter scrutiny. For discussion, see L Sossin, "Discretion Unbound: Reconciling the Charter and Soft Law" (2003) 45 Canadian Public Administration 465.

51   "159 (1) The Chairperson is, by virtue of holding that office, a member of each Division of the Board and is the chief executive officer of the Board. In that capacity, the Chairperson ... (h) may issue guidelines in writing to members of the Board and identify decisions of the Board as jurisprudential guides."

and as such, be in a position to control the conduct of the hearing in order to ensure efficient and speedy determinations of claims. Guideline 7 "changes the order of questioning by having the Refugee Protection Division (RPD) leading the inquiry in the hearing room. The purpose of this change is to allow the RPD to make the best use of its expertise as a specialist tribunal by focusing on the issues which it has identified as determinative."[52]

In *Thamotharem v Canada (Minister of Citizenship and Immigration)*,[53] Guideline 7 was challenged as a breach of procedural fairness and on the grounds that it fettered the discretion of board members to decide the order of questioning appropriate to a particular claim. It was raised in the context of a refugee application involving a Tamil student claiming persecution if returned to Sri Lanka. The Federal Court held that Guideline 7 did not violate the board's duty of fairness but was an unlawful fetter on the exercise of discretion because board members often operate as if they are bound by it. The denial of Mr Thamotharem's refugee status was quashed on this basis. The IRB appealed and the Federal Court of Appeal affirmed the court's finding with regards to Guideline 7 and the duty of fairness but reversed the aspect of the decision dealing with administrative discretion. It dismissed Thamotharem's application for judicial review on the basis that Guideline 7 expressly directs members to consider the facts of the particular case before them in order to determine whether there are circumstances warranting a deviation from the standard order of questioning. Also, it was not evident that board members generally disregarded this aspect of Guideline 7 and unthinkingly adhered to the standard order of questioning. Thus, while transparency calls for tribunals to develop and publicize guidelines on which parties before a tribunal may rely, the principles of administrative law may limit the effectiveness of that reliance by requiring that a tribunal not treat its own guidelines as binding.

While guidelines may not be binding, they frequently represent a distillation, simplification, and operationalization of existing case law and legal principles. So while the guidelines may not be binding *as guidelines*, decision-makers who stray from them may be found to have committed legal errors in doing so. This may be particularly clear in respect of guidelines, such as the IRB's Guidelines 7 and 8 (both discussed above), that set out procedural standards to ensure the fairness of proceedings. Recall that questions of fairness tend to be assessed by reviewing courts on a correctness standard. This suggests that decision-makers may have little latitude in straying from procedural guidelines where the guidelines set out baseline expectations as to what the tribunal considers to be the requirements of procedural fairness in the particular proceedings that come before it. That said, decision-makers cannot allow guidelines to take the place of their own consideration of the legal questions that must be resolved.[54] In other words, guidelines serve as a minimal set of content for what procedural fairness requires but will not be sufficient in all cases.

Additionally, tribunals often have the authority to issue rules of practice. BC's *Administrative Tribunals Act* (ATA) provides authority for tribunals to make rules and issue practice

---

52 Immigration and Refugee Board, *Chairperson Guideline 7: Concerning Preparation and Conduct of a Hearing in the Refugee Protection Division*, online: <http://www.irb-cisr.gc.ca/Eng/BoaCom/references/pol/GuiDir/Pages/GuideDir07.aspx>.

53 2007 FCA 198, [2008] 1 FCR 385; see also *Benitez v Canada (Minister of Citizenship and Immigration)*, 2007 FCA 199, [2008] 1 FCR 155.

54 See, for example, the court overturning an immigration officer's complete reliance on a guideline in *Kanthasamy v Canada (Citizenship and Immigration)*, 2015 SCC 61.

directions (on any matters consistent with its empowering legislation, so long as these practice directions are made public).[55] In Ontario, the SPPA provides that "a tribunal may make rules governing the practice and procedure before it" and also stipulates that where a tribunal does so, it must make those rules available to the public.[56]

By these rules, tribunals exercise significant discretion with respect to access, limited only by the requirement that rules of practice be consistent with a tribunal's enabling statute and, where applicable, general procedural statutes such as the SPPA. Rules of practice will, as a practical matter, determine whether the tribunal is easy or difficult to access. These rules set out the applicable time limits for filing material, the extent of material and disclosure provided, and whether hearings will be in writing, in person, or by electronic means.

Whether guidelines or rules, the question to be considered is not just the legal sufficiency of such instruments, or the legality of how they are used, but also the context within which they are used. Are they publicly available? Has the decision-maker made clear the role such instruments will play in the decision? These contextual questions form the backdrop against which people experience administrative justice.

B. Simplification

As another setting for our focus on the lived experience with administrative justice, the intelligibility of a process is vital to parties' ability to access it. Being provided with forms that are unduly complex or with guidelines that are inscrutable is equivalent to closing the doors to the tribunal. According to the Council of Canadian Administrative Tribunal's report, *Literacy and Access to Administrative Justice*, tribunals should adopt the following approach in order to address the question of access:

> Administrative tribunals, like other courts, have to follow the standards set in case law. We can:
> - make sure, as much as is possible, that our clients understand all the proceedings;
> - examine how we deal with low literacy clients and how this can affect fair administration of justice;
> - follow the lead of many organizations and use "plain language" in all our communications, written, visual, and spoken.[57]

Most tribunals are committed to simple and user-friendly forms. Some are going further and investigating services which provide assistance to individuals in completing forms and understanding the basic process requirements of the tribunal.[58] In some contexts, non-governmental organizations can play an important role in helping to simplify and clarify legal processes that may otherwise seem dizzying to the uninitiated. In Ontario, a legal aid clinic—Community Legal Education Ontario (CLEO)—exists for the sole purpose of providing

---

55 SBC 2004, c 45, ss 11-13.

56 SPPA, s 25.1.

57 Council of Canadian Administrative Tribunals, *Literacy and Access to Administrative Justice: The Promotion of Plain Language* (2005) at 12, online: <http://www.ccat-ctac.org/CMFiles/Publication/Literacyandjustice.pdf>.

58 Often, this role will fall to the registrar or other front-line staff of tribunals, but in 2006, Pro Bono Students Canada established an "Administrative Justice" initiative under which law students are recruited to work with tribunals on providing such services.

plain-language and simple instruction to individuals in a wide variety of legal settings.[59] In the refugee context, a national program has been created to assist refugee claimants in preparing for their hearings by offering tours that take them inside an actual refugee hearing room at the Immigration and Refugee Board of Canada and provide instruction as to what happens in the hearing room and who the participants in the process will be.[60]

While most administrative tribunals are less formal than courts, they too can be intimidating to those who come before them. Some of these individuals will have never appeared in a legal setting before. For others, their only experience with government officials may have been negative, as in, for example, refugee claimants who assert that they have been persecuted by the state in their country of origin.

People who appear before administrative tribunals frequently have experienced trauma and anxiety, both of which may impede their ability to make their case.[61] Efforts by tribunals, counsel, and non-profit organizations can play an important role in demystifying and simplifying administrative proceedings in ways that can tangibly enhance both access and fairness.

C. Language

Just as "plain language" may facilitate access, so may the capacity of tribunals to provide services and adjudication in the language spoken by those seeking out the tribunal.

Since *R v Tran*,[62] the Supreme Court of Canada has adopted a contextual approach to s 14 of the Charter, which provides, "A party or witness in any proceedings who does not understand or speak the language in which the proceedings are conducted or who is deaf has the right to the assistance of an interpreter." The court noted that this Charter right is closely linked to the common law right to a fair hearing. The right to be heard, in other words, implies a right to understand the case to be met, which in some circumstances will not be possible unless interpretation and translation services are available.

Even in the criminal context, however, it is clear that the right to an interpreter is not absolute. To establish a violation of s 14, the claimant of the right must prove on a balance of probabilities not only that he or she was in need of assistance, but also that the interpretation received fell below the basic, guaranteed standard and did so in the course of the case being advanced. Then, unless the Crown is able to show, on a balance of probabilities, that there was a valid and effective waiver of the right that accounts for the lack of or lapse in interpretation, a violation of the right to interpreter assistance guaranteed by s 14 of the Charter will have been made out. In terms of the guaranteed standard, it is not one of "perfection" but rather one of continuity, precision, impartiality, competency, and contemporaneousness.

In *Tran*, the court makes it clear that not every error of translation or interpretation provided to an accused individual will constitute a violation of the Charter. Further, the court holds that the error must be one that goes to the "vital interests" of the accused and, therefore, even a serious problem with translation on a minor point (e.g., a scheduling motion) will not constitute a violation.

---

59 See online: <http://www.cleo.on.ca/en>.

60 See READY Tours, online: <http://refugeeclaim.ca/ready-tours/>.

61 See, generally, Sarah Katz & Deeya Haldar, "The Pedagogy of Trauma-Informed Lawyering" (2016) 22 Clinical L Rev 359.

62 [1994] 2 SCR 951 [*Tran*].

It is clear that the standards developed in *Tran* had to be modified to the particular contexts of various administrative proceedings and that a spectrum of interpretation/translation rights might be more appropriate to these contexts. In *Tran*, while the court specifically acknowledged the application of s 14 of the Charter to civil and administrative proceedings, it limited its analysis to the criminal context: "I leave open for future consideration the possibility that different rules may have to be developed and applied to other situations which properly arise under s 14 of the Charter—for instance, where the proceedings in question are civil or administrative in nature."[63]

The right to an interpreter (and, by extension, to translation of relevant material) in the administrative context was considered in *Filgueira v Garfield Container Transport Inc*.[64] In that case, the Canadian Human Rights Tribunal considered its own obligation to provide an interpreter to a complainant alleging discrimination in the workplace. The tribunal noted that the complainant had a bilingual agent assisting with his case. While this mitigated the complainant's need, and while it was acknowledged that the ruling would have an impact on scarce resources, the tribunal nonetheless ordered that fairness required that the complainant be provided with an interpreter (for at least part of the hearing).

A judicial review application of the tribunal's decision in *Filgueira* was dismissed.[65] In upholding the aspect of *Filgueira* dealing with the right to an interpreter, Hughes J concluded:

> Thus, both the complainant and Respondent/employer, while parties before the Tribunal, are players in a larger endeavour, that of seeking to the removal of discrimination. It is within the discretion of the Tribunal to determine whether such an objective can be fairly achieved in the absence of providing, in whole or during part of the process, translation services into a language other than an official language, at taxpayer's expense, to one or more of the parties.[66]

Filgueira is an example of the principles in *Tran* being applied flexibly to the realm of administrative adjudication. While the case law answers the question, in part, as to the legal requirements of interpretation and translation services, it raises a host of others, such as whether tribunals or legal aid or the government or some other service providers should be responsible for interpreter and translation services, and which languages should be available for which tribunals. Should a government-sponsored or administered roster of approved interpreters and translators be established? Some tribunals have undertaken initiatives to translate brochures into languages used by user groups,[67] but linguistic access remains a significant hurdle for almost all tribunals.

Perhaps not surprisingly, given its constitutionally protected status, one exception is in the area of refugee determination where the Immigration and Refugee Board provides access to interpreters at all hearings. Interpretation in relation to hearing preparation is also generally (though not universally) covered by provincial legal aid plans.

Another exception to this observation involves access to one of Canada's official languages—in other words, access to French-language tribunal services in English

---

63 *Ibid* at 961.
64 2005 CHRT 32 [*Filgueira*].
65 *Filgueira v Garfield Container Transport Inc*, 2006 FC 785.
66 *Ibid* at para 38.
67 The Ontario Landlord and Tenant Tribunal, for example, translates its brochures into Arabic, Chinese, Farsi, Korean, Punjabi, Spanish, Urdu, Tamil, Russian, and Vietnamese.

communities, and vice versa, is governed by an additional layer of statutory, and in some cases, constitutional, entitlement.[68]

D. Prior Decisions

One of the most controversial aspects of access is how parties may learn about previous decisions of a tribunal. While privacy concerns make it difficult for some administrative bodies to publish their decisions, in most cases, making available a tribunal's past decisions is seen as a key aspect of its public interest function. In this sense, it is analogous to the rule that, absent circumstances justifying confidentiality, all tribunal proceedings should be open to the public, and documents used in those proceedings should be available to the public.[69] The practice with respect to publishing decisions is not uniform. Some tribunals publish all of their decisions in an easily searchable form.[70] Still others publish anonymized versions of only those previous decisions determined to be of general significance.[71] There are at least some tribunals who charge a fee to access earlier decisions, which obviously presents a financial burden, and in some circumstances a barrier, to those who need to understand the standards applied by a tribunal.

Unlike a court, tribunals are not bound by their earlier decisions. Many tribunals in practice, however, aim for consistency and will treat previous decisions as strongly influential over similar disputes. For this reason, making prior decisions available could plausibly be seen as an element of fairness and as part of the requirement that parties before the tribunal should know the "case to meet."

For all of these reasons, access to administrative justice includes access to sufficient legal and institutional knowledge.

E. People

Access to legal and institutional knowledge is vital but may not be enough to address the barriers that vulnerable parties may face. It is equally important to focus on the people who make up the administrative justice system, including both adjudicators and staff. Sandra Nishikawa, for example, has argued that both the legitimacy and public confidence enjoyed by tribunals depends on their appointments reflecting the demographic makeup of the communities they serve.[72] The importance of the makeup of tribunals is particularly salient in tribunals serving diverse communities, such as an immigration and refugee board, or human rights tribunal.

---

68 For discussion, see *Caron v Alberta (Human Rights and Citizenship Commission)*, 2007 ABQB 525.

69 See e.g. ss 41 and 42 of British Columbia's ATA. See also Cristie Ford's discussion of this legislation in Chapter 2 of this volume.

70 See e.g. the Alberta Labour Relations Board, online: <http://www.alrb.gov.ab.ca/decisions.html>, or the Ontario Information and Privacy Commission, online: <http://decisions.ipc.on.ca/ipc-cipvp/en/nav.do>, which allows for the public to search prior decisions both by subject and by name.

71 See e.g. Ontario's Social Benefits Tribunal, online: <http://www.sbt.gov.on.ca/userfiles/HTML/nts_1_7_1.html>.

72 Sandra Nishikawa, *Diversity on Adjudicative Administrative Tribunals: An Integrative Conception* (2009) (University of Toronto, LLM Thesis), online: <https://tspace.library.utoronto.ca/bitstream/1807/18937/6/nishikawa_sandra_y_200911_LLM_thesis.pdf>.

The focus on people is not only a focus on the background and experiences of the individuals who perform key roles in administrative justice, but also a focus on those individuals' skills, capacity, and competencies. Cross-cultural competency, for example, is a key component of merit-based appointments in a host of administrative justice settings.[73] More specifically, the Truth and Reconciliation Commission includes in its Calls to Action specific expectations that those involved in the justice system receive education in the experience of Indigenous communities, conflict resolution, and anti-racism training.[74]

While the focus on people in the context of fairness is appropriately on the staff of tribunals, similar scrutiny may be applicable to the agents, advocates, and organizational staff who interact with and support individuals in the midst of administrative justice proceedings.[75]

In all of these contexts, a party's interaction with the specific people encountered as part of administrative justice can make the difference between an accessible or inaccessible form of justice, from communicative skills to compassion and empathy in the context of impartial decision-making. Whether virtually or physically, administrative justice is an interpersonal setting, in which the capacities, conduct, attitudes, values, and actions of the people who make up a tribunal matter as much (and sometimes more) as the legal structures and formal rules that govern a tribunal's process and decision-making.

IV. ACCESS TO RESOURCES NEEDED TO NAVIGATE THE TRIBUNAL SYSTEM

Access to administrative justice is not just a matter of obtaining the necessary information, of course, but as noted above, access is also a matter of resources. This attention to financial barriers is particularly important in the context of vulnerable parties without other access to representation or advocacy services. There are several ways in which an absence of resources may create barriers to access and impede the fairness of proceedings. Below, we address three potential barriers: legal representation, fees and costs, and the budgeting and staffing of tribunals.

A. Legal Representation

The first and most significant impact of resources is the availability of adequate legal representation.

---

73 This concern has given rise to a number of initiatives, including the project on "Building Capacity Together: Enhancing Relationships Between Racialized Communities and Administrative Tribunals in Ontario," which brings together OCASI—Ontario Council of Agencies Serving Immigrants, Colour of Poverty—Colour of Change Network, Metro Toronto Chinese & Southeast Asian Legal Clinic, South Asian Legal Clinic of Ontario, and Rexdale Community Legal Services.

74 See e.g. Truth and Reconciliation Commission of Canada, *Truth and Reconciliation Commission of Canada: Call to Action* (2015), online: <http://www.trc.ca/websites/trcinstitution/File/2015/Findings/Calls_to_ Action_English2.pdf>.

75 For one innovative attempt at connecting individuals with disabilities with others who have navigated the tribunal system, see the resources of the Administrative Justice Support Network, online: <http:// asjn.communitylivingontario.ca>.

In the criminal justice sphere, a right to state-funded legal representation has been long recognized. In *New Brunswick (Minister of Health and Community Services) v G (J)*,[76] the Supreme Court of Canada affirmed that the constitutional right to legal assistance extends beyond the correctional context. In that case, the New Brunswick Minister of Health and Community Services was seeking an extension of custody of a mother's three children for a six-month period. The mother was poor and receiving social assistance. She applied for legal aid but was turned down because, at the time, custody applications were not covered under the legal aid guidelines in New Brunswick. The court recognized a constitutional obligation on the New Brunswick government to provide state-funded counsel in the particular circumstances of that case.

While the principle in *G (J)* has potential application in the context of administrative tribunals, at least where Charter rights are at stake, the reach of constitutionally mandated legal aid may be modest. That said, many provincial legal aid statutes mandate funding of legal representation before administrative tribunals. For example, in Ontario, those committed to psychiatric facilities who appear before the Ontario Review Board to argue for release are covered by legal aid certificates, while specialty clinics provide limited representation for eligible claimants before the Social Benefits Tribunal, the Landlord and Tenant Board, and other administrative bodies.

It is important to recognize that the right to counsel is not the same as the right to *state-funded* counsel. For example, the *Immigration and Refugee Protection Act* expressly provides that any person who is the subject of proceedings before the Immigration and Refugee Board may be represented by "legal or other counsel," but the applicable provision also makes it clear that such representation is at the person's own expense.[77] This said, many (though not all) provincial legal aid plans do provide coverage for immigration and refugee services, principally directed toward refugee determination claims and appeals and judicial review matters arising from these claims.

Implicit in any right to legal representation in administrative proceedings is the assumption that such representation be competent. When legal representation is incompetent, it gives rise to one of the very few scenarios in which an individual's rights to procedural fairness may be infringed for reasons completely unrelated to the actions (or omissions) of the administrative tribunal. In *R v GDB*, the Supreme Court of Canada endorsed the view that where counsel fails to provide effective representation, the legitimacy of an ensuing decision—in both outcome and process—is compromised and may result in a miscarriage of justice.[78] For this ground to succeed, however, "it must be established, first, that counsel's acts or omissions constituted incompetence and second, that a miscarriage of justice resulted."[79]

Although *GDB* was a criminal case, it has found application in the administrative context, particularly in immigration and refugee law.[80] Generally, however, the courts have concluded

---

76   [1999] 3 SCR 46 [G *(J)*]

77   *Immigration and Refugee Protection Act*, s 167(1).

78   *R v GDB*, 2000 SCC 22 [*GDB*].

79   *Ibid* at para 26.

80   *Memari v Canada (Minister of Citizenship and Immigration)*, 2010 FC 1196 [*Memari*]; *Gulishvili v Canada (Minister of Citizenship and Immigration)*, 2002 FCT 1200; *Shirwa v Canada (Minister of Employment and Immigration)* (1993), [1994] 2 FCR 51; *Huynh v Minister of Employment and Immigration* (1993), 65 FTR 11 (TD) [*Huynh*].

that the incompetence of counsel will only constitute a breach of natural justice in "extra-ordinary circumstances."[81] Such circumstances were found to arise in *Memari*, where a lawyer representing an unsuccessful refugee claimant swore an affidavit in support of the subsequent judicial review in which she acknowledged that she had not represented the applicant to an acceptable standard.[82]

Of course, allegations of counsel incompetency are easy to make and potentially difficult to assess in the absence of the counsel who has been accused of incompetence. They are also made with sufficient frequency that the Federal Court has issued a "Procedural Protocol" setting out a number of steps that must be followed, including notice to the allegedly incompetent counsel, before an argument can be made on judicial review that an applicant's right to a fair hearing has been compromised through the actions or inaction of a former lawyer.[83]

However, in the myriad contexts of administrative law, it is also important to recognize that access to fair procedures will not always depend on access to lawyers. The availability of paralegal assistance and the development of self-help support networks and resources all may play a role in the administrative justice sphere. For example, a pro bono initiative involving Pro Bono Students Canada and the Medico-Legal Society of Toronto enables law students to provide limited legal services to unrepresented parties appearing before the Health Professions Appeal and Review Board in Ontario.[84]

In the civil context, the Supreme Court of Canada has recently endorsed the Canadian Judicial Council's *Statement of Principles on Self-Represented Litigants and Accused Persons*.[85] Among other recommendations, this statement provides that judges "should do whatever is possible to provide a fair and impartial process and prevent an unfair disadvantage to self-represented persons."[86] Importantly, this includes the specific principle that "judges, court administrators and other participants in the legal system" should, among other things, inform self-represented parties of the potential consequences and responsibilities of proceeding without a lawyer and refer self-represented persons to available sources of representation, including those available from legal aid plans, pro bono assistance, and community and other services.[87]

---

81 *Memari, supra* note 80 at para 36; *Huynh, supra* note 80 at 15.

82 *Ibid* at paras 39-40.

83 Federal Court, *Procedural Protocol Re: Allegations Against Counsel or Other Authorized Representative in Citizenship, Immigration and Protected Person Cases Before the Federal Court* (7 March 2014), online: <http://cas-cdc-www02.cas-satj.gc.ca/portal/page/portal/fc_cf_en/Notices/procedural-protocol_7mar2014>.

84 See online: <https://www.law.utoronto.ca/programs-centres/programs/pbsc-pro-bono-students-canada>.

85 *Pintea v Johns*, 2017 SCC 23.

86 Canadian Judicial Council, *Statement of Principles on Self-Represented Litigants and Accused Persons* (2006) at 4, online: <https://www.cjc-ccm.gc.ca/cmslib/general/news_pub_other_PrinciplesStatement_2006_en.pdf>. The term "self-represented litigants" is not uncontroversial. Specifically, some criticize the term as connoting that there is an element of choice associated with litigants who appear in court without legal representation. In fact, most individuals who do not have counsel would opt to have legal representation, but for economic or other reasons cannot obtain a representative. As such, these critics prefer the term "unrepresented"; see, for example, Russell Engler, "And Justice for All—Including the Unrepresented Poor: Revisiting the Roles of Judges, Mediators and Clerks" 67 Fordham L Rev 1987.

87 Canadian Judicial Council, *supra* note 86 at 2.

The Canadian Judicial Council's *Statement of Principles on Self-Represented Litigants* only applies to court proceedings. This said, the principles articulated in them, particularly those related to basic fairness principles, have clear application in the administrative law context.

While there are a host of reasons why access to administrative justice is imperative, this should not be confused with a constitutional obligation to provide a particular kind of access. In *Christie v British Columbia*[88] it was argued that a tax on legal services prevents people from accessing the courts and tribunals and thus violates the right to access justice. The trial judge held that access to justice is a fundamental constitutional right and that taxation on a fundamental right which denies service to low-income persons unjustifiably violates s 7 of the Charter. The Court of Appeal affirmed this decision and, in fact, went further, holding that, because the right to access justice is held by all, the tax should not be levied on *any* legal services which determine rights and obligations, whether before courts or tribunals, and should be struck down for *all* citizens, not just the less affluent.

The provincial attorney general successfully appealed this decision to the Supreme Court of Canada, which held that not every limit on access is unconstitutional. The Constitution does not mandate a *general* right to legal representation as an aspect of, or precondition to, the rule of law. Rather, the right to counsel is limited to instances where life, liberty, and security of the person are affected, as is demonstrated by ss 7 and 10(b) of the Charter.[89] The decisions of the lower courts were reversed, and as a consequence, the scope of access to justice with respect to non-criminal proceedings remains unsettled.

The one area where the Supreme Court has taken a more interventionist role to access is around financial barriers in the forms of fees and costs, which we turn to next.

B. Fees and Costs

The second way in which resources may affect access is through user fees or other costs associated with a tribunal's process.

1. Fees

Tribunals may be funded in a variety of ways. Regulatory tribunals are sometimes self-funded, whereby the tribunal levies an assessment on regulated individuals or organizations and funds its adjudicative operations on the basis of these levies. Consider the example of energy boards. The National Energy Board received 90 percent of its funding from industry levies, with the remaining 10 percent coming from the federal government. In Alberta, the government pays for close to 50 percent of the Alberta Energy and Utilities Board's operations while industry levies pay the rest. In British Columbia and Ontario, energy boards are entirely self-funded.[90]

---

88   2005 BCCA 631, 262 DLR (4th) 51.

89   Section 10(b) of the Charter provides that everyone has the right to retain and instruct counsel, and to be informed of that right "on arrest or detention."

90   See Ontario Energy Board, *Survey of Regulatory Cost Measures* (September 2006), online: <https://www.oeb.ca/documents/abouttheoeb/corpinfo_reports/rcm_surveyreport-elenchus_120906.pdf>.

While most adjudicative tribunals are free for the parties,[91] the practice of charging fees is attracting increasing attention. These fees can range from the $25 per complaint filing fee charged by the Ontario Assessment Review Board to the $50,000 per merger notification filing fee charged by the federal Competition Bureau. The British Columbia ATA provides the government with the power to make regulations setting out the fees associated with filing applications before tribunals.[92]

Fees of any size have the potential to pose a barrier to access to justice. This is even more relevant in the field of administrative justice since low-income individuals are more likely to have interactions with administrative decision-makers than courts. In *Polewsky v Home Hardware Stores Ltd*,[93] the Ontario Divisional Court recognized that the constitutional principle of access to justice required that small claims court fees be waived in the context of an individual who otherwise would not be able to bring a case to court. Similarly, in *Pearson v R*,[94] the Federal Court held that the provision of the *Federal Courts Act*, which, in special circumstances, allows the court to disregard its rules,[95] should be interpreted so as to allow the court to exempt impecunious parties from having to pay filing fees. In so doing, Muldoon J observed:

> The rule of law is a feature of the law, of at least the common-law parts of Canada, and has been such since long before the adoption of the Charter, as demonstrated in part by Prof. Dicey's learned writings. So, indeed, is that precept of the rule of law—the equality of civil rights among all who claim the benefit of the sovereign's peace, in truth all the inhabitants, whether citizens or not. That which is by law reserved for poor folk—taking Court proceedings "in forma pauperis"— is a civil right and therefore available to the plaintiff herein, on even the bare evidence which he has provided in order to qualify for taking his court proceedings "in forma pauperis."[96]

More recently, a majority of the Supreme Court of Canada examined the nexus between court fees and access to justice from a somewhat different constitutional perspective. In *Trial Lawyers Association of British Columbia v British Columbia (Attorney General)*, the court considered a challenge to the fees levied against litigants in civil matters in British Columbia. The majority concluded that while courts may certainly impose fees, the quantum of fees imposed in this case amounted to an unconstitutional impeding of access to the superior courts, contrary to s 96 of the *Constitution Act, 1867*.[97] The majority further reasoned that, given the role played by s 96 in preserving the rule of law, and given the connections between the rule of law and access to justice, "it is only natural that s. 96 provide some degree

---

91 Canadian Human Rights Commission, "Filing a Complaint" online: <http://www.chrc-ccdp.gc.ca/sites/default/files/howtofileacomplaint.pdf>. The Social Benefits Tribunal, "Videos and FAQs," online: <http://www.sjto.gov.on.ca/sbt/faqs/>; The Ontario Workplace Safety and Insurance Board, "Worker Forms," online: <http://www.wsib.on.ca>; Ontario Pay Equity Hearings Tribunal, "Forms and Rules: Form 1—Application," online: <http://www.olrb.gov.on.ca/pec/peht/forms/peht_form01_e.pdf>.

92 ATA, s 60(c).

93 (2003), 109 CRR (2d) 189 (Ont Div Ct).

94 (2000), 195 FTR 31 [*Pearson*].

95 *Federal Courts Act*, s 55.

96 *Pearson, supra* note 94 at para 14. The principle in *Pearson* recently received positive treatment in both *Spatling v Canada (Solicitor General)*, [2003] FCJ No 620 (QL), and *Pieters v Canada (Attorney General)*, 2004 FC 1418.

97 *Trial Lawyers Association of British Columbia v British Columbia (Attorney General)*, 2014 SCC 59, [2014] 3 SCR 31.

of constitutional protection for access to justice."[98] Put in context, this means that legislation that effectively denies people the right of access to the courts, such as the court fees scheme under consideration, infringes the s 96 concern with preserving the rule of law.

Writing for himself, Cromwell J concurred with the majority in the result, but arrived at this conclusion for reasons related to the common law right of access to civil justice, as articulated for example in *Polewsky v Home Hardware Stores Ltd*. According to Cromwell J, the governing legislation—the *Court Rules Act*—did not contain sufficiently clear language to oust the common law right of access to the courts. Indeed, the Attorney General for British Columbia asserted that the Act preserved the common law right.[99]

This being the case, Cromwell J went on to examine the fee exemption contained in the applicable Court Rules that were created under the governing *Court Rules Act*. These rules provided that an exemption of court fees was available to persons who are "impoverished" and "indigent." The rules could not be interpreted to cover people who, while not indigent, are of modest means and may be prevented from having a trial because of the substantial hearing fees. As neither the imposition of fees, nor the exemption provision, met the standard required by the common law right of access, Cromwell J would have found the fees to be *ultra vires* the regulation-making authority conferred by the *Court Rules Act*.

In a dissenting opinion, Rothstein J would have upheld the fees on the basis that there is no express constitutional right to access the civil courts without hearing fees and because the hearing fee scheme in this case cannot be struck down on the basis of a "novel" (and incorrect) extension of the reach of s 96 of the *Constitution Act, 1867*.[100]

This finding may have limited implications for administrative law, because the rationale of the majority—that the main constraint on imposing filing fees relates solely to concerns over access to superior courts—does not find clear application to administrative tribunals as "mere creatures of statute."

While administrative tribunals do not necessarily give rise to these same common law civil rights, the court's approach of interpreting its statutory rules so as to provide discretion to ensure that fees do not bar access to justice could be applied in an analogous fashion to the rules or enabling statute of a tribunal. Consider, for example, the Landlord and Tenant Board, which charges filing fees but provides fee waivers in certain cases.[101]

In the immigration context, the federal government has imposed "cost recovery" fees for a variety of applications, including applications for special relief on humanitarian and compassionate grounds. In *Toussaint v Canada*, an individual challenged these fees, arguing that on a proper reading of the applicable legislation, a waiver of fees could be read in to the general humanitarian and compassionate waiver provision found at s 25(1) of the *Immigration and Refugee Protection Act*, which at the time read in part:

> The Minister shall ... examine the circumstances concerning the foreign national and may grant the foreign national permanent resident status or an exemption from any applicable criteria or obligation of this Act if the Minister is of the opinion that it is justified by humanitarian and compassionate considerations ... .

---

98   *Ibid* at para 40.
99   *Ibid* at para 72.
100 *Ibid* at para 86.
101 Landlord and Tenant Board, "Practice Direction on Fee Waiver," online: <http://www.sjto.gov.on.ca/documents/ltb/Practice%20Directions/Practice%20Direction%20on%20Fee%20Waiver%20(Jan%2016%202017).html>.

If such a fee waiver could not be found at s 25(1), the applicant argued in the alternative that the failure on the part of the state to provide a fee waiver in appropriate cases violated the common law constitutional right of access to the courts discussed in *Polewsky v Home Hardware Stores Ltd* and infringed ss 7 and 15 of the Charter.[102] The Federal Court rejected these arguments, but on appeal to the Federal Court of Appeal, the court found that the broad wording of s 25(1) ("may grant ... an exemption from *any* applicable obligation under the Act") clearly extended to the discretionary waiver of fees where justified by humanitarian and compassionate considerations.[103] While this was sufficient to dispose of the appeal, the court went on to reject Toussaint's further arguments on the applicability of the Charter and on the common law principle of access to the courts. The court's rationale in respect of the latter was tied to the discretionary nature of the relief that Toussaint was seeking. Sharlow JA stated in this regard:

> The absence of a provision for the waiver of fees is not contrary to the common law constitutional right of access to the courts or to the rule of law. Access to the Minister under subsection 25(1) of the IRPA is not the same as, or analogous to, access to the courts because the Minister's authority under subsection 25(1) is limited to providing an exceptional discretionary benefit. In the context of the immigration provisions of the IRPA, the rule of law cannot be used to create a fee waiver where none exists in the legislation.

Of interest, following the *Toussaint* matter, the government amended s 25 of the *Immigration and Refugee Protection Act* by making the payment of fees a clear prerequisite to humanitarian and compassionate consideration. Subsection 25(1.1) of the *Immigration and Refugee Protection Act* now states:

> (1.1) The Minister is seized of a request referred to in subsection (1) only if the applicable fees in respect of that request have been paid.

The unwritten constitutional principle of "access to justice" was described by Dickson CJ in *British Columbia Government Employees' Union v British Columbia (Attorney General)* (a case concerning the constitutional validity of an injunction issued by the court to clear the courthouse steps of picketers during a public service strike) in the following terms:

> Let us turn then to s. 52(1) of the *Constitution Act, 1982* which states that the Constitution of Canada is the supreme law of Canada and any law that is inconsistent with the provisions of the Constitution is, to the extent of the inconsistency, of no force or effect. Earlier sections of the Charter assure, in clear and specific terms, certain fundamental freedoms, democratic rights, mobility rights, legal rights and equality rights of utmost importance to each and every Canadian. ... Of what value are the rights and freedoms guaranteed by the Charter if a person is denied or delayed access to a court of competent jurisdiction in order to vindicate them? How can the courts independently maintain the rule of law and effectively discharge the duties imposed by the Charter if court access is hindered, impeded or denied? The Charter protections would become merely illusory, the entire Charter undermined.
>
> There cannot be a rule of law without access, otherwise the rule of law is replaced by a rule of men and women who decide who shall and who shall not have access to justice.[104]

---

102 *Toussaint v Canada (Minister of Citizenship and Immigration)*, 2009 FC 873 [*Toussaint*].
103 *Toussaint v Canada (Citizenship and Immigration)*, 2011 FCA 146.
104 *British Columbia Government Employees' Union v British Columbia (Attorney General)*, [1988] 2 SCR 214 at 229-30.

Access to justice is no less imperative in tribunals than courts. Unlike judicial independence, which is an unwritten constitutional principle applying uniquely to courts,[105] access to justice has broader application to all adjudicative proceedings in which rights and interests are at stake, and especially to those with jurisdiction over the Charter.

2. Costs

In addition to the question of fees, there has also been growing concern over the issue of costs in the context of tribunal adjudication and the effect of costs on access to administrative justice. Where a tribunal is deciding a dispute between two or more parties, should the winning parties be able to claim costs against the losing parties as in civil courts? Should the tribunal itself ever be in a position to recover costs? What should the consequences be where a party is unable to pay costs?

The British Columbia ATA expressly provides for tribunals to develop their own costs regimes:

Power to award costs

47(1) Subject to the regulations, the tribunal may make orders for payment as follows:

(a) requiring a party to pay part of the costs of another party or an intervener in connection with the application;

(b) requiring an intervener to pay part of the costs of a party or another intervener in connection with the application;

(c) if the tribunal considers the conduct of a party has been improper, vexatious, frivolous or abusive, requiring the party to pay part of the actual costs and expenses of the tribunal in connection with the application.

(2) An order under subsection (1), after filing in the court registry, has the same effect as an order of the court for the recovery of a debt in the amount stated in the order against the person named in it, and all proceedings may be taken on it as if it were an order of the court.[106]

One of the first decisions of a tribunal considering a costs regime developed pursuant to this section was *BC Vegetable Greenhouse I, LP v BC Vegetable Marketing Commission*.[107] This case concerned an application to the British Columbia Farm Industry Review Board (FIRB) by the BC Vegetable Marketing Commission (the Commission) and BC Hot House Foods Inc (BC Hot House) for an order that BC Vegetable Greenhouse I, LP (BC Vegetable) pay their costs incurred during BC Vegetable's appeal of a commission order that required BC Vegetable to remit to the commission $376,642 in outstanding levies. Some of BC Vegetable's grounds of appeal were unsuccessful or abandoned during the proceeding and the tribunal generally found the conduct of the company to have rendered the proceeding more costly than it should have been. The FIRB panel ordered BC Vegetable to pay the costs of the other parties (but not the FIRB's, although that option would have been open to the board as well). This decision suggests that where costs are available, unless otherwise circumscribed by a tribunal's enabling legislation, the applicable principles will be similar to those developed

---

105 See *Ocean Port Hotel Ltd v British Columbia (General Manager, Liquor Control and Licensing Branch)*, 2001 SCC 52, [2001] SCR 781, at para 24.

106 See also s 17.1 of the SPPA.

107 *BC Vegetable Greenhouse I, L P v BC Vegetable Marketing Commission* (20 May 2005), Farm Industry Review Board.

in the civil courts, with the exception of the potential for liability on the part of losing parties to pay costs directly to the tribunal.

By contrast, in *Canada (Canadian Human Rights Commission) v Canada (Attorney General)*, the Canadian Human Rights Tribunal awarded substantial costs to a complainant based on its interpretation of its enabling statute. The Federal Court upheld the costs award, but this determination was overturned on appeal.[108] On further appeal, the Supreme Court of Canada held that no reasonable interpretation of the relevant statutory provisions could support the view that the tribunal had the authority to award legal costs in matters that come before it.[109] As such, it would appear that tribunals will generally only have the authority to award costs where such authority is explicitly set out in its enabling legislation.

What remains undeveloped is whether the availability of costs will discourage parties from bringing disputes to tribunals or dilute the notion of the public interest jurisdiction underlying all administrative tribunal mandates.

C. Budget and Staffing

The third area where resources play a role is with respect to the budget and staff allocation of the tribunal. This is a controversial area for administrative law, as budgetary issues are usually categorized under the rubric of public administration rather than within the sphere of administrative law. Could a court ever compel the government to fund or organize a tribunal differently? The notion seems paradoxical. After all, tribunals are established as a matter of government policy through empowering legislation. There is nothing preventing a government from changing the mandate of a tribunal or repealing it altogether. How, then, could it be unlawful for the government to decide its level of funding or staffing?

While the government may not be under a legal obligation to create tribunals, once it has chosen to do so, it may well be under a legal obligation to provide adequate funding to ensure fairness, the rule of law, and access to justice before these tribunals. For example, in *Khan v University of Ottawa*,[110] the Ontario Court of Appeal held that an oral hearing was required in the context of a university proceeding, which would determine whether a student would fail a course. The court found that where a decision affecting significant interests of an individual turns on credibility, fairness requires that the individual have an opportunity to put forward her case in person before the decision-maker. What if the body in question is not a university, however, but a province-wide licensing body located in the capital city and the person affected lives in a remote rural community? What if an oral hearing is simply not practicable in the context of a high-volume tribunal? As discussed by Kate Glover in Chapter 5, the standard of procedural fairness required in a particular case will vary, but not (at least expressly) based on questions of resources.[111]

---

108   *Canada (Attorney General) v Mowat*, 2009 FCA 309.

109   *Canada (Canadian Human Rights Commission) v Canada (Attorney General)*, 2011 SCC 53.

110   (1997), 34 OR (3d) 535, 148 DLR (4th) 577 (CA).

111   See the discussion of *Baker* in Chapter 5 of this volume: in *Baker*, the Supreme Court held that the content of procedural fairness will vary depending on the nature of the decision being made, nature of the statutory scheme, importance of the decision to the people affected, legitimate expectations, and the agency's choice of procedures.

While it is true that tribunals are creatures of public policy, once established, and once the rights and interests of people depend on the fairness and reasonableness of that body's decision-making, then the duty of fairness clearly imposes constraints on government, as discussed above in the context of the requirement to hold an oral hearing in *Khan*. Perhaps the best known example of this dynamic is *Singh v Canada*,[112] in which the duty of fairness was held to require that the federal government provide oral hearings for refugee claimants. This decision resulted in significant expenditures for government and the reorganization of the entire refugee determination process. In rejecting the government's warning that requiring oral hearings for all refugee claims would be costly, Wilson J stated:

> I have considerable doubt that the type of utilitarian consideration brought forward by Mr Bowie [as counsel for the Minister of Immigration] can constitute a justification for a limitation on the rights set out in the Charter. Certainly the guarantees of the Charter would be illusory if they could be ignored because it was administratively convenient to do so. No doubt considerable time and money can be saved by adopting administrative procedures which ignore the principles of fundamental justice but such an argument, in my view, misses the point of the exercise under s. 1 [of the Charter].[113]

More recently, changes implemented in the refugee determination process created rigid statutory timelines for the determination of all new claims. Because of a lack of resources, however, these changes meant that the claims that predated (and were not subject to) the timelines were essentially shelved. In response, several of these so-called "legacy" refugee claimants have brought *mandamus* applications before the Federal Court, in which they are essentially seeking an order from the courts to force the government to provide the Immigration and Refugee Board with sufficient resources to determine their cases without undue further delay.[114]

In *2747-3174 Quebec Inc v Quebec (Regie des permis d'alcool)*,[115] the Supreme Court of Canada contemplated ordering the Government of Quebec to reorganize a liquor board on independence grounds. In *Suresh v Canada*,[116] dealing with security certificates, fairness obligations were said to constrain the ability of the government to shield disclosure of national security documents. All of these constraints may implicitly impose resource obligations on governments. Courts have yet to consider the corollary issue of whether fairness requirements in common law could be compromised by a tribunal, which is provided inadequate funding to fulfill its statutory mandate and/or to provide fair proceedings.

Some years ago, while conducting research on how administrative independence is experienced by decision-makers in the field of humanitarian and compassionate exemptions under the *Immigration and Refugee Protection Act*, it was learned that from the perspective of decision-makers, independence could be compromised by the requirement that a certain number of cases be "cleared" each week. This clearance rate was a product of the volume of applications and the limited number of staff assigned to these units within Citizenship and Immigration Canada. The result, these decision-makers asserted, was to limit

---

112   *Supra* note 39.
113   *Ibid* at 218-19.
114   See *Idris v Canada (Minister of Citizenship and Immigration)*, Court File No IMM-3802-16.
115   [1996] 3 SCR 919.
116   2002 SCC 1.

their ability to conduct interviews, to research files, and to consider and deliberate on the evidence provided.[117]

This focus on the lived experience of decision-makers also raises the broader issue of how decision-makers are selected (whether on a merit principle, by political appointment, or some hybrid of the two). Is access to a tribunal compromised where decision-makers are viewed as extensions of the government of the day? Is access enhanced where a tribunal is representative, in the sense that the demographic makeup of members and staff reflects the community and/or user groups of the tribunal?

The line between public administration and administrative law is clearly blurring. It is no longer possible (or desirable) to exclude significant government discretion over how administrative bodies are designed, funded, and governed from the purview of administrative law principles. Where these dynamics can be tied to the fairness of a decision-making process or the reasonableness of a decision, they cease to be matters of policy preference alone.

V. CONCLUSIONS

Administrative tribunals are established for a variety of purposes, including the following:

- to resolve disputes or reach decisions on the basis of specialized expertise;
- to resolve disputes or reach decisions in a more informal and expeditious fashion than is possible in the courts, thereby reducing costs to the parties; and
- to resolve disputes at an arm's length from the government and advancing the policy mandates set out in the applicable legislation.

Underpinning these purposes is a very basic presumption: that tribunals can achieve their objectives in a manner that is substantively fair and accessible to those subject to their decisions. Concerns over accessibility and fairness may, however, raise another key consideration, that being the scarce resources of government. Accessibility, whether in the form of more and better facilities, more and better information for parties, or more and better representation services, requires resources, and given the high volume of some tribunals, the resource implications may be quite substantial.

In addition to resources, a fulsome approach to fairness may also depend on how a tribunal accommodates unequal power and resources between parties. For example, consider a social benefits tribunal, where often unrepresented welfare recipients face ministry representatives. How can a decision-maker remain impartial on the one hand while insuring a sufficiently level field on the other? This is a challenge familiar to courts as well, particularly in areas such as family law where power imbalances and self-represented litigants are common. An aspect of this balancing exercise that is unique to administrative tribunals is the added feature that many tribunals are established precisely so as to empower vulnerable individuals. In the case of social benefits tribunals, for example, the whole purpose of these tribunals would be undermined if those whose benefits were wrongfully taken away could not, in practice, access the tribunal.

---

117 For a discussion of this research and its findings, see L Sossin, "From Neutrality to Compassion: The Place of Civil Service Values and Legal Norms in the Exercise of Administrative Discretion" (2005) 55 UTLJ 427.

Access also involves the balance between fairness and efficiency. It might be optimal for a high-volume tribunal, such as a landlord and tenant tribunal, to have facilities in every major population centre. It will be more efficient, of course, to maintain fewer facilities but invest in new technologies, such as videoconferencing, which allow for far greater numbers to have access to dispute resolution. At what point does the pursuit of efficiency erode the fairness of the proceeding? This is precisely the question which administrative law will increasingly have to address.

As important as access is to the parties in administrative justice, it is largely uncharted territory for administrative law. As we have observed above, the duty of fairness, for example, typically has not included a concern for the simplicity of forms, the transparency of guidelines, or the adequacy of a tribunal's database of prior decisions. The logic of fairness, however, is that it must be viewed from the standpoint of those affected by decision-making, and from this perspective, accessibility and fairness are inextricably linked.

Finally, the analysis thus far has assumed that access relates to process. Access to justice, however, includes not just being able to understand, navigate, and participate in a tribunal's decision-making, but also presupposes that the tribunal will deliver administrative justice of high quality. In this sense, access to administrative justice includes not just standing, guidelines, fees, and representation, but also extends to whether decisions are well reasoned and delivered in a timely fashion. Access in this sense may also extend to whether decision-makers are appointed under a competitive merit-based process, and whether decision-makers are able to access appropriate training and education (as substantive expertise in subject areas of a tribunal may not include expertise in the conduct of a hearing or vice versa).

The purpose of this chapter has been to introduce issues of access to administrative justice and to show how integrated such questions are with the broader principles of fairness on the one hand, and the everyday practice of diverse tribunals on the other hand. Ultimately, this analysis leads to a challenge for administrative law, to do justice to questions of access both as part of traditional fairness determinations and as an emerging, independent aspect of the legal framework within which tribunals are established and operate. The many implications of this new focus on access to administrative justice remain to be elaborated.

CHAPTER TEN

Crown Liability for Negligent Administrative Action

Alexander Pless*
Department of Justice, Government of Canada

I. INTRODUCTION

As we observed at the outset of this text, the administrative state plays a significant role in our lives. There is scarcely a single area of the law that does not require *any* state intervention. Sometimes, however, the administrative state interferes in our lives in a way that causes harm. Sometimes this is a necessary consequence of the state's goals (e.g., taxation to pay for social policies), but sometimes it is unauthorized (e.g., Duplessis's revocation of Roncarelli's liquor licence).[1] This chapter explores the general criteria that must be satisfied for the Crown to be held liable in damages for causing that harm.

Typically, the liability of public authorities in tort (or extracontractual liability in Quebec) is evaluated using the same principles as those that apply to the liability of private entities.

---

* The views expressed in this text are my own and not necessarily those of my employer, the Department of Justice of Canada. I am grateful to Sara Gauthier and Evan Fox-Decent for their rigorous and patient editing and to Elisabeth for everything else.

1 For discussion of *Roncarelli v Duplessis*, [1959] SCR 121 [*Roncarelli*], see Chapter 4, Administering the Canadian Rule of Law, by Mary Liston.

They are little adapted to the public context.[2] However, when the state regulates and acts in its public capacity, private tort law is often an awkward fit, forcing the court to rely on ad hoc solutions to account for public law considerations.

The common law of judicial review of administrative action largely comprises principles for assessing the legality of administrative decisions. Intuitively, one might think that these principles would be the first place courts would look to evaluate the liability of public authorities. In *Roncarelli*, for example, the majority relied on the administrative law doctrine of improper purposes en route to finding Duplessis liable in damages for the harm he caused Roncarelli.

However, the courts have been reluctant to rely on administrative law principles in the analysis of Crown tort liability,[3] even though the constitutional requirements of the rule of law and the separation of powers mean that similar considerations of deference will arise when the court is faced with a question of Crown liability.[4]

This chapter has two aims. In Section II, it sets out the law of Crown liability in tort as it is. In Section III, it offers a critical examination of the existing case law—especially the hesitation to incorporate public law principles into liability. I suggest that the incorporation of those principles into Crown liability law would improve that law's coherence and predictability, and, most importantly, enhance access to justice.

II. LIABILITY OF PUBLIC AUTHORITIES—BASIC PRINCIPLES

At common law, the Crown is immune from tort liability.[5] That immunity has largely been replaced by statutory conditions of liability. The federal government, for example, has enacted the *Crown Liability and Proceedings Act*.[6] Each province has enacted similar legislation to allow parties injured by the Crown to sue.[7]

Other than setting aside the Crown's immunity, none of the Crown liability statutes are particularly helpful in determining the precise conditions under which the Crown is liable for harm produced by administrative action. In the federal *Crown Liability and Proceedings Act*, for example, Parliament has established that the "Crown is liable for the damages for which, if it were a person, it would be liable."[8]

---

2   The exception being the narrow tort of misfeasance in public office discussed by Cristie Ford in Chapter 2.

3   *Entreprises Sibeca Inc v Frelighsburg (Municipality)*, 2004 SCC 61, [2004] 3 SCR 304 at para 15 [*Sibeca*].

4   Stephen Allan Scott, "The Supreme Court and Civil Liberties" (1976) 14 Alta L Rev 97; see also *Cooper v Hobart*, 2001 SCC 79, [2001] 3 SCR 537 at para 38, [*Cooper*]; *R v Power*, [1994] 1 SCR 601.

5   *Conseil des Ports Nationaux v Langelier*, [1969] SCR 60 at 71-72. See also PW Hogg, PJ Monahan & WK Wright, *Liability of the Crown*, 4th ed (Toronto: Carswell, 2011) at 7.

6   RSC 1985, c C-50.

7   *Crown Proceeding Act*, RSBC 1996, c 89 (British Columbia); *Proceedings Against the Crown Act*, RSA 2000, c P-25 (Alberta); *Proceedings Against the Crown Act*, RSS 1978, c P-27 (Saskatchewan); *Proceedings Against the Crown Act*, CCSM c P140 (Manitoba); *Proceedings Against the Crown Act*, RSO 1990, c P.27 (Ontario); Article 1376 of the *Civil Code of Quebec* (Quebec); *Proceedings Against the Crown Act*, RSNB 1973, c P-18 (New Brunswick); *Proceedings against the Crown Act*, RSNS 1989, c 360 (Nova Scotia); *Crown Proceedings Act*, RSPEI 1988, c C-32 (Prince Edward Island); *Proceedings Against the Crown Act*, RSNL 1990, c P-26 (Newfoundland and Labrador).

8   *Crown Liability and Proceedings Act*, s 3. This section further distinguishes between the conditions of liability in Quebec (fault of a servant) and the rest of Canada (tort of a servant).

In many cases the state acts in ways that are identical to private entities. If the activity at issue is something ordinary people do—like driving a car, maintaining a building, or contracting with private parties[9]—there is no special framework of analysis applicable to the state's conduct. The public official is usually liable under the same circumstances we as individuals are.

Of course, the Crown does lots of things that ordinary people do not do (like regulate professions, pardon criminals, issue fishing licences, or inspect trains). These are the interesting and difficult cases of Crown liability. The general body of tort law is ill-suited to the administrative context, but our courts have nonetheless tried to adapt it to public law concerns. The result, discussed below, leaves room for improvement.

A. The Anns Test

The House of Lords decision in *Anns v Merton London Borough Council* is the leading Crown liability case in Canada.[10] The *Anns* test was first applied by the Supreme Court of Canada in *Kamloops v Nielsen*,[11] where the City of Kamloops was held responsible for a negligent building inspection. While the approach in *Anns* has since been abandoned in the UK, it remains, with some modification, the preferred approach in Canada.

The test was summarized by the Supreme Court with a modest restatement in *R v Imperial Tobacco Canada Ltd*:[12]

> At the first stage of this test, the question is whether the facts disclose a relationship of proximity in which failure to take reasonable care might foreseeably cause loss or harm to the plaintiff. If this is established, a *prima facie* duty of care arises and the analysis proceeds to the second stage, which asks whether there are policy reasons why this *prima facie* duty of care should not be recognized.[13]

1. The First Stage—Foreseeability and Proximity

The first step considers the relationship between the plaintiff and the state. Was harm foreseeable, and was the person injured sufficiently proximate such that it can be said that a duty was owed to that particular person? This first step is common to any negligence analysis in common law. It is not tailored to the public law context, but where the defendant is a public authority, public law principles will inevitably inform the proximity analysis.[14] The

---

9 For a period time, the court applied public law principles to the Crown in contract. So, for example, in *Knight v Indian Head School Division No 19*, [1990] 1 SCR 653, the court found that the duties of procedural fairness applied. In *Dunsmuir v New Brunswick*, 2008 SCC 9, [2008] 1 SCR 190 at para 114, however, the court rejected that approach and affirmed that only the rules of contract govern the relationship. See also *Peter G White Management Ltd v Canada*, 2007 FC 686 at para 9. But see *Canada (Attorney General) v Mavi*, 2011 SCC 30, [2011] 2 SCR 504 at para 47, where the Supreme Court reminds us that a contract that incorporates a public law obligation does not displace it.

10 [1978] AC 728 [*Anns*].

11 *Kamloops (City of) v Nielsen*, [1984] 2 SCR 2 [*Kamloops*].

12 2011 SCC 42, [2011] 3 SCR 45 [*Imperial Tobacco*].

13 *Ibid* at para 39.

14 *Cooper, supra* note 4 at para 30.

requirement of proximity means that there will be cases where harm is foreseeable, but no duty of care because there is insufficient connection between the individual and the state.

Cooper is the leading case on the application of the proximity test to public authorities. In that case, investors who suffered substantial investment losses following the collapse of Eron Mortgage Corporation sued the Registrar of Mortgages Brokers for failing to protect them. They argued that the regulator was aware of serious violations of the Act committed by Eron but that they failed to suspend Eron's licence in a timely manner or even to alert investors that Eron was under investigation. The Supreme Court rejected this argument on the grounds that even though harm was foreseeable, the relationship between the regulator and the investors was not sufficiently proximate or direct. In *Finney*, where the Barreau du Québec was exercising similar supervisory powers, the fact that the plaintiff had made a complaint to the Barreau that was handled negligently was sufficient to establish a proximate relationship.[15]

2. The Second Stage—Policy/Operational

The second step of the *Anns* test offers a further opportunity for the courts to relieve public authorities from a duty of care, this time for policy reasons. The court in *Cooper* mentions two: first, does the law already provide a remedy? and, second, would recognition of the duty of care create the spectre of unlimited liability to an unlimited class? In addition, the court allows generally that the inquiry should focus "the effect of recognizing a duty of care on ... society more generally."[16] The court concludes that even had they found that a *prima facie* duty exists at the first stage, they would have negated it at the second stage for policy reasons. McLaughlin CJ and Major J, writing for a unanimous court, conclude that "to impose a duty of care in these circumstances would be to effectively create an insurance scheme for investors at great cost to the taxpaying public. There is no indication that the Legislature intended that result."[17]

But by far the most common consideration relied on at the second stage is the recognition that certain types of decisions are immune from liability. A true policy decision, one taken on the basis of "social, political or economic factors,"[18] will be immune from liability, while the implementation or the operation of such decisions may give rise to liability if executed negligently. As the court explains in *Cooper*, "[t]he basis of this immunity is that policy is the prerogative of the elected Legislature. It is inappropriate for courts to impose liability for the consequences of a particular policy decision."[19] This is the core of what is commonly referred to as the "policy/operational" distinction. A policy decision is immune from liability, while an operational decision is not. Again, we see the same concerns about the institutional role and competence of the judiciary—ever-present in judicial review—establishing the boundaries of Crown liability.

Determining whether a particular action was policy or operational has proven difficult. In *Imperial Tobacco*, McLachlin CJ takes on a comprehensive review of the test. She considers

---

15   *Finney v Barreau du Québec*, 2004 SCC 36, [2004] 2 SCR 17 at para 46 [*Finney*].

16   *Cooper, supra* note 4 at para 37.

17   *Ibid* at para 55.

18   *Brown v British Columbia (Minister of Transportation and Highways)*, [1994] 1 SCR 420; *Swinamer v Nova Scotia (Attorney General)*, [1994] 1 SCR 445; *Just v British Columbia*, [1989] 2 SCR 1228.

19   *Cooper, supra* note 4 at para 38.

the jurisprudence in the United Kingdom, Australia, and the United States. She observes that there is common ground with Canada that certain types of government activities are beyond the reach of the court because of economic, political, or social considerations that are not justiciable by the courts. She recognizes that other jurisdictions have tended to rely on the discretionary character of decisions as the hallmark of immunity, but prefers a slightly restated version of policy immunity:

> I conclude that "core policy" government decisions protected from suit are decisions as to a course or principle of action that are based on public policy considerations, such as economic, social and political factors, provided they are neither irrational nor taken in bad faith. ... [M]ost government decisions that represent a course or principle of action based on a balancing of economic, social, and political considerations will be readily identifiable.[20]

While the *Imperial Tobacco* test immunizes "core policy decisions" from liability, it leaves a great deal of government activity exposed to liability. But it doesn't tell us much about how to assess liability in the vast sphere of government activity that is not core policy. Once done applying *Anns* and *Imperial Tobacco*, courts only have ordinary private law tools of tort or extracontractual liability to assess the legal quality of government action. While public law considerations are inevitably in the background given the presence of a government plaintiff and concerns regarding the proper reach of the judiciary, public law plays no clear role. Stratas J of the Federal Court of Appeal offers this description of the state of the law: "To make this analytical framework suitable for determining the liability of public authorities, courts have tried gamely to adapt it. And then, dissatisfied with the adaptations, they have adapted the adaptations, and then have adapted them even more, to no good end."[21]

B. A Role for Administrative Law

Whether sitting in judicial review or assessing a claim in damages, the constitutional requirements of the separation of powers and the requirements of the rule of law must inform the proper role of the judiciary.[22] This is the province of administrative law. Nonetheless, the Supreme Court has resisted embracing administrative law principles in assessing the liability of public authorities primarily because the court resists the view that the legality of administrative actions is relevant to assessing liability. This section questions that reluctance.

1. *It Is Necessary to Distinguish Between the Crown's Public and Private Activities*

When Supreme Court judgments deny that administrative law principles are relevant to questions of liability, they tend to rely on examples of the Crown acting like a private party. For example, in *Imperial Tobacco* McLachlin CJ mentions that even driving a government vehicle involves discretion,[23] and in *TeleZone* Binnie J says the government could be liable *in contract* for damages even though, from an administrative law perspective, the conduct is authorized by statute.[24] They are of course correct that public law principles are of no

---

20 *Imperial Tobacco, supra* note 12 at para 90.
21 *Paradis Honey Ltd v Canada*, 2015 FCA 89 at para 121 [*Paradis Honey*].
22 *Supra* note 2. See also Chapter 4 of this text, Administering the Canadian Rule of Law, by Mary Liston.
23 *Imperial Tobacco, supra* note 12 at para 84.
24 *Canada (Attorney General) v TeleZone Inc*, 2010 SCC 62, [2010] 3 SCR 585 at para 28 [*TeleZone*].

assistance in such cases. As a result, in approaching a question of Crown liability, it is useful to establish at the outset whether the state action is public in nature. If it is not, the Crown can and should be subject to private tort law.

One method of drawing the public/private distinction would be to ask whether the matter is *susceptible* to judicial review of the administrative law variety. The Federal Court of Appeal decision in *Air Canada v Toronto Port Authority*[25] provides a comprehensive review of the jurisprudence on that question. The Supreme Court's reasons in *Des Champs v Conseil des écoles séparées catholiques de langue française de Prescott-Russell*[26] provide another useful guide. Binnie J distinguishes between functions that are "inherently of a public nature" or ones that are of "an internal or operational nature having a predominantly private aspect." But a detailed analysis will not usually be necessary. Simply answering one question—could the matter have been the subject of judicial review?—will be easy and resolve the vast majority of cases. You don't seek judicial review for bad driving, for example.

Importantly, this does not introduce a new question into the analysis. Even on the existing approach, there are at least two moments where the availability of judicial review must be considered. Recall that at the second stage of the *Anns* test one of the "policy" considerations to provide an immunity to the public authority is that "the law already provides a remedy."[27] As a result, in cases where judicial review *is* available, this in itself could establish immunity.[28] In the same vein, in any question of assessment of damages there is a general duty to mitigate.[29] Where an application for judicial review might have reduced the harm caused by an illegal decision, ordinary principles of restitution dictate that it should be pursued or liability reduced accordingly.

2. Can a Legal Exercise of Authority Be a Tort or Fault?

If we correctly identify occasions where the Crown is acting in a public capacity, the first thing that an administrative law approach would resolve is that legal government action cannot give rise to liability.

Professors Hogg and Monahan observe that "a lawful act by the Crown, even if it causes injury, is not tortious, and therefore gives rise to no liability to pay damages."[30] If a court cannot substitute its opinion for a reasonable exercise of authority in judicial review, how can it award damages against the same conduct? As Professor Stephen Scott pointed out writing about *Roncarelli* nearly 40 years ago, the central question must always be what in truth the legislature actually authorized its servant to do.[31] In a recent decision concerning the liability of the Crown for an allegedly unreasonable refusal to grant a pardon, Gascon J writing for the court explains:

---

25   2011 FCA 347.

26   [1999] 3 SCR 281 at paras 21-51. A five-part test is set out at para 51.

27   *Cooper, supra* note 4 at para 37.

28   *Comeau's Sea Foods Ltd v Canada (Minister of Fisheries and Oceans)*, [1995] 2 FCR 467.

29   *Janiak v Ippolito*, [1985] 1 SCR 146.

30   See also PW Hogg, PJ Monahan & WK Wright, *Liability of the Crown*, 4th ed (Toronto: Carswell, 2011) at 32 and 188. See also *Crown Liability and Proceedings Act*, s 8, and *TeleZone, supra* note 24 at para 46.

31   *Supra* note 2.

[I]t would be paradoxical if the exercise of the Minister's power of mercy were subject to a reasonableness standard on judicial review while being considered from the standpoint of a simple
fault in extracontractual liability.[32]

Put another way, a finding of fault must be at least as high as the bar for quashing the
decision on judicial review. If we respect the threshold question of identifying when the
defendant public authority is acting in a public capacity, legality will always be relevant and
obviate the need for the policy/operational debate.

3. What About Illegal Government Action?

The tougher question is how the illegality should be treated. There is a fairly consistent line
of jurisprudence that illegality cannot be equated with fault.[33] One line of cases concerns
private parties that act contrary to the law.[34] In private law, the breach of a statutory obligation is not necessarily a tort or fault. That distinction is understandable for private parties,
but not obviously the same when the state exercises public authority over a person, causes
harm, and it is subsequently determined that the authority was illegally exercised. Why
shouldn't the innocent bystander, illegally injured, be compensated?

Perhaps the clearest explanation comes from the doctrine that no liability flows from the
harm associated with the good faith application of an unconstitutional law. Where section
52 of the Constitution Act, 1982 applies, remedies under s 24 are generally not available.[35] But
the rationale for this rule is unpersuasive. The Supreme Court cites with approval Professor
ML Pilkington's theory that "if the official acts reasonably in the light of the current state of
the law and it is only subsequently determined that the action was unconstitutional, there
will be no liability. To hold the official liable in this latter situation might 'deter his willingness
to execute his office with the decisiveness and judgment required by the public good.'"[36]

If it were true that assessing liability for unconstitutional or illegal actions would "deter the
willingness" of public officials to do their jobs for fear of liability, this would be a serious basis to
immunize their actions. This reasoning fails to appreciate that government officials are not
personally liable for the harm they cause in the execution of their functions. The Crown is vicari-
ously liable. It is unlikely that the ordinary civil servant would be reluctant to do their job for fear
that their employer may be liable to pay in the case that a law is declared unconstitutional.

In Kingstreet,[37] the Supreme Court rejected similar reasoning to Pilkington's that supported the long-standing rule limiting recovery of unconstitutional taxes.[38] The court quotes
with approval Wilson J's reasons in Air Canada:

---

32 Hinse v Canada (Attorney General), 2015 SCC 35, [2015] 2 SCR 621 at 52.

33 Sibeca, supra note 3 at para 15.

34 The Queen (Can) v Saskatchewan Wheat Pool, [1983] 1 SCR 205; Holland v Saskatchewan, 2008 SCC 42,
    [2008] 2 SCR 551 at para 10.

35 Schachter v Canada, [1992] 2 SCR 679 at 720; Guimond v Québec (Attorney General), [1996] 3 SCR 347 at
    para 19 [Guimond]. See also Mackin v New Brunswick (Minister of Finance), 2002 SCC 13, [2002] 1 SCR 405.

36 Guimond, supra note 35 at para 15.

37 Kingstreet Investments Ltd v New Brunswick (Finance), 2007 SCC 1, [2007] 1 SCR 3 [Kingstreet].

38 The bar against recovery of ultra vires taxes was proposed by La Forest J in Air Canada v British
    Columbia, [1989] 1 SCR 1161 [Air Canada].

Why should the individual taxpayer, as opposed to taxpayers as a whole, bear the burden of government's mistake? ... If it is appropriate for the courts to adopt some kind of policy in order to protect government against itself (and I cannot say that the idea particularly appeals to me) it should be one which distributes the loss fairly across the public. The loss should not fall on the totally innocent taxpayer whose only fault is that it paid what the legislature improperly said was due.[39]

The same might be said of the harm associated with unreasonable or illegal government action. The consequence was not what the legislature intended. Why should the individual rather than society as a whole bear the burden of the error? Crown immunity doesn't eliminate the cost; it just prefers one distribution over another. The cost actually exists; the question is who must pay. A system that accounts for or internalizes the cost associated with errors is more likely to correct them. At the very least, internalizing the cost of error allows people designing the administrative process to have access to a realistic assessment of the overall costs and benefits of different administrative designs. For example, improving procedural fairness often imposes a financial burden on the state, but if it reduces costly errors, further expense made be justified.

4. A Fresh Approach?

Both the Federal Court of Appeal and the Quebec Court of Appeal have proposed approaches that assess Crown liability through the lens of public law. In *Montambault c Hôpital Maisonneuve-Rosemont*, Deschamps JA (as she then was) rejected the policy/operational approach to assessing Crown liability and adopted an approach that mirrors judicial review.[40] More recently, in *Paradis Honey*, Stratas JA held that questions of tort liability of public authorities should be addressed through administrative law principles. Moreover, he concludes that a court sitting in judicial review of administrative action should be able to award damages in appropriate cases where the court quashes the administrative action. He is critical of the existing approach saying we have been "using a screwdriver to turn a bolt."[41]

While at first blush his proposal seems revolutionary, he observes that it is the preferred approach when an applicant for judicial review *chooses* to combine an application for judicial review with an action for damages.[42] So, he suggests, why not provide for it in the ordinary course? There can be little doubt that where damages are an appropriate remedy, principles of judicial economy and access to justice support resolving the matter in a single case rather than two separate actions. One is reminded of Binnie J's reasons in *TeleZone* that "[p]eople who claim to be injured by government action should have whatever redress the

---

39   Kingstreet, *supra* note 37 at para 28.
40   [2001] RJQ 893 at paras 76-77. The decision is endorsed by the Supreme Court in *Canadian Food Inspection Agency v Professional Institute of the Public Service of Canada*, 2010 SCC 66, [2010] 3 SCR 657 at para 28 but indirectly questioned in *Finney, supra* note 15, at para 31. Nonetheless, the approach is regularly applied in Quebec. See recently: *Agence du revenu du Québec c Groupe Enico inc*, 2016 QCCA 76 at para 81.
41   *Paradis Hone*, *supra* note 21, at para 127.
42   In support of this proposition, Stratas J cites *Hinton v Canada (Minister of Citizenship and Immigration)*, 2008 FCA 215, [2009] 1 FCR 476. *Hinton* is also cited by the SCC in *TeleZone, supra* note 24, at para 37 in support of the view that a single direct approach is to be preferred.

legal system permits through procedures that minimize unnecessary cost and complexity. The court's approach should be practical and pragmatic with that objective in mind."[43] *TeleZone* stands for the principle that a party should not be forced to go through judicial review if all they want is damages, but in a case where a party wants both public law and private law remedies, they should be allowed to combine them, and the court should rely on the teachings of administrative law to guide them.

In *Doré*,[44] the court adopts an administrative law approach for assessing administrative action affecting Charter[45] rights rather than the traditional *Oakes*[46] test. The court's reason for turning to administrative law in this context is that a failure to do so would risk the loss of "a rich source of thought and experience about law and government" and would have the effect of "undermining a more robust conception of administrative law."[47] The same observation could be made with respect to questions of Crown liability. The presence of a damages claim should not cause a reviewing court to disregard the teachings of administrative law, and in particular the role of the judiciary in relation to administrative law's twin pillars: legislative supremacy and the rule of law.

III. CONCLUSION

Despite the presence of public law concerns in Crown liability jurisprudence, the Supreme Court has been reluctant to use administrative law principles to address some of the more difficult public law issues in tort. However, in the ordinary case, a person who comes into contact with the administrative state and is injured is not best placed to justly bear the cost of administrative error. Generally, the community (or the state) should bear these costs. This is especially true when the administrative process deals with marginalized groups. Accessible compensation for administrative error can thus enhance access to justice, since the ordinary remedies of judicial review may not adequately address the harm caused by illegal action.[48]

Providing compensation for illegal Crown acts has a further benefit: the costs of administrative error are internalized, allowing persons responsible for administrative design to assess better the costs and benefits of the relevant administrative process. The reform proposed thus interlocks and advances together the public goods of access to justice and administrative efficiency.

---

43   *TeleZone, supra* note 24 at para 18.
44   *Doré v Barreau du Québec*, 2012 SCC 12, [2012] 1 SCR 395.
45   *Canadian Charter of Rights and Freedoms*, Part I of the *Constitution Act, 1982*, being Schedule B to the *Canada Act 1982* (UK), 1982, c 11.
46   *R v Oakes*, [1986] 1 SCR 103 at paras 69-71.
47   *Doré, supra* note 44, at para 34.
48   *Parrish & Heimbecker Ltd v Canada (Agriculture and Agri-Food)*, 2010 SCC 64, [2010] 3 SCR 639 at para 6.

CHAPTER ELEVEN

Standard of Review: Back to the Future?

Audrey Macklin*

Centre for Criminology and Sociolegal Studies and
Faculty of Law, University of Toronto

* Thanks to Lorne Sossin for his editorial assistance and to the other contributors in the volume who kindly offered insights and corrections. I am also grateful to David Dyzenhaus for his constructive suggestions for the first edition, Jennifer Nedelsky for her helpful comments on the second edition, and Sheila Wildeman for her careful and incisive analysis and generous encouragement throughout.

I. INTRODUCTION

When judges hear appeals from decisions made by other judges, their task is straight-forward: ask whether the lower court got the answer "right" or "wrong." If the answer is "wrong," the appellate judges will substitute the "correct" answer. The scare quotes used here alert us to the unstated premise that there is always a single correct answer, and it consists of the one given by judges perched on the higher rung of the judicial ladder. Appellate courts will depart from the premise where they are called upon to review findings of fact. Here, higher courts may hesitate to intervene because they lack the trial judge's advantage of first-hand exposure to the evidence, especially *viva voce* testimony, and be-cause revisiting factual determinations of little precedential value constitutes a poor use of judicial resources.

Judicial review of administrative action elicits a different set of questions that do not generally arise in ordinary appellate jurisprudence, and includes the following:

- Is there always a single correct answer?
- Who is better situated to determine the answer, the first-level specialist decision-maker or the generalist reviewing judge?
- What criteria can assist in determining who is better situated?
- What doctrinal consequences flow from that determination for judges tasked with reviewing administrative action?
- How do courts operationalize the doctrine in their review of administrative decisions?

The last of these questions is the subject of Chapter 12. This chapter tackles the remaining questions, and bundles them together under the rubric "choice of standard of review." The overarching dilemma concerns whether and why courts should defer to the decision of the original decision-maker, rather than just proceed under the traditional assumption that judges always know best. (It is not without significance that courts sometimes refer to ad-ministrative decision-makers as "inferior tribunals.")

Over the last 50 years, administrative law jurisprudence has grappled with standard of review. There have been pitched debates at the level of principle: what should the rules say about when, why, and how courts intervene in administrative decisions? Even if those ques-tions are provisionally settled, considerable disagreement arises about practice—namely whether judges actually do what the rules they created say they should do. For instance, a judge may say she is deferring when it looks more like she is simply rubber-stamping. Or a judge may say he is deferring to the decision-maker when what he is really doing is endorsing a decision that conveniently happens to align with the result that the judge thinks is correct. A judge may say she is adopting a deferential posture, but the actual mechanics of the judicial review may show no actual respect for the original decision-maker's reason-ing. These gambits are often difficult to detect, much less police, but they have a distorting impact on jurisprudence and make the quest for coherence in the case law a frustrating enterprise.

The following is a short and deceptively clear description of the current rules governing standard of review: A court that is called upon to review the interpretation or application of a statutory provision by an administrative decision-maker will usually (but not always) deter-mine that the decision made by the agency, board, or tribunal that is assigned primary responsibility under the statute merits deference from the reviewing court. This means that a court should hesitate to set aside the decision even if it might have arrived at a different result had it been the original decision-maker. In *Baker*, the Supreme Court of Canada endorsed David Dyzenhaus's articulation of deference as respect, stating, "Deference as respect requires not submission but a respectful attention to the reasons offered or which could be offered in support of a decision."[1]

Deference entails attaching weight to the fact that the administrative actor (and not the court) was delegated the initial task by the legislator and/or may be better qualified than a court to perform the task. We are familiar with this in our daily lives. We often defer to the opinion of a health professional (even in the face of private doubts) because we believe she has greater expertise than us; when we divide up labour for a group project, we generally refrain from interfering in our colleague's choice of how to complete his task (even if we disagree) because it's his job to do, not ours. Put differently, deference means that, in certain circumstances, the identity of the original decision-maker sways a court away from interfering with the decision, quite apart from whatever persuasive force the decision itself exerts.

In administrative law, a court will ask whether it should defer to the recommendations of an environmental review board regarding the construction of a pipeline, the appointment of labour arbitrators by a minister, a securities tribunal's interpretation of a limitation period in the *Securities Act*, or the exercise of humanitarian and compassionate discretion by an immigration officer. If the answer is yes, a court must then operationalize deference through a method of scrutiny that is somehow distinct from simply asking what outcome it would have reached had it been charged with making the original decision. And courts must do this across a vast range of subject areas, involving a staggering array of administrative actors, types of decisions, and affected interests.

In administrative law doctrine, the standard of review inquiry proceeds in two steps. First, should the court defer? Second, if the answer is yes, how does the court defer—how does a court *do* deference? If a court decides it need not defer, then it will judge the administrative decision on the basis of its correctness, and will set it aside if it disagrees with the decision-maker. If the court decides it ought to defer (which the Supreme Court of Canada currently thinks it should do in the overwhelming majority of cases), then a court will only set aside the original decision if it is unreasonable. For reasons that will be explained below, the label "correctness" is unfortunate, and should not be interpreted literally. Rather, a "correct" answer is best understood as the court's preferred outcome, where no credit or weight is given to the original decision-maker on the basis of the latter's competence or authority. Under the contemporary doctrine of standard of review, courts never completely relinquish their entitlement to have the last word, and so no decision can be completely immunized from judicial scrutiny. The issue is how closely and in what manner the decision will be scrutinized.

The remainder of this chapter provides a genealogy of standard of review. How did we get to where we are now and how does that path guide current doctrine? The jurisprudential history matters for several reasons. First, the underlying tensions around the rule of law, and the role of judicial review in the contemporary administrative state, are endemic and possibly intractable; it is important to be aware of how different doctrinal schema have

---

1 *Baker v Canada (Minister of Citizenship & Immigration)*, [1999] 2 SCR 817 at para 65, 174 DLR (4th) 193 [*Baker*], quoting David Dyzenhaus, "The Politics of Deference: Judicial Review and Democracy" in M Taggert, ed, *The Provinces of Administrative Law* (Oxford: Hart Publishing, 1997) 279 at 286; for the facts of *Baker*, see Kate Glover, Chapter 5, The Principles and Practices of Procedural Fairness.

grappled with them over time. Secondly, the past is never over in Supreme Court of Canada jurisprudence. Landmark cases seldom wipe the slate completely clean, and traces of past doctrines often linger or go dormant, only to reappear later. Understanding what the courts said in the past aids in understanding what they are saying now (and why). Thirdly, comparing past and present jurisprudence also illustrates an oscillation between two methodologies that pervade the common law: one, a defeasible rule (rule + exceptions) and the other, a multi-factorial balancing test. Appreciating the virtues and limitations of each in relation to standard of review offers an opportunity to consider more broadly the operation and effects of common law methodologies.

This chapter is best read as a very long introduction to the next chapter. But you should hesitate before skipping it. The jurisprudence is volatile, and the Supreme Court of Canada may yet hit the "reset" button again, as it did in 1979 (*CUPE v NB Liquor Corporation*),[2] 1998 (*Pushpanathan v Canada (Minister of Citizenship and Immigration)*),[3] and 2008 (*Dunsmuir v New Brunswick*).[4] At present, the standard of review is almost always "reasonableness," but the court has been reticent to provide guidance on how to apply this deferential standard across the wide range of situations that reviewing courts encounter. One resource for thinking about how to give context to the application of reasonableness under the current model is to look to past jurisprudence that formally addressed a different question (what is the standard of review?) but identified considerations that might be helpful to answering the current question (how does one defer in a given case?).

II. THE PREQUEL

In Chapter 1, A Historical Map for Administrative Law: There Be Dragons, Colleen M Flood and Jennifer Dolling surveyed the diverse reasons for the creation of administrative agencies, tribunals, and commissions. Certain functions—for example, licensing, distribution of goods or resources, and polycentric disputes—are ill-suited to resolution in a bipolar or adversarial judicial process. Some domains, such as engineering, the environment, securities, and telecommunications, require a level and type of technical or experiential expertise that judges lack. Other areas—for example, immigration, social assistance, and workers' compensation—generate a high volume of cases (usually involving people of limited means) that would overwhelm the ordinary courts and judicial processes. Concerns of efficiency, cost, and specialization militate in favour of an administrative regime. In the 20th century, ideological conflict between the expanding administrative state and the courts (incisively and passionately critiqued by the legal realists) led governments in the Anglo-American legal world to withdraw certain tasks from courts and allocate them to newly created, specialized agencies. The iconic case is labour law. Judicial deployment of traditional common law doctrines of freedom of contract, protection of private property, privity of contract, and prohibition on contracts in restraint of trade consistently thwarted legislation designed to provide a measure of protection to workers, standardize minimum terms

---

2 [1979] 2 SCR 227, 25 NBR (2d) 237 [*CUPE*].
3 [1998] 1 SCR 982, 160 DLR (4th) 193 [*Pushpanathan*].
4 2008 SCC 9, [2008] 1 SCR 190 [*Dunsmuir*].

of employment, and enable the emergence of an industrial relations regime based on union representation.

Frustrated with judicial hostility toward the objectives of labour relations legislation, the government not only established a parallel administrative regime of labour relations boards, but also enacted statutory provisions, known as privative or preclusive clauses, that purported to oust entirely judicial review of the legality of administrative action. Ordinarily, judicial review is available for breaches of procedural fairness, errors of law, abuse of discretion, or factual findings made in the absence of evidence.

So-called privative clauses were originally intended to prevent courts from interfering with substantive outcomes of administrative action through the doctrines of error of law or absence of evidence for findings of fact. A primary, but not exclusive, motive behind privative clauses was to direct the judiciary to respect the relative expertise of the administrative or regulatory body. Other reasons for privative clauses included the promotion of prompt and final resolution of disputes and the rationing of scarce judicial resources. Moreover, although the dominant narrative of the 20th century depicted a progressive administrative state using privative clauses to shield social welfare legislation from the conservative grasp of a retrograde judiciary, one should not assume that the politics of judicial review are uniform or static. In recent years, for example, the Australian government has perfected the use of the privative clause in the service of precluding judicial review of the interpretation and application of draconian legislation directed at asylum seekers.

Privative clauses vary in wording, but usually include a grant of exclusive jurisdiction over the subject matter, a declaration of finality with respect to the outcome, and a prohibition on any court proceedings to set the outcome aside. The following example from the Saskatchewan *Workers' Compensation Act, 1979* is typical:

> The board shall have exclusive jurisdiction to examine, hear and determine all matters and questions arising under this Act and any other matter in respect of which a power, authority or discretion is conferred upon the board .... The decision and finding of the board under this Act upon all questions of fact and law are final and conclusive and no proceedings by or before the board shall be restrained by injunction, prohibition, or other proceeding or removable by *certiorari* or otherwise in any court.[5]

The privative clause poses a conundrum for the traditional conception of the rule of law. On the one hand, a legislative grant of authority is always circumscribed by the terms of the statute. The common law presumes that citizens retain access to the ordinary courts in order to ensure that creatures of statute do not exceed or abuse the power granted to them. Making government actors accountable to the ordinary (and independent) courts is a principle that Dicey espoused as essential to the rule of law. As the British jurist HWR Wade wrote, the rule of law demands that "administrative agencies and tribunals must at all costs be prevented from being sole judges of the validity of their own acts."[6] As discussed below, the Supreme Court of Canada has even elevated judicial review to a constitutionally protected principle under s 96 of the *Constitution Act, 1867*.

---

5 *Workers' Compensation Act, 1979*, SS 1979, c W-17.1, s 22, quoted in *Pasiechnyk v Saskatchewan (Workers' Compensation Board)*, [1997] 2 SCR 890 at para 5 [*Pasiechnyk*].

6 HWR Wade, *Administrative Law*, 4th ed (Oxford: Clarendon Press, 1977).

On the other hand, the doctrine of parliamentary supremacy dictates that the legislator enacts the law, and the court must interpret and apply the law in accordance with the legislator's intent. A privative clause pits the second principle against the first by stating rather clearly and unambiguously that the legislator intends to oust the courts from supervising the actions of the administrative decision-maker.

Not surprisingly, judges historically resisted the privative clause's "plain meaning" and circumvented it through the following chain of reasoning, most powerfully articulated in the House of Lords' *Anisminic*[7] case: decision-makers' jurisdiction (authority to act) is demarcated by statute. This authority can be represented visually as a circle, where the line marks the boundary of the decision-maker's jurisdiction. Actions that exceed jurisdiction *purport* to be decisions or findings, but in actuality are nullities because they are not authorized by the statute. Therefore, "decisions" or "findings" that are insulated by a privative clause do not include actions that exceed the jurisdiction granted to the decision-maker.

If a college of physicians and surgeons purported to suspend the licence of a dentist to practise dentistry, we might all agree that the putative suspension was beyond the jurisdiction of the college and not protected by a privative clause. However, few real cases present such starkly deviant administrative behaviour. Typically, the issue is the interpretation of a statutory provision, inferences from evidence whose relevance to the outcome depends on a particular statutory construction, or the exercise of discretion. Judges faced with a privative clause assigned themselves the task of determining whether the issue fell "within jurisdiction" and, therefore, within the ambit of the privative clause or was a "jurisdictional question" that determined the outer boundary of the decision-maker's authority. In a case of the latter, a court was entitled to review the decision. At this juncture, and before the emergence of a variable standard of review, correctness was the implicit and exclusive standard of review. Rather like the early approach to natural justice, review in the face of a privative clause was an all-or-nothing affair; either the issue was a jurisdictional question, and the courts treated it as they would an issue on appeal, or it was virtually immunized from judicial oversight.

The effectiveness of privative clauses in deterring judicial intervention depended on the ease and frequency with which courts could designate an issue as determinative of jurisdiction, therefore warranting strict judicial scrutiny. Two techniques deployed by the courts were the "preliminary or collateral question" doctrine, and the "asking the wrong question" doctrine.

In the 1971 case of *Bell v Ontario (Human Rights Commission)*,[8] the Supreme Court of Canada considered the interpretation of s 3 of the Ontario *Human Rights Code*,[9] which, *inter alia*, proscribed discrimination on the basis of race in the provision of rental housing. The provision applied to rental of a "self-contained dwelling unit," and the landlord argued that the flat for rent in his house did not fall within the meaning of "self-contained dwelling unit." The landlord sought an order of prohibition to prevent the board of inquiry law professor Walter Tarnopolsky from investigating the complaint on the ground that the board had no jurisdiction under the *Human Rights Code* over the rental of his unit. The Supreme Court of Canada held that ascertaining the meaning of "self-contained dwelling unit" was

---

7 *Anisminic Ltd v Foreign Compensation Commission*, [1969] 2 AC 147 (HL).

8 [1971] SCR 756, rev'g *R v Tarnopolsky, Ex parte Bell*, [1970] 2 OR 672 (CA) [*Bell*].

9 RSO 1990, c H.19.

preliminary to the question of whether the landlord had engaged in discrimination contrary to the *Human Rights Code*. According to Martland J, the definition of "self-contained dwelling unit" was "an issue of law respecting the scope of the operation of the Act, and on the answer to that question depends the authority of the board to inquire into the complaint of discrimination at all … and a wrong decision on it would not enable the board to proceed further."[10] On the basis of the landlord's affidavit and photographs of his house, the majority of the court determined that the rental unit was not "self-contained." The landlord "was not compelled to await the decision of the board on that issue before seeking to have it determined in a court of law."[11] In so stating, the majority tacitly communicated that there could be no benefit in permitting the board of inquiry to first offer its own interpretation of "self-contained dwelling unit," and that the court could make its own determination based on looking at the blueprints of the house.

In *Metropolitan Life Insurance Company v International Union of Operating Engineers, Local 796*,[12] the Supreme Court of Canada addressed an Ontario Labour Relations Board certification of a union as the sole bargaining agent for a group of employees engaged in janitorial and building maintenance work. The union constitution provided for membership by "operating engineers" alone, but, in practice, the union had signed up workers from many occupational classifications. For almost two decades, the Ontario Labour Relations Board applied a policy of imposing a uniform set of criteria for determining whether employees were members of a union applicant for certification, where eligibility under the union constitution was only one factor and, even then, only an explicit constitutional exclusion from membership status (along with its rights and privileges) would be determinative. The board's reasons explained at length the rationale for its approach and specifically addressed why reliance on union constitutions as the determinant of union membership would produce incongruous outcomes and confer unfair advantages on some unions over others. The Ontario *Labour Relations Act*[13] contained a form of privative clause. The employer sought judicial review and ultimately appealed to the Supreme Court of Canada.

The court ruled that the determination by the board was not protected by the privative clause, because the board had "asked itself the wrong question." Although the question of whether enough employees were members of the union was undoubtedly an issue within the exclusive jurisdiction of the board, the board lost jurisdiction because it employed a faulty reasoning process. According to the court, "the Board [had] failed to deal with the question remitted to it (i.e. whether the employees in question were members of the union at the relevant date) and instead [had] decided a question which was not remitted to it (i.e., whether in regard to those employees there [had] been fulfillment of the conditions [for membership devised by the board])."[14] Implicit in the court's reasoning was the assumption that the union constitution was determinative of membership; indeed, the court did not engage at all with the rationale of the board in employing different criteria. The upshot of "asking the wrong question" was that even matters otherwise within the jurisdiction of a decision-maker (and thus protected by a privative clause) could become jurisdictional and

---

10 *Bell, supra* note 8 at para 775.
11 *Ibid* at para 769.
12 [1970] SCR 425 [*Metropolitan Life*].
13 SO 1995, c 1, Schedule A.
14 *Metropolitan Life, supra* note 12 at para 435.

subject to judicial ·scrutiny if the decision-maker engaged in a reasoning process that the court deemed defective.

The doctrines of "preliminary or collateral question" and "asking the wrong question" were derided by academic commentators as formalistic, malleable, and instrumental devices manufactured by the courts to meddle in spheres where the legislature had deliberately and explicitly excluded them. Courts inclined to disagree with a decision could, with little effort, transform almost any issue into a preliminary or collateral question, or depict the tribunal as asking the wrong question, in order to impugn a decision as the product of a flawed chain of reasoning.

The doctrines described above have largely been discarded, but the language of jurisdiction lives on. Familiarity with the jurisprudential history of privative clauses and jurisdiction remains important for two reasons. First, the sources of judicial anxiety about jurisdiction, rooted in the rule of law, remain salient. Second, it is arguable that traces of the "preliminary or collateral question" and "asking the wrong question" doctrines have been largely forgotten but have not disappeared entirely. For example, the assertion that a statutory provision is properly understood according to the principles of another area of law survives in the stricter scrutiny of legal questions deemed of "central importance to the legal system as a whole."[15] A reasoning process that inquires into the effect of a given interpretation on advancing the broader objectives of the statute may be rejected as a flawed and self-aggrandizing attempt to expand the jurisdiction of the decision-maker.[16]

III. THE BLOCKBUSTER: CUPE V NEW BRUNSWICK LIQUOR CORPORATION

CUPE v NB Liquor Corporation[17] is to the standard of review what *Nicholson*[18] is to procedure and *Baker* is to discretion: a judgment that shifted the legal landscape onto new terrain.[19] The facts are straightforward. A public sector union, Canadian Union of Public Employees (CUPE), went on strike. Under the terms of the New Brunswick *Public Service Labour Relations Act*,[20] striking employees were prohibited from picketing and employers were prohibited from using replacement workers. Section 102(3) of the Act stated:

> 102(3) ... during the continuance of the strike
> (a) the employer shall not replace the striking employees or fill their position with any other employee, and
> (b) no employee shall picket, parade or in any manner demonstrate in or near any place of business of the employer.[21]

---

15   *Toronto (City) v CUPE, Local 79, infra* note 102 at para 62, LeBel J; see also *UES, Local 298 v Bibeault*, [1988] 2 SCR 1048 [*Bibeault*].

16   *Barrie Public Utilities v Canadian Cable Television Association*, 2003 SCC 28, [2003] 1 SCR 476 [*Barrie Utilities*].

17   *Supra* note 2.

18   *Nicholson v Haldimand-Norfolk (Regional) Police Commissioners*, [1979] 1 SCR 311 [*Nicholson*].

19   See Glover, *supra* note 1; Sheila Wildeman, Chapter 12, Making Sense of Reasonableness.

20   RSNB 1973, c P-25 [PSLRA].

21   PSLRA, s 102(3); *CUPE, supra* note 2 at para 4.

Section 101 of the Act contained a lengthy privative clause declaring, *inter alia*, that every "award, direction, decision, declaration, or ruling of the Board … is final and shall not be questioned or reviewed in any court."[22]

The employer complained to the NB Public Service Labour Relations Board that the union was picketing, contrary to s 102(3)(b), and the union complained that the employer was filling striking employees' positions with management personnel, contrary to s 102(3)(a). The board upheld the employer's complaint and ordered the union to cease and desist picketing. It also upheld the complaint against the employer and ordered it to refrain from using management personnel to do work ordinarily performed by bargaining unit employees. The employer successfully sought judicial review of the board's order against it and, eventually, the union appealed to the Supreme Court of Canada.

The issue in the case was the interpretation of s 102(3)(a). The employer argued that the provision should be interpreted to prohibit the temporary replacement of employees "with any other employee" or permanently filling their positions "with any other employee." Management personnel were not employees as defined in the Act, and therefore s 102(3)(a) was not breached by the use of management personnel to replace employees during the strike. The employer argued that the objective of the provision was to preserve the positions of the employees once the strike was over. The union argued that the phrase "with any other employee" only applied to permanently filling positions, and not to temporarily replacing employees during the strike.[23] Therefore, s 102(3) also precluded the temporary replacement of employees by management personnel.

Writing for the Supreme Court of Canada, Dickson J (as he then was) paraphrased the board's approach to interpreting s 102(3) as follows:

> It was the opinion of the board that when the Legislature saw fit to grant the right to strike to public employees, it intended through the enactment of s. 102(3) to restrict the possibility of picket-line violence by prohibiting strikebreaking, on the one hand, and picketing, on the other. This apparent intention, the board held, would be frustrated [by the employer's interpretation]. The result of such an interpretation would be that strikers would have been deprived of their right to picket, but the employer would not have been deprived of the right to employ strike-breakers.[24]

The court allowed the union's appeal. However, it did not follow the extant analytical framework toward the conclusion that the interpretation of s 102(3) was a question within the jurisdiction of the board and thus immunized from judicial review by the privative clause. Instead, Dickson J canvassed the reasons for the existence of privative clauses, emphasizing the legislative choice to confer certain tasks onto administrative actors, the specialized expertise and accumulated experience of administrative bodies, and the virtues of judicial restraint. In the case at bar, the interpretation of s 102(3) "would seem to lie logically at the heart of the specialized jurisdiction confided to the Board."[25] Consequently, a court should only interfere if (by labelling as jurisdictional error) an interpretation of the provision

---

22 PSLRA, s 101(1); *CUPE, supra* note 2 at para 14.
23 *CUPE, supra* note 2 at paras 5-6.
24 *Ibid* at para 7.
25 *Ibid* at para 15.

is "so patently unreasonable that its construction cannot be rationally supported by the relevant legislation."[26]

The court's judgment in *CUPE* did not make a clean break with earlier jurisprudence that invoked jurisdictional error to circumvent privative clauses. Rather, it reconfigured the analysis of when, why, and how the doctrine of jurisdictional error ought to be deployed. Most importantly, it conveyed a spirit of curial deference, a recognition that administrative decision-makers are not merely "inferior tribunals" but specialized bodies that possess a legislative mandate to apply their expertise and experience to matters that they may be better suited to address than an "ordinary court." This change of heart regarding the appropriate role of judicial review eventually transcended the confines of privative clauses to encompass substantive judicial review in general, including the exercise of discretion.

A reading of *CUPE* reveals three sources of the Supreme Court of Canada's doctrinal change. First, the court situates the case in a broader reappraisal of the respective roles assigned by the legislature to the courts and to administrative bodies in the implementation of regulatory regimes.[27] According to Dickson J, courts should recognize and respect the fact that these specialized decision-makers bear primary responsibility for implementing their statutory mandate and may be better suited to the interpretive task than the generalist judge.

Second, the judgment candidly admits that, because the provision in dispute "bristles with ambiguities,"[28] no single interpretation could lay claim to being "correct." Instead, there were several plausible interpretations, including that of the board, the majority of the New Brunswick Court of Appeal, and a minority opinion of the Court of Appeal. Dickson J canvassed at length the basis for each possible interpretation, not in order to discern which one was correct, but to demonstrate why the board's interpretation "would seem at least as reasonable as the alternative interpretations suggested in the Court of Appeal" and, in any event, could not be described as patently unreasonable.[29] Although *CUPE* was concerned with a statutory provision whose ambiguity was attributable to poor drafting, it was amplified in subsequent cases, such as by Wilson J in *Corn Growers*[30] and L'Heureux-Dubé J in *Domtar*,[31] into a more radical critique of the conceit that there is always only one correct interpretation of a statutory provision. Ambiguity, gaps, silences, and contradictions can rarely (if ever) be completely excised from text. This ineluctable interpretive choice makes it possible to ask who is better placed to make the choice—the tribunal or the court? In other words, indeterminacy of meaning also underwrites the plea for judicial humility that is at the heart of *CUPE*. Moreover, Dickson J's interpretive survey notably focused on the meaning of the provision in the context of the statute, its purpose, and the consequences of various interpretive options for the fulfillment of the legislative scheme's objectives. He did not resort to dictionary definitions of "fill" or "replace," invoke common law presumptions about access to the courts, or employ mechanistic canons of statutory construction.

---

26 *Ibid* at para 16.
27 *Ibid* at para 15.
28 *Ibid* at para 4.
29 *Ibid* at para 29.
30 *National Corn Growers Assn v Canada (Import Tribunal)*, [1990] 2 SCR 1324 [*Corn Growers*].
31 *Domtar Inc v Quebec (Commission d'appel en matière de lésions professionnelles)*, [1993] 2 SCR 756 [*Domtar*].

Finally, Dickson J acknowledged the failure of prior judicial efforts to construct a coherent, principled means of distinguishing reviewable questions from those insulated by a privative clause. He noted that the "preliminary or collateral question" method is not helpful because one can, with little effort, characterize just about anything as preliminary or collateral. He admitted that identifying what is and is not jurisdictional can also be difficult, but counselled that "courts ... should not be alert to brand as jurisdictional, and therefore subject to broader curial review, that which may be doubtfully so."[32] Unfortunately, the judgment did not offer any technique, except to suggest that "jurisdiction is, typically, to be determined at the outset of the inquiry"[33] and, in the case at bar, the board's statutory authority over the parties (in this case, the union and the employer) and the subject matter (the conduct of a lawful strike) indisputably conferred jurisdiction "in the narrow sense of authority to enter upon an inquiry."[34] The issue then became whether the board did "something which takes the exercise of its powers outside the protection of the privative or preclusive clause."[35] According to Dickson J, short of a patently unreasonable interpretation of a statutory provision, courts should not interfere with the result reached by the administrative decision-maker. The shorthand description of *CUPE*'s outcome is that a jurisdictional question is assessed according to a standard of "correctness," while questions within jurisdiction are evaluated against a standard of "patent unreasonableness."

CUPE destabilized the idea that statutory provisions have a single, correct meaning that judges are uniquely qualified to discern. Yet, labelling the non-deferential standard of review "correctness" seems to convey exactly the opposite message. Even if one rejects a thesis of radical indeterminacy of meaning in favour of the contention that some (or many) statutory provisions do have a single correct meaning, one cannot know prior to the interpretive exercise which provisions do and which do not have a single correct meaning. Yet, the choice of standard of review necessarily precedes that interpretive exercise. Recall that a standard of review analysis proceeds in two steps: first, choose the appropriate standard of review; second, apply it. Only after performing the second step can one form an opinion about whether there is a single "correct" meaning (and maybe not even then). That is why using the term "correctness" at the first step of a standard of review analysis is premature and misleading. The better view is that "correctness" as a standard of review means that the judge's task is to reach what she considers the optimal resolution of the issue, and the reasoning or outcome of the original decision-maker exerts no distinctive influence on how the judge performs that task. It is worth as little (or as much) as the opinion of a lawyer arguing the case, or an academic writing about the issue, or a court in another jurisdiction.

CUPE transformed the conceptual basis of substantive review through a reformulation of the institutional relationship between courts and the administrative state. As Dyzenhaus and Fox-Decent[36] observed, however, there is a certain irony in the fact that *CUPE* was decided only a year after *Nicholson*. The latter heralded a new era in procedural review by vastly expanding the range of administrative action subject to judicial scrutiny on grounds of

---

32 *CUPE*, *supra* note 2 at paras 9-10.
33 *Ibid* at para 9.
34 *Ibid* at para 12.
35 *Ibid* at para 16.
36 David Dyzenhaus & Evan Fox-Decent, "Rethinking the Process/Substance Distinction: Baker v Canada" (2001) 51 UTLJ 193.

procedural fairness. Meanwhile, *CUPE* signalled a radical break from the existing modes of substantive review by advocating judicial retreat from the interventionism of the past. Interestingly, both *Nicholson* and *CUPE* were and continue to be hailed by most commentators as progressive and forward-looking judgments.

IV. THE SEQUELS

A. The Retreat

In the aftermath of *CUPE*, many provincial superior courts embraced the message of curial deference, although the Supreme Court of Canada itself displayed more diffidence. One indication was a line of cases that endowed judicial review with constitutional protection under s 96 of the *Constitution Act, 1867*.[37] This meant that no privative clause, no matter how carefully drafted, could entirely insulate an administrative decision from judicial review.[38] In terms of the rule of law tension between fidelity to parliamentary intent and the common law presumption of access to the ordinary courts, the court's expansive interpretation of s 96 of the *Constitution Act, 1867* ensures that the latter trumps the former.[39]

Another sign of retrenchment was the disregard of Dickson J's admonition against labelling issues as jurisdictional in order to subject them to the more stringent correctness review.[40] The Supreme Court of Canada post-*CUPE* showed no reluctance in labelling issues as jurisdictional, even (or especially) in labour law. The absence of methodological guidance about how to identify "jurisdictional" questions stoked a certain skepticism that the court

---

37 (UK), 30 & 31 Vict, c 3. Section 96 grants jurisdiction over the appointment of superior court judges to the federal government, but has been interpreted to protect "essential" judicial functions associated with superior court judges.

38 *Crevier v Quebec (Attorney General)*, [1981] 2 SCR 220; *Bibeault, supra* note 15; *Pasiechnyk, supra* note 5; *Royal Oak Mines Inc v Canada (Labour Relations Board)*, [1996] 1 SCR 369 [*Royal Oak*].

39 The court's devotion to the primacy of access to the ordinary courts remains to be tested where courts themselves (rather than the legislature) police access to first-level judicial review. As we have seen in *Baker* and will see in *Pushpanathan*, below, the *Immigration and Refugee Protection Act* imposes a written leave requirement on first-level judicial review. Whereas legislatures purport to limit access to judicial review via a privative clause, a leave requirement endows Federal Court judges with authority to restrict access to judicial review by denying leave. The jurisprudence indicates that the threshold for leave is low and ought to be granted where the applicant makes "an arguable case," and denied only where it is "plain and obvious that the applicant would have no reasonable chance of succeeding." Apart from descriptions of a quantitative threshold, there are no discernible qualitative criteria, no reasons requirement, and no appeal from a denial of leave. In practice, about 85 percent of applications for leave to seek judicial review of refugee decisions are denied, although there is radical variation in grant rates between judges. One might contend that judicial consideration of a leave application constitutes a perfunctory form of access to the ordinary courts, but the fact that the leave process operates in an opaque and unaccountable manner makes this characterization difficult to defend from a rule of law perspective. See Sean Rehaag, "Judicial Review of Refugee Determinations: The Luck of the Draw?" (2012) 38 Queens LJ 1.

40 See e.g. *L'Acadie* (*Syndicat des employés de production du Québec et de l'Acadie v Canada (Canadian Human Rights Commission)*, [1989] 2 SCR 879. Elsewhere in the jurisprudence, when addressing the capacity of tribunals to entertain Charter challenges to their constitutive statute, the Supreme Court of Canada described tribunal "jurisdiction over the whole of the matter" as jurisdiction over parties, subject matter, and remedy: *Cuddy Chicks Ltd v Ontario (Labour Relations Board)*, [1991] 2 SCR 5 at para 12.

was reverting to a result-oriented analysis driven by agreement or disagreement with the ultimate outcome.

From *Bibeault*[41] onwards, the Supreme Court of Canada attempted to develop and refine a test for distinguishing a jurisdictional question (subject to correctness) and those falling within a tribunal's jurisdiction (subject to patent unreasonableness). Beetz J's innovation was to propose what he called a "pragmatic and functional" analysis for distinguishing between jurisdictional and non-jurisdiction-conferring provisions. The central question posed by the analysis was not whether a question was preliminary or collateral, but whether "the legislator [intended] the question to be within the jurisdiction conferred on the tribunal."[42]

Responding to this question involved an examination not only of "the wording of the enactment conferring jurisdiction on the administrative tribunal, but the purpose of the statute creating the tribunal, the reasons for its existence, the area of expertise of its members and the nature of the problem before the tribunal."[43] By framing the question in terms of legislative intent, and by requiring a privative clause in order to trigger a departure from the usual approach to judicial review, Beetz J retained a formal commitment to parliamentary supremacy. He also invoked the expertise of the tribunal as a relevant factor in the analysis, which hearkened back to *CUPE*'s plea for judicial humility in relation to so-called "inferior tribunals." Nevertheless, in his application of the criteria, Beetz J swiftly concluded that the issue before the court was indeed a jurisdictional question that the commissioner failed to answer correctly.[44]

B. The Advance

The Supreme Court of Canada demonstrated its most enthusiastic endorsement of *CUPE* by making "should the court defer?" a question asked not only where statutes contain privative clauses, but also where statutes contain finality clauses,[45] or leave intact the option of judicial review, or even provide a full appeal to the courts on questions of law and fact.

Pezim v British Columbia (Superintendent of Brokers)[46] is noteworthy because the issue concerned a question of law and the enabling statute provided for a right of appeal to a court. Writing for the court, Iacobucci J's judgment offers a time-lapse photograph of the rapid shift in the jurisprudence from the language of "jurisdiction" and "privative clause" to "expertise" and "deference."[47] The issue was whether newly acquired information about asset value constituted a "material change" requiring disclosure by a reporting issuer. At the outset of his review of principles of judicial review, Iacobucci J hewed closely to *Bibeault*, and stated:

> The central question in ascertaining the standard of review is to determine the legislative intent in conferring jurisdiction on the administrative tribunal. … Included in the analysis is an examination

---

41   *Supra* note 15.
42   *Ibid* at para 120.
43   *Ibid* at para 123.
44   But compare *Ivanhoe Inc v UFCW, Local 500*, 2001 SCC 47, [2001] 2 SCR 565 [*Ivanhoe*], where the court adopted a standard of patent unreasonableness for the interpretation of the same phrase in a slightly revised statute.
45   A finality clause typically states that the decision of the agency is final and binding on the parties, but the clause says nothing about judicial review.
46   [1994] 2 SCR 557 [*Pezim*].
47   See also *Canada (Director of Investigation and Research) v Southam Inc*, [1997] 1 SCR 748 at para 31, 144 DLR (4th) 1 [*Southam*]: "There is no privative clause, and so jurisdiction is not at issue."

of the tribunal's role or function. Also crucial is whether or not the agency's decisions are protected by a privative clause. Finally, of fundamental importance is whether or not the question goes to the jurisdiction of the tribunal involved.[48]

A few paragraphs later, Iacobucci J declared that "even where there is no privative clause and where there is a statutory right of appeal, the concept of the specialization of duties requires that deference be shown to decisions of specialized tribunals on matters which fall squarely within the tribunal's expertise."[49]

The presence of a privative clause was apparently not so crucial after all, and the fundamentally important "jurisdictional question" was supplanted by "expertise" as the key determinant of standard of review.[50]

In *Pezim*, there was no doubt that the BC Securities Commission had jurisdiction over the parties (members of the board of directors of reporting issuers on the Vancouver Stock Exchange), the subject matter (disclosure of material change), and the remedy (suspension of trading). The court identified several factors that contributed to the conclusion that the BC Securities Commission was a highly specialized tribunal and that an interpretation of material change in the BC *Securities Act*[51] "arguably goes to the core of its regulatory mandate and expertise" in regulating the securities market in the public interest.[52]

Although the court concluded that the interpretation of the statutory provision warranted curial deference, it conspicuously failed to describe the applicable standard of review as "patently unreasonable." Instead, Iacobucci J simply adverted to the need for considerable deference. Three years later, in *Canada (Director of Investigation and Research) v Southam Inc*,[53] Iacobucci J made explicit what he had only hinted at in *Pezim*—namely, an intermediate standard of review between patent unreasonableness and correctness. He labelled the standard "reasonableness *simpliciter*" and declared it (retrospectively) as the standard of review applied in *Pezim*. To understand how the perceived need for a "middle ground" emerged, one must return to *Pezim*'s shift in emphasis from privative clauses to relative expertise. A binary focus on the presence or absence of a privative clause (and the attendant jurisdictional/non-jurisdictional question) aligns with two standards of review embodying the presence or absence of deference. Shifting to an emphasis on relative expertise does not map easily onto a dichotomy, which may help to explain the impetus driving the court to insert reasonableness *simpliciter* into the spectrum.

Southam concerned a finding by the Competition Tribunal that Southam's acquisition of various newspapers within a given advertising market substantially lessened competition. By way of remedy, the tribunal gave Southam the option of divesting itself of one of two community papers. The relevant statute provided for an appeal directly to the Federal Court of Appeal. Two aspects of the tribunal's decision were the subject of appeal to the Supreme Court of Canada: the dimensions of the relevant market within which to assess impact on competition and the remedy of divestment.

---

48   *Pezim*, *supra* note 46 at paras 589-90.

49   *Ibid* at para 591.

50   See also *United Brotherhood of Carpenters and Joiners of America, Local 579 v Bradco Construction Ltd*, [1993] 2 SCR 316.

51   SBC 1985, c 83.

52   *Pezim*, *supra* note 46 at para 591.

53   *Southam*, *supra* note 47.

After reviewing various factors pertinent to the standard of review, Iacobucci J concluded that some factors pointed toward deference and some away from it:

> Several considerations counsel deference: the fact that the dispute is over a question of mixed law and fact; the fact that the purpose of the *Competition Act* is broadly economic, and so is better served by the exercise of economic judgment; and the fact that the application of principles of competition law falls squarely within the area of the Tribunal's expertise. Other considerations counsel a more exacting form of review: the existence of an unfettered statutory right of appeal from decisions of the Tribunal and the presence of judges on the Tribunal. Because there are indications both ways, the proper standard of review falls somewhere between the ends of the spectrum. Because the expertise of the Tribunal, which is the most important consideration, suggests deference, a posture more deferential than exacting is warranted.[54]

The new middle ground was reasonableness *simpliciter*: "an unreasonable decision is one that, in the main, is not supported by any reasons that can stand up to a somewhat probing examination." This examination entails an inquiry into the "evidentiary foundation or the logical process by which conclusions are sought to be drawn from it."[55] Although Iacobucci J was not entirely clear on this point, he seems to have regarded the most deferential standard of patent unreasonableness as appropriate only in the presence of a privative clause, where intervention must formally be justified by resort to the concept of jurisdiction.

The insertion of an intermediate standard of review did little to promote predictability or determinacy in this area of administrative law. Moreover, some contended that if three standards were better than two, four standards must be better than three, five better than four, and so on. Others suggested that standard of review should be conceptualized as a spectrum—sometimes closer to correctness, sometimes closer to patent unreasonableness—depending on the balance of factors for and against deference in the particular case. The Supreme Court of Canada squelched both propositions in *Law Society of New Brunswick v Ryan*[56] and stood firm on three standards of review rather than a spectrum.

V. PRAGMATIC AND FUNCTIONAL REDUX: PUSHPANATHAN V CANADA

Shortly after *Southam*, the Supreme Court of Canada took the opportunity to consolidate and summarize the factors to be taken into account in determining the appropriate standard of review. *Pushpanathan*[57] concerned the interpretation of a provision in the *Immigration Act*[58] (incorporating art 1F(c) of the UN Convention Relating to the Status of Refugees) that excludes from refugee status those persons "guilty of acts contrary to the purposes and principles of the United Nations." Pushpanathan had made a refugee claim in Canada. Before his claim was heard, he was convicted in Canada of the offence of conspiracy to traffic narcotics. He was subsequently excluded from refugee protection under art 1F(c) on the basis

---

54 *Southam, supra* note 47 at para 54.
55 *Ibid* at para 56.
56 2003 SCC 20, [2003] 1 SCR 247 [*Ryan*].
57 *Supra* note 3.
58 *Immigration Act*, RSC 1985, c I-2.

of his conviction. The issue in the case concerned whether "acts contrary to the purposes and principles of the United Nations" included a criminal conviction for drug trafficking in the country of asylum.[59] A distinctive feature of the *Immigration Act* (also applicable in *Baker*) was the mechanism for judicial review. The statute contained no privative clause or right of appeal. Instead, judicial review could only commence with leave of a judge of the Federal Court, and no reasons were required where leave was denied. If leave was granted and the case heard, the losing party could only appeal to the Federal Court of Appeal if the trial judge certified "a serious question of general importance."

Writing for the court, Bastarache J reformulated *Bibeault*'s pragmatic and functional question "Did the legislator intend this to be within the tribunal's jurisdiction?" into "Did the legislator intend this question to attract judicial deference?" The significance of this semantic shift was to regard a jurisdictional question as equivalent to a question to which no deference was owed, which would be determined through the pragmatic and functional analysis. He organized the factors relevant to discerning this legislative intent into four categories: (1) privative clause, (2) expertise, (3) purpose of the act as a whole and of the provision in particular, and (4) nature of the problem (question of law, fact, or mixed law and fact). Jurisprudence after *Pushpanathan* routinely relied on these four categories. The *Dunsmuir* decision, discussed below, does not completely reject *Pushpanathan*, but post-*Dunsmuir* judgments have tended to write *Pushpanathan* out of the story. Whether that will continue remains unclear.

Although the *Pushpanathan* court identified four separate factors, there are arguably only two ingredients in the deference calculus: the legislator's direct or indirect pronouncement about judicial supervision (privative clause, finality clause, common law judicial review, statutory judicial review, appeal) and the reviewing court's assessment of the agency's relative expertise. The inquiry into statutory purpose and the nature of the problem seem to address specific indicia of expertise. In *Pushpanathan* itself, the court admitted that "purpose and expertise often overlap,"[60] and that the rationale for greater scrutiny of general questions of law than questions of fact relates to the relative expertise of courts versus agencies.[61] A year after *Pushpanathan*, *Baker* expanded the reach of the standard of review inquiry to encompass judicial review of discretion, as well as questions of fact, mixed fact and law, and law. The outcome of the pragmatic and functional test would direct a reviewing court to the appropriate stance toward the substantive fairness of the decision before it: don't defer (correctness); defer a little (reasonableness *simpliciter*); defer a lot (patent unreasonableness).

The following survey summarizes the meaning ascribed to the four elements of the *Pushpanathan* test and provides examples of their application in various cases, bearing in mind the substantial overlap just described.

A. Privative Clause

Pushpanathan furthered the project of detaching the rationale of deference from privative clauses. By the time the court reached *Pushpanathan*, the formal category of "jurisdiction" had been hollowed out: "a question which 'goes to jurisdiction' is simply descriptive of a

---

59 *Pushpanathan*, *supra* note 3 at para 22.

60 *Ibid* at para 36.

61 *Ibid* at para 37.

provision for which the proper standard of review is correctness, based upon the outcome of the pragmatic and functional analysis."[62]

Privative clauses are not all identical, though the differences between them can be overstated by courts. In any event, as La Forest J unhelpfully stated in *Ross v New Brunswick School District No 15*, "there are privative clauses and there are privative clauses."[63]

Under the pragmatic and functional test, the presence of a privative clause weighed in favour of curial deference. It never played a determinative role, however. The court often said that lack of expertise could outweigh a privative clause; the court never said that a privative clause could outweigh the court's estimation of the decision-maker's relative lack of expertise.

B. Expertise

The case law was clear that relative expertise was the most important factor in determining the standard of review. In *Pushpanathan*, the court identified three steps in evaluating expertise: "the court must characterize the expertise of the tribunal in question; it must consider its own expertise relative to that of the tribunal; and it must identify the nature of the specific issue before the administrative decision-maker relative to this expertise."[64] Where the tribunal possesses "broad relative expertise" that it brings to bear "in some degree" on the interpretation of highly general questions, the court would show considerable deference, despite the generality of the issue.[65] Such was the case in *Southam* ("material change") and *Corn Growers* (interpretation of a treaty provision), where the court applied the standard of patent unreasonableness in view of the tribunal's specialized expertise. In *Southam*, Iacobucci J described the objectives of the *Competition Act* as more economic than "strictly legal." Business people and economists possess greater expertise than a "typical judge," who is more "likely to encounter difficulties in understanding the economic and commercial ramifications of the Tribunal's decisions and consequently … less able to secure the fulfillment of the purpose of the *Competition Act* than is the Tribunal."[66] This judicial modesty in relation to certain regulatory domains was presaged in an earlier concurring judgment of L'Heureux-Dubé J in *Corn Growers*, where she identified "labour relations, telecommunications, financial markets and international economic relations" as examples where courts "may simply not be as well equipped as administrative tribunals or agencies to deal with issues which Parliament has chosen to regulate through bodies exercising delegated power."[67]

Unfortunately, the case law provided scant guidance on when the court would valorize the agency's expertise as relevant to the interpretation of a question of law and when it would discount it. When describing the broad expertise of an agency, the Supreme Court of Canada attended to the agency's composition and specialized knowledge in comparison to a court. Evidence of distinctive expertise could come from statutory criteria for appointment

---

62 *Ibid* at para 28.
63 [1996] 1 SCR 825 at para 26.
64 *Pushpanathan, supra* note 3 at para 33.
65 *Ibid* at para 34.
66 *Southam, supra* note 47 at para 49.
67 *Corn Growers, supra* note 30 at para 80.

(for example, non-legal qualifications, length of term, and security of tenure), a policy-making function, or a "non-judicial means of implementing the Act."[68]

Bodies that deal with economic, financial, or technical matters seem to sit at the apex of the court's estimation of expertise. Members of securities commissions, international trade tribunals, and telecommunications bodies have all been recognized by the court as possessing experience, expertise, and specialized knowledge that courts lack.

Labour boards, often protected by privative clauses, are in some ways the paradigmatic example of expert administrative tribunals. Indeed, the Supreme Court of Canada would typically acknowledge their specialized knowledge and expertise in relation to industrial relations.[69] Yet labour boards tend not to benefit as consistently from curial deference as some other bodies. Labour arbitrators are considered less expert than labour boards (even though the same people often engage in both decision-making activities), because arbitrators are usually appointed by the parties on an ad hoc basis, and the arbitrator's task is confined to the interpretation and application of a particular collective agreement, rather than administration of the entire regime of industrial relations.[70] The ad hoc nature of the appointment usually counts against the expertise of certain human rights tribunals as well. More generally, the majority of the Supreme Court of Canada consistently deprecated the expertise of human rights tribunals and commissions, which they confined to fact-finding in the human rights context. The divergent judgments of La Forest J (concurring) and L'Heureux-Dubé J (dissenting) in *Canada (Attorney General) v Mossop*[71] vividly illustrate this point.

To the extent that expertise was the animating principle of the pragmatic and functional test, it is perhaps unsurprising that the court resisted deferring to human rights tribunals. Rights adjudication lies at the heart of the judicial function and institutional self-understanding. The court has found it difficult to concede anything but a narrow compass of relative expertise to another body charged with tasks that so closely resemble its own.

On the other hand, in both *Ryan*,[72] a case involving the sanction for misconduct imposed on a miscreant lawyer, and *Moreau-Bérubé v New Brunswick (Judicial Council)*,[73] involving allegations of judicial misconduct, the court went to some length to defend the superior expertise of professional discipline committees composed of lawyers and judges. Unlike a securities commission or a competition tribunal, the expertise of a law society or judicial council discipline committee could hardly be described as beyond the ken of most judges. Nevertheless, the *Ryan* majority explained that practising lawyers "may be more intimately acquainted with the ways that these [professional] standards play out in the everyday practice of law than judges who no longer take part in the solicitor–client relationship."[74] To the extent that at least one member of the committee was a layperson, the fact that the member was not a lawyer could even place him or her "in a better position to understand how par-

---

68   *Ibid* at para 32.

69   See e.g. *Canada (Attorney General) v Public Service Alliance of Canada*, [1993] 1 SCR 941; *Ivanhoe, supra* note 44; *Royal Oak, supra* note 38; *Toronto (City) Board of Education v OSSTF, District 15*, [1997] 1 SCR 487.

70   See e.g. *Dayco (Canada) Ltd v CAW-Canada*, [1993] 2 SCR 230.

71   [1993] 1 SCR 554 [*Mossop*].

72   *Supra* note 56.

73   2002 SCC 11, [2002] 1 SCR 249 [*Moreau-Bérubé*].

74   *Supra* note 56 at para 31.

ticular forms of conduct and choice of sanctions would affect the general public's perception of the profession and confidence in the administration of justice."[75] Ultimately, "owing to its composition and its familiarity with the particular issue of imposing a sanction for professional misconduct in a variety of settings, the Discipline Committee arguably has more expertise than courts on the sanction to apply to the misconduct."[76] As for the New Brunswick Judicial Council, Arbour J concluded that a "council composed primarily of judges, alive to the delicate balance between judicial independence and judicial integrity, must ... attract in general a high degree of deference."[77] The court eventually decided on the intermediate standard of reasonableness in both cases.

Decision-making bodies staffed by elected officials have proven problematic subjects for the evaluation of expertise (and for the application of the pragmatic and functional test as a whole). In *Baker*, the court dealt with the humanitarian and compassionate discretion that was statutorily conferred on the minister of citizenship and immigration, but delegated to a civil servant. The court found that the "fact that the formal decision-maker is the Minister is a factor militating in favour of deference. The Minister has some expertise relative to courts in immigration matters, particularly with respect to when exemptions should be given from the requirements that normally apply."[78]

In *Chamberlain v Surrey School District No 36*,[79] a local school board composed of elected trustees passed a resolution against authorizing three books depicting same-sex-parented families to be used in the classroom. One challenge to the resolution was that the board acted outside its mandate under the *School Act*[80] in passing the resolution—that is, it exceeded its jurisdiction. The majority of the court applied the pragmatic and functional test to arrive at a reasonableness standard of review, and found the resolution unreasonable. Writing for the majority, McLachlin CJ described the board as expert in balancing "the interests of different groups, such as parents with widely differing moral outlooks, and children from many types of families," and acknowledged that, as locally elected representatives, the board is better placed to understand community concerns than the court."[81] However, McLachlin CJ went on to find that, because the decision in question "has a human rights dimension" in which courts are more expert than administrative bodies, less deference is owed. Writing in dissent, Gonthier J commented that, although the board's decision clearly had a human rights aspect, "courts should be reluctant to assume that they possess greater expertise than administrative decision-makers with respect to all questions having a human rights component,"[82] especially in the context of local democracy. LeBel J's dissent challenged the premise that expertise ought to be the basis of curial deference toward elected officials in their legislative (as opposed to adjudicative) capacity. He noted that, in judicial review of municipal actors, "our court has always focused on whether the action in question

---

75 *Ibid* at para 32.
76 *Ibid* at para 34.
77 *Moreau-Bérubé, supra* note 73 at para 60.
78 *Baker, supra* note 1 at para 59.
79 2002 SCC 86, [2002] 4 SCR 710 [*Chamberlain*].
80 RSBC 1996, c 412.
81 *Chamberlain, supra* note 79 at para 10.
82 *Ibid* at para 143.

was authorized, not on whether it was reasonable."[83] In LeBel J's view, the animating principle is the separation of the judiciary and representative government and the need to protect each from illegitimate interference by the other. Application of the pragmatic and functional test, with the possible result of a reasonableness standard,

> fails to give due recognition to the board's role as a local government body accountable to the electorate. As long as it acts pursuant to its statutory powers, it is carrying out the will of the community it serves and in general is answerable to the community, not the courts. But if it purports to exercise powers it does not have, its actions are invalid.[84]

One way of understanding LeBel J's position is to posit that elected officials merit deference because they represent the will of the majority, not because of any expertise they may possess. The *ultra vires–intra vires* dichotomy (familiar from division of powers jurisprudence) is analogous to the inside–outside jurisdiction dichotomy, but is even more deferential to matters deemed *intra vires*. In certain respects, the disagreement between the majority and LeBel J on this issue mirrors a similar debate about the application of the doctrine of reasonable apprehension of bias. It brings to the surface the recurring dilemma about when elected officials should be held accountable through judicial review versus the ballot box.

Although the Supreme Court of Canada prioritized expertise in formulating the standard of review, its inquiry was limited to the statutory role of the administrative actor, not to the particular individual occupying it. Courts gleaned evidence of expertise from statute and surrounding context, but did not scrutinize the qualifications, competence, training, or experience of a specific decision-maker. Administrative law does not provide a mechanism for directly imposing on the state an obligation to adopt a merit-based appointment process for non-elected decision-makers. Consider the *Back to School Act, 2001* (Toronto and Windsor),[85] wherein the statute empowered the minister of labour to appoint as arbitrator a person who "has no previous experience as an arbitrator" and who is not "mutually acceptable to both trade unions and employers."[86] Even the doctrine of independence of decision-makers adopts narrow and formal criteria for assessing independence from inappropriate government influence on decision-makers. In other words, independence identifies formal indicia of susceptibility to government influence, and standard of review evaluates the presence or absence of expertise according to different formal criteria, but neither body of law requires or promotes actual expertise. One might consider whether merit and competence ought to matter to courts and, if so, how these concerns could be addressed in administrative law doctrine.[87]

C. Purpose of the Statute as a Whole and the Provision in Particular

What aspect of statutory purpose is relevant to the standard of review? In *Pushpanathan*, the court distilled prior jurisprudence into the following proposition: where the statute or provision can be described as "polycentric"—that is, engages a balancing of multiple interests,

---

83 *Ibid* at para 197.
84 *Ibid* at para 201.
85 SO 2001, c 1, cited in *CUPE v Ontario (Minister of Labour)*, 2003 SCC 29, [2003] 1 SCR 539 at para 81 [*Retired Judges*]. Note: This Act was repealed on December 15, 2009 (SO 2009, c 33, Schedule 20, ss 5(1), 6).
86 *Back to School Act, 2001*, s 11(4).
87 *Retired Judges, supra* note 85.

constituencies, and factors or contains a significant policy element, or articulates the legal standards in vague or open-textured language—more judicial restraint is warranted. Disputes that more closely resemble the bipolar, adversarial model of opposition between discrete parties and interests attract less curial deference. The rationale is that judges have less relative expertise in the former and more relative expertise in the latter. When discretion was added to the mix of provisions subject to review, courts tended to regard discretion-granting provisions as polycentric insofar as the exercise of discretion engaged the consideration of multiple factors. Note, however, that discretionary decisions (such as the humanitarian and compassionate decision in *Baker*) may directly affect only a single individual or identifiable group of individuals, in contrast to the more diffuse benefits and burdens associated with conventional "polycentric" provisions. Courts have also identified provisions that confer positive discretion (a beneficial exemption from a rule) as attracting more deference than negative discretion.

D. The Nature of the Problem

Appellate and judicial review jurisprudence have long divided legal issues into questions of law, questions of mixed law and fact, and questions of fact. In administrative law, these conveniently map onto the spectrum of deference as less deference, neutral, and more deference, in accordance with courts' declining relative expertise: "without an implied or express legislative intent to the contrary ... legislatures should be assumed to have left highly generalized propositions of law to courts."[88]

The characterization of a matter as a question of law or as a question of mixed law and fact may not be straightforward.[89] It is complicated by the fact that identifying an issue as a question of law does not necessarily preclude the possibility that the tribunal may possess greater expertise than a court in interpreting it, especially if the court otherwise regards the agency as highly expert, and the legal question involves interpretation of a provision in the agency's enabling statute.[90]

One clue that judges have looked for in distinguishing legal questions confided to the tribunal from those better resolved by the courts is the extent to which the determination will have precedential value in subsequent cases. The greater the precedential impact, the greater the assessment of expertise tilted toward the courts. Labelling the issue as a "pure" question of law (*Barrie Utilities*),[91] a "concept derived from the common law or Civil Code" (*Bibeault*),[92] a general question of law (*Mossop*),[93] not scientific or technical (*Mattel*),[94] or a human rights issue (*Pushpanathan*[95] *Chamberlain*[96]) was usually a reliable signal that the Supreme Court of Canada had concluded that the legal issue was one in which it believed itself to have superior expertise. In *Pushpanathan*, the court relied on the unique provision

---

88   *Ibid* at para 38.
89   *Southam, supra* note 47 at paras 34-35.
90   See *Retired Judges, supra* note 85.
91   *Supra* note 16.
92   *Supra* note 15.
93   *Supra* note 71.
94   *Mattel Inc v 3894207 Canada Inc*, 2006 SCC 22, [2006] 1 SCR 772 [*Mattel*].
95   *Supra* note 3.
96   *Supra* note 79.

in the *Immigration Act* (now the *Immigration and Refugee Protection Act*)[97] whereby a Federal Court judge must certify a "serious question of general importance"[98] in order for the litigants to proceed to the Federal Court of Appeal. The statutory requirement of generality and serious importance (as determined by the Federal Court judge) allowed the court to declare that "s. 83(1) would be incoherent if the standard of review were anything other than correctness. The key to the legislative intention as to the standard of review is the use of the words 'a serious question of *general* importance.'"[99]

In *Baker*, decided a year later, the court reiterated that s 83(1) inclined away from deference, but quickly added that "this is only one of the factors involved in determining the standard of review."[100] Indeed, the Supreme Court of Canada in *Baker* also held that once leave to appeal was granted, appellate courts were not restricted to the certified question. In *Baker* itself, the court addressed only obliquely the question identified by the Federal Court as a "serious question of general importance," even though the *Pushpanathan* court regarded the certified question provision as virtually irreconcilable with deference. Instead, the fact that the decision in *Baker* was discretionary seemed to exert the most significant influence in favour of deference. The court ultimately arrived at the intermediate standard of reasonableness *simpliciter*.[101]

VI. DUNSMUIR: AND THEN THERE WERE TWO

Ever since *Southam* ushered in the intermediate standard of review—reasonableness *simpliciter*—commentators, practitioners, and even some lower court judges complained about the indeterminacy, impracticability, unpredictability, and sheer confusion generated by three standards of review. The balancing test for determining which of three standards of review should apply often produced indicators pointing both toward and away from deference, thereby failing to provide predictable or reliable guidance to lawyers and litigants. Identifying criteria to distinguish the merely "unreasonable" from the "patently unreasonable" decision proved frustrating and elusive. In short, the "pragmatic and functional" test was neither.

In his concurring judgment in *Toronto (City) v CUPE, Local 79*,[102] LeBel J canvassed the widespread discontent with the direction of Supreme Court of Canada jurisprudence. He provided a thorough and thoughtful analysis of the sordid history of the rise and application of three standards and issued a plea for the abandonment of three standards in favour of a

---

97   SC 2001, c 27.

98   *Pushpanathan, supra* note 3 at para 87 (*Immigration Act*, s 83(1); *Immigration and Refugee Protection Act*, s 82.3).

99   *Pushpanathan, supra* note 3 at para 43 (emphasis added by the court).

100 *Baker, supra* note 1 at para 58.

101 The court in *Baker* also undercut the logic of its own reasoning in *Pushpanathan* regarding s 83(1). In *Baker, supra* note 1, the court ruled that, once a question was "certified," the Federal Court of Appeal (and, *a fortiori*, the Supreme Court of Canada) was free to consider any other issue that was apposite to the disposition of the case, without filtering it through the s 83(1) criterion of "serious question of general importance."

102 2003 SCC 63, [2003] 3 SCR 77 [*Toronto v CUPE*].

return to "a two standard system of review, correctness and a revised unified standard of reasonableness."[103]

Five years later, the *Dunsmuir* case gave the court the occasion to heed LeBel J's *cri de coeur*.[104] Like *CUPE*, *Dunsmuir* arose out of New Brunswick, involved employment, and featured confounding statutory text.

Mr Dunsmuir was dismissed from his civil service position in the Department of Justice. He received severance, but insisted that he was also owed a duty of fairness prior to termination. He grieved unsuccessfully, and then appealed to an adjudicator. (The procedural fairness aspects of the case are discussed by Kate Glover in Chapter 5, The Principles and Practices of Procedural Fairness.) The adjudicator appointed to address Mr Dunsmuir's grievance interpreted the relevant statutory provisions in a manner that allowed him to consider the reasons for discharge, even though the employer did not assert that Mr Dunsmuir was dismissed for cause. The question of law was whether the adjudicator was entitled to inquire into whether the employer actually dismissed Mr Dunsmuir for cause and, by extension, whether just cause existed. The adjudicator determined that the statute authorized him to inquire into the reasons for discharge as part of the grievance arbitration, but then went on to find that the dismissal was, on the facts, not for cause. One issue before the Supreme Court of Canada was the appropriate standard of review for the question of law concerning the adjudicator's authority to inquire into the reasons for dismissal.

The *Dunsmuir* majority acknowledged that its pragmatic and functional approach had attracted criticism for its "theoretical and practical difficulties" and that it had "proven difficult to implement." Binnie J, concurring, described it less charitably as "distracting" and "unproductive."

Despite the deficiencies of past jurisprudence, the court did not resile from its post-*CUPE* endorsement of deference as an animating principle of substantive judicial review. En route to introducing the new standard of review analysis, the majority rehearsed the rationale for deference:

> Deference in the context of the reasonableness standard therefore implies that courts will give due consideration to the determinations of decision makers. As Mullan explains, a policy of deference "recognizes the reality that, in many instances, those working day to day in the implementation of frequently complex administrative schemes have or will develop a considerable degree of expertise or field sensitivity to the imperatives and nuances of the legislative regime."[105] In short, deference requires respect for the legislative choices to leave some matters in the hands of administrative decision makers, for the processes and determinations that draw on particular expertise and experiences, and for the different roles of the courts and administrative bodies within the Canadian constitutional system.[106]

For the court, the problem lay not in the concept of deference or its virtues, but in the challenge of putting it into operation. After surveying the evolution of judicial review over the past 50 years, the majority offered the following diagnosis:

---

103   *Ibid* at para 134.

104   *Supra* note 4.

105   DJ Mullan, "Establishing the Standard of Review: The Struggle for Complexity?" (2004) 17 Can J Admin L & Prac 59 at 93.

106   *Dunsmuir, supra* note 4 at para 49.

The court has moved from a highly formalistic, artificial "jurisdiction" test that could easily be manipulated, to a highly contextual "functional" test that provides great flexibility but little real on-the-ground guidance, and offers too many standards of review. What is needed is a test that offers guidance, is not formalistic or artificial, and permits review where justice requires it, but not otherwise. A simpler test is needed.[107]

The Supreme Court of Canada followed the lead of LeBel J and walked the legal test back from three to two standards of review—correctness and reasonableness. It rebranded the pragmatic and functional test as the standard of review analysis. It also adopted a different methodology for choosing between correctness and reasonableness.

The pragmatic and functional test, as synopsized in *Pushpanathan* and applied thereafter, laid out four factors to be evaluated and weighed. Although the *Dunsmuir* judgment is not without ambiguity, the pattern of subsequent jurisprudence thus far suggests that the new standard of review methodology is no longer a balancing test, but more closely resembles a defeasible rule: the default position is deference, unless one of the exceptions applies.

The court began by casting the net of deference widely over a range of issues and situations: "Where the question is one of fact, discretion or policy, deference will usually apply automatically. We believe that the same standard must apply to the review of questions where the legal and factual issues are intertwined with and cannot be readily separated."[108] The majority explained that the court ought to defer to the interpretation of a "discrete and special administrative regime in which the decision maker has special expertise."[109] On the basis of the pattern of past jurisprudence, the court anticipated that "[d]eference will usually result where a tribunal is interpreting its own statute or statutes closely connected to its function, with which it will have particular familiarity."[110] Deference will even be warranted "where an administrative tribunal has developed particular expertise in the application of a general common law or civil law rule in relation to a specific statutory context."[111] The majority paused to genuflect briefly before the privative clause, acknowledging it as "a statutory direction from Parliament or a legislature indicating the need for deference."[112]

Given all the situations that incline toward deference, when is deference not warranted? The majority stated that a standard of correctness would apply to:

1. a question of law "of central importance to the legal system as a whole and outside the adjudicator's specialized area of expertise";[113]

---

107 *Ibid* at para 43.

108 *Ibid* at para 53. As Paul Daly wryly notes, "It is worth pausing for a moment to consider the linguistic wonder that is 'the thing that usually happens automatically.' A sliding door that 'usually opens automatically' is likely to lead to puzzled pedestrians at best and bruised noses at worst. A company which 'usually deposits paychecks automatically' is unlikely to gain the trust of its employees. ... At the same time as it purported to establish presumptive categories to which either reasonableness or correctness would appropriately be applied, ... [the *Dunsmuir* court] gave no guidance as to when the presumptions would be rebutted or displaced, or what weight the presumptions should be given": Paul Daly, "The Unfortunate Triumph of Form Over Substance in Canadian Administrative Law"(2012) 50 Osgoode Hall LJ 317 at 326-27.

109 *Dunsmuir, supra* note 4 at para 54.

110 *Ibid.*

111 *Ibid.*

112 *Ibid* at para 55.

113 *Ibid* at para 60; see also para 55.

2. constitutional questions;
3. "true" questions of jurisdiction: "where the tribunal must explicitly determine whether its statutory grant of power gives it the authority to decide a particular matter";[114]
4. "questions regarding the jurisdictional lines between two or more competing specialized tribunals."[115]

Much like *CUPE*, the majority in *Dunsmuir* broke with the past, but not entirely. For instance, the majority counselled a two-step process for judicial review: first, courts "ascertain whether the jurisprudence has already determined in a satisfactory manner the degree of deference to be accorded with regard to a particular category of question."[116] If no precedent exists, then a court should proceed to applying the standard of review analysis. In so stating, the majority seemed to assume that the new standard of review methodology would yield the same result as the old pragmatic and functional analysis. The court also indicated that the application of the new standard of reasonableness would not undermine decisions that might have withstood the less exacting standard of patent unreasonableness. The court addressed this concern directly when it reiterated that deference is "central to judicial review in administrative law," and affirmed that "[t]he move towards a single reasonableness standard does not pave the way for a more intrusive review by courts."[117]

When applying its new standard of review analysis to the legal issue raised in *Dunsmuir*, the majority proceeded swiftly to a deferential standard of review: the statute contained a full privative clause; the arbitrator was administering a discrete and specialized labour law regime that provided for prompt and final non-judicial remediation:

> Although the adjudicator was appointed on an ad hoc basis, he was selected by the mutual agreement of the parties and, at an institutional level, adjudicators acting under the PSLRA can be presumed to hold relative expertise in the interpretation of the legislation that gives them their mandate, as well as related legislation that they might often encounter in the course of their functions. ... The remedial nature of s. 100.1 and its provision for timely and binding settlements of disputes also imply that a reasonableness review is appropriate.[118]

While *Dunsmuir* engaged a question of law, it was not one of central importance to the legal system, and so the standard of reasonableness applied.

This deferential tenor of *Dunsmuir* might have assuaged the concern that decisions previously sheltered under the standard of patent unreasonableness might henceforth be set aside as unreasonable. But does this mean that the new reasonableness is the same as the old "patent unreasonableness"? That seems unlikely. Yet the court seems determined to change the test without overruling any prior decisions. One way of finessing the dilemma is to imagine that the new technique for evaluating reasonableness will be neither the "somewhat probing" analysis proposed under reasonableness *simpliciter*, nor the "clearly irrational" benchmark of patent unreasonableness, but something qualitatively different.

---

114 *Ibid* at para 59.
115 *Ibid* at para 61.
116 *Ibid* at para 62.
117 *Ibid* at para 48.
118 *Ibid* at paras 68-69.

The way in which reasonableness is measured is the subject of Chapter 12, Making Sense of Reasonableness, by Sheila Wildeman.

The *Dunsmuir* majority equivocated on the role of *Pushpanathan's* pragmatic and functional balancing approach, describing it as a kind of backup to the defeasible rule method of the standard of review analysis.[119] It is not clear how these two methodologies can co-exist, or what advantage exists in maintaining both. Over time, the majority of the court quietly jettisoned *Pushpanathan's* four factors in favour of exclusive reliance on the defeasible rule methodology, though minority and dissenting judgments occasionally attempt to revive the factors in mounting an argument that deference is not warranted in a particular case.[120] One cannot discount the possibility that today's dissent might be tomorrow's majority. In any case, the decision tree in Figure 11.1 illustrates the dominant rendition of *Dunsmuir*, as distilled by majority judgments up to 2017.

The concurring judgment by Binnie J aligns with the majority judgment in most respects, though a close reading suggests a somewhat less deferential posture. Compare his approach to questions of law with that of the majority:

> It should be sufficient to frame a rule exempting from the correctness standard the provisions of the home statute and closely related statutes which require the expertise of the administrative decision maker (as in the labour board example). Apart from that exception, we should prefer clarity to needless complexity and hold that the last word on questions of general law should be left to judges.[121]

Binnie J also foreclosed the application of the standard of review analysis to questions of procedural fairness,[122] although his dictum has not entirely laid the matter to rest. Perhaps the most enduring and notable features of Binnie J's judgment are those passages where he plays the role of Cassandra, cautioning that the majority judgment leaves various issues unresolved, which will eventually come home to roost in the application of the new and improved standard of review analysis. We return to those below.

Deschamps J delivered separate concurring reasons along with Charron and Rothstein JJ. While they share the same concern about the complexity and unwieldiness of existing doctrine, their proposed solution departed significantly from the other six judges:

> By focusing first on "the nature of the question," to use what has become familiar parlance, it will become apparent that all four [*Pushpanathan*] factors need not be considered in every case and that the judicial review of administrative action is often not distinguishable from the appellate review of court decisions.[123]

Deschamps J explained that in the absence of a privative clause (and definitely in the presence of a statutory appeal), the same principles that govern an appeal court hearing an appeal from a lower court should govern judicial review on questions of law, mixed law and

---

119   *Ibid* at para 64. For other examples of equivocation, see *Nolan v Kerry (Canada) Inc*, 2009 SCC 39, [2009] 2 SCR 678; *Nor-Man Regional Health Authority Inc v Manitoba Association of Health Care Professionals*, 2011 SCC 59, [2011] 3 SCR 616.

120   See e.g. *Edmonton (City) v Edmonton East (Capilano) Shopping Centres Ltd*, 2016 SCC 47, [2016] 2 SCR 293 [*Capilano Shopping Centres*], McLachlin CJ and Moldaver, Côté, and Brown JJ, dissenting.

121   *Dunsmuir*, *supra* note 4 at para 128.

122   *Ibid* at para 129.

123   *Ibid* at para 168.

Figure 11.1

Standard of Review Decision tree in *Dunsmuir* (Majority)
SoR = Standard of Review
R = reasonableness (deference)
C = correctness (no deference)

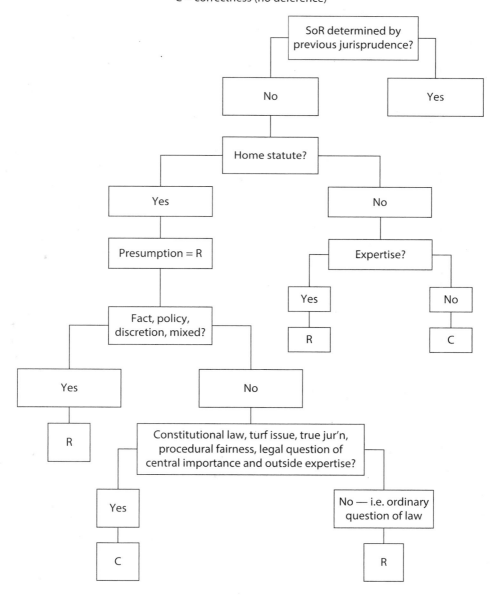

fact, and fact. This would mean no deference on questions of law, and greater deference on questions of mixed law and fact, and questions of fact. She would also extend deference to administrative bodies' exercise of statutory discretion.

In the presence of a privative clause, Deschamps J would counsel deference to questions of law as well, unless they did fall outside the decision-maker's "core expertise." In such cases, the court has a constitutional responsibility "as guardians of the rule of law" to ensure a correct interpretation of the law.[124] Deschamps J explained:

> This reduced deference insures that laws of general application, such as the Constitution, the common law and the *Civil Code*, are interpreted correctly and consistently. Consistency of the law is of prime societal importance.[125]

Deschamps J's concurring judgment borrows from various time periods: its insistence that judicial review by a court is not qualitatively different than an appeal from one court to a higher court hearkens back to the pre-*CUPE* period, where the nature of the superior courts' superiority was qualitatively the same in respect of lower courts and "inferior tribunals." Treating the presence or absence of a privative clause as determinative of legislative intent regarding deference is reminiscent of the post-*CUPE*, pre-*Pezim* era. Prioritizing expertise is consistent with the *Pushpanathan* test. Deschamps J's solution to "keeping it simple" is to treat judicial review in the same manner as appellate review by calibrating the standard of review according to the nature of the problem (law, fact, mixed law/fact, discretion). Only in the presence of a privative clause is deference on questions of law warranted and only to the extent of the decision-maker's expertise.

Deschamps J's minority judgment is rarely cited in subsequent jurisprudence. Nevertheless, it is important to revisit its underlying logic when considering how, in practice, the Supreme Court of Canada has applied "reasonableness" to questions of law, questions of mixed law and fact, and questions of fact and discretion.

The court's new standard of review analysis seems refreshingly uncluttered. The choice is simply to defer (reasonableness) or not to defer (correctness) according to the following rule: presume reasonableness where an administrative actor is interpreting or applying a provision of the home statute or closely allied statute, subject to the four enumerated exceptions.

In *Capilano Shopping Centres*, the majority reiterated why a rebuttable presumption in favour of deference advances democratic objectives:

> This presumption of deference on judicial review respects the principle of legislative supremacy and the choice made to delegate decision making to a tribunal, rather than the courts. A presumption of deference on judicial review also fosters access to justice to the extent the legislative choice to delegate a matter to a flexible and expert tribunal provides parties with a speedier and less expensive form of decision making.[126]

The reference to access to justice seems almost ironic. While providing parties with faster and cheaper decision-making may have been a goal of legislators in setting up agencies, boards, and tribunals in the first place, judicial review of those decisions remains slow and

---

124   *Ibid* at para 171.
125   *Ibid*.
126   *Capilano Shopping Centres, supra* note 120 at para 22.

expensive, and the confusion generated by standard of review jurisprudence up to the present only reduces predictability and creates incentives to litigate.

If the defect of the pragmatic and functional test was that it asked the right questions but delivered few determinate answers, the weakness of the new standard of analysis is that it delivers clear answers but at the expense of leaving various conceptual loose ends dangling. In this respect, the two methodologies exemplify the attractions and limitations of functional versus formal analysis.

The remainder of this chapter spins out *Dunsmuir*'s progeny, focusing almost exclusively on Supreme Court of Canada jurisprudence on the choice between correctness and reasonableness as the standard of review. Superficially, it seems simple: it's (almost) all reasonableness, (almost) all the time. But the volatility of standard of review compared to other areas of administrative law makes complacency risky. Abella J has signalled a desire to jettison correctness altogether and apply deference to all decisions by all administrative decision-makers all the time.[127] Another faction of the court seems more intent on moving the jurisprudence in the opposite direction. One can find evidence sprinkled in the case law where one or more of the *Pushpanathan* factors are invoked to justify deviation from deference, but they remain exceptional, ad hoc, and often the minority view—at least for now.

While the *Dunsmuir* court genuinely endeavoured to clarify and streamline standard of review analysis when it delivered its judgment in 2008, seven years later, Slatter JA of the Alberta Court of Appeal still felt constrained to commence his judgment with the following words: "the day may come when it is possible to write a judgment like this without a lengthy discussion of the standard of review. Today is not that day."[128]

A. Punting the Problem

Dunsmuir reduced the forms of deference from two (patent unreasonableness, reasonableness *simpliciter*) to one (reasonableness). Justice Binnie was preoccupied with the problem of how a single, invariant standard of deference could manage the diverse range of actors, issues, statutory review provisions and expertise that the pragmatic and functional test previously identified and calibrated according to two standards of deference. He opined that the majority decision simply shifts the problem downstream from the selection of the standard of review to its application in the individual case. He contended that the new reasonableness standard would inevitably devolve into a spectrum of deference, where the assessment of what constituted an (un)reasonable decision would vary according to the four factors that *Pushpanathan* previously used to select between more and less deference.

The majority of the court has resolutely resisted repeated pleas to acknowledge reasonableness as a sliding scale or spectrum, repeating often this dictum from *Khosa*: "reasonableness is a single standard that takes its colour from the context."[129] Over the course of a decade of post-*Dunsmuir* jurisprudence, the court has declined to share the contextual

---

127   *Wilson v Atomic Energy, infra* note 191, Abella J; *Capilano Shopping Centres, supra* note 120 (dissent).

128   *Edmonton East (Capilano) Shopping Centres Limited v Edmonton (City)*, 2015 ABCA 85, 382 DLR (4th) 85 at para 11. In its judgment on appeal from the Alberta Court of Appeal, the SCC optimistically replied, "That day has not come, but it may be approaching": *Capilano Shopping Centres, supra* note 120 at para 20.

129   *Canada (Citizenship and Immigration) v Khosa*, 2009 SCC 12, [2009] 1 SCR 339 at para 59 [*Khosa*].

crayons it uses to colour reasonableness from one case to the next. The court's reticence means that students, lawyers, academics, and lower courts must read between the lines of individual judgments, look for patterns in the case law, and seek guidance from pre-*Dunsmuir* jurisprudence (including the *Pushpanathan* factors) to divine what is (or is not) contextually relevant. The next chapter addresses this central challenge directly.

B. What About the Privative Clause?

Up to and including *CUPE*, the privative clause operated as the requisite legislative signal for deference. Under the pragmatic and functional test, the privative clause was demoted to one among many factors that a reviewing court would consider in determining whether to defer and, if so, how much to defer. In *Dunsmuir*, the privative clause becomes superfluous. The default position is deference irrespective of the presence or absence of a privative clause, there is only a single standard of reasonableness, and the privative clause does not trump the countervailing force of the exceptions to the presumption of deference. So where is the value added by the privative clause? In his concurring judgment, Binnie J delivers a tribute—or perhaps a requiem—for the unique heft of the privative clause:

> The existence of a privative clause is currently subsumed within the "pragmatic and functional" test as one factor among others to be considered in determining the appropriate standard of review, where it supports the choice of the patent unreasonableness standard. ... A system of judicial review based on the rule of law ought not to treat a privative clause as conclusive, but it is more than just another "factor" in the hopper of pragmatism and functionality. Its existence should presumptively foreclose judicial review on the basis of *outcome* on substantive grounds unless the applicant can show that the clause, properly interpreted, permits it or there is some legal reason why it cannot be given effect.[130]

Binnie J's insistence on the distinctiveness of privative clauses can be linked to his prediction of the inevitable emergence of a spectrum of deference under the rubric of reasonableness. Thus he asserted that "[a] single standard of 'reasonableness' cannot mean that the degree of deference is unaffected by the existence of a suitably worded privative clause. It is certainly a relevant contextual circumstance that helps to calibrate the intrusiveness of a court's review. It signals the level of respect that must be shown."[131] Perhaps this means that the presence of a privative clause should "colour" how reasonableness is applied.

C. What About Statutory Appeals?

Just as the privative clause has become superfluous as a legislative signal in favour of deference, the statutory appeal is no longer an impediment to deference. Before *Pezim* and *Southam*, the availability of a statutory appeal to the courts signalled that no curial deference was owed to the decision under appeal, and according to *Pushpanathan*, it was a relevant factor in choosing between the three standards of review. *Dunsmuir* did not explicitly address the significance of the statutory appeal, and in *Khosa*, Binnie J unhelpfully remarked that "[w]hile privative clauses deter judicial intervention, a statutory right of appeal may be

---

130 *Dunsmuir, supra* note 4 at para 143.

131 *Ibid.* In *Khosa, supra* note 129 at para 55, Binnie J reiterates that a "privative clause is an important indicator of legislative intent" to "deter judicial intervention."

at ease with it, depending on its terms."[132] Binnie J did not elaborate on the kind of terms that would put a statutory right of appeal more or less at ease with judicial intervention.

In general, the court continued to rule that that administrative decisions subject to statutory appeal to a court still attracted deference.[133] In *Capilano Shopping Centres*,[134] the Alberta Court of Appeal held that a statutory right of appeal should be another exception to the presumption of reasonableness. A five-judge majority of the Supreme Court of Canada swiftly rejected the proposition: "recognizing issues arising on statutory appeals as a new category to which the correctness standard applies—as the Court of Appeal did in this case—would go against strong jurisprudence from this court."[135] The majority then listed six post-*Dunsmuir* cases where the court applied a reasonableness standard of review in the presence of a statutory appeal provision.[136]

The four dissenting judges objected to framing the issue as the recognition of a new category of correctness review. Rather, they contended that "[i]n every case, a court must determine what the appropriate standard of review is for *this* question by *this* decision-maker."[137] Taking up Binnie J's unfinished business, the dissent set out to explain why the particular appeal provision before it sent a strong signal in favour of correctness review. First, the statutory appeal was limited to questions of law and jurisdiction "of sufficient importance to merit an appeal." The limited right of appeal and the criterion of importance "[indicated] that the legislature intended these questions to be reviewed by the Court of Queen's Bench for correctness."[138] Secondly, where a statutory appeal is allowed and the court sets aside the original decision, it must send it back to the original decision-maker to re-hear and decide in accordance with the opinion or direction by the court "on the question of law or the question of jurisdiction." In the dissent's view, this militated in favour of correctness: "the fundamental premise of [the provision] is that pure questions of law and jurisdiction appealed to the Court of Queen's Bench do lend themselves to one specific, particular result because the Court of Queen's Bench is bound to provide *direction* on these pure questions of law and jurisdiction and the board is prohibited from reaching a different result on those questions when the matter is remitted to it.[139]

D. Whatever Happened to Jurisdiction?

Recall that the "jurisdictional question" arose as a judicial escape hatch from the strictures of privative clauses: a decision, determination, or order that exceeded the jurisdictional boundaries conferred by statute was a nullity and, therefore, not a genuine decision, determination,

---

132   *Ibid* at para 55.
133   The lone exception was *Tervita Corp v Canada (Commissioner of Competition)*, 2015 SCC 3, [2015] 1 SCR 161 at paras 34-40, where the statutory provision governing appeal from the tribunal directly to the Federal Court of Appeal stated that the decision was appealable as of right on a question of law as if "it were a judgment of the Federal Court." The Supreme Court ruled that this signalled a correctness standard, because that is the standard applicable to an ordinary appeal from the Federal Court to the Federal Court of Appeal.
134   *Supra* note 128.
135   *Ibid* at para 28.
136   *Ibid* at para 29.
137   *Ibid* at para 71 (dissent).
138   *Ibid* at para 77 (dissent).
139   *Ibid* at para 79 (dissent).

or order insulated from judicial review. But the demotion of privative clauses cast into question the raison d'être of its foil, the jurisdictional question. After *Southam*, a court could both justify deference in the absence of a privative clause and justify correctness scrutiny in the presence of a privative clause. Eventually, the jurisdictional question lost its formal, conceptual moorings and became merely a label affixed to the outcome reached by a judicial balancing of the four factors summarized in *Pushpanathan*. Serious attention to formal attributes of jurisdiction (authority over subject matter, parties, or remedy) virtually disappeared.

As applied by subsequent courts, *Dunsmuir* seemed to relinquish the *Pushpanathan* balancing test, but the judgment also revived the formal idea of jurisdiction as a boundary-drawing concept capable of rebutting a presumption of deference. The majority also invoked the dictum in *CUPE* that urged the courts to be sparing in their resort to the formal claim of jurisdiction. Thus far, the post-*Dunsmuir* Supreme Court of Canada seems committed to exercising restraint in labelling an issue as jurisdictional and thereby subject to the stricter standard of correctness. The best proof lies in *Dunsmuir* itself. Without expending much effort, the court could have transformed the question "Does the statute authorize the adjudicator to inquire into the existence of cause for dismissal?" into "Does the adjudicator have jurisdiction to inquire into the existence of cause for dismissal?" Yet, the court refrained from even posing the question in jurisdictional terms. The adjudicator had jurisdiction over the parties (the employer and employee) and over the subject matter (discharge, suspension, or other financial penalty), and that sufficed.[140]

Later, in *Alberta (Information and Privacy Commissioner) v Alberta Teachers' Association*,[141] the court directly confronted the post-*Dunsmuir* endurance of jurisdictional questions in relation to the standard of review analysis.

Writing for six judges, Rothstein J ventured that "the time [had] come to reconsider whether, for purposes of judicial review, the category of true questions of jurisdiction [existed] and [whether it was] necessary to identifying the appropriate standard of review."[142] The core of Rothstein J's proposal resides in the admission that decades of administrative law jurisprudence had left him "unable to provide a definition of what might constitute a true question of jurisdiction."[143] Preserving a concept that is theoretically compelling but practically unworkable and even superfluous seems only to invite the type of arcane and indeterminate legal wrangling that *Dunsmuir* sought to avoid. Because the Supreme Court of Canada had already cast the cloak of constitutional protection over judicial review (thereby foreclosing any literal application of a privative clause), and *Dunsmuir* had identified other criteria for applying the correctness standard, extinguishing the category of jurisdictional question jeopardized neither the resilience of judicial review nor

---

140   See also *Smith v Alliance Pipeline Ltd*, 2011 SCC 7, [2011] 1 SCR 160 [*Smith*]. In *Northrop Grumman Overseas Services Corp v Canada (Attorney General)*, 2009 SCC 50, [2009] 3 SCR 309 at para 10, the court avoided engaging the question by noting that the parties all accepted that earlier case law remained authoritative in imposing a standard of correctness. Because the earlier jurisprudence determined the standard of review in "a satisfactory manner," the court was relieved of the task of conducting a fresh standard of review analysis.

141   2011 SCC 61, [2011] 3 SCR 654 [*Alberta Information and Privacy Commissioner*].

142   *Ibid* at para 34.

143   *Ibid* at para 42.

correctness scrutiny. Technically though, the majority does not deal the fatal blow to jurisdiction as a basis of correctness view, concluding instead that jurisdictional questions are
exceptional and none had come before it since *Dunsmuir*.[144]

A sympathetic reading of the majority judgment might suggest that the other post-
Dunsmuir grounds for correctness review really amount to exemplars of situations typically
regarded as "jurisdictional" in pre-*Dunsmuir* case law. In a jurisprudence chiefly notable for
its lack of predictability, the correctness standard was most consistently applied to issues of
procedural fairness, constitutionality, the "jurisdictional lines between competing specialized
tribunals," and questions of law elevated to "central importance to the legal system as a
whole and … outside the adjudicator's expertise."[145] One could argue that the work done by
"jurisdiction" pre-*Dunsmuir* is performed post-*Dunsmuir* by these exceptions to the default
presumption of *Dunsmuir* reasonableness, thereby rendering "jurisdiction" itself otiose.

Cromwell J emphatically disagreed with the majority on the fate of jurisdiction, warning
that the position espoused by Rothstein J threatened to "undermine the foundation of judicial review of administrative action."[146] As Rothstein J notes, however, Cromwell J's objection
fails to take into account the bases for application of a correctness standard apart from the
jurisdictional question.

Cromwell J's version of the standard of review analysis tempers the inclination toward
reasonableness with "a more thorough examination of legislative intent when a plausible
argument is advanced that a particular provision falls outside the 'presumption' of reasonableness review and into the 'exceptional' category of correctness review."[147] Cromwell J
does not actually conduct a thorough examination of legislative intent in the case, or indicate what a plausible argument should contain, confining himself to the conclusory statement that the legislature did not intend a correctness standard to apply because "the power
to extend time is granted in broad terms in the context of a detailed and highly specialized
statutory scheme which it is the Commissioner's duty to administer and under which he is
required to exercise many broadly granted discretions."[148] This quick concession seems
curious, because Cromwell J could have identified the fact that the interpretation of a statutory provision about timelines essentially concerns the process of investigation and adjudication, and the court has consistently applied a correctness standard to matters of
procedural fairness.

Binnie J (Deschamps J concurring) staked out a conciliatory middle position between
Rothstein J and Cromwell J. He agreed with the latter that the concept of jurisdiction is
"fundamental," but endorsed Rothstein J's initiative "to euthanize the issue" on account of
its practical disutility.[149] Binnie J's middle ground consists of two propositions. The first is a
reiteration of his prediction that reasonableness will entail a spectrum of intensity of scrutiny, with the implication that the application of a reasonableness review may, in appropriate
cases, look very similar to correctness review. The second is a revision of the "question of

---

144 See also *Canadian Broadcasting Corp v SODRAC 2003 Inc*, 2015 SCC 57, [2015] 3 SCR 615 at para 39.
145 *Ibid* at para 30.
146 *Ibid* at para 92.
147 *Ibid* at para 99.
148 *Ibid* at para 101.
149 *Ibid* at para 88.

central importance to the legal system as a whole" exception to deference. Here, Binnie J offered a broader and more generic exception for questions of law that "raise matters of legal importance beyond administrative aspects of the statutory scheme under review" and which do not lie "within the core function and expertise of the decision maker."[150] If adopted, Binnie J's reformulation would appear to enlarge the scope of questions of law subject to the correctness standard of review.

The boundary metaphor that underwrites jurisdiction is at once irresistible and impracticable. Perhaps it is no coincidence that the vocabulary of jurisdiction feels most natural when invoked in respect of entities that also happen to be geographically bounded, such as municipalities, provinces, and states. This makes all the more notable the 2012 judgment in *Catalyst Paper Corp v North Cowichan (District)*,[151] which concerned a municipal tax by-law. The court resolutely avoided the term "jurisdiction," or its close cousin (*ultra*) *vires*, and couched its analysis of the by-law within the standard of review framework of reasonableness. The court did the same for Manitoba Law Society rules, but retained the *ultra vires* framework (with its implicit correctness standard) for evaluating the legality of subordinate legislation enacted by the Ontario Cabinet to regulate the sale of generic drugs.[152] The rationale for the disparity is not apparent, yet the court still avoided using the term "jurisdiction" in the latter case.

Yet it seems that reports of jurisdiction's death as a ground of correctness review may be premature. Like a true B-movie zombie, it lumbered back to life in the dissenting judgment in *Quebec (Attorney General) v Guérin*.[153] The case concerned a framework agreement between the province of Quebec and the provincial federation of physicians regulating, *inter alia*, fees that physicians could charge the government. The agreement also empowered the two negotiating parties to recognize (according to stipulated criteria) laboratories eligible to bill the government for certain fees under the framework agreement. The parties recognized the appellant's laboratory but did not make the recognition retroactive (which they could do on an exceptional basis). The appellant submitted a dispute to the arbitrator of the framework agreement alleging that his clinic should have received retroactive recogntion, and that it was entitled to bill for the contested fee. Section 54 of the *Health Insurance Act*[154] provided that "[a] dispute resulting from the interpretation or application of an agreement [like the Framework Agreement] is submitted to a council of arbitration, to the exclusion of any court of civil jurisdiction."[155]

The arbitrator ruled that he did not have authority to rule on whether the appellant's laboratory should have been recognized retroactively, because recognition of laboratories was reserved to the negotiating parties in the framework agreement and, in any case, the

---

150   *Ibid* at para 89.
151   2012 SCC 2, [2012] 1 SCR 5 [*Catalyst*].
152   Compare *Green v Law Society of Manitoba*, 2017 SCC 20; *Katz Group Canada Inc v Ontario (Health and Long-Term Care)*, 2013 SCC 64, [2013] 3 SCR 810.
153   2017 SCC 42 [*Guérin*].
154   CQLR, c A-29.
155   *Guérin*, supra note 152 at para 6.

appellant did not have standing as an individual to submit the dispute to arbitration.[156] At issue was whether certain radiology clinics fell within the terms of the agreement such that they could claim a certain type of fee. The majority of the court regarded both the issue of arbitrability and standing under s 54 as subject to reasonableness, and found the arbitrator's decision on each issue to be reasonable. Brown and Rowe JJ (dissenting) agreed that the issue of standing attracted deference, but insisted that the question of whether the arbitrator could rule on the recognition of the laboratory was jurisdictional because it concerned the authority of the arbitrator to decide a matter submitted to it.

> Our colleagues Wagner and Gascon JJ, however, say that jurisdiction was not at issue here; rather, they view the matter as one of arbitrability. It is true that an issue is not arbitrable before a tribunal that has no jurisdiction to hear it. That said, arbitrability is distinct from jurisdiction and standing. Jurisdiction is about who has competence to decide what issues. Standing is about who can participate in the proceedings. Arbitrability, however, is akin to justiciability, in that it goes to whether the issue is capable of being considered legally and determined by the application of legal principles and techniques (by, in this case, the arbitrator). In our respectful view, the majority risks undermining the coherence of the analytical structure in administrative law by mischaracterizing questions of jurisdiction and standing as questions of arbitrability. The question of whether the arbitrator had the authority to decide on Dr. Guérin's matter was, as we say and as this Court's own jurisprudence demonstrates, clearly jurisdictional.[157]

It is too early to predict whether the dissent will succeed in reviving jurisdiction as a ground of correctness review, or whether their judgment is rather more like a rear guard action in a lost battle.

E. Whatever Happened to Patent Unreasonableness?

Pity the legislators: long ago, they gave up trying to refine the privative clause in order to persuade judges that when they told the courts to "get out and stay out," they really meant it. If the privative clause was an exercise in communicating legislative intent about the role of the courts, suffice to say that the message was, if not lost, then reformulated in translation. The Supreme Court of Canada rationalized this through the constitutionalization of judicial review, and a negotiation between the rule of law and an idea of parliamentary sovereignty counterpoised against the rule of law.

Sometime after *Southam*, a few legislators switched tactics and decided instead to direct the courts on the legislature's intended standard of review by explicitly stating whether a reviewing court should apply correctness, unreasonableness *simpliciter*, or patent unreasonableness. For example, the BC *Administrative Tribunals Act*[158] (ATA) itemizes grounds of judicial review applicable to the tribunals subject to the ATA and matches each ground with a standard of review. In the case of judicial review of discretion, the ATA also lists factors

---

156 *Ibid* at para 3.

157 *Ibid* at para 70. Note that even if the arbitrator erred by refusing to arbitrate the issue, the outcome of the case does not change if the appellant had no standing to bring the issue to arbitration in the first place.

158 SBC 2004, c 45 [ATA].

relevant to determining whether discretion was exercised in a patently unreasonable way.[159] In Ontario, the *Human Rights Code* contains a privative clause stipulating that "a decision of the [Human Rights] Tribunal is final and not subject to appeal and shall not be altered or set aside in an application for judicial review or in any other proceeding unless the decision is patently unreasonable."[160]

And then *Dunsmuir* came along, and out went patent unreasonableness.

The court in *Khosa* acknowledged the predicament for parties dealing with statutes that incorporate the now obsolete common law standard of "patent unreasonableness":

> Generally speaking, most if not all judicial review statutes are drafted against the background of the common law of judicial review. Even the more comprehensive among them, such as the British Columbia *Administrative Tribunals Act*, can only sensibly be interpreted in the common law context because, for example, it provides in s 58(2)(a) that "a finding of fact or law or an exercise of discretion by the tribunal in respect of a matter over which it has exclusive jurisdic- tion under a privative clause must not be interfered with *unless it is patently unreasonable.*" The expression "patently unreasonable" did not spring unassisted from the mind of the legislator. It was obviously intended to be understood in the context of the common law jurisprudence, al- though a number of indicia of patent unreasonableness are given in s 58(3). Despite *Dunsmuir*, "patent unreasonableness" will live on in British Columbia, but the *content* of the expression, and the precise degree of deference it commands in the diverse circumstances of a large prov- incial administration, will necessarily continue to be calibrated according to general principles of administrative law. That said, of course, the legislature in s 58 was and is directing the BC courts to afford administrators a high degree of deference on issues of fact, and effect must be given to this clearly expressed legislative intention.[161]

How have courts interpreted statutory standards of "patent unreasonableness" post-*Dunsmuir*?

In *British Columbia (Workers' Compensation Board) v Figliola*,[162] the Supreme Court of Canada considered whether the BC Human Rights Tribunal exercised its discretion in a pat- ently unreasonable fashion when it decided to adjudicate a *Human Rights Code* complaint that had already been rejected by a review officer of the BC Workers' Compensation Board. The court was not required to interpret the term "patently unreasonable" post-*Dunsmuir*, because the ATA already defined it according to the traditional indicia of abuse of

---

159 If a tribunal's enabling statute has a privative clause, the standard of review is patent unreasonableness for questions of law and fact or the exercise of discretion for all matters over which "the tribunal has ex- clusive jurisdiction" (ATA, s 58(1)). Common law rules of natural justice and procedural fairness must be decided "having regard to whether, in all of the circumstances, the tribunal acted fairly" (ATA, s 58(2)(b)), and a standard of correctness applies to "all other matters." Where the enabling statute has no privative clause, findings of fact are reviewable on the basis of no evidence or unreasonableness, questions of law are reviewable on correctness, the exercise of discretion is subject to a standard of patent unreasonableness, and procedural fairness is decided "having regard to whether, in all of the circum- stances," the tribunal acted fairly (ATA, s 59(5)).

160 *Human Rights Code*, s 45.8.

161 *Khosa, supra* note 129 at para 19.

162 2011 SCC 52, [2011] 3 SCR 422 [*Figliola*].

discretion.[163] In *Shaw v Phipps*,[164] the Ontario Divisional Court held that "patently unreasonable" in the Ontario *Human Rights Code* should be interpreted against the legislative intent at the time of enactment. The Divisional Court reasoned that the Ontario legislature's intent was to confer the highest level of deference available under general principles of administrative law on the Human Rights Tribunal. In 2006, that standard was patent unreasonableness. The Supreme Court of Canada subsequently declared the highest level of deference available under general principles of administrative law to be reasonableness. Therefore, according the highest degree of deference to the tribunal's determination of liability and remedy post-*Dunsmuir* meant respecting those "questions within the specialized expertise of the Tribunal" unless "they are not rationally supported—in other words, they are unreasonable."[165]

F. What Is a Question of Central Importance to the Legal System as a Whole (and Outside the Decision-Maker's Area of Expertise)?

This category of correctness review contains two elements that figured prominently in pre-*Dunsmuir* jurisprudence. The first is expertise, which was the guiding principle animating *Pushpanathan*. The second is consistency, which is both a virtue of good administration and valorized by the rule of law. In *Dunsmuir*, questions of jurisdiction and constitutionality might be understood as matters that lie outside the expertise of administrative decision-makers. Issues concerning the jurisdictional boundaries between different administrative tribunals seem more ambiguously tied to expertise, but also link back to the allocation of questions of true jurisdiction to the correctness standard. Questions of "central importance to the legal system as a whole" are assigned to correctness review only if they are also "outside the specialized area of expertise of the administrative decision-maker."[166] The *Dunsmuir* majority is also concerned about precedent: "Because of their impact on the administration of justice as a whole, such questions require uniform and consistent answers."[167]

The particular wording of this exception appears to come from the pre-*Dunsmuir* case of *Toronto v CUPE*.[168] In that case, the Supreme Court of Canada considered the standard of review applicable to the relitigation of a criminal conviction in the course of a grievance arbitration. LeBel J concurred with the majority's assessment that the question concerned common law doctrines that went to the administration of justice. He agreed that the appropriate standard of review was correctness, because the issue concerned "a question of law

---

163 ATA, s 59(4) defines a patently unreasonable exercise of discretion as one where the discretion

    (a) is exercised arbitrarily or in bad faith,

    (b) is exercised for an improper purpose,

    (c) is based entirely or predominantly on irrelevant factors, or

    (d) fails to take statutory requirements into account.

164 2010 ONSC 3884.

165 *Ibid* at para 42.

166 *Dunsmuir, supra* note 4 at para 60.

167 *Ibid*.

168 *Supra* note 102.

that is both of central importance to the legal system as a whole and outside the adjudicator's specialized area of expertise."[169]

By relegating the only explicit mention of expertise to a subclause of one exception, the standard of review approach articulated in *Dunsmuir* arguably decentres expertise as relevant to the choice of standard of review. The court routinely mentions delegation and expertise as part of the overall rationale for curial deference, but it is unclear whether demonstrated lack of expertise is capable of rebutting a presumption of reasonableness, or useful in calibrating how reasonableness is applied. In its post-*Dunsmuir* jurisprudence, the court has largely ducked the issue of consistency as a practical matter without actually disputing it as a virtue of legality.

Prior to *CUPE*, the privative clause was a necessary signal that the legislator regarded the administrative actor as expert. Post-*Southam*, other factors could also demonstrate expertise, with or without a privative clause. One reading of *Dunsmuir* is that it does not disavow the relevance of expertise; rather, it simply deems administrative decision-makers as expert in doing whatever is involved in administering the statutory scheme by virtue of their existence (unless one of the exceptions applies). This posture contrasts with the view expressed by former US appellate judge (and scholar) Richard Posner, whose critique of poor-quality decision-making by US immigration adjudicators commenced with the declaration, "deference is earned; it is not a birthright."[170] The Supreme Court of Canada comes close to affirming deference as a birthright in the following passage from *Capilano Shopping Centres*:

> Expertise arises from the specialization of functions of administrative tribunals like the Board which have a habitual familiarity with the legislative scheme they administer ... . Expertise may also arise where legislation requires that members of a given tribunal possess certain qualifications. However, as with judges, expertise is not a matter of the qualifications or experience of any particular tribunal member. Rather, *expertise is something that inheres in a tribunal itself as an institution.*[171]

This deemed expertise reaches its zenith (or nadir, depending on one's perspective) in the Federal Court of Appeal decision in *Tran*.[172] A minister's delegate (Canada Border Services Agency (CBSA) officer) had discretion to refer a permanent resident to an inadmissibility hearing on grounds of serious criminality, which is defined under immigration law according to, *inter alia*, the length of the penal sentence potentially or actually imposed on the offender. The complications in Mr Tran's case were that he was given a conditional rather than carceral sentence, and the minimum potential sentence was raised by amendments to the *Criminal Code* between the time he was charged and his trial. Counsel for Mr Tran made lengthy legal submissions to the minister's delegate about whether a conditional sentence should be counted as the equivalent of a carceral sentence, and the significance of retrospectivity in criminal sentencing. In the reasons for his decision to refer Mr Tran to an inadmissibility hearing, the minister's delegate, "I have reviewed counsel's submissions carefully and thoroughly, and given thought to each relevant point. Many are legal arguments that do

---

169 *Ibid* at para 62.
170 *Kadia v Gonzales*, 501 F (3d) 817 (7th Cir 2007) at 821.
171 *Capilano Shopping Centres*, *supra* note 120 at para 33 (emphasis added).
172 *Canada (Public Safety and Emergency Preparedness) v Tran*, 2015 FCA 237, 392 DLR (4th) 351.

not fall within the scope of my duties in this matter."[173] The minister's delegate then proceeded by ignoring Mr Tran's legal arguments, which had the same practical effect as considering and rejecting them. Despite the delegate's own admission that he lacked competence to address questions of statutory interpretation relating to penal law, the Federal Court and the Federal Court of Appeal extended deference to his decision. It seems difficult to impute to the minister's delegate an expertise in statutory interpretation that he expressly disavowed. The judgments in *Tran* thus bring to the fore the questions of what it means for expertise to inhere in an institution as opposed to those who exercise power in the name of the institution, and whether expertise actually matters at all.

In a unanimous judgment, the Supreme Court of Canada allowed Mr Tran's appeal.[174] But to the surprise and disappointment of observers, the Supreme Court of Canada did not even advert to the standard of review issues that the Federal Court of Appeal called on the court to address, much less resolve them. The court confined its reasoning exclusively to statutory interpretation of the contested provisions.

The other prong of this exception to deference is that the question of law be of "central importance to the legal system as a whole." Over 40 years ago, Peter Hogg made the case for administrative decision-makers' lack of expertise in making determinations of this nature:

> The very qualities which make the Agency well-suited to determine questions within its area of specialization may lead it to overlook or underestimate general values which are fundamental to the legal order as a whole. The generalist court is ideally suited to check the specialist Agency at the point where these general values are threatened.[175]

The *Dunsmuir* majority's requirement that the question be of "central importance" to the legal system and outside the expertise of the decision-maker caused Binnie J to worry that these qualifications would unleash needless and distracting debate in the lower courts. In his view, deference on questions of law should be interpreted narrowly or, to put it the other way, the exception to deference on questions of law should be interpreted broadly to cover all general questions of law.[176]

It is difficult to identify what the post-*Dunsmuir* court considers to be a question of central importance to the legal system because it has rejected virtually every attempt to designate one. In *Pushpanathan*, the Immigration and Refugee Board was interpreting art 1F(c) of the *UN Convention Relating to the Status of Refugees*. The court determined that a correctness standard of review applied to that interpretation, using the four "pragmatic and functional" factors identified in that judgment. Although it could not be said that the *UN Convention* as such was outside the expertise of refugee adjudicators, art 1F(c) required identification of the "purposes and principles of the United Nations," an issue that Immigration and Refugee Board members would have little occasion and no training or experience to address. And, as noted earlier, the court in *Toronto v CUPE* identified abuse of process as a question of law of central importance to the legal system as a whole and beyond the expertise of a labour adjudicator.

---

173   Subsection 44(1) Decision of CBSA Officer, on file with author.
174   *Tran v Canada (Public Safety and Emergency Preparedness)*, 2017 SCC 50.
175   Peter W Hogg, "Judicial Review in Canada: How Much Do We Need It?" (1974) 26 Admin L Rev 337 at 344.
176   *Alberta Information and Privacy Commissioner*, *supra* note 141 at para 89.

The court has only invoked the exception post-*Dunsmuir* on two occasions. In *Alberta (Information and Privacy Commissioner) v University of Calgary*,[177] the Alberta Information and Privacy Commissioner exercised statutory authority to issue a Notice to Produce Records to University of Calgary as a public employer subject to a constructive dismissal claim. Section 56(3) of the *Freedom of Information and Protection of Privacy Act*[178] requires a public body to disclose records to the commissioner "[d]espite ... any privilege of the law of evidence" applied to records over which the body asserts solicitor–client privilege. Like *Toronto v CUPE*, the issue concerned a general litigation doctrine. The majority identified several factors in favour of characterizing both the interpretation and application of s 56(3) as questions of central importance to the legal system as a whole and outside the commissioner's expertise:[179] solicitor–client privilege is "fundamental to the proper functioning of our legal system";[180] it has acquired constitutional dimensions as a principle of fundamental justice and client privacy;[181] the interpretation of the statutory language has "potentially wide implications on other statutes";[182] and, finally, the commissioner has "no particular expertise with respect to solicitor–client expertise, an issue which has been traditionally adjudicated by the courts."[183]

The second case is *Mouvement laïque québécois v Saguenay (City)*,[184] in which the Quebec Human Rights Tribunal determined that a by-law permitting recitation of a religious prayer prior to council meetings infringed the Quebec Charter's freedom of conscience and religion.

After quoting with approval the dictum from *Canada (Attorney General) v Mowat*[185] that "not all questions of general law entrusted to the Tribunal rise to the level of issues of central importance to the legal system or fall outside the adjudicator's specialized area of expertise," the court asserted that the issue in the case at bar crossed the threshold:

> In my opinion, in the context of this appeal, this court's decisions, more specifically *Dunsmuir*, *Mowat* and *Rogers*, to which I have referred, support a separate application of the standard of correctness to the question of law concerning the scope of the state's duty of neutrality that flows from freedom of conscience and religion. I find that the importance of this question to the legal system, its broad and general scope and the need to decide it in a uniform and consistent manner are undeniable.[186]

Reading *Dunsmuir*, *Mowat*, and *Rogers*[187] does not immediately illuminate how the outcome in *Saguenay* was undeniable. Perhaps the explanation lies in the historic reluctance of the court to defer to human rights tribunals in the interpretation of substantive anti-

---

177 2016 SCC 53, [2016] 2 SCR 555 [*AIPC v University of Calgary*].
178 RSA 2000, c F-25.
179 *AIPC v University of Calgary*, *supra* note 177 at para 22.
180 *Ibid* at para 20 (quoting *Canada (Privacy Commissioner) v Blood Tribe Department of Health*, 2008 SCC 44 at para 9).
181 *Ibid* at para 20.
182 *Ibid*.
183 *Ibid* at para 22.
184 2015 SCC 16, [2015] 2 SCR 3 [*Saguenay*].
185 2009 FCA 309, [2010] 4 FCR 579 [*Mowat*].
186 *Saguenay*, *supra* note 184 at para 51.
187 *Infra* note 190.

discrimination provisions, which lie close to the heart of the judicial task of interpreting s 15 of the Charter.[188] Indeed, it is noteworthy that in *Saguenay*[189] and *Rogers Communications Inc v Society of Composers, Authors and Music Publishers of Canada*,[190] a separate rationale for correctness was that the relevant legislation provided the courts with concurrent jurisdiction at first instance over the contested legal question. Where tribunals perform a task similar or identical to a task courts understand as a core judicial function, courts seem less inclined to defer.

One motive for adopting a correctness standard on certain questions of law is to promote consistency. Conflicting interpretations of the same rule give the appearance of arbitrariness and undermine public confidence in the legal system. Some judges regard the fact of inconsistency in the interpretation of a given statutory provision as a reason to treat it as a question of central importance to the legal system as a whole, while others treat inconsistency as an independent basis for correctness review.

The Supreme Court of Canada directly addressed the issue of inconsistency in 1993, after *CUPE* but before *Pushpanathan*. *Domtar*[191] concerned the disparate interpretation of a common phrase by two administrative bodies constituted under different statutes. The court rejected the assertion that the precedential value of resolving inconsistency within or between tribunals constituted an independent basis for adopting a correctness standard of review, where deference would otherwise be warranted. The court conceded that judicial intervention would be justified if the divergent decisions created an operational conflict, whereby compliance with one order would necessitate breach of the other. A significant concern for the court in *Domtar* was the risk that real or apparent inconsistencies within or between tribunal decisions might become a pretext for undermining fidelity to the principles underlying curial deference. The court also adverted to internal mechanisms available to tribunals to encourage consistency, and downplayed the virtues of consistency in relation to other important values served by deference. In *Domtar*, the reach of the court's dictum was limited only by the possibility of direct operational conflict.

In *Mowat*, the Federal Court of Appeal was presented with conflicting interpretations of the same statutory provision by different panels of the same tribunal and, subsequently, by different Federal Court judges on judicial review. The Federal Court of Appeal described the problem as follows:

> The question has not been answered consistently by the Tribunal and is the subject of diverse opinions in the Federal Court. It comes before the court for the first time. It is difficult, if not impossible, to conclude that the answer (either yes or no) can be said to fall within a range of possible acceptable outcomes. There is much to be said for the argument that where there are two conflicting lines of authority interpreting the same statutory provision, even if each on its own could be found to be reasonable, it would not be reasonable for a court to uphold both.[192]

---

188   Note that in *Mowat*, where the court applied a reasonableness standard *de jure* (if not *de facto*), the issue concerned expenses, not the interpretation of a substantive anti-discrimination provision.

189   *Saguenay, supra* note 184 at paras 46, 51.

190   2012 SCC 35, [2012] 2 SCR 283 at paras 14-20 [*Rogers*].

191   *Domtar, supra* note 31.

192   *Mowat, supra* note 185 at para 45 (FCA).

The values of certainty and consistency for the affected parties and the public at large led the Court of Appeal to characterize the question of whether a human rights tribunal can order the losing party to pay the legal costs of the complainant as a "general question of law of central importance to the legal system as a whole and one that is outside the specialized area of the Tribunal's expertise."[193] It set aside the Human Rights Tribunal's affirmative response to the question as incorrect.

The Supreme Court of Canada in *Mowat* suppressed the issue of conflicting decisions and did not advert to it. It decided that the Human Rights Tribunal's inclusion of legal costs as "expenses" was unreasonable. The judgment had the convenient effect of ruling out one of only two possible interpretations of the statutory provision. The court thus provided definitive guidance to subsequent decision-makers without adverting to the inconsistency.

In *McLean v British Columbia (Securities Commission)*,[194] the court rejected an argument for correctness based on potential inconsistency in the interpretation of similarly worded statutory limitation periods between provincial securities commissions. The majority observed that "[i]f there is a problem with such a hypothetical outcome, it is a function of our Constitution's federalist structure—not the administrative law standards of review."[195]

The court addressed inconsistency again in *Wilson v Atomic Energy of Canada Ltd*.[196] The issue was whether the *Canada Labour Code* permitted dismissals only for cause. The Federal Court of Appeal depicted this as a matter of long-standing disagreement among labour adjudicators and, on that basis, made a principled case for intervening on a correctness standard to resolve the disputed point, declaring that "we have to act as a tie-breaker."[197] The Federal Court of Appeal's decision was endorsed by two dissenting judges at the Supreme Court of Canada, who insisted that as long as there is even "one conflicting but reasonable decision, its very existence undermines the rule of law."[198] The dissent's rather extravagant rhetoric about the menace of inconsistency might have been spurred by the uncontested evidence that among thousands of decisions on unjust dismissal rendered in the previous 35 years, only eight diverged from the overwhelming consensus that dismissal must be for cause.[199] The Federal Court of Appeal and the dissenters on the Supreme Court of Canada ruled that this inconsistency warranted a correctness standard of review and, furthermore, that the interpretation adopted in the eight decisions was the correct one. Abella J, speaking for the majority on this point, dismissed the concern about inconsistency by acknowledging that "[i]t is true that a handful of adjudicators have taken a different approach to the interpretation of the *Code*, but … this does not justify deviating from a reasonableness standard."[200]

How a court should address conflicting jurisprudence remains a vexing and unanswered question. Does or should it matter how frequent or long-standing the inconsistency, or what the stakes are for those affected? How does inconsistency convert a question that is not

---

193   *Ibid* at para 47.
194   [2013] 3 SCR 895, 2013 SCC 67.
195   *Ibid* at para 11.
196   2016 SCC 29, [2016] 1 SCR 770 [*Wilson*].
197   *Wilson v Atomic Energy of Canada Ltd*, 2015 FCA 17, [2015] 4 FCR 467 at para 55.
198   *Wilson*, *supra* note 196 at para 89, Moldaver, Côté and Brown JJ, dissenting.
199   *Wilson v Atomic Energy of Canada Ltd*, Factum of the Appellant in the Supreme Court of Canada at para 46, online: <http://www.scc-csc.ca/WebDocuments-DocumentsWeb/36354/FM010_Appellant_Joseph-Wilson.pdf>.
200   *Wilson*, *supra* note 196 at para 17.

otherwise of central importance to the legal system into one that is? If you were a member of a tribunal, would you prefer that it be left to your peers to address divergent interpretations through institutional mechanisms within the administrative agency, or would you rather that the courts resolve the matter definitively by applying a correctness standard? Does it matter whether such institutional mechanisms exist and whether they have been deployed? Would it be legitimate to pre-empt future conflict by asserting a standard of correctness the first time the interpretation of a legal provision is contested? If not, when does it become appropriate to do so?

G. Reasonable Charter Violations

Dunsmuir preserves correctness review for constitutional questions, and this seems like an easy case: The Constitution is the supreme law of Canada, constitutional decisions reverberate widely through the legal system, judges possess expertise in constitutional adjudication, the Charter protects fundamental rights, and adjudication by independent judges ensures protection of individual rights from majoritarian tyranny.

At the same time, discretionary decisions attract deference, ostensibly because there is, *ex hypothesi*, no uniquely correct answer to how discretion should be exercised. As Evan Fox-Decent and Alexander Pless explain in Chapter 13, The Charter and Administrative Law Part II: Substantive Review, the court has vacillated in how to manage this tension. Currently, a wobbly majority endorses deference to Charter determinations conducted in the course of discretionary decisions. This significantly retracts the scope of correctness review for constitutional questions.

In *Doré v Barreau du Québec*,[201] the Supreme Court of Canada addressed the discretionary decision by the Barreau to sanction Doré for an intemperate letter he wrote to a judge. Doré argued that doing so infringed his expressive rights under the Charter. The court rebranded Doré's freedom of expression under s 2(a) as a Charter "value," and then explained why deference should apply to judicial review of a discretionary infringement of this "value," stating, "when Charter values are applied to an individual administrative decision, they are being applied in relation to a particular set of facts. *Dunsmuir* tells us this should attract deference."[202] The majority explained that courts should recognize "the distinct advantage that administrative bodies have in applying the Charter to a specific set of facts and in the context of their enabling legislation."[203] Rather than adapt the s 1 *Oakes* test to the exercise of a case-specific discretion (the approach taken in the earlier case of *Multani*),[204] the court proposed a "proportionality" analysis that balances "the severity of the interference of the Charter protection with the statutory objectives."[205] If the outcome of that balancing "falls within a range of possible, acceptable outcomes," then it merits deference. The concluding declaration of the court is that "[i]f, in exercising its statutory discretion, the decision-maker

---

201 2012 SCC 12, [2012] 1 SCR 395 [*Doré*]. But see also *Loyola High School v Quebec (Attorney General)*, 2015 SCC 12, [2015] 1 SCR 613, where three of seven judges effectively applied the *Oakes* (*R v Oakes*, [1986] 1 SCR 103) test to the exercise of discretion affecting freedom of religion.
202 *Doré, supra* note 201 at para 36.
203 *Ibid* at para 48.
204 *Multani v Commission scolaire Marguerite-Bourgeoys*, 2006 SCC 6.
205 *Doré, supra* note 201 at para 56.

has properly balanced the relevant *Charter* values with the statutory objectives, the decision will be found to be reasonable."[206]

Abella J, the author of *Doré* and its chief proponent, insists that her administrative proportionality approach is compatible with the *Oakes* test, and will ensure a comparable level of rights (or "values") protection delivered via a methodology more appropriate to discretionary decision-making. These are crucial and contestable claims. Unlike the procedural fairness doctrine, standard of review analysis historically has been indifferent to the nature of the interests or the impact of a decision on the affected party.[207] The fact that an important interest was affected or that a decision would have a profound impact on a party did not strengthen the case for a correctness standard of review. However, correctness review for constitutional questions comes closest to tacitly doing this, insofar as part of the justification for more stringent judicial scrutiny turns on the weight we attach to Charter rights. If *Doré*'s administrative law proportionality test does not ascribe Charter rights (or "values") the unique weight that a more traditional *Oakes* test does, then rights protection will differ according to whether the Charter is infringed via a rule or via discretion.

We live in an era where most governments take advice from government lawyers in drafting legislation in order to avoid flagrant unconstitutionality. It is also the case that many contemporary statutes look increasingly "skeletal." What goes on the bones of the statute is fleshed out through regulatory authority delegated to the governor in council or through expansive and broad grants of statutory discretion to administrative decision-makers (including ministers). If Charter issues are increasingly likely to emerge in the exercise of discretion rather than in the text of a legal rule, the scope and intensity of judicial oversight of Charter-impacting discretion will have implications for the level of rights protection within the Canadian legal order.[208]

VII. SPIN-OFFS

A. Segmentation

Where a judicial review application raises several discrete issues, reviewing courts have sometimes calibrated the standard of review separately for each issue. Segmentation arises whenever one link in a decision chain attracts a different standard of review from other links in the chain. *Dunsmuir* offers relief from the complexity of this process by expanding the range of

---

206   *Ibid* at para 58.
207   For a pre-*Dunsmuir* argument in favour of taking impact into account, see Lorne Sossin and Colleen Flood, "The Contextual Turn: Iacobucci's Legacy and the Standard of Review in Administrative Law" (2007) 57 UTLJ 581.
208   See Audrey Macklin, "Charter Right or Charter Lite? Administrative Discretion and the Charter" (2014) 67 SCLR (2d) 561. In *Gehl v Canada (Attorney General)*, 2017 ONCA 319, the Ontario Court of Appeal split on the question of how to sequence judicial review of Charter-impacting discretion. The case concerned the discretionary refusal by the Registrar for Aboriginal Affairs to register Dr Gehl as a status Indian because she could not prove the status of her paternal grandfather. Applying *Doré*, Sharpe JA ruled that the Registrar's discretion was exercised unreasonably in light of s 15 of the Charter. Lauwers and Miller JJA ruled that the Charter should not be considered, even in an administrative law analysis, unless and until non-Charter bases of review were exhausted.

decisional steps to which deference will presumptively apply, but the problem remains where one or more elements of the decision attracts a standard of review of correctness.

In *Dunsmuir*, Binnie J described segmentation in the following terms:

> Mention should be made of a further feature that also reflects the complexity of the subject matter of judicial review. An applicant may advance several grounds for quashing an administrative decision. He or she may contend that the decision maker has misinterpreted the general law. He or she may argue, in the alternative, that even if the decision maker got the general law straight (an issue on which the court's view of what is correct will prevail), the decision maker did not properly apply it to the facts (an issue on which the decision maker is entitled to deference). In a challenge under the *Canadian Charter of Rights and Freedoms* to a surrender for extradition, for example, the minister will have to comply with the court's view of Charter principles (the "correctness" standard), but if he or she correctly appreciates the applicable law, the court will properly recognize a wide discretion in the application of those principles to the particular facts. The same approach is taken to less exalted decision makers.... In the jargon of the judicial review bar, this is known as "segmentation."[209]

Unfortunately, neither Binnie J nor his colleagues say anything further in *Dunsmuir* (or in subsequent cases) about the dilemmas posed by segmentation, or how to resolve them. As a practical matter, however, the problem has diminished owing to the decline in instances where the court considers a correctness standard of review appropriate. It may reappear.

B. Standard of Review and Procedural Fairness

The *Dunsmuir* majority says nothing about the standard of review for questions of procedural fairness, but Binnie J plugs that hole by confirming that a standard of correctness will continue to apply, stating, "On such matters ... the courts have the final say. The need for such procedural safeguards is obvious. Nobody should have his or her rights, interests, or privileges adversely dealt with by an unjust process."[210] In a brief obiter in *Khela*, a unanimous court reiterated that "the standard for determining whether the decision maker complied with the duty of procedural fairness will continue to be 'correctness.'"[211] Another way of stating this principle is to deny that standard of review is apposite to questions of procedural fairness. The only metric is whether the proceedings were conducted fairly.[212]

Despite the Supreme Court of Canada's cursory rejection of deference on questions of procedural fairness, a lively discussion persists among academic commentators and some lower court judges about the desirability of extending the logic that underpins deference to matters of procedure.[213]

---

209 *Dunsmuir, supra* note 4 at para 142.
210 *Ibid* at para 129.
211 *Mission Institution v Khela*, 2014 SCC 24, [2014] 1 SCR 502 at para 79.
212 See e.g. *Gismondi v Ontario (Human Rights Commission)* (2003), 50 Admin LR (3d) 302, [2003] OJ No 419 (QL) (Div Ct).
213 See e.g. *Bergeron v Canada (Attorney General)*, 2015 FCA 160; Paul Daly, "Canada's Bipolar Administrative Law: Time for Fusion" (2014) 40:1 Queen's LJ 213; John Evans, "Fair's Fair: Judging Administrative Procedures" (2015) 28 CJALP 111.

1. Reasoning About Reasons

Reasons straddle procedure and substance. As Kate Glover explains in Chapter 5, The Principles and Practices of Procedural Fairness, *Baker* recognized that a common law duty to give reasons is a component of fairness. Reasons serve a number of purposes, not the least of which is to communicate that the decision-maker has genuinely heard and considered the evidence and arguments presented.

Reasons also disclose the findings of fact, interpretations of law, applications of law to fact, and exercises of discretion that are the substance of the decision. Reasons contain the evidence of the reasonableness (or correctness, as the case may be) of those exercises of statutory authority. As you will see in the next chapter, measuring the substantive reasonableness of a decision post-*Dunsmuir* includes assessing the quality of the reasoning process, as measured against criteria of justification, transparency, and intelligibility.

There is obvious potential for overlap between assessing the formal adequacy of reasons as a matter of procedural fairness and evaluating the substantive content of reasons as a matter of merits review. Framing the ground of review in terms of procedure rather than substance potentially invites a greater degree of judicial intervention via the correctness standard. The more a court demands of reasons in order to satisfy the procedural duty of fairness, the greater the scope for expansive and intrusive judicial review.

Finding a consistent "break point" between the form of reasons and the content of reasons proved challenging for lower courts, but the Supreme Court of Canada abruptly terminated the debate in its decision in *Newfoundland and Labrador Nurses' Union v Newfoundland and Labrador (Treasury Board)*.[214] Abella J, writing for the court, stated: "I do not see *Dunsmuir* as standing for the proposition that the 'adequacy' of reasons is a stand-alone basis for quashing a decision, or as advocating that a reviewing court undertake two discrete analyses—one for the reasons and a separate one for the result."[215] Later, she explicitly minimized the procedural aspect to a mere formal requirement:

> It strikes me as an unhelpful elaboration on *Baker* to suggest that alleged deficiencies or flaws in the reasons fall under the category of a breach of the duty of procedural fairness and that they are subject to a correctness review. As Professor Philip Bryden has warned, "courts must be careful not to confuse a finding that a tribunal's reasoning process is inadequately revealed with disagreement over the conclusions reached by the tribunal on the evidence before it" … . It is true that the breach of a duty of procedural fairness is an error in law. Where there are no reasons in circumstances where they are required, there is nothing to review. But where, as here, there *are* reasons, there is no such breach. Any challenge to the reasoning/result of the decision should therefore be made within the reasonableness analysis.[216]

A scenario not identified in the judgment arises where the reasons are deficient because they fail to address a particular issue. So, there are some reasons for the ultimate decision, but effectively no reasons at all with respect to the particular issue. The problem surfaced in *Alberta Information and Privacy Commissioner.* The statute required the commissioner (or delegated adjudicator) to complete an inquiry within 90 days of receiving a complaint, unless the commissioner (or delegate) notified the parties that the period was being extended

---

214   2011 SCC 62, [2011] 3 SCR 708 [*Newfoundland Nurses*].
215   *Ibid* at para 14.
216   *Ibid* at paras 21-22.

to an estimated date. The issue was whether the inquiry automatically terminated after 90 days if no notice was given, or whether the commissioner (or delegate) could notify the parties of the extension after expiry of the 90 days. As described above, the court ruled that the timelines issue was not jurisdictional, and so the standard of review was, in principle, reasonableness.[217] But applying reasonableness to the decision was hampered by the fact that the timelines issue was not raised before the adjudicator and was first raised on judicial review. The fact that the adjudicator finally notified the parties 22 months after the complaint was filed was taken as conveying an implicit decision about the timelines issue.

Quoting from David Dyzenhaus, the court reiterated that the concept of "'deference as respect' requires of the courts 'not submission but a respectful attention to the reasons offered or which could be offered in support of a decision.'"[218] The court observed that since no reasons were offered on the timelines issue, there was nothing to which respectful attention could be given:

> However, the direction that a reviewing court should give respectful attention to the reasons "which could be offered in support of a decision" is apposite when the decision concerns an issue that was not raised before the decision maker. In such circumstances, it may well be that the administrative decision maker did not provide reasons *because* the issue was not raised and it was not viewed as contentious. If there exists a reasonable basis upon which the decision-maker could have decided as it did, the court must not interfere.[219]

A court might embark on its own search for reasons that "could be offered" in circumstances where the original decision-maker did not address the issue because it was not raised, or there was no duty to give reasons, or where "only limited reasons" were required.[220] In contrast to *Newfoundland Nurses*, which some interpret as an invitation to reviewing courts to rummage around in the record for additional indicia of reasonableness (even where reasons are provided),[221] the court in *Alberta Information and Privacy Commissioners* was more circumspect:

> I should not be taken here as suggesting that courts should not give due regard to the reasons provided by a tribunal when such reasons are available. The direction that courts are to give respectful attention to the reasons "which could be offered in support of a decision" is not a "carte blanche to reformulate a tribunal's decision in a way that casts aside an unreasonable chain of analysis in favour of the court's own rationale for the result." Moreover, this direction should not "be taken as diluting the importance of giving proper reasons for an administrative decision." On the contrary, deference under the reasonableness standard is best given effect when administrative decision makers provide intelligible and transparent justification for their decisions, and when courts ground their review of the decision in the reasons provided.[222]

---

217 *Alberta Information and Privacy Commissioner, supra* note 141. Arguably, timelines are an issue of procedural fairness, but none of the judgments advert to this possibility.

218 *Alberta Information and Privacy Commissioner, supra* note 141 at para 52.

219 *Ibid* at para 53.

220 *Ibid* at para 54. Note that Dyzenhaus urged courts to consider reasons that "could be offered" prior to *Baker*, and was presumably addressing situations where the statute did not require reasons and no common law duty existed to furnish reasons.

221 *Newfoundland Nurses, supra* note 214 at para 15.

222 *Alberta Information and Privacy Commissioner, supra* note 141 at para 54 (citations omitted).

But what happens where no reasons are provided on a given issue in circumstances where the decision-maker could have, but did not, supply reasons? In some cases, like *Alberta Information and Privacy Commissioners*, the tribunal may have other precedents that address the issue. In other cases, it might be appropriate to remit a decision back to the original decision-maker to supply the missing reasons. But if these options are unavailable, what does it mean for a court to defer to a decision on an issue where reasons could have been provided but were not? In *Agraira*,[223] the court deferred to an "implied" interpretation of "national interest" under s 34(2) of the *Immigration and Refugee Protection Act* by the minister of public safety. In *McLean*, the court deferred to an "implied" interpretation by the BC Securities Commission of a statutory limitation period. And in *Tran*, discussed earlier, the Federal Court of Appeal deferred to an "implied" interpretation of IRPA criminality provisions by a CBSA officer with no legal expertise, who expressly stated in his reasons that he would not—and did not—consider relevant legal arguments about the interpretation of the statutory provision he was applying.

In effect, the court's approach to "implied" reasons seeks to retrofit the outcome reached by the decision-maker with judicially created reasons. It is difficult to reconcile this exercise with the idea of deference as respect. When courts step in and supply reasons that a decision-maker could have but did not provide, they are not demonstrating respect for the decision-maker: they are doing the job that the decision-maker was supposed to do. More worrying is the pervrse incentive that this practice creates for administrative decision-makers: instead of crafting thorough reasons that risk being set aside as "unreasonable," why not write the bare minimum to satisfy *Newfoundland Nurses'* low standard, and let a reviewing court fill in any gaps? This tactic would seem inimical to the "culture of justification" that administrative law aspires to promote in the administrative state. Were courts to demand more from decision-makers to satisfy their reason-giving requirement, it is possible that decision-makers would be motivated to provide more careful reasons in order to demonstrate the reasonableness of their outcomes.

C. Standard of Review and Internal Appeals

Some administrative regimes provide for an internal appeal from a first-level decision-maker to an internal appellate body. Should the same principles applicable to judicial review or statutory appeal apply to an internal administrative appeal?

The issue was litigated in *Huruglica v Canada (Citizenship and Immigration)*.[224] In 2013, the Refugee Appeal Division (RAD) was introduced to hear appeals from first-level refugee determinations by the Refugee Protection Division (RPD) of the Immigration and Refugee Board. The RAD was constituted and governed by provisions of the *Immigration and Refugee Protection Act*. The expectation was that most appeals would be conducted in writing, though oral hearings were possible. The statutory provisions, *inter alia*, authorized the RAD to confirm the RPD decision, set it aside and "substitute a determination that, in its opinion, should have been made," or remit to the RPD with directions if it is of the opinion that "the decision of the Refugee Protection Division is wrong in law, in fact, or in mixed law and fact."[225]

---

223 *Canada (Public Safety and Emergency Preparedness) v Agraira*, 2011 FCA 103 [*Agraira*]
224 2016 FCA 93, [2016] 4 FCR 157, aff'g, 2014 FC 799, [2014] 4 FCR 811.
225 See *Immigration and Refugee Protection Act*, ss 110-111, quoted in *Huruglica* (FCA), *supra* note 224 at para 25.

One of the first questions addressed by the RAD was the scope of its mandate. As stated by the Federal Court of Appeal, the "controversy … can be more accurately described as a disagreement over whether to import either the standard from a judicial review of an administrative action (*Dunsmuir*) or an appellate court's review of a lower court decision (*Housen*)[226] into the RAD's review of an RPD decision."[227] The Federal Court of Appeal concluded that it was a mistake to analogize an internal appeal to either a judicial review or an appeal from lower to higher court:

> The principles which guided and shaped the role of courts on judicial review of decisions made by administrative decision-makers (as set out in *Dunsmuir* at paras. 27-33) have no application here. Indeed, the role and organization of various levels of administrative decision-makers do not put into play the tension between the legislative intent to confer jurisdiction on administrative decision-makers and the constitutional imperative of preserving the rule of law. [I]t would also be inappropriate to import the considerations set out in *Housen*, since the adoption of the high level of deference afforded by appellate courts of law to lower courts of law on questions of fact and mixed fact and law was mainly guided by judicial policy.[228]

The important insight for present purposes is that the nature of the relationship between two administrative bodies does not generate the same institutional concerns that animate curial deference by courts toward administrative decision-makers. Rather than import common law techniques for resolving the question, the Federal Court of Appeal instructed the RAD to look to its statute for the answer: "the textual, contextual and purposive approach mandated by modern statutory interpretation principles provides us with all the necessary tools to determine the legislative intent in respect of the relevant provisions of the *IRPA* and the role of the RAD."[229] In other words, internal appeal bodies should just do what their statute tells them to do. This may or may not resemble what courts do on judicial review or on appeal from a lower court.

D. Are Ministers Different?

Tacitly or explicitly, courts are often inclined to defer to Cabinet ministers across the span of administrative law, and so the routine application of a standard of review of reasonableness seems unproblematic. The reasons for this posture are various: ministers sit at the apex of the executive (the Cabinet), and may attract deference because of their "prominence in the administrative food chain."[230] A minister, who is almost always a politician, is more able to "respond to the political, economic and social concerns of the moment"[231] that are relevant to making broad policy decisions under law. Ministers, because of their leadership of a government department, may be deemed expert in all aspects of their portfolio by virtue of the position or because of their access to advisers with actual expertise. Finally, because virtually all ministers are elected officials, their actions carry a democratic

---

226   *Housen v Nikolaisen*, 2002 SCC 33.
227   *Huruglica* (FCA), *supra* note 224 at para 44.
228   *Ibid* at paras 47-48.
229   *Ibid* at para 46.
230   *Dunsmuir, supra* note 4 at para 145, Binnie J.
231   *Canada (Attorney General) v Inuit Tapirisat of Canada*, [1980] 2 SCR 735 at 755; *R v Advance Cutting & Coring Ltd*, 2001 SCC 70, [2001] 3 SCR 209 at para 239.

imprimatur that courts both lack and respect. *Suresh v Canada (Minister of Citizenship and Immigration)*[232] challenged, *inter alia*, ministerial discretion to deport non-citizen terror suspects to countries where they could face torture. A unanimous court stated that "[i]f the people are to accept the consequences of such decisions, they must be made by persons whom the people have elected and whom they can remove."[233]

The foregoing may seem relevant only to how the court actually applies the deferential reasonableness to ministerial actions, not to the appropriateness of deference as such. But in at least two circumstances, one might question whether the presumption of deference should apply to ministers.

The first case arises where ministers interpret statutes that they are responsible for implementing. This was the scenario in *Agraira*, where the court not only applied a deferential standard of review, but applied it to "implied" non-existent reasons for an interpretation of "national interest." In an earlier Federal Court of Appeal judgment that *Agraira* did not consider, *Minister of Fisheries and Oceans v David Suzuki Foundation*,[234] the Federal Court of Appeal ruled that ministers' interpretations of their own statutes did not attract deference in a non-adjudicatory context.[235]

The Federal Court of Appeal reached back for support past *Pushpanathan*, beyond *CUPE*, all the way to the Glorious Revolution of 1688, the *Bill of Rights* of 1689, and the *Act of Settlement* of 1701. The Court of Appeal invoked these as the historic touchstones for the principles of parliamentary sovereignty, the separation of powers, and the rule of law: "the Crown and its officials would thereafter be bound by Parliament's laws as interpreted by the independent common law courts."[236] After tracking the evolution of substantive review forward to *Dunsmuir*, the Court of Appeal emphasized that *Dunsmuir's* presumption of deference was directed at independent adjudicative bodies, whose core and explicitly delegated tasks include statutory interpretation, which in turn approximates the judicial function. The Court of Appeal vigorously resisted the expansion of *Dunsmuir's* presumption to all administrative actors who administer a federal statute:

> The Minister thus seeks to establish a new constitutional paradigm under which the Executive's interpretation of Parliament's laws would prevail insofar as such interpretation is not unreasonable. This harks back to the time before the *Bill of Rights* of 1689 where the Crown reserved the right to interpret and apply Parliament's laws to suit its own policy objectives. It would take a very explicit grant of authority from Parliament in order for this court to reach such a far-reaching conclusion.
>
> The issues in this appeal concern the interpretation of a statute by a minister who is not acting as an adjudicator and who thus has no implicit power to decide questions of law. Of course, the Minister must take a view on what the statute means in order to act. But this is not

---

232 2002 SCC 1, [2002] 1 SCR 3.

233 *Dunsmuir, supra* note 4 at para 145; see also *Retired Judges, supra* note 85 at para 18, Bastarache J, dissenting: "Furthermore, empowering the Minister, as opposed to an apolitical figure such as the Chief Justice of the province [to appoint arbitrators], suggests a legislative intent that political accountability also play a role in policing appointments and the integrity of hospitals interest arbitration."

234 2012 FCA 40, 427 NR 110 [*David Suzuki*].

235 The Federal Court of Appeal in *Agraira* also ruled that the interpretation of "national interest" was subject to a standard of review of correctness.

236 *David Suzuki, supra* note 234 at para 73.

the same as having a power delegated by Parliament to decide questions of law. The presumption of deference resulting from *Dunsmuir* … does not extend to these circumstances.[237]

The Supreme Court of Canada has not taken up the Federal Court of Appeal's challenge. A similar issue arises with respect to ministerial determinations of whether their own actions violate the Charter. In *Lake v Canada (Minister of Justice)*,[238] the court deferred to the Minister of Justice's determination that surrender of a fugitive for extradition would not violate the fugitive's ss 6 and 7 rights under the Charter. The court regarded the discretionary power to order extradition as "largely a political decision, not a legal one" and "a fact-driven inquiry."[239] Deferring to a minister's assessment of the constitutionality of his or her own conduct risks eroding individual rights protection, bearing in mind that the democratic legitimacy that ministers enjoy entails responsiveness to majoritarian will. The judgment in *Lake* preceded *Doré*, but seems consistent with it. Many, if not most, individualized exercises of discretion can easily be characterized as "fact-driven." The claim that a decision is political rather than legal is conclusory and unhelpful, insofar as many "political" decisions have a legal dimension. Moreover, it is precisely because the violation of individual rights may be politically expedient that the Charter places legal limits on the exercise of governmental power.[240]

E. Aboriginal Law and Standard of Review

In Chapter 3, Realizing Aboriginal Administrative Law, Janna Promislow and Naiomi Metallic survey the intersections between Aboriginal and administrative law. Emerging case law on the Specific Claims Tribunal (SCT) and the duty to consult provide occasions for attending to the role of standard of review. As with all such intersections between public law and the claims of Indigenous Peoples, an underlying question concerns whether the conventional doctrinal tools used to ensure accountability for the exercise of executive power over the individual are really transposable to the relationship between Canada and Indigenous Peoples.

The SCT was established by the federal government in 2008 to deal with historic Indigenous claims about the Crown's duties and failures in relation to setting aside of reserve lands, and the management of assets and moneys from reserve lands. Prior to the establishment of the SCT, claims were decided by the minister without any mechanism for adjudication. The SCT is the key venue for adjudicating breaches of fiduciary duty in Crown–Indigenous relations, especially in relation to historical claims. The members of the SCT are drawn from a roster of Superior Court judges. In the first case to reach the Federal Court of Appeal, *Kitselas First Nation v The Queen*,[241] the court ruled that the standard of review applicable to SCT interpretation of fiduciary law was correctness. The Court of Appeal reasoned that superior courts have concurrent jurisdiction over fiduciary law, and the members of the SCT are, in fact, superior judges. Relying on the Supreme Court of Canada judgment in *Rogers*,[242] the Court of Appeal reasoned that it would not make sense to defer to the SCT's

---

237 *Ibid* at paras 98-99. The Court of Appeal then proceeds to apply *Pushpanathan*'s four factors, and concludes that correctness is the appropriate standard of review: paras 101-105.

238 2008 SCC 23, [2008] 1 SCR 761 [*Lake*].

239 *Ibid* at paras 37-38.

240 See generally, "Charter Right or Charter Lite," *supra* note 208.

241 2014 FCA 150, 460 NR 185.

242 *Ibid* at para 33.

interpretation of fiduciary law when an appellate court would apply a correctness standard to the same issue arising from a trial court. Even though this was the first case to come before a reviewing court, the Court of Appeal also invoked the importance of consistency, stating, "Inconsistency on such fundamental matters would be unseemly and give rise to significant practical consequences."[243]

Although ordinary courts do address fiduciary law in Crown-Indigenous relations, the SCT is unique in its legislative mandate and its focus on historic claims about the setting aside of reserve lands. In litigation before ordinary courts, limitation periods sharply curtail the ability to bring historic claims forward, and often bar them. The SCT operates within a framework where addressing historic claims is neither marginal nor exceptional, but is central to its specific mandate. Interestingly, in the first appeal from the SCT to reach the Supreme Court of Canada, *Canada v Williams Lake Indian Band*,[244] all parties (including the government) agreed that the appropriate standard of review was reasonableness, notwithstanding the Federal Court of Appeal's endorsement of correctness on questions of law. The parties disagreed, of course, on the reasonableness of the SCT's resolution of the contested questions of law, mixed law and fact, and fact.

Chapter 3 sets out the contours of the duty to consult. In the pre-*Dunsmuir* case of *Haida Nation v British Columbia (Minister of Forests)*,[245] the Supreme Court of Canada applied extant principles that allocated the standard of review according to the type of question at stake: on factual assessments, including those relevant to the existence or extent of the duty to consult, courts should defer; to the extent that the legal elements of the duty to consult can be extricated from the factual questions, the standard would be correctness, but, if not, the standard would be reasonableness; on the actual implementation of consultation, the standard would be reasonableness; "the government is required to make reasonable efforts to inform and consult. This suffices to discharge the duty [to consult]."[246] Note that the adequacy of consultation is measured according to reasonableness, whereas the court's stance on procedural fairness is correctness. What explanation lies behind the apparent disparity in scrutiny of the duty of fairness owed by a state actor to a legal subject and the duty of the state to consult Indigenous People?

Another question concerns the relationship between fulfillment of the duty to consult and the ultimate decision that is the subject of consultation. In *Gitxaala Nation v Canada*,[247] the Federal Court of Appeal determined that the standard of review applicable to a Cabinet order approving the Northern Gateway pipeline project was reasonableness.[248] That order was the culmination of a very lengthy and complex process that engaged, *inter alia*, a duty to consult with Indigenous Peoples. The Court of Appeal ruled that reasonableness was also the appropriate standard for reviewing the adequacy of consultation. But the sequence of

---

243 *Ibid* at para 34.
244 2016 FCA 63, leave to appeal to the SCC granted, 2016 CanLII 68008.
245 2004 SCC 73, [2004] 3 SCR 511. The standard of review in respect of the duty to consult has not been revised by the Supreme Court of Canada in light of *Dunsmuir*. See *Beckman v Little Salmon/Carmacks First Nation*, 2010 SCC 53, [2010] 3 SCR 103 at para 48.
246 *Ibid* at para 62.
247 2016 FCA 187.
248 *Ibid* at para 145: "The standard of review for decisions such as this—discretionary decisions founded upon the widest considerations of policy and public interest—is reasonableness."

the Court of Appeal's judgment was unusual: it began with the reasonableness of Cabinet's order. The Court of Appeal ruled that the Cabinet order approving the pipeline was reasonable. Then the Court of Appeal proceeded to consider the duty to consult on a deferential standard of reasonableness, and concluded that Cabinet had not fulfilled its duty to consult Indigenous People. In administrative law jurisprudence, courts typically refrain from commenting on the substantive merits of an outcome produced by a process that fails to meet the requirements of procedural fairness. A court usually begins with the procedural grounds of review and, if the process was defective, the court orders a remedy, which typically involves setting aside the decision and remitting it back to the original decision-maker. The Federal Court of Appeal in *Gitxaala* proceeded by finding an outcome reasonable even though the process leading to it was not.

VIII. REVIEW OF STANDARD OF REVIEW: PAST AS PROLOGUE

The tensions lying at the heart of jurisprudence about the standard of review have not changed and will not go away. In its recent jurisprudence, the majority of the Supreme Court of Canada has staked out a position that, in principle, inclines toward deference. It has told and retold the story about why and when courts ought to defer to the decisions of administrative decision-makers. Each major iteration reveals shifts in emphasis, additional nuances, glosses on past recitations, and attempts to reconcile, distinguish, or conceal apparent anomalies. On rare occasions, we get a new plot twist: from two standards of review to three, then back to two (but not the same two); from the formalism of "preliminary or collateral question" to multifactor balancing to a defeasible rule (or maybe not). Lower court resistance to current trends and dissenting voices on the court may yet provoke another change of course.

The job of discerning the appropriate standard of review became simpler after *Dunsmuir*, and for this students and practitioners of administrative law should feel relieved. But they should also attend to the prediction of Binnie J in *Dunsmuir*. By streamlining the standard of review analysis and winnowing deference down to a single standard of reasonableness, the court has not resolved the challenge of operationalizing deference in all its multifarious applications. Rather, it has shifted the task downstream to the next stage of judicial review—namely, the application of correctness or (more commonly) reasonableness review to actual decisions. And once in the land of reasonableness, all depends on "context." But since the court has declined thus far to articulate what counts as context, students, lawyers, scholars, and lower court judges must search for clues where they can find them. Pre-*Dunsmuir* jurisprudence is one place to look. And so, the conclusion of this chapter is a prologue to the next, where the real action unfolds.

SUGGESTED ADDITIONAL READINGS

BOOKS AND ARTICLES

CANADIAN

Daly, P, "Struggling Towards Coherence in Canadian Administrative Law? Recent Cases on Standard of Review and Reasonableness" (10 August 2016). McGill LJ, online: <https://ssrn.com/abstract=2821099>.

Daly, P, "The Signal and the Noise in Administrative Law" (22 November 2016). Forthcoming, University of New Brunswick Law Journal; online: <https://ssrn.com/abstract=2874310>.

Dyzenhaus, D, "The Politics of Deference: Judicial Review and Democracy" in M Taggart, ed, *The Province of Administrative Law* (Oxford: Hart Publishing, 1997).

Green, A, "Can There Be Too Much Context in Administrative Law? Setting the Standard of Review in Canadian Administrative Law" (2014) 47 UBC L Rev 443.

Hutchinson, A, "Why I Don't Teach Administrative Law (And Perhaps Why I Should?)" (27 June 2016). Osgoode Legal Studies Research Paper No 54/2016, online: <https://ssrn.com/abstract=2801258>.

Lewans, M, "Deference and Reasonableness Since Dunsuir" (2012) 38 Queens LJ 59.

Mullan, D, "Dunsmuir v New Brunswick, Standard of Review and Procedural Fairness: Let's Try Again!" (2008) 21 Can J Admin L & Prac 117.

Mullan, D, "Unresolved Issues on Standard of Review in Canadian Judicial Review of Administrative Action—the Top Fifteen!" (2013) 42 Adv Q 1.

Sossin, L, & C Flood, "The Contextual Turn: Iacobucci's Legacy and the Standard of Review in Administrative Law" (2007) 57 UTLJ 581.

Stratas, D, "The Canadian Law of Judicial Review: A Plea for Doctrinal Coherence and Consistency" (17 February 2016), online: <https://ssrn.com/abstract=2733751>.

CASES

Alberta (Information and Privacy Commissioner) v Alberta Teachers' Association, 2011 SCC 61, [2011] 3 SCR 654.

Alberta (Information and Privacy Commissioner) v University of Calgary, 2016 SCC 53, [2016] 2 SCR 555.

Baker v Canada (Minister of Citizenship and Immigration), [1999] 2 SCR 817, 174 DLR (4th) 193.

Canada v Williams Lake Indian Band, 2016 FCA 63, leave to appeal to the SCC granted, 2016 CanLII 68008.

Canada (Canadian Human Rights Commission) v Canada (Attorney General), 2011 SCC 53, [2011] 3 SCR 471.

Canada (Citizenship and Immigration) v Khosa, 2009 SCC 12, [2009] 1 SCR 339.

Canada (Director of Investigation and Research) v Southam Inc, [1997] 1 SCR 748, 144 DLR (4th) 1.

Canada (Public Safety and Emergency Preparedness) v Tran, 2015 FCA 237, 392 DLR (4th) 351.

CUPE v NB Liquor Corporation, [1979] 2 SCR 227, 25 NBR (2d) 237.

Doré v Barreau du Québec, 2012 SCC 12, [2012] 1 SCR 395.

Dunsmuir v New Brunswick, 2008 SCC 9, [2008] 1 SCR 190.

Edmonton (City) v Edmonton East (Capilano) Shopping Centres Ltd, 2016 SCC 47, [2016] 2 SCR 293.

Huruglica v Canada (Citizenship and Immigration), 2014 FC 799, 3 [2014] 4 FCR 811, aff'd 2016 FCA 93.

Minister of Fisheries and Oceans v David Suzuki Foundation, 2012 FCA 40, 427 NR 110.

Newfoundland and Labrador Nurses' Union v Newfoundland and Labrador (Treasury Board), 2011 SCC 62, [2011] 3 SCR 708.

Pushpanathan v Canada (Minister of Citizenship and Immigration), [1998] 1 SCR 982, 160 DLR (4th) 193.

Wilson v Atomic Energy of Canada Ltd, 2016 SCC 29, [2016] 1 SCR 770.

CHAPTER TWELVE

Making Sense of Reasonableness

Sheila Wildeman*

Schulich School of Law, Dalhousie University

---

* Thanks to Lorne Sossin and Audrey Macklin for assistance with this chapter. The chapter includes revised passages from my chapter in the 2nd edition of this text, Pas de Deux: Deference and Non-Deference in Action.

I. INTRODUCTION

When the Supreme Court of Canada released its judgment in *Dunsmuir v New Brunswick*[1] in 2008, there was general (if cautious) agreement that this development was likely to simplify substantive review. That is, *Dunsmuir*'s downsizing of the standards from three to two (cutting out patent unreasonableness and leaving only reasonableness and correctness), together with its streamlining of the work of selecting the standard (by way of a set of categorical presumptions), was regarded, not least by the judges issuing the decision, as a win for efficiency and judicial economy.[2] What the implications of *Dunsmuir* would be for judicial deference was another question. Some raised the obvious worry that loss of the most deferential standard would mean more (unjustified) judicial intervention.[3] But it was difficult to argue with the reasons for cutting patent unreasonableness loose. The *Dunsmuir* majority had affirmed a strong line of criticism on the conceptual incoherence and pragmatic unworkability of the distinction between the two deferential standards.[4] This, plus the majority's rule-of-law-based rejection of the idea that *some* unreasonableness was good enough for administrative law (so long as it was not "patent") pulled the common law rug out from patent unreasonableness as a respectable legal standard.

Yet, in this, the *Dunsmuir* majority hinted at a further prospect, beyond the attractive prospect of simplifying the standard of review analysis: that of freeing up judicial energies to engage more directly and seriously with the meaning of reasonableness, and deference, and how these should interact in administrative law.[5] The newly consolidated reasonableness standard called out for this kind of attention, uniting as it did the imperative of judicial deference to administrative decisions and the expectation that administrative decisions be justified. Now that deference no longer required judges to conduct review according to fictional distinctions about the permissible "depth of probing" or "magnitude of error"— asking "how much deference?" or "how much error?" in an effort to distinguish patent unreasonableness from reasonableness review[6]—one anticipated that further guidance would be forthcoming on how the imperatives of deference and justification should work together. But would the courts follow through and invest more intellectual resources into clarifying the purposes, structure, and implications of reasonableness review, and how exactly it differs from correctness review? That was, and is, no idle question; rather, it goes to a project central to repairing the legitimacy crisis (the growing sense that the standards of review are a waste of time) that provoked *Dunsmuir*'s refashioned standards in the first place.

---

1   2008 SCC 9, [2008] 1 SCR 190 [*Dunsmuir*].

2   See Chapter 11 by Audrey Macklin.

3   See David Mullan, "Dunsmuir v New Brunswick, Standard of Review and Procedural Fairness for Public Servants: Let's Try Again!" (2008) 21 Can J Admin L & Prac 117 at 133, 137-40 ["Let's Try Again!"]; Ron Goltz, "'Patent Unreasonableness Is Dead. And We Have Killed It.' A Critique of the Supreme Court of Canada's Decision in *Dunsmuir*" (2008) 46 Alta LR 253 at paras 1, 31. Both authors suggest that the worry is eased because the newly unified reasonableness standard is likely to incorporate a spectrum of deference, shading into something like patent unreasonableness review at one extreme.

4   See *Toronto (City) v CUPE, Local 79*, 2003 SCC 63, [2003] 3 SCR 77 at paras 60-135, LeBel J and *Dunsmuir*, *supra* note 1 at paras 40-42.

5   This shift in emphasis is brought out most clearly in the concurring opinion of Binnie J in *Dunsmuir*, *supra* note 1 at para 145. See also, *Alberta (Information and Privacy Commissioner) v Alberta Teachers' Association*, 2011 SCC 61, [2001] 3 SCR 654 at para 38, Rothstein J for the majority [*ATA*].

6   *Dunsmuir*, *supra* note 1 at paras 40-42.

Nearly ten years on from *Dunsmuir*, there is general agreement that the work of selecting the standard to be applied in judicial review of substantive administrative decisions has been nicely economized.[7] Moreover, it is quite clear that *Dunsmuir*'s categorical approach to selecting the standard has shifted substantive review away from correctness as the default on questions of law (including questions involving the limits of discretion) toward reasonableness as the presumptive standard on all categories of question—with rare exceptions.[8] That is, *Dunsmuir*'s "standard of review analysis" and the principles it identifies as scaffolding have precipitated a fundamental shift toward selecting a deferential standard of review in matters that, for much of the history of judicial review, were presumed to rest within the exclusive constitutional authority of the courts.

One may be forgiven, then, for thinking that the twisting paths of the standards of review in Canadian administrative law have finally reached their proper terminus: the "triumph of reasonableness,"[9] and with this, a new understanding of administrative decision-makers as institutionally and constitutionally equipped (and expected) to justify their decisions in law. But as Binnie J predicted in his concurring judgment in *Dunsmuir*,[10] neither the majority's simplification of the standard of review analysis nor the rise of reasonableness as default standard means that we are done fighting about substantive review—in particular, as applied to questions of law. Setting aside the emerging schisms among members of the Supreme Court of Canada about whether or how *Dunsmuir*'s presumptions may be rebutted,[11] much of the instability and contestation once expressed at the stage of selecting the standard has, as Audrey Macklin noted in Chapter 11, moved downstream to the stage of application—more specifically, to application of the reasonableness standard.

The question that drives this chapter's inquiry into reasonableness review—now the presumptive standard on questions of law (or nearly all such questions),[12] fact, mixed law and fact, and discretion—is whether or how deference to administrative decision may be reconciled with the expectation that those decisions be justified. This raises a host of sub-questions. For instance, how important is the quality of reasons, or reasoning, to the assessment of reasonableness? More specifically, if reasons for decision may sometimes be implicit rather than express (as the Supreme Court of Canada has indicated),[13] how far can this principle be extended before it undermines the duty of public authorities to justify their decisions? Moreover, is inconsistency among administrative decisions or interpretations an unavoidable byproduct of deference (given the lack of *stare decisis* among administrative

---

7   See Lauren J Wihak, "Wither the Correctness Standard of Review? Dunsmuir, Six Years Later" (2014) 173 Can J Admin L & Prac at 182; Robert Danay, "Quantifying Dunsmuir: An Empirical Analysis of the Supreme Court of Canada's Jurisprudence on Standard of Review" (2016) 66 UTLJ 555 ["Quantifying Dunsmuir"].

8   *Ibid*.

9   The Hon John M Evans, "Triumph of Reasonableness: But How Much Does It Really Matter?" (2014) 27:1 Can J Admin L & Prac 101 ["Triumph of Reasonableness"]; Paul Daly, "The Scope and Meaning of Reasonableness Review" (2015) 52 Alta L Rev 799 at 800 ["Scope and Meaning of Reasonableness Review"].

10 *Dunsmuir, supra* note 1 at para 139, Binnie J.

11 See Chapter 11 by Audrey Macklin.

12 See the discussion of the narrowing of the *Dunsmuir* categories said to attract correctness review in Chapter 11.

13 See the discussion of implicit reasons in Chapter 11 and Section III.B of this chapter.

decision-makers)?[14] Is such inconsistency as may be promoted by deference consistent with a principled approach to reasonableness—or the rule of law?

In recent years, leading commentators have decried the thinness of Supreme Court guidance on these and other matters.[15] The economizing ethos of *Dunsmuir*, commentators have argued, has failed to produce a coherent and workable set of guiding principles on how to conduct substantive review. This is particularly true of reasonableness review, where the Supreme Court's decisions seem to shuttle unpredictably between postures of judicial supremacy ("disguised correctness review")[16] and judicial abdication.[17] All this does little to alleviate the suspicions of administrative lawyers that reasonableness, like correctness, means nothing more or less than agreement with the opinion of the reviewing court.

This chapter takes a back-to-basics approach and asks: how does one begin to make sense of reasonableness in administrative law? Relatedly, how does one engage in effective administration and advocacy under the cloud of confusion (or is it a context-saturated rainbow[18]) that has settled around the application of this now-dominant standard? Given the high stakes of administrative decisions that come before the courts on review—whether one is dealing with the decision of a front-line immigration officer to refuse humanitarian and compassionate grounds relief to one who wishes to avoid deportation and apply for permanent residency from within Canada (as in *Baker*[19] and *Kanthasamy*[20]) or the decision of the governor in council to approve a pipeline argued to jeopardize the environment as well as the rights and interests of Indigenous communities (*Gitxaala Nation v Canada*)[21]—the

---

14   See Section III.C.1 of this chapter. And see *Altus Group Limited v Calgary (City)*, 2015 ABCA 86 at paras 16-18 [*Altus Group*].

15   See e.g. David Mullan, "Unresolved Issues on Standard of Review in Canadian Judicial Review of Administrative Action—The Top Fifteen!" (2013), 42 Adv Q 1 ["The Top Fifteen!"]; David Mullan, "2015 Developments in Administrative Law Relevant to Energy Law and Regulation" (2016) 4:1 Energy Regulation Quarterly ["2015 Developments"]; The Hon David W Stratas, "The Canadian Law of Judicial Review: A Plea for Doctrinal Coherence and Consistency" (2016) 42:1 Queen's LJ 27 ["A Plea for Doctrinal Coherence"]; Paul Daly, "Struggling Towards Coherence in Canadian Administrative Law? Recent Cases on Standard of Review and Reasonableness" (2016) 62:2 McGill LJ 527 ["Struggling Towards Coherence"]; "Scope and Meaning of Reasonableness Review," *supra* note 9; John M Evans, "Triumph of Reasonableness," *supra* note 9; Matthew Lewans, "Deference and Reasonableness Since Dunsmuir" (2012) 38 Queen's LJ 59 ["Deference and Reasonableness"].

16   See Mullan, "The Top Fifteen!," *supra* note 15 at 76-81, and *Wilson v Atomic Energy of Canada Ltd*, 2016 SCC 29, [2016] 1 SCR 770 at para 27, n8 [*Wilson*].

17   See the sources cited *supra* note 15.

18   The metaphor of reasonableness as rainbow (a context-sensitive spectrum, or continuum, of expectations or levels of intensity on review) was famously put into play in common law judicial review theory by Michael Taggart in "Proportionality, Deference, Wednesbury" (2008) NZL Rev 423 at 451 ff ("We must get beyond simply talking about context and actually contextualize in a way that can generate generalizable conclusions ... [W]e need a map of the rainbow of review that is reliable and helpful, and we need willing cartographers" (at 454).). See also, e.g., Dean Knight, "Mapping the Rainbow of Review: Recognizing Variable Intensity" (2010) NZL Rev 393.

19   *Baker v Canada (Minister of Citizenship and Immigration)*, [1999] 2 SCR 817 [*Baker*].

20   *Kanthasamy v Canada (Citizenship and Immigration)*, 2015 SCC 61, [2015] 3 SCR 909 [*Kanthasamy*].

21   *Gitxaala Nation v Canada*, 2016 FCA 187, [2016] 4 FCR 418 [*Gitxaala*].

question of what courts should expect under the heading of "reasonableness" is likely to provoke intense disagreement. Is the legal doctrine (or for that matter the model of constitutional democracy) underlying the standard robust enough to support all the weight the standard must bear?

Section II addresses in brief three key elements that continue to shape and inform the law on reasonableness review: (1) shifting and competing views on the proper roles and relationships of administrative decision-makers and courts; (2) shifting and competing approaches to statutory interpretation; and (3) shifting and competing rationales (related to both (1) and (2) on the nature and function of the correctness standard of review. The section concludes with Abella J's recent endorsement of the proposal that the correctness standard be retired.[22] The question this raises is whether reasonableness review is or could be adequate to the institutional and constitutional imperatives that correctness review has been understood to serve.

Section III turns more squarely to *Dunsmuir* reasonableness. Section A sets out the leading judicial statements on the standard. Section B offers a critical assessment of how the standard has been applied, with attention to judgments argued to represent "disguised correctness review" on the one hand and abdication of the proper supervisory role of the courts (particularly with regard to implied decisions and reasoning) on the other. Section C takes up developments in the case law and commentary through which it has been suggested that the principled structure of reasonableness review may be enhanced, by paying more attention to context—while at the same time heightening vigilance concerning certain common indicia or markers of *un*reasonableness.

A central point of the final section, and indeed the chapter as a whole, is that understanding reasonableness review is not a matter of memorizing ready-made tests or categories of error, or, for that matter, of unreasonableness. Rather, it requires that one develop a critical appreciation of—even a theory about—the proper function of administrative decision-making in the constitutional order. In accordance with the central commitment of this text to understanding administrative law in context, one should be prepared to critically evaluate administrative decisions, as well as judgments on review, not only on the basis of their consistency with existing legal doctrine, but also and more fundamentally on the basis of their theoretical and ideological underpinnings and material effects. Yet such critiques are likely to be most effective, and coherent, when grounded in a positive account of how the work of administrative decision-makers and judges *should* be distributed and coordinated in a constitutional democracy, that is, a theory of how administrative law may best advance the dual values of democracy and the rule of law.

The chapter approaches reasonableness review in light of such a theory, or thesis—one that centres on the proposition (put in play by David Dyzenhaus 20 years ago) that deference, and so review for reasonableness, requires judicial "respect for," but not "submission"

---

22 *Wilson, supra* note 16.

to, the decisions and reasons of administrative decision-makers.[23] To conceive of deference "as respect" is to displace the traditional approach to selection and application of the standards of review, as a kind of rarified turf war between courts and administrative decision-makers—an approach focused on identifying zones of exclusive jurisdiction. Instead, the approach positions judicial review as an opportunity for inter-institutional dialogue (or conversation, requiring the participation of all three branches along with affected legal subjects) on the justified uses of public power.[24] In other words, deference as respect conveys the expectation, internal to law or to the rule of law and arguably also internal to democracy, that administrative decision-makers (along with courts and legislatures) can and must actively contribute to forging a "culture of justification."[25]

The deep challenge of reasonableness review is to build in sensitivity or responsiveness to the unique democratic and rule-of-law imperatives arising across the array of decision-making contexts that make up the contemporary administrative state. In particular, the challenge is to ensure that judges respect the purposive insights of administrative decision-makers legally mandated to advance important public ends while also ensuring that those decision-makers show respect for law, including the rights and significant interests of those who find themselves at the "sharp end" of law's administration. Or this is broadly the challenge of substantive review, which at present includes two standards: correctness and reasonableness. Whether reasonableness review is able to internally coordinate these imperatives is a central question of this chapter.

---

23   D Dyzenhaus, "The Politics of Deference: Judicial Review and Democracy" in M Taggart, ed, *The Province of Administrative Law* (Oxford: Hart Publishing, 1997) 279 at 286 ["The Politics of Deference"]. As noted later in this chapter, the phraseology from Dyzenhaus quoted in numerous Supreme Court decisions, beginning with *Baker*, is: "Deference as respect requires not submission but a respectful attention to the reasons offered or which could be offered in support of a decision." (*Baker*, *supra* note 19 at para 65.

24   Geneviève Cartier builds on Dyzenhaus's ideas to arrive at a conception of administrative discretion not as a site of unconstrained or unidirectional power but rather as a site of relationship and reasoned dialogue: Geneviève Cartier, "Administrative Discretion as Dialogue: A Response to John Willis (or; From Theology to Secularization)" (2005) 55:3 UTLJ 629. Evan Fox-Decent, *Sovereignty's Promise: The State as Fiduciary* (Oxford: Oxford University Press, 2012) theorizes the state–subject relationship in a manner that foregrounds the critical relational and normative function of the administrative state.

25   For development of the idea of a culture of justification, see David Dyzenhaus, "Law as Justification: Etienne Mureinik's Conception of Legal Culture" (1998) 14 SAJHR 11; D Dyzenhaus & E Fox-Decent, "Rethinking the Process/Substance Distinction: Baker v Canada" (2001) 51 UTLJ 193 ["Process/Substance"]; D Dyzenhaus, "Constituting the Rule of Law: Fundamental Values in Administrative Law" (2002) 27 Queen's LJ 445 ["Constituting the Rule of Law"]. See also The Hon Justice B McLachlin, "The Roles of Administrative Tribunals and Courts in Maintaining the Rule of Law" (1999) 12 Can J Admin L & Prac 171 at 174-75):

     [S]ocieties governed by the Rule of Law are marked by a certain ethos of justification. ... Where a society is marked by a culture of justification, an exercise of public power is only appropriate where it can be justified to citizens in terms of rationality and fairness. ... A culture of justification shifts the analysis from the institutions themselves to, more subtly, what those institutions are capable of doing for the rational advancement of civil society. The Rule of Law, in short, can speak in several voices so long as the resulting chorus echoes its underlying values of rationality and fairness.

II. GETTING TO REASONABLENESS

A. Old Habits Die Hard: Jurisdictional Zombies, Discretionary Doughnuts, and the Legacy of AV Dicey

While the standards of review in administrative law bear some similarities to those that apply on appellate review,[26] they have arisen out of a distinct institutional and constitutional context, or set of contexts, which present unique reasons for courts to adopt the principle of restraint on review known as deference. In short, whether judicial oversight of administrative decision-making is formally grounded in the inherent supervisory powers of the s 96 courts or in a statutory right of appeal, considerations of democratic legitimacy as well as institutional capacity are brought to bear to inform analysis of the standard of review. Most importantly, unlike the direction taken in the English law on judicial review,[27] and in Canadian doctrine on appellate review of the decisions of lower courts, this is the case in Canadian administrative law even where the challenge on review is to a question of law. That is, the Canadian law of substantive review requires that no matter what category of question is in issue, there must first be an inquiry (however truncated) into the rationales for and/or against deference: an analysis aimed at identifying the standard of review.

But in order to begin to understand the meaning and function of deference in administrative law, we must take a moment to reflect on the origins and evolution of the Canadian law on substantive review.

1. Successive Eras of Substantive Review: Pre-CUPE to Dunsmuir

The law on judicial review and, in particular, review of substantive administrative decisions, was troubled from the start by the question of whether or in what sense administrative decision-makers were a legitimate part of the constitutional order. As Colleen M Flood explains in Chapter 1, the rise of the administrative state in the 19th and 20th centuries in Canada took the form of Parliament's conferring an increasing range of statutory powers upon decision-makers who were neither democratically elected nor steeped in

---

26 The leading authority on appellate review is *Housen v Nikolaisen*, 2002 SCC 33, [2002] 2 SCR 235. In short, the appellate standards of review are: correctness on questions of law, "palpable and overriding error" on questions of fact, and a murkier territory (sometimes referred to as a "spectrum" of standards) on questions of mixed law and fact. See also *L (H) v Canada (Attorney General)*, 2005 SCC 25, [2005] 1 SCR 401. For a cogent argument that the appellate standards of review are, or should be, collapsed from their current state to just two—correctness and reasonableness—following *Dunsmuir's* two-standard model, see Mike Madden, "Conquering the Common Law Hydra: A Probably Correct and Reasonable Overview of Current Standards of Appellate and Judicial Review" (2010) 36:3 Adv Q 269. See also the judgment of Deschamps J in *Dunsmuir, supra* note 1 at para 158.

27 See *Anisminic Ltd v Foreign Compensation Commission*, [1969] 2 AC 147; Mark D Walters, "Jurisdiction, Functionalism, and Constitutionalism in Canadian Administrative Law" in Christopher Forsyth et al, eds, *Effective Judicial Review: A Cornerstone of Good Governance* (Oxford: Oxford University Press, 2010) 300 at 302.

the traditions and conventions of the common law. This provoked deep anxieties on the part of judges.[28]

From the point of view of the judiciary, this new concentration of state power, including powers of adjudication, in the executive and administrative branch was tantamount to putting the fox (the executive) in charge of the chickens (legal subjects—or, more properly, legal powers fundamentally affecting individual rights, including rights in contract and property). But, from the point of view of government, it was necessary to create administrative institutions, often with broad discretionary powers, in order to advance government mandates in the face of unanticipated and shifting regulatory challenges. Indeed, key administrative institutions were created precisely to overcome judge-made law actively obstructing the social welfare state.

There are two apparently contradictory ways that the deep thesis of administrative illegitimacy manifested historically (and arguably continues to manifest) in the law on substantive review. On the one hand, it manifested as reflexive, exclusive prioritization of judicial over administrative judgments on questions given to administrative decision-makers to decide.[29] On the other, it manifested as an unwillingness to oversee administrative decisions, or some subset of these (in particular, decisions classed as discretionary and/or those protected by a privative clause) at all—decisions thereby assigned the status of politics or policy, not law.[30] Finding a principled form of judicial review and moreover a theory of administrative legitimacy that avoided these extremes—judicial supremacy on the one side, and judicial abdication on the other—remains the central challenge posed to the law on substantive review.

Matthew Lewans distinguishes three broad eras in the Canadian law on judicial review, each of which illustrates in different ways a pattern of unpredictable veering between extremes of judicial supremacy and abdication.[31] First was the Formal and Conceptual Era, which ran from the turn of the 20th century to the decision in *CUPE v New Brunswick Liquor* in 1979.[32] The era was marked by legal formalism in that it was committed to an idea of the common law (including principles of statutory interpretation) as a self-contained, internally coherent body of concepts, wholly removed from moral or political controversy and

---

28 For a careful examination of how different schools of thought about the nature of law and its place in society informed administrative law theory and practice over the 20th century, see Matthew Lewans, *Administrative Law and Judicial Deference* (Oxford and Portland: Hart Publishing, 2016). See also Mark D Walters, *supra* note 27.

29 See Audrey Macklin's discussion of the "preliminary or collateral question" doctrine in Chapter 11.

30 See the judgment of Cartwright J in *Roncarelli v Duplessis*, [1959] SCR 121, 16 DLR (2d) 689 (discretion untrammelled unless clear statutory limits are stated). Contrast this with the judgment of Rand J in that case. For a hands-off approach to administrative jurisdiction (or errors deemed to fall within jurisdiction), see the judgment of Lord Sumner in *R v Nat Bell Liquors*, [1922] 2 AC 128.

31 Lewans, *Administrative Law and Judicial Deference*, *supra* note 28, ch 5. See also Paul Daly, "The Struggle for Deference in Canada" in Mark Elliott and Hanna Wilberg, eds, *The Scope and Intensity of Substantive Review: Traversing Taggart's Rainbow* (Oxford and Portland: Hart Publishing, 2015) 297.

32 [1979] 2 SCR 227 [*CUPE*]. Lewans, *supra* note 28 at 141-56. For an historically and biographically contextualized reading of Dicey's *Law of the Constitution* against the grain of more conventional (two-dimensional) portraitures of Dicey's thought, see Mark D Walters, "Dicey on Reading the Law of the Constitution" (2012) 32:1 Oxford J Leg Stud 21.

presided over by neutral judges.[33] A key expression of the formalist era was the common law judiciary's devising a range of formal or nominate grounds of review (e.g., "asking the wrong question," or the "preliminary or collateral question" doctrine that Audrey Macklin describes in Chapter 11), which judges applied to administrative decisions otherwise protected from correctness review (e.g. discretionary decisions, or decisions shielded by a privative clause) as if to root out self-evident excesses of statutory power or jurisdiction. This approach tended to relieve courts from having to justify, in a more contextualized and responsive manner, their decisions to displace administrative judgments with the alternative value-laden judgments or interpretations they favoured.

This era was also marked by what scholars have characterized as a uniquely Diceyan constitutionalism, centring upon the separation of powers and a profound suspicion of the administrative state (you met AV Dicey in Chapter 1 by Colleen M Flood).[34] On the Diceyan model, constitutionally sound governance required a clear division of labour among the legislature (with exclusive responsibility for making law), the judiciary (with exclusive responsibility for interpreting law), and the executive and administrative state (effectively the "transmission belt" or vehicle for law's application, lacking legitimate authority either to make or interpret law).[35] Among the primary responsibilities of judges was to discipline administration in the name of the legislature's will.

However, Diceyan judges struggled with how to accommodate the broad, discretionary powers often conferred on administrative decision-makers. That is, discretion presented a conundrum precisely because it (unlike law interpretation, conceived by the Diceyan as the opposite of discretion) resisted top-down judicial supervision in the name of a clear legislative intent. It was, by definition, a form of legal power that lacked express, determinate conditions or controls.[36] Here the Diceyan judge was wracked by conflicting constitutional imperatives: On the one hand, recognition of parliamentary supremacy (and with this, respect for Parliament's intent to confer broad decision-making authority on administration—in some cases, reinforced through the formal mechanism of the privative clause),[37] and on the other, recognition of the judge's duty to protect the rule of law and to ensure that the executive remained within the limits of law. In effect, the judge was torn between impulses of relinquishing and asserting supervisory power over Parliament's administrative delegates.

---

33 Katrina Wyman surveys some of the diverse uses of the term "formalism" in legal academia in her article "Is Formalism Inevitable?" (2007) 57 UTLJ 685. See especially 688, n7. Compare Dyzenhaus: "Formalism is formal in that it requires judges to operate with categories and distinctions that determine results without the judges having to deploy the substantive arguments that underpin the categories and distinctions." ("Constituting the Rule of Law," *supra* note 25 at 450.)

34 See also Chapter 4 by Mary Liston.

35 See Dyzenhaus, "Constituting the Rule of Law," *supra* note 25 at 453-57.

36 See *Baker*, *supra* note 19 at para 54.

37 Dyzenhaus, "The Politics of Deference," *supra* note 23 at 281. Dyzenhaus adds: "Dicey reconciled [the judiciary's] interpretative authority with the sovereignty of the legislature by adverting to the fact that the English Parliament did not generally use legislation as a blunt instrument to overrule judges' interpretation of statutes in the light of the common law." Yet the "pre-emptive" legislative device of the privative clause, identifying certain administrative decisions as "immune to judicial supervision," threw a wrench in the Diceyan effort to reconcile parliamentary and judicial rule.

The pre-*CUPE* doctrine on substantive review attempted to negotiate these tensions by carving out separate, watertight spheres of exclusive authority for courts and administration, roughly along the lines of "law" versus "policy." But the frustrating thing for the Diceyan judge was that these separate spheres—law/policy, law/discretion, legality/merits, and matters falling within and outside administrative jurisdiction—were and are based on inherently unstable categories.[38]

The next era in the Canadian law on substantive review, the central features of which are described by Audrey Macklin in Chapter 11, was the Pragmatic and Functional Era.[39] This period extended from *CUPE* in 1979 through the consolidation of the four-factor analysis in *Pushpanathan v Canada (Minister of Citizenship and Immigration)*[40] in 1998, until it reached its rough terminus in *Dunsmuir*, in 2008. Over the course of this period, the Canadian law on substantive review began to detach, albeit gradually and unevenly, from the core Diceyan idea that the judiciary holds exclusive authority to interpret law. This was supported by a turn in the doctrine on the standards of review "from formal questions of power, authority or mandate to pragmatic questions about function, perspective, and relative ability."[41]

As you saw in Chapter 11, judges during this period engaged in meticulous efforts to determine how to approach administrative decisions on review—that is, what standard of review to apply—by attending to multiple (sometimes conflicting) contextual signals said to be expressive of legislative intent, an analysis that ultimately centred on relative expertise. The court adopted correctness review where the legislative signals were said to indicate that the matter on review fell within the proper authority or institutional capacities of the judiciary, and deferential review where the matter was deemed more properly to engage the authority or institutional capacities of administration. As such the Pragmatic and Functional Era was organized, like the prior period, around the idea of competing zones of exclusive jurisdiction. The governing question was: "Who should decide?" What was not clear was what exactly courts should do when called upon to oversee those decisions that commanded deference—particularly where the challenge was to administrative law interpretation.

Indeed, deep debates arose around this question, beginning with debates on how courts should operationalize the standard through which Dickson J in *CUPE* first gave expression to the ethos of deference in Canadian administrative law in 1979, using the language of "patent unreasonableness."[42] As Audrey Macklin has described in Chapter 11, the judgment in *CUPE* marked a revolution in substantive review in recognizing that not all questions of law give rise to a single correct answer, and moreover, that there are good reasons, both pragmatic and democratic, to defer to administrative decision-makers even on questions of law. The manner in which Dickson J conducted review in *CUPE* was in key ways consistent with this new understanding of the legitimate role of the administrative branch in the legal order. That is, Dickson J's analysis was anchored not in tribunal-independent scrutiny of the

---

38   See D Dyzenhaus, "Formalism's Hollow Victory" (2002) NZL Rev 525 at 530-39; "The Politics of Deference," *supra* note 23 at 280-82; "Constituting the Rule of Law," *supra* note 25 at 448-51 and 454-58; Dyzenhaus and Evan Fox-Decent, "Process/Substance," *supra* note 25 at 197-200 and 204-5. See also David Mullan, "A Proportionate Response to an Emerging Crisis in Canadian Judicial Review Law?" (2010) NZL Rev 233 at 251-53 ["A Proportionate Response?"].

39   See Lewans, *Administrative Law and Judicial Deference, supra* note 28 at 156-75.

40   [1998] 1 SCR 982 [*Pushpanathan*].

41   See Walters, *supra* note 27 at 305-6.

42   *CUPE, supra* note 32.

statutory text in context, but rather in attentiveness to the decision and reasoning of the tribunal, drawing on and building on its purposive interpretation of the disputed statutory term in dialogical fashion[43] to arrive at the conclusion that it was "no less reasonable than"[44] the conflicting interpretations preferred at the Court of Appeal.

Yet this approach to substantive review raised new questions for reviewing courts. How should they deal with situations where an administrative decision-maker adopted an interpretation that differed from the judge's own understanding of the statutory text in context? This became particularly tricky where the difference lay in competing conceptions of the statutory purpose, or the significance or priority to be given to different and potentially warring elements of the statutory text or mandate. Was it appropriate to allow that competing, even contradictory, approaches to an interpretive problem were equally reasonable? And if (as in *CUPE*) it was recognized that this may sometimes be the case, what were the justified limits of that principle? When should the court's, or for that matter the decision-maker's, opinion trump?

Three competing approaches emerged after *CUPE*, which continue to be discernible in the contemporary law on deference (or reasonableness). These were exemplified in *Caimaw v Paccar of Canada Ltd.*[45] The first approach (illustrated in the concurring majority judgment of Sopinka J) was rooted in the idea that problems of statutory interpretation tend to deliver up one right answer, which courts are best positioned to identify. Sopinka J counselled that courts reviewing a disputed interpretation of law should first seek the correct answer, and only then, if the opinion of the decision-maker differed, grant the decision-maker a "margin of error."[46] This approach has since largely been rejected as overly judge-centric. In practical terms, judges are highly unlikely to give credence to administrative interpretations after deeming them incorrect. More broadly, the approach is inconsistent with what has become a core principle of deferential review: that reviewing courts must pay respectful attention to the reasons and decisions of administrative decision-makers, and, moreover, must assess administrative law interpretations in a manner that is informed and enriched by such respectful attention. However, as we will see, the idea that judges engaged in reasonableness review must first apply "the ordinary tools of statutory interpretation"[47] to determine whether there is a single right (or reasonable) answer, before even broaching the possibility of deference (understood, on this approach, as defaulting to the administrator's interpretation where it falls among competing reasonable options), remains prominent in the law on reasonableness review today.[48]

The second approach articulated in *Paccar* (in the concurring majority judgment of La Forest J) was rooted in a more decidedly pluralist understanding of law or of administrative law. That approach regarded administrative law interpretation (or more specifically those interpretations deemed to fall under the protection of a privative clause) as the expression of policy choices within the proper authority of administrators and not courts. The

---

43   *Ibid.*
44   *Ibid* at 242.
45   [1989] 2 SCR 983 [*Paccar*].
46   *Ibid* at 1017-20, Sopinka J. *Contra* this approach, see e.g. *Law Society of New Brunswick v Ryan*, 2003 SCC 20, [2003] 1 SCR 247 at paras 52-53 [*Ryan*]: "Even if there could be, notionally, a single best answer, it is not the court's role to seek this out when deciding if the decision was unreasonable."
47   *McLean v British Columbia (Securities Commission)*, 2013 SCC 67, [2013] 3 SCR 895 at para 38, Moldaver J [*McLean*].
48   *Ibid* at paras 38-40.

approach counselled broad tolerance for such policy choices, including (indeed, in particular) where they conflicted sharply with the judge's construction of statutory purposes. This approach, too, continues to have influence, and may be discerned in contemporary judgments on the ability of reasonableness review to accommodate multiple, even starkly contradictory administrative interpretations and applications of law as so many instantiations of reasonableness.

Finally, a third approach articulated in *Paccar* (most clearly in the dissenting judgment of L'Heureux-Dubé J, and supported in that of Wilson J) centred upon attention to, and acknowledgment of, the reasons for deference to, tribunal reasoning. At the same time, this approach allowed for evaluation of administrative decision-makers' interpretive reasoning in light of the wider interpretive field, and invalidation of those interpretations on the basis that they were incompatible with (and/or inattentive to) the judge's best construction of statutory purposes (and/or wider legal norms).[49] On applying this approach in *Paccar*, L'Heureux-Dubé J concluded that the statutory purpose animating the collective bargaining regime in issue—namely, advancement of peaceable labour relations through promotion of equality of bargaining power—had been ignored and therefore defeated by the tribunal's interpretation; thus, the interpretation was patently unreasonable.

The question of how exactly to express deference on review was in many ways still unresolved when the third standard, "reasonableness *simpliciter*," was interposed between correctness and patent unreasonableness in the mid-1990s.[50] As Audrey Macklin explains in Chapter 11, this standard reflected an effort on the part of the courts to respond to conflicting signals gleaned from pragmatic and functional analysis (e.g., cases in which there was a statutory right of appeal and yet relative administrative expertise relevant to the question in issue). In other words, reasonableness *simpliciter* was fashioned out of a kind of Goldilocks logic: it was to be neither too interventionist nor too deferential. The new standard also reflected the concern that deference should not (at least, not in the situations attracting this middle standard) allow *any* tolerance of unreasonableness, regardless of whether it might take significant "searching" to root out.[51]

Ensuing efforts to distinguish the two deferential standards tended to take one of two forms: reference to "the magnitude of the defect" or reference to its "'immediacy or obviousness' … and thus the relative invasiveness of the review necessary to find it."[52] Neither approach managed to stabilize the practices of courts or the expectations of parties on review. Indeed, the failure of the case law to produce a distinction of any conceptual or practical value as between review for reasonableness *simpliciter* and review for patent unreasonableness led the court in *Dunsmuir* to conclude that the efficiency-based merits of reducing the standards to just two (representing deference and non-deference, respectively) were not outweighed by any competing considerations.

---

49   *Paccar, supra* note 45 at 1042-44, L'Heureux Dubé J.

50   *Canada (Director of Investigation and Research) v Southam Inc*, [1997] 1 SCR 748, 144 DLR (4th) 1 [*Southam*]; there, the newly articulated standard is said to have also been engaged in *Pezim v British Columbia (Superintendent of Brokers)*, [1994] 2 SCR 557, 114 DLR (4th) 385 [*Pezim*].

51   See the decision of Gonthier J in *National Corn Growers Assn v Canada (Import Tribunal)*, [1990] 2 SCR 1324, 74 DLR (4th) 449.

52   *Toronto (City) v CUPE, Local 79, supra* note 4 at para 78, LeBel J.

The contemporary era (Lewans calls it "the Dis-Functional Era"—we might also call it the era of Neo-Formalism) was consolidated with *Dunsmuir* in 2008.[53] As Audrey Macklin explained in Chapter 11, the *Dunsmuir* majority observed that the four-factor pragmatic and functional approach to selecting the standard of review had become both overly complicated and, at the same time, unpredictable. The solution offered involved a partial return to formalism, in a bid to attain the certainty that had been missing from the previous era's multi-dimensional contextual analysis. Thus, *Dunsmuir*'s standard of review analysis focuses on categories of question typically, or presumptively[54]—or in the case of the correctness categories, always—attracting one of just two standards: reasonableness (deference) or correctness (no deference). *Dunsmuir* also reflects an intensified focus on the democratic and pragmatic bases for deference, such that questions of law (arising under the home statute or closely connected statutes) are said to "usually"[55] attract reasonableness review and so deference. Such categorical shortcuts, however, sit uneasily with continuing anxieties about whether or how the diverse functions and capacities of *particular* administrative decision-makers (elements of the decision-making context once canvassed through the pragmatic and functional analysis) should inform the approach taken to particular questions on review. Which brings us to the present moment, which is marked by signs and portents of another imminent revolution in the law on the standards of review, likely to bring renewed attention to contextually informed reasons *not* to defer (or to defer … differently, in different contexts).

In sum, for much of the history of substantive review in Canada, courts sought to negotiate the felt tensions between democracy (conceived as legislative supremacy) and the rule of law through efforts to carve out competing zones of exclusive jurisdiction for courts and administrative decision-makers. Those competing zones were constructed and manipulated in ways that expressed the Diceyan judge's unease at the prospect of legislatively constructed "black holes," whether in the form of broad discretionary administrative powers or privative clauses ostensibly immunizing administrators' interpretations and applications of law. The contemporary law on substantive review since *CUPE* has struggled against this history to affirm the legitimacy of the administrative state, and so to acknowledge the democratic as well as pragmatic reasons for respecting administrative decisions while preserving a meaningful role for courts in upholding the rule of law.

This is where we now sit: with two standards of review, one of which (reasonableness) is nearly always applied in the review of substantive administrative decisions. The pressing question is: what does (or what should) reasonableness mean in any given case? Or more precisely: how should the imperatives of deference (and so the constitutional and institutional rationales for deference) be reconciled with the expectations of public justification—again, in any given case?

With this recap of the evolution of the law on the standards of review and the gradual rise to dominance of the reasonableness standard in mind, that central question can now be pursued. We start with a word on statutory interpretation, which is both the engine of

---

53   Lewans, *Administrative Law and Judicial Deference, supra* note 28 at 175-80.
54   See Chapter 11 by Audrey Macklin.
55   *Dunsmuir, supra* note 1 at para 54.

substantive review and the site of deep controversies about the nature of law, and the role of judges and of administrative decision-makers in advancing and protecting the rule of law.

2. *Statutory Interpretation and Substantive Review: Getting Past "One Right Answer"*

Assessment of the substantive legality of an administrative decision is steeped in the work of statutory interpretation.[56] Interpretation assists in selecting the standard of review, and in resolving discrete disputes about the meaning of statutory terms, whether classed as questions of law or questions concerning the limits on discretion.

It may be difficult to reconcile the ubiquity of statutory interpretation in substantive review with the deference required under the now-dominant standard of reasonableness review, for the principles of statutory interpretation have been crafted by—and tend to be understood as falling within the exclusive institutional and constitutional capacities of—judges. Thus, before moving on to take a closer look at the two standards of review in play post-*Dunsmuir*, it is worth pausing to consider what is involved in statutory interpretation as it arises in administrative settings and on review.[57] The objective is not to attempt an exhaustive account of the relevant principles,[58] but rather to make a few basic observations aimed at disrupting the common assumption that statutory interpretation necessarily or regularly yields a single correct answer that judges are best placed to discern.

The natural starting point is the "modern principle" of statutory interpretation, articulated in the second edition of Driedger's *Construction of Statutes* and repeatedly endorsed by the Supreme Court:

> Today there is only one principle or approach [to statutory interpretation], namely, the words of an Act are to be read in their entire context and in their grammatical and ordinary sense harmoniously with the scheme of the Act, the object of the Act, and the intention of Parliament.[59]

General judicial acceptance of this principle tends to obscure continuing conflicts among judges (and sometimes even among decisions of a single judge) as to the factors that should be deemed of primary relevance when interpreting contested statutory texts.[60] As Ruth Sullivan states: "the modern principle has been used in Canada to justify every

---

56   "To a large extent judicial review of administrative action is a specialized branch of statutory interpretation": *UES, Local 298 v Bibeault*, [1988] 2 SCR 1048 at 1087. Beetz J (writing for the court) is quoting SA de Smith, H Street & R Brazier, *Constitutional and Administrative Law*, 4th ed (Harmondsworth, UK: Penguin, 1981) at 588. Compare JM Keyes, "Judicial Review and the Interpretation of Legislation: Who Gets the Last Word?" (2006) 19 Can J Admin L & Prac 119.

57   A further question of interest, not explored here, is whether administrators do or should approach statutory interpretation differently than judges. See S Slinn, "Untamed Tribunal? Of Dynamic Interpretation and Purpose Clauses" (2009) 42 UBCL Rev 125; JL Mashaw, "Small Things like Reasons Are Put in a Jar: Reason and Legitimacy in the Administrative State" (2001) 70 Fordham L Rev 17.

58   An excellent introduction to statutory interpretation in public law is found in C Forcese et al, *Public Law: Cases, Commentary and Analysis*, 3rd ed (Toronto: Emond Montgomery, 2015) at 425-523.

59   EA Driedger, *Construction of Statutes*, 2nd ed (Toronto: Butterworths, 1983) at 87.

60   See R Sullivan, "Statutory Interpretation in the Supreme Court of Canada" (1998) 30 Ottawa L Rev 175 ["Statutory Interpretation in the Supreme Court of Canada"]; S Beaulac & P Côté, "Driedger's 'Modern Principle' at the Supreme Court of Canada: Interpretation, Justification, Legitimization" (2006) 40 RJT 131.

possible approach to interpretation and, more importantly, has been used as a substitute for real justification."[61]

Of course, statutory texts do not always give rise to significant disagreement. But the cases that tend to come before tribunals and courts as contests about interpretation are typically "hard cases." That is, these disputes tend to require the adjudicator to make a contestable judgment involving selection among competing elements of the text or context, or potentially competing fundamental legal norms or values (the rule of law, democracy, equality, liberty). Sullivan observes: "While most cases that come before tribunals and courts are hard, Driedger's modern principle does not acknowledge this problem and offers no guidance on how to resolve it."[62]

It is worth underlining this point so as to correct the misconception that statutory interpretation is in many or most cases simply a matter of finding the right answer by expertly applying the right tools. But does this mean that it is "all subjective"—that is, a matter of the judge's or administrator's personal moral or political preferences? Sullivan advances an approach to hard cases that she presents as a form of "pragmatism." The approach requires decision-makers to prioritize and choose among competing bases for stabilizing interpretation (statutory text, legislative purposes and history, and the wider normative context of interpretive presumptions and legal values). Such strategies are necessarily contestable, and may give rise to deep disagreement even (and perhaps particularly) among those accorded the status of experts. Competing interpretations may admit of ranking as better or worse, or more or less appropriate—based, for instance, on whether a given interpretation is able to account for a wider or narrower range of considerations arising under the different modes of analysis. But the ranking of interpretive judgments, too, is contestable, and so is similarly steeped in the effort to persuade.

Sometimes interpretive conflicts may be mediated by reference to meta-rules, such as the rule that statutory terms must be determined to be ambiguous at the level of text and legislative–historical context before they may be interpreted in light of the values or norms of the Charter or international law.[63] But even these meta-rules require contestable judgments—for instance, on what counts as ambiguity.

a. Competing Approaches to Interpretation and Implications for Substantive Review

As noted above, contemporary understandings of statutory interpretation have mostly outgrown the simple thesis that statute law necessarily or even often yields a singular and determinate legislative intent. However, it is still possible to identify in the contemporary case law—including the case law on substantive review—what we may call positivist (and

---

61 R Sullivan, "Statutory Interpretation in Canada: The Legacy of Elmer Driedger" in T Gotsis, ed, *Statutory Interpretation: Principles and Pragmatism for a New Age* (Sydney: Judicial Commission of New South Wales, 2007) 105 ["Statutory Interpretation in Canada"]. The question of what "real justification" is, is of course at the heart of review for reasonableness.

62 *Ibid* at 123. Critical examination of the function of Driedger's modern principle in Canadian law is provided in Nicholas Hooper, "Notes Toward a Postmodern Principle," Can JL & Jur (forthcoming, 2018).

63 *Bell ExpressVu Ltd Partnership v Rex*, 2002 SCC 42, [2002] 2 SCR 559 [*Bell ExpressVu*]; *Gitxaala, supra* note 21. For a critique, see Sullivan, "Statutory Interpretation in Canada," *supra* note 61 at 119-22.

static) approaches to statutory interpretation, and to distinguish these from normative (and dynamic) approaches.[64]

A positivist approach to statutory interpretation flows from the presumption, long debunked in linguistic theory, and increasingly marginalized in law, that statutory language contains a singular and unified meaning that is stable over time.[65] Judges adhering to that presumption tend to assume (or to appear to assume) that this stable meaning may be ascertained through interpretive techniques proper to and perfected by the judiciary.[66] Those techniques may involve a strict focus on the statutory text or efforts to situate the text in its legislative–historical context. On either variant of this approach, the objective is to "find" a determinate legislative intent.[67]

A general criticism raised against the positivist approach to law interpretation is that it smuggles into legal judgment contestable value-driven choices, where those choices should be explicitly submitted for public justification.[68] In administrative law, a positivist approach may further be argued to work against deference, in that it restricts the potential for judges to acknowledge their own value-laden presumptions in the face of the potentially competing values or perspectives of administrative decision-makers.

In contrast, it is the explicit submission of the value-laden bases of legal judgment for public justification that marks a normative (and dynamic) approach to statutory interpretation.[69] Such an approach proceeds on the assumption that contested matters of statutory interpretation cannot be resolved by exclusive reference to the text,[70] or even by situating the text in its social or legislative–historical context,[71] but also require judgments about the competing values or social priorities informing alternative statutory constructions. This approach is reflected in the acknowledgment of L'Heureux-Dubé J, in her judgment in the

---

64 Ruth Sullivan in "Statutory Interpretation in the Supreme Court of Canada," *supra* note 61, distinguishes textualist and intentionalist (which I am loosely calling "positivist") from pragmatic (which I am calling "normative") approaches to statutory interpretation. On the static/dynamic descriptors, see Forcese, *supra* note 58 at 429-32, and William Eskridge, *Dynamic Statutory Interpretation* (Cambridge, Mass: Harvard University Press, 1994). I adopt the "positivist"/"normative" dichotomy because it puts the claim to value-neutrality at the centre of the distinction.

65 *Cf* N Hooper, *supra* note 62. See also David Dyzenhaus, "David Mullan's Theory of the Rule of (Common) Law" in G Huscroft & M Taggart, eds, *Inside and Outside Administrative Law: Essays in Honour of David Mullan* (Toronto: University of Toronto Press, 2006) 448 at 474 [*Inside and Outside*]: "[T]he point of the positivist conception of law is to insist that real law is the determinate content of valid law, where determinate means determinable in accordance with tests that do not rely on moral considerations and arguments, including arguments about the principles of an internal morality of law."

66 This approach is therefore consistent with a Diceyan or formalist approach to the rule of law, focused on the separation of powers. See the discussion of Diceyan formalism in Section II.A.

67 Compare J Gardner, "Legal Positivism: 5½ Myths" (2001) 46 Am J Juris 199 at 218-22. Gardner argues that legal positivism is not committed to either textualism or originalism in statutory interpretation. Again, see "Statutory Interpretation in the Supreme Court of Canada," *supra* note 61.

68 "Statutory Interpretation in the Supreme Court of Canada," *supra* note 61 at 220-25.

69 *Ibid* at 184-87 and 220-27 (on the "pragmatic" approach to interpretation).

70 Sullivan, *ibid* at 185, makes this point, and canvasses a set of standard critiques of textualist and intentionalist approaches: "[C]ommunication through natural language is never a sure thing; rules drafted by legislatures tend to be general and are often abstract; and legislatures cannot form intentions with respect to how these rules should apply to every possible set of facts."

71 See Hanoch Dagan, "The Realist Conception of Law" (2007) 57 UTLJ 607 at 649.

Baker case,[72] that law interpretation is continuous with and not strictly distinct from the exercise of discretion.[73] That is not to say that, on this model, law is without any anchor beyond the whim of the judge—or the administrative decision-maker. Rather, the normative model of law interpretation implies a conception of the rule of law in which the legitimacy of state action (including law interpretation) depends on the efforts of judges and administrative decision-makers alike to justify their decisions in light of the important public values inscribed in our social and legal traditions.[74] Yet just as these values and traditions are not monolithic or static, so does a normative approach to interpretation tend to be dynamic—approaching interpretation as an opportunity for ongoing public deliberation about the nature and relative priority of legal norms.

The distinction between positivist and normative approaches to statutory interpretation sheds light on the tension between correctness and reasonableness review. If there is a right and wrong way to interpret a statute, independent of contestable value judgments, then it follows that the rule of law should empower expert, independent courts to correct the errors of administrative decision-makers. Alternatively, if interpreting statutes necessarily involves contestable value judgments, then it follows that administrative decision-makers, steeped in the policy imperatives of particular governments and specialized fields of government activity, are (sometimes? often?) best placed to decide—or, in any case, that their decisions should be accorded respectful attention and even presumptive weight by the courts on review.

A further refinement of the normative model of statutory interpretation, and of the relationship between statutory interpretation and judicial review, is suggested by David Dyzenhaus in his account of "the politics of deference."[75] Dyzenhaus traces the erratic reviewing habits of the Diceyan judge (shuttling between postures of abdication of supervisory authority and supremacist interventionism) to irreconcilable commitments to "democratic positivism" or law-as-legislative-will on the one side (respect for the legislature's will to confer broad discretion on administration), and "liberal anti-positivism" or law-as-liberal-morality on the other (as expressed through the commitment to individual rights). Dyzenhaus suggests a way past these contradictory commitments that turns upon an understanding of judicial review, and deference, not as a zero-sum game of warring claims

---

72 *Supra* note 19.

73 L'Heureux-Dubé J writes (for the majority) in *Baker, supra* note 19 at para 54:

> It is, however, inaccurate to speak of a rigid dichotomy of "discretionary" or "non-discretionary" decisions. Most administrative decisions involve the exercise of implicit discretion in relation to many aspects of decision making. To give just one example, decision-makers may have considerable discretion as to the remedies they order. In addition, there is no easy distinction to be made between interpretation and the exercise of discretion; interpreting legal rules involves considerable discretion to clarify, fill in legislative gaps, and make choices among various options.

74 The function of moral values in law and in the claim to legitimate rule (or to the rule of law) is recognized in the following statement of McLachlin CJ for the court in *Reference re Secession of Quebec*, [1998] 2 SCR 217 at para 67, 161 DLR (4th) 385 [*Secession Reference*]: "[A] system of government ... must be capable of reflecting the aspirations of the people. But there is more. Our law's claim to legitimacy also rests on an appeal to moral values, many of which are embedded in our constitutional structure. It would be a grave mistake to equate legitimacy with the "sovereign will" or majority rule alone, to the exclusion of other constitutional values." See also Mary Liston's discussion of the *Secession Reference* in Chapter 4 of this text.

75 Dyzenhaus, "The Politics of Deference," *supra* note 23.

to exclusive jurisdiction, but rather as a dialogical encounter based on "respect."[76] More generally, deference "as respect" (an idea that we will see has been adopted by the Supreme Court of Canada) forms part of a wider account in Dyzenhaus's work of the relationship of law or the rule of law to legitimate, or morally justified, governance. On this account, governance according to the rule of law requires the fostering of a "culture of justification"[77]—a legal culture that enacts and is expressive of a moral relationship of reciprocity as between legal authorities and legal subjects.[78]

Consistent with this purposive understanding of law or the rule of law, Dyzenhaus conceives of statutory interpretation, and, in particular, the interpretive work of the administrative state, may be regarded as an opportunity for activating inclusive deliberation about how the deep moral and political values inscribed in our social and legal traditions should inform the proper exercise of public power. For Dyzenhaus, this has bearing on the expectations of judges on review. That is, given the critical role of administrative decision-makers in enabling the participation of legal subjects in the interpretation and application of law, and so in ensuring that state action is publicly justified in a way that takes account of and indeed speaks to those directly affected, judges must both hold decision-makers to account in light of the participatory and justificatory norms through which the rule of law is secured, and be respectful of the purposive reasoning through which decision-makers demonstrate their adherence to those norms.[79]

One does not have to accept Dyzenhaus's account of the broad functions of administrative statutory interpretation and judicial review in securing a culture of justification in order to engage seriously with this area of law. However, one's approach to statutory interpretation in the context of judicial review necessarily depends upon and reflects a thesis or theory about the nature and purposes both of law and of the administrative state. That thesis, or theory, will affect one's approach to the central challenge for judicial review as it is expressed through the reasonableness standard: to recognize the capacities and responsibilities of administrative decision-makers to engage in statutory interpretation, without wholly surrendering the work of delimiting executive and administrative powers (or of identifying the deeper legal values of relevance to the legitimate exercise of those powers) to the executive and administrative branch. This is the challenge referred to above as coordinating the imperatives of deference and public justification.

B. Correctness: The Antithesis of Reasonableness?

As the exploration of statutory interpretation above has begun to suggest, one way of making sense of reasonableness review is to ask whether or how it is distinct from correctness review. But is there a practical difference between these standards? If so, what exactly is that difference?

76　*Ibid* at 286, cited e.g. in *Baker, supra* note 19 at para 65.

77　Dyzanhaus, "Law as Justification," *supra* note 25, on the concept of a "culture of justification."

78　See Dyzenhaus, "Constituting the Rule of Law," *supra* note 25 at 501 and Fox-Decent, *Sovereignty's Promise, supra* note 25. And see Geneviève Cartier, "The Baker Effect: A New Interface Between the Canadian Charter of Rights and Freedoms and Administrative Law—The Case of Discretion" in David Dyzenhaus, ed, *The Unity of Public Law* (Oxford: Hart Publishing, 2004) 61 at 79-85 ["The Baker Effect"].

79　Mark D Walters "Respecting Deference as Respect: Rights, Reasonableness and Proportionality in Canadian Administrative Law" in Wilberg & Elliott, eds, *The Scope and Intensity of Substantive Review* at 418 ["Respecting Deference as Respect"]. And see Dyzenhaus, "The Politics of Deference," *supra* note 23 at 305, 307.

1. Correctness in Theory

As discussed by Audrey Macklin in Chapter 11, the majority in *Dunsmuir* indicates that a correctness standard will presumptively apply in certain types of cases, including those that raise constitutional questions,[80] "true questions of jurisdiction or *vires*,"[81] questions about the relative jurisdictional scope of different tribunals,[82] and questions of law that are "of central importance to the legal system as a whole and outside the adjudicator's specialized area of expertise."[83] From the start, *Dunsmuir* reduced the reach of correctness review by lending increased specificity to the broad category of questions of "general" law previously attracting this standard, and indicating that a narrow approach should be taken to the category of jurisdictional questions. The subsequent case law has reduced the reach of these categories even further. Consequently, as Audrey Macklin relates, correctness review has only rarely been applied at the Supreme Court of Canada in the years since *Dunsmuir*. It has mostly been overtaken by the presumption of deference to administrative decision-makers' interpretations of their home statutes.[84]

But what does correctness imply in the context of substantive review? Review for correctness may at first appear so obvious or plain in meaning as to need no further explanation. That is, asserting a requirement of correctness appears to amount merely to an insistence that the decision-maker get it right, full stop. On reflection, however, the meaning of "getting it right" and the method by which this should be evaluated are less than transparent; indeed, as suggested in the previous section, these matters open onto fundamental questions about law, interpretation, and the roles and responsibilities of the three branches of government.

Guidance from the courts has focused on a very basic, and important, feature of correctness review as distinguished from review for reasonableness. Thus, in *Ryan*,[85] Iacobucci J wrote that where a correctness standard is imposed, "the court may undertake its own reasoning process to arrive at the result it judges correct."[86] This may be contrasted with what is arguably the most important feature of deferential review—that is, the requirement that judges make an effort to consider the administrative decision-maker's reasoning on its own terms.

The *Dunsmuir* majority confirms this point:

> When applying the correctness standard, a reviewing court will not show deference to the decision maker's reasoning process; it will rather undertake its own analysis of the question. The analysis will bring the court to decide whether it agrees with the determination of the decision maker; if not, the court will substitute its own view and provide the correct answer. From the outset, the court must ask whether the tribunal's decision was correct.[87]

Beyond this rather perfunctory description of what it means to review administrative decisions on a correctness standard, the majority in *Dunsmuir* further gestures at the standard's underlying rationale. Thus, the standard is said to find its foundation in a commitment to the rule of law. More specifically, maintaining a correctness standard of review in relation to

---

80 *Dunsmuir, supra* note 1 at para 58.
81 *Ibid* at para 59.
82 *Ibid* at para 61.
83 *Ibid* at para 60.
84 *Ibid* at para 41. And see Danay, *supra* note 7.
85 *Supra* note 46.
86 *Ibid* at para 50.
87 *Dunsmuir, supra* note 1 at para 50.

"jurisdictional questions and some other questions of law" is asserted to be essential in order to "promot[e] just decisions and avoi[d] inconsistent and unauthorized application of law."[88] Implicit in this statement is the suggestion that the reasonableness standard conflicts with these imperatives—at least where the categories of question referred to are in issue. This is a proposition we will have occasion to pursue.

2. Correctness in Practice

To better understand the distinction between correctness and reasonableness review, consider briefly three examples of correctness review in action. First is the pre-*Dunsmuir* case *Barrie Public Utilities v Canadian Cable Television Assn*.[89] *Barrie Public Utilities* involved review of a decision of the Canadian Radio-Television and Telecommunications Commission (CRTC), which had granted the applicant cable television companies access to the power poles of certain provincially regulated electrical power utilities. The CRTC's authority to make that order had turned upon its determination that the poles in question constituted "the supporting structure of a transmission line."[90]

In his judgment for the majority, Gonthier J characterized this determination as a matter of "pure statutory interpretation"[91] outside the CRTC's expertise, thereby attracting correctness review. He then proceeded to identify the plain meaning of the phrase in question and of other elements of the statutory scheme,[92] with an emphasis on elements of the text and context suggesting that power poles did not qualify as "supporting structures of a transmission line." The contrary interpretation, favoured by the CRTC, had been based on objectives that it considered fundamental to its mandate. That is, while the CRTC had taken account of various elements of the statutory scheme, its primary focus had been to avoid "the construction of duplicative distribution infrastructures," a consequence that it determined "was not in the public interest."

Bastarache J criticized the majority's approach, in comments that drew on the reasons of L'Heureux-Dubé J for a unanimous court in *Domtar Inc v Quebec (Commission d'appel en matière de lésions professionnelles)*:[93]

> Substituting one's opinion for that of an administrative tribunal in order to develop one's own interpretation of a legislative provision eliminates its decision-making autonomy and special expertise. Since such intervention occurs in circumstances where the legislature has determined that the administrative tribunal is the one in the best position to rule on the disputed decision, it risks, at the same time, thwarting the original intention of the legislature. For the purposes of judicial review, statutory interpretation has ceased to be a necessarily "exact" science and this Court has, again recently, confirmed the rule of curial deference set forth for the first time in *Canadian Union of Public Employees, Local 963 v New Brunswick Liquor Corp*.[94]

The thesis that statutory interpretation is not (or is "no longer") an exact science has gained increasing acceptance in law, and in particular in the law on judicial review, since *Barrie Public Utilities*. Moreover, post-*Dunsmuir* there are few circumstances in which challenges to

---

88 *Ibid.*
89 2003 SCC 28, [2003] 1 SCR 476 [*Barrie Public Utilities*].
90 *Telecommunications Act*, SC 1993, c 38, s 43(5).
91 *Barrie Public Utilities, supra* note 89 at para 16.
92 *Ibid* at para 42.
93 [1993] 2 SCR 756, 105 DLR (4th) 385 [*Domtar*].
94 *Barrie Public Utilities, supra* note 89 at para 128, Bastarache J, quoting *Domtar, ibid* at 775.

decisions under the home statute will attract correctness review.[95] Yet correctness review may continue to apply to interpretation of the home statute in some circumstances (for instance, where the courts and decision-maker have concurrent jurisdiction over the question at first instance).[96] Moreover, correctness-style approaches to statutory interpretation may at times be discerned in instances of ostensible reasonableness review (a prospect discussed below). Therefore, it is important to remain alert to the sorts of deep disputes evident in a case like *Barrie Public Utilities*, on whether or in what circumstances it is appropriate to conclude that there is just one right answer to an interpretive dispute concerning the proper exercise of administrative powers—and whether or in what circumstances the courts should be confident in their ability to discover that answer in a manner that ignores, or otherwise departs starkly from, the reasoning and with this the value-laden priorities reflected in the decision on review.

A second notable case of correctness review—again, pre-*Dunsmuir*—is *Pushpanathan v Canada (Minister of Citizenship and Immigration)*.[97] In *Pushpanathan*, the court applied correctness review to a decision of the Convention Refugee Determination Division of the Immigration and Refugee Board. The board had determined that a provision of the *Immigration Act* excluding from refugee status persons who have "been guilty of acts contrary to the purposes and principles of the United Nations" functioned to exclude persons convicted of drug trafficking. Correctness review was justified on the basis that the decision engaged a "general legal principle," a characterization supported by the formal certification of the question in issue by the Federal Court (Trial Division) as a "serious question of general importance."[98]

Ultimately, the majority and dissent in *Pushpanathan* differed fundamentally on how best to assemble and prioritize the evidence and arguments concerning whether drug trafficking was contrary to the purposes and principles of the UN, and reached contradictory conclusions. Thus, *Pushpanathan* reminds us that application of the correctness standard does not necessarily mean that there is an obvious or uncontroversial answer to the interpretive dispute; rather, the standard may apply in situations in which the right or best answer is highly contested, even among the nation's top judges. In such cases, it is the need for finality and for system-wide normative and doctrinal coherence that appears to recommend the standard. The question is again whether or when it is defensible for reviewing courts to approach such matters without any engagement with the reasoning of the decision-maker—that is, simply asking what the right answer is, rather than inquiring specifically into the strength or justification of the decision-maker's approach.

Finally, *Mouvement laïque québécois v Saguenay (City)*[99] is a post-*Dunsmuir* example of correctness review that, like *Pushpanathan*, reflects rule of law imperatives that appear

---

95   For empirical support for this claim, see Danay, *supra* note 7 at 595-97. However, there remain important exceptions—justified, for instance, by anomalous language in the statutory right of appeal (*Tervita Corp v Canada (Commissioner of Competition)*, 2015 SCC 3, [2015] 1 SCR 161), concurrent jurisdiction as between the courts and tribunal at first instance (*Rogers Communications Inc v Society of Composers, Authors and Music Publishers of Canada*, 2012 SCC 35, [2012] 2 SCR 283 [*Rogers*]), and/or classification of the matter on review as a question of general law of central importance to the legal system as a whole and outside the decision-maker's expertise (*Mouvement laïque québécois v Saguenay (City)*, 2015 SCC 16, [2015] 2 SCR 3 [*Saguenay*]).

96   See *Rogers*, *supra* note 95.

97   *Supra* note 40.

98   Per s 83(1) of the then *Immigration Act*, RSC 1985, c I-2.

99   *Supra* note 98.

to spring not from positivistic expectations that law interpretation necessarily yields clear and determinate answers, but rather from the institutional imperative that questions of system-wide legal importance yield consistent interpretations, informed by and coherent with the wider fabric of general or fundamental (system-wide) legal norms.

In *Saguenay*, the Supreme Court of Canada upheld a decision of the Quebec Human Rights Tribunal that a municipality's practice of reading a prayer prior to municipal council meetings (and its display of religious symbols in council chambers) constituted a discriminatory breach of freedom of religion and conscience, contrary to Quebec's *Charter of Human Rights and Freedoms*. The majority segmented the decision into a few discrete elements. It identified correctness review as appropriate to what it identified as the first step in the required analysis: ascertaining "the scope of the state's duty of religious neutrality that flows from the freedom of conscience and religion protected by the Quebec Charter."[100] Correctness review was adopted for this issue in light of its importance "to the legal system, its broad and general scope and the need to decide it in a uniform and consistent manner."[101] Added to this was the argument that the tribunal's jurisdiction on this question was exercised concurrently with the first-instance jurisdiction of the courts.[102]

On applying the correctness standard, Gascon J, for the majority, drew on case law precedents as well as academic sources. He concluded that "the state's duty to protect every person's freedom of conscience and religion means that it may not use its powers in such a way as to promote the participation of certain believers or non-believers in public life to the detriment of others."[103] Notably, this brought the court into full agreement with the tribunal: "The Tribunal was therefore correct in holding that the state's duty of neutrality means that a state authority cannot make use of its powers to promote or impose a religious belief."[104] In contrast, the Court of Appeal, which had rejected the tribunal's conclusion as "excessively radical,"[105] was deemed to have been incorrect.

In short, the majority in *Saguenay* indicated that, while Quebec's Human Rights Tribunal got it right on the scope of the state's duty of religious neutrality, its reasoning and conclusion were inessential and so superfluous to the reasoning and conclusion of the court. Audrey Macklin has discussed in Chapter 11 the historical controversy around whether human rights tribunals should be accorded deference, given the system-wide importance (and constitutional status) of human rights norms. The judgment in *Saguenay* serves as a reminder that even decision-makers with express authority to deal with system-wide norms may be susceptible to correctness review, and so to relegation of their reasoning to inconsequentiality on review. The question is: is this consistent with the purposes of judicial review—or with the proper institutional and constitutional relationships of judges and administrative decision-makers?

---

100   *Ibid* at paras 23, 49.
101   *Ibid* at para 51.
102   *Ibid*.
103   *Ibid* at para 76.
104   *Ibid*.
105   *Ibid* at para 77, citing the Court of Appeal in 2013 QCCA 936 at paras 70, 74.

3. *The Demise of Correctness Review?*

In *Wilson*,[106] Abella J made the bold suggestion that the correctness standard should be retired in favour of a single standard of reasonableness. She advanced two primary rationales in support of this proposal. First, parties and courts continue to spend too much time in disagreement over the standard of review. Second, Abella J suggested, once one grasps the proper nature and function of contemporary reasonableness review, it becomes clear that the correctness standard is redundant, or in any case that it "can live comfortably under a more broadly conceived understanding of reasonableness."[107] That is, reasonableness has become a big tent with "the ability to continue to protect both deference *and* the possibility of a single answer where the rule of law demands it, as in the four categories singled out for correctness review in *Dunsmuir*."[108]

To these arguments, Abella J added the fallback position that if the rest of the court rejected her proposal for a single (reasonableness) standard of review, it should nonetheless refrain from expanding the reach of correctness review beyond the preset categories of question expressly said to attract the standard in *Dunsmuir*.[109]

What difference would a shift to a single standard make? While Abella J suggests that efficiency gains may accrue as there would be no need for argument on which standard to adopt, it is nonetheless likely that similar disputes would surface downstream in the form of efforts to adjust the expectations of reasonableness to the context at hand.[110]

Yet beyond the debatable efficiency gains, adoption of a single standard of (reasonableness) review holds out the possibility of extending the ethos of deference "as respect" (i.e., respectful attention to administrative reasoning and evaluation of administrative decisions against a presumption of reasonableness) to all administrative decisions, including those engaging system-wide norms. Such a shift would convey the expectation that administrative decision-makers function as both capable and responsible participants in the rule-of-law project of public justification. The dangers, however, are twofold. On the one hand, (depending on the care taken reasonableness review to distinguish deference from submission), the approach may weaken fundamental legal protections.[111] On the other hand, the ethos of deference as respectful attention may itself be weakened by intensified incursions of correctness-style reasoning into a more sharply differentiated or "contextualized" reasonableness review. The question is: are there ways of conceiving of or applying big-tent reasonableness that are likely to avoid both these dangers while maintaining the commitment to deference "as respect"?

---

106   *Wilson, supra* note 16.
107   *Ibid* at para 24.
108   *Ibid* at para 31.
109   *Ibid* at para 38.
110   See the discussion in Section III.C of this chapter.
111   See the discussion of *Doré v Barreau du Québec*, 2012 SCC 12, [2012] 1 SCR 395 [*Doré*] in Section III.C of this chapter.

4. Conclusion—Correctness

Examination of how correctness review has been described and applied reveals tensions between a positivist approach to statutory interpretation, which looks to statutory text (or perhaps text in historical context) as a closed system indicative of a determinate legislative intent, and a dynamic, normative approach, which views problems of statutory interpretation in light of shifting, contestable social facts and value-laden purposes. Arguably, the normative approach, taken seriously, begins to erode the idea that courts need not give any weight or respect to the justificatory efforts of tribunals on the matters traditionally reserved for correctness review.

This proposition is further supported by the observation that it may be difficult, if not impossible, ever to achieve a surgical separation of fact and law or policy and law. That is, if it is accepted that questions of law are unlikely ever to be fully disengaged from the factual as well as normative dimensions of interpretation—that is, from judgment calls about the likely effects of a given interpretive decision and the relative importance of the values and interests engaged by alternative interpretations—then it is unclear why the opinions of administrative decision-makers on these matters would ever be relegated to the status of legal irrelevance. That is, if one is prepared to recognize that administrative decision-makers are often likely, empirically speaking, to be uniquely attuned to the sectors in which they carry out their mandates, and, moreover, that they should be expected, normatively speaking, to strive to identify and implement the best ways of carrying out those mandates, then it does not make sense to dismiss administrative reasoning as superfluous to the deliberative work of law interpretation.

The implicit bedrock of correctness review remains the concept of jurisdiction, and the corresponding imperative that administrative decision-makers must not be permitted to exceed their legislatively conferred authority. Further, the correctness standard reflects the rule-of-law concern for stability in legal ordering, and moreover for impartial and even-handed justice, particularly in matters of general legal (including constitutional) significance. For all that, the standard sits uneasily with the democratic and rule-of-law aspiration of integrating the work of administrative tribunals more fully into the constitutional order. For signals that this is an aspiration that is central to the modern law on substantive review, we turn to the now-dominant standard: *Dunsmuir* reasonableness.

III. DUNSMUIR REASONABLENESS

The question at the heart of reasonableness review—indeed, one that has troubled the standard even in its pre-history as review for "patent unreasonableness"—is how the imperative of judicial deference and the expectation that administrative decisions must be reasonably justified may be integrated or reconciled. As described above, this question has driven successive transformations in this area of law over the past three decades, as courts have struggled to strike a principled understanding of the relationship between these imperatives. The question is whether *Dunsmuir*'s unified standard of reasonableness will assist in achieving equilibrium where prior doctrine has not.

A. Dunsmuir Reasonableness in Theory

Having ousted patent unreasonableness from the menu of common law standards of review—on the basis that it lacked practical utility, conceptual coherence, and normative (rule of law-based) justification—the majority in *Dunsmuir* frames its discussion of the two remaining standards with reference to a fundamental tension in the principled foundations of judicial review. The model of judicial review the majority adopts is based on an understanding of constitutional democracy in which the rule of law (conceived in terms of the supervisory role of judges) is in tension with democracy (conceived as parliamentary supremacy).[112] The question is whether this endorsement of the Diceyan idea that democracy threatens the rule of law, and vice versa, is bound to perpetuate the historical pattern of courts veering between these ostensibly competing commitments, or whether, instead, the approach adopted in *Dunsmuir* or the ensuing case law offers a coherent and practicable means of reconciling them.

1. Expectations of Reasonableness: Reasoned Justification

The *Dunsmuir* majority begins its discussion of reasonableness review with the oft-quoted lead-in to the oft-quoted 47th paragraph:

> Reasonableness is a deferential standard animated by the principle that underlies the development of the two previous standards of reasonableness: certain questions that come before administrative tribunals do not lend themselves to one specific, particular result. Instead, they may give rise to a number of possible, reasonable conclusions. Tribunals have a margin of appreciation within the range of acceptable and rational solutions.

Recognition that the questions brought to administrative decision-makers do not necessarily yield a single right answer appears to support the proposition that reviewing courts should not oversee *all* decisions on a standard of correctness. It also invites speculation about which questions do and which do not lend themselves to one right answer. Relatedly, the statement invites speculation, and, potentially, dispute, about whether or how deference will inform the "margin of appreciation within the range of acceptable and rational solutions." Just how, one may ask, will establishing the margin of appreciation be distinguished from the traditional (manipulable, judge-centric) exercise of delimiting administrative "jurisdiction"?

a. Practising Reasonableness Review: Deference as Respect

The passages in *Dunsmuir* offering guidance on the newly unified standard of reasonableness are constructed around the central imperative of judicial deference to administrative reasoning and decisions. More specifically, the majority affirms prior case law endorsing David Dyzenhaus's idea of deference "as respect"—or, to quote more fully from Dyzenhaus's

---

112 *Dunsmuir, supra* note 1 at paras 27-32.

statement on which the majority relies: deference as "not submission but a respectful attention to the reasons offered or which could be offered in support of a decision."[113]

Two key elements of Dyzenhaus's conception of deference as respect ("not submission") have been repeatedly affirmed: (1) reviewing courts must pay close (respectful) attention to the reasoning of administrative decision-makers (deference requires "respect"); and (2) administrative decision-makers must ensure their decisions are reasonably justified in light of the relevant law and facts (deference does not mean "submission").

The first imperative has been confirmed and elaborated in a few key cases. In *Ryan*, Iacobucci J urged judges to "stay close to the reasons" for an administrative decision, while searching for "a line of analysis within the given reasons that could reasonably lead the tribunal from the evidence before it to the conclusion at which it arrived."[114] In *Egg Films Inc v Nova Scotia (Labour Board)*, Fichaud JA elaborated upon this statement:

> Reasonableness isn't the judge's quest for truth with a margin of tolerable error around the judge's ideal outcome. Instead, the judge follows the tribunal's analytical path and decides whether the tribunal's outcome is reasonable. [*Law Society v Ryan* … .] That itinerary requires a "respectful attention" to the tribunal's reasons … .[115]

However, just what is required in order to meet the second imperative—justification—and relatedly, what is meant by deference to reasons that have not been but "could be offered" are questions that continue to attract significant controversy.

b. Expectations Placed on Administrative Decision-Makers: Reasons and Outcomes

The *Dunsmuir* majority devotes a brief discussion to "the qualities that make a decision reasonable, referring both to the process of articulating the reasons and to outcomes."[116] The majority states:

> In judicial review, reasonableness is concerned mostly with the existence of justification, transparency, and intelligibility within the decision-making process. But it is also concerned with whether the decision falls within a range of possible, acceptable outcomes which are defensible in respect of the facts and law.[117]

This passage offers three conceptual touchstones for the assessment of administrative reasoning: "justification, transparency and intelligibility."[118] The first of these terms arguably falls more toward the substantive end of judicial review (even carrying connotations of s 1 of the Charter, and its allowance for limitations on Charter rights where these may be "demonstrably justified in a free and democratic society"). The second two terms are more suggestive of the procedural fairness side of judicial review. Together, these touchstones suggest a coordination of traditional process and substance values in support of reasoned justification.

---

113   *Dunsmuir, supra* note 1 at para 48, citing Dyzenhaus, "The Politics of Deference," *supra* note 23 at 286. The passage is also cited with approval in *Baker, supra* note 19 at para 65.

114   *Ryan, supra* note 46 at paras 49, 55

115   *Egg Films Inc v Nova Scotia (Labour Board)*, 2014 NSCA 33 at para 30.

116   *Dunsmuir, supra* note 1 at para 47.

117   *Ibid.*

118   *Ibid.*

However, the terms are stipulated rather than explained—and have, since *Dunsmuir*, received little to no elaboration.

Also more suggestive than elucidative is the way the statement aligns these three guiding concepts with the "process of reasoning" while apparently consigning the evaluation of administrative conclusions to a distinct analysis of the "possible, acceptable outcomes which are defensible in respect of the facts and the law." On this description, administrative conclusions are isolated from the strength or weakness of administrative reasoning rather than evaluated in light of that reasoning.[119]

Some provincial courts of appeal subsequently interpreted *Dunsmuir*'s statements on reasonableness as mandating a distinct, two-stage inquiry, first into the reasoning process and then into whether the decision falls into the range of reasonable outcomes.[120] But in 2011, Abella J, writing for a unanimous court in *Newfoundland and Labrador Nurses' Union v Newfoundland and Labrador (Treasury Board)*,[121] rejected the suggestion that *Dunsmuir* stood "for the proposition that a reviewing court undertake two discrete analyses—one for reasons and a separate one for the result."[122] Rather, the assessment of reasonableness was said to be "a more organic exercise—the reasons must be read together with the outcome and serve the purpose of showing whether the result falls within a range of possible outcomes."[123]

This is a sensible enough proposition: A reviewing court should inquire into whether the reasons and conclusion are mutually supportive. To this, the court in *Nurses' Union* added that "the 'adequacy' of reasons" is not "a stand-alone basis for quashing a decision."[124] That is, judges on review should not fixate overly upon flaws (including apparent gaps) in reasoning, and should instead assess reasons in light of the wider decision-making context including the relevant law and the supporting evidence and arguments on the record.[125] All this is consistent with deference "as respect." However, in drawing back from the idea that administrative reasoning may serve as an independent basis for invalidation, *Nurses' Union* arguably risks weakening the expectations of reasoned justification articulated in *Dunsmuir*. This occurs through the judgment's emphasis on the imperative (drawn from the well-worn statement on deference from Dyzenhaus) that courts should "supplement" gaps in administrative reasoning.[126] This imperative has been applied in the ensuing case law in a manner that, as

---

119 However, the application of all three criteria to both reasons and outcomes is suggested in the majority judgment in *Canada (Citizenship and Immigration) v Khosa*, 2009 SCC 12, [2009] 1 SCR 339 [*Khosa*] in the statement that "as long as the process and the outcome fit comfortably with the principles of justification, transparency, and intelligibility, it is not open to a reviewing court to substitute its own view of a preferable outcome" (at para 59).

120 See *Casino Nova Scotia v Nova Scotia (Labour Relations Board)*, 2009 NSCA 4, 307 DLR (4th) 99; *Communications, Energy and Paperworkers' Union, Local 1520 v Maritime Paper Products Ltd*, 2009 NSCA 60 278 NSR (2d) 381; *Taub v Investment Dealers Association of Canada*, 2009 ONCA 628, 311 DLR (4th) 389.

121 *Newfoundland and Labrador Nurses' Union v Newfoundland and Labrador (Treasury Board)*, 2011 SCC 62, [2011] 3 SCR 708 [*Nurses' Union*].

122 *Ibid* at para 14.

123 *Ibid*.

124 *Ibid* at para 27.

125 See *Ryan*, *supra* note 46 at para 55. See also *Canadian Broadcasting Corp v Canada (Labour Relations Board)*, [1995] 1 SCR 157 at paras 48-49.

126 *Nurses' Union*, *supra* note 121.

explored in Section III.B, has arguably gone some distance to erode the expectation that administrative decision-makers justify their decisions in light of the relevant law and facts.

c. Conclusion: Dunsmuir Reasonableness in Theory

So far, a few principles of *Dunsmuir* reasonableness are clear. Courts should avoid an approach to judicial review that starts with the court's view of the right answer; instead, they should give respectful attention to administrative reasoning. Moreover, respectful attention is distinct from submission; that is, courts must evaluate administrative decisions and reasons and be prepared to invalidate these where they are unreasonable. But the central question remains: How may courts ensure that their evaluation of administrative decisions and reasons is consistent with deference? What exactly does it mean to give respectful attention (or as one judgment elaborates, "considerable weight"[127]) to those decisions and reasons while maintaining principled expectations of legality?

In what follows, it is argued that the principles from *Dunsmuir* have been extended and applied in the post-*Dunsmuir* case law in ways that conflict with the idea of deference "as respect." That idea, as described earlier, was plucked from a wider theory of constitutional legitimacy (most prominently advanced in the work of David Dyzenhaus), which centres upon the co-participation of all three branches, in interaction with legal subjects, in enacting a "culture of justification." The administrative branch plays a special role in this theory, functioning as a kind of constitutional feedback loop by informing the interpretation and application of law with the diverse interests and views of affected legal subjects. One of the themes in the following section is that the central expectation underpinning the deference owed by judges to administrative reasoning and decisions—namely, that administrative decision-makers *demonstrate* expertise, and so justify their decisions in ways that evince responsiveness to the relevant context including the significant interests of those directly affected—has as yet failed to find adequate traction in the law on reasonableness review.[128] Another related theme is that judges have failed to consistently pay respectful attention to administrative reasoning.

B. Dunsmuir Reasonableness in Practice

While, in theory, *Dunsmuir* reasonableness aims at reconciling the imperatives of justification (identified with the rule of law) with the imperatives of judicial deference (identified with respect for the legislature's intent to confer significant decision-making powers on administrative decision-makers), in practice, review for *Dunsmuir* reasonableness has expressed the same contradictory impulses toward judicial supremacy and judicial abdication that have long marked the law on judicial review.

---

127 See *Southam, supra* note 50 at para 62: "In the final result, the standard of reasonableness simply instructs reviewing courts to accord considerable weight to the views of tribunals about matters with respect to which they have significant expertise."

128 See Walters, "Respecting Deference as Respect," *supra* note 79 at 417.

1. Deference as Supremacy? Disguised Correctness Review

a. Dunsmuir: Judicial Supremacy in Practice?

A number of decisions issued post-*Dunsmuir* that ostensibly adopt a reasonableness standard have proven susceptible to the argument that they are better characterized as examples of "disguised correctness" review.[129] That is, they are said to be marked by a lack of concern for the reasoning of the decision-maker on review, and instead apply a standard of simple concordance with the court's favoured reasoning and conclusion. Two prominent examples of decisions vulnerable to this critique are *Dunsmuir* itself, and *Mowat*.[130]

In Chapter 11, Audrey Macklin discussed the facts of *Dunsmuir*, along with the central question posed in that case. This was whether a labour arbitrator's interpretation of certain statutory provisions governing the employment relationship between public servants and the government of New Brunswick—provisions located primarily in two provincial statutes, the *Civil Service Act*[131] and the *Public Service Labour Relations Act*[132]—was reasonable. Was the Supreme Court's unanimous conclusion that the decision was unreasonable a good example of *Dunsmuir* reasonableness in action?

The arbitrator in *Dunsmuir* determined that the two statutes could be read together so as to give a non-unionized public employee a right to inquire into whether ostensibly no-cause dismissal was in fact dismissal for cause, potentially triggering a greater range of remedies from government than would be available under the common law of employment. According to the Supreme Court, this interpretation was unsupportable. In coming to this conclusion, the majority judgment entered briefly into an analysis of the statutory scheme, focusing primarily on a term of the *Civil Service Act* preserving the common law of contract in the public employment relationship. The majority concluded that to allow a non-unionized employee to go behind no-cause dismissal would disrupt this statutory guarantee of an employment relationship structured in accordance with private law, in the absence of a clear statutory basis.[133]

Despite the *Dunsmuir* majority's stated commitment to deference to administrative decision-makers' field-sensitive interpretations of statutes they encounter on a frequent basis,[134] its application of a reasonableness standard to the arbitrator's decision proceeded quickly

---

129 See Mullan, "The Top Fifteen!," *supra* note 15. And see P Daly, "Dunsmuir's Flaws Exposed: Recent Decisions on the Standard of Review" (2012) 58:2 McGill LJ 483 at 496-501 ["Dunsmuir's Flaws Exposed"]. Arguable "disguised correctness" cases include examples in which correctness-style reasoning ends up in agreement with the decision-maker: *Plourde v Wal-Mart Canada Corp*, 2009 SCC 54; *Agraira v Canada (Public Safety and Emergency Preparedness)*, 2013 SCC 36, [2013] 2 SCR 559 [*Agraira*]; *ATCO Gas and Pipelines Ltd v Alberta (Utilities Commission)*, 2015 SCC 45. In other examples, correctness-style reasoning sets the court's opinion in opposition to that of the decision-maker: beyond *Dunsmuir* and *Mowat* (both discussed below), see *British Columbia (Workers' Compensation Board) v Figliola*, 2011 SCC 52; *Halifax (Regional Municipality) v Canada (Public Works and Government Services)*, 2012 SCC 29, [2012] 2 SCR 108 [*Halifax*]; *John Doe v Ontario (Finance)*, 2014 SCC 36, [2014] 2 SCR 3.

130 *Canada (Canadian Human Rights Commission) v Canada (Attorney General)*, 2011 SCC 53, [2011] 3 SCR 471 [*Mowat*].

131 SNB 1984, c C-5.1.

132 RSNB 1973, c P-25.

133 *Dunsmuir, supra* note 1 at paras 72-76, especially para 74.

134 *Ibid* at para 54.

to the conclusion above. What is most disturbing, according to David Mullan,[135] is that the majority's reasoning is seemingly driven by an automatic or reflexive prioritization of common law values (specifically, freedom of contract) over the competing remedial purposes (securing comparable protections for non-unionized civil servants to those afforded unionized civil servants) that the administrator appears to have privileged in his construction of the statutory regime.

Mullan asks: was the arbitrator's decision properly construed as outside the range of reasonableness?[136] Or did the decision instead fail to pass muster because of its starkly different weighting of the competing norms and interests engaged by this problem of law interpretation than was preferred by the Supreme Court?

Revisited in this manner, it is arguable that in *Dunsmuir* the court failed to adhere to the very expectations for reasonableness review (deference "as respect") it had just set out.

b. Mowat: Displacing Purposive Reasoning in Favour of the "Right Answer"

A second example of a Supreme Court of Canada decision that may be characterized as "disguised correctness review" is *Mowat*.[137] The case originated in a determination by the Canadian Human Rights Tribunal that it could order a respondent to pay the legal costs of a successful complainant. This turned upon interpretation of ss 53(2)(c) and (d) of the *Canadian Human Rights Act*,[138] which granted the tribunal authority to "compensate the victim ... for any expenses incurred by the victim as a result of the discriminatory practice." In support of its interpretation, the tribunal canvased five Federal Court decisions, three of which had held that the sections in question empowered it to award costs and two of which had come to the opposite conclusion. The tribunal went with what was then the "predominance of authority from the Federal Court." More substantively, it adopted from these decisions the proposition that the absence of the term "legal costs" or "costs of counsel" in s 53(2)(c) was not determinative, and that the language of the section in the Act was broad enough to include the power to award costs. According to the tribunal, this conclusion was further supported by policy reasons; indeed, in its opinion, the contrary interpretation would defeat the remedial purposes of the Act.[139]

The unanimous decision of the Supreme Court of Canada on review adopted a reasonableness standard, as interpretation of the compensation clause was "inextricably intertwined with the tribunal's mandate and expertise to make factual findings relating to discrimination." That is, this was "a fact-intensive inquiry" that "afforded the Tribunal a certain margin of discretion."[140] LeBel and Cromwell JJ, for the court, further acknowledged that human rights legislation expresses fundamental values and pursues fundamental goals, and

---

135   "Let's Try Again!," *supra* note 3 at 137-40.
136   *Ibid* at 139.
137   *Supra* note 130. Again, see the discussion in Mullan, "The Top Fifteen!," *supra* note 15; Daly, "Dunsmuir's Flaws Exposed," *supra* note 129 at 496-501.
138   RSC 1985, c H-6.
139   *Mowat, supra* note 130 at paras 22-23.
140   *Ibid* at para 26.

"must therefore be interpreted liberally and purposively so that the rights enunciated are given their full recognition and effect."[141] However, they continued, it was essential to adopt "an interpretation of the text of the statute which respects the words chosen by Parliament."[142]

The judgment of LeBel and Cromwell JJ in *Mowat* then turned briefly to the tribunal's reasoning. In two sentences, the judges noted that the tribunal had relied in part on judicial precedents and in part on policy rationales "relating to access to the human rights adjudication process."[143] However, they stated: "[O]ur view is that these points do not reasonably support the conclusion that the Tribunal may award legal costs." The judges concluded, rather, that there was but one reasonable answer to this interpretive problem, taking account of the statutory text and the legislative–historical context, which together weighed against the purposive reasoning of the tribunal.

First, the judges reasoned, had Parliament intended to allow costs awards as part of compensation for expenses arising from discrimination, it would have included a clause expressly indicating this.[144] The logic flows as follows: typically, authority to award costs is expressly conferred; thus, if the legislature intended a departure from this convention, it would have done so expressly. However, a counterargument is available, rooted in the competing convention of broad, liberal, purposive interpretation of human rights statutes, and the complementary convention that where the legislature intends to circumscribe or limit human rights, it must do so expressly.[145] A second argument raised by LeBel and Cromwell JJ focused on redundancy, as two separate sections of the Act (dealing respectively with employment-related and goods-and-services-related discrimination) referred to compensation for "expenses."[146] Similar counterarguments (based on liberal, purposive interpretations) apply.

Perhaps the strongest argument offered in *Mowat* in support of the determination that there is but one reasonable conclusion to this interpretive problem is based on legislative history. LeBel and Cromwell JJ observe that the *Canadian Human Rights Act*, as originally drafted, included a provision contemplating costs awards to the successful party—but this was removed before the bill became law. This, they suggest, indicates an intention to preclude costs awards. Similarly, a later proposed amendment allowing the tribunal to award costs against the commission failed to be passed into law. And further, at another point, the commission itself recommended that the Act be reformed to give the tribunal the express power to award costs—and this recommendation, too, failed to be acted upon. However, none of these proposals was specifically focused on costs awards against respondents, or, therefore, on promotion of the interests of complainants. Moreover, failure of a recommended reform to become law does not settle the interpretive question, as the recommended reform may be understood to simply make explicit what was already implicit.

---

141 *Ibid*, citing R Sullivan, *Sullivan on the Construction of Statutes*, 5th ed (Markham, Ont: LexisNexis, 2008) at 497-500.

142 *Mowat, supra* note 130 at 497-500.

143 *Ibid*.

144 The discussion of *Mowat* in this section draws significantly on a note on the judgment written by Denise Réaume (on file with author). My thanks to Professor Réaume for sharing her work and permitting me to cite it here.

145 See *Canada (Attorney General) v Mossop*, [1993] 1 SCR 554, L'Heureux-Dubé J, in dissent.

146 *Mowat, supra* note 130 at para 37.

A related argument accepted by the judges was that because the statute confers power on the commission to take carriage of complaints before the tribunal "in the public interest," interpretation of the Act should reflect a presumption that the commission will fulfill that function. Yet the Act does not require this of the commission; it confers a discretion. Denise Réaume comments:

> In *Mowat*, the government, as respondent, argues that because Parliament intended that the Commission is supposed to play an active role (which it can't do because government, as government, doesn't provide sufficient funds), the Act should be read not to permit damage awards to be levied against respondents, mainly the government, that include legal fees. How does that honour the parliamentary intent behind the anticipated active role of the Commission?[147]

These counterarguments challenge the Supreme Court's conclusion that the tribunal's interpretation was unreasonable. As Réaume observes: "To uphold the Tribunal's decision, one does not need to show that it is right, or even better, just that it's reasonable."[148] Recent judgments of the Supreme Court have been clear in stating that there may in some cases be just one reasonable answer to an interpretive problem—a claim that has been specifically illustrated through reference to *Mowat*. And yet it is not at all clear that the reviewing court in *Mowat* accorded the kind of respectful attention or presumptive weight that is demanded on review for reasonableness. Rather, the judgment de-centres the tribunal's decision and reasoning in favour of a detailed accounting of controversial textual and contextual considerations. As a result, the judgment arguably not only fails to produce an indisputably right answer, it produces an unreasonable answer, one that defeats the human rights-promoting purposes of the Act.

2. Deference as Abdication?

If one extreme of the post-*Dunsmuir* case law on reasonableness review has taken the form of disguised correctness, the other flirts with judicial abdication.

a. Review of Implicit Administrative Reasoning

i. Nurses' Union: Deference or Abdication?

The Supreme Court judgment in *Nurses' Union*[149] was noted above for the principle that reasonableness review is an organic exercise in which "the reasons must be read together with the outcome and serve the purpose of showing whether the result falls within a range of possible outcomes."[150] This and other principles stated in the judgment were directed at how a court should proceed where it is alleged that administrative reasoning is fatally flawed. The allegation may be that the decision-maker has failed to address an issue potentially determinative of the outcome, or has otherwise failed to lay down a clear reasoning path from the relevant evidence or law to the conclusions reached. The guidance provided by Abella J for the court (and the application of this guidance in subsequent cases) aims to advance the

---

147 Réaume, *supra* note 144 at 3.
148 *Ibid.*
149 *Supra* note 121.
150 *Ibid* at para 14.

cause of deference. However, the principles stated, which converge on the imperative that courts must attempt to "supplement" obscure or conspicuously absent administrative reasoning before arriving at a conclusion of unreasonableness, have spawned questions about whether the post-*Dunsmuir* case law has gone too far in downplaying the responsibility of courts on review to discipline failures on the part of administration to adhere to conventions of reasoned justification.

Writing on behalf of the court in *Nurses' Union*, Abella J first addressed whether allegations of incomplete or inadequate reasons should be decided through an inquiry into substantive reasonableness, or alternatively, an inquiry into whether the duty to provide reasons was met as a matter of procedural fairness. Abella J concluded that the question of whether any (as opposed to no) reasons have been given should be decided on procedural fairness grounds (i.e., the law on the duty to give reasons). But where questions arise about "the *quality*" of reasons, this is a matter for substantive review. This alleviates the prospect of inefficient doubling of efforts to address sufficiency of reasons on both procedural and substantive grounds. It also ensures that the imperatives of deference will not be subverted by review of tribunal reasoning under the head of procedural fairness, where the standard applied has conventionally been understood to be correctness.[151]

However, the approach gives rise to new questions. First, there will inevitably be borderline cases in which there is uncertainty about whether the appropriate allegation is that no reasons were given, or that the reasons, while given, are of very poor or overly perfunctory quality. For instance, what if the decision-writer simply states: "I have considered the evidence and arguments, and conclude that the application must fail"? Or what if reasons are given on some issues but not others? There is law suggesting that the right approach in such cases (or some subset of these) is to select reasonableness review.[152] A second question arises where the quality of reasons is indeed determined to be in issue, and reasonableness review is applied. What limits should the reviewing court place on deference to reasons that are incomplete, or difficult to follow, or that otherwise fail to fully or clearly support the conclusion reached? As we will see, this is the central question raised in the wake of *Nurses' Union*.

Nurses' Union arose out of a grievance decision challenged by the union on the basis that the arbitrator had failed to clearly articulate the reasoning path from certain agreed-upon statements of fact and law to the conclusion reached. The chambers judge agreed that the arbitrator had failed to directly address or resolve the central interpretive issue in dispute. In contrast, Abella J, writing for the Supreme Court, concurred with the Court of Appeal that "'a more comprehensive explanation' would have been preferable,"[153] and affirmed that the decision was reasonable. According to Abella J, the reasoning could be discerned, when the passages in question were read in light of the background information the arbitrator had supplied (for instance, the relevant terms of the collective agreement and applicable interpretive principles), along with "a plain reading of the agreement itself."[154]

---

151 See *Nurses' Union*, *supra* note 121 at para 21. And see Alice Woolley, "The Continued Complexity of Administrative Law Post-Dunsmuir" (14 December 2010), *ABlawg: The University of Calgary Faculty of Law Blog*, online: <http://ablawg.ca/wp-content/uploads/2010/12/blog_aw_mitzel_dec2010.pdf>.

152 See *Agraira*, *supra* note 129.

153 *Nurses' Union*, *supra* note 121 at para 9.

154 *Ibid* at para 7.

Was this deference, or abdication? Importantly, Abella J in *Nurses' Union* gave particular attention both to efficiency concerns and to what the parties affected by the decision would have likely understood to be the basis for the decision. She stated: "[Labour arbitrators] are not writing for the courts, they are writing for the parties who have to live together for the duration of the agreement. Though not always easily realizable, the goal is to be as expeditious as possible."[155]

Thus, Abella J suggested that the chambers judge had focused overly myopically on a few passages in the written reasons, rather than asking whether the basis for the decision would have been apparent to the parties, viewed in light of the wider legal, institutional, and factual context, and the arguments on which the parties had relied.

Abella J uses this occasion to state some general principles on reading administrative reasons in context. She first affirms that reasons must, in order to meet the bar of reasonableness, "allow the reviewing court to understand why the tribunal made its decision and permit it to determine whether the conclusion is within the range of acceptable outcomes."[156] However, "[p]erfection is not the standard."[157] Here Abella J draws on the now-authoritative statement from David Dyzenhaus on deference as respect, which indicates that the requisite respect must be directed at "the reasons offered *or which could be offered* in support of a decision."[158] To this is appended an expectation (again rooted in Dyzenhaus's 1997 statement)[159] that "[a] court must first seek to *supplement* [administrative reasons] before it seeks to subvert them."[160] Abella J elaborates: "This means that courts *should not substitute their own reasons*, but they may, if they find it necessary, look to the record for the purpose of assessing the reasonableness of the outcome."[161]

More generally, Abella J adds, a reviewing court may (or, if no reasonable basis for the decision is otherwise apparent, should) situate the decision-maker's conclusions in "the context of the evidence, the parties' submissions and the process."[162] Thus, it is not simply reasons and conclusions that are to be read together on the organic approach to reasonableness review promoted in *Nurses' Union*, but reasons, conclusions, and other contextual information available from the record (and perhaps other contextual sources).

In sum, *Nurses' Union* affirms that reasons (read in context) must explain why the decision-maker arrived at its conclusion, and affirms, moreover, that courts must refrain from substituting their reasoning for that required of decision-makers. However, the judgment—specifically, its emphasis on the duty of reviewing courts to supplement facially inadequate administrative reasons—lays the groundwork for an approach to reasonableness review that marginalizes (and potentially even renders obsolete) the expectation that decision-makers give reasons that meet the criteria of "justification, transparency, and intelligibility." Precisely this marginalizing effect may be discerned in the subsequent case law. However, to understand

---

155 *Ibid* at para 23.
156 *Ibid* at para 16.
157 *Ibid* at para 18, citing Evans JA in *Public Service Alliance of Canada v Canada Post Corporation*, 2010 FCA 56, [2011] 2 FCR 221.
158 *Ibid* at para 12 (emphasis added), citing Dyzenhaus, "The Politics of Deference" *supra* note 23.
159 Dyzenhaus made this statement (on deference to reasons that "could be offered") prior to the Supreme Court of Canada's endorsement of a common law duty to give reasons.
160 *Nurses' Union, supra* note 121 at para 12, citing Dyzenhaus, "The Politics of Deference," *supra* note 23.
161 *Nurses' Union, supra* note 121 at para 15 (emphasis added).
162 *Ibid* at para 44.

these developments, one must also be apprised of the closely related yet distinct principles stated in *Alberta (Information and Privacy Commissioner) v Alberta Teachers' Association*.[163]

ii.   Deference to Implicit Decisions

The judgment of Rothstein J for the majority in *ATA*,[164] released the day before *Nurses' Union*, offers a more delimited pronouncement on the sort of case in which judges may speculate on the reasons that "could be offered" in support of an administrative decision. At the same time, the judgment expands the set of supplementary sources that may be drawn upon by reviewing courts faced with an absence of or alleged gaps in tribunal reasoning.

The decision in issue in *ATA* involved interpretation of a section of Alberta's *Personal Information Protection Act* stating that an inquiry must be completed within 90 days unless the commissioner gives notice of an extension of time. The commissioner had not given notice until months after the 90-day period had expired. No arguments were raised concerning the commissioner's power to extend time in this fashion; however, such an argument was raised on review.

Thus, *ATA* presented a situation in which a question (here, involving law interpretation) that was potentially of determinative importance to the outcome of a wider administrative decision-making process was implicitly decided, but was not expressly addressed in reasons. Critically, the situation was moreover one in which the party raising the issue on review had failed to alert the decision-maker that the question was in dispute, and so failed to put the decision-maker on notice about the importance of taking account of the arguments on both sides, and of giving reasons on point.

In such cases, the reviewing judge has discretion concerning whether to deal with the issue.[165] Indeed, Rothstein J indicates that ordinarily, the judge should refuse to deal with such after-the-fact challenges,[166] for three reasons: (1) deference to the expertise of the tribunal, which should have an opportunity to address such matters in the first instance; (2) the potential for prejudice to other parties, who will not have had the opportunity to put relevant evidence or argument on the record; and (3) the related prospect that the matter raised on review will lack a sufficient evidentiary foundation.[167] Accompanying these rationales is disapproval of those who sleep on their rights, whether strategically or out of sheer lassitude or both.

However, Rothstein J recognized that exceptions may be made to the general principle of refusing to hear such challenges (raised for the first time on review). These exceptions arise where (1) there are alternative ways of ascertaining the decision-maker's reasoning on point, and (2) there is no prejudicial effect to other parties (e.g., where the issue is a "straightforward determination of law," not requiring a detailed evidentiary record).[168] In *ATA*, Rothstein J determined that the interpretive issue raised was indeed a straightforward question of law, and moreover that there was an adequate alternative way of ascertaining

---

163   *Supra* note 5.
164   *Ibid.*
165   *Ibid* at paras 22-28.
166   *Ibid* at para 23.
167   *Ibid* at paras 24-26.
168   *Ibid* at paras 26-28.

the decision-maker's reasoning. Specifically, the court was supplied with past decisions of the commissioner and "his delegated adjudicators," dealing with the same interpretive question as it arose under the provision in issue and a similarly worded provision.[169] Rothstein J stated: "[I]n the circumstances here, it is safe to assume that the numerous and consistent reasons in these decisions would have been the reasons of the adjudicator in this case."[170] Those decisions "easily" established "that a reasonable basis exists for the adjudicator's implied decision."[171]

Justice Rothstein further emphasized that adverting to the reasons that "could be offered" in such cases must not collapse into submission to defective reasoning, or substitution of judicial for (again, defective) administrative reasoning.[172] The question in *ATA* was rather how to deal with *absent* reasoning. Rothstein J acknowledged that "deference under the reasonableness standard is best given effect when administrative decision-makers provide intelligible and transparent justification for their decisions, and when courts ground their review of the decision in the reasons provided."[173] But, he added, "[w]hen there is no duty to give reasons ... or when only limited reasons are required, it is entirely appropriate for courts to consider the reasons that could be offered for the decision when conducting a reasonableness review."[174] In *ATA*, only "limited reasons [were] required," it seems, specifically because of the failure of the applicant to raise the question before the decision-maker. One key issue emerging out of *ATA* is what other situations may give rise to the conclusion that only "limited reasons are required."

Rothstein J further indicates that where the exceptional conditions are met for review of an implied decision (on a question not argued before the decision-maker), the first question is whether "a reasonable basis for the decision is apparent to the reviewing court." If a reasonable basis is apparent—even if it is not certain that this would be the reasoning path of the decision-maker—reasonableness should generally be affirmed on that basis. For, Rothstein J adds, remitting for reasons may "undermine the goal of expedient and cost-efficient decision making."[175] However, where no such reasonable basis is apparent, it is more consistent with deference to remit the question to the decision-maker for reasons on the point in issue than to quash the decision and require a full redetermination.[176]

In sum, *ATA* addresses a situation in which administrative reasoning is not merely flawed, as in *Nurses' Union*, but rather is wholly absent in support of a decision (or subdecision) of potentially determinative relevance. The situation addressed is moreover one in which the applicant could have, but did not, make arguments on point to the administrative decision-maker. *ATA* responds with two important principles on the review of what it calls implicit decisions: one, on when such decisions may be heard despite a failure to raise the matter before the decision-maker, and the other, on the sources that may stand

---

169   *Ibid* at para 56.
170   *Ibid*.
171   *Ibid*.
172   *Ibid* at para 54. See also *Khosa, supra* note 119 at para 63.
173   *ATA, supra* note 4 at para 54.
174   *Ibid*.
175   *Ibid* at para 55.
176   *Ibid*.

in for or supplement the missing reasoning. These principles seek to rationalize review of implicit decisions in a manner that neither subverts deference nor abdicates the responsibilities of legal oversight. However, following the 2011 decisions in *ATA* and *Nurses' Union*, the cracks have begun to show in judicial efforts to express both deference and expectations of public justification in the review of implicit (or absent) decisions and reasons.

iii. Cracks in the Foundations: McLean, Agraira, and Tran

Briefly, three further decisions suggest that the principles out of *Nurses' Union* and *ATA* are susceptible to application in ways that are in tension with the duty of administrative decision-makers to publicly justify their decisions.

The dispute that gave rise to the 2013 Supreme Court judgment in *McLean v British Columbia (Securities Commission)*,[177] involved a fight about interpretation of a provision of the BC *Securities Act* stating a limitation period applicable to "secondary proceedings"—that is, proceedings commenced by the commission against persons who had entered into settlement agreements with securities regulators in other jurisdictions. The question was whether the limitation period stated in the Act was triggered by the misconduct giving rise to the proceedings or, alternatively, the individual's entry into such a settlement agreement. In contrast to the situation in *ATA*, arguments on the interpretive question raised on review had been put to the commission (indeed, these were the only arguments made by McLean at that stage). Therefore, the principles from *ATA* on when a court should exercise its discretion to refuse review of an implicit decision were not in issue. Rather, the question was whether the decision of the commission to commence secondary proceedings despite the arguments made—and with no express reasons given on point—should be upheld as reasonable.

Given that, as noted, the applicant in *McLean* had made arguments to the commission that the proceedings were time barred and received no reasons on point, there appears to have been justification for the court to quash the decision or remit for reasons.[178] However, the majority determined that the decision was reasonable (as did the concurrence of Karakatsanis J). This was informed in significant part by the interpretive reasoning advanced by the respondent executive director of the commission. Moldaver J commented:

> Unlike *Alberta Teachers*, in the case at bar, we do not have the benefit of the Commission's reasoning from its decisions in other cases involving the same issue (see paras 56-57). However, a basis for the Commission's interpretation is apparent from the arguments advanced by the respondent, who is also empowered to make orders under (and thus to interpret) s 161(1) and (6). These arguments follow from established principles of statutory interpretation. Accordingly,

---

177   *Supra* note 47.

178   The Court of Appeal (2011 BCCA 455) had dismissed McLean's argument that the secondary proceedings in BC were time barred. In contrast, that court concluded that the question of whether BC's order against McLean was in the public interest (a question that McLean had not argued before the commission) should be remitted to the commission for a "brief explanation" (at para 31).

though reasons would have been preferable, there is nothing to be gained here from requiring the Commission to explain on remand what is readily apparent now.[179]

Moldaver J here omits the distinguishing fact that McLean *had* made arguments on point to the commission. However, efficiency considerations appear to win out over the expectation that decision-makers give (reasonable) reasons for their decisions. There is "nothing to be gained" by remitting the question to the decision-maker for reasons, as it is anticipated that those reasons would simply mirror the arguments of the executive director on review. Yet it is important to note that the majority in *McLean* determined that *both* the interpretation advanced by the respondent and the contradictory interpretation advanced by McLean were "reasonable." That is, there was apparently room for policy choices in this interpretive field. Moreover, the decision was not the executive director's to make. Finally, what is missing from the statement above is consideration of the principle that agency representatives should not be permitted to shoehorn (or "bootstrap") after-the-fact reasons through arguments on review in this fashion. It is a practice that erodes the duty to give reasons.[180] In short, the approach taken to the review of implicit reasons in *McLean* arguably undermines the expectation from *Dunsmuir* that administrative reasoning be expressive of justification, transparency, and intelligibility.

A second example of post-*Dunsmuir* application of the law on implicit reasons and decisions is the 2013 Supreme Court of Canada decision in *Agraira v Canada (Public Safety and Emergency Preparedness)*.[181] This case involved a review of a ministerial decision under s 34(2) of *Immigration and Refugee Protection Act*,[182] which provides that "a permanent resident or a foreign national who satisfies the Minister that their presence in Canada would not be detrimental to the national interest"[183] may be treated as admissible, despite engagement of one or more grounds of inadmissibility. The minister rejected Agraira's application under s 34(2) on grounds that the Supreme Court characterized as resting primarily or exclusively on national security and public safety. The focus of review became the minister's implied interpretation of the term "national interest." While the minister had given no express reasons on this interpretive issue, and there were no prior ministerial decisions on point, LeBel J, writing for the court, read the minister's reasons in light of the applicable guidelines and drew the highly speculative conclusion that,

> had the Minister expressly provided a definition of the term "national interest" in support of his decision on the merits, it would have been one which related predominantly to national security and public safety, but did not exclude the other important considerations outlined in the Guidelines or any analogous considerations.[184]

---

179 *McLean, supra* note 47 at para 72.

180 On the general condemnation of tribunal "bootstrapping" of reasons for decision—along with a canvassing of the rationales for granting standing to administrative decision-makers in certain circumstances—see *Ontario (Energy Board) v Ontario Power Generation Inc*, 2015 SCC 44, [2015] 2 SCR 147. For further criticism of *McLean* along these lines, see Daly, "Scope and Meaning of Reasonableness Review," *supra* note 9 at 817-18.

181 *Supra* note 129.

182 SC 2001, c 27

183 *Supra* note 129 at para 42.

184 *Ibid* at para 62.

In this way, LeBel J imputed to the minister an interpretation that accorded with the judge's own appraisal of the text, legislative history, "evident purpose," and statutory/soft law context.

As Paul Daly has observed, among the many surprising things about *Agraira* is that the interpretation imputed to the minister is contrary to that which the minister argued on review was the proper, or reasonable, interpretation.[185] That is, the court rejected the interpretation advanced by the minister in favour of an interpretation it first stipulated to have been the minister's and then relied upon to affirm the decision's reasonableness.

The line of case law on review of implicit decisions and reasoning in which *McLean* and *Agraira* participate puts reviewing courts in a difficult position when faced with decisions that lack express supporting interpretations of the relevant law. Consider the 2015 Federal Court of Appeal decision in *Canada (Public Safety and Emergency Preparedness) v Tran*,[186] heard on appeal at the Supreme Court of Canada in December of 2016 and discussed by Audrey Macklin in Chapter 11. In *Tran*, an officer with the Canadian Border Services Agency had refused to engage with key interpretive questions raised by the applicant (including questions involving the relevance of Charter values to the interpretive problem) on the basis that he lacked competence to address questions of law. Based in part on the officer's reasoning (and without further interpretive analysis), a ministerial delegate referred Tran's case to an admissibility hearing. Gauthier JA, who upheld the decision of the minister's delegate, commented on the difficulties presented to reviewing judges by the state of the law on deference to implicit reasons:

> In cases, like this, where it is not evident that only one interpretation is defensible, it is quite difficult to do what the Supreme Court of Canada mandates us to do given the number of interpretative presumptions and principles that can be considered and applied. Some further guidance would certainly be welcomed in that respect, especially when the relative weight to be given to competing presumptions and interpretative tools has never been clearly dealt with by the Supreme Court of Canada.[187]

Daly argues that in a situation like *Tran*, the appropriate response must be to remit the matter to the decision-maker to squarely address the statutory and/or Charter arguments.[188] More generally, where the reasoning of a decision-maker is not clear to the reviewing court (and not likely to be clear to the parties) despite attentiveness to the evidence and argument on the record, the principles out of both *Nurses' Union* and *ATA* indicate that the court should remit the matter to the decision-maker for reasons—short of compelling counterarguments like those entertained in *ATA* (where no arguments were made on point in the first instance).[189] This would be most consistent with "deference as respect." However, the examples above suggest a turn in the substantive review jurisprudence toward deference as abdication—or, rather, a concerning

---

185 See Daly, "Scope and Meaning of Reasonableness Review," *supra* note 9 at 817-18.

186 2015 FCA 237, [2015] 2 FCR 459 [*Tran*]. The judgment of the Supreme Court of Canada in *Tran* was issued just as this chapter was going to press: 2017 SCC 50. Côté J for the court determines that "on either standard of review" the "assumed interpretation" of the minister's delegate could not be sustained. The court does not address the concerns about implicit reasons raised by Gauthier JA.

187 *Tran, supra* note 186 at para 46.

188 See Paul Daly, "A Snapshot of What's Wrong with Canadian Administrative Law: MPSEP v Tran, 2015 FCA 237" (13 November 2015), *Administrative Law Matters,* online: <http://www.administrativelawmatters.com/blog/2015/11/13/a-snapshot-of-whats-wrong-with-canadian-administrative-law-mpsep-v-tran-2015-fca-237>.

189 See Paul A Warchuk, "The Role of Administrative Reasons in Judicial Review: Adequacy and Reasonableness" (2016) 29 CJALP 87.

confluence of abdication and supremacy, as judges absolve decision-makers of expectations of public justification while at the same time filling the void with their own reasoning on review.

3. The Rule Against Revisiting the Weight Accorded Factors of Legal Relevance

A more controversial claim regarding judicial abdication centres on reasonableness review of discretion: specifically, the principle that judges should not revisit the weight that administrative decision-makers place on the factors of legal relevance to discretion.[190] The question is: *should* judicial reassessment of the importance of factors relevant to discretion (including the significant interests of those affected by discretionary action) be discouraged as contrary to deference, or is this sort of evaluation required by a defensible conception of reasonableness?

The rule against revisiting the weight placed on factors of relevance sits uneasily with another line of case law, in which unreasonableness takes the form of unreasonable "failure *to consider*" a factor of legal relevance (an analysis ostensibly putting aside contestable questions of weight). The tension arises because it is not uncommon for the "failure to consider" analysis to be impugned, by commentators or dissenting judges, as a disguised reassessment of the weight or relative importance of the considerations said to have been (expressly and/or implicitly) ignored.[191]

The tension between the rule against revisiting the weight placed on factors relevant to discretion and the law on "failure to consider" came to a head in *Baker*—a case you have already encountered in this text. In *Baker*, the decision of an immigration officer to deny Mavis Baker humanitarian and compassionate grounds-based relief from imminent deportation was deemed unreasonable for "failure to give serious weight and consideration"[192] to the best interests of Baker's children. This ruling was presented as consistent with deference—understood (in accordance with Dyzenhaus's phraseology) as requiring respectful attention, but not submission, to the reasons offered or that could be offered for the exercise of ministerial discretion.[193] At the same time, the ruling was based on the expectation that discretion be exercised consistent with "the values underlying the grant of discretion."[194]

In elaborating on what it means to defer to discretionary decisions, L'Heureux-Dubé J indicated that judges "may give substantial leeway to the discretionary decision-maker in determining the 'proper purposes' or 'relevant considerations' involved in making a given determination."[195] This extends the parameters of deference to discretion beyond the traditional Diceyan division of labour, whereby judges were understood to have exclusive responsibility for identifying the legal limits on discretion (i.e., the considerations of mandatory legal relevance) while administrative decision-makers were given free rein within those limits. Attentiveness to the views of the decision-maker on the factors of mandatory relevance is

---

190   See e.g. *Southam, supra* note 50 at para 43, and the cases discussed below.
191   See e.g. the majority and dissenting reasons in *CUPE v Ontario (Minister of Labour)*, 2003 SCC 29.
192   *Baker, supra* note 19 at para 65.
193   *Ibid.*
194   *Ibid.* The legal and factual background to the case, along with a more complete analysis, is provided by Geneviève Cartier in Chapter 11 of the second edition of this textbook, Administrative Discretion: Between Exercising Power and Conducting Dialogue, online: <www.emond.ca/adminlaw3e>.
195   *Baker, supra* note 19 at para 56.

exhibited in *Baker* through the special attentiveness given to ministerial guidelines—although the attention paid to those guidelines is as demanding as it is (respectfully) attentive.

In elaborating on where or how the "values underlying the grant of discretion" may be discerned, L'Heureux-Dubé J lists a formidable array of sources: the decision-maker's enabling legislation and associated regulations, instruments of soft law such as departmental policies and guidelines, the common law ("the principles of administrative law"), the Constitution ("the principles of the rule of law" and "the principles of the *Charter*"), international law, and the "fundamental values of Canadian society."[196] This list of sources of legal limits on discretion has arguably been under-interpreted and under-applied in the years since *Baker*—although, as we will see, the spirit behind it has been revived in some measure (in controversial and partial fashion) in *Doré*.[197]

The values relevant to the grant of discretion exercised in *Baker* were inferred from the statute, an international convention ratified but not incorporated into domestic legislation, and the applicable ministerial guidelines. Together, held L'Heureux-Dubé J, these sources established that "the rights, interests, and needs of children and special attention to childhood are important values that should be considered in reasonably interpreting the 'humanitarian' and 'compassionate' considerations that guide the exercise of the discretion."[198] Contrary to this principle, the officer's notes failed to reflect that the decision-maker was "alive, attentive, or sensitive to the interests of Ms. Baker's children," and moreover established that he "did not consider [those interests] an important factor in making the decision."[199] Therefore, the decision failed to meet the standard of reasonableness *simpliciter*. Notably, L'Heureux-Dubé J added that "the reasons for decision failed to give sufficient weight or consideration to the hardship that a return to Jamaica might cause Ms Baker, given the fact that she had been in Canada for 12 years, was ill and might not be able to obtain treatment in Jamaica, and would necessarily be separated from at least some of her children."[200] That is, failure of the decision-maker to accord appropriate weight to Mavis Baker's lack of sociological attachment to Jamaica, her disability, and her interest in maintaining her relationship with her children constituted independent bases for deeming the exercise of discretion unreasonable. These considerations, however, are not typically brought out in the case law and commentary on *Baker*, which has tended to focus on failure to consider the best interests of the child.[201]

The judgment in *Baker* was followed by uncertainty in the case law and commentary as to whether this marked a radical departure from the reigning principles on review of

---

196 *Ibid* at paras 56, 67.

197 *Supra* note 111.

198 *Baker, supra* note 19 at para 73.

199 *Ibid*.

200 *Ibid* at para 73.

201 As Pless and Fox-Decent explain in Chapter 6, the Supreme Court expressly opted to deal with Baker's claim on administrative law bases rather than the Charter, despite the fact that Charter arguments had been raised by Mavis Baker and various interveners. Alyssa Clutterbuck argues that the judicial preferencing of administrative law analysis in *Baker* functioned to construct the claim as one of individualized arbitrariness—that is, a decision-making anomaly on the part of a single officer—thereby obscuring the structural violence of immigration norms that, as a matter of course, exclude applicants on intersecting bases of disability, poverty, race, and gender. See Alyssa Clutterbuck, "Rethinking Baker: A Critical Race Feminist Theory of Disability" (2015) 20 Appeal 51.

discretion, or this was just an unusual application of those principles. In *Suresh v Canada (Minister of Citizenship and Immigration)*,[202] the court responded by stating that *Baker* "does not authorize courts reviewing decisions on the discretionary end of the spectrum to engage in a new weighing process." Rather, the majority in *Baker* had drawn "on an established line of cases concerning the failure of ministerial delegates to consider and weigh implied limitations or patently relevant factors."[203] The court in *Suresh* added:

> To the extent this Court reviewed the Minister's discretion in that case, its decision was based on the ministerial delegate's failure to comply with self-imposed ministerial guidelines, as reflected in the objectives of the Act, international treaty obligations and, most importantly, a set of published instructions to immigration officers.[204]

That is, the problem with the decision on review in *Baker* (according to the court in *Suresh*) was the decision-maker's *failure to consider* the best interests of the child, rather than a failure to accord that factor sufficient weight. Or if an element of weight was involved, this reflected the unusual nature of the consideration in issue: one that arguably carried inherent "elements of weight or degree"[205] and, moreover (apparently most important to the court in *Suresh*), one that was, after all, self-imposed (by way of "published instructions" to immigration officers).

In *Canada (Citizenship and Immigration) v Khosa*,[206] a majority of the court again confirmed the traditional prohibition. *Khosa* was a judicial review of a decision of the Immigration and Refugee Board (Immigration Appeal Division) to deny Sukhvir Singh Khosa's application for humanitarian and compassionate relief from deportation following completion of his sentence for criminal negligence causing death. The majority wrote: "The weight to be given the respondent's evidence of remorse and his prospects for rehabilitation [factors of mandatory relevance under the applicable legal test] depended on an assessment of his evidence in light of all the circumstances of the case."[207] This assessment was to be left to the tribunal.

In dissent, Fish J argued that the tribunal had placed irrational or inordinate weight on one consideration (Khosa's failure to admit that he had been street racing), which, Fish J argued, had caused it to ignore the importance of other legally relevant considerations that favoured granting the application.[208] Despite these strong objections, the traditional prohibition was held to apply: the majority refrained from second-guessing the tribunal's

---

202 2002 SCC 1, [2002] 1 SCR 3 [*Suresh*].

203 *Ibid* at para 37.

204 *Ibid* at para 36.

205 See David Mullan, "Deference from Baker to Suresh and Beyond—Interpreting the Conflicting Signals" in David Dyzenhaus, ed, *The Unity of Public Law* (Portland, OR: Hart Publishing, 2004) 21 at 31-37.

206 *Supra* note 119 at para 61, Binnie J for the majority: "I do not believe that it is the function of the reviewing court to reweigh the evidence." And see para 64: "It seems evident that this is the sort of factual dispute which should be resolved by the IAD in the application of immigration policy, and not reweighed in the courts."

207 *Ibid* at para 66.

208 *Ibid* at para 159, Fish J: "To be sure, the majority at the IAD stated that even if it were to have found that Mr Khosa did not present a risk to the public 'in balancing all the relevant factors, I determine the scale does not tip in [Mr Khosa's] favour and decline to exercise favourable discretion' (para. 23). This sort of conclusory statement, however, cannot insulate the IAD's decision from review when the rest of its reasons demonstrate that its decision rests on an unreasonable determination of central importance, as in this case."

assessment of the relative weight of the various considerations of legal relevance to the tribunal's decision.

The question raised by the dissent of Fish J in *Khosa*, and raised more generally under this line of case law, is whether the prohibition on revisiting the weight or importance placed on factors of relevance to discretion fits with the importance placed on justification in *Dunsmuir*—or, more broadly, in a political and legal order committed to a "culture of justification."

The tension is further illustrated by the 2015 judgment in *Kanthasamy v Canada (Citizenship and Immigration)*.[209] There, the decision on review again involved a humanitarian and compassionate grounds-based exemption under the *Immigration and Refugee Protection Act*.[210] The statutory grant of discretion (reformed since *Baker*) now expressly required that the decision-maker take "into account the best interests of a child directly affected." The applicant in *Kanthasamy* was a 17-year old Tamil from Sri Lanka who had come to Canada out of fear for his safety, following his arrest and questioning by Sri Lankan authorities. He had been unsuccessful in establishing a refugee claim, and again at the stage of pre-removal risk assessment. In his humanitarian and compassionate grounds application, he sought an exemption from the ordinary requirement to apply for permanent residency from outside Canada.

An immigration officer rejected the application. In this she expressly relied on factors set out in guidelines developed to assist in interpreting the Act[211]—in particular, a section stating that humanitarian and compassionate grounds decisions require applicants to demonstrate either "unusual and undeserved" or "disproportionate" hardship.[212]

A majority of the Supreme Court of Canada held that the officer had unreasonably applied the guidelines as if they imposed "three new thresholds for relief," rather than being merely "descriptive" of the types of hardship qualifying for relief. The officer's fixation on these terms had diminished her "ability to consider and give weight to all relevant humanitarian and compassionate considerations in [the] particular case."[213] In particular, the officer had "failed to give sufficiently serious consideration to [the applicant's] youth, his mental health, and the evidence that he would suffer discrimination if he were returned to Sri Lanka."[214] All this supported the majority's conclusion that the decision was unreasonable, and in particular that it had failed to meet the requirement under s 25(1) of taking into account the best interests of a child directly affected.

---

209 *Supra* note 20.

210 The section provides:

> 25. (1) The Minister must, on request of a foreign national in Canada who is inadmissible or who does not meet the requirements of this Act, and may, on request of a foreign national outside Canada, examine the circumstances concerning the foreign national and may grant the foreign national permanent resident status or an exemption from any applicable criteria or obligations of this Act if the Minister is of the opinion that *it is justified by humanitarian and compassionate considerations relating to the foreign national, taking into account the best interests of a child directly affected*. [Emphasis added.]

211 *Guidelines on International Protection No 8: Child Asylum Claims under Articles 1(A)2 and 1(F) of the 1951 Convention and/or 1967 Protocol relating to the Status of Refugees*, HCR/GIP/09/08, 22 December 2009.

212 *Ibid*, s 5.10. See also s 5.11, cited in *Kanthasamy, supra* note 20 at para 27.

213 *Kanthasamy, supra* note 20 at para 33.

214 *Ibid* at para 45.

The dissent in *Kanthasamy* argued that the majority had failed to accord the officer's decision the requisite deference.[215] According to the dissent, the majority "parse[d] the Officer's decision for legal errors, resolve[d] ambiguities against the officer, and reweigh[ed] the evidence." The dissent added:

> Lest we be accused of adopting a "do as we say, not what we do" approach to reasonableness review, this approach fails to heed the admonition in *Newfoundland and Labrador Nurses*—that reviewing courts must be cautious about substituting their own view of the proper outcome by designating certain omissions in the reasons to be fatal (para 17). As is the case with every other court, this Court has no licence to find an officer's decision unreasonable simply because it considers the result unpalatable and would itself have come to a different result.[216]

Kanthasamy raises important questions. Is the majority judgment a good example of "deference as respect"? Or is it disguised correctness? The difficulty one may have in answering this arguably reflects the instability in the law on reasonableness review concerning whether courts should revisit the weight placed by decision-makers on factors of legal relevance. The Diceyan approach classes the attribution of weight or importance as a function of policy, not law. But is that approach coherent with the purposes or ambitions of reasonableness review, as the dominant tool in administrative law for ensuring that the exercise of public power is justified?

Two recent judgments of appellate and lower courts have attempted in different ways to walk the line between *Baker*'s insistence that administrative decision-makers exercising discretion take account of fundamental legal values and the caution stated in *Suresh* and *Khosa* that reviewing courts not revisit the weight accorded considerations of legal relevance to discretion. They also walk the line between constitutional and administrative law. That is, one employs "failure to consider a relevant factor" to support a determination of unreasonableness, while the other employs a variant of the "failure to consider" analysis (given specific expression in the law on the obligations of government in its relations with Indigenous Peoples) to support a determination of unconstitutionality.

The first case is *Kainaiwa/Blood Tribe v Alberta (Energy)*,[217] a decision of the Alberta Court of Queen's Bench. This was a judicial review of a ministerial refusal to transfer to the Kainaiwa/Blood Tribe Band subsurface rights to lands the band had previously acquired through a settlement with the Crown, pursuant to the Specific Claims process. Justice Jeffrey held that the Crown was under no legal duty to transfer the subsurface rights; moreover, given the absence of express statutory limits on the minister's discretion and the hands-off approach of the courts to rights in property, the discretion was deemed so broad as to be "almost unfettered."[218] Yet the decision was nonetheless invalidated as unreasonable.

---

215 *Ibid* at para 111.

216 *Ibid* at para 112. The dissent adds, in response to the conclusion of the majority that the officer fettered her discretion by overly meticulously focusing on the considerations set out in the guidelines:

> [H]ad the Officer *failed* to discuss each factor individually, and instead simply listed the facts and stated her conclusion on the evidence as a whole, this appeal might well have been before us on the basis of insufficient reasons [at para 114].

217 2017 ABQB 107 [*Kainaiwa*]. I thank Janna Promislow for bringing this decision to my attention. Nigel Bankes provides a useful summary and reflections in his blog post "Reasons, Respect and Reconciliation" (3 March 2017), *ABlawg: The University of Calgary Faculty of Law Blog*, online: <https://ablawg.ca/2017/03/03/reasons-respect-and-reconciliation/>.

218 *Kainaiwa, supra* note 217 at paras 109, 130.

That determination was based in part on the minister's failure to give intelligible and transparent reasons (express or implicit) for the decision.[219] The minister's position had been inconsistent over time, and the communications on the record failed to evince a rational connection between the reasons given and the outcome.[220] Moreover, while failure to meet the duty to give reasons had not been argued as a basis for quashing the decision on procedural fairness grounds, the duty to give reasons in a manner and form expressive of *respect* was suggested by the judge to have been heightened by the special context of this decision, which engaged the constitutional principle of the honour of the Crown.[221] That is, this principle had the effect of informing and so enhancing the expectations of reasonableness— intelligibility, transparency, justifiction—applied to the minister's decision. That said, the reasons that could be ascertained from the record were deemed to be so flawed as to dash even low expectations.

The determination of unreasonableness in *Kainaiwa* also rested more specifically—in what was arguably the boldest element of the judgment—on the minister's *failure to consider* the constitutionally mandated objective of reconciliation between Aboriginal peoples and the Crown.[222] More specifically, the minister failed to consider "the importance his decision might play in promoting the process of reconciliation with the Band."[223] Just how the objective of reconciliation should be weighed against competing considerations was a matter that, according to the judge, fell within the minister's discretion; thus, the judge remitted the matter to the minister for redetermination.[224] But the narrowness of the range of reasonable options (even the potential that that range might include expectations of proportionality)

---

219 *Ibid* at paras 115, 122-25, 128, 131. It seems the band did not argue that the honour of the Crown supported a duty to give reasons or more specifically that failure to do so in this case was a breach of procedural fairness.

220 *Ibid* at para 128.

221 *Ibid* at para 117:

> Even though the honour of the Crown does not require that the Minister grant the Band's request, it does extend to the nature and manner of the Minister's communications with the Band. Communicating reasons to the Band is a sign of respect. Providing reasons displays the requisite comity and courtesy becoming the Crown as Sovereign toward a prior occupying nation. Providing reasons is also important for a decision holding such significance to the Band as does this one. Of course there are also here the more common benefits from proper reasons, of revealing to the losing party whether they were properly understood, of the losing party learning why their thinking was not persuasive, and of enabling the losing party to consider whether to challenge the decision by legal process.

The statements of Jeffrey J on the importance of reason-giving where the Crown makes decisions affecting First Nations is affirmed in the recent decision of the Supreme Court of Canada in *Chippewas of the Thames First Nation v Enbridge Pipelines Inc*, 2017 SCC 41 at para 62.

222 *Kainaiwa, supra* note 217 at para 129:

> Opportunities to advance and promote this "process of reconciliation" warrant attention and consideration with that in mind. It is constitutionally mandated by Section 35 of the Constitution Act, 1982: *Taku River Tlingit First Nation v British Columbia (Project Assessment Director)*, 2004 SCC 74 at para 24. At paragraph 42 of that decision the Court states:
>
> > The purpose of s. 35(1) of the Constitution Act, 1982 is to facilitate the ultimate reconciliation of prior Aboriginal occupation with *de facto* Crown sovereignty.

223 *Supra* note 217 at para 130: "His considering that possibility might not have changed the outcome, but it was a mandatory consideration given the circumstances presented."

224 *Ibid* at paras 130, 133.

was suggested by the judge's observation that transfer of the subsurface rights would have "at most [a] nominal adverse impact" on the province's interests.

In keeping with this volume's case study on pipelines, consider the additional example of the Federal Court of Appeal's decision in *Gitxaala Nation v Canada*.[225] This was a judicial review of a decision of the federal governor in council (by way of order in council) to approve the Northern Gateway Pipeline project.[226] That decision marked the final stage of a complex, multi-phased process of consultation and deliberation informed, *inter alia*, by constitutional obligations to affected Indigenous groups. The process had included oral hearings convened by a joint review panel acting under authority of the *Canadian Environmental Assessment Act* and the *National Energy Board Act*, submission of a report and recommendations from the joint review panel to the governor in council, and ultimately the decision of the governor in council on whether to accept the recommendations. The application for judicial review rested on a number of bases, including failure of the Crown to meet its constitutional obligations to consult and accommodate Indigenous communities, and alleged unreasonableness of the governor in council's decision.

In dealing with the common law administrative law issue of unreasonableness, the majority focused on the polycentric nature of the decision. It observed: "[T]he Governor in Council's discretionary decision was based on the widest considerations of policy and public interest assessed on the basis of polycentric, subjective or indistinct criteria and shaped by its view of economics, cultural considerations, environmental considerations, and the broader public interest."[227] Thus, the majority concluded that a "very broad margin of appreciation"[228] was due. Correspondingly, after devoting much of its judgment to the complex multi-staged processes through which the proposed project was evaluated, the majority dealt with the decision's reasonableness in remarkably light-touch fashion: in two brief paragraphs that in the main pointed back to the preceding discussion of the scope and complexity of the project approval process, thus reinforcing the rationales for deference (or, for refraining from closely scrutinizing the governor in council's reasoning or the joint review report on which it relied).[229]

However, the majority dealt quite differently with the arguments that government had breached its constitutionally grounded responsibilities. Here, "failure to consider" was determinative. More properly there were two main bases for invalidation. On the one hand, government officials had failed to satisfy their constitutionally mandated duty to consult, specifically during the final phase of the process.[230] On the other hand, the governor in council's reasons (even when read in light of the joint review panel's report and the record of communications from Canadian officials) had failed to address the core question of whether the Crown's duty to consult had been fulfilled. In these circumstances—where the rights and interests of affected Indigenous communities were significant enough to require a duty of "deep consultation"—reasons responsive to those communities' affected rights

---

225 *Supra* note 21 leave to appeal to the SCC refused (21 September 2016), File 37201.
226 Subsequently, the government under Justin Trudeau withdrew Cabinet support in November of 2016.
227 *Gitxaala, supra* note 21 at para 154.
228 *Ibid* at para 152. On contextual analysis of the "margin of appreciation" or "range of reasonable outcomes," see Section III.C, below.
229 *Ibid* at paras 156-57.
230 *Ibid* at para 279.

and interests and to their concerns about the consultation process were constitutionally required. That duty was enhanced, rather than diminished, by the polycentric nature of the decision; that is, "where, as in this case, the Crown must balance multiple interests, a safeguard requiring the Crown to set out the impacts of Aboriginal concerns on decision-making becomes more important. In the absence of this safeguard, other issues may overshadow or displace the issue of the impacts on Aboriginal rights."[231]

Both *Kainaiwa* and *Gitxaala* thus reflect special, constitutionally grounded expectations imposed on the Crown in its relationship with Indigenous Peoples.[232] Yet in *Kainaiwa*, the constitutional obligation of the Crown to advance reconciliation is integrated into an administrative law analysis of the minister's broad ("almost unfettered") discretionary powers, such that failure to consider this constitutionally mandated objective takes on special normative force, even as the reviewing court leaves the common law prohibition against revisiting the importance or weight of factors relevant to discretion formally undisturbed. In *Gitxaala*, the discretion of the governor in council is, for the purpose of common law administrative law, so broad as to be *de facto* unfettered; unlike the situation in *Kainaiwa*, the analysis of reasonableness is not informed or delimited by constitutional values or objectives. Accordingly, that analysis refrains from overt scrutiny of the reasoning offered or whether it justifies the conclusion. Yet on switching gears to constitutional obligations, the expectations placed on the governor in council's reasoning, both express and implicit, are comparatively robust.

Is it appropriate that expectations of public justification are bifurcated across constitutional and administrative law in the manner illustrated in *Gitxaala*? Is it better or worse for constitutionally mandated norms[233] to expect that they be integrated into common law administrative law reasoning? This question goes to the implications of the *Baker* judgment or its core principle that discretion must be exercised in accordance with "the values underlying the grant of discretion." How should this principle inform strategies of argumentation and justification in administrative law—or the relationship between administrative and constitutional law?

C. Dunsmuir Reasonableness in Context

So far, this chapter's discussion of the theory and practice of reasonableness review has focused mostly on the frequency with which theory and practice diverge. This final section inquires into recent and evolving developments in the case law and commentary that reflect efforts to give more structure, predictability, and coherence to reasonableness review. The first development builds on the idea that reasonableness takes its "colour from context" by using contextual analysis to inform the "range of reasonable outcomes." The second

---

231 *Ibid* at para 315. See further Chapter 3 by Janna Promislow and Naiomi Metallic in this text.

232 Another important recent example is *Twins v Canada (Attorney General)*, 2016 FC 537, [2017] 1 FCR 79 [*Twins*]. There, Southcott J overturned a decision of the Parole Board of Canada revoking an Indigenous woman's parole on the basis that the board failed to take into account principles derived from *R v Gladue* [1999] 1 SCR 688. Those principles require consideration of the effects of colonialism and systemic discrimination in producing the overrepresentation of Indigenous Peoples in Canada's prisons and jails, and consideration of how alternatives to incarceration may be promoted in the case at hand.

233 It is also worth carefully considering the proposition that the *constitutional* expectations placed on reason-giving in *Gitxaala* (and the related case law) are unduly informed by the minimalist common law expectation that fundamental rights and values must simply be "considered."

(related) development, formally endorsed by the Supreme Court but attracting increasing critical scrutiny in the case law and commentary, contextualizes reasonableness specifically by imposing an expectation of proportionality where discretion engages Charter values. The third development, reflected in case law at the Federal Court of Appeal and in academic commentary,[234] seeks to add a dash more formalism to reasonableness review by articulating discrete indicia or markers of unreasonableness, in order to guide and in some respects standardize the analysis.

1. Assessing the "Range of Possible, Acceptable Outcomes Which Are Defensible in Respect of the Facts and Law"

A subject of growing controversy in the post-*Dunsmuir* case law is what should be expected of courts by way of contextual analysis in order to set the expectations of reasonableness for the decision at hand. In what sense (if any) are courts supposed to operationalize the idea that reasonableness "takes its colour from context,"[235] or that each decision carries a variable, context-sensitive "range of reasonable outcomes" marking off acceptable from unacceptable decisions? Should these and other statements be taken to support a dedicated pragmatic and functional-type inquiry at the outset of reasonableness review? And is there a danger that an analysis of this sort may conflict with the imperative of deference (as respect)?

a. Degrees of Deference, Scope of Authority: What's the Difference?

Binnie J, in his concurring reasons in *Dunsmuir*, suggested that adoption of a single standard of reasonableness would require context-sensitive adjustment of the level of deference appropriate to the specific decision on review.[236] He added that the considerations likely to be of relevance would include those that had informed the pragmatic and functional analysis for selecting the standard of review. To these, Binnie J added the significance of the interests affected (not historically entertained among the pragmatic and functional factors), which in certain circumstances, he said, should attract an expectation of "proportionality."[237]

Binnie J's position in this regard was rejected in the majority reasons of Rothstein J in *ATA*. Rothstein J wrote:

> Once it is determined that a review is to be conducted on a reasonableness standard, there is no second assessment of how intensely the review is to be conducted. The judicial review is simply concerned with the question at issue. A review of a question of statutory interpretation is different from a review of the exercise of discretion. Each will be governed by the context. But there is no determination of the intensity of the review with some reviews closer to a correctness review and others not.[238]

---

234 See the sources in note 15 (particularly the work of Stratas JA and Paul Daly). See also *Canada (Minister of Transport, Infrastructure and Communities) v Farwaha*, 2014 FCA 56, [2015] 2 FCR 1006 at para 100 [*Farwaha*]; and *Workplace Health, Safety and Compensation Commission v Allen*, 2014 NLCA 42 at para 67.

235 *Khosa, supra* note 119.

236 *Dunsmuir, supra* note 1 at para 139.

237 *Ibid* at para 151, Binnie J. And see L Sossin & CM Flood, "The Contextual Turn: Iacobucci's Legacy and the Standard of Review in Administrative Law" (2007) 57 UTLJ 581 at 596.

238 *ATA, supra* note 5 at para 47.

Rothstein J's rejection of the idea of degrees of deference reaches back to the dual thesis of conceptual incoherence and practical unworkability relied upon by the *Dunsmuir* majority in rejecting two separate reasonableness standards. In short, if it was not possible to distinguish between patent unreasonableness and reasonableness review without sending courts on fruitless quests to adjust for the allowable "depth of probing" or "magnitude of error," then further attempts to fine-tune deference into infinite degrees are likely to be of little use—and worse, may distract courts from the central work of explaining why the decision on review is or is not reasonable.[239]

Rothstein J's comments were recently echoed in the judgments of Abella and Cromwell JJ in *Wilson*.[240] Their disapproval of the idea of variable degrees of deference was provoked by the observation of Stratas JA in the Court of Appeal decision below that the statutory interpretation problem in issue had involved "relatively little specialized labour insight beyond the means the courts have at hand," such that, were a reasonableness standard to be applied, it would afford "only a narrow margin of appreciation."[241] The disapproving comments of Abella and Cromwell JJ appear to be informed at least in part by the worry that judicial reappraisal of such factors as relative expertise subsequent to settling on reasonableness review will undercut the commitment to deference.

Yet Abella J simultaneously gave strong support, in *Wilson*, to the notion that reasonableness review does and should include context-sensitive evaluation of the range of reasonable outcomes supportable on the law and facts. Indeed that proposition (which, after all, was endorsed in *Dunsmuir*) was at the heart of Abella J's proposal in *Wilson* to retire the correctness standard. As explored earlier, that proposal was grounded in the idea that the expectations of reasonableness may be adjusted to reflect the legitimate scope of the decision-maker's authority in any particular case—and, in some cases, will admit of only one reasonable interpretation or outcome.

Even if we accept, for the sake of argument, that contextualization of reasonableness review aims at illuminating the scope of authority and not adjusting the degree of deference (setting aside the question of whether this is a meaningful distinction), questions remain. For one: what considerations or contextual factors are relevant to the analysis of the "range"? And second: in what sense, if any, is this analysis to reflect the imperative of deference "as respect"?

b. What Context? And Whither Deference?

The statements above from members of the Supreme Court in rejecting the idea of degrees of deference suggest that contextual assessment of the range or scope of authority is to be guided primarily or perhaps exclusively by the nature of the question—its classification as law, discretion, fact-finding, or application of law to fact. However, as explored below, there is also Supreme Court precedent supportive of the proposition that other contextual factors, relating, for instance, to relative institutional capacities as well as (at least in the case of Charter-protected interests or "Charter values") the significance of the interest at stake, may play an important role in informing the expectations of reasonableness appropriate to the

---

239 *Ryan, supra* note 46 at para 46.
240 *Supra* note 16.
241 *Wilson v Atomic Energy of Canada Ltd*, 2015 FCA 17 at para 58, Stratas JA.

case at hand. The Federal Court of Appeal has gone the farthest to formalize the contextual factors informing the range of reasonableness (or margin of appreciation), taking account of the significance of the interest at stake (including non-Charter-protected interests such as the interest in employment) as well as relative expertise, in addition to the nature of the question, in order to orient the court to the breadth or narrowness of acceptable or justified approaches to the decision on review.[242] Given the support of a powerful four-judge dissent in *Edmonton (City) v Edmonton East (Capilano) Shopping Centres Ltd*[243] for recognizing the full set of pragmatic and functional factors as relevant to contextualizing reasonableness review, this is a debate that one should continue to watch.

c. Discretion and the Range of Reasonable Outcomes: Catalyst Paper

Where a decision is classed as *discretionary*, it appears that analysis of the contextual factors or signals informing the range of reasonable outcomes should take account of factors that are not (or not as obviously) engaged where the question is classed as law or law interpretation—where (as noted below) the range appears to be set through application of the "ordinary" tools of statutory interpretation.[244] (Of course, this turns on a bright-line distinction between law and discretion, which, as suggested earlier, is under increasing attack in and beyond administrative law.)

A key Supreme Court precedent illustrating contextualized reasonableness review of discretion is *Catalyst Paper Corp v North Cowichan (District)*.[245] This case involved review of a municipal by-law that imposed a markedly higher rate of property tax on industrial ratepayers in comparison with residents. McLachlin CJ, writing for the court, affirmed that a review for reasonableness "must be assessed in the context of the particular type of decision making involved and all relevant factors," and is therefore "an essentially contextual inquiry."[246]

---

242 See *Farwaha, supra* note 234.

243 2016 SCC 47, [2016] 2 SCR 293. The four-judge dissent wrote at para 89:

> [C]ontext does not cease to be relevant once the standard of review is selected. Even if the applicable standard of review were reasonableness, it is a contextual analysis—guided by the principles of legislative supremacy and the rule of law—that defines the range of reasonable outcomes in any given case .... In short, "context simply cannot be eliminated from judicial review."

> The dissent relies heavily (as have other courts on this point) on the work of Paul Daly, specifically "Struggling Towards Coherence," *supra* note 15. See also the contribution of Jonathan M Coady on this issue: "The Time Has Come: Standard of Review in Canadian Administrative Law" (2017) 68 UNBLJ 79 especially at 104-5 (suggesting that the contextual factors giving content to a single standard of (reasonableness) review should address: (1) "[t]he nature of the decision-maker"; (2) the nature of the question; (3) "[t]he content of the statutory scheme" (including statutory purposes as well as existence of a private clause or right of appeal); and (4) relative expertise. Just how, and why, institutional considerations like relative expertise should inform substantive expectations of reasoned justification is a question that requires further attention in the Canadian case law and commentary.

244 The phrase is from Moldaver J in *McLean, supra* note 49, and is used to describe the approach to be taken to assessing the range of reasonable outcomes where the question centres upon statutory interpretation.

245 2012 SCC 2, [2012] 1 SCR 5 [*Catalyst Paper*].

246 *Ibid* at para 18.

To this she added: "The fundamental question is the scope of decision-making power conferred on the decision-maker by the governing legislation."[247]

The contextual factors that came together to inform recognition of a broad "range of reasonable outcomes"[248] (and permissible considerations)[249] in *Catalyst Paper* included:

1. the nature of the decision (an exercise of discretionary authority lacking express statutory constraints, indeed described as "virtually unfettered");[250]
2. the statutory purpose or function of the decision-maker (characterized as "legislative" and as allowing for consideration of "an array of social, economic, political and other non-legal considerations"); and
3. the municipality's democratic legitimacy or more specifically electoral accountability.[251]

These contextual considerations informed the approach taken by the court to the process as well as the substance of the municipality's decision. On process, McLachlin CJ observed that municipal by-law-making need not be supported by formal reasons; rather, reasons may be reconstructed through attention to the record of municipal debates and any ensuing policy statements.[252] On substance, the chief justice articulated a sub-species of reasonableness review that drew expressly on the English judgment *Associated Provincial Picture Houses, Ltd v Wednesbury Corp*,[253] and its highly forgiving concept of "Wednesbury unreasonableness."[254] In *Wednesbury*, Lord Greene stated that the decision of a public authority on a matter within its competence should be upheld unless it is "so unreasonable that no reasonable authority could ever have come to it"—demonstration of which, he further indicated, "would require something overwhelming."[255] Following this approach, McLachlin CJ stated (modifying the test slightly, in light of "the wide variety of factors that elected municipal councillors may legitimately consider in enacting bylaws"):[256] "The applicable test is this: only if the by-law is one no reasonable body informed by these factors could have taken will the by-law be set aside."[257] Thus, the expectations of reasonableness are adjusted to reflect the particular nature (and institutional context) of this highly political, quasi-legislative decision.

---

247 *Ibid* at para 18.
248 *Ibid* at para 25.
249 *Ibid* at paras 17, 19.
250 *Ibid* at para 26.
251 *Ibid* at para 19.
252 *Ibid* at para 28.
253 [1948] 1 KB 223 (CA) [*Wednesbury*].
254 For contrasting accounts of the nature and cogency of (variegated) *Wednesbury* analysis, compare Paul Daly, "Wednesbury's Reason and Structure" (2011) Pub L 238 with Andrew Le Sueur, "The Rise and Ruin of Unreasonableness?" (2005) 10 Jud Rev 32 at 32-33. Daly follows in the tradition of Jowell and the other editors of De Smith's *Judicial Review*, 7th ed (London: Sweet & Maxwell, 2013) in identifying implicit structuring principles or forms of unreasonableness in *Wednesbury* unreasonableness. In contrast, Le Sueur states the major criticisms of and proposals for common law reform of *Wednesbury* unreasonableness. Dyzenhaus subjects the judgment of Lord Greene to critique of a form similar to that raised to patent unreasonableness review in *Dunsmuir* in "Formalism's Hollow Victory," *supra* note 38 at 542-48.
255 *Wednesbury*, *supra* note 253 at 230, Lord Greene.
256 *Catalyst Paper*, *supra* note 245 at para 24.
257 *Ibid*.

McLachlin CJ was quick to add that the discretionary power of municipalities to make by-laws is not wholly untrammelled. Indeed, she built in further traditional common law parameters, drawing now on the nominate grounds of review for abuse of discretion:

> If, for instance, [by-laws] were found to be partial and unequal in their operation as between different classes; if they were manifestly unjust; if they disclosed bad faith; if they involved such oppressive or gratuitous interference with the rights of those subject to them as could find no justification in the minds of reasonable men, the court might well say, "Parliament never intended to give authority to make such rules; they are unreasonable and ultra vires."[258]

If it was surprising to unearth *Wednesbury* unreasonableness to inform review of municipal by-law-making in *Catalyst Paper*, it is perhaps even more surprising to reprise the nominate grounds from English law, traditionally applied without concern for deference.

Yet for all its casting lines back to old English precedents, the judgment in *Catalyst Paper* is arguably a good example of deference "as respect." First, it confirms that there are always legal limits on the decision-making powers of statutory decision-makers—regardless of whether those decision-makers are democratically accountable, or their decisions are deemed policy-rich.[259] Second, it carefully and respectfully explores the rationales for the decision (reconstructed from the municipal debates), and, in accordance with the relatively recent principle that courts should show deference to a discretionary decision-maker's opinions on what considerations are relevant,[260] confirms the relevance of the array of social, economic, and political considerations that the municipality identified as critically important. Finally, rather than moving to correct the property tax differential on the basis of intuitive perceptions of injustice, or disproportionality, the judgment affirmed the distributive justice rationale relied on by the municipality: its concern to ensure that long-time residents on fixed incomes were not forced out of their homes by steeply rising property taxes. It took account, as well, of the municipality's efforts to gradually reduce the burdens placed on the industrial class.[261] These elements of deferential reasoning are arguably informed by the earlier contextual analysis through which the court was apprised of the municipality's legitimate role and function.

d. Law Interpretation and the Range of Reasonable Outcomes: Return of the Jurisdictional Zombie?

If *Catalyst Paper* approaches analysis of the range of reasonable outcomes in a manner that aims to be fit for discretion (or, more specifically, for municipal by-law-making), Moldaver J in *McLean*[262] articulates an approach that aims to be fit for law, or law interpretation. The

---

258   *Kruse v Johnson* (1898), 2 QB 91 at 99-100 (Div Ct), Lord Russell CJ, cited in *Catalyst Paper, supra* note 245 at para 21 (emphasis in original).

259   The judgment in *Catalyst Paper* importantly rejects the principle from *Thorne's Hardware Ltd v The Queen*, [1983] 1 SCR 106 at 115 that matters of municipal policy-making are not subject to judicial review. *Catalyst Paper, supra* note 245 at paras 14-15.

260   See *Baker, supra* note 19 at para 56. And see *Canada (National Revenue) v JP Morgan Asset Management (Canada) Inc*, 2013 FCA 250 at para 74 [*JP Morgan*].

261   So perhaps there is an analysis of proportionality in the background, after all. I would argue that the decision centres upon this principle—and exemplifies its context-sensitive and deferential application. This is supported by McLachlin CJ's affirmation of the nominate grounds from *Kruse v Johnson*.

262   *Supra* note 49.

question is whether the approach advanced moves beyond the old habits of shuttling between supremacy and abdication.

Moldaver J, writing for the majority in *McLean*, devotes his judgment in part to offering general guidance on analysis of the "range of reasonable outcomes" in cases involving law interpretation. He frames these statements by recalling from *Dunsmuir* the possibility that some interpretive problems engaged by administrative decisions may admit of multiple reasonable interpretations. However, he takes pains to convey that instances in which multiple interpretations are supportable in law are rare (statute law, he says, "will on occasion be susceptible to multiple *reasonable* interpretations"[263]). Against this background, Moldaver J states:

> Where the ordinary tools of statutory interpretation lead to a single reasonable interpretation and the administrative decision-maker adopts a different interpretation, its interpretation will necessarily be unreasonable—no degree of deference can justify its acceptance .... In those cases, the "range of reasonable outcomes" ... will necessarily be limited to a single reasonable interpretation—and the administrative decision-maker must adopt it.[264]

On this approach, the "ordinary tools of statutory interpretation" are what circumscribe the range of reasonable outcomes; no other contextual factors are in view. Moldaver J cites *Mowat* as exemplary of the form of analysis he has in mind.[265] As we have seen, in *Mowat*, the process of narrowing the range of reasonable outcomes to just one was effected primarily, if not exclusively, though statutory interpretation principles and strategies.[266] However, what was not apparent in the court's approach was adherence to the imperative of deference. That is, the court made little to no discernible effort to supplement the tribunal's framework of reasoning, or to entertain counterarguments to the court's preferred reasoning—or otherwise to position the decision in its best light.

As Paul Daly has suggested,[267] the approach to questions of law interpretation counselled by Moldaver J in *McLean* arguably marks the introduction into Canadian law of the approach adopted in the US in *Chevron USA Ltd v Natural Resources Defence Council Inc.*[268] Under that doctrine, courts reviewing an administrative interpretation of law must first determine whether a disputed statutory provision is or is not ambiguous (i.e., whether there are two or more "plausible" interpretations). Only if ambiguity is established do they move on to adopt the posture of deference, specifically by asking whether the administrative interpretation falls among the plausible options. This approach to deference, that is, first ascertaining whether there is one "right answer" and then moving to a posture of deference

---

263   *Ibid* at para 32 (emphasis on "reasonable" in original, emphasis on "on occasion" added).

264   *Ibid* at para 38.

265   *Ibid*.

266   See *Mowat, supra* note 130 at para 34. The use of statutory interpretation principles to identify the existence of just one reasonable interpretation was also in play in *Wilson v British Columbia (Superintendent of Motor Vehicles)*, 2015 SCC 47, [2015] 3 SCR 300—although in a manner that confirmed the interpretation taken by the decision-maker.

267   Paul Daly, "Deference and Reasonablenes" (23 March 2013), *Administrative Law Matters* online: <http://administrativelawmatters.blogspot.ca/2013/03/deference-and-reasonableness.html>. See also Daly, "Scope and Meaning of Reasonableness Review," *supra* note 9 at 824-25.

268   467 US 837 at 842-43 (1984).

only if there is not, is similar in key respects to the position of Sopinka J in *Paccar,*[269] an approach widely condemned in the case law and commentary as overly judge-centric.

Yet while the approach to setting the range of reasonable outcomes counselled in *McLean* veers on the one hand toward judicial supremacy, it arguably also veers on the other toward judicial abdication. Specifically, Moldaver J indicates that where the framing analysis of the range of reasonable outcomes suggests that there is *more than one* plausible interpretation—that is, that more than one interpretation has "*some* support in the text, context, and purpose of the statute"[270]—and the tribunal's interpretation is among those, then deference requires that the court simply affirm the decision's reasonableness: the tribunal wins by default. What the court should not do is inquire into whether the interpretation favoured by the tribunal (or some competing interpretation) was the best.[271] This reflects the concern, pervasive in judicial review and especially in substantive review, to ensure that courts do not bump aside the field-sensitive interpretations of democratically mandated administrative decision-makers in favour of their own policy preferences. The question is whether the baseline criterion of merely having "some support" in the statutory text, context, and purposes is sufficient to govern the evaluation of reasonableness. For instance, is an interpretation that fails to reflect Charter values or values at international law (and yet meets the baseline requirement of "plausibility") "as reasonable" as an interpretation that accords with those values? Here it is worth recalling that one of the dominant principles of statutory interpretation states that statutory ambiguity (and so baseline "plausibility") is to be assessed without reference to Charter values or the values reflected in international human rights law.[272]

Further concerns arise where competing interpretations (recognized as reasonable on a minimalist assessment of interpretive plausibility) produce contradictory conclusions and result in differential treatment of similarly situated individuals. For instance, in *Tran,*[273] (which, as discussed above, involved review of a decision to refer Tran's case to an admissibility hearing on grounds of "serious criminality"), one of the interpretive questions was whether the phrase "a term of imprisonment"[274] included a conditional sentence (i.e., a sentence with no jail time). Was it appropriate—or concordant with a defensible understanding of reasonableness review—that the Federal Court of Appeal deemed the officer's (implicit)[275] interpretation, whereby Tran's 12-month conditional sentence did so

---

269 *Supra* note 45. (And see the discussion above.)

270 *McLean, supra* note 47 at para 39.

271 See *ibid* at paras 38-41.

272 See *Bell ExpressVu, supra* note 63 at para 62; *Gitxaala Nation v Canada*, 2015 FCA 73 at para 17 ("As a practical matter, this canon of construction [the principle that interpretation should be consistent with Canada's obligations at international law] is seldom applied because most legislative provisions do not suffer from ambiguity and, thus, 'must be followed even if they are contrary to international law': *Daniels v White*, [1968] SCR 517 at 541, 2 DLR (3d) 1.") For critical commentary on the requisite determination of "ambiguity" prior to informing interpretation with wider legal and constitutional values (including those at international law), see Sullivan, "Statutory Interpretation in Canada," *supra* note 60 at 119-21.

273 *Supra* note 186.

274 Per s 36(1)(a) of the IRPA.

275 On the separate difficulties raised by *Tran* in connection with review of implicit decisions, see Section III.B.2.

qualify, *as reasonable as* the alternative interpretation argued by Tran?[276] Or would it be more appropriate in such a case for the court to weigh in—in light of Charter values, say—on the *best* interpretation?

In *McLean*, the competing interpretations before the court also produced inconsistent conclusions. The statutory limitation period for commencing secondary proceedings was triggered either by the underlying misconduct, or by the person's entering into a settlement agreement with another provincial securities commission. The majority recognized that the commission's approach (using the settlement agreement as the baseline) clearly advanced the statutory purpose of interprovincial cooperation of securities regulators. It added that the appellant's competing approach, while not clearly "inconsistent with" this purpose, was less clearly supportive of it. Karakatsanis J, in her concurrence, disagreed: she argued that the appellant's approach was inconsistent with the statutory purpose and so was unreasonable. She added that the majority's legitimizing both interpretations had produced a result that was itself counterproductive to the fundamental statutory purpose of interjurisdictional cooperation. That is, the majority's conclusion served to exacerbate the uncertainty and so lack of coordination around when secondary proceedings may be launched.

It is important to note that the Supreme Court has repeatedly rejected arguments for the imposition of correctness review on the basis of alleged inconsistency among administrative decisions.[277] The concern is that this would fundamentally undercut deference.[278] That is, it would allow judges to sidestep deference by finding inconsistency or threatened inconsistency under every interpretive dispute. Moreover, it would undercut the institutional objective of ensuring that administrative decision-makers have "flexibility to adjust to new arguments and circumstances"[279]—indeed, in some settings, to adjust to the shifting policy objectives of the governments of the day.

Notably, however, recent developments in the appellate case law have been more circumspect about inconsistency among administrative decisions. These judgments advance the principle that the presence of "directly conflicting"[280] tribunal precedents may *narrow the range of reasonable outcomes*. That is, in such circumstances, the courts will inquire into "whether both interpretations can reasonably stand together under the principles of

---

276 *Tran, supra* note 186 at para 87: "In the circumstances, considering the current teachings of the Supreme Court of Canada and although there may clearly be other defensible interpretations, I cannot conclude that the interpretation adopted by the Minister's delegate in this case is unreasonable. Obviously the deference granted to administrative decision-makers is in part meant to give them flexibility to adjust to new arguments and circumstances." On the response of the Supreme Court of Canada, see *supra* note 189.

277 *Domtar, supra* note 93; *Wilson, supra* note 16.

278 *Domtar, supra* note 93. The court in *Domtar* also makes the important observation that "internal mechanisms developed by administrative tribunals to ensure the consistency of their own decisions" may be employed as an alternative to judges' having the last word. However, as pointed out by the dissents in *Wilson, supra* note 16 at para 82, and in *Edmonton (City) v Edmonton East (Capilano) Shopping Centres Ltd, supra* note 243 at para 80, this is not a possibility in all administrative decision-making regimes. For further discussion, see Paul Daly's blog, "Threats to Stare Decisis: The Consistency Problem" (19 May 2015), *Administrative Law Matters*, online: <http://www.administrativelawmatters.com/blog/2015/05/19/threats-to-stare-decisis-the-consistency-problem/>.

279 *Tran, supra* note 186 at para 87.

280 *Altus Group, supra* note 14 at para 31.

statutory interpretation and the rule of law."[281] Is this any different from correctness review? Assuming that the reviewing court gives respectful attention to the reasoning informing the competing interpretive approaches, does it instead represent a defensible way of reconciling deference with the rule of law?

The approach to inconsistency above among administrative decisions has yet to be confirmed at the Supreme Court. Indeed, it arguably runs against the grain of key precedents[282]—including the judgment of Moldaver J in *McLean*. For, again, on that approach, once vying (including inconsistent) interpretations have attained the minimal status of plausibility, they are to be treated as so many policy choices, immune from assessment on a standard of better or worse.

Arguably, the principles stated by Moldaver J on evaluating the range of reasonable interpretations of law straddle both poles of the Diceyan dialectic: supremacy and abdication. On the one side (in particular, at the stage of determining whether or not there is "ambiguity") is an affirmation of the judge's supremacy in relation to law. On the other (following a judge's discerning ambiguity) is an understanding of the role of administrative decision-makers as one of making choices within a relatively undifferentiated field of policy preferences. Does this approach to review of law interpretation strengthen, or weaken, the system-wide commitment to a "culture of justification"? Is it the best we can make of deference?

e. Conclusion: Home on the Range?

Whether or how deference may be reconciled with (or may perhaps require) a discrete contextual analysis within reasonableness review aimed at setting the expectations of reasonableness, or the range of reasonable outcomes, has yet to be firmly settled at the Supreme Court.

But as long as reviewing courts prioritize respectful attention to the reasoning of administrative decision-makers,[283] it is arguably perfectly appropriate to inform the expectations of reasonableness with attention to contextual factors, including not only the nature of the question, but also the decision-maker's function viewed in light of the statutory purposes and wider statutory scheme, and the nature and significance of the affected interests. Such an analysis amounts to methodically taking account of the legal and factual context in light of which the decision must be evaluated. The more difficult question is how a court may legitimately, and so consistent with deference "as respect," distinguish (in light of these and/ or other factors) questions that give rise to just one reasonable conclusion from those that support more than one; that is, how to ensure that courts do not simply substitute their own

---

281   *Ibid* at para 31. Contrary to this proposition, see *McLean, supra* note 47 at para 39. See also *Communications, Energy and Paperworkers Union of Canada, Local 30 v Irving Pulp & Paper, Ltd*, 2013 SCC 34, [2013] 2 SCR 458 at para 79, per the dissent. See also LJ Wihak, "Wither the Correctness Standard of Review? Dunsmuir, Six Years Later" (2014) 27 Can J Admin L & Prac 173; Evans, "Triumph of Reasonableness," *supra* note 9 at 105.

282   See *Domtar, supra* note 93, and see also *McLean, supra* note 47 at para 39.

283   See Fichaud JA's integrating the dicta on the range of reasonableness from McLean with the law mandating a deferential approach (prioritizing the decision-maker's reasoning) in *Ghosn v Halifax (Regional Municipality)*, 2016 NSCA 90 especially at paras 22-23.

preferred interpretations and conclusions for those of administrators, while ensuring that they (and those whose decisions they review) follow through on their responsibility to uphold the rule of law.

2. Reasonableness, Proportionality, and "The Charter Context"

An alternative approach to contextualizing reasonableness counters the dominant spatial metaphors that have had such a hold on the judicial imagination for so long ("range," "scope," "margin," "jurisdiction") with the "balancing" metaphor of proportionality. Yet recent limited moves of the Supreme Court to inform reasonableness review with proportionality analysis have so far produced more questions than answers.

a. Background

For over two decades, common law jurisdictions throughout the world have debated whether or how proportionality has a place in common law judicial review.[284] Should the analysis be reserved for evaluating state action under dedicated human rights instruments? Or should it be integrated into common law judicial review to deal with a special subset of rights, values, or interests deemed "fundamental"?[285] Or, on yet another alternative, should proportionality analysis be introduced more pervasively into common law judicial review, to deal with a wider range of decisions and interests, beyond those associated with fundamental rights?[286] Further, if some form of proportionality analysis is admitted, what form should it take?[287] A simple "balancing" test? Or a more structured inquiry, along the lines of Canada's *Oakes* test[288]—that is, taking account of the importance of state purposes, means-end rationality, and minimal impairment, in addition to the relative weight of salutary and deleterious effects?

---

284 See e.g. David Dyzenhaus, M Hunt, & M Taggart, "The Principle of Legality in Administrative Law: Internationalisation as Constitutionalisation" (2001) 1 Oxford University Commonwealth Law Journal; M Taggart, "Proportionality, Deference, Wednesbury" (2008) NZL Rev 423 ["Proportionality, Deference, Wednesbury"]. In the Canadian context, the thesis that proportionality is an essential component of the legal expectations internal to reasonableness review was advanced by some scholars prior to the Supreme Court's decision in *Doré*. See Guy Régimbald, "Correctness, Reasonableness and Proportionality: A New Standard of Judicial Review" (2005) 31 Man LJ 239 ["A New Standard"]; Mullan, "A Proportionate Response?," *supra* note 38; Evan Fox-Decent, "The Internal Morality of Administration" in *The Unity of Public Law, supra* note 78 at 143 ["The Internal Morality"]; Cartier, "The Baker Effect," *supra* note 81. Also see Dyzenhaus, "The Politics of Deference," *supra* note 23 and "Constituting the Rule of Law," *supra* note 25.

285 See Taggart, "Proportionality, Deference, Wednesbury," *supra* note 284.

286 See Mark Elliott & Hanna Wilberg, "Modern Extensions of Substantive Review: A Survey of Themes in Taggart's Work and in the Wider Literature" in Wilbert & Elliott, eds, *The Scope and Intensity of Substantive Review, supra* note 31 at 24-30.

287 See Sir Jeffrey Jowell, "Proportionality and Unreasonableness: Neither Merger nor Takeover" in Wilberg & Elliott, eds, *The Scope and Intensity of Substantive Review, supra* note 31 at 54-55.

288 Section 1 of the Charter has been the subject of extensive case law elaboration, beginning with Dickson J's 1986 judgment in *R v Oakes*, [1986] 1 SCR 103 [*Oakes*]. See further Chapter 6 by Evan Fox-Decent and Alexander Pless.

In the United Kingdom, where proportionality analysis has been used for some time to deal with matters arising under the *Human Rights Act 1998*[289] and the *European Convention on Human Rights*,[290] the law remains unsettled on whether proportionality has a place in common law judicial review; however, there is increasing support for the idea at the UK Supreme Court.[291] In Canada, proportionality analysis has for some time been applied at the s 1 justification stage of Charter rights claims. But it has not, until recently, been endorsed as part of common law judicial review.

Some commentators in the United Kingdom and Canada argue that expectations of proportionality are already implicit in common law (reasonableness) review—for example, in cases concerned with the onerousness of a decision's effects, or with whether certain considerations in a multifactor balancing test have been given disproportionate weight.[292] Yet the deeper conflict is less about the kind of reasoning that already informs reasonableness review and more about the kind of reasoning that should inform it.[293]

The core purposive rationale in favour of integrating proportionality analysis into common law reasonableness review complements that which animates the idea of deference "as respect"—that is, the goal of fostering a culture of justification.[294] In this, the proposal reflects the thesis that public law, and with it law's administration, is not just about getting the job of governing done: it is a central mechanism for promoting the moral relationship of reciprocity that marks legitimate governance.[295] More concretely, the proposal reflects the view that administrative law should be sensitive to the moral relevance of the interests of those affected by administrative decisions. That view, or aspiration, was at least part of what moved the Supreme Court to recognize a place for proportionality review in administrative law, in *Doré*.[296] As Abella J remarked, referencing *Baker*: empowering administrative decision-makers to interpret and apply fundamental values, while at the same time holding them to account in light of those values, "allows the Charter to 'nurture' administrative law, by emphasizing that Charter values infuse the inquiry."[297]

However, once again the rift between aspiration (or the integration of the Charter and administrative law in theory) and reality (the many institutional and constitutional puzzles produced by *Doré*) is painfully in evidence.

---

289 1998, c 42.

290 ETS 5; 213 UNTS 221.

291 *Kennedy v Charity Commission (Secretary of State for Justice intervening)*, [2014] UKSC 20, per Lord Mance; *Pham v Home Secretary*, [2015] 1 WLR 1591.

292 See e.g. Jeffrey Jowell, *supra* note 287, especially at 52-57; Mullan, "A Proportionate Response?," *supra* note 38 at 254; Régimbald, "A New Standard," *supra* note 284 at para 80; Evan Fox-Decent, "The Internal Morality," *supra* note 284; Geneviève Cartier, "The Baker Effect," *supra* note 81. But see also *Khosa*, *supra* note 119.

293 See e.g. Paul Craig, "The Nature of Reasonableness" (2013) 66 CLP 131.

294 See the sources cited in note 25 (on the concept or ideal of a "culture of justification").

295 Dyzenhaus, "Constituting the Rule of Law," *supra* note 25.

296 *Doré*, *supra* note 111.

297 *Doré*, *supra* note 111 at para 29, citing Dyzenhaus and Fox-Decent, "Process/Substance," *supra* note 25 at 240.

b. Doré Proportionality

In Chapter 6, Evan Fox-Decent and Alexander Pless situate *Doré* within a wider set of doctrinal developments on the interaction of the Charter and administrative law. They offer a critical foundation on which to assess the increasingly prominent arguments that the approach advanced in *Doré* weakens or disrupts the normative, institutional, and doctrinal coherence of Charter law. Here, I briefly assess the implications of the decision for reasonableness review.

First, a few basics. In *Doré*, Abella J, writing for a unanimous court, took the opportunity to revisit the principles that apply to judicial review of discretionary decisions where these engage, or limit, Charter guarantees.[298] Inquiry into whether such limitations are justified, indicates Abella J, is from *Doré* forward to be analyzed not by way of application of s 1 of the Charter (with its attendant *Oakes* test), but rather application of common law reasonableness review.

More specifically, Abella J states that where administrative decisions engage Charter values, "the reasonableness analysis is one that centres on proportionality, that is, on ensuring that the decision interferes with the relevant *Charter* guarantee no more than is necessary given the statutory objectives." She adds: "If the decision is disproportionately impairing of the guarantee, it is unreasonable. If, on the other hand, it reflects a proper balance of the mandate with *Charter* protection, it is a reasonable one."[299] Requiring proportionality analysis in such cases, Abella J observes, is merely an expression of the principle recognized in *Catalyst Paper* that the nature of the reasonableness analysis is always contingent on its context—the context here being "the *Charter* context."[300]

But what is a "proper balance" and how is disproportionate impairment to be ascertained? Abella J offers a little further guidance—here speaking directly to the work of administrative decision-makers, and the critical question of how they are to avoid illegal intrusions on Charter-protected interests in the first place. Decision-makers, she states, are to "balanc[e] the *Charter* values with the statutory objectives." She continues: "In effecting this balancing, the decision-maker should first consider the statutory objectives."[301] Next, the decision-maker "should ask how the *Charter* value at issue will best be protected in view of the statutory objectives." Abella J adds: "This is at the core of the proportionality exercise, and requires the decision-maker to balance the severity of the interference of the *Charter* protection with the statutory objectives."[302]

---

298 Abella J refers a few times to Charter guarantees, but more commonly refers to the Charter-based triggers for proportionality analysis as *Charter values*. Just what is a Charter value, and whether or how it relates to a Charter right, is addressed in Lorne Sossin & Mark Friedman, "Charter Values and Administrative Justice" (2014) 67 SCLR (2d) 391. See also Peter Hogg, "Equality as Charter Value in Constitutional Interpretation" (2003) 20 SCLR 113 at 116-17.

299 *Doré, supra* note 111 at para 7.

300 *Ibid* at para 7, citing *Catalyst Paper, supra* note 245.

301 *Doré, supra* note 111 at para 55.

302 *Ibid* at para 56. Note the phrasing: the severity of the interference "of" (not "with") the Charter protection. The premise appears to be that the Charter interferes with the discretionary decision, rather than vice versa.

Abella J then addresses the role of the court on review, stating that where a court applies a reasonableness standard to decisions of this sort, "the question becomes whether, in assessing the impact of the relevant *Charter* protection and given the nature of the decision and the statutory and factual contexts, the decision reflects a proportionate balancing of the *Charter* protections at play."[303] Here we arrive at the issue of deference. Abella J states that just as, in the review of impugned laws for justification under s 1, courts must accord some leeway to the legislator (such that the proportionality test will be satisfied if the measure "falls within a range of reasonable alternatives"),[304] so, in common law review of discretionary decisions engaging Charter values, decision-makers are entitled to a measure of deference so long as the decision (in the words of *Dunsmuir*) "falls within a range of possible, acceptable outcomes."[305]

Extending deference to discretionary decisions that engage Charter values is suggested by Abella J to reflect a rationale similar to that supporting deference to administrative interpretations of law: "An administrative decision-maker exercising a discretionary power under his or her home statute, has, by virtue of expertise and specialization, particular familiarity with the competing considerations at play in weighing *Charter* values."[306] The counterargument, however, is that government and state-appointed actors may be too embedded in sector-specific values or majoritarian interests to warrant deference on matters involving fundamental human rights.[307] The question is whether such concerns may be met, in the context of reasonableness review, through an approach to deference as "respect," not "submission." That is, is reasonableness review able to meaningfully incorporate the heightened expectations of justification appropriate to the seriousness of Charter rights?[308]

Abella J attempts to stave off the anticipated concern that the deference accorded on reasonableness review will compromise Charter rights through an appeal to parity with the analysis under s 1 of the Charter, which, as noted, also contemplates "giving a 'margin of appreciation'" to government.[309] But there are at least four reasons for doubting the claimed parity:

1. The s 1 analysis involves a shift in onus to government following the applicant's establishing rights infringement, while the reasonableness analysis does not (indeed, *Doré* does not even clearly make rights infringement analytically prior to the analysis of "balancing");

---

303 *Ibid* at para 57.

304 *Ibid* at para 56, citing *RJR-MacDonald Inc v Canada (Attorney General)*, [1995] 3 SCR 199 at para 160.

305 *Doré, supra* note 111 at para 56, citing *Dunsmuir, supra* note 1 at para 47.

306 *Doré, supra* note 111 at para 47.

307 See Ruth Sullivan, *Sullivan on the Construction of Statutes*, 5th ed (Markham, Ont: LexisNexis, 2009) at 625: Most "non-judicial interpreters have little training in legal interpretation. Their focus tends to be narrow and coloured by the concerns and possibly by the biases of their own professional culture. They may have particular interests to promote on behalf of their department or agency, or they may have strong views respecting the groups or problems regulated by their legislation. This may put them into an adversarial position with other interested parties."

308 Audrey Macklin answers with a resounding "no" (or at least, not without major repairs). See Audrey Macklin, "Charter Right or Charter-Lite? Administrative Discretion and the Charter" (2014) 67 SCLR (2d) 561 ["Charter Right or Charter-Lite?"].

309 *Doré, supra* note 111 at para 56.

2. Significant weight is conventionally accorded to public or regulatory purposes in administrative law, a phenomenon arguably distinct from but adding to the hurdles (for applicants) posed by the doctrine of deference and bearing of the burden;

3. Common law judicial review has (as discussed above) traditionally prohibited judges from revisiting the weight placed by administrative decision-makers on factors of relevance to their discretionary decisions, including the significant interests of legal subjects. *Doré* runs against that grain; and

4. Moving from breach to remedy, it is not clear that administrative law remedies are as flexible or as responsive to Charter rights infringements as those available under s 24(1) of the Charter.[310]

These concerns represent just a few of the deep institutional and constitutional worries raised in the wake of *Doré*.[311]

c. A Future Together?

I conclude with a note on the prospect (signalled, for instance, in the way the minority in *Loyola High School v Quebec (Attorney General)*[312] simply ignored *Doré* in favour of a more conventional Charter analysis) that reasonableness and proportionality may not have much of a future together. Acknowledging that there may be good reasons for maintaining distinct institutional pathways to vindicating Charter rights claims and claims in common law judicial review (similar to the parallel options of statutory and Charter-based discrimination claims), there arguably remain good reasons, too, for persisting with (and even extending) the integration of proportionality analysis into common law reasonableness review.

That proposition turns upon the claim that the most compelling reason for integrating proportionality analysis into reasonableness review in *Doré* was not, as Abella J suggested, the doctrinal incoherence of Charter-based review of discretion. Rather, it was the importance of enhancing, or "nurturing"—or addressing the moral vacuum at the heart of—reasonableness review. It is the stark contrast between the respect accorded the significant interests of legal subjects in human rights law and the lack of any equivalent in common law

---

310 On the remedies question, see Hoi Kong, "Doré, Proportionality and the Virtues of Judicial Craft" (2013) 63 SCLR (2d) at 517-18. On the required responsiveness of s 24(1) Charter remedies to a Charter breach, see *Doucet-Boudreau v Nova Scotia (Minister of Education)*, 2003 SCC 62, [2003] 3 SCR 3 at paras 55-59. See also *Vancouver (City) v Ward*, 2010 SCC 27, [2010] 2 SCR 28.

311 Important critical discussions of the reasoning in and implications of *Doré*, beyond the work of Fox-Decent and Pless in this text, include Hoi Kong, *supra* note 310. See also the general arguments against collapsing human rights-based proportionality analysis into common law judicial review in Jason NE Varuhas, "Against Unification" in Wilbert & Elliott, eds, *The Scope and Intensity of Substantive Review, supra* note 31 at 92. For a guardedly positive reception of *Doré*, see Matthew Lewans, "Administrative Law, Judicial Deference, and the Charter" Constitutional Forum at 29; and Lorne Sossin & Mark Friedman, "Charter Values and Administrative Justice," *supra* note 298.

312 2015 SCC 12, [2015] 1 SCR 613 [*Loyola*] (the minority adopts a conventional Charter analysis and fails even to advert to the *Doré* principles applied by the majority). For a highly critical judicial appraisal of *Doré*, see the reasons of Lauwers and Miller JJA in *Gehl v Canada (Attorney General)*, 2017 ONCA 319.

judicial review that has fuelled the debates in common law countries around bringing pro-portionality into administrative law. At the same time, carving out an explicit place (or places) for proportionality analysis in reasonableness review promises to bring the values already informing the judgments of administrators and judges alike to the surface, where they may be publicly contemplated (and challenged).

The problem with *Doré* is that it functions (or threatens to function) to subordinate Charter-based judicial review to a relatively unrehabilitated model of common law judicial review.[313] One way to strengthen the normative resources of reasonableness review may be to extend proportionality, as an expectation of reasonableness, beyond Charter rights (or their shadowy cousin, Charter values) to become a generalized expectation in all cases in which administrative action (or specifically, discretion) affects the significant interests of legal subjects. As Mullan suggests, the analysis may also sensibly apply to cases in which it is alleged that disproportionate weight has been placed on one or more factors in a multi-factor balancing test.[314]

This need not mean reducing all rights and interests to an undifferentiated sea of values. Rather, as both Mullan and Macklin have argued, proportionality analysis in administrative law may be and should be adjusted to context, including (most obviously) the significance of the interest at stake. Macklin adds to this the compelling suggestion that the expectations placed on administrative decision-makers to justify their decisions on reasonableness review should be especially heightened where the decision engages Charter rights, and, moreover, the decision-maker lacks independence—effectively standing with government in an adver-sarial relationship with the affected party.[315] That is, the harnessing of decision-makers to majoritarian impulses should arguably narrow the range of reasonableness where the deci-sion affects the rights or significant interests of a marginalized individual or group.

In short, the claim is that contextualizing reasonableness review should be about more than assembling background information about the statutory text and context, or, for that matter, about comparative institutional competencies potentially supplying prudential reasons for judges to back off (or not). It should (also) be about ensuring that the weight assigned to the important values and interests engaged by administrative action is reason-ably justified. In this, common law proportionality review need not wholly displace the op-tion of pursuing Charter remedies by way of a formal Charter challenge to administrative discretion. Yet neither should existence of the Charter route wholly displace or diminish common law reasonableness-as-proportionality.

3. *Indicia of Unreasonableness*

Last in this survey of developments oriented to contextualizing reasonableness is a proposal (most prominent as yet in the commentary, but gaining some traction in the appellate case law) to add structure to reasonableness review by formally identifying certain indicia or markers of *un*reasonableness.

The concern that judges post-*Dunsmuir* have been falling prey both to the mistake of judicial supremacy (whereby judges illegitimately substitute their opinions for those of

---

313   See Walters, "Respecting Deference as Respect," *supra* note 79 at 422.
314   Mullan, "A Proportionate Response," *supra* note 38.
315   Macklin, "Charter Right or Charter-Lite?," *supra* note 308 at 587.

administrative decision-makers) and to the mistake of judicial abdication (whereby judges illegitimately refrain from holding administrative decision-makers to expectations of reasoned justification) has led a few commentators to propose consolidation of certain indicia[316] (or "badges"[317]—or markers) of unreasonableness. The idea is to pull together some common bases on which unreasonableness has been discerned in the precedents, and designate these as *prima facie* indicators of unreasonableness, identification of which should trigger further inquiry into whether the reasons taken in context overcome the suspicions raised.

The point is to give more structure, and so consistency and predictability, to reasonableness review.[318] At the same time, it is argued that inquiry guided by designated indicia of unreasonableness may avoid the errors of formalism through an emphasis, both in articulating the indicia and in their application, on the deep values animating judicial review: the values of democracy and the rule of law.[319]

Justice Stratas summarizes the approach in one of a few recent decisions in which it has been applied at the Federal Court of Appeal:

> For example, a decision whose effects appear to conflict with the purpose of the provision under which the administrator is operating may well raise an apprehension of unreasonableness ... . In that sort of case, the quality of the explanations given by the administrator in its reasons on that point may matter a great deal. Another badge of unreasonableness is the making of key factual findings with no rational basis or entirely at odds with the evidence. But care must be taken not to allow acceptability and defensibility in the administrative law sense to reduce itself to the application of rules founded upon badges. Acceptability and defensibility is a nuanced concept informed by the real-life problems and solutions recounted in the administrative law cases, not a jumble of rough-and-ready, hard-and-fast rules.[320]

The following list consolidates a few common forms of—or, to follow this line of analysis, indicia of—unreasonableness. Some have featured already in this chapter; consequently, this assembling of indicia affords an opportunity for review. Others are suggested, for instance, in the work of Paul Daly, Justice David Stratas, and Sir Jeffrey Jowell.[321] As Stratas JA cautions, it is important to emphasize that these are not self-executing heads of error, but rather aids for context-sensitive inquiry into justification, to be applied in a way that reflects deference "as respect."[322]

---

316 See Paul Daly, *A Theory of Deference in Administrative Law: Basis, Application and Scope* (Cambridge: Cambridge University Press, 2012), ch 4.

317 See Mullan, "A Proportionate Response?" *supra* note 38.

318 See Stratas JA in *Farwaha*, *supra* note 234 at para 100; *Delios v Canada (Attorney General)*, 2015 FCA 117 at para 37 [*Delios*].

319 See Daly, "Struggling Toward Coherence," *supra* note 15.

320 *Delios*, *supra* note 318 at para 27.

321 Daly, *A Theory of Deference*, *supra* note 316; Daly, "Struggling Towards Coherence," *supra* note 15 at 557-58; Stratas, "A Plea for Doctrinal Coherence," *supra* note 15 at 63-67; *Delios*, *supra* note 318; *Farwaha*, *supra* note 234.

322 As Stratas JA states, the analysis is to be subordinated to the principle that the reviewing court must focus on the reasoning of the decision-maker, rather than "developing, asserting and enforcing its own view of the matter" (*Delios, ibid* at para 28).

4. *Indicia or Markers of Unreasonableness: A Few Examples to Consider*

1. **Unintelligibility**: "Unintelligibility" may be understood to describe situations in which it is not clear why or how the decision-maker arrived at the decision it did. It may take the form of incoherent or illogical reasoning,[323] gaps in reasoning (i.e., missing inferences or logical links),[324] or other situations in which it is simply not clear how the decision-maker intended to support its conclusions of fact or law.[325] In review of discretion, unintelligibility may include failure to explain how competing factors of relevance were weighed against each other, where it is not otherwise clear how the decision was supported on the law and facts.[326]

   As explored in Section III.B (on review of implicit reasoning and decisions), evaluation of alleged unintelligibility once a legitimate basis (i.e., a *prima facie* case) for the allegation has been established requires the reviewing court to supplement express reasons (if any) through attention to the record[327] or other sources, including other decisions from within the administrative regime on the same issue.[328] However, such efforts should not extend to substituting judicial for defective administrative reasoning.[329] (For tensions in the case law on this principle, see the discussion in Section III.B, above). Query whether the reviewing court should supplement (or backfill) absent reasoning where it is not clear which of a few alternative reasoning paths the decision-maker would have taken.[330]

2. **Inconsistency:** Where an administrative decision-maker fails to explain inconsistency with the decision of an internal administrative appeal body that has remitted a matter to the decision-maker for reconsideration,[331] or inconsistency with advice of a designated adviser,[332] this may give rise to an apprehension of (or *prima facie* case of) unreasonableness. Again, this should spur further inquiry into the administrator's reasoning, viewed in light of the wider legal and factual context, in order to determine whether the decision is nonetheless justified.

---

323 See *Reed v Nova Scotia (Human Rights Commission)*, 2017 NSSC 85 at para 13 [*Reed*]: "[T]he second HRO's decision letter offers eloquent reasons why the first HRO was in error; (while stating the opposite—that she was correct?? [*sic*])."

324 This was the allegation in *Nurses' Union, supra* note 121, discussed in Section III.A.1.

325 An illustration of review oriented to analysis of gaps in reasoning is *Canada v Kabul Farms Inc*, 2016 FCA 143 at para 34:

> Here, the Director has provided no rationale for the base amounts or reductions he chose [in imposing an administrative monetary penalty]. The evidentiary record before the Director also sheds no light on the matter. To conduct reasonableness review here, we would have to simply assume or trust that the Director had good reasons for the numbers he chose. As this Court said in *Leahy* (at para 137), that "is inconsistent with our role on judicial review." We are to review, not trust or assume.

326 *LeBon v Canada (Attorney General)*, 2012 FCA 132 at para 25 [*LeBon*]; *Canada (Public Safety and Emergency Preparedness) v LeBon*, 2013 FCA 55.

327 *Nurses' Union, supra* note 121.

328 *ATA, supra* note 5.

329 *Nurses' Union, supra* note 121 and *ATA, supra* note 5.

330 See the discussion of *Tran, supra* note 186.

331 *RP v Alberta (Director of Child, Youth and Family Enhancement)*, 2015 ABCA 171.

332 See *LeBon, supra* note 326.

As discussed in Section III.C.1, above, more controversial is inconsistency among administrative decisions made under the same statutory grant of authority, resulting in differential treatment of similarly situated subjects. Despite rule of law concerns about consistency, predictability, and even-handedness in the administration of law, the courts will not impose a standard of correctness based solely on the alleged prospect of inconsistency.[333] However, as noted above, recent appellate case law has recognized inconsistency as a factor that may narrow the range of reasonable outcomes, raising the question of "whether both interpretations can reasonably stand together under the principles of statutory interpretation and the rule of law."[334] This line of authority has yet to receive approval from the Supreme Court.

3. **No evidence (lack of a reasonable basis in the evidence):** Reasonableness review of questions of fact or fact-finding is typically framed as an inquiry into whether there was "some" or alternatively "no evidence" (or no legally probative evidence) in support of the conclusion of fact.[335] This is also the standard adopted on patent unreasonableness review where that standard applies by operation of statute.[336] There is some support for the proposition that reasonableness review imposes the more demanding expectation that conclusions of fact require a *sufficient* basis in the evidence.[337] However, the Supreme Court has repeatedly confirmed that it is not "the function of the reviewing court to reweigh the evidence."[338] On a separate but important note, decision-makers are precluded from immunizing themselves from review by withholding material evidence.[339]

4. **Unreasonable interpretations or applications of law—defeating the purpose:** Perhaps the deepest challenge presented to reasonableness review (and so deference) is that of overseeing the consistency of administrative decision-making with statutory purposes and/or wider legal norms. Courts cannot be understood to fulfill their constitutional role, whether as guardians of the rule of law or as partners in a culture of justification, unless judicial review is guided by expectations of concordance with statutory purposes.[340] At the same time, in view of the imperative of deference ("as respect"), courts must inquire into suspected lack of concordance in a

---

333 *Domtar Inc, supra* note 93; *Wilson, supra* note 16.

334 *Altus Group, supra* note 14.

335 *Dr Q v College of Physicians and Surgeons of British Columbia*, 2003 SCC 19, [2003] 1 SCR 226 [Dr Q]. See also *Quebec (Commission des droits de la personne et des droits de la jeunesse) v Bombardier Inc (Bombardier Aerospace Training Center)*, 2015 SCC 39, [2015] 2 SCR 789 at paras 72-99

336 *British Columbia (Workers' Compensation Appeal Tribunal) v Fraser Health Authority*, 2016 SCC 25, [2016] 1 SCR 587; *Toronto (City) Board of Education v Ontario Secondary School Teachers' Federation, District 15*, [1997] 1 SCR 487.

337 *Hartwig v Saskatoon (City) Police Assn*, 2007 SKCA 74 at paras 27-29. For counterargument, see *142445 Ontario Limited (Utilities Kingston) v International Brotherhood of Electrical Workers, Local 636*, 2009 CanLII 24643 (Ont Sup Ct J (Div Ct)): "Generally speaking, in the absence of a statutory right of appeal, the courts are confined to ensuring that the findings on which the decision is based are supported by some logically probative evidence on which the decision-maker may lawfully rely," citing Brown & Evans, *Judicial Review of Administrative Action in Canada* at 12:3100.

338 *Khosa, supra* note 119 at para 61.

339 *Tsleil-Waututh Nation v Canada (Attorney General)*, 2017 FCA 128 at paras 77-78.

340 See e.g. the reasoning of L'Heureux-Dubé J in dissent in *Paccar, supra* note 47 (discussed in Section II.A, above).

manner that is led by tribunal reasoning. Courts must not simply displace the purposive reasoning of decision-makers for their own preferred interpretations.

So long as the principles of deferential review are adhered to, unreasonableness may be established on the basis that the decision-maker's interpretation or application of the law was inconsistent with, or defeated, statutory purposes.[341]

5. **Lack of reasonable support in the legislative text/context:** Where purposive reasoning is argued to stretch interpretation of the legislative text beyond its plausible meaning (taking account of the wider statutory scheme and legislative–historical context), this too raises an apprehension of unreasonableness.[342] Again, the ensuing inquiry should pay respectful attention to the tribunal's reasoning, supplementing that reasoning through efforts to place it in its best, purposive light.

6. **(Unreasonable) failure to consider a relevant factor:** There is a line of appellate authority indicating that this and other traditional or nominate grounds of review for abuse of discretion have been integrated into reasonableness review.[343] Where a (*prima facie*) case is made that a factor of potentially determinative relevance to the decision was not considered—whether the consideration in question involves evidence, law, or a legal argument put to the decision-maker—this should trigger (deferential) inquiry into whether the factor was indeed expressly or implicitly considered, and whether failure to consider the factor in question would be unreasonable.

It is important to note, however, that the principles out of *Newfoundland Nurses' Union* (on supplementing reasons before subverting them) conflict with automatic correctness-style invalidation for failure to expressly address the factors deemed by the reviewing court to be of mandatory legal relevance.[344]

Examples of "failure to consider" that may give rise to an apprehension of unreasonableness include: (1) failure to consider or address evidence or argument of potentially determinative legal importance;[345] (2) failure to apply a legal test of mandatory relevance (traditionally dealt with on a correctness standard);[346] and (3) failure

---

341   Again, see the reasoning of L'Heureux-Dubé J in dissent in *Paccar, ibid*. An example in which a decision-maker's interpretation was deemed contrary to statutory purposes (indeed, contrary to "plain and grammatical meaning of the words; statutory and international contexts; and legislative intent" (at para 76)) is *B010 v Canada (Citizenship and Immigration)*, 2015 SCC 58, [2015] 3 SCR 704. However, it is debatable whether the process of reasoning that the court adopts on review in that case is consistent with deference "as respect." See also *Montréal (City) v Montreal Port Authority*, 2010 SCC 14, [2010] 1 SCR 427. A recent Nova Scotia decision that focused in part on unintelligibility (or lack of coherence in the reasoning) and in part on defiance of the statutory mandate is *Reed, supra* note 323.

342   See *Mowat, supra* note 130 at para 33; *Wilson v British Columbia (Superintendent of Motor Vehicles), supra* note 266 at paras 26-29; *Izaak Walton Killam Health Centre v Nova Scotia (Human Rights Commission)*, 2014 NSCA 18.

343   See *Dr Q, supra* note 335 at paras 22, 24; *Baker, supra* note 19 at para 56; *JP Morgan, supra* note 260 at para 74.

344   *Nurses' Union, supra* note 121. See also *Agraira, supra* note 129 at paras 18, 60-61; *Antrim Truck Centre Ltd v Ontario (Transportation)*, 2013 SCC 13, [2013] 1 SCR 594 [*Antrim Truck Centre*].

345   *Turner v Canada (Attorney General)*, 2012 FCA 159 [*Turner*] (Human Rights Tribunal failed to consider one of the grounds of discrimination alleged); *Lemus v Canada (Citizenship and Immigration)*, 2014 FCA 114 (officer deciding application for humanitarian and compassionate grounds exemption determined that she lacked jurisdiction to consider evidence and argument properly before her and of central importance to the application).

346   *Halifax, supra* note 129 at para 43; *Lake v Canada (Minister of Justice)*, 2008 SCC 23, [2008] 1 SCR 761 at para 41.

to take account of an element of a multifactor balancing test. But, again, see the law on deference to implicit reasoning, which joins with the traditional prohibition on revisiting the weight accorded factors of relevance to present significant challenges to establishing unreasonableness on this basis.[347]

Discretion may also be challenged on the basis of failure to take account of a fundamental legal value or principle (including those reflected in the Constitution or in international law) argued to be of mandatory relevance to a decision.[348] In such cases, the principles from *ATA* on the expectation that the issue must have been raised before the decision-maker may apply;[349] however, query whether or in what circumstances the decision-maker is expected to take account of such factors regardless of whether they are raised in argument, on the basis that they are "values underlying the grant of discretion" that administrative decisions must "always" consider.[350] The argument may be strengthened where the value or principle in question is reflected in applicable policies or guidelines.[351]

7. **Consideration of an irrelevant factor:** Here "the appropriate question will be: 'Was it reasonable for the tribunal to treat this factor as relevant?'"[352] This ground (along with bad faith) was engaged in *Roncarelli v Duplessis*, although the challenge was formally framed as an action for damages at civil law.[353] Even where a decision-maker has taken account of a consideration deemed to be irrelevant, the reviewing court must adopt a holistic analysis and assure itself that the consideration was potentially determinative of the result.[354]

8. **Disproportionality:** See the discussion of *Doré* proportionality in Section III.C.2, above. Where an "adjudicated," "individual" discretionary discretion engages "Charter values," reasonableness requires proportionality as between pursuit of the statutory mandate and harm to the relevant Charter right or value. The applicant may argue that the decision was not minimally impairing of a Charter right or value, and/or that it failed to reflect a proportionate balancing of the purposes informing the decision and the effects on the Charter guarantee.[355] Query whether proportionality analysis should be engaged also in cases where administrative decisions affect significant interests that are not plausibly constructed as engaging Charter rights or values (e.g., interests in employment), or where it is alleged that undue weight was placed on one or more factors in a multifactor balancing test.

---

347   See the principles stated by Mainville JA in *Turner, supra* note 345 at paras 41, 42; see also *Agraira, supra* note 129 at para 18; *Antrim Truck Centre, supra* note 345 at paras 53-54.

348   See the discussion of *Baker, supra* note 19; *Kainaiwa, supra* note 217; *Twins, supra* note 232.

349   See e.g. *Mikail v Canada (Attorney General)*, 2012 FC 940 at para 34.

350   See *Baker, supra* note 19 at para 56; *Doré, supra* note 111 at para 35.

351   *Baker, supra* note 19 (taking account of the fact that the value placed on the best interests of the child was reflected in the Act as well as the minister's own guidelines); *Suresh, supra* note 202.

352   Mullan, "The Top Fifteen!," *supra* note 15 at 58.

353   See David Mullan, "Roncarelli v Duplessis and Damages for Abuse of Power: For What Did It Stand in 1959 and For What Does It Stand in 2009?" (2010) 53 McGill LJ 587.

354   *Canadian Association of Regulated Importers v Canada (Attorney General)*, [1994] 2 FC 247 at 260 (CA).

355   *Doré, supra* note 111; *Loyola, supra* note 312 at para 40.

IV. CONCLUSION: MAKING SENSE OF REASONABLENESS

This chapter has explored the contemporary doctrine on reasonableness review, approaching that body of law as an effort, over time and across frequent changes of the judicial guard, to meet the challenge of reconciling the imperative of deference to administrative decisions with the expectation that those decisions be justified. The success of the efforts in *Dunsmuir* to simplify the standard of review analysis have placed this challenge at the forefront of contemporary debates on judicial review. And yet, as we have seen, the case law following *Dunsmuir* has exhibited many of the tendencies common to judicial review since the start of the 20th century—tendencies to revert on the one side to the posture of judicial supremacy, and on the other, the posture of judicial abdication. Is there a middle way? Or rather, is there a way to ensure robust protections for those affected by administrative action, while leaving room for the important work of state regulation and governance in the public interest?

The developments discussed in Section III.C under the theme of contextualizing reasonableness may assist in giving more determinate and so predictable shape to the expectations of reasoned justification appropriate to specific administrative contexts. These developments arguably reinforce the proposal made by Abella J in *Wilson* to finally retire the correctness standard of review. Yet it is essential not to simply build correctness-style review back into the reasonableness standard; rather, the question is how deference "as respect" would or should transform review of matters now attracting that standard. It is essential, more broadly, not to lose sight either of the imperative of deference (and its underlying ethic of respectful attention to administrative decisions and reasons) or of the expectation that those decisions be justified. It is only through a constant effort to demonstrate the mutually reinforcing nature of these imperatives, and with them, the values of democracy and the rule of law, that judges and administrative decision-makers may effectively join forces in creating a culture of justification.

In this regard, among the most important developments in the law on reasonableness review since *Dunsmuir* are those that assert the legitimacy of the expectation on review—and at the front lines of administration—that decision-makers take account of the legal values that express the fundamental commitments of constitutional democracy. As Mary Liston has stated, the expectation that decision-makers identify and give appropriate weight to those fundamental values expresses a shift from a "command-and-control"[356] model of administrative law to a model based on reasoned dialogue about the values that make the legal order worth protecting. Here constitutional law and administrative law meet.

In recent years, the decision in *Doré* has been the most prominent and prominently critiqued expression of the Supreme Court of Canada's commitment to the idea that administrative law is an integral part of, and should not be dislocated from, the deep values of the legal order. That decision, for all the important criticisms it has elicited on its institutional destabilization and common law-ification of Charter rights, should nonetheless be regarded as the start of further conversations aimed at ensuring the integrity and protection of fundamental rights under the Charter *and* under common law administrative law—even if these paths are maintained as distinct institutional options. It should be regarded, more concretely, as an effort to invite legal subjects to assert the relevance and indeed central

---

356   Liston, as cited in *Doré, supra* note 111.

importance of Charter guarantees (and, arguably, other morally significant interests) in the context of "ordinary" administrative processes. Ensuring that Charter guarantees, along with other constitutional guarantees and principles such as the duty of the Crown to promote reconciliation with Indigenous Peoples, are identified and given protection in administrative settings while at the same time ensuring that the public purposes of regulatory regimes are also respected is arguably the greatest challenge of contemporary administrative law.

In the end, you may not be satisfied that the shifting approaches to substantive review in judicial review doctrine over the past 40 years—and with this, the veering of courts between attitudes of judicial supremacy and judicial abdication—are best chalked up to a problem at the level of constitutional theory, that is, a failure to settle upon a coherent model of the proper roles of Parliament, the judiciary, and the executive/administrative state in securing the rule of law. You may find more convincing the thesis that the phenomenon of wave after wave of successive substantive review doctrines and unpredictable applications of those doctrines is instead an elaborate cover for the hard truth that substantive review is only ever end-driven reasoning, through which the reviewing court reaches the conclusion it thinks is right—a working out of the "inarticulate first premises" that Oliver Wendell Holmes suggested spring from sources outside law. Alternatively, the doctrinal niceties of substantive review may be argued to be but shifting tactics in an ongoing array of institutional power struggles: struggles for supremacy around who has the last word on the proper exercise of state power, with judges ingeniously couching their bids for dominance in the language of respect for the other two branches.

There is likely to be some truth in all these hypotheses. But it is important to be clear not only about your favoured diagnoses of administrative law's various pathologies, but also about your favoured prescriptions: your views on the proper aspirations of the constitutional order and how these should inform administrative law. That is how to start making sense of reasonableness review, and, more generally, the project of substantive review in administrative law.

SUGGESTED ADDITIONAL READINGS

ARTICLES

Daly, Paul, "Struggling Towards Coherence in Canadian Administrative Law? Recent Cases on Standard of Review and Reasonableness" (2016) 62:2 McGill LJ 527.

Dyzenhaus, David, "The Politics of Deference: Judicial Review and Democracy" in M Taggart, ed, *The Province of Administrative Law* (Oxford: Hart Publishing, 1997) 279.

Fox-Decent, Evan, "The Internal Morality of Administration: The Form and Structure of Reasonableness" in David Dyzenhaus, ed, *The Unity of Public Law* (Oxford: Hart Publishing, 2004) 143.

Stratas, The Hon David W, "The Canadian Law of Judicial Review: A Plea for Doctrinal Coherence and Consistency" (2016) 42:1 Queen's LJ 27.

Walters, Mark D, "Respecting Deference as Respect: Rights, Reasonableness and Proportionality in Canadian Administrative Law" in Mark Elliott & Hanna Wilberg eds, *The*

Scope and Intensity of Substantive Review: Traversing Taggart's Rainbow (Oxford: Hart Publishing, 2015) 395.

CASES

Alberta (Information and Privacy Commissioner) v Alberta Teachers' Association, 2011 SCC 61, [2011] 3 SCR 654.

Catalyst Paper Corp v North Cowichan (District), 2012 SCC 2, [2012] 1 SCR 5.

CUPE v NB Liquor Corporation, [1979] 2 SCR 227.

Doré v Barreau du Québec, 2012 SCC 12, [2012] 1 SCR 395.

Dunsmuir v New Brunswick, 2008 SCC 9, [2008] 1 SCR 190.

McLean v British Columbia (Securities Commission), 2013 SCC 67, [2013] 3 SCR 895.

Newfoundland and Labrador Nurses' Union v Newfoundland and Labrador (Treasury Board), 2011 SCC 62, [2011] 3 SCR 708.

CHAPTER THIRTEEN

The Charter and Administrative Law Part II: Substantive Review

Faculty of Law, McGill University

Alexander Pless**
Department of Justice, Government of Canada

I. INTRODUCTION

We turn now to examine how Canadian public law deals with administrative decisions that appear to engage rights guaranteed by the Charter. Such cases are common. Indeed, the Supreme Court has considered dozens of them since the Charter came into force.

For most of the Charter's history, the court's approach has been less than constant. This inconstancy stemmed from differing views and approaches as to whether, when, and how

  * We are indebted to Colleen Flood, Robert Leckey, Mary Liston, Sara Gauthier, Vincent Marquis, Patrick Baud, and Lorne Sossin for valuable comments and suggestions, either on past versions of this chapter or on this one, or both.
  ** The views expressed in this chapter are my own and do not necessarily reflect those of my employer, the Department of Justice.

to conduct a s 1 analysis of an administrative decision that infringes a protected right. Should only the legislation that authorizes the decision be subject to review for its consistency with Charter rights and (in the event of an infringement) s 1 of the Charter? On this view, the decision itself is subject to only administrative law analysis, which usually means a determination of whether it is reasonable or correct, depending on whether reasonableness or correctness is selected as the standard of review. Or should both the decision and the authorizing legislation be subject to review for consistency with Charter rights and (if there is an infringement) s 1 of the Charter? Or should courts seek a methodological halfway house that deploys administrative law to assess the decision but that takes into consideration Charter rights and values?

All these approaches have been endorsed by the Supreme Court or members of the court in recent years. Table 13.1 at the end of this chapter sets out the diversity of views in the cases discussed. However, it is the last approach that more recently won favour with the Supreme Court in *Doré v Barreau du Québec*.[1] Abella J, writing for a unanimous court, squarely addressed the unsettled nature of this area of law and laid the foundation for an administrative law approach adapted to consider Charter values. While the new approach is still experiencing some growing pains, Charter values now play a prominent role in administrative decision-making. As in the case of procedural review that implicates Charter concerns, the relationship between Charter jurisprudence and administrative law suggests that each is porous to the other. Put generously, the relationship between constitutional law and administrative law exhibits a cross-fertilization of principles and approaches that inform judicial review of administrative action. Put somewhat less generously, the courts have yet to develop a consistent framework for the precise role that Charter rights and Charter values play in the administrative state. The continued uncertainty risks undermining the laudable goals of the new approach.

Many of the tensions that *Doré* aims to resolve are not fully resolved. In *Loyola High School v Quebec (Attorney General)*,[2] the court's next opportunity to apply its new approach, the court split 4–3, with two judges who had supported *Doré* demurring from the new approach. Despite this uncertainty, the court's approach in *Doré* remains a binding precedent and has been applied by the lower courts hundreds of times. It seems likely that *Doré* will be the dominant approach in the years to come, but clarifications and adjustment will be required to ensure that it delivers on its promise of robust protection for Charter rights and values.

This chapter examines the different approaches courts have used to review decisions when a Charter right is at issue. With the decision in *Doré*, the court has made clear that ideas and concepts developed at common law for substantive review of administrative action should be respected even when Charter rights are at issue. It is best to read Audrey Macklin's discussion in Chapter 11, Standard of Review: Back to the Future?, and Sheila Wildeman's discussion in Chapter 12, Making Sense of Reasonableness, prior to reading this chapter.

A distinct issue raised by the advent of the Charter is whether administrative tribunals and agencies have jurisdiction to apply the Charter to their enabling statutes. The issue is controversial because administrative decision-makers, as creatures of statute belonging to the executive branch, are not normally viewed as having authority to refuse to apply the

---

1 2012 SCC 12 [*Doré*].
2 2015 SCC 12, [2015] 1 SCR 613 [*Loyola*].

very legislation the legislature has entrusted them to implement. Nonetheless, the Supreme Court has affirmed that the Charter is "not some holy grail which only judicial initiates of the superior courts may touch,"[3] and has found that administrative bodies may have jurisdiction to apply the Charter if they have authority to decide questions of law. We discuss the legal basis and practical effects of administrative bodies' jurisdiction over the Charter. These questions take on newfound importance post-*Doré* because part of the Supreme Court's prior justification for recognizing administrative tribunals' authority to apply the Charter was the fact that such decisions would ultimately be reviewed on the standard of correctness. *Doré* now requires deference to these administrative decision-makers. It remains to be seen what impact this development may have on the court's approach to administrative tribunals' jurisdiction over Charter issues.

This chapter is divided into several parts. In the first part, we examine the history up to *Doré* of the law applying the Charter to an administrative decision. Second, we examine *Doré* itself. Following that, we explore two important questions raised by *Doré*. First, does the new approach change anything? And second, what is the role of Charter values in administrative decision-making and judicial review? Finally, we examine *Loyola*, the Supreme Court's first application of *Doré*. The division of the court in *Loyola* raises questions about how the court will apply *Doré* in the future.

A. From Slaight to Doré—A Brief History

The Supreme Court first considered the application of the Charter to an administrative decision in *Slaight*.[4] Mr Davidson worked for Slaight Communications as a salesperson for almost four years prior to his termination. A labour adjudicator found that he had been dismissed unjustly. The adjudicator enjoyed broad discretionary authority under the *Canada Labour Code* to impose a remedy. Part of the remedy consisted of a "positive order" that required the employer to write an unembellished, factual letter of reference setting out Mr Davidson's success relative to annual sales targets, as well as the fact that the adjudicator had found Mr Davidson's dismissal to be unjust. The adjudicator also made a "negative order" requiring Slaight to provide the letter, and only the letter, to prospective employers making inquiries about Mr Davidson's employment. In other words, to protect the integrity of the positive order, Slaight was forbidden from making any negative comments about Mr Davidson's work performance to possible future employers. Slaight sought judicial review, arguing that both the positive and the negative order infringed its freedom of expression guaranteed under s 2(b) of the Charter, and that the infringement could not be justified under s 1.

Although the majority reasons are written by Dickson CJ, he expressly adopts Lamer J's (as he then was, dissenting in part) analytic framework.[5] The first step in Lamer J's framework is to determine whether the disputed order was made pursuant to legislation that confers "either expressly or by necessary implication, the power to infringe a

---

3 *Nova Scotia (Workers' Compensation Board) v Martin; Nova Scotia (Workers' Compensation Board) v Laseur*, 2003 SCC 54, [2003] 2 SCR 504 at para 29 [*Martin*], Gonthier J, citing with approval McLachlin J's (as she then was) dissenting dictum in *Cooper v Canada (Human Rights Commission)*, [1996] 3 SCR 854 at para 70 [*Cooper*].

4 *Slaight Communications Inc v Davidson*, [1989] 1 SCR 1038 [*Slaight*].

5 *Ibid* at 1048.

protected right."[6] If the legislation does confer such a power, then the legislation itself must satisfy the requirements of s 1 of the Charter. However, the fact that the legislation is thus justified does not guarantee that the Supreme Court will not also subject the decision itself to the requirements of s 1.

The *Extradition Act*[7] is a paradigmatic example of legislation that expressly authorizes the infringement of a Charter right. In its usual application, the decision-maker is authorized to infringe a citizen's right to remain in Canada guaranteed by s 6 of the Charter. Courts have consistently found that ordinary exercises of this right-infringing authority are justified under s 1. It does not follow, of course, that any and every case of extradition is immunized from Charter review. On the contrary, every extradition order is a *prima facie* infringement of a protected right, so the decision-maker must show in each particular case that the decision is a justified limitation on the individual's s 6 right.[8]

If, however, the legislation provides broad or imprecise discretion, and the authority to infringe a protected right is not express, as was the case in *Slaight*, then the order alone must be justified in accordance with s 1. If the order cannot be justified under s 1, the administrative tribunal has necessarily exceeded its jurisdiction. If, on the other hand, the order can be justified under s 1, then the administrative tribunal has acted within its jurisdiction.

The framework set out in *Slaight* proved difficult to apply, and the Supreme Court attempted to clarify it in *Multani v Commission scolaire Marguerite-Bourgeoys*.[9]

Multani dealt with a decision by a school board to prohibit an orthodox Sikh student from wearing a kirpan, a religious object that resembles a dagger. The carrying of weapons at school was prohibited by the school's *Code de vie*. The school board considered the object a weapon despite the student's promise to wear it sewn into his clothing. Multani and his father applied for judicial review of the school board's decision, arguing that the decision infringed their freedom of religion guaranteed under s 2(a) of the Charter.

Charron J, for a majority of the court, followed the *Slaight* framework and applied an *Oakes*[10] analysis to the decision to determine if the decision was justified under s 1.[11] In powerful concurring reasons, Deschamps and Abella JJ rejected the *Oakes* analysis altogether and insisted that the matter be analyzed through the lens of administrative law alone.[12] LeBel J, in separate concurring reasons, offered a further variation on the theme, proposing a modified s 1 analysis adapted to the administrative context.[13]

According to the majority in *Multani*, the reviewing judge of a Charter case is to conduct a traditional Charter analysis without evaluating the decision through an administrative law framework. The two concurring judgments in *Multani* point to certain tensions the majority's deployment of the *Slaight* framework leave unresolved. As we will see below, those tensions came to the fore in *Doré*, where a unanimous Supreme Court rejects the *Slaight–Multani* approach.

---

6   *Ibid* at 1079.
7   SC 1999, c 18.
8   *United States of America v Cotroni; United States of America v El Zein*, [1989] 1 SCR 1469. Consider also *Little Sisters Book and Art Emporium v Canada (Minister of Justice)*, 2000 SCC 69, [2000] 2 SCR 1120 [*Little Sisters*].
9   2006 SCC 6, [2006] 1 SCR 256 [*Multani*].
10   *R v Oakes*, [1986] 1 SCR 103.
11   *Ibid* at paras 42-80.
12   *Ibid* at paras 84-139.
13   *Ibid* at paras 140-155.

B. Doré

Mr Doré was a lawyer practising in Quebec. After a difficult day in court in front of Boilard J, Mr Doré returned to his office and wrote Boilard J a letter "man to man." With what might be described charitably as colourful prose, Mr Doré expressed reservations as to Boilard J's suitability for the office of a judge. Boilard J did not read the letter "man to man" but rather "lawyer to judge." Boilard J forwarded a copy of the letter to the Chief Justice of the Quebec Superior Court, who in turn forwarded a copy to the Barreau du Québec, the professional order responsible for the discipline of lawyers in Quebec. The Barreau found that Mr Doré ran afoul of Quebec's *Code of ethics of advocates*—in particular s 2.03, which requires that "[t]he conduct of an advocate must bear the stamp of objectivity, moderation, and dignity."[14] The Barreau suspended Mr Doré from the practice of law for three weeks. The Barreau accepted that s 2.03 and its decision infringed s 2(b) of the Charter, but found that the infringement was justified under s 1.

Mr Doré appealed the decision to Quebec's Tribunal des professions, an appellate tribunal for all professional orders. Mr Doré abandoned his argument that s 2.03 of the *Code of ethics of advocates* itself violated s 2(b) of the Charter, pursuing instead a complaint that the *decision* taken under s 2.03 violated the Charter. The Tribunal des professions applied a standard of correctness to the decision. Relying on LeBel J's separate concurring reasons in *Multani*, the Tribunal des professions upheld the decision. Instead of formally applying the *Oakes* test, the tribunal focused, as LeBel J had proposed, on whether the decision-maker has achieved "proportionality or, more specifically, minimal limitation of the guaranteed right."[15] The decision of the Tribunal des professions was upheld on judicial review. The Quebec Court of Appeal also upheld the decision, but only after applying the *Oakes* test to the decision.[16]

A unanimous Supreme Court upheld the Barreau's decision and took the opportunity to set out a new approach that explicitly rejects application of the *Oakes* test to administrative decisions. The *Oakes* test, Abella J explained, is appropriate for dealing with a "law" or rules of general application that infringe on rights and freedoms guaranteed in the Charter, but not for deciding whether an administrative decision infringes the rights and freedoms of a particular individual.[17]

Where an individual decision is at issue, the decision will be reviewed on the reasonableness standard, adjusted for context, such that the decision will be affirmed as reasonable only if "the decision reflects a proportionate balancing of the Charter protections at play."[18] Abella J assigns to the decision-maker the task of determining "how the *Charter* value at issue will best be protected in view of the statutory objectives."[19] The decision-maker "balances the *Charter* values with the statutory objectives."[20] The challenges of applying this approach to different cases are discussed below, but we note immediately two critical

---

14 *Code of Ethics of Advocates*, CQLR, c B-1, r 3, s 2.03, replaced by *Code of Professional Conduct of Lawyers*, CQLR, c B-1, r 3.1, s 4 ("A lawyer must act with honour, dignity, integrity, respect, moderation and courtesy.")

15 *Doré, supra* note 1 at para 19. See also *Multani, supra* note 9 at para 155.

16 *Ibid* at para 21.

17 *Ibid* at para 36.

18 *Ibid* at para 57.

19 *Ibid* at para 56

20 *Ibid* at para 55.

features of the new approach. First, the decision is reviewed on the standard of reasonableness and, second, Charter values, which may be different from Charter rights, are the focus of the review.

In many respects the *Doré* approach is not as revolutionary as it might appear. As the court points out, it builds on approaches that have been adopted from time to time throughout the history of the Charter. With respect to the shift from correctness review to a reasonableness standard, the critical step of the *Oakes* analysis (minimal impairment) has always required deference to legislative choice. Although the *Oakes* test contains four distinct steps, almost every piece of legislation that fails the test stumbles at the minimal impairment stage,[21] where the Supreme Court shows deference to the legislature's choices. Indeed, under both the *Oakes* test and reasonableness review in administrative law, the court says that the government's action must fall within a range of reasonable alternatives.[22]

It is not clear from *Doré*, however, whether deference is owed to an administrative decision-maker's assessment of whether the decision infringes a Charter right, and thereby triggers the balancing exercise described above. In *Doré*, the disciplinary action plainly infringed Mr Doré's s 2(b) right to freedom of speech. But there are lots of cases, such as *Baker*,[23] where the infringement will not be obvious. *Dunsmuir* suggests that this is a question of law to be evaluated on the correctness standard,[24] but *Doré* casts doubt on whether *any* constitutional question is to be determined on a standard of correctness. In *Loyola*, the only Supreme Court case to apply *Doré* at the time of writing, the court does not expressly address the question.

C. Do the Different Approaches Produce Different Results?

Do the differences between these approaches matter? Put another way, faced with the same decision, is it possible that a traditional s 1 analysis would lead a court to intervene whereas an administrative law analysis on a standard of reasonableness would not (or vice versa)? The evidence from the cases is mixed. In *Loyola*, the Superior Court of Quebec applied *Oakes* on a correctness standard and found the decision incorrect, striking it down. The Quebec Court of Appeal, writing after *Doré*, review the decision on a reasonableness standard and upheld the decision. And the Supreme Court, also applying *Doré*, reversed the Court of Appeal and reached the same decision as the Superior Court.[25] One could be forgiven for thinking that the standard of review or approach applied is unlikely to influence the outcome.

Multani nonetheless provides a good example of how the different approaches might produce different results, even though, in *Multani*, they converged on the same result. Deschamps and Abella JJ concluded that the decision was unreasonable because, among other things, the school board failed to take into consideration Multani's Charter rights.

---

21   Peter W Hogg, *Constitutional Law of Canada*, 5th ed Supp (Toronto: Carswell, 2007) at 38 (updated 2015, release 1).

22   Compare *RJR-MacDonald Inc v Canada (Attorney General)*, [1995] 3 SCR 199 at para 160 and *Dunsmuir v New Brunswick*, 2008 SCC 9, [2008] 1 SCR 190 at para 47 [*Dunsmuir*].

23   *Infra* note 35.

24   *Dunsmuir*, *supra* note 21 at para 58 ("constitutional [questions] are necessarily subject to correctness review because of the unique role of s. 96 courts as interpreters of the Constitution").

25   *Loyola*, *supra* note 2 at paras 29-30.

Suppose the school board *had* seriously considered the applicant's Charter rights and *had* wrestled with the practical considerations and dangers of allowing him to wear the kirpan, and yet *still* concluded that the kirpan should be prohibited. This would have all the trappings of a reasonable decision and presumably have been owed deference. Judges will strike down a decision where the decision-maker fails to take account of relevant considerations (for example, Charter rights), but according to one line of cases they are not to "reweigh" the weight the decision-maker gives to those considerations.[26] It seems possible, then, that the hypothetical school board decision could have been upheld under Deschamps and Abella JJ's approach. For Charron J, on the other hand, the decision would be unlawful because it would remain an unjustified infringement on the child's right to freedom of religion, as assessed on a standard of correctness that is indifferent to the way the decision-maker made the decision.

It bears emphasizing, however, that Abella J's judgment in *Doré* puts pressure on the purported rule against reweighing. Indeed, according to *Doré*, a decision is reasonable *only* when the decision-maker has struck the "appropriate balance" between its statutory mandate and the Charter rights at issue.[27] Testing whether an appropriate balance has been struck necessarily involves an inquiry into the weight accorded the countervailing considerations.

This problem is of more than merely academic interest because *Doré* does not disturb the ordinary approach to examining a law or other rule that infringes a Charter right (what the court in *Slaight* calls express authority to infringe). This approach still requires the government to meet the burdens of the *Oakes* test in order to satisfy the requirements of s 1 of the Charter.

If there is a difference between the two approaches, one can legitimately question why, when the Constitution is the supreme law of Canada, there would be two different approaches to determining the constitutionality of government action depending on whether that action is expressly authorized by legislation or not. One can easily imagine a legal power being codified in such a way as to contain in the statute an express power to do the very same thing that an administrator had done previously under an imprecise or general grant of discretion. Indeed, if it had not been for the school board's "decision" in *Multani* to reject the proposed accommodation of Multani's freedom of religion, Multani's constitutional challenge would have been directed toward the absolute rule prohibiting "weapons" from school grounds (i.e., a rule that did include the possibility of an exemption on religious grounds). Why should the strength of an individual's constitutional rights depend on the manner in which legislation invites the government to infringe them?

In *Doré*, Abella J does not squarely address whether the new approach will yield a more relaxed standard of scrutiny for rules, though the introduction of the reasonableness standard points in this direction. Recall that Abella J says that the integrity of both s 1 of the Charter and administrative law can be respected with the approach she adopts.[28] Much of

---

26 *Canada (Citizenship and Immigration) v Khosa*, 2009 SCC 12, [2009] 1 SCR 339 at paras 60-64. But see *Kanthasamy v Canada (Citizenship and Immigration)*, 2015 SCC 61, [2015] 3 SCR 909, Abella J, for the majority, finding that the decision-maker must treat certain considerations, such as a child's best interests, as especially significant.

27 *Doré, supra* note 1 at paras 7, 57, and 58. Note also that in *Lake v Canada (Minister of Justice)*, 2008 SCC 23 at para 41, [2008] 1 SCR 761, the court says the minister must identify the "correct test," but is owed deference in the application of the test.

28 *Doré, supra* note 1 at para 3.

Abella J's explanation would lead one to think that she perceives the new approach as merely adapting the same requirements (those of s 1) to different types of problems, but without diminishing scrutiny. For Abella J, the *Oakes* test is suitable for assessing "principles of general application," and not "individual administrative decision[s]" that are "in relation to a particular set of facts."[29] This is a puzzling distinction because, ever since the early days of the Charter, the court has consistently resisted analyzing Charter questions in the abstract, and has insisted that a law be tested in its actual application. So, arguably, every s 1 analysis we have ever seen has dealt with individual cases "in relation to a particular set of facts."[30] It is true that in many cases a rule of general application is at issue, but it is tested in light of how it is or could be applied to a particular case.

As a result, *Doré* might be read to blur the line between the *Oakes* analysis as an analytic tool on the one hand and compliance with s 1 of the Charter on the other. It is one thing to say that individual discretionary decisions are "ill-suited" to the *Oakes* test; it is quite another to say that they are a type of government action that can legally infringe a Charter right without needing to satisfy s 1 of the Charter. The requirements of *Oakes* and s 1 are not identical. Section 1 provides that "[t]he *Canadian Charter of Rights and Freedoms guarantees the rights and freedoms set out in it* subject only to such reasonable limits prescribed by law as can be demonstrably justified in a free and democratic society" (emphasis added). *Oakes* provides an analytic framework to assess whether a given rule satisfies these requirements. Its components—a pressing and substantial objective, rationally connected to a minimally impairing infringement whose benefits are not outweighed by its interference with a protected right—are not provided for in s 1. However, s 1 *does* require that the limit be reasonable, that it be prescribed by law, and, importantly, that its reasonableness be *demonstrably justified*.

Admittedly, Abella J's reasons in *Doré* do not expressly distinguish between the requirements of s 1 and the requirements of *Oakes*. For example, to demonstrate that a s 1 analysis of an individual decision is "awkward," Abella J asks rhetorically: "On whom does the onus lie, for example, to formulate and assert the pressing and substantial objective of an adjudicated decision, let alone justify it as rationally connected to, minimally impairing of and proportional to that objective?"[31] In constitutional review of legislation, from which the *Slaight–Multani* approach was derived, the answer is clear: the party that seeks to uphold the infringement of a right guaranteed by the Charter (i.e., the government) bears the burden of *demonstrating* that the infringement constitutes a reasonable limit.[32] There is no analogue in administrative law that imposes a similar burden on the government when a Charter right is infringed. This is significant because under the Charter, its rights and freedoms are absolutely guaranteed *except* where the infringement can be demonstrably justified to be a reasonable limit prescribed by law in a free and democratic society. This justificatory requirement and the burden of proof it imposes on the government slips into the background—if not out of sight—under the *Doré* approach. The government seems to be relieved of its considerable burden of explicitly justifying the decision in accordance with s 1.

---

29   *Ibid* at para 36.

30   See e.g. *Reference re Same-Sex Marriage*, 2004 SCC 79, [2004] 3 SCR 698 at para 51; *Danson v Ontario (Attorney General)*, [1990] 2 SCR 1086 at 1093; *MacKay v Manitoba*, [1989] 2 SCR 357 at 361-62; *Hy and Zel's Inc v Ontario (Attorney General); Paul Magder Furs Ltd v Ontario (Attorney General)*, [1993] 3 SCR 675.

31   *Doré, supra* note 1 at para 4.

32   See e.g. *Irwin Toy Ltd v Quebec (Attorney General)*, [1989] 1 SCR 927 at 986.

While it seems unlikely that the court intended *Doré* to provide less protection of Charter rights than the *Oakes* test, that is a possible result. As we see in the next section, the risk that *Doré* lessens the protections of the Charter also arises from its expansive reliance on Charter values. In our view, however, the risk can be mitigated.

D. The Role of Charter Values Post-Doré

In *Doré*, the court uses the terms "Charter values" and "Charter rights" almost interchangeably. As a result, it is not clear how consideration of Charter values fits within the constitutional requirements to respect Charter rights. On one view, the requirement to consider broad Charter values is all-encompassing and obviates the need to identify infringements of specific Charter rights. It replaces a structured or formal analysis of Charter rights with a diffuse and less precise inquiry. If this is a correct reading of *Doré*, there is a risk that it leads to a weakening of the protection of Charter rights. Treating fundamental constitutional rights on the same footing as values may lead to a watering down of the burden on the government to justify the infringement of those rights.

On another view, the requirement to consider Charter values is an additional command, above and beyond the constitutional requirement to respect Charter rights. In our view, this would be a positive development. It would be helpful if the Supreme Court were to clarify the role of Charter values in the analysis and, ideally, distinguish the requirement to consider Charter values from the constitutional obligation to respect Charter rights and the requirements of s 1.

The view that Charter values and Charter rights are two different things is supported by the role Charter values have played in previous cases. It is worth observing that almost every case cited by Abella J in *Doré* in support of the new approach is a case where the court concluded that Charter rights were *not* engaged or not addressed. Abella J refers to those cases saying that they "applied an administrative law/judicial review analysis in assessing whether the decision-maker took sufficient account of *Charter* values."[33] That characterization is puzzling because, in many of the cases that she mentions, the court expressly resists addressing Charter arguments. In *Baker*, for example, L'Heureux-Dubé J expressly states that "[b]ecause, in my view, the issues raised can be resolved under the principles of administrative law and statutory interpretation, I find it unnecessary to consider the various *Charter* issues raised by the appellant."[34] While L'Heureux-Dubé J states that any exercise of discretion must be consistent with Charter values, she does not consider whether a Charter right is engaged by the decision, or whether the decision-maker "took sufficient account of Charter values."[35] *Baker* was decided in the same year as *G (J)*, and in *G (J)* the court found that a forced separation of a mother from her children would trigger s 7.[36]

---

33 *Doré, supra* note 1 at para 32.
34 *Baker v British Columbia Canada (Minister of Citizenship and Immigration)*, [1999] 2 SCR 817 at para 11 [*Baker*].
35 *Ibid* at para 56.
36 *New Brunswick (Minister of Health and Community Services) v G (J)*, [1993] 3 SCR 46 at para 61.

Abella J also cites *Trinity*[37] in support of the idea that courts can use administrative law to examine whether "the decision-maker took sufficient account of *Charter* values."[38] Again, Charter values were relied on in that case because the court considered that no violation of Charter rights had been proven. The case came before the court because the BC College of Teachers refused to grant the evangelical Trinity Western University (TWU) permission to assume full responsibility for its educational program. TWU required faculty and students to sign its TWU Community Standards code, which described same-sex relations as a "sexual sin." The BC College of Teachers worried that TWU was promoting a culture of discrimination that could be passed from TWU teacher-graduates to children attending public school. Iacobucci and Bastarache JJ, writing for the majority, found that analysis under the Charter was inappropriate because there was no evidence that s 15 equality interests of school children were affected. The decision of the BC College of Teachers, they held, punished TWU for its religious beliefs alone, and not for any wrong it had committed. The proper subject of censure, the majority said, is conduct rather than belief, such as discriminatory conduct in the classroom. Because there was no evidence that TWU graduates had engaged in dis-criminatory conduct, the majority could not conclude that TWU graduates would adversely affect the s 15 interests of BC school children.

However, the majority clearly thought that the impugned decision infringed TWU's free-dom of religion by declining TWU's request to assume full responsibility for its program on the basis of its beliefs. Contending values—freedom of religion versus equality—were un-deniably at stake. Nonetheless, the majority declined to apply the Charter despite a power-ful dissent by L'Heureux-Dubé J that Charter rights were engaged. They disagreed and did not review the decision under ss 2(a) and 1 of the Charter. They resolved the issue on an administrative law analysis where Charter values weighed heavily in the balance. Once again, judges in both the majority and minority treated and understood Charter values as something different from Charter rights.

As a distinct consideration from Charter rights, there is plenty of room for Charter values in administrative decision-making. Much of the history of the role of the Charter in adminis-trative decision-making has been concerned with the capacity of administrative deci-sion-makers and parties appearing before tribunals to adequately address complex Charter questions. One view of the rise to prominence of Charter values in *Doré* is that they represent an effort to move away from the language and structures of Charter rights.[39] The point of doing so tracks access to justice concerns and the fact that it is unrealistic to think that Charter rights will be adequately pleaded and adjudicated in administrative settings where parties are unrepresented and adjudicators are not necessarily legally trained. Moreover, this Charter values approach imposes on decision-makers a general duty to respect the funda-mental values of Canadian society expressed in the Charter.

Courts must be vigilant, however, to ensure that administrative decision-makers properly balance Charter values against statutory objectives. As the British Columbia Court of Appeal stated in the recent case concerning the bar association's refusal to recognize graduates from TWU's proposed law school: "a tribunal's preoccupation with its own statutory regime [might] lead it to value the statutory objectives of that regime too highly against *Charter*

---

37   *Trinity Western University v British Columbia College of Teachers*, 2001 SCC 31, [2001] 1 SCR 772 [*Trinity*].

38   *Doré, supra* note 1 at para 32.

39   Lorne Sossin & Mark Friedman, "Charter Values and Administrative Justice" (2014) 67 SCLR (2d) 391.

values."[40] The Supreme Court majority in *Trinity* did not perceive the decision-maker as especially well placed to evaluate the Charter claims. In determining the standard of review, Iacobucci and Basterache JJ concluded that "the [College of Teachers'] Council is not particularly well equipped to determine the scope of freedom of religion and conscience and to weigh these rights against the right to equality in the context of a pluralistic society. All this to say that even if it was open to the [College of Teachers] to base its decision on perception rather than evidence of actual discrimination or of a real risk of discrimination, there is no reason to give any deference to that decision."[41]

Another challenge posed by the *Doré* approach is that the content and scope of this inchoate collection of values is largely undefined. This problem came squarely before the Ontario Court of Appeal in *Gehl*.[42] The case concerned whether Dr Lynn Gehl was entitled to be registered as an Indian under the *Indian Act*. Sharp JA would have quashed the Registrar of Indian Status's decision because the government policy failed to respect Charter values. Lauwers and Miller JJA concurred in the result but disagreed with Sharp JA's analysis on the grounds that Charter values must maintain a "modest role" in judicial reasoning, particularly because there is no established "doctrinal structure to guide their identification or application."[43] Lauwers and Miller JJA expressed particular concern that a party that comes to court seeking a determination of their Charter rights should not have the question set aside in favour of a diffuse consideration of Charter values.

It seems we can have the best of both worlds. The Supreme Court could help by making clear that Charter values do not replace Charter rights. They are distinct. Charter values arguably include ideals such as equality, liberty, and respect for minorities and the vulnerable. They tend to be general and fundamental principles that can help explain and interpret both statutory provisions and Charter rights. Because they inform statutory interpretation, they play a role in all administrative decision-making that engages them.

Where Charter rights are plainly at stake, however, courts have a duty to address them as such and explicitly.[44] A Charter values analysis should not replace or obscure the question of whether a Charter right has been infringed. If a Charter right has been infringed, the government bears the burden of s 1 to demonstrate that the limit on that right is justified.

Loyola raises questions about the strength of the Supreme Court's commitment to the *Doré* approach.[45] At issue was Loyola High School's request for a partial exemption from a mandatory curricular program called "Ethics and Religious Culture," which teaches about the ethics and beliefs of various religions from a secular and neutral perspective. As a Catholic high school, Loyola sought to teach the ethics of other religions from a Catholic perspective. The minister denied Loyola's request.

While a majority of four led by Abella J followed *Doré*, three members did not, including McLachlin CJ and Rothstein J as well as Moldaver J. Interestingly, McLachlin CJ and Rothstein J were part of the unanimous bench that decided *Doré*. The dissent's reasons do not disavow

---

40 *Trinity Western University v The Law Society of British Columbia*, 2016 BCCA 423 at para 82, leave to appeal to SCC granted, 2017 CanLII 8574.

41 *Trinity*, *supra* note 37 at para 19.

42 *Gehl v Canada (Attorney General)*, 2017 ONCA 319 at paras 78-83.

43 *Ibid* at para 79. See also *Trinity Western University v The Law Society of British Columbia*, *supra* note 40 at para 82.

44 *Symes v Canada*, [1993] 4 SCR 695 at 752.

45 *Loyola*, *supra* note 2.

Doré. Nor do they rely on the *Oakes* test in every detail. However, they employ language that sounds very much like the traditional s 1 analysis that the approach from *Doré* was supposed to supplant.

McLachlin CJ and Moldaver J make it clear that the government bears the burden of showing that Loyola's freedom of religion is limited no more than is reasonably necessary to achieve the goals of the Ethics and Religious Culture program.[46] As noted above, the Court in *Doré* does not say with whom the burden lies, and in the ordinary administrative law case, it is the complainant who must show that the decision is unreasonable. Furthermore, McLachlin CJ and Moldaver J require the government to demonstrate that the decision was "minimally impairing,"[47] echoing the critical step in the *Oakes* test.

A third indicator that the minority from *Loyola* departs from *Doré* is that they relied on evidence filed before the Superior Court of Quebec on the application for judicial review.[48] The Superior Court even heard experts. On an ordinary application for judicial review, further evidence, much less testimony, is not admissible. Judicial review on a reasonableness standard is based on the record that was before the decision-maker. The evidence was admissible in this case because *Loyola* was heard by the Superior Court *before Doré* was rendered and so was heard on the assumption that *Oakes* applied, and the standard of review was correctness.[49] McLachlin CJ and Moldaver J's reliance on this evidence *after Doré* suggests that they are reviewing the decision on a correctness standard.[50]

E. Conclusion

In *Doré*, the Supreme Court purports to end the debate over whether to apply the *Oakes* analysis to administrative decisions that infringe Charter rights. *Doré* is clear that the administrative law approach and the standard of reasonableness will apply. The court emphasized that this approach will work "the same justificatory muscles: balance and proportionality," as in ordinary administrative law.[51] Whether this approach will provide the same protection for parties as they would have received with the *Oakes* test remains to be seen in future cases. Abella J suggests that it should, but aspects of the decision remain to be clarified, such as the role of Charter values in the analysis.

Some questions to watch for:

- What is the burden on a party defending a decision that infringes a Charter right? What does the party need to demonstrate?
- What is the standard of review on the issue of whether a Charter right is engaged by an administrative action? For example, is deference owed to an administrative decision-maker who decides that a Charter right is not engaged (or what if they don't consider the issue at all)?
- Are Charter values the same as Charter rights within the new approach from *Doré*?
- Will deference apply when a decision-maker's Charter analysis does not fall within the expertise of its "home statute"?

---

46   *Ibid* at para 146.
47   *Ibid* at paras 88 and 151.
48   *Ibid* at paras 141-142, 144, 153.
49   *Ibid* at para 29.
50   *Ibid* at para 57.
51   *Doré, supra* note 1 at para 5.

II. AGENCY JURISDICTION OVER THE CHARTER

It is a commonplace principle of statutory interpretation that administrative tribunals and courts alike should endeavour to interpret legislation in light of the Charter and its underlying values. Sometimes, however, unambiguous statutory provisions may appear to infringe Charter rights under any reasonable interpretation. This section examines whether administrative agencies, as creatures of statute, have authority to interpret and apply the Charter to their enabling legislation for the purpose of refusing to give effect to provisions found to violate the Charter. The section then considers the authority of administrative bodies to grant remedies under s 24(1) of the Charter.

A. The Old Trilogy and "Jurisdiction over the Whole Matter"

The Supreme Court initially considered the first issue in a trilogy of cases: *Douglas/Kwantlen Faculty Assn v Douglas College*,[52] *Cuddy Chicks Ltd v Ontario (Labour Relations Board)*,[53] and *Tétreault-Gadoury v Canada (Employment and Immigration Commission)*.[54] La Forest J wrote the majority reasons in each of these decisions. He held that because s 52(1) of the *Constitution Act, 1982* declares the Constitution, including the Charter, to be the supreme law of the land, and any law inconsistent with it to be of no force and effect, administrative decision-makers with the power to interpret law must also interpret and respect this supreme law. Therefore, although administrative decision-makers cannot declare infringing statutory provisions to be invalid (this power is reserved for the courts), s 52(1) authorizes them to both apply the Charter to their enabling legislation and refuse to give effect to provisions they determine to be inconsistent with it.

The Supreme Court pointed out that it retained authority to review agency determinations of Charter issues on a standard of correctness. Perhaps more significantly, however, the court deployed a restrictive understanding of what it would mean for an agency to have authority to interpret law, and thus authority to apply the Charter. In *Cooper*, the court later characterized this authority as one that must evince a "general power to consider questions of law."[55] This power had to be conferred by the enabling legislation because agencies have no inherent authority to decide questions of law, but it could be granted explicitly or implicitly. In *Cuddy Chicks*, the court described this authority as "jurisdiction over the whole of the matter before it, namely, the parties, subject matter and remedy sought."[56] Specifically, the authority to interpret law had to be more than the authority required to implement the legislation's basic policies and programs, because all public officials had to be capable of this much interpretation, and the court was not prepared to say that all public officials had jurisdiction to apply the Charter.

Although the majority in *Douglas College* were careful to insist that their recognition of agency jurisdiction over the Charter did not offend the separation of powers, their restrictive understanding of authority to consider questions of law is grounded in the same separation of powers concerns raised by Lamer CJ in his concurring judgment in *Cooper*. Lamer CJ

---

52 [1990] 3 SCR 570 [*Douglas College*].
53 [1991] 2 SCR 5 [*Cuddy Chicks*].
54 [1991] 2 SCR 22.
55 *Cooper, supra* note 3 at para 46.
56 *Cuddy Chicks, supra* note 52 at 14.

thought that recognizing agency jurisdiction over the Charter undermined the separation of powers according to which the legislature makes law and the executive applies it: permitting agencies to apply the Charter to their enabling legislation appeared, he said, to let the executive decide the limits of its own jurisdiction. Conventional wisdom has the legislature determining those limits at first instance through legislation, and the judiciary policing those limits through judicial review. Lamer CJ held that allowing tribunals to hear Charter challenges to their enabling legislation means that "the executive can defeat the laws of the legislature,"[57] thus inverting the relationship between the legislature and the executive.

The court's restrictive view of authority to consider questions of law led to the much-criticized *Cooper* decision. The case turned on whether the Canadian Human Rights Commission or a tribunal struck under it had jurisdiction to apply s 15 of the Charter to s 15(c) of the *Canadian Human Rights Act.*[58] Section 15(c) of the Act provided that it was not a discriminatory practice for an employer to terminate an individual if the individual reached the normal age of retirement for employees occupying a similar position. La Forest J, for the majority, held that the legislation did not confer on the commission an explicit power to consider questions of law, and that no such power was implicit to the statutory scheme because the commission's role within it was to screen complaints rather than adjudicate them. Thus, the commission had to apply s 15(c) of the Act to the appellants in *Cooper,* disqualifying their case as one that could be sent to a tribunal for adjudication. As a consequence, neither the commission nor a tribunal could review the constitutional validity of the impugned provision. McLachlin J (as she then was, and with L'Heureux-Dubé J) dissented, insisting that "[a]ll law and law-makers that touch the people must conform to [the Charter]"[59] and that the commission had the power to consider questions of law.

B. Vindication of the Dissent in Cooper?

Seven years later, a series of unanimous decisions emerged that confirmed the dissenters' more generous understanding of what it means for a tribunal to have authority to consider questions of law. As we shall see, however, the vindication of the dissent in *Cooper* may not be complete. Two judgments were released together, *Nova Scotia (Workers' Compensation Board) v Martin; Nova Scotia (Workers' Compensation Board) v Laseur;*[60] the third is *Paul v British Columbia (Forest Appeals Commission).*[61] The leading case is *Martin.*

In *Martin,* the Nova Scotia *Workers' Compensation Act* and its regulations excluded chronic pain sufferers from receiving benefits under the regular workers' compensation system and provided, in lieu of benefits usually available to injured workers, a four-week functional restoration program beyond which no further benefits were available. As a result of the statutory exclusion, the Workers' Compensation Board denied benefits to two workers suffering chronic pain. The workers appealed the board's decision to the Workers' Compensation Appeals Tribunal. They alleged that the legislation infringed

---

57   *Cooper, supra* note 3 at para 25.
58   RSC 1985, c H-6.
59   *Cooper, supra* note 3 at para 70.
60   *Supra* note 3.
61   2003 SCC 55, [2003] 2 SCR 585 (agency jurisdiction extends to determinations of Aboriginal rights enshrined in s 35 of the *Constitution Act, 1982*).

s 15(1) of the Charter by denying them equality under the law and discriminating against them on the basis of their disabilities. The Appeals Tribunal held that it had jurisdiction to hear the Charter argument, and concluded that the statutory exclusion violated the Charter as the complainants alleged. The Appeals Tribunal then went on to adjudicate the claims without giving effect to the infringing legislation. The board challenged the Appeals Tribunal's jurisdiction to hear the Charter argument.

Gonthier J wrote for the court and rejected the board's challenge, finding that "[a]dministrative tribunals which have jurisdiction—whether explicit or implied—to decide questions of law arising under a legislative provision are presumed to have concomitant jurisdiction to decide the constitutional validity of that provision,"[62] and that the Appeals Tribunal had such jurisdiction. He relied on the old trilogy and overruled *Cooper* to the extent that it went the other way.

Martin's most important novelty is that it eschewed the prior restrictive understanding of what it means for an agency or tribunal to have authority to consider questions of law. The inquiry into legislative intent on this matter does not rely on whether the legislature intended the tribunal to apply the Charter. The question is "whether the empowering legislation implicitly or explicitly grants to the tribunal the jurisdiction to interpret or decide *any* question of law."[63] Gonthier J rejected the distinction made in *Cooper* between "general" and "limited" questions of law. However, he restricted the inquiry to one that must focus on whether the tribunal has the power "to decide questions of law arising under the challenged provision."[64] These powers typically reside in tribunals with adjudicative functions, but Gonthier J made it clear that the presence or absence of adjudicative authority is not necessarily determinative.

If the legislation does not expressly grant jurisdiction to consider questions of law, the jurisdiction may still be present implicitly and inferred from a series of factors: "the statutory mandate of the tribunal in issue and whether deciding questions of law is necessary to fulfilling this mandate effectively; the interaction of the tribunal in question with other elements of the administrative system; whether the tribunal is adjudicative in nature; and practical considerations, including the tribunal's capacity to consider questions of law."[65] The guiding principle that informs the application of these factors (save perhaps practical considerations) is whether the legislature intended the tribunal to have jurisdiction to decide questions of law.

The presence of such an intent does not, however, end the inquiry; it merely establishes a rebuttable presumption that the agency has jurisdiction to apply the Charter. The presumption can be rebutted, Gonthier J said, by pointing to an explicit or implied statutory withdrawal of authority to determine constitutional questions.

---

62 *Martin, supra* note 3 at para 3.

63 *Ibid* at para 36 (emphasis in original).

64 *Ibid* at para 37.

65 *Ibid* at para 41. For an insightful discussion of the explicit/implicit distinction in *Martin*, and possible uncertainties regarding its application, see JM Evans, "Principle and Pragmatism: Administrative Agencies' Jurisdiction over Constitutional Issues" in G Huscroft & M Taggart, eds, *Inside and Outside Canadian Administrative Law: Essays in Honour of David Mullan* (Toronto: University of Toronto Press, 2006) 377-420.

Despite the court's unequivocal recognition of agency jurisdiction to hear Charter challenges, some tension remains. The tension arises from the requirement of legislative intent and one of its immediate consequences: legislatures can amend and enact law to withdraw tribunal jurisdiction over the Charter. Various provincial legislatures have enacted omnibus legislation that insulates their statutes from agency scrutiny of constitutional matters. For example, in 2004 the British Columbia legislature enacted the *Administrative Tribunals Act*,[66] a comprehensive justice reform measure that expressly denies most provincial administrative tribunals jurisdiction over Charter issues. The Attorney General justified the jurisdiction-depriving sections of the Act on several grounds.[67] In his second reading speech to the legislative assembly, he claimed that courts are more expert than most tribunals with respect to complex and far-reaching Charter questions. He also worried that permitting agencies to resolve these questions would require laypersons to hire (costly) legal counsel where they would not otherwise have to do so. He expressed concern over the drain on resources and the additional time required to settle Charter challenges at the agency level. These resource and access to justice problems, he said, would be exacerbated by the non-binding nature of tribunal decisions over Charter issues, because similar questions would have to be decided anew in subsequent proceedings.

Both proponents and critics of agency jurisdiction over the Charter claim that their policy is the one that, overall, minimizes the expense and time required to settle an administrative dispute involving a Charter challenge. No one denies that if the tribunal does not have jurisdiction to hear a Charter challenge, separate judicial review proceedings must be launched. Critics of agency jurisdiction reply that these constitutional issues are likely to come before the courts in any event, and thus addressing them in the tribunal adds considerable cost and time to the final resolution of the matter. As yet, no comparative empirical studies examine similar cases before similar tribunals in which one jurisdiction's tribunals have competence to consider Charter issues while the others do not. Studies of this nature are needed to advance this aspect of the debate past the current speculation.

The unchallenged doctrinal assumption that merits further reflection is that agency jurisdiction to apply the Charter depends on legislative intent. Recall that the idea underlying this assumption is that tribunals have no inherent jurisdiction to decide questions of law (including constitutional questions), and so all such jurisdiction must issue from the legislature. However, the mere fact that tribunals rely on the legislature for jurisdiction to decide questions of law does not imply that the legislature has authority to deprive them of jurisdiction to apply the Charter to their enabling legislation.

---

66   SBC 2004, c 45, ss 43-45. The Labour Relations Board and the Securities Commission are exceptions to the rule and can decide Charter questions: *Labour Relations Act*, RSBC 1996, c 244, s 115.1(e); *Securities Act*, RSBC 1996, c 418, s 4.1(c). Other BC tribunals can determine constitutional issues related to federalism, but cannot apply the Charter: e.g. *Human Rights Code*, RSBC 1996, c 210, s 32. Yet others cannot determine any constitutional issues: e.g. *Residential Tenancy Act*, SBC 2002, c 78, s 78.1. Alberta has similar legislation: *Administrative Procedures and Jurisdiction Act*, RSA 2000, c A-3, ss 11, 16. In *Tranchemontagne v Ontario (Director, Disability Support Program)*, 2006 SCC 14, [2006] 1 SCR 513, the Supreme Court reaffirmed that legislatures can preclude tribunals from considering Charter questions through clear legislation, though the bar in that case was specific to the relevant statute.

67   British Columbia, Legislative Assembly, *Official Report of Debates*, vol 25, no 15 (18 May 2004) at 11193 et seq, as cited in Deborah K Lovett, "Administrative Tribunal Jurisdiction over Constitutional Issues and the New Administrative Tribunals Act" (2005) 63 Advocate 177 at 191-92.

Arguably, respect for the supremacy of the Constitution requires agencies to have due regard for the Charter—independently of legislative intent—whenever they interpret ordinary legislation to decide questions of law. Otherwise, tribunals are not treating the Constitution as the supreme law with which all other law must conform.[68] Put another way, a plausible interpretation of the principle of constitutional supremacy is that the legislature cannot confer on agencies the authority to decide questions of law without necessarily conferring on them the authority to apply the Charter. This is entirely consistent with the idea that tribunals have no inherent jurisdiction and so must receive all their legal powers from statute. The issue is whether those legal powers can be exercised without regard for the Charter. Yet, as we shall now see, the legislative intent basis of agency jurisdiction over the Charter became more deeply entrenched in the Supreme Court's most recent ruling on agency jurisdiction to grant remedies under s 24(1) in *R v Conway*.[69]

C. Remedies Under Section 24(1)

Section 24(1) provides that anyone whose Charter rights have been infringed may apply to a "court of competent jurisdiction" to obtain a remedy that is appropriate and just in the circumstances." In *Conway*, Abella J, writing for the court, built on the rationale in *Martin* to develop a "new approach" for determining when a board or tribunal can grant a specific remedy under s 24(1) of the Charter.[70] There is a sense in which *Conway* is to s 24(1) what *Martin* is to s 52(1) of the *Constitution Act, 1982*: in both cases, the court relaxes the prior test for determining whether a board or tribunal has jurisdiction to grant the relevant remedy.

Conway has spent most of his adult life in mental health institutions. In 1984 he was found not guilty by reason of insanity of sexual assault with a weapon. In 2006 he complained of various abuses and Charter rights violations. He sought an absolute discharge under s 24(1) before the Ontario Review Board. After an eight-day hearing, the board rejected Conway's request for discharge, finding that he was "an egocentric, impulsive bully" with "continued paranoid and delusional ideation," and that he would pose a risk to public safety if released.[71]

On review, Abella J held that the board had jurisdiction to grant Charter remedies generally, but not the remedy of an absolute discharge. The first stage of the analysis, she said, is to determine whether the board is a "court of competent jurisdiction" within the meaning of s 24(1). Whereas the prior case law, originating with *Mills v The Queen*,[72] called for an inquiry into whether the agency had jurisdiction over the particular s 24(1) remedy sought, Abella J held that the time had come to ground the initial inquiry on a more general and institutional question: "Does this particular tribunal have the jurisdiction to grant *Charter* remedies generally?"[73] She held that the test for resolving this question is precisely the test from *Martin*, which asks whether the tribunal has jurisdiction to decide questions of law, and, if so, whether that jurisdiction has been removed by the legislature. The advantage of this

---

68   Charter, s 32(1); *Constitution Act, 1982*, s 52(1).
69   2010 SCC 22, [2010] 1 SCR 765 [*Conway*].
70   *Ibid* at para 18.
71   *Ibid* at para 13.
72   [1986] 1 SCR 863.
73   *Conway, supra* note 69 at para 22.

approach, Abella J said, is that it attributes Charter jurisdiction "to the tribunal as an institution, rather than requiring litigants to test, remedy by remedy, whether it is a court of competent jurisdiction."[74] If the board is found to be a court of competent jurisdiction, then the
inquiry moves to whether the board has jurisdiction to grant the remedy sought. This issue
is to be determined by legislative intent, as discerned from the board's statutory mandate,
structure, and function.[75]

In *Conway*, the court found that the board was a quasi-judicial body authorized to decide
questions of law in relation to persons detained for wrongful acts for which they were not
criminally responsible (NCR patients). The board is established by, and operates under,
part XX.1 of the *Criminal Code*.[76] Section 672(1) of the *Criminal Code* provides for appeals from
the board's decisions on questions of law. So, as a general matter, Abella J found the board to
be a court of competent jurisdiction for purposes of s 24(1). She then had to determine
whether the remedy of an absolute discharge was available to Conway in light of the board's
mandate and function. At its annual review hearings of NCR patients, the board is required
under part XX.1 to weigh and consider the public's interest in protection from dangerous
persons, the patient's mental condition, and the patient's liberty interest and other needs. If
the NCR patient poses a significant risk to the public, the board is barred by statute from
granting the individual an absolute discharge. Because the board found that Conway continued to pose a risk to public safety, it could not grant him an absolute discharge under s
24(1) of the Charter. Nor could the board grant Conway specific treatment orders and amel-
iorative detention conditions, as he had requested in the alternative, because these too lay
beyond the board's statutory authority. In the result, the court denied Conway's application
for s 24(1) remedies.

While the "new approach" from *Conway* is intended to avoid forcing litigants to "test,
remedy by remedy, whether [the board] is a court of competent jurisdiction,"[77] its method
still forces litigants to "test, remedy by remedy," whether the board has jurisdiction with respect to the remedy sought. Because this has always been the critical question at issue in
s 24(1) cases, in practice the "new approach" may turn out to be old wine in new bottles.[78] It
is also unclear whether the new approach will result, as it is intended to do, in a lessening of
the bifurcation of proceedings. Boards and tribunals after *Conway*, when petitioned for a
s 24(1) remedy, are not to begin with an assessment of the Charter claim that there has been
a rights violation. At no point in *Conway* does the court consider this matter. The inquiry is
directed solely to the availability of the remedy. Presumably, if the remedy were available in
Conway, a consideration of the merits would have been necessary. But because the remedy
is unavailable, the board would never get to the merits of the case, and so Conway would

---

74   *Ibid* at para 23.
75   Sometimes the legislature makes this task easy by expressly *excluding* authority to consider Charter
     questions. See e.g. s 45 of the BC *Administrative Tribunals Act*.
76   RSC 1985, c C-46.
77   *Conway*, *supra* note 69 at para 23.
78   Lorne Sossin & Andrea Hill, "Social Rights and Administrative Justice" in *Reconceiving Human Rights
     Practice for the New Social Rights Paradigm*, research project, Social Rights in Canada online: <http://
     socialrightscura.ca>; see also: Steve Coughlan, "Tribunal Jurisdiction over Charter Remedies: Now You
     See It, Now You Don't" (2010) 75 CR (6th) 238.

have to go to court if he wished to have a public institution determine whether his Charter rights had been violated.

Less clear still is the content of s 24(1), as a constitutional remedial provision, given that provision's strict dependence on the board's statutory scheme. The court could have read s 24(1) as conferring on all "courts of competent jurisdiction" a statute-independent jurisdiction to do whatever is "appropriate and just in the circumstances" to remedy a Charter violation. As with all administrative action, exercise of this jurisdiction would be subject to judicial review. But by grounding jurisdiction over s 24(1) on the statutory scheme alone, rather than on the statutory scheme *and* the Charter considered as a power-conferring enactment, it appears that applicants are entitled to petition boards for only those remedies and orders that are already available under the statute. Additional cases will be needed to determine whether agency jurisdiction to grant remedies under s 24(1) has any independent substance.

III. CONCLUSION

The relationship between administrative law and the Charter is sometimes uncertain, but important. There are significant areas of overlap and the constitutional role of the judiciary is similar whether or not judges refer to the Charter when they review administrative decisions. As a result, there is considerable cross-pollination such that developments in one area will often, and even necessarily, give rise to changes in the other.

Cases involving judicial review of administrative action that may affect Charter rights are common. The courts have had numerous occasions to address such issues in a diversity of circumstances. The court's recent decision in *Doré* is a strong indication that the future will be more stable than the past. While there was considerable uncertainty as to when a traditional s 1 analysis would be engaged, the court has now identified a vast area of decision-making that engages Charter rights where the *Oakes* analysis will not be relied on. The court has prudently reserved the challenges of determining precisely how this will play out for later cases.

Finally, the scope of authority of administrative tribunals to apply the Charter is increasingly clear and arguably more generous. The authority of administrative tribunals to grant remedies under s 24 of the Charter is also better defined and possibly more extensive than it ever has been. Although it is too early to say, this may give rise to an increase in applications for such relief before administrative tribunals, which in turn will give the court occasion to determine whether s 24 can ground remedies not already available under the tribunal's enabling statute.

Table 13.1   Different Approaches to Reviewing Administrative Decisions That Engage Charter Rights

Case	Administrative analysis, Charter, both, or hybrid?	If administrative analysis, was the decision reasonable?	Was a Charter right infringed by the legislation or the decision?	Justified under s 1?
Doré	hybrid administrative and Charter	reasonable	decision	yes, reasonable decision
Slaight (Dickson CJ +3)	Charter	n/a	decision	yes, both
Slaight (Lamer J)	both	unreasonable	decision	one yes, one no
Slaight (Beetz J)	Charter	n/a	decision	no, both
Baker (L'Heureux-Dubé J +4)	administrative	unreasonable	n/a	n/a
Little Sisters (Binnie J +5)	Charter	n/a	decision	no
Little Sisters (Iacobucci J +2)	Charter	n/a	both	no
Trinity Western (Iacobucci, Bastarache JJ)	administrative	unreasonable	n/a	n/a
Trinity Western (L'Heureux-Dubé J)	both	reasonable	decision	no
Chamberlain (McLachlin CJ +5)	administrative	unreasonable	n/a	n/a
Chamberlain (Gonthier, Bastarache JJ)	hybrid administrative and Charter	reasonable	n/a	n/a
Chamberlain (LeBel J)	administrative with reserve	unreasonable	n/a	n/a
Multani (Charron J +4)	Charter	n/a	yes	no
Multani (Abella, Deschamps JJ)	hybrid administrative and Charter	unreasonable	n/a	n/a
Multani (LeBel J)	Charter, not all factors of s 1	n/a	decision	no
Lake (LeBel J +8)	Charter, but with deference s 1	unclear	both	yes
PHS (McLachlin CJ +8)	Charter	n/a	both	legislation yes, decision no

SUGGESTED ADDITIONAL READINGS

BOOKS AND ARTICLES

Choudhry, S, & K Roach, "Racial and Ethnic Profiling: Statutory Discretion, Constitutional Remedies, and Democratic Accountability" (2003) 41 Osgoode Hall LJ 1.

Evans, JM, "Principle and Pragmatism: Administrative Agencies' Jurisdiction over Constitutional Issues" in G Huscroft & M Taggart, eds, *Inside and Outside Canadian Administrative Law: Essays in Honour of David Mullan* (Toronto: University of Toronto Press, 2006) 377-420.

Evans, JM, "The Principles of Fundamental Justice: The Constitution and the Common Law" (1991) 29 Osgoode Hall LJ 51.

Leckey, Robert, "Prescribed by Law/Une règle de droit" (2007) 45:3 Osgoode Hall LJ 571.

Lovett, DK, "Administrative Tribunal Jurisdiction over Constitutional Issues and the New Administrative Tribunals Act" (2005) 63 Advocate 177.

Van Harten, G, G Heckman & D Mullan, *Administrative Law: Cases, Text, and Materials*, 6th ed (Toronto: Emond Montgomery, 2010) 276-80.

Sossin, Lorne, "Discretion Unbound: Reconciling the Charter and Soft Law" (2002) 45 Can Public Admin 465.

CASES

Canada (Attorney General) v PHS Community Services Society, 2011 SCC 44, [2011] 3 SCR 134.

Canada (Prime Minister) v Khadr, 2010 SCC 3, [2010] 1 SCR 44.

Charkaoui v Canada (Citizenship and Immigration), 2007 SCC 9, [2007] 1 SCR 350.

Conway, R v, 2010 SCC 22, [2010] 1 SCR 765.

Doré v Barreau du Québec, 2012 SCC 12.

Lake v Canada (Minister of Justice), 2008 SCC 23, [2008] 1 SCR 761.

Mills v The Queen, [1986] 1 SCR 863.

Multani v Commission scolaire Marguerite-Bourgeoys, 2006 SCC 6, [2006] 1 SCR 256.

Newfoundland and Labrador Nurses' Union v Newfoundland and Labrador (Treasury Board), 2011 SCC 62, [2011] 3 SCR 708.

Nova Scotia (Workers' Compensation Board) v Martin; Nova Scotia (Workers' Compensation Board) v Laseur, 2003 SCC 54, [2003] 2 SCR 504.

Singh v Canada (Minister of Employment and Immigration), [1985] 1 SCR 177.

Slaight Communications Inc v Davidson, [1989] 1 SCR 1038.

Suresh v Canada (Minister of Citizenship and Immigration), 2002 SCC 1, [2002] 1 SCR 3.

Wareham v Ontario (Ministry of Community and Social Services), 2008 ONCA 771.

CHAPTER FOURTEEN

Top Ten Questions (and a Few Answers) About Substantive Review

Peter J Carver

Faculty of Law, University of Alberta

I. INTRODUCTION

Law professors live good lives—don't let them tell you otherwise. However, into these charmed lives, certain seasonal raindrops fall. One of the stormier moments occurs when the law professor is called to come up with good exam questions. This is especially true in administrative law. Since the subject matter of administrative law is "statutorily delegated decision-making," the first problem is fairly easy to understand. Hypothetical fact patterns in administrative law must generally include statutory provisions, and often provisions that delegate, describe, and give context to decision-making powers exercised by government officials or tribunals. The instructor knows that no one likes reading statutes and few people are good at it, and that these things are only truer under the time pressures produced by exams.

Finding a statutory setting is just the first difficulty. If an exam question is going to test students' abilities to perform a standard of review analysis, then other features need to be built into the problem: factors that make the choice between "reasonableness" and "correctness" somewhat arguable; an issue (of law, or of fact, or—oh no—of mixed fact and law) that can be identified and discussed, even if briefly; and reasons given by the decision-maker that are both plausible and flawed. Writing an administrative law problem dealing with substantive review is a job that calls for Lewis Carroll, performed by people like Homer Simpson.

This chapter is intended to give you some insight into how an instructor—perhaps even your instructor—goes about putting together a fact pattern exam question dealing with substantive review, and how you can go about answering it. The way in which this will be done is by raising and answering ten commonly asked questions about substantive review. The first five questions go to the first stage of analyzing a substantive review problem: "What is the applicable standard of review?" Questions 6 through 10 go to the second analytical step: "How should the appropriate standard of review be applied to a set of facts?" With each question, we provide a short description of what you can expect in an exam question that touches on the points raised. Before getting to this task, we first need to establish common ground about what "substantive review" means.

The term "substantive review" refers to judicial review of the merits, or substance, of administrative decision-making. The area of "procedural review" goes to the fairness of the processes leading to the making of a decision, including that the decision-maker be impartial. Administrative law is concerned with other matters going to the lawfulness of decision-making, including proper delegation of authority, the process of appointing decision-makers, and the evidence to be received and weighed in a hearing. However, substantive review deals with the actual decision or outcome of the process, and the bases on which it can be questioned in a superior court. The theoretical problem or dilemma for substantive review derives from the following contextual feature: in every instance of substantive review, legislators (either at the federal or provincial level) have delegated the making of a decision on the merits to a person or a tribunal *other than* a court. In a 1979 case called *CUPE v NB Liquor Commission*,[1] the Supreme Court of Canada decided that this context called on the judiciary to accord deference to the substantive decisions of statutory delegates, at least in some circumstances. The issues of what those circumstances are, and how to operationalize deference, have remained the central concerns of substantive review in Canada since that time.

---

1   [1979] 2 SCR 227 [*CUPE*].

II. SELECTING THE APPROPRIATE STANDARD OF REVIEW

The Supreme Court of Canada (SCC) set out the contemporary approach to substantive review in 2008 in *Dunsmuir v New Brunswick*.[2] Although the justices wrote three separate opinions in *Dunsmuir*, they all agreed that there should be two standards of review applicable to statutorily delegated decision-making: (1) a standard of *reasonableness*, or of deference to the decision-maker; and (2) a standard of *correctness*, or no deference. The first issue in any substantive review case is that of identifying which of these two standards of review is appropriate to the decision-making in question. The stated hope of the SCC in *Dunsmuir* was to simplify the law of substantive review, in part by reducing the number of possible standards of review from three to two by eliminating a standard of high deference, known as "patent unreasonableness." However, almost a decade after *Dunsmuir*, the court's hope has not come to fruition. Lawyers and courts, including the SCC, continue to spend considerable time wrestling with the question of when to accord deference to a delegated decision-maker.

This ongoing difficulty is reflected in a decision by the SCC from late 2016, *Edmonton (City) v Edmonton East (Capilano) Shopping Centres Ltd*.[3] The case concerned the annual property tax assessment of a shopping mall in Edmonton. No, not THAT mall. Here, the Capilano Shopping Mall in southeast Edmonton was assessed as being worth $31 million. The owners of the mall exercised their right under the provincial *Municipal Government Act* (MGA)[4] to file a "complaint" to the Assessment Review Board, seeking a lower valuation. In its response to the board, the City of Edmonton submitted that the original assessment had been made on a mistaken classification of the property, and the assessment should be *raised*. The board agreed with the city, and raised the assessed value to $41 million.

The mall owners appealed the board's decision to the Alberta Court of Queen's Bench, pursuant to a statutory right of appeal in s 470 of the MGA. The owners argued that the statute did not empower the board to *raise* an assessment on a complaint filed by a taxpayer. The argument turned on interpreting the following provisions of the MGA:

> 460(1) A person wishing to make a complaint about any assessment or tax must do so in accordance with this section....
>
> (3) A complaint may be made only by an assessed person or a taxpayer.
>
> 467(1) An assessment review board may, with respect to [a complaint], make a change to an assessment roll or tax roll or decide that no change is required.

Rooke J of the Court of Queen's Bench, affirmed by the Alberta Court of Appeal, ruled that the appropriate standard of review to apply to the board's decision was correctness, and went on to quash the decision. The City of Edmonton appealed to the Supreme Court of Canada. In a 5–4 decision, the court ruled that the appropriate standard of review was reasonableness, and found the board's decision reasonable. The four justices in the minority would have found the appropriate standard of review to be correctness, and set the board's decision aside.

---

2 2008 SCC 9, [2008] 1 SCR 190 [*Dunsmuir*].
3 2016 SCC 47, [2016] 2 SCR 293 [*Edmonton East*].
4 RSA 2000, c M-26.

It may be useful to have the facts of *Edmonton East* in mind as we move through a series of five questions that students (and lawyers) often ask when confronted with the task of identifying the appropriate standard of review. Like a good exam question, the statutory and other facts are relatively straightforward, but the issues they give rise to are eminently arguable.

1. Are we dealing with judicial review or a statutory right of appeal?

There are two ways in which the decisions of statutorily delegated decision-makers can be challenged in superior courts—either through judicial review, or on appeal. Administrative law professors really want you to know the difference. Fortunately, it is fairly easy to tell the difference. Appeals to court exist only where granted expressly in a statute. Judicial review, on the other hand, is available to a party affected by an administrative decision as a matter of common law (or, more precisely, as part of the inherent jurisdiction of superior courts). If no reference is made in a statute to a right to appeal a delegated decision, then there will nevertheless still be recourse to judicial review. A legislature may grant an appeal right for a limited set of issues; if it does so, then issues not listed should be subject to judicial review.

For exam purposes, a question will give you enough to know whether you are dealing with an appeal or judicial review. If you are asked only to "challenge" a decision, then look to see if the fact pattern refers to a statutory appeal provision. If there is none, then any recourse will lie in judicial review.

Why does the difference between an appeal and judicial review matter for substantive review? In the 1990s, the SCC decided that regardless of which process is employed, the judiciary should apply the same analysis to determine the appropriate standard of review to apply to the decision in question.[5] The court made the question of whether the process was by appeal or by review into one of several contextual factors for determining the standard of review: if the matter arose by way of a statutory appeal, this pointed toward correctness review; if by judicial review, and especially if the tribunal's jurisdiction was protected by a "privative clause," this pointed to reasonableness review. In *Edmonton East*, the mall owners brought their challenge to the assessment board's decision by way of the appeal right set out in s 470 of the MGA. The discussion of the weight to be given this factor was a significant issue in the *Edmonton East* case, and will be discussed further below.

One more note about appeals: once a superior court makes a ruling with respect to an administrative decision, the court's ruling can be appealed to a higher court in the usual fashion. In *Edmonton East*, the first judicial decision was made by the Court of Queen's Bench. It decided on the applicable standard of review for the board's decision, and applied that standard. On appeal to the Alberta Court of Appeal, the latter court dealt with the standard of review issue as a legal issue subject to correctness. The same applied with respect to the appeal to the Supreme Court of Canada. Neither a standard of review analysis, nor any degree of deference, is owed by a higher to a lower court on legal questions.

---

5   *Canada (Director of Investigation and Research) v Southam Inc*, [1997] 1 SCR 748 [*Southam*].

2. What is the decision being challenged (the "impugned decision")? Is there only one decision or two?

The "impugned decision" refers, of course, to the administrative decision that is being or has been challenged, whether in an appeal or by judicial review. In an exam setting, just as in legal practice, it is important to be clear about what the impugned decision is (as well as who is supposed to make it, and under what authority). This is not always straightforward.

For example, it can be important to determine whether one is dealing with a single issue, or with multiple issues, each deserving separate analysis. The impugned decision in *Edmonton East* was that of the Assessment Review Board, which decided to raise the assessment of the Capilano Shopping Centre from $31 million to $41 million. However, neither the parties nor the Supreme Court addressed the question of what the precise assessment amount should be. Instead, the argument in the case concerned whether the board had the power or jurisdiction to award *any* increase in assessed value on a complaint by a taxpayer. The majority described this decision as "implicit" in the overall assessment appeal.[6]

This approach, of breaking a single overall outcome into multiple component issues, called "disaggregation" by some commentators, has generally been discouraged by the Supreme Court of Canada.[7] In moving to a position that favours deference in most instances of substantive review, the court has rejected the "preliminary questions" and related doctrines that imply a statutory delegate must "correctly" confirm its statutory jurisdiction before moving on to make a decision on the facts before them in an individual case. On occasion, however, it may make sense to identify a single decision as having distinct components. Is *Edmonton East* such a case? The issue of whether the board had the power to raise assessments did lie to some extent on the face of the statute. The provision giving the right to file a "complaint" with the board stated a "complaint may be made only by an assessed person or a taxpayer." This provided the basis for an argument, accepted by the minority justices, that since the city had no right to file a complaint saying that an assessment was too low, the board should not be able to rule on that basis.

For exam purposes, an instructor will not usually want students to be unnecessarily tangled up in the question of multiple, or implicit, decisions. Fact patterns will generally identify a single decision, and it will be up to you to characterize the nature of the issue as one of law, fact, or mixed fact and law. On occasion, however, a fact pattern may contain clues that there is more than one decision involved. This can be done, for instance, by separating a statutory provision that deals with liability from a provision that deals with remedy. The purpose of creating two issues in this way will almost always be to have you distinguish between the standard of review applicable to each issue, and explain why.

---

6   *Edmonton East, supra* note 3 at para 13.
7   See majority judgment in *Council of Canadians with Disabilities v VIA Rail Canada Inc*, 2007 SCC 15, [2007] 1 SCR 650.

A second vexed question concerns the nature of the issue being decided: is it an issue of law, fact, or mixed law and fact? The best statement on the question remains that made by Iacobucci J in *Southam* in 1997:

> Briefly stated, questions of law are questions about what the correct legal test is; questions of fact are questions about what actually took place between the parties; and questions of mixed law and fact are questions about whether the facts satisfy the legal tests. A simple example will illustrate these concepts. In the law of tort, the question what "negligence" means is a question of law. The question whether the defendant did this or that is a question of fact. And, once it has been decided that the applicable standard is one of negligence, the question whether the defendant satisfied the appropriate standard of care is a question of mixed law and fact. I recognize, however, that the distinction between law on the one hand and mixed law and fact on the other is difficult.[8]

Perhaps we can all take some comfort from that last sentence. In any event, there is one issue that is almost always understood to be a "question of law": the interpretation of a statutory provision. For that reason, instructors frequently base standard of review questions around situations in which an administrative decision-maker is engaged in interpreting a statutory provision.

3. Which approach should we use in selecting the appropriate standard of review to apply?

In *Dunsmuir*, agreement between the nine justices ended with the idea that correctness and reasonableness were the two available standards of review. The court divided over the method to be employed in choosing between these two standards in any particular case. The division reflected the fact that the court was caught between two approaches. The first, known by the ungainly name of the "pragmatic and functional" (P&F) approach had predominated since the mid-1990s. The P&F approach involved balancing four factors to determine the degree of deference owed to an administrative decision-maker:

1. the existence of a privative clause or, by contrast, a right of appeal;
2. the degree of expertise of the decision-maker relative to the issue being decided;
3. whether the decision was one of law, or fact, or mixed law and fact; and
4. whether the role of the decision-maker was more adjudicative, or policy-making.

In *Dunsmuir*, the court affirmed that these continued to be relevant factors. However, a majority of the justices also suggested that reasonableness would be the appropriate standard of review in most cases, with correctness being an exception.

Over the next several years, the court came to endorse the latter position in the form of a "presumption of reasonableness." In *Edmonton East*, Karakatsanis J, writing for the majority, described how the presumption should operate on these terms:

> Unless the jurisprudence has already settled the applicable standard of review (*Dunsmuir*, at para. 62), the reviewing court should begin by considering whether the issue involves the interpretation by an administrative body of its own statute or statutes closely connected to its function. If so, the standard of review is presumed to be reasonableness (*Mouvement laïque*

---

8   *Southam, supra* note 5 at para 35.

québécois v. Saguenay (City), 2015 SCC 16 (CanLII), [2015] 2 S.C.R. 3, at para. 46). This presumption of deference on judicial review respects the principle of legislative supremacy and the choice made to delegate decision making to a tribunal, rather than the courts.[9]

She went on to cite four exceptional categories of issues that may rebut the presumption of reasonableness: constitutional questions regarding the division of powers; issues of central importance to the legal system as a whole and outside the adjudicator's specialized area of expertise, true questions of jurisdiction, and issues regarding the jurisdictional lines between two or more competing specialized tribunals. In applying the presumption of reasonableness approach, then, we need to know something about the scope and meaning of these exceptions. We return to this discussion shortly.

The dissenting justices in *Edmonton East*, however, adopted an alternative approach to choosing the standard of review. In an opinion written by Brown and Côté JJ, the minority termed the alternative the "contextual approach." In some ways, the contextual approach can be viewed as a return to the multi-factoral approach (the "pragmatic and functional" approach) that predominated before *Dunsmuir*. The main purpose of the contextual approach, according to Brown and Côté JJ, is to identify what the legislature *intended* with respect to the standard of review to be applied to any particular decision-making power. Several contextual factors (related to the context of the statutory power) assist in revealing legislative intent. Chief among relevant factors in the *Edmonton East* case, according to the minority, was the appeal provision in s 470 of the MGA.[10]

The idea is that if the legislature has created a right of appeal to a court, and authorized the court to "give direction" to the administrative body as to how to deal with the issue in question, then this is tantamount to the legislators saying that the court should apply correctness review. In making this point, the minority was relying heavily on a 2014 decision by the SCC in a case called *Tervita Corp v Canada*.[11] In that case, a majority had concluded that an appeal clause represented a clear legislative preference for correctness review. The appeal clause read:

> 13(1) Subject to subsection (2), an appeal lies to the Federal Court of Appeal from any decision or order, whether final, interlocutory, or interim, of the Tribunal *as if it were a judgment of the Federal Court*.[12]

In *Edmonton East*, the majority distinguished *Tervita* on the basis that the appeal clause in the latter case was unambiguous with respect to legislative intent concerning standard of review. The majority found the kind of appeal right in the MGA insufficient to rebut the presumption of reasonableness.

What is going on here? The first thing to acknowledge is that there is a significant division on the SCC with respect to the degree to which correctness review should survive (or perhaps, even prosper) in Canadian administrative law. Justices who support the "presumption

---

9   *Edmonton East*, *supra* note 3 at para 22.

10 Following the decision in *Edmonton East*, the Legislative Assembly of Alberta replaced these appeal provisions with an express right of judicial review from the board to the Court of Queen's bench. In the circumstances, should this amendment be understood as the legislators' endorsing a deferential standard of review for board decisions?

11 *Tervita Corp v Canada (Commissioner of Competition)*, 2015 SCC 3, [2015] 1 SCR 161 [*Tervita*].

12 *Competition Tribunal Act*, RSC 1985, c 19 (2nd Supp), s 13(1) (emphasis added).

of reasonableness" approach believe that deference should be shown in the great majority of substantive review cases, with correctness being reserved for a tightly circumscribed list of exceptional circumstances. In recent years, Rosalie Abella J has been the strongest proponent of this position. Justices who support the "contextual approach" believe that courts should accord deference to administrative law-makers less frequently, and that there are numerous factors (including the existence of a broad appeal right) that point to correctness review.

The second thing to note is that the current Canadian approach to substantive review is the presumption of reasonableness approach. Applying the presumptive approach calls on us to understand the "exceptional circumstances," to which we turn momentarily. One benefit of the presumptive approach is its greater predictability. As the majority noted in *Edmonton East*, the contextual approach tends to throw the doors to argument open, and to draw in a number of possibly relevant factors.

For exam purposes, and until further notice, use the "presumption of reasonableness" approach. Almost certainly, this means that your analysis should address whether one or more of the four recognized exceptions to the presumption is arguable on the facts given. In addition, you should consider whether an argument could be made for one of the alternative approaches for determining standard of review. The principal alternatives are precedent, and the contextual approach. The latter might appear arguable where there is a strong indicator of legislative intent (such as a broad appeal right or a strong privative clause), or of another factor that has been important in the case law.

---

4. What are "issues of central importance to the legal system as distinct from those viewed as falling within the adjudicator's specialized area of expertise?"

The presumption of reasonableness applies, subject to the four exceptions listed earlier. Only two of the four exceptions will be discussed here. The other two—constitutional issues involving the division of powers, and issues going to the drawing of jurisdictional boundaries between two tribunals—are relatively discrete and thus easier to identify. For this very reason, they make for good hypothetical facts tucked into exam questions, and so must not be forgotten. The discussion in this and the next question, however, address the two more ambiguous exceptions to the presumption of reasonableness: "issues of central importance to the legal system," and "true questions of jurisdiction."

In *Edmonton East*, Karakatsanis J termed one exception to the presumption of reasonableness as issues of central importance to the legal system as distinct from those viewed as falling within the adjudicator's specialized area of expertise. This phrasing draws then on two ideas, and puts them in opposition to each other: "issues of central importance to the legal system" versus "issues falling within the adjudicator's specialized area of expertise."

a. Issues of central importance to the legal system

In general, the Supreme Court has drawn a high threshold for identifying an issue of law as being of "central importance to the legal system," and so calling for application of correctness review. This can best be seen in the case *Canada (Canadian Human Rights Commission) v Canada (Attorney General)*,[13] where the issue in question was whether the statutory provision that authorized a tribunal to award compensation to a successful complainant "for any expenses incurred by the victim [complainant] as a result of the discriminatory practice" should be understood to include an order for legal costs. In finding that this question of costs was not one of central importance to the legal system, the court said:

> In addition, a decision as to whether a particular tribunal will grant a particular type of compensation—in this case, legal costs—can hardly be said to be a question of central importance for the Canadian legal system and outside the specialized expertise of the adjudicator. Compensation is frequently awarded in various circumstances and under many schemes. It cannot be said that a decision on whether to grant legal costs as an element of that compensation and about their amount *would subvert the legal system*, even if a reviewing court found it to be in error.[14]

The idea that to be "central to the legal system" an issue of law must be one whose misapplication would "subvert the legal system" suggests few issues will rise to this level. The court in *Mowat* applied reasonableness to the tribunal's decision that the statute allowed it to award legal costs, but found this interpretation of the statute unreasonable.

The idea of "subverting the legal system" seems somewhat narrow. Another way of looking at "questions of central importance to the legal system" might involve the seriousness of the interest at stake, not so much for the individual parties in a case, but for others more generally. Issues of liberty, discrimination, immigration status, and other forms of personal status, might speak to that idea.

For exam purposes, the following things might be used to indicate "centrality to the legal system": interpretation of a phrase that is known to be, or said to be, used commonly in another area of law, such as contracts, torts, or damages; interpretation of a statutory phrase that appears in various statutes; interpretation of a term used in human rights law or international law; and matters going to interests, such as liberty, for which courts have traditionally been viewed as important protectors. If the issue involves interpreting a statute, then be clear whether this is the tribunal's "home statute" or one the tribunal does not usually consider.

---

b. Specialized expertise

In *Southam*,[15] the SCC identified expertise of the decision-maker as the single most important factor for deciding whether deference was owed. In the ensuing years, expertise has

---

13   2011 SCC 53, [2011] 3 SCR 471 [*Mowat*].
14   *Ibid* at para 25 (emphasis added).
15   *Supra* note 5.

ceased to be viewed as determinative. For one thing, the court made clear that "expertise" means expertise "relative to the judiciary," meaning that there must be grounds for believing the administrative decision-makers have an advantage over judges themselves. This connects up with a difficulty in defining what the sources of such expertise might be, and in what circumstances it can be recognized. The clearest indicator of expertise is likely where the governing statute requires that appointees to a tribunal have a certain professional or educational background. If the issue before the tribunal relates to that background, then this will strongly support the idea of expertise. However, instances of required backgrounds for appointment as a decision-maker are infrequent. Courts have looked instead at the function of the tribunal, in terms of the specialized area of its activity, and the volume of cases, as an experiential basis for finding tribunal members to have expertise. In *Edmonton East*, Karakatsanis J said the following about the expertise:

> Expertise arises from the specialization of functions of administrative tribunals like the Board which have a habitual familiarity with the legislative scheme they administer: "… in many instances, those working day to day in the implementation of frequently complex administrative schemes have or will develop a considerable degree of expertise or field sensitivity to the imperatives and nuances of the legislative regime" (*Dunsmuir*, at para. 49, quoting D. J. Mullan, "Establishing the Standard of Review: The Struggle for Complexity?" (2004), 17 *C.J.A.L.P.* 59, at p. 93 …. [E]xpertise is something that inheres in a tribunal itself as an institution: "… at an institutional level, adjudicators … can be presumed to hold relative expertise in the interpretation of the legislation that gives them their mandate, as well as related legislation that they might often encounter in the course of their functions" (*Dunsmuir*, at para. 68).[16]

This approach places emphasis on the institutional source of expertise. It links expertise to the other aspect of the "exceptional category" in question, whether the issue arises from the "home statute" or from a more general area of law. The minority in *Edmonton East* found the institutional approach to result too easily in findings of expertise:

> The majority's view that "expertise is something that inheres in a tribunal itself as an institution" risks transforming the presumption of deference into an irrebuttable rule. Courts must not infer from the mere creation of an administrative tribunal that it necessarily possesses greater relative expertise in all matters it decides, especially on questions of law.[17]

For exam purposes, identify what in the facts shows a degree of expertise on the part of the decision-makers. Is it a requirement that they have a certain educational or professional background, or is it simply that they would be expected to acquire experience by operating under their "home statute?" The former can be a stronger indicator of expertise, so long as the issue in question calls on that background. If the facts suggest the decision-makers have a role of developing policy, this supports the idea of a specialized or expert function.

---

16   *Edmonton East, supra* note 3 at para 33.
17   *Ibid* at para 85.

5. *What are true questions of jurisdiction?*

The concept of what is a "jurisdictional issue," or an issue that is "within a tribunal's jurisdiction" or outside that jurisdiction, has been one of the most fraught questions in substantive review in Canada. From *CUPE*[18] in 1979 to the mid-1990s, the question served as the starting place for assessing whether a statutory delegate's decision-making was entitled to deference. In 1998 with *Pushpanathan v Canada*,[19] the Supreme Court appeared to dispense with the question of jurisdiction in favour of moving directly to the issue of deference, to be determined by a series of contextual factors. Then, somewhat surprisingly, in its attempt to streamline and simplify the law of substantive review in *Dunsmuir*, the court revived the idea that some issues of law are "true questions of jurisdiction" in nature, calling for correctness review. Just three years later in *Alberta Teachers*,[20] a majority of the court all but finished off "true questions of jurisdiction" as a category for analysis. Rothstein J put it this way:

> As I have explained, I am unable to provide a definition of what might constitute a true question of jurisdiction. The difficulty with maintaining the category of true questions of jurisdiction is that without a clear definition or content to the category, courts will continue, unnecessarily, to be in doubt on this question. However, at this stage, I do not rule out, in our adversarial system, counsel raising an argument that might satisfy a court that a true question of jurisdiction exists and applies in a particular case. The practical approach is to direct the courts and counsel that at this time, true questions of jurisdiction will be exceptional and, should the occasion arise, to address in a future case whether such category is indeed helpful or necessary.[21]

This kind of an invitation coming from a high court judge has more the character of a warning, even a dare, rather than encouragement to give it a try. Nevertheless, the court's having left the door open to the "exceptional" appearance of a true question of jurisdiction creates a major temptation for law professors: to conceive of fact patterns that might look like such an exception.

The problem with which the court has been concerned in trying to reduce the analytical importance of "jurisdiction" is that most examples of statutory interpretation can be easily transformed into a basis for casting doubt on the jurisdiction of a delegate to even answer the question. Getting the interpretive answer "right" can look very much like a necessary first step to the delegate's acquiring the jurisdiction to make a decision. This can be seen in *Mowat*, where the tribunal's interpretation of the phrase "any expenses" is, from one perspective, the necessary basis for its awarding legal costs for the complainant. The underlying concern of those advancing this perspective is that administrative decision-makers like the tribunal will, if unchecked by the courts, make decisions that expand their own statutory power. The Supreme Court in *Mowat*, of course, declined to view this as a "true question of jurisdiction." Similarly, in *Edmonton East*, the majority gave short shrift to the idea the board was dealing with a true question of jurisdiction:

> This category is "narrow" and these questions, assuming they indeed exist, are rare …. It is clear here that the Board may hear a complaint about a municipal assessment. The issue is simply one

---

18 *Supra* note 1.

19 *Pushpanathan v Canada (Minister of Citizenship and Immigration)*, [1998] 1 SCR 982.

20 *Alberta (Information and Privacy Commissioner) v Alberta Teachers' Association*, 2011 SCC 61, [2011] 3 SCR 654 [*Alberta Teachers*].

21 *Ibid* at para 42.

of interpreting the Board's home statute in the course of carrying out its mandate of hearing and deciding assessment complaints. No true question of jurisdiction arises.[22]

The dissenting justices rested their conclusion that the appropriate standard of review was correctness on the wording of the appeal provisions and what they disclosed of legislative intent, and declined to rule on the true question of jurisdiction issue.

It is possible the SCC could make the definitive ruling that true questions of jurisdiction do not exist for analytical purposes, but they have not yet done so. Unless and until they do so, this remains an area rife for speculation about what might constitute such a jurisdictional question. One possibility that comes to mind is where the outcome of the impugned decision forms the basis for a *different* decision-maker to assume its statutory authority. In the non-administrative sphere, an example might be the finding of guilt on a driving offence serving as a basis for a director of motor vehicle licensing deciding to suspend a licence. The first decision is jurisdictional for the second. The same concept might apply between two administrative decisions.[23] However, there could be another way to approach this relationship between overlapping authorities. The first decision-maker might be viewed not so much as the decision-maker in the statutory scheme but as a "screener" or referring agent. This would be similar to the analysis given by the court in *Halifax (Regional Municipality) v Nova Scotia (Human Rights Commission)*.[24] In that case, the City of Halifax applied for judicial review to have the commission's decision to refer a complaint of discrimination against the city to a hearing tribunal set aside. The trial court applied correctness review to what it described as a jurisdictional issue. The Supreme Court, however, viewed the commission's ruling as merely preliminary to the final determination that would be made by a tribunal. In such circumstances, it was appropriate to apply the standard of reasonableness review, such that a reviewing court would intervene to stop the proceedings only where the referral decision was unreasonable:

> The Commission's referral decision did not involve the sort of determinations that the chambers judge thought it did. Instead, the Commission's function was simply one of exercising its statutory discretion to decide whether it was satisfied that, having regard to all of the circumstances of the complaint, an inquiry by a board of inquiry was warranted, a function "more administrative than judicial in nature."[25]

For exam purposes, it is appropriate to note that the SCC has questioned whether true questions of jurisdiction exist. Nevertheless, you should be prepared to identify what might make the grade as such a rare creature. Due to its presumed rarity, a possible "true question of

---

22 *Supra* note 3 at para 26.
23 For an example of such a situation, see *Canada (Public Safety and Emergency Preparedness) v Tran*, 2015 FCA 237, [2016] 2 FCR 459. In this case, judicial review was taken of a decision by a departmental official—a decision that arguably foreclosed the statutory jurisdiction of the Immigration and Refugee Board. The appeal of the Federal Court of Appeal decision was heard by the Supreme Court of Canada on January 19, 2017. This case, in simplified form, serves as the basis for the "Sample Exam Question" in the accompanying online materials.
24 2012 SCC 10, [2012] 1 SCR 364.
25 *Ibid* at para 26, Cromwell J.

jurisdiction" in an exam will usually be highlighted. This might be done using the word "juris-diction," or similar terms like "provide the authority to" or "the power to." Or, the facts might show that the impugned decision must be made before a second process of decision-making can be undertaken. Ways to highlight this include separating the decisions into different statutory provisions, or, even better, having them made by different decision-makers.

III. APPLYING CORRECTNESS AND REASONABLENESS REVIEW

The second stage of substantive review involves assessing the "merits" of the decision being reviewed, and deciding whether the decision meets the applicable standard. Here is a secret: the most challenging aspect of putting together a substantive review question for an exam in administrative law occurs at this second stage. This is so for two reasons. First, it can take a lot of exam space to create a factual matrix to which students can apply skills of interpreting language and applying and distinguishing case law—the usual tools of legal analysis—in order to form a view on the merits; moreover, an instructor is leery of creating a problem on the merits that deals with an area of law that is more familiar to some students than others. Those are drafting issues. The second problem is more serious, because it derives from the state of Canadian administrative law itself: the judiciary has largely been unable to articulate how deference, or reasonableness review, should operate.

6. What is the difference between correctness and reasonableness review?

The difference between the two standards of review is simply that of whether the reviewing body (a superior court) should show deference, or no deference, to a statutory delegate's decision. The standard of deference is called "reasonableness review," and the no-deference position is called "correctness review." The position of deference does not mean that the reviewing court will accept the administrative decision, but rather that the decision will be accepted so long as it is found to be "reasonable," or, in other words, not "unreasonable."

Correctness review is easy to define. The standard of correctness means that a reviewing court will uphold an administrative decision that it agrees with—that is, the decision is the one that the court itself would have made.

For exam purposes, should you decide that the appropriate standard of review is correct-ness, you may well not find a lot of material in the fact pattern that allows you to assess whether the impugned decision was correct or not. Be on the lookout for references to es-tablished case law on the issue, or to what appear to be clear dictionary definitions of words in dispute.

All the difficulty we encounter in this area comes with trying to define the meaning of "reasonableness" review. By differentiating between the "correct" and the "reasonable," the law implies that there is a space or a margin between them. In that margin fall decisions that a reviewing court would not itself have made, but that it finds to be "reasonable." As some have put it, this means that in according deference, reviewing courts must be prepared to allow decisions to stand that they view as "incorrect," so long as they are not outside the scope of what is reasonable, or acceptable. This is a difficult distinction to articulate.

7. Are the reasons given by a decision-maker important to reasonableness review?

The short answer is that reasons are important, if given, but not necessary.

In *Dunsmuir*, the majority of the court made justification and transparency the hallmarks of a decision that would withstand scrutiny under a deferential standard—in other words, if administrative decision-makers explain and justify their decisions in a transparent fashion, those decisions will generally be found to be reasonable. This would seem to go beyond encouraging decision-makers to provide reasons, and to imply that in the absence of reasons, it will be difficult to find a decision to be reasonable. However, in the same passage, the court said that reasons for a decision are not the only matter under scrutiny:

> A court conducting a review for reasonableness inquires into the qualities that make a decision reasonable, referring both to the process of articulating the reasons and to outcomes. In judicial review, reasonableness is concerned mostly with the existence of justification, transparency, and intelligibility within the decision-making process. *But it is also concerned with whether the decision falls within a range of possible, acceptable outcomes which are defensible in respect of the facts and law.*[26]

Accordingly, a reviewing court can uphold a decision or outcome as reasonable even when that decision is accompanied by poor reasons, or by no reasons at all. This concept has taken on more significance in the post-*Dunsmuir* years. In *Newfoundland Nurses*, the court found that the (in-)adequacy of reasons does not in itself constitute a ground of substantive review—that is, a decision could be upheld as reasonable even where the reasons given by the administrative official failed to justify it. The reviewing court can look to the evidence, the process, and other sources to find justification for the outcome reached by the official. Abella J quoted with approval this passage by Professor David Dyzenhaus: "[E]ven if the reasons in fact given do not seem wholly adequate to support the decision, the court must first seek to supplement them before it seeks to subvert them."[27]

The idea that reasons are not needed for a decision to be reasonable has been taken at least one step further—there also may not be a need for a decision, or at least an express decision. In *Alberta Teachers*, the impugned decision was described as an "implied decision" by the Privacy and Information Commissioner in Alberta, who proceeded with a hearing into a complaint under the applicable provincial application after the lapsing of a limitation period. The commissioner did not advert to, much less give reasons for "ignoring" the limitation provision. The Supreme Court found the "decision" (perhaps better described as the

---

26 *Dunsmuir, supra* note 2 at para 47, Bastarache and Lebel JJ (emphasis added).

27 *Newfoundland and Labrador Nurses' Union v Newfoundland and Labrador (Treasury Board)*, 2011 SCC 62, [2011] 3 SCR 708 at para 12.

"action" or "outcome") to be reasonable, in that it corresponded with a justifiable interpretation of the statute as not having imposed a mandatory limitation period, an interpretation that the commissioner had given in earlier cases.

Similarly, in *Edmonton East*, the Assessment Review Board gave no reasons for deciding that it had the power to raise the assessed value on the complaint made by the shopping centre owners. It simply proceeded to do so. The majority at the SCC looked at the record, and found that counsel for the owners had conceded that the board had this jurisdiction. The majority continued:

> Therefore, it is hardly surprising the Board did not explain why it was of the view that it could increase the assessment: the Company expressly conceded the point. Parties "cannot gut the deference owed to a tribunal by failing to raise the issue before the tribunal and thereby mislead the tribunal on the necessity of providing reasons" (*Alberta Teachers*, at para. 54). Accordingly, I shall review the Board's decision in light of the reasons which *could be* offered in support of it.[28]

For exam purposes, *read any reasons for decision carefully*. This is certainly what reviewing courts do. Any reasons for decision provided in an exam fact pattern are there to disclose an arguable issue or issues with respect to whether the decision is "correct" or "reasonable," depending on the standard applied. If no reasons are given, or scant reasons that appear not to explain anything, then this may raise the procedural fairness of a breach of the duty to provide reasons. However, the absence of reasons will not in itself answer the question of substantive "reasonableness."

---

8. What does "reasonableness" review mean?

This is the most difficult question to answer in our list of the "Top Ten." We know that to be the case because the Supreme Court of Canada has not been able to answer the question satisfactorily. We can see this from looking again at *Dunsmuir*. The SCC's judgment in *Dunsmuir* was intended to introduce a new era of simplified substantive review into Canadian administrative law. By all accounts, this has failed to occur. One reason for this might be described as the "original sin" of the *Dunsmuir* case.[29] The majority sought to expand the basis for deference in judicial review. It made the first intimations of a presumption of reasonableness, which was later expressly adopted by the court. The majority found that the issue before the labour arbitrator—whether statutory provisions gave a non-union public employee the same right to challenge the cause given for dismissal from his job that a union employee had—was an issue that fell within the well-recognized expertise of labour

---

28 *Edmonton East, supra* note 3 at para 40.
29 Some might say the original sin of *Dunsmuir* was that of a 6–3 division in the court (with three strong opinions going in different directions). It seems difficult to simplify the law with other than a unanimous judgment on that law.

arbitrators. The majority ruled that the appropriate standard of review was reasonableness. The majority then went on to find the arbitrator's decision to be unreasonable and set it aside. The justices said:

> The decision of the adjudicator treated the appellant, a non-unionized employee, as a unionized employee. His interpretation of the PSLRA [*Public Services and Labour Relations Act*], which permits an adjudicator to inquire into the reasons for discharge where notice is given and, under s. 97(2.1), substitute a penalty that he or she determines just and reasonable in the circumstances, creates a requirement that the employer show cause before dismissal. *There can be no justification for this; no reasonable interpretation can lead to that result* …. Therefore, the combined effect of s. 97(2.1) and s. 100.1 cannot, *on any reasonable interpretation*, remove the employer's right under contract law to discharge an employee with reasonable notice or pay in lieu of notice.[30]

This statement effectively means that there was only one reasonable, or defensible, answer to the question asked of the arbitrator. The answer he gave could not be justified on the basis of any defensible reasons or logic. Nor is there any hint in the case that there was a "middle ground" result available that the arbitrator might have reached. In short, *Dunsmuir* is a case in which there was no "range of possible, acceptable answers." Where that is the case, it would not seem that "deference" can operate in any meaningful way.

This raises a serious problem for conceiving of reasonableness review with respect to issues of law, particularly of statutory interpretation. There is no doubt that deferential review is available for these issues. In fact, the major impetus for the contemporary Canadian approach to substantive review is to restrain superior courts from too readily interfering with the decisions of tribunals on issues of law and statutory interpretation within their spheres of specialized activity—in short, to give administrative decision-makers the scope to develop the law in those areas. But how does this fit with our general understanding of how courts approach the task of interpreting statutes?

The Supreme Court of Canada established a standard approach to that task in *Rizzo & Rizzo Shoes Ltd (Re)*.[31] Statutory interpretation entails discerning legislative intent by examining the words of a statute in their entire context and in their grammatical and ordinary sense, in harmony with the statute's schemes and objects. The principle underlying *Rizzo & Rizzo* is that the judiciary is capable of ascertaining the proper meaning of any statutory language, no matter how convoluted. This may be a fiction, but it is a useful fiction. For one thing, it has permitted our courts to limit the concept of unconstitutional "vagueness" in Canadian statutes to a disappearingly small number of instances, virtually removing this argument from the lawyer's toolbox. In short, statutory interpretation does not give rise to "a range of reasonable alternative interpretations."

If we accept this last point (and, if needed, please take it on faith for the moment), and if issues of statutory interpretation generally arrive at a dichotomous or "yes/no" decision point, it becomes difficult to describe a process of thinking or a set of techniques that can distinguish between a "reasonable" outcome and a "correct" outcome.

Allow me to set out three ways in which courts seem to have addressed this dilemma (this is by no means to say these are the only three ways). Each of them is, in my view, more

---

30   *Dunsmuir, supra* note 2 at para 75, Lebel and Bastarache JJ (emphasis added).
31   [1998] 1 SCR 27 [*Rizzo & Rizzo*].

metaphorical than prescriptive about how to conduct reasonableness review of issues of law. They may nevertheless give some guidance.

First, there is the idea of ambiguity in the law. The Supreme Court referred to ambiguity in statutory language as both explaining and providing a basis for according deference to administrative decision-makers in the formative case of *CUPE*. Dickson CJ noted that the wording of the statutory provisions in question was "very badly drafted" and "bristles with ambiguities."[32] In such circumstances, he said, superior court judges should not insist on their preferred interpretation over that of an expert tribunal, in that case a labour relations board. This idea of leaving ambiguous questions of law to be decided by statutory delegates is appealing, but it has flaws. For one thing, it takes considerable legal analysis or "searching" to get to the point where two alternative answers could be seen as plausible; and, second, from a practical standpoint, one can find few if any instances (including *CUPE*) where a reviewing court let a decision stand without implying that it was the better decision. Truly ambiguous problems, where more than one solution is plausible or reasonable, are rare, for conceptually strong reasons.

Second, the Supreme Court has described deference as a kind of mental posture that reviewing courts should take to the decisions of administrative officials. One of the more commonly mentioned approaches is the idea of a "deference of respect," a term coined by Professor David Dyzenhaus. The court cited Dyzenhaus's idea with approval in *Dunsmuir*:

> Deference is both an attitude of the court and a requirement of the law of judicial review. It does not mean that courts are subservient to the determinations of decision makers, or that courts must show blind reverence to their interpretations, or that they may be content to pay lip service to the concept of reasonableness review while in fact imposing their own view. Rather, deference imports respect for the decision-making process of adjudicative bodies with regard to both the facts and the law .... We agree with David Dyzenhaus where he states that the concept of "deference as respect" requires of the courts "not submission but a respectful attention to the reasons offered or which could be offered in support of a decision."[33]

The description of a deferential state of mind is perhaps most helpful as a reminder of tone, and of making sure a decision-maker's written reasons for decision are treated seriously and carefully. It does not go very far toward saying what makes a decision "unreasonable." One cannot help wondering if the judgment in *Dunsmuir* itself reflected a "deference of respect" when it came to dealing with (or, more aptly, not dealing with) the arbitrator's lengthy reasons for decision.

Third, reasonableness review when applied to statutory interpretation and other questions of law may mean that on certain questions, superior courts simply cede interpretive authority to administrative decision-makers. That is, deference would best be understood as a "hands-off" operation, that once a court determined the appropriate standard of review was deference, it should not examine the issue any further. The law in the protected area would be left to be developed by decision-makers delegated by the legislators. However, judicial review in Canada has never been based on a full-scale cession of the authority to interpret law. As stated in *Crevier*[34] and confirmed in *Dunsmuir*, judicial review serves the rule

---

32   *CUPE, supra* note 1 at 230.
33   *Dunsmuir, supra* note 2 at para 48.
34   *Crevier v Quebec (Attorney General)*, [1981] 2 SCR 220.

of law principle by ensuring that the courts will supervise and prevent government action outside its lawful boundaries. This requires that even if deferring to administrative interpretations of statutory statements, the courts must be prepared to intervene where any such interpretation is so improper, or unreasonable, as to threaten the rule of law.

For exam purposes, if called on to assess whether a particular administrative decision is reasonable or unreasonable, feel free to note that reasonableness review is different from correctness review, and that it involves deference to the decision-maker. Be able to articulate briefly an understanding of what deference means. Then apply this understanding to whatever facts are available, including apparent ambiguity (or its absence), thoughtfulness of written reasons, or a history of well-established tribunal jurisprudence. Don't be surprised or disappointed if you find little to go on for this part of an answer.

---

9. How does one identify whether a particular issue gives rise to a "range of reasonable answers," and is that important?

In mid-2016, the Supreme Court of Canada released an intriguing judgment in substantive review, *Wilson v Atomic Energy of Canada Ltd*.[35] The case is notable for two principal reasons: (1) the 6–3 division in the court on the issue of standard of review, going to fundamental issues of jurisdiction and rule of law;[36] and (2) the *obiter* opinion of Abella J in which she set out a possible new approach to standard of review analysis. On the second point, Abella J, the strongest proponent of judicial deference on the court, suggested in *Wilson* that the court move from two to only a single standard of review, reasonableness, for all administrative decisions. This would, of course, dispense with the initial question of choosing between reasonableness and correctness review. On the other hand, it would seem to lead to an intensified inquiry into what reasonableness review means, including whether it could possibly be conceived as representing a single standard of review, and of how it could incorporate situations that previously were addressed as calling for correctness review. Abella J sought to answer these doubts:

> A single standard of reasonableness still invites the approach outlined in *Dunsmuir*, namely:
> ... reasonableness is concerned ... with whether the decision falls within a range of possible, acceptable outcomes which are defensible in respect of the facts and law.
> [para 47]
> Approaching the analysis from the perspective of whether the outcome falls within a range of defensible outcomes has the advantage of being able to embrace comfortably the animating

---

35   2016 SCC 29, [2016] 1 SCR 770 [*Wilson*].

36   In *Wilson*, the majority found reasonableness to be the appropriate standard of review to apply to a labour arbitrator's interpretation of provisions of the *Canada Labour Code*, RSC 1985, c L-2. The minority found that the legislation was open only to a single interpretation. In circumstances where legal certainty was called for because of differing opinions by different arbitrators, the minority ruled that the appropriate standard should be correctness. This is, of course, similar to the points raised in the discussion of Question 7, above.

principles of both former categories of judicial review. Courts can apply a wider range for those kinds of issues and decision-makers traditionally given a measure of deference, and a narrow one of only one "defensible" outcome for those which formerly attracted a correctness review.[37]

Would it have been helpful in *Dunsmuir* for the court to ask as a first question: in the matter before us, is there a range of available outcomes? Possibly so. This approach would not foreshorten legal analysis in any particular case, as in many instances it might require a full argument on the merits to conclude whether such a range of answers exists. However, there may be some situations where one could say fairly quickly that a range of defensible outcomes is available. Such situations might include statutory powers to grant remedies, assess damages, or render evaluations. This suggestion appears, in one sense, to turn substantive review on its head. It replaces the question "What is the appropriate standard of review?" with the question "Does the issue involved in the particular case give rise to a range of reasonable (or defensible) outcomes?" If the answer to this question is "yes," then an adjudicator's decision should be upheld if it falls within that range; if the answer is "no, there is only a single defensible answer," then the adjudicator is upheld only if she gives that answer. Abella J believes that both situations can fall within the rubric of reasonableness review. Leaving aside that arguable point, the idea that multiplicity of possible outcomes is the basis for exercising deference may be helpful.

The existence of "multiplicity" may not inhere so much in a statutory statement of different possible outcomes as in the nature of the decision-making power. In a couple of post-*Dunsmuir* cases, the SCC has engaged in substantive review of delegated law-making powers. Legislative powers represent the height of discretionary action. The very nature of making laws or binding rules and regulations involves decision-makers taking in all the information they wish to gather by way of informing themselves, and then making what they deem to be the best rule to govern prospective circumstances. Law-making is policy-making, and by definition is open to disagreement. If any form of delegated decision-making calls to be reviewed on a standard of deference, it should be delegated law-making. In *Catalyst Paper Corp v North Cowichan (District)*,[38] the court dealt with a property tax assessment by-law enacted by the municipality. The paper company challenged the by-law for being unreasonable. The company agreed that deferential review applied to the making of by-laws, but argued that since *Dunsmuir*, reasonableness should be understood as a single standard that did not allow for a "high degree" of deference. The court disagreed, ruling that reasonableness review took on a different character depending on the decision-making context. In the law-making context at hand, this meant considerable leeway for the North Cowichan council:

> The applicable test is this: *only if the bylaw is one no reasonable body informed by these factors could have taken will the bylaw be set aside*. The fact that wide deference is owed to municipal councils does not mean that they have *carte blanche*.[39]

Similarly, in *Green v Law Society of Manitoba*,[40] where a lawyer sought judicial review of a decision to discipline him for breach of a rule dealing with continuing legal education

---

37   *Wilson, supra* note 35 at paras 32-33.
38   2012 SCC 2, [2012] 1 SCR 5.
39   *Ibid* at para 24 (per McLachlin CJ) (emphasis added).
40   2017 SCC 20.

adopted by the Society, the court identified the threshold for unreasonableness as "so long as no reasonable person could have come to the rule."

A statutory power to make subordinate legislation might often be described as a "discretionary" power. Discretion is a famous word in administrative law—it is perhaps shocking that it has not appeared earlier in this chapter. The notion of discretion as "choice," the power to select among different options, is often viewed as a near-automatic basis for according deference in substantive review. When talking about discretion, however, we are not necessarily talking about a multiplicity of outcomes. A discretionary decision, such as the approval of a licence, or the outcome of an environmental review process, may well come down to a "yes" or "no" result. Any "range of reasonable answers" would not lie so much in the outcomes, as in the reasons for decision—that is, the idea that there are a range of acceptable explanations or justifications for a decision, very much including the wisdom or judgment of the decision-maker. With this important caveat, we can fairly safely add powers that are described in discretionary terms—"in his or her opinion," "as they see fit," "should they be satisfied," and so on—to the class of issues that give rise to a range of possible answers.

For exam purposes, consider whether the impugned decision gives rise to a "range of alternative answers," including a range created by the submissions of the parties (e.g., one party submits that damages should be $250,000, while the other party argues for $1 million in damages) or whether it involves a question that can be answered only "yes" or "no." If the former, look for facts or factors that suggest the decision-maker has gone outside the accepted range. Also, be attuned to statutory language that implies or expressly calls for discretion on the part of the decision-maker. The presence of discretion implies a "range of alternative reasons, if not answers," on the part of a decision-maker.

---

10. What role does the concept of "abuse of discretion" play in contemporary standard of review analysis?

The most celebrated decision in Canadian administrative law is *Roncarelli v Duplessis*.[41] The circumstances, the parties, the lawyers, the Supreme Court justices, and the ruling all contributed to the drama of the case. Frank Roncarelli was the owner of a restaurant in Montreal, and a member of the Jehovah's Witnesses. Maurice Duplessis was premier and attorney general of Quebec. In the mid- to late 1950s, government officials, at the behest of the Catholic Church, became concerned with proselytization by Jehovah's Witnesses in Montreal. On numerous occasions, adherents of that faith were arrested on public nuisance charges while handing out their literature. As a successful businessperson, Roncarelli posted their bail so they could be released from jail. Frustrated with this, Premier Duplessis instructed the provincial liquor commissioner to revoke the liquor licence for Roncarelli's restaurant. The commissioner did so under a statutory power that merely said the

---

41   [1959] SCR 121.

"Commission may cancel any permit at its discretion." Roncarelli challenged the decision to revoke the licence. At the Supreme Court of Canada, Rand J famously said:

> In public regulation of this sort there is no such thing as absolute and untrammeled "discretion," that is that action can be taken on any ground or for any reason that can be suggested to the mind of the administrator; no legislative Act can, without express language, be taken to contemplate an unlimited arbitrary power exercisable for any purpose, however capricious or irrelevant, regardless of the nature or purpose of the statute.[42]

The court ruled that Duplessis and the commissioner had exercised the statutory power for an "improper purpose," that is, a purpose unrelated to those intended by the legislature in granting the power. This ruling is a classic example of one kind of "abuse of discretion," long known in Canadian administrative law as a substantive ground of judicial review. Other kinds of abuse of discretion included basing a decision on irrelevant considerations, failing to take into account relevant considerations, and fettering discretion. What these named abuses of discretion tend to have in common is a focus on *relevance*—what is relevant, and what is not relevant, for a decision-maker to take into account.

In the hallmark case of *Baker v Canada (Minister of Citizenship and Immigration)*[43] in 1999, the Supreme Court of Canada decided that "abuse of discretion" should no longer be a stand-alone ground of judicial review, but instead be brought within the standard of review analysis. That is, in judicial review of discretionary powers, just as with powers to decide issues of law, fact, and mixed law and fact, the first question to be answered is "What is the applicable standard of review—correctness or reasonableness?" Four years later, the court went a step further. It described the abuse of discretion categories as "nominate grounds" of judicial review that no longer played a principal analytical role:

> To determine standard of review ... it is not enough for a reviewing court to interpret an isolated statutory provision relating to judicial review. Nor is it sufficient merely to identify a categorical or nominate error, such as bad faith, error on collateral or preliminary matters, ulterior or improper purpose, no evidence, or the consideration of an irrelevant factor .... The nominate grounds, language of jurisdiction, and ossified interpretations of statutory formulae, while still useful as familiar landmarks, no longer dictate the journey.[44]

Since that time, it has been difficult to say what role the former abuses of discretion should play in substantive review. It seems clear that they no longer constitute, as they once did, a basis in and of themselves for setting aside an administrative decision.

In my view, however, the nominate abuses of discretion remain hallmarks for identifying faulty reasoning. In particular, where reasonableness is found to be the appropriate standard of review (which, as the court has stated on numerous occasions, including in *Baker*, will usually be the case with powers of a discretionary nature), an "abuse" such as failing to consider a relevant factor or deciding for an improper purpose constitutes a species of unreasonableness. In this way, the pre-*Baker* jurisprudence, including *Roncarelli v Duplessis*, remains relevant and helpful. For exam purposes, the suggested approach to substantive review—where the facts disclose a form of abuse of discretion—is to (1) perform a standard

---

42 *Ibid* at 140.
43 [1999] 2 SCR 817, 174 DLR (4th) 193 [*Baker*].
44 *Dr Q v College of Physicians and Surgeons of British Columbia*, 2003 SCC 19, [2003] 1 SCR 226 at paras 22-24.

of review analysis; (2) having identified reasonableness as the appropriate standard, cite the "abuse" as a basis for finding the impugned decision to be unreasonable; (3) recognize that this may not be conclusive, as deference may call for recognizing the decision-maker as having a role in deciding what is relevant to the decision.

One more point. The nominate abuses of discretion serve a purpose that goes beyond that of helping to analyze whether a certain administrative decision should be upheld or set aside. They also give guidance to administrative decision-makers about how to do their jobs, and how to avoid mistakes. They show what constitutes being "unreasonable." This is not something that is otherwise easily found in contemporary Canadian law of substantive review. That takes us to the tenth and last question to be addressed in this discussion.

For exam purposes, the nominate abuses of discretion remain among the easiest "flaws" in reasoning by decision-makers to build into an exam question. For this reason, they are not at all uncommon. As stated, these "abuses" go mostly to matters of relevance—whether the decision-maker has failed to take into account something that is relevant (especially if stated to be relevant by the statute) or, conversely, has drawn an arguably irrelevant factor into his thinking. An "improper purpose" may be denoted by a contrast between a statutory statement of purpose and the tribunal's reasons for decision.

IV. CONCLUSION: SUBSTANTIVE REVIEW, WHAT IS IT GOOD FOR?

A different way for an administrative law instructor to ask about substantive review is through a short essay question rather than a fact pattern question. That question—which might be politely phrased as "How does the jurisprudence on standard of review affect decision-makers?"—is a form of essay question. It is a way of asking about the contribution standard of review analysis makes to the administrative justice system as a whole. If we ask the same question of procedural justice law, we would say that it reminds decision-makers to employ fair processes in assembling evidence and hearing from affected parties, and eliminating bias from their consideration of the relevant issues. An individual judgment in judicial review dealing with fairness will provide guidance to the tribunal involved, and perhaps others, about how to handle a tricky problem in the future.

This idea of guidance for decision-makers is more ambiguous when it comes to substantive review. As has been noted, substantive review generally has two components: selection of the appropriate standard of review, and application of the standard to the merits of the case to ascertain if the impugned decision was "reasonable" or "correct." With respect to the first, the choice of standard of review provides little guidance to administrative decision-makers. The choice is done *ex post facto*, after the decision has been made. Every tribunal and tribunal member would likely *prefer* to be reviewed on a deferential standard, for a number of reasons, including that deferential review should mean a reduced scope for a tribunal's decisions to be overturned, relieving it both of the embarrassment that comes with reversal, and the additional workload of revisiting a case for a second time. In addition, being reviewed on a reasonableness basis betokens a degree of respect from the superior courts, a recognition that the tribunal has specialized business to do, and, perhaps, that it seems to know how to do that business. However, a decision-maker can do little to influence the selection of a standard of review. That will largely follow from the statutory context, and the nature of the issue in an impugned decision. The one thing a decision-maker might be able to do to win the respect of reviewing courts is consistently to produce thoughtful reasons for decision. This, it goes without saying, is difficult to do, and is also no guarantee.

Further, the selection of one standard of review over the other would not seem likely to have any impact on future decision-making of the tribunal in question. Knowing that one's decisions will or will not be deferred to does not lead to a different approach to making decisions. Always presuming good faith, every statutory decision-maker wants to make the best decision it can on the information available to it. None are satisfied with merely making a "reasonable" decision, that is, a decision that will pass muster at a lower standard of reasoning. That's as it should be.

The Canadian law of substantive review should be able to do a better job of providing guidance about good decision-making. It might be useful, for instance, to restore the language of "abuse of discretion" to its former place of honour as a way of pinpointing failures of logic. Identifying other types of flawed reasoning would be welcome. However, the law of substantive review has other important purposes as well. The main purpose is to provide substantive answers to difficult questions, and to do so in a principled way that respects a system of diverse governmental decision-making.

No one said this was supposed to be easy. What they frequently say, at the end of the last class of a term, is "Good luck with your exams!" Just know that in saying that, administrative law instructors mean that as much for themselves as for their audience.

CHAPTER FIFTEEN

Making a Federal Case Out of It: The Federal Court and Administrative Law

Craig Forcese
Faculty of Law, University of Ottawa

I. INTRODUCTION

Earlier chapters in this book have focused on the broad sweep of administrative law. This chapter shifts focus and concentrates instead on one particular venue of administrative law practice: the Federal Courts of Canada. It is, of course, true that the Federal Courts of Canada are not the only superior courts in which administrative law issues arise. The provincial superior courts and the Supreme Court of Canada are generalist courts and have jurisdiction to deal with administrative law matters.

The Federal Courts, however, are distinguished by two qualities. First, they exercise a virtual monopoly on the administrative judicial review function in relation to the federal executive. Second, that monopoly makes Federal Courts mostly administrative law courts. Federal Court judges are, in other words, the closest things to administrative law specialists in the Canadian judicial system. For both these reasons, Federal Courts deserve special attention in a volume on administrative law.

The chapter begins with a review of the structure and jurisdiction of the Federal Courts. It then canvasses a series of fundamental issues related to federal judicial review, including basic judicial review procedure and issues surrounding the grounds of review and remedies at the federal level.

II. STRUCTURE AND JURISDICTION OF THE FEDERAL COURTS

A. Federal Courts as Statutory Courts

The Federal Courts are "statutory courts"—that is, they are created by federal statute and have only the jurisdiction conferred on them by that statute. Constitutionally, the authority to create the Federal Courts lies in Parliament under s 101 of the *Constitution Act, 1867*.[1] In addition to authorizing a national supreme appeal court, that provision empowers Parliament to "provide for the Constitution, Maintenance, and Organization ... any additional Courts for the better Administration of the Laws of Canada."[2]

As s 101 "statutory courts," the Federal Courts differ from the provincial superior courts. The latter—also known as "s 96" courts, in reference to s 96 of the *Constitution Act, 1867*—are courts of inherent jurisdiction. "Jurisdiction" "is shorthand for the collection of attributes that enables a court or tribunal to issue an enforceable order or judgment."[3] "Inherent," in this context, means automatic or default jurisdiction. Although provincial statutes prescribe their structural attributes, the ultimate origin of s 96 courts lies in the *Constitution Act, 1867*, and their jurisdiction is inherited from courts in the United Kingdom. In an ancient maxim recently cited with approval by the Supreme Court of Canada, "nothing shall be intended to be out of the jurisdiction of a Superior Court, but that which specially appears to be so; and, on the contrary, nothing shall be intended to be within the jurisdiction of an Inferior Court [in this context, courts other than the Royal Courts and their successors] but that which is so expressly alleged."[4]

---

1   30 & 31 Vict, c 3 (UK).

2   *Ibid*, s 101. Other s 101 courts include the Tax Court of Canada and the Court Martial Appeal Court of Canada. The first court deals with tax matters and is, essentially, a special, tax-specific, administrative court. The second hears appeals from court martials applying the Code of Service Discipline to members of the Canadian Forces. As such, it is principally a criminal law court, albeit one that applies rules more extensively than those applicable to civilians. This chapter does not deal with either of these specific bodies.

3   *Canada (Attorney General) v TeleZone Inc*, 2010 SCC 62, [2010] 3 SCR 585 at para 44 [*TeleZone*].

4   *Peacock v Bell* (1667), 1 Wms Saund 73, 85 ER 84 at 87-88, cited with approval in *TeleZone*, *supra* note 3 at para 43.

Thus, while the Federal Courts have only those powers given to them by their constituting (or other) federal statute, the provincial superior courts have all judicial powers not expressly removed from them. Moreover, it is no small thing to strip judicial powers from provincial superior courts. Parliament does have the power to give exclusive federal administrative judicial review jurisdiction to the Federal Courts.[5] However, in the Supreme Court's words, the "ouster of jurisdiction from the provincial superior courts in favour of vesting exclusive jurisdiction in a statutory court ... requires clear and explicit statutory wording to this effect."[6]

In the result, the actual jurisdiction of the Federal Courts is anemic relative to that of the provincial superior courts, and the Federal Courts must have regard to statutory authorization in the exercise of their judicial powers. As the Federal Court has itself warned repeatedly: "The Federal Court is a statutory court whose jurisdiction cannot be presumed, unlike provincial superior courts, whose jurisdiction is both general and inherent. There must be a statutory basis for the Federal Court to have jurisdiction in a given case."[7] As discussed below, the key statutory basis for Federal Court jurisdiction is the *Federal Courts Act*.[8]

B. Administrative Law Jurisdiction of the Federal Courts

1. The Federal Court of Canada and the Federal Court of Appeal

The *Federal Courts Act* constitutes the Federal Courts. Specifically, it creates both a Federal Court of Canada (FCC), once known as the Federal Court—Trial Division, and a Federal Court of Appeal (FCA). The FCC is principally a court of first instance—that is, it is the first court that hears a dispute. The FCA is an appellate court, hearing appeals from the FCC and other federal judicial bodies, such as the Tax Court of Canada.

In some areas of Federal Courts jurisdiction, this pattern of trial court and court of appeal operates much as it would in any superior court. Thus, the FCC has concurrent jurisdiction with the provincial superior courts to hear civil claims brought against the federal government. This means that plaintiffs may choose to bring their action before either the FCC or a s 96 court. If they opt for the FCC as the court with original jurisdiction, any appeal from the trial of that action is to the FCA and, from there, with leave, to the Supreme Court of Canada. (Whether counsel selects the federal court or provincial superior court for civil actions is a question more of strategy than of law. Many civil litigators will have limited experience with the federal court, and will gravitate toward provincial superior court.)

This simple description does not, however, adequately capture the jurisdictional division of labour between the FCC and the FCA. In the administrative law area, it is not always the case that the FCC is inevitably the court of first instance. Most notably, there are several administrative tribunals enumerated in s 28 of the *Federal Courts Act* for whom the FCA is the

---

5 *TeleZone, supra* note 3 at para 45, citing *Canada Labour Relations Board v Paul L'Anglais Inc*, [1983] 1 SCR 147 at 154.

6 *Ordon Estate v Grail*, [1998] 3 SCR 437 at para 46, cited with approval in *TeleZone, supra* note 3 at para 42.

7 *Pontbriand v Federal Public Service Health Care Plan Administration Authority*, 2011 FC 1029, [2011] 4 FCR D-11 at para 2. See also *DRL Vacations Ltd v Halifax Port Authority*, 2005 FC 860, [2006] 3 FCR 516 at para 6.

8 RSC 1985, c F-7.

court of first instance on judicial review. These special tribunals include, among others, the Canadian International Trade Tribunal, the Public Service Labour Relations Board, the Copyright Board, and the Competition Tribunal. And they also include "the National Energy Board [NEB] established by the *National Energy Board Act.*" As discussed below, the NEB is the quasi-judicial body charged, among other things, with pipeline approvals.

This division of labour between FCC and FCA has much to do with history. Basically, the FCA was given a special role in relation to quasi-judicial tribunals when the federal court system was created. That history lingers in the present s 28—the entities listed in it are formalized tribunals with court-like qualities. But the list is a closed one and so deciding whether one goes to the FCC or the FCA obliges nothing more than a reading of the statute.

And any applicant should read s 28, or risk filing their application for judicial review in the wrong court. That said, the clear majority of applications for judicial review are not in relation to administrative bodies listed in s 28, and thus it is the FCC that has exclusive "original" jurisdiction—that is, it is the place you start your proceeding. In part, this is because the bulk of federal judicial review work stems from immigration disputes and not from decisions issued by the finite list of tribunals listed in s 28. The balance of this chapter focuses mostly on this more common FCC judicial review route.

2. The Federal Court's Exclusive Jurisdiction

Section 18 of the *Federal Courts Act* specifies that, subject to the above-discussed s 28, the FCC has "exclusive original jurisdiction":

> (a) to issue an injunction, writ of *certiorari*, writ of prohibition, writ of *mandamus* or writ of *quo warranto*, or grant declaratory relief, against any federal board, commission or other tribunal; and
>
> (b) to hear and determine any application or other proceeding for relief in the nature of relief contemplated by paragraph (a), including any proceeding brought against the Attorney General of Canada, to obtain relief against a federal board, commission or other tribunal.

Section 18 is the source of the FCC's considerable role in Canadian administrative law. It purports to give the FCC "exclusive" powers to issue classic administrative law remedies (and hear any application in relation to these) for any "federal board, commission or other tribunal." "Exclusive" means, essentially, a monopoly, subject to considerations discussed below.

For its part, "federal board, commission or other tribunal" is expansively defined in s 2 of the Act as:

> any body, person or persons having, exercising or purporting to exercise jurisdiction or powers conferred by or under an Act of Parliament or by or under an order made pursuant to a prerogative of the Crown, other than the Tax Court of Canada or any of its judges, any such body constituted or established by or under a law of a province or any such person or persons appointed under or in accordance with a law of a province or under s. 96 of the *Constitution Act, 1867.*

Note the sweep of this paragraph. Somewhat counterintuitively, "board, commission or other tribunal" need only be a single "person." So long as that person is deploying powers conferred by a federal statute *or* under the royal prerogative, administrative judicial review jurisdiction lies with the FCC.

Because, as a practical matter, all the powers that matter in federal administrative action are conferred by statute or under royal prerogative, the FCC has administrative judicial review authority over all federal administrative action. As the Supreme Court noted recently, "[t]he federal decision makers that are included [by s 2] run the gamut from the Prime Minister and major boards and agencies to the local border guard and customs official and everybody in between."[9]

The question has occasionally arisen as to how exclusive the FCC exclusive jurisdiction really is. As already noted, s 96 courts guard their jurisdictional prerogatives closely. Parliament can assign Federal Courts powers to conduct administrative judicial review authority. But Parliament cannot assign Federal Courts exclusive federal *constitutional* judicial review authority: as the Supreme Court noted recently, Parliament "cannot operate to prevent provincial superior court scrutiny of the constitutionality of the conduct of federal officials."[10] Constitutional review jurisdiction is concurrent, shared by both provincial superior courts and Federal Courts. Accordingly, an attack on administrative action that is, in turn, grounded in an attack on an allegedly unconstitutional statute or unconstitutional conduct can be brought in either s 96 courts or Federal Courts.

Further, the Federal Courts' s 18 jurisdiction does not include issuance of the remedy of *habeas corpus*, except in narrow circumstances.[11] For this reason, the provincial superior courts retain *habeas corpus* jurisdiction in relation to federal administrative action in circumstances where that remedy's own requirements are met.[12]

III. JUDICIAL REVIEW BEFORE THE FEDERAL COURTS

In addition to defining the Federal Courts' jurisdiction, the *Federal Courts Act* creates a relatively comprehensive guide to the manner of, and basis for, judicial review of federal administrative action. This includes special rules relating to certain types of statutory appeals, standing, limitation periods, grounds of review, and remedies.

A. Statutory Appeals

As discussed earlier by Cristie Ford in Chapter 2, applicants must exhaust all other remedies—such as statutory appeals—before applying for judicial review. Failure to exhaust this administrative appeal option may be a basis for the denial of a remedy on judicial review, a concept as true at the federal level as it is at the provincial.[13]

---

9   *TeleZone, supra* note 3 at para 3. Section 2 does exempt other judges from FCC supervision and those provincial agencies constituted by a provincial law who might have occasion to apply federal law. But these are limited exceptions.

10   *Canada (Attorney General) v McArthur*, 2010 SCC 63, [2010] 3 SCR 626 at para 14.

11   Section 18 gives the FCC "exclusive original jurisdiction to hear and determine every application for a writ of *habeas corpus ad subjiciendum*, writ of *certiorari*, writ of prohibition or writ of *mandamus* in relation to any member of the Canadian Forces serving outside Canada." This power is obviously less sweeping than that found in other parts of s 18, being limited to members of the Canadian Forces overseas.

12   *May v Ferndale Institution*, 2005 SCC 82, [2005] 3 SCR 809 at para 32.

13   See e.g. *Fast v Canada (Minister of Citizenship and Immigration)*, 2001 FCA 368.

To take one example, many pipeline disputes—a recurring theme in this book—come to the Federal Court of Appeal via statutory appeals. The NEB is the quasi-judicial tribunal charged with issuing certificates for pipeline construction under the *National Energy Board Act*.[14] That statute creates an appeal for such decisions directly to the Federal Court of Appeal "on a question of law or of jurisdiction, after leave to appeal is obtained from that Court."[15]

Attentive readers may wonder why, given this statutory appeal, Parliament also listed the NEB in s 28 of the *Federal Courts Act* as a tribunal for which judicial review applications go straight to the FCA? Why is there any need for judicial review of the NEB if the *National Energy Board Act* creates a statutory right of appeal? There are two simple answers: first, the NEB performs functions under other statutes as well as the *National Energy Board Act*. And, second, there may be instances where judicial review applications are brought in advance of an actual decision of the NEB, on interlocutory grounds. In these latter circumstances, the statutory appeal mechanism is not yet available, and judicial review is the correct path.

Of course, review of interlocutory decisions is generally disfavoured by the courts. But they can arise—the *Forest Ethics Advocacy* case discussed below is one example.

1. Section 18.5

The *Federal Courts Act* adds an even more robust bar to judicial review where there are certain statutory appeals:

> [I]f an Act of Parliament expressly provides for an appeal to the Federal Court, the Federal Court of Appeal, the Supreme Court of Canada, the Court Martial Appeal Court, the Tax Court of Canada, the Governor in Council or the Treasury Board from a decision or an order of a federal board, commission or other tribunal made by or in the course of proceedings before that board, commission or tribunal, that decision or order is not, to the extent that it may be so appealed, subject to review or to be restrained, prohibited, removed, set aside or otherwise dealt with, except in accordance with that Act.[16]

Put simply, where a statutory appeal from an administrative decision-maker lies in one of the bodies listed in the section, there can be no judicial review of the same subject matter covered by that appeal.

A point to be carefully underscored: s 18.5 is a rigid bar on judicial review. Where it applies, there is no further analysis required. As the Federal Court has noted, "Parliament's clear intention ousts judicial review by the Federal Court under s 18.1 of the *Federal Courts Act* and this intention also removes the necessity for this Court to test whether the prescribed review route provides for an adequate alternative remedy."[17]

This bar to judicial review for certain statutory appeals is a sensible and unsurprising limitation for those statutory appeals that go from an administrative body to a court itself. It would make little sense, for example, for judicial review to be available before the Federal Court when the same issue may be statutorily appealed to the FCA. Section 18.5 also reaches

---

14   RSC 1985, c N-7 [NEBA].

15   NEBA, ss 22; 31.

16   *Federal Courts Act*, s 18.5.

17   *Abbott Laboratories Ltd v Canada (Minister of National Revenue)*, 2004 FC 140, [2005] 1 FCR D-40 at para 40.

more than courts, however, and includes circumstances where an appeal lies to the governor in council (GIC) or the Treasury Board. The result may create some confusing situations.

2. The Sometimes Tricky Operation of Section 18.5

There are circumstances where statutory appeals may be available to *both* the FCA *and* the GIC. The *Telecommunications Act* authorizes the GIC to "vary or rescind" a decision of the Canadian Radio and Telecommunications Commission (CRTC) made under that statute.[18] That same Act creates an appeal from the CRTC to the FCA "on any question of law or of jurisdiction."[19]

Both the common law doctrine of exhaustion and s 18.5 demand that any challenge to a decision of the CRTC under the *Telecommunications Act* must come in the form of an appeal to the FCA or to the GIC.[20] Presumably, an applicant would select the FCA where questions of "law or jurisdiction" are at issue. In other instances, where the challenge is to the policy wisdom of the CRTC decision, recourse to the GIC would likely be preferred. What happens next varies between these two sorts of appeals.

In instances where an appeal is brought to the FCA, there will *never* be judicial review. Section 18.5 of the *Federal Courts Act* bars judicial review of the CRTC matter that is on appeal. Once the FCA issues its statutory appeal decision, that decision is not amenable to judicial review—the FCA is not a federal "board, commission or other tribunal" under the *Federal Courts Act*. Instead, it is a court, and any further challenge to any of its determinations are simply taken up the regular court appeal chain to the Supreme Court of Canada, with leave.

If the CRTC decision were instead appealed to the GIC under s 12 of the *Telecommunications Act*, the pattern would be slightly different. Again, s 18.5 would preclude judicial review of a CRTC matter that is subject to appeal to the GIC—that GIC appeal must be exhausted. Once it is exhausted, and the GIC issues its determination, judicial review now become a possibility: the GIC decision is not subject to any additional statutory appeal. Because the GIC is a "federal board, commission or other tribunal," it is itself subject to judicial review before the Federal Court. Thus the FCC could judicially review the GIC appeal decision. A litigant unhappy with the outcome of that FCC judicial review could then appeal that decision up the regular court appeal chain to the FCA and from there to the Supreme Court of Canada, with leave.

Note the differential impact of s 18.5 in these two scenarios. In the first, where the statutory appeal is to the FCA, s 18.5 has the end effect of creating an appeal-*only* route. In the second, where the statutory appeal is to the GIC, s 18.5 prioritizes that GIC appeal over judicial review. Then, once the GIC completes its task, judicial review re-emerges as a sort of "one step removed from the CRTC decision" possibility.

---

18 SC 1993, c 38, s 12.

19 *Ibid*, s 64.

20 Note that the CRTC has roles under other statutes as well; readers should thus be attentive to the appeal rules that may exist under these other instruments. The pattern may not be the same as described for the *Telecommunications Act*. To add an extra layer of complexity, in those statutes where the CRTC is amenable to judicial review (that is, where there is no statutory appeal triggering s 18.5), judicial review would go first to the FCA because the CRTC is one of the bodies listed in s 28 of the *Federal Courts Act*.

This discussion conveys one recurring caution: any administrative lawyer must passionately embrace the close reading of statutes, and federal administrative lawyers should be particularly zealous lest they miss signals directing them down one review path or another.

3. Leave Requirements and Judicial Review

Generally speaking, there is no requirement that the Federal Court give leave before an applicant brings an application for judicial review. One significant exception to this observation relates to immigration matters. Under the *Immigration and Refugee Protection Act*,[21] judicial review must be commenced via an application for leave brought before the Federal Court.[22] These may or may not be granted and constitute an extra hurdle for judicial review applications in the immigration context.

B. Standing

The *Federal Courts Act* provides that "[a]n application for judicial review may be made by the Attorney General of Canada or by anyone directly affected by the matter in respect of which relief is sought."[23] This provision provides standing as of right to the government of Canada and standing to persons "directly affected" by federal, administrative decision-making.

For a person to be directly affected, "the decision at issue must be one which directly affects the party's rights, imposes legal obligations on it, or prejudicially affects it directly."[24] There are, however, some decisions so general that it is difficult to envisage them being of sufficient direct affect vis-à-vis any single person. Pipeline projects may fall into this category—there may not be a natural applicant with enough individual interest to meet the directly affected standard. And public interest groups may seek to fill the vacuum. But they themselves are not "directly affected." For example, during an NEB pipeline assessment process, a group called "Forest Ethics Advocacy" was denied participation opportunities. It challenged the board's decision on judicial review, instantly raising standing issues. The Federal Court of Appeal concluded the "Board's decisions do not affect [the group's] legal rights, impose legal obligations upon it, or prejudicially affect it in any way."[25]

If standing rules were not relaxed in these circumstances, the government would be immunized from challenge. Accordingly, the Federal Courts do recognize "public interest standing," something that exists where the three-part test established by the Supreme Court in *Canadian Council of Churches v Canada (Minister of Employment and Immigration)*[26] is met. The applicant must show that a serious issue has been raised; it must have a genuine or

---

21   SC 2001, c 27.

22   *Ibid*, s 72.

23   *Federal Courts Act*, s 18.1(1).

24   *League for Human Rights of B'Nai Brith Canada v Canada*, 2008 FC 732 at para 24, cited with approval in *Friends of the Canadian Wheat Board v Canada (Attorney General)*, 2011 FCA 101, [2011] 2 FCR D-1 at para 21.

25   *Forest Ethics Advocacy Assn v Canada (National Energy Board)*, 2014 FCA 245 at para 30 [*Forest Ethics Advocacy*].

26   [1992] 1 SCR 236.

direct interest in the outcome of the litigation; and there must be no other reasonable and effective way to bring the matter to court.

Seriousness of the issue "encompasses both the importance of the issues and the likelihood of their being resolved in favour of the applicant," with the latter measured by considering whether the applicant has a "fairly arguable case."[27] The requirement of genuine or direct interest sufficient to satisfy the test for public interest standing relates, at least in part, to the experience and expertise of the applicant in relation to the subject matter of the litigation.[28] Last, the "reasonable and effective means" threshold once focused on whether there is a more appropriate applicant. As discussed in Chapter 9, *Fairness in Context: Achieving Fairness Through Access to Administrative Justice*, the Supreme Court has since relaxed this prong of the test and now requires consideration of "whether the proposed suit is, in all of the circumstances, a reasonable and effective means of bringing the matter before the court."[29] The court has also emphasized:

> These factors, and especially the third one, should not be treated as hard and fast requirements or free-standing, independently operating tests. Rather, they should be assessed and weighed cumulatively, in light of the underlying purposes of limiting standing and applied in a flexible and generous manner that best serves those underlying purposes.[30]

But even this more flexible public interest standing test still presents a hurdle. In the *Forest Ethics Advocacy* case noted above, the Federal Court of Appeal was rather stern:

> 33 Forest Ethics is a classic "busybody," as that term is understood in the jurisprudence. Forest Ethics asks this Court to review an administrative decision it had nothing to do with. ...
>
> 34 The record filed by Forest Ethics does not show that it has a real stake or a genuine interest in freedom of expression issues similar to the one in this case. Further, a judicial review brought by Forest Ethics is not a reasonable and effective way to bring the issue before this Court. Forest Ethics' presence is not necessary—Ms. Sinclair, represented by Forest Ethics' counsel, is present and is directly affected by the Board's decision to deny her an opportunity to participate in its proceedings.
>
> 35 Also, ... the issue before this Court is not evasive of review—others can be expected to raise the issue and, indeed, are now raising it.
>
> 36 If Forest Ethics were allowed to bring an application for judicial review in these circumstances, it and similar organizations would be able to bring an application for judicial review against any sort of decision anywhere at any time, pre-empting those who might later have a direct and vital interest in the matter. That is not the state of our law.[31]

In sum, federal standing rules open the door wide to applicants, but there is still a door, and courts will not hear matters brought by those with no demonstrable interest in the government decision.

---

27 *Sierra Club of Canada v Canada (Minister of Finance)*, [1999] 2 FC 211 at paras 38 and 39 (TD) [*Sierra Club*].

28 *Ibid* at para 53.

29 *Canada (Attorney General) v Downtown Eastside Sex Workers United Against Violence Society*, 2012 SCC 45, [2012] 2 SCR 524 at para 52.

30 *Ibid* at para 20.

31 *Forest Ethics Advocacy*, *supra* note 25 at paras 33-36.

C. Limitation Periods

The *Federal Courts Act* also establishes an unusually demanding limitation period on applications for judicial review: "An application for judicial review in respect of a decision or an order of a federal board, commission or other tribunal shall be made within 30 days after the time the decision or order was first communicated by the federal board, commission or other tribunal to the office of the Deputy Attorney General of Canada or to the party directly affected by it."[32] A judge may extend this time either before or after its expiry, but, to receive such an extension, the applicant must "show a continuing intention to pursue the application, that the application has some merit, that no prejudice to the respondent arises from the delay, and that a reasonable explanation for the delay exists."[33]

Note that even if a court accepts an extension on the statutory limitation period, the court retains a discretion to deny a remedy because of unreasonable delay.[34]

We should also note that the limitation period applies only to circumstances where there has been an actual administrative decision, as opposed to a challenge to a persisting situation. The limitations clock does not, for example, attach to a circumstance in which "an application for judicial review is sought for an order in the nature of mandamus, prohibition or declaratory relief for redress against a state of affairs that is by its very nature continuing and on-going and is alleged to be invalid or unlawful."[35]

D. Grounds of Review

Among the most difficult issues raised by the Federal Court's administrative law role are the grounds of review available to applicants challenging federal executive decisions. The *Federal Courts Act* specifies that

> [t]he Federal Court may grant relief … if it is satisfied that the federal board, commission or other tribunal
>
> (a) acted without jurisdiction, acted beyond its jurisdiction or refused to exercise its jurisdiction;
>
> (b) failed to observe a principle of natural justice, procedural fairness or other procedure that it was required by law to observe;
>
> (c) erred in law in making a decision or an order, whether or not the error appears on the face of the record;
>
> (d) based its decision or order on an erroneous finding of fact that it made in a perverse or capricious manner or without regard for the material before it;
>
> (e) acted, or failed to act, by reason of fraud or perjured evidence; or
>
> (f) acted in any other way that was contrary to law.[36]

Great care is required in reading this language. In the past, some courts have interpreted the grounds of review listed in s 18.1(4) as also prescribing the standard of review,[37] although

---

32 *Federal Courts Act*, s 18.1(2).

33 *Stanfield v Canada*, 2005 FCA 107 at para 3, applied to s 18.1 by, *inter alia*, *Sander Holdings Ltd v Canada (Minister of Agriculture)*, 2006 FC 327, 289 FTR 221 at para 29, aff'd 2007 FCA 322, 370 NR 274.

34 *Sander*, *supra* note 33 at para 34.

35 *Maple Leaf Foods Inc v Consorzio Del Prosciutto Di Parma*, 2009 FC 1035 at para 19.

36 *Federal Courts Act*, s 18.1(4).

37 See *Mugesera v Canada (Minister of Citizenship and Immigration)*, 2005 SCC 40, [2005] 2 SCR 100 at paras 37 and 38 [*Mugesera*].

that reasoning has not survived the Supreme Court's decision of *Canada (Citizenship and Immigration) v Khosa*,[38] an immigration case. The exact matter before the court in the latter case was "the extent to which, if at all, the exercise by judges of statutory powers of judicial review (such as those established by ss. 18 and 18.1 of the *Federal Courts Act* …) is governed by the common law principles lately analysed by our Court in *Dunsmuir v. New Brunswick*."[39] A majority of the court concluded that s 18.1(4), although clearly prescribing grounds of review, was largely silent on the standard of review to be applied. Accordingly, it was entirely proper for the court in *Khosa* to turn to the common law (as had been recently by *Dunsmuir*) in determining what standard of review it would apply to the ground of review in question.

Extrapolating from *Khosa*, we might make the following observations about the key grounds enumerated in s 18.1(4).

1. *Acting Without Jurisdiction*

As the Supreme Court noted in *Khosa*, "jurisdictional issues command a correctness standard."[40] Once again, however, special caution is warranted because jurisdictional issues are virtually non-existent in the common law administrative law jurisprudence, and their invocation in the *Federal Courts Act* has, so far, not resuscitated them. Although, in *Dunsmuir*, the Supreme Court appeared to open the door a crack to a new creature known as a "true question of jurisdiction," it has held its shoulder against that door to prevent any further embellishment of the concept. As the court observed in 2011, "our Court has held since *Dunsmuir* that issues which in other days might have been considered by some to be jurisdictional, should now be dealt with under the standard of review analysis in order to determine whether a standard of correctness or of reasonableness should apply."[41]

2. *Procedural Fairness*

In *Khosa*, the Supreme Court observed "procedural issues (subject to competent legislative override) are to be determined by a court on the basis of a correctness standard of review."[42] More generally, there is usually nothing unusual or unique in the Federal Court approach to common law procedural fairness. The procedural fairness described elsewhere in this book is that applied at the Federal Court. Indeed, Federal Court jurisprudence is the source of much of that general law on procedural fairness. This reflects, in part, the fact that, at the federal level, there is no codified procedural statute intended to apply to all or some significant part of federal administrative action. This places federal administrative decision-making on a very different procedural footing than, for instance, Ontario provincial equivalents governed by the *Statutory Powers Procedures Act*.[43] (Note that it is an error to assert that the

---

38   2009 SCC 12, [2009] 1 SCR 339 [*Khosa*].
39   *Ibid* at para 1, citing *Dunsmuir v New Brunswick*, 2008 SCC 9 [*Dunsmuir*].
40   *Khosa, supra* note 38 at para 42.
41   *Canada (Canadian Human Rights Commission) v Canada (Attorney General)*, 2011 SCC 53, [2011] 3 SCR 471 at para 24 [*Canada v Canada*].
42   *Khosa, supra* note 38 at para 43.
43   RSO 1990, c S.22.

Federal Court may or can apply these provincial laws—they *do not apply* to federal administrative decision-making.)

But it is necessary to add two caveats to the claim that there is nothing much unique in Federal Court approaches to procedural fairness. First, there is now a line of cases associated from the Federal Court of Appeal that, while applying a correctness standard of review to procedural fairness, talks also about deference and a "margin of appreciation." Thus, in the *Forest Ethics Advocacy* case discussed above, the FCA held that the NEB was "entitled to a significant margin of appreciation in the circumstances of this case."[44] These circumstances included expertise and experience, a general deference to the NEB's procedural choices, statutory language supporting deference on the procedural matter at issue (whether someone can participate in an NEB proceeding) and the existence of a privative clause. Some of these considerations echo those listed in the *Baker* test[45] for the content of procedural fairness. But this is not at all the *Baker* test—it is a hybrid between *Baker* and *Dunsmuir*, and its fate remains uncertain. (See Chapters 5, 11, and 12, for a discussion on *Dunsmuir* and its aftermath.)

Second, one due process area that is distinctly federal is the *Canadian Bill of Rights*.[46] The procedural guarantees found in ss 1(a) and 2(e) of that instrument apply exclusively to the federal level. Thus, to the extent there is a jurisprudence interpreting these provisions (and it is a slender jurisprudence), it originates in the Federal Courts.

Sections 1(a) and 2(e) of the *Bill of Rights* read:

> 1. It is hereby recognized and declared that in Canada there have existed and shall continue to exist without discrimination by reason of race, national origin, colour, religion or sex, the following human rights and fundamental freedoms, namely,
>
> (a) the right of the individual to life, liberty, security of the person and enjoyment of property, and the right not to be deprived thereof except by due process of law. ...
>
> 2. Every law of Canada shall, unless it is expressly declared by an Act of the Parliament of Canada that it shall operate notwithstanding the *Canadian Bill of Rights*, be so construed and applied as not to abrogate, abridge or infringe or to authorize the abrogation, abridgment or infringement of any of the rights or freedoms herein recognized and declared, and in particular, no law of Canada shall be construed or applied so as to ...
>
> (e) deprive a person of the right to a fair hearing in accordance with the principles of fundamental justice for the determination of his rights and obligations.[47]

One reason that these provisions have received relatively little treatment by the courts is because of their overlap with both common law procedural fairness and s 7 of the Charter. For the most part, the jurisprudence seems to treat the *Bill of Rights* provisions as alternative sources of the same sorts of procedural protections offered by the common law and the Charter—that is, procedural rights under the Bill are different in source but not in kind from those found at common law or in s 7 of the Charter. There are, however, several caveats to this point.

First, unlike the common law (but like the Charter), a statute does not displace *Bill of Rights* procedural entitlements (unless the *Bill of Rights* is expressly excluded by that statute). Like the Charter, therefore, the *Bill of Rights* is available to challenge *statutory* provisions that curtail procedural rights.

---

44   *Forest Ethics Advocacy*, *supra* note 25, at para 72.
45   *Baker v Canada (Minister of Citizenship and Immigration)*, [1999] 2 SCR 817 [*Baker*].
46   SC 1960, c 44.
47   *Canadian Bill of Rights*, ss 1(a) and 2(e).

However, unlike the Charter, the trigger for the application of s 1(a) of the *Bill of Rights* includes more than simply life, liberty, and security of the person. It also includes property. This gives it a much more expansive reach than s 7 of the Charter.

For both these reasons, the *Bill of Rights* may be the sole source of procedural rights available to litigants presented with a statutory annulment of procedural rights in circumstances where property interests (but not life, liberty, or security of the person) are engaged.

A second caveat to the observation that the *Bill of Rights* procedural rights dovetail with those provided by common law and the Charter flows from some slender jurisprudence on the concept of "due process" in s 1(a). There is a hint in the jurisprudence that "due process" in this context may reach "substantive due process," a concept that is not truly explored to date.[48] In a somewhat antiquated case, one Federal Court judge concluded that "due process requires, in addition to a fair hearing, a total process which provides for the making of a decision authorized by law, a means for rationally relating the facts in the case to criteria legally prescribed, as in this case, by Parliament."[49] This definition has never caught on, but it is notable that, were it to do so, it would give s 1(a) coverage more closely associated with substantive grounds for administrative judicial review. Specifically, rationally relating fact to applicable legal standards is the sort of decision-making process one would associate with reasonable exercises of discretion.

Lawyers who ignore the *Bill of Rights* do so at considerable disservice to their clients. As this book goes to press, the FCC has pointed to the *Bill of Rights* in invalidating portions of the *Citizenship Act* process for denaturalizations. It did so in circumstances where it concluded that s 7 of the Charter did not apply.[50] Put another way, but for the *Bill of Rights*, counsel would have lost this case.

3. *Error of Law*

Again, there is nothing unique about Federal Court application of this ground. Despite quite different language in a predecessor case,[51] *Khosa* establishes that an error of law may be reviewable on correctness *or* reasonableness grounds. Which standard applies depends on consideration of the sorts of issues raised by *Dunsmuir* and its successors—for example, the Supreme Court has emphasized as a justification for reasonableness review the fact that the statute in question involved "the home statute or a closely related statute" applied "by an expert decision-maker."[52] The other variables that point toward correctness versus reasonableness review of errors of law are discussed elsewhere in this book.

But I shall highlight one example: *Smith v Alliance Pipelines Ltd*[53] involved an arbitration panel established to adjudicate compensation for the expropriation of land for pipeline purposes. At issue was what "costs" could be awarded under the *National Energy Board Act*

---

48 *Authorson v Canada (Attorney General)*, 2003 SCC 39, [2003] 2 SCR 40 at para 51.

49 *Smith, Kline & French Laboratories v Canada (Attorney General)*, [1986] 1 FC 274 (TD), aff'd [1987] 2 FC 359 (CA).

50 *Hassouna v Canada (Minister of Citizenship and Immigration)*, 2017 FC 473.

51 See *Mugesera, supra* note 37 at para 37, asserting that errors of law under s 18.1(4) are reviewable on a standard of correctness.

52 *Canada v Canada, supra* note 41 at para 44.

53 2011 SCC 7, [2011] 1 SCR 160.

to a successful claimant. In deciding this matter, the Supreme Court applied a reasonableness standard. And it also articulated the clearest expression of its *Dunsmuir* approach (sadly, since muddied by unnecessary complexity of the sort discussed elsewhere in this book):

> Under *Dunsmuir*, the identified categories are subject to review for either correctness or reasonableness. The standard of correctness governs: (1) a constitutional issue; (2) a question of "general law 'that is both of central importance to the legal system as a whole and outside the adjudicator's specialized area of expertise'" ...; (3) the drawing of jurisdictional lines between two or more competing specialized tribunals; and (4) a "true question of jurisdiction or *vires*". ... On the other hand, reasonableness is normally the governing standard where the question: (1) relates to the interpretation of the tribunal's enabling (or "home") statute or "statutes closely connected to its function, with which it will have particular familiarity" ...; (2) raises issues of fact, discretion or policy; or (3) involves inextricably intertwined legal and factual issues ... .[54]

Often, there is now little real contest over standard of review, given the extent to which the Supreme Court has emphasized reasonableness review. In the *Forest Ethics Advocacy* case noted above, all the parties agreed that the standard of review for the NEB in its pipeline decisions under the *National Energy Board Act* was reasonableness.[55]

4. Erroneous Finding of Fact

As with errors of law, there is an earlier jurisprudence assigning standard of review significance to the phrase "perverse and capricious manner or without regard for the material before it."[56] Some courts envisaged this language as connoting "patent unreasonableness" under the pre-*Dunsmuir* tripartite standard-of-review approach, while others applied a reasonableness *simpliciter* concept. This debate fell away after *Dunsmuir* and, for its part, *Khosa* holds that "it is clear from s. 18.1(4)(d) that Parliament intended administrative fact finding to command a high degree of deference. This is quite consistent with *Dunsmuir*. It provides legislative precision to the reasonableness standard of review of factual issues in cases falling under the *Federal Courts Act*."[57]

5. Other Way Contrary to Law

This provision serves as a basket clause allowing the evolution of new grounds of review. Error of discretion is an obvious ground of review not expressly mentioned elsewhere in s 18.1(4) that reasonably falls within this category.[58] As Audrey Macklin observes in Chapter 11, Standard of Review: Back to the Future?, *Dunsmuir* establishes that courts will generally review errors of discretion using the reasonableness standard.

One final note on grounds of review relates to the nature of proceedings before the Federal Court. Judicial review applications are heard on the record—that is, they do not involve the presentation of *viva voce* evidence by, for example, witnesses testifying in court. Instead, at issue before the court is the record of decision made by the decision-maker in

---

54   *Ibid* at para 26.
55   *Forest Ethics Advocacy*, *supra* note 25 at para 60.
56   See again *Mugesera*, *supra* note 37 at para 38.
57   *Khosa*, *supra* note 38 at para 46.
58   *Telfer v Canada (Revenue Agency)*, 2009 FCA 23, [2009] 2 FCR D-15 at para 23.

question, as demonstrated either by the documents produced by that decision-maker in rendering its decision or, for more informal decisions, by affidavits describing the decision. Therefore, judicial review applications bear more resemblance to appellate court proceedings than to trial-like proceedings.

E. Remedies

A last issue relating to administrative judicial review before the Federal Courts is remedies. As already noted, the Federal Court has exclusive, original jurisdiction under s 18 "to issue an injunction, writ of *certiorari*, writ of prohibition, writ of *mandamus* or writ of *quo warranto*, or grant declaratory relief, against any federal board, commission or other tribunal."[59] A more formal remedies section is found at s 18.1:

> (3) On an application for judicial review, the Federal Court may
>   (a) order a federal board, commission or other tribunal to do any act or thing it has unlawfully failed or refused to do or has unreasonably delayed in doing; or
>   (b) declare invalid or unlawful, or quash, set aside or set aside and refer back for determination in accordance with such directions as it considers to be appropriate, prohibit or restrain, a decision, order, act or proceeding of a federal board, commission or other tribunal.[60]

In essence, this language simply encapsulates in textual form the meaning of the prerogative writs of *certiorari*, *mandamus*, and prohibition and the ordinary remedies of declaration and injunction discussed by Cristie Ford in Chapter 2. In this respect, it equips the Federal Courts with the same remedies as the provincial superior courts, operating under an unmodified common law administrative remedy regime. Further, like these common law remedies, the Federal Courts' power to award remedies is purely discretionary: s 18.1(3) uses the word "may." As a consequence, the Act "preserves the traditionally discretionary nature of judicial review."[61]

In practice, therefore, the circumstances in which the Federal Courts will award relief are not greatly different from those in which provincial superior courts will now act. For instance, in deciding whether to "order a federal board, commission or other tribunal to do any act or thing it has unlawfully failed or refused to do or has unreasonably delayed in doing,"[62] the Federal Court has employed the common law tests for the writ of *mandamus*. Likewise, in deciding whether to exercise its discretion to deny a remedy, the Federal Court has looked to considerations like those contemplated by provincial superior courts, including "prematurity, mootness, waiver, impermissible collateral attack, conduct, the existence of an alternate remedy, or on the basis of a broader assessment of the balance of convenience between the parties."[63]

That said, there are a few potential differences between the federal and provincial remedies systems. First, relief under s 18.1(3), "while doubtless modelled on the forms of relief available under the prerogative orders and the declaration and injunction, are not necessarily encrusted with the same technicalities that at one time hampered the development of

---

59 *Federal Courts Act*, s 18(1)(a).
60 *Ibid*, ss 18.1(3)(a) and (b).
61 *Canadian Pacific Ltd v Matsqui Indian Band*, [1995] 1 SCR 3 at para 31.
62 See e.g. *Vaziri v Canada (Minister of Citizenship and Immigration)*, 2006 FC 1159, [2007] 2 FCR D-2 at para 38.
63 *Mwesigwa v Canada (Minister of Citizenship and Immigration)*, 2011 FC 1367 at para 15.

the common law remedies of judicial review."[64] This is particularly true in the area of standing and procedure. To the extent that different common law remedy rules had embedded in them distinct rules of procedure and standing, the Federal Court regime abolishes those in favour of the system established in the *Federal Courts Act*. Put another way, one follows the same process regardless of the administrative law remedy one is seeking. That hasn't always been the case at the provincial level, although modern provincial judicial review statutes echo the *Federal Courts Act* in consolidating judicial review procedure into a single process, irrespective of the remedy sought.

Second, there is a modest statutory embellishment on the common law remedies standard found in s 18.1:

> (5) If the sole ground for relief established on an application for judicial review is a defect in form or a technical irregularity, the Federal Court may
>> (a) refuse the relief if it finds that no substantial wrong or miscarriage of justice has occurred; and
>> (b) in the case of a defect in form or a technical irregularity in a decision or an order, make an order validating the decision or order, to have effect from any time and on any terms that it considers appropriate.[65]

IV. CONCLUSION

In summary, the federal system of administrative law is a variant to that applied provincially. The Federal Court issues a large number of administrative law cases every year, and as a close perusal of the cases cited elsewhere in this book suggests, federal cases have been the source of many important developments in administrative law. This is particularly the case in common law procedural fairness.

However, both students and practitioners of administrative law must be wary of several important considerations in approaching administrative practice in front of Federal Courts. First, because the Federal Courts are statutory bodies, they are unusually attentive to a statutory basis for their authority. Second, that statutory basis simplifies matters to an important extent by prescribing in detail guidance on issues such as standing, limitation periods, grounds of review, and remedies.

Nevertheless, we should exercise caution in relation to these statutory prescriptions. For one thing, the *Federal Courts Act*'s limitation period is unusually brief, and inattentive applicants may quickly find their applications dismissed as untimely. For another, the statutory codification of grounds of review does not in any real way answer the question of standard of review. Accordingly, Federal Court practitioners, like other administrative lawyers, must pay close attention to Supreme Court machinations on standard of review. Likewise, the codification of remedies in the statute is incomplete, in the sense that much of the common law on remedies remains relevant, as are the discretionary bases for declining to issue a remedy.

Put another way, the *Federal Courts Act* is the place to start in understanding administrative judicial review at the federal level. It is not, however, the final answer in any judicial review analysis.

---

64 *Sierra Club, supra* note 27 at para 47.
65 *Federal Courts Act*, ss 18.1(5)(a) and (b).

CHAPTER SIXTEEN

International Human Rights Norms and Administrative Law

Gerald Heckman*

Faculty of Law, University of Manitoba

* I would like to thank Loretta Choi, Melanie Wire, and Gwen Muirhead for their able research assistance and the Manitoba Legal Research Institute for its financial support. I would also like to thank the editors: Colleen Flood and Lorne Sossin.

I. INTRODUCTION

If we define administrative law as the set of principles and rules that govern the exercise by administrative decision-makers of their statutory powers, then international human rights law is, and has long been, relevant to administrative lawyers. However, it only garnered significant attention as a source of administrative law in Canada following the Supreme Court of Canada's judgment in *Baker v Canada (Minister of Citizenship and Immigration)*, released in 1999.[1] More recently, the court has focused on the role of international human rights norms in defining *constitutional* limits to governmental power and, in particular, to state encroachments on freedom of association in the collective bargaining context.[2]

Canadian decision-makers must exercise discretionary powers and interpret each of their enabling statutes "in accordance with the boundaries imposed in the statute, the principles of the rule of law, the principles of administrative law, the fundamental values of Canadian society, and the principles of the *Charter*."[3] This chapter will show that international human rights norms are relevant to defining several of these boundaries. First, the interpretation of a statutory provision may be influenced by a relevant international right or obligation, especially when the statute was enacted to implement this right or obligation in Canadian law. Second, the fundamental values of Canadian society may be reflected in the international rights and obligations that bind Canada's governments through custom or convention. Finally, the meaning of rights and freedoms under the *Canadian Charter of Rights and Freedoms*,[4] which must be taken into account in administrative decision-making, may be influenced by the scope and content of Canada's international human rights obligations, many of which the Charter was intended to implement.[5] In sum, public officials and administrative agencies may be required, in a variety of circumstances, to exercise their statutory discretion or interpret their enabling legislation in a manner that conforms with or sufficiently accounts for international human rights norms or the values underlying these norms.

The provisions of international human rights treaties may also have an impact on the review of administrative decisions for procedural defects. In *Baker*, the Supreme Court recognized the legitimate expectations of the person affected by a decision as a factor in determining what procedures are required by the common law duty of procedural fairness.

---

1   [1999] 2 SCR 817 [*Baker*]. For the facts of *Baker*, see Kate Glover, Chapter 5, The Principles and Practices of Procedural Fairness.

2   See e.g. *Health Services and Support—Facilities Subsector Bargaining Assn v British Columbia*, 2007 SCC 27, [2007] 2 SCR 391 [*Health Services*]; *Ontario (Attorney General) v Fraser*, 2011 SCC 20, [2011] 2 SCR 3 [*Fraser*]; and *Saskatchewan Federation of Labour v Saskatchewan*, 2015 SCC 4, [2015] 1 SCR 245 [*SFL*] discussed in Section IV.B.

3   *Baker, supra* note 1 at para 56. The Supreme Court used these words to describe the boundaries applicable to the exercise of discretionary power, but in doing so, rejected any rigid dichotomy of "discretionary" or "non-discretionary" decisions.

4   Part I of the *Constitution Act, 1982*, being Schedule B to the *Canada Act 1982* (UK), 1982, c 11 [Charter].

5   That an official's discretionary decision could frustrate proceedings initiated by an individual before an international treaty body to clarify his or her rights under the treaty may also be a relevant consideration to the official's exercise of the discretionary power. This channel of influence, which will not be discussed further here, was explored in the second edition of this text: see Gerald Heckman, "The Role of International Human Rights Norms in Administrative Law" in Colleen M Flood and Lorne Sossin, eds, *Administrative Law in Context*, 2nd ed (Toronto: Emond Montgomery, 2013) 489 at 517-20, available online at <www.emond.ca/adminlaw3e>.

Moreover, the court left open the possibility that the terms of an international instrument ratified by Canada could give rise to a legitimate expectation,[6] an approach it later adopted in *Suresh*[7] to define the content of fundamental justice under s 7 of the Charter. In that case, the court confirmed that it would look to international law as evidence of the principles of fundamental justice. Thus, international human rights treaties may be relevant to defining the content of procedural fairness and fundamental justice and, in the latter case, may factor into a challenge of the constitutionality of statutory procedures.

Many of the materials referred to in this chapter to describe the influence of international law on administrative law in Canada—including judicial decisions, statutes, regulations, and guidelines—are from the immigration and refugee law context. While international human rights law is relevant in other spheres of administrative decision-making, it is a key source of state obligations toward non-citizens. Absent sufficient express legal protections for their clients, immigration and refugee lawyers have frequently and consistently raised international human rights norms when arguing before administrative decision-makers and reviewing courts.[8] As advocates,[9] judges, and administrative decision-makers pay more attention to these norms,[10] opportunities to apply them in other administrative contexts can only multiply.[11]

Because many readers may not be familiar with public international law and, in particular, international human rights law, Section II of this chapter sets out a brief synopsis of the sources of international law. Section III describes the rules that govern the reception of international law into Canada's domestic legal order. Section IV of this chapter examines how international human rights norms affect the courts' review of officials' and agencies' interpretation of their enabling legislation, including discretionary powers, and whether this

---

6   *Baker, supra* note 1 at para 29.

7   *Suresh v Canada (Minister of Citizenship and Immigration)*, 2002 SCC 1, [2002] 1 SCR 3 at para 60 [*Suresh*].

8   Audrey Macklin, "The State of Law's Borders and the Law of States' Borders" in David Dyzenhaus, ed, *The Unity of Public Law* (Oxford: Hart Publishing, 2004) 173 at 174.

9   Amnesty International intervenes before administrative tribunals and courts to explain the relevance of Canada's international human rights obligations to their proceedings: see e.g. *First Nations Child and Family Caring Society of Canada v Canada (Minister of Indian Affairs and Northern Development)*, 2016 CHRT 2 at paras 13 and 428-55 [*First Nations Child and Family Caring Society*]; *Gitxaala Nation v Canada*, 2015 FCA 73 at para 25 [*Gitxaala Nation*].

10   See e.g. *Erickson v Ontario (Ministry of the Environment)*, [2011] OERTD No 29 at para 520 (QL), where the Ontario Environmental Review Tribunal accepted that the precautionary principle, as developed at international law, was relevant to the interpretation and application of Ontario's *Environmental Protection Act*, RSO 1990, c E.19. See also *First Nations Child and Family Caring Society, supra* note 9, where the Canadian Human Rights Tribunal reviewed the provisions of several international human rights conventions to which Canada is a party relating to the equality rights of Indigenous Peoples. It concluded that by failing to ensure that the child and family services it provided to on-reserve First Nations children were of comparable quality and accessibility to those provided to Canadian children off-reserve, the Canadian government had violated the principles of substantive equality guaranteed in these international conventions. But see Catherine Dauvergne, "International Human Rights in Canadian Immigration Law—The Case of the Immigration and Refugee Board of Canada" (2012) 19 Ind J Global Legal Stud 305 at 315-16, concluding that the Immigration and Refugee Board made scant use of international law from 2002 to 2010, with only 43 of close to 10,000 decisions revealing a robust discussion of international law.

11   See e.g. Russell J Juriansz, "International Law and Canadian Courts: A Work in Progress" (2009) 25 NJCL 171 at 179. And see Gerald Heckman & Lorne Sossin, "How Do Canadian Administrative Law Protections Measure Up to International Human Rights Standards?" (2005) 50 McGill LJ 193.

legislation complies with the Charter. Section V describes the role of international human rights law in shaping the content of the duty of procedural fairness and the principles of fundamental justice.

II. A SHORT INTRODUCTION TO INTERNATIONAL HUMAN RIGHTS LAW

International law is derived from several sources.[12] The most important of these are international custom (customary international law) and international treaties (conventional international law).

Rules of customary international law are "reflected in the practice or conduct of states" and "accepted by them, expressly or tacitly, as being legally binding on the international plane."[13] A practice that meets these two requirements and qualifies as customary law is obligatory for all states that have not consistently objected to it.[14] To establish that a legal norm is a rule of customary international law, there must be evidence that states have consistently and generally followed the rule[15] and that they have acted in this manner because they are of the view that they were obliged to do so under international law rather than for reasons of political expediency.[16] Some norms expressed in international instruments of "universal" character may eventually give rise to customary rules of international law. Whether a rule of customary law has crystallized from a treaty norm depends on whether ratification of the treaty is widespread among interested states and whether these states extensively and uniformly accept that the treaty provision sets out a rule of law that is binding as custom.[17]

Customary law is not static, and groups of states may create new customary regimes by introducing new rules backed up with consistent and general practice. Moreover, an international treaty may displace otherwise applicable customary rules as between the parties to

---

12   Statute of the International Court of Justice, as found in the *Charter of the United Nations*, 26 June 1945, Can TS 1945 No 7, c 14 [UN Charter].

13   Thomas Buergenthal & Sean D Murphy, *Public International Law in a Nutshell*, 5th ed (St Paul, Minn: West Academic Publishing, 2013) at 27. See also *Kazemi Estate v Islamic Republic of Iran*, 2014 SCC 62, [2014] 3 SCR 176 at para 38 [*Kazemi Estate*].

14   A state may "contract out of a custom in the process of formation" by persistently objecting to it: James Crawford, *Brownlie's Principles of Public International Law*, 8th ed (Oxford: Oxford University Press, 2012) at 28.

15   *Ibid* at 24-25. Universality is not required. Evidence of official state conduct could include diplomatic correspondence, state policies and legislation, executive decisions, treaties, and UN General Assembly resolutions.

16   *Opinio juris* (opinion of justice), the sense among states that they are obligated under international law to follow a certain practice, is sometimes implied on the basis of the evidence of a consistent and general practice: *Asylum Case* (1950), 17 ILR 280 at 285.

17   Alan Brudner, "The Domestic Enforcement of International Covenants on Human Rights: A Theoretical Framework" (1985) 35 UTLJ 219 at 248. Crawford, *supra* note 14 at 31-32, notes that non-parties may, by their conduct, accept the provisions of an international convention as representing customary international law.

that treaty.[18] However, this is not true of *jus cogens*, or peremptory norms of customary international law, which are recognized by the international community of states as norms "from which no derogation is permitted and which can be modified only by . . . subsequent [norms] of general international law having the same character."[19] States cannot contract out of peremptory norms by acquiescing to their breach or by ratifying inconsistent treaties. Accordingly, the burden of proof to establish the existence of a peremptory norm is high. The International Court of Justice has held that peremptory norms derive "from the outlawing of acts of aggression, and of genocide, as also from the principles and rules concerning the basic rights of the human person including protection from slavery and racial discrimination."[20] The Supreme Court of Canada has recognized that the prohibition against torture is a peremptory norm.[21]

Most international human rights norms find their source in conventional, rather than customary, international law. Following the Second World War, to further their pledge under the United Nations (UN) Charter to promote "universal respect for, and observance of, human rights and fundamental freedoms for all,"[22] states engaged in an intense international effort, coordinated by the UN, to codify human rights and fundamental freedoms in declarations and treaties. Regional international organizations—the Organization of American States (OAS), the Council of Europe, and the Organization of African Unity—also developed treaty-based systems for the protection of human rights. These instruments form "a vast body of legal norms, a veritable human rights code, that gives meaning to the phrase 'human rights and fundamental freedoms.'"[23] Canada is a party to many important multilateral and regional international treaties that bind Canada at international law, some of which are discussed below.[24] Canada has also adopted important declarations, including the *Universal*

---

18   Buergenthal & Murphy, *supra* note 13 at 24. In this sense, conventions play a role analogous to that of statutory law in common law domestic legal systems.

19   *Vienna Convention on the Law of Treaties*, 23 May 1969, Can TS 1980 No 37, UN Doc A/Conf 39/26, art 53 [Vienna Convention]; *Kazemi Estate, supra* note 13 at para 151.

20   *Barcelona Traction*, [1970] ICJ Rep 33 at para 34.

21   *Kazemi Estate, supra* note 13 at para 152.

22   UN Charter, arts 55(c), 56.

23   Thomas Buergenthal, Dinah Shelton & David Stewart, *International Human Rights*, 4th ed (St Paul, Minn: West Publishing, 2009) at 35.

24   These include the UN Charter; the *International Covenant on Civil and Political Rights*, 16 December 1966, [1976] Can TS No 47 [ICCPR]; the *International Covenant on Economic, Social and Cultural Rights*, 16 December 1966, [1976] Can TS No 46 [ICESCR]; the *Convention Against Torture and Other Cruel, Inhuman or Degrading Treatment or Punishment*, 25 May 2000, [2002] Can TS No 5 [CAT]; the 1951 *Convention Relating to the Status of Refugees*, 28 July 1951, [1969] Can TS No 6 [1951 Convention]; the *International Convention on the Elimination of All Forms of Racial Discrimination*, 21 December 1965, [1970] Can TS No 28; the *Convention on the Rights of the Child*, 20 November 1989, [1992] Can TS No 3 [CRC]; the *Convention on the Elimination of All Forms of Discrimination Against Women*, 18 December 1989, [1982] Can TS No 31 [CEAFDAW]; the *Convention on the Rights of Persons with Disabilities*, 13 December 2006, [2010] Can TS No 8 [CRPD]; *Convention (No 87) Concerning Freedom of Association and Protection of the Right to Organize*, 68 UNTS 17 [ILO Convention No 87]; and the *Charter of the Organization of American States*, 30 April 1948, [1990] Can TS No 23 [OAS Charter].

Declaration of Human Rights (UDHR),[25] which, while not formally binding at international law, may "have solemn effects as the formal act of a deliberative body of global importance."[26] International treaties to which Canada is not a party are also important sources of human rights norms that can eventually bind Canada if they become customary international law.[27]

Broadly speaking, international human rights treaties contain several kinds of provisions that may be relevant to Canadian administrative decision-makers, reviewing courts, and public lawyers. Some guarantee substantive rights at international law to individuals. These range from the right to freedom from torture or cruel, inhumane, or degrading treatment, conferred by the *International Covenant on Civil and Political Rights* (ICCPR) and the Convention Against Torture (CAT),[28] to the right to the opportunity to earn one's living through work that one freely chooses or accepts, granted by the *International Covenant on Economic, Social and Cultural Rights* (ICESCR).[29] Others impose substantive obligations on states parties at international law. The *Convention on the Rights of the Child* (CRC) requires states' social welfare institutions, courts of law, administrative authorities, and legislative bodies to take into account the best interests of the child as a primary consideration in all actions concerning children.[30] Many treaties require states to provide an "effective remedy" to persons whose

---

25 GA Res 217(III), UN GAOR, 3d Sess, Supp No 13, UN Doc A/810 (1948) [UDHR]. The UDHR has acquired a moral and normative status unlike that of any other declaration. The repeated reliance of state governments and international organizations on the UDHR as an authoritative expression of human rights has likely given to some of its provisions the status of customary international law: Buergenthal, Shelton & Stewart, *supra* note 23 at 44-46. See also the *American Declaration of the Rights and Duties of Man*, 2 May 1948, 43 AJIL 133, art 2 [ADRDM]. The ADRDM contains and defines the fundamental rights proclaimed by OAS member states in art 3(I) of the OAS Charter: *Interpretation of the American Declaration of the Rights and Duties of Man Within the Framework of Article 64 of the American Convention on Human Rights* (1989), Advisory Opinion OC-10/89, Inter-Am Ct HR (Ser A), No 10 at paras 45-46. Finally, see the *United Nations Declaration on the Rights of Indigenous Peoples*, 13 September 2007, GA Res A/61/295, UNGAOR, 61st Sess, Supp No 49, Vol III, UN Doc A/61/49 (2007) [UNDRIP].

26 HJ Steiner & P Alston, *International Human Rights in Context: Law, Politics, Morals*, 2nd ed (Oxford: Oxford University Press, 2000) at 142, describing the impact of UN General Assembly declarations.

27 These include the *American Convention on Human Rights*, 22 November 1969, 65 AJIL 679 [American Convention]; the *European Convention for the Protection of Human Rights and Fundamental Freedoms*, 4 November 1950, 213 UNTS 221 [ECHR]; and the *African Charter of Human and Peoples' Rights*, 27 June 1981, 1520 UNTS 217 [African Charter]. In interpreting a state's human rights obligations under the ADRDM, the Inter-American Commission on Human Rights takes the American Convention into account even if the state has not ratified it because it represents, in many cases, "an authoritative expression of the fundamental principles set forth in the American Declaration": OAS, Inter-American Commission on Human Rights, *Report on the Situation of Human Rights of Asylum Seekers Within the Canadian Refugee Determination System*, OEA/Ser.L/V/II.106/Doc 40, rev 28 February 2000 at para 38 [IACHR Report]. The ECHR is a particularly important source of international norms for Canada because it is historically and conceptually related to the ICCPR, a treaty ratified by Canada. The drafting of these treaties was conducted, in part, contemporaneously, and important linkages can be drawn between their respective provisions: see P van Dijk, "'The Interpretation of Civil Rights and Obligations' by the European Court of Human Rights—One More Step to Take" in F Matscher & H Petzold, eds, *Protecting Human Rights: The European Dimension—Studies in Honour of Gérard Wiarda*, 2nd ed (Berlin: Carl Heymans Verlag KG, 1990) 137.

28 CAT; ICCPR, art 7. These provisions were considered by the Supreme Court of Canada in *Suresh, supra* note 7. Compare ECHR, art 3; American Convention, art 5.

29 ICESCR, art 6(1). This provision was considered by the Supreme Court of Canada in *Slaight Communications, infra* note 160.

30 CRC, art 3.

substantive treaty rights are violated.[31] In conjunction with the right to an effective remedy, substantive rights may imply institutional or procedural safeguards without which the substantive rights cannot be effectively implemented. Other treaty provisions expressly guarantee institutional and procedural rights at international law, such as the ICCPR right to a fair and public hearing by a competent, independent, and impartial tribunal established by law in the determination of one's rights and obligations in a suit at law,[32] or the CRC right of children, in expressing their own views on matters affecting them, to be heard in any judicial and administrative proceedings affecting them, either directly, or through a representative or an appropriate body.[33] The rights and obligations set out in the international treaties to which Canada is a party are clearly binding on Canada at international law. The more difficult question of the extent to which these treaties are sources of domestic law that bind Canadian courts and constrain the powers of administrative decision-makers is addressed below.

Although many international human rights treaties comprise enforcement mechanisms, they rely primarily on the institutions of the signatory states to enforce their guarantees in domestic law. For example, most of the major UN treaties establish treaty bodies charged with the task of supervising states parties' implementation of the rights set out in their constituent treaties. Treaty bodies carry out several supervisory functions, including reviewing periodic reports submitted by states parties regarding their implementation efforts,[34] issuing interpretive guidelines (general comments) that give meaning to specific treaty provisions, investigating systemic violations of treaty rights,[35] and reviewing petitions alleging treaty violations by a state party filed by other states[36] or by individuals.[37] However, consistent with the primacy of state laws and institutions in protecting human rights, individual petitions are admissible before UN treaty bodies only if the petitioners have exhausted all domestic remedies available to vindicate the rights in question.[38] Canadian institutions may enforce the rights and obligations expressed in international human rights treaties or in customary international law in one of several ways.[39] For example, Parliament or the provincial legislatures may draft laws to achieve compliance with international human rights norms. In turn, administrative decision-makers may, if possible, interpret their statutory powers in a manner consistent with international human rights norms. Canadian courts may also give effect to such norms in individual cases, including those that involve procedural or substantive challenges to the decisions of administrative decision-makers. The principles governing whether courts may give effect to a norm of international law—the rules of reception—are discussed in the next section.

---

31   ICCPR, art 2(3). Compare ECHR, art 13; American Convention, art 25; ADRDM, art XVIII.

32   ICCPR, art 14.

33   CRC, art 12.

34   ICCPR, art 40.

35   CAT, art 20.

36   ICCPR, art 41.

37   *Optional Protocol to the International Covenant on Civil and Political Rights*, 16 December 1966, [1976] Can TS No 47, art 1 [Optional Protocol].

38   *Ibid*, art 5(2)(b).

39   For a full listing, see Armand de Mestral & Evan Fox-Decent, "Implementation and Reception: The Congeniality of Canada's Legal Order to International Law" in Oonagh E Fitzgerald, ed, *The Globalized Rule of Law* (Toronto: Irwin Law, 2006) 31 at 42-56 [de Mestral & Fox-Decent, "Implementation and Reception"].

III. RULES OF RECEPTION OF INTERNATIONAL LAW

Which rules govern whether and in what circumstances Canadian courts may take international norms into account and how these norms can shape the interpretation of statutes and constitutional provisions? Despite significant efforts by the Supreme Court of Canada to clarify the rules of reception of international law into domestic law,[40] some uncertainty remains, particularly with regard to the role of conventional international law in Charter interpretation.[41] In this section, the reception of both customary and conventional international human rights law is examined.

A. Reception of Customary International Human Rights Law

After a lengthy period of relative uncertainty, the Supreme Court of Canada confirmed, in its 2007 decision in *R v Hape*, that the reception of customary international law into Canadian law is governed by the doctrine of adoption, whereby customary rules of international law are incorporated automatically, as they evolve, into domestic law:

> [F]ollowing the common law tradition, it appears that the doctrine of adoption operates in Canada such that prohibitive rules of customary international law should be incorporated into domestic law in the absence of conflicting legislation. The automatic incorporation of such rules is justified on the basis that international custom, as the law of nations, is also the law of Canada unless, in a valid exercise of its sovereignty, Canada declares that its law is to the contrary. Parliamentary sovereignty dictates that a legislature may violate international law, but that it must do so expressly. Absent an express derogation, the courts may look to prohibitive rules of customary international law to aid in the interpretation of Canadian law and the development of the common law.[42]

The court's use of the word "should" (rather than "are") and its seemingly tentative conclusion that courts "may" look to customary international law to "aid" in the interpretation of Canadian law and the development of the common law caused some observers[43] to question whether it had indeed adopted a rule of automatic incorporation under which, absent an express statutory derogation, customary international law *is* Canadian law and thus directly binding on Canadian courts.[44] Writing extrajudicially, Justice Louis LeBel, who authored the majority opinion in *Hape*, has stated that when it is read in context, "the gist of [this opinion] was that accepting incorporation of customary international [law] was the right approach."[45] Thus, "the law in Canada today appears to be settled on this point: prohibitive

---

40 See, notably, *R v Hape*, 2007 SCC 26 and *Kazemi Estate, supra* note 13.

41 See e.g. Patrick Macklem, "The International Constitution" in Fay Faraday, Judy Fudge & Eric Tucker, eds, *Constitutional Labour Rights in Canada* (Toronto: Irwin Law, 2014) 261 at 285; John Currie, "International Human Rights Law in the Supreme Court's Charter Jurisprudence: Commitment, Retrenchment and Retreat—In No Particular Order" (2010) 50 SCLR (2d) 423.

42 *Hape, supra* note 40 at para 39.

43 John Currie, *Public International Law*, 2nd ed (Toronto: Irwin Law, 2008) at 232.

44 See Armand de Mestral & Evan Fox-Decent, "Rethinking the Relationship Between International and Domestic Law" (2008) 53 McGill LJ 573 at 583 et seq [de Mestral & Fox-Decent, "Rethinking the Relationship"].

45 Louis LeBel, "A Common Law of the World? The Reception of Customary International Law in the Canadian Common Law" (2014) 65 UNBLJ 3 at 15.

customary norms are directly incorporated into our common law and must be followed by courts absent legislation which clearly overrules them."[46] As John Currie notes, the power of the legislative branch to override customary international law "flows from the basic constitutional principle of legislative supremacy which, although subject to constitutional imperatives, is not subject to any requirement of compliance with international law, whether of a customary or conventional nature."[47]

This and other aspects of the doctrine of adoption, including the distinction between prohibitive (or mandatory) and permissive rules of customary international law, were considered by the Supreme Court of Canada in *Kazemi Estate v Islamic Republic of Iran*.[48] In 2013, Zahra Kazemi, a Canadian photographer and journalist, was detained, tortured, and killed in Iran. Her son filed legal proceedings on his own behalf and on behalf of his mother's estate seeking damages from the Islamic Republic of Iran, Iran's head of state, and other Iranian officials allegedly tied to Kazemi's death. The defendants asked that the action be dismissed on the basis of state immunity. Canada's *State Immunity Act*[49] provides that "except as provided by this Act," foreign states are immune from the jurisdiction of Canadian courts. Subsequent provisions of the Act specify that foreign states are not immune from the jurisdiction of Canadian courts in proceedings relating to commercial activity in the foreign state or to death, personal or bodily injury, or damage or loss of property that occur in Canada. The estate argued that international customary law provided a further exception to state immunity for acts of torture conducted in Iran by Iranian government officials. LeBel J, writing for a majority of the Supreme Court, held that even if such an exception had reached the status of a customary rule of international law, it could not be adopted into Canadian law as a common law exception to s 3(1) of the SIA as it would be in "clear conflict with the SIA."[50] Section 3(1) exhaustively established the parameters for state immunity from civil proceedings and its exceptions:[51]

> [T]he words of s. 3(1) of the SIA completely oust the common law and international law as a source of potential exceptions to the immunity which it provides. The plain and ordinary meaning of the words "except as provided by this Act" is that it is the Act, and the Act alone, that may provide exceptions to the immunity granted pursuant to s. 3(1) of the SIA.[52]

Moreover, LeBel J was of the view that "should an exception to state immunity for acts of torture have become customary international law, such a rule could likely be *permissive*— and not *mandatory*—thereby, requiring legislative action to become Canadian law."[53] In other words, a rule of customary international law providing that states *could* choose to further relax the bar on bringing civil proceedings against a foreign state in domestic courts in cases involving allegations of torture committed abroad would not, through the doctrine of adoption, lead to the incorporation into domestic law of a directly enforceable obligation on Canada to exempt civil proceedings from state immunity.

---

46 *Ibid.*
47 Currie, *supra* note 43 at 234-35.
48 *Supra* note 13.
49 RSC 1985, c S-18, s 3(1) [SIA].
50 *Kazemi Estate, supra* note 13 at para 61.
51 *Ibid* at para 54.
52 *Ibid* at para 58.
53 *Ibid* at para 61.

B. Reception of Conventional International Human Rights Law

As a matter of international law, an international treaty is binding on Canada if it is signed and ratified by Canada and has entered into force.[54] The effect of a ratified treaty on Canada's domestic law is another question entirely. Traditionally, conventional international law and Canadian domestic law have been conceived of as two separate regimes residing on entirely distinct planes. This "dualist" relationship is founded on the doctrine of separation of powers between the executive and legislature, which underpins the legal sovereignty of Parliament. Under this traditionalist account, the federal executive may exercise its prerogative power to sign and ratify international treaties that bind Canada on the international plane, but only Parliament or the provincial legislatures can enact laws that affect legal rights and obligations within Canada.[55] If treaties created legally enforceable rights and obligations without the need to enact enabling legislation, the federal executive could legislate without the consent of Parliament or the provincial legislatures.[56] Thus, international treaty provisions must be "implemented" or "transformed" into domestic law to impose obligations or confer rights legally enforceable in domestic courts.[57] From the traditionalist perspective, an "automatic" domestic application of treaty norms by courts leads to a "democratic deficit," which must be cured by legislative or constitutional reforms to enhance legislatures' involvement in the decision to ratify international treaties.[58] In 2008, the Government of Canada adopted a policy to table the text of treaties in the House of Commons for 21 sitting days to allow Parliament to debate the treaties and request votes on motions recommending action, including ratification.[59] While the government undertakes to consider any concerns with ratification raised during the tabling process, it retains full author-

---

54   By signing a treaty, the state expresses its intent to be bound by the treaty obligations in the future. The state formally expresses its final consent to be bound by a treaty by ratifying the treaty, usually by depositing a declaration to this effect with other states parties or an agreed-upon depository like the UN Secretariat. Typically, a treaty provides that it comes into force once a specified number of states have ratified it: see e.g. ICCPR, arts 48, 49. See, generally, Mark Freeman & Gibran van Ert, *International Human Rights Law* (Toronto: Irwin Law, 2004) at 57-58.

55   *Baker, supra* note 1 at paras 80-83, Iacobucci J, dissenting. See also *Baker v Canada (Minister of Citizenship and Immigration)* (1996), [1997] 2 FC 127, 142 DLR (4th) 554 at 563-64 (FCA) [*Baker* (FCA)].

56   *Attorney General for Canada v Attorney General for Ontario (Labour Conventions)*, [1937] AC 326 (PC) [*Labour Conventions*]; Hugh M Kindred, *International Law: Chiefly as Interpreted and Applied in Canada*, 7th ed (Toronto: Emond Montgomery, 2006) at 206 [Kindred, *International Law*]. The jurisdiction to enact laws to implement a treaty resides with Parliament or the provincial legislatures, depending on the treaty's subject matter.

57   *Kazemi Estate, supra* note 13 at para 149.

58   Joanna Harrington, "Redressing the Democratic Deficit in Treaty Law Making: (Re-)Establishing a Role for Parliament" (2005) McGill LJ 465 at 468. For a detailed description of Canadian practice regarding the negotiation and implementation of treaties and a proposal for a federal *Canada Treaties Act* to bring greater unity to the relationship between international and domestic law, see de Mestral & Fox-Decent, "Rethinking the Relationship," *supra* note 44 at 538 et seq.

59   Global Affairs Canada, *Policy on Tabling of Treaties in Parliament* at para 6.2, online: <www.treaty-accord.gc.ca/procedures.aspx?lang=eng>. To facilitate consideration of a treaty, the government also provides Parliament an "explanatory memorandum" that explains, among other things, its subject matter, the main obligations that Canada will assume, how the treaty will be implemented, to what extent the treaty relates to federal and provincial constitutional jurisdiction and reasons why Canada should be a party.

ity and responsibility for the decision of whether to ratify a treaty. A distinct but related objection to the domestic application of international treaty norms without specific legislative implementation is that federal treaty-making may affect areas of provincial legislative jurisdiction and lead to violations of Canada's constitutional division of powers.[60]

The traditionalist view that a treaty obligation binding on Canada at international law is irrelevant or "has no domestic, internal consequence"[61] unless implemented by specific legislation following the treaty's ratification is an oversimplification.[62] First, "not all implementing legislation is obviously so."[63] For example, Parliament may enact statutes for the purpose of implementing a treaty obligation without referring to the treaty. Moreover, "legislation that was not originally intended to implement a treaty may later be relied upon by the federal government as its means of doing so."[64] Canada ratifies most international human rights treaties without adopting implementing legislation, on the assumption that Canadian constitutional, statutory, and common law regimes already conform with the treaty norms.[65] Controversially, despite this claim of conformity, the Canadian government has resisted attempts to enforce human rights treaty norms in Canadian courts on the ground that, absent implementing legislation, they are not binding in Canadian law.[66] Many convincingly argue that express statutory implementation of a treaty is required only if the treaty purports to alter existing domestic law,[67] and that implementation should be inferred where Canada premises its ratification on the prior conformity of Canadian legislation, common law, and administrative policy.[68] Indeed, Canada's Department of Foreign

---

60 See *Labour Conventions, supra* note 56.

61 *Capital Cities Communications Inc v Canadian Radio-Television Commission*, [1978] 2 SCR 141 at 173 per Laskin CJ.

62 *Ibid* at 188, Pigeon J.

63 Freeman & van Ert, *supra* note 54 at 166.

64 *Ibid* at 167. Canada's government claims that "many laws and policies, adopted by the federal, provincial and territorial governments, assist in the implementation of Canada's international human rights obligations": *ibid*, n 94. For an enumeration of the different modes of treaty implementation used in Canada, see de Mestral & Fox-Decent, "Rethinking the Relationship," *supra* note 44 at 617 et seq.

65 Irit Weiser, "Effect of International Human Rights Treaties Ratified Without Implementing Legislation" in *The Impact of International Law in the Practice of Law in Canada* (The Hague: Kluwer Law, 1999) 132 at 132; Stephen J Toope, "The Uses of Metaphor: International Law and the Supreme Court of Canada" (2001) 80 Can Bar Rev 534 at 538.

66 See *Baker* (FCA), *supra* note 55; *Ahani v Canada (Attorney General)* (2002), 58 OR (3d) 107 (CA), leave to appeal denied, 2002 SCC 2 [*Ahani*]. See also K Norman, "Taking Human Rights Lightly: The Canadian Approach" (2001) 12 NJCL 2 at 291.

67 S Toope & J Brunnée, "A Hesitant Embrace: The Application of International Law by Canadian Courts" (2002) 40 Can YB Int'l Law 3 at 26-27 [Toope & Brunnée, "Hesitant"]. See *Labour Conventions, supra* note 56 at 347, Lord Atkin: the performance of treaty obligations requires legislative action "if they entail alterations of existing domestic law." See also *Francis v The Queen*, [1956] SCR 618 at 626, Rand J: statutory action is needed if treaties "purport to change existing law" or restrict future legislative action.

68 Toope & Brunnée, "Hesitant," *supra* note 67 at 26; J Brunnée & S Toope, "A Hesitant Embrace: Baker and the Application of International Law by Canadian Courts" in Dyzenhaus, *supra* note 8, 357 at 363 [Brunnée & Toope, "Embrace"]. See also Hugh M Kindred, "The Use and Abuse of International Legal Sources by Canadian Courts: Searching for a Principled Approach" in Fitzgerald, *supra* note 39, 5 at 15-17; de Mestral & Fox-Decent, "Implementation and Reception," *supra* note 39 at 54-55.

Affairs states that "the government can accept the obligations within many treaties without new legislation."[69]

Others challenge the traditionalist view by questioning the very basis of the formal separation of powers doctrine—the legislature's monopoly over the production of domestic legal norms. These critics point out that courts have long constrained the administrative state's exercise of statutory powers by insisting that it conform with "fundamental" or "constitutional" common law values,[70] including the duty of procedural fairness in administrative law.[71] In their view, courts' increasing reliance on norms expressed in international human rights treaties (whether implemented by statute or not) is best understood as "the judicial updating of the catalogue of values to which the common law subjects the administrative state" from "pre-democratic, property-based values, to a more modern set of democratic values, including fundamental human rights."[72]

C. The Presumption of Conformity with International Law

The rules of reception may govern how customary and conventional international laws are given direct effect in Canada's domestic law, but international law, including "unimplemented" treaties, indirectly influences Canadian law through the well-established principle of statutory interpretation that domestic legislation[73] will be presumed to conform with international law, including customary international law and treaty obligations:

> The presumption of conformity is based on the rule of judicial policy that, as a matter of law, courts will strive to avoid constructions of domestic law pursuant to which the state would be in violation of its international obligations, unless the wording of the statute clearly compels that result.... [T]he presumption has two aspects. First, the legislature is presumed to act in compliance with Canada's obligations as a signatory of international treaties and as a member of the international community. In deciding between possible interpretations, courts will avoid a construction that would place Canada in breach of those obligations. The second aspect is that the legislature is presumed to comply with the values and principles of customary and conventional international law. Those values form part of the context in which statutes are enacted, and courts will therefore prefer a construction that reflects them. The presumption is

---

69 (2008), Canada Treaty Information online: <http://www.treaty-accord.gc.ca/procedures.aspx> at para 6.2. For a contrary view reflecting the traditionalist approach to implementation, see William A Schabas & Stéphane Beaulac, *International Human Rights and Canadian Law—Legal Commitment, Implementation and the Charter*, 3rd ed (Toronto: Thomson Carswell, 2007) at 60.

70 David Dyzenhaus, Murray Hunt & Michael Taggart, "The Principle of Legality in Administrative Law: Internationalisation as Constitutionalisation" (2001) 1 OUCLJ 5 at 7, 34 ["Principle of Legality"]. See also John Mark Keyes & Ruth Sullivan, "A Legislative Perspective on the Interaction of International and Domestic Law" in Fitzgerald, *supra* note 39, 277 at 292 et seq.

71 de Mestral & Fox-Decent, "Implementation and Reception," *supra* note 39 at 57-58; *Knight v Indian Head School Division No 19*, [1990] 1 SCR 653 at paras 22 and 24.

72 "Principle of Legality," *supra* note 70 at 7, 34.

73 The presumption of conformity applies to secondary legislation such as regulations, including Rules of Court, as well as primary legislation: *Xela Enterprises Ltd v Castillo*, 2016 ONCA 437 at para 23; *Wang v Lin*, 2016 ONSC 3967 (Div Ct).

rebuttable, however. Parliamentary sovereignty requires courts to give effect to a statute that demonstrates an unequivocal legislative intent to default on an international obligation.[74]

Courts should even apply the presumption of conformity with international law when interpreting legislation that does not necessarily implement a treaty ratified by Canada because the underlying rationale of the presumption—to avoid an unintended breach of Canada's international obligations through judicial misconstruction of a statute—applies as much to ordinary laws as it does to implementing legislation.[75] The Supreme Court of Canada has indeed applied the presumption of conformity as a "general principle" of statutory interpretation on several occasions.[76]

More recently, the Supreme Court of Canada reiterated the central role played by the presumption in ensuring that international law is considered in the interpretation of Canadian legislation:

> This Court has previously explained that the values and principles of customary and conventional international law form part of the context in which Canadian laws are enacted: *R. v Hape* .... This follows from the fact that to interpret a Canadian law in a way that conflicts with Canada's international obligations risks incursion by the courts in the executive's conduct of foreign affairs and censure under international law. The contextual significance of international law is all the more clear where the provision to be construed "has been enacted with a view towards implementing international obligations": *National Corn Growers Assn v Canada (Import Tribunal)*. ...
>
> In keeping with the international context in which Canadian legislation is enacted, this Court has repeatedly endorsed and applied the interpretive presumption that legislation conforms with the state's international obligations .... This interpretive presumption is not peculiar to Canada. It is a feature of legal interpretation around the world. ...
>
> These principles, derived from the case law, direct us to relevant international instruments at the context stage of statutory interpretation. ...[77]

---

74 *Hape, supra* note 40 at para 53.

75 Freeman & van Ert, *supra* note 54 at 156. Toope & Brunnée, "Hesitant," *supra* note 67 at 32.

76 See e.g. *Canadian Foundation for Children, Youth and the Law v Canada (Attorney General)*, 2004 SCC 4, [2004] 1 SCR 76 [*Canadian Foundation*], where the Supreme Court interpreted in conformity with the CRC and ICCPR a provision of the *Criminal Code* that predated these treaties and was thus not enacted to implement them. See also *Thibodeau v Air Canada*, 2014 SCC 67, [2014] 3 SCR 340 at para 113 [*Thibodeau*], where the appellant asked the Federal Court to exercise its broad remedial power under s 77(4) of the *Official Languages Act*, RSC 1985, c 31 [OLA] (allowing it to grant "such remedy as it considers appropriate and just in the circumstances") to order Air Canada to pay punitive and exemplary damages for breaching his right to French-language services. Air Canada argued that such an order breached art 29 of the *Convention for the Unification of Certain Rules for International Carriage by Air*, 2242 UNTS 309 [*Montreal Convention*], which precluded, in this context, an award of punitive, exemplary, or any other non-compensatory damages. This convention was part of Canadian law by virtue of the *Carriage by Air Act*, RSC 1985, c C-26, s 2. The Supreme Court of Canada held, at para 113, that the appellant's position "that Parliament, through s 77(4), intended that courts should be able to grant damages even though doing so would be in violation of Canada's international undertakings as incorporated into federal statute law" would "run afoul of the principle of interpretation that Parliament is presumed not to intend to legislate in breach of Canada's international law obligations." Thus, it applied this presumption to interpret the OLA, a statute clearly not intended to implement the *Montreal Convention*.

77 *B010 v Canada (Citizenship and Immigration)*, 2015 SCC 58, [2015] 3 SCR 704 at paras 47-49 [*B010*].

This passage is significant for at least two reasons. First, it confirms that the presumption of conformity does have general application, since international law is contextually significant for the interpretation of all legislation, albeit "more clearly so" for legislation that implements the relevant treaty. Second, the fact that the interpretive presumption directs courts to "relevant international instruments at the context stage of statutory interpretation" confirms that consideration of international law, as part and parcel of the exercise of statutory interpretation, is not contingent on a prior finding that a statutory provision is grammatically ambiguous. Courts should consider these treaties from the outset of the interpretation process rather than having to ensure that the relevant statute is ambiguous before bringing in relevant treaties.[78]

The presumption of conformity will be rebutted by a statute that is unambiguously contrary to international law. In *Kazemi Estate*, several interveners claimed that the SIA did not unambiguously extend state immunity to cases involving the breach of the prohibition of torture at international law, and invited the court to apply the presumption of conformity to read down the statute. It declined this invitation:

> International law cannot be used to support an interpretation that is not permitted by the words of the statute. Likewise, the presumption of conformity does not overthrow clear legislative intent ... Indeed, the presumption that legislation will conform to international law remains just that—merely a presumption. This Court has cautioned that the presumption can be rebutted by the clear words of the statute under consideration (*Hape*, at paras. 53-54). In the present case, the SIA lists the exceptions to state immunity exhaustively. Canada's domestic legal order, as Parliament has framed it, prevails.[79]

Through the rules of reception and the presumption of conformity, international law can influence administrative decision-makers' interpretation of the scope of their statutory powers and impact the substantive review of administrative decisions, an influence examined in the next section.

IV. INTERNATIONAL HUMAN RIGHTS NORMS AND THE SUBSTANTIVE REVIEW OF ADMINISTRATIVE DECISION-MAKING

International human rights norms influence the substantive review of administrative decision-making in at least two ways. First, public officials and administrative agencies exercise decision-making powers that are defined in legislation. International law may be relevant to their interpretation of the scope of these powers. In assessing the correctness or reasonableness of administrative decisions, reviewing courts will consider whether administrative decision-makers have appropriately accounted for the influence of international law in interpreting the scope of their statutory powers. Second, administrative decisions must be consistent with

---

78   See Gib van Ert, *Using International Law in Canadian Courts*, 2nd ed (Irwin Law: Toronto, 2008) at 170. The Federal Court of Appeal's view, in *Gitxaala Nation, supra* note 9 at paras 16-17, that courts may not resort to international treaties to interpret legislation before demonstrating grammatical ambiguity is inconsistent with the Supreme Court of Canada's broader view of the presumption's applicability.

79   *Kazemi Estate, supra* note 13 at para 60.

the Charter. By influencing the scope of Charter protections, international human rights norms shape courts' assessment of the lawfulness and reasonableness of administrative decisions that engage the Charter.

A. International Human Rights Norms, Statutory Interpretation, and Substantive Review

The Supreme Court of Canada's recent jurisprudence supports a general duty to interpret legislation, including administrative decision-makers' enabling statutes, in conformity with Canada's international law obligations—both conventional and customary. The following section focuses first on the substantive review of administrative decisions involving implemented treaty norms before addressing unimplemented treaty norms. The discussion then turns to the substantive review of decisions involving customary norms of international law.

1. Conventional International Human Rights Norms and Substantive Review

In interpreting a statute that expressly implements an international treaty, courts must rely on the provisions of that treaty.[80] In *Pushpanathan v Canada (Minister of Citizenship and Immigration)*,[81] the court reviewed the interpretation by the Immigration and Refugee Board (IRB) of a provision in the *Immigration Act* that implemented article 1(F)(c) of the 1951 *Convention Relating to the Status of Refugees*, excluding from refugee protection individuals "guilty of acts contrary to the purposes and principles of the United Nations."[82] Since the statutory provision sought to implement the 1951 Convention, the court was bound to "adopt an interpretation consistent with Canada's obligations under the Convention,"[83] which it determined by analyzing the Convention's text and applying the rules of treaty interpretation articulated in the Vienna Convention.[84] The court reviewed the IRB's determination on a correctness basis, largely because the interpretation of an international human rights convention was a pure question of law of precedential value over which it could claim more expertise

---

80 Traditionally, courts would not resort to the text of an underlying treaty as an aid to interpreting the provisions of implementing legislation unless they were satisfied that the text was patently ambiguous: Kindred, *International Law, supra* note 56 at 202-3. In *National Corn Growers Assn v Canada (Import Tribunal)*, [1990] 2 SCR 1324 at 1371 [*National Corn Growers*], the Supreme Court jettisoned this requirement and held that it was proper to refer to the treaty at the outset of the interpretive inquiry, because implementing statutes can reveal latent ambiguities. But see Stéphane Beaulac, "International Law and Statutory Interpretation: Up with Context, Down with Presumption" in Fitzgerald, *supra* note 39, 331 at 349-51.

81 [1998] 1 SCR 982 [*Pushpanathan*].

82 1951 Convention, art 1(F)(c).

83 *Pushpanathan, supra* note 81 at para 51.

84 Article 31 of the Vienna Convention requires that a treaty be "interpreted in good faith in accordance with the ordinary meaning to be given to the terms of the treaty in their context and in light of its object and purpose." Article 32 recognizes that if this approach to interpretation leaves the meaning of a treaty provision ambiguous or obscure or leads to manifestly absurd or unreasonable results, recourse may be had to supplementary means of interpretation, including the preparatory work of the treaty and the circumstances of its conclusion.

than the IRB.[85] It decided that the IRB had erred in denying Mr Pushpanathan Convention refugee status under the exclusion clause in article 1F(c) on the grounds that conspiring to traffic in a narcotic was an act "contrary to the purposes and principles of the United Nations." In the court's view, article 1F(c) applied where there was a consensus in international law that particular acts constituted sufficiently serious and sustained violations of fundamental human rights as to amount to persecution or were explicitly recognized as contrary to UN purposes and principles. The crime of conspiracy to traffic a narcotic satisfied neither prerequisite.[86]

In *Németh v Canada (Justice)*,[87] the Supreme Court of Canada's interpretation of several provisions of the *Immigration and Refugee Protection Act*[88] and *Extradition Act*[89] defining the scope of the justice minister's authority to extradite a refugee was heavily influenced by its analysis of how Parliament had chosen to implement in these statutes the prohibition at international law against the refoulement of Convention refugees. A few years after the Némeths, Hungarian Roma, had been recognized by the IRB as refugees, Hungary sought their extradition to face fraud charges. Canada's minister of justice ordered their surrender despite claims that they feared persecution in Hungary. He determined that to successfully resist their extradition, they had to establish that they would face persecution on their return to Hungary. The Némeths claimed that s 115 of the IRPA implemented the principle of non-refoulement from the 1951 Convention by providing that a person recognized as a Convention refugee shall not be removed from Canada to a country where he or she would be at risk of persecution. In particular, they argued that an interpretation of s 115 that precluded removal by extradition until their refugee status had ceased or been revoked through the processes set out under the IRPA was necessary to implement Canada's obligations under the Convention. Cromwell J, writing for a unanimous court, agreed that "where possible, statutes should be interpreted in a way which makes their provisions consistent with Canada's international treaty obligations and principles of international law."[90] However, he determined that, properly construed, "removal" in s 115 was used solely in connection with "removal orders" under the IRPA and did not extend to removal by extradition.[91] Accordingly, the presumption that s 115 implemented Canada's

---

85 *Pushpanathan, supra* note 81 at para 45 et seq. But see *National Corn Growers, supra* note 80, where the court applied a deferential standard in its review of the Canadian Import Tribunal's interpretation of the *Special Import Measures Act*, RSC 1985, c S-15, including the tribunal's decision to refer to the General Agreement on Tariffs and Trade (GATT), which the Act was intended to implement. Such a standard was appropriate in light of the presence, in the specialized tribunal's enabling statute, of a privative clause.

86 See also *Ezokola v Canada (Citizenship and Immigration)*, 2013 SCC 40, [2013] 2 SCR 678, where, reviewing a decision of the IRB's Refugee Protection Division, the Supreme Court interpreted article 1F(a) of the 1951 Convention, also implemented by the *Immigration and Refugee Protection Act*, in light of relevant sources of international law, including the *Rome Statute of the International Criminal Court*, UN Doc A/CONF 183/9, 17 July 1998, to clarify under what circumstances an individual would be excluded from refugee status for complicity in crimes against peace, war crimes or crimes against humanity.

87 2010 SCC 56, [2010] 3 SCR 281 [*Németh*].

88 SC 2001, c 27 [IRPA].

89 SC 1999, c 18.

90 *Németh, supra* note 87 at para 34.

91 *Ibid* at paras 26-31.

international obligations in the context of extradition was rebutted by the unambiguous and clear meaning of that statutory provision.[92] Cromwell J held that "the *IRPA* does not and was not intended to implement Canada's international obligations against *refoulement* in the context of expulsion by extradition,"[93] a role assigned in his view to s 44 of the *Extradition Act*, which required the minister to refuse to make a surrender order in certain circumstances. Similarities in language and legislative history leading to its enactment showed that s 44(1)(b) was inspired by the provisions of the European Convention on Extradition and the UN Model Treaty on Extradition. It was thus reasonable to infer that s 44(1)(b) was adopted to serve the purpose identified for these provisions—"protection against prejudice in the requesting state, particularly when extradition would constitute a violation of the requested state's obligations in relation to *non-refoulement*"[94]—and was Canada's "primary legislative vehicle to give effect to Canada's *non-refoulement* obligations when a refugee is sought for extradition."[95] Accordingly, the international norms governing refugee protection played an important role in the interpretation of the provision:

> This clear link between s 44(1)(b) and Canada's international obligations under the Refugee Convention has important implications for its interpretation and application in the refugee context. The Refugee Convention has an "overarching and clear human rights object and purpose," and domestic law aimed at implementing the Refugee Convention, such as s. 44(1)(b), must be interpreted in light of that human rights object and purpose: *Pushpanathan* .... Section 44(1)(b), when applied to the situation of a refugee whose extradition is sought, must be understood in the full context of refugee protection.[96]

The court decided that the closing words of s 44(1)(b), which provide that the minister shall refuse surrender if satisfied that "the request for extradition is made for the purpose of prosecuting or punishing the person by reason of their race [or other Convention grounds] ... or [if] the person's position may be prejudiced for any of those reasons,"[97] should be interpreted broadly as "protecting a refugee against *refoulement* which risks prejudice to him or her on the listed grounds in the requesting state whether or not the prejudice is strictly linked to prosecution or punishment."[98] Moreover, imposing on a

---

92 Similarly, the Némeths' claim that extradition could be ordered only if a previous finding that a person was a refugee had been formally set aside was inconsistent with the temporal nature of refugee status under the 1951 Convention and not supported by more specific international norms: *ibid* at paras 50-52.

93 *Ibid* at para 41.

94 *Ibid* at para 81.

95 *Ibid* at para 77. But see Catherine Dauvergne, "The Troublesome Intersection of Refugee Law and Criminal Law" in Katja Franko Aas and Mary Bosworth, eds, *The Borders of Punishment: Migration, Citizenship and Social Exclusion* (Oxford: Oxford University Press, 2013) 76. Dauvergne argues, at 85-86, that Canada's *Extradition Act* provides less protection against refoulement than the 1951 Convention and that the court erred in finding that domestic law provided "a complete reflection of Canada's non-refoulement obligations."

96 *Németh, supra* note 87 at para 86.

97 *Ibid* at para 56.

98 *Ibid* at para 96.

refugee the burden of proving that persecution would in fact occur and that the conditions that led to the conferral of refugee protection had not changed was "not compatible with Canada's international undertakings with respect to *non-refoulement* or with the requirements of fundamental fairness to the refugee."[99] In the opinion of the court, by imposing such a burden on the Némeths and by failing to address s 44(1)(b) in his decision to surrender them, the minister had made an unreasonable decision.[100]

Németh illustrates that before a court relies on the terms of an international treaty to interpret a statutory provision, it first ascertains whether the legislature in fact intended for the specific provision to implement that treaty. However, one of the Supreme Court's most notable decisions raising the role of international law in the substantive review of administrative decisions involved the CRC, a treaty considered by the court to be unimplemented in Canadian law. Ms Baker, an illegal overstayer facing removal to Jamaica by Canadian immigration authorities, asked the minister of citizenship and immigration to exercise her discretion under the *Immigration Act*[101] to allow her, on humanitarian and compassionate grounds, to remain in Canada where she could care for her Canadian-born children and continue treatment for paranoid schizophrenia. The minister denied her application. Although the court decided *Baker* on the procedural issue of bias, it also held that this was an unreasonable exercise of discretion because the immigration officer who had examined Baker's case had not shown attentiveness and sensitivity to the best interests of Baker's children. The court's assessment of the reasonableness of the decision was informed by the objectives of the *Immigration Act* including family reunification, ministerial guidelines that emphasized preserving family connections, and the values underlying the CRC. The Act, the guidelines, and the CRC indicated that emphasis on the rights, interests, and needs of children, and special attention to childhood were "important values that should be considered in reasonably interpreting 'humanitarian' and 'compassionate' considerations that guide the exercise of the discretion."[102] The court did reject Baker's claim that in assessing her application, the minister should have given *primacy* to the best interests of her children as required by article 3(1) of the CRC[103] because, in its view, the CRC was not implemented by statute and article 3(1) was thus not part of Canadian law and could not apply directly to structure the minister's discretion under the Act.[104] However, L'Heureux-Dubé J, for the majority, ruled that the CRC still played an important role:

99   *Ibid* at para 105.

100   Catherine Dauvergne argues that, properly interpreted, the 1951 Convention "provided a full and complete answer" in *Németh*, and required that the minister refuse the extradition request: Dauvergne, *supra* note 95 at 85. The Supreme Court's interpretation of the 1951 Convention failed to recognize the very limited scope of the exceptions to Canada's obligation of non-refoulement in art 33: only a refugee for whom there are reasonable grounds to regard him as a danger to the security of the country in which he is or who, following a conviction for a particularly serious crime, constitutes a danger to the community of that country, may not claim the benefit of the prohibition on refoulement. Németh fell into neither of these categories.

101   RSC 1985, c I-2 (repealed).

102   *Baker*, *supra* note 1 at para 73.

103   Article 3(1) of the CRC reads: "In all actions concerning children . . . the best interests of the child shall be a primary consideration."

104   But see de Mestral & Fox-Decent, "Implementation and Reception," *supra* note 39 at 54-55 for the argument that the CRC had in fact been implemented into Canadian law.

[T]he values reflected in international human rights law may help inform the contextual approach to statutory interpretation and judicial review. As stated in R. Sullivan, *Driedger on the Construction of Statutes* (3rd ed 1994) at 330:

> [T]he legislature is presumed to respect the values and principles enshrined in international law, both customary and conventional. These constitute a part of the legal context in which legislation is enacted and read. *In so far as possible, therefore, interpretations that reflect these values and principles are preferred.*[105]

The decision that values reflected in an unimplemented international treaty may help inform the interpretation, exercise, and judicial review of statutory discretion sparked an animated debate. Iacobucci and Cory JJ dissented on this point, arguing that allowing reference to an unincorporated treaty during the process of statutory interpretation allowed *Baker* to "achieve indirectly what cannot be achieved directly, namely, to give force and effect within the domestic legal system to international obligations undertaken by the executive alone that have yet to be subject to the democratic will of Parliament."[106] Arguably, however, the majority did not go far enough in giving effect to the CRC, which is ratified, in force, and thus binding on Canada. Unlike other international norms, the CRC is not "potentially persuasive," but obligatory: the court should have applied the presumption of conformity of domestic law with Canada's international obligations, requiring it to strive, as far as possible, to interpret the *Immigration Act* in conformity with Canada's obligations under article 3 of the CRC. Instead, *Baker* prescribes only that the values underlying the CRC "may help inform" courts' "interpretive effort,"[107] an arguably less demanding interpretive onus, appropriate in relation to international norms not binding on Canada.[108] Curiously, when the court reaffirmed the presumption of conformity and its application to treaty norms in *Hape*, it did not mention *Baker* or acknowledge this inconsistency.

Craig Scott argues that *Baker* changed courts' focus from the "bindingness" to the "persuasiveness" of international norms:

> [I]t is not simply a rule-of-law concern with the formal legal status of Canada's international legal commitments that determines the depth of interpretive influence of international norms on statutory interpretation but also (and more so) those commitments' resonance with Canadian law and society's fundamental constitutive values and principles. . . .

---

105 *Baker*, *supra* note 1 at para 70 (emphasis in original).

106 *Ibid* at para 80.

107 Brunnée & Toope, "Embrace," *supra* note 68 at 372.

108 John Currie characterized *Baker* as setting out "a permissive rule allowing courts to have regard to Canada's treaty obligations as an aid to statutory interpretation": John Currie, *Public International Law* (Toronto: Irwin Law, 2001) at 226. Gib van Ert, *supra* note 78 at 299 argues that *Baker* was "in effect, an application of the presumption of conformity to the enabling provision: the discretion conferred by the statute was presumed to be consistent with the requirements of international law." In his view, "there is no convincing reason to distinguish *Baker*'s use of an unimplemented treaty from the ordinary presumption of conformity." For an example of the application of the less demanding interpretive onus applicable to non-binding international norms, see *R v Hamm*, 2016 ABQB at para 95, where, on a *habeas corpus* application, the court held that the *United Nations Standard Minimum Rules for the Treatment of Prisoners*, GA Res 70/175, UNGAOR, 2015, UN Doc A/Res/70/175 adopted by the UN General Assembly but not implemented by Canada informed but did not dictate whether the decision to place the applicant inmates in solitary confinement was reasonable.

While the [interpretive presumption of legislative conformity with international law] . . . is generally applicable to Canada's international commitments, the normative force of any given commitment being called in aid must vary with the subject matter of the international norms and with some appreciation of how the context in which it has been produced relates to our "free and democratic" ideals. In other words, *Baker* helps us understand how international human rights law has a special interpretive force within Canada's legal order.[109]

Following *Baker*, Parliament amended Canada's immigration laws to expressly require officials to take into account the best interests of children directly affected by their decisions, consistent with Canada's obligations under the CRC.[110] It also enacted s 3(3)(f) of the IRPA, which provides that the Act "is to be construed and applied in a manner that . . . complies with international human rights instruments to which Canada is a signatory." Interpreting s 3(3)(f) for the first time, Evans JA, writing for the Federal Court of Appeal in *De Guzman v Canada (Minister of Citizenship and Immigration)*, drew upon the "expanding role that the common law has given to international law in the interpretation of domestic law," which he characterized as "one of the signal legal developments of the last 15 years."[111] Accordingly, the salience of this decision is not limited to the interpretation of Canada's immigration laws:

Paragraph 3(3)(f) should be interpreted in light of the modern developments in the courts' use of international human rights law as interpretative aids. Thus, *like other statutes*, the IRPA must be interpreted and applied in a manner that complies with "international human rights instruments to which Canada is signatory" that are binding because they do not require ratification or because Canada has signed and ratified them. . . . Thus, a legally binding international human rights instrument to which Canada is signatory is determinative of how the IRPA must be interpreted and applied, in the absence of a contrary legislative intention.[112]

Indeed, after describing the principles governing the common law presumption of conformity with international law, the Supreme Court of Canada stated that s 3(3)(f) "make[s] Parliament's presumed intent to conform to Canada's international obligations explicit."[113] Significantly, Evans J held that by interpreting s 3(3)(f) as merely requiring the court to consider relevant international human rights instruments as context when interpreting ambiguous provisions of the IRPA, the motions judge had adopted an overly limited view of the recent developments in the common law regarding the interpretive use of international human rights law.[114] In his view, s 3(3)(f) attached more than mere ambiguity-resolving, contextual significance to international human rights instruments to which Canada is signatory:

If only available to resolve an ambiguity in the IRPA, an international human rights instrument might not be able to be used to expose a latent ambiguity in a statute (see *National Corn Growers*), or to bring specificity to a vague statutory provision: for the distinction between

---

109 Craig Scott, "Canada's International Human Rights Obligations and Disadvantaged Members of Society: Finally into the Spotlight?" (1999) 10 Const Forum Const 97 at 100, 101. See also "Principle of Legality," *supra* note 70 at 33.

110 IRPA, ss 28(2)(c), 60, 67(1)(c), 68(1), 69(2).

111 *De Guzman v Canada (Minister of Citizenship and Immigration)*, 2005 FCA 436 at para 62 [*De Guzman*], leave to appeal refused, [2006] SCCA No 70.

112 *Ibid* (FCA) at para 87 (italics added, underlining in the original).

113 *B010, supra* note 77 at para 49.

114 *Ibid* at para 61.

ambiguous and vague, see Randal N Graham, *Statutory Interpretation: Theory and Practice* (Toronto: Emond Montgomery, 2001), Chapter 4.[115]

The Federal Court of Appeal noted that s 3(3)(f) applied to a broad range of international instruments, including non-binding instruments and instruments that were not signed by Canada or even in existence when the IRPA was enacted.[116] It acknowledged the concerns expressed by the dissenting judges in *Baker* about giving domestic effect to international norms recognized by the federal executive without Parliamentary approval, and recognized the value of their point in respect of the use of non-binding instruments as persuasive and contextual factors in statutory interpretation. In its view, however, these concerns were attenuated by the fact that, in the case of s 3(3)(f), Parliament had approved such a role for non-binding international instruments.[117] Significantly, the court's reservations focused on the role of non-binding instruments rather than on that of binding international obligations, governed by the common law presumption of conformity.

De Guzman is significant not only for its thorough exposition of the common law presumption of conformity and for reading it into s 3(3)(f); it illustrates how recourse to the presumption can shape the boundaries of broad statutory discretion, including the governor in council's power to promulgate regulations. De Guzman, a citizen of the Philippines who had successfully applied for permanent residence, established herself in Canada, became a citizen, and applied to sponsor the admission of her two sons as members of the family class. Her application was denied because she had failed to disclose that she had dependent sons

---

115 *Ibid* at para 82. According to Graham, an ambiguous provision supports two or more specific meanings that cannot be resolved by context whereas a vague provision uses open-textured language of a breadth that supports a continuum of meanings: Randal N Graham, *Statutory Interpretation: Theory and Practice* (Toronto: Emond Montgomery, 2001) at 120-26. But see *Gitxaala Nation, supra* note 9, where the Federal Court of Appeal, in the context of an application by Amnesty International to intervene on an application for judicial review of a decision by the National Energy Board to approve a pipeline, described how international law could enter a court's assessment of the reasonableness or correctness of an administrative decision. Stratas J stated, at paras 15 and 17, that "international law can enter the analysis where the meaning of the legislative provision is unclear" and that the presumption of conformity was "seldom applied because most legislative provisions do not suffer from ambiguity." He also stated, at para 17, that the Supreme Court had resorted to international law in *Baker* because it "considered the statutory words 'humanitarian and compassionate' to be ambiguous and so it used international law to resolve the ambiguity." With respect, while the court recognized the "open-textured" nature of the language that defined the boundaries of the immigration officer's discretion, it did not characterize it as "ambiguous." Rather, it interpreted these words using a contextual approach, with international norms in the CRC making up an important part of the interpretive context. In the words of Evans JA in *De Guzman*, international law was appropriately used to bring specificity to a vague statutory provision. To the extent that *Gitxaala Nation* and decisions following it (see *Prophet River First Nation v Canada (Attorney General)*, 2016 FCA 120) condition courts' reference to international law on a prior finding of statutory ambiguity, they are inconsistent with *De Guzman* and with the Supreme Court's approach to the presumption of conformity: see *B010, supra* note 77 at para 49: the principles governing the interpretive presumption "direct us to relevant international instruments at the context stage of statutory interpretation." See e.g. *Najafi v Canada (Public Safety and Emergency Preparedness)*, 2014 FCA 262 at para 61, where the Federal Court of Appeal stated that "relevant international law, like other relevant elements of the legal context, should ideally be taken into account before concluding whether or not a text is clear or ambiguous."

116 *De Guzman* (FCA), *supra* note 11 at para 86.

117 *Ibid* at para 89.

to Canadian immigration officials when she had applied for permanent residence. Under s 117(9)(d) of the *Immigration and Refugee Protection Regulations*,[118] her sons could not be considered members of the family class because at the time of her application for permanent residence, they were "non-accompanying family members" who, due to her misrepresentation, had not been examined by immigration officials. De Guzman argued, *inter alia*, that s 117(9), promulgated by the governor in council under a regulation-making power framed in broad, discretionary language,[119] was inconsistent with the CRC and ICCPR, which protected the best interests of children and the right of families to live together. The court applied the statutory presumption of conformity to the IRPA provisions defining the governor in council's regulation-making power. Where a regulation, considered in the context of the entire legislative scheme, rendered the IRPA non-compliant with Canada's international law obligations,

> the Court must determine whether, properly construed, the relevant enabling section of the IRPA authorizes the Governor in Council to enact a regulation which renders the IRPA non-compliant with a binding international human rights instrument to which Canada is signatory. In view of paragraph 3(3)(f), only a clear legislative intention to the contrary will warrant a conclusion that the regulation-making power could lawfully be exercised in this manner.[120]

Though the court determined that s 117(9)(d) of the IRP Regulations did not conflict with the ICCPR or CRC, making an examination of these enabling sections unnecessary, *De Guzman* illustrates the potential reach of international law in the substantive review of exercises of discretion. Broad, discretionary regulation-making powers are to be interpreted in conformity with Canada's international obligations; absent clear legislative intent to the contrary, they should be read as authorizing only the promulgation of regulations that comply with these obligations. Regulations that render a statutory scheme non-compliant with Canada's international obligations would be *ultra vires*.

Canadian courts have clarified what it means for the IRPA to be interpreted and applied in a manner that complies with Canada's binding international obligations. It does not require a decision-maker to cite specific international instruments in a decision,[121] so long as the analysis of the underlying international norms is "cogent, considered and thoughtful."[122] Moreover, an assessment of whether the interpretation or application of a specific statutory

---

118   SOR/2002-227 [IRP Regulations].

119   IRPA, ss 5(1), 12(1), 14(2).

120   *De Guzman* (FCA), *supra* note 111 at para 92.

121   *Thiara v Canada (Citizenship and Immigration)*, 2007 FC 387, upheld on appeal, 2008 FCA 151 [*Thiara*]. The discretionary decision of an immigration officer to deny a non-citizen's application, on humanitarian and compassionate grounds, to remain in Canada so that she could raise her Canadian-born daughters free from the poverty, poor educational opportunities, and other problems faced by young girls in her home country was not unreasonable solely because she had not cited the CRC, UDHR, and other specific international instruments in her decision. The applicant had argued that forcing her to return to India would be inconsistent with the UDHR guarantee of parental choice in children's education (art 26) and the CEAFDAW obligation on states parties to eliminate discrimination against women in education (art 10), and would also violate the ICESCR and CRC, which required states parties to support family unity and parents' child-rearing responsibilities (ICESCR, art 10; CRC, art 18).

122   *Thaira* (FC), *supra* note 121 at para 41. The officer's analysis of the best interests of the children was "cogent, considered and thoughtful, signifying that she was sensitive to the issues raised" in these international instruments. See also *Okoloubu v Canada (Minister of Citizenship and Immigration)*, 2008 FCA 326, [2009] 3 FCR 294 at para 60.

provision violates Canada's international legal obligations has to "be made on the basis of the statute as a whole."[123] For example, the fact that a decision-maker was not authorized by a specific provision of the IRPA to consider the best interests of children was cured by the existence of subsequent statutory opportunities to do so.[124] Finally, where several international instruments are relevant to determining the purpose of a statutory provision, an interpretation "which harmonizes obligations in the international instruments to which Canada is a party in a way that avoids conflict and gives expression to each of the various commitments" should be favoured.[125]

The interpretive presumption that legislation conform with Canada's international obligations has been invoked in statutory contexts other than immigration law, including the right to services in Canada's official languages, commercial arbitration, and criminal law.[126] The social and economic rights set out in international conventions ratified by Canada, which are largely concerned with individuals' entitlement to public goods and services provided or regulated by the modern state, could have a significant impact on administrative decision-making.[127] Under the ICESCR, individuals are entitled to "the enjoyment of the highest attainable standard of physical and mental health," and states parties must create conditions to "assure to all medical service and medical attention in the event of sickness."[128]

---

123   *Idahosa v Canada (Minister of Public Safety and Emergency Preparedness)*, 2008 FCA 418 at para 54 [*Idahosa*].

124   *Ibid*. While s 50 of the IRPA, which stays a removal order "if a decision that was made in a judicial proceeding . . . would be directly contravened by the enforcement of a removal order," did not, interpreted contextually, enable non-citizens to defer their removal by obtaining custody orders for their children when there was no genuine dispute about custody, this did not mean that the IRPA, as a whole, failed to comply with the provisions of the UDHR, ICCPR, and CRC that protect the best interests of children and the parent–child relationship. The IRPA provided opportunities for the consideration of the best interests of the children subject to deportation such as humanitarian and compassionate applications and pre-removal risk assessments.

125   *R v Appulonappa*, 2015 SCC 59, [2015] 3 SCR 754 at para 45. Looking to both the 1951 Convention and the *Protocol against the Smuggling of Migrants by Land, Sea and Air, supplementing the United Nations Convention against Transnational Organized Crime*, 2241 UNTS 480, the Supreme Court determined that s 117 of the IRPA, which prohibited persons from aiding the coming into Canada of one or more undocumented persons, sought to permit a robust fight against people smuggling in the context of organized crime, not to criminalize conduct amounting solely to humanitarian, mutual, or family aid.

126   See *Thibodeau, supra* note 76 at para 113 where the presumption was invoked to support an interpretation of the *Official Languages Act* that constrained a broad remedial power by excluding damages awards in the context of international air travel in conformity with the *Convention for the Unification of Certain Rules for International Carriage by Air*. See also *GreCon Dimter Inc v JR Normand Inc*, 2005 SCC 46, [2005] 2 SCR 401 at paras 39 et seq where the presumption was invoked to confirm the primacy of an article of Quebec's *Civil Code* relating to the jurisdiction of a Quebec authority over a commercial dispute over another provision of that Code based on the *Convention on the Reception and Enforcement of Foreign Arbitral Awards*, 330 UNTS 3. Finally, see *Canadian Foundation, supra* note 76 at para 31 et seq., where the Supreme Court relied on the CRC and ICCPR to restrictively interpret a provision of Canada's *Criminal Code*, RSC 1985, c C-64, s 265 excluding from criminal sanction for assault "reasonable" physical correction of children by parents and teachers.

127   My consideration of provisions of the ICCPR and ICESCR at this point in this section to illustrate the potential influence of international human rights norms on substantive review does not indicate that I consider these treaties to be unimplemented in Canadian law. Indeed, strong arguments can be made that many of Canada's obligations under these instruments were implemented, notably through enactment of the Charter: see Section IV.B, below.

128   ICESCR, art 12.

The Committee on Economic, Social and Cultural Rights has noted that health facilities, goods, and services must be affordable for all, and that all are entitled to equal and timely access to appropriate treatment for prevalent diseases, illnesses, injuries, and disabilities, including the provision of essential drugs.[129] There is a strong presumption that retrogressive measures in relation to the right to health are not permissible, and that the state party has the burden of proving that such measures "have been introduced after the most careful consideration of all alternatives and that they are duly justified by reference to the totality of the rights provided for in the Covenant in the context of the full use of the State party's maximum available resources."[130] The committee also defines as a core obligation of states parties to "provide essential drugs as from time to time defined under the WHO Action Programme on Essential Drugs."[131] ICESCR norms, as developed by the committee in its general comment, could be argued to be relevant considerations for the exercise of provincial officials' discretion to list or delist, in the public interest, specific drugs from provincial drug formularies or treatments from provincial Medicare schedules of benefits.[132] The ICESCR's "right to health" arguably resonates with Canadian legal values, and although the Supreme Court of Canada has not recognized a free-standing constitutional right to health care,[133] it has determined that state interference with Canadians' ability to access vital health care engages constitutionally protected life and security of the person interests.[134]

Another area of administrative decision-making that could be influenced by international norms is the state regulation of residential tenancies. Article 11(1) of the ICESCR guarantees to all the right to adequate housing, which is interpreted by the committee as including a right to security of tenure that guarantees legal protection against forced eviction: "Evictions should not result in rendering individuals homeless or vulnerable to the violation of other human rights."[135] Before it was repealed and replaced by the Ontario legislature in 2006, the Ontario *Tenant Protection Act* allowed for expedited evictions without a hearing and did not require adjudicators with the Ontario Rental Housing Tribunal to consider the risk that evicted households could become homeless. In its review of Canada's fifth periodic report, the committee noted that "many evictions occurred on account of minimal arrears of rent

---

129 Committee on Economic, Social and Cultural Rights, *General Comment 14—The Right to the Highest Attainable Standard of Health (Art 12)*, UN Doc E/C.12/2000/4 at paras 12(b)(iii), 17.

130 *Ibid* at para 32.

131 *Ibid* at para 43(d).

132 See e.g. *Ontario Drug Benefit Act*, RSO 1990, c O.10, ss 16-20; *Ontario Drug Benefit Regulations*, O Reg 201/96, s 11 et seq. The Ontario Drug Benefit Program covers most of the cost of prescription drug products listed on the Ontario Drug Benefit Formulary for over 2 million Ontarians who are seniors or who receive social assistance or provincial disability support.

133 *Chaoulli v Quebec (Attorney General)*, 2005 SCC 35, [2005] 1 SCR 791 at para 104.

134 *Ibid* at para 124. International norms could be relevant factors in assessing the reasonableness of the decisions of provincial authorities to refuse to reimburse patients for out-of-province care that is not available to them in a timely manner in their home province. These reimbursement schemes were described by the dissenting judges, at para 264, as an important "safety valve," the administration of which could be supervised under s 7 of the Charter. See e.g. *Flora v Ontario (Health Insurance Plan, General Manager)*, 2008 ONCA 538.

135 Committee on Economic, Social and Cultural Rights, *General Comment 7—The Right to Adequate Housing (Art 11(1) of the Covenant): Forced Evictions*, UN Doc E/1998/22, annex IV at para 17.

without due consideration of [Canada's] obligations under the Covenant."[136] Based on the committee's interpretation of article 11 of the ICESCR, it can be argued that any decision by the Landlord and Tenant Board to grant an application for eviction that failed to consider the risk of homelessness would be unreasonable.[137] These and other sources of international norms were considered in the successful challenge of the constitutionality of a municipal by-law's prohibition against erecting temporary shelter on public property, which had been used to evict homeless persons from a public park.[138]

As described in the following section, the duty to interpret statutes and regulations in conformity with Canada's international obligations extends beyond obligations defined in international conventions to customary norms of international law.

2. Norms of Customary International Law and Substantive Review

Norms of customary international law, particularly in the area of environmental protection, have also influenced the substantive review of the decisions of public bodies, including municipal councils. In *114957 Canada Ltée (Spraytech, Société d'arrosage) v Hudson (Town)*,[139] the Supreme Court of Canada sought to determine whether a by-law enacted by the town of Hudson restricting the use of pesticides was authorized by municipalities' general power under the Quebec *Cities and Towns Act*[140] to enact by-laws to "secure peace, order, good government, health and general welfare" in the municipality. Applying the purposive approach to statutory interpretation, a majority of the court found that the purpose of the town's by-law fell squarely within its power under the CTA to secure citizens' health. In support of this interpretation of the CTA and of the by-law, L'Heureux-Dubé J, writing for the majority, turned to principles of international law and the presumption of conformity. Relying on *Baker*, she noted that the majority's expansive interpretation of the scope of municipal powers under the CTA respected international law's "precautionary principle,"[141] a principle codified in several Canadian federal and provincial statutes, included in conventional international law, and, in the majority's estimation, likely a principle of customary international law.[142] Concurring in the result, LeBel J held that "references to international sources had little relevance" to the "principles governing the interpretation and application of the laws governing cities and towns ... in the Province of Québec."[143] This concurring opinion does not appropriately acknowledge the role of international law. If the precautionary principle is indeed a principle of customary international law, it is binding on Canada at

---

136 Concluding Observations on Canada's 4th and 5th Periodic Reports, E/C.12/CAN/CO/5, 22 May 2006, 36th Sess.

137 *Residential Tenancies Act, 2006*, SO 2006, c 17, s 83.

138 *Victoria (City) v Adams*, 2008 BCSC 1363, aff'd 2009 BCCA 563 [*Adams*]. But see *Abbotsford (City) v Shantz*, 2015 BCSC 1909 at para 173.

139 2001 SCC 40, [2001] 2 SCR 241 [*Spraytech*].

140 RSQ, c C-19 [CTA].

141 The principle holds that "[w]here there are threats of serious or irreversible damage, lack of full scientific certainty should not be used as a reason for postponing measures to prevent environmental degradation": *Spraytech, supra* note 139 at para 31.

142 *Ibid* at para 32.

143 *Ibid* at para 48.

international law and, absent express language or other indications of contrary legislative intent, the CTA should be construed in a manner that reflects the precautionary principle.[144] Even if the precautionary principle has not yet crystallized into a principle of customary international law and remains a non-binding international norm, it is not "irrelevant" but can still inform the court's interpretive effort.[145] *Spraytech* clearly stands for the proposition that courts will interpret the scope of delegated authority consistently with norms of customary international law. Like norms of conventional international law, customary international law can constrain the discretionary powers of municipalities, government officials, and administrative decision-makers.[146]

In summary, conventional and customary international human rights norms may play a significant role in the substantive review of decisions involving government officials and tribunals interpreting and applying their statutory powers, including their regulation-making powers. Under a reasonableness review, courts will examine whether a decision-maker's interpretation of its enabling statute or statutes closely connected to its function falls within a range of acceptable and rational solutions derived from the application of the modern approach to statutory interpretation.[147] This approach involves reading the words of the provision in their entire context and according to their grammatical and ordinary sense, harmoniously with the scheme and object of the Act and the intention of the legislature.[148] As demonstrated by the emerging general duty to interpret legislation, including statutes conferring discretionary powers, in conformity with Canada's international law obligations— customary and conventional—these obligations are undoubtedly an important aspect of the "context in which statutes are enacted." An interpretation of a statutory provision that is inconsistent with applicable and relevant international norms absent express language or clear legislative intent supporting such an interpretation arguably falls outside of the range

---

144   Van Ert, *supra* note 78 at 153; Brunnée & Toope, Embrace, *supra* note 68 at 378-79.

145   Brunnée & Toope, "Embrace," *supra* note 68 at 379. There is some disagreement about whether the majority was applying the presumption of conformity in *Spraytech*. Van Ert observes that L'Heureux-Dubé J's invocation, in the same breath, of *Baker* and the presumption of conformity indicates that the court's use of international law in *Baker* amounted to an application of the presumption: van Ert, *supra* note 78 at 151. Viewing *Baker* as setting out a permissive rule *allowing* courts to take into account the values underlying international law to inform their interpretive effort, Toope and Brunnée were critical of its application to a purported customary norm of international law, which as a binding international norm directly applicable in Canadian law was more than "potentially relevant" to statutory interpretation. For further discussion of the precautionary principle at international law and its relevance to the exercise of discretionary power by administrative decision-makers, see Chris Tollefson & Jamie Thornback, "Litigating the Precautionary Principle in Domestic Courts" (2008) 19 J Envtl L & Prac 33.

146   For example, Neil Craik argues that the federal government's statutory discretion to initiate an environmental assessment must be exercised consistently with an emergent international customary obligation to undertake such an assessment where proposed industrial activity may have a significant adverse impact in a transboundary (international) context, in particular, on a shared resource: Neil Craik, "Transboundary Environmental Assessment in Canada: International and Constitutional Dimensions" (2010) 21 J Envtl L & Prac 107 at 134.

147   The application of the reasonableness standard of review is discussed by Sheila Wildeman in Chapter 12, Making Sense of Reasonableness.

148   *Canada (Canadian Human Rights Commission) v Canada (Attorney General)*, 2011 SCC 53, [2011] 3 SCR 471 at para 33; *Alberta (Information and Privacy Commissioner) v Alberta Teachers' Association*, 2011 SCC 61, [2011] 3 SCR 654 at para 85, Binnie J.

of possible, acceptable outcomes defensible in respect of the facts and the law and is therefore, unreasonable.[149] The Federal Court of Appeal has applied the presumption of conformity codified under the IRPA flexibly, upholding decisions as reasonable that are in substance consistent with applicable and binding international human rights norms and assessing compliance with such norms based on the statute as a whole.

In addition to respecting the boundaries imposed by relevant legislation, administrative decisions must also comply with Charter principles.[150] As described in the following section, the Supreme Court of Canada looks to international human rights law to interpret the Charter. By influencing the scope of Charter protections, international human rights norms inform courts' review of the lawfulness and reasonableness of administrative decisions.

B. International Human Rights Norms, Charter Interpretation, and Substantive Review

Administrative decisions that engage Charter protections may be set aside as unreasonable by reviewing courts if they do not give effect as fully as possible to the Charter protections at stake given the decision-maker's statutory mandate.[151] To the extent that they influence the scope and content of Charter protections, international human rights norms can impact the substantive review of administrative decisions. This section first describes Canadian courts' evolving approach to the use of international human rights norms in Charter interpretation. It then turns to how these norms might impact the substantive review of administrative decisions engaging the Charter.

1. International Human Rights Norms and Charter Interpretation

The Charter is an important locus of reception of international law norms in Canada's legal system. Fulfilling Canada's obligations under the UDHR and ICCPR was a major impetus to drafting and adopting the Charter: the language of the general limitation clause in s 1, the legal rights in ss 7-14, and the right to equality in s 15 were derived from analogous provisions in the ICCPR.[152] Moreover, Canada represents to domestic audiences and international

---

149 See *Najafi, supra* note 115 at paras 79, 90-91, where the Federal Court of Appeal upheld as reasonable a decision of the Immigration Division of the IRB broadly interpreting a provision designating as inadmissible to Canada a foreign national who "engaged in the subversion by force of any government" because, although such an interpretation may be inconsistent with the *Protocol Additional to the Geneva Conventions of 12 August, 1949, and relating to the Protection of Victims of International Armed Conflicts* (Protocol I), 8 June 1977, other factors of the relevant context to the provision's interpretation (including its legislative history) supported the Immigration Division's decision.

150 The role of the Charter in administrative law is discussed by Evan Fox-Decent and Alexander Pless in Chapter 6, The Charter and Administrative Law Part I: Procedural Fairness, and Chapter 13, The Charter and Administrative Law Part II: Substantive Review.

151 *Loyola High School v Quebec (Attorney General)*, 2015 SCC 12, [2015] 1 SCR 613 at para 39 [*Loyola*].

152 Anne Bayefsky, *International Human Rights Law—Use in Canadian Charter of Rights and Freedoms Litigation* (Toronto: Butterworths, 1992) at 49. See also GV La Forest, "The Expanding Role of the Supreme Court of Canada in International Law Issues" (1996) 34 Can YB Int'l Law 89 at 97. The same can be said for Quebec's *Charter of human rights and freedoms*, CQLR c C-12: *Imperial Tobacco Canada Ltd v Quebec (Attorney General)*, 2015 QCCA 1554 at para 56.

treaty bodies that the Charter gives effect to provisions of these treaties.[153] Accordingly, it would be open to courts or administrative decision-makers to recognize the Charter as legislation intended to implement these and other important international human rights instruments. Some academics argue that the Supreme Court of Canada should treat binding international human rights norms, whether customary or conventional, as "presumptively protected" by the Charter, while non-binding international instruments, such as General Assembly declarations, and the views of UN treaty bodies should be treated as "relevant and persuasive sources for *Charter* interpretation."[154] Others object to applying the presumption of conformity to Charter interpretation because it would allow the federal executive to "unilaterally amend" Canada's Constitution.[155]

In *Reference Re Public Service Employee Relations Act (Alta)*, Dickson CJ recognized that, as a party to international human rights treaties with provisions similar or identical to those in the Charter, Canada had "obliged itself internationally to ensure within its borders the protection of certain fundamental rights and freedoms which are also contained in the *Charter*."[156] Consequently, "[t]he general principles of constitutional interpretation require that these international obligations be a relevant and persuasive factor in *Charter* interpretation":[157]

> The content of Canada's international human rights obligations is, in my view, an important indicia of the meaning of "the full benefit of the *Charter*'s protection." I believe that the *Charter* should generally be presumed to provide protection at least as great as that afforded by similar provisions in international human rights documents which Canada has ratified.
>
> In short, though I do not believe the judiciary is bound by the norms of international law in interpreting the *Charter*, these norms provide a relevant and persuasive source for interpretation of the provisions of the *Charter*, especially when they arise out of Canada's international obligations under human rights conventions.[158]

Freeman and van Ert claimed that this passage reveals two conflicting approaches to the use of international law in Charter interpretation.[159] The first paragraph speaks of a

---

153   Presenting Canada's fourth periodic report regarding the ICCPR's implementation to the UN Committee on Human Rights, Canada's representative stated that the Charter "was the primary mechanism" for implementing the ICCPR and that the Charter's provisions "were based on the Covenant": UN Human Rights Committee, Summary Record of the 1738th Meeting: Canada (17 March 1999), UN Doc CCPR/C/SR.1738. See also UN Human Rights Committee, *Consideration of Reports Submitted by States Parties Under Article 40 of the Covenant, Sixth Periodic Reports of States Parties due in October 2010: Canada* (9 April 2013), UN Doc CCPR/C/CAN/6 at para 8, online: <http://www.refworld.org/cgi-bin/texis/vtx/rwmain?docid=559e3ba24>, where Canada noted in its sixth periodic report to the Committee on Human Rights that "many of the rights contained in the Covenant are constitutionally protected by the [Charter]." Similarly, the Canadian government informed the Inter-American Commission on Human Rights that the Charter shared many of the ADHR's principles: IACHR Report, *supra* note 27 at para 36. Finally, as noted by Ross J in *Adams*, *supra* note 138 at para 98, Canada informed the Committee on Economic, Social and Cultural Rights that s 7 of the Charter must be interpreted consistently with Canada's obligations under the ICESCR not to deprive persons of the basic necessities of life: Summary Record of the 5th Meeting, ESC, 8th Sess, 5th Mtg, UN Doc E/C.12/1993/SR.5 (25 May 1993).

154   Freeman & van Ert, *supra* note 54 at 194-95.

155   Irit Weiser, "Undressing the Window: Treating International Human Rights Law Meaningfully in the Canadian Commonwealth System" (2004) 37 UBC L Rev 113 at 148. See also Benjamin Oliphant, "Interpreting the Charter with International Law: Pitfalls and Principles" (2014) 19 Appeal 105 at para 28. But see Toope & Brunnée, "Hesitant," *supra* note 67 at 45, n 140 and 49, n 200.

156   [1987] 1 SCR 313 at para 59 [*Alberta Reference*].

157   *Ibid.*

158   *Ibid* at paras 59-60, dissenting on another point.

159   Freeman & van Ert, *supra* note 54 at 193.

presumption that the Charter should be interpreted in conformity with Canada's international obligations. The second holds that international norms should be viewed by courts as relevant and persuasive, but not binding. In contrast, Currie argues that these statements set out a single "hierarchical interpretive approach":

> [T]he minimum content prescription, applicable to international human rights treaties which Canada has ratified, is simply a particularization—rather than a contradiction—of the relevant and persuasive influence that all international human rights law (whether internationally binding on Canada or not) should have in Charter interpretation.[160]

In subsequent decisions,[161] the Supreme Court of Canada appeared to emphasize that international norms provide a broader context within which to determine the scope and content of Charter rights, a "weaker version" of the presumption of conformity that does not require the court to "strive for an interpretation that is consistent with international norms."[162]

In *Suresh*, the court extended this approach to norms of customary international law. The *Immigration Act* gave the minister of citizenship and immigration the discretion to decide that a refugee, on the ground of membership in a terrorist organization, was a danger to the security of Canada and could be removed to a country where his or her life or freedom would be threatened. The court held that its inquiry into whether Mr Suresh's deportation to a country where he faced a substantial risk of torture violated the principles of fundamental justice under s 7 would be "informed not only by Canadian experience and jurisprudence, but also by international law, including *jus cogens*":[163]

> [T]he principles of fundamental justice expressed in s. 7 . . . and the limits on rights that may be justified under s. 1 . . . cannot be considered in isolation from the international norms which they reflect. A complete understanding of the [*Immigration Act*] and the *Charter* requires consideration of the international perspective.[164]

However, international norms were not treated as binding or even determinative by the court. In "seeking the meaning of the Constitution," courts were not bound by international law but could be "informed" by it:

> Our concern is not with Canada's international obligations *qua* obligations; rather our concern is with the principles of fundamental justice. We look to international law as evidence of these principles and not as controlling in itself.[165]

---

160 John H Currie, "International Human Rights Law in the Supreme Court's Charter Jurisprudence: Commitment, Retrenchment and Retreat—In No Particular Order" (2010) 50 SCLR (2d) 423 at 429 [Currie, "Commitment"]. In *Slaight Communications Inc v Davidson*, [1989] 1 SCR 1038 at 1056-57 [*Slaight Communications*], speaking for a majority of the court, Dickson CJ reiterated the minimum content prescription and the principle that Canada's international human rights obligations (whether arising from custom or treaty) should "inform" not only the interpretation of Charter rights but what can constitute reasonable limits to these rights under s 1 of the Charter.

161 *Slaight Communications, supra* note 60. See also *Kindler v Canada (Minister of Justice)*, [1991] 2 SCR 779; and *United States v Burns*, 2001 SCC 7, [2001] 1 SCR 283 [*Burns*].

162 Toope & Brunnée, "Hesitant," *supra* note 67 at 33.

163 *Suresh, supra* note 7 at para 46.

164 *Ibid*, at para 59. To properly review the international perspective, courts should consider "the various sources of international human rights law—declarations, covenants, conventions, judicial and quasi-judicial decisions of international tribunals, [and] customary norms": *ibid* at para 46.

165 *Ibid* at para 60.

Despite international law's "virtually categoric" rejection of deportation to torture, the court concluded that under Canadian law, the minister retained an exceptional discretion to deport to torture after balancing the probability of prejudice to national security and the importance of the security interest at stake with the serious consequences of deportation to the deportee.[166] As long as the minister considered the correct factors in the balancing exercise, courts could not question the weight she accorded to them.[167]

Suresh sent a mixed message regarding the potential of international human rights norms to shape the interpretation of Charter rights.[168] The court did hold that decision-makers must consider the influence of international norms in determining the procedural and substantive content of fundamental justice under s 7, a more onerous duty than its direction in *Slaight Communications* that Canada's international human rights obligations "should" inform Charter interpretation.[169] On the other hand, its "international norms as evidence" approach to the role of international law in Charter interpretation allowed the court to sidestep the question of whether the prohibition on torture is a peremptory norm of customary international law. Peremptory norms of international customary law are more than "evidence" of fundamental justice; they are automatically incorporated and directly enforceable in Canadian law to the extent that they are not incompatible with a contrary statute or established principle of common law. Applying the presumption of conformity, the court could have read down the minister's statutory discretion in a manner consistent with the international customary prohibition on torture.[170] Alternatively, it could have decided that the prohibition on torture, incorporated into Canada's common law, was a fundamental tenet of Canada's legal system, and hence a substantive principle of fundamental justice under s 7 of the Charter. The prohibition on torture would have constitutional force; the *Immigration Act* would have been inoperative to the extent that it conflicted with the prohibition.[171] Instead, looking at international law merely as "evidence" of the content of fundamental justice, the court came to a conclusion that seems extraordinary: although "international law rejects deportation to torture even where national security interests are at stake,"[172] fundamental justice nevertheless permits the minister to exercise an extraordinary discretion to deport refugees to torture.

Twelve years after *Suresh*, in *Kazemi Estate*, the court altered its position on the role of peremptory norms in the task of establishing the existence of a principle of fundamental justice. The Kazemi Estate had challenged the statutory immunity from civil proceedings conferred on foreign states and government officials for acts of torture committed abroad, arguing that it was a principle of fundamental justice that Canada ensure a civil remedy for victims of torture committed in foreign countries. It relied chiefly on art 14 of the CAT, a treaty ratified by and binding on Canada at international law, which states that "each State Party shall ensure in its legal system that the victim of an act of torture obtains redress and has an enforceable right to fair and adequate compensation." Another basis for the

---

166 *Ibid* at paras 76-78.
167 *Ibid* at para 41.
168 For a full discussion, see Gerald Heckman, "International Human Rights Law Norms and Discretionary Powers: Recent Developments" (2003) 16 Can J Admin L & Prac 31 [Heckman, "Recent Developments"].
169 *Supra* note 126.
170 Evan Fox-Decent, "Suresh and Canada's Obligations Regarding Torture" (2001) 12 NCLJ 425 at 446.
171 Neither s 7 nor s 1 balancing was appropriate in *Suresh* because the *jus cogens* norm prohibiting torture "should have been directly controlling within Canadian law to preclude deportation": Toope & Brunnée, "Hesitant," *supra* note 67 at 49.
172 *Suresh, supra* note 7 at para 75.

proposed principle of fundamental justice was that the prohibition on torture, arguably a peremptory norm of international law, required a civil remedy for torture committed in a foreign state. The court held that while the prohibition of torture is "certainly a *jus cogens* norm from which Canada cannot derogate (and also is very likely a principle of fundamental justice),"[173] the peremptory norm prohibiting torture had not yet created an exception to state immunity from civil liability in cases of torture committed abroad.[174]

This greater openness to the role of peremptory norms in establishing principles of fundamental justice is consistent with the rules of reception of customary international law and for that reason preferable to the restrictive approach adopted in *Suresh*. It is a welcome development, even though the likely impact of peremptory norms on Charter interpretation is small, since few such norms have been recognized. The court was much more guarded in allowing treaty norms to shape the content of the principles of fundamental justice, setting out a two-part test:

> When a party points to a provision in an international treaty as evidence of a principle of fundamental justice, a court must determine (a) whether there is significant international consensus regarding the interpretation of the treaty, and (b) whether there is consensus that the particular interpretation is fundamental to the way in which the international legal system ought to fairly operate .... The absence of such consensus weighs against finding that the principle is fundamental to the operation of the legal system.[175]

Article 14 of the CAT failed this two-part test because there was a lack of consensus on its scope.[176] The court sounded a note of caution about reliance on treaty norms to establish principles of fundamental justice:

> [T]he existence of an article in a treaty ratified by Canada does not automatically transform that article into a principle of fundamental justice. Canada remains a dualist system in respect of treaty and conventional law .... This means that, unless a treaty provision expresses a rule of customary international law or a peremptory norm, that provision will only be binding in Canadian law if it is given effect through Canada's domestic law-making process .... The appellants have not argued, let alone established, that their interpretation of art. 14 reflects customary international law, or that it has been incorporated into Canadian law through legislation.
>
> It is true that the *Charter* will often be understood to provide protection at least as great as that afforded by similar provisions in international human rights documents to which Canada is a party .... In my view, however, this presumption operates principally as an interpretive tool in assisting the courts in delineating the breadth and scope of *Charter* rights .... International Conventions may also assist in establishing the elements of the *Malmo-Levine* test for recognition of new principles of fundamental justice .... But not all commitments in international agreements amount to principles of fundamental justice. Their nature is very diverse. International law is ever changing. The interaction between domestic and international law must be managed carefully in light of the principles governing what remains a dualist system of application of international law and a constitutional and parliamentary democracy. The mere existence of an international obligation is not sufficient to establish a principle of fundamental justice. Were we to equate all the protections or commitments in international human rights documents with principles of fundamental

---

173 *Kazemi Estate, supra* note 13 at para 152.
174 *Ibid* para 153.
175 *Ibid* at para 147.
176 Many states parties, including Canada, and international and domestic courts interpret art 14 as guaranteeing redress solely for acts of torture committed within the forum state's own territorial jurisdiction.

justice, we might in effect be destroying Canada's dualist system of reception of international law and casting aside the principles of parliamentary sovereignty and democracy.[177]

In contrast to its cautious stance with regard to the role of conventional international norms in defining principles of fundamental justice, the court has with increasing enthusiasm applied the presumption of conformity with international law to define the scope of Charter rights, such as freedom of association. Its decisions in *Hape* and *Health Services* marked the beginning of an approach to Charter interpretation more open to the influence of international norms. In *Hape*, a majority of the court held that s 8 of the Charter, which protects individuals from unreasonable search and seizure, could not be enforced in criminal investigations carried out in another state's territory unless that state consented to the Charter's application.[178] It found support for this narrow construction of the Charter's application in the jurisdictional principles of customary international law,[179] declaring that "[i]n interpreting the scope of application of the *Charter*, the courts should seek to ensure compliance with Canada's binding obligations under international law where the express words are capable of supporting such a construction."[180] *Hape* illustrates that the application of the presumption of conformity may sometimes support a less generous interpretation of Charter protection. In contrast, under the minimum content presumption, international norms, including international human rights norms of a relatively rudimentary or retrograde nature, establish a floor—not a ceiling—for the content of Charter protections.[181]

In *Health Services*,[182] released a day after *Hape*, the court found support for its conclusion that workers' access to collective bargaining was protected by the Charter's guarantee of freedom of association in Canadian labour history, Charter values, and international norms. Reiterating the traditionalist view that "the incorporation of international agreements into domestic law is properly the role of the federal Parliament or the provincial legislatures,"[183] it noted that "Canada's international obligations can assist courts charged with interpreting the *Charter*'s guarantees." The court's analysis gave prominence to the impact of *ratified* conventions and the international *obligations* they create:

> Canada's *adherence* to international documents recognizing a right to collective bargaining supports recognition of the right in s. 2(d) of the *Charter*. As Dickson C.J. observed in the *Alberta*

---

177   *Kazemi Estate, supra* note 13 at paras 149-50 (citations omitted). In *India v Badesha*, 2017 SCC 44 at para 38, the Supreme Court held that in extradition cases, s 7 of the Charter should be presumed to provide at least as great a level of protection as found in Canada's international commitments regarding non-*refoulement* to torture or other gross human rights violations. Since art 3(1) of the CAT prohibited the removal of a person to a state where there are substantial grounds for believing that he or she would be in danger of being subjected to torture, it followed that in the extradition context, "surrendering a person to face a substantial risk of torture or mistreatment in the requesting state" violated the principles of fundamental justice. The Supreme Court did not refer to its decision in *Kazemi Estate, ibid*, at para 149 where it held that "*unless a treaty provision expresses a rule of customary law or a peremptory norm*, that provision will only be binding in Canadian law if it is given effect through Canada's domestic law-making process" (emphasis added). As noted in *Kazemi Estate*, art 3(1) of the CAT expresses a peremptory norm.

178   *Hape, supra* note 40 at para 69.

179   *Ibid* at para 56.

180   *Ibid*.

181   For this reason, Currie prefers the minimum content presumption: Currie, "Commitment," *supra* note 160 at 441 and 459.

182   *Supra* note 2.

183   *Ibid* at para 69.

Reference, at p. 349, the *Charter* should be presumed to provide at least as great a level of protection as is found in the international human rights documents *that Canada has ratified.*

The sources most important to the understanding of s. 2(d) of the *Charter* are the . . . [ICESCR],
the . . . [ICCPR], and the (ILO's) Convention (No. 87) . . . *Canada has endorsed all three of these
documents, acceding to both the ICESCR and the ICCPR, and ratifying Convention No. 87 in 1972. This
means that these documents reflect not only international consensus, but also principles that
Canada has committed itself to uphold.*

The ICESCR, the ICCPR and Convention No. 87 extend protection to the functioning of trade
unions in a manner suggesting that a right to collective bargaining is part of freedom of association. The interpretation of these conventions, in Canada and internationally, not only supports
the proposition that there is a right to collective bargaining in international law, but also
suggests that such a right should be recognized in the Canadian context under s. 2(d).[184]

However, it also relied on treaty bodies' interpretations of these conventions,[185] on the
Declaration on Fundamental Principles and Rights at Work,[186] a soft law instrument, and on
non-authoritative summaries of applicable "principles of international law" to discern a
"global consensus" on the meaning of freedom of association. It explained its reliance on the
1998 Declaration in interpreting s 2(d) as follows:

For one thing, the Declaration was made on the basis of interpretations of international instruments, such as *Convention No. 87*, many of which were adopted by the ILO prior to the advent of
the *Charter* and were within the contemplation of the framers of the *Charter*. For another, the
Charter, as a living document, grows with society and speaks to the current situations and needs
of Canadians. Thus Canada's current international law commitments and the current state of
international thought on human rights provide a persuasive source for interpreting the scope of
the *Charter*.[187]

By concluding that both "international law commitments" and "the current state of international thought on human rights" provide "persuasive sources" for Charter interpretation,
the court appeared to suggest that international norms that are binding on Canada have the
same degree of influence on Charter interpretation as non-binding norms.

The court's use of international norms to support the constitutional protection of a right
to engage in collective bargaining and a concomitant duty on employers to bargain in good
faith was criticized by some academics[188] and by members of the court who had not participated in the *Health Services* decision. In *Fraser*,[189] Rothstein J (joined by Charron J) argued
that *Health Services* should be overturned in part because international law did not support

---

184 *Ibid* at paras 70-72 (emphasis added).
185 These included the UN Human Rights Committee, the ILO Committee of Experts on the Application of
Conventions and Recommendations, and the ILO Committee on Freedom of Association. Significantly,
the court did not engage with the reasoning underlying the treaty bodies' interpretations.
186 6 IHRR 285 (1999).
187 *Health Services, supra* note 2 at para 78. The court's preoccupation with whether specific international
norms were elaborated before or after the Charter's entrenchment sits uncomfortably with its description of the Charter as a living document whose meaning evolves with Canadian society: see Oliphant,
supra note 155 at para 35.
188 See, notably, Brian Langille and Benjamin Oliphant, "From the Frying Pan into the Fire: Fraser and the Shift
from International Law to 'International Thought' in Charter Cases" (2012) 16 CLELJ 181 at 208.
189 *Supra* note 2. *Fraser* involved a constitutional challenge to an Ontario law that granted farmworkers the
right to form and join an employees' association, participate in its activities, assemble, and make representations to their employers on their terms and conditions of employment. The associations argued,
inter alia, that the law did not sufficiently protect farmworkers' rights to organize and bargain collectively.

constitutionalizing bargaining rights. He noted that the majority had inappropriately inter-preted the scope of Canada's international obligations by relying on an academic summary of ILO principles, which was based mostly on a convention not ratified by Canada[190] and under which it had no obligations.[191] The majority replied that its interpretation of s 2(d) was con-sistent with conventions ratified by Canada and defended its reliance on the academic sum-mary of principles by claiming that it reflected the "current state of international thought on human rights" in the context of freedom of association and collective bargaining.[192] It did not elaborate on how "current international thought on human rights" was to be ascertained, and how its persuasive value measured up to that of binding international human rights norms. Significantly, the majority confirmed that "*Charter* rights must be interpreted in light of . . . Canada's international and human rights commitments"; an analysis of these commit-ments is therefore an obligatory—not optional—part of Charter interpretation. The majority buttressed its decision in *Health Services* by pointing to a finding by the ILO Committee on Freedom of Association (CFA), applying ILO Convention No 87, that the very legislation scrutin-ized in *Health Services* violated employees' right of freedom of association. However, it did not discuss the authoritativeness of the CFA's interpretations of ILO conventions within the ILO system or any of the reasoning leading to the CFA's conclusion.[193] Remarkably, in upholding the constitutionality of the impugned statute in *Fraser*, the majority failed to acknowledge that the CFA had found that this statute breached international principles.[194]

The debate on the role of international norms in Charter interpretation continued in *SFL v Saskatchewan*.[195] A majority of the court held that a statute authorizing the provincial government to declare that certain public sector union members provided essential services and to suspend their right to strike violated s 2(d) because the right to strike was a necessary component of the process through which workers could participate meaningfully in the pursuit of their collective workplace goals. Writing for the majority, Abella J established, through a historical account of the right to strike in Canadian labour relations[196] and a review of relevant Canadian jurisprudence and academic commentary, that the right to strike played a crucial role in a meaningful process of collective bargaining.[197] International norms also played a key role. Invoking the presumption that the Charter provided "at least as great a level of protection as is found in the international human rights documents that Canada has ratified,"[198] which she described as a "magnetic guide" for the court, Abella J found that Canada's international obligations clearly argued for the recognition of a right to strike within s 2(d).[199] In particular, art 8(1) of the ICESCR and art 45(c) of the Charter of the

---

190 ILO *Convention (No 98) Concerning the Application of the Principles of the Right to Organize and Bargain Collectively,* 96 UNTS 257.

191 *Fraser, supra* note 2 at para 248.   .

192 *Ibid* at paras 92-93.

193 *Ibid* at para 94.

194 Langille & Oliphant, *supra* note 188 at para 52; Case No 2704, Report No 358: complaint against the Government of Canada presented by the United Food and Commercial Workers' Union—Canada (UFCW Canada) (2010).

195 *Supra* note 2.

196 *Ibid* at paras 34-51.

197 *Ibid* at paras 52-61.

198 *Ibid* at para 64.

199 *Ibid* at para 65.

Organization of American States[200] explicitly protected the right to strike.[201] Abella J also looked beyond these "explicit commitments" to "other sources" that "tend to confirm" the protection of the right to strike at international law.[202] First, she relied on the recognition by the CFA and Committee of Experts of the right to strike as "an indissociable corollary" of the right of trade union association protected in ILO Convention No 87, a convention ratified by Canada and whose obligations are incorporated into the ICCPR.[203] Though CFA decisions were not strictly binding, they had

> considerable persuasive weight and have been favourably cited and widely adopted by courts, tribunals and other adjudicative boards around the world, including our Court . . . . The relevant and persuasive nature of the Committee on Freedom of Association jurisprudence has developed over time through custom and practice and, within the ILO, it has been the leading interpreter of the contours of the right to strike.[204]

Second, she invoked an "emerging international consensus that, if it is to be meaningful, collective bargaining requires a right to strike."[205] For evidence of this consensus, she looked to the European Court of Human Rights' interpretation of the right to freedom of association under art 11 of the ECHR,[206] the decisions of German and Israeli courts, the express protection of the right to strike in the constitutions of several European states, and recognition in the European Social Charter of the importance of the freedom to strike for meaningful collective bargaining.[207]

Rothstein and Wagner JJ penned a vigourous dissent, arguing that "the current state of international law on the right to strike [was] unclear" and could provide no guidance on the question of whether the right to strike was protected by s 2(d) of the Charter:[208]

> Caution must be exercised where the current state of international law is subject to conflicting interpretations. As explained below, international bodies disagree as to whether the right to strike is protected under international labour and human rights instruments. Where this Court opts to rely on non-binding interpretations of international conventions, it should not cherry pick interpretations to support its conclusions.[209]

The dissenting judges reviewed, in turn, the ILO Convention No 87, the ICCPR, and the ICESCR. They noted that while the CFA and Committee of Experts were of the view that Convention No 87 protected a right to strike, these bodies "do not perform judicial functions and do not enforce obligations under ILO Conventions" and that a third ILO body, the Conference Committee on the Application of Standards, had not reached a consensus on whether freedom of association included the right to strike.[210] Second, they observed that a majority of the UN Human Rights Committee had determined, in *JB v Canada*,[211] that the

---

200 *Supra* note 24.
201 *SFL, supra* note 2 at paras 65-66.
202 *Ibid* at para 67.
203 ICCPR, art 22(3).
204 *SFL, supra* note 2 at para 69 (citations omitted).
205 *Ibid* at para 71.
206 *Supra* note 27.
207 *SFL, supra* note 2 at paras 71-79.
208 *Ibid* at para 150.
209 *Ibid* at para 151.
210 *Ibid* at para 153.
211 Communication No 118/1982 (1986) [*JB*].

guarantee of freedom of association in art 22 of the ICCPR did not protect the right to strike.[212] Finally, the dissenting judges pointed out that the right to strike expressly provided for by art 8(1)(d) of the ICESCR was qualified by art 8(2), which allowed for "lawful restrictions" on the exercise of the rights guaranteed by art 8(1), including the right to strike, by members of the Armed Forces, police, or administration of the state. This demonstrated that "the measures at issue are not precluded."[213] The dissenting judges concluded that there was "no clear consensus under international law that the right to strike is an essential element of freedom of association."[214] Turning their attention to the other sources of international law relied upon by the majority, the dissenting judges noted that while these could have some persuasive value in appropriate circumstances, they should be granted "much less weight than sources under which Canada is bound," which alone engaged the minimum content presumption.[215] In their view, the express inclusion of the right to strike in the domestic constitutions of other countries had "little relevance" to the interpretation of s 2(d) of the Charter and little weight should be accorded to international instruments, like the ECHR, to which Canada was not a party.[216] In sum, international law was "of no help" in determining whether freedom of association in s 2(d) of the Charter included a right to strike.[217]

In the wake of the Supreme Court of Canada's freedom of association jurisprudence, what is the role of international human rights norms in Charter interpretation? The court has held that "the *Charter* should be presumed to provide at least as great a level of protection as is found in the international rights documents that Canada has ratified."[218] In applying this presumption, the court has identified relevant international human rights instruments ratified by Canada that create binding legal obligations.[219] It has looked to treaty bodies' interpretation of these instruments that, while not strictly binding, it has accepted as relevant and

---

212 Dissenting, Rosalyn Higgins and four other Committee members would have interpreted art 22 as protecting the right to strike—an interpretation that several commentators have agreed "corresponds more to the wording, object, purpose and historical background of the provision": Ben Saul, David Kinley & Jacqueline Moubray, *The International Covenant on Economic, Social and Cultural Rights: Commentary, Cases, and Materials* (Oxford University Press: Oxford, 2014) at 593. By failing to directly address the dissent's objection and engage with the reasoning of the UN Committee, if only to agree with the dissenting Committee members' views because these were more persuasive, the majority in *SFL* invited the dissenting judges' accusation of "cherry-picking" of interpretations to support its conclusions. Ironically, this charge could also be levelled at the dissent, which curiously omitted to mention that the UN Human Rights Committee had reversed its position on art 22 after *JB* and now accepts that art 22 protects workers' right to strike: Patrick Macklem, "The Right to Bargain Collectively in International Law: Workers' Right, Human Right, International Right?" in Philip Alston, ed, *Labour Rights as Human Rights* (Oxford: Oxford University Press, 2005) 61 at 72-73. See also KD Ewing, "The Lady Doth Protest Too Much, Methinks—The Right to Strike, International Standards and the Supreme Court of Canada" (2015) 18 CLELJ 517 at para 31. Concluding observations on Estonia, UN Doc CCPR/C/EST/CO/3 at para 15.
213 *SFL, supra* note 2 at para 155.
214 *Ibid* at para 156.
215 *Ibid* at para 157.
216 *Ibid* at para 159.
217 *Ibid* at para 160.
218 *Health Services, supra* note 2 at para 70. See also *Divito v Canada (Public Safety and Emergency Preparedness)*, 2013 SCC 47, [2013] 3 SCR 157.
219 Some argue that the court omitted relevant obligations, including those assumed by Canada by virtue of its membership in the ILO: KD Ewing & John Hendy, "Giving Life to the ILO—Two Cheers for the SCC" in Faraday, Fudge & Tucker, *supra* note 41, 286 at 303-4. For an exhaustive review of international norms pertaining to freedom of association in the context of back to work legislation in Canada, see Renée-Claude Drouin & Gilles Trudeau, "Les lois spéciales de retour au travail: enjeux institutionnels et constitutionnels" (2015) 61:2 McGill LJ 387.

persuasive in its task of Charter interpretation. However, beyond adverting to the fact that treaty bodies' interpretations have, over time, commanded the respect of other courts and tribunals, the court has not generally explained why they should be persuasive in interpreting the Charter. It did not directly respond to the arguments of dissenting judges and academics[220] questioning the legitimacy of taking into account treaty body interpretations given these bodies' representative or "non-judicial" nature and the fact that they do not have the power to issue final or authoritative interpretations of treaty provisions. It has not examined the reasons offered by treaty bodies in defence of their interpretive role, including the legitimacy derived from, amongst other factors, their independence, experience, and expertise. It has typically not examined in any detail the reasons offered by the treaty bodies for their interpretations and applications of specific provisions. It has sometimes even failed to examine the views of treaty bodies that interpret and apply international provisions similar to the Charter right at issue in a manner that could be read as contradicting its own conclusions.[221] In the face of charges of cherry-picking and of calls for the court to explain "exactly when and why international law matters to constitutional interpretation,"[222] the court would do well to engage with international human rights norms and their interpretation by treaty bodies more deeply and more consistently. As a participant in a dialogue on the scope and meaning of human rights norms,[223] it must strive to provide a principled account of whether a particular interlocutor's views matter to the task of Charter interpretation, to what extent, and why. Clear governing principles would likely encourage litigants and their counsel to appeal to international human rights norms and trial courts to rely on them.[224]

In addition to considering international human rights documents ratified by Canada that, under the minimum content presumption, are relevant and persuasive factors in Charter interpretation, the court has consistently considered "non-binding" international instruments, including declarations and unratified conventions, non-authoritative academic summaries of applicable principles of international law, the decisions of international courts interpreting treaties to which Canada is not a party, the decisions of national courts interpreting the same or similar norms, and the terms of national constitutions. Although it has

---

220 Langille and Oliphant, *supra* note 187 at 205.

221 The majority in *Fraser, supra* note 2 did not address the CFA's decision finding that Ontario's *Agricultural Employees Protection Act* violated principles of freedom of association. The majority in *SFL, supra* note 2 did not comment on the UN Human Rights Committee's interpretation of the guarantee of "freedom of association" in art 22 of the ICCPR in *JB, supra* note 211. In assessing the constitutionality of the security certificate provisions under Canada's IRPA, the Court in *Charkaoui v Canada (Citizenship and Immigration)*, 2007 SCC 9, [2007] 1 SCR 350 did not comment on the UN Human Rights Committee's review of this process in *Ahani v Canada*, Communication No 1051/2002, UN Doc CCPR/C/80/D/1051/2002 (2004). But see *Kazemi Estate, supra* note 13, where the court discussed an interpretation of art 14 of the CAT by the Committee Against Torture that was contrary to its own.

222 Macklem, "The International Constitution" at 285; see also Oliphant, *supra* note 155 at para 37.

223 *Kazemi Estate, supra* note 13 at para 148.

224 Currie, "Commitment" at 457. In some cases, courts describe relevant international norms but do not incorporate them into the Charter analysis: *Adams, supra* note 138; *Inglis v British Columbia (Minister of Public Safety)*, 2013 BCSC 2309, [2013] BCJ No 2708 (QL) at para 364. In others, international norms play a confirmatory role by reinforcing a conclusion already arrived at based on the application of Canadian law: see e.g. *Canadian Doctors for Refugee Care v Canada (Attorney General)*, 2014 FC 651 at paras 590-92 (ECHR, article 3 case law supporting the conclusion that the denial of refugee claimants' access to health care is "treatment" under s 12 of the Charter), paras 659-60 (CRC, art 6(2) supporting the conclusion that this denial is cruel and unusual), and para 768 (1951 Convention, art 3 supporting the conclusion that discrimination against refugees based on national origin is prohibited under s 15 of the Charter).

stated that "the fundamental question" remains whether "Canada's international obligations" support a particular interpretation of a Charter right or freedom, the court has not determined the degree to which such sources of international human rights law are persuasive compared to international human rights instruments ratified by Canada. It has marshalled these other sources of human rights law—international and foreign (comparative)—to discern "the current state of international thought on human rights" or evidence of an "emerging international consensus" on the meaning and scope of a particular human rights norm without carefully explaining its methodology for selecting and weighting (in terms of persuasiveness) the sources that should be considered to ascertain international "thought" or "consensus." Are binding international obligations more persuasive or deserving of greater weight (by virtue of their bindingness) than other normative sources in the interpretation of Charter rights and freedoms? Alternatively, are all international and "foreign" or comparative law norms potentially relevant and persuasive, with an influence on Charter interpretation that depends only on their pertinence to the Charter right in question and the quality of the reasons underlying the norm?

The court's enthusiastic reliance on Canada's international human rights obligations in defining the scope of freedom of association under the Charter led one observer to posit that it had adopted a post-dualist conception of Canada's constitutional relationship with international law where "the current state of international thought on human rights"— whether expressed in hard or soft legal norms—is relevant to determining the contours of Canada's constitutional order.[225] Though supported by the *SFL* decision, the force of this prediction must be tempered in light of the court's cautious approach to the role of conventional international norms in defining principles of fundamental justice under s 7 of the Charter. In *Kazemi Estate*, the court expressed concern that equating all of Canada's commitments in international human rights documents with principles of fundamental justice would destroy Canada's dualist system of reception of international law and cast aside the principles of parliamentary sovereignty and democracy.[226] It should be recalled that the application of the *Alberta Reference* presumption is premised on the existence of provisions in international human rights documents ratified by Canada that are *similar* to the relevant Charter provision. In *Health Services* and *SFL*, the court used the presumption as an interpretive tool to assist it in delineating the scope of "freedom of association," a freedom protected in similar provisions in the ICCPR, ICESCR, and ILO Convention No 87, which also guarantee "freedom of association" but with a greater degree of particularity and in the specific con-

---

225   Patrick Macklem, "The International Constitution" in Faraday, Fudge & Tucker, *supra* note 41 at 279.

226   *Kazemi Estate*, *supra* note 13 at para 150. But see *India v Badesha*, 2017 SCC 44 at para 38, where the Supreme Court held that in extradition cases, s 7 of the Charter should be presumed to provide at least as great a level of protection as found in Canada's international commitments regarding non-*refoulement* to torture or other gross human rights violations. Since art 3(1) of the CAT prohibited the removal of a person to a state where there are substantial grounds for believing that he or she would be in danger of being subjected to torture, "it follows that in the extradition context, surrendering a person to face a substantial risk of torture or mistreatment in the requesting state will violate the principles of fundamental justice." As the Court noted in *Kazemi Estate, supra* note 13 at para 149, "*unless a treaty provision expresses a rule of customary law or a peremptory norm*, that provision will only be binding in Canadian law if it is given effect through Canada's domestic law-making process" (emphasis added). Art 3(1) of the CAT certainly expresses a peremptory norm.

text of industrial relations. These decisions do not support the indiscriminate application of the minimum content presumption to elevate all manner of differently worded substantive human rights commitments in international instruments to the status of principles of fundamental justice under s 7 of the Charter.

International human rights norms are clearly relevant to defining the scope and content of Charter rights. The next section explores how these norms have been brought to bear on the substantive review of administrative decisions that engage the Charter.

2. International Human Rights and the Substantive Review of Decisions Engaging Charter Protections

Administrative decisions, including those involving the exercise of discretion, may in some circumstances engage rights protected by the Charter, such as freedom of expression,[227] freedom of religion[228] or the right not to be deprived of life, liberty, and security of the person except in accordance with the principles of fundamental justice.[229] As discussed in greater detail by Evan Fox-Decent and Alexander Pless in Chapter 13, The Charter and Administrative Law Part II: Substantive Review, the Supreme Court of Canada's approach to the judicial review of discretionary decisions touching on Charter rights has shifted over time. Initially, it reviewed such decisions as it would the constitutionality of legislation. Where it found that a decision infringed the Charter right of an affected party, it ascertained whether the infringement was nevertheless justified under s 1 by applying the *Oakes* test.[230] More recently, in *Doré v Barreau du Québec*,[231] the court unanimously adopted an "administrative law" approach to the review of discretionary administrative decisions that engage the Charter:

> The preliminary issue is whether the decision engages the *Charter* by limiting its protections. If such a limitation has occurred, then "the question becomes whether, in assessing the impact of the relevant *Charter* protection and given the nature of the decision and the statutory and factual contexts, the decision reflects a proportionate balancing of the *Charter* protections at play" .... A proportionate balancing is one that gives effect, as fully as possible to the *Charter* protections at stake given the particular statutory mandate. Such a balancing will be found to be reasonable on judicial review.[232]

While a majority of the court applied this approach in the subsequent case of *Loyola*, in their concurring judgment, McLachlin CJ and Moldaver J (joined by Rothstein J) adopted a different framework more closely aligned with the conventional "constitutional law" approach, which required courts to ask, first, whether a Charter right or freedom was infringed and, second, whether the administrative decision limited the right or freedom proportionately—that is, no more than was reasonably necessary.[233] *Loyola* concerned a decision by

---

227 *Doré v Barreau du Québec*, 2012 SCC 12, [2012] 1 SCR 395 [*Doré*]; *Slaight Communications, supra* note 160.
228 *Multani v Commission scolaire Marguerite-Bourgeoys*, 2006 SCC 6, [2006] 1 SCR 256; *Loyola, supra* note 151.
229 *Suresh, supra* note 7.
230 See e.g. *Slaight Communications, supra* note 161.
231 *Supra* note 227.
232 *Loyola, supra* note 151 at para 39 (citations omitted).
233 *Ibid* at para 114. For further analysis of this decision, see Gerald Heckman, "Developments in Administrative Law: The 2014-2015 Term" (2016) 72 SCLR (2d) 1.

Quebec's minister of education, recreation, and sports denying Loyola High School's application to be exempted from the mandatory Ethics and Religious Culture (ERC) Program designed to teach students about the beliefs and ethics of different world religions from a neutral and objective perspective and to encourage among students respect for and openness to others. In the minister's view, Loyola's proposed alternative program, which would have allowed students to learn about world religions and ethical approaches with the doctrine and belief system of the Catholic Church as the normative core of the curriculum, was not "equivalent" to the ERC program, with its secular and cultural orientation. Both the majority and partially concurring opinion invoked conventional international human rights norms to support their conclusion that the minister's decision engaged s 2(a) of the Charter.

In the majority's view, the minister was bound to exercise her discretion whether to exempt Loyola from the mandatory curriculum "in a way that respects the values underlying the grant of her decision-making authority, including the *Charter*-protected religious freedom of the members of the Loyola community who seek to offer and wish to receive a Catholic education."[234] By preventing a Catholic discussion of Catholicism at Loyola, the minister's decision interfered with parents' rights to transmit their Catholic faith to their children, an essential ingredient of the vitality of a religious community, and profoundly interfered with religious freedom.[235] The majority found support in international human rights law for the importance to religious freedom of the ability of parents to pass on their beliefs to their children. In particular, art 18(4) of the ICCPR requires states parties to "have respect for the liberty of parents and, when applicable, legal guardians to ensure the religious and moral education of their children in conformity with their own convictions."[236] In the majority's view, the minister's decision did not reflect a proportionate balancing of religious freedom and was unreasonable because it presumed that engagement with an individual's own religion on his or her own terms impaired respect for others, an assumption that ran counter to the objectives of the regulatory scheme and had "a disproportionate impact on the values underlying religious freedom in this context."[237]

Notably absent from the majority's treatment of international law is any mention of the presumption of conformity or any other explanation of how and why art 18(4) of the ICCPR should exert a persuasive influence on the scope of religious freedom under s 2(a) of the Charter. By contrast, the concurring judges invoked the minimum content presumption to interpret the scope of s 2(a) in light of international norms. They first considered whether Loyola, as a religious non-profit corporation or organization, enjoyed freedom of religion under s 2(a). The attorney general of Quebec had argued that religious freedom protected sincerely held beliefs, and that corporations were capable of neither sincerity nor belief. After canvassing the Supreme Court's own jurisprudence, which indicated that the individual and collective aspect of freedom of religion were indissolubly intertwined, the concurring judges, highlighting provisions of the UDHR,[238] ICCPR, [239] and ECHR,[240] observed that "international human rights instruments recognize the communal character of religion and

---

234 *Loyola, supra* note 151 at para 34.
235 *Ibid* at paras 64 and 67.
236 *Ibid* at para 65.
237 *Ibid* at para 69.
238 UDHR, art 18.
239 ICCPR, arts 18(1), (4).
240 ECHR, art 9.

support the extension of constitutional protection to the organizations through which congregants worship and teach their faith."[241] Because "the *Charter* should be presumed to provide at least as great a level of protection as is found in the international human rights documents that Canada has ratified," it followed that "the collective aspect of freedom of religion should find protection under the *Charter*."[242] As an organization constituted primarily for religious purposes and whose operation accorded with these purposes, Loyola could claim the protection of s 2(a). The concurring judges found that the minister's decision infringed on Loyola's freedom of religion by requiring it to teach Catholicism and ethics from a neutral, secular perspective rather than a Catholic perspective.[243] Moreover, it was not minimally impairing under s 1 of the Charter because in assuming that only a secular approach to teaching religious beliefs and ethics could qualify as equivalent and meet the objectives of the ERC Program, it eschewed the flexible, case-by-case assessment of proposed programs that was contemplated by the legislation.[244]

Loyola demonstrates that, by influencing the scope of Charter protections, international human rights norms can play an important role in assessing the reasonableness or constitutionality (depending on the analytical framework selected by the reviewing court) of exercises of administrative discretion that engage the Charter. While only the concurring judges expressly invoked the *Alberta Reference* presumption of conformity with Canada's international human rights obligations, it would have been appropriate and indeed preferable, for reasons of consistency and transparency, for the majority to do so too since it also relied on the protection of religious freedom in art 18 of the ICCPR, a convention ratified by and binding on Canada at international law.

International norms have also been invoked by reviewing courts in support of the reasonableness of a decision-maker's balancing of Charter protections and statutory objectives under the *Doré* framework. In *Trinity Western University v The Law Society of Upper Canada*,[245] the Ontario Court of Appeal reviewed the decision of the Law Society that it would not be in the public interest to accredit a private evangelical Christian university's proposed law school program because the university's requirement that prospective students sign and adhere to a Community Covenant forbidding sexual intimacy except between married heterosexual couples discriminated against members of the LGBTQ community. The court determined that this decision balanced the statutory objectives of "promoting a legal profession based on merit and excluding discriminatory classifications with the limit that denying accreditation would place on Trinity Western University's religious freedom."[246] The outcome was reasonable, *inter alia*, because this balancing was faithful to art 18(3) of the ICCPR, which provides that "freedom to manifest one's religion or beliefs may be subject only to such limitations as are prescribed by law and are necessary to protect . . . the fundamental rights and freedoms of others."[247]

International human rights norms—customary and conventional—clearly have a role to play in the substantive review of administrative decision-making. Decisions resting on the

---

241　*Loyola*, *supra* note 151 at para 97.
242　*Ibid*.
243　*Ibid* at para 143.
244　*Ibid* at para 151.
245　2016 ONCA 518, 131 OR (3d) 113, leave to appeal granted, [2016] SCCA No 418.
246　*Ibid* (CA) at paras 112 and 118.
247　*Ibid* at paras 139-40.

interpretation of a statutory provision intended to implement an international human rights treaty obligation may be reviewed on the basis that the decision-maker incorrectly or un-reasonably[248] interpreted the statute by giving it a meaning inconsistent with the imple-mented treaty. More generally, given the presumption that statutes should be interpreted in conformity with Canada's international law obligations, a decision-maker who interprets a statutory provision in a manner inconsistent with applicable and relevant international human rights norms, absent express language or clear legislative intent supporting such an interpretation, renders a decision that arguably falls outside of the range of possible, acceptable outcomes defensible in respect of the facts and the law and is thus unreason-able. Broad, discretionary regulation-making powers should also be read, absent clear legislative intent to the contrary, as authorizing only the promulgation of regulations that comply with Canada's international obligations. Finally, a discretionary decision that en-gages Charter protections may also be challenged as unreasonable on the basis that it does not reflect a proportionate balancing of the Charter protections at play given the decision-maker's statutory mandate. Canada's international human rights obligations are relevant to such challenges because they presumptively define the minimum content of similar Charter protections.

The following section shows that some international human rights norms guarantee basic procedural safeguards in the context of state decision-making affecting fundamental interests, including the rights to life, liberty, and security of the person. As explained in the following section, they may also serve to challenge administrative decision-making—but on procedural rather than substantive grounds.

V. INTERNATIONAL HUMAN RIGHTS NORMS AND THE PROCEDURAL REVIEW OF ADMINISTRATIVE DECISIONS

The procedural norms set out in international human rights treaties resonate deeply with Canadian legal values. As Evan Fox-Decent and Alexander Pless discuss in Chapter 6, The Charter and Administrative Law Part I: Procedural Fairness, procedural fairness is a basic tenet of Canada's legal system and a principle of fundamental justice under s 7 of the Charter. International norms can also be called upon to influence the development of pro-cedural safeguards in Canada. In *Baker*, the applicant had invited the Federal Court of Appeal and the Supreme Court of Canada to find that she had a legitimate expectation, based on the terms of the CRC, that her children would be afforded a hearing by the immigration of-ficer considering her humanitarian and compassionate application. In particular, art 12 of the CRC provides that children have the right "to be heard in any judicial or administrative pro-ceedings affecting the child, either directly or through a representative or an appropriate body." This provision appeared to entitle Ms Baker's children to participate directly in the humanitarian and compassionate application process. In fact, the interests of Baker's

---

248 While courts will presumptively review an administrative decision-maker's interpretation of its enabling statute on a reasonableness standard, it may be possible to characterize some questions touching on the scope of fundamental human rights as general questions of law of central importance to the legal system and outside the decision-maker's expertise and reviewable on a correctness standard: see Audrey Macklin, Chapter 11, Standard of Review: Back to the Future?

children had only been considered through the written submissions of Baker's own counsel. The court decided that the CRC's terms did not give rise to a legitimate expectation on Baker's part that specific procedural rights above what would normally be required under the duty of fairness would be accorded.[249] The CRC was not "the equivalent of a government representation about how [humanitarian and compassionate] applications will be decided, nor does it suggest that any rights beyond the participatory rights [afforded by common law procedural fairness] will be accorded."[250] The Federal Court of Appeal more clearly explained its concerns at the prospect of giving effect to the right of Baker's children to direct representation in the humanitarian and compassionate application. It warned that giving judicial force to the procedural provisions of the CRC, a treaty ratified by the federal executive but not formally implemented by the legislative branches, would have a significant impact on decision-making by provincial authorities involving children, notably the administration of family law and the provision of legal aid for family law and child custody proceedings—matters of provincial jurisdiction.[251]

Curiously, in rejecting Baker's legitimate expectations argument, the court made no mention of the High Court of Australia's judgment in *Minister for Immigration and Ethnic Affairs v Teoh*,[252] which was raised by the applicant and discussed at length by the Federal Court of Appeal. In *Teoh*, the High Court had recognized that ratified but unimplemented international treaties could influence administrative decision-making through the doctrine of legitimate expectations. The minister's delegate had decided that there were insufficient compassionate grounds to allow Teoh's application for a permanent entry permit, despite the fact that his deportation jeopardized the livelihood of his Australian children. A majority of the High Court decided that Australia's ratification of the CRC gave rise to a legitimate expectation that the minister's delegate would, in conformity with the CRC, treat the best interests of Teoh's children as a primary consideration in his decision. His failure to do this, or to allow Teoh to argue against a decision inconsistent with his legitimate expectation, breached procedural fairness. The majority held that Australia's ratification of the CRC was

> not to be dismissed as a merely platitudinous or ineffectual act, particularly when the [CRC] evidences internationally accepted standards to be applied by courts and administrative authorities in dealing with basic human rights affecting the family and children. Rather, [it] is a positive statement by the executive government of this country to the world and to the Australian people that the executive government and its agencies will act in accordance with the Convention. That positive statement is an adequate foundation for a legitimate expectation, absent statutory or executive indications to the contrary, that administrative decision-makers will act in conformity with the Convention and treat the best interests of the children as "a primary consideration."[253]

Dissenting, McHugh J complained that the majority's ruling effectively allowed the executive to amend Australian law by ratifying an international convention without involving the political branches of government, a view accepted by the Federal Court of Appeal in

---

249 The doctrine of legitimate expectations is discussed further by Kate Glover in Chapter 5, The Principles and Practices of Procedural Fairness.
250 *Baker, supra* note 1 at para 29.
251 *Baker* (FCA), *supra* note 55 at para 30.
252 (1995), 183 CLR 273 [*Teoh*].
253 *Ibid* at 291.

Baker.[254] For this reason, successive Australian governments rejected *Teoh*'s holding,[255] and publicly declared that the act of entering into a treaty did not give rise to legitimate expectations that could form the basis for challenging administrative decisions.[256]

Although the Supreme Court of Canada dismissed Baker's legitimate expectations argument, it left open the possibility that an international instrument ratified by Canada could, in other circumstances, give rise to a legitimate expectation.[257] In *Suresh*, a refugee facing deportation to his country of origin successfully argued that fundamental justice under s 7 entitled him to procedures over and above those provided by the *Immigration Act* based in part on a legitimate expectation raised by the terms of the CAT. To determine the procedural requirements of fundamental justice, the Supreme Court of Canada applied the common law approach to determining the content of the duty of procedural fairness.[258] Several factors weighed in favour of substantial procedural safeguards, including the absence of any appeal procedure, the determinative nature of the minister's decision, and the serious personal, financial, and emotional consequences for Suresh if he were to be deported from Canada. The court also considered whether Suresh had a legitimate expectation of additional procedure. It noted that the CAT prohibits the deportation of persons to states where there are "substantial grounds" for believing they would be "in danger of being subjected to torture." In the court's view, it was "only reasonable that the same executive that bound itself to the CAT intends to act in accordance with the CAT's plain meaning."[259] Given "Canada's commitment to the CAT," and the requirement of "substantial grounds" to trigger the obligation of non-refoulement, the court found that Suresh was entitled to an opportunity to demonstrate and defend those grounds.[260] Suresh was not owed a full hearing or complete judicial process, but was entitled to examine the material upon which the minister based her decision to deport (subject to claims of privilege), respond to the minister's case, and challenge her information regarding the threat he posed to national security, the risk of torture,

---

254   *Ibid* at 316. See *Baker* (FCA), *supra* note 55 at para 39.

255   H Charlesworth et al, "Deep Anxieties: Australia and the International Legal Order" (2003) 25 Sydney L Rev 423 at 437.

256   Attempts to enact legislation to counteract *Teoh* were unsuccessful: Charlesworth et al, *ibid* at 449. However, controversy over the decision led to important reforms to enhance parliamentary participation in the treaty-making process: Harrington, *supra* note 58 at 491-97. Several High Court judges called for *Teoh* to be revisited in *Re Minister for Immigration and Multicultural Affairs; ex parte Lam*, [2003] HCA 6 at para 102, McHugh and Gummow JJ, and para 145, Callinan J. The High Court now appears to have repudiated legitimate expectations altogether as a basis for determining whether and to what extent procedural fairness is owed to individuals: *Minister for Immigration and Border Protection v WZARH*, (2015) HCA 40 at para 30. Academics also criticized *Teoh* as a disingenuous application of the legitimate expectations doctrine: Michael Taggart, "Legitimate Expectation and Treaties in the High Court of Australia" (1996) 112 LQR 50; Murray Hunt, *Using Human Rights Law in English Courts* (Oxford: Hart Publishing, 1997) at 251-59.

257   *Baker*, *supra* note 1 at para 29.

258   *Suresh*, *supra* note 7 at paras 113-15. For a description of the common law approach, see Kate Glover, Chapter 5, The Principles and Practices of Procedural Fairness, and for a detailed discussion of the interface between s 7 and administrative law, see Evan Fox-Decent and Alexander Pless, Chapter 6, The Charter and Administrative Law Part I: Procedural Fairness.

259   *Suresh*, supra note 7 para 119.

260   *Ibid.*

and the value of assurances from foreign governments that he would not be tortured. Finally, he was entitled to written reasons from the minister justifying her final decision.[261]

Although *Suresh* indicates that it is possible to seek procedural review of administrative decisions on the grounds that the procedures provided by the decision-maker did not live up to the legitimate expectations of the applicant based on the terms of a ratified international treaty, it is unclear when such an argument will be successful given its dramatically different treatment by the court in *Baker* and *Suresh*. More guidance is needed from the courts as to when state obligations in ratified conventions can or cannot raise legitimate expectations.[262]

VI. CONCLUSION

There is no doubt that international human rights norms from binding international treaties, customary international law, or non-binding international instruments can play an important role in the substantive and procedural review of administrative decisions. More work remains to be done to precisely delineate that role and to strengthen it. It is incumbent on public lawyers to familiarize themselves with the international human rights norms relevant to their area of practice and to raise them in individual cases.[263] Administrative decision-makers, reviewing courts, and, ultimately, the Supreme Court of Canada must seize the opportunities so created to bring greater clarity and certainty to the relationship between international law and Canadian administrative and constitutional law: no less than the effective domestic enforcement of international human rights depends on it.

---

261 *Ibid* at paras 121-27.

262 In Canada, the doctrine of legitimate expectations cannot lead to substantive results outside of the procedural domain: *Baker, supra* note 1 at para 26. Thus, the Ontario Court of Appeal rejected a non-citizen's attempt to invoke the doctrine to secure an injunction against the Canadian government's attempts to remove him to Iran, where he alleged he would be tortured, until such time as the UN Human Rights Committee had delivered its views on a petition he had filed claiming a violation of his rights under the ICCPR. The right to remain in Canada was a substantive outcome which the doctrine of legitimate expectations did not support: *Ahani, supra* note 66 at para 63. Arguably, however, Canada's failure to consider the impact of Ahani's removal on the effectiveness of his right under the Optional Protocol, *supra* note 37, to communicate with the committee rendered the removal decision unreasonable: Gerald Heckman, "The Role of International Human Rights Norms in Administrative Law" in Colleen M Flood and Lorne Sossin, eds, *Administrative Law in Context*, 2nd ed (Toronto: Emond Montgomery, 2013) 489 at 517-20, online: <www.emond.ca/adminlaw3e>.

263 But see Stephen Meili, "When Do Human Rights Treaties Help Asylum Seekers? A Study of Theory and Practice in Canadian Jurisprudence Since 1990" (2014) 51 OHLJ 627 at paras 57, 59, and 93, where he warns against the "indiscriminate" invocation of human rights treaties before tribunals and courts that may trigger "human rights fatigue" in these decision-makers and be interpreted as a sign of counsels' "desperation."

SUGGESTED ADDITIONAL READINGS

BOOKS AND ARTICLES

Brunnée, Jutta, & Stephen Toope, "A Hesitant Embrace: Baker and the Application of International Law by Canadian Courts" in David Dyzenhaus, ed, *The Unity of Public Law* (Oxford: Hart Publishing, 2004).

Currie, John H, "International Human Rights Law in the Supreme Court's Charter Jurisprudence: Commitment, Retrenchment and Retreat—In No Particular Order" (2010) 50 SCLR (2d) 423.

de Mestral, Armand, & Evan Fox-Decent, "Rethinking the Relationship Between International and Domestic Law" (2008) 53 McGill LJ 573.

Fitzgerald, Oonagh E, ed, *The Globalized Rule of Law* (Toronto: Irwin Law, 2006).

Freeman, Mark, & Gibran van Ert, *International Human Rights Law* (Toronto: Irwin Law, 2004).

Heckman, Gerald, "International Human Rights Law Norms and Discretionary Powers: Recent Developments" (2003) 16 Can J Admin L & Prac 31.

Schabas, William A, & Stéphane Beaulac, *International Human Rights and Canadian Law— Legal Commitment, Implementation and the Charter*, 3rd ed (Toronto: Thomson Carswell, 2007).

Stéphane Beaulac, "'Texture ouverte,' droit international et interprétation de la Charte cana-dienne" in Errol Mendes & Stéphane Beaulac, eds, *Canadian Charter of Rights and Freedoms*, 5th ed (Markham: LexisNexis, 2013) 191.

van Ert, Gibran, *Using International Law in Canadian Courts*, 2nd ed (Toronto: Irwin Law, 2008).

CASES

Baker v Canada (Minister of Citizenship and Immigration), [1999] 2 SCR 817.

De Guzman v Canada (Minister of Citizenship and Immigration), 2005 FCA 436.

Minister for Immigration and Ethnic Affairs v Teoh (1995), 183 CLR 273.

R v Hape, 2007 SCC 26, [2007] 2 SCR 292.

Suresh v Canada (Minister of Citizenship and Immigration), 2002 SCC 1, [2002] 1 SCR 3.

Kazemi Estate v Islamic Republic of Iran, 2014 SCC 62, [2014] 3 SCR 176.

Saskatchewan Federation of Labour v Saskatchewan, 2015 SCC 4, [2015] 1 SCR 245.

Table of Selected Federal and Provincial Administrative Boards and Tribunals

Jurisdiction	Name	Legislation
Canada (Federal)	Canada Industrial Relations Board <http://www.cirb-ccri.gc.ca/eic/site/047.nsf/eng/home>	*Status of the Artist Act* (SAA) (1992) *Canada Labour Code* (1985)
	Canada Agricultural Review Tribunal <http://cart-crac.gc.ca/index-en.html>	*Canada Agricultural Products Act* (CAPA) (1985)
		Rules of the Review Tribunal (Canada Agricultural Review Tribunal)
		Agriculture and Agri-Food Administrative Monetary Penalties Act (AA-FAMPA) (1995)
		Agriculture and Agri-Food Administrative Monetary Penalties Regulations [respecting animals and plants] (AA-FAMPA)
		Agriculture and Agri-Food Administrative Monetary Regulations respecting the Pest Control Products Act and Regulations (AA-FAMPA)
		Health of Animals Act (HAA) (1990)
		Health of Animals Regulations (HAA)
		Plant Protection Act (PPA) (1990)
		Plant Protection Regulations (PPA)
		Pest Control Products Act (PCPA) (2002)
		Pest Control Products Regulations (PCPA)

Jurisdiction	Name	Legislation
Canada (Federal) (continued)	Canadian Forces Grievance Board <http://www.cfgb-cgfc.gc.ca>	*National Defence Act* (NDA) (1985) Canadian Forces Grievance Board Rules of Procedure (Review of a Grievance by Way of a Hearing) (NDA)
	Commission for Public Complaints Against the RCMP <http://www.cpc-cpp.gc.ca>	*Royal Canadian Mounted Police Act* (RCMPA) (1985) Commissioner's Standing Orders (General Administration) Royal Canadian Mounted Police Public Complaints Commission Rules of Practice (RCMPA)
	Federal Public Sector Labour Relations and Employment Board <http://pslreb-crtefp.gc.ca/index_e.asp>	*Federal Public Sector Labour Relations and Employment Board Act* (FPSLREA) (2014) Public Service Labour Relations Regulations (2005) PSSRB Regulations and Rules of Procedure (PSLRA) *Federal Public Sector Labour Relations Act* (2003) *Financial Administration Act* (1985) *Canada Labour Code* (1985) *Canadian Human Rights Act* (1985) *Parliamentary Employment and Staff Relations Act* (PESRA) (1985) PESRA Regulations and Rules of Procedure (PESRA)
	Hazardous Materials Information Review Commission <http://www.hmirc-ccrmd.gc.ca>	*Hazardous Materials Information Review Act* (HMIRA) (1985) Hazardous Materials Information Review Act Appeal Board Procedures Regulations (HMIRA)
		Hazardous Materials Information Review Regulations (HMIRA) *Hazardous Products Act* (1985)

Jurisdiction	Name	Legislation
Canada (Federal) (continued)	Military Police Complaints Commission of Canada <http://www.mpcc-cppm.gc.ca>	*National Defence Act* (1985)
	National Parole Board <http://pbc-clcc.gc.ca>	*Corrections and Conditional Release Act* (CCRA) (1992) Corrections and Conditional Release Regulations (CCRA) *Criminal Code* (1985) *Criminal Records Act* (1985) *Access to Information Act* (1985) *Privacy Act* (1985) *Canadian Multiculturalism Act* (1985)
	Patented Medicine Prices Review Board <http://www.pmprb-cepmb.gc.ca>	*Patent Act* (1985) Patented Medicines Regulations (*Patent Act*)
	Social Security Tribunal of Canada <https://www1.canada.ca/en/sst/index.html>	*Old Age Security Act* (OASA) (1985) Old Age Security Regulations (OASA) *Canada Pension Plan* (CPP) (1985) Canada Pension Plan Regulations (CPP) *Pension Benefits Standards Act* (PBSA) (1985) Pension Benefits Standards Regulations (PBSA)
	Specific Claims Tribunal Canada <http://www.sct-trp.ca>	*Specific Claims Tribunal Act* (SCTA) (2008) Specific Claims Tribunal Rules of Practice and Procedure (SCTA)
British Columbia	British Columbia Securities Commission <http://www.bcsc.bc.ca>	*Securities Act* (1996) Note: The Commission administers 44 regulations, BC Instruments and National Instruments, all enacted pursuant to the *Securities Act*.

Jurisdiction	Name	Legislation
British Columbia (continued)	Building Code Appeal Board <http://www.housing.gov.bc.ca/bcab>	*Building Act* (2015) British Columbia Building Code Regulation (LGA)
	Community Care and Assisted Living Appeal Board <http://www.ccalab.gov.bc.ca>	*Community Care and Assisted Living Act* (2002)
	Expropriation Compensation Board <http://www.ecb.gov.bc.ca>	*Expropriation Act* (EA) (1996) Expropriation Act General Regulation (EA) Expropriation Proceeding Cost Regulation (EA) Tariff of Costs Regulation (EA) The Compensation Action Procedure Rule (EA)
	Forest Appeals Commission <http://www.fac.gov.bc.ca>	*Forest Practices Code of British Columbia Act* (FPCBCA) (1996) *Forest and Range Practices Act* (FRPA) (2002) Administrative Orders and Remedies Regulation (FRPA) Administrative Review and Appeal Procedure Regulation (FPCBCA and FRPA) *Forest Act* (1996) *Private Managed Forest Land Act* (2003) *Range Act* (2004) *Wildfire Act* (2004)
	Hospital Appeal Board <http://www.hab.gov.bc.ca>	*Hospital Act* (HA) (1996) Hospital Act Regulation (HA)
	Office of the Information and Privacy Commissioner <http://www.oipc.bc.ca>	Freedom of Information and Protection of Privacy Act (1996) *Personal Information Protection Act* (2003)

Jurisdiction	Name	Legislation
British Columbia (continued)	Real Estate Council of British Columbia <http://www.recbc.ca>	*Real Estate Services Act* (RESA) (2004) Real Estate Services Regulation (RESA) *Real Estate Development Marketing Act* (REDMA) (2004) Real Estate Development Marketing Regulation (REDMA)
Alberta	Agricultural Products Marketing Council Appeal Tribunal <http://www1.agric.gov.ab.ca/ general/progserv.nsf/all/pgmsrv109>	*Marketing of Agricultural Products Act* (MAPA) (2000) Review and Appeal Regulation
	Alberta Barley Commission <http://www.albertabarley.com>	*Marketing of Agricultural Products Act* (MAPA) (2000) Alberta Barley Commission Authorization Regulation (MAPA) Alberta Barley Commission Regulation (MAPA) Alberta Barley Plan Regulation (MAPA)
	Alberta College of Medical Diagnostic & Therapeutic Technologists <http://www.acmdtt.com>	*Health Professions Act* (HPA) (2000) Medical Diagnostic and Therapeutic Technologists and Electroneurophysiologists Profession Regulation (HPA)
	Alberta Gaming and Liquor Commission <http://aglc.ca>	*Gaming and Liquor Act* (GLA) (2000) Gaming and Liquor Regulation (GLA) *Criminal Code* (1985) *Tobacco Tax Act* (2000) *Horse Racing Alberta Act* (2000)
	Alberta Irrigation Council <http://www1.agric.gov.ab.ca/$ department/deptdocs.nsf/all/irc9440>	*Irrigation Districts Act* (2000)
	Alberta Podiatry Association <http://www.albertapodiatry.com>	*Health Professions Act* (2000) Podiatrists Profession Regulation

Jurisdiction	Name	Legislation
Alberta (continued)	Environmental Appeals Board <http://www.eab.gov.ab.ca>	*Environmental Protection and Enhancement Act* (EPEA) (2000)
		Environmental Appeal Board Regulation (EPEA)
		Environmental Protection and Enhancement (Miscellaneous) Regulation (EPEA)
		Water Act (2000)
		Climate Change and Emissions Management Act (2003)
		Government Organization Act (2000)
	Metis Settlements Appeal Tribunal <http://www.msat.gov.ab.ca>	*Metis Settlements Act* (MSA) (2000)
		Metis Settlements Land Registry Regulation (MSA)
		Land Interests Conversion Regulation (MSA)
		Metis Settlements Subdivision Regulation (MSA)
Saskatchewan	Board of Revenue Commissioners <http://www.gov.sk.ca/BRC>	*Revenue and Financial Services Act* (1983)
		The Freehold Oil and Gas Production Tax Act, 2010
		Mineral Taxation Act (1983)
		Crown Minerals Act (1984)
		Municipal Employees' Pension Act (1978)
		The Cities Act (2002)
		The Municipalities Act (2005)
		The Northern Municipalities Act (2010)
		The Lloydminster Charter (*City of Lloydminster Act*, 2005)
	Denturist Society of Saskatchewan <http://saskdenturists.com>	*Dental Disciplines Act* (1997)

Jurisdiction	Name	Legislation
Saskatchewan (continued)	Registered Psychiatric Nurses of Saskatchewan <https://www.rpnas.com>	*Registered Psychiatric Nurses Act* (1993)
	Saskatchewan Association of Licensed Practical Nurses <http://www.salpn.com>	*Licensed Practical Nurses Act, 2000*
	Saskatchewan Real Estate Commission <http://www.srec.ca/legis.asp>	*Real Estate Act* (REA) (1995) Real Estate Regulations (REA)
	Saskatchewan Registered Nurses' Association <http://www.srna.org>	*Registered Nurses Act* (1988)
Manitoba	Automobile Injury Compensation Appeal Commission <http://www.gov.mb.ca/fs/cca/auto/index.html>	*The Manitoba Public Insurance Corporation Act* (1987)
	Clean Environment Commission <http://www.cecmanitoba.ca>	*The Environment Act* (TEA) (1988) Participant Assistance Regulation 125/91 (TEA) *The Contaminated Sites Remediation Act* (1996) *The Drinking Water Safety Act* (2004) *The Sustainable Development Act* (1997)
	Manitoba Boxing Commission <http://www.manitobaboxingcommission.com>	*The Combative Sports Act* (1993) Boxing Regulation (TBCA)
	Manitoba Film Classification Board <http://www.gov.mb.ca/chc/mfcb>	*The Amusements Act* (TAA) (1991-1992) Film Classification and Licensing Regulation (TAA)
	Manitoba Horse Racing Commission <http://www.manitobahorsecomm.org>	*The Horse Racing Commission Act* (THRCA) (1991-1992) Horse Racing Commission Regulation 10/91 (THRCA) Racing Days Regulation (THRCA)

Jurisdiction	Name	Legislation
Ontario	Bereavement Authority of Ontario <https://thebao.ca>	*Funeral, Burial and Cremation Services Act, 2002*
	Board of Negotiation (under the *Environmental Protection Act*) <http://www.pas.gov.on.ca/scripts/en/boardDetails.asp?boardID=754>	*Environmental Protection Act* (EPA) (1990) Note: There are 81 specific environmental regulations enacted pursuant to the EPA.
	Child and Family Services Review Board <http://www.cfsrb.ca>	*Child, Youth and Family Services Act, 2017* *Intercountry Adoption Act, 1998* *Education Act* (1990)
	College of Naturopaths of Ontario < http://www.collegeofnaturopaths .on.ca/>	*Regulated Health Professions Act, 1991* *Naturopathy Act, 2007* *Health Care Consent Act* (1996) *Drugs and Pharmacies Regulation Act* (1990) *Laboratory and Specimen Collection Centre Licensing Act* (1990) General (Regulations) (DPA)
	College of Respiratory Therapists of Ontario <http://www.crto.on.ca>	*Respiratory Therapy Act, 1991* (RTA, 1991) *Regulated Health Professions Act, 1991* *Personal Health Information Protection Act, 2004* Professional Misconduct (Regulations) (RTA, 1991) General (Regulations) (RTA, 1991) *Controlled Drugs and Substances Act* (CDSA) (1996) Narcotic Control Regulations (CDSA) *Personal Information Protection and Electronic Documents Act* (2000)
	Environment & Land Tribunals Ontario <http://elto.gov.on.ca>	*Ontario Heritage Act* (1990)

Jurisdiction	Name	Legislation
Ontario (continued)	Financial Services Tribunal <http://www.fstontario.ca>	*Financial Services Commission of Ontario Act, 1997* *Pension Benefits Act* (1990) *Insurance Act* (1990) *Mortgage Brokerages, Lenders and Administrators Act, 2006* *Loan and Trust Corporations Act* (1990) *Credit Unions and Caisses Populaires Act, 1994* *Co-operative Corporations Act* (1990)
	Health Services Appeal and Review Board <http://www.hsarb.on.ca>	Ministry of Health and Long-Term Care Appeal and Review Boards Act (1998) Note: Monitors 14 different statutes.
	Landlord and Tenant Board <http://www.ltb.gov.on.ca>	*Residential Tenancies Act, 2006* (RTA, 2006) General (Regulations) (RTA, 2006)
	Ontario Special Education Tribunal <http://www.oset-tedo.ca>	*Education Act* (EA) (1990) Identification and Placement of Exceptional Pupils (Regulations) (EA) *Freedom of Information and Protection of Privacy Act* (1990)
	Tarion Warranty Authority <http://www.tarion.com>	*Ontario New Home Warranties Plan Act* (ONHWPA) (1990) Designation of Corporation (Regulations) (ONHWPA) Terms and Conditions of Registration of Builders and Vendors (Regulations) (ONHWPA) Warranty for Delayed Closing or Delayed Occupancy (Regulations) (ONHWPA) Building Code (Regulations) (*Building Code Act, 1992*)

Jurisdiction	Name	Legislation
Ontario (continued)	Technical Standards and Safety Authority <http://www.tssa.org>	*Technical Standards and Safety Act, 2000* (TSSA, 2000)
		Amusement Devices (Regulations) (TSSA, 2000)
		Boilers and Pressure Vessels (Regulations) (TSSA, 2000)
		Certification and Training of Amusement Device Mechanics (Regulations) (TSSA, 2000)
		Certification and Training of Elevating Device Mechanics (Regulations) (TSSA, 2000)
		Certification of Petroleum Equipment Mechanics (Regulations) (TSSA, 2000)
		Codes and Standards Adopted by Reference (Regulations) (TSSA, 2000)
		Compressed Gas (Regulations) (TSSA, 2000)
		Elevating Devices (Regulations) (TSSA, 2000)
		Fuel Industry Certificates (Regulations) (TSSA, 2000)
		Fuel Oil (Regulations) (TSSA, 2000)
		Gaseous Fuels (Regulations) (TSSA, 2000)
		Liquid Fuels (Regulations) (TSSA, 2000)
		Oil and Gas Pipeline Systems (Regulations) (TSSA, 2000)
		Operating Engineers (Regulations) (TSSA, 2000)
		Propane Storage and Handling (Regulations) (TSSA, 2000)
		Upholstered and Stuffed Articles (Regulations) (TSSA, 2000)
Quebec	Chambre des notaires du Québec— Committee on Discipline <http://www.cnq.org>	*Notaries Act* (NA) (2012) *Loi sur le notariat* (2012)

Jurisdiction	Name	Legislation
Quebec (continued)	Commission des droits de la personne et des droits de la jeunesse (Human Rights Tribunal) <http://www.justice.gouv.qc.ca/english/tribunaux/trib-droi-a.htm>	Quebec *Charter of Human Rights and Freedoms* (Quebec Charter) (1975)
		Code of ethics of the members of the Human Rights Tribunal (Quebec Charter)
		Regulation respecting the procedure for the recruitment and selection of persons apt for designation to the function of arbitrator or appointment to the function of assessor with the Human Rights Tribunal (Quebec Charter)
		Regulation respecting the handling of complaints and the procedure applicable to the investigations of the Commission des droits de la personne et des droits de la jeunesse (Quebec Charter)
		Regulation of the Human Rights Tribunal
	Cree Naskapi Commission <http://www.creenaskapicommission.net>	*Loi sur les Cris et les Naskapis du Québec* (LCNQ) (1984)
		Désignation de la ville d'Ottawa comme le lieu du siège de la Commission crie-naskapie (Regulations) (LCNQ)
	Régie des marchés agricoles et alimentaires du Québec <http://www.rmaaq.gouv.qc.ca>	*An Act respecting the marketing of agricultural, food and fish products* (1990)
	Tribunal administratif du Québec <http://www.taq.gouv.qc.ca/en>	*An Act Respecting Administrative Justice* (ARAJ) (1996)
		Rules of procedure of the Administrative Tribunal of Quebec (ARAJ)
		Code of ethics applicable to the members of the Administrative Tribunal of Quebec (ARAJ)
		Regulation respecting the procedure for the recruitment and selection of persons apt for appointment as members of the Administrative Tribunal of Quebec (ARAJ)

Jurisdiction	Name	Legislation
Quebec (continued)	Tribunal des professions <http://www.justice.gouv.qc.ca/english/tribunaux/trib-prof-a.htm> <http://www.tribunaux.qc.ca/Tribunal_professions/index_professions.html>	*Professional Code* (PC) (1973) Regulation of the Professions Tribunal (PC)
New Brunswick	Consumer Advocate for Insurance <http://www.insurance-assurance.ca>	*Consumer Advocate for Insurance Act* (2004) *Insurance Act* (1973)
	Farm Land Identification Appeal Board, New Brunswick Agriculture and Aquaculture <http://www2.gnb.ca/content/gnb/en/services/services_renderer.14296.html>	*Real Property Tax Act* (RPTA) (1988) Farm Land Identification Regulation 84-75 (RPTA)
	New Brunswick Dental Society <http://www.nbdental.com>	*New Brunswick Dental Act, 1985*
Nova Scotia	Adoption Appeal Committee <https://novascotia.ca/apps/abc/BoardProfile.aspx>	*Adoption Information Act* (1996)
	Crop and Livestock Insurance Arbitration Board <https://novascotia.ca/apps/abc/BoardProfile.aspx>	*Crop and Livestock Insurance Act* (CLIA) (1989) Arbitration Proceedings Regulations (CLIA)
	Dairy Farmers of Nova Scotia organization (previously the Diary Commission) <http://www.dfns.ca>	*Dairy Industry Act* (DIA) (2000) Dairy Farmers of Nova Scotia By-laws (DIA)
	The Disabled Persons Commission (Nova Scotia) <http://www.gov.ns.ca/disa>	*Disabled Persons Commission Act* (1989)
	Elevators and Lifts Appeal Board <http://www.gov.ns.ca/lae/elab>	*Elevators and Lifts Act* (ELA) (2002) Elevators and Lifts General Regulations (ELA)

Jurisdiction	Name	Legislation
Nova Scotia (continued)	Freedom of Information and Protection of Privacy Review Office <http://foipop.ns.ca>	*Freedom of Information and Protection of Privacy Act* (FOIPOPA) (1993)
		Part XX of the *Municipal Government Act* (1998)
		Privacy Review Officer Act (2008)
		Freedom of Information and Protection of Privacy Regulations (FOIPOPA)
	Pay Equity Commission <http://www.gov.ns.ca/lae/payequity>	*Pay Equity Act* (PEA) (1989)
		Pay Equity Commission Procedures Regulations (PEA)
	Private Career Colleges Division <http://pcc.ednet.ns.ca/>	*Private Career Colleges Regulation Act* (PCCRA) (1998)
		Private Career Colleges General Regulations (PCCRA)
	Student Aid Appeal Committee (aka Student Assistance Higher Appeal Board) <http://studentloans.ednet.ns.ca/content/appeal-boards>	*Student Aid Act* (SAA) (1989)
		Nova Scotia Student Aid Appeal Committee Regulations (SAA)
		Prince Edward Island
		Industrial Relations Council
		Labour Act (1988)
Prince Edward Island	Industrial Relations Council	*Labour Act* (1988)
	Prince Edward Island Social Work Registration Board <http://peiasw.ca>	*Social Work Act* (SWA) (1988)
		Certification Regulations (SWA)
		Standards and Discipline Regulations (SWA)
	Regulatory and Appeals Commission <http://www.irac.pe.ca>	*Island Regulatory and Appeals Commission Act* (1988)
Newfoundland and Labrador	Income and Employment Support Appeal Board <http://www.hrle.gov.nl.ca/hrle/income-support/appealprocess.html>	*Income and Employment Support Act* (IESA) (2002)
		Income and Employment Support Regulations (IESA)
	Newfoundland Board of Dispensing Opticians	*Dispensing Opticians Act* (DOA) (2005)
		Dispensing Opticians Regulations (DOA)

Jurisdiction	Name	Legislation
Newfoundland and Labrador (continued)	Royal Newfoundland Constabulary Public Complaints Commission <http://www.justice.gov.nl.ca/rncpcc>	*Royal Newfoundland Constabulary Act* (RNCA) (1992) Royal Newfoundland Constabulary Public Complaints Regulations (RNCA)
Yukon	Social Assistance Review Committee, Yukon Health and Social Services <http://www.hss.gov.yk.ca/sarc.php>	*Social Assistance Act* (SAA) (2002) Social Assistance Regulation (SAA) Social Assistance Review Committee Remuneration Regulation (SAA)
	Yukon Surface Rights Board <http://www.yukonsurfacerights.com>	*Yukon Surface Rights Board Act* (1994) *Placer Mining Act* (2003) *Quartz Mining Act* (2003) Individual Yukon First Nation Final Agreements
	Yukon Utilities Board <http://www.yukonutilitiesboard.yk.ca>	*Public Utilities Act* (2002) Note: There are a dozen regulations and directives issued pursuant to the *Public Utilities Act*, most focused at specific utilities projects.
Northwest Territories	Aboriginal Languages Revitalization Board	*Official Languages Act* (OLA) (1988) Aboriginal Languages Revitalization Board Regulations (OLA)
	Inuvialuit Environmental Impact Review Board <http://www.eirb.ca>	Inuvialuit Final Agreement (1984)
	Mackenzie Valley Environmental Impact Review Board <http://www.reviewboard.ca>	*Mackenzie Valley Resource Management Act* (MVRMA) (1998) Mackenzie Valley Land Use Regulations (MVRMA) *Canadian Environmental Assessment Act, 2012*
	Territorial Board of Revision	*Property Assessment and Taxation Act* (1988)

Jurisdiction	Name	Legislation
Nunavut	Criminal Code Review Board	*Criminal Code* (1985)
	Discipline Board	*Corrections Act* (1988)
	Nunavut Planning Commission <http://www.nunavut.ca>	*Nunavut Land Claims Agreement* (1993)
	Water Board <http://www.nwb-oen.ca>	*Nunavut Waters and Nunavut Surface Rights Tribunal Act* (NWNSRTA) (2002) Application of Regulations made under paragraph 33(1)(m) or (n) of the Northwest Territories Waters Act in Nunavut Order (NWNSRTA)

Index